"The best all-around guide for North America, hands down."

Thanks

No project as complex as this can be completed by
a single person or team without help from others.

•

Thank you to the public relations personnel at each of the ski resorts
reviewed in these pages: they carefully check facts,
phone numbers, prices and programs
even though they don't always agree with our reviews.

•

Thank you to Auto Europe for arranging automobile rentals
for the Ski Snowboard America and Canada and Ski Snowboard Europe staff
whenever they travel to Canada or Europe.
If you are planning to rent a car abroad,
this company is a secret all travelers
should know about—(800) 223-5555.

•

And thank you to the Salt Lake City Convention and Visitors Bureau,
Alta, Brighton, Snowbird and Solitude resorts in Utah
for hosting our 2006 editorial conference.

SKI SNOWBOARD AMERICA

by Charles A. Leocha

Steve Giordano, Editor
Mitch Kaplan, Eastern Editor
Lynn Rosen, Western Editor

with

Peggy McKay Shinn, Karen Cummings

Claudia Carbone, Hilary Nangle, James Kitfield

Andrew Bill, Chris Elliott, Kari Haugeto

Roger Lohr, Tom Patterson, Phil Johnson,

Susan Staples, Diane Scholfield, Vanessa Reese

WORLD LEISURE CORPORATION

Hampstead, NH

Help us do a better job

Research for this book is an ongoing process. We have been at it for almost two decades. Each year we revisit many of these resorts, and every winter we speak with locals from every resort.

If you find a new restaurant, hotel, bar or dance club that you feel we should include, please let us know. If you find anything in these pages that is misleading or has changed, please let us know. If we use your suggestion, we will send you a copy of next year's edition.

Send your suggestions and comments to:
Charlie Leocha, *Ski Snowboard America*
World Leisure Corporation
Box 160, Hampstead NH 03841, USA

Distributed to the trade in the U.S.A. by
Midpoint Trade Books, Inc., 27 W. 20th Street, Suite 1102,
New York, NY 10011, Tel. (212) 727-0190, fax (212) 727-0195.
Internet: www.midpt.com; E-mail sales: midpointny@aol.com

Distributed to the trade in the U.K. by
Portfolio, Unit 5, Perivale Industrial Park, Perivale, Middlesex UB6 7RL
Tel. (020) 8997-9000, fax (020) 8997-9097.
Internet: www.portfoliobooks.com

Mail Order, Catalog, other International sales and rights, and Special Sales by
World Leisure Corporation, PO Box 160, Hampstead, NH 03841.
Tel. (877) 863-1966, fax (614) 388-2305.
E-mail: admin@worldleisure.com; Internet: www.skisnowboard.com.

ISBN: 0-915009-84-6   ISSN: 1072-8988   LCCN: 93-643936

Contents
by geographical regions

Western U.S. Resorts

Contributors

Charlie Leocha has skied virtually every major international resort. He writes about travel and skiing for magazines, newspapers and the Internet. Charlie is a black-diamond skier, but a double-diamond apres-skier. The rest of us bow to his energy and dancing ability. He's also the only staffer who knows which resorts have the best wine lists *and* the best bacon-and-eggs breakfasts. He is a member of the North American Snowsports Journalists Association (NASJA).

Steve Giordano is a veteran ski and travel journalist whose work has appeared in newspapers, magazines, books, radio and television. He used to be a ski patroller, but switched to ski journalism after pulling one too many drunks out of snowy creeks. A skier for more than 20 years, he switched to snowboarding long after reaching adulthood. He is a member of NASJA and SATW. He's also married to Lynn Rosen, and together they make sure our Northwest entries are up to date.

Lynn Rosen, an Emmy award-winning television and radio broadcaster, producer and director, is on the Journalism faculty at Western Washington University in Bellingham. She's also a theater critic and travel writer. Mountain scenery is quite dramatic, so it's fitting that Lynn belongs to the American Theater Critics Association as well as NASJA. She is one of the staff champion shoppers, an advocate for unique jewelry, shoes and clothing.

Mitch Kaplan took up the pen to support his inexhaustible ski habit and has been covering skiing, adventure and family travel ever since. He holds the unofficial New Jersey state record for the most consecutive days spent dreaming about playing in the snow. The author of several books and a member of NASJA, SATW and ASJA, he writes a ski column for *The Record*, New Jersey's second-largest daily. Mitch lives with his non-skiing wife, Penny, and two college-age children who won't empty the nest.

Claudia Carbone lives in the woods, minutes from Breckenridge in her native state of Colorado. For her, a great day is dancing through knee-deep powder. Claudia writes for many publications. Her groundbreaking book, *WomenSki*, established her as an authority on women's skiing. Claudia is a founder of Snow Sports Association for Women and is the recipient of the Lowell Thomas Award from Colorado Ski Country and NASJA's Excellence in Snowsports Journalism–Writing award. She also is past president of NASJA.

Hilary Nangle realized early in life that work didn't have to be drudgery. Much to her parents' dismay, she spent years working for whitewater rafting companies and ski resorts, before finally landing a real job as a journalist. She now freelances for travel and ski publications and appears as a TV travel expert. She's a member of NASJA (and has won its Excellence in Snowsports Journalism award), and the Society of American Travel Writers (SATW). Hilary lives in Maine with her husband, Tom, a photographer.

Peggy McKay Shinn, a Westerner at heart, is now a resident Vermonter. She has skied at most major U.S. resorts, where she seeks out terrain that makes the rest of us grow weak in the knees. A NASJA member, she cast aside a graduate degree in environmental engineering to write full time. She gives us the real scoop on child-care and nursery facilities. Much to her mother's dismay, motherhood has not slowed Peggy down.

Karen Cummings has been writing about skiing for more than a decade. She lives life, balanced between Boston and Maine, with a smile. Karen began skiing at the tender age of 25 and immediately discovered apres-ski—her specialty. These days her nightlife forays are "research." Karen is an expert shopper and has bought something at every resort she visits. She is also our cross-country aficionado who loves a workout with skating skis.

Andy Bill has been fighting with, and losing to, his inner nomad for at least 25 years—working as a journalist on three continents. Along the way he has contributed to America's leading travel publications. Recent exploits include becoming the 12,161st member of the Sourtoe Cocktail Club (an august, if unsavory, society based out of Dawson City in the Yukon), surviving another ski season, and picking up a Northern Lights award. As an avid, if erratic skier, he has left his mark on many a tree.

James Kitfield is an expert apres-skier who first met Charlie dancing in a conga line through a bar in Verbier, Switzerland. Life has been downhill since, at least as often as he can manage trips to the mountains. On the slopes he points his skis down double diamonds. Amazingly, he has a serious side. He has been awarded the Gerald R. Ford prize twice for distinguished defense reporting, and the Jesse H. Neal award for excellence in reporting.

Kari Haugeto and **Christopher Elliott** live in Florida, but spend all winter dreaming about powder days in the mountains. Kari writes about apres-ski and nightlife activities as the editor of Cocktail.com. And Christopher, who writes about consumer and business travel issues for publications such as *The New York Times, National Geographic Traveler* and *Forbes*, covers mountain activities.

Tom Patterson spends equal time on his board, skis and skinny skis, the latter usually with daughter Ella in a baby carrier. He is a NASJA member and skis all over northern New England and Quebec. He spends his days in the exciting world of student loans, but his passion includes regular snowsports contributions to weekly and monthly publications near his home in Portland, Maine.

Roger Lohr, our cross-country skiing guru, lives in New Hampshire. His claim to fame: He's traveled and been on the snow either cross-country skiing, telemarking or snowboarding in 27 different states or provinces in North America. He edits our sister website, XCSkiResorts.com, which provides information about where to go cross-country skiing, Top 10 lists and promotional news for cross-country ski resorts and product suppliers. He also conducts the industry statistics for the Cross Country Ski Areas Association; and writes for *Ski Area Management, Nordic Network* and many regional fitness and parenting magazines.

Vanessa Reese considers herself to be the world's first "black-diamond virtual skier." She works on *Ski Snowboard America and Canada* and *Ski Europe* and helped develop our website. Until a few years ago, the closest this Harvard graduate had ever come to a ski slope was Boston's blizzard of '78. Now she's visited several Western resorts, taken her first halting glides on cross-country skis, and discovered snow tubing and dogsledding.

Laurie Fullerton is a full-time journalist specializing in skiing and yatching — nice combination. She has edited magazines and newspapers and authored three guidebooks covering the Canadian Maritimes, New Caledonia and the Philipines. Her byline has appeared in the *South China Morning Post, New York Times, Miami Herald, Yatching Magazine, Sailing Magazine, Torronto Globe and Post* and others.

Phil Johnson is the president of NASJA, lives in upstate New York and has written travel, outdoor and ski columns for the regional papers for years.

Katy Keck, our gourmet consultant, is recognized as one of the Top 30 Women Chefs in The World. **Karuna Eberl, Bob Aubrey, Gavin Forbes Ehringer, Ammon Smith, Wade Nelson,** and **Erica Williams,** wrote some of our snowboarding coverage. Both **Susan Staples** and **Diane Scholfield** the ex-editors and proof readers, have their fingerprints and commas all over this book.

Plan your winter vacation
with Ski Snowboard America

Here's a book to help you branch out and to find the perfect ski resort (plus accommodations, restaurants and nightlife) to match your ability, your pocketbook and your interests. For overseas skiers, *Ski Snowboard America* offers insights to help you locate the resort that matches your dream of a North American ski vacation.

Not surprisingly, people take ski vacations for different reasons—for a romantic getaway, to have quality time with the family, to ski all-out with buddies, to ski a little and maybe shop a lot. And what happens when a hotshot skier travels with a first-timer or beginner? The average ski resort's brochure indicates that their resort is all things to all skiers—this is definitely not the case.

Ski Snowboard America is as straightforward and honest a guide to North America's top resorts as you can buy. Our goal is to match you with the right vacation spot. Our staff includes experts and intermediates (including some who learned as adults), Generation Xers and Baby Boomers, skiers and snowboarders, eggs-and-bacon breakfast eaters and gourmet-coffee-and-bagel fans. Each skier and snowboarder has various likes and dislikes, and resorts have different personalities. We recognize this—that's why we include our opinions and personal observations. We detail the personality of each resort: where we found the best skiing and snowboarding, where we liked to eat and where we enjoyed the liveliest off-slope fun. And we give you the facts and current prices, plus hotel and restaurant descriptions, lift ticket and lesson prices, children's programs, nightlife hot spots, and where to call, e-mail or write for more information.

What's new in this edition

Of course, prices, programs, lessons and facilities have been updated to provide the most accurate information available at press time about each resort. Some resorts have been completely transformed through new developments and new hotels.

The six Utah chapters covering Salt Lake City and ten nearby ski areas have been rewritten

---

A note about prices and older editions of this book

We make every attempt to include prices for the current ski season. Unfortunately, as of late August many resorts had not announced their new prices. Current prices have the 2006/07 notation. Where there is no notation, assume prices are from last season (2005/06). The text will normally specify which season. In recent years, ski resorts have created lift ticket prices for every occasion: prices for various age groups, various days, various times of the season, supermarket discounts, ad infinitum. It's getting to be just as complicated to purchase lift tickets as it is to buy your airline tickets.

Prices provided in this guidebook are in no way official and are subject to change at any time. In fact, prices do change with high and low seasons; and resorts sometimes announce one price in July, change it by November, and change prices again during the season.

Ski Snowboard America is published every fall, but sometimes bookstores have older copies in their inventory. If you are reading this book in Fall 2007 or after, get the latest edition. It can be found in most major bookstores or order it through www.amazon.com or www.barnesandnoble.com. Or, send a check for $24.95 plus $3.00 for

---

after our staff held its annual editorial meeting in the region this past winter. We stayed at five resorts as a group and individually fanned out to the rest. During the rest of winter, staff visited more than two dozen other resorts and updated and rewrote those chapters accordingly.

Keeping up with area code, resort, hotel, restaurant and price changes always keeps us busy. There are literally thousands of changes to the book each year.

Using the Internet—SkiSnowboard.com and XCSkiResorts.com

The development of the Internet has significantly changed the way people research and make reservations at ski resorts. Every world-class resort now has a website with basic information including statistics, lift tickets, ski school prices, and how to contact them. You even can book online on some of the more savvy resort sites.

We have gathered more information than we can possibly stuff into this guidebook, so if you want to know more about any of the resorts we review here, visit our websites, SkiSnowboard.com and XCSkiResorts.com. There you'll find additional facts, advice and words of wisdom; often you'll find out more about a resort than at the resort's own site. Indeed, few resorts work to promote the surrounding areas, but SkiSnowboard.com offers details about the surrounding areas as well as much more economical lodging and dining options. As prices change at each resort, we'll post that information.

We have included the Web addresses for every resort listed in this book. Use them as well as SkiSnowboard.com and XCSkiResorts.com to get the information you need.

Chapter organization

Each resort chapter has several sections. We begin by sketching the personality of the place—is it old and quaint, or modern and high-rise? Clustered at the base of the slopes, or a few miles down the road? Remote and isolated, or freeway-close? Family-oriented or catering to singles? Filled with friendly faces or an aloof herd of "beautiful" skiers?

The basic statistics of each resort include **addresses and phone numbers:** postal, e-mail, Internet, snow phones, toll-free—all of them that we could find.

A few important notes: The resort's **area code** is listed in the fact box and at the bottom of each even-numbered page. We don't list the local area code for every number in the chapter because you probably will use local numbers most often while you're at the resort (in the case of restaurants, for instance). Some of the fax numbers we list are for the ski area; others are for the central reservations office; some resorts don't have public fax numbers. In every instance, the Internet address we list is the officially sanctioned one maintained by the resort.

The **base and summit altitudes** are important for those with altitude-related medical difficulties or for sea-level dwellers who plan to hit the slopes the same day they arrive. **Vertical drop, skiable acreage** and **number and types of lifts** provide a good idea of the resort's size.

Our terrain stats reflect *lift-served* terrain. Examples: Keystone, Colo., lists its vertical as 3,128 feet; we list it as 2,630. If you want that maximum vertical, you must take a snowcat or hike the extra 498 feet to the in-bounds summit. Grand Targhee has two mountains totaling 3,000 acres, but 1,000 of that acreage is reserved for snowcat skiing and snowboarding. Exceptions like these are explained where they occur.

Uphill lift capacity is the number of riders the lift system can carry each hour. **Bed base** is the approximate number of people who can be accommodated overnight near the resort. If the uphill capacity is much bigger than the bed base, the result is usually shorter lift lines. (Resorts with great uphill capacity/bed base ratios may still have long weekend lines if they are near major cities—we try to identify these.)

We tell you how close the **nearest lodging** is, if the resort has **child care** and the youngest age accepted, and the number of **terrain parks and pipes**. The **lift ticket** price in the fact box tells the per-day range of the adult lift ticket. The lower price usually is the per-day cost of the adult five-day ticket, or it is the midweek price. The higher price is the weekend walk-up-to-the-window cost. Ticket prices in the stat box are intended as an approximation; look in the chapter for more details.

Finally, **we rate the slopes** (based on five ability levels), the **dining**, the **nightlife** and the **other activities**. One star means it's poor, two is OK, three is good, four is very good and five is outstanding. Ratings are quite subjective, but they are a general consensus of the *Ski Snowboard America and Canada* staff. We are simply trying to point you in the right direction.

Following the fact box is a detailed description of the mountain. **Mountain layout** describes various sections of the mountain best for skiers at each of five ability levels. The Ride Guide at the end of this section tells riders where to go and where the flats are. **Parks and pipes** gives you the inside scoop on terrain parks, snowcross courses, jib parks, rail parks, superpipes, halfpipes, minipipes and quarterpipes so you know which resorts are the most fun for skiers and riders who like to play on manmade terrain. We also point you in the direction of natural terrain features that will make your day on the mountain complete.

Cross-country and snowshoeing information will tell you which resorts have Nordic trails, as well as significant cross-country and backcountry skiing opportunities nearby, and snowshoe rental and tour information.

Lessons details instructional programs for adults, including any special programs and recreational racing. "First-timer package" refers to a package with a half-day or full-day first-time lesson, a lift ticket (often just for the beginner lift) and use of rental equipment.

KidStuff covers non-skiing nursery and day-care programs, children's ski and snowboard lesson programs, and special supervised activities available after the lifts close.

Lift tickets are listed using the age categories resorts use, such as adults, seniors, teens, juniors and children. We've organized them in a chart with one-day, three-day and five-day prices, followed by "Who skis free" and "Who skis at a discount" listed in paragraph form. Where prices are from last season, assume an increase of a couple of dollars.

Under **Accommodations** we list both the most luxurious places and many of the budget lodges, including features such as slopeside location, pools and hot tubs, health clubs and intra-resort transportation. We also suggest lodging that is particularly suited to families, and our favorite B&Bs and inns.

Dining always includes the gourmet restaurants, but we don't leave out affordable places where a hungry family or a snowboarder on a budget can chow down and relax. We have compiled these suggestions from dozens of interviews with locals and tourists, plus our own dining experiences.

Apres-ski/nightlife describes places to go when the lifts close, and where to find entertainment later in the evening. We tell you which bars are loud, which are quiet, what kind of music they play and whether they have live music.

Other activities covers off-slope activities—such as dogsledding, snowmobiling, ice skating, sleigh rides, shopping, fitness clubs and spas.

Getting there and getting around tells you how to get to the resort by air and car (and sometimes by train or bus), and whether a car is optional or necessary at the resort.

Types of accommodations

A **hotel** is relatively large, with 25 rooms or more, and comes without meals. If hotel rates include any meals, that is noted.

A **mountain inn** usually has fewer rooms than a hotel. Many have packages that include breakfast and dinner.

A **bed & breakfast (B&B)** tends to be even smaller, with just a few rooms. Most B&Bs have private baths now, so if guests must share a bath, we say so. Breakfast is included and some B&Bs also offer dinner.

Motels don't have the amenities of a hotel or the ambiance of a B&B, and often are farther from the slopes. Motels are good for families and budget-minded skiers.

Condominiums are the most affordable group lodging at North American ski resorts. They usually have a central check-in facility, and most have daily maid service for everything but the kitchen.

When you call the resort's central reservations number, ask for suggestions. Most of the staff have been on lodging tours and can make honest recommendations based on your needs. In the Canadian chapters, we note that prices are in Canadian currency, so take into account the exchange rate. Many higher-end accommodations and restaurants in Canada may actually be affordable for budget-conscious visitors from the U.S. and Europe, so at least consider them.

Where you find $$$ signs, refer to this legend (also found on the bottom of pages in each chapter):

Dining: $$$$-Entrees $30+; $$$-$20-$30; $$-$10-$20; $-less than $10.

Accommodations: (double room) $$$$-$200+; $$$-$141-$200; $$-$81-$140; $-$80 and less.

Regional resorts

Throughout the book you'll find coverage of regional resorts too. These resorts are best for weekend or short midweek visits by skiers and snowboarders who live in that region. When a regional resort can be a side trip from a destination resort, we have included the description within that chapter. Regional resorts that are not near a large destination resort are in separate mini-chapters throughout the book.

These ski areas all have the following common features, *unless otherwise noted:*

• lodging within a 20-mile radius (Note: Some of the phone numbers listed for lodging are reservations services; others just provide information about lodging in the area. If no phone number is listed for lodging, call the ski area.)

  • a day lodge with food service
  • adult and child ski and snowboard lessons (children usually start at age 4)
  • equipment rentals

We list toll-free phone numbers where available, plus the resort's recorded information line and website address. If you can't get a live voice from the info line, try the ski area's office number. (The toll-free numbers may not be applicable nationwide, since these resorts draw visitors primarily from the nearest urban areas.)

Ability levels

These are the terms we use in the "Mountain layout" and other sections:

● **First-timers** are just what the name implies. We apply the term to novices during their first couple of days on skis or a snowboard.

●● **Beginners** can turn and stop (more or less) when they choose, but still rely on snow-plow turns if on skis and sideslipping if on a snowboard. This group feels most comfortable on wide, fairly flat terrain.

■ **Intermediates** generally head for blue trails and parallel ski or link snowboard turns (more or less) on the smooth stuff. They return to survival technique on advanced trails, and struggle in heavy powder and crud.

♦**Advanced** skiers and boarders can descend virtually any trail with carved turns, but are still intimidated by deep powder, crud and super steeps. Advanced terrain by our definition includes moguls and glade skiing.

♦♦**Experts** favor chutes, tight trees on steep slopes, deep-powder bowls and off-piste exploration. True experts are few and far between.

Skiing at altitude

People who visit resorts at higher elevations should be aware of health symptoms specific to altitude and preventative measures that can make acclimating more tolerable. The reduced oxygen at altitude may cause shortness of breath, a rapid pulse, increased blood pressure, and foot and ankle swelling. Dehydration is also an issue, since humidity is low. Dehydration can sap energy, cause headaches and affect athletic performance. Drink enough water to cause urination at least every three hours.

The effects of alcohol and other drugs are dramatically increased at altitude. At 6,200 feet, the effect of alcohol doubles for those living at sea level. Hangovers also will be worse at altitude. Avoid alcohol for at least the first 24 hours.

Acute Mountain Sickness (AMS) ranges from mild headaches to incapacitating illness. Although it generally occurs when sleeping above 8,000 feet, some will develop symptoms at lower elevations. Symptoms include headache, nausea, insomnia, fatigue, lack of appetite and light-headedness. Symptoms should improve with a lower elevation, rest and fluids over 24 to 48 hours. A prescription called Diamox, if taken prior to arrival at elevation, might help prevent AMS. Alcohol, tranquilizers, sleep medications and antihistamines may make AMS worse. AMS can progress to a much more serious illness known as High Altitude Cerebral Edema (HACE). This medical emergency presents incapacitating headaches, neurological symptoms such as a "drunken" gait, and may proceed to a coma. Prompt emergency help is critical.

Altitude sickness is quite common among children during the first few days, especially for those who live at sea level. Be sure to have lots of water available and be sensitive to a child's complaints of discomfort.

Because there's less atmosphere to filter out ultraviolet rays, high altitude predisposes people to sunburn and snow blindness (sunburn of the eyes). Sun block is imperative, even if it's not a blue-sky day. Don't forget to protect ears and scalp. Use UV-filtering sunglasses.

Nosebleeds occur more frequently at high altitude due to the dry air, particularly in the early morning. Humidifiers and petroleum jelly usually help prevent this problem. Pinching the nose for five to 10 minutes should stop the bleeding.

Sugarloaf/USA
Maine

Summit elevation:	4,237 feet
Vertical drop:	2,820 feet
Base elevation:	1,417 feet

Address: 5092 Access Road
Carrabassett Valley, ME 04947
Area code: 207
Ski area phone: 237-2000
Snow report: 237-6808
Toll-free reservations: (800) 843-5623
or (800) 843-2732
Fax: 237-3768
E-mail: info@sugarloaf.com
Internet: www.sugarloaf.com
Expert:★★★★★
Advanced:★★★★★
Intermediate:★★★★
Beginner:★★★ **First-timer:**★★

Number and types of lifts: 15—2 high-speed
quads, 2 quads, 1 triple, 8 doubles, 2 surface
Skiable acreage: 1,400 acres
Snowmaking: 94 percent
Uphill capacity: 21,810 per hour
Parks & pipes: 3 parks, 3 pipes
Bed base: 5,400
Nearest lodging: Slopeside, condos and hotel
Resort child care: Yes, 10 weeks–5 years
Adult ticket, per day: $61 (05/06)

Dining:★★★
Apres-ski/nightlife:★★
Other activities:★★

Sugarloaf is unpretentious, genuinely friendly and as unaffected as an L.L. Bean boot. Although trend-conscious sophisticates might find it rough around the edges, Sugarloaf delivers the best alpine skiing and riding in New England. Just ask Torino Olympians—snowboard cross gold medalist Seth Wescott and alpine skiers Bode Miller and Kirsten Clark—who trained here as students at Carrabassett Valley Academy.

Narrow, serpentine Route 27 rounds Oh My Gosh corner and delivers the gasp-producing views of the mountain that earned the corner its name. It would be hard to find another ski area in North America with such presence. It commands the landscape, a perfect white-capped pyramid piercing the sky and laced with ribbons of trails. Sugarloaf is an oasis in the wilderness. While there are the requisite condominiums and a growing number of timber, glass and stone trophy homes, the compact base village and handful of restaurants and stores clustered near the access road and strewn along Route 27 are about it for shopping and dining. The good news is that because most of the restaurants are independently owned, the food is very good.

Sugarloaf's renowned for the only lift-serviced above-treeline terrain in the East, but don't let that scare you away. It is well-rounded, boundary-to-boundary, and will keep most anyone happy. That's no real surprise: With 1,400 acres, it's the largest resort in the East and, with the exception of Killington, it's about twice the size of the East's other largest resorts, Better yet: all that terrain is on one peak. Although some of the lifts need updating, the network is well planned. On all but the most crowded days, you can find lifts with short or no lines.

Like other northern New England resorts, the weather can be brutally cold, especially if the wind is honking. And during January, days seem almost cruelly short. But when the sun begins to peak over the mountaintop and things warm up, you won't find a better place to ski or party. The annual Reggae Weekend in April, when name bands play outdoors by The Beach, always sells out.

Mountain layout

The key to enjoying the 'Loaf is knowing how to move around the mountain without descending to the base. To do that, use the cross-cuts, which run more horizontally than vertically. Key cross-cut trails are Spillway, running east and west from the Spillway East chair apex; Peavy, which cuts across the mountain's midsection, running east, from Tote Road to Whiffletree; Mid-station, which cuts from Sluice, at the mountain's core, to Ramdown, connecting to King Pine area; and Lombard, which connects the top of Whiffletree with the base of Spillway. There are others, but locating these on your trail map will make navigating easier. Then there are the goat paths, which bisect glades and woods. If you want to avoid the occasional lift lines, use the Whiffletree and Bucksaw chairs and work your way over to the mid-mountain lifts that take you up higher.

♦♦**Expert:** This is a good all-around mountain for any level of skier, but what sets it apart is that it has enough steep and challenging runs to keep experts happily banging the boards all day. In addition to more than 500 acres of classic wooded New England ski trails, Sugarloaf also has 80 to 100 acres of treeless snowfields at the summit, where experts can experience Western-style, open-bowl skiing. Powder collects on the Backside, but the Front Face has some of the steepest terrain in New England; White Nitro literally falls away beneath you, and Gondi Line is a favorite for its consistent fall line. The downside is that only one lift, a fixed-grip quad, services the summit. Although it is much more reliable than the gondola it replaced, it still shuts down on occasion due to high winds.

Experts can easily figure out where to ski. Double-diamond on the trail map is the honest truth. Steep black runs beckon from the summit, and most also can be accessed from the East Spillway double chair. Bubble Cuffer, Winter's Way and Ripsaw are designated Wild Thing trails. They're rarely touched by a grooming machine, dependent upon natural snow and littered with moguls and natural obstacles. Misery Whip is an old T-bar line, cut straight and steep and rarely groomed. For serious bumps, head to Skidder, a training ground for the future Olympians attending Carrabasset Valley Academy.

With its boundary-to-boundary policy, Sugarloaf has glades too, and chances are you'll have them to yourself. Locals can be found almost anywhere in glades where they have spent the summers working with their own chainsaws.

♦**Advanced:** The blacks down to the King Pine quad are all sweet and steep, if a little short. Bump monkeys should head for Choker, a natural snow trail on this side of the mountain. Widowmaker to Flume is usually groomed, but best early in the day. Narrow Gauge is perhaps the 'Loaf's most famous trail. It's the only trail in the East that's FIS approved for all four World Cup Alpine disciplines. Usually groomed, but seldom seeing traffic, are Lower Gondi Line and Lower Wedge.

■ **Intermediate:** Advanced-intermediates will find that they can handle some of the single-diamond blacks on this mountain. With a few exceptions, the western half of the mountain is an intermediate playground. Tote Road and Timberline to Scoot are long (Tote Road is 3.5 miles) and wide cruisers that wind from the summit to the base—skiers can be on these trails for a half hour, notes one regular. Hayburner and King's Landing both swoop down a continuous fall line, making them ideal for cruising.

Ramdown, off the King Pine chair, has an often nasty first 25 yards, but work through it and be rewarded with a lovely cruise no matter which direction you choose. Ditto for Boomauger, when groomed.

Blueberry's Grove, between Cruiser and Whiffletree, and Ram Pasture Glade, off the lower part of Tote Road, are good introductions to tree skiing. Adventurous kids and playful adults duck off Lombard Cross-cut into Rookie River, where you work your way down a small frozen waterfall before following a winding riverbed. Don't be surprised if the kids have more gumption than the adults; they have shorter skis and boards.

●● **Beginner:** At the base of the mountain, beginners will find the very broad and very gentle Boardwalk run. Those looking for a little more challenge graduate to Lower Winter's Way (secluded with little traffic), off the Double Runner chairs, and from there to the Whiffletree quad. When you're comfortable on the Whiffletree trails, head for the summit and take a run leisurely run down Timberline, a wide scenic trail that eases down the mountain's western edge before it connects with Tote Road. Be forewarned: The Chicken Pitch section of Tote Road is a notorious trouble spot, especially later in the day, when it becomes a body slalom.

Terrain off the pokey Bucksaw chair offers a bit more challenge: a steeper pitch or narrower trails. The plus here is that these trails get very little traffic.

● **First-timer:** First-timers start on the long, gentle Birches slope, served by two chairlifts, Snubber and Sawduster. This is a great learning slope with only one caveat: It also is the access slope for a lot of slopeside lodging, so first-timers should quit a little early.

Ride Guide: SuperQuad area: Double Bitter or Wedge are winding and narrow, with natural bank turns and drop-offs. Skidder has a natural quarterpipe, rider's right. King's Landing and Hayburner have natural knolls. West Mountain is ideal for novices and lower intermediates, with long, gentle cruising trails that incorporate some steeps at the beginning. West Mountain trail also has some nice banks on the rider's left, but beware of the clearance underneath the double chair and be sure to cut right toward Windrow near the end of the steeps.

King Pine area: Misery Whip is at most 9 feet wide and usually ungroomed and full of huge whale-size bumps of stored-up snow. Take Boomauger to gain speed and lay down huge carves. Rip Saw and the Rip Saw Glades have nice drop-offs on rider's left at the beginning. Try to avoid returning to the base via Cross Haul from here. Some sections are pretty darn flat and you could end up hoofing it. Best choice is to ride the lift up and work your way back towards the middle of the mountain.

Parks and pipes

Riders who visit Sugarloaf continue to reap the rewards of the resort's mutually beneficial relationship with Carrabassett Valley Academy (CVA). In partnership with CVA, Sugarloaf built a piece de resistance of Alpine terrain elements on the lower mountain between Lower Winter's Way and the former gondola lift line. The park is an extension of the prestigious ski and snowboard academy's off-mountain Anti-Gravity Complex, a multimillion-dollar training facility for all race disciplines. The park also is the site of Sugarloaf's competition superpipe—Pipe Dreams—which is more than 400 feet long with 16-foot walls. This location provides the consistent 22-degree pitch preferred for world-class pipe events. The superpipe is named in recognition of U.S. Snowboard Team member Seth Wescott. Wescott is a graduate of CVA and is living his dreams by competing on the FIS World Cup circuit and will lead the U.S. team in the latest Olympic event: the snowboard cross. In addition to the Pipe Dreams Superpipe, the Pipeline trail, which leads to the superpipe, hosts a rail park that includes up to 5 rails to test jibbers' skills. CVA's freeride and snowboard teams designed both the superpipe and park elements in what is being touted as an expert-only terrain playground. Access to the park is easy and efficient via the Double Runner East (Short Side) chairlift.

Upper-immediate and advanced freeriders will still find plenty of air in The Stomping

Grounds, where challenging elements and a mellowed version of the superpipe provide a place for up-and-coming snowboarders to perfect tricks. The learning pipe is also nearly 400 feet long, but the 10-foot walls are more forgiving of mistakes. The Stomping Grounds and learning pipe are on Chaser, accessible via either the Sugarloaf SuperQuad or the Double Runner West (Long Side) chairlift. For newbie tricksters, the Quarantine Zone, on Cruiser under the Whiffletree SuperQuad, offers a number of non-intimidating terrain elements to get the hang of air time. Just for kids is Moose Alley, a wiggle through the woods off Cruiser.

 ## Cross-country and snowshoeing (visit xcskiresorts.com for more details)

The **Sugarloaf/USA Outdoor Center** (237-6830) is the largest and most complete in Maine, with 105 km. of trails groomed with double tracks and lanes for skating. The center is off Rte. 27, south of the resort access road. Three trails reach it from the resort's lodging facilities and the village area. The center also has a lighted Olympic-sized outdoor skating rink and a 6,000-square-foot lodge with a giant fireplace, a south-facing deck, and food and drink at the Bull Moose Café, a locals' favorite.

Group and private lessons are available, as are equipment rentals. Multiday ticket holders may exchange a day of downhill for a day of cross-country including trail fee, lesson and equipment. Exchange tickets at the guest services desk in the base lodge.

Snowshoers may use the machine-packed portion of all the cross-country trails as well as access backcountry trails. Snowshoe programs include the guided Snowshoe Safari, Women's Stew & Shoe Tour and moonlight tours. Snowshoe rentals are available.

 ## Lessons (05/06 prices)

Group lessons: The ski school uses the Perfect Turn ® program, which has 10 levels of clinics. For lower-intermediates and above, the clinics normally last 90 minutes with a maximum of 11 clients. Enrollees watch a short video that demonstrates various ability levels. This eliminates the "ski-off," which can take up 40 minutes of a two-hour lesson. Clinics meet three times each morning and cost $30.

First-timer package: Perfect Turn clinics for first-timers to beginners are 90 minutes to two hours. Reservations are requested. The $75 Level 1 package includes the clinic, equipment, and a lift ticket for learning lifts. The resort guarantees Level 1 skiers that they will be able to ride a lift, turn and stop by the end of the clinic, or they can repeat it free or get their money back. Levels 2–3 cost $75 per clinic, or three for $165.

Learn-to-Ride programs start at $75 and include coaching, equipment and a lift ticket.

Private lessons: $75 for one hour, with discounts for multiple hours.

Special programs: The Women's Turn program offers three- and five-day programs with at least five instruction hours on the snow and after-ski activities. The cost is $399 for three days and $699 for five, which includes clinics, lift tickets, lunch and activities. Special 90-minute Women's Turn clinics are $30.

 ## KidStuff (05/06 prices)

Childcare: Child care and children's programs are far from an afterthought at the Loaf; it is obvious that a positive overall experience for visiting families is the number-one priority. The child care center is conveniently located trailside in Gondola Village, adjacent to the Base Lodge and on the primary on-mountain shuttle route. The facility is sizable, accommodating as many as 82 children, including up to 12 infants and 15 toddlers. Staff members are seasoned, averaging more than 10 years at Sugarloaf. Many of the seasonal employees are students in the early childhood education program at the University of Maine in Farmington. The center is licensed and maintains more staff than required by state law — one care provider for every three infants or four toddlers. Sugarloaf's spacious child center is staffed by caring and nurturing workers. Some vacationers come here specifically because it is so good. The center takes children ages 10 weeks to 5 years. A full day costs $55, a half day is $35; full day with skiing is $68, half day with skiing is $52. Reservations are required; call (207) 237-6959.

Special activities: Younger children will be thrilled to see one of four mascots in the child care center or skiing with them on-mountain. Amos the Moose, Pierre the Lumberjack, Blueberry the Bear and Lemon the Yellow-Nosed Vole all have fascinating stories behind them. The mountain provides age-appropriate programmed activities almost every night for children ages 5 to 12. Older kids enjoy tubing, snowshoeing or the Antigravity complex, while game, movie and pizza nights appeal to all ages.

Children's lessons: Perfect Kids programs are available for ages 3–14. Ages 3–6 get lessons, lift tickets and lunch for $68; a half day without lunch is $52. Rentals are extra. Ages 7–14 pay $60 for a full-day lesson and lunch, and $45 for a half day without lunch; lift tickets and rentals are extra. Reservations are required at least 48 hours in advance. Teens ages 15–18 can join the Mountain Experience clinic program or take adult lessons. Moose Alley is a special kids-and-instructors-only section of the mountain where kids can do some controlled tree skiing.

Lift tickets (05/06 prices)

	Adult	Junior (6-12)	Young Adult (13-18)
One day	$61	$39	$55
Three days	$171($57/day)	$102($34/day)	$150 ($50/day)
Five days	$275 ($55/day)	$165($33/day)	$245($49/day)

Who skis free: Children ages 5 and younger; however, they must have a lift ticket, which can be obtained at a ticket window.

Who skis at a discount: Seniors 65 and older pay junior prices. Purchase tickets online more than 14 days in advance and receive a 10-percent discount. College students with ID card can ski or ride for $30 during special college breaks; call for details.

Note: Holiday prices are higher.

Accommodations

Sugarloaf is a condominium community. Packages at the Grand Summit include adult group lessons and use of its private health spa, while the condos and Sugarloaf Inn include adult group lessons and use of the Sugarloaf Sports & Fitness Club (see *Other Activities*). Make reservations at (800) 843-5623.

The **Grand Summit Resort Hotel** ($$–$$$$) is the centerpiece of the Alpine village. It has a small health club with indoor pool, restaurant and lounge. The slopeside **Sugarloaf Inn** ($$–$$$) has a New England inn ambiance.

More than 900 condo units are designed so skiers and snowboarders can slide back to their lodging. Not all have lift access, but a shuttle runs from the lodging to the lifts. Families like the **Gondola Village** units because they are close to the child-care facility and designated family skiing trails are right outside the door. The **Bigelow, Snowflower** and **Commons** units are more luxurious. **Sugartree** units offer easy access to the health club, and **Snowbrook** has its own indoor pool. **Timberwind** has rather small units but boasts its own outdoor hot tub,

Dining: $$$$-Entrees $30+; $$$-$20-$30; $$-$10-$20; $-less than $10.
Accommodations: (double room) $$$$-$200+; $$$-$141-$200; $$-$81-$140; $-$80 and less.

is across from the fitness club and right next to the Snubber chairlift.

There is an RV area serviced by lifts. It costs $10 per night, with electrical hook-up.

For more affordable lodging, try Kingfield, 15 miles south of the mountain, or Stratton, 7 miles north. **Three Stanley Avenue Bed & Breakfast** (265-5541; $), in Kingfield, is a Victorian-style B&B, where six rooms have private or shared bath. In Stratton, the **Spillover Motel** (246-6571; $) has clean rooms at reasonable rates. For budget accommodations, call The **Widow's Walk** (800-943-6995 or 246-6901; $), a no-frills bed and breakfast.

Dining

Sugarloaf is compact, but it has 18 eateries that range from pizza and burgers to fine dining. The best part is many offer ski-in/ski-out lunches, a big plus for those who dislike crowded base lodges. If you're visiting Sunday through Thursday, ask where the two-for-one specials are that night.

On Wednesdays, Saturdays and more often during holiday time, Sugarloaf's on-mountain restaurant, **Bullwinkle's** (237-6939; $$$$) is transformed into an almost-elegant retreat. The price includes a snowcat ride to the restaurant and a four-course candlelight dinner.

While food in the base lodge is pretty good, it adds up very quickly. However, the independent restaurants in the base village provide more bang for the buck. Both **Gepetto's** (237-2192; $–$$) and **The Bag** (237-2451; $–$$) are perennial favorites for lunch and dinner. Gepetto's has the more varied menu, with soups, salads, sandwiches and entrees. The Bag, a brewpub, is THE place for soups, burgers and pizzas. Rate the local talent on Blues Monday, while scarfing down a Bag-burger. **D'Ellie's** (237-2490; $), a small, mostly take-out bakery/deli, serves excellent homemade soups, huge sandwiches (on homemade bread) and good salads. Avoid lunch crowds by ordering in the morning for later pick-up at the Express Lane. It also serves the best full breakfast on the mountain. For the region's best cuppa Joe and a bagel, head to **Java Joes** (237-3330; $). **The Rack** (237-2211; $–$$$) has pretty good barbecue fare.

If any restaurant gives meaning to the phrase "don't judge a restaurant by its exterior," it's **Hug's** (237-2392; $–$$), a hole-in-the-wall about 2 miles from the mountain's access road. Go for northern Italian food, accompanied by betcha-can't-eat-just-one-piece pesto bread and a family-style salad. **Tufulio's** (235-2010; $–$$), in Carrabassett Valley has huge portions and a family friendly atmosphere). Also in the valley is the **Carrabassett Inn** (235-3888; $–$$), a good choice for burgers and pizza anytime or passable Mexican fare on Mondays.

In Kingfield, **One Stanley Avenue** (265-5541; $$$) is the most expensive restaurant in the region and offers the only true fine dining experience in the area. **The Herbert** (265-2000; $$–$$$) is hit or miss, a better bet is fireside dining at **Julia's** (265-5421; $$), in **The Inn on Winter's Hill**; ask about wine tastings. Far less fancy is **Longfellow's Restaurant & Riverside Pub** (265-4394, $–$$) with its wide-ranging menu and good, filling food. For lighter fare, head to **The Orange Cat** (265-2860; $) or the **Old School House Cafe & Bakery** (265-2323; $). Both serve tasty homemade soups, creative sandwiches and baked goods. For a serious breakfast, fill up at **The Kingfield Woodsman** (265-2561; $).

About 15 minutes north of the Access Road, in the wilds of Eustis, the **Porter House** (246-7932; $$) draws diners from Rangeley to Quebec. New, locally renowned chef-owners in 2005 kept the fancier fare downstairs. Upstairs is now the **Heron Pub**, serving lighter fare. In Stratton, the $7.95 Friday night Fish Fry at the White Wolf Restaurant (246-2922, $–$$) satisfies the tummy grumblings of those on a lean budget; good burgers, too.

Stock up on groceries at Hannaford's in Farmington for the best selection and price. Tranten's, in Kingfield, is a small grocery store with an o.k. meat and deli department. Fill in the cracks at one of three smaller grocery stores, all under the same ownership: Sugarloaf Groceries in the base village, Mountainside Grocers at the base of the access road, which has the biggest selection of the three, and Ayotte's, down valley.

 ## Apres-ski/nightlife

On sunny days, apres-skiers crowd the decks of The **Beach**, in front of the base lodge. **Gepetto's** Side Bar and **The Bag** are also lively on weekends. The hot spot for live music and dancing at night is the **Widowmaker Lounge**. For a more subdued atmosphere, try the **Sugarloaf Inn**, home of the **Shipyard Brewhouse** or The **Double Diamond Steakhouse and Pub** in the Grand Summit Resort Hotel.

Judson's, on Rte. 27, is a favorite with locals as well as UMaine and Colby College students. **Tufulio's** has a popular happy hour with locals and the middle-aged set.

Preteens have **Pinocchio's**, downstairs from Gepetto's, with video games, pinball and board games.

 ## Other activities

Sugarloaf has a **Turbo Tubing** park with its own lift and four 1,000-foot chutes. The park is open various days depending on the season, with one session midweek and two on weekends. The fee is $12 per session. The **Anti-Gravity Complex** (referred to as the AGC), at the base of the access road, provides a place to work off any energy not burned on the slopes. It boasts one of the highest **indoor climbing walls** in New England as well as an **indoor skating park, basketball court, track, weight room, trampolines, aerobic programs** and more. The **Sugarloaf Sports & Fitness Club**, free to on-mountain guests, has an **indoor pool, indoor and outdoor hot tubs, steam room, sauna, weight room, racquetball courts, indoor climbing wall, Internet cafe and massage services.**

Dogsledding, horse-drawn sleigh rides, snowmobiling, ice fishing and **skating** are among the activities that Sugarloaf Guest Services can arrange (237-2000).

Special events: Sugarloaf rolls back prices during **White White World Week**, held in late January. The annual **Reggae Weekend**, usually in mid-April, is a two-day bash with indoor and outdoor reggae bands. Book well in advance, as it usually sells out.

The village has just a few **shops**. Goldsmith Gallery sells gold and silver jewelry, photo frames, and similar items.

 ## Getting there and getting around

By air: The closest commercial airport is the Portland International Jetport. There's also a small regional airport in Augusta. Bangor International Airport is also an access point. Guests who fly into Bangor or Portland and who reserve lodging and lift stays through Sugarloaf/USA reservations can reserve transportation at the time of booking. There is an airstrip for private planes in Carrabassett Valley.

By car: Take I-95 north to Augusta, Rte. 27 north through Farmington and Kingfield. Or take the Maine Turnpike to the Auburn exit, Rte. 4 to Farmington and Rte. 27 through Kingfield. The drive is about 2.5 hours from Portland.

Getting around: A car is optional—nearly everything in the resort is within walking distance. A free on-mountain shuttle runs on weekends and during holiday periods and is on call during the week. To do anything away from the resort complex, you will need a car.

Dining: $$$$–Entrees $30+; $$$–$20-$30; $$–$10-$20; $–less than $10.
Accommodations: (double room) $$$$–$200+; $$$–$141-$200; $$–$81-$140; $–$80 and less.

Nearby resort

Maine Saddleback, Rangeley, ME; (207) 864-5671

Internet: www.saddlebackmaine.com

5 lifts: 1 quad, 2 doubles, 2 tows; 58 trails; 132 acres; 2,000 vertical feet; 1 terrain park

What a sleeper! Underdeveloped, uncrowded, untamed are the words most often used to describe this area just 45 minutes from Sugarloaf, but that's changing. Since purchasing the resort in 2003, the Berry family, longtime Saddlebackers and area residents, have been infusing much-needed cash into improvements, upgrades and expansion.

For starters, rates were lowered and trail names reverted to their original ones, honoring fly-fishing lures. The past seasons saw a new quad servicing a new beginner area, the much-needed renovation and expansion of the base lodge (now with espresso bar and humongous stone fireplace), improved snowmaking and grooming, a halfpipe, paving of the access road (yippee!), new intermediate and expert trails and kiddie and expert glades.

Still, Saddleback remains an old-fashioned, family area, where it seems everyone knows just about everyone else. The base lodge is filled with brown-bags at lunch, and this isn't discouraged. Smiles are genuine; greetings warm.

Even in a bad snow year, Saddleback is blessed with an abundance of snow, an average of 200 inches each year. You can find powder stashes here long after they've been exhausted at nearby Sugarloaf or Sunday River.

In general, trails get progressively more difficult as you progress from east to west, with the most expert terrain, including some serious glades, on the top third of the mountain. Most trails are narrow, winding through birches and hardwoods and offering views of Saddleback Lake and the surrounding wilderness. From the summit (accessed via T-bar), you can gaze over the wind-stunted trees across the Rangeley Lakes to the Presidential Range and Mt. Washington. The middle chunk of the mountain is ideal for intermediates.

The lower third, especially the new terrain below the base lodge, is designed for beginners. The gentle learning area with its own chairlift and choice of trails attracts young families, first-timers and the not-yet confident.

The drawback to Saddleback is the lift system. The double chair serving the main core of the mountain is aged and slow. The only way to the summit is a T-bar, with a steep, often-icy track with no escape hatches. What is planned is an expansion of intermediate terrain and the eventual addition of another quad chair servicing it from a new base.

Saddleback has on-mountain condominium lodging, but you'll have to make your own entertainment here when the lifts close. Rangeley, 7 miles from the base, is a good-sized town with at least a dozen restaurants and a good range of lodging. There's an excellent Thai restaurant at the base of the Access Road.

Child care is available for children ages 8 weeks to 8 years.

Lift tickets (05/06): Adults, $39; ages 13–18 and college students, $31; ages 7–12, $29. Seniors 70 and older and children 6 and younger, free. Half-day tickets are available.

Distance from Boston: About 5-plus hours. Take I-95 North to the Maine Turnpike, get off at Exit 12 and follow Rte. 4 north through Farmington to Rangeley.

Lodging information: For the limited number of condos on the mountain (400 trailside), call the ski area number, (207) 864-5671. To reach the Rangeley Chamber of Commerce, call (800) 685-2537.

Sunday River
Maine

Summit elevation:	**3,140 feet**
Vertical drop:	**2,340 feet**
Base elevation:	**800 feet**

Address: P.O. Box 450
Bethel, ME 04217
Area code: 207
Ski area phone: 824-3000
Fax: 824-5110
Snow report: (207) 824-5200;
Toll-free reservations: (800) 543-2754
E-mail: info@sundayriver.com
Internet: www.sundayriver.com
Expert: ★★
Advanced: ★★★
Intermediate: ★★★★
Beginner: ★★★★★
Never-ever: ★★★★★

Number of lifts: 18—4 high-speed quads,
5 quads, 4 triples, 2 doubles, 3 surface lifts
Snowmaking: 92 percent
Skiable acreage: 663 acres
Uphill capacity: 32,000 per hour
Parks & Pipes: 4 parks, 3 pipes
Bed base: 6,000 on mountain; 2,000 nearby
Nearest lodging: Slopeside
Resort child care: Yes, 6 weeks to 6 years
Adult ticket, per day: $56 (04/05 price)
Dining: ★★
Apres-ski/nightlife: ★★
Other activities: ★★

In the beginning, there was the mountain, and God made snow and taught Les Otten to make snow and brought him to Bethel, Maine, and commanded him to make the mountain white. And Otten came. He carpeted the slopes with guaranteed snow, expanded the terrain to adjacent peaks, added high-speed lifts to access them and built condos to house the masses that followed The True Way. So begins the gospel of Sunday River. Les Otten is gone, but the True Believers remain, and Sunday River continues to prosper, despite benign neglect by distant owner American Ski Company.

The "Rivah" sprawls across eight connected mountains in the Sunday River Valley. For all its vertical, Sunday River is very horizontal, spreading more than 3.5 miles across those peaks. Those unfamiliar with the terrain can feel as if they're spending more time getting from one place to another than skiing. Keep a trail map handy, because you're going to need it.

Sunday River can suffer from its own popularity. Its trails can be crowded, and the frequent intersections are accidents waiting to happen. Hint: To avoid crowds, consider starting the day at Jordan Bowl and working back across the general flow of traffic (an ideal scenario for those staying at the Jordan Grand Hotel). Still, the plusses far outweigh the drawbacks. Sunday River's impressive size yields plentiful and varied terrain; its efficient lift system makes it pretty easy to get around; and its stellar snowmaking and grooming make skiing and riding here a delight.

Sunday River lacks a true center. It has three separate base lodges: South Ridge, Barker Mountain and White Cap and the on-mountain North Peak Lodge. Six miles south is the antidote to the on-mountain modernity, the lovely town of Bethel, with its white-steepled churches and Victorian homes. Classic country inns and historical houses-turned-B&Bs provide lodging for those seeking New England charm. Bethel has a surprising variety of restaurants, from Korean to Texas-style barbecue. The free Mountain Explorer shuttle bus operates between village and mountain, and a free, on-mountain trolley connects base lodges and hotels .

Mountain layout

♦♦Expert ♦Advanced: Oz is a playground for high-level sliders. Served by a fixed-grip quad, it features a 500-yard-wide steep swath with tree islands and glades.

Aurora Peak, served by a quad chair and a triple chair, is still the spot to find tough skiing. Northern Lights provides an easier way down the mountain though it's no stroll through the park. Celestial, reached from Lights Out, is one of the nicest gladed trails.

From the top of Barker Mountain, a steep trio—Right Stuff, Top Gun and Agony—provide advanced skiers long, sustained pitches. Agony and Top Gun are premier bump runs. Right Stuff is a cruiser early in the day after it's been groomed, but normally develops moguls by afternoon. Tree-skiing fans will find the Last Tango glade between Right Stuff and Risky Business to be a natural-slalom area. It's the gentlest and most spacious of the resort's nine mapped glades. From the top of Locke Mountain, T2 plunges down the tracks of an old T-bar.

White Heat is a wide swath straight down the mountain from White Cap. Double-diamond Shockwave, considered by many as tougher than White Heat, has 975 vertical feet of bumps and steep pitches. Two gladed areas, Hardbal and Chutzpah, start out deceptively mellow and open-spaced, but watch out. Technically, they are the most demanding on the mountain.

■ **Intermediate:** Advanced intermediates are at home at Sunday River. The top of North Peak has the largest concentration of blue runs, though there's an intermediate way down from the top of every peak. For the most part, these are wide, undulating trails, such as Obsession off White Cap. Jordan Bowl provides some of the best blue-square cruising in New England down Excalibur and Rogue Angel, with the wide-open Blind Ambition glade accessed by the mellow cruiser Lollapalooza. An advanced-intermediate trail is Monday Mourning, which starts out steep and wide but mellows near the end where the race arena is located. Lower intermediates can head to the White Cap quad (far left on the map) and enjoy the relatively mellow Moonstruck, Starburst and Starlight runs. Off Barker Mountain, Lazy River is narrow by Sunday River standards and a fun cruise, but it can be strewn with people during busy times, since it's the main route to adjoining Spruce Peak.

●● **Beginner:** Once a skier is past the basic snowplow and into easy turns, much of Sunday River beckons. The North Peak triple chair reaches long practice runs like Dream Maker. Lollapalooza, the green-circle trail in Jordan Bowl, is "like Dream Maker on steroids," as one frequent visitor said. It's long and wide with great views, but not a trail that beginners should start out on; the upper part can get bumped up on busy days and probably should have a blue rating. Farther down it's quite mellow.

● **First-timer:** First-timers start on Sundance and then have the entire South Ridge area to practice their turns. Twelve beginner runs in the South Ridge area are serviced by a high-speed quad, a triple, a double and a surface lift. Beware, this area can become very busy.

Ride Guide: Some favorite riders' trails are on Jordan Bowl, but it's a pain in the glutes, calves and feet to get there and back. You either have to hike to the #13 lift, which brings you to a somewhat maneuverable pitch, or chance the possibility of having to unstrap and skate your way over the dreaded Kansas trail, a long and almost uphill traverse. We're definitely a long way from home, Toto. The Aurora basin, where the Jordan Mountain double drops you, also is a trek across a couple football fields to the North Peak triple chairlift. Instead, jump on the Aurora Quad and ride back to the main mountain from the top. Other flat spots to avoid at all costs are Three Mile Trail, Southway and Easy Street. For bumps, try Agony; for trees, head into Wizard's Gulch; for cruising, you can't beat Cascades or Obsession.

Parks and pipes

Sunday River's commitment to Alpine terrain playgrounds is as strong as any major resort, as evidenced by a full-time parks and pipes manager on the operations staff. The resort consistently responds to its freeriders with innovative park designs and new or larger elements. The park plan mirrors the trail plan with something for every level of rider, in a progression of four parks spread across different mountain peaks.

Whoville on South Ridge is designed for kids with many snow features like bank turns, a 10-foot jump, and a few rollers and small rails. The South Ridge Jib Park, near the minipipe on Easy Street is still perfect for novices, but with a bit bigger rails. Next on the difficulty scale is 3D Park on the 3D trail on North Peak. It's served by a high-speed quad, making it easy to do laps in the park. The hits here are larger and the rails and flat boxes longer for the upper-intermediate rider. It also has a mini mogul course with airs. The premier expert park is Rocking Chair Park, directly beneath the Barker quad and in plain view of thousands. The park features a little bit of everything, including 40-foot jumps, a 48-foot C box and S box, 24-foot connectable boxes, saddle boxes, 30-foot flat-down boxes, rainbow and battleship rails, and a wall ride. Rocking Chair finishes up with a nice quarterpipe. The superpipe is near the Locke Mountain triple chair. The Starlight Park at White Cap is a boardercross course.

The parks and pipes benefit from state-of-the-art maintenance equipment and the mountain's legendary snowmaking system. The superpipe, across from the Locke Mountain triple chairlift, gets carved frequently by a Zaugg Pipe Monster. A Terrain Master Park Cat is also put to use by a seasoned crew that samples its work daily and demands excellent results. Sunday River commit early-season snowmaking to opening its parks as early as possible. In most seasons, the mountain operates its superpipe and a couple of parks by Christmas.

 ## Cross-country and snowshoeing (visit xcskiresorts.com for more details)

Sunday River lacks a dedicated cross-country center, but some of New England's best Nordic skiing and snowshoeing can be found within an hour's drive. Golf-course skiing, with some wooded trails, is available at the Bethel Inn Cross-Country Ski Center (824-2175). The center has 40 km. of trails, 30 km. are groomed for both diagonal and skate skiing. Rentals, lessons and evening sleigh rides are available. The many gentle trails make this a great place for novices to learn. Midweek, the trail fee allows entrance to the outdoor heated pool, sauna and fitness center, until 4 p.m.

The Sunday River Inn's Sunday River Ski Touring Center (824-2410), on the Sunday River access road, has 40 km. of trails, with 2 km. lit for night skiing. It's family oriented, with warming shelters, an overnight yurt, a groomed dog trail, a downhill practice area and instruction, plus ice skating, snowshoeing, sleigh rides, and an outdoor hot tub and sauna .

Owned by an ex-cross-country ski racer, Carter's Cross-Country Ski Center (539-4848) has two locations. One, on Intervale Road, just 5 miles from Sunday River, has great views of the downhill area. It has 60 km. of trails for all levels (half groomed) and a backcountry experience with rustic get-away cabins. Carter's Cross-Country Center in Oxford, off Rte. 26, is an alternative, with 25 km. of tracks. Forty-five minutes from Bethel is the **Jackson Ski Touring Center** (603-383-9355) in New Hampshire's Mt. Washington Valley.

Snowshoe tours and guided fireworks snowshoe treks depart from the Nite Cap Fun Center at Sunday River; snowshoe rentals are available. Bethel Outdoor Adventures (824-4224) also offers snowshoeing tours.

Lessons (05/06 prices)

Group lessons: This resort created the innovative teaching program called Perfect Turn®. It combines state-of-the-art ski technique with state-of-the-art educational theory. The Sprint Perfect Turn Discovery Center offers one-stop shopping: Lift tickets, lessons and rental equipment are all in one spot.

Perfect Turn has eight levels. For lower intermediates and higher, the clinics normally last 90 minutes with a maximum of six skiers. Skiers watch a short video that demonstrates various levels of skiing ability. The video eliminates the "ski-off," which usually takes up about 40 minutes of a two-hour lesson. Clinics run about every half hour and cost $30.

First-timer package: The Learn-to-Ski and Ride package includes the clinic, equipment rental and a lift ticket for the South Ridge and North Peak. It costs $80 for Level 1. Sunday River guarantees Level 1 skiers will be able to ride a lift, turn and stop by the end of the clinic, or they can either repeat it free or get their money back. A two-day clinic costs $125.

Private lessons: $75 per hour, additional person is $40; $200 for a half day; $380 for a full day. Discounts available for a second person in the lesson.

KidStuff (05/06 prices)

Child care: Available for children 6 weeks to 6 years. All-day programs are $55, including lunch; half-day programs are $35. Bring diapers, formula and food for infants. Reservations are required. Call 824-5959. The main child care facility is at South Ridge. Child care, day and evening, is also available at the Grand Summit Resort Hotel and the Jordan Grand Resort Hotel.

Children's lessons: Sunday River's children's programs are among the best-organized and smoothest-running at any resort. The flow from equipment rental to classes is outstanding and all facilities are separate, which makes dealing with youngsters much easier.

Tiny Turns is a one-hour private lesson for 3-year-olds that's part of a half- or full-day session in day care. Cost is $62 for a half day; $78 for a full day.

Mogul Munchkins is for ages 3–6 (skiing only). A full-day clinic with lunch costs $68; $78 with rentals. Half-day clinics are $52; $62 with rentals. Lift tickets are included.

Mogul Meisters is for ages 7–14 (skiing and snowboarding). Full-day costs $65; $80 with rentals. Half-day clinics cost $48; $63 with rentals. Lift tickets are extra.

Lift tickets (05/06 prices)

	Adult	Young adult (13-18	Jnrs.(6-12) Srs. (65+)
One day	$59	$54	$41
Three days	$156 ($52/day)	$147 ($49/day)	$102 ($34/day)
Five days	$250 ($50/day)	$230 ($46/day)	$165 ($33/day)

Note: No midweek discounts; holiday tickets are $1 to $2 more for adults and young adults.

Who skis free: Children ages 5 and younger with parent.

Ages 65 and older pay junior rates.

Multiresort discounts: Sunday River is one of the American Skiing Company (ASC) resorts. ASC has set up a discount lift ticket website at www.sundayriver.com/metickets.html.

Accommodations

The Summit hotels and condominiums are the most convenient to the slopes. But Bethel also has a group of excellent B&Bs and old country inns. Call central reservations (800-543-2754) for any of the resort condos and hotels.

The Jordan Grand Resort Hotel and Conference Center ($$–$$$$) is slopeside to Jordan Bowl, but miles by car or shuttle to the rest of the resort. Enjoy spa, indoor/outdoor pool, full-service health club, child care. Be forewarned: The walls are not well soundproofed.

The Grand Summit Resort Hotel and Conference Center ($$–$$$$) is trailside with a 25-meter heated outdoor pool, athletic club and one of the resort's better restaurants. The Snow Cap Inn is a short walk from the slopes; the Snow Cap Ski Dorm next door offers affordable digs. All but the dorm offer packages with lift tickets.

Sunday River has nine condominium complexes; all are convenient to the slopes and have trolley service. Locke Mountain Townhouses are the most upscale, but hard to book. The ideally situated Merrill Brook condominiums are not far behind.

Less than a mile from the area, the **Sunday River Inn** (824-2410; $–$$$) is a traditional lodge with large living room with fireplace. Family-style breakfast and dinner are included. There is ice skating, ski-jouring (harnessed dogs pull a Nordic skier), plus a wood-fired hot tub and sauna. Choose among dorms or rooms with shared or private baths. Shuttles take guests to Sunday River. (NOTE: As of Summer, 2006, this inn is for sale, and most locals think it will no longer operate as an inn when sold.)

In Bethel, the Bethel Inn and Country Club (824-2175; $$$$) has an old-style atmosphere. Renovated rooms are first-rate; others barely make the grade. The rates include breakfast and dinner. The inn also has a cross-country center, health club and a shuttle to the ski area.

L'Auberge (800-760-2774; 824-2774; $$), in a renovated barn off the Bethel Common, has a French country-style flavor, boasts an excellent restaurant and welcomes kids and dogs. The innkeepers will help arrange a pizza/movie party for kids, while their parents enjoy a leisurely dinner. Guest rooms are spacious and some well configured for families.

The Sudbury Inn (824-2174; $$$$), one of our favorites, has comfy rooms, one of the best restaurants in town and Sud's Pub, a popular watering hole; some pet-friendly rooms. The **Gideon Hastings House** (824-3496; $$–$$$) has four rooms as well as two suites with whirlpool tubs and a casual restaurant downstairs.

Just east of Bethel, on the road to the mountain, the **Briar Lea** (877-311-1299; 824-4714; $$) is an unstuffy B&B with an English accent and six guest rooms decorated with floral wallpapers and antique furnishings. All have TV/DVD and Wifi. Some can be connected as suites for families. Well-behaved dogs and children are welcome. Rates include an English-style breakfast. The inn also has a good, authentic, English pub-style restaurant.

A Prodigal Inn and Gallery (800-320-920; 824-8884; $$$) is a bit more upscale than other Bethel-area B&Bs. Bronze sculptures by innkeeper Tom White accent the public spaces, including a TV room with video/DVD library and a living room with fireplace. Some guest rooms have jetted tubs; all have CD players. Breakfasts are elegant, delicious and huge. Coffee and tea are always available, and yummy snacks welcome guests each afternoon.

At the **Inn at the Rostay** (207-824-3111 or 888-754-0072, $-$$), motel-style rooms ooze charm, with homemade quilts and country themes. All have TV, VCR (library available) and phone; some have refrigerators and microwaves. Free Wifi, an outdoor hot tub, afternoon snacks and a reasonably priced hot breakfast are provided. There's also a quilt shop on the premises. The budget conscious can't do better than the **Andover Roadhouse** (207-392-1209, $) a restored 18th-century Colonial-style village home with seven private rooms (shared baths) and a 10-bed bunkhouse. Guests have use of a kitchen, free Internet access, and a common living room.

Dining: $$$$-Entrees $30+; $$$-$20-$30; $$-$10-$20; $-less than $10.
Accommodations: (double room) $$$$-$200+; $$$-$141-$200; $$-$81-$140; $-$80 and less.

Information about **other lodging** is available through Sunday River's central reservation line (800-543-2754) or the Bethel Area Chamber of Commerce (824-3585).Information about **other lodging** is available through Sunday River's central reservation line (800-543-2754) or the Bethel Area Chamber of Commerce (824-3585).

 Dining

Sunday River continues to strive to improve its dining and, although still no culinary capital, the options for good food are improving. Phoenix House (842-2222; $$$) adds significantly to that effort with truly fine dining in an expansive arts-and-crafts setting highlighted by floor-to-ceiling windows that look onto the ski hill. A superb New Zealand rack of lamb highlights the menu. The more budget-minded eat downstairs at The Well ($-$$), serving a pub menu of soups, salads, stews and grill items. Legends (824-3500, ext. 5858; $$$), in the Summit Hotel, ranks next in the mountain's fine-food realm.

Foggy Goggle ($$$), in the South Ridge base, is packed for lunch, with good reason. The Peak Lodge and Skiing Center ($$$) at the summit of North Peak, is a popular lunch spot with a giant deck. **Shipyard BrewHaus Restaurant** (824-5269; $$–$$$), in the White Cap Lodge, serves an upscale pub menu that includes cedar-plank sesame tuna, lamb kabob and chili made with Shipyard beer. There's a good kids' menu, too. In the Jordan Grand Hotel, Sliders ($$) is good for lunch, especially for deck dining on sunny spring days. **Gringo Harry's** (824-4000, $$), in the Fall Line Condominiums, earns locals' high marks for its upscale Tex-Mex fare.

Off-mountain, the very popular Matterhorn/ Great Grizzly American Steakhouse (824-6836), set in a ski artifact filled barn on the access road, serves brick-oven-baked pizza, fresh pasta and steak along with nightly specials. At the base of the access road, the Moose's Tale (824-3541; $$$), in the Sunday River Brewing Company, serves decent pub grub.

For fine dining in Bethel, the Sudbury Inn (824-6558; $$$) and the Bethel Inn (824-2175; $$$) earn accolades for their food as well as their refined dining rooms. L'Auberge Bistro (824-2774 or 800-760-2774; $$-$$$) is country French with some multicultural accents.

The English Pub **The Jolly Drayman at the** Briar Lea (877-311-1299 or 824-4714; $$$) is a good choice for a nice meal in an unfussy setting, and it also has a children's menu. More lively is **Suds Pub** (824-6558, $--$$), in the Sudbury Inn, serving pizzas, burgers, sandwiches, steaks and pizzas *and* 29 beers on tap, in a family friendly atmosphere. Cafe Di Cocoa (824-5282; $-$$) serves authentic ethnic dinners on Friday and Saturday nights; call to check the menu and for reservations. Cho-Sun (824-7370; $$-$$$) serves fabulous, authentic Korean dishes as well as sushi and other Asian foods in a renovated Victorian house on Main Street. Reservations on weekends or holidays are a must.

A good source for prepared foods to go, as well as natural and gourmet groceries, is the Good Food Store (824-3754). Although there's a small grocery store on-mountain, it's best to stock up on staples before arriving in Bethel. The Foodliner supermarket on Main Street is a good option for that, as well, and it has a surprisingly nice wine selection.

 Apres-ski/nightlife

If you strike it rich, you may find midweek action at Sunday River and in Bethel, but the real fun heats up on weekends.

Immediate apres-ski is at the base of the slopes. **Foggy Goggle**, in the South Ridge base area, is the liveliest of the mountain spots. Try the **Barker Pub** in the Barker Mountain base area **The Well**, opposite the South Ridge Base Lodge, has big-screen TVs and live entertainment on Saturdays. Off mountain, head to the **Sunday River Brewery**, at the base of the access road. The **Matterhorn** is the place for 48-ounce Glacier Big Bowl drinks and extensive beer choices, including Guinness. **Sud's Pub** in town has 29 beers on tap .

At night, the **Matterhorn** rocks until the wee hours of the morning, with great bands; if you've been seated for dinner, you don't pay the cover. The **Sunday River Brewery** has live music and excellent homemade brew. Downtown, the very-local **Funky Red Barn** has the only pool tables in town. At the Sudbury Inn, **Suds Pub** has bands ranging from blues to bluegrass on weekends, but for local flavor, nothing beats Thursday for Hoot Nite, an open-mike forum that has been running for about 20 years. A sedate crowd fills **Legends** at the Summit Hotel for acoustic music and family entertainment on Saturday.

Other activities

Swimming pools and saunas are in virtually every resort condominium complex. Guests staying at the few condos without them get privileges at nearby complexes. The ski dorm has **video games** and **pool tables.**

The White Cap Base Lodge houses the **Nite Cap Fun Center** for families. Activities include an arcade, lighted tubing park and skating rink with skate rentals. Fireworks blast off here most Thursday and Saturday evenings.

Bethel Station, about four miles from Sunday River, has a four-screen **movie theater**. Arrange **snowmobile** rentals and tours through Sun Valley Sports (824-7533) or Bethel Outdoor Adventures (824-4224). **Indoor laser tag, miniature golf and rock climbing** are available at B.I.G. Adventure Center (824-0929). For one-day or multiday, fully-outfitted **dogsledding** trips, call Mahoosuc Guide Service (824-2073), in Grafton Notch.

Bethel has unusual **shops**. Bonnema Potters sells pottery depicting the Maine landscape. Mt. Mann is a native gemstone shop. Samuel Timberlake makes fine reproduction Shaker-style furniture. Ruthie's Dress Shop sells unique clothes.

Public Internet Access is available at the Bethel Chamber of Commerce Office (824-2282), at the railroad station next to the Casablanca Cinema.

Getting there and getting around

By air: Portland International Jetport is 75 miles from Sunday River. Private planes can land in Bethel. Bethel Express Corporation will pick up from either airport by reservation (824-4646).

By car: Sunday River is in western Maine, 1.5 hours northwest of Portland and about 3.5 north from Boston. From I-95, take the Gray exit in Maine to Rte. 26 north, continue to Bethel, then take Rte. 2 north 6 miles to Sunday River.

RV parking, no hookups, is allowed in designated parking areas at the resort. An RV park is also at White Birch Camping, in Shelburne on Rte. 2.

Getting around: The Mountain Explorer public transit system provides free transportation between the resort and the village of Bethel. It operates weekends from Thanksgiving to Christmas, then daily through March, from 7 a.m.–midnight. Pick up a schedule at the resort or local lodgings.

During the regular season, the on-mountain, trolley-car transport between the base areas is quite good. The shuttle loop expands to include the condos at night. In shoulder season, the mountain shuttles are by request only. Several off-mountain properties have shuttle service to and from the slopes. Midwinter, you can get along without a car, but they're nice to have, especially if traveling into Bethel. Early or late season, you'll need one.

Dining: $$$$-Entrees $30+; $$$-$20-$30; $$-$10-$20; $-less than $10.
Accommodations: (double room) $$$$-$200+; $$$-$141-$200; $$-$81-$140; $-$80 and less.

Mt. Washington Valley

New Hampshire
Attitash, Cranmore and Wildcat and five touring centers
Also: Black, King Pine and Shawnee Peak

Mt. Washington Valley Facts

Address: Chamber of Commerce
P.O. Box 2300, N. Conway, NH 03860
Toll-free information: (800) 367-3364
Dining: ★★★★★
Apres-ski/nightlife: ★★★★
Other activities: ★★★★★

Area code: 603
Phone: 356-5701 **Fax:** 356-7069
E-mail: info@mtwashingtonvalley.org
World Wide Web: www.mtwashingtonvalley.org
Bed base: 7,500+

Variety — that's what the skiing region of Mt. Washington Valley is known for, as skiers and riders can choose from the intimate feel of Mt. Cranmore to the splendid isolation of Wildcat with something in between for everyone. The Valley, as locals call it, has many bests. These include spectacular scenery, a long history of hospitality, extensive shopping, diverse nightlife and plentiful choices in skiing, dining, lodging and fun things to do.

Home to the main ski areas of Cranmore, Attitash and Wildcat, the Valley also has the smaller, but great beginner/family resorts of King Pine and Black Mountain within its confines. On a clear day, all but King Pine offer spectacular views of the Northeast's highest peak, the 6,288-foot Mt. Washington, and the surrounding Presidentials. And, if you need more skiing choices, just an hour's ride reaches Bretton Woods and Sunday River, while Shawnee Peak is located a half-hour drive east from North Conway. As if these choices weren't enough, some of the Northeast's best cross-country ski centers are here.

The few remaining grand old hotels attest to the fact that Mt. Washington Valley was a destination resort long before anyone came here to ski. In the 1930s, the variety of terrain in what was then called the Eastern Slope Region was a magnet to early skiers. Depression-era work crews cut trails (the Wildcat Trail was one of the first), and enterprising young men started ski schools bringing Austrian instructors and the famous Arlberg method.

If this ski history means nothing to you, no matter, Mt. Washington Valley has the best of now, too. Wide fall-line cruisers complement the classic, narrow winding trails of yesteryear. Modern condos, motels and hotels mix with country inns and B&Bs throughout the region, which encompasses the Conways, Bartlett, Jackson and extends through Pinkham Notch. Outlying towns, from Gorham to Snowville, N.H., to Bridgton, Maine, figure in the mix.

Some of the region's New England charm has been lost over the years as retail outlets and development moved in. However, shoppers flock here because of that evolution. Locals and longtime visitors know that the commercialization is condensed to the North Conway strip. They head to the villages outside the hub of North Conway for the quiet, and then come to the village and the strip for its many good bargains, pubs and restaurants.

Attitash
Mountain layout

Just west of Glen on Rte. 302 in Bartlett, Attitash is an all-around, two-mountain resort with a few expert touches. On the Attitash side is a warren of narrow New England trails and the newer Bear Peak trails provide great cruising terrain.

Ptarmigan, on Attitash, is one of the steepest trails in New England, but it is manageable for good intermediates, too. The rest of the mountain will keep 80 percent of skiers satisfied with Northwest Passage to Cathedral and Saco to Ammonoosuc providing inspired cruising, while Idiot's Option and Grandstand are favorites for their bump runs. The Attitash side of the mountain lacks a high-speed, base-to-summit lift but on the Bear Peak side there's a high-speed quad backed by several other chairlifts. Bear Peak features Illusion, Avenger, Kachina and Myth Maker: a foursome of cruising delights. Seeking more challenge? Jump into the Peak's ever-expanding glades.

The Attitash base has the primary lodge where you'll find the Adventure Center, the Learn to Ski and Ride programs and children's programs. Lessons, rentals and child care are all under one roof, and just outside, beginners have a "Snowbelt" lift. First-timers graduate from that to the adjacent learning slope served by a triple chair. From there, they move on to beginner trails around the nearby Double-Double lifts.

Ride Guide: The transitions between Attitash and Bear Peak are the only flat areas. When riding from Attitash to Bear Peak, avoid Bearback and ride the quad instead. When riding from Bear Peak to Attitash, avoid Bear Right to Stonybrook. Instead, when you see the bridge, take Bear Notch Pass to Stonybrook Bypass. Here, it's worth it to unstrap and walk the 50 feet to the top of the bypass. From there on, it's all downhill.

Parks and pipes

Attitash has a terrain park on Thad's Choice, and a Superpipe on Lower Ptarmigan. The park has jumps, hits and rails that are maintained daily. There's an early-season park on Far Out Trail. A dedicated park and superpipe groomer is used, and park rangers patrol these areas.

Lessons (05/06 prices)

Group lessons: $30 per 90-minute session for levels 2-8.
Never-ever packages: The Guaranteed Learn to Ski and Learn to Ride package includes rentals, lifts and lessons for $155.

Private lessons: $69 per hour for one student. Early bird/last run (before 9 a.m. or after 2 p.m.) is $55.

KidStuff (05/06 prices)

Child care: Available for ages 6 months to 6 years for $45 per day, including lunch, or $40 half day. Tiny Turns, an intro-to-skiing program designed for kids ages 3-5, costs $74 an hour, $50 for children enrolled in child care. Reservations are recommended, call 374-2368.

Children's lessons: ages 4-6, $79 full day (with lunch), $59 half day; includes lessons, and lift ticket; rentals cost $15.

Lift tickets (05/06 prices)

	Adult	Young Adult (13-18)	Child (6-12)
One day	$55*	$39	$39
Three days	$139	$120	$75
Five days	$219	$190	$125

*Note: Adult one-day tickets cost $59, young adult $49, child $37 on Saturdays and during the holiday periods. **Who skis at a discount:** Students with college ID ski for same price as Young Adults. Seniors (65+) ski for $39 any day. Multiday E-tickets and midweek tickets purchased online at www.attitash.com at least seven days in advance offer an additional 10 percent off the already discounted multiday price.

Cranmore Mountain Resort

Mountain layout

Cranmore is one of the oldest ski resorts in the nation. The good, balanced terrain, modest size (yet with an extensive trail system) and convenient location make it an ideal mountain for families. The sunbathed slopes (predominantly south facing) and lower elevation means it's the warmest of all the valley resorts. Cranmore skis larger than it is, and has both open slopes (don't miss the back or east side of the mountain) as well as classic, narrower trails. This is a resort for beginners and intermediates. Experts and advanced skiers can have a good time, but they shouldn't expect anything too challenging.

A favorite is the old Rattlesnake Trail, to the skier's right off the summit. The Ledges and Koessler trails down the center and to the skier's left offer some challenge, as do the tight, but not too steep, Black Forest and Tree Meister glades from Rattlesnake and Kandahar.

In addition to the standard skiing and snowboarding, Cranmore offers night skiing on weekends as well as Cranapalooza on Saturday nights - a family-oriented event featuring fireworks, torchlight parades, jugglers, clowns, and fire eaters. Cranmore also offers tubing and snow toys with lift-serviced tubing on eight groomed lanes Fridays, Saturdays and during holiday weeks.

Pipes and parks

The Darkside Terrain Park has rails, jibs, jumps and boxes designed by the same folks who make the parks for the U.S. Open. The Darkside is home to the Jib Saw Massacre, a series of three snowboard competitions and one skiing competition. The newly-expanded progression park to help ease newbies into the terrain park scene.

Lessons (05/06 prices)

Group lessons: A 90-minute group lesson costs $39; or $99 with lifts, and equipment as well.

First-timer package: Adult two-hour Getting Started lesson, with lift ticket and rental equipment, is $79 for the first day; and $60 for days two and three.

Private lessons: $85 for 90 minutes; $150 for a half day.

Kids Stuff

Child Care: Cranmore's Penguin Park Day Care provides care for children ages 3 months to 6 years. There are indoor and outdoor creative play areas and nap areas. The cost is $35 for a half day, $65 for a full day or $12 per

Attitash Facts
Summit elevation: 2,350 feet
Vertical drop: 1,750 feet
Base elevation: 600 feet
Expert:★★ **Advanced:**★★★
Intermediate:★★★★
Beginner:★★★★★
First-timer:★★★★★
Address: P.O. Box 308, Barlett, NH 03812
Ski area phone: 374-2368
Snow report: (877)677-SNOW
Toll-free reservations: (800) 223-7669
E-mail: info@attitash.com
Internet: www.attitash.com
Number and types of lifts: 12–2 high-speed quads, 1 quad, 3 triples, 3 doubles, 3 surface lifts
Skiable acreage: 280 acres
Snowmaking: 97 percent
Uphill capacity: 14,385 per hour
Parks & pipes: 2 parks; 1 pipe
Bed base: 1,600 Nearest lodging: Slopeside
Resort child care: Yes, 6 months and older
Adult ticket, per day: $44-59 (05/06)

Wildcat Facts
Summit elevation: 4,062 feet
Vertical drop: 2,112 feet
Base elevation: 1,950 feet
Expert:★★★ **Advanced:**★★★★
Intermediate:★★★★
Beginner:★★★
First-timer:★★★
Address: Rte. 16, Pinkham Notch Jackson, NH 03846
Ski area phone: (800) 255-6439; 466-3326
Snow report: (888) 754-9453
E-mail: through website
Internet: www.skiwildcat.com
Number and types of lifts: 4–1 high-speed quad, 3 triples
Skiable acreage: 225 acres
Snowmaking: 90 percent
Uphill capacity: 7,200 per hour
Bed base: None at the area
Nearest lodging: About a quarter-mile
Resort child care: Yes, 2 months and older
Adult ticket, per day: $55 (05/06)

hour. Introductory ski and snow play programs are available. Reservations are recommended, call (603) 356-5544, ext. 245.

Children's lessons: Intro to Ski, a 60-minute lesson for 3-year-olds, including equipment and lift, is $60. Penguin Camp, for ages 4-7, a full-day ski program including lift, lesson and equipment is $89; half day is $79. Intro to Snowboard for ages 5-7 is $65 for an hour, with lift, lesson and equipment.

Adventure Camp for skiers and snowboarders ages 8–14 includes lift ticket, lesson and equipment. A full day is $89, with lunch; half day is $79. Private instruction for children is $85 for 90 minutes; $150 for three hours; lift ticket and equipment required.

Lift tickets (05/06 prices)
Adult tickets cost $45; teens (13–18) $29; kids (6–12) and seniors (65+) cost $25. Children 5 and younger ski free. These prices are good any day of the season.

Wildcat Mountain

Wildcat Mountain features back-to-basics skiing with old-style trails that ebb and flow with the mountain's contours. It's a true skiers' mountain but with no residential development allowed in the protected wilderness area, Wildcat struggles financially compared to the fully-

Cranmore Facts

Summit elevation:	1,700 feet
Vertical drop:	1,200 feet
Base elevation:	500 feet

Expert:★ Advanced:★★
Intermediate:★★★★
Beginner:★★★★
First-timer:★★★
Address: 1 Skimobile Road
N. Conway, NH 03860
Ski area phone: 356-5544
Snow report: 356-7070

Toll-free reservations: (800) 786-6754
Internet: www.cranmore.com
Number and types of lifts: 12–1 high-speed quad, 1 triple, 3 doubles, 5 surface lifts, 2 moving carpets
Skiable acreage: 192 acres
Snowmaking: 100 percent
Uphill capacity: 7,500 skiers per hour
Parks & pipe: 3 terrain parks
Bed base: 250
Nearest lodging: Slopeside
Resort child care: Yes, 6 months and older
Adult ticket, per day: $39 (04/05)

developed resorts. However, skiers and riders who frequent this mountain are fiercely loyal and the varied and challenging terrain give Wildcat a true heart and soul, and through investments in snowmaking, grooming equipment, a high-speed lift and trail widening, Wildcat has made major progress in the past few years.

Wildcat sits across a narrow ribbon of highway from Mt. Washington, home to some of the highest recorded winds in the world. While Mt. Washington's summit, at 6,288 feet, is higher than Wildcat's, at 4,062, and the mountain can be windy and cold. However, the location and elevation does have a silver lining: the scenery is consistently voted the best in the East by a major ski magazine and snow is plentiful — an average year yields at least 15 feet — that comes early and stays late, often well into May. Spring skiing at Wildcat is an event and every skier in the Valley looks forward to it.

Mountain layout

Wildcat deserves its reputation as an experts' mountain. Upper Wildcat (a trail that just passed its 70th birthday), to the left and Top Cat and Lift Lion in the middle can get your heart pounding. New for 06-07 are bigger and better gladed runs that create a change of pace from the huge vertical steeps and cruisers.

Beginners are not forgotten here. The Snowcat area, with its own triple chair, is an ideal place for first-timers and the 2.75-mile cruise down Polecat from the summit gives advanced beginners an authentic Alpine experience. Another favorite for those who want a nice glide in the woods is the Wild Kitten off the Bobcat triple.

Intermediates have plenty to play on here, too. The Tomcat triple reaches about two-thirds of the way up the mountain and is a good retreat when the wind blows hard on the summit quad. The Bobcat triple reaches a little below mid-mountain and provides access to the narrow trails at Wildcat's core, two glades and the Bobcat slope and the Cheetah slope, which is often used for races.

For a religious experience, try Lynx from top to bottom: It might just convince you that Wildcat is God's chosen mountain. For decades, Lynx has been the 'Cat's most popular trail. It's easy to see why. Lynx plays with you, dropping quickly at the summit, then rolling around a few bends before dropping and rolling again. When taken from summit to base, there are few trails in New England that can compare for range of terrain and the sheer joy of skiing.

Lessons (05/06 prices)

Group lessons: $35 per session.

First-timer packages: $65, including rentals, lifts and lessons. Extra days $75, including lift ticket. **The First Impressions Program**, limited to five students, includes an all-day lesson, lift ticket, rentals, plus lunch and apres-ski hot chocolate with your instructor for $90; reservations required.

Private lessons: $62 for one hour; up to five people can share a private lesson, with each additional person paying $42.

KidStuff (05/06 prices)

Child Care: Available for ages 2 months to 5 years old. Cost is $55 for a full day (with lunch); $35 for a half day (without lunch). The Cubs Nursery & Snowplay program is a combination of child care and snow play instruction for ages 3 to 5 (must be toilet-trained). Cost is $79 for a full day (with lunch); $59 for a half day (without lunch). Reservations are recommended on weekends and required midweek, and are required for children 18 months and younger; call (888) 754-9453.

Children's lessons: Ski lessons are for ages 5–12, snowboard lessons are for ages 8–12. Program including lessons, lift ticket and rentals costs $89 for a full day (includes lunch); $69 for a half day. Reservations are strongly suggested for all kids' programs.

Lift tickets (05/06 prices)

	Adult	Teen (13-17)	Jr. (6-12)/Sr.65+
One day	$59	$49	$25
Two-day	$80	$67	$50

Who skis free: Children age 5 and younger with a ticket-holding parent. Anyone on his or her birthday, with valid ID.

Who skis at a discount: College students ski for teen prices. Everyone on Sunday afternoons: noon to close is $20. Two ski for $59 on non-holiday Wednesdays. Ages 50+ get a lift ticket and 10 a.m. lesson on non-holiday Tuesdays. Ladies get a lift ticket and 10 a.m. ski lesson on non-holiday Thursdays, plus a 10% discount on the children's programs (reservations required). A second consecutive day is $25 for anyone.

Mt. Washington

A trip to Tuckerman Ravine on the east side of Mt. Washington is a rite of spring for New England's skiers and riders. Called the birthplace of extreme skiing, skiers have hiked into this snow-filled glacial cirque since 1914, and in the 1930s, races were held here. In fact, the first giant slalom in the United States was held at Tuckerman, as well as the American Inferno, which started at the very summit of Mt. Washington and ended 4,200 feet lower at Pinkham Notch.

Today the Tuckerman Inferno Pentathlon every April continues as a fund-raiser for the non-profit Friends of Tuckerman organization.

To reach the ravine from the Pinkham Notch Visitor's Center, hike a wide trail two miles to HoJo's shelter. From here, the floor of the Ravine is reached via a steep hike.

Although skiing Tuck's is only for experts, less experienced folks still make the trek to watch or to ski and snow tube the shallower terrain close to the ravine floor. Most spectators of this unique spring scene head straight for Lunch Rocks, an outcropping on the right as you hike into the ravine. From here, you can rest and then kick step into the snow and hike up any of the gullies or the famous headwall. At day's end, you either ski down the Sherburne Trail or, if snow is thin, hike down the way you came. For weather and trail info, call 466-2721.

Cross-country and snowshoeing (visit xcskiresorts.com for more details)

Jackson Ski Touring Foundation (383-9355 or 800-927-6697; Box 216, Jackson, N.H. 03846), on Rte. 16A in Jackson Village, is a mecca for Nordic skiers with more than 150 km. of trails (93 km. are groomed, 80 km. are skate groomed). It has lessons, rentals and snowshoeing.

Mt. Washington Valley Ski Touring and Snowshoe Center (356-3042; Box 130, Intervale, N.H. 03845) has 65 km. of inn-to-inn trails (60 km. tracked, 20 km. skate groomed), plus ski school and rentals. It offers guided star-gazing tours and animal-tracking clinics.

The Appalachian Mountain Club (466-2721) maintains a network of touring trails radiating from the AMC Camp at Pinkham Notch. About 7 km. are rated Easiest or More Difficult (requiring skills up to a strong snowplow and step-turn), but about 40 km. are rated Most Difficult, with long challenging hills and narrow trails. **Great Glen Trails** (466-2333) has 40 km. of cross-country skiing (14 km. tracked, 20 km. skate groomed) and snowshoeing trails at the base of Mt. Washington, which translates into jaw-dropping scenery all around you. Telemarkers, cross-country skiers and snowshoers can take a snowcat partly up the Mt. Washington Auto Road, then ski down; sightseers also are welcome. It also has a snowtubing park.

Bear Notch Ski Touring Center (374-2277) is one of the Valley's best kept secrets. With a truly beautiful setting just north of Bartlett Village (Rte. 302), the 70 km. (60 km. tracked and skate groomed) of trails offer uncrowded, wooded scenery. **The Nestlenook Recreation Center** (383-9443), also in Jackson, has 35 km. of touring tracks that wind through its 65-acre farm. **Purity Spring Resort** (800-373-3754 or 367-8896), near Madison, has 15 km. of groomed and tracked trails. Rentals and lessons are available. **Purity Spring Resort** (367-8896 or 800-373-3754), near Madison, has 15 km. of groomed and tracked trails. Rentals and lessons are available.

Accommodations

If you like romantic country inns and B&Bs, you're in the right spot. The Valley also has plenty of moderately priced motels suitable for families.

For condominiums, chalets and motel suites, call **Top Notch Vacation Rentals** (800-762-6636; 383-4133; $–$$$$), which works with properties all up and down the Valley. **Luxury Mountain Getaways** (800-472-5207; 383-9101; $$–$$$$) has everything from one-bedroom condos to luxury villas. **Attitash Mountain Village** (800-862-1600; 374-6500; $–$$$$), across the road from the ski area, has inexpensive to upscale packages. For lodging information (but no reservations), call the **Mt. Washington Valley Chamber of Commerce** at (800) 367-3364 or visit its website. Lodgings are listed by region:

Bartlett (Attitash Resort): Right at the base of Bear Peak, the ski-in/ski-out **Grand Summit Resort Hotel** (800-223-7669; $$–$$$$) provides all amenities from saunas and hot tubs to fitness rooms and restaurants. A visit to the **Covered Bridge House** (800-232-9109; 383-9109; $–$$) resembles a visit to Grandma's. Bed-cover quilts, braided rugs and stenciling characterize the decor. A family suite is available; rates include breakfast and use of the outdoor hot tub.

Active folks who don't need fancy digs will appreciate the warmth of **The Bartlett Inn**

(800-292-2353; 374-2353; $–$$$). Choose from shared-bath rooms in the main inn or cottages with private baths, some with fireplaces and kitchenettes. When lodging in same room with two adults, kids younger than 12 stay free, teenagers stay for $19. Cross-country trails are out the back door.

Gorham (Wildcat): If you are skiing at Wildcat, this town, just to the north of the Valley, is where to stay. The **Royalty Inn** (800-437-3529; 466-3312; $–$$) has 88 rooms that are all very spacious and well kept. Kitchenettes are available. The family-owned **Town & Country Motor Inn** (800-325-4386; 466-3315; $) is a bit simpler, with recently upgraded rooms. Families will want to stay in the same building that houses the pool, video games and sauna. Children ages 13 and younger stay free. Dorm-style accommodations start at $15 per person.

Pinkham Notch (Wildcat): To be really close to Wildcat or to get a head start if you're climbing, skiing, or using Mt. Washington's cross-country trails, try the **Joe Dodge Lodge** (466-2727; $) at Pinkham Notch, run by the Appalachian Mountain Club. The two-, four- and five-bunk rooms are simple, and rates include either one or two meals. Three public rooms have fireplaces; one has a well-used piano, another is stocked with games and activities for children and the third has a library.

Jackson Village: This town is home to a collection of old-time mansions, hotels, farms and houses that have grown into upscale B&Bs. Many offer dining on premises. **Luxury Mountain Getaways/Nestlenook Farm on the River** (383-9443; $$$–$$$$) is an elegant Victorian fantasy land, with pastel colors and gingerbread trim. A full breakfast and snacks mean you never go hungry. The extensive grounds are peppered with ornate bridges and fanciful gazebos. Ask about add-on fees—they're steep.

The Inn at Thorn Hill (800-289-8990; 383-4242; $$$–$$$$), with views of Mt. Washington, is rebuilt in the style of Stanford White following a fire. Now offering spa services, the inn gets top ratings from both travel and dining publications. Rates include breakfast and a three-course dinner. Practically next door is a more affordable choice, **The Inn at Jackson** (800-289-8600; 383-4321; $–$$), a gem. It's an easy walk to Jackson's restaurants and shops. The Inn at **Ellis River** (800-233-8309; 383-9339; $$–$$$$) is an elegant, country retreat furnished with antiques; many rooms have fireplaces and whirlpool baths. Unlike many B&Bs, each room has TV and phone. A gourmet breakfast is included.

The Wentworth Resort Hotel (800-637-0013; 383-9700; $$$–$$$$) is an historic hotel and one of the area's best values. It has spacious rooms with big hot tubs as well as a top-notch dining room and a nice lounge. Rates include a full breakfast and a multi-course dinner.

The nearby **Snowflake Inn** (888-383-1020; 383-8259; $$$) includes king-size beds and two-person jetted tubs, Internet access and flat screen TVs with DVDs. Afternoon refreshments and a continental breakfast are included in the rate.

The **Eagle Mountain House** (800-966-5779; 383-9111; $–$$$) is a restored, rambling 19th-century resort hotel that welcomes families. Children age 17 and younger stay free if sleeping in existing beds. **The Christmas Farm Inn & Spa** (800-443-5837; 383-4313; $$–$$$), added a full-service spa in 2004. The rate includes breakfast and a 15-percent service charge and taxes will be added to your bill.

Whitneys' Inn (800-677-5737; 383-8916; $$–$$$), is a restored, 1840s farmhouse at the base of Black Mountain, allowing Alpine and cross-country skiing from the door.

Intervale: The 1785 Inn (800-421-1785; 356-9025; $–$$$) is a country inn with what has been called the best view of the Valley. You can cross-country ski or snowshoe right out the back door of **The Forest Inn** (800-448-3534; 356-9772; $$), a cozy B&B on Rte. 16A,

Dining: $$$$-Entrees $30+; $$$-$20-$30; $$-$10-$20; $-less than $10.
Accommodations: (double room) $$$$-$200+; $$$-$141-$200; $$-$81-$140; $-$80 and less.

and **The New England Inn** (800-826-3466; 356-5541; $$–$$$$), in the same vicinity, has everything from inn rooms to romantic cabins and a deluxe lodge, plus a lively pub.

North Conway: With a few exceptions, North Conway's lodging is more motels and hotels including national chains. **Stonehurst Manor** (800-525-9100; 356-3113; $$–$$$), created from a turn-of-the-century mansion has the setting, rooms and restaurant that are pure elegance. Breakfast and dinner meal plans are optional.

Less than a 10-minute walk to downtown is **The Victorian Harvest Inn** (800-642-0749; $$–$$$$). Amenities include in-room hot tubs, fireplaces, TV and connecting rooms that are ideal for families with older children. A full breakfast is included.

The **Wildflower Inn** (866-945-3357; 356-7567; $–$$$$) is a Victorian showplace. It boasts to-die-for views of Mt. Washington and the Presidential Range, comfy public rooms and spacious guest rooms and suites, all with fireplace. Only suites have private hot tubs, but there's a communal one on the deck. Rates include a full country breakfast.

The **Buttonwood Inn** (800-258-2625; 356-2625; $$–$$$) is tucked in the woods with cross-country skiing from the door. Ask about the family suites. Rates include a full breakfast and afternoon snacks. The **Eastman Inn** (800-626-5855; 356-6707; $–$$) delivers warm hospitality with a Southern accent. Breakfast is superb.

White Mountain Hotel and Resort (800-533-6301; 356-7100; $–$$), is at the foot of Whitehorse Ledge, the enormous granite cliff you see from all North Conway. The views back across the Valley toward Cranmore are unmatched, and the food is excellent.

The Eastern Slope Inn Resort (800-862-1600; 356-6321; $$), in the heart of North Conway, is a classic New England inn with an indoor pool. The **Green Granite Inn** (800-468-3666; 356-6901; $–$$) is on Rte. 16 on the 1.5-mile shopping strip. It has an indoor pool and a hot tub; evening movies and children's programs at weekends and vacation periods. **Mt. Washington Valley Motor Lodge** (800-634-2382; 356-5486; $$) is a pleasant surprise for families with basic rooms and a swimming pool.

The **Red Jacket Mountain View** (800-752-2538; 356-5411; $$–$$$$), is a rambling building with some loft rooms and townhouses, both good for families. It has panoramic views and an indoor pool and hot tub. **The Briarcliff** (800-338-4291; 356-5584; $–$$), is affordable and convenient. For rock-bottom prices, head to **Hostelling International-White Mountains** in Conway (447-1001; $).

Dining

The Rare Bear Bistro and Black Bear Pub are at The Bernerhof (383-4414; $$–$$$; right), in Bartlett on Rte. 302. It has its own nationally famous cooking school. **Stonehurst** (356-3113; $$) and **The 1785 Inn**, in North Conway (356-9025; $$–$$$;*left*), have excellent cuisine.

In Jackson, **The Christmas Farm Inn** (383-4313; $$–$$$), **The Inn at Thorn Hill** (383-4242; $$$;), **Wentworth Resort Hotel** (383-9700; $$–$$$), and **Wildcat Inn and Tavern** (383-4245; $$) are all fairly expensive but renowned for their fine dining.

For more down-to-earth meals, in Glen, try the **Red Parka Pub** (383-4344; $$), near the junction of Rtes. 16 and 302. They don't take reservations; come early or expect up to an hour wait on Saturday nights.

In North Conway, **Moat Mountain Smoke House & Brewing Co.** (356-6381, $$), is a family favorite for wood-grilled or smoked entrees as well as lighter fare such as pizza and quesadillas. It brews its own beer on premises.

Monte Bello (356-6668; $$–$$$) serves the best Italian meals in town. **Coyote Rose**

(356-7673; $$) earns raves for Southwestern fare and margaritas. **Horsefeathers** (356-6862; $–$$) is perhaps the most popular spot in town. For a good time and plenty to eat, it's hard to beat, although the menu promises more than it can deliver.

The Flatbread Company (356-6321, $–$$), in the Eastern Slope Inn, is great for families. **Delaney's Hole-in-the-Wall** (356-7776; $–$$), a locals' haunt, inexplicably has Southwestern flair. **Maestro's Café and Deli** (356-8790; $–$$) offers pasta specialties.

On the Rte. 16 strip, the **Red Jacket Mountain View** (356-5411; $–$$) serves very good food. The **Muddy Moose** (356-7696; $$) has affordable prices, as well as some exotic choices, such as Wild Boar Marsala or Venison Pasta.

Ethnic fare is plentiful. Head to the **Shannon Door Pub** (383-4211; $), in Jackson, for Irish entertainment and good thin-crust pizzas. Pizza, from thin-crust to deep-dish, is found at **Elvio's** (356-3208; $), in North Conway. For Mexican, locals head to **Margarita Grille** (383-6556; $–$$), just beyond the Red Parka, on Rte. 302, in Glen, or to **Cafe Noche** (447-5050; $), on Main Street, Conway.

On particularly crowded weekends in the Valley, head to spacious quarters of the **Red Fox Pub & Restaurant** (383-6659; $$), just south of the covered bridge in Jackson, which seats 200. The Sunday Jazz Brunch here is a locals' favorite and a bargain at $5.95 per person. Or try the new Western-themed **White Horse Saloon** (356-9745; $$) on West Side Road for great ribs and wild game at reasonable prices.

For breakfast, head to **Peaches** (356-5860; $) on the main drag in North Conway. In Jackson, we recommend **Yesterday's** (383-4457; $) or the **Wentworth Resort Hotel** (383-9700), which serves an exceptionally good breakfast for $8. For lighter fare, stop by **Jackson Bistro** or **As You Like It** in Jackson. These also good places to pick up fat sandwiches and fancy confections to stash for lunch.

In Gorham, **Welsh's** (466-2206; $) serves hearty breakfasts and lunches. The oversized muffins and charbroiled burgers are delicious. **Libby's Bistro** (466-5330; $$) earns high marks for its ever-changing menu of creative entrees, such as duck au poivre with a balsamic rhubarb sauce. For down-to-earth fare, you can't beat **Wilfred's** ($–$$), where turkey is a specialty. At the **Appalachian Mountain Club** (466-2727; $$), meals are served family-style: a great way to meet people.

Apres-ski/nightlife

The legendary **Red Parka Pub** offers lively après-ski and then nightlife activity into the wee hours. Something is happening every night, and its informal style runs to beer served in Mason jars to vintage skis and creative license plates covering the walls. Live music, live comedy or a movie is often featured; Open Mic Nights on Mondays.

The place to be in Jackson is the **Wildcat Tavern**, where folk rock keeps the place hopping on weekends.

For a mellow time and sipping a few beers, **Tuckerman's** at the New England Inn, on Rte. 16A in Intervale, is gaining in popularity, as is the **Moat Mountain Smokehouse and Brewery** on Rte. 16 on the northern edge of North Conway. On Friday and Saturday nights, **Horsefeathers**, in the center of North Conway, is standing-room only, and the **Up Country Saloon** and Red Jacket have live dance music. Locals hang out in **Hooligans, Horsefeathers** and **Delaney's Hole-in-the-Wall,** all in North Conway.

Other activities

The **Cranmore Sports Center** (356-6301), at the Cranmore base, is a huge all-season facility, with indoor tennis courts, pool, aerobics classes, steam-room and sauna. It is also home to a huge (30 by 40 feet) indoor climbing wall. Classes are available through **International Mountain Climbing School** (356-6316). The owner, Rick Wilcox, has climbed Mt. Everest. **Eastern Mountain Sports** (356-5433) is in the Eastern Slope Inn. Both offer a range of winter climbing and hiking programs, including ice-climbing instruction, ascents of Mt. Washington and traverses of the Presidential Range.

The **Appalachian Mountain Club** (466-2721) has an active schedule of courses and workshops on ski touring, snowshoeing, avalanches and more.

Take a **sleigh ride** in the Valley. Try Nestlenook's horse-drawn sleigh (383-0845) or The Stables at the Farm off West Side Road (356-6640). Sleigh rides can be combined with dinner at the Darby Field Inn (800-426-4147 or 383-2181), in Conway.

Cranmore, Black Mountain, King Pine and Shawnee Peak have active **tubing** hills.

The Ham Arena (447-5886), in Conway, has indoor **ice skating**. Two-hour skating lessons start at $4 for children and $5 for adults. Call ahead for public skating hours. You can ice skate in Jackson, North Conway and at King Pine's covered ice arena (free with a lift ticket).

At the **Weather Discovery Center** (356-2137) experience what it felt like to be atop Mt. Washington in high winds or practice being a weather reporter and see yourself on TV.

For bargain hunters, Mt. Washington Valley may have the best **shopping** of any ski resort in the nation, with more than 100 factory outlets and no sales tax. The area also has many unusual boutiques with creative gift items. For a chance to meet local authors and some national ones, stop by **White Birch Books** in North Conway Village. The Chamber of Commerce in North Conway has Visitor Guides; as well as a map and guide to shopping.

Getting there and getting around

By air: Portland, Maine, less than 90 minutes from North Conway, is the closest major airport. Manchester, N.H., airport is about two hours by car.

By car: The Mt. Washington Valley is 140 miles north of Boston. Take I-95 to Rte. 16, then north on 16/302. An alternate route is I-93 north to Rte. 104 to Rte. 25 to Rte. 16 and on to North Conway. From Portland, follow Rte. 302.

North Conway has been notorious for its weekend traffic jams going through town. The new North-South connector road has taken some of the pressure off and is a good alternate route for those coming from the north or the south, but it's not well marked. Find it from the south by heading straight at all lights through Conway, turning left onto Route 302 about a mile out of town, and then turning right at the Wal-Mart (there's a light here, too).

It leaves you out right in the middle of North Conway, practically on Cranmore's doorstep. If you are driving from the Jackson/Wildcat/Attitash Bear Peak end of town to the south, the West Side Road lets you avoid most of the shopping traffic and the North Conway crowds. In any case, be patient if you're behind the wheel at 4 p.m., when the lifts close.

Getting around: Bring a car.

Other Mount Washington Valley Resorts

Black Mountain, Jackson, NH

(800) 698-4490; (603) 383-4490
Internet: www.blackmt.com
4 lifts: 1 triple, 1 double, 2 surface lifts; 140 trail acres; 1,100 vertical feet

Black Mountain, a compact ski area at the top of Jackson Village on Rte. 16B, may be the best place in the valley for beginner lessons and family skiing. Wide-open Whitneys' Hill was the site of the first ski lessons in the Valley in 1936. Black is still an ideal place to take your first turns or have your children take theirs. The best beginner trails down the mountain are Sugarbush and Black Beauty, while Upper Galloping Goose and Mr. Rew offer some short expert fun. Upper-intermediate or expert skiers can play in the glades.

On the Jackson Ski Touring trail system, Black has more than its share of telemark skiers, both beginner and experts; with its top-to-bottom Skinny Ski Inferno, a classic event. Additionally, Black Mountain's southern exposure provides a warmer place to ski when it's just too cold at other Valley areas.

Lift tickets (05/06 prices): Adults, $32 weekends and $22 midweek; juniors (17 and younger) and seniors (65+), $24 weekends and $17 midweek; ages 5 and younger, free. The Passport, a day ticket valid for two adults and two juniors, is $89 weekends/holidays and $70 midweek.

Lessons: Group lessons cost $25 for a one-hour session.

Learn to Ski or Ride is $49. Price includes rentals, lifts and lessons. Private lessons cost $42 per hour for one student.

Lodging information: (800) 698-4490.

Purity Spring Resort/King Pine Ski Area, East Madison, NH;

(800) 373-3754; (603) 367-8896
Internet: www.kingpine.com
5 lifts: 2 triples, 1 double, 2 surface lifts; 350 vertical feet; 35 skiable acres

This small area, part of family-run Purity Spring Resort, has a modest vertical drop, but for those just starting out and parents who want to keep an eye on young children, it is an ideal resort. On-mountain lodging, a health club with indoor pool and packages that include lodging, skiing, meals and full use of the resort's facilities make this a good value for young families. King Pine does have one short, steep trail, reportedly one of the steepest in the state, but top-level skiers are better off somewhere else. Night skiing is available Tuesdays, Fridays, Saturdays and holidays, and the resort also has 15 km. of groomed and tracked cross-country trails. Other activities include snow tubing, snowshoeing and ice skating.

Lift tickets (05/06prices): Adults, $36 weekends and $28 midweek; kids (6–12) and seniors (65-69), $24 weekends and $18 midweek; seniors 70 and older, $10 weekends and $5 midweek; kids 5 and younger, free. Night skiing is available. Tubing is $14 for two hours. **Lessons:** Group lesson cost $25 for 90 minutes. Private lessons cost $55 per hour. A First Time package is $53 adult/$43 junior (6-12)/$31 junior (4-5) for skiing or snowboarding; and first-tme junior snowboarders must be at least 8 years old. Package includes beginner lift ticket, rentals and lesson.

Distance from Boston: About 2-1/2 hours via I-95, Rte. 16, Rte. 25 and Rte. 153.

Lodging information: (800) 373-3754.

Shawnee Peak, Bridgton, ME

(207) 647-8444

Internet: www.shawneepeak.com

5 lifts; 40 trails; 233 acres; 1,300 vertical feet; 2 terrain parks; 1 halfpipe

About a 30-minute drive from North Conway via Rte. 302, this family resort offers fantastic views across Maine's flatlands and lakes to the White Mountains. It has excellent snowmaking and a twice-a-day grooming program that allows for "first tracks" twice daily, if you're lucky. Its terrain offers a bit of something for everyone, and it's very popular with families. The toughest runs are at the top and left side of the mountain as you look at the trail map, and wide-open beginner slopes are to the right (or west).

Excellent, tight, gladed areas are nestled between the two sides of the mountain. Most of the trails to the left are New England-narrow. Upper/Lower Appalachian is a great steep cruiser with fabulous views that uses almost all of the mountain's vertical. Shawnee has the most extensive night skiing in New England with a lighted drop of 1,300 feet covered by 17 trails. It also has a 68,000-square-foot learning area, a terrain park and a 400-foot-long halfpipe, and a beginner terrain park.

Lift tickets (05/06 prices): Adults, $44 weekends/holidays and $34 midweek; ages 6–12 and 65 and older, $31 on weekends/holidays and $23 midweek; ages 5 and younger ski free when accompanied by a paying adult. Night skiing also is available until 9 p.m. Mon-Thurs and 10 p.m. Friday and Saturday.

Lessons: 3-2-1-Snow Fun, for first-time skiers or riders ages 8 and older, costs $179. It includes three days of lessons, lifts and rental equipment. For $299, you get a FREE season pass upon graduation. Individually, GET Skiing or Riding I offers two hours for $59; GET Skiing or Riding II is two hours for $69. A one-hour private is $55.

Child Care: The **Peak-A-Boo Day Care** is a state-licensed (required in Maine) child care facility for children aged three months to six years. All-day programs are $60, including lunch; half-day programs are $40. Bring diapers, formula and food for infants. Reservations using a credit card are required at all times; call (207) 824-5959. The child care facility is located beneath the Main Base Lodge

Children's lessons: Shawnee Peak offers skiing and riding instruction for children aged 4 through 12 (13 & above go to ski school). All clinic participants are required to wear helmets, which are available to rent. Programs include a lift ticket, and equipment rentals are $15 a day and helmet rental is $7 a day.

SkiWee – 4 & 5 year olds. Half-day (two-hour program) only Weekends and holidays only $50. Junior Mountaineers – ages 6-12. Half-day $65, Full-day $80. Includes lessons and lift ticket. Full-day includes lunch. Mini Riders – ages 7-12. Half-day $65, Full-day $80. Includes lessons and lift ticket. Full-day includes lunch. Private lessons – one-hour one-on-one programs start at age 3 (must be potty trained). $55 for ages 3-5, $65 for ages 6-12.

SKIwee, Junior Mountaineers, and Mini Riders programs are offered on weekends and holiday periods only. Reservations required. Call (207) 647-8444 ext. 26.

Distance from Boston: About three hours. Take 95 North to Rte. 295 to the Forest Avenue/Rte. 302 West exit and follow Rte. 302 through Bridgton. The access road is about 6 miles beyond downtown.

Lodging information: For the limited number of condos on the mountain, call the ski area, (207) 647-8444. For lodging in North Conway, call the Mt. Washington Valley Chamber of Commerce, (800) 367-3364.

Bretton Woods
New Hampshire

Summit elevation:	2,800 feet
Vertical drop:	1,500 feet
Base elevation:	1,600 feet

Address: Route 302
Bretton Woods, NH 03575
Area code: 603
Ski area phone: 278-3320
Snow report: 278-3333
Toll-free reservations: (800) 258-0330
E-mail: skiinfo@brettonwoods.com
Internet: www.brettonwoods.com
Expert:★
Advanced:★
Intermediate:★★★
Beginner:★★★★★
First-timer:★★★★

Number and types of lifts: 9–4 high-speed quads, 1 quad, 1 triple, 1 double, 2 surface lifts
Acreage: 431 trail acres
Snowmaking: 92 percent
Uphill capacity: 13,700 per hour
Parks & pipes: 1 park; 1 pipe
Bed base: 3,400+
Nearest lodging: Slopeside
Resort child care: Yes, 2 months and older
Adult ticket, per day: $57-64(06/07 prices)
Dining: ★★★★
Apres-ski/nightlife:★★
Other activities:★★★

Bretton Woods is a relatively new ski area by New Hampshire standards, having been started in 1973. In close proximity to the famed Mount Washington Hotel, and joining it as part of the Bretton Woods Mountain Resort complex, it has grown over the past 10 years to become New Hampshire's largest ski area in terms of acreage.

Long known as a destination for beginner and intermediate skiers—its gentle pitch and mostly wide-open terrain makes it a perfect place for all to feel like "boy, can I ski!"—recent expansions into West Mountain and Rosebrook Canyon have added much-needed challenge for upper intermediate and expert skiers. Now dotted with glades—from wide-open gentle tree runs to gnarly stump- and tree-ridden precipices—this is not your father's Bretton Woods. Everyone from troll-hunting third graders to their arboreal-thrill-seeking parents will find a smorgasbord of gladed terrain.

When the nearby Mount Washington Hotel began welcoming winter guests in late 1999, Bretton Woods became more than a regional ski area. It became a grand resort. Although the ski industry often overuses the word—with "grand" tacked onto the name of many new large hotels—the Mount Washington is the real deal. The colossal turn-of-the-20th-century Spanish Renaissance structure, with its Tiffany glass, one-sixth-mile-long wrap-around verandah, and plasterwork sculpted by Italian craftsmen, is what every other grand hotel wants to be. John F. Kennedy, Joan Crawford and Bjorn Borg all slept here (to name just a few) and, oh yes, there was that monetary conference there in 1944.

Bretton Woods touts itself as a family ski resort and it really is. With one base area, it's difficult to get lost, although at times in the deep woods, you might feel lost. The free Learning Center quad serves a dedicated slope that's long enough and gentle enough that beginners can easily link turns without knee-shaking fear. The renovated base lodge is expansive. The children's center, which is expanded for the 2006-'07 season to streamline the process for children whether they are going to day care or off to lessons, is convenient and well-equipped. If you're waiting for the shuttle back to the hotel or other area lodging, it's great to hang out in front of the fire in the large curbside gazebo and even roast marshmallows!

Skiing isn't the only activity at Bretton Woods. The Mount Washington Hotel has a list of daily activities reminiscent of a cruise ship: culinary demonstrations, martini tasting and bead workshops, just to name a few. Or hit the hotel during one of its many theme weekends, such as the Food & Wine Festival or Mardi Gras.

When darkness falls at Bretton Woods, the skiing and riding fun continues. The Bethlehem Express high-speed detachable quad accesses the Bigger Ben, Big Ben and Bretton's Wood trails. Bretton's Wood also is home to the Lumber Yard Terrain Park, which hosts a "freestyle frenzy" informal jam session every Friday night. The Learning Center Quad services the lighted Rosebrook Meadow trail, ideal for the first-time skier or snowboarder.

Mountain layout

♦♦**Expert** ♦**Advanced** : Glades, glades, glades. Head to West Mountain and warm up on Peppersass or Cherry Mountain Slide, wide-open glades that aren't steep. The double-diamond glades on West Mountain have short steep pitches with varying density of trees. The most challenging terrain is now Rosebrook Canyon, an almost entirely gladed area on the resort's eastern side. With such thick, dark woods, this canyon feels like a backcountry experience. Only extreme-skiing junkies will be out of place and probably won't be found here unless they are skiing the trees out of bounds.

■ **Intermediate**: Strong intermediates may enjoy any of the single-black diamond trails such as MacIntire's Ride or Bode's Run. To sample glade skiing, try Peppersass, Cherry Mountain Slide or Millennium Maze on West Mountain. You can pop out on easier trails if the trees seem daunting. Cruising here is ideal. Coos Caper, Herb's Secret, Granny's Grit and Crawford's Blaze are great for just rolling those edges side-to-side.

●● **Beginner**: The Zephyr and Bethlehem express quads serve long beginner runs — perhaps the longest beginner runs you'll find anywhere. The traditional Bretton Woods trails, such as Sawyer's Swoop, Big Ben and Range View, are ideal for cruising. This is a good place for strong beginners to test their skills on blue runs such as Coos Caper and Granny's Grit.

● **First-timer:** The Learning Center quad serves Rosebrook Meadow and Rosebrook Lane, both dedicated learning slopes.

Ride Guide: When riding back from West Mountain to the main base area, snowboarders can avoid the Crawford Ridge, where it's difficult to maintain momentum and impossible for beginner snowboarders. About two-thirds of the way down Avalon, before a big rock on the right, take a right into the woods and cross over to Aggassiz. Then take the Coos Connector off to the right and go down Coos Caper. To get to West Mountain off of Fabyan's Triple chair, speed and momentum are necessary to make it to the top of Avalon.

Parks and pipes

Experienced riders might find the Accelerator Halfpipe and Terrain Park a bit of a yawn, but it suits the intermediates who favor this resort. At night, they're lit for riding. Whether it's skis, boards or blades, all are welcome to take on the hits, ride the rails or go for big air on the professionally groomed pipe and terrain elements contrived by the resort's newest groomer attachment, the Pipe Magician. This patented grooming tool is the latest invention of Piston Bully, the German manufacturer of groomers that are the demand for worldwide FIS and World Cup events.

Cross-country and snowshoeing (visit xcskiresorts.com for more details)

This area averages 200 inches of snow every year. The 100 km. of cross-country and snowshoeing trails are on the grounds of the **Mount Washington Hotel** and offer 1,700 acres of spectacular scenery. The trail system is dotted with a series of restaurants and lounges. Intrepid cross-country skiers can glide from the top of the Bretton Woods ski area back to the hotel. Snowshoers can use the skate lanes of the cross-country trails with a trail pass. The variety and extent of trails rivals that of the nearby Jackson Ski Touring and Vermont's Stowe system.

There is a cross-country ski school and a telemark ski school as well. with rentals at the Bretton Woods alspine shop. Snowshoes are available for sale or rent as well.

Lessons [06/07 prices]

Group lessons: $35 for 90 minutes.

First-timer package: First-timer package: First-timers' lesson package, Red Carpet Learn-to-Ski, includes equipment, all-day lessons and a limited lift ticket for $69 per day.

Private lessons: $75 per hour, $175 for half-day and $275 for full-day.

Special programs: Intermediate clinics include equipment, lessons and lifts for $95.

KidStuff [06/07 prices]

Child care: The Babes in the Woods program, with stories, crafts and games for ages 2 months to 5 years, is $69 for a full day (8 a.m.–4:30 p.m.) with lunch; $45 for a half day, morning or afternoon. Hourly prices are $12 with a two-hour minimum. Ski and Snow Play Program, a gentle introduction to skiing for children ages 3–5, is $95 for a full day (8 a.m.–4:30 p.m.) with lunch or $69 for the morning only. Reservations are required; call 278-3325.

Children's lessons: The Hobbit Ski and Snowboard School (ages 4–12) has ski and snowboard lessons including lunch and rentals for $95 full day; $69 half day. Snowboard clinics are for ages 6–12. Reservations are required for snowboard programs; call (800) 278-3345.

Lift tickets [06/07 prices]

	Adult	Teen (13-18)	Junior (6-12)	Senior 65+
One day (weekend/holiday)	$64	$52	$39	$64
One day (midweek non-holiday)	$57	$45	$34	$16
Three days (holiday)	$164	$133	$100	$164
Three days (midweek)	$121	$100	$82	$48
Five days (holiday)	$239	$195	$147	$239
Five days (midweek)	$192	$156	$123	$80

Who skis free: Age 5 and younger ski free. The Learning Center Quad chair is free for everyone.

Who skis at a discount: Seniors 65 and older ski for $16 midweek, non-holiday. On non-holiday Wednesdays, two ski or ride for $57. The $249 Bold and the Beautiful Midweek Season Pass is an interchangeable pass good at Bretton Woods or Cannon Mountain. It's on sale at the Bretton Woods ticket offices throughout the season. College students save $10 on weekend lift tickets and $15 on midweek with the College Card.

Accommodations at the resort

All Bretton Woods properties can be reached through (877) 873-0626 or 278-1000. In winter, a complimentary shuttle operates to and from the slopes. Be sure to ask about packages, as Bretton Woods offers plenty, including themed weekends such as ballroom dancing, a food and wine festival, Mardi Gras and more.

At first sight of the **Mount Washington Hotel** ($$$–$$$$), children will gasp, "It's a castle!" And it is. Flags fly from the two octagonal towers that anchor the huge hotel—the largest wooden structure in New England—set on a knoll overlooking the Presidential Range. From the antique light poles on the meandering drive to the expansive lobby defined by its rows of square Corinthian columns to the classic operator-run elevator, the hotel is the very definition of Old World Charm. Staying here is a step back in time, with excellent service and a touch of class: an orchestra plays on weekends in the dining room, and guests are asked to dress appropriately (that means jackets for gentlemen) in the dining room after 6 p.m. Shops, massage rooms and a great bar are on the lower level, while the first floor has sitting areas in the main lobby and several private rooms for smaller functions or quiet reading. The cross-country center, indoor and outdoor heated pools, ice skating and tubing hill are all at the hotel or right nearby; the Alpine area is across the street.

The restored 1896 **Bretton Arms Country Inn** ($$–$$$), a National Historic Landmark, is more intimate. It has spacious rooms, old-fashioned charm and an excellent dining room. Guests have full use of all Mt. Washington resort facilities. The **Lodge at Bretton Woods** ($–$$) is a good choice for those on a budget. Rooms are nice but not fancy; there's an indoor pool; and guests have full use of all Bretton Woods facilities, including the shuttlebus and the sports center. Bretton Woods also has a grouping of **townhouses.**

Other area accommodations

Built of granite, the romantic and isolated **Notchland Inn** (800-866-6131; 374-6131; $$–$$$$), in Hart's Location, has 13 rooms, all with fireplaces. It has a hot tub, skating, and cross-country skiing from the door. **The Mulburn Inn** (800-457-9440; 869-3389; $$–$$$) is an elegant Tudor-style B&B with oak staircase and stained glass windows. It's located in Bethlehem, once considered one of the fresh-air centers of New England, only about 10 minutes from Bretton Woods.

The Appalachian Mountain Club's beautiful **Highland Center** (466-2727; $–$$) at Crawford Notch combines state-of-the-art environmental engineering and green policies with grand architecture. Rates include a hot buffet breakfast and a multi-course, all-you-can-eat supper. The lodge has 45 rooms for 122 people, including private and family rooms (with private baths), and shared rooms/baths. Educational programs are offered.

Dining

Unless otherwise noted, phone number for all restaurants listed is 278-1000.

The opulent **Dining Room at the Mount Washington Hotel** ($$–$$$) provides a unique and grand setting for any meal complete with serenading orchestra, daily menus and an extensive wine list. Breakfast in the expansive dining room with Mt. Washington presiding outside the massive windows is an inspirational experience. Proper attire is required in the evenings (gentlemen, that means jackets). For a more intimate, century-old atmosphere, try the **Bretton Arms Dining Room** ($$–$$$)—recommended for its superb cuisine. For casual dining, head to **Stickney's** ($$) on the patio level of the Hotel for a nightly dinner buffet. Another spot recommended by locals for fine dining is **Notchland Inn** (800-866-6131; 374-6131; $$–$$$) in Hart's Location.

On the mountain, the **Top o' Quad Restaurant** ($$) with views of Mt. Washington's summit serves casual lunches daily. In the renovated base lodge, there's the **Slopeside Restaurant and Lounge** ($–$$) on the second floor. Also in the base lodge is **Lucy Crawford's Food Court** ($–$$), a typical base-lodge cafeteria.

Only a quarter-mile from the slopes, try **Darby's Diner** ($–$$) for pizza and subs. **Fabyans Station** ($–$$) serves lunch and dinner daily. The **Nordic Cafe** ($–$$) in the Bretton Woods Nordic Center is also a good place for a quick meal. For cheap eats try the AMC's **Highland Center** ($–$$), which serves a hot buffet breakfast and a family style dinner.

 ## Apres-ski/nightlife

Bretton Woods is not known for wild nightlife. Still there's enough to keep most guests happy. Enjoy a pre-dinner cocktail in the **Princess Lounge** adjacent to the fabulous Mount Washington Hotel dining room. You can dance to a dinner orchestra or head down into the stone depths of the hotel to the **Cave Lounge**. Occasional theme weekends provide other options.

 ## Other activities

The Mount Washington Hotel has plenty of non-skiing activities including **horse-drawn sleigh rides**, a **skating rink**, an **indoor pool** and **outdoor heated pool**. It's a cold walk from one to the other. **Massage** is available at the hotel. Don't miss the historic **hotel tour** offered daily. The south end of the resort also has a **snow tubing** area and a separate sports center with indoor pool, racquetball courts, exercise and weight rooms, whirlpool tubs and sauna. Nearby Cannon is home to the **New England Ski Museum,** a collection of ski memorabilia well worth a brief visit. **Cannon's tram** is open for non-skiing sightseers too.

The Rocks Estate, owned by the Society For The Protection of New Hampshire Forests, in Bethlehem (800-639-5373) has **sleigh rides** and offers some **forestry-related activities**. Nearby Twin Mountain is one of New England's top **snowmobiling** areas.

The AMC's **Highland Center** (466-2727) offers a full-range of outdoor and educational programs including rock climbing, snowshoeing, slide shows and natural history programs.

Then there's the "don't miss" activity that you won't find anywhere else in ski country: The historic **Cog Railway** takes skiers and riders one mile up (1,100 vertical feet) the flanks of Mt. Washing-ton, New England's highest peak. It may sound intimidating, but it's not. From the drop-off station above the Waumbek water tank, an intermediate groomed trail adjacent to the tracks takes you back to the base.

 ## Getting there and getting around

By air: Boston's Logan Airport is 150 miles away from the area. Manchester Airport (624-6556; www.flymanchester.com) 100 miles south, is serviced by most major carriers as well as Southwest.

By car: From I-93 heading north, Bretton Woods is on Rte. 302. Take Exit 35 to Rte. 3, which meets Rte. 302 at Twin Mountain.

Getting around: A car is a necessity to conveniently reach the resort but a shuttlebus operates throughout the resort.

Dining: $$$$-Entrees $30+; $$$-$20-$30; $$-$10-$20; $-less than $10.
Accommodations: (double room) $$$$-$200+; $$$-$141-$200; $$-$81-$140; $-$80 and less.

Cannon Mountain
New Hampshire

Summit elevation:	**4,146 feet**
Vertical drop:	**2,146 feet**
Base elevation:	**2,000 feet**

Address: Franconia Notch State Park
Franconia, NH 03580
Area code: 603
Ski area phone: 823-8800
Snow report: 823-7771
Fax: 823-8088
Toll-free reservations: None
E-mail: info@cannonmt.com
Internet: www.cannonmt.com
Expert:★★
Advanced:★★
Intermediate:★★★★
Beginner:★★★
First-timer:★★★

Number and types of lifts: 9–1 70-person aerial tram, 1 high-speed quad, 2 quads, 3 triples, 2 surface lifts
Acreage: 165 skiable acres
Snowmaking: 97 percent
Uphill capacity: 11,000 per hour
Parks & pipes: 1 park
Bed base: 13,000 nearby
Nearest lodging: about 1/2 mile
Resort child care: Yes, 6 weeks and older
Adult ticket, per day: $42-54 (05/06)

Dining:★★
Apres-ski/nightlife:★
Other activities:★★

In the early 1930s, people came to Franconia Notch in winter for one reason: to ski Cannon Mountain. More than 70 years later, they're still coming for that very same reason, and to snowboard, too. Like other historic ski areas, Cannon is a mountain with a strong New England flavor. Trails make narrow, sinuous turns through the pine forest, and the famous Front Five, the seemingly vertical shafts visible from the highway, are as steep as you'll find in the East.

But that's not to say that beginners and intermediates should head elsewhere. As much hard-core terrain as there is at Cannon, there are even more intermediate and beginner trails. More than two-thirds of the trails off the summit are smooth, wide, blue runs with stunning views. From the top, you can see the Presidential Range of the White Mountains and no signs of civilization except for the highway and base lodges.

Cannon embraces its history. The mountain is home to the New England Ski Museum, located adjacent to the Tram base. It's well worth a visit. The Taft Slalom is part of the first racing trail in North America, cut in 1933. And when the original 1938 aerial tramway was replaced in 1980, Cannon didn't tear down the base or summit stations. On a quiet day, you half-expect the ghost-of-skiing-past to fly out of the woods. Cannon also embraces its present. World Cup winner Bode Miller grew up skiing at Cannon Mountain. The Millers still ski Cannon to this day and Bode is a local legend.

Mountain layout

♦♦**Expert:** True experts will want to try the extreme terrain on Tramline Trail, and we're not misusing the word "extreme" here. The narrow trail is a series of cliff steps. One of the longest glades in the East is Kinsman Glade, on skier's right of the tramline. The Front Five, as known to locals, are the intimidating-looking trails that appear to plunge into Echo Lake. These are accessed via Paulie's Extension or Lower Cannon. Three of them, Avalanche, Paulie's Folly and Zoomer, are marked black and rightfully so. The other two, Rocket and Gary's, have less pitch and no bumps. Lakeview Glade is under the Zoomer triple chair. For a backcountry experience, take the Taft Slalom straight across the ridge, then hike the remaining 100 yards to Mittersill, Cannon's defunct neighbor. Skiers and riders can use Mittersill's trails on a don't-ask, don't-tell basis, but it's unpatrolled and you're on your own.

♦**Advanced:** From the summit, experience New England skiing the way it used to be by winding down Upper Cannon, Skylight or Upper Ravine. To test your mettle on the Front Five, start on skier's left (Gary's) and work right until you feel you've hit your limit.

■ **Intermediate:** Intermediates will find plenty of terrain to suit their skills. From the summit, you can take Vista Way, Tramway or Upper Cannon, which swoops down through the forest. These feed into a collection of intermediate runs, including Middle Cannon and Middle Ravine. Or from the top of the Cannonball Express Quad, treat yourself to Upper Ravine, another swooping trail. Intermediates wishing to return to the tram without scaring themselves on the Front Five can follow the Tram Cutback from Gary's, the easiest of the Front Five.

●● **Beginner:** The Tuckerbrook quad chair serves beginner trails—Bear Paw, Deer Run, Fleitman and Coyote Crossing—that are segregated from the upper mountain. From the Peabody Base Area, take Brookside to the Tuckerbrook area. The bottom half of Cannon has four long runs that will suit beginners: Lower Cannon, Parkway, Gremlin and Turnpike, but be forewarned that a slew of intermediate runs feed into them. The Eagle Triple Chair, from the Peabody Base Area, is the best way to access this terrain. More daring beginners can take the Peabody Express Quad.

● **First-timer:** The Brookside learning area adjacent to the Peabody Base Area is ideal for first-timers. The area is segregated from the rest of the mountain, and is serviced by its own triple chairlift, as well as two surface lifts. First-timers can then progress to the short beginner trails off the Tuckerbrook quad chair.

Ride Guide: If you stray into Mittersill, the adjacent defunct area, be aware that you *can* run into flats.

Parks and pipes

Cannon's terrain park is on the lower section of Toss-Up. Cannon is now committed to having snowboarders design the park, and it encourages feedback from those who use it, which has greatly enhanced the experience.

Cross-country and snowshoeing (visit xcskiresorts.com for more details)

The **Franconia Village X-C Ski Center** (800-473-5299) has 105 km. of trails, 65 km. of which are groomed and tracked; 5 km. are skate groomed. Ski, stay and sleigh packages are available through the Franconia Inn at the same telephone number.

Lessons (05/06 prices)

Group lessons: $32 per session; second lesson on the same day costs $10.
First-timer package: The all-day learn-to-ski or -ride program costs $54 and includes lessons, rentals and a Brookside lift ticket.

Private lessons: $50 for one hour, $75 for two hours, $100 for three hours, $175 for full day. Semi-private instruction for up to five people costs $85 for one hour, $105 for two hours, $155 for three hours, and $245 for full day.

Special programs: A guide for up to five people is $295 for a full day; $150 half day.

Workshops: Three workshops are available at 1:30 p.m. on weekends and holidays: Mastering bumps, mastering Cannon's famous Front Five, and women's groups. Cost is $29.

KidStuff [05/06 prices]

Child care: For ages 12 months and older, $9 per hour; $28 for a half day; $55 for a half day with skiing; $50 for full day with lunch; $70 for full day with lunch and skiing. For ages 6 weeks to 12 months, $10 hourly; $30 half day; $60 full day. Hourly rates require two-hour minimum. Reservations advised; call (603) 823-8800.

Children's lessons: Cannon Tykes, for ages 3–4, costs $50 for a lesson with rentals. Cannon Kids is for skiers ages 4–7; Mountain Explorers is for skiers and riders ages 8–12. Rates include lift tickets. An all-day session is $70; morning session is $55; afternoon session is $45. Five-day program with two sessions daily is $300. Five-day program with one session daily is $225. Rental equipment for all programs is $10.

Lift tickets [05/06 prices]

	Adult	Teen (13-19)	Child (6-12)	Seniors 65+
(weekend/midweek)	$54/$42	$39/$25	$30/25	

Who skis free: Ages 5 and younger when with a ticketed adult.

Who skis at a discount: On non-holiday Tuesdays and Thursdays, two people can ski for $54. The Brookside beginner lift is $20 any time. Ages 65 and older pay junior rates. College students with ID pay teen rates. The Brookside beginner lift is $25 any time. Anyone who comes to the ticket window with the previous day's lift ticket from Cannon or Bretton Woods still attached to their clothing gets a $5 discount.

Accommodations

Cannon has no slopeside lodging, but nearby Lincoln and Woodstock (about 15 minutes south) and Franconia (about 5 minutes north) have accommodations to suit just about any needs. Plus, Bretton Woods is within striking distance. See the Loon chapter for recommended accommodations in the Lincoln/Woodstock area, or call Lincoln/Woodstock Central Reservations at 745-6221.

Long known as a ski town, Franconia has several quaint New England Inns, the nicest being the Sunset Hill House (800-786-4455; 823-5522; $–$$) and the Franconia Inn (800-473-5299; 823-5542; $$-$$$). Just outside Franconia on historic Sugar Hill (the site of the first ski school in North America), sits the Sunset Hill House, a restored farmhouse built in 1789 that has wonderful views of the Presidential Range and nearby Mt. Lafayette. The Franconia Inn is a lovely turn-of-the-century inn with hand-hewn beams in the cozy lobby and a sunny dining room. Some of the rooms have been recently renovated; others still have quaint old bathrooms with claw-foot tubs.

The Inn at Forest Hills (823-9550; $–$$) is a beautifully restored, English Tudor-style B&B built into a house that was once part of the grand Forest Hills Hotel. It's about a mile from the village of Franconia, on Rte. 142, heading toward Bethlehem.

The modern Franconia Hotel (888-669-6777; 823-7422; $–$$) has an indoor heated pool, fitness and games rooms, and a full-service restaurant .

Among the least expensive places to stay are the Hillwinds Lodge (800-473-5299; 823-5551; $); the Cannon Mountain View Inn (800-823-9577; 823-9577; $), with rooms renovated in early 2004; and **The Eastgate Motor Inn** (866-640-3561; 444-3971; $) just off I-93. The **Kinsman Lodge** (866-546-7626; 823-5686; $) is a casual and affordable B&B.

About 30 minutes north is the newly renovated and reopened **Mountain View Grand** (866-484-3843; 837-2100; $$–$$$$). This sprawling historical hotel now houses a European-style spa on the fourth floor, and has a fitness center, indoor pool and steamroom.

 ## Dining

For elegant dining the **Sunset Hill House** (823-5522; $$), with views of the Franconia Range, and the **Franconia Inn** (823-5542; $$–$$$), with a sunny dining room, are the best. Both establishments require reservations, even if you're a guest.

The Pub with Mexican Grub ($–$$) recently opened in the Franconia Hotel. For more traditional fare, head to the **Village House** (823-5405; $-$$) in downtown Franconia, where prime rib is the Saturday-night special, or **The Eastgate Restaurant** (444-3971; $–$$), considered one of the better local restaurants. For breakfast, don't miss **Polly's Pancake Parlor** (823-5575; $) up Sugar Hill outside Franconia. Or drive a few miles up I-93 to Littleton and the **Littleton Diner** (444-3994; $), a traditional old diner car where you can get a great breakfast.

See the Loon chapter for more dining recommendations in the area.

 ## Apres-ski/nightlife

With no restaurants nearby, Cannon is not exactly bustling with apres-ski activities. But down the road in Franconia, try **Village House**, a comfortable lounge with a lot of classic ski history. Or head back down I-93 and catch up with Loon skiers partying at **Woodstock Station** or the **Indian Head Resort**, where there are live bands Wednesday through Sunday.

 ## Other activities

The **New England Ski Museum** sits adjacent to Cannon's Tramway Base Station and has a collection of ski memorabilia well worth a visit; open noon-5 p.m. Friday-Monday, free admission. **Cannon's tram** is open for non-skiing sightseers for $10 a ride. **Snowtubing** at Cannon's tubing park on weekends and holidays costs $10 per session.

The Franconia Inn (800-473-5299; 823-5542) has an **ice skating** pond, **sledding hill**, winter **horseback riding**, and **sleigh rides** and equipment rentals.

The **Rocks Estate** in Bethlehem, on a hilltop about 10 miles from Cannon, has **sleigh rides** and offers some **forestry-related activities,** since it's owned by the Society For The Protection of New Hampshire Forests.

 ## Getting there and getting around

By air: Boston's Logan Airport is about 145 miles south from Cannon and the Franconia area. Manchester Airport is 85 miles south.

By car: From I-93 heading north, Cannon is visible just north of Franconia Notch State Park. Take Exit 34B for the Tramway Base Station, Exit 34C for the Peabody Base Area.

Getting around: Since there is no on-mountain lodging, a car is a necessity.

Dining: $$$$-Entrees $30+; $$$-$20-$30; $$-$10-$20; $-less than $10.
Accommodations: (double room) $$$$-$200+; $$$-$141-$200; $$-$81-$140; $-$80 and less.

Loon Mountain
New Hampshire

Summit elevation:	3,050 feet
Vertical drop:	2,100 feet
Base elevation:	950 feet

Address: RR1, Box 41
Lincoln, NH 03251
Area code: 603
Ski area phone: 745-8111
Snow report: 745-8100
Fax: 745-8214
Toll-free reservations:
(800) 229-LOON (5666)
E-mail: info@loonmtn.com
Internet: www.loonmtn.com
Expert:★ **Advanced:**★★
Intermediate:★★★★
Beginner:★★★★
First-timer:★★★

Number and types of lifts: 10–1 gondola,
2 high-speed quads, 1 triple, 3 doubles,
2 surface lifts, 1 moving carpet
Acreage: 275 skiable acres
Snowmaking: 99 percent
Uphill capacity: 11,865 per hour
Parks & pipes: 6 parks; 2 pipes
Bed base: 13,000 **Nearest lodging:** slopeside
Resort child care: Yes, 6 weeks - 8 years
Adult ticket, per day: $54-$65 (05/06)
Dining:★★★
Apres-ski/nightlife:★★★
Other activities:★★★

Like many of the other ski resorts in the White Mountains, Loon has decent vertical. Many of the runs maintain their pitch from top to bottom (unlike some resorts, where most of the runs wash out to beginner terrain near the base). The mountain's black-diamond terrain will keep experts entertained, but, for the most part, Loon is an intermediate's mountain. The blue-square runs are true-blue friends for intermediates; beginners who venture onto them may find their limits tested.

The resort has some of the friendliest staff around, which keeps skiers and riders coming back. It also offers plenty of family-friendly activities, including snow tubing (both day and night), snow toys, a climbing wall, and an ice skating rink. The two base areas are separated by a parking lot, but connected by a steam train that shuttles skiers and riders back and forth, a real hit with children.

The resort has some of the friendliest staff around, which keeps skiers and riders coming back. It also offers plenty of family-friendly activities, including snow tubing (both day and night), snow toys, a climbing wall, and an ice skating rink. The two base areas are separated by a parking lot, but connected by a steam train that shuttles skiers and riders back and forth, a real hit with children.

When it comes to lodging, the resort is a behemoth. It's one of the few resorts where the bed base is larger than the lift capacity. Combined with easy access off I-93 from Boston and other points south, can create crowded conditions at times. Fortunately, Loon has made a number of improvements during the past few years. Among these are trail improvements to relieve congestion in high-traffic stretches, new lifts to get people up the mountain faster, more snowmaking coverage and a dedicated learning area.

Mountain layout

♦♦**Expert** ♦**Advanced:** North Peak runs are challenging and well removed from lower-intermediate traffic. The steeps are there, but half the bumps are groomed out. To reach North Peak, take the gondola, then ski down Big Dipper, Triple Trouble or Angel Street to the North Peak Triple Chair. In fresh snow, experts will like the three tree-skiing areas: One is accessed off Upper Flying Fox, another off Angel Street and the third off Haulback, between Lower Flume and Lower Walking Boss.

■ **Intermediate:** The intermediate runs are good and solid, with no expert surprises around the next clump of trees. The upper trails are a bit twisted, narrow and seemingly un-directed, but they open onto a series of wide intermediate pistes. Flying Fox is a delightful cruise, with old-fashioned twists and turns through the trees and granite boulders. Depending on snow conditions, skiers can link up with the West Side trails via Upper Speakeasy, or they can drop down to the parking lot on any of the wide cruising runs (Rumrunner is a good choice, if there isn't a race on it), and ride the steam train the 100 yards to the adjacent base area and the gondola. Perhaps the sweetest and longest cruise on the mountain is the perimeter-hugging Sunset to Bear Claw Extension to Upper Speakeasy to Lower Speakeasy, which descends from the summit of North Peak to the Governor's base.

If you want to sample trees, try Misgiving Link or Scaler, off Grand Junction.

●● **Beginner:** The center of the mountain, serviced by the Seven Brothers triple chair, has good intermediate trails that advanced beginners can handle. The east side of the chair has beginner runs such as Grand Junction, The Link, Brookway, and Lower Bear Claw.

● **First-timer:** There's a nice learning area next to the Governor Adams Base Lodge.

Parks and pipes

The Kanc Quad and the Seven Brothers lift provide easy access to the Loon Mountain Park. The gondola is also an option, if you don't mind the long run from the summit to the top of the park, between Lower Picked Rock and Picaroon. Jumps range in difficulty from little ones that give newbies just a few inches of air under their boards to hit-it-for-all-you're-worth-and-hope-you-make-it-to-the-landing kickers. Our riders found good transitions and smooth landings in the park, but the superpipe could use more frequent grooming. Loon also has three Pocket Parks: Both Lower Picked Rock (with tabletops and a rail) and Bear Island Bypass (with berms and rollers) are designed for beginners. Little Sister is a boardercross with berms and rollers. Rounding out Loon's parks is The Junkyard, off the Little Sister lift, created as a playground for those using snowplay toys such as snowdecks, skibikes and snowscoots.

Cross-country and snowshoeing (visit xcskiresorts.com for more details)

The **Loon Mountain Adventure Center** (745-8111, ext. 5568) has 35 km. of trails, 25 tracked and 20 skate groomed, that wind along the Pemigewasset River. Children ages 6 and younger and seniors 70 and older ski free.

Lessons (05/06 prices)

Group lessons: $35-$39 for 2 hours.

First-timer package: For skiers or riders, this includes equipment, all-day lessons and a limited lift ticket for $89 per day. A follow-up package is $99.

The Burton Method Center pairs snowboard instruction with equipment progression.

Private lessons: $59–$79 an hour. **Racing:** The course is served by the Seven Brothers lift.

KidStuff (05/06 prices)

Child care: Loon has a spacious Children's Center near the Governor Adams Lodge. Child care is available for ages 6 weeks to 8 years. Hours are 8 a.m. to 4 p.m. A half day is $50 midweek and $55 weekends; a full day is $60 weekdays and $65 weekends. Reservations are required; call 745-8111.

Children's lessons: Kids' Ski & Snowboard Day Camps for ages 3–6 and Adventure Camp for ages 7–12 are $89–$94 full day, including lunch; half day $69–$74. All children's lessons are run out of the Children's Center, which also houses a rental shop for skiers and boarders to age 6. Reservations are required for all programs, call 745-6281, ext. 5160 or 5162. Camps are not available during holidays or peak periods.

Special activities: The Kids Night Out program lets parents enjoy a night on the town. Bring kids ages 6 weeks to 12 years to the Loon Children's Center for a supervised evening of games, snowtubing, ice skating and other activities. The cost is $35 for the first child, and $19 for each additional sibling. The program operates every Saturday evening, beginning after Christmas, from 5:30–9 p.m., as well as nightly during the Christmas and February vacation weeks. Reservations are required, call 745-6291 ext. 5166 or 5163.

Lift tickets (05/06 prices)

	Adult	Young Adult	Child (6–12)
One day (holiday/weekend)	$65	$55	$45
One day (weekday)	$58	$48	$38
Three days	$164 ($55/day)	$117	$104
Five days (midweek)	$270 ($54/day)	$195	$170

Who skis free: Children ages 5 and younger.

Who skis at a discount: Ages 65 and older pay $15 midweek (non-holiday), but pay the regular adult price on Saturday, Sunday and holidays.

Note: Ticket sales are cut off after approximately 6,000 have been sold. To reserve tickets, parking or ski rentals in advance call or visit the website.

Loon is owned by Booth Creek Ski Holdings, which owns nearby Waterville Valley, Mt. Cranmore in the Mt. Washington Valley and several Western resorts. The three New Hampshire areas have interchangeable lift tickets and season passes.

Accommodations

The Mountain Club on Loon (800-229-7829; 745-2244) is a ski-in/ski-out property with everything under one roof, from parking to pool, fitness club to restaurants. A full-service spa opened in late 2003. Note: Many of its rooms have a double Murphy bed with two small day beds along the windows. This arrangement is fine for couples, or for a family with young children, but it is awkward for two adults who don't want to sleep in the same bed. Instead, request two rooms that, when adjoined, make a suite. Loon also has condominiums. Make reservations through the Mountain Club.

The **Comfort Inn** (800-228-5150; 745-6700; $$) is right off I-93 at Hobo Railroad. It has both regular hotel rooms and one-bedroom suites with kitchenettes. Two prominent properties on the Kancamagus Highway (Main Street) in Lincoln are **The Mill House Inn** (800-654-6183; 745-6261; $–$$$) at The Mill and the **Nordic Inn** (800-536-1038; $–$$), which has studio to three-bedroom condos. The **Rivergreen Resort Hotel** (800-654-6183; 745-2450; $$–$$$), owned by the same group that owns The Mill House Inn, is another condominium hotel. The last in a trio of "Mill" properties is **The Lodge at Lincoln Station** (800-654-6188; 745-3441; $$–$$$), a hotel on the Pemigewasset River. Accommodations range from studios to one-bedroom suites. They are about 1 mile west of Loon.

Another couple of miles away from Loon is **The Woodstock Inn B&B** (800-321-3985; 745-3951; $–$$), a typical New England lodge. The main building is more than 100 years old, and no two rooms are alike. The restaurant in the front of the inn is one of North Woodstock's most elegant; the one in the station at the rear is one of the town's liveliest.

Wilderness Inn B&B (745-3890; $–$$) welcomes families with youngsters. Parents note: This place has laundry facilities. The B&B is only steps from the center of North Woodstock, which is filled with shops and restaurants.

Three motelish properties along Rte. 3 in Lincoln, one exit up I-93 from Loon, have similar accommodations and prices, but slightly different amenities. **Indian Head Motel Resort** (800-343-8000; 745-8000; $$) is one of the centers of apres-ski action, with live bands and a great ice-skating and cross-country. **The Beacon** (800-258-8934; 745-8118; $–$$$) has indoor tennis and large indoor pools, but attracts the bus-tour crowd. **Woodward's Motor Inn** (800-635-8968; 745-8141; $–$$) is the most family-oriented. It has the area's only racquetball court and the best steaks in the region. Another reasonably priced motel along this stretch of Rte. 3 is the **Drummer Boy Motor Inn** (800-762-7275; 745-3661; $–$$$), with an indoor pool, guest laundry and free continental breakfast.

 ## Dining

The most elegant dining experience in the Lincoln/Woodstock area is found at the **Woodstock Inn's Clement Room Grille** (745-3951; $$–$$$). It gets high ratings from locals for its informal dining with style. The Woodstock Inn also serves great daily breakfast as well as a fabulous weekend brunch.

The Common Man (745-3463; $$–$$$) serves excellent food, with a menu ranging from lobster-corn chowder and rock-crab cakes to hazelnut-crusted chicken and double-thick pork chops.

For convenient, on-mountain dining, there are two choices: the **Mountain Club on Loon** (745-2244; $$) and **The Black Diamond Bar** ($–$$), both at the Mountain Club.

Locals claim the **Open Hearth Steak House** (745-8141; $$), at Woodward's Motor Inn, has the best steaks. The wide-ranging menu at **Gordi's Fish and Steak House** (745-6635; $–$$) includes steaks, Maine lobster, chicken, pasta and fish; a pub menu serves lighter fare.

Truant's Tavern (745-2239; $–$$) serves clever dinner entrees in a mock schoolhouse atmosphere; drinking in class was never so much fun. The bar hops on weekends. For a reasonably priced meal, head to **Woodstock Station** (745-3951; $–$$), located in an old train station on Main Street. Options range from meatloaf to Mexican fare, and the restaurant brews its own beer. Locals agree that the best pizza in town is found at **Elvio's Pizzeria** (745-8817; $). The **Gypsy Cafe** (745-4395; $), on the Kancamagus Highway, across the street from The Mill. is a good choice for either lunch or dinner, and don't miss the margaritas.

If you're off-mountain for lunch, **KimberLee's Deli** (745-3354; $), in Depot Plaza just outside the Loon Mountain entrance, has a good choice of sandwiches, soups and salads. It also serves breakfast bagel-wiches. In the Kancamagus Motor Lodge, **Brittany's Cafe** (745-3365; $–$$) is a good choice for either breakfast or dinner and **CJ's Penalty Box** (745-4899; $–$$) is a sports pub with light fare.

Winners in the breakfast category include the **Sunny Day Diner** (745-4833: $) and

Dining: $$$$-Entrees $30+; $$$-$21-$30; $$-$10-20; $-less than $10.
Accommodations: (double room) $$$$-$200+; $$$-$141-$200; $$-$81-$140; $-$80 and less.

Peg's Family Restaurant (745-2740; $), both in North Woodstock. Sunny Day also serves inexpensive homestyle dinners, such as salisbury steak and fried chicken.

Apres-ski/nightlife

After skiing at Loon, head to the **Black Diamond Bar** in the Mountain Club for good weekend entertainment and a quiet après-ski spot. The **Paul Bunyan Lounge** at the Octagon base has a young, rowdy crowd and really rocks. Another on-mountain choice is **Babe's**, in the Governor Adams Lodge.

Off mountain, near Loon, those with romance on their minds should head to the fireplace at the **Common Man**. Otherwise, **Gordi's Fish and Steak**, in Lincoln, is a local favorite while across the street, **CJ's Penalty Box Sports Bar and Pub**, in the basement of the Kancamagus Motor Lodge, is usually hopping. Down Main Street, towards I-93, the **Olde Timbermill** in the Millfront Marketplace, has good singles action, with bands on weekends.

From Wednesday through Sunday, live bands rock the **Indian Head Resort**, in Lincoln. The **Tavern Sports Bar** is a low-key darts, video game and pool hall.

Locals set up party camp at **Truant's Tavern** and the **Woodstock Station.**

Other activities

Loon Mountain has **ice skating**, day and night tubing (10 a.m. to 10 p.m. daily on Little Sister Trail on the Octagon side of the mountain), and apres-ski entertainment for families.

Profile Mountaineering, in Lincoln, offers introductory **ice climbing and winter mountaineering**. Alpine Village has a **rock-climbing wall**, as does the Pemi Valley Rock Gym (745-9800) in Woodstock. Alpine Adventures (745-9911) in Lincoln offers guided **snowmobile tours**. Creations in The Depot has **make-your-own pottery**. Lincoln also has one **movie theater** with four screens.

The town of Lincoln has several specialty **shops** worth a look, including some factory outlets, along the Kancamagus Highway in town. The factory outlet bonanza of tax-free North Conway is 35 miles east of town, but the drive takes about an hour in winter.

Getting there and getting around

By air: Boston's Logan Airport is 140 miles away from Loon. Manchester Airport, 80 miles south, is serviced by Southwest as well as most major carriers and numerous discount ones. The airport phone number is 624-6556; its Internet address is www.flymanchester.com.

By car: From I-93 heading north, Loon Mountain is about two miles up the Kancamagus Highway (Rte. 112) from Exit 32 in Lincoln.

Getting around: A car is a necessity unless you stay in the Lincoln-Woodstock area. Lincoln-Woodstock has a shuttle service and taxi, available anytime.

Waterville Valley
New Hampshire

Summit elevation:	4,004 feet
Vertical drop:	2,020 feet
Base elevation:	1,984 feet

Address: One Ski Area Rd., Waterville Valley, NH 03215
Area code: 603
Ski area phone: 236-8311
Snow report: 236-4144
Fax: 236-4344
Toll-free reservations: (800) 468-2553
E-mail: info@waterville.com
Internet: www.waterville.com
Expert:★
Advanced:★★
Intermediate:★★★
Beginner:★★★ **First-timer:**★★★

Number and types of lifts: 11–2 high-speed quads, 2 triples, 3 doubles, 4 surface lifts
Skiable acreage: 255 acres
Snowmaking: 100 percent
Uphill capacity: 15,187 per hour
Parks & pipes: 3 parks; 3 pipes
Bed base: 2,500
Nearest lodging: quarter mile
Resort child care: Yes, 6 months - 4 years
Adult ticket, per day: $47-$55 (05/06 prices)
Dining:★★★
Apres-ski/nightlife:★★★
Other activities:★★★

Waterville Valley is the first "big" resort when heading north on I-93, making it one of the most popular in New Hampshire. Its relatively low ticket prices add to its appeal. The resort built its reputation by staging more than 10 World Cup ski races, but the emphasis now is on family. That has resulted in it becoming a more well-rounded area, as seen by its bountiful terrain parks.

A planned community/resort, Waterville Valley is sufficiently self-contained so that most visitors, once they enter, do not venture any farther than the slopes, just a short shuttlebus ride away from the lodging in and around Town Square, where there are a variety of shops, restaurants and bars. Most of the off-slope activities are in Town Square, including cross-country skiing, sleigh rides, ice skating, and a huge sports complex with pools, tennis, squash and racquetball courts and indoor track. Visitors can enroll in the town's numerous family-oriented recreation programs, such as ice cream socials.

At the mountain, the single base area is ideal for families who don't want to get separated amidst multiple base lodges. Two high-speed quads start right outside the base lodge, one being Quadzilla. Despite its scary name, the lift is decorated like a happy dog wearing a whirly-bird beanie. You can tell how windy it is by how fast the propeller turns.

New for the 2006-'07 season, an expanded unload area at the top of Quadzilla will give skiers and snowboarders more room to prepare to head down the mountain or meet for snowsports lessons. The other quad, White Peak Express, takes skiers and riders almost to the summit. The High Country Double services the three uppermost intermediate slopes when wind (and snow) conditions are right.

Mountain Layout

♦♦**Expert** ♦**Advanced:** One of the toughest runs, True Grit, develops big moguls and drops down the Sunnyside face. With several tough rollers and steep pitches, the World Cup Slalom Hill is a good place for experts to test carving skills. Lower Bobby's Run is a double-diamond mogul field with two glades for diversion: The one on the right is rated more difficult than the one below it, off the left. An interesting note—Bobby's Run (both Upper and Lower) was named after the late Senator Robert Kennedy, who frequented the resort after it opened in 1966.

■ **Intermediate:** Waterville's trails are not New England's typical steep and narrow pistes. Most are wide swaths through the trees, and there's elbow room and a chance to check out the slope before committing to the fall line again.

Such trails as White Caps, Sel's Choice, Old Tecumseh and Tippecanoe are intermediate and advanced playthings. Upper Bobby's Run is a great intermediate trail. But if you don't want to find yourself on a black diamond or double-diamond mogul trail (Lower Bobby's), make sure you take a strong left to Terry's Trail or Old Tecumseh. The natural hits on Oblivion, on the resort's north side, are popular with snowboarders.

Something more resorts should do: Waterville has a designated "easier mogul field." For those wanting to move to the next level, this is great practice.

●● **Beginner:** Beginner terrain at Waterville is limited. Beginners who have skied blue runs at other resorts might find Waterville's intermediate terrain challenging. But the Valley Run is a beginner/lower intermediate haven with enough width to allow skiing for a couple of days down different sections. This run is served by Quadzilla, a high-speed quad that takes skiers to the top of the run in 4.5 minutes.

● **First-timer:** There's a small area with a separate lift.

Parks and pipes

Waterville Valley has three terrain parks, including one for younger aficionados, a Boarder Cross that's open to the public, and a 400-foot-long superpipe. Based on the resort's dedication to the freestyle snowboarding scene, Burton Snowboards has selected Waterville Valley as an Eastern site for the latest creative idea in snowboard progression.

The Exhibition Terrain Park & Halfpipe, located right above the base area, has a 16-foot superpipe, rails, tabletops, hips, trannies and kickers. The signature rail is a shaped C that's 22 feet long. The Hubba Street Course includes elements such as stairs and is at the base of Exhibition. While Exhibition has its own surface lift, if you access the top of the park from Psyched, you'll gain extra hits. There's a yurt at the park's summit where you can get warm. Younger kids can train for the big stuff in their own terrain park, Little Slammer, with mini-pipe, smaller tables, rails and boxes. Waterville also has a dedicated snowskate park next to the Quadzilla lift and an indoor skate ramp at the base lodge, tucked under the heated deck, with five-foot miniramp and lighted night sessions.

Cross-country and snowshoeing (visit xcskiresorts.com for more details)

There are 76 km. of classic and skating trails with some of the best grooming in New England, as well as more than 35 km. of backcountry trails. New this year are the addition of another groomer, a yurt warming hut and picnic spot out on the trail system.The center has a couch, tables and a fireplace and a full retail shop. Rentals and lessons are available, as are guided cross-country and snowshoe tours for all levels and ages. Call 236-4666 for more information.

Lessons [05/06 prices]

Group lessons: $35 for two hours. Waterville also offers free from-the-summit clinics for upper-intermediate and advanced skiers. The one-hour clinics meet twice daily in the afternoon.

First-timer package: Skiing $69 or snowboarding $74, For ages 7 and up, includes a two hour lesson in the morning **and** afternoon (total of 4 hours of instruction), quality rental equipment, and a learning area lift ticket. Register at the Rental Shop. Lessons at 10:00 and 1:30 daily.

Private lessons: $79 an hour and up.

Racing: A course on Utter Abandon has races Wednesdays and Friday to Sundays.

Signature Clinics: Three-day Women's Retreats include lessons, video analysis, apres-ski parties and other special events. Call for dates and prices.

KidStuff (05/06 prices)

Child care: Waterville has two nurseries at its base area. Child care is available for ages 6 months to 4 years. All day is $65, with multiday discounts. Half day is $50, hourly is $17. Lunch is $7, or children may bring their own. Reservations required to ensure a space. Call (603) 236-8311.

Children's lessons: Mogul Mites, for ages 3-4; Explorers, for ages 4-6; and Scouts, for ages 7-12; are all $75 for a full day. Rental equipment, lunch and lift ticket are extra.

Lift tickets (05/06 prices)

	Adult	Teen (13-18)	Youth (6-12)
One day	$55	$45	$35
Three days	$145	$115	$85
Five days	$235	$185	$135

Note: Lift tickets may be used at Loon and Mt. Cranmore.

Who skis free: Kids 5 and younger ski free anytime. Waterville often runs a Kids Ski Free promotion (for ages up to 12) when parents buy multiday lodging packages; ask about it.

Who skis at a discount: Ages 65 and older ski at youth rates non-holiday weekdays.

Accommodations

Waterville Valley has 2,500 beds in its Village, about 1.5 miles from the slopes. To make reservations at any of the Waterville Valley accommodations listed below, call (800) 468-2553 or 236-8311. The "Winter Unlimited" package is all inclusive, offering all of Waterville's winter activities plus lodging for one price.

The **Golden Eagle Lodge**, with condominium suites, features a distinctive design reminiscent of the turn-of-the-century grand hotels. Additionally, Waterville has three hotel properties and four groups of condominiums, all in the valley. **The Valley Inn and Tavern** operates as a country inn with rates that can include meals, and the **Black Bear Lodge** is more hotel-like. All are in the same price range. **The Best Western/Silver Fox** offers continental breakfast and is the most economical place to stay. Condominiums also are available.

Dining

The most elegant dining experience can be found at the **William Tell** (726-3618; $$–$$$) on Rte. 49, just down the valley from the resort. The William Tell has a strong Swiss-German accent with excellent wines.

On Saturday nights, take a 30-minute snowcat ride up the slopes to the **Schwendi Hutte** (236-8311, Ext. 3000). The food is some of the best in the valley, as is the ambiance. Reservations are required, and the snowcat ride and meal cost $65 per person.

The **Wild Coyote Grill** (236-4919; $–$$), in the White Mountain Athletic Club, offers nouveau cuisine with a Southwestern flair, and the calamari is a specialty. For moderately

Dining: $$$$-Entrees $30+; $$$-$20-$30; $$-$10-$20; $-less than $10.
Accommodations: (double room) $$$$-$200+; $$$-$141-$200; $$-$81-$140; $-$80 and less.

priced family fare, head to **Aglio** (236-4646; $) or call **Olde Waterville Valley Pizza Co.** (236-3663; $). **Diamond's Edge North** (236-2006; $$) also in Town Square, offers classier meals with nicer presentations.

The **Schwendi Hutte,** at the top of the White Peak Express Quad, has the best lunch on the mountain. Here you can slip off your boots and warm your tootsies in the slippers provided. On sunny spring days, head for barbecue on the deck of **Sunnyside Up** on Valley Run. The base area has a cafeteria, pizza corner and **T-Bars**. For breakfast, pick up coffee and pastries at the **Waterville Coffee Emporium** (236-4021; $) or the **Jugtown Sandwich Shop and Country Store** (236-8662; $). The Coffee Emporium also cooks omelets, eggs, French toast and waffles. Both are in Town Square. **Buckets Bones and Brews**, on the top level of the base lodge, offers an outdoor deck with barbecue served in buckets.

 ## Apres-ski/nightlife

Waterville now has a collection of bars in Town Square, each with slightly different apres-ski. They are all within a few steps of each other. **Legends 1291, Latitudes** and **Diamond's Edge** deliver a good time, and later in the evening music ranges from loud disco and rock to quieter music. **T-Bars**, at the mountain, has the normal collection of skiers for apres-ski until 5:30 p.m.

Just down the road from Waterville, on the way back to the interstate, try the **William Tell**, for a cozy quiet apres-ski, or the **Mad River Tavern**, for a more raucous setting.

 ## Other activities

Waterville Valley has **sleigh rides** and an **indoor fitness center** with pool, track, weight rooms and more, as well as an indoor ice arena for **skating.**

The resort also offers a full recreation program that includes activities for toddlers, youngsters and teens such as ice cream socials, basketball and dances.

Waterville Valley's Town Square has several specialty **shops** selling books, souvenirs, gifts, clothing and jewelry. Free Internet access is available at the check-in office. Wi-Fi is available in the base lodge, at Town Square and in the Conference Center.

 ## Getting there and getting around

By air: Boston is 130 miles south and Manchester is 70 miles south.

By car: From I-93 heading north take Exit 28. . Then go 11 miles on Rte. 49 and turn left on Tripoli Rd.

Getting around: Waterville Valley offers a shuttle from the village to the slopes. It's wise to take the shuttle, since parking at the ski area can be a nightmare. Valet parking is available for $15. If you plan to venture away from the village or want to try to Loon, Cannon and Bretton Woods farther north, a car is a necessity.

New Hampshire Regional Resorts

The Balsams Wilderness, Dixville Notch, NH

(603) 255-3400; (800) 255-0800 within NH; (800) 255-0600 outside NH

Internet: www.thebalsams.com

4 lifts; 87 acres; 1,000 vertical feet; 1 terrain park

When you need to be pampered, owe your loved one a romantic weekend or want a family vacation without hassle, The Balsams Wilderness delivers. This remote resort, situated on a private, 15,000-acre estate in far northern New Hampshire, easily earns its four-star rating. This is not, however, a ski resort. Rather, it's a resort where skiing is just one of many amenities. The mountain is small, but crowds here are rare.

The Balsams Wilderness is one of New Hampshire's surviving Grand Resort Hotels and the first to be winterized. It resembles a Disney Castle, with turrets and towers, porches and balconies, and huge public rooms rambling from one to another. It's also the site of the first-in-the-nation primary, and the Ballot Room is a history lesson in itself. Guestrooms are mostly understated with an old-fashioned charm complemented with some amenities. Only a few rooms have televisions, but there is a big screen in the TV room.

In a break with the original Balsams tradition, rooms are available with only breakfast and with limited activities for those who do not want to participate in skiing and snowboarding. Award-winning chefs prepare a full breakfast buffet (or you can order from the menu) and five-course dinner daily. You can put your car keys away once you check in, and you don't even need to carry your wallet. Children's programs include meals as well as skiing The hotel offers movies in a full-size theater, dancing and entertainment nightly in two lounges and often in the ballroom.

The Wilderness Alpine trails are varied, the people are very friendly and the area gets lots—and we mean lots—of snow. A triple chair accesses the summit. The terrain is primarily intermediate, but these long winding trails—up to 2 miles in length—just invite leisurely cruising. Expert skiers will not be tested at the Balsams, but will enjoy the narrow twisting Notch and mountain's five gladed areas. Another triple serves the sunbathed beginner slope that is completely separate from the main mountain and has a perfect learning grade with a continuous slope. There's also a terrain park.

The Balsams has 95 km. of cross-country trails. One circuit that has a vertical drop of 1,000 feet on trails 20 and 19. There are less daunting loops on the golf course. Trails are 12 feet wide and have two diagonal lanes and one skate lane. The resort also has a topographical trail map so you can avoid that big drop if you want. An ice-skating rink, 30 km. of designated snowshoeing trails, horse-drawn sleigh rides and a natural-history program with guided tours round out the outdoor experience. If you still have energy to burn, there's a small fitness center, and the hotel usually offers a morning exercise program and limited spa treatments.

Lift tickets (06/07): $38 for adults weekends/holidays, $35 midweek; $35 for teens 13-18 weekends/holidays, $30 midweek; $27 for children 6–12 and younger weekends/holidays, $25 midweek. (Skiing is complimentary for hotel guests.)

Distance from Boston: About 220 miles north via I-93 (to Exit 35) then Rte. 3 to Colebrook and Rte. 26 to Dixville Notch.

Lodging information: (800) 255-0800 within NH; (800) 255-0600, U.S. and Canada.

Ragged Mountain, Danbury, NH; (603) 768-3475 or (603) 768-3600

Internet: www.raggedmountainresort.com

9 lifts; 1,250 vertical feet; 220 skiable acres; 1 terrain park; 1 snowcross course

Ragged is an affordable resort experience for families that provides an excellent value with varied terrain on seven peaks. Ragged boasts New Hampshire's only high-speed, six-passenger chairlift, which takes skiers and riders from base to summit in just five minutes.

Spooks Gorge, on Ragged Mountain, provides advanced skiers with an extensive gladed area with trails long enough to leave skiers and riders huffing and puffing by the time they get out of the trees and bumps. For more glades, the Devil's Den on Spear Mountain give more challenge.

Intermediate cruisers head to Upper and Lower Exhibition, the widest and longest non-beginner run at Ragged. Sweepstakes or Birches are tighter and winding. The Glades run, reached by the Northeast Peak double chair, is a good choice.

Beginners will enjoy Juniper Meadows, a separate learning area, with seven gentle trails and four lifts, adjacent to the base area. There's no cross traffic from more advanced skiers and riders, which means less congestion and safer conditions for first timers. The runs are flat and the lifts are appropriately slow and non-intimidating.

Ragged provides one of the only consistently open boarder/skiercross courses in New Hampshire and a terrain park with 28 elements, including a halfpipe. The park is more than half a mile long, with no cross-traffic or intersections to break the flow. It's served by the Six Pack lift and by its own triple, too. Snowboarders might want to be wary of the perimeter beginner runs (Easy Winder, Cardigan Turnpike), as these are generally flat.

The resort has two New England colonial-style base lodges with a small resort feel. The food is basic ski area fare with burgers, fries, soups, and soft drinks. There is a bar and more seating on the upper floor. Tubing, ski school, equipment rentals and child care are available.

On-mountain lodging includes new, two-bedroom condos as well as the Ridgeline Cabin that tops Northeast Peak. This rustic rental cabin ($750 per night) accommodates up to 30 people and has a wood stove, bunks, TV/VCR, cooking facilities, full bath, an outhouse and a wraparound deck with panoramic views of the White Mountains. Area lodging is limited to a few bed & breakfast inns and small lodges.

Lift tickets (05/06): Adults, $52 weekends/holidays and $45 midweek; teens (13–18), $42 weekends/holidays and $32 midweek; juniors (6–12) and seniors (65–71), $32 weekends/holidays and $22 midweek; seniors 72 and older, $16 everyday. Ages 5 and younger ski free.

Distance from Boston: About 100 miles via I-93 to Exit 17/Rte. 4 West to 104 East.

Lodging information: (800) 887-5464; Ragged Mountain condos: (800) 400-3911.

Mount Sunapee, Newbury, NH; (603) 763-2356

Internet: www.mountsunapee.com

10 lifts; 61 trails; 1,510 vertical feet; 220 skiable acres; 1 terrain park; 1 superpipe

Offering views over the lake of the same name, Mount Sunapee has a loyal following of skiers who like its New England feel and close proximity to Boston (just 90 minutes for a Massachusetts-style driver). This mountain has seen a real renaissance since 1999 when the state of New Hampshire, which had run the mountain as part of its parks system, transferred operations and development responsibilities to the same family that owns and operates Okemo Mountain in Vermont.

This new management brought a proven recipe of maximum snowmaking, new lifts, new base lodge, and a focus on family amenities to Mount Sunapee. Plans are afoot to add snowmaking to two more trails for the 2006-2007 season: Elliot Slope and Portage.

Today Mount Sunapee has been ranked as the second most popular ski and snowboard resort in New Hampshire, and has also received high grades in the East for snow quality, grooming, family programs, weather (while no one really has control over Mother Nature, the orientation of many of the slopes helps skiers find the sun), and accessibility.

The mountain is not giant when compared with some of its brethren, however, it makes the most of its size. The trails are cut to use as much of the mountain as possible, and from top to bottom, skiers and snowboarders can drop more than 1,500 feet and enjoy runs more than a mile long.

Most of Mount Sunapee's skiers are day trippers due to its proximity to several of the Northeast's largest cities, but the nearby small towns of Charlestown, Bradford, New London, and North Sutton offer interesting dining. Lodging options are growing too.

Sunapee has also long been the base for the New England Handicapped Sports Association (NEHSA), which provides programs for skiers with physical and mental challenges.

Lift tickets (05/06): Adults, $58 weekend/holiday and $54 midweek; young adult (13–18) and senior (65–69), $48 weekend and $41 weekday; junior (6–12) and super senior (70+), $37 weekend and $33 weekday. Children 5 and younger ski free with a ticketed adult. A day ticket for the South Peak Beginner Area is $6 for ages 6 and older.

Distance from Boston: About 90 miles northwest via I-93, I-89 and Rte. 103.

Lodging information: A selection of B&Bs, inns, hotels/motels and condos is available through the Mount Sunapee website and on skisnowboard.com/sunnapee/index.html.

Gunstock, Gilford, NH; (800) 486-7802 or (603) 293-4341

Internet: www.gunstock.com

8 lifts; 220 acres; 1,400 vertical feet; 1 terrain park; 1 halfpipe; 2 tubing tows

Gunstock is a family-friendly resort with an excellent learn-to-ski program, great cruising trails and plentiful winter sports, day and night. With the new Panorama High Speed quad you have access from the base to the summit in 6 minutes. Other improvements include snowmaking enhancements, increasing the size of the terrain park and new lighting that will add about 25 acres of terrain for night skiing.

The trails are kept in good condition thanks to Gunstock's Groom On Demand program: When the mountain needs attention, the cats go out. Advanced skiers can ski through glades on Middle Trigger and find bumps on Red Hat or Flintlock Extension. Intermediate glades can be found on Middle Recoil. Beginners have their own separate area at the Ski Learning Center, with handletow, conveyor lift and the Gunshy chairlift. The Gunstock Freestyle Academy offers Freestyle Ski or Snowboard camp sessions where you can learn to ride the Park and the Pipe with some of the best freestyle riders in the Lakes Region. These coaches design, build, and maintain the Gunstock Park, giving them home court advantage. There's also a 600-foot halfpipe and a terrain park. Night skiing is open on 17 trails served by four lifts. Snow tubing is available day and night. Snowshoers and cross-country skiers can enjoy 52 km. of trails for hiking, skating and gliding. The surrounding N.H. Lakes Region has ample accommodation and plenty of restaurants, as well as other activities such as ice fishing and snowmobiling.

Lift tickets (05/06): Adults, $52 weekend and $45 weekday; teens (13–18), $42 weekend and $35 midweek; Child (6–12), $32 weekend and $25 weekday; seniors (69+), $42 weekend and $25 midweek. Night tickets are available. Skiers and riders ages 5 and younger and 70 and older ski free. Gunstock also has a Flex half-day ticket.

Distance from Boston: About 90 miles north via I-93 and Rtes. 3 and 11A.

Lodging information: (603) 293-4341 or (800) 754-7819.

Tenney Mountain Ski & Snowboard Resort; Plymouth, NH; Tel. 603-536-4125

Internet: www.tenneymtn.com; info@tenneymtn.com

6 lifts; 46 trails (including glades); 110 skiable acres; 1,400 vertical feet; 1 terrain park

In this day of high-speed quads, cushy gondolas, wide cruising runs, and luxurious base lodges, we'll be kind and say Tenney keeps the feel of genuine, old-time skiing. However, Tenney entered a veritable time machine last summer: Its fun, top-to-bottom, winding classic New England trails haven't changed, but they've been catapulted into the world of ultra-modern snowmaking and perhaps the ultimate future of skiing.

SnowMagic bought Tenney to showcase and test its technology of snowmaking in warmer weather. Now for those New Englanders wanting to get on the boards in October or even earlier, Tenney's new system of "monster" snowmaking will lengthen the mountain's ski season. Called ICS and developed by Piste Industries Co. Ltd. of Japan, the system is dubbed as the "world's first temperature independent snow creating system." Yes, you read that right—temperature independent.

According to SnowMagic's website (SnowMagic.com), the "patented process produces high quality snow as close to Mother Nature's as you can get. You can even confuse Old Man Winter with the ability to make snow in temperatures up to 60 degrees Fahrenheit." It's all done differently than conventional snowmaking. The ICS system (a veritable snow manufacturing plant) freezes water into tiny crystals within itself, then the already made snow crystals are blown out. In any 24-hour period, SnowMagic claims they can make 150 tons of snow or 10,600 cubic feet of environmentally friendly snow with a natural feel and texture that can be recycled and reused after use.

Tenney is an uncrowded day-trip area. Trails start out mellow, but end with a nice pitch. With exteme-skier Dan Egan as the general manager, there has to be a playground for expert skiers and the glades are it. Egan is out there skiing almost every day; follow him for a fun ride down the mountain. The first trail at Tenney was Edelweiss; it remains its longest and its most popular. Tenny has a terrain park and a tubing park. Both parks are open under the lights from 5:30–9 p.m. Thursdays through Saturdays during the winter season.

Lift tickets (04/05): Adults, $39 weekend and $15 weekday; teens (13–19), $32 weekend and $15 midweek; child (6–12) and senior (65–69), $21 weekend and $15 weekday; 5 and younger and 70 and older ski free.

Distance from Boston: 115 miles north.

Lodging/Dining information: There's a cafeteria and a small, very friendly pub in the base lodge at Tenney for lunches or apres-ski. At the same exit (26) off I-93, the Common Man (536-2764; $$) is the most popular restaurant in the area for either pub fare or a full meal. For lodging log into the resort's website.

Lake Placid/Whiteface

New York

Summit elevation:	4,386 feet
Vertical drop:	3,166 feet
Base elevation:	1,220 feet

Address: Olympic Regional Development Authority (ORDA), Olympic Center, Lake Placid, NY 12946
Area code: 518
Ski area phone: 946-2223
ORDA phone: 523-1655
Coca Cola Snow Phone: 946-7171
Toll-free information: 800-462-6236
Fax: 523-9275
E-mail: info@orda.org
Toll-free reservations:
(800) 447-5224
Internet: www.whitefacelakeplacid.com
Expert:★★★
Advanced:★★★★★
Intermediate:★★★
Beginner:★★★★★ **First-timer:**★★★★★

Number and types of lifts: 10–1 eight-passenger gondola, 1 high-speed quad, 1 quad, 1 triple, 5 doubles, 1 surface lift
Skiable acreage: 221 acres
Snowmaking: 98 percent
Uphill capacity: 13,270 skiers per hour
Parks & pipes: 2 parks; 1 pipe
Bed base: 5,000
Nearest lodging: 1/2 mile in Wilmington, about 9 miles in Lake Placid
Resort child care: Yes, 12 months and older
Adult ticket, per day: $45-$67 (05/06 price)
Dining:★★★★
Apres-ski/nightlife:★★★
Other activities:★★★★★

A quarter century after it hosted the Olympics, Lake Placid is still all about winter games. Race down the ice chute feet first on a luge sled and try not to stretch your toes to save that extra .001 of a second on the clock...try not to push just a little harder as you ski into the cross country finish stadium...try not to put a little extra lean into the scoreboard turn under the lights at the speedskating oval...look down the in-run of the 120-meter ski jump and...well, let's not go overboard here! You get the picture. This is not your average ski town.

Welcome to Lake Placid, the surprisingly unspoiled and quiet village that has been host to two Winter Olympics, 1932 and 1980, and the 2000 Winter Goodwill Games. The memories these stir, combined with the plethora of winter sports activities available, set Lake Placid apart as a winter sports mecca.

As you drive past the dramatic Olympic jumps, just south of the village, you'll know this isn't an ordinary winter vacation spot. The Olympic Regional Development Authority (ORDA) operates the multifacility recreational area. More world-class winter sports athletes train and compete here than anywhere else in North America. The facilities also attract competitions in all of the Olympic winter sports, so athletes of all ages, nationalities and abilities fill the town throughout the season, constantly refreshing the village's Olympic atmosphere.

Even in non-Olympic years, there is always lots of top level competition in Lake Placid. For instance, winter 2006-07 starts off with World Cup Bobsled and Skeleton races in December. There is a World Cup Freestyle competition in January and World Cup Snowboarding in

March. The NCAA Women's Ice Hockey Championships will be held at the Olympic Arena in March. These events are a great opportunity to see Olympic-level competitors, up close, at neighborhood prices. A Kodak Sites passport, available at the ORDA Store on Main Street and at ORDA Facilities, will gain you access to venues and activities at a reduced cost.

The town of Lake Placid, situated between two Adirondack lakes, is home to the ice arena where America watched its Cinderella hockey team enter the history books with the "Do you believe in miracles?" victory over the heavily favored Russian team in 1980. The Mt. Van-Hoevenberg Sports Complex Sports Complex, 6 miles to the southeast, has the bobsled and luge runs as well as 50 km (31 miles) of cross-country ski trails. The MacKenzie-Intervale Ski Jumping Complex is on the edge of town where jumping and freestyle aerials take place.

The Alpine trails are 9 miles to the northeast, at Whiteface Mountain, officially in the town of Wilmington. Whiteface is one of those rare mountains that has more to offer experts and beginners, but it still has plenty for intermediates. Experts will find the upper half of the mountain challenging. Beginners will find almost everything accessed by the Face Lift high-speed quad much to their liking. Intermediates probably will find plenty of cruising and opportunities to advance their skills from the top of the mountain. The trails, for the most part, are wide, making some black-rated steep runs manageable for solid intermediates.

Lake Placid's Main Street makes up in charm and bustle what it lacks in quaintness. Day or evening, people find both relaxation and exercise on the Olympic oval (where Eric Heiden won five gold medals), on a dogsled ride across the lake or a 3-mile walk-around. Another favorite, is the nighttime toboggan slide down a floodlit ramp onto the darkness of frozen Mirror Lake. A word of caution: Wear old clothes!

 ## Mountain layout

Whiteface has the biggest vertical drop in the East at 3,430 feet if you count hiking to the Slides. It stands majestic and unshielded, lording over a vast valley of forests and frozen lakes. Its position makes for spectacular views but winter winds do whip across the valley and up the walls of Whiteface with regularity. Veteran Eastern skiers do complain that Whiteface is often windblown, cold and icy. Of course, you can't fault any area for bad weather, and the addition of the Cloudsplitter gondola provides relief, as well as comfort. On an ideal day, Whiteface is as good as it gets in the East.

♦♦**Expert** ♦**Advanced**: For some of the best expert skiing in the East, take the Summit Quad and test your legs on Cloudspin and Skyward, where the Olympic downhill races started. For certifiable experts who don't mind a hike to reach the best terrain, the Slides is the real deal on days when conditions permit. The black-diamond trails off Little Whiteface—Approach, Upper Northway, Empire and Essex—are often left to bump up, providing great terrain for advanced skiers. Whiteface has serious tree skiing, too: 13 acres of black and double-black glades can be found off Little Whiteface Mountain

■ **Intermediate**: Take the Cloudsplitter gondola from the base or the Little Whiteface double from the midstation to the top of Little Whiteface. An observation platform, off to the left at the top, gives you an unparalleled view of the lakes and valley. Then try the snaking Excelsior run, which twists down to the midstation. You can cut the rounded corners of this baby like a bobsled, choosing your own pace. After that warm-up, tackle Paron's Run or The Follies from the top of the Summit Quad. This run allows intermediates to enjoy the awe-inspiring view and the best-in-the-East vertical available from the top of the mountain. Virtually the entire lower half of this mountain is a delight for intermediates. High-speed lifts have eliminated the old bottlenecks, and there is plenty of space to cruise.

●● **Beginner** ● **First-timer:** These levels have two secluded areas, the Mixing Bowl to the left and Kids Kampus at Easy Acres to the right. The Mixing Bowl allows adult beginners to progress out of the way of more accomplished skiers using Bear lift. Novices and families will enjoy Easy Acres, below the midstation lodge, with its own secluded lift and a series of beginner glades. Brookside and Boreen also are good choices for beginners.

Ride Guide: When cruising down Excelsior, keep up your momentum when you hit the eighth and ninth corners so you can ride out the short flat.

Parks and pipes

Terrain parks are located on Brookside, Lower Thruway and portions of Lower Valley and Bronze. There's a superpipe on Bear trail. Whiteface grooms the 400-foot pipe with a Zaugg Pipe Monster. The halfpipe has hosted events such as the Winter Goodwill Games and the Paul Mitchell Board Frenzy Tour. The resort will offer World Cup snowboarding March 10-11, 2007 with events in superpipe and snowboardcross.

Cross-country and snowshoeing (visit xcskiresorts.com for more details)

Lake Placid stands as a major cross-country destination with 455 km. of trails. Foremost is the **Mt. VanHoevenberg Sports Complex** (523-2811), site of the Nordic and biathlon races during the 1980 Olympics. It has cross-country skiing you are unlikely to find elsewhere: 50 km. of marked trails that average 15 ft. wide, regularly groomed and patrolled; bridges built especially for cross-country skiers, so you don't have to worry about traffic; snowmaking (5 km.); and emergency phones. The complex has 10 marked loops: one expert, six intermediate and three novice tours, with additional expert skiing on the Porter Mountain racing loops. Snowshoeing is allowed.

The **Lake Placid Resort** (523-2556) has 25 km. of trails and connects with the more secluded **Jackrabbit Trail** (ski conditions: 523-1365): 50 km. that run from Keene through Lake Placid and Saranac Lake.

Snowshoeing trails crisscross the entire **High Peaks Wilderness** area; get maps and advice at the Eastern Mountain Sports Store on Lake Placid's Main Street. **Dewey Mt. Ski Center** has snowshoe trails in addition to cross-country skiing. For a more controlled snowshoe experience, complete with bonfires to roast marshmallows and educational stops on the trail, stop at the **High Falls Gorge** center (946-2278). Here you can follow a marked trek around the Ausable River gorge and be welcomed back with free hot chocolate or coffee. Reservations are recommended on weekends.

Lessons (05/06 prices)

Group lessons: $30 for two hours; $70 for three sessions.

First-timer package: A Parallel from the Start group lesson with pass and equipment rental is $80 for skiers or riders for one day, $140 for two days and $335 for five days. It puts new skiers on the short skis called Snowblades and guarantees that in five days they'll be able to ski from the top of Little Whiteface.

The Burton Learn-to-Ride program includes lift ticket, two-hour lesson each day and rental equipment; cost is $80 for one day, $140 for two days and $205 for three days. More days available, includes rentals, lifts and lessons; The Ski/Ride to Perfection program includes rentals, lifts and lessons; cost is $90 for one day, $179 two days; and $79 each additional day.

Private lessons: $77 an hour, with $40 for an additional person. Full day (five hours) costs $225 for one person, or $395 for two to five people.

KidStuff (05/06 prices)

Child care: The Kids Kampus at Easy Acres (946-2223) has its own parking area, base lodge, lifts (including Magic Carpet surface lift) and trails and is completely separate from the main ski trails of Whiteface while still connected with the lift and trail network allowing parents to ski or ride to and from it. The Bear's Den Nursery accepts children ages 1–6 years for $30 per half day or $55 per day, with lunch in full-day price. Reservations are recommended; call 946-2223.

Children's programs: Play 'n Ski is for children ages 4–6. It includes ski lessons, lift ticket and indoor activities and costs $90 for a full day (with lunch), $55 for a half day. Lessons for ages 7–12 are $60 2 hours and $90 full day, lunch included in full-day program.

Lift tickets (05/06 prices)

	Adult	Junior (7-12)	Teen (13-19)
One day	$63	$34	$52
Three days	$163 ($54+/day)	$94 ($31+/day)	$136 ($45+/day)
Five days	$263 ($52+/day)	$154 ($31/day)	$226 ($45+/day)

Who skis free: Children aged 6 and younger when accompanied by an adult, and ages 70 and older.

Who skis at a discount: Seniors 64–69 pay teen prices. Active military pay $39 any day. Super Sunday Specials pricing is $45 per adult and $25 for juniors (check the website for dates). Ask about lodging packages. Holiday pricing is about $4/day higher.

Accommodations

The **Mirror Lake Inn** (523-2544; $$$$), a traditional lodge right on the lake shore, is one of the finest hotels in the area. The New England-style exterior continues inside with antiques, chandeliers and mahogany walls. The inn also has an indoor pool, whirlpool, sauna, health spa and game room. The two restaurants include one of the best in town, with candlelight dining overlooking the lake.

If you want to experience the traditional Adirondack Lodge atmosphere, try the **Lake Placid Lodge** (523-2700; $$$$), an exclusive Relais & Chateau property, However, the main building, including the highly regarded dining room, was destroyed by fire in December, 2005. The resort will remain only partially open until mid-2007. **The Whiteface Lodge** (800-523-3387; 523-3400) is an elegant inn on Saranac Avenue built to replicate the classic Adirondack style. It features rooms and suites, an indoor/outdoor pool, spa, movie theater, ice skating rink, and fine dining in the vaulted ceiling, beam-butressed Great Room. It also features its own shuttle service to downtown and to Whiteface.

The **Lake Placid Crowne Plaza** (800-874-1980; 523-2556; $–$$$), in the town center, is Lake Placid's largest hotel. All 209 rooms have refrigerators and microwaves, and some have a Jacuzzi tub and fireplace. It has a large indoor pool and complete health club, cross-country trails and two restaurants, including one of the area's finest. The **Best Western Golden Arrow** (800-582-5540; 523-3353; $$–$$$) is on the lake with spectacular views. It has an indoor pool, hot tub, sauna, weight room, and racquetball courts. With similar amenities, the **Lake Placid Hilton Resort** (800-755-5598; 523-4411; $$–$$$), has two indoor pools and private balconies for each room with a view of the lake. The hotel's bed & breakfast package is quite popular. There is also an excellent **Howard Johnson Resort Inn** (800-858-4656; 523-9555; $$–$$$).

The **Mt. VanHoevenberg B&B and Cabins** (523-9572; $$), with an outdoor sauna and a games room, and **Trail's End Inn** (576-9860; $–$$$), with a hot tub, are both excellent choices for cross-country skiers and snowshoers.

Skiers on a budget should try the **Edge of the Lake Motor Inn** (523-9430; $$), **Art Devlin's Motor Inn** (523-3700; $$–$$$), **Town House Lodge by the Lake** (523-2532; $–$$$), **Alpine Air Motel** (523-9261; $–$$$), the **Placid Bay Inn** (523-2001; $$) the **Econo Lodge** (523-2817; $–$$$) or the **Wildwood on the Lake** (523-2624; $–$$$).

To stay right by Whiteface, book at the **Ledge Rock** (800-336-4754; 946-2379; $–$$$), the **Hungry Trout** (946-2217; $$–$$$) or **Huntington's** (946-2332; $–$$$) .

 ## Dining

The newest fine dining spot in town is **The Great Room** at The Whiteface Lodge (523-3400; $$$$) where the menu is impressive and so is the setting. Across the street, **The Caffe Rustica** (523-3400; $$$) has earned a loyal following in just the past few years. In the village, The Averil Conwell Dining Room, at The Mirror Lake Inn (523-2544; $$$–$$$$), has fine dining in a very elegant atmosphere. Sadly, the main lodge, including the dining room, at the **Lake Placid Lodge**, was destroyed by fire and is not scheduled to reopen until at least mid-2007.

Richard's Freestyle Cuisine (523-5900; $$$) serves some excellent creative dishes. **The Brown Dog** (523-3036; $–$$$) is a deli by day but offers fine dining with wine by night. The **Great Adirondack Steak and Seafood Company** (523-0233; $$) serves beer brewed on premises and hearty food. **The Cottage** (523-2544; $$–$$$), at the Mirror Lake Inn, delivers good burgers and pub fare at water's edge. Locals swear by the **Caribbean Cowboy** (523-3836; $–$$).

Every Wednesday, January through March, the **Alpine Cellar** restaurant has a Bratwurst Night with traditional German fare and oom-pah-pah accordion music. Wash it all down with your choice of 80 different beers. The **Charcoal Pit** (523-3050; $$–$$$) has been charbroiling steaks and chops for 25 years. **Veranda** (523-3339; $$), next to the Crowne Plaza, has a great view to go with fine food. **Desperados** (523-1507; $–$$) is the Mexican place in town. **Mykonos'** (523-1164; $$–$$$) has good Greek fare.

On the way into the village, there are a trio of good spots lined up in a row. The **Downhill Grill** (523-9510 $-$$), **Lisa G's** (523-2093, $-$$) and **The Station Street Grill** (523-9963, $-$$) are all solid choices for lunch or an informal evening meal. No ski town is complete without an inexpensive Italian restaurant featuring pizza—**Mr. Mike's Pizza** (523-9770; $) takes care of that craving. Original soups and arguably the best burger in town can be found at **Cameron's Restaurant** (no reservations; $–$$$). For sushi, **Aki Sushi** (523-5826, $$–$$$) on lower Main Street is the choice. For breakfast, head to the **City Diner**, **Saranac Sourdough**, **Aroma Round** or **Hojos**.

In Wilmington, the upscale and excellent **Hungry Trout** (946-2217; $$) specializes in, you guessed it, fish. In the same neighborhood is the **Wilderness Inn** (946-2391; $$–$$$), where steak lovers will want to try the sandwich on the bar menu.

Apres-ski/nightlife

Lake Placid is large enough to generate its own heat as a nightlife center for out-of-towners and locals. Because Whiteface is separated from the town, however, most of the apres-ski action is in the base lodge. **Steinhoff's** and **R.F. McDougall's**, at the **Hungry Trout**, just down the road from Whiteface, are also good for an apres-ski drink.

Dining: $$$$-Entrees $30+; $$$-$20-$30; $$-$10-$20; $-less than $10.
Accommodations: (double room) $$$$-$200+; $$$-$141-$200; $$-$81-$140; $-$80 and less.

Wise Guys, next to the speed skating oval, is a sports bar upstairs, a dance club downstairs, and serves pub grub into the wee hours. Roomers, next to the Best Western, the Dancing Bears Lounge at the Hilton and the Zig Zag's are popular spots along Main Street. The Lake Placid Pub and Brewery, with its downstairs companion P.J. O'Neils, is on Mirror Lake Drive, offering outstanding pub fare. For a quieter nightspot, stop by The Cottage, by the Mirror Lake Inn. The fire's always on, and the lake-and-mountains sunset view is postcard perfect. It also serves good burgers.

Other activities

Lake Placid has fantastic *winter* activities. The half-mile **bobsled rides** at Verizon Sports Complex (six miles from the village) are $40 per person and a must for any Lake Placid visitor. Rides on the combination bobsled/luge track are by reservation only (523-4436). Try the Luge Rocket too.

Tours of the MacKenzie-Intervale Ski Jumping Complex, with chairlift and elevator ride, cost $9 for adults, $5 for children and seniors. Hours are 9 a.m. to 4 p.m.

The Olympic Speed Skating Oval is open for public skating 7–9 p.m. daily and 1–3 p.m. on Saturdays and Sundays (523-1655). The cost is $5 for adults and $3 for juniors. Operating hours for the toboggan run on Mirror Lake are Wednesday, 7–9 p.m.; Friday, 7–10 p.m.; Saturday, noon–4 p.m. and 7–10 p.m.; and Sunday, noon–4 p.m. The charge is $3 for adults, $2 for children, and $3 for the toboggan rental. The Kodak Winter Passport includes a day of cross-country or snowshoeing and admission to the jumping complex, museums and public skating. The passport also qualifies you for a $10 discount on the half-mile bobsled ride and a 10-percent discount at the ORDA Store.

Don't miss the Lake Placid Winter Olympic Museum, with displays from the 1932 and 1980 Winter Olympics. Open daily, admission is $3 for adults and $2 for juniors. Call 523-1655 ext. 226 for more information.

Getting there and getting around

By air: Flights will arrive in Burlington, Vt., or Albany, N.Y. Organized transportation from the airports to the resort is sporadic. Rent a car. Commuter service is available into the Adirondack Regional Airport in Lake Clear, about 30 minutes from Lake Placid.

By train: Trains stop at Westport on the New York City–Montreal line. There has been a shuttle bus from the train station to the resort in the past, but in our experience this is not a convenient way to reach Lake Placid; ask the Lake Placid Visitors Bureau (800-447-5224) for info. Amtrak has ski packages; call (800-872-7245; spells USA-RAIL) for more info.

By car: From the south, take Exit 24 (Albany) off the New York State Thruway (I-87). Take Northway (still I-87) to Exit 30, follow Rte. 9 north two miles to Rte. 73 and continue 28 miles to Lake Placid. From the west, take I-90 (N.Y. State Thruway) to Exit 36 (Syracuse) for I-81. Follow I-81 north to Watertown, go east on Rte. 3 to Saranac Lake, then take Rte. 86 east to Lake Placid.

Getting around: It's about a 10-mile drive to Whiteface and 6 miles to Mt. VanHoevenberg from the center of Lake Placid. A free shuttlebus connects the town with Whiteface from Christmas until April 1, but having a car available makes moving around town and to the activity venues more convenient.

Jay Peak
Vermont

Summit elevation:	3,968 feet
Vertical drop:	2,153 feet
Base elevation:	1,815 feet

Address: 4850 VT. Rte. 242, Jay, VT 05859
Area code: 802
Ski area phone: 988-2611
Snow report: 988-9601
Toll-free reservations: (800) 451-4449 (outside Vermont) or 988-2611
Fax: 988-4049
E-mail: info@jaypeakresort.com
World Wide Web: www.jaypeakresort.com

Expert:★★★★★
Advanced:★★★★★
Intermediate:★★★
Beginner:★★
First-timer:★★

Number and types of lifts: 8–1 60-passenger aerial tramway, 1 high-speed quad, 2 quads, 1 triple, 1 double, 1 T-bar, 1 moving carpet
Skiable acreage: 385 (plus 200 acres off-piste)
Snowmaking: 85 percent
Uphill capacity: 12,175 per hour
Parks & pipes: 4 parks
Bed base: 1,300 slopeside; 1,800 in area
Nearest lodging: slopeside
Resort child care: Yes, 2-7 years; infant care for on-property guests available
Adult ticket, per day: $58 (05/06 price)
Dining:★★
Apres-ski/nightlife:★
Other activities:★

They call it the "Jay Peak Cloud." It hovers over the mountain, and dumps a foot or more of snow on days when skies are clear just five miles away. Jay averages 355 inches of snow a year and that's at least 100 inches more than others in the region. Some years, more snow falls here than anywhere east of the Sierras. One year, 571 inches blanketed the mountain. Even in a "poor" snow year, Jay receives several feet more than other resorts in the Green Mountains. If you're looking for (almost) guaranteed snow, Jay is your safest bet.

While it's a bit of a trek and a lot of back roads to get to Jay, it's well worth the effort. Most of the time, you have the mountain practically to yourself. Even on powder days, you can find untracked snow all day long. During holiday weekends, you'll wonder why you ever went anywhere else.

People come to Jay for more than just the snow though. Many of the trails, particularly the glades, hold more challenge than you'll find at most Eastern resorts. Long before it was popular for Eastern resorts to cut glades, Jay's locals were sneaking into the woods to cut their own lines. Since 1987, the resort has cut 21 glades and two extreme chutes.

For this terrain, hardcore skiers and riders drive the distance to test themselves, and sometimes their friends. The focus here is the outdoors and all it has to offer, for better or worse. Come if you want to ski or ride your legs off, sink into a hot tub as the sun sets, then go to sleep early to get up early in the morning and do it all over again. It isn't a good vacation for a group that includes non-skiers and non-riders. There's not a whole lot to do in the area. This is rural Vermont at its best, quiet and relaxing, with a focus on outdoor activities and recreation.

Mountain layout

The biggest drawback to Jay's layout is that there are only three ways to work your way between the two peaks—Northway, Goat Run and Vermonter. These can get crowded, and the snow gets skied off, so stay alert, especially later in the day. Locals refer to the Green Mountain Flyer chair as the Green Mountain Freezer. You'll understand once you crest the ridge and get a full blast of the wind off the lake. It's best to avoid this lift if you're prone to getting cold quickly.

♦♦**Expert** ♦**Advanced:** Experts who have never been here may very well quake in their boots when they see what Jay considers single-diamond terrain. The Face, The Saddle and Tuckermans Chutes are rock-and-tree-stub strewn, forcing you to pick your way over some gnarly stuff to get to the goods. All this is in full view of the folks riding up the Tram. But, the real challenge is in the woods. Warm up in Hell's Woods, Buckaroo Bonzai, Everglade and Beaver Pond Glade, then head to Timbuktu and Valhalla. Locals groaned loudly when Jay officially opened Beyond Beaver Pond Glade because it was just about the only piece of "unofficial woods" left on the mountain, but it remains pretty much untouched since you have to hike a bit to get there. Keep an eye out for locals, who are more than willing to share their secret stashes, *if* they see that you know what you're doing in the trees. There's plenty of in-bounds woods skiing to keep you grinning for a week, so we don't recommend going out of bounds, unless you're with someone who knows the area.

Kitzbuehl is a tight bumped run that'll leave you huffing and puffing. River Quai and Green Beret (when it's open) are both truly hairy trails. The monster moguls and double fall line on Powerline will give you a run for your money.

Advanced skiers ready to push themselves will want to take a glade technique lesson and head into the woods. You can always try out the "kiddie" glades mentioned below and see if you're ready first

■ **Intermediate:** Jay is a great place for intermediates who are comfortable with their ability and are seeking a challenge. Most intermediate trails here would be rated for advanced skiers elsewhere. One writer's niece and nephew, who are used to skiing at Mount Snow, found the narrower trails and wide-open "kiddie" glades (Kokomo, Moon Walk and Bushwacker) to be great fun.

Warm up on Ullr's Dream (slip into Kokomo if you want to avoid the long flat at the end), JFK or Northway to Angel's Wiggle. To take in the amazing 360-degree views from the top to Mt. Mansfield, Quebec's Eastern Townships, Lake Champlain, Mt. Washington and Montreal, ride up the tram and head down Vermonter. Goat Run is another fun trail, but the top gets icy and moguled on heavy-traffic days.

Most advanced-intermediates will enjoy the groomed black-diamond trails off the Jet Triple Chair, once you make it past the somewhat-steep top sections. A favorite is Derick Hot Shot, a narrow winding trail that gets moderate bumps on high-traffic days. If you're looking to make sweeping arcs, head to wide-open Jet and Haynes. If you get to the top of the Jet and decide the terrain looks too steep, take Montrealer to Angel's Wiggle, then take the Wiggle all the way down or choose from some wonderful intermediate terrain like Lower Milk Run, Paradise Meadows and Hell's Crossing. (We wish this area of the mountain were served by its own chair.)

●● **Beginner:** All of the beginner terrain is at the bottom of the mountain. A quad chair replaced the Metro T-bar, completely recreating the beginner experience. All the beginner trails are now connected, making it easier to move around the mountain to play. A fabulous beginner run that doesn't get much traffic is Deer Run, to the right as you get off the lift and a short traverse across the mountain. It's also fun to cut over to Queen's Highway. Bushwacker and Moon Walk Woods are great "kiddie glades," with Moon Walk being wide open enough to groom. Or try Racoon Run, which accesses some of the newer condos and has its own chair. Higher-level skiers and riders use some of the beginner trails to reach the Tram and Green Mountain Flyer, so keep an eye out for them. If you're adventurous and want to try the intermediate terrain at the top of the mountain, it's wise to return to the base by mid-afternoon, before the snow on the major trails is skied off.

● **First-timer:** There is a dedicated learning center with a moving carpet at the base of Tramside, giving first-timers their very own piece of the mountain.

Ride Guide: Ullr's Dream is a great run, but duck into Kokomo to avoid the lo-o-ong flat at the bottom. Riders coming out of Beaver Pond Glade and Beyond Beaver Pond Glade hook back up to Ullr's, so you'll also want to heed that warning (plus Beyond has its own unavoidable flat that will have you hoofing back to the trails).

Parks and pipes

While most skiers and riders still come to Jay for the glades, chutes and off-piste terrain, the freestyle scene continues to evolve, with a big boost coming from the resort's decision to hire a park manager, who treats the parks as a labor of love. It's not unusual to see the park manager and his crew out hand-sculpting features to perfection. Jay now has four terrain parks and hosts several freestyle events. The terrain park for experienced park riders, called The Park, is on Lower Can Am. Features change throughout the season, but on any given day, you'll find rails (including a rainbow rail, an "S" rail and a rollercoaster rail), boxes (including a straight box and a "C" box), tables and step-ups. The Progression Park is on Rabbit Trail (rider's left of Lower Can Am). Tabletops range in size from small ones for beginners to huge hits for experts, allowing riders to practice new moves before heading to the main park.

Tramside is where you'll find the two other parks. The Rail Garden is next to the moving carpet near the base lodge. Six to 10 rails, smaller versions than in The Park, help you learn the basics and improve your moves. Barrels, picnic tables, chairs and other random features mix it up for some extra fun. It's lighted for night riding, so head here after the lifts close. The Grom Park is on Harmony Lane and accessed by the Metro Quad. Small features make it perfect for those just learning moves in the park.

 ## Cross-country and snowshoeing (visit xcskiresorts.com for more details)

Jay Peak has 20 km. of cross-country skiing that networks into 200 km. of touring trails in the area. Instruction and rentals are available. Included in the Nordic trail system are more than 5 km. of snowshoe trails. Naturalist-led tours on snowshoes are scheduled Tuesdays, Wednesdays and Saturdays from 4:30 – 6:30 p.m.; cost, $15. Check with the Ski School Desk to register. Extended or group tours also can be arranged. If you want to head out on their own, snowshoe rentals are available anytime through the rental shop.

Hazen's Notch Cross-Country Ski & Snowshoe Center (802-326-4799), about 10 miles away in Hazen's Notch, is owned and operated by the nonprofit Hazen's Notch Association. The 64 km. of groomed and backcountry trails include 16 km. of snowshoe-only trails. The views alone are worth the trip, plus the high elevation ensures bountiful snow. You'll find ski and snowshoe rentals, and instruction by appointment. Ask about naturalist-guided snowshoe tours and full-moon snowshoe tours.

Lessons (05/06 prices)

Group lessons: Two-hour lesson, $30. Multiday packages available.

First-timer package: The Learn to Ski/Ride program includes a two-hour ski or snowboard lesson with rental and use of beginner lifts for $49. Multiday packages available. First-time snowboarders are taught using Burton Method Center techniques and ride on Burton's specially designed learn-to-ride equipment.

Private lessons: One-hour ski or snowboard session, $50; half day, $120; full day, $230. Telemark also available.

Special programs: Glade Techniques, two-hour sessions offered during primo conditions, are for advanced skiers and riders only, $30. Backcountry Adventure gives guided tours of popular off-piste areas. You must be a very experienced skier or rider; the ski school has the option to disqualify participants, $50. Women's Clinics are offered on two separate weekends each winter. Cost is $110 for one day, $210 for two days, lift ticket included. For information or to register, call 800-451-4449.

Advanced skiers can go for the First Tracks program with a ticket purchased the day before, getting you up the first tram at 8:15 a.m. weekdays (and 7:45 a.m. weekends) for a guided tour down the untouched mountain.

Racing: Racing Camps feature gate running and on-hill training. NASTAR races at 1 p.m. on Thursday, Friday and Saturday, $5 for two runs. Special NASTAR Clinic available.

KidStuff (05/06 prices)

Child care: Ages 2 to 7 years old. All ski and stay packages at Jay include free day care from 9 a.m.-9 p.m. Pre-registration is advised. Call 802-988-2611. Those staying off-resort can put their children in Jay's day care on a walk-up first come, first served basis only. Cost is $45 all day ($6 extra for lunch); $25 half day. Infant care for on-property guests is available on a fee basis with advanced reservations.

Children's lessons: The Kinderschool Ski Program is for ages 3–5 and costs $40 for a half-day, $80 full day (includes lift ticket). Preregistration is required. Rentals are $5 extra (half-day) or $10 extra (full-day); lunch costs $6. Mini-Learn-to-Ride is the same program for snowboarders ages 5–6 and costs the same. Pre-registration is required for both.

Jay Explorers, a full-day program for ages 6–10, costs $59 (lift tickets, rentals and lunch are extra). Miniriders is the same program for snowboarders ages 7-10.

Mountain Adventures is a full-day program for ages 8 and older who want to not only ski and snowboard, but try alternatives such as snowshoeing, apprenticing with instructors, telemarking and getting First Tracks before the resort opens to the public in the morning. Cost is $59 (lift tickets, rentals and lunch are extra).

Special activities: There is nightly supervised dining in Hotel Jay for ages 2-7; sign up by 2 p.m. There's an activity room with ping pong, video games and pool table in the Hotel Jay. Movies are shown nightly at 7 p.m. (for kids) and 9 p.m. (for adults) on all on-property TVs as well as in the family room of the Hotel Jay.

Lift tickets (05/06 prices)

	Adult	Junior (7-17)	Toddler (6 and younger)
One day	$58	$42	$8
Three day	$150	$108	$24
Five day	$215	$160	$40

Who skis at a discount: Seniors 65 and older ski for $15. College students with an ID ski for $35. A Beginner Zone ticket is $22 adult, $12 junior. Vermont and Clinton County, NY, residents with ID ski and ride for $38 adult and $32 junior.

Accommodations

Jay Peak Resort assists guests in arranging lodging, air travel, train travel, shuttle van service to the airport and train station and rental cars. Jay Peak is overall a bargain. The best deal is to stay in the slopeside hotel or condos. During non-holiday weeks, children 14 and younger stay and ski free, and teens 15–18 stay and ski for $50 per day when sharing the same room or condo with their parents (meals are extra). Children 6 and younger always stay and ski free (and eat free in the Hotel Jay).

If you have kids ages 2–7, stay at Hotel Jay or the on-mountain condos, and you'll receive complimentary child care from 9 a.m. to 9 p.m., including a supervised dinner. Five-day stays and longer include a half-day complimentary ticket that can be used on the day of arrival beginning at 12:30 p.m.

The **Hotel Jay** (800-451-4449; 988-9601; $–$$) offers a sauna, family room with fireplace and game room are available. Five-day packages for a family with two adults cost $649 per adult (includes meals for adults).

Slopeside condos range from luxury to economy. Five-day packages, including lodging and lift tickets, range from $479 to $869 per adult. Meal plans are available. The ski-in/ski-out **Village Townhouses and Condominums** have two to five bedrooms, are wonderfully spacious and some units have a steam bath and sauna. What the resort calls "deluxe" accommodations can be found at the older **Mountainside, Trailside** and **Slopeside** condos. Many units in Slopeside are ski-in/ski-out, though some require a short walk. Mountainside and Trailside units are about a five-minute walk to the lifts, have kitchenettes instead of full kitchens, and are value priced. **Stoney Path,** the resort's economy condo lodging, is a five-minute walk to the lifts.

The **Lodge at Jay,** in the town of Jay, (800-204-7039; 988-4459; $–$$$$), a 27-room inn, was refurbished in 2002 with warm Southwestern hues and handcrafted furniture. Rooms range from economy to family suites. A restaurant, steam room, sauna, fitness facilities, spa services, movie room and fireside lounges are on the premises. Prices include breakfast; kids younger than 14 stay free.

The European-influenced **Inglenook Lodge** (800-331-4346; 988-2880; $$–$$$$) is a bit worn but owned by a friendly couple who warmly welcome families and kids. Amenities include an indoor pool, hot tub, sauna, game room, restaurant and lounge. Prices include breakfast and dinner. Children 6 and younger stay free; kids 7–16 have reduced rates.

The **Black Lantern Inn** (800-255-8661; 326-4507; $$–$$$$), about 20 minutes down the road in Montgomery, is a beautifully restored stagecoach stop originally built in 1803 and now listed on the National Historic Register. The inn has eight rooms and seven suites, all with private baths and decorated with Vermont antiques, some with gas fireplace stoves and jetted tubs. An outdoor hot tub, a sitting room warmed by a wood stove, and a bountiful breakfast add extra creature comforts.

Two Victorian inns can be found in Montgomery Center. **Phineas Swann Bed & Breakfast** (326-4306; $$–$$$), has three bedrooms, plus four suites with fireplaces, jetted tubs en suite, and four-poster queen-size beds. Guests enjoy a gourmet breakfast and afternoon tea. **The Inn on Trout River** (800-338-7049; 326-4391; $–$$) pampers guests with queen-size beds covered with down quilts, feather pillows and flannel sheets. A fancy breakfast is served.

Dining: $$$$-Entrees $30+; $$$-$20-$30; $$-$10-$20; $-less than $10.
Accommodations: (double room) $$$$-$200+; $$$-$141-$200; $$-$81-$140; $-$80 and less.

Dining

Each lodge has a **cafeteria** that serves breakfast and lunch, and the food is quite good. **Hotel Jay's Alpine Room Restaurant** serves breakfast and dinner. The atmosphere is rustic, the food is not. Entrees like grilled maple mesquite pork loin and tequila roast duckling fill the menu.

Two local inns are renowned for their fine dining. Top dog is **The Black Lantern Inn** (326-4507; $$), where candlelight sets the mood and the menu changes frequently. The elegant cuisine, cozy atmosphere and wallet-friendly prices here rival any you'll find across the border in Quebec. **Lemoine's**, at The Inn on Trout River (326-4391; $$), is an intimate restaurant with a country Victorian theme. For simpler fare, consider the pub menu at **Hobo's Cafe**, also at The Inn on Trout River (326-4391; $$).

Ask at the hotel front desk to find out about favorite restaurants in nearby Quebec. You'll find French cuisine at affordable prices because of the Canadian dollar exchange rate.

Apres-ski/nightlife

On-mountain, head to the **Golden Eagle Sports Bar** and the **International Bar,** both in the Tram base lodge, and the **Sport Lounge at Hotel Jay** when you quit the slopes. taste-test the Vermont microbrews. Live entertainment, Karaoke nights and theme parties are frequently scheduled. **The Belfry**, just down the mountain road toward Montgomery Center, has a good selection of beers and local microbrews.

Other activities

The idea here is to enjoy the great outdoors. The **ice skating rink** is sometimes the site of impromptu ice hockey games. Bring your own skates. The **ice skating rink** is sometimes the site of impromptu ice hockey games. But you'll need to bring your own skates. Rent a snowmobile and book a guided tour through the Jay Village Inn (802-988-2306). Try **night sledding** behind Hotel Jay; ask the front desk for sleds. Sleighride at Phil & Karen's Sleighrides (744-9928) in Westfield.

Jay has a few **shops** worth visiting, including The Snow Job (where you'll get the best tunes around) and the Jay Country Store, but for a shopping excursion, we suggest heading to Burlington, Montreal or Magog. In the spring, visit one of the nearby maple sugar shacks.

Getting there and getting around

By air: Burlington International Airport is a 1.5-hour drive from the base.

By car: Jay Peak Resort is on Rte. 242 in northern-central Vermont, just below the Canadian border, about equidistant between I-91 and I-89. Sample driving times: Boston, 3.5 hours; Albany, 4.5 hours; New York City, 6.5 hours; Toronto, 7 hours; Montreal, 1.5 hours.

By bus: Vermont Transit serves nearby Newport from all major New England points. Ground transportation available.

By train: Amtrak Vermonter to St. Albans, 45 minutes away. Ground transfers available to Jay Peak.

Getting around: Bring a car if you want to venture off-mountain.

Killington/Pico
Vermont

Summit elevation: 4,215 feet
Vertical drop: 3,050 feet
Base elevation: 1,165 feet

Address: Killington Road
Killington, VT 05751
Area code: 802
Ski area phone: 422-3333
Snow report: 422-3261
Toll-free reservations: (800) 621-6867
E-mail: info@killington.com
Internet: www.killington.com

Expert: ★ ★
Advanced: ★ ★ ★
Intermediate: ★ ★ ★ ★
Beginner: ★ ★ ★ ★
First-timer: ★ ★ ★

Number and types of lifts: 33-3 gondolas,
6 high-speed quads, 6 quads, 6 triples,
4 doubles, 8 surface lifts
Skiable acreage: 1,215 acres
Snowmaking: 70 percent
Uphill capacity: 52,973 per hour
Parks & pipes: 6 parks; 2 pipes
Bed base: 5,500 (base); 18,000 (region)
Nearest lodging: Walking distance
Resort child care: Yes, 6 weeks to 6 years
Adult ticket, per day: $69-72 (05/06)
Dining: ★ ★ ★
Apres-ski/nightlife: ★ ★ ★ ★
Other activities: ★ ★ ★

Tucked beneath Vermont's second-highest peak, the Killington Basin is a natural place for a ski resort. The K-1 gondola carries skiers and riders to the highest lift-served skiing in the state (yes, even higher than on Stowe's Mt. Mansfield).

Killington Ski Resort with Pico Mountain Vermont The basin receives, on average, 250 inches of snow each year. If the snow doesn't fall from the sky, Killington/Pico makes it fall from its guns. With one of the world's largest snowmaking systems, the resort literally blankets its seven mountains in white. Thanks to this prodigious snowmaking capacity, Killington/Pico is usually open longer than any resort in the East, sometimes as long as eight months. The resort is huge, by Eastern standards, and truly has terrain for all abilities, including some super bumps, nice glades, old-time narrow trails and plenty of blue squares for easing down the mountain.

From the cool days of autumn, when skiers and snowboarders make a few turns down a white strip high on the mountain, framed by colorful fall foliage, to the carefree days of late spring, long after mud season, Killington attracts those who can't wait for winter and are sad when it's over. Spring is probably the best time to ski or ride at Killington/Pico. Crowds gather on the deck of the Bear Mountain Lodge, hooting and hollering as up-and-coming bump skiers rip it up—or flail—on the legendary Outer Limits trail, the longest, steepest mogul slope in the East. The smell of burgers on the grill wafts into the air, beer is plentiful (for age 21 or older), and everyone is having a good time. It's like a giant frat party on the slopes.

Or you can ski Pico, a physically separate mountain from Killington's other six. The resort added Pico to the "family" in 1996. Even though it's 10 minutes away by car, Pico is still worth visiting. Considered by many locals as a feather in the Mother Ship's cap, Pico has 2,000 feet of vertical, 48 trails and some very interesting (and often uncrowded) terrain.

Mountain layout

Killington's five base areas (six, if you count Pico) disperse skier and riders across the seven peaks rather quickly, even on the busiest of days. Three are clustered within striking distance at the top of Killington Road—Snowshed and Rams Head are across the street from one another, and Killington base is just a bit up the road. Bear Mountain, home of the famed Outer Limits bump run, is on Bear Mountain Road off Rte. 4 (note: occasionally, four-wheel drive, snowtires or chains are required on the Bear Mountain Access Road). Also off Rte. 4 is the Skyeship Base Station, a good choice for those who don't want the hassle of the Access Road.

◆◆**Expert** ◆**Advanced:** Some of the toughest terrain is Between Snowdon Mountain and Killington Peak. The Canyon quad chair services this area for access to double-diamond Cascade, Downdraft, Double Dipper and Big Dipper Glade.

Skye Peak is one of the most popular sections. Skylark and Bittersweet are fairly easy expert trails, while Superstar and Ovation—the steepest trail on the mountain—will test any expert's legs. With plenty of machine-made snow, Superstar is the last trail to close in spring and is the scene of the downhill ski leg of Killington's annual triathlon.

Bear Mountain is another popular haven for experts with double-diamond drops such as Devil's Fiddle and the infamous Outer Limits, where bumps are the name of the game. If you ski it on one of the rare days it's groomed, and if you fall, you may slide all the way to the bottom, much to the amusement of the crowd watching from the base and the chairlift.

After a good snowfall, head to Pico and get fresh tracks down the gnarly Giant Killer or Upper Pike. Upper KA and Sunset 71, narrow trails reminiscent of the early days of New England skiing, wind down from the top of Pico and offer interesting knolls, twists and turns.

■ **Intermediate:** Many of the single-black diamond runs would be blue cruisers at other resorts, and indeed, we've been told that many of them have been relabeled as such. The Rams Head high-speed quad covers beginner and intermediate trails. Caper is a good warm-up cruiser. The Snowdon area is another mellow delight. It's served by two chairs from the base area and a mid-mountain Poma lift on Bunny Buster. Highline is an advanced cruising run with excellent pitch. Bunny Buster and Chute have less of a grade.

Needle's Eye, a wide run, drops beneath the second leg of the Skyeship gondola. Another cruiser is the aptly named Cruise Control. A trip back up the Needle's Eye Express quad will put you back on Bittersweet for wide turns to the Killington Base Lodge or Snowshed.

Pico is home to 49-ner, a cruiser that offers superb views from the top of Pico. Beginners will find the top part of this blue square challenging, though.

●● **Beginner:** Green trails lead from all six interconnected peaks, which allows beginners the panoramic vistas and thrill of skiing from the summit, not possible at areas where the upper-mountain trails are reserved for seasoned skiers. Beginners beware: It's easy to get lost at Killington on these meandering trails. If it's the end of the day, consult your map frequently to make sure you'll end up at the same base area as your car, or be prepared to hop on the shuttle. The new signage should help with directional issues.

● **First-timer:** Killington, in theory, has a perfect learning area: Snowshed. Served by three chairlifts, this gentle slope is a segregated beginning area. But the top of the trail is accessible from the upper part of the mountain, which can make Snowshed exceedingly crowded and not just with other beginners. Experts often fly down the slope. Consider learning at another resort or head to Pico, where beginners learn at the more isolated Bonanza area.

Ride guide: This is quite a confusing mountain for first-time Killington riders. Half of our snowboard writer's day was spent stopped and studying the trail map, trying to figure out where she was and how she got there, when she wanted to be two peaks over. If you're going to make the most of your time here, either take a free "Meet the Mountains" tour or befriend a local. Be aware that some roped-off trails are not visibly marked until it's too late—around a bend or over a knoll—which means you'll have to hike a few feet back to the open trail.

Parks and pipes

Killington's signature terrain park on Bear Mountain has a 425-foot long superpipe featuring 18-foot walls cut by a Silver Zaugg, a boardercross course and numerous hits, rails and boxes on Bear Trap and Wildfire. There's a good chance you'll see Killington's Park and Pipe crew, who are serious riders and hardcore jibbers, buttering up the transitions between jumps and hand-grooming park features or testing the product. Many park features have two differently sized approaches, one for the intermediate jumpers and one for advanced. The park has six rails, eight jumps, a quarterpipe and other features. Transitions between jumps are smooth, and the crew works harder on the landings than average.

The intermediate-oriented Timberline Terrain Park, at Rams Head, has a halfpipe, along with its numerous rails, hits and boxes. The minipark on Reason is usually the first to open each season and generally has a few rails, boxes and a few hits. Easy Street is a beginner park.

Pico has a terrain park on upper Triple Slope with one rail and a few

Cross country and snowshoeing (see xcskiresorts.com for more details)

Near the base of the Killington Access Road, **Mountain Meadows Cross-Country Ski Resort** (775-7077) has 57 km. of trails meandering across Kent Lake and through surrounding forests. The Center also has a 1.2-km. loop with an extensive snowmaking system. Killington's new **Winter Adventure Center** (422-6200) at the golf course (across the road from the Grand Resort Hotel) is great for snowshoeing. When snow is lean, Mountain Meadows is one of the few cross-country ski resorts that opens. **Mountain Top Cross-Country Ski Resort** (483-2311), in Chittenden, has 110 km. of trails, 40 km. of dual-set tracks and 0.5 km. of trails with snowmaking. Both areas have rentals, lessons, ski shops and warming huts. Mountain Top offers sledding and horse-drawn sleigh rides. In Woodstock, the **Ski Touring Center** (457-2114) has 75 km. of trails, lessons and rentals.

Lessons [05/06 prices]

Group lessons: The Killington Skier Development Program uses the innovative teaching program called Perfect Turn®. Perfect Turn has 10 levels. For lower intermediates and higher, the two-hour clinics are offered at 9:45 a.m. and 12:45 p.m. and cost $45 for one day. There are also five-day programs.

First-timer package: A well-designed Perfect Turn Learn-to-Ski Center at Snowshed. for five-days ($320) includes lift, clinic and equipment.

Private lessons: A one-hour clinic is $95 for one person, $155 for two. A two-hour lesson is $159 for one, $275 for two. Three- and six-hour clinics also are available.

Special programs: Among the topics are moguls, women's instruction, racing, adaptive instruction for the disabled and even instruction for instructors.

Racing: None for public participation. Call the Alpine Training Center (422-6797) near the Killington Base Lodge for information on clinics and programs.

KidStuff [05/06 prices]

Child care: The Friendly Penguin Children's Center is in the Rams Head Family Center and provides care for ages 6 weeks to 6 years. Cost is $70 per day and $55 per half day (both with lunch). Parents must supply food and beverage for children 23 months and younger. Multiday discounts available. Reservations are required; call (800) 621-6867. All-day programs run from 7:45 a.m. to 4:30 p.m

Children's lessons: First Tracks is a combination of day care and lessons for ages 2–6 that includes lessons, lunch, lift tickets and rentals; cost is $85 for a full day with a one-hour lesson and $100 for a full day with two one-hour lessons. Programs for ages 7–12 cost $75 for a full day (with lunch) and $45 for a half day; rentals and lift tickets are extra; lunch can be added to the half-day program. Teens 13–18 can take part in The SnowZone, which offers skiing, snowboarding and skiboarding, for the same price. One-, three- and five-day courses are also available.

Lift tickets [05/06 prices]

	Adult	Young Adult (13-18)	Junior (6-12)
One day	$69/$72 holiday	$59	$40
Three days	$180 ($60/day)	$162 ($54/day)	$105 ($35/day)
Five days	$275 ($55/day)	$250 ($50/day)	$160 ($32 day)

Who skis free: Children ages 12 and younger ski free when accompanied by an adult who buys a Monday-Friday five-day pass or longer.

Who skis at a discount: Ages 65 and older, same price as juniors. Pico Card holders ski for $10 off the Pico-only lift ticket price of $48 Sunday and $45 Monday through Friday, nonholiday. To order a free Pico Card, log onto www.killington.com.

Killington tickets are valid at Pico, but if you plan to ski just Pico, you can buy a Pico-only pass that's about $15 cheaper than the full pass. Public transportation between the two is on The Bus ($2) and it stops along the Access Road. Catch it at the Snowshed Base Lodge.

Accommodations

Killington has very little slopeside lodging and no real ski-in/ski-out options; on-mountain condos are ski-in, but not ski-out. To make reservations for the **Killington Grand Resort Hotel, Killington Resort Villages** and most properties, call the **Killington Lodging Bureau** (800-621-6867).

Killington Resort Villages has good values, with nearby athletic club facilities, some nightlife and an excellent shuttlebus system. Of the condo complexes here, **Highridge** units are by far the most desirable. **Sunrise**, at the base of Bear Mountain, is another good choice. Other condos include **The Woods at Killington**, which boasts whirlpool tubs, saunas and a complete spa, and **Mountain Inn** and the **Cascades Lodge**, which are convenient but basic. The Cascades has a nice indoor pool, and the Mountain Inn has some of the best nightlife.

The **Killington Grand Resort Hotel** ($$–$$$$), near the base of Snowshed, has a full-service restaurant, outdoor heated swimming pool, health club and "slopeside" location. (In truth, you have to walk across a long pedestrian bridge to reach the slopes.) What you're paying for here is that location. The top hotel on the mountain road at Killington is **The Inn of the Six Mountains** (800-228-4676; 422-4302; $$–$$$), with a 65-foot indoor lap pool, exercise room and frequent shuttles to the slopes. Rates include breakfast. **The Red Clover Inn** (800-752-0571; 775-2290; $$$–$$$$) is 5 miles west of the Killington Access Road, hard to find, but it's the best in the area. Set on 13 acres, this farm estate has private baths and country decor. Room rates include breakfast and dinner, and the food is superb. Another favorite is **The Inn at Long Trail** (800-325-2540; 775-7181; $–$$). One of Vermont's first ski lodges, the inn still maintains its cozy, rustic feel. The 19 rooms are small, but the inn has a devoted following. Rates include breakfast and dinner.

Mountain Meadows Lodge (800-370-4567; 775-1010; $$–$$$$) is a good choice for families. Adjacent to the Mountain Meadows Cross-Country Ski Resort (but separately owned), this country inn—a converted 19th century dairy barn and farmhouse—has an in-house children's program, game and video rooms and a small petting farm.

The **Birch Ridge Inn** (422-4293; $$$–$$$$) was created from a former executive retreat. The A-frame design gives it a 1960s flair, and the cuisine gets high marks. Near the base of the Killington Road is the **North Star Lodge** (422-4040; $–$$), which has a pool and shuttle service and is surrounded by good restaurants.

The Grey Bonnet (775-2537; $–$$), on Rte. 100 north, received numerous recommendations. There is a nice indoor pool, sauna and pub. Rates include breakfast and dinner.

The Cortina Inn (800-451-6108; 773-3333; $$$–$$$$), on Rte. 4, a mile past Pico, has a health club, pool, spa, two restaurants, children's activities on holiday weekends, and many large suites. **The Vermont Inn** (800-541-7795 ; 775-0708; $$–$$$$) is a charming New England country inn with fireside dining. Homemade breakfast and dinner are included.

For pampering, stay at the **Woodstock Inn and Resort** (800-448-7900; $$$–$$$$), about 17 miles east of Killington. (*See Nearby Skiing at end of this chapter*).

Dining

The Killington area has more than 100 restaurants and bars. The best is **Hemingway's** (422-3886; $$$$), one of only two four-star restaurants in Vermont. The fixed-price, four-course menu ranges from $50–$65.

Our other favorites are **Maxwell's Restaurant** at The Summit (422-3535; $$$$), an award-winning restaurant with a menu that changes nightly and a great wine list; the top-rated **The Vermont Inn** (800-541-7795 or 775-0708; $$$$), with fine formal dining; and the award-winning **Red Clover Inn** (775-2290; $$$–$$$$), where the rack of lamb is exceptional; and **Cafe Toast** (422-5777; $$$), which serves exceptional cuisine in an intimate setting.

The **Birch Ridge Inn** (422-4293; $$$) has a small, but highly acclaimed restaurant. **Jason's** (422-3303; $$$), in The Red Rob, has excellent Northern Italian food, and **Zola's Grille,** at the Cortina Inn (773-3333; $$$), serves an eclectic blend of Northern Italian, French bistro and Mediterranean cuisine in a casual atmosphere. **McGrath's Irish Pub** (775-7181; $$), at The Inn at Long Trail, serves Guinness stew and shepherd's pie in its funky pub and restaurant built into a cliff. Service can be slow, but the food is hearty and tasty. At **Charity's** (422-3800; $$), the bar is cozy and welcoming, the portions healthy and the menu of steaks, barbecue and Italian dishes appease any appetite.

How often do you get to dine in a restored circa-1900 railroad car? **Casey's Caboose** (422-3795; $$–$$$) is a good choice for affordable steaks, seafood and pasta. The rambling **Grist Mill Restaurant** (422-3970; $$) sits beside a tranquil pond and has a rustic interior.

For spots kinder to the budget: **The Wobbly Barn** (422-3392; $$) is known for steaks and a great salad bar. **Mrs. Brady's** (422-2020; $–$$) serves the "basics" (salads, burgers, roast turkey and monster sandwiches). **Pizza Jerks** (422-4111) and the **Outback Pizza** (422-9885; $), both on the Killington Road, serve decent pizza.

Sushi Yoshi and Hibachi Steakhouse (422-4241; $–$$$) has the best—and only—Jap-

Dining: $$$$–Entrees $30+; $$$–$20-$30; $$–$10-$20; $-less than $10.
Accommodations: (double room) $$$$–$200+; $$$–$141-$200; $$–$81-$140; $–$80 and less.

anese and Chinese food on the mountain, including a sushi bar.

For breakfast, locals head to **Ppeppers** ($), yes that's how it's spelled, at the nightspot Outback. Portions are massive, and it caters to the hung-over. **Johnny Boy's Pancake House** ($), a breakfast haunt on the Killington Road in front of the Comfort Inn, serves regular homestyle before-noon fare. If you're looking for a good cup of coffee or a quick breakfast, head to the **Sun-up Bakery** ($), but be forewarned: If there're 10 inches of fresh snow, the staff often shuts the doors and skis for a few runs.

Apres-ski/nightlife

Killington's apres-ski scene, strung out along the Killington Road, is often voted number one in the nation, with the atmosphere generally raucous and young, and festivities often driven by excellent bands, some nationally known. Apres-ski at the mountain includes the **Mahogany Ridge** at the Killington Base Lodge, the **Long Trail Brew Pub** at Snowshed and the **Bear Mountain Lounge** at the Bear Mountain Base Lodge.

Apres-ski action on the Killington Road can be found in the **Lookout Bar & Grille** or **Charity's**. **Outback Pizza** is recommended for its happy hour. It's a favorite locals' hangout on weekdays, with $5 all-you-can-eat pizza on Monday nights; entertainment and dancing extend into the evening on weekends. For rowdy apres-ski and then dancing to loud music, head to the **Wobbly Barn Steakhouse**. Big name bands often lead the line-up at **The Pickle Barrel**, which has a lively happy hour with dancing later in the evening. It's a favorite among the young college crowd. **Casey's Caboose** is a favorite locals' haunt with killer spicy buffalo wings that are free during happy hour. An older, quieter set meets at the **Summit** for happy hour.

Those older than 30 may want to opt out of the mosh pit at the Pickle Barrel, and head down the road to **The Grist Mill.** This restaurant/bar has earned a reputation as the place for slightly "more mature" skiers, but don't let that fool you: Maturity at Killington is strictly relative. The place rocks on weekends, when live music and dancing is featured, and its circular bar and layout is perfect for checking out the action and general people-watching. Plus, for our money, the Grist Mill makes the area's most toe-curling Goombays, a local concoction of fruit juices and various flavors of rum. Two Goombays and you'll understand why this rates as the unofficial drink of the official apres-ski/nightlife capital of the East.

From Pico, head a few yards up Rte. 4 to **The Inn at Long Trail**, nestled right into the apex of Killington Pass. **McGrath's Irish Pub** here serves Guinness ale on tap. Live entertainment, performing on a stage built right into the cliff, keeps the bar full on weekends.

Other activities

Killington's new **Winter Adventure Center** (422-6200) at the golf course (across the road from the Grand Resort Hotel) is a hub for tubing and arcade games. An **outdoor skating rink** can be found below the Summit Lodge on Grist Mill Pond. For **snowmobiling information** call the Cortina Inn, 773-3333, or Killington Snowmobile Tours, 422-2121.

The **Spa at The Woods** (422-3139) is a full-service European spa at The Woods Resort & Spa. Treatments include hot stone therapy, citrus body polish and seaweed body mask.

Shopping is plentiful, but as spread out as the resort. The Killington Shops at the Shack, several outlet-style stores, are at the intersection of Rte. 4 and the Killington Road.

Getting there and getting around

By air: Major airports are in Burlington, Vt., Albany, N.Y., and Manchester, N.H. Burlington is about a 90-minute drive from Killington, while Albany and Manchester are each about two hours. Green Mountain Limousine Service (773-1313) runs transfers from the Burlington airport for $330 for two, round-trip, plus 15-percent driver gratuity. Thrifty Rental Cars has an office at the Inn of the Six Mountains. Major car rental companies are also available at the airports.

By car: Killington is at the intersection of Rtes. 4 and 100 near Rutland, about three hours northwest of Boston. Pico is about 3 miles west of the Access Road on Rte. 4.

By train: Daily service is available on Amtrak's Ethan Allen Express from New York City to Rutland, with bus service or car rental to Killington. Call (800) 872-7245 for train information, or Killington Central Reservations (800-621-6867) for package information.

Getting around: Bring or rent a car or use the Killington Shuttle bus service. Though you might not use your car to move between your lodging and the slopes, Killington is very spread out, and you may want to visit the attractions nearby.

Nearby resorts

Suicide Six, Woodstock Vt;[802] 457-6661

Internet: www.woodstockinn.com
2 chairlifts; 1 J-bar; 23 trails; 650 vertical feet

Don't let the name discourage you from visiting this family-friendly mountain that's owned by the Woodstock Inn and Resort. It's ideal for young families, sun-seekers and those who've wasted their legs at Killington the previous day. Suicide Six makes up for its small size with a nice range of terrain. There's just enough here to test most skiers for at least a few runs, but the emphasis is on laid back skiing and riding. No high-speed quads, but there are seldom crowds either. The views are of rural Vermont—no condos or development to speak of, just barns, farmhouses, rolling fields and forests.

Lodging: The elegant **Woodstock Inn** (800-448-7900; 457-1100; $$$$), in downtown Woodstock, is *the* place to stay. Tickets and equipment rentals are free for inn guests during midweek and non-holiday periods. The inn boasts one of the state's better cross-country skiing trail systems, with 60 km. of trails. It also has an excellent indoor sports facility, a well-respected dining room and a more casual restaurant. Woodstock has plenty of other lodging, too, including an especially nice choice of small inns and B&Bs. These include the Ardmore Inn (800-497-9652; 457-3887; $$-$$), a lovely intown B&B; The Village Inn of Woodstock (800-722-4571; $$-$$$) on the eastern edge of town; and The Jackson House Inn and Restaurant (800-448-1890; 457-2065; $$$$), heading west toward Killington, with its renowned dining room (reservations essential).

Lift tickets (05/06): Adults, $52 weekends, $30 midweek; children (14 and younger) and seniors (65+), $35/$24. Half-day tickets are available. A J-bar-only ticket is $7 and a single ride ticket is $8. Lodging and lift packages are the way to go here; call the Woodstock Inn for more information.

Distance from Burlington: About 100 miles via I-89 and Rte. 4. Suicide Six is about 125 miles from Albany and about 150 miles from Boston.

Lodging information: Woodstock Inn, (800) 448-7900 or (802) 457-1100.

Dining: $$$$-Entrees $30+; $$$-$20-$30; $$-$10-$20; $-less than $10.
Accommodations: (double room) $$$$-$200+; $$$-$141-$200; $$-$81-$140; $-$80 and less.

Mad River Valley
Sugarbush & Mad River Glen

Waitsfield/Warren Region
Vermont

Dining:★★★★
Apres-ski/nightlife:★★
Other activities:★★
Toll free reservations: (800) 828-4748
Internet: www.madrivervalley.com

Sugarbush

Summit elevation:	4,083 feet
Vertical drop:	2,600 feet
Base elevation:	1,483 feet

Address: 1840 Sugarbush Access Road
Warren, VT 05674-9572
Area code: 802
Ski area phone: 583-6300
Snow report: 583-SNOW
Toll-free reservations: (800) 537-8427
Fax: 583-6303
Internet: www.sugarbush.com
Number and types of lifts: 16—5 high-speed quads, 2 quad chairs, 2 triples, 4 double chairs, 3 surface lifts
Skiable acreage: 508 acres
Snowmaking: 68 percent
Uphill capacity: 25,463 per hour
Parks & pipes: 9 parks; 1 pipe
Bed base: 6,600 (2,200 on mountain)
Nearest lodging: Slopeside
Resort child care: Yes, 6 weeks and older
Adult ticket, per day: $49-$64 (04/05)

Expert: ★★
Advanced: ★★★
Intermediate:★★★★
Beginner: ★★★★
First-timer:★★★★

Mad River Glen

Summit elevation:	3,637 feet
Vertical drop:	2,037 feet
Base elevation:	1,600 feet

Address: PO Box 1089
Waitsfield, VT 05673
Area code: 802
Ski area phone: 496-3551
Snow report: 496-3551
Toll-free information: (800) 850-6742 (area Chamber)
Fax: 496-3562
E-mail: ski@madriverglen.com
Internet: www.madriverglen.com
Number and types of lifts: 5—3 double chairs, 1 single chair, 1 surface lift
Skiable acreage: about 115 acres
Snowmaking: 15 percent
Uphill capacity: 3,000 per hour
Snowboarding: Not allowed
Bed base: 6,600
Nearest lodging: About a quarter-mile
Resort child care: Yes, 6 weeks to 6 years
Adult ticket, per day: $50 (05/06)

Expert: ★★★★
Advanced: ★★★★
Intermediate:★★★
Beginner: ★★
First-timer: ★

Conjure up a Hollywood-influenced image of Vermont, and chances are you'll picture the Mad River Valley. It's equal parts Bing Crosby's White Christmas and the Bob Newhart Show. The rolling, pastoral countryside is dotted with clapboard farmhouses, restored barns, restored inns and those iconic Vermont cows. The mountains rise sharply, and sideroads to ski areas wind through ledges cutting the landscape.

Once the playground for the well-to-do, the out-of-the-way Mad River Valley gradually fell out of favor with the "in" crowd and became the place that time forgot. This is a good thing. The valley remains free of large chain hotels, fast-food restaurants and other sprawl. Two small towns, Waitsfield and Warren, provide everything a visitor might need, and do so in that oh-so-Vermont, New York-accented country-store fashion. You may be rusticating, but you needn't do without a fine wine and a fancy meal.

Sugarbush and Mad River are the yin and yang of the Alpine world. They balance each other and manage to entertain everyone from just-happy-to-be-together families to death-defying extreme skiers. Sugarbush has lots of snowmaking and plenty of condos and relatively wide trails—from an Eastern point of view.

Mad River Glen is the way skiing used to be, because, well, little has changed here over the years. Home to one of the few single chairs left in the country, Mad River has almost no snowmaking and no condos. Narrow trails cut down the thickly wooded mountain are merely suggestions of where to ski. Diehards ski all over Mad River Glen, through trees, over frozen waterfalls and down cliffs. Its terrain attracts such a devoted following that Mad River is America's only skier-owned, nonprofit cooperative.

Sugarbush

Mountain layout

Sugarbush is divided into two separate areas, Lincoln Peak and Mt. Ellen, connected by a 10-minute ride on rollercoaster-like, high-speed quad chairlift. Each of these mountains has subareas with its own distinct flavors. With over 4,000 acres spilling from a five-mile wide ridgeline, this season is the inaugural year for Lincoln Peak Village, the most ambitious project in the resort's almost 50-year history. It features three new facilities including Clay Brook, the cornerstone of the revitalizationand the brand new Gate House lodge, double the size of the old building from11,000 square feet to 23,000 square feet.

◆◆**Expert ◆Advanced:** At Lincoln Peak, the runs served by Castlerock lift are serious blacks and no place for the timid. The entire Castlerock area offers narrow New England-style steeps, and if you're lucky the Castlerock run will occasionally be groomed, making for a heavenly smooth steep. The Castlerock double chair is popular with those in this ability level, so be aware that sometimes there is a wait, usually not more than eight to 10 minutes. The benefit is that these narrow trails do not fill up with yahoo skiers. You have to *want* to be there to end up at Castlerock.

From the summit of Lincoln Peak and the top of the Heaven's Gate triple, experts can drop down Ripcord or Paradise, two double-black-diamond runs that frequently bump up. The more wide-open Organgrinder (the old gondola lift line), which we dubbed "Organ Donor," is a wide, steep run that dares you to ski fast. Stein's Run, accessible by either the Super Bravo Express or the Valley House Double chairlifts, is another long, steep, mogul run. Egan's Woods, to skier's left of Stein's Run, is no doubt where extreme skier John Egan plays.

Mt. Ellen is primarily an intermediate playground, though the double blacks at the top—F.I.S., Black Diamond, Exterminator and Bravo (the latter a single diamond)—are among the toughest in New England. The Green Mountain Express high-speed quad from the base connects to the Summit Quad, allowing easy access to the top.

■ **Intermediate:** Intermediates should start at the Super Bravo chair on Lincoln Peak, then traverse to the Heaven's Gate triple. Once at the summit, take Upper Jester, a run full of fun switchbacks that take you back to the top of the Super Bravo lift. From here, choose from Downspout, Domino, Snowball, Murphy's Glades or Lower Jester. On a busy day, these runs are crowded with skiers. Intermediates also tend to flock to the North Lynx triple on the upper part of North Lynx Peak. Here, the views are good, and the runs sometimes bump up.

The slopes tend to be less crowded on the lower part of North Lynx Peak and parts of Gadd Peak. Eden, a tree-skiing area on Gadd Peak, is the place to learn to navigate glades. Spring Fling is wide-open and attracts few skiers and is great for long, fast turns.

Mt. Ellen has wide-open cruising runs. On the map, the intermediate runs from the top of the Summit quad chair seem relatively short, but the map is misleading. The Rim Run, connecting to Upper Lookin' Good, Lower Rim Run, Cruiser and Straight Shot, is a classic cruising run. The other intermediate section is Inverness, served by a quad chair.

●● **Beginner:** North Lynx Peak on the far right side, of the Lincoln Peak is a good place for beginners. Start on Pushover and Easy Rider and then graduate to Slowpoke and Sleeper. At Mt. Ellen, Walt's Trail is a long green run from the top of the Inverness chair.

● **First-timer:** Lincoln Peak has Easy Rider, a gentle slope served by a double chair. Mt. Ellen has Graduation, Riemergasse and Sugar Run, also served by a double chair.

Ride Guide: The only trail that will leave you hiking here is Lower FIS; even if you hold speed you'll be booting out and kicking. It's worth it on a powder day, because this is a quiet trail that holds freshies late, but you will have to hike out. There are a few traverses where you'll need to keep up speed: Bailout from Castlerock Run to Heaven's Gate is not all that bad, a little speed will get the job done. The Northway, from Exterminator to the Inverness lift at Mt. Ellen, is long and somewhat flat as well, but speed should carry you, provided the surface is groomed; otherwise, you'll hike. Reverse Traverse, from the top of Stein's Run over to Murphy's Glades, is tough because you really can't get a lot of speed to go the distance. Instead, head down Snowball to Spring Fling.

Parks and pipes

Five of the resort's nine terrain parks and the superpipe are located at the Mt. Ellen base. Getting to the park from Lincoln Peak requires a cold ride on the Slide Brook Express or a warmer ride on the base-to-base trolley. The upper section of the park is on Whichway. The lower section is on Crackerjack. Maintain your speed when crossing the flats between Whichway and Crackerjack, but watch for the Slide Brook quad that unloads just before the flattest section. All of Sugarbush's park rangers are professionally trained coaches.

Lessons (05/06 prices)

Group lessons: $39 for all levels except first-timers. A Value Pak of five two-hour clinics costs $160.

First-timer package: Learn-to-Ski or Ride clinics include lesson, lifts and rentals and cost $70 for the first day, $75 for the second, with mid-mountain access, and $80 for the third. Call (888) 651-4827 for details.

Private lessons: $92 an hour; $50 for each added hour; $20 for each additional person.

Special programs: The Sugarbush Ski & Ride School offers multiday clinics for snowboarders, women and expert skiers or riders, and specialty classes (powder, bumps, etc.) in private lessons. Outback Tours take advanced skiers/riders off-piste into Lincoln Peak's Slide Brook Wilderness area for 2.5 hours at 10 a.m. and 1 p.m. Saturday, Sunday, and holidays when the natural snow coverage allows. Book through the Guest Service at Lincoln Peak. Cost: $40. Call 888-651-4827 for reservations.

KidStuff (06/07 prices)

Child care: Available for ages 6 weeks to 6 years in Sugarbush Village, a group of condos to the far right past the main parking lot at Lincoln Peak. Day Care Cubs (6 weeks–6 years) get a non-ski program for $70 full day, $50 half day. Multiday pricing is available. Reservations required; call 583-6717.

Note: You can park at Sugarbush Village and buy lift tickets at the day school. Access the slopes by skiing or walking or taking the shuttlebus.

Children's lessons: For instruction children are divided into age groups. Microbears for 3-year-olds combines day care with ski play: $95 full day, $75 half day weekends and holidays; $85 full day/$65 half day midweek. Minibears (ages 4-6) and Sugarbears (ages 7–12) combines lessons with snow fun: $85 full day, $65 half day Monday–Friday; $95 full day, $75 half day, weekends and holidays. Full-day children's programs include lunch and lift tickets. Equipment is extra. Reservations required; call (888) 651-4827. Lessons for every group but Microbears start at the Gate House Lodge at Lincoln Peak. Microbears are at the child care center in Sugarbush Village.

Lift tickets (06/07 prices)

	Adult	Young Adult (13-18)
One day	$62	$55
Three days	$165 ($55/day)	$135 ($45)
Five days	$240 ($48/day)	$105 ($41)

Note: Three- and five-day rates are rounded to the closest dollar.

Who skis free: Children ages 6 and younger.

Who skis at a discount: Sugarbush lowers ticket prices for adults in its Value Season, opening through mid-December and in April. Children, ages 7–12, pay $32 for a midweek day, $90 for three days and $150 for five days. Ages 65 and older ski for the child's price. Sugarbush also offers a Mt. Ellen-only ticket for $45—a smart buy for terrain park enthusiasts.

Note: The Ski the Valley, a joint ticket for Mad River Glen and Sugarbush, is available when skiers purchase accommodation for three nights or more in the valley. The joint lift ticket allows skiers to choose where they want to ski in the valley each day. Make sure to ask about this special lift ticket when you make reservations.

Mad River Glen

Mad River Glen is a throwback to earlier ski days, and as one of our contributors put it, "It's the type of skiing that made my mother give up the sport." The ski area prides itself on being tough, and the bumper sticker, "Mad River Glen: Ski It If You Can," is all too true. Trail ratings are not inflated. Even the beginner trails here might be graded intermediate elsewhere. But MRG fans love this area and have shown their devotion by buying shares of this now skier-owned resort. And yes, we mean *ski* resort; snowboards are not allowed. MRG is traditional (it's one of two areas in the nation with a chairlift for solo riders), natural (little snowmaking, combined with plenty of tight tree skiing), hard-corps (the ski shop at the base sells T-shirts with the slogan, "Friends don't let friends get first tracks") and homey (skiers with serious tracks to carve have got to love a cafeteria with peanut-butter-and-jelly sandwiches to go). It's a mountain for serious skiers, not poseurs. Leave your Bogner suit on the hanger and don some wool pants. You'll fit right in. Free guided mountain tours are offered on weekends and holidays at 10 a.m. and 1 p.m.

 ## Mountain layout

♦♦**Expert** ♦**Advanced:** Experts will be happy just about anywhere at Mad River Glen, especially after a snowstorm when the bumps become gigantic. One nice feature that's a throwback to tradition is the area's refusal to make much snow. All of the expert terrain is covered with natural snow (when it falls), so it bumps up nicely and doesn't get as icy as the East's other resorts.

While the line for the single chair is usually about 10 minutes long, it can approach 45 minutes on peak holidays and good powder days. Experts happily wait. From the top of this lift, then can immediately drop down the Chute under the lift or traverse to Catamount Bowl, one of the most wide-open runs on the mountain. For more of a challenge, find a guide or hook up with a local and venture into the area called Paradise, entered by dropping down a five-foot waterfall. Ask around for Octopus's Garden and the 19th and 20th Holes. If you look like you know how to ski, a local may direct you to these. At the single chair's midstation, tree skiing beckons through the Glades to the right as you ski off the chair.

■ **Intermediate:** Mad River Glen is not known for its cruiser runs. If intermediates find themselves at the top of the single chair, they have only one route down upper Antelope, which splits into Catamount after a few turns. Both runs are quite narrow and intermediates should beware: About halfway down, Antelope veers off into the woods, gets steeper, and, hard to believe, even narrower. Unless you're up for a challenge, follow Broadway under the lift, and head to the other side of the mountain.

Intermediates will find a better selection of terrain off the Sunnyside Chair. Quacky to Porcupine is a nice run. Bunny will also take you from Quacky to the base. To the right of the chair is a series of expert trails, Panther, Partridge, Slalom Hill and Gazelle, most of which empty into Birdland. Confident intermediates will find these runs challenging, if not downright scary. A missed turn may mean you have to sideslip into a trail.

If you feel like you're ready to tackle MRG's classic terrain (i.e., the woods), give yourself a sampler. From the top of the Sunnyside chair, take Fox to the big intersection and traverse straight into the woods. The trees soon open up into the Glades. If this trail seems fun, congratulations! You're ready for the tough stuff. If you're intimidated, bail out on Bunny.

●● **Beginner:** Birdland is ostensibly the beginner area, but to get there, you have to have good route-finding skills. Otherwise, you'll find yourself at the top of an overly-moguled expert pitch vowing to give up the sport. Take the Sunnyside chair to the top, then follow Fox to Snail, catwalks that will take you to the land of green circles. Granted, Duck, Lark, Robin, Wren and Loon are for beginners. Learn to ski here, and little will daunt you elsewhere. But be aware that the Birdland Chair runs only on weekends and holidays. During those times, however, a novice-level skier can spend an entire day here, dine at the Birdcage lodge at the bottom of Birdland, and avoiding the sometimes long base-area lift lines. Mad River's old-fashioned lifts also mean less on-trail skier traffic that beginners will welcome.

● **First-timer:** While few think of Mad River Glen as the best place for a first-timer, the Callie's Corner rope tow is isolated at the base and provides a nice venue for an easy intro.

Lessons [06/07 prices]

Mad River Glen has a ski school that, like the area, marches to its own drummer.

Group lessons: The Create Your Own Group is $125 for a one-hour lesson. A second two-hour Create Your Own Group on the same day is $100.

First-timer package: The Beginner "You Can" Learn to Ski Package, including lifts, two-hour lesson and rentals, is $65 for either Alpine or telemark. A follow-up two-hour lesson on the same day costs $35. A nice touch for beginners—so few come here to learn that classes almost always end up being private lessons.

Private lessons: Cost is $55 for an hour, plus $20 per additional person; $90 for two hours, plus $35 per extra person. The "I Can" card delivers three one-hour private lessons for $125

Special programs: Free Heel Fridays is a two-hour telemark lesson, at either 10 a.m. or 1 p.m., for $40 ($65 with lift ticket).

KidStuff [06/07 prices]

Child care: The Cricket Club Nursery (496-3551 ext. 20) offers infant care for children 6 weeks to 18 months for $60 for a full day, $45 for a half day, $115 for two days. Child care for children ages 18 months to 6 years costs $55 for a full day and $40 for a half day, $105 for two days. The Ski and Play introduction to skiing program is $70 for a full day with lunch and two lessons, $135 for two days. A half day with one ski lesson is $50. Children ready for more advanced skiing should register in the lesson programs (*see below*). The nursery takes no reservations, but if you check your child into the nursery on Friday and pay for two days, you're guaranteed a spot on Saturday. Or, if you call at 8:15 a.m. and say you're coming, they'll hold a spot for your kid.

Lessons: Programs run from 10 a.m. to 3 p.m. A full day is $95 with lunch, half-day is $40, without lunch. Mad River offers a number of options for kids and teens: Rockin' Robins is for kids ages 4-12 who are learning to ski for the first time; class size is limited to three. Chipmunks is for ages 4-7 who have had some ski experience and are able to ride lifts. Kids 7 and older can chose from Panthers, Development Team, Freestyle Team, Telemark Team and Junior Race Program.

Private lessons: for kids 3-12 cost $40 per hour, $25 for each additional child; $70 for two hours; $35 for each additional child. Weekdays, the lack of volume means that kids' groups lessons are offered as privates at weekend junior group rates.

Lift tickets [06/07 prices]

	Adult	Junior (6-15)/Senior (65-69)
One day	$54	$40
Three days*	$140 ($47/day)	$100 ($33/day)
Five days*	$222 ($44/day)	$156 ($31/day)

*Weekend and holiday rates: Three-day midweek is $97 adult, $70 junior or senior; five-day is $137 and $110.

Mad River offers a number of deals including the Mad Card which offers ***three days of skiing for $119*** good any time during the 2006-2007 ski season Season-long midweek passes running from Monday to Friday are $320.

Who skis free: Ages 70 and older ski free five days per season. Children 5 and younger are issued a free ticket when skiing with a paying adult.

Note: Ski the Valley is a joint ticket for Mad River Glen and Sugarbush available when skiers purchase accommodation for at least three nights over a weekend or two nights mid-week in the valley.

Cross-country and snowshoeing (visit xcskiresorts.com for more details)

The **Blueberry Lake Cross-Country Ski Center** (496-6687) has 23 km. of trails, beginner to expert, groomed for skate skiing and classic. Dogs are permitted. **Ole's Cross-Country Center** (496-3430; near the airport) has 50 km. of groomed trails on rolling terrain. Ole's also has snowshoeing and a Rossignol demo center. The **Inn at the Round Barn Farm** (496-2276) cross-country area, with 15 km. of groomed trails, is linked with Ole's.

Snowshoe treks (583-6537) are available in Sugarbush's **Slidebrook Wilderness Area**, a remote 2,000-acre wilderness between Mt. Ellen and Lincoln Peak. **Mad River Glen** (496-3551) has nearly 5 miles of snowshoe trails on the mountain, which connect with Vermont's famed Long Trail. Guided naturalist programs are offered every weekend. These include full-moon snowshoe treks, an evening naturalist series, slide shows and other events. You can arrange snowshoe treks through **Clearwater Sports** (496-2708). Carol Thompson of **Out Back Tracks** (496-3153) tells how to recognize animal tracks and interpret animal behaviors on personalized, guided snowshoe expeditions. Snowshoers who want to strike out on their own can take advantage of a variety of backcountry trails in the region. A trail map is available from the Sugarbush Chamber of Commerce.

Accommodations

Excellent country inns and B&Bs can all be booked through Mad River Valley Chamber of Commerce (800-828-4748 or www.madrivervalley.com), Sugarbush Central Reservations (800-537-8427) or call the inns directly. The chamber website offers info on current availability and online reservations for 23 properties.

It is easy to be spoiled at **The Pitcher Inn** (888-867-4824; 496-6350; $$$$), a Relais and Chateaux member property in Warren. We especially liked the Ski, Mountain and Trout rooms. Many rooms have fireplaces, whirlpool tubs and steam rooms. Full breakfasts are served in the light-filled dining room, where gourmet meals are served at night. Afternoon tea and treats are served in the library. Drinks are served in the comfy downstairs lounge and adjacent games room. Owners Win and Margaret Smith are also part owners of Sugarbush.

The Inn at the Round Barn Farm (496-2276; $$–$$$$), a mile from Rte. 100, across the covered bridge on East Warren Road, is one of the country's best B&Bs. The farmhouse has been turned into an elegant, spacious, peaceful 11-room bed & breakfast. Children's stays are discouraged. The Richardson Room with Vermont-made canopied bed, skylights, gas fireplace, oversized jetted tub and steam shower is tops. Out back are 30 km. of Nordic tracks.

Tucker Hill Inn (800-543-7841; 496-3983; $-$$), 2 miles from the lifts, has 18 rooms and a fine dining restaurant. **The Waitsfield Inn** (800-758-3801; 496-3979; $-$$), in the center of Waitsfield Village, started life in the 1820s as a parsonage, was a sleeping-bag dorm for young skiers in the '60s and '70s and is now a quaintly elegant 14-bedroom B&B.

The Sugartree Inn (583-3211; $$) has award-winning breakfasts. Rooms range from large with canopied beds and/or fireplace to small. The inn is only a quarter mile from Sugarbush's slopes. **The Featherbed Inn** (496-7151; $$), on Rte. 100 only a stone's throw from the resort access road, is a restored 1806 house and cottage with nine spacious individually decorated guest rooms, all with private baths and luxurious featherbeds, plenty of space to spread out and to-die-for gourmet breakfasts. **West Hill House B&B** (496-7162; $$-$$$) is an 1850s farmhouse with eight guest rooms, all with fireplaces, DSL Internet access and either jetted tub or steamroom. **Beaver Pond Farm Inn** (583-2861; $-$$) is right on the cross-country trails of the Sugarbush golf course. The **1824 House Inn** (496-7555; $) has eight rooms just north of town, with featherbeds and an outdoor hot tub. It's chef-owned and offers intimate, gourmet dinners, by reservation only, to both lodgers and the public.

The nicest full-service hotel property is the **Sugarbush Inn** (800-537-8427; 583-6100; $$) on the access road. The inn and its 42 rooms are well-kept but nondescript. Closer to Sugarbush resort, you'll find **Sugar Lodge** at Sugarbush (800-982-3465; $-$$), only a half mile from Lincoln Peak. It parallels good-quality chain lodging with a hot tub and lounge.

The **Weathertop Mountain Inn** (800-800-3625; 496-4909; $-$$), on Rte. 17 between town and Mad River Glen, is an affordable B&B. The **Inn At The Mad River Barn** (496-3310; $-$$) has rustic but spacious rooms and some of the best lodging food in the valley (both in quantity and quality). To stay here is to step into a wonderful 1940s ski lodge. Families, and the budget-minded, will want to check into the **Hyde Away Inn and Restaurant** (496-2322; $-$$) on Rte. 17. Both are great spots for children and close to the slopes.

Of the condominiums in the **Village at Sugarbush** (800-53-SUGAR), the most luxurious are the **Southface Condominiums** with hot tubs in each unit and a shuttlebus ride from the slopes. **The Snow Creek** condos are ski-in/ski-out but are plagued by the noise of snow guns out the back window. **Paradise** condos are newer but a good walk from the slopes; however, they have a free shuttle service. The **Summit** units are roomy, and **Castle Rock** condos are close to the slopes. **Trailside,** previously called Unihab, looks like boxes stacked on one another, and the small **North Lynx** condos, previously called Middle Earth, are 10 minutes from the lifts. Rates range from $145 for a one-bedroom in value season to $635 for a four-bedroom during holidays. Guests may use the indoor pool, tennis, racquetball, squash courts, aerobics, whirlpool tubs, steam room and Nautilus equipment at the Sugarbush Health and Racquet Club for an additional fee.

The Bridges Resort and Racquet Club (800-453-2922; 583-2922; $$-$$$$), with tennis courts and an indoor pool, is across the street from the ski area parking lot. These units are quieter than the mountain units and have wonderful amenities as well as a regular shuttle.

Skiers heading for Mad River Glen should check into the unfortunately named **Battle-ground** condos on Rte. 17 (800-248-2102; 496-2288).

 Dining

The Mad River Valley has more than 40 restaurants, many of which offer excellent food. Most require reservations, so call before venturing out. Valley residents are quite proud of having no fast-food chain restaurants. At Sugarbush, great food, light and wide open spaces are some of the features in the new Gate House Food Court opening this 2007 season in Lincoln Peak featuring a revamped Castlerock Pub. It will be the apres-ski place to be this season in Lincoln Peak Village

For top of the line dining try **Chez Henri** (583-2600; $$-$$$) in Sugarbush Village at the base area of Lincoln Peak. The oldest restaurant in the valley, it captures a true French bistro feeling, with low ceilings and a flickering fire. The owner, Henri Borel, personally greets guests and makes them feel at home. He also supervises the excellent wine selection. Chez Henri features lunch, fondue in the late afternoon, then dinner until 10 p.m.

The **Pitcher Inn Restaurant** (496-6350; $$$$) serves contemporary American fare

Dining: $$$$-Entrees $30+; $$$-$20-$30; $$-$10-$20; $-less than $10.
Accommodations: (double room) $$$$-$200+; $$$-$141-$200; $$-$81-$140; $-$80 and less.

with a New England accent. The understated dining room has a huge fireplace and windows overlooking the Mad River. You may also make reservations to have an intimate dinner in the wine cellar. The **Spotted Cow** (496-5151; $$-$$$$), run by Jay and Renata Young, has gained a reputation for some of the best food in the valley. Pricey to be sure. Don't miss the Bermuda fish chowder; it's worth the trip to Waitsfield. The **Common Man** (583-2800; $$-$$$) has attracted a faithful clientele and has a reputation for good food, but for the money, it's not quite as "common" as the name implies. The atmosphere is what might be called a New England Baroque barn with crystal chandeliers.

The **Warren House** (583-2421; $$), down a driveway to the left as you approach the Sugarbush parking lot, has developed lots of fans and offers an eclectic menu rivaling any in the area, along with a good wine list. The **Tucker Hill Inn & Restaurant** (496-3025; $$) serves meals in front of a flickering fireplace under a beamed ceiling. It also has light apres-ski and late-night fare. **Millbrook Country Inn** (496-2405; $$), on Rte. 17, has a small dining room with a fireplace, original art and antiques. The meals are prepared from local organic produce. **Mad River Barn Restaurant** (496-3310; $) has a popular Saturday buffet and serves dinners Sunday to Friday from 6:30 to 8 p.m.

Worth the effort is the clay-oven wood-fired, organic flatbread pizza at **American Flatbread** (496-8856; $), open only on weekends, at the Lareau Farm Country Inn. A toasty bonfire is a nice distraction during the long wait (anywhere from 30 to 90 minutes).

John Egan's New Pub & Grill (496-3033; $$) serves excellent food and is a great place to bring the family. For families out to stretch the budget and still get good wholesome food, try the **Hyde Away** (496-2322; $-$$), on Rte. 17. **BonGiorno**'s (496-6265; $), also on Rte. 17, is the place to head for pizza and affordable pasta, with delivery as well. For simple quick food, try **The Den** (496-8880; $-$$) on Waitsfield's main street. **Jay's** (496-8282; $) doesn't claim to be anything fancy but is a good spot for family fare.

Michael's Good to Go (496-3832; $$), at the Village Square Shopping Center, prepares fine gourmet dinners to go such as Ants Climbing a Tree (organic pork and thin noodles stir-fry) and Jamaican Jerk Chicken. The **Easy Street Café and Market** (496-7234; $-$$), on Rte. 100 north of the Sugarbush Access Road, an eat-in/take-out gourmet deli serving breakfast and lunch, plus frozen dinners, prepares excellent homemade soups, hot dishes, salads and sandwiches. The **Valley Pizzeria** (496-9200; $) makes real brick-oven, hand-thrown pizza. It's as close to Jersey pizza as you'll ever find in Vermont, one local tells us.

For breakfast, locals tell us **Easy Street** is far and away the breakfast place in town, and that the **Warren Store** makes great breakfast burritos. Also try the **Hyde Away** or **Pepper's Restaurant** (583-2202; $) at Pepper's Lodge.

Condo dwellers can pick up basic staples, baked goods, beer and wine at the **Paradise Deli & Market** (583-2757) on the access road. The deli also has dinners-to-go. Also pick up goodies to go at the **Warren Store** (496-3864). There are two supermarkets in town: **Shaw's** and **Mehuron's Market**. Shaw's has the better produce. Mehuron's is the local's choice, the bonuses here are the butcher and fish departments.

Apres-ski/nightlife

Après-ski starts at the base lodges that do booming business at the bar as the lifts close. **Chez Henri's Back Room** is the on-mountain apres-ski hangout and can rock all evening. **The Hyde Away** is where you will find the locals; the **Blue Tooth** on the access road is most popular with tourists. On weekends try the **Sugarbush Inn** for a more upscale, older crowd. The base area bar at Mad River Glen, **General Stark's Pub**, follows the retro atmosphere of the area with plenty of fun in an old-time bar. After leaving Mad River Glen, the next place to stop is the **Mad River Barn**. The bar there looks like an old Vermont bar should look: moose head hanging over the fireplace, hunting scenes on every wall, big couches and stuffed chairs, wood paneling and bumper pool or shuffleboard. **Local Folk Smokehouse** is a great bbq, tex mex and family friendly bar. **The Purple Moon Pub**, next door to the Easy Street Café, is a non-smoking spot for live music and apres-ski snacking.

Other activities

The Sugarbush Health & Racquet Club and the Bridges Resort and Racquet Club have various **sports and exercise facilities**.

Sleigh rides and skijoring (496-7141) can be arranged at the Vermont Icelandic Horse Farm in Waitsfield. (Skijoring here involves being pulled behind a horse while on skis.) Also offering sleigh rides is the Mountain Valley Farm (496-9255). **Ice skating** at the Mad River the Skatium, is next to Shaw's Supermarket, in Waitsfield.

The **Alta Day Spa** (496-2582), renovated in 2004, is an Aveda concept day spa in Warren providing massages, exfoliations, wraps, masques and facials. Their signature treatment is the Dead Sea Full-Body Masque, $110 for 1.5 hours. Massage rates begin at $75 for one hour; stone massage is $125 for 1.5 hours. Salon services, manicures and pedicures also are available. **Mad River Massage** (496-5638) on Rte. 100 just south of the intersection with Rte. 17, in Waitsfield, offers nine different 60-minute massages, including relaxation, shiatsu, reflexology, sea salt and Reiki, at $55–$65.

Waitsfield and Warren have **art galleries**, **country stores** and **antique and collectible shops** that are fun for browsing and buying. Most shops in tiny Warren Village are within easy walking-distance of each other.

Getting there and around

Getting there: Sugarbush is off Rte. 100, about 20 miles south of Waterbury. Burlington airport is about a 45-minute drive. Amtrak offers train-ski-lodging packages, with daily service from New York, Philadelphia and Washington, D.C.; call (800) 237-7547; (800) 872-7245 for train only.

Getting around: The Mad Cab (793-2320) offers airport pickups and transportation throughout the valley. The Mad Bus (496-7433) provides free, round-trip travel between designated stops in Warren and Waitsfield, including the Sugarbush base areas and Mad River Glen (weekends and holidays only). Two buses leave Lincoln Peak consecutively, on the hour and half hour. Schedules can be obtained from your lodging or online at www.madrivervalley.com/transportation. For a one-time visit to town it's OK, but for more frequent visits, drive or rent a car. Valley Rent-All (496-5440) rents cars locally.

Dining: $$$$-Entrees $30+; $$$-$20-$30; $$-$10-$20; $-less than $10.
Accommodations: (double room) $$$$-$200+; $$$-$141-$200; $$-$81-$140; $-$80 and less.

Mount Snow
Vermont

Summit elevation:	3,600 feet
Vertical drop:	1,700 feet
Base elevation:	1,900 feet

Pisagah Road
Mount Snow, VT 05356
Area code: 802
Ski area phone: 464-3333
Snow report: 464-2151 **Weather:** 464-4131
Toll-free reservations:
(800) 245-7669
E-mail: info@mountsnow.com
World Wide Web: www.mountsnow.com
Expert: ★
Advanced: ★
Intermediate: ★★★★
Beginner: ★★★★
First-timer: ★★

Number of lifts: 19–3 high-speed quads,
3 quad, 7 triples, 4 doubles, 3 surface lifts, 1 tow rope
Snowmaking: 76 percent
Trail acreage: 598 acres
Uphill capacity: 30,370 per hour
Parks & pipes: 4 parks; 1 pipe
Bed Base: 10,000
Nearest lodging: Base area, condos, hotel
Resort child care: Yes, 6 weeks to 6 years old
Adult ticket, per day: $67 (05 price)

Dining: ★★★★
Apres-ski/nightlife: ★★
Other activities: ★★

For those living in the Northeast's major metropolitan areas such as New York, Albany and Hartford, Mount Snow, in southern Vermont, with a summit elevation of 3,600 feet, is renowned as the closest big-mountain resort.

Mount Snow is a big draw for families for both the terrain and the price. The mountain's ego-boosting trails are long, undulating cruiser runs, where kids can learn and parents can enjoy their turns. The nine sections of gladed terrain—regularly thinned and pruned—mean even intermediates can feel "extreme." And most packages include free skiing for all kids age 12 and under, as long as they are with a parent.

This resort is also a favorite with snowboarders and has created excellent terrain parks and half-pipes that are getting snowboarder raves.

Mountain layout

♦♦Expert ♦Advanced: Aggressive skiers and snowboarders looking for a shot of adrenaline should head straight for the North Face, a group of isolated steeper runs, such as Ripcord, with a 37-degree pitch. On the opposite side of Mount Snow, Beartrap is a haven for bump skiers, because of its sunny face and snowmaking coverage. Beartrap has its own double lift. Along the trail music pumps out from 900-watt speakers to get you in the spirit.

■ **Intermediate:** Other than the North Face, the rest of Mount Snow is cruising paradise. You can carve hero turns down just about any trail on the mountain. Be sure not to miss Snow-dance, a trail as wide as a football field off the Canyon Express chairlift. The Sunbrook area, located off the south side of the summit, is an ideal spot for lower intermediates. Beware, the Sunbrook quad is s-l-o-w. Although the resort's glades are all marked with black diamonds, they're great for practicing in the trees.

●● **Beginner** ● **First-timer:** First-timers can start at the Launch Pad area outside the Perfect Turn® Discovery Center on the right side (looking up the mountain) of Mount Snow's main base area. This well-staffed area is segregated and has its own lifts: two moving carpets, a rope tow and a triple chair. From the summit, beginners will feel comfortable on Deer Run and Long John, two trails that make 2.5-mile-wide traverses of the mountain. At the south end of the resort is Carinthia, which offers long mellow runs for advanced beginners, lower intermediates and anyone else who wants to have a playful cruise. There are enough zigs, zags and small drops to keep you awake. Beginners beware: terrain park athletes flock to this area and will soar past slower skiers, unnerving those who are still learning.

Parks and pipes

New for 2007, Mount Snow has combined the best of two parks into one. The new "un-named" park, on the former Nitro trail at Carinthia, is the longest park in the East. At 4940 feet, it's nearly a mile of hits, jibs and rails. It's serviced by the Nitro Express, a high-speed quad that drops freestylers right at the top of the park. The park is also right under the lift, so those who want an audience for their tricks will have one. The park empties out into the superpipe, so freestylers can include the pipe in their park run. As for the name, Mount Snow will be running a season-long contest to name the new park. Go to their website for more details.

Un Blanco Gulch, on the mountain's Main Face, is a terrain park built for experienced riders who are not quite ready for the big leagues. Quickest access is via the Canyon Express. Take the Canyon Trail, and watch for the park—it sneaks up on you—about halfway down on rider's left. This park is all about options: Almost all of the jumps have two takeoffs of different size and approach. It opens with a few tabletops, then there's a nice hip jump off to the left, which offers a perfect segue into the lower rail section. These smaller sized rails are almost identical to those of the larger park, and offer a great way to practice for the expert park.

Grommet Park, located on Cooper's Junction trail, is a specially designed park for kids age 12 & under. With kid-sized hits, jumps and slides, it's the perfect spot for youngsters to experience the thrill of freestyling in a park just their size.

The Gut Superpipe, big enough for competition, yet not overpowering, offers smooth transitions and well-shaped walls. It's big – 460 feet long, with 18-foot walls and 17-foot transitions. Located at Carinthia, it's easily accessible via two lifts and is a nice finisher after a run through the "Un-Named" park.

Cross-country and snowshoeing (visit xcskiresorts.com for more details)

The Mount Snow Valley has three major ski touring centers. The largest is **Hermitage Cross-Country Touring Center** (464-3511), on Coldbrook Road in Wilmington, with 50 km. of trails that form a circle from the warming hut to Mount Snow and back. **Timber Creek** (464-0999) and the **White House of Wilmington Cross Country Ski Center** (464-2135) offer more than 60 km. of trails skewed toward the intermediate Nordic skier.

Lessons (06/07 prices)

Group clinics: Morning and afternoon sessions are offered and cost $43.

First-timer package: Learn n' Turn, a package geared for first-time skiers and snowboarders includes lodging, a lower mountain lift ticket, equipment rental and daily morning clinic. Participants learn at Mount Snow's Discovery

Center, an area reserved exclusively for beginners with its own slow-moving lifts, teaching terrain, rental shop and lodge. Packages start at $99 per day and are available Nov. 25 – Dec. 15, 2006, and Jan. 2 – March 25, 2007 (excluding holidays). Call: 800-498-0479.

Private clinics: $92 an hour.

Special Programs: adaptive program, family ski/snowboard clinics are available. There are also separate clinics available for advanced skiers and snowboarders. Call the resort.

KidStuff [06/07 prices]

Child care: Open 8 a.m.–4:30 p.m. daily for ages 6 weeks to 6 years. The cost is $70 for a full day with lunch. Cub Camp, an introductory two-hour ski program for 3-year-olds, costs $60 and includes equipment during the session. Reservations are required. Call (800) 889-4411 or 464-4152.

Other options: Mount Snow Child Care has babysitter referral service. Sitters will come to your vacation home, condo or hotel room. Cost is $10 per hour for one child, $1 per hour for each additional child (rates do not apply New Year's Eve). Call (800) 889-4411 or 464-4152. **Baby on the Go** (464-5475) rents baby needs, such as cribs, strollers, car seats and high chairs. Delivery and set-up are available at an additional charge.

Children's clinics: Perfect Kids programs are for ages 4-14. Kids 4-6 enroll in Snow Camp, $97 for a full day, including lift ticket, clinic and lunch. Rental equipment is available at an additional charge. Ages 7–14 enroll in Mountain Camp or Mountain Riders, $83 for full day with clinic and lunch. A lift ticket is required, but not included, and rental equipment is extra. A half-day clinic is $48 for Mountain Camp or Mountain Riders, including a snack.

Lift tickets [05/06 prices]

	Adult	Junior (6-12)/Sr65+
One day midweek	$61	$41
One day weekend/holiday	$69	$47
Three days*	$192	$126
Five days*	$305	$190

*Note: Prices are rounded to the nearest dollar to include the 6% Vermont sales tax. These are 06/07 prices.)

Who skis free: Children ages 5 and younger. Children 12 and younger ski free when their parent buys a three- to five-day midweek non-holiday lift and lodging package.

Who skis at a discount: Check the website for occasional deals such as "Youth Pay Their Age Day."

Accommodations

Condominums and several lodges at the base area have shuttle service to the slopes. Most of the other lodging lines Rte. 100 between the slopes and Wilmington, with some tucked on side roads back into the foothills.

Five-day midweek packages (Sunday through Thursday nights) are a bargain—some as low as around $50 per person per day. A one-night package combines one hotel night with a day of skiing starting at $68 a day (another bargain). For a **vacation planner** with descriptions of most area properties, write: Mount Snow, Pisgah Road, Mount Snow, Vermont 05356, or call (800) 245-7669.

Condominium rates are based on the size of the unit and number of bathrooms. They start at about $305 on the weekends; half that midweek.

The Mount Snow Condominiums (800-451-4211; 464-7788; $$$–$$$$) are at the base of the lifts. **The Seasons** complex is ski-in/ski-out with an athletic center, pools, saunas and hot tubs. Two-bedroom/two-bath units cost around $900 for a weekend.

Timber Creek Townhomes (800-982-8922; 464-1222; $$$$) are luxury condos across Rte. 100 from the ski area. They have a fitness center and 18 km. of cross-country trails just outside. **Greenspring at Mount Snow** (800-247-7833; 464-7111; $$$-$$$$) are upscale condos a mile from the slopes. This complex has the best athletic center in the area. Both complexes are served by frequent shuttle buses.

The **Grand Summit Resort Hotel & Conference Center** (800-845-7690; 464-6600; $$$-$$$$) is a ski-in/ski-out resort hotel, in the Main Base Area, with 200 rooms.

The region has numerous inns. **Snow Lake Lodge** (800-451-4211; 464-7788; $$-$$$) is a sprawling 197-room mountain lodge near the base of Mount Snow. The lodge has sauna and hot tubs.

The Inn at Sawmill Farm (800-493-1133; 464-8131; $$$$) is one of the nation's top country inns. Secluded in a renovated dairy barn and outbuildings, the inn coddles guests with spacious rooms decorated in a country chic style. Fresh flowers, wood-burning fires, meticulous service and an excellent dining room complete the picture. The inn is not suitable for children.

The White House of Wilmington (464-2135; $$-$$$), Rte. 9, Wilmington, is an upscale, romantic 23-room inn serving breakfast and dinner. It has an indoor pool.

Less than a quarter-mile from Mount Snow, the **Big Bear Lodge** (800-388-5591; 464-5591; $$$$) is family-friendly and comes highly recommended by the locals. **Andirons Lodge** (800-445-7669; 464-2114; $$), on Rte. 100 in West Dover, is just two miles from the lifts. While somewhat short on hospitality, this motel offers low-cost lodging in simple paneled rooms with double beds; an indoor pool, sauna and game room. The attached Dover Forge restaurant serves affordable meals. **Nordic Hills Lodge** (800-326-5130; 464-5130; $$$$), on 179 Coldbrook Road in Wilmington, is friendly and clean.

Gray Ghost Inn (800-745-3615; 464-2474; $$-$$$) on Rte. 100, West Dover, is a large country inn. Many rooms have smaller beds or bunk beds for children, and there is a game room. Rates include a continental breakfast. **Trail's End** (800-859-2585; 464-2727; $$-$$$), Smith Road, Wilmington, has 15 country-style rooms. **Old Red Mill** (877-733-6455; 464-7767; $-$$), Rte. 100 in Wilmington, was created from a former sawmill and is one of the bargains in the region. Rooms are small, only about 7 by 12 feet with a double bed, but all have TV. Good for families. Common areas are rustic.

Horizon Inn (800-336-5513; 464-2131; $-$$$), Rte. 9 in Wilmington, 13 miles from Mount Snow, has an indoor heated pool, whirlpool, sauna and game room.

Mount Snow also has a group of charming and elegant B&Bs with rates starting at about $125 per night on weekends and $70 midweek. These B&Bs are smaller, most with fewer than 15 rooms.

In West Dover: The Doveberry Inn (800-722-3204; 464-5652; $$) on Rte. 100, is run by culinary-school-trained chefs. This inn is not suitable for young children. **West Dover Inn** (800-732-0745; 464-5207; $$), Rte. 100, is an historic country inn built in 1846 with 12 elegant, antique-furnished rooms, hand-sewn quilts and color TVs, as well as two suites with fireplaces and whirlpool tubs. **Deerhill Inn** (800-993-3379; 464-3100; $$-$$$$), Valley View Road, is a chef-owned romantic hillside inn with panoramic views of Mount Snow and Haystack.

The Four Seasons Inn (877-531-4500, $$$-$$$$), recently renovated, is a beautiful inn run by an English couple. Catering to couples, it's a romantic and cozy getaway and offers in-room massage and spa services with English afternoon tea and full Vermont breakfasts.

In Wilmington: The Red Shutter Inn (800-845-7548; 464-3768; $$-$$$) on Rte. 9,

Dining: $$$$-Entrees $30+; $$$-$20-$30; $$-$10-$20; $-less than $10.
Accommodations: (double room) $$$$-$200+; $$$-$141-$200; $$-$81-$140; $-$80 and less.

is an 1894 country home that has been converted into an elegant country inn with nine guest rooms. **The Nutmeg Inn** (800-277-5402; 464-3351; $$–$$$) on Rte. 9W, built in the 1770s, is decorated with country accents, quilts and has 10 rooms and four fireplace suites. **The Inn at Quail Run** (800-343-7227; 464-3362; $$$) welcomes both children and pets. Special weekends for crafters, women only, cooking and quilting.

Dining

The top dining experience and the most expensive is the **Inn at Sawmill Farm** (464-8131; $$$–$$$$), which holds a Wine Spectator Grand Award. Ask to see the wine cellar. **The Hermitage** (464-3511; $$$) serves an eclectic menu with entrees such as angel hair and pesto topped with a red-wine roasted duck and shiitake mushrooms or hand-cut Black Angus steak.

Ravello's (464-8437; $$–$$$) serves Italian food in a 19th-century farmhouse. Another fine dining choice is **Two Tannery Road** (464-2707; $$$). **Doveberry Restaurant** (464-5652; $$$) is small and intimate with a Northern Italian menu; the husband-and-wife chefs have worked in Nantucket and San Francisco. **The Deerhill Inn and Restaurant** (464-3100; $$$) in West Dover, has won awards for its American cuisine and boasts a strong wine list.

The White House (464-2135; $$) with its 30-foot buffet table, is the choice for Sunday brunch, but the French-accented dinners are excellent too.

The Roadhouse (464-5017; $$) is normally packed. It serves large portions at a menu price and attracts lots of locals. **Dot's of Dover** (464-6476; $), in the Mountain Park Plaza, serves breakfast and lunch daily, plus an excellent Sunday brunch. The chili has won awards. Also enjoy dinner daily at **Dot's Restaurant** on Rte. 9 in Wilmington (464-7284; $).

For economical eats, try **Poncho's Wreck** (464-9320; $$), a local institution with an eclectic dining room serving Mexican food, steaks, lobsters and fresh fish. **Anchor Seafood** (464-2112; $$), specializes in surf and turf. **The Vermont House** (464-9360; $–$$) on Wilmington's main street, serves good food for cheap prices and is another of the locals' favorites.

The **Maple Leaf Brewery** (464-9900; $–$$) also on Main Street in Wilmington, brews 16 types of beer on-site and serves pub fare. **TC's Family Restaurant** (464-9316; $–$$), owned by 2002 Olympic gold medalist Kelly Clark's parents, has inexpensive family fare.

For groceries, head to Shaw's on Rte. 9 in Wilmington, east of Rte. 100.

Apres-ski/nightlife

The **Snow Barn** features live music most weekends, sometimes with up-and-coming national acts. It has a separate area for pool and other games, with a central stone fireplace and a pizza window. Both Snow Barn and **Deacon's Den** have cover charges on weekends.

Apres-ski at **Cuzzins** is a wild affair where the DJ gets folk up and dancing on the tables. The line is long, but the fun is worth it.

One of the most popular nightspots, the **Silo**, is actually in a converted grain silo in the Silo Family Restaurant on Rt. 100. Under new management, it caters to a young crowd and has practically a monopoly on nightlife for the snowboarding set. Locals head to the Silo every Monday for 10-cent wings from 4-6 p.m. The **Dover Bar & Grille** (464-2689), across Rte. 100 from the Silo, is a local hangout. **Billiard Sanctuary** is also a very popular haunt with billiard tables and a great bar.

In Wilmington, the **Maple Leaf Brewery** and the **Wilmington Village Pub** offer entertainment on weekends.

Other activities

The Mount Snow Valley is reportedly the busiest area for **snowmobiling** in Vermont. Try High Country Snowmobile Tours (800-627-7533; 464-2108) that operates from the base of Mount Snow, Wheeler Farm snowmobile tours (464-5225) in Wilmington and Stizmark (464-3384).

The **Adams Family Farm** (464-3762), 4 miles south on Higley Hill Rd. (off Rte. 100), has an indoor petting farm where kids help milk goats and find eggs to take home for breakfast. Sleigh rides are available. Open Wednesday, Friday, Saturday and Sunday, 10 a.m.–5 p.m.

Mount Snow runs a lift-served **tubing** hill open Friday and Saturday evenings.

The Grand Summit Resort Hotel now has a **spa** offering massage therapy, facials and body treatments. Reservations are required; call 464-6606. Wilmington Village has **boutiques**, **galleries** highlighting local and national artists and intriguing shops.

 Getting there and getting around

By air: The closest airports are in Albany, N.Y., and Hartford's (Ct.) Bradley International, both less than a two-hour drive.

By car: Mount Snow is the closest major Vermont ski resort to New York and Boston. It is on Rte. 100, just 9 miles north of Wilmington.

Getting Around: A car isn't necessary, but is convenient, especially at night. During the day, take shuttle buses to and from the lifts; at night, take the MOOver, a free shuttle that serves much of the Mount Snow Valley from the resort down into Wilmington. It runs late on weekends. You can't miss it: The buses are painted like Holstein cows.

Dining: $$$$–Entrees $30+; $$$–$20–$30; $$–$10–$20; $–less than $10.
Accommodations: (double room) $$$$–$200+; $$$–$141–$200; $$–$81–$140; $–$80 and less.

Okemo Mountain

Vermont

Summit elevation:	3,344 feet
Vertical drop:	2,200 feet
Base elevation:	1,194 feet

Address: 77 Okemo Ridge Road
Ludlow, VT 05149-9708
Area code: 802
Ski area phone: 228-4041
Snow report: 228-5222
Fax: 228-4558
Toll-free reservations:
(800) 786-5366
E-mail: info@okemo.com
Internet: www.okemo.com

Number of lifts: 18–5 high-speed quads,
4 quads, 3 triple chairs, 6 surface lifts
Snowmaking: 95 percent
Skiable acreage: 620 acres
Uphill capacity: 32,050 per hour
Parks & pipes: 6 parks; 2 pipes
Bed base: 10,000
Nearest lodging: Slopeside
Resort child care: Yes, 6 weeks to 6 years
Adult ticket, per day: $63-69(05/06 prices)

Expert: ★
Advanced: ★
Intermediate: ★★★★★
Beginner: ★★★
First-timer: ★★

Dining: ★★★
Apres-ski/nightlife: ★★
Other activities: ★★

With five mountain areas, including Jackson Gore, the resort is one of the largest in New England. Rising more than 2,200 feet above the bustling village of Ludlow, Okemo's mostly intermediate trails run down the mountainside like ribbons of white flowing down the fall line.

With the addition of Jackson Gore, the Big O is now one of the largest resorts in New England with five mountain areas: Jackson Gore, Solitude, Northeast Summit/Glades, South Face and South Ridge. In 2004, the base area at Jackson Gore, featuring New England Colonial architecture, made its debut. Included are the 117-room Jackson Gore Inn, a day lodge with a cafeteria and restaurant, guest services like day care, ski school and shops and amenities like heated walkways. Also new is a high-speed quad chairlift, a 500-foot moving carpet servicing a new beginners' area, sixteen trails and a snowskate park. The nine new trails added in the Jackson Gore expansion fit right in. They're cut in the old New England style, winding down the mountain's natural undulations.

More than just terrain, Okemo is about service and snow quality. The resort covers 95 percent of the terrain with machine-made snow, groomed until it feels like brand new wall-to-wall carpeting. Some call it "Hero snow." A few laps off the Northstar Express Quad on blue runs such as World Cup, and you may start to feel as if you could, well, ski on the World Cup.

Okemo's hands-on owners Tim and Diane Mueller can often be found loading lifts or busing trays in the cafeteria on busy weekends. Everyone smiles, says good morning, and asks how your day is going. Because Okemo's main base area has limited parking, once on the mountain, you have to take one of two lifts to get to the more wide-open terrain on the mountain proper. On busy weekends, these two lifts are a bottleneck. Jackson Gore presents a better option for day skiers—although reaching the base lodge from its parking lot also requires some hiking (or the shuttle). Still, it's much less crowded, easier to handle, radiates a more pleasant, less frenetic atmosphere and features all of the amenities and services found at the Okemo base area with lessons, day care, ticket windows, rental/repair shop and sundries shop.. It's on Route 103 North, just past the junction of Rte. 100/103 North.

Mountain layout

The mellow skiing and much of the beginning ski-school action take place on the gentle rise served by two sister lifts, South Ridge Quads A and B. These two quads also provide access to several clusters of slopeside condos and townhouses, as well as serving as the gateway to the rest of Okemo's lift system from the base lodge. There can be a logjam at these two lifts, but once up on the mountain you can choose among several lifts to reach the upper trails. The Jackson Gore base area is a more laid-back alternative. The Coleman Brook Express serves beginner terrain and accesses the Jackson Gore Express, which takes you to 2,725-foot Jackson Gore Peak. It also links you to the main mountain. The Northstar Express is always the most popular on weekends and holidays. To save time, take the Black Ridge Triple to the Green Ridge Triple. Both Green Ridge and Northstar unload by the Summit Lodge. Another well-kept secret: Ride the Sachem Quad to the Glades Peak Quad and head to the South Face Area in the morning to enjoy the glades and long cruisers. With the Jackson Gore base area fully active, weekend crowds should be more dispersed at Okemo. Park here and take the two new chairs to the Jackson Gore summit. Then throw yourself down trails such as Quantum Leap or head south toward the rest of Okemo.

♦♦**Expert ♦Advanced:** There are no true double-black trails on the mountain. Outrage and Double Black Diamond are both gladed and not particularly precipitous, but enjoyable and challenging with proper snow conditions. Black Hole, at the top of Jackson Gore, has tight trees and a healthy pitch. Quantum Leap and Vortex, on Jackson Gore, have a good pitch at the top but quickly mellow out. Wild Thing, Blind Faith and Punch Line are often left to bump up; and you can often find manmade bumps on Sel's Choice and the Ledges.

■ **Intermediate:** Overall, the pitch on this mountain is so consistent and the trails are so similarly cut, a skier would be hard pressed to describe the difference between Dream Weaver at one side of the mountain and Sidewinder on the opposite side. This is not a negative, just a fact of life. Intermediates should choose their trails based on crowds. Our experience has been that while a cruise down groomed Punch Line and Blind Faith may be crowded, wide arcing turns can be made down Upper and Lower Tomahawk and Screamin' Demon without another person in sight. As its name implies, the Solitude area is often the least crowded and has loads of intermediate terrain.

●● **Beginner:** The 4.5-mile Upper and Lower Mountain Roads are the easiest route from the top. But beginners can ski virtually anywhere marked intermediate on this mountain. The Green Ridge triple and the Solitude Peak high-speed quad have many runs for beginners. The trails are wide enough to allow traverses and the pitch is mellow enough for them to maintain control. The gentle and undulating Sachem and Kettle Brook trails have tunnels to glide through. On Jackson Gore Peak, try Tuckered for a long, winding slide, punctuated by gentle undulations and fine views.

● **First-timer:** Again, Jackson Gore has changed everything. The area, with its two moving carpets for novices and a high-speed quad serving gentle terrain, is tailor-made for novice and beginner skiers and riders. The rental shop, Learning Center and kids' programs are all in the same building. Choose to start here, if possible. That said, we'll tell you about the learning area near the original base lodge. It's served by two quads and two free surface lifts. Unfortunately, the first novice lessons take place in an area that is crisscrossed by more advanced skiers moving between lifts and condos. Fortunately, the children's learning area is tucked away from other skiers.

Ride Guide: When playing in the double-diamond Forest Bump glades off the South Face quad, keep your speed up, because it dumps into the oh-so-flat Catnap trail.

Parks and pipes

If you're an expert or advanced rider, Okemo won't offer enough of a challenge unless you're happiest in the park and pipe. But the resort, home to 2006 Olympic halfpipe gold medalist Hannah Teter, has a large snowboarding community not confined to the young and restless. Gray-haired ski patrollers and instructors foster a pro-boarding attitude. Okemo's 500-foot-long Zaugg-maintained SoBe superpipe has 18.5-foot walls. For those seeking a bit less air, there a mini-halfpipe at Hot Dog Hill.

In addition, Okemo has five terrain parks. Blind Faith Terrain Park, in South Face, has rollers, bank turns and tabletops. The Dew Zone, next to the superpipe, is loaded with rails, including rainbows, Cs, rollercoasters, flat-to-down and flat stock rails. The Nor'Easter Terrain Park, the longest, contains rails, step downs, spines, S-turns, tabletops, funboxes, hips, double tabletops, hit tables, rollers and pyramid jumps. Hot Dog Hill, below the Sugar House, is geared to beginners. The constantly evolving parks are groomed nightly. They're designed by Park Rangers and have staggered take-offs to accommodate various abilities and comfort levels.

Cross-country and snowshoeing (visit xcskiresorts.com for more details)

The Okemo Valley Nordic Center (288-1396), set along the Black River, a half-mile from Okemo Mountain, has fine facilities that include a rental and repair shop, a restaurant, 26 km. of trails. Twenty are groomed for skate skiing. Instruction is available. It also has 10 km. of dedicated snowshoe trails. Changing rooms with showers are available. The center is open from 8 a.m.-4 p.m. on weekends and holidays; Monday through Friday, it opens at 9 a.m. The **Okemo Express Rental Shop** (228-1780) at Okemo Mountain also rents snowshoes. Guided snowshoe tours are planned for during the Christmas, Martin Luther King and Presidents Week holidays. Tours leave the Okemo base area at 7 p.m.

Lessons (06/07 prices)

Group lessons: $45 for a two-hour lesson. Seniors pay half price. For more advanced skiers and riders, morning specialty clinics ($45) and afternoon adventure workshops ($60) are more popular choices. Workshops focus on specific topics and trends, such as powder, bumps and cruisers.

First-timer package: For skiing or snowboarding, First Tracks packages include lesson, rental equipment and beginner lifts and cost $95 for adults. Double Tracks builds upon the skills learned in the first day by getting students back for a second straight day. It includes three lessons, two on the first day and one on the morning of the second day. The second day's lift ticket can be upgraded to a full-day, all-mountain lift ticket. Double Tracks is $150 for adults.

Private lessons: $85 per hour, ; discounts available for additional hours and students.

Early- and late-day privates are offered at 8:30 a.m. and 2:30 p.m. for $69. Parent and Tot private lessons, as well as adaptive private lessons, are also available.

Special programs: Women's Alpine Adventure Clinics are a popular multiday indulgence for women of all abilities. Cost is $639 for the five-day program, $479 for the three-day weekend and $319 for a two-day midweek program.

KidStuff [06/07 prices]

Child care: Ages 6 months to 6 years at the Penguin Playground Day Care Center. Parents can choose between facilities at the Okemo base area and the Jackson Gore base area: $75 for a full day with lunch; $49 half day. Sunday morning, 8 a.m.–1 p.m., $61, with lunch. Special Mini Stars lessons are available for kids ages 3–4 and are taught by professional Okemo instructors; cost is $55 for 1-1/2 hour session ($40 as an add-on to day care). Rentals are extra. Reservations are required, call 228-1780.

Special activities: Kids' Night Out, for ages 6 months to 12 years, includes evening care from 6–9:30 p.m. on Saturdays. Kids eat pizza, watch movies and play games. Call (802) 228-1780 for price and reservations.

Okemo also has **Snow Monsters,** a program for children, families and educators that stresses on-slope safety, courtesy and protecting the environment while having fun. Kids can take a monster quiz, earn points, send a postcard to a friend, play online games and more.

Children's lessons: Ages 4–7 (skiing) and 5–7 (snowboarding) enroll in Snow Stars at the Okemo base area or the Jackson Gore base area: $95 for a full day with lunch, $65 for a half day; $75 for Sunday morning. Rentals are extra. Half-hour private "Starbooster" lessons are available for children ages 3-7 for $45. Young Mountain Explorers and Young Riders, ages 7–14, have supervised lesson programs for $82 a day. Rentals and lift tickets are extra.

First Tracks is a packages for first-timers that includes lesson, rentals and beginner lifts; cost is $85 for ages 7–12 and $95 for ages 13–18. Double Tracks is a two-day first-timer package; cost is $135 for ages 7–12 and $150 for ages 13–14.

Lift tickets [05/06 prices]

	Adult (13-18)/Sr.	Young Adult/Sr. (65-69)	Junior/Sr.+ (7-12)/(70+)
One day midweek	$63	$53	$41
One day weekend/holiday	$69	$59	$45
Three days midweek	$162	$138	$105
Three days weekend/holiday	$168/186	$142/159	$109/123
Five days midweek	$250	$215	$165
Five days weekend/holiday	$254/290	$217/250	$167/190

Who skis free: Children ages 6 and younger may get a free lift ticket at any window.

Sunday morning discount: The Sunday Solution is available every Sunday as well as Jan. 16 and Feb. 22, 2006: Ski from 8 a.m.-1:30 p.m. for $55 adult; $46 young adult/senior and $36 junior/super-senior and hit the road before the rest of the traffic.

Accommodations

First-class hotel amenities are available at the full-service, 117-room **Jackson Gore Inn** (800-786-5366 $$$-$$$$). Accommodations are high-quality and comfortable, ranging from standard hotel rooms to one- to three-bedroom units, with full kitchen and whirlpool baths. There's an indoor-outdoor heated pool, restaurant and lounge, health club and underground parking.

Okemo has many **slopeside condos and townhouses** (800-786-5366). Per-person rates vary widely depending on proximity to the slopes and size, but a range would be $375–$850 off-mountain to $450–$1,000+ slopeside for a five-night ski week. Kids ages 12 and younger stay free at Okemo Mountain Resort condos. Always ask about packages.

The Okemo/Ludlow area, including Chester, Springfield, Weston, Plymouth and Proctorsville, has more than 50 country inns, B&Bs and motels. **The Governor's Inn** (800-468-3766; 228-8830; $$–$$$$) is on Main Street and is one of Ludlow's nicest lodges. All rooms have private baths and are furnished in Victorian fashion, complete with puffy comforters. Rates include breakfast only or breakfast and dinner. The six-course dinners are preceded by hors d'oeuvres in the den. At the base of Okemo's Mountain Road is the **Andrie Rose Inn** (800-223-4846; 228-4846; $$$–$$$$) considered one of the most romantic inns in Vermont. Most rooms have jetted tubs and the suites have fireplaces. The inn also has well-appointed condos.

The Echo Lake Inn (800-356-6844; 228-3075; $$–$$$$), north on Rte. 100, is a rambling New England inn. It has been completely refurbished with an excellent dining room and cozy public rooms. Presidents Coolidge and McKinley slept here. Rates with breakfast only or with breakfast and dinner are available. **The Inn at Water's Edge** (228-8143; $$$–$$$$), north on Rte. 100 on the shores of Echo Lake, is a completely refurbished 150-year-old Victorian home. It has a traditional English pub and 11 small, antique-furnished rooms. Rates include breakfast, dinner served fireside and afternoon tea. Of note, the inn caters to couples without children as guests.

The Hawk Inn and Mountain Resort (800-685-4295; 672-3811; $$$$), 9 miles north of Okemo on Rte. 100, has luxury country inn and townhouse facilities. This complex features an indoor/outdoor pool, sauna, sleigh rides and fine dining. Rates include breakfast. **Castle Hill Resort & Spa** (800-438-7908; 226-7688; $$$$) is a gracious, turn-of-the-century former Governor's mansion. The owners have painstakingly preserved the old-world standard for luxury and ambiance, and have furnished the entire mansion with period furniture. The food is exceptional and the dining room extremely romantic. In 2004, the inn added a full-service Aveda Fitness Center and Spa.

The **Clarion Cavendish Pointe Hotel** (800-438-7908; 226-7688; $$–$$$), 2 miles from Okemo, is a full service, 70-room country-style hotel, with restaurant, indoor pool, lounge and game room. The **Best Western Colonial Motel** (228-8188; $$–$$$) offers very affordable lodging within walking distance of Ludlow's shopping, nightlife and dining. **Happy Trails Motel** (800-228-9984; 228-8888; $$–$$$) in Ludlow offers great bargains with a good hot tub. The **Timber Inn Motel** (228-8666; $–$$) has the cheapest rates in town.

Dining

On mountain, don't miss **Gables** ($–$$), in the Solitude Day Lodge. The menu was created by the New England Culinary Institute and puts typical ski lodge fare to shame. Lunch delicacies include Tuscan bruschetta, butternut squash ravioli and portobello mushroom sandwiches. The Jackson Gore Base Lodge has the **Roundhouse** food court, including the **Vermont Pizza Company.** **Smokey Joes** has fine prime rib sandwiches, **Jump** has Chinese food at the Summit Cafe, **Sitting Bull** offers sit-down wraps, chicken tenders and fries and **Amigos** serves Tex-Mex.

Coleman Brook Tavern (228-1435; $$$–$$$$), at Jackson Gore, is the resort's best restaurant and has full-service, all-day dining. It also has an adults-only wine room that allows a quiet, sophisticated dining experience with Vermont's most exclusive restaurant wine list.

Upscale restaurants serving dinner in the area include the **Echo Lake Inn** (228-3075; $$–$$$) north of town where Chef Kevin Barnes has been creating gourmet delicacies for more than a decade. **The River Tavern Restaurant,** at the Hawk Inn and Mountain Resort (672-3811; $$–$$$), serves delicious meals like tortilla-crusted lamb chops with tart cherry chipotle sauce. **Castle Hill** (226-7361; $$–$$$) offers fine dining in a romantic setting. **The Inn at Water's Edge** (228-8143; $$$$) serves fixed-price dinners for $30 per person each evening at 7 p.m. Make reservations and select your dinner by noon that day. A must visit is the **Old Town Farm Inn** (888-232-1089, $–$$$), a charming, family friendly, restored 1861 Vermont farmhouse, in Chester. What really makes this unique is the Japanese dinners prepared by owner, Chef Michiko, a sixth-generation chef. Everything is made to order, so be sure to allow plenty of time for a leisurely meal. Bring your own bottle.

The following restaurants are not as upper crust, but serve excellent affordable meals perfect for families. **Willie Dunn's Grille** (228-1387; $$), at the Okemo Valley Golf & Nordic Center, offers superb affordable meals. The Shrimp Puttanesca with capers and olives in a red sauce is excellent. **Sam's Steakhouse,** (228-2087; $$), on Rte. 103, serves a filet mignon so tender it can be cut with a butter knife, as well as seafood, chicken, sinful desserts and an incredible salad bar; first come, first served. **D.J.'s Restaurant** (228-5374; $–$$) gets high marks from locals for its prime rib, steak, seafood, pasta and fabulous salad bar. **Cappuccino's** (228-7566; $$) has a strong local following. The pastas and veal dishes are worth the visit.

The Killarney (228-7797; $$), located at the bottom of the Okemo access road features classic Irish pub fare, like bangers and mash, shepards pie, corned beef and cabbage, plus traditional American fare and a variety of draught beers.

The Combes Family Inn (228-8799; $$$) serves a home-cooked single-entree dinner at 7 p.m. each evening. Call for the day's menu and to make reservations. **Java Baba's** (228-2326; $) at the base of the access road has over-stuffed chairs and couches, and serves fresh-baked muffins, pastries, homemade soups, sandwiches, salads, desserts and, of course, a variety of coffee drinks. North of Ludlow on Rte. 103 is **Harry's** (259-2996; $–$$), an understated place that has a high repeat business because of its moderate prices and international cuisine.

In nearby Chester, stop and have a meal at **Raspberries and Thyme** (875-4486; $–$$). Breakfast and lunch are always good; dinner is served Wednesday to Sunday. **The Inn at Weathersfield** (263-9217; $$$$), in the nearby town of Perkinsville, has been a winner of the Wine Spectator Award and many other culinary awards.

On Main Street in Ludlow, **Trappers Restaurant** (228-5477) and **The Hatchery** (228-2311) are the locals' recommendations for breakfast. **Wicked Good Pizza** (228-4131; $) has good pie (pizza pie, that is). **Chef Mei** (228-4355; $–$$) offers Chinese specialties that you can eat in or take out.

Apres-ski/nightlife

The **Sitting Bull Bar & Restaurant** is Okemo's apres-ski epicenter, with regularly scheduled parties, a wide-screen TV, apres-ski parties, $1 draft beer days on non-holiday Wednesdays and live music on weekends. **Coleman Brook Tavern,** at Jackson Gore, has comfy chairs and couches and a wide selection of martinis, exclusive wines and premium liquors. Down mountain, **Archie's Steakhouse** has chicken wings and draft beer specials. Later in the evening, **The Pot Belly** has country rock, '60s and '70s classics with a great bar and a big TV. Beware their wines by the glass—they recork leftover bottles

Dining: $$$$-Entrees $30+; $$$-$20-$30; $$-$10-$20; $-less than $10.
Accommodations: (double room) $$$$-$200+; $$$-$141-$200; $$-$81-$140; $-$80 and less.

each night and save them for the next day; order the wine only if you can see them open a new bottle. **The Black River Brewing Company**, on Rte. 103 outside Ludlow, is among the best deals in town. The home-brew is good and other local microbrews are available, as is pub food. **Christopher's** in the basement of the Old Mill, has bands and nightlife as well.

Other activities

The **Fitness and Aquatic Center at Jackson Gore**, new in October 2006, is an 18,000-square-foot multi-use facility with a **two-lane lap pool, small kids' pool with frog slide and splash/fountain features, 10-person hot tub, racquetball court, weight and cardio room**, and **aerobics and yoga classroom**. The center is open to resort guests and the public on a membership basis.

The Okemo Valley **Winter Indoor Golf** Academy (228-1396), at the country club, has a 700-square-foot putting green, swing stations, a full-swing golf simulator and a pro shop. Golf clinics are offered year round. **Ice skating** is free under the lights at Dorsey Park; bring your own skates. Take a weekend course at the **Fletcher Farm School for the Arts and Crafts** (228-8770), offering courses like watercolor, funky felted hats, decoupage and rug hooking.

Ludlow also has a wide array of specialty **shops** with clothing, antiques and gifts. **Chapter XIV** is a book-lovers dream, mixed with women's clothing and jewelry, children's clothing and toys and other fun and artsy items. Blue Sky Trading has a nice selection of Vermont-made pottery and jewelry. There's great browsing at the **Vermont Country Store** in nearby Weston, on Rte. 100. It's jam-packed with clothing, housewares, funky specialty foods (go hungry and sample everything) and hard-to-find but useful little items; things you never knew you wanted but once you see them, you wonder how you've lived without them. A more genuine country store experience is had at **Singleton's**, about three miles south of the mountain, just off Rte. 103 on Rt. 131, in Proctorsville. You can purchase antique guns as well as some of the best bacon and ham we've ever tasted. As for the cheese: Singleton's goes through four or five *wheels* a week! **The Green Mountain Sugarhouse**, three miles north on Rte. 100, is another spot to get Vermont cheese and maple syrup gifts.

Bentley Snow Sports provides a full line of **video and digital picture programs**. Guests choose their favorite music customize their video on a complimentary take-home DVD.

Public Internet Access is available at **Java Baba's** (*see Dining*) and **The Fletcher Memorial Library**, on Main Street, provides access on five computers.

Getting there and getting around

By air: The nearest major airports are Burlington, Vt.; Manchester, N.H.; or Hartford, Conn., all about two hours away. Regional service is available from Rutland (25 miles from Okemo) to Boston or from West Lebanon, N.H.

By car: Okemo is in south-central Vermont on Rte. 103 in Ludlow, about two hours from Albany, N.Y.; three hours from Boston; and 4.5 hours from New York City.

By train: Amtrak has service from New York's Penn Station to Rutland, 25 miles to Okemo. Thrifty has a car rental office at the train station in Rutland.

Getting around: We recommend a car. Unless you are staying on-mountain, parking can be a bear. If you're staying in town, use the free Village Shuttle that operates four routes through Ludlow and Proctorsville on weekends and holidays, from 7:30 a.m.-5:30 p.m. An on-mountain shuttle runs daily mid-December through March connecting all on-mountain properties with the base area and the Nordic Center.

Smugglers' Notch
Vermont

Summit elevation:	3,640 feet
Vertical drop:	2,610 feet
Base elevation:	1,030 feet

Address: 4323 Vermont Rte. 108 South Smugglers' Notch, VT 05464-9537
Area code: 802
Ski area phone: 644-8851
Snow report: 644-1111
Toll-free reservations and information: (800) 451-8752
Toll-free from the United Kingdom: 0800-169-8219
E-mail: smuggs@smuggs.com
Internet: www.smuggs.com
Expert:★★★★
Advanced:★★★★
Intermediate:★★★
Beginner:★★★★
Never-ever:★★★★★

Number and types of lifts: 8–6 double chairs, 2 surface lifts
Skiable acreage: 310 acres marked trails; access to 750 acres of woods
Snowmaking: 62 percent
Uphill capacity: 7,400 per hour
Parks & pipes: 4 parks; 1 pipe
Bed base: 2,400; 565 condominiums
Nearest lodging: Walking distance, condos
Resort child care: Yes, 6 weeks to 3 years
Adult ticket, per day: $58 (05/06)

Dining:★★
Apres-ski/nightlife:★
Other activities:★★★

Ah, the glory of being Number One. For years, Smugglers' Notch has taken home the prize for the best family ski resort from scores of magazines. In fact, Smuggs (as it is familiarly known) has won surveys for the Best Family Programs in North America a total of six times - five times in the past five years. As the accolades roll in, Smuggs just gets more family-friendly.

Treasures, the resort's new child-care center, built alongside the bunny slope and surrounded by a 4,000-square-foot outdoor playground, is a beautiful facility with a staff trained in first aid, CPR, child development and behavior management. Smuggs understands small children—and their sometimes nervous parents—very well. Kid-level fish tanks, one-way viewing mirrors, radiant floor heating, and remote-access cameras are just a few special touches here. Treasures joins a long list of family amenities at the resort that include a tubing hill, outdoor ice rink, indoor pool, hot tubs, three fun centers with indoor miniature golf and organized dances for teens—even a weekly study hall for kids who need to keep up with their schoolwork.

There's plenty here for adults too, starting with the resort's three mountains. The big one, Madonna, has a 2,610-foot vertical drop and has glades, bumps and really steep steeps. (Anyone with the mistaken impression that Smuggs is just for kids needs only to peer over the ledge of the trail named F.I.S. and take in the 41-percent gradient.) To the west, Sterling Mountain offers a wide range of terrain for skiers of all levels, while Morse, to the east, is for first-timers to get going downhill.

Some visitors may be discouraged to find that, in an age when many resorts are adding lifts that seat six across, Smuggs still relies on double chairs to take riders to the top. Management says this is a deliberate choice designed to keep crowds off the top of the mountain and to preserve the resort's "classic mountain feel." For the skier, it's a tradeoff: there are occasionally long waits at the lift loading area on weekends and holidays, but the trails are rarely crowded. The Madonna I lift has been reconditioned for a smoother ride, and the lift has been lowered below the treeline to screen the chairs from the wind, making for a somewhat warmer ride and fewer wind outages. It's still a slow ascent. Just sit back and enjoy the prospect of the excellent downhill ride to come.

At Smuggs, "family fun" is guaranteed: If any family member fails to have fun in one of the resort's snowsports university programs, Smuggs will refund the entire program portion of that family member's stay.

Mountain layout

♦♦**Expert** ♦**Advanced:** The real challenge is from the top of Madonna Mountain. Five double-black-diamond trails beckon. The Black Hole, which is between Liftline and Freefall, adds trees to the steeps. The icefalls, ledges and stumps on Upper Liftline will make even true experts hold their breath. Freefall is just that: The turns come quickly and you drop 10 to 15 feet with each turn. Upper F.I.S. sports a 41-percent gradient, and with the addition of top-to-bottom snowmaking, it has become a tad more civilized than in the past.

If you're hooked on glades, you'll want to check out Doc Dempsey's. It lost some trees in an ice storm awhile back, which just gives it more character: It's become a winding, narrow New England trail dotted with groves of trees, and the bumps in spring make it extra fun. We just wish it were longer. A quick adrenaline rush is Highlander Glades on Sterling Mountain. Tree skiers will be awed by the amount of uncut terrain within the resort's boundaries: keep an eye out for locals who might share their secret stashes.

The best bump runs are F.I.S., the middle portion of Upper Liftline, Smugglers' Alley and Exhibition. The snow on Madonna Mountain takes longer to soften, so warm up on Sterling and head to the Madonna Summit chair after 11:30 a.m. or so.

■ **Intermediate:** Fifty-five percent of the trails are rated intermediate, and many are well suited to recent ski-school grads. Intermediate runs are concentrated on Madonna and Sterling peaks. Two favorite routes for lower intermediates who want to get a sense of big-mountain skiing are off Sterling: Upper Rumrunner to Lower Rumrunner, and Upper Rumrunner to Black Snake to the bottom of Treasure Run to Lower Exhibition. The views are spectacular both ways. An unofficial easy glade that makes for a great first foray into the woods for kids is off the top of the Practice Slope Extension.

For advanced-intermediates who want to test their mettle, try Chute on Sterling Mountain—a short advanced run that's steep with some bumps and stumps, but it only takes15 to 20 turns to get down make, in case you decide you're in over your head.

●● **Beginner** ● **First-timer:** The third mountain at Smuggs is Morse, with 17 trails ranging from beginner to expert. It is the ski schooler's mountain. Kids swarm over Morse Mountain, center of apres-ski bonfires, hot chocolate and almost all Smuggs' condos , making it a magnet for those who revel in a family atmosphere. It's also home to Mogul Mouse's Magic Lift, a half-speed double chair especially kind to beginners and young children. From the top of the lift winds the Magic Learning Trail, with nature stations, exploration paths and ski-through "caves." Morse Bowl is served by the Highlands double chair and has five trails for beginners and advanced beginners and a separate base lodge.

Ride Guide: One drawback for boarders is occasional difficulty riding back to Morse (and your condo) from Madonna and Sterling. Meadowlark trail from the upper base lodge back to the Village has a gentle grade, if the snow is fast, it's fine; if it's spring and sticky, take the shuttlebus. Same goes for visitors staying in the condos around Morse Highlands, whose ski-in, ski-out access is too flat for boarding home. Happily, the shuttlebus operation is excellent. Just make sure everyone keeps a map and schedule handy.

Parks and pipes

Beginners stick to the two Children's Terrain Gardens on Morse, and at Morse Highlands, then graduate to Birch Run Park, on Sterling Mountain, which offers 1,000 feet of small thrills. Intermediate and expert riders looking for bigger air head to Prohibition Park on Madonna. It connects to a 425-foot superpipe with a 16.5-foot radius and has piped-in music and multiple hits, including table tops, hips and spines. A Bombardier Super HalfPipe Grinder and the Zaugg Groomer keeps the pipe, jumps, rails and jibs in tip-top shape. The Zone on Sterling offers the biggest hits and is the site for the open-to-anyone Superpipe Jam and Altitude Adjustment events, which alternate every Saturday throughout the season.

Smugglers' Night School of Boarding meets twice a week at Sir Henry's Hill & Fun Park at the base of Morse Mountain. The three-hour sessions are open to novices ages 6 and older, who can take advice from coaches positioned strategically on the hill.

Cross-country and snowshoeing (visit xcskiresorts.com for more details)

Thirty-four km. of scenic, groomed and tracked, cross-country skiing trails, plus 20 km. of dedicated snowshoe trails, are on site. **The Nordic Ski and Snowshoe Adventure Center** offers rentals, lessons, backcountry and night tours as well as snowshoe rentals and tours including kids' rentals and tours for the whole family. Winter Walking Tours are also offered.

Lessons (05/06 prices)

Smuggs calls its ski school Snow Sport University, and its director, Peter Ingvoldstad, has been acclaimed as one of the most innovative teachers in the country. Lessons for children and beginning adults are included with the Club Smugglers' Advantage Package. Lessons for skiing and snowboarding can be purchased separately. Lesson for ski registration is taken when you make your reservations, or can be purchased separately.

Group lessons: A 90-minute lesson is $36. When five or more consecutive lessons are purchased, an additional day's lesson is free.

A four-day Mountain Experience for Adults program gives big kids a chance to accomplish the unexpected. It is available weekly for $380.

First-timer package: The daily First Timer One-Day Package is $59 and includes a 90-minute coaching session, rentals and lift ticket valid on Morse Mountain. A three-day package costs $119.

Private lessons: $70–$85 per hour for the first person, $40–$50 for each additional; 6-hour private instruction or guided tour, $299 per person or $399 for up to five people. Lessons with Peter Ingvoldstad, $150 per hour.

Special programs: Classes on style, terrain park tactics, jibs & jumps, parents teaching children to ski, halfpipe tricks, night snowboarding and programs for skiers 55 and older.

Racing: The race course is on Lower Liftline on Madonna Mountain; $1 a run, open four days a week.

KidStuff (05/06 prices)

Child care: Ages 6 weeks to 3 years old. Children are separated into three age groups. Cost is $66 per day or $15 per hour. The Treasures Child Care Center just puts this resort at the top of the child-care world. The state-of-the-art facility, fully licensed by the state of Vermont, is staffed by 20 professionals. Reservations are required; make them when you book your vacation. Given 24 hours notice, Treasures also will arrange for a babysitter. Little Rascals on Snow, a skiing program for 2.5-3 year-olds, is run from Treasures. Ski time, quiet time, and play time are combined for a low pressure introduction to skiing and winter fun. The daily fee is $95.

Children's lessons: Kids and teens are divided into four age groups: 3–5 (4–5 for snowboarding), 6–10, 11–15 and 16–17. The teen programs allow kids to meet new friends with whom they can hang out at the supervised evening teen activities. Full-day programs (9–4 daily except Thursday, 9–2:30) can be purchased separately, for $95 per child per day, or can be included in ski-and-lodging packages for considerably less for those ages 3–14. Programs include ski or boarding lessons, science discovery, hot lunch and indoor entertainment. Ninety-minute programs are offered for ages 6–17 at $36 for kids who don't want a full-day program.

Special programs: Mom & Me/Dad & Me program teaches parents how to teach their younsters to ski or board for $70 per parent/child session. Scouts Honored allows scouts to earn snowsport merit badges. Other special programs include terrain park tactics, recreational racing and night school for boarding.

Special activities: Kids' Night Out, with dinner and activities for ages 3–11, is offered three nights a week (Wednesday, Thursday and Saturday). Cost is $25 per child.

Lift tickets (05/06 prices)

	Adult	Youth (6-18)
One day	$58	$44
Multiday	*	*

Who skis free: Ages 6 and younger and 70 and older.

Who skis at a discount: Those 65–69 pay youth prices.

* **Note:** If you're staying for more than one day here, the wise move is to buy a lodging package that includes tickets and lessons.

Accommodations

Resort Village is all within walking distance of the lifts. Prices start at $495 per adult and $425 per youth for a five-day Club Smugglers' package, which includes lifts and lessons (packages for fewer days can be arranged). Children ages 6 and younger ski and stay free. Free off-slope activities such as a welcome party, use of the pool and hot tub, family game nights, outdoor ice skating, family sledding parties, a weekly torchlight parade with fireworks finale and a party will keep most everyone entertained. Showtime Theatre, nightly teen activities and entertainment is also available. Call (800) 451-8752.

Condos at Smuggs are spacious, clean and family-furnished. Kitchens come well equipped. Condos closer to the Village tend to be older; condos further away are newer, with good amenities, but less conveniently located. Daily housekeeping and Internet access through a local provider are both available for an extra fee.

Smugglers' central check-in area is designed around the concept that once you check in, you have everything you need—lift tickets, instruction vouchers, rentals and child-care arrangements. Smuggs continues to improve the check-in system. The lines at check-in have been greatly reduced thanks to online preregistration for many activities and the addition of a property owners' check-in, removing them from the line.

 ## Dining

You never have to leave the Village to eat. In fact, many people just eat in their condo.

For home-baked breakfast treats and giant cookies, try **The Green Mountain Deli and Sweet Shoppe** (644-8851; ext. 1141; $) with fresh-roasted coffee, espresso or cappuccino. Lunch favorites include chili in a bread bowl, spinach salads and made-to-order deli sandwiches. The **Riga-Bello's Pizzeria** (644-8851; ext. 1142; $–$$) offers daily specials, pizza, salads, calzones and stuffed breads with meat and vegetable fillings. The **Mountain Grille** (644-8851; ext. 1247; $–$$), with a view of the slopes, is open for breakfast, lunch and dinner. The **Hearth and Candle** (644-8090 $–$$$) is a privately operated restaurant in the Village with a friendly, though more formal, atmosphere. Families are served in the cozy Hearth Room, and couples desiring a quiet atmosphere are escorted upstairs to the adults-only Birch Room. Entrees range from steak and pasta to exotic preparations of fish and game.

Ben & Jerry's Scoop Shop in the Village Lodge serves more than 15 flavors of its famous ice cream, low-fat ice cream and sorbet everyday.

Restaurants dot the route between the resort and Jeffersonville, 5 miles away. Some examples: **Stella Notte Restaurant** (644-8884; $–$$), across the road from the resort entrance, offers authentic Italian cuisine. The **Three Mountain Lodge** (644-5736; $$) serves an eclectic menu in a classic log-lodge atmosphere. The night we were there, an acoustic blues guitarist provided entertainment. **158 Main Restaurant and Bakery** (644-8100; $–$$), housed in the historic Windridge Farms Building, has brought nouveau cuisine to the valley. Tasty premise-baked breads surround favorite sandwich stuffings, as well as unexpected pairings of fresh vegetables and meats in hot and cold dishes for breakfast, lunch and dinner. **Angelina's** (644-2011; $–$$) in Cambridge has great pizza, with a thin crust that's crispy on the bottom, soft on the top and loaded with sauce. Our kids, who consider themselves pizza connoisseurs, gave it an 8 out of 10.

The **Tuesday-night Snowshoe Adventure Dinner** takes adults to the top of Sterling Mountain for a gourmet meal in a cabin lit only by candles, then sends the whole crowd back downhill on snowshoes to work off the calories.

 ## Apres-ski/nightlife

Smuggs has lots to do once the slopes close down. It's family-oriented activity, but even our childless staffers who have visited here end up having more fun than they expected. Activities provide fun for all ages; for example, tubing on lighted Sir Henry's Hill, outdoor ice skating, evening snowmobile tours, weekly torchlight parade and fireworks display, bingo blast and a pizza-and-ice-cream-sundae party.

Even very young children flock to the **FunZone** — an indoor play area for guests of all ages that offers inflatable attractions such as bouncing platforms, crawl-through spaces, a 22-foot giant double-lane slide and a kid-sized climbing wall. Teens love Smuggs, too. The resort offers two teen centers, and while both are supervised, there is a strict No Parents Allowed policy, which pleases the kids. Teens 16 and older have the **Outer Limits Teen Center**, with music videos, Internet access, snacks, lava lamps, Nightspiker and the like. Younger teens

Dining: $$$$–Entrees $30+; $$$–$20–$30; $$–$10–$20; $–less than $10.
Accommodations: (double room) $$$$–$200+; $$$–$141–$200; $$–$81–$140; $–$80 and less.

(13–15) have **Teen Alley**, with similar amenities; video games and pool are especially popular. Recent efforts to entertain adults more fully have been very successful, with a nightly roster of events in the new adult-only **Bootlegger's Lounge**: Comedy Night, Live Music Jam, Marko's Magic Hypnosis Show, Adult Karaoke Party, Night at the Movies, and more.

Nearby, those looking for off-the-resort fun can head to the **Brewski Bar.** The **Boyden Valley Winery** can be a type of apres-ski adventure if you go for the bargain wine tasting.

Other activities

Smuggs has **day trips** on its activity roster—A Wednesday trip to Montreal that takes in numerous city highlights; and A Taste of Vermont tour on Thursday that includes Ben & Jerry's Ice Cream Factory, Cold Hollow Cider Mill, Lake Champlain Chocolates, Cabot Creamery Annex and the Trapp Family Lodge.

Don't miss a visit to the **Boyden Valley Winery**, 8 miles down the road in Cambridge. This fourth-generation Vermont farmer makes award-winning wines using Vermont apples and berries and his own grapes and maple syrup. They have tours and free wine tastings and you'll find Vermont specialty products, an artisans' gallery, handmade furniture and gift baskets.

If you want handmade Vermont crafts, you also can make your own. Smugglers' has an unusual activity, **Artists in the Mountains**. Local artisans teach classes in traditional New England crafts, such as tin punching, basket weaving, stenciling and dried flower arranging. The classes include materials and cost $10–$48.

Getting there and getting around

By air: Burlington International Airport is 40 minutes away. Shuttles are available (24-hour notice required; book it when you book lodging).

By car: Smugglers' Notch is on Rte. 108 near Jeffersonville in northwest Vermont. *Note that the stretch of Rte. 108 between Stowe and Smugglers' is closed in winter. If you are coming from the south, you must drive around the mountain and come in from the north.*

Getting around: Everything is within walking distance at the resort or ride the free resort shuttle. If you want to visit some of the restaurants in or on the way to Jeffersonville, you'll need a car. A local taxi service also is available.

Stowe
Vermont

Summit elevation:	3,640 feet
Vertical drop:	2,360 feet
Base elevation:	1,280 feet

Address: 5781 Mountain Rd.
Stowe, VT 05672
Area code: 802
Ski area phone: 253-3000
Snow report: 253-3600
Toll-free reservations:
(800) 247-8693;
for slopeside lodging only, (800) 253-4754
Advance Ticket Sales: (888)253-4849
Fax: 253-3406 **E-mail:** info@stowe.com
Internet: www.stowe.com; www.ridestowe.com;
www.13pitch.com
Expert:★★★★ **Advanced:**★★★★
Intermediate:★★★★
Beginner:★★★★
First-timer:★★★

Number and types of lifts: 12–4 high-speed
quad, 3 detachable quads, 1 eight-passenger gondola, 2
triples, 4 doubles, and 4 surface lifts
Skiable acreage: 490 acres
Snowmaking: 90 percent
Uphill capacity: 15,000 per hour
Parks & pipes: 4 parks; 1 pipe
Bed base: 5,000+
Nearest lodging: Slopeside, hotel
Resort child care: Yes, 6 weeks - 6 years
Adult ticket, per day: $64 (04/05)

Dining:★★★★
Apres-ski/nightlife:★★
Other activities:★★★

Site of Vermont's first racing trail—Nose Dive, cut in the early 1930s by the Civilian Conservation Corps—Stowe Resort has retained its old-time New England feel. Its trails zig-zag along forest contours, or drop precipitously straight down the fall line. Across from Mt. Mansfield, is Spruce Peak, with kinder, gentler terrain and a sunnier exposure. Both Mansfield and Spruce are vintage Vermont. But vintage doesn't mean stodgy, and Stowe is on the move. The revitalization of Stowe Mountain resort, which began in 2005 with the addition of two new lifts, enhanced snowmaking and additional terrain at Spruce Peak, is just the beginning of many "big" things to come on the sleepy side of Stowe's two mountains. The old Big Spruce Double chair has been replaced with a state of the art high-speed quad, top to bottom snowmaking coverage, and new trails. The construction gives Stowe a true base village between Spruce Peak and Mt. Mansfield.

The town of Stowe, with its white-steepled church and Main Street lined with historic buildings, is the epitome of how most folks picture Vermont. Between the village and the mountain are historic inns and swanky resorts, two world-class spas, and restaurants to serve every appetite and palate. But, the trails, with very little run-out at the bottom, keep you turning to the liftline. Those are just some of many reasons that Stowe has so many diehard fans

Mountain layout

♦♦**Expert:** Part of the legend of Stowe revolves around its Front Four, and the fact that it features some of the steepest and most difficult runs in skidom. Having descended the Front Four is a badge of honor for Northeast skiers and deservedly so, given the nature of Goat, Starr, Liftline and National. Besides being steep, the headwalls are frequently draped with vintage New England hardpack, and the trails are liberally moguled. For off-piste terrain, try the woods off Bypass, where there's a steep, tight drop-in that opens into perfectly spaced trees. Once you dump out on Nosedive, you'll find more wide-open trees to skier's left off the main trail. Skiers are known to hike The Chin (4,395 feet) and put their mettle to the test on its out-of-bounds terrain, but we suggest you hook up with someone who's familiar with the area. The cliff bands and tight chutes are really nasty stuff, plus you can easily end up on the backside of the mountain with no clue how to return to civilization.

♦**Advanced:** A very nice section of glade skiing through well-spaced trees is just off the top section of Nosedive. Chin Clip from the top of the gondola is long, moguled, and moderately narrow, but it does not have quite the steep grade that the Front Four boast.

■ **Intermediate:** At Mt. Mansfield, ski to the right or left of the Front Four. Advanced-intermediates will probably want to chance the tricky top part of Nosedive for the pleasure of skiing the long, sweeping cruiser that beckons further down. Going left from the top of the FourRunner Quad, take Upper Lord until it leads you to a handful of long excellent intermediate runs all the way to the bottom in Lower Lord, North Slope, Standard and Gulch.

From the quad, reaching the intermediate skiing under the gondola presents a problem. The connection between these two parts of the mountain is not convenient unless you are willing to take a run down Nosedive, rated double-black at its top. If you don't want to chance Nosedive, it's a hike from the quad area over to the gondola, or you can take the green-circle Crossover trail toward the bottom of the mountain and traverse directly across the Front Four to the gondola base. To work your way back from the gondola to the quad, take the Cliff Trail, which eventually hooks up with Lower Nosedive and dumps you at the base of the high-speed chair.

Try Perry Merrill or Gondolier from the gondola to cut turns about as wide as you want. The resort has changed the entire experience on Upper Spruce Peak by replacing the old and cold Big Spruce double chair with a high-speed quad and adding snowmaking. The mountain is a cruiser's delight, and powder days are a real treat.

Intermediates may also enjoy Stowe's night skiing. The upper portion of Perry Merrill and about 85 percent of Gondolier are lit Thursday through Saturday until 9 p.m. The ride up is in the warm gondola.

●● **Beginner:** There are very nice beginner trails off the lower lifts on Spruce Peak and off the Toll House chair on Mt. Mansfield. You won't find yourself worrying about faster skiers, so you'll be able to enjoy the experience.

One route we would recommend to all levels is the 4-mile-long, green-circle Toll Road, which starts at the top of the FourRunner Quad. This is a marvelous trail for lower-level skiers, but it is beautiful for all. Pass under a canopy of trees, where you can hear birds chirping or snow plopping from the branches. A little later you'll find the small wood and stone Mountain Chapel, where on Sundays at 1 p.m. you can attend an informal church service. You just won't find this type of intimate ski trail out West.

●**First-timer:** First-timers should start at Spruce Peak base area, then work up to the runs off the Toll House chair (Chair 5), then advance to Chair 4.

Ride Guide: Rimrock, which takes you from Nosedive over to the trails off the gondola, requires snowboarders to carry their speed (but don't miss those nice tree shots). Crossover, which takes you from the quad trails to the gondola trails, also has some pretty flat parts. And be ready for the flats coming from Tyro, site of the terrain park, and Standard back to the lifts. Avoid the Toll Road, it's way too long and has too many flats

Parks and pipes

At the mountain that Burton founder Jake Burton Carpenter now calls home, snowboarding is one of the top priorities. Tyro, the biggest of the resort's three terrain parks, attracts many Burton employees and features more than a dozen different elements, including boxes, rails, jibs, tabletops, rollers and a quarterpipe. If you haven't had enough after the top half of Tyro, stay the course: the lower section has so many rails you can't hit them in one run. (In the early season, when Tyro isn't yet open, Stowe sets up rails on lower North Slope, an area locals call Jib Nation.)

For a change of pace, hit the top of Tyro then use Crossover to access Stowe's superpipe, a competition-caliber pipe on North Slope. Both are best accessed by the Mountain Triple. There is great freeriding to Tyro from the top of the Lookout Double or FourRunner Quad.

Stowe's two other terrain parks are designed for learners or less hardcore aerialists. The Midway Mini Park, near the Midway Lodge features its own surface lift and hits that are out in the open for everyone to see. Demos are often staged here because of the visibility. The Spruce Terrain Park directly beneath the Alpine Double chairlift on Spruce Mountain offers more easy elements and fewer riders lined up to hit them.

 Cross-country and snowshoeing (visit xcskiresorts.com for more details)

Stowe has one of the top cross-country networks in the country. Four touring areas all interconnect to provide roughly 150 km. of groomed trails, and an additional 110 km. in the backcountry, plus a slew of trails for snowshoeing.

The Trapp Family Lodge (253-5719; 800-826-7000) organized America's first touring center and has 60 km. of groomed and machine-tracked trails that connect to another 100 km. in the Mt. Mansfield and Topnotch Resort networks. Trapp's also has 45 km. of backcountry trails. Rentals and instruction are available. **The Edson Hill Touring Center** (253-7371) has about 50 km. of trails with 25 km. of them groomed. Elevation varies from 1,400 to 2,100 feet. **Stowe Mountain Resort** (253-3000) has 80 km. of trails, 35 km. of which are groomed. The daily fee is $14 for adults and $7 for children. **The Topnotch Resort** (253-8585) has 30 km. of trails, most of which are groomed and tracked. Trail fee is $10 for adults, $6 for children.

Snowshoe rentals and tours are available at Umiak Outdoor Outfitters (253-2317).

Lessons [05/06 prices]

Telephone extensions for the ski school are 3680 and 3681.

Group lessons: $39 for 90 minutes.

First-timer package: Stowe for Starters ,for up to Level 6, includes up to two 90-minute group lessons, rentals and a Spruce Mountain lift ticket for $116 ($124 weekends/holidays). Levels 6–9 can take two-hour semi-privates for $63.

Private lessons: Multilingual, telemark, racing, pipe/park and handicapped-specific pros are available. For one person, one-hour lessons are $102; before 8:30 a.m. or after 3 p.m., $81; two hours, $164; half day (three hours), $238; full day, $374. For two to five people, one-hour lessons are $153; before 8:30 a.m. or after 3 p.m., $114; two hours, $232; half day (three hours), $323; full day, $543. Midweek/non-holiday prices are a lower.

Special programs: The Women in Motion three-day program is offered on specific dates for intermediates and up. It costs approximately $478 and includes lessons and lunch.

KidStuff (05/06 prices)

Child care: The Cubs Infant Care Center near the base of the Little Spruce double chairlift is convenient for folks skiing on Spruce Peak, but its use requires a little planning if you ski at Mount Mansfield. The center is just one minute away by car from the Mansfield Base Lodge, or the mountain shuttle runs continuously throughout the day. The center is state licensed and features a small but friendly staff that averages a decade or more at Stowe. The facility is not very large, and reservations are highly recommended. From the main playroom, floor to ceiling windows provide what has to be the valley's best view of Mansfield and the Front Four.

The center takes children ages 6 weeks through 6 years. Full day with lunch is $80 ($86 on weekends/holidays). Half day with snack is $56/$61. with a morning ski session for 3-year-olds is $100/$108. Parents must provide formula and food for infants. Toddlers are served lunch and offered snacks throughout the day. A beeper rental is $5 per day. Security cards are issued to parents and are required for pick-up at day's end. Late pick-up charge is $20 per child, applicable after 4:30 p.m. Call 253-3000, ext. 3686 for reservations.

Children's lessons: Headquartered at Spruce Peak, full-day programs for skiing (ages 4–12) and snowboarding (ages 6–12) include lunch. Cost is $100 ($108 weekends/holidays). The Big Easy is a two-hour group lesson with lift ticket for first-time skiers (ages 4–12) and snowboarders (ages 7–12) for $64 ($69 weekends/holidays). A program called 3 Ski is a two-hour lesson with lift ticket for 3-year-olds.

Lift tickets (05/06 prices)

	Adult	Child (6-12)
One day	$74 ($76/holiday)	$54 ($56 /holiday)
Three days	$177/$198 $107/$1126	
Five days	$275/$305 $164/$192	

Who skis free: Children ages 5 and younger with paid adult.

Who skis at a discount: Ages 65 and older pay junior prices.

Note: The Vacation Rewards Program provides discounted advance purchase multiday tickets. Call (888) 253-4849. Non-holiday night skiing is $24 for adults and $18 for children. A twilight ticket, valid from 1 to 9 p.m., is $52 for adults, $48 for children. All prices include Vermont sales tax.

Accommodations

When staying at least three days, ask about the Stowe Vacation Program. Extras include night skiing, extra half days, lessons, and more. Your lift tickets will be waiting for you with your room key, so there's no need to stop at the ticket window on your way to the trails the next morning. Call (800) 247-8693.

Topnotch at Stowe Resort & Spa (800-451-8686; 253-8585; in Canada 800-228-8686; $$$$) is the top spa and fitness center destination in the area. Rooms range from doubles in the main hotel to surrounding condominiums. The experience is all about comfort and luxury, from the overstuffed chairs in the lobby to the amazingly comfortable bed pillows in the rooms. The spa is world-class, and the resort has the only indoor tennis courts in Stowe.

The Trapp Family Lodge (800-826-7000; 253-8511; $$$$), was established by the Trapp family of The Sound of Music fame upon their arrival in the United States during WWII and is a legend in its own right. The Lodge is still in the family and is a self-contained resort with an excellent cross-country center, excellent restaurants and modern pool and fitness center. Make reservations early because this lodge is normally full throughout the season (Christmas reservations should be made about a year in advance). Rates include breakfast and dinner.

Green Mountain Inn (800-253-7302; 253-7301; $$–$$$$), on Main Street, is a charming old inn in the middle of town. In the original inn, the wide-planked floors are pine, as is the furniture, with many antique, four-poster canopied beds. Room in the annex are away from the main road noise; most rooms there have whirlpool tubs.

The Inn at the Mountain (800-253-4754; 253-3656; $$–$$$$) is part of the Stowe Mountain Resort. The flavor is country New England, and the inn surrounding condos have the only ski-in/ski-out facilities. The modern Fitness Center is free to all guests. The Fireside Tavern perfect for unwinding at day's end. Room and condo unit rates include breakfast and dinner.

The Stoweflake Mountain Resort and Spa (800-253-2232; 253-7355; $$$–$$$$), about halfway between the mountain and the town, has a trendy spa and sports club. This property has had continual upgrades over past years in its quest to match Topnotch. Rates include breakfast and dinner. The Stoweflake also manages a nice group of townhouse condos with studio to three-bedroom units.

Stowe Inn (800-546-4030; 253-4030; $$-$$$) is a renovated 17th-century landmark on the Mountain Road. Some deluxe inn rooms in the main lodge feature four-posted sleigh or panel beds. Standard doubles in the carriage house are a good value yet well-adorned. There is plenty of common space to unwind next to an open fire after skiing. Breakfast and afternoon snacks are included, and dinner is available downstairs in Harrison's Tavern.

The best family accommodations in Stowe are at the **Golden Eagle Resort** (800-626-1010; 253-4811; $$–$$$). This sprawling complex has more than a dozen buildings and facilities, from motel rooms with kitchenettes to apartments. **Ye Olde England Inne** (800-477-3771; 0800-962-684 toll-free from the U.K.; 253-7558; $$–$$$$), is on the Mountain Road. The Bluff House, perched on the hill behind the inn, has luxury suites. Rates include breakfast.

Ten Acres Lodge (800-327-7357; 253-7638; $$-$$$$) on Luce Hill Road was converted from an 1840s farm house. Rooms vary in size; those in the main lodge are relatively simple, but the common areas are beautiful. Eight modern units, called the Hill House, all have fireplaces in the rooms and share an outdoor hot tub. Rates include breakfast.

The Gables Inn (800-422-5371; 253-7730; $$–$$$$), on Mountain Road, is a real lived-in house; breakfasts are among Stowe's best, and guests wouldn't think of eating dinner anywhere else, either. Rates include two meals.

The **Stone Hill Inn** (253-6282; $$$$) is a luxurious getaway designed for romance and comfort; no kids allowed. Each of the nine rooms has a king-size bed, a cozy sitting area, a fireplace in the bedroom *and* in the bathroom and a jetted tub for two. Breakfast, evening hors d'oeuvres and unlimited soft drinks included.

 Dining

Stowe has long been famous for its cuisine. **Ten Acres** (253-7638; $$$), **Mes Amis** (253-7751; $$$) and **Blue Moon Cafe** (253-7006; $$–$$$) are considered tops for fine dining. **Maxwell's at Topnotch** (253-8585; $$$), known nationally for its innovative spa cuisine, is one of the signature Stowe dining experiences.

Winfield's Bistro (253-7355; $$$), at the Stoweflake, serves nicely gussied-up New American fare with an international flair and has an excellent wine list.

Michael's on the Hill (244-7476; $$-$$$), in nearby Waterbury, is a chef-owned res-

Dining: $$$$-Entrees $30+; $$$-$20-$30; $$-$10-$20; $-less than $10.
Accommodations: (double room) $$$$-$200+; $$$-$141-$200; $$-$81-$140; $-$80 and less.

taurant in an 1820s farmhouse with spectacular mountain views. The European-influenced menu is sophisticated and changes seasonally. **Harrison's Restaurant and Bar** (253-7773; $$-$$$), in the Stowe Inn, features New American cuisine in a glass-enclosed setting overlooking Stowe village. Sit near the bar, a mahogany masterpiece relocated from an authentic Bronx neighborhood bar.

The **Trapp Family Lodge** (253-8511; $$–$$$) traditionally has put on an excellent Austrian-style meal for a fixed price of about $42. Or, chose among a dozen a la carte entrees. Live harp music accompanies dinner.

The **Whip Bar and Grill** (253-7301; $$), in the lower level of the Green Mountain Inn, is a good place for a light dinner or sandwiches. **The Shed** (253-4364; $-$$) has a microbrewery and is a great spot for steaks and prime rib. **Foxfire** (253-4887; $$) has good Italian food, as does **Trattoria La Festa** (253-8480; $$). **Mr. Pickwicks Polo Pub** in the Ye Olde England Inne (253-7558; $$) serves excellent game. **Red Basil** (253-4478; $-$$) specializes in fantastic Thai food and has a great martini menu. There's a sushi bar, too.

For alternatives that aren't budget-busters, try **Miguel's Stowe Away** (253-7574; $-$$) or the **Cactus Café** (253-7770; $-$$) for Mexican food; **Restaurant Swisspot** (253-4622; $-$$) for fondues and decadent Swiss chocolate pie; **The Depot Street Malt Shoppe** (253-4269; $) for a 1950s-style fountain shop; and **Gracie's** (253-8741) for great burgers and meatloaf. **GiGi's Deli** (253-0340; $) on South Main is a best-bet option for breakfast and lunch. It is owned and operated by New England Culinary Institute grad Joey Buttendorf. Also, the country breakfasts at **The Gables** (253-7730; $) shouldn't be missed, especially on weekends.

On-mountain, there are several choices for lunch and snacks as well as cafeterias in all base lodges. The **Fireside Tavern** (235-3000; $$), in the Inn at the Mountain, at the base of the Toll House lift, hearty breakfasts and lunches. The **Midway Café** ($) in the Midway Lodge has good pizza and paninis. The **Cliff House Restaurant** ($-$$) at the gondola top has a nice upscale atmosphere and great views.

Apres-ski/nightlife

The ingredients that make the perfect apres-ski spot are all here in just the right measure and to excess at the **Matterhorn Bar**. On the mountain road, this raucous little roadhouse is packed and rollicking after the lifts close. There's a dance floor, a disc jockey, loud music, pool tables, a big-screen TV and a sushi bar. A more low-key apres-ski at the mountain is in the **Fireside Tavern** at the Inn at the Mountain.

The **Rusty Nail** is the "in" spot for dancing and live music, frequently blues. **The Shed** brews its own beer. **Mr. Pickwick's** at Ye Olde England Inne gets a good pub crowd with its 150-plus different beers, and the bar at **Miguel's Stowe Away** seems to be a singles meeting place. **The Back Yard** is small and normally has plenty of beer to drink around a fire.

Other activities

Stowe is home to two world-class **spas**: the Spa at Topnotch Resort (253-6463) and the Spa at Stoweflake Mountain Resort (253-7355). With booklets full of treatments, massaging waterfalls, and gender-specific hot tubs, saunas, and steamrooms, you could easily forget about skiing and spend the entire day at either spa.

Indoor tennis can be played at the Topnotch Tennis Center (253-9649) on the Mountain Road. The center has four indoor courts and offers lessons, round robins, and Boomer, a computer-guided ball machine that let's you play actual matches. In the Village, Jackson Arena has an Olympic-size **ice skating** rink (253-6148). The Swimming Hole (253-9229) has a 25-meter **indoor pool, kids pool with waterslide, fitness classes** and **weight training equipment.**

Rent **snowmobiles** at Nichols Snowmobiles (253-7239) or from Farm Resort (888-3525). The Sterling Ridge Inn (644-8265), in Jeffersonville, offers snowmobile tours of Smugglers' Notch. **Horse-drawn sleigh rides** take place at Edson Hill Manor (253-7371), Stowehof Inn (253-9722), Pristine Meadows (253-9901), Charlie Horse (253-2215), Stoweflake (253-7355), the Trapp Family Lodge (253-8511) and Topnotch (253-8585). Stowe also has **horseback riding** at Edson Hill Manor (253-7371) and Stowehof Inn (253-9722). Umiak Outdoor Outfitters (253-2317) on South Main provides **snowshoe** rentals, instruction and tours on private and public trails. Snowmobile tours in the Green Mountain National Forest also are available. In the Village, Jackson Arena has an Olympic-size **ice skating** rink (253-6148).

The **Vermont Ski Museum** is on Main Street in Stowe Village. Tours of **Ben and Jerry's ice cream factory** (244-5641), just down the road in Waterbury, include samples. **The Cabot Cheese Factory** (563-2231) is also open.

Stowe has more than a hundred **shops** and **art galleries** for browsing, most in town. Shaw's General Store is a century old and was the town's first ski shop. Other unusual shops are Moriarty Hats & Sweaters, for knitted goods, and the Stowe Craft Gallery for handcrafted, contemporary works. At the Cabot Annex complex, in Waterbury, you can purchase a wide variety of Vermont specialty foods. The complex also is home to Lake Champlain Chocolates (Yum!), Vermont Teddy Bears and Mesa International, which sells home furnishings.

Special events include the Stowe Winter Carnival in January, the country's oldest winter party; the Mountain Adventure Fest Tour de Stowe cross-country races as well as the Stowe Derby — the country's oldest combination downhill/cross-country event — both held in February; a Sugar Slalom race with maple-sugar-on-snow at the finish line and the Stowe Snow Beach Party, both in April.

Internet Access: You can check your email at the Octagon Web Cafe at the top of the Forerunner express quad.

 ## Getting there and getting around

By air: Flights arrive at Burlington International Airport, 45 minutes from Stowe. Most hotels have a transfer service; you can also rent a car. The Stowe Area Association provides discounts on flights and rental cars when you make your hotel reservations.

By train: A romantic trip aboard Amtrak's Vermonter offers private berths where you arrive in Waterbury, 15 miles from Stowe, early in the morning (the Stowe trolley meets each daily arrival and departure). Reservations required. The Stowe Area Association offers 10 percent off Amtrak tickets with no date restrictions.

By car: Distance from Boston is about 205 miles; from New York, 325 miles. The resort is a few miles north of Waterbury Exit 10 on I-89.

Getting around: You can manage without a car, but we recommend one. The Town Trolley runs between the village of Stowe and Mt. Mansfield. It provides, in the words of a British journalist who begged a ride back into town with us, "an epic voyage." But it's free and runs from the village from 7:30 a.m. to 4:30 p.m., and from the mountain from 8 a.m. to 5 p.m. at 30-minute intervals.

Dining: $$$$-Entrees $30+; $$$-$20-$30; $$-$10-$20; $-less than $10.
Accommodations: (double room) $$$$-$200+; $$$-$141-$200; $$-$81-$140; $-$80 and less.

Stratton Mountain

and the Manchester area

Stratton Facts

Summit elevation: 3,875 feet
Vertical drop: 2,003 feet
Base elevation: 1,872 feet

Address: RR1 Box 145,
Stratton Mountain, VT 05155
Area code: 802
Ski area phone: 297-2200
Snow report: 297-4211
Toll-free reservations: (800) 787-2886
Fax: 297-4300
E-mail: skistratton@intrawest.com
Internet: www.stratton.com
Number and types of lifts: 16 –
1 12-passenger gondola, 4 high-speed six-pax,
4 quads, 1 triple, 1 double, 2 surface lifts, 3 moving
carpets

Skiable acreage: 600 acres
Snowmaking: 90 percent
Uphill capacity: 29,550 per hour
Parks & pipes: 6 parks; 2 pipes
Bed base: 8,000 in region
Nearest lodging: Slopeside
Resort child care: Yes, 6 weeks and older
Adult ticket, per day: $59-$72 (05/06 prices)
Expert: ★
Advanced: ★★★
Intermediate: ★★★★
Beginner: ★★★★
First-timer: ★★★★

Manchester Region
Dining: ★★★★
Apres-ski/nightlife: ★★★
Other activities: ★★★

Stratton seems to be moving in two distinct directions. On the one hand, the self-proclaimed "Snowboarding Capital of the East" offers truly inexpensive midweek deals. On the other hand, the resort has invested significant money in high-end lodging, built an exclusive members-only club and imposes one of the most expensive single-day lift tickets in the nation. Go figure. The bottom line, however, is this: Radical dudes, easy-going intermediates, professionals on hiatus and families can all find their place at Stratton.

Stratton's base area has always been a helter-skelter affair, with various lodging and condominum complexes scattered amidst private homes. Due to poor signage and a snake-pit road layout, arriving—especially after dark—can be confusing.

However, the recent completion of the Commons and the surrounding lodging properties, Rising Bear and Long Trail House make it quite easy to check in, wander up to the village, and get out to the lifts. Additionally, the development in recent years of a car-free base village has really improved the ambiance. The village creates a centralized locale for swanky shops, gourmet and not-so-gourmet restaurants, slopeside condos and even a Bavarian-style clock tower—all linked by a heated cobblestone walkway. Jitney service does connect the dots and getting around has improved.

Other base-area improvements include an expanded base-lodge cafeteria that can now handle the weekend lunchtime crowds; a self-contained, slopeside kids' ski and snowboard school facility; and an under-21 club that's open weekends and holiday weeks.

Stratton was the first Eastern resort to permit snowboarding, and few resorts equal its dedication to the sport, specifically terrain parks. Parks serve every ability level and the resort has pioneered a required certification program to ride its most advanced park. On the other end of the spectrum, Stratton is a Burton Method Center, offering Burton Learn to Ride, the Cadillac of introductory snowboarding programs. The resort now matches its snowboarding commitment with freeskiing zeal; it hosts the annual Vermont Freeskiing Open and the winter-long Friday and Saturday night Cold Wars Rail Jam Series.

Outside the parks, the full variety of downhill choices can be found on 90 trails and 500 skiable acres. A 12-passenger, high-speed gondola and four six-packs swiftly move everyone out of the base areas and out onto the mountain. For those who crave a less frenetic ambiance, the Sun Bowl base lodge is low-key and more "small ski area" in ambiance. A smattering of gladed runs completes the picture. It's not all wine and roses on the hill, however. Traffic at some of the convoluted, multi-trail intersections creates havoc on crowded days.

The resort is 20 miles outside Manchester and its access highways, Rtes. 11 and 30, are lined with shops, accommodations and some pretty good restaurants. Manchester and its twin, Manchester Center, project a Currier & Ives vision of the quintessential Vermont village, complete with white-spire churches and manorial hotels. The nearby Orvis fly-fishing store and school offer fly-fishing lessons on the Battenkill River in season. The lavish Sunday brunch at the Equinox Hotel or a visit to the Southern Vermont Arts Center can gild a ski weekend or vacation.

 ## Mountain layout

One of few Eastern resorts with its own base village, Stratton caters to a tony down-country clientele who want convenient amenities and manicured slopes. Excellent grooming on the mostly intermediate terrain makes Stratton one of America's best ego-inflating resorts. Experts can find some good challenges, but don't expect to be pushed; come here to get pampered and feel good about your skiing. This mountain is also great for wide-open, top-to-bottom cruising.

◆◆**Expert ◆Advanced:** The pitch for cruising here is nice enough that no expert or advanced skier will complain. For the more challenging terrain, head straight to the summit on the gondola. Polar Bear, Grizzly Bear and Upper Tamarack are narrow runs in fine New-England tradition with good vertical. Do laps on the Ursa Express six-pack chair. Upper Kidderbrook to Freefall provides another good advanced cruiser on the Sun Bowl side. Upper Standard, right under the gondola, starts steep but mellows at the bottom. Upper Spruce is the easiest of the double-diamond trails, with tempting glades to the right, but none of the double diamonds is really worthy of that rating. For bumps, head to World Cup.

■ **Intermediate:** The upper mountain has some steeps for advanced-intermediates. Upper Lift Line to Lower Lift Line, the longest fall-line trail on the mountain, is made for big giant-slalom turns, and Upper Drifter to Lower Drifter is the same. Racers from the Stratton Mountain School are often carving turns on these trails, as well as North American, off the Ursa Express. The Sun Bowl chair has excellent cruisers down Rowley's Run and Sunriser. On the lower mountain, Yodeler is a good warm-up run.

●● **Beginner:** Stratton has a Ski Learning Park with 10 gentle trails and its own lift. This park includes a terrain garden, where the mountain staff sculpts bumps and rolls, so beginners can practice their balance and independent leg action. A long top-to-bottom trail, West Meadow to Lower Wanderer, makes beginners feel like champs. In the Sun Bowl area, head to Lower Middlebrook. The other beginner trails, 91, Big Ben and Main Line, are only reached from intermediate trails.

● **First-timer:** Stick to the Teddy Bear, Club and Villager lifts on the far left of the base area. Stage I and Village Walk are unintimidating places to learn to ski or ride.

Ride Guide: Avoid cutting across the mountain via Black Bear and Old 8. It's better to just go straight down to the Sun Bowl and avoid the flats. Also avoid Old Log Rd. on the other side of the mountain, because you'll have to take off your board and hike it.

Parks and pipes

Stratton, one of the pioneers in snowboarding, demonstrates its commitment to the sport with six terrain parks filled with many unique features and by hosting the annual U.S. Open. Indeed, no matter where riders go here, there's bound to be a park nearby.

The Power Park on Suntanner was designed and built with the stamp of approval of two-time Olympic-medalist Ross Powers, a Stratton regular. It's Stratton's biggest, best and most extreme terrain park, has the highest visibility and gets the most traffic. It's also home to the superpipe. With a new mandatory safety and educational video, the park has finally achieved perfection. Expert riders can do their thing without being bothered by uneducated beginners. The 20-minute class includes a video presentation, question & answer period, park-and-pipe etiquette and safety tips. Afterwards, skiers and riders are issued a card—valid all season—to use the park.

Only one word can describe the jumps and rails in the Power Park, and that is HUGE. The park starts off with two massive hips that can be hit back to back; both have smooth transitions and nice landings. After that there are a couple ramp jumps that let you drop the sickest tricks you have. Next is a jib fest served with everything from kinked rails to fun boxes. The rails are set up in excellent lines and allow for many back-to-back jibs. The park also contains a 420-foot superpipe with 20-foot walls. After the halfpipe and a couple more rails, it's a fast smooth ride to the top of the park aboard the American Express six-pack. The park is well groomed and offers a day of fun to the most extreme riders around.

East Byrneside Park, on the other side of the gondola from Suntanner, is Stratton's intermediate park. It has seven rails of different variety set up in good lines that allow for optimal jibbing. The only problem with this park is the lack of jumps. With only one slightly icy hip jump, it is hard to work on your air moves before attempting the Power Park.

Take the Janeway Junction, far rider's left, to East Meadow, a beginner freestyler's park. The upper section has a few rollers and a small spine; the lower section is set up boardercross style, with rollers, banked turns and a jump. Our rider found it small and not well maintained, but still fun. A kids' learning park on Tyrolienne has small rollers, spines and a minipipe.

If you time your visit to Stratton to about a week before the U.S. Open, head to the Sunriser Supertrail on the other side of the mountain to check out what the competitors trick off. This park and pipe are built about a week before the Open and aren't maintained afterwards. The huge U.S. Open superpipe, under the Sunrise Express chair, is also used by the Ross Powers Snowboard Camp for training a week after the Open.

Lessons (06/07 prices)

Stratton has an on-mountain Adventure Center where you can try telemark skis, a snowboard, Snowblades or freeride skis designed for fun and tricks, in the halfpipe and terrain parks. Begin at Village Rentals in the Village Lodge. From here, go to the rental tent to pick up your equipment, then finally up to the Ski & Snowboard School. Give yourself time or you'll miss your lesson.

Group lessons: $39 for 1.75 hours. Learn to Freestyle lessons for snowboarders start at $45 and progress to $79 for lessons and rental. This series of lessons will get you grooving in the terrain park and the halfpipe.

First-timer package: For skiers, $98 includes beginner lift ticket, two lessons and equipment. Burton Method Center Learn to Ride program is $98.

Private lessons: $98 per hour. One hour costs $98 on weekends/holidays and $89 midweek. A half day costs $285 weekends/holidays and $230 midweek. A full day costs $480 weekends/holidays and $380 midweek.

Special programs: Stratton has women's ski and snowboard camps during the season designed to boost confidence and enhance strength, style and technique.

KidStuff [06/07 prices]

Child care: Stratton's Childcare Center, located in the Village Lodge, takes children ages 6 weeks to 5 years and is open 8 a.m. to 5 p.m. Drop-off is under the upper parking deck. A full day costs $95 midweek, $110 weekend holidays, lunch and snack included; half-day morning costs $79 ($65 midweek); afternoons cost $65. Reservations required; call (800) 787-2886.

Children's lessons: An all-day Little Cub snow school program for ages 4–6 costs $105; half day costs $60. The program for ages 7–12 is all day and costs $130 with lift ticket. A first-timer package for ages 7–12 including beginner ticket, rentals and lesson costs $105.

Lift tickets [05/06 prices]

	Adult	Child (7-12)	13-17/65+
One day (holiday/weekend)	$72	$51	$60
One day (weekday)	$59	$46	$52
Three days (holiday/weekend)	$186/$162	$123/$116	$165/$137
Three days (weekday)	$144	$106	$125
Five days (holiday/weekend)	$288/$215	$185/$166	$249/$188
Five days (weekday)	$198	$158	$176

Who skis at a discount: Children younger than age 7 are $5.

Stratton and Okemo have joined forces on a multiday lift ticket plan that permits skiing or riding at either resort. For details, call either resort.

Cross-country and snowshoeing (see xcskiresorts.com for more details)

The Stratton Ski Touring Center (297-4114) has two locations: the country club and Sun Bowl. Both offer groomed trails for diagonal and skate skiing, but trails at the country club are easier (fewer hills). Lessons and rentals are available. At the country club center, Stratton also has snowshoe rentals.

Viking Ski Touring Center (824-3933), in Londonderry, has 30 km. of groomed trails through woods and open fields. The terrain is best suited for intermediates but advanced skiers won't be bored. This is one of the oldest cross-country centers in North America.

Wild Wings Ski Touring Center (824-6793) in Peru is noted for its wooded terrain and the fact that it offers only classical cross-country skiing on 24 km. of groomed trails.

Down in Manchester Village, **Hildene** (362-1788) has 17 km. of trails through the pine-covered estate of Robert Todd Lincoln. There is a warming hut in the carriage barn with rentals, trail tickets and light refreshments.

Accommodations

The town of Manchester is a tourist town with accommodations from giant resorts and B&Bs to a slew of lesser-priced roadside motels. The Manchester and Mountains Chamber (362-2100) and the **Londonderry Chamber** (824-8178) can help with arrangements. The hotels and B&Bs listed below are near the ski areas.

At Stratton: Lift-and-lodging packages (midweek, non-holiday) begin at $59 per person, per night, based on double occupancy. For reservations at any of Stratton's lodges, call (800) 787-2886. The **Long Trail House** units will comfortably house a family for an extended stay, with an outdoor heated pool, hot tubs and underground climate-controlled parking. The **Stratton Mountain Inn** is a full-service lodge that's also good for families. The **Liftline Lodge** provides Stratton's most economical lodging on the mountain and has many of the resort's restaurants. Stratton Reservations also has plenty of condos all within easy reach of the slopes.

Down the road in Jamaica (the town, not the Caribbean island), we highly recommend the elegant colonial **Three Mountain Inn** (800-532-9399; 874-4140; $$-$$$). On the Select Registry of distinguished inns, the Three Mountain is both cozy and elegant where the innkeepers strive to exceed your expectations.

These property management companies deal with condos throughout the area: Bondville Real Estate (800-856-8388; 297-3316) or Winhill Real Estate (800-214-5648; 297-1550).

Dining

Verde (297-9200; $$-$$$) is the latest rave spot at Stratton. Entrees from the Mediterranean grill include wild mushroom crespelle and zarzuella, a Spanish fish stew. Great Italian food is the main theme on the mountain where **Mulberry Street** (297-3065; $$) serves basic pastas and pizzas. **Mulligan's** (297-9293; $$) serves moderately priced, basic American fare with a good kids' menu in a loud, TV-in-every-corner atmosphere. **Luna** (297-4036; $$-$$$) at the Stratton Mountain Club is open to the public for dinner by reservation.

Stratton offers mid-mountain **snowcat dinners** on Tuesdays and Saturdays at **Aunt Chiladas**. Cats leave every half-hour from 6-8:30 p.m. and are restricted to 12 passengers per trip. The menu is preset with a choice of three entrees, grilled meat, seafood, and pasta. Not recommended for children. No reservations are needed.

The **Stone Chimney Grille** (297-2500), in the Stratton Mountain Inn specializes in family dining, with steaks, seafood, and a salad bar. At the **Blue Moon Cafe** (297-2093; $), breakfast goes nouveau with an assortment of crepes and blue pancakes called Full Moons.

The **OutBack** (297-3663; $$$), just south of the access road, has phenomenal lobster bisque along with other casual fare. Nearby, **The Red Fox** (297-2488; $$-$$$) serves Vermont-style nouveau cuisine in a restored barn.

The award-winning **Three Clock Inn** (824-6327; $$$) in South Londonderry, brings a bit of authentic Provence to the hills of Vermont. An upscale favorite for Stratton regulars — many of whom owner/chef Serge Roche knows by name — the inn has a wine collection in keeping with its gourmet menu. Fine food can also be found at the **Three Mountain Inn** (800-532-9399 or 874-4140; $$$) in Jamaica. The lobster with saffron-champagne butter and mushroom risotto is not to be missed.

The **Frog's Leap Inn** (824-3019; $$$) serves creative meals by candlelight. **The Garden Cafe** (824-9574; $$$) has been serving upscale meals for more than 15 years. **Jake's Cafe** (824-6614; $) serves pizzas and sandwiches. **Johnny Seesaw's** (824-5533), just down the road from Bromley, serves enormous portions and is a perfect family spot.

Apres-ski/nightlife

Catch apres-ski is on the deck of **Grizzly's** with entertainment almost every weekend; in **Mulligan's,** with its 50 different types of beer; or **Bear Bottom Pum,** in the Stratton Mountain Inn. In the evenings, the action on the mountain continues in the **Green Door Pub** in Mulligan's with live entertainment on Saturdays and big-screen football on Sundays, plus pool and foosball. **Snyder's** is the newest hot spot in the base area. The no-smoking bar has patio seating, daily drink specials, and 10-cent wings on Fridays. Off the mountain, try the locals' hangout, **Red Fox** in Bondville, for live music on weekends. The **Foggy Goggle** also in Bondville gets packed as well. If you're into cigars and martinis, head to **Mulberry Street.** The **Perfect Wife** has live bands every weekend in season.

 Other activities

Phoenix, **an under-21 club** in Liftline, has games, big-screen video, a DJ, snacks and smoothies. It's open from 6 p.m. on weekends and holidays. The Riley Rink (362-0150), in Manchester, has **ice skating**.

The Stratton Sports Center (297-4230) offers **indoor tennis, racquetball, indoor pool, hot tubs, saunas, fitness center, tanning salons** and **massages.**

A fixed-up **movie theater** in Manchester has two screens. **Sleigh rides** are offered by Horses for Hire (297-1468) in Rawsonville, just south of Bondville on Rte. 30; Sun Bowl Ranch (297-9210) at Stratton; and Taylor Farm Sleigh Rides (824-5690) in Londonderry.

The Avanyu Spa (362-7881), at the Equinox Resort in Manchester, offers everything from Reiki to arnica sports massages to maple-leaf scrubs. Or try **The Spa at Stratton Mountain** (297-3339), a full-service day spa open from 8 a.m.–9 p.m.

Shopping is a major activity in the Manchester region. About 40 factory outlet stores are spread throughout Manchester, alongside boutiques and shops with handcrafted gift items and unique clothing.

 Getting there and getting around

By air: Manchester is about 90 minutes from the Albany, N.Y. airport and requires a car for easy access.

By car: Manchester Center is at the intersection of Rtes. 7A and 30 in southwestern Vermont, about 140 miles northwest of Boston and 235 miles north of New York City. Stratton is on Rte. 30, about 20 miles east of Manchester. Look for the Stratton Mountain Road from Rte. 30. If you're heading straight for Stratton from I-91, take Exit 2 at Brattleboro, follow signs to Rte. 30, then drive 38 miles to Bondville and the Stratton Mountain Road.

Getting around: Drive a car.

Dining: $$$$-Entrees $30+; $$$-$20-$30; $$-$10-$20; $-less than $10.
Accommodations: (double room) $$$$-$200+; $$$-$141-$200; $$-$81-$140; $-$80 and less.

Nearby resorts

Bromley, Manchester Center, VT; (802) 824-5522

Internet: www.bromley.com

9 lifts; 300 skiable acres; 1,334 vertical feet; 3 terrain parks; 1 halfpipe

Bromley, 6 miles east of Manchester, is a no-nonsense, function-over-fashion ski resort. Its base area consists of a lodge. Period. Slopeside are a hotel, some condos and a few private homes, but no stores or restaurants. People come to Bromley to ski, ride and hang out with their friends and families on its usually sun-drenched slopes. Although significantly smaller than Stratton, Bromley has trails for everyone, from gentle beginner runs that wind down the mountain through the woods to expert pistes with shots through the trees.

Lift tickets (06/07): One day for adults, $64/$61 weekend/holiday and $25 midweek; ages 7–12, $42/$39; ages 13–17, $56/$53.

Lodging: For slopeside lodging stay at **Bromley Sun Lodge** (800-722-2159; 824-6941 ; $-$$$). Condos and private homes (up to four bedrooms) are either slopeside or fed by a shuttle to the base lodge.

Distance from Boston: Manchester Center is at the intersection of Rtes. 7A and 30 in southwestern Vermont, about 140 miles from Boston and 235 miles from New York City. Bromley is 6 miles from Manchester traveling on Rte. 11, just 8 miles west of Londonderry.

Vermont Regional Resorts

Ascutney Mountain Resort, Brownsville, VT; (802) 484-7711; (800) 243-0011

Internet: www.ascutney.com

5 lifts; 55 trails; 1,800 vertical feet

Ascutney, off I-91 on the New Hampshire/Vermont border, is a mid-sized resort that appeals to young families with a variety of activities both on and off the hill, including tubing, ice skating, pizza parties, torchlight parades and a good children's ski school. Recent years have seen big improvements here, including a high-speed quad to a new summit, improved snowmaking and an enhanced children's learning area. Ascutney's terrain is a good mix for advanced and intermediate skiers and riders, with plenty of narrow, twisting old-style New England trails. There's a separate beginner area that's perfect for learning or for skiing with little ones. The base area is anchored by a 240-room ski-in/ski-out hotel.

Lift tickets (06/07): Adults, $58 weekend/holiday and $56 weekday; juniors (7–16) and seniors (65–69), $44 weekend/holiday and $39 midweek. Those 6 and younger, and 70 and older, ski free. Half-day tickets are available.

Distance from Burlington: About 105 miles south I-89, I-91, Rte. 5 and Rte. 44. Ascutney is about 130 miles from Albany, NY, and about 130 miles from Boston or Hartford, Ct.

Lodging information/reservations: (800) 243-0011.

Snowshoe Mountain

West Virginia

Summit elevation:	4,800 feet
Vertical drop:	1,500 feet
Base elevation:	3,200 feet

Address: 1 Snowshoe Drive, Snowshoe, WV, 26209
Area code: 304
Ski area phone: (877) 441-4386
Snow report: 572-4636
Reservations: (877) 441-4386
Fax: 572-5664
E-mail: info@snowshoemtn.com
Internet: www.snowshoemtn.com
Expert:★
Advanced:★★
Intermediate:★★★★★
Beginner:★★★★★
First-timer:★★★

Number and types of lifts: 14–3high-speed quads, 2 quads, 6 triples, 3 surface lifts
Acreage: 234 acres
Snowmaking: 100 percent
Uphill capacity: 22,900 per hour
Parks & pipes: 4 parks, 1 pipe
Bed base: 1,800 condo and lodge rooms
Nearest lodging: Slopeside
Resort child care: Yes
Adult ticket, per day: $60-$65 (06 price)
Dining: ★★★★
Apres-ski/nightlife:★★
Other activities:★★★

"Northern exposure with southern hospitality" is the way Snowshoe Mountain folks like to describe this unique resort. This southern ski area gets nearly 200 inches of annual snowfall, so they can lay claim to a northern orientation, yet the vast majority of the nearly half million skiers who come here annually live south of the Mason-Dixon line.

Snowshoe Resort is the closest "big mountain" skiing to be found in the South. It's the most elaborate and extensive resort in the region, and it does very well by its core customers. It attracts a curious blend of D.C. bureaucrats, Nashville nurses and Atlanta attorneys. Most are drawn here because of its location and great facilities. Soome may come just to experience snow, struggle through skiing and party up a storm. The terrain is approachable with superb snowmaking and snow grooming that allows beginners and intermediates to have a good time. Pickings are slim for the truly advanced and expert skier.

The resort comprises three areas: Snowshoe, Silver Creek and the Western Territory, each with its own personality. The Silver Creek section presents an excellent venue for families, especially those with younger children, with its combination of single-facility, ski-in/out lodging, night skiing, terrain park and snow tubing. It's also less crowded than the other areas, and the slopes are wider and better designed than at the Snowshoe area, but the skiing is less challenging.

This is an "upside down" resort: the base facilities are at the summit. A mountaintop village has been under construction for several years, and a lodge, condominiums, restaurants, shops and a new conference hall have been and continue to be added including Seneca Lodge, a 62-unit facility, at the Village at Snowshoe. Additionally, a 100-unit condo complex, Expedition Station, was completed in February, 2006. New for '06-'07 is the replacement of the Widow-maker chairlift by a high-speed quad adjacent to the new ('06-'07) Soaring Eagle Lodge.

Mountain layout

♦♦Expert ♦Advanced: The Western Territory is home to Snowshoe's expert terrain. It's literally across the street from Snowshoe. A shuttle bus transports skiers between Silver Creek and the Snowshoe/Western Territory areas. Given the predominance of southern, once-a-year ski-weekers among the clientele, this section is usually the least crowded, but it comprises only two runs — Cupp Run and Shay's Revenge. Both take advantage of Snowshoe's total vertical drop, and both are worthy of their black-diamond rating. At moments along Cupp, nifty little places can be found to zip into the trees. Lower Shay's is significantly steep and often bumps up.

Silver Creek has two trails marked black — Flying Eagle and Bear Creek. While these have short sections that present some pitch, competent intermediates can handle them.

■ **Intermediate:** Snowshoe is an intermediate skier's delight. At the Snowshoe area, the best runs are Ball Hooter and Skip Jack, which lead down to the Ball Hooter and Grabhammer chairs respectively. On packed weekends, traffic can be a problem here. Another interesting, less-traveled option is the Upper Flume/J Hook/Lower Widowmaker route, found to skier's far right off the Widowmaker chair. Even though the Northern Tract is rated beginner, it is a great place to find untracked powder after a storm.

At Silver Creek, Fox Chase-to-Laurel Run is the most extended blue-rated run. Cascade and Slaymaker-to-Spur are also good cruisers, but none is particularly long. An intermediate will have a blast at Silver Creek and find much smaller crowds compared to Snowshoe.

●● **Beginner:** The resort caters to green-level skiers and riders. At the far left, off Snowshoe's top ridge, the Northern Tract, a comfortably isolated group of a half-dozen easy trails gives green-trail skiers their own lift-served real estate off the Powderidge chair. These trails are wide enough to be reassuring, but meander a bit to lend variety.

Silver Creek's green-rated runs are generally short but very welcoming, presenting a good place for first-timers to begin the transition to more general terrain. Cubb Run gently hugs the far right edge of the area and allows access to three chairlifts.

● **First-timer:** The good news is that the Skidder area for first-timers is just a few steps from the Shavers Center, home to the ski school and rental shop. The bad news is that it's laid out laterally on the ridge top and can become a bit frenzied and turbulent with skiers and riders passing through en route to other parts of the hill. The terrain itself is conducive to learning: short, wide and gentle.

Ride Guide: The resort's terrain is generally snowboarder-friendly, with a minimum of crossover trails and relatively few spots that require unstrapping and pushing.

Parks and pipes

The Super Park at Silver Creek is spread across seven trails: Timberjack, Mountaineer, Cascade, Fox Chase, Laurel Run, Bear Claw and Buck Saw. It holds a variety of aerial features, rails and boxes, plus a 400-foot halfpipe. A boardercross course on Slaymaker and Spur includes gates, berms and rollers.

On the Snowshoe side, skiers and boarders can hit the Pro Park at Spruce Glades near the top of the Ballhooter lift. A $5 park pass, received after watching a safety video, is required. The park has rails, spines and steps, plus tabletops and jumps that range from 35 to 50 feet.

The Spruce Glades Terrain Garden at Snowshoe, a beginner terrain park, has a few small rails, a funbox and small snow features for aerials. Silver Creek's Mountaineer Terrain Garden provides an introduction to riding rails and getting air for the novice.

Cross-country and snowshoeing

The resort's cross-country skiing operates out of the **Snowshoe Outdoor Adventure Center** (572-5477), between Snowshoe and Silver Creek. The trail system covers 40 km. along the Cheat Mountain Ridge Trail, as well as through the nearby backcountry. The center is fully equipped with rentals and offers instruction.

The **Elk River Inn** (572-3771) in Slatyfork, about 5 miles from the bottom of the Snowshoe access road, has a touring center and immediate access to 5 km. of adjacent groomed trails. Another 35 km. can be accessed nearby. The Inn offers ski rentals and will give instruction by appointment.

Lessons [05/06 prices]

The Snowshoe Ski and Snowboard School is in the main resort complex's Shavers Center, and adjacent to Silver Creek's Silver Creek Lodge.

Group Lessons: Lessons for ages 13 and older (skiing or snowboarding) are 1.75 hours long. Beginners pay $35 in the morning and $30 in the afternoon; intermediates and better pay $40/morning and $35/afternoon. Advanced Bump Clinics cost $35. Snowboarders, intermediates and better, can take a parks and pipes lesson for $35.

First-timer packages: Snowboarders can take the Burton Learn to Ride program, which includes a morning and afternoon lesson, rentals and novice-area trail pass for $69.

Private Lessons: All-day costs $400 ($450 weekends/holidays); half-day, $250/$270; 1-hour session, $75/$90. Additional people, $25 each. Up to 5 people can take all-day and half-day privates; up to 2 people can take 1-hour privates. Reservations recommended; call (877) 441-4386 or (304) 572-1000.

KidStuff [05/06 prices]

Child care: For ages 12 weeks to 10 years old. Ages 12 weeks up to 2 years old cost $70 all day with lunch; $40 half day without lunch; $15 per hour with a two-hour minimum. Ages 2–10 cost $60 all day with lunch; $35 half day without lunch; $12 per hour with two-hour minimum. Reservations required; call (877) 441-4386 or (304) 572-1000

Children's lessons: Lessons for ages 4–12 have two groups: ages 4–6 (skiers only) and 7–12 (skiers and snowboarders), based also on ability level. Full-day programs run from 9 a.m. to 3:45 p.m. Cost is $85 per day ($90 weekends/holidays). Half-day sessions run from 9–11:45 a.m. and 1–3:45 p.m. Cost is $55 per day ($60 weekends/holidays). Rates do not include lift tickets or equipment rental, but all-day sessions include lunch. Reservations recommended.

Special activities: The Kids' Night Out program is offered Wednesdays and Saturdays from 6–9 p.m. for ages 5–12 for $45. Activities includes arts and crafts, snowshoeing, bonfires, story telling, and other indoor and outdoor activities.

Lift tickets [05/06 prices]

	Adult	Junior (7-12)	Student/Sr. (65+)
One day*	$65	$45	$60
Multiday	$60	$41	$55

*Snowshoe has a variety of pricing modes; these are weekend prices. Valid 8:30 a.m.-10 p.m.

Who skis free: Children 6 and younger.

Who skis at a discount: Weekdays are $50 for adults, $35 for juniors and $40 for students and seniors (65+).

Note: Snowshoe sells tickets for night skiing, 4:30–10 p.m., and a Twilight Skiing pass valid 12:30–10 p.m.

 ## Accommodations

The resort is in the process of creating one a signature base villages (in this case, at the mountain's top) at Snowshoe. It holds a vast array of housing of all types, including 1,500 condominium and lodge units and, at the base of the access road, a nice but basic motel. Call (877) 441-4386 or 572-5262.

Allegheny Springs ($$–$$$$) is the poshest lodging in the Village at Snowshoe. It has a fresh-water thermal pool in the courtyard, as well as a full-service restaurant and a day spa.

Rimfire Lodge ($$–$$$$) is set in the heart of the pedestrian village with hotel rooms, plus studio, one- and two-bedroom units. Accommodations are comfortable, but smaller units can be a bit cramped. Most units have kitchens, all have gas-fired fireplaces, and guests get the advantage of underground parking. The intra-resort shuttle stops at the door.

Highland House ($$–$$$$) overlooks the Ball Hooter lift. Units range from hotel rooms and so-called deluxe hotel rooms to two-bedroom condos.

Silver Creek Lodge ($$–$$$$) is the 240-unit, self-contained base facility at Silver Creek. Accommodations range from studios to four-bedroom condos, plus a penthouse. This is an ideal site for families with young children, as the tubing hill, night skiing, terrain park, kids' ski school, child care, rental shop, pool and other amenities are right there.

Expedition Station ($$-$$$) is the resort's second newest condo development, 100 units that opened in February, 2006. Set right in the heart of things-and at the top of the resort's main trails-units run from studios to three-bedrooms, and feature all the expected amenities. The newest development is **Soaring Eagle Lodge ($$-$$$$)**; the first phase of this eventual 140-unit collection, opens for the 2006-07 season. It features luxury condos ranging from studios to three-bedrooms, with such amenities as flat screen televisions, high-speed Internet and direct access to the new high-speed Widowmaker quad lift.

Inn at Snowshoe ($–$$) sits at the base of the access road, 6 miles from the summit village. It has 150 rooms, including some one-bedroom suites.

Off the mountain are a handful of nice B&Bs. The **Elk River Inn** (572-3771; $–$$) is comprised of a 10-room inn, a five-room farmhouse with three shared baths and kitchen, and five kitchen-equipped cabins. It's 5 miles from the access road and offers breakfast, an excellent restaurant and on-site Nordic skiing as well as its own snowboard shop. **The Morning Glory Inn** (572-5000; $–$$$) is located just 3 miles from the access road. It has six large bedrooms with oversized jetted-tub bathrooms, a large, homey public living room and a full breakfast that's substantial and homemade. The **Brazen Head Inn** (339-6917; $–$$$), 7 miles north of the mountain on Rte. 219, offers comfortable B&B lodging and dining. This 20-room roadside inn also offers daily dining and features an Irish style pub.

Dining

This resort has traditionally been a beacon of creative, gourmet dining in West Virginia, but it recently lost the Red Fox, one of the top ski resort restaurants in the country. Still, the resort offers some fine choices.

The **Foxfire Grill** (572-5555; $$–$$$), puts fun into the dining experience. The menu is irreverent and hillbilly tasty. Make sure to try the southern barbecue, fried bologna sammich, ribs or a fried PB&J sandwich for dessert. Modeled after the Harris Grille in Charlotte, North Carolina, **The Village Bistro (572-2213; $$-$$$)** prides itself on offering "international cuisine with a southern-American flair" and features daily blue-plate specials. The large bar area has great views of Snowshoe Mountain.

The decor at the **Junction Restaurant** (572-5800; $$) harkens back to the early days of logging and steam locomotives, with memorabilia from the nearby Cass Scenic Railroad. The food is classic American fare and reasonably good. **Yodeler's Pub** (572-1111; $$) serves sushi once a week from 4:30-9:30 p.m. as well as soup and sandwiches. **The Cheat Mountain Pizza Company** (572-5757; $-$$) serves uninspired pizza, as well as salads, calzones and other Italian fare. For a unique dining adventure, head to the **Sunrise Country Hut** (572-5477; $$$+). After a two-mile ride on a snowmobile or all-terrain vehicle, enjoy an elegant meal in a beautiful, isolated rustic setting for $175 per couple. Also in the village is a Starbucks.

Off mountain, the **Restaurant at the Elk River Inn** (572-3771; $$$) serves a changing menu of truly gourmet regional and international dishes, superb desserts and a nice selection of local microbrews. Reservations are recommended.

The terrific waffle breakfast at **The Boathouse** (572-1000; $), a rustic day lodge set at the base of the Ballhooter Lift, is a great way to start the day. Lunch is also available. At Silver Creek, the **Black Run Sugar House** (572-5746; $) serves fine flapjacks slathered with West Virginia maple syrup.

Apres-ski/nightlife

There's plenty to do here after dark, including night skiing.

For immediate apres-ski head to **The Junction**, packed with tourists, or to **Foxfire Grill** and hang out with patrollers and instructors. Foxfire keeps heating up and the crowd stays late. **Yodeler's Pub** also draws a good bar crowd as the day skiing ends, and then again late in the evening. **Rosa's Cantina**, found a bit out of the way at the top of the Widowmaker lift, serves unremarkable burgers and Mexican fare, but somehow manages to have one fine bar. Gregarious bartenders, good brew and an altogether very friendly locals' atmosphere make it a good spot for a drink.

Later on Snowshoe keeps rocking. **The Connection** is the hottest spot on the mountain. Yes, it's in the Shavers Centre base facility, so there's nothing exotic about it, but the upstairs club scene really does rock. Live bands and a DJ are a regular feature, plus there's pool, foosball, some video games and a large-screen TV. The partying usually lasts well into the night.

Comedy Cellar Bar (572-5440 for performance information) is squirreled away in the basement of the almost dorm-like Mountain Lodge. The bar itself is small and intimate and open Tuesdays–Saturdays at 9 p.m. Local Roy Riley (an good alright performer himself) shares the small stage with one or two pros who frequent the national circuit for a full evening of stand-up comedy. It's definitely adult entertainment, and it's lots of fun.

If you're staying over on the family-oriented Silver Creek side, you have two choices right in Silver Creek Lodge. The **Bear's Den** is on the second floor, a fine spot to take in a quiet beer or hot drink on a cold day. At the **Misty's Sports Bar**, you can quench your thirst while playing billiards or foosball.

Other activities

The **Big Top at Snowshoe Mountain**, located adjacent to the Shavers Centre base lodge is a 15,000 square foot family fun center. Indoors, it houses

Dining: $$$$-Entrees $30+; $$$-$20-$30; $$-$10-$20; $-less than $10.
Accommodations: (double room) $$$$-$200+; $$$-$141-$200; $$-$81-$140; $-$80 and less.

an arcade area with more than 60 video games, table games, billiards and a video cafe. Outdoors, is a Eurobungy. And, there's a stage and performance area, as well. Snowshoe Resort offers **snowmobiling tours.** Reservations can be made at the Adventure Center in the base village. The cost for a one-hour tour is $50 per driver, plus $15 per passenger.

The spectacular **Split Rock Pools**, just across from Allegheny Springs, has an exceptional water slide for the kids and hot tubs for the adults. Entrance is included with packages booked through Snowshoe Central Reservations.

The tubing hill at **Ruckus Ridge Adventure Park** is found at Silver Creek. The cost runs $12 per person for two hours, or $15 for an all-day pass.

Spa Vantage (572-0804)**,** at the Vantage, offers massages, manicures and pedicures, waxing, facials, hair salon, workout facility, men's and women's saunas and outdoor hot tubs. The spa offers the only fitness center open to the public. Prices range from $15 for waxing to $120 for an 80-minute Swedish massage or stone therapy. Guests can purchase day, week, month or year passes to the fitness center.

Nobody is going to mistake this place for a shopper's paradise. The expanding base village represents an attempt to bring in some interesting **shops,** but it's minimal at best. We like **The Chocolate Factory** (572-1289) because, well, who doesn't love a store that sells chocolate? **Wildcat Provisions** sells provisions for your condo, but beware the high-elevation prices. If you're heading to a condo, best to pack in supplies from your local supermarket, then add absolute necessities, or must-be-fresh stuff here. It also rents videos and VCRs, sells gas and makes some pretty good sandwiches.

Getting there and getting around

By car: You're going to end up driving here, even if you fly, since the nearest sizable airport is nearly three hours away. The resort is on Rte. 66 off Rte. 219, about 45 miles south of Elkins, W.V. It's rather remote no matter from which direction you approach. From the south or the west, take I-64, exit at White Sulphur Springs, then take Hwy. 92 and 39 to Marlinton, until you see the Snowshoe signs. From the north, take I-79, exit at Weston (Highway 33 at exit 9), go to Elkins, then south on Hwy. 219. From the East, it's I-81 to Staunton, Rte. 42/39 west to Rte. 28 south; or, from Harrisonburg, Va., take Rte. 33 west to Rte. 28 south.

By plane: Roanoke, Va., airport is about three hours from the resort. Yeager Airport in Charleston, W.V., is about three-and-a-half hours away. Greenbrier Valley Airport in Lewisburg, W.V., about 1.5 hours from Snowshoe, is only served by US Airways, but offers the Greenbrier Valley Airport Shuttle (304-536-1193) for those who choose not to drive.

Getting around: As long as you stay on the mountain, the shuttlebus will reliably get you where you need to go. If you want to go off-mountain, you're going to need a car. Parking is a bit chaotic; however, Rimfire Lodge has underground parking.

Alyeska
Alaska

Summit elevation (lift-served):	**2,750 feet**
Vertical drop:	**2,500 feet**
Base elevation:	**250 feet**

Address: P.O. Box 249
Girdwood, AK 99587
Area code: 907
Ski area phone: 754-1111 or (800) 880-3880
Snow report: 754-7669
Toll-free reservations: (800) 880-3880
Fax: 754-2200
E-mail: info@alyeskaresort.com
Internet: www.alyeskaresort.com
Expert:★★★
Advanced:★★
Intermediate:★★★★
Beginner:★★
First-timer:★★

Number and types of lifts: 9
1 60-passenger tram, 1 high-speed quad, 2 quads, 3 doubles, 2 surface lifts
Skiable acreage: 1,000 acres
Snowmaking: 42 percent
Uphill capacity: 11,416 per hour
Parks & pipes: 2 parks, 1 pipe
Bed base: 533
Nearest lodging: Slopeside, hotel
Resort child care: Babysitting services
Adult ticket, per day: $55 (06/07)
Dining:★★★★
Apres-ski/nightlife:★★
Other activities:★★★

It's easy to miss the turn off Seward Highway to Alyeska. Chances are you'll be mesmerized by the jaw-dropping views over fjord-like Turnagain Arm, where the mountains literally plunge to the sea. What makes it even more unusual is that at this low elevation, the summits—and often much more—of these mountains are above treeline. If you cast your eyes eastward at just the right moment, you can detect a lift on Alyeska, looking like a neat surgical scar on the treeless peak. From the mountain, the view is even more spectacular, perhaps even hazardous.

Just 40 miles southeast of Anchorage, Alyeska offers big-mountain skiing without the threat of altitude sickness. A 60-passenger tram and the high-speed quad that services the summit mean lift lines are short on weekends, nonexistent midweek. Alyeska averages more than 700 inches of snow each season, and had a high of 1,116 inches a couple years back.

The Alyeska Prince Hotel provides luxurious accommodations at the resort's tram base. The tram zips up 2,028 feet of Alyeska's 2,500-foot rise in just 3.5 minutes, rising over the forested lower half to the glaciers and open bowls near the summit and providing a birds-eye view of the mountain's two faces, the original main face and the North Face.

Contrary to popular opinion, the weather in this part of Alaska is quite tolerable in winter, with temperatures an average of 10 to 30 degrees Fahrenheit. What can make it seem colder here is the darkness that prevails during the heart of winter. By mid-February, however, Alyeska boasts more daylight hours than any other ski area in North America. And here's a real bonus for late-night revelers: Lifts don't even open until 10:30 a.m., meaning you can sleep in, have breakfast *and* get first tracks. Normal closing time is 5:30 p.m., but on Friday and Saturday nights from mid-December until mid-March, the lifts remain open to 9:30 p.m.

When Alyeska's skies are clear, the skiing is great. But the slopes sometimes are blanketed with severe whiteout or flat light conditions. Such conditions can be unnerving, especially above treeline, and can cause vertigo in susceptible skiers. Locals advise skiing at night (or late in the day) when visibility is better.

One of Alyeska's pluses during ski season is its proximity to Anchorage, a bustling city with plenty to keep residents entertained through the long winter nights. Alaskans are particularly good at winter celebrations. The U.S. Alpine Skiing Championships will return to the slopes this spring on March 27 to April 3. The 2007 races will feature some of the best alpine ski racers in the United States, including Olympic gold medal winners Ted Ligety (Park City, UT) and Julia Mancuso (Olympic Valley, CA), along with other members of the 2006 U.S. Olympic Ski Team and hopefully newly-crowned FIS World champions. This event always draws a diverse crowd with some great skiing.

We recommend visiting in late February during Fur Rendezvous, Anchorage's winter festival (see *Other Activities*), or early March, to coincide with the Anchorage start of The Iditarod dogsled race. By that time of year, the temperatures start to rise (average high is 30 degrees Fahrenheit; -1 degrees Centigrade) and daylight hours increase (almost 13 hours).

Alaska is one of the most spectacularly beautiful spots on Earth. The incentives for a winter visit are it is low season, so the price is right; crowds are light; and you can ski. Just keep in mind that Anchorage and Alyeska are one time zone beyond the West Coast of the United States. So if it's 9 a.m. in Los Angeles and noon in New York City, it's 8 a.m. at Alyeska.

Mountain layout

♦♦**Expert** ♦**Advanced:** The high-speed Spirit of Alyeska quad carries skiers 1,411 vertical feet to the top of the lift-serviced terrain, which is at the base of the Alyeska Glacier. Up here it's wide-open, above-treeline skiing. The entire 2,500 feet of vertical is skiable in one continuous run, with intermediate to super-expert pitch depending on your choice of route. The adventurous hike to the 3,939-foot summit of Mt. Alyeska, where expert-level Glacier Bowl and the Headwall await.

From the quad, experts can go right and drop down Gail's Gully or Prospector and take a gully left or right of Eagle Rock, then back to the quad. Experts willing to work can take the High Traverse from the quad, arcing through The Shadows between Mt. Alyeska and Max's Mountain, and dropping down through new snow and open steeps; or continue over the ridge to find good steeps and a short section of gladed skiing on Max's Mountain.

The lower half of the steep North Face makes it possible to ski double-black terrain from the upper to the lower tram terminal. You can scout out this gnarly area while you ride up the tram. The upper part (called Tram Pocket) is above treeline; the lower part is heavily forested with two trails—Jim's Branch and Last Chance. Descend Tram Pocket, then cut over to the rest of Alyeska's runs if you want to avoid the gladed area below.

■ **Intermediate:** Alyeska has an unusual combination of open-bowl skiing and trails through the trees directly under Chairs 1 and 4. Take the quad chair, drop into the bowl and ski whatever you can see. It doesn't take much judgment to figure out whether you're getting in over your head, and this bowl gives you plenty of room to traverse out of trouble. The bowl funnels into Waterfall and ends on Cabbage Patch before reaching the base area.

If you take the Spirit quad to the top of the resort, swing left when you get off the chair and follow the Mighty Mite. This takes you past the Glacier Express restaurant in the Glacier Tram Terminal, and back to the quad by three intermediate routes, or tip down South Face (very steep and ungroomed).

●● **Beginner:** Beginners should stick to the area served by Chairs 3 and 7. The area is pretty big, but unfortunately used by everyone on their way home, so it's busy.

● **First-timer:** Don't make the long trip to Alyeska solely to learn to ski. Not a huge amount of easy terrain, plus the flat light problem, could put a serious crimp in those plans.

If "the Alaska experience" (scenery, dogsledding in Iditarod country, being able to brag you "survived" Alaska in winter) is your main goal, then definitely make the trip. You can find some great things to do off the slopes while everyone else skis.

Ride Guide: Because of Mt. Alyeska's natural topography—with its steep vertical and rocky slopes—the entire mountain becomes a natural terrain park. Cat tracks cut across several sections of the upper part of the mountain, creating a series of exhilarating cat-track jumps. You can also catch great air coming off the cat track just above Gun Mount 2. Jumps in "The Fridays" on North Face are a snowboarder's dream, as are hits on Half Moon and Horseshoe off the Silvertip Run. Many aren't on the trail map, so ask the locals and they'll gladly share some secret spots. Heading down the mountain is Lolo's Leap, with 10- to 30-foot drops into the trees. Keep your speed up going into Ego Flats in the bowl area and on the Prince Run heading back to the tram base and the Alyeska Prince Hotel or you'll be walking. In spring, wait until after noontime for the snow to soften for the best riding. The best-kept locals' secret at Alyeska is anytime it's raining on the bottom, you can count on lots of fresh powder up top!

Parks and pipes

Alyeska's two machine-built terrain parks below Eagle Rock and at Chair 7 have several tabletops, rails and quarterpipes. They're the best bets on icy days. Throughout the season, the resort builds one or two halfpipes near the base of Tanaka Hill that are well maintained with a halfpipe groomer.

Cross-country and snowshoeing (visit xcskiresorts.com for more details)

The 10-km. **Winner Creek trail** leaves from Alyeska's base and wanders through woods, across meadows and up and down gentle hills. The trail is not groomed, and locals recommend it for snowshoeing. Groomed and tracked trails are in the nearby **Moose Meadow** area—locals will point you there. It's maintained by volunteers. Rental equipment is available at the Alyeska Prince Hotel's rental shop. In spring you need to wait late enough into the morning for the ice cover to melt. Lessons are not regularly scheduled, so make advance reservations with the ski school by calling 754-2280.

If you are a serious cross-country enthusiast, Anchorage is the place to go. About 115 km. of groomed cross-country trails are in **Kincaid, Russian Jack** and **Far North Bicentennial parks**. Kincaid Park is the best, with more than 1,500 acres covered by trails for all abilities. The Nordic Skiing Association of Anchorage (561-0949; grooming report, 248-6667) maintains the trails, all supported by donations and volunteer labor (Hint: If you use the trails, please make a donation.). NSAA puts out a great map of the trails, printed on a water-resistant paper.

Lessons (06/07 prices)

Group lessons: Alyeska packages its ski and snowboard lessons, a real benefit for those traveling from the Lower 48. For example, adult intermediate and advanced skiers can get a lesson, lift ticket and rentals for $60, or the lesson alone for $35. (The snowboard price is $65 for the package, $35 just for the lesson.)

First-timer package: First-timers pay $50 for a lift ticket-lesson-rental package, snowboard novices pay $55; for the lesson alone for both groups, it's $35.

Private lessons: Skiing, telemarking or snowboarding cost $60 an hour, $30 for extra students. Telemark lessons are not regularly scheduled, so make reservations with the ski school, 754-2280. If you're enrolled in a private lesson, ask about discounted lift and rental prices.

Special programs: The Challenge Alaska Adaptive Ski School, a chapter of Disabled Sports USA, provides skiing for the disabled: all disabilities, all ages, by reservation only. A skier with a disability, and buddy, may buy discount lift tickets and rent adaptive ski equipment. Open daily, usually December 15 to April 15. The Alyeska Price Hotel and Tramway are fully wheelchair-accessible, and Challenge Alaska has material on other wheelchair-accessible accommodations and amenities. Challenge Alaska, 3350 Commercial Drive, Suite 208, Anchorage AK 99501; 344-7399; fax 344-7349.

Racing: A $1-per-run race course is open on selected dates.

KidStuff [06/07 prices]

Child care: Ages 6 months to 10 years. At Little Bears Playhouse in nearby Girdwood, children ages 6 to 14 months cost $25 for a half day and $40 for a full day. Kids 15 months to 35 months are $22 for a half day, $36 for a full day. For children ages 3 to 10, the cost is $21 for a half-day, $34 for a full day. An up-to-date immunization record and a complete physical exam signed by a doctor are required. Reservations are a must; call 783-2116 or ask when you reserve lodging. Little Bears is open 7 a.m. to 6 p.m. weekdays, 10 a.m. to 6 p.m. on Saturdays, through the ski season (closed on Sundays). Babysitting service may be available by appointment during ski season, three days in advance, through the Alyeska Prince Hotel's guest service desk; call (800) 880-3880 or 754-1111.

Children's lessons: Cubs and Super-Cubs caters to ages 3–4 learning to ski; Mini-Riders is for ages 5–7 learning to snowboard. Cost is $40, including lift ticket, one-hour lesson and rental; available only on weekends and Anchorage School District holidays. Group lessons for ages 5–13 for skiing and 8-13 for snowboarding are offered daily and during Anchorage School District holidays. A two-hour lesson, all-day lift ticket and rental package ranges from $45–$55, depending on ability level. If you don't need rentals, ask about discounted pricing.

Lift tickets [06/07 prices]

	Adult	Child (8-13)
One day	$50	$25
Three days*	$126 ($42/day)	$60 ($20/day)

*The best deal on multiday tickets comes with lodging-lift packages.

Who skis free: Children 7 and younger when skiing with a ticketed adult.

Who skis at a discount: Students with ID (14–17) and seniors (60-69) pay $33 for one day; $84 for three days, $39 for half day. Ages 70 and older pay $10. Adult guests of the Alyeska Prince Hotel pay $40 per day for all lifts and all hours. A family of four skis for $119 per day.

Note: Keep in mind that winter days here, are shorter than they are farther south. The lifts don't start running until mid-morning at 10:30 a.m., but the "ski day" ends at 5:30 p.m. (Daylight lingers for about 90 minutes after sunset in early February, and you can see very well.) Night skiing on 27 trails covering 2,000 vertical feet runs Fridays and Saturdays 4:30–9:30 p.m. mid-December through mid-March: Adults cost $24; children, $16; seniors $21.

Accommodations

The **Alyeska Prince Hotel** (800-880-3880; 754-1111; $$$–$$$$) is a self-contained resort. Package rates begin at $229 per room per night, single or double occupancy and include lodging, breakfast and lift tickets. There is no charge for up to two children younger than 18 who are staying in the same room in existing bedding with a maximum of two adults. The hotel is a Prince hotel, but its architecture is faintly reminiscent of the grand Fairmont hotels, such as the Fairmont Banff Springs Hotel and

Fairmont Chateau Lake Louise. Though the hotel has 307 spacious rooms, several restaurants, shops and other guest facilities, it has a very intimate feel. The Alyeska Tramway is right outside the door, or you can ride Chair 7 to the lower-elevation terrain at the ski area's base.

Other than the hotel, lodging is in condos or bed-and-breakfast inns. The **Winner Creek Bed & Breakfast** (783-5501; $–$$) is a log lodge owned by 30-year Alaska residents Victor and Kim Duncan. It's within walking distance of Alyeska. **The Gingerbread House** (783-1952; $-$$) in Girdwood is open year-round and offers suites with private fireplaces. **The Carriage House B&B and Stables** (783-9464; $-$$) is a timber-frame lodge in a secluded part of Girdwood, and just a short walk from the best dining in town. **Alyeska Accommodations** (783-2000) is a place to start, or you can get a list of B&Bs on the Girdwood community website, www.girdwoodalaska.com. B&B rates range from $45-$125 per night, based on double occupancy; condos range from $125-$250.

The larger bed base is in **Anchorage**, a 35- to 55-minute drive depending on weather: Major hotels include the **Anchorage Hilton** (800-445-8667; 272-7411; $$$–$$$$), with views of the Chugach Mountains and Cook Inlet; **Holiday Inn** (800-465-4329; 279-8671; $–$$); **Sheraton Anchorage** (800-478-8700; 276-8700; $$–$$$$); and **Westmark Anchorage** (800-544-0970; 276-7676; $-$$). The **Hotel Captain Cook** (800-843-1950; 276-6000; $$$–$$$$) has a great downtown location, very convenient to the Fur Rendezvous festivities, shopping and restaurants. It also has one of the best hotel health clubs we've come across. Another place we like downtown is the **Historic Anchorage Hotel** (800-544-0988; 272-4553; $$–$$$$). It's quietly elegant, with 10 suites (each different), 16 standard rooms and complimentary continental breakfast.

We've listed a small portion of the lodging that's available. We expected lodging prices to be rock bottom in winter, but Anchorage does a steady convention business then. Prices aren't as high as they are in summer, but most are in the $100 to $200 per night range. More options are listed in the excellent free Visitors Guide, available by writing to the **Anchorage Convention & Visitors Bureau**, 524 W. Fourth Ave., Anchorage, AK 99501-2212. Phone, 276-4118; fax 278-5559; website: www.anchorage.net. Or call **ACVB's Log Cabin Visitor Center** at 274-3531 to get travel advice from a real, live person. But remember the time difference and try to call mid-day in Alaska.

 ## Dining

These are some of our favorite restaurants; see the Visitors Guide for more selections.

In the Alyeska Prince Hotel the **Pond Cafe** ($-$$) serves breakfast, lunch and dinner with a California-Alaskan menu—try the caribou stew with a big sourdough cheese roll and lots of vegetables. Elegant dinners are the Prince's forté. We heartily recommend the **Katsura Teppanyaki** ($$$), open for dinner five nights a week. It seats about 20 diners around a U-shaped table facing the chefs who prepare the meals in front of you. The four-diamond **Seven Glaciers Restaurant and Lounge** ($$$), on the second level of the Glacier Terminal at 2,300 feet, gives you a view that's beyond belief and the gourmet meals are excellent. Call 754-2237 for reservations at all three.

The Bake Shop (783-2831; $) in the ski area base lodge has superb soups, sandwiches, and energy-filled, buttered sticky buns. Lots of locals, ski instructors and patrollers eat here. **Jack Sprat** (754-5225; $$) right next to Chair 3 offers an eclectic selection of world cuisine—everything from brie quesadillas to a black-bean burger.

Alyeska vicinity:

Dining: $$$$-Entrees $30+; $$$-$20-$30; $$-$10-$20; $-less than $10.
Accommodations: (double room) $$$$-$200+; $$$-$141-$200; $$-$81-$140; $-$80 and less.

Perhaps the best restaurant in the area is the **Double Musky Inn** (783-2822; $$$), a mile from the lifts on Crow Creek Road. It's mind-boggling to find great Cajun food in Alaska (go for the French Pepper Steak). Service is excellent and the decor is a delight—Mardi Gras beads everywhere and posters on the ceiling. Dress is casual—some Alaskans wear muddy boots to dinner. Busy nights may require a two-hour wait, but it's worth it. No reservations, opens at 5 p.m. Tuesday through Thursday, 4:30 p.m. Friday through Sunday; closed Mondays.

Chair Five (783-2500; $-$$) is casual and big on burgers and pizza, but also offers an interesting and changing menu of pasta, meats and fresh pasta. A favorite is pasta primavera with sundried tomatoes. It's in the Girdwood business district next to the Post Office. **Turnagain House** (653-7500; $$-$$$), a white-tablecloth restaurant looking out on Turnagain Arm halfway to Anchorage, has a reputation for fine seafood and other dishes with excellent service.

Anchorage:

A special-occasion restaurant for locals is **Simon & Seafort's Saloon & Grill** (274-3502; $$-$$$). It specializes in seafood and steak. Take a walk through the bar and try to find the on-purpose errors in the paintings. Ask for a table next to the large picture window, and get there before dark so you can admire the view across Knik Arm. **Marx Brothers Cafe** (278-2133, reservations required; $$$) is known for inventive continental cuisine, a notable wine list and impeccable service in a cozy frame-house setting that reminds us of a small New England inn. **Southside Bistro** (348-0888, reservations recommended; $$-$$$), with its highly inventive Italian and fusion cuisine, has frequent menu changes, a huge wine list, a bright and open atmosphere, excellent service and white tablecloths (but wear whatever you want).

For great views, especially at cocktail time, try the top-floor **Crow's Nest** (276-6000; $$$) at the Hotel Captain Cook, or **Top of the World** (265-7111; $$$) in the Hilton. **Josephine's** (276-8700; $$$) in the Sheraton also has a view, and is a good choice for Sunday brunch. Make reservations if dining at any of these restaurants.

Many Japanese have settled in Anchorage, and restaurants such as **Akaihana** (276-2215; $$) and **Tempura Kitchen** (277-2741; $$) are among the Asian eateries. They offer tempura, sukiyaki and other cooked dishes as well as sushi and sashimi. Anchorage also has Thai, Chinese and Korean restaurants.

For moderately priced, delicious food—and great beer—head to **Glacier Brewhouse** (274-2739; $$) on Fifth Avenue. For a hearty breakfast, check out **Gwennie's Old Alaska Restaurant** (243-2090; $), which serves generous omelets with thick-cut bacon and toasted sourdough bread.

Families should head to **Sourdough Mining Co.** (563-2272; $) for great ribs and corn fritters; **Hogg Brothers Cafe** (276-9649; $) for wow omelets; and the **Royal Fork Buffet** (276-0089; $) or **Lucky Wishbone** (272-3454; $) for the best fried chicken.

Apres-ski/nightlife

The **Aurora Bar and Lounge** in the Alyeska Prince Hotel has a somewhat lively atmosphere in the bar, where skiers can watch sports on TV. Patrons may play the piano, sing and dance, and make the evening as lively as they want. The lounge is quieter, with a stone fireplace and comfortable sofas and chairs. For apres-ski, head to the **Sitzmark Bar** at the DayLodge for burgers and live bands on Friday and Saturday nights during ski season. The **Double Musky** and **Chair 5** also have taverns.

Anchorage has a highly developed nightlife and cultural scene, a legacy of pipeline days, long winter nights, and generous doses of oil-patch money. The city reportedly had an orchestra before it had paved streets.

We love wacky watering holes that have unique character. Anchorage has two great ones, but unfortunately, one is closed most of the winter. For loud rock and dancing try **Chilkoot Charlie's**, 2435 Spenard Rd., "where we cheat the other guy and pass the savings on to you." (They sell T-shirts with that slogan—it's a great souvenir.) Chilkoot's is huge—six bars with about 30 beers on tap, two stages (the night we were there during Fur Rondy, one stage had a rockin' band and the other had the Fur Bikini contest), pool tables and games, and sports on TV (though it's impossible to hear the audio). Generally, the ratio of men to women is about seven to one, and any attire goes—one February night, we saw people dressed in gym shorts; others in business suits and cocktail dresses. The other unique nightclub is **Mr. Whitekeys' Fly By Night Club**, famed for its Spam appetizers and satirical, summertime Whale Fat Follies show. The club does a "Christmas in Spenard" show, but after that, it's closed for the winter, much to our disappointment. (We've seen the summer show; it's a hoot.)

Humpy's on Sixth Avenue has 36 beers on tap and occasional live entertainment. For quieter dancing and a slightly older clientele try **Legends** at the Sheraton, **Whale's Tail** at the Hotel Captain Cook, or the lounge at the **Golden Lion Best Western**. For country music, head to **Last Frontier Bar** or **Buckaroo Club.**

For theater, opera, drama and movies, buy the local newspaper (*Anchorage Daily News*). There's a Thursday entertainment tabloid that's very helpful too (*Anchorage Press*). You may be surprised at the visiting artists and productions at the **Alaska Center for the Performing Arts** downtown. For recorded information, call 263-2901.

Other activities

The variety of winter activities is staggering. We have room to list just a sampling. We encourage you to get the excellent free Visitors Guide from the **Anchorage Convention & Visitors Bureau**, 524 W. Fourth Ave., Anchorage, AK 99501-2212. Phone, 276-4118; website, www.anchorage.net.

At Alyeska Resort, **Glacier Tubing Park** is fun for the entire family. It's at the base of Tanaka Hill, offers lighted terrain and surface lift service, and is open Friday–Sunday.

Think of Alaska in winter and you think of **dogsleds.** Call Chugach Dog Sled Tours in Girdwood near the ski area (783-2266 for reservations, last-minute calls don't work; or make reservations through the guest services desk at the Alyeska Prince Hotel). If you're staying in Anchorage, drive about 20 minutes to the hamlet of Chugiak to Mush a Dog Team-Gold Rush Days (688-1391). As you travel the trail, you'll see a recreation of an Alaskan gold miner's camp. You'll be amazed at how cramped and cold those unheated tents must have been.

Dogsled races are a focal point of **Fur Rendezvous,** held annually in mid-February. The World Championship Sled Dog Race is the sprint (some sprint—25 miles a day for three days) counterpart to the more famous endurance race, **The Iditarod**, which follows Fur Rondy on the first Saturday in March. Fur Rondy also has fireworks, a snow sculpture contest, a small carnival, a snowshoe softball tournament (hilarious for spectators) and the World Champion-ship Dog Weight Pull, a contest detailed in Jack London's book, *Call of the Wild.* Alaskan Natives come from all parts of the state for Fur Rondy, and many wear traditional fur parkas, stunning works of art with intricate patterns. By the way, if seeing people wearing fur offends you, don't come at this time. You'll only work yourself into a lather over something that has kept native Alaskans warm for centuries. If you're a dog lover, don't miss the start of The Iditarod, when about 1,500 sled dogs are parked on the main street in downtown Anchorage. Early in the morning, you can visit with the dogs and the mushers.

Several companies offer **flightseeing tours** via helicopter or fixed-wing planes. It is

Dining: $$$$-Entrees $30+; $$$-$20-$30; $$-$10-$20; $-less than $10.
Accommodations: (double room) $$$$-$200+; $$$-$141-$200; $$-$81-$140; $-$80 and less.

the best way to see Alaska's spectacular mountains and glaciers and well worth the cost. We flew with Era Helicopters (800-478-1947; 248-4422; www.eraaviation.com) into the rugged Chugach Mountains that border Anchorage. On an overcast day, you'll gain an appreciation for the arduous conditions that 19th-century mushers endured to bring supplies over mountain passes from Seward to Anchorage. On a clear day, you'll see Mt. McKinley off in the distance, its broad hulk standing apart from surrounding mountains. Alpine Air (783-2360) operates tours out of Girdwood. They will pick up at the Alyeska Prince Hotel.

Alyeska offers **snowcat skiing and heliskiing** with more than 750 square miles of back-country slopes. Chugach Powder Guides (783-4355) operates out of the Alyeska Prince Hotel. A full-day heli-skiing package is $675, with a guarantee of 16,000–20,000 vertical. A full-day snowcat package is $195. Reservations required. **Tandem paragliding** with a certified pilot 2,300 feet above the ski area is another thrill for visitors. Available daily in summer and by appointment in winter. Call Alyeska for more details, 754-2275.

In Anchorage, the **Anchorage Museum of History and Art** (343-4326) is a must-see, with excellent displays that show 10,000 years of Alaskan civilization, from ancient days through the Gold Rush and the great earthquake of 1964. The **Alaska Native Heritage Center** (800-315-6608; 330-8000) provides an introduction to Alaska's native population. Although it's not fully open in winter, special events such as cultural gatherings and art shows are reason enough to visit. If you're in law enforcement, don't miss the **Alaska State Trooper Museum** (800-770-5050), which tells the history of the state's law enforcement through exhibits, memorabilia and photographs.

The **Northern Lights** are awesome. If you've ever seen photos of the aurora borealis, with its green, blue and red streaks of light across an ink-black sky, you have an inkling of how magnificent this phenomenon is. For forecasts on when to plan your trip to maximize the chances of seeing the Northern Lights, go to this Internet site: www.geo.mtu.edu/weather/aurora. The Alyeska Prince Hotel has a unique Northern Lights wake-up service and a seven-minute electronic display of the aurora on the ceiling of the hotel's three-story lobby.

Getting there and getting around

By air: Anchorage International Airport is served by many major airlines. East Coast skiers who want to make the trek to Alyeska would be well advised to find a travel agent who specializes in Alaska in order to find the best airfares and packages.

By car: Alyeska Resort is 45 miles south of downtown Anchorage. Get on Gambell Street south, which becomes the Seward Highway, Rte. 1, along Turnagain Arm, which has one of the highest tides in the world. The drive is quite scenic; try to alternate drivers so everyone can admire the view. Bring your camera and lots of film for the Dall sheep, moose and bald eagles often seen along the way. Turn left at the Girdwood/Alyeska highway turn-off, the resort is 3 miles up the road.

Getting around: If you stay in Anchorage or at the Alyeska Prince Hotel, you can get by without a car. Alaska Sightseeing or The Magic Bus (268-6311) can take you from the city to the resort with advance reservations. Ask at the hotel desk. Otherwise, you'll need a car. The Alyeska area (town of Girdwood) doesn't have a local transportation system, but the hotel runs a continuous free shuttle during mountain operations and evenings by request. If you want to try restaurants we listed, such as the Double Musky, make arrangements with the bell desk.

North Lake Tahoe Area

Alpine Meadows
Squaw Valley USA
Northstar-at-Tahoe
Diamond Peak
Mt. Rose
Sugar Bowl
with Reno, Nevada

Toll-free reservations:
(888) 434-1262, North Lake Tahoe
(800) 468-2463, Incline Village/Crystal Bay
(888) 448-7366, Reno
Internet: www.mytahoevacation.com (North Lake Tahoe)
www.renolaketahoe.com (Reno)
E-mail: info@mytahoevacation.com (North Lake Tahoe) or
info@renolaketahoe.com (Reno)
Dining:★★★
Apres-ski/nightlife:★★(near the lake) ★★★★(Reno)
Other activities:★★★

Few regions on the North American continent have the ski-resort diversity of the Lake Tahoe region. When you consider the elements of a perfect ski vacation—variety of terrain, good snow, comfortable lodging, beautiful scenery, a wide choice of restaurants and nightlife, myriad other activities, accessibility—Lake Tahoe would rank near the top in all but a couple of categories (and it would be above the median in those).

Lake Tahoe, one of the largest and most stunningly beautiful mountain lakes in the world, straddles the border of California and Nevada about 200 miles east of San Francisco. Tahoe has received accolades from travel writers for more than a century. Mark Twain was one of the first to note its beauty. In 1861, he wrote in "Roughing It," Tahoe was "the fairest picture the whole earth affords." Because the lake is so deep and doesn't freeze, it retains its sapphire-blue color throughout the winter. Its name comes from a Washoe Indian word meaning "lake in the sky"—the lake is about 6,200 feet above sea level.

Tahoe is best divided into two regions for vacation purposes. Though you can run yourself ragged by trying to visit every major area in a week, it's better to concentrate on the North Shore or the South Shore. The two regions provide very different vacation experiences.

South Tahoe is densely developed, with high-rise casino-hotels hugging the state line, frequent big-name entertainment and non-stop, apres-ski activity. It has three ski/snowboard resorts, one of which overlooks the twin towns of Stateline and South Lake Tahoe. Speaking in general terms, South Shore tends to attract first-time visitors who live outside California and Nevada, while the North Shore attracts fewer first-time visitors, but loads of Californians.

North Shore has history, is more spread out and a lot quieter, and has an amazing concentration of excellent skiing and snowboarding facilities. Resort skiing in California started in the North Lake Tahoe region in the late 1930s, when a group of investors, including Walt Disney, started Sugar Bowl. The 1960 Winter Olympics were staged at another North Tahoe resort, Squaw Valley USA. North Tahoe isn't as densely developed as the South Shore, but it covers a lot more miles of the lakeshore. Its Nevada side has casinos, but they are not as prominent as the ones at South Shore. The California side of North Tahoe is dominated by condos that are vacation homes for Northern Californians. There are restaurants and nightlife, but things get quiet once the sun goes down. The North Tahoe region has 12 Alpine ski facilities (the lake is visible from five of them) and six cross-country areas. The five largest Alpine resorts are Squaw Valley USA, Alpine Meadows, Northstar-at-Tahoe, Diamond Peak, Mt. Rose and Sugar Bowl. More and more visitors are staying nearby in Reno. It is the air hub and has far more dining and lodging opportunities than the towns on the lake. However, Reno is a relatively long drive from these areas, except Mt. Rose, which is its neighborhood mountain.

Note: If you need child care for your infant, ski elsewhere. None of the North Lake Tahoe resorts offers child care for children younger than age 2. Resorts that accept children 2 and older require toddlers to be toilet-trained. They also require a birth certificate with proof of age.

Squaw Valley USA

Squaw Valley USA is the best-known resort in the region, because it hosted the 1960 Winter Olympics. It offers some of the finest skiing in the United States. There aren't many trail-cut runs here, just wide-open snowfields—4,000 acres of them. In fact, Squaw boasts no named runs—the lifts have names and then skiers and riders can pick their own way down the mountain. Some might say "mountains," since Squaw skis more like a series of smaller resorts rather than one large entity. Anything within the boundaries can be skied by anyone daring enough to challenge the mountain. All levels can push their limits here—experts and beginners alike ride side by side on the cable car to the top.

Access starts at the base with the 28-person Funitel. Or board the 110-person cable car. Or start with the Squaw One high-speed quad and then connect to other lifts. Six separate peaks, each with every conceivable exposure, overlook Lake Tahoe.

The Funitel, which carries 15 people seated and 13 standing, replaced Squaw Valley's gondola and follows its course from the base to the Gold Coast facility. The Pulse, a custom gondola, connects the resort's two mid-mountain complexes at High Camp and Gold Coast. It has five cabins that operate with the push of a button. These lifts enable guests to take a mountain tour without putting on skis or a snowboard (of course, skiers and boarders will use them, too). You can ride the cable car to High Camp, the Pulse lift to Gold Coast, then download on the Funitel to the mountain's base.

If you haven't been to Squaw recently, you won't recognize it. The first two phases of Intrawest's new $250-million Village at Squaw Valley—First Ascent and 22 Station—are now open. The European-style pedestrian village has a total of 286 slopeside condominiums, 17 boutique shops and seven restaurants.

 ## Mountain layout

♦♦ **Expert** ♦ **Advanced:** Extreme skiers will be in heaven at Squaw. Thirty percent of the runs are either single- or double-black diamond. Two popular spots are the Palisades above Siberia Bowl and Eagle's Nest at the top of KT-22. In fact, KT-22 has such a variety of terrain that some season-pass holders ski the peak exclusively. The Granite Chief, Headwall and Silverado lifts access some of the most challenging terrain in the world. Locals will take you to terrain that resembles an elevator shaft.

■ **Intermediate:** Intermediate terrain has challenge and variety. Siberia Express accesses the largest intermediate bowl, advanced levels turn left getting off the lift, intermediates traverse to the right, which feeds into the Gold Coast terrain and other wide-open slopes. Newport, Gold Coast and Emigrant lifts offer acres of open-bowl intermediate terrain. Intermediates will like the Shirley Lake area served by a high-speed quad and a triple chair. For tougher runs, take the Headwall Express Lift, then opt for Chicken Bowl or drop over the back of the ridge to Sun Bowl, a beauty if conditions are right. Or, ride the KT-22 chair, head west on the Saddle Traverse, then drop into the Saddle, which is groomed.

Squaw Valley USA

Summit elevation:	**9,050 feet**
Vertical drop:	**2,850 feet**
Base elevation:	**6,200 feet**

Address: Box 2007, Olympic Valley CA 96146
Area code: 530
Ski area phone: 583-6985
Snow report: 583-6955
Toll-free reservations: (888) 766-9321
or (800) 545-4350
Fax: 581-7106
E-mail: squaw@squaw.com
Internet: www.squaw.com

Number of lifts: 34–1 cable car, 1 Funitel,
1 Pulse, 3 high-speed six-packs, 4 high-speed quads,
1 quad, 8 triples, 10 doubles, 3 surface lifts,
2 moving carpets
Snowmaking: 10 percent
Skiable acreage: 4,000 lift-served acres
Uphill capacity: 49,000 per hour
Parks & pipes: 3 terrain parks, 1 superpipe,
1 halfpipe
Bed base: 3,500 within 3 miles
Nearest lodging: Slopeside
Resort child care: Yes, 3 years and older
Adult ticket, per day: $53-S65 (05/06 prices)
Expert:★★★★★
Advanced:★★★★★ **Intermediate:**★★★
Beginner:★★★ **First-timer:**★★★

The Mountain Run is a crowded end-of-the-day cruise: Top to bottom, it's a hefty 3-mile run. Another great cruise is Home Run. Or give the Olympic High ski run a try. It follows the route of the original 1960 Olympic men's downhill. It begins above the bottom shack of Headwall and heads to the base, bypassing the Mountain Run entirely.

●● **Beginner** ● **First-timer:** Though Squaw Valley's well publicized steep terrain has given it a menacing reputation, it has a little-known surprise: This is a great spot to learn. Squaw has a gentle bowl at the top of the cable car known as Bailey's Beach, served by two slow-moving lifts. Though Bailey's Beach is not physically separated from the other terrain, better skiers rarely use it. Beginners usually long to head toward any summit just like the big boys and girls, and here they can. They just ride the cable car up to High Camp (where they'll also find restaurants, shelter and an outdoor ice rink), and at the end of the day, ride the cable car back down. The Papoose Learning Area is tucked away on the lower mountain near the Far East lift and has a double chairlift and three surface lifts for first-timers.

Ride Guide: As much fun as Squaw's manmade features are, Mother Nature's features still can't be beat here. The in-bounds riding gets insane and, unfortunately, gets tracked up quickly by hordes of riders who know all the mountain's secrets. When you have Sierra Cement at the lower elevations, book it to Granite Chief, where you'll find powder instead. And when it's freshies all over, you just can't go wrong, especially since they can be accompanied by bluebird days that make you swear you've died and gone to heaven. On those days, make sure to hike Granite Chief, hightail it to the cornice on Siberia or seek out the Hanging Gardens. Gotta huck cliffs? Head to Palisades. If you don't like bumps, skip Headwall.

Parks and pipes

Let's just say that Squaw is monstrous, and so are its parks and pipes. In various locations you'll find a superpipe, halfpipes, quarterpipes, plus terrain features such as tabletops, rails, rollers and volcanoes. All parks and pipes are cut daily and the Riviera halfpipe is cut twice, once for night sessions and again after night operations so the pipe is fresh in the morning.

The pipe sessions can definitely get heated—prepare to be humbled by locals.

The Mainline Terrain Park is the home of Squaw's legendary Mainline Superpipe, a 550-plus-foot-long pipe with 17-foot walls that overlooks Lake Tahoe. You won't know whether you're catching your breath because of the exertion or the view. Just below the pipe are an assortment of rails—a 30-foot single-kink rail, a 40-foot S rail, a 52-foot S box, a 40-foot double-kink rail, and the massive 78-foot swirly rail—and a wide-open area of tabletops and jumps. Throughout the season, depending upon weather, additional features may include hips, rollers, a snowcross course and volcanoes.

Central Park, in the Riviera area just below the top terminal of the Funitel, is the heart of Squaw's intermediate parks and pipes. Intermediate riders and freeskiers will find a standard halfpipe, tables, jumps, rails, boxes, and whatever the park designers feel like putting in here, all accessed by a dedicated lift. You can reach it from the High Camp lift too. Riviera is lit until 9 p.m. and has a pumping sound system to keep you going.

Belmont Park is for kids and people new to parks and pipes. It has small berms, rolls, and bumps to help you get used to catching air.

 ## Lessons (05/06 prices)

Group lessons: Beginner to intermediate skiers and snowboarders get instruction through a "Ski Your Pro" format, where instructors are assigned to training areas on the mountain, and skiers/riders can join in on the hour for $47. Higher-level skiers/riders get two-hour workshops on specific skills, such as moguls, powder, gate training, freeriding, halfpipe and terrain park, also for $47. A book of five two-hour lessons is $185.

First-timer package: A Fun in the Sun Adventure Package that includes a beginner lift ticket, rentals and a two-hour lesson is $84 for skiing or snowboarding. The same package for just the Papoose Learning Area is $65.

Private lessons: $99 for one hour; $50 for each additional person.

Special programs: An introduction to telemarking lesson includes beginner lift ticket, rentals and two-hour lesson for $84; reservations required, call (530) 581-7263. Advanced Ski Clinics are one-day, three-day and five-day programs to help you become an all-mountain skier. Go to Squaw's website for dates, prices and to make online reservations. Squaw Valley also has a full-service adaptive ski school.

Racing: A coin-op course is at the top of the Shirley Lake Express.

 ## KidStuff (05/06 prices)

Child care: Ages 3–5 years. All-day care at the licensed SquawKids' Children's Center costs $99 ($105 holidays) with lunch, activities and supervision, while half-day care is $63 (no lunch; $85 holidays). Reservations are highly recommended; call (530) 581-7166. Parents must provide current immunization records and a birth certificate for 3-4 year olds.

Other options: Baby's Away (800-446-9030; 530-544-2229) rents and will deliver baby items (cribs, strollers, toys, etc.) to your hotel or condo. For **babysitting referrals,** call North Lake Tahoe Resort Association (800-434-1262; 530-583-3494).

Children's lessons: Ages 4–12 can take an all-day lesson, with lunch, lift ticket, activities and instruction for $99 ($129 holidays). The half-day price is $99 ($129 holidays) and includes a snack instead of lunch. Snowboard lessons start at age 8. Reservations strongly recommended; call (530) 581-7166.

Lift tickets (05/06 prices)

	Adult	Child (Up to 12)
One day	$65	$5
Three days	$166 ($55/day)	$15 ($5/day)
Five days	$267 ($53/day)	$25 ($5/day)

Who skis free: Ages 76 and older. Those older than 85 are paid $5 in resort script.

Who skis at a discount: Tickets for ages 65-75 are $39 and youth ages 13-15 are $49. Non-skiers can ride the cable car and gondolas for $19 for adults, $15 for seniors and youth, $5 for children 4-12, and free for ages 3 and younger. Full-day lift tickets include night skiing until 9 p.m. (mid-December through mid-March). Night skiing costs $20 for adults, $15 for seniors/youth and $5 for children.

Accommodations–Squaw Valley

The resort has several lodging choices. All have easy access to the slopes. If you're staying here, it is best to rent a car if you'd like to explore dining and nightlife in Truckee and Tahoe City. For **central reservations at Squaw Valley** call (800) 545-4350.

The Village at Squaw Valley (866-818-6963; $$$$) has a brand new collection of luxury one-, two- and three-bedroom condominiums across from the lifts, each with kitchen, fireplace and balcony. Other amenities are laundry facilities and underground parking. Four outdoor hot tubs are reached by heated sidewalks.

The **PlumpJack Squaw Valley Inn** (800-323-7666; 530-583-1576; $$$–$$$$), with 61 rooms, is right across from the cable car building. The remodeled rooms have down comforters, hooded bathrobes and VCRs. A lap pool and two hot tubs further pamper the guest. The lodging blends intimate country charm with the style and service of a grand European hotel. Its name honors Sir John Falstaff, Shakespeare's swaggering, high-living character. Its restaurant is excellent (see *Dining*).

Resort at Squaw Creek (800-327-3353; 530-583-6300; $$$$) is a luxury hotel that blends well with the valley. It connects with the ski area by its own lift, and is a self-contained resort, with five restaurants and three pools (one of which is open in winter), several hot tubs, health and fitness center, full-service spa, cross-country skiing and an ice-skating rink.

Squaw Valley Lodge (800-992-9920; in California, 800-922-9970; $$$–$$$$) is only a few yards' walk from the lifts. The lodge boasts a fully equipped health club, free covered parking and kitchenettes in the units.

The Olympic Village Inn (800-845-5243; 530-583-1501; $$$–$$$$) has five hot tubs, and all units have kitchens. **Red Wolf Lodge** (800-791-0081; $$$$) at the base of Red Dog Chair next to the Children's Center has studio, one- and two-bedroom units with full kitchenettes.

Alpine Meadows

It's hard not to like Alpine Meadows. For every level, particularly intermediate and advanced, Alpine Meadows has something to offer. It has expert terrain, sweeping intermediate bowls and scenic trails, and a good beginner area. The view from the base lodge suggests that Alpine is a relatively small area. Not so. You'll see just how big it is when you take the Summit Six (a six-seater) and see it expand beneath you. In the Lake Tahoe area, Alpine Meadows has traditionally been the ski area with the earliest and longest season (it's open well into May and some years, until July 4).

Mountain layout

♦♦ Expert: This level has plenty of great bowl skiing and riding and enough steeps to keep hearts in throats. Scott Chair, which accesses expert terrain, was upgraded from a double to a triple. The added weight of the triple chairs allows it to run more often in bad weather—good news for experts who want to get to this area during a snowfall.

Here's a route suggestion: Take the Summit Six and descend into the expert Wolverine Bowl, Beaver Bowl and Estelle Bowl (they're to the right as you ascend), then take the Summit Six again and cruise into the upper-blue territory of the Alpine Bowl. Finally, take the Alpine Bowl Chair and traverse to the Sherwood Bowls on the back side of the area or take the High Yellow Traverse to the Saddle Bowl. When you come up the Sherwood high-speed quad, drop down Our Father—and you can say a few en route—then head to Scott Chair and try out Scott Chute for a direct plunge, or take it easy on tree-lined roundabouts. By then your knees will have earned a cruise. The Promised Land has great tree skiing for top skiers.

♦ Advanced: Take your warm-up in Alpine Bowl, staying to skier's right on Rock Garden and Yellow Trail as you cruise down to the Hot Wheels chair. Then head for the Back Bowls. If there's a line at Hot Wheels, you also can reach the bowls via the Scott Chair through the blue-square Lakeview area to Ray's Rut. Depending on your mood, you can stay on the groomed Sherwood run to check out the scene, or traverse to the steeper Sherwood Face or South Face. You may want to stay here all day—one of our staffers did.

■ Intermediate: Plenty of terrain for this level off these lifts: Alpine Bowl, Roundhouse and Lakeview. The Lakeview Chair is appropriately named—it has great views of Lake Tahoe from the top. The terrain off the Kangaroo lift is a short intermediate run, but much of it is devoted to race programs and the terrain park. All this activity creates a narrow descent, something many intermediates are uncomfortable with.

●● Beginner ● First-timer: Beginners have good terrain under the Meadows and Subway chairs. First-timers have a small but sheltered area close to the base lodge. The terrain is quite gentle and seldom used by better skiers and riders.

Alpine Meadows Facts

Summit elevation:	**8,637 feet**	**E-mail:** info@skialpine.com
Vertical drop:	**1,802 feet**	**Internet:** www.skialpine.com
Base elevation:	**6,835 feet**	

Expert: ★★★★
Advanced: ★★★★★
Intermediate: ★★★★
Beginner: ★★★
First-timer: ★★★

Number of lifts: 12–1 high-speed six-pack, 2 high-speed quads, 3 triples, 5 doubles, 1 surface lift
Snowmaking: 12 percent
Skiable acreage: 2,000 acres
Uphill capacity: 18,400 per hour
Parks & pipes: 1 terrain park, 1 superpipe

Address: Box 5279, Tahoe City CA 95730
Area code: 530
Ski area phone: 583-4232
Snow report: 581-8374
Toll-free information: (800) 441-4423

Bed base: 10,000 (N. Lake Tahoe Area)
Nearest lodging: Tahoe City, 6 miles
Resort child care: None
Adult ticket, per day: $41-49 (05/06 prices)

www.skisnowboard.com

Ride Guide: Even though Alpine Meadows is paying more attention to its manmade features, most riders agree that the natural terrain is the real reason to come here. If you like in-bounds hiking, this is the place for you. Unfortunately, you might be doing some hiking even if you're *not* looking for it: There are some flat spots and traverses that you might just find yourself cursing about. The biggest beware is traveling back from the Lakeview and Sherwood lifts to the front side. It never hurts to ask one of the liftees; many of them snowboard and have helpful tips to make the trip less grueling.

The Bowls are great powder runs—with special kudos to Upper Beaver and Estelle Bowl—and there are plenty of steeps, gullies and nutty drops if you go looking for them. Mix it up with some of the tree runs such as Hot Wheels Gully; you'll be happy you did. If you're there after a fresh dump, look for the wind lips—you'll find yourself airborne for days—and see if you can find Munchkins and Outer Outer.

If you favor groomers, don't panic. Alpine does a real nice job and there's plenty to choose from all over the mountain.

Parks and pipes

Riders and skiers will jump for joy when they see the nicely kept superpipe. It's together with the terrain park—Roo's Ride—and the boardercross course off the Kangaroo lift. The park includes rails, tabletops, funboxes and quarterpipes. The pipe and terrain park are open for riding 5 to 9 p.m. nightly, complete with a speaker system for tunes. If you only want to ride the parks and pipe, consider buying a Kangaroo lift ticket (see *Lift Tickets* for details).

Lessons [05/06 prices]

Group lessons: $42 for 2.25 hours.

First-timer package: A 1-3/4-hour adult learn-to-ski or -snowboard program includes beginner lifts, equipment and instruction for $69. A full-day program is $95. Same prices for lessons geared toward beginner-refresher and anyone still skiing or riding green runs.

Private lessons: For one person, $90 for one hour; $250 ffor three hours; all day is $450. For two to four people, one hour is $135; all day is $550.

Special programs: Tahoe Adaptive Ski School offers adaptive lessons in half-day increments, $50 (includes beginner lift ticket and adaptive ski gear); reservations required, call (530) 581-4161. Multiday clinics for women, early-season warm-up, snowboarding, and various advanced skills such as racing, powder, telemark, moguls and trees are also available. Call for details, dates and prices.

Racing: Daily race-training clinics are offered for around $55, or you can buy a book of five sessions for $235. There is a race every Thursday, which costs about $8 for two runs for all abilities with special prizes. Alpine Meadows also has coin-op racing.

KidStuff [05/06 prices]

Child care: Alpine Meadows has no child care.

Other options: Baby's Away (800-446-9030; 530-544-2229) rents and will deliver baby itemsto your hotel or condo. For **babysitting referrals,** call North Lake Tahoe Resort Association (800-434-1262; 530-583-3494).

Children's lessons: Little Mountaineers for children ages 4–6 costs $105 for a full day on weekends and holidays, and $95 midweek/non-holiday (including lunch, snack, equipment, lift ticket and two 2-hour lessons). A half day costs $79 weekends and holidays, $69 midweek/non-

Dining: $$$$-Entrees $30+; $$$-$20-$30; $$-$10-$20; $-less than $10.
Accommodations: (double room) $$$$-$200+; $$$-$141-$200; $$-$81-$140; $-$80 and less.

holiday. Reservations required, (530) 581-8240. Private lessons are available and snowboard lessons for ages 4–6 are by private lesson only; call for reservations and prices.

Junior Mountaineers is for children 7–12, skiing or snowboarding. A full-day program includes lunch, lift ticket, rentals and lessons, $105 weekends and holidays, $95 midweek/non-holiday. A half day costs $79 weekends and holidays, $69 midweek/non-holiday.

Lift tickets (05/06 prices)

	Adult	Child (7–12)
One day (non-holiday)	$41	$15
One day (holiday)	$49	$15

Who skis free: Children ages 6 and younger.

Who skis at a discount: Ages 65–69 pay $39 ($59 holidays); teens 13–18 pay $39 ($49 holidays); seniors 70 and older pay $15 all the time. Parents can get an interchangeable ticket that can be traded between them for $41 a day ($49 holidays).

Note: Holiday periods are Christmas/New Year's week, Martin Luther King, Jr. weekend, and Presidents' Day weekend. The resort does not offer multiday discounts. On holidays and midwinter weekends, the resort limits the number of tickets sold to keep the slopes from becoming too crowded. You can reserve lift tickets in advance.

Accommodations–Alpine Meadows

Alpine Meadows doesn't have accommodations at the base, but has lodging-lift packages in the region. Call **Alpine Meadows** at (800) 949-3296. A bed & breakfast package includes some two-dozen North Shore lodges, some starting at $59 per person, double occupancy, for lodging and a lift ticket.

Northstar-at-Tahoe Resort

After a massive reconstruction, Northstar is maintaining its reputation as a family-oriented resort. Kids will still find the hidden Adventure Parks, kid-friendly menus in the on-slope restaurants and cafeterias, and nonskiing fun like snowtubing and the bungee trampoline.

You won't find bowls and cornices at Northstar. Instead the skiing is all trail-cut with a bunch of awesome tree skiing. The tree skiing on Lookout Mountain rivals any found in the region. Combined with the widely spaced trees on the Backside, Northstar provides an excellent variety of tree skiing for everyone, from intermediates making their first forays into the woods to experts looking for the tightest glades they can ski.

Mountain layout

◆◆ **Expert** ◆ **Advanced:** Lookout Mountain, with 200 acres of terrain and a high-speed quad, is heralded as the expert section. Experts who expect a real challenge should go elsewhere, you won't find any scare-the-pants-off-you terrain here. There are five advanced/expert runs, named after the surrounding reservoirs: Prosser, Stampede, Gooseneck, Boca and Martis. The trails can be classified as advanced, but trees are clearly expert. Stampede, Gooseneck and Boca are left to bump up while Prosser and Martis are groomed regularly. After a storm, Northstar is one of the prime areas where you can enjoy powder through the trees long after Alpine and Squaw's powder has been skied off.

On the Backside, you'll find long rides with moderately steep and sustained pitch off the back side via the Comstock Express. These runs make you feel as though you're in another mountain range, far away from crowds. Though they're all labeled advanced runs, a strong intermediate will have no difficulty in good conditions. Sawtooth Ridge, off Challenger on the Backside, has steep off-piste terrain. It's open at select times during the season and only advanced skiers are allowed.

Advanced skiers or those aspiring to the upper levels of intermediate will find some challenge in the drops off the East Ridge (labeled as black diamonds, but the mapmaker was being generous). Most of the runs in this section are groomed or have moderate bumps.

■ **Intermediate:** This group will enjoy 50 percent of the mountain, particularly the smooth blues that descend from the two ridges into Main Street, an intermediate run that nearly every other run on the mountain feeds into. Avoid Main Street except when you need to get to a lift. Strong intermediates should try some of the black runs here. They will provide a good challenge to an intermediate looking to improve.

●● **Beginner** ● **First-timer:** Northstar is the best first-timer and beginner resort in the region because its gentlest terrain is below the gondola, while all other runs are above it. Better skiers leave this area to the learners except at day's end, when some of them use it to race back to the car. Luckily for everyone, it's fairly flat, so no one can keep up excessive speed.

Ride Guide: If you're craving serious steeps with sick air, you'll need to go somewhere else. Northstar is really geared more towards groomed cruising and woods riding with some good bumps through the center of Lookout Mountain.

After a storm, this is one of the prime areas where you can enjoy powder through the trees long after it's been tracked out at other Tahoe areas. On Lookout Mountain, riders claim Stampede, Gooseneck and Boca are divine. On the Backside, stick to the right side of the area where the trails drop right to the Backside Express Chair. If riders swing to the left down Challenger, they will face a long runout at the bottom of the area. Jibboom and Powder Bowl are some other favorites.

Stay on the front side if you're like wide-open groomed runs for intermediates and beginners. The terrain here is mellow and will boost your ego. This is a good resort for learning to ride, too.

Northstar-at-Tahoe Facts

Summit elevation:	**8,610 feet**
Vertical drop:	**2,280 feet**
Base elevation:	**6,330 feet**

Expert:★★
Advanced:★★★★
Intermediate:★★★★★
Beginner:★★★★★
First-timer:★★★★
Address: Box 129, Truckee, CA 96160
Area code: 530
Ski area phone: 562-1010
Snow report: 562-1330
Toll-free reservations:
(800) 466-6784

E-mail: northstar@boothcreek.com
Internet: www.northstarattahoe.com
Number of lifts: 17–1 gondola, 5 high-speed quads, 2 triples, 2 doubles, 3 surface lifts, 4 moving carpets
Snowmaking: 50% of developed acres
Total acreage: 2,420 acres
Uphill capacity: 21,800 per hour
Parks & pipes: 7 terrain parks, 1 snowskate park, 1 superpipe, 1 halfpipe
Bed base: 5,500 at resort
Nearest lodging: Ski-in/ski-out, slopeside
Resort child care: Yes, 2 years and older (toilet-trained)
Adult ticket, per day: $55-$63 (05/06)

Dining: $$$$-Entrees $30+; $$$-$20-$30; $$-$10-$20; $-less than $10.
Accommodations: (double room) $$$$-$200+; $$$-$141-$200; $$-$81-$140; $-$80 and less.

Parks and pipes

If you like terrain parks and pipes, Northstar is right up your alley. You'll find six terrain parks (not counting the kids' Adventure Parks), a 17-foot superpipe and a halfpipe. Some of the parks have scaled-down features for beginners; Magic Moguls will remind you of a parking lot full of snow-covered VW bugs; another is a snake-run with high walls; and Sidewinder and Forerunner runs will now be host to the Burton Progression Park with hits and rails made especially for those learning to ride in the park. The superpipe is on Pipeline. Get a good view of it from the Launch Pad, a patio restaurant where parents can drink microbrews and watch their kids get serious airtime. As for Adventure Parks, they're adventure zones for kids—pint-size terrain parks scattered across the mountain that include bumps, jumps, hideaways and snow play areas. Look for the paw prints on the trail map.

Lessons [05/06 prices]

These are prices for regular season. Peak/holiday prices are higher.

Group lessons: Free 75-minute skill improvement clinics are held in the afternoons, Sunday–Friday, for intermediate and higher levels, skiing and snowboarding, ages 13 and older (not available during holiday/peak periods). Other group lessons are $49 for ages 13 and older.

First-timer package: First-time ski and snowboard students ages 13 and older get a 2.5-hour lesson, with beginner lift access and rental equipment, for $85. A three-day package costs $159, and days do not have to be consecutive.

Private lessons: For ages 13 and older, $199 for one hour; $304 for a half day; $339 for a full day. Take a one-hour lesson at 8:30 a.m. or 9 a.m. and pay $69. Semi-private lessons (up to five people) cost $154 for one hour; $280 for a half day; $429 for a full day. Three- and six-hour privates include free use of demo equipment. Reservations are recommended.

Special programs: Three-day clinics for women are offered a few times per year; call for specifics and pricing.

KidStuff [05/06 prices]

Child care: Ages 2–6 years (toilet-trained). All day costs $85 (with lunch and snacks); half day costs $45. All-day program including a one-hour ski lesson (ages 3-6) costs $98. Prices are higher during holiday periods. Activities include art, snow play, science, drama and language development. Reservations recommended; call (530) 562-2278. Hours are 8:30 a.m. to 4:30 p.m. Northstar is repeatedly recognized as one of the nation's best resorts for children's programs.

Other options: Baby's Away (800-446-9030; 530-544-2229) rents and will deliver baby items (cribs, strollers, toys, etc.) to your hotel or condo. For **babysitting referrals,** call North Lake Tahoe Resort Association (800-434-1262; 530-583-3494).

Children's lessons: All-day program for children ages 7–12 is $102 with lifts, lessons, equipment and lunch. An afternoon-only program is $82. Ages 4–6 get indoor activities as part of the program. Holiday rates are higher. Meet at the Children's Teaching Area at mid-mountain. Children 13 and older enroll in adult programs.

Here's something you shouldn't pass up: Northstar's instructors will teach parents how to teach their 3- and 4-year-olds in a free program called Mommy, Daddy & Me, offered Sunday through Friday (non-holidays) at 1:30 p.m. Meet at midmountain at the Ski & Snowboard School.

Lift tickets (05/06 prices)

	Adult	Child (5-12)
Any day	$63	$16
Three days	$165 ($55/day)	$36 ($12/day)
Five days	$275 ($55/day)	$60 ($12/day)

Who skis free: Children 4 and younger ski free with a paying adult.

Who skis at a discount: Ages 13–22 pay $46 for one day. Ages 65–69 pay $40 for one day; 70 and older pay $16 for single day and $12/day for multiday. Unlimited gondola rides for nonskiers cost $10.

Note: Prices are higher during holiday periods. Northstar limits its daily ticket sales; cars will be turned away once sellout has occurred. If a sellout occurs in the morning, afternoon tickets will not be sold.

 ## Accommodations–Northstar-at-Tahoe

The village area was created for condo living. The village has a convenient lodge, with rooms from $209 a night, two-night minimum. The condo rates range from $184 a night for a studio to $395 for a two-bedroom, two-bath unit. Northstar also has full-sized homes for rent, accommodating six to 14 people for $449 to $1,175 per night. Packages can be arranged for whatever resort amenities you need—airfare, lifts, rentals and lessons are just some of the choices. **For reservations,** call (800) 466-6784.

Diamond Peak

Bigger is not always better, nor desirable. For skiers and snowboarders who don't want the expansive terrain of most Lake Tahoe resorts, let us recommend Diamond Peak, a medium-sized but exquisite jewel that destination vacationers too often overlook.

Diamond Peak often is less crowded than the other large Tahoe areas and perfect for families. Visitors remark that this is a very friendly area. Take a camera—the view is beautiful.

With runs knifing down through Ponderosa Pines along a long single ridge, Diamond Peak offers an excellent family mountain where all trails funnel to a single base area. The views down toward the lake are spectacular and the early-morning groomed corduroy alongside powder seems to drop right into the water.

The tougher trails drop from the crest of the ridge traced by Crystal Ridge and the intermediate trails are clustered within sight of the base lodge. Intermediates can't go too far wrong at this resort and advanced skiers will have a good time at the higher reaches of the resort.

 ## Mountain layout

Diamond Peak was the first U.S. resort to install a "launch pad" loading system, a conveyor belt covered with a skiable felt surface. All of its quad chairs, except for the high-speed quad, have this family-friendly system.

♦♦ **Expert ♦ Advanced:** Here's one of Diamond Peak's best-kept secrets: the tree skiing and riding in Solitude Canyon and elsewhere throughout the ski area. Solitude is reached by a short hike over a knoll at the top of the Crystal high-speed quad. The rest of the resort's terrain falls from a single ridge that starts at the summit and ends at the octagonal Snowflake Lodge overlooking Lake Tahoe. The canyons, glades and gullies off Crystal Ridge (a long blue run) are labeled advanced, but strong intermediates will have a blast on them; however, the tree skiing is definitely expert. At the other end of the resort, below the Snowflake Lodge,

Diamond Peak Facts

Summit elevation:	8,540 feet
Vertical drop:	1,840 feet
Base elevation:	6,700 feet

Expert:★ Advanced:★★★
Intermediate:★★★★
Beginner:★★★
First-timer:★★★
Address: 1210 Ski Way, Incline Village, NV 89451
Area code: 775
Ski area phone: 832-1177
Snow report: 831-3211
Toll-free reservations: (800) 468-2463

Fax: 832-1281
E-mail: info@diamondpeak.com
Internet: www.diamondpeak.com
Number of lifts: 6–1 high-speed quad, 2 quads, 3 doubles
Snowmaking: 75 percent
Skiable acreage: 655 acres
Uphill capacity: 9,800 per hour
Parks & pipes: 1 terrain park
Bed base: 6,000
Nearest lodging: About 1/4 mile away
Resort child care: Yes, 3 years and older (toilet-trained)
Adult ticket, per day: $46 (05/06 price)

Oh God and G.S. provide some steep ungroomed pitches and good tree skiing.

■ **Intermediate:** This is a wonderful area for intermediates, especially families who don't want to worry about the kids taking a wrong turn and getting lost. The aforementioned Crystal Ridge is a 2.5-mile-long blue from the summit, with a stunning view of the lake. Golden Eagle Bowl provides intermediates a place to test their tree skiing. The lower-mountain runs off Red Fox also have a nice intermediate pitch.

●● **Beginner** ● **First-timer:** This is a great learner's mountain more because of its friendly atmosphere and manageable size rather than its terrain (unfortunately, the amount of beginner terrain is a bit limited). Diamond Peak employs about 100 instructors—equal to much larger areas—another indication that it's a good place to learn.

Ride Guide: The resort's terrain features attract boarders at every skill level, from first-timers to the most advanced. This is an excellent resort for riders who are ready to test themselves on the more adventurous terrain of canyons and gullies, since nothing here will give you the heebie-jeebies. Snowboarders also can find some alone time in the "Glades," in the trees between The Great Flume and Thunder. Enjoy fantastic tree riding and untapped powder stashes.

Parks and pipes

For skiers and riders who like pulling some tricks, check out the terrain park. The park is on Spillway (at the bottom of The Great Flume) and includes tabletops, spines, hits and jumps—all overlooking beautiful Lake Tahoe.

Lessons (06/07 prices)

Group lessons: Lessons are one hour and 45 minutes long. Cost is $30 (ski or snowboard); two sessions in the same day cost $45.

First-timer package: Learn-to-Ski/Snowboard including beginner lifts, rentals and 105-minute lesson is $72. Kids 7–12 pay $66. Followup lessons are $80 for adults and $66 for kids.

Private lessons: $72–$86 an hour, depending on the time you take your lesson. The Family & Friends Private Lessons is for two to five people in a lesson, with prices starting at $100 an hour. Reservations recommended, call (775) 832-1135.

KidStuff (06/07 prices)

Child care: There is no child care without lessons. Ages 3–7 (toilet-trained). Cost is $62 for a half day (10:30 a.m.–12:30 p.m. or 2–4 p.m.); $110 for all day. Diamond Peak's Bee Ferrato is a New Zealand native every kid will want to adopt. Reservations required; call (775) 832-1130.

For **babysitting referrals,** call North Lake Tahoe Resort Association (800-434-1262; 530-583-3494).

Children's lessons: All-day group lesson, rentals, ticket and supervised lunch for children 8–12 costs $110. A similar program for kids 4–7 costs $10 plus $20 for skis and $30 for snowboards. Children ages 3 and up can enroll in Diamond Pete's Special: two-hour private lesson, two-hours of child care, rentals, lift and lunch for $220. Three to seven-year-olds can also take private lessons: $90 for one hour, $130 for 1.5 hours. Reservations are required for private children's lessons, call (775) 832-1298.

Lift tickets (06/07 prices)

	Adult	Child (6-12)
One day	$46	$17

Who skis free: Ages 5 and younger, and 80 and older.

Who skis at a discount: Ages 13–17 pay $36; ages 60–79 pay $17. Parents can buy an interchangeable adult ticket for $46 that either of them can use—a good deal for those with toddlers. If you are planning on skiing more than just one day, consider the Diamond Peak Mini Pass program, where you can buy tickets in combinations of two, three, five or seven days, starting at $81 (tickets are valid any day of the season). Purchase tickets at any ticket window. Beginners ski for $20 all day on the two beginner lifts. Last but not least, the ever-affordable Family Special Package starting at just $60 is one deal that parents simply cannot pass up. The offer lets families customize a ticket package designed just for them. Packages available daily at any ticket window and valid for up to six persons with a maximum of two adults. Believe it or not, a family of four can hit the slopes for $115.

Accommodations—Diamond Peak

Incline Village has several hotels and condo complexes. It also has private homes that can easily sleep 12–16 people. For **Incline Village** accommodations, call (800) 468-2463.

The **Hyatt Regency Lake Tahoe Resort, Spa and Casino** (888-591-1234; 775-832-1234; $$$$) is a four-star luxury hotel that resembles the grand homes built in the 1920s. After a multimillion dollar renovation, the lobby and rooms are wonderful, with natural pine, leather furnishings and autumn colors. The **Cal-Neva Resort, Spa & Casino** (800-225-6382; 775-832-4000; $$-$$$$) is split by the state line and once was owned by Frank Sinatra and visited by Marilyn Monroe. Every room has a lake view. There are also honeymoon bungalows with heart-shaped tubs, round beds and mirrored ceilings. The **Tahoe Biltmore Casino** (800-245-8667; 775-831-0660; $$) in Crystal Bay has midweek ski packages with Diamond Peak, including a lift ticket, lodging, a full breakfast and transportation to and from the slopes.

The **Inn at Incline Motor Lodge and Condominiums** (800-824-6391; $$) has more modest facilities but rooms are comfortable and there's an indoor pool and hot tub. **Haus Bavaria** (800-731-6222; $$-$$$$) is a European-style guest house with five rooms and **Crystal Bay Motel** (775-831-0287; $-$$) is an economy property near casinos.

Mt. Rose Facts

Summit elevation:	**9,700 feet**
Vertical drop:	**1,800 feet**
Base elevation:	**8,260 feet**

Expert:★★★★★
Advanced:★★★★★
Intermediate:★★★★★
Beginner:★★★
First-timer:★★★
Address: 22222 Mt. Rose Hwy., Reno, NV 89511
Area code: 775
Ski area phone/reservations: 849-0704
Snow report: (800) SKI-ROSE (754-7673)
E-mail: deepsnow@skirose.com

Internet: www.skirose.com
Number of lifts: 7–2 high-speed 6-pax, 2 quads, 2 triples, 1 surface lift
Snowmaking: 28 percent
Skiable acreage: 1,200 acres
Uphill capacity: 13,400 per hour
Parks & pipes: 2 terrain parks
Bed base: thousands in Reno
Nearest lodging: Reno, NV 25 miles
Resort child care: No
Adult ticket, per day: $54 (05/06 price)

Mt. Rose

At the top of the mountain from Reno to Lake Tahoe, sits one of America's undiscovered gems, Mt. Rose. This area has long been the mountain of choice for Reno natives who can reach the slopes in abour a half hour. It was a collection of enjoyable cruising and beginner trails that caught the early-morning sun and then the last rays of the sun on the other side of the mountain. All of that still remains, but the super-steep north-facing chutes, which were recently opened have changed everything.

Today Mt. Rose now has perhaps the largest selection of lift-served steep terrain in the country. This is the real thing, but with an escape valve. There are few places in the ski world where these kinds of steeps are nestled side-by-side with rolling cruisers. From the top of the Northwest Magnum six-pax, skiers and riders have choices to drop into the steep and deep, head to the east or to the west.

Mountain layout

♦♦ **Expert** ♦ **Advanced:** The Chutes have changed everything for Mt. Rose. These double-diamond steeps are long but most importantly, accessible. The 16 chutes all drop down to the Chuter quad, which then delivers skiers and riders to the the East Bowl where the Blazing Zephyr six-pax takes them back to the top to drop in again.

The Chutes basically are steepest on the eastern side of the Chutes. Start with Nightmare. If you can handle that move over to Chaos. El Cap and Jackpot are considered two of the toughest fall lines.

■ **Intermediate:** This is a wonderful area for intermediates. The Slide side (eastern side) of the mountain has delightfully long cruisers that inspires song. Though some of the trails are marked with diamonds, there is nothing here that will get any intermediate in trouble. Swing to the far eastern runs such as South Rim and Washoe Zephyr. Cruise down Big Bonanza and Bruce's. Bash you way straignt down the face along Silver Dollar. No matter what route you ski or ride, it will be about 1,500 feet of non-stop vertical.

Later in the day after the sun has softened up the easters side, head to the west. Take the Kit Carson Traverse over to Ramsey's and the Kit Carson Bowl. Any confident intermediate can drop into one of a half-dozen black-diamond trails. When groomed, they are smooth and easy, when bumped up, it will take a little more time to get down, but none are dangerous.

●● **Beginner** ● **First-timer:** Beginners have a secluded area to the far west section of the resort. Take the Ponderosa lift then the Galena lift to a web of trails that serve as great learning terrain. North Rim, Galena, Bronco, Mustang and Ski Off are all good beginner trails. Nearby there are runs that go through the trees.

Ride Guide: The resort's terrain features attract boarders at every skill level, from first-timers to the most advanced. This is an excellent resort for riders who are ready to test themselves in the Chutes.

Parks and pipes

There are two terrain parks. Double Down, a massive one on the east side under the Zephyr lift with more hits, spines and jumps than I could count riding over it. The second park, Badlands, is smaller on the Little Red Bowl off Fremont.

Lessons [05/06 prices]

Group lessons: Lessons are one hour and a half long. Cost is $39 (ski or snowboard). Sessions start at 10 a.m. and 2 p.m..

First-timer package: Learn-to-Ski/Snowboard including beginner lifts, rentals and 90-minute lesson is $49. Rookie lessons, the next step costs $59 and includes rentals.

Private lessons: $59–$99 an hour, depending on the time you take your lesson. Each additional person costs $29.

KidStuff [05/06 prices]

Child care: There is no nursery program.

Children's lessons: The Rosebuds Ski and Snowboard Camp teaches children how to turn the mountain into their playgrouns. Children ages 4–10 can take ski lessons and those ages 7–10 can take snowboard lessons.

A two-hour session costs $55 and a full day is $110. This includes lift ticket and rental equipment. Class levels range from turtles who have never skied or boarded, to squirrels who can stop, to foxes who can turn, to bears who are confident on all blue trails.

Private lessons cost $90 for an hour and $60 for each additional person or hour.

Lift tickets [06/07 prices]

	Adult	Child (6-12)	Teen(13-17)
Half day	$88	$12	$38
One day	$58	$12	$38

Who skis free: Ages 5 and younger, and 75 and older.

Who skis at a discount: Seniors (60–74) pay a flat rate of $38.

Accommodations–Mt. Rose

The hotel base for Mt. Rose is Reno, about a half hour away. The town has a phenomenal collection of major casino hotels, regular establishments and plenty of motels. Arrangements at all price points are available. The highway system cuts through Reno, so getting to the resort is easy from just about any part of the city. Every major online travel agent has scores of packages for the Reno/Tahoe area or see you travel agent.

Silver Legacy Resort Casino (1-800-687-8733 or 775-325-7401) in the heart of downtown sports a lush Victorian theme. It has six restaurants of all levels and plenty of nightlife and entertainment as well.

John Ascuaga's Nugget (800-648-1177) in Sparks, sits off by itself, but features a wonderful Basque restaurant, Orozko, as well as Trader Dick's with a Polynesian theme.

Peppermill Casino (800-282-2444) is in the part of the city closest to Mt. Rose. It has eight restaurants, 14 themed bars and a waterfall pool.

Atlantis Casino (800-723-6500) has a spa, wonderful buffet restaurants, a great seafood place and wonderful sushi on the Sky Terrace.

All of these properties have ski and snowboard packages and all are served by a shuttle bus that brings skiers and riders to Mt. Rose. Lift and shuttle cost $54. Buses leave the major hotels to arrive at Mt. Rose at either 9 or 11 a.m.

Dining and Nightlife

Dining in Reno ranges from the casino restaurants that are run by top chefs from around the country to traditional family-style Basque restaurants. Check out the **Santa Fe** (775-323-1891) and **Louis' Basque Corner** (775-323-7203) for two of the most famous. I suggest lunch at Louis' and dinner at the Santa Fe.

Reno is one of the centers of nightlife in North America. Everything from big-name musical performers, to symphony orchestras, to broadway plays, to top comedians play in Reno.

Sugar Bowl

Founded by Walt Disney, Sugar Bowl is one of the oldest resorts in the U.S. Although it is keeping pace with the modern ski era—with high-speed lifts, excellent grooming, and a plethora of terrain parks and features—the resort is, ironically, not suffering from "Disneyfication." From the moment you step out of your car and board the gondola to ride *down* across a valley to the lifts, you feel like you're stepping back in time. The snowbound Village is a small collection of old ski chalets, the Inn at Sugar Bowl (which also serves as a base lodge), the child-care center, and a ski shop. Period. No Starbucks. No fancy truffle shop. You can feel your body clock slow as soon as you step off the gondola.

People come to Sugar Bowl for one reason: To ski and ride. And those who aren't spending the night at the Inn should park at the Mt. Judah parking area, thus avoiding the slow Village Gondola. From Mt. Judah, your mountain adventure begins quickly thanks to two high-speed quads. If you're looking for the classic Sugar Bowl experience, head to the top of Mt. Lincoln and ski Silver Belt to Steilhang. As you dive under the first cliff and into the natural gully, imagine yourself racing the infamous Silver Belt giant slalom, which attracted the world's best skiers from 1940-1975. In 2000, the race was revived as a very gnarly invitation-only skiercross event.

Sugar Bowl is another of Tahoe's overlooked ski areas. We recommend Sugar Bowl for a day's change of pace from the larger Tahoe resorts. However, remember that it's one of the first ski areas on the drive from San Francisco, Oakland and Sacramento and gets its big crowds on weekends. Visit midweek if you can and take advantage of their $44 Monday through Friday ticket price (excluding holidays).

Sugar Bowl has three peaks—Mt. Judah, with its own parking lot and base lodge; Mt. Lincoln; and Mt. Disney, reached initially by the Village Gondola. The three peaks are con-

Sugar Bowl Facts

Summit elevation:	8,383 feet
Vertical drop:	1,500 feet
Base elevation:	6,883 feet

Expert:★★
Advanced:★★★
Intermediate:★★★★★
Beginner:★★★★
First-timer:★★★
Address: P.O. Box 5, Norden, CA 95724
Area code: 530
Ski area phone/reservations: 426-9000
Snow report: 426-1111
E-mail: info@sugarbowl.com

Internet: www.sugarbowl.com
Number of lifts: 13–1 gondola, 4 high-speed quads, 3 quads, 3 doubles, 2 surface lifts
Snowmaking: 25 percent
Skiable acreage: 1,500 acres
Uphill capacity: 13,755 per hour
Parks & pipes: 4 terrain parks, 1 superpipe, 1 halfpipe, 2 quarterpipes
Bed base: 460
Nearest lodging: Slopeside
Resort child care: Yes, 3 years and older (toilet-trained)
Adult ticket, per day: $46-$59 (05/06 price)

nected. This is one of the few ski areas where we agree with virtually all their trail ratings. All lifts are high-speed so that a skier can pack in lots of vertical very quickly.

Mountain layout

♦♦ Expert ♦ Advanced: Mt. Disney, one of three peaks at Sugar Bowl, has advanced runs off either side of a ridge. Mt. Lincoln also has advanced terrain dropping directly beneath the lift. There's an expert, very steep cliff area, The '58 and The Palisades, to the right of the Mt. Lincoln Express that's double-diamond and comparable to the jumps at Squaw. There is some good tree skiing off Crow's Nest peak down the face or through Strawberry Fields.

■ **Intermediate:** From the top of the Disney Express, head down the left side of the ridge along Crow's Traverse then drop down Pony Express, Montgomery and Upper Mac into Disney Meadows. Keep up your speed and stay high at the end of the run to avoid having to push to the lift. From the top of the Mt. Lincoln Express head to the right down Crowley's Run, Rahlves' Run and eventually head back top the base of the lift along Ridge Run or Silver Belt Finger. The entire area served by Mt. Judah Express and Jerome Hill Express is an intermediate paradise, perfect for long cruising with occasional short steeps.

●● **Beginner ● First-timer:** Beginners have beautiful long runs off the Christmas Tree and Mt. Judah chairs. White Pine at Mt. Judah is an excellent teaching area, segregated from the main ski trails. Beginners staying at the Inn at Sugar Bowl can reach the Christmas Tree and Mt. Judah chairs via the Nob Hill chairlift.

Ride Guide: Strawberry Fields and Crow's Nest Face are not to be missed on powder days. The groomers off the Jerome Hill Express are great for high-speed arcs. Remember to keep your speed up for the flat between the Mid Mountain Lodge and Village Lodge and at the bottom of the runs down from Crow's Nest.

Parks and pipes

Sugar Bowl has incredible natural hits and quarterpipes. Real experts should check out The 58s and The Palisades off Mt. Lincoln, and the Sugar Bowl off the Disney Express. On Sunset (off the Mt. Judah Express lift), the resort takes advantage of the natural gully-like terrain

Dining: $$$$-Entrees $30+; $$$-$20-$30; $$-$10-$20; $-less than $10.
Accommodations: (double room) $$$$-$200+; $$$-$141-$200; $$-$81-$140; $-$80 and less.

with added banks, whoops, gullies and drops. The natural terrain features have been the site of the X-Game Qualifer for skiercross and boardercross.

If that isn't enough there are manmade terrain parks to suit every ability level. Sugar Bowl has two major parks, Golden Gate and SnowBomb Terrain Park, both off the Mt. Judah Express lift. Both parks have quarterpipes, tabletops, spines and hips. Buena Vista has an intermediate fun-for-all park. For beginners and children, a dedicated family park on Nob Hill is within eyesight of the Village Lodge deck. For experts, head to the superpipe near the base of the Mt. Lincoln Express.

Lessons (05/06 prices)

Group lessons: $45 for two hours.
First-timer package: Fast Track packages of lift ticket, two-hour lesson and rental (ski or snowboard) is $85 for adults, $75 for young adults (13–22).
Private lessons: $90 an hour. A sunrise special from 9–10 a.m. costs $60.

KidStuff (05/06 prices)

Child care: Ages 3–6 years (toilet-trained). All day costs $100; half day is $70 (no lunch). Sugar Bears Child Care is a licensed center with educational and recreational activities as well as skiing and quiet time. The program includes snacks, lunch and ski equipment. Reservations suggested; call (530) 426-6776 well in advance. The child-care center is in the Village, reached only via the gondola.

Other options: Baby's Away (800-446-9030; 530-544-2229) rents and will deliver baby items (cribs, strollers, toys, etc.) to your hotel or condo. For **babysitting referrals,** call North Lake Tahoe Resort Association (800-434-1262; 530-583-3494).

Children's lessons: Base Camp is a fully supervised program for 4–5-year-olds Choose morning (10 a.m.–noon) or afternoon (1–3 p.m.) for $70. Summit Adventure Camp for ages 6–12 is a half- or full-day ski or snowboard program. A full day costs $100 and includes lifts, equipment, lessons and lunch; half-day costs $70 (no lunch). The Fast Track package for teens who are first-timers includes lift ticket, two-hour lesson and rental (ski or snowboard) and costs $75. Lessons are only available from the Learning Center at the Mt. Judah base area.

Lift tickets (05/06 prices)

	Adult	Child (5-12)
One day Holiday	$59	$15
Midweek, non-holiday	$46	$15

Who skis free: Children 5 and younger.
Who skis at a discount: Skiers 70+ pay $5.

Accommodations–Sugar Bowl

The Inn at Sugar Bowl ($$$$; 530-426-6742) was built at the base of Mt. Disney in 1939 and is one of the most unusual ski lodges in North America. A seven-minute gondola ride from the Donner Pass Road (where you parked your car), the inn—and the gondola, for that matter—take you back to a time gone by. Lying in bed at this isolated inn, you only hear the wind in the treetops outside the snowbound three-story, shed-like building, a utilitarian structure constructed to withstand the heavy Sierra snows. The rooms are bright and comfortable, but except for a private bath and TV, there are no frills. You are paying for the location (slopeside) and intimacy. Breakfast and dinner (and lunch on the weekends) are served in the inn's small elegant dining room, and people often gather in the bar or comfortable lobby outside the dining room where it's easy to strike up conversations with fellow guests. The lobby and bar also are hotspots for the inn's wireless Internet connection. Room rates start at $200 per night, double occupancy. Bed-breakfast-lift packages, available Sunday through Thursday, non-holiday, are $255 double occupancy, per night. Five-day ski weeks with two meals a day also are available. Make reservations well in advance.

Nearby resorts

Homewood Mountain Resort, Homewood, CA; (530) 525-2992

Internet: www.skihomewood.com

8 lifts; 1,260 skiable acres; 1,650 vertical feet; 1 terrain park; 1 halfpipe

Homewood Mountain Resort, on the west shore of Lake Tahoe, is one of three Tahoe ski areas that can qualify for Best View Of The Lake honors. This area, though smallish by Tahoe standards, has more than 1,200 skiable acres accessible from either of two base areas called North Side and South Side.

Lift tickets (05/06): Adults, $45 ($48 holidays); junior (11–18), $33; seniors (62–69), $22; super seniors (70+), $10; kids 10 and younger, free. Value days (Monday through Thursday, non-holiday), adults and juniors, $27; seniors, $15; super seniors, $10.

Distance from Reno: About 50 miles from Reno via I-80 west and Hwy. 89 south.

Distance from Sacramento: About 120 miles via I-80 east and Hwy. 89 south.

Lodging information: (877) 525-7669 or (800) 824-6348.

Boreal, Truckee, CA; (530) 426-3666

Internet: www.borealski.com

9 lifts; 380 skiable acres; 500 vertical feet; 7 terrain parks; 1 superpipe

You can't miss Boreal when you're driving toward Tahoe from Sacramento. It is a wide ridge of fairly short ski trails right off I-80 on the Donner Pass. It's the closest resort to Sacramento and San Francisco. Boreal, purchased in 1995 by the company that owns Alpine Meadows, is very popular with riders, who like the short, straight runs off the summit and the eight Vans-sponsored terrain parks. Boreal also has runs down its back side.

Boreal has night skiing and a night halfpipe and terrain park. It is the home of the Western Ski Sport Museum, generally open during Boreal's ski hours.

Lift tickets (05/06): Adults, $38; adult night skiing, $22; children (5–12), $10; seniors (60–69), $25; children 4 and younger, free; seniors 70+, $5. Parent shared ticket, $38.

Distance from Reno: About 45 miles west on I-80.

Distance from Sacramento: About 80 miles east on I-80.

Lodging information: (530) 426-1012.

Dining: $$$$-Entrees $30+; $$$-$20-$30; $$-$10-$20; $-less than $10.
Accommodations: (double room) $$$$-$200+; $$$-$141-$200; $$-$81-$140; $-$80 and less.

Cross-country and snowshoeing

The Lake Tahoe region may have the greatest concentration of large cross-country ski areas in the U.S., with more than 800 km. of groomed trails. We have listed the bigger operations; local tourist offices can direct you to smaller and less expensive centers. Many of the ones we list here also have full-moon tours and snowshoe rentals and tours, so call for information.

The largest private trail system in North America is in California at **Royal Gorge** (530-426-3871; 800-500-3871, nationwide; 800-666-3871, Northern California only) just off I-80, west of Donner Summit at the Soda Springs exit. Royal Gorge has nearly 9,000 acres of terrain, and more than 300 km. of trails with a skating lane inside the tracks. They also make snow on some trails and use modern snowcats. Royal Gorge has four surface lifts to help skiers up the tougher inclines. It is a full-service ski area, with rental equipment, ski school, ten warming huts, four cafes and a full-time ski patrol. Trailside lodging is at **Rainbow Lodge**, an historic 1920s B&B, or at **Wilderness Lodge,** a rustic retreat in the middle of the trail system. Book either through the ski area.

Northstar-at-Tahoe (530-562-2475) has 50 km. of groomed and marked trails. All are near the day lodge and downhill slopes. This is one of the gentler trail systems in the area—very good for families and those just learning. Lessons and rentals are available, as are snowshoe rentals. Full-moon Nordic Tours are a must-do if you time your trip at the right point in the lunar cycle.

The Tahoe Donner Cross-Country Area (530-587-9484) is off I-80 at Donner State Park exit. This area has 100 km. of trails, all double-tracked with wide skating lanes, and a day lodge with cafe. Tahoe Donner has California's only lighted night cross-country skiing, Wednesdays and Saturdays. Cross-country gear, snowshoes and pulk sleds are available for rental.

Squaw Creek Cross-Country Ski Center (530-583-6300) is a small area at the Resort at Squaw Creek, which has rentals and lessons. Trails cover 18 km., are groomed daily, and range from beginner to expert. Child care is available for kids ages 4 and older.

Tahoe Cross-Country Ski Area (530-583-5475), 2 miles east of Tahoe City, is now a non-profit ski foundation. It has 65 km. of groomed skating lanes and tracks, a day lodge, cafe, lessons and rentals. Call to inquire about bringing your dog. Snowshoes and pulk sleds also are available for rental.

Spooner Lake Cross-Country (775-887-8844, recording; 755-749-5349, live voice) on Hwy. 28, about a half-mile north of Hwy. 50, has more than 80 km. of trails, nearly all of which are machine groomed, with one 19-km. backcountry trail. Lessons and cross-country gear, snowshoe and pulk sled rentals are available; you also can rent a backcountry cabin.

Accommodations

The North Shore is relatively quiet. The accommodations below generally run less than $150; however, the more luxurious lodging will top out closer to $200. The North Shore has B&Bss, cabins on the lake, plush or spartan condominiums, and medium-sized casino hotels—a place for everyone. The best source for lodging-and-lift packages is **North Lake Tahoe Resort Association Lodging Information & Reservations,** (888) 434-1262 or (530) 583-3494.

The most upscale bed-and-breakfast is the **Rockwood Lodge** (800-538-2463; 530-525-5273; $$–$$$$), originally built in the mid-1930s. There are four rooms, two with private bath. It has antique furnishings, plush carpet, brass-and-porcelain bath fixtures, and down comforters. It is about 7 miles south of Tahoe City, no-smoking inn and no children.

Mayfield House at Lake Tahoe (888-518-8898; $$$), a B&B, is elegant and romantic, and full breakfasts come with the rate. Each of the rooms has a private bath.

Other B&Bs that are recommended are **The Cottage Inn** (800-581-4073; 530-581-4073; $$$) in Tahoe City; **The Shore House** (800-207-5160; 530-546-7270; $$$) in Tahoe Vista; or **Tahoma Meadows Bed & Breakfast** (530-525-1553; $$–$$$$) in Homewood.

Just south of Tahoe City is the **Sunnyside Lodge** (530-583-7200, or in California only, 800-822-2754; $$$), directly on the lake. There are 23 rooms, all with a lake view and a few rooms have fireplaces. No. 39 makes a great honeymoon suite—it has a four- to six-week waiting list. There's a lively apres-ski bar and a good restaurant, the Chris Craft.

The **Granlibakken Resort & Conference Center** (800-543-3221; $$–$$$$) in Tahoe City is a great place to stay. Lodging is in 160 privately owned suites and townhouses. Sizes start at one bedroom and top out at a six-bedroom, six-bath townhouse. Two saunas and an outdoor spa are on site. The lovely complex sits on a hill among towering pines and red firs. Two cross-country ski trails and a beginner's Alpine hill also can be found here. Ski packages are available with Squaw Valley and Alpine Meadows.

For families or anyone looking for a great deal, **North Lake Lodge** (530-546-2731; $$), in Kings Beach only a few feet from the shore, is one of the oldest hotels but still in great shape. Continental breakfast is included and the shuttles stop just across the street.

River Ranch (530-583-4264; $$) on Hwy. 89 near Alpine Meadows is another moderately priced lodge. This historic ski lodge sits on the banks of the Truckee River and rooms are furnished with early American antiques. Continental breakfast is included, and the shuttles for Squaw Valley and Alpine Meadows are nearby. A rushing river lulls you to sleep.

Truckee

The town of Truckee is convenient to Northstar and Sugar Bowl. For real Western authenticity, try **The Truckee Hotel** (800-659-6921; 530-587-4444; $$), open since 1873. Mostly it housed timber and railroad workers, but one of the residents was a madam. It was renovated in 1992, but you'll still feel like you're sleeping in the Old West. Eight of the 37 rooms have private baths, including old-fashioned, claw-footed tubs. Some rooms are large enough to sleep six. Breakfast and afternoon tea served in the parlor are included with the B&B rates.

The **Richardson House** (888-229-0365; 530-587-5388; $$$) is a B&B in Truckee that was built in the 1880s as a private residence. It has been fully restored. Six of the eight rooms have private baths. A full breakfast buffet is included, as well as 24-hour access to the "refreshment center." Beds and comforters are feather-filled.

Another recommended lodge is the **Best Western Truckee Tahoe Inn** (800-824-6385; 530-587-4525; $$), about a mile outside downtown Truckee, with 100 rooms and large complimentary breakfast.

Nevada Northeast

Reno offers big-time casino atmosphere closer to the North Shore and at lower prices than you'll find surrounding the lake. Reno also has a planetarium and two major museums, and is 30–45 minutes by car from the North Shore resorts. It is only a half hour from Mt. Rose. This is a good place to stay if you want to save some serious money and have a big enough group to split a rental car cost. Some hotels have ski shuttles, but most visitors here probably will want a car. **Reno Central Reservations** is at (888) 448-7366.

Incline Village is a quiet upscale community that is home to Diamond Peak ski area. It has several very fine hotels and condo units, some of which we list in the Diamond Peak section. It also has private homes that can easily sleep 12–16 people. For **Incline Village** accommodations, call (800) 468-2463.

Dining: $$$$-Entrees $30+; $$$–$20-$30; $$-$10-$20; $-less than $10.
Accommodations: (double room) $$$$-$200+; $$$-$141-$200; $$-$81-$140; $-$80 and less.

Dining (530 area code unless noted)

Dining is in the midst of a renaissance in North Lake Tahoe. The old mom-and-pop places are giving way to some upscale gourmet eateries. All restaurants are within a half-hour drive of each other. They are listed geographically—Very North Tahoe, Tahoe City, Truckee, Incline Village and Squaw Valley.

Very North Lake Tahoe (Carnelian Bay, Tahoe Vista, King's Beach, Crystal Bay)

Le Petit Pier (546-4464; $$$$) in Tahoe Vista presents upscale French cuisine. Locals refer to this restaurant as "where to go on a very special date." Reservations needed.

In Spring 2003 the **Wild Goose** (546-3640; $$$–$$$$) made its debut with an interior that's reminiscent of the lake cruisers of the 1920s, replete with mahogany, leather and polished steel, plus lake views. The Paris-educated chef, whose mantra is "nuances and simplicity," uses fresh seasonal and regional ingredients to create Contemporary American cuisine that showcases a sophisticated combination of flavors and textures.

Spindleshanks (546-2191; $$$), also in Tahoe Vista, has been awarded "Best Wine List" several years in a row. The food matches at somewhat reasonable prices. The place gets packed. Call for reservations or go early. On Wednesdays, when the appetizers are half price all evening at the bar, get a spot there and order a couple to make a nice light dinner.

The Soule Domain (546-7529 or 775-833-0399; $$$) in Crystal Bay receives consistent raves from people at both ends of the lake. The menu has changed for years but it seems to work. **Gar Woods Grill & Pier** (546-3366; $$-$$$) in Carnelian Bay serves a California grill menu.

Lake Tahoe Brewing Company (775-831-5822; $-$$) in Crystal Bay serves the usual pub fare and fresh-brewed beer. The casinos on the Nevada border serve inexpensive breakfasts, lunches and dinners. Try **Lakeview Dining Room** at the Cal-Neva Resort (775-832-4000; $-$$) or the **Cafe Biltmore** at the Tahoe Biltmore (775-831-0660; $-$$).

In Kings Beach, **Jason's Beachside Grill** (546-3315; $$) has moderate fare with lots of burgers to choose from. In Tahoe Vista, **Boulevard Cafe** (546-7213; $$) gets regular mention from locals for good Italian-influenced meals.

For sushi head to **Hiro Sushi** (546-4476; $$) in Kings Beach, where you should order the all-you-can-eat menu (you only have an hour to stuff it in). The caterpillar rolls, made with eel, look just like caterpillars down to the antenna. The best Mexican in the area is **La Mexicana** (546-0310; $$) in Kings Beach.

Lanza's (546-2434; $–$$), an institution in Kings Beach, has excellent Italian fare at family prices. **Steamer's Beachside Bar and Oven** (546-2218; $-$$) has been voted best pizza on the North Shore. Other good places for pizza are **C.B's Pizza** (546-4738; $) in Kings Beach and **Jiffy's Pizza** (546-3244; $) in Tahoe Vista.

For breakfast try the **Old Post Office** (546-3205; $) at Carnelian Bay and order the deluxe French toast or create your own omelet, or the **Log Cabin** (546-7109; $$) in Kings Beach where you can get lobster and shrimp scrambles, trout Benedict and fancy pancakes. The price bargain is breakfast at the **Tahoe Biltmore** ($) served 24/7.

Tahoe City and nearby

Wolfdales (583-5700; $$$$) with its frequently changing menu is superb. Claiming the food is "cuisine unique," it's essentially Asian and European with a taste of California mixed in. Reservations are suggested.

Christy Hill (583-8551; $$$$) is a real find. Christy Hill offers superb lake views in an intimate, casually elegant atmosphere. The menu, which changes several times each week, is loaded with the freshest fish and specialty produce. The restaurant is open for dinner only from Tuesday through Sunday. Call for reservations.

Jakes on the Lake (530/583-0188; $$) has good basic cooking and a great location.

Black Bear Tavern (583-8626; $$–$$$) is in an historic A-frame log building with a large stone fireplace. South of Tahoe City on Hwy. 89, with top-rate dining at moderate prices—steak, chicken, and fresh salmon and swordfish when available. Portions are large, but save room for apple crisp, an old German recipe smothered in vanilla ice cream.

Swiss Lakewood Restaurant (525-5211; $$$) in Homewood is Lake Tahoe's oldest and one of its finest dining experiences with impeccable service. Cuisine is French-Swiss and classic continental. Closed Mondays, except holidays. **Sunnyside** (583-7200; $$$) has good meals and a great setting. The crab legs are wonderful and on Wednesdays fish tacos rule.

Yama Sushi and Robata Grill (583-9262; $$-$$$) in the Lighthouse Shopping Center is a classic sushi restaurant but it also includes grilled meats, fish and vegetables. **Coyotes Mexican Grill** (583-6653; $$-$$$) is recommended by return visitors and locals alike.

River Ranch (583-4264; $$–$$$), at the access road to Alpine Meadows, has been there for years and still gets great reviews. In the spring, sitting by the river is a joy. Another Tahoe original is the **Old European Restaurant and Bar/Pfeifer House** (583-3102; $$), just north of Tahoe City on the road to Alpine and Squaw, with its traditional German meals.

Fiamma (581-1416; $$), in the middle of town, has a wood-fired pizza oven. Also try **Lakehouse Pizza** (583-2222; $$) for a great lake view. **Za's** (583-1812; $$) serves moderately priced Italian.

For Mexican with a big dose of margaritas and a shoulder-to-shoulder crowd on weekends, a good choice is the **Hacienda del Lago** (583-0358; $) in the Boatworks Mall. If you want lots of good food at very reasonable prices, try **Bacchi's** (583-3324; $) for Italian or **Bridgetender** (583-3342; $) for great half-pound burgers and an extensive beer selection.

For breakfast head to **The Fire Sign** (583-0871; $), about 2 miles south of Tahoe City, where many believe the best breakfasts and lunches in the region are served, or go to **Rosie's Cafe** (583-8504; $), where breakfast is a locals' affair. Near Alpine Meadows, try **The Alpine Riverside Cafe** (583-6896; $–$$) for breakfast and lunch.

Truckee

Moody's Bistro and Lounge (587-7619; $$$$) in the Truckee Hotel is run by a locally well-known chef. **Pianeta** (587-4694; $$$) serves an excellent Italian menu. **Dragonfly** (587-0557; $$$), upstairs on Truckee Row, has an interesting Asian menu with dishes from Japan, Thailand, China and Vietnam.

OB's (587-4164; $$), decorated with old farm antiques, serves prime rib as its house specialty. **Java Sushi** (582-1144; $$) serves what its name implies. Try the Friday Night Special served every night. They also serve tempura, teriyaki and broiled salmon.

El Toro Bravo (587-3557; $) is known for outstanding Mexican cuisine, with fajitas topping the menu. Head to **Pacific Crest** (587-2626; $-$$) for a wood-fired pizza. For simple meals, try **Andy's Diner** (582-6925; $).

For breakfast, go early to the **Squeeze In** (587-9814; $$) in Truckee, where the list of omelets requires a speed-reading course. The Squeeze In has all the atmosphere you could want in a breakfast joint, built in a former alley and only 10 feet wide. On weekends, expect to wait a while—this place is popular.

Northstar-at-Tahoe Resort

Not content to rest on their laurels, the chefs at Northstar's restaurant, **True North Res-**

Dining: $$$$-Entrees $30+; $$$-$20-$30; $$-$10-$20; $-less than $10.
Accommodations: (double room) $$$$-$200+; $$$-$141-$200; $$-$81-$140; $-$80 and less.

taurant and Bar (562-2250; $$$), decided to reinvent themselves with a new menu, new name and refurbished interior. Consistently one of Tahoe's best restaurants and recipient of the "Wine Spectator" Award of Excellence, it now showcases sustainable food choices using Niman Ranch all-natural beef and pork, fresh organic produce and Monterey Bay Aquarium-approved seafood flown in daily from Honolulu. Wine recommendations are listed with each entree.

Incline Village

On the northeastern side of the lake, in Incline Village, go to **The Lone Eagle Grill** at the Hyatt Regency (775-832-3250; $$$$) for some of the best food on the Nevada lakeshore. The soaring stone and timber and the massive fireplace blend with magnificent views across the lake at sunset, and the cuisine and wine list provide accomplished accompaniment. **Le Bistro** (775-831-0800; $$$$), across the street from the Hyatt Regency, is considered the best restaurant on the lake by some locals. As the name implies, the focus is on French fare.

Also in Incline Village, try **The Big Water Grille** (775-833-0606; $$$), at the bottom of the hill at Diamond Peak. A Native American name for Lake Tahoe, the Big Water features an eclectic menu and spectacular lake views—the perfect setting for romantic dinners, apres-ski relaxation and group gatherings. The menu features American Contemporary cuisine with Mediterranean and Pacific-Rim influences.

Cafe 333 (775-832-7333; $$$) in Incline Village, written up in "Bon Appetit" several times, is favored by Incline locals. It has French country decor and a moderately priced menu. **The Wild Alaskan Fish Company** (775-832-6777; $$) is one of the top spots for excellent seafood on the lake. It's just plain good.

Ciao Mein Trattoria (775-832-3275; $$) in the Hyatt Regency has a menu that is half Italian and half Chinese. **Azzara's** (775-831-0346; $–$$) in Incline Village serves good, reasonable Italian food. **Austin's** (775-832-7778; $) gets raves for meatloaf and homemade soups. **T's Rotisserie** (775-831-2832; $–$$) gets the nod from knowledgeable locals for chicken and burritos. **Hacienda de La Sierra** (775-831-8300; $) is a top Mexican spot. **China Wok** (775-833-3633; $-$$) is the only true Chinese place in town. **Wildfire Cafe** (702-831-8072; $) is an Incline institution for breakfast.

Squaw Valley

With the new restaurants in Squaw Valley's pedestrian village added to the excellent upscale choices at the lodges here, you don't have to leave the resort to get a good meal.

PlumpJack Squaw Valley (583-1576; $$$$) is an extraordinary dining experience in a style that is as unique as the cuisine is delicious. The wine list is carefully selected and prices are very reasonable, given the high quality. Reservations suggested.

Plumpjack Balboa Cafe Squaw Valley (583-5850; $$$$) in the Village at Squaw Valley is an American bistro with San-Francisco-style dining. It's owned by the same team who own PlumpJack Squaw Valley (if you're familiar with San Francisco, you'll also be familiar with the fine reputation of their two restaurants there).

Glissandi at the Resort at Squaw Creek (581-6621; $$$$) brings New York and San Francisco style and service, all overlooking Squaw Valley. Reservations suggested. Also in the hotel, **Ristorante Montagna's** (581-6619) serves a California/Italian fusion cuisine. Try **Graham's** (581-0454; $$$) at the Christy Inn for gourmet southern European meals.

Alexander's Cafe (581-7278; $$$) at High Camp requires that guests ride the scenic cable car up 2,000 vertical feet to the top of the mountain, where they dine on a fixed-price, three-course meal overlooking Lake Tahoe. The sushi restaurant in the village, **Mamasake** (584-0110; $-$$$), has become a new hotspot. It could be just because the "Eat Raw at

Squaw" proposition is hard to skip but it's more likely because the food here really is good. **High Sierra Grill** (584-6100; $-$$$) has "awesome" steaks and other grilled items; **Tantara Bakery, Bistro and Beyond** ($-$$) transforms itself from a bakery for breakfast to a deli and bistro for lunch and dinner; **Fireside Pizza Co.** (584-6150; $$) bakes fancy pizzas made with sourdough crust and farm-fresh ingredients; and **Chamois** ($) has good basic pizza.

Apres-ski/nightlife

Squaw is a party place. There are 27 bars from Squaw Creek to High Camp. One person commented that the total length of bars at Squaw was longer than the resort's vertical drop. At Squaw apres-ski is hot at at **Le Chamois**, the **Loft Bar** and the **Red Dog Bar & Grill**. **Bar One** has live music, dancing and pool tables, while the **Plaza Bar** is where sports fans go to see sporting events on the big screen TV. For a more intimate apres-ski, the bar at **the PlumpJack Squaw Valley Inn** has a cozy fireplace and an excellent selection of wine. The newest apres-ski spot in the Squaw scene is the **Balboa Cafe**, with its tasty appetizers and a variety of drinks.

River Ranch on the Alpine Meadows access road was voted to have the top apres-ski in North Lake Tahoe. Go before sunset to enjoy the winter wonderland scene across the Truckee River. Northstar-at-Tahoe often has live entertainment in its **Village Pavillion** on weekends.

In Tahoe City, places to head include **Pete 'N Peters, Bridgetender, Rosie's Cafe, Pierce Street Annex** (behind Safeway near the Boatworks Mall, voted best pick-up place), or **Jake's on the Lake. Hacienda del Lago** in the Boatworks has nachos 'til 6 p.m. **Sunnyside,** just a couple of miles south of Tahoe City on the lake, has a lively bar. For the best live music, try **Sierra Vista,** adjacent to the Boatworks Mall.

In Truckee, you can find music at **Bar of America** and the **Pastime Club** on Commercial Row. The **Cottonwood Restaurant** overlooking Truckee on Hwy. 267 has jazz.

Spindleshanks bar in Tahoe Vista is a great apres-ski spot where drinks and appetizers are half price every day during happy hour. On Wednesdays the appetizers are half price all evening. The lakefront **Gar Woods Grill & Pier** in Cornelian Bay is worth an apres-ski visit not just for the view, but for the clever laugh-out-loud names and descriptions of the drinks.

Incline locals hang at **Bigwater Grill, Frederick's** at the 7/11 Plaza, **Hacienda de la Sierra, Rookie's Sports Grill, Crosby's** and **Legends. Cutthroats** in the Hyatt Regency also gets rocking apres-ski.

With all these bars check the local papers for their half-price appetizer days.

Other activities

Squaw Valley's High Camp at the top of the cable car has **ice skating, snow-tubing, dining** and more. Polaris Park, mid-mountain at Northstar, has lighted snow play areas for **tubing, snowbiking and other activities.** It is open noon to 4 p.m. Friday, 10 a.m.–4 p.m. Saturday and Sunday. **Sleigh rides** are available at Northstar-at-Tahoe (530-562-2480) and in the Squaw Valley meadow (530-583-6300). The region also has **snowmobiling, dogsledding, scenic flights, hot-air balloon rides, horseback riding, bowling, movies** and **health clubs.**

Alpine Meadows Ski Patrol's **search and rescue dogs** put on a fascinating demonstration every Saturday and Sunday at 1:30 p.m. at the bottom of the Tiegel Poma. **Snow Festival** is North Tahoe's winter carnival, usually in late February/early March. Call (800) 824-6348 or (530) 583-3494 for a complete list of things to do.

At Diamond Peak, check out the Incline Village Recreation Center, which has **aerobics,**

Dining: $$$$–Entrees $30+; $$$–$20-$30; $$–$10-$20; $–less than $10.
Accommodations: (double room) $$$$–$200+; $$$–$141-$200; $$–$81-$140; $–$80 and less.

basketball court, weight room, European sauna and an **indoor pool** among its amenities. Visitors can use the facilities for either daily or weekly rates. Discounts are available for children, teens, seniors and families. Another spot for family fun is Bowl Incline with more than **bowling.** You'll find **pool tables, other pinball gizmos, video poker built into the bar** and a **golf simulator** where you can play seven world-class courses. Greens fees are by the hour and it takes about an hour to play 18 holes. The Incline Village Cinema is an excellent **movie theater.**

The **casinos** on North Lake Tahoe have gambling and entertainment every night. Call to see what **shows** are currently performing. Sure bets are the Cal-Neva Lodge (775-832-4000), Hyatt Regency Lake Tahoe (775-832-1234) and the Tahoe Biltmore (775-831-0660). The Tahoe Biltmore has an excellent **pool hall** and is a favorite of locals for **slots** and **poker.** The Hyatt Lake Tahoe is also an excellent casino and has perhaps the best shows.

The best **shopping** is in Tahoe City, especially in the Boatworks Mall. The new pedestrian village at Squaw Valley has some delightful shops too.

Getting there and getting around

By air: Reno-Tahoe International Airport has dozens of nonstop flights a day from various parts of the country. Resorts are about an hour away.

By train: Amtrak (800-872-7245) serves Truckee and Reno on the California Zephyr line, running from Oakland to Chicago.

By bus: Shuttles run from almost every major hotel to each major ski resort. Check for schedules when you arrive.

Sierra Nevada Gray Lines (800-822-6009; 775-329-1147) operates a daily ski shuttle between Reno and Alpine Meadows as well as Northstar-at-Tahoe (except Saturdays). Squaw Valley USA (800-446-2928) operates a Reno/South Lake Tahoe Shuttle from mid-December through the end of March. Tahoe Casino Express (800-446-6128) runs between Reno airport and South Shore.

By car: Driving time from Reno is about an hour via I-80 to any major North Shore resort. San Francisco is about four hours away via I-80 to the North Shore. During storms, the California Highway Patrol doesn't let drivers come up the mountains without chains or a four-wheel-drive vehicle, so be prepared.

The only resort with signs on the interstate is Squaw Valley. Alpine Meadows and Squaw Valley are both on Hwy. 89 (runs between I-80 and Hwy. 28, which hugs the North Shore). It's the last Truckee exit on Hwy. 80 coming from Reno and the first coming from San Francisco. Sugar Bowl is off I-80 just west of Donner Lake. Northstar-at-Tahoe is on Hwy. 267 (it also runs between I-80 and Hwy. 28, which hugs the North Shore). Diamond Peak is on Hwy. 28 in Nevada on the lake's east side.

Tip: If you are driving a rental car from Reno on I-80, headed west toward Northstar, Squaw or Alpine, you may pass through a California agricultural checkpoint. If you do, get off the freeway at the next stop and turn around. That checkpoint means you just missed the turnoff for Hwy. 89, just like one of our staffers did. The signs are dimly lit at night and tough to see a couple of hours before sunset.

Getting around: As much as we hate to recommend adding more auto pollution to this pristine location, rent a car. Public transportation is getting better, but not yet to the point where we can honestly recommend using it exclusively. If you stay near one of the ski resorts, your dining and evening options would be limited. Alpine Meadows, Squaw Valley, Sugar Bowl, Diamond Peak, Northstar and Homewood all have shuttles from North Tahoe towns.

South Lake Tahoe Area

Heavenly Mountain Resort

Kirkwood

Sierra-at-Tahoe

Toll-free reservations:
(800) 288-2463
Internet: www.bluelaketahoe.com
Dining:★★★
Apres-ski/nightlife:★★★★★
Other activities:★★★

Few regions in the world have what South Lake Tahoe does: almost 10,000 acres of lift-served terrain that annually receives an average of 40 feet of snow, a stunning Alpine lake—72 miles of shoreline—that never freezes, and sunny skies for more than 300 days a year. Add to this entertainment such as Chris Isaak, Sammy Hagar, Jonny Lang, Macy Gray and Toby Keith (all musicians who played here regularly), 24-hour access to slot machines and casino table games, and lots of great food. And did we mention that South Lake Tahoe is slightly more than an hour from a major international airport? Paradise, eh?

Better still, you can pick your style of vacation. Part of the town lies in Nevada, so if you like to stay up late dancing and gambling, you can book a room at one of four giant, high-rise casino hotels. A few steps across the Nevada/California state line, which runs right through town, life is quieter. But the new gondola has stretched the modern part of the city about half a mile to the west. Here in Alpine-style Heavenly Village you can take a the gondola right to the top of the mountain, enjoy the hustle and bustle of the South Shore's casino nightlife, shop in one of the village's stores, or sit back and quietly soak in the area's innate beauty. Across the Hwy. 50 or a hundred yards towards the setting sun, The Tahoe world changes back to the way it was in the 80s with smaller inns and motels, and maybe a water bed or two.

When you're ready for the slopes, you can pick from three resorts: Heavenly and Kirkwood, two of the largest Tahoe resorts, and Sierra-at-Tahoe, just 12 miles down the road. Heavenly is the most popular Tahoe resort with out-of-towners, probably because you can see its runs rising above town. Kirkwood has a well-deserved reputation for awesome terrain and massive amounts of snow, and the near completion of the mountain village at its base is metamorphosing it into a year-round resort. You also shouldn't miss Sierra-at-Tahoe, a locals' favorite known for its tree skiing and incredible backcountry terrain.

A word on phone numbers: Though the South Shore appears to be one big town, it's two towns in two states. If you're staying on the Nevada side, you'll need to dial the area code before all California phone numbers, and vice versa. Kirkwood is in another area code, 209.

Heavenly Mountain Resort

Heavenly is big. It ranks Number One at Lake Tahoe for highest summit elevation (10,067 feet), greatest vertical rise (3,500 feet, though not all of it is "working vertical") and longest run (5.5 miles). Heavenly has some excellent expert terrain—Mott and Killebrew Canyons on the Nevada side, and its famous face run, Gunbarrel, on the California side. New tree skiing and riding is now open on the California side as well, making Heavenly much more of af an expert's resort.

Heavenly is also the only two-state mountain resort—you can start out from either California or Nevada. The gondola provides direct access from the center of the South Lake Tahoe/Stateline district to the resort, and the 12-minute ride gives skiers and riders a killer view of the lake. There's a public parking garage at the Heavenly Village, near the base of the gondola, available to skiers and riders. More parking is available at the California base just up Ski Run Blvd. On busy weekends, to avoid crowds, start from the Nevada side; take Hwy. 207 (Kingsbury Grade) to either the Stagecoach or Boulder bases.

But mostly, Heavenly is the most spectacular view of Lake Tahoe—perhaps the most awesome view from a ski area summit anywhere—is at the top of the Sky Express. From here on a sunny day just after a storm, the lake looks like a brilliant blue sapphire, nesting in soft folds of white velvet. Pack a camera or stop at one of the photographers lining Ridge Run.

 Mountain layout

You can't ski down to Heavenly Village and the gondola stops downloading people at 4 p.m., so be sure you wind your way back to the top of the gondola before then (via 49'er, Sam's Dream, Cascade, or the California Trail). Signage is good at Heavenly, so you shouldn't have trouble finding it.

◆◆**Expert:** The California base strikes awe in all but the best skiers because the world seems to drop straight down into Lake Tahoe. Gunbarrel and East Bowl are 1,700-vertical-foot-high straight ladders of bumps, often with dangerous-looking rocky protrusions in early winter or late spring. The trees are wonderful on the California side as well.

But true experts looking for more steeps should head to the Nevada side. From the gondola, take the Tamarack Express chair, then cruise down to the Dipper Express. From here, traverse to Milky Way Bowl, which has arguably the best snow at the resort. Then enter Mott Canyon via designated gates 5 or 6. Hully Gully and Pinenuts are double-diamond runs and will allow you to do some reconnaissance on the canyon's north-facing chutes. But if you're already uncomfortable, don't try Bill's, Snakepit, or The Y—listed in order of difficulty and accessed via gate 1. They are three of the steepest lift-served runs in the west. Killebrew Canyon is even more treacherous. Only venture here if you have a change of underwear.

◆**Advanced:** If the bumps on the California face look too menacing, head to the Sky Express chair, right off the gondola down Von Schmidt's Trail. From the top of the Sky Express, the best of the California side opens up. After you have admired the view of Lake Tahoe, drop down Ellie's if you are looking for bumps. When Ellie's is groomed, it's a screaming Mach 3 ride. Or drop into the sweet powder stashes in the trees that used to be exclusive local territory. Northbowl Woods, Powderbowl Woods, Skiways Glades, Scorpion Woods and Dipper Knob Trees will test experts and advanced skiers on the California side.

Then strike out for Nevada, where 50 percent of the terrain is. You get to the Nevada side from the top of Sky Express; go left along the Skyline Trail. As you near Milky Way Bowl, look to your right for tracks leading into the trees and follow them. After a short traverse you will end up near the top of the bowl. Those coming off the Dipper chair on the Nevada side can use the same traverse. The daring may want to test their mettle in Mott Canyon. But if the view of the canyon makes you tremble, return instead to the Dipper Express for a run in the Dipper Bowl. Avoid the Galaxy chair; it's a slow lift that serves relatively flat terrain.

■ **Intermediate:** If you want long smooth cruising, head to the right from the Sky Express when you get off the chair and steam down Liz's, Canyon, Betty's or Ridge Run.

The Nevada side has even better cruisers. From the top of the Dipper Express are the Big Dipper and Orion's. The Galaxy Chair is a good spot for low intermediates to gain confidence. With its meandering intermediate runs, it also is a great hideaway for families with small children. For a cruise that seems to take forever, take Olympic Downhill to Stagecoach Base.

●● **Beginner** ● **First-timer:** In the past, Heavenly's green terrain was smack in the middle of the boarding area for four lifts. People dart in every direction, making a most intimidating scene for many beginners. Now the resort has isolated a 15-acre learning area at the top of the gondola that has improved the learning experience here. The new learning area is served by three lifts — a quad, a mighty might tow and a moving carpet. There is a ski school yurt and nearby food service. Plus, the trip to the lesson area up the gondola is (ahem) heavenly.

Ride Guide: Riders flock to Heavenly for its steeps, powder-filled canyons and powder stashes in the woods. The biggest bummer is the terrain layout isn't exactly snowboarder-friendly — the traverses are flat, flat, flat, and you have to do a lot of strapping and unstrapping to move around the mountain. But, all that work is worth it, especially after a powder dump.

General consensus among riders is the California side is too bumped up (stay away from Gunbarrel and East Bowl if you hate bumps like most riders do), so the Nevada side is the place to play. Mott Canyon and Killebrew Canyon have the steepest terrain at Heavenly. But beware: by steep, we mean *way* steep. For strictly trees, head to Dipper Knob Trees and the area known as the "western perimeter" (off Olympic Chair, ride the ridge to the trees, where you'll find natural hits, waves and lots of powder). On the California side, the best woods are Skiways and Maggie's Canyon (both reached by the Sky Express lift).

Other playgrounds include the numerous hits in Sand Dunes, the waterfall in North Bowl trees and the natural pipe left of Sky chair. Stick to Stagecoach and Olympic lifts if you want to carve your brains out.

Parks and pipes

You'll find four terrain parks, one lighted for night riding. The resort boasts one of the pre-eminent park builders on the West Coast.

The advanced park, High Roller California, is on the upper California side off the Canyon chair. The High Roller Superpipe is at the top of the Powderbowl chair on the California side.

Heavenly Mountain Resort Facts

California Side—
Summit elevation: 10,067 feet
Vertical drop: 3,500 feet
Base elevation: 6,540 feet

Nevada Side—
Summit elevation: 10,067 feet
Vertical drop: 2,840 feet
Base elevation: 7,200 feet

Address: Box 2180, Stateline, NV 89449
Area code: 775   **Ski area phone:** 586-7000
Snow report: 586-7000, press 1
Toll-free reservations: (800) 432-8365
E-mail: info@skiheavenly.com
Internet: www.skiheavenly.com

Number of lifts: 29–1 aerial tram, 1 gondola, 2 high-speed six-packs, 6 high-speed quads, 6 triples, 5 doubles, 6 surface lifts, 2 moving carpets
Snowmaking: 70 percent of trails
Total acreage: 4,800 patrolled acres (1,084 skiable trail acres)
Uphill capacity: 41,000 per hour
Parks & pipes: 3 terrain parks, 1 superpipe
Bed base: 22,000 in S. Lake Tahoe
Nearest lodging: At base of gondola
Resort child care: Yes, 6 weeks and older
Adult ticket, per day: $65 (04/05)

Expert:★★★★
Advanced:★★★★★
Intermediate:★★★★
Beginner:★★★
First-timer:★★★

The intermediate park, High Roller Stateline, is off the Tamarack chair on the California/Nevada border. The beginner park, Low Roller, is between Groove and Patsy's chairs on the California side. Heavenly has South Lake Tahoe's only after-hours terrain park—with hits, rails and funboxes—lighted 5–9 p.m. every Thursday through Saturday.

 ## Lessons (05/06 prices)

Group lessons: Levels 3–9 (skiers and snowboarders) choose from a 2.75-hour lesson for $70 or an all-day clinic with lift ticket and lesson for $126.

First-timer package: A 2.75-hour lesson, rentals and access to the beginner lifts costs $115, ski or snowboard. Same offer applies to novices with some experience on snow. Ask about multiday savings.

Private lessons: $295 for two hours; $485 for all day (six hours). Additional people cost $50 each for any lesson shorter than six hours, but six-hour privates can have up to six people at no extra charge. Reservations suggested, call (775) 586-4400.

Special programs: Heavenly has adaptive clinics and clinics for women. First Tracks gets you on the mountain a half-hour before the lifts open and includes breakfast at Lakeview Lodge. Call for prices, dates and reservations on all these programs.

 ## KidStuff (05/06 prices)

Child care: Ages 6 weeks to 6 years. Full-day program costs $105; half-day, morning or afternoon, costs $90. Lunch included except in afternoon class. Ski instruction/day-care combo programs also are available for ages 3 and older. Reservations required; call (775) 586-7000. The child-care center is at the California base.

Children's lessons: Full-day lessons (ages 4-13 for skiers, 7-13 for snowboarders) start at $145 and includes lift tickets, rentals, helmet and lunch.

 ## Lift tickets (05/06 prices)

	Adult	Child (5-12)
One day	$70	$36
Three days	$210 ($70/day)	$108 ($36/day)
Five days	$350 ($70/day)	$180 ($36/day)

Who skis free: Children ages 4 and younger ski free with a paying adult.

Who skis at a discount: Teens (ages 13–18) cost $58 per day; ages 65 and older pay $45 per day (see Notes below for explanation of one-day ticket prices). Heavenly offers PEAKS discounted multiday tickets purchased in advance. Membership in PEAKS is free and you are automatically enrolled when you make your early purchase. A gondola ride for sightseers costs $24 for adults, $22 for teens and seniors, $15 for children, free for ages 4 and younger. PEAKS discounts available.

Kirkwood

The lovely drive through Hope Valley to Kirkwood from South Lake Tahoe takes only about 45 minutes, but it is light-years away in altitude and ambiance. Kirkwood has no bright lights, no ringing jackpots, no wide blue lake, no high-rise buildings and no urban noise. Instead, you have the feeling that you are entering a special secret place, known to a select few. Yet you're at one of Tahoe's "big six" resorts.

As you drive up the access road from Hwy. 88, it's easy to see why these giant bowls were chosen for a ski resort. Skiers and snowboarders have left their tracks on every slope leading down to Kirkwood Village. No town existed before the resort came to fruition in 1972, and whatever you see was built (and is still being built) for a purpose: to improve the skiing and riding experience. Not that there was much to improve. Kirkwood sits in a natural basin with a base elevation of 7,800 feet—the highest in the Tahoe area. In a mountain range known for heavy powder (a.k.a. Sierra cement), Kirkwood's snow is often lighter and fluffier and more abundant than the other Tahoe resorts. Consequently, the resort frequently stays open into May with good late-season conditions.

Terrain-wise, Kirkwood is the most balanced resort in the Tahoe region. It has one of the best learning areas in the country; several gentle runs off to one side, away from the main traffic, are served by their own lifts. Kirkwood will thrill any expert, even super-expert, with its steeps and dozens of chutes. And it offers great terrain for all ability levels between those extremes. The only complaint we've ever heard about Kirkwood is its slow lifts. Of its 10 chairlifts, only two are express quads. The new TC lift replaces Hole "n" Wall.

Mountain layout

Kirkwood has both named and numbered its lifts. Locals and staff tend to use the numbers, so we list those in parentheses in the following terrain description.

♦♦**Expert:** Kirkwood locals know to follow the sun. Take The Reut (Chair 11) and traverse under Norm's Nose. Make a few turns down this wall and head to Caples Crest (Chair 2). Then drop into the backside (watch for Bud's Alley to the right or you'll end up below

Kirkwood Facts

Summit elevation:	**9,800 feet**
Vertical drop:	**2,000 feet**
Base elevation:	**7,800 feet**

Address: Box 1, Kirkwood, CA 95646
Area code: 209
Ski area phone: 258-6000
Snow report: (877) 547-5966
Toll-free reservations: (800) 967-7500
Fax: 258-8899
E-mail: info@kirkwood.com
Internet: www.kirkwood.com

Number of lifts: 12–2 quads, 7 triples, 1 double, 2 surface lifts
Snowmaking: 5 percent
Skiable acreage: 2,300 acres
Uphill capacity: 17,905 per hour
Parks & pipes: 3 terrain pipes, 1 superpipe, 1 quarterpipe
Bed base: 2,000 in resort, 22,000 in S. Lake Tahoe
Nearest lodging: Slopeside, ski-in/ski-out
Resort child care: Yes, 2 years and older
Adult ticket, per day: $59–$62 (05/06)
Expert:★★★★★
Advanced:★★★★★
Intermediate:★★★★★
Beginner:★★★★ **First-timer:**★★★★★

the Sunrise lift). As you ride up the painfully slow Sunrise chair, you can scout for untracked powder (or read the historical trivia posted on the lift towers). Since it takes three chairs to get here (four if you miss Bud's Alley), and the Sunrise chair closes when it's too windy, powder often remains for days after a storm. But beware, it can be heavy too. To return to the front side, drop down to Thunder Saddle and pick one of four north-facing chutes to return to the main base area.

Then, pick from the Wagonwheel/The Wall (Chair 10) or Cornice (Chair 6) lifts. Both serve steep, wide-open bowls and white-knuckle chutes. For a real thrill, traverse from Chair 10 to the top of Notch Chute in The Sisters. If you can handle the "step" that's been carved into the chute, you're there. Cornice serves single-diamond runs that feel like double-diamonds (e.g., Lost Cabin). From the top of Cornice, you can also traverse right to Palisades Bowl for some good powder shots. One final note: Pay attention to signs warning of cliffs. A run that looks like a simple trail on the map may in reality be a tight plunge through a cliff band.

♦**Advanced:** Both Sentinel Bowl and Zachary are groomed every day, a draw for anyone looking for super-smooth steeps. If you want bumps, try Olympic, Look-Out Janek, or Monte Wolfe, on either side of the Cornice Chair. The Reut (Chair 11) has some great cruisers—black on the map, but a solid intermediate could handle them. Don't miss runs on the back side, served by the Sunrise chair. Return to the front side via the Iron Horse chair.

■ **Intermediate:** Intermediates can stay on the lower sections of the face, using Hole'n'Wall (Chair 7) and Solitude (Chair 5), or work their way over Caples Crest (Chair 2) to the Sunrise section, where there's plenty of groomed terrain. The entire lower mountain, with just a couple of exceptions, is perfectly suited for intermediates. When you're ready to test your black-diamond skills, try the runs off Chair 11.

●● **Beginner:** Beginners will find gentle trails served by Snowkirk Chair (Chair 1) to the east, and Bunny Chair (Chair 9) and Hole 'n' Wall (Chair 7) at the far west.

● **First-timer:** First-timers should head straight for the Timber Creek Lodge, a right-hand turn before you reach the main parking lot (there's a sign). Here novices will find a rental shop and ticket window, plus Chairs 9 and 7 (Bunny and Hole'n'Wall) that serve novice and low-intermediate terrain. Experienced skiers should park in the main lot and get their tickets in the main lodge farther down the road, but if there's a novice in your group, you can get to the main area using Chair 7. Kirkwood has—by far—the best setup for novices in the South Tahoe region.

Ride Guide: Kirkwood has the best pow in Tahoe—sick, dry and fluffy. Besides the obvious double-black shots off Wagonwheel/The Wall (Chair 10) and the back side just waiting to be explored, experts will find some of the best riding off the Cornice chair (Chair 6), which also serves Palisades Bowl, to the far right on the trail map. Getting here requires a bit of a traverse and some hoofing, but you'll find great powder shots. Some favorite spots on the back side served by Sunrise (Chair 4): Drop the cornice at the spot called The Wave or float the chutes to the right of Thunder Saddle. Beware of the long flat back to the lifts after dropping off the saddle.

Parks and pipes

Kirkwood has loads of gullies that are Mother Nature's very own halfpipes and quarterpipes. Kirkwood also gets high marks for its three freestyle terrain parks and superpipe. Skilled skiers and riders should head straight to the much-admired Superpark. You'll be challenged on everything from Hollywood-sized tabletops and gap jumps to custom rail slides, fun boxes and a 23-foot quarterpipe. In order to enter the park, you must obtain a special pass, available free of charge at the Season Pass Office on the Plaza. Stomping Grounds Terrain Park, off the Plaza on Chair 5, is a pro-style park with terrain features designed for advanced ability levels. Multiple-level tabletops, rail slides, fun boxes and the massive Sierra Mist Superpipe are waiting for you to show off your stuff. Just learning to catch air? Then head to the The Playground off the new highspeed lift. There are easy jumps, rollers and banked turns, along with easy to moderate rails here just for you. Kids will have a ball getting familiar with man-made features in AdventureLand, off Chair 9 — rail slides, rollers and banked turns.

Lessons [05/06 prices]

We provide regular season rates. Holiday rates are higher.

Group lessons: Lessons are 90 minutes long and cost $40.

First-timer package: A First Time ski or snowboard package including lesson, beginner lift ticket and rental equipment costs $69.

Private lessons: Start at $95 an hour.

Special programs: Programs include clinics for women, all-mountain day camps, parks and pipes, and tackling non-groomed terrain. Call for dates and prices.

KidStuff [05/06 prices]

Child care: Ages 2–6, toilet-trained. All day costs $95 with lunch, a half day costs $75. Kids ages 4–6 get day care and ski lesson for $100. Holiday rates are $5 more. The child-care center is slopeside, across from Red Cliffs Lodge. Reservations recommended; call (209) 258-7274. Licensed child care for infants can be arranged with an outside agency at (209) 258-8783.

Children's lessons: Ski lessons for ages 4–12 and snowboard lessons for ages 7–12 include rental equipment, lunch, lessons and lifts for $105 for a full day and $90 for a half day package and $75 for a half-day lesson (no lunch). Multiday discounts are available. Ages 14 and older are considered young adults and enroll in the adult lessons. Helmets are encouraged for all children; rentals available. The children's ski and snowboard school is in the Timber Creek novice area, the first right-hand turn before you reach the main parking lot.

Lift tickets [05/06 prices]

	Adult	Child (6–12) and Seniors (70+)
One day	$62	$13
Three days	$177 ($59/day)	$39 ($13/day)
Five days	$295 ($59/day)	$65 ($13/day)

Who skis free: Children ski free on Sundays when accompanied by a paying adult.

Who skis at a discount: Ages 5 and younger pay $6; young adults 13–18, $46; ages 60–69, $31; seniors 70 and older, $13. On Sundays, children 12 and younger ski free when accompanied by a paying adult; two children per paid adult lift ticket, holidays excluded.

Note: Holiday rates are higher.

Accommodations–Kirkwood

If you want big-mountain skiing and a get-away-from-it-all location, stay slopeside at Kirkwood. The village has many recently built condos, shops, and services such as an ice rink and recreation center/swim complex. Phase One of the village is now complete and includes **Snowcrest Lodge, The Mountain Club** and the **Lodge at Kirkwood. Meadow Stone Lodge** is just steps from the lifts. Perhaps the best part about the new village is that it's, well—new. All the rooms feature modern interiors, have a prime location on the slopes and make efficient use of space. Of the other condo-complexes on the Meadow Side, the top choice is **Sun Meadows**, which is across from the Solitude and Cornice chairs and about as centrally located as you can get in Kirkwood. The second choice is **The Meadows**, between Timber Creek and the Cornice Chair. Rates range from $160-299 for a studio to $555-699 for a three-bedroom condo. Packages—particularly midweek stays—bring down the cost. Reservations: (209) 258-7000 or (800) 967-7500.

For a classic Sierra experience, book a cabin at **Sorensen's Resort** (800-423-9949; 530-694-2203; $$–$$$$). Nestled beneath a cliff in the Hope Valley 14 miles from Kirkwood, Sorensen's is a secluded, quiet camp bustling with winter activity, including cross-country skiing.

Sierra-at-Tahoe

Sierra-at-Tahoe often is overlooked by destination skiers to the South Shore. What a shame. Sierra-at-Tahoe has more than 2,000 vertical feet and 2,000 acres, and the tree skiing is some of the best in the country. Roughly 1,500 of the 2,000 acres are in the trees, old growth fir trees that, as one local put it, seem "strategically placed."

Just 12 miles south of South Lake Tahoe (about 30 minutes), this fun, big resort has an intimate feel. The resort has opted to invest its money into on-mountain upgrades; consequently you won't find any lodging or even a mountain village at its base. You *will* find a compact base area that's easy to get around, fabulous terrain, an efficient lift network, and great customer service, thank you very much.

Mountain layout

♦♦**Expert:** Forget trails. Head for the trees, particularly on a powder day. In West Bowl, the trees between Horsetail and Clipper hold almost unlimited stashes. When you hit the lift line, don't bail. Head back into the trees on the other side for a secret area of more untracked, creamy powder. The terrain around the Grandview Express gets tracked quickly, but you can still find fun in the trees between Preacher's Passion and the Tahoe King lift. It's steep and littered with giant boulders that, when covered with 10 feet of snow, resemble giant gnomes. Consider it nature's terrain park. Higher up, dive into the trees before Upper Dynamite. An opening referred to as Daylight Chute isn't on the map. Five backcountry access gates are still one of the resort's best-kept secrets. You can find fresh powder here a week after a storm. Access is free with the purchase of a lift ticket and guided tours are available daily.

♦**Advanced:** Sierra-at-Tahoe has a good collection of bumped-up black-diamond trails off the Grand View Express. Eastabout, Castle, Preacher's Passion and Dynamite all cascade roughly 1,300 vertical feet. Also try Clipper and Horsetail in the West Bowl.

■ **Intermediate:** This is a wonderful area for intermediates. West Bowl will fast become the favorite area of the mountain for this level. Lower Main is a steep, groomed run that rises above the day lodge. It's gotta be the toughest blue run here. If you see this trail and gulp, don't worry. Fun awaits in West Bowl. The Backside is another good spot for intermediates looking to test their powder skills.

●● **Beginner:** Sugar 'n' Spice is a 2.5-mile, easy cruise from the summit. Ride the

Grand View Express chair and take a moment to look at the view of the lake (much better on the roof deck of the Grand View Grill). As you descend Sugar 'n' Spice, stay a good distance from the snowbank on the left edge of the run, especially when it gets to be head-high. Hot shots like to shoot out of the trees between this run and Upper Snowshoe. Fortunately, Sugar 'n' Spice is plenty wide. Stay to the middle or the right and give the idiots some room.

Upper Snowshoe is another good beginner run, but be sure to turn right at Marten to meet up with Sugar 'n' Spice, or you'll be on Lower Snowshoe, a blue run. Another chair that serves good beginner terrain is Rock Garden.

● **First-timer:** This is a great learner's mountain. Sierra-at-Tahoe has a super learning slope called Broadway, right at the day lodge and served by its own quad chair.

Ride Guide: Like riding in the trees? Powder stashes often stay hidden in the old-growth forest for days after a storm. Ride the Grand View Express or West Bowl Express and just jump into the trees—anywhere. If you need a clue where to start, Jack's Bowl and Avalanche Bowl are two favorites for snowboarders. Five backcountry access gates open up a dreamland. Like chutes? Rock drops? Endless powder fields? You'll find it all here.

Lower Main is a steep, groomed intermediate run that begs you to work on your high-speed carving technique. West Bowl will become the favorite intermediate area of the mountain.

Parks and pipes

Sierra-at-Tahoe has five terrain parks, all marked with icons on the trail map. One of the most well-known parks is on The Alley and has five rail slides, two hits, two tabletops (with multiple hits) and a sound system. Aspen West is home to the 17-foot superpipe, which attracts some incredible skiers and riders and is highly regarded. Advanced tricksters, hear this: Head to Sierra's new super-sized terrain park on Bashful to test your mettle on the 40-foot Wall of Fortune. Intermediates should go to the park on Upper Main or Broadway, where you'll find rail gardens for jibbing, tables of all sizes and plenty of fun boxes. Beginners will find the Boardercross track on Smokey is the perfect place to test your speed on berms, rollers and banked turns.

Sierra-at-Tahoe Facts

Summit elevation:	**8,852 feet**
Vertical drop:	**2,212 feet**
Base elevation:	**6,640 feet**

Address: 1111 Sierra-at-Tahoe Rd.
Twin Bridges, CA 95735
Area code: 530
Ski area phone: 659-7453
Snow report: 659-7475
Toll-free reservations: (800) 288-2463
Fax: 659-7749
E-mail: sierra@boothcreek.com
Internet: www.sierratahoe.com
Number of lifts: 12–3 high-speed quads, 1 triple, 5 doubles, 2 moving carpet, tube tow

Snowmaking: 10 percent
Skiable acreage: 2,000 acres
Uphill capacity: 14,921 per hour
Parks & pipes: 5 terrain parks, 1 superpipe, 1 halfpipe
Bed base: 22,000 in S. Lake Tahoe
Nearest lodging: About 12 miles away
Resort child care: Yes, 18 months and older
Adult ticket, per day: $39-$59 (05/06 prices)

Expert: ★★
Advanced: ★★★★
Intermediate: ★★★★
Beginner: ★★★★
First-timer: ★★★★

Lessons (05/06 prices)

Group lessons: Two-hour lessons for advanced-beginners through advanced skiers and snowboarders cost $41 for lessons only; $96 with lifts, ticket and rentals. Buy a 3-Pak and pay $27 per day for lessons only and $52 per day with lifts, ticket and rentals.

First-timer package: A First Time package including beginner lifts, rentals and a two-hour lesson is $75 for skiers or snowboarders; all day costs $93. A three-day Ride or Ski Guarantee includes three days of lessons, lifts and rentals, and a guarantee that you'll be able to ski/ride top-to-bottom on a beginner trail or a fourth lesson is free; cost is $129.

Snowboarders can opt for the Burton Learn To Ride program, which uses specially designed snowboards to make learning easier. Two-hour lesson with ticket and rental costs $75; all day costs $93; three-days cost $129.

Private lessons: $152 for two hours; $190 for three hours; $270 for all day. Semi-privates for up to five people are $189 for two hours; $235 for three hours; $315 for all day. Reservations required, call (530) 659-7453.

KidStuff (05/06 prices)

Child care: Ages 18 months to 5 years. Cost is $98 for full day (includes lunch); $80 for half day. Reservations recommended; call (530) 659-7453.

Children's lessons: All-day ski or snowboard instruction (including rentals and lift ticket) is $98 for ages 4–12. A special all-day program for 3-year-olds combines ski lessons and daycare, $98 (includes lunch, snacks, lift ticket, lessons and day care).

Lift tickets (05/06 prices)

	Adult	Child (5-12)
One day	$59	$14
Three of five days	$117 ($39/day)	$42 ($14/day)

Who skis free: Ages 4 and younger.

Who skis at a discount: Young adults ages 13-22 pay $47 for one day; ages 65-69 pay $33; ages 70 and older pay $16.

Cross-country and snowshoeing (visit xcskiresorts.com for more details)

The Lake Tahoe region may have the greatest concentration of large cross-country ski areas in the U.S., with more than 800 km. of groomed trails. Most of that is on the north end of the lake, but South Shore has a good network of trails, too. Most also allow snowshoes.

Heavenly's Adventure Peak (775-586-7000) at the top of the gondola includes a cross-country skiing and snowshoeing center. You'll find 5 km. of groomed trails that meander through the forest and provide awesome views from nearly 3,000 feet above Lake Tahoe.

Spooner Lake Cross-Country (775-887-8844, recording; 775-749-5349, live voice) on Hwy. 28, about a half-mile north of Hwy. 50, has more than 80 km. of trails, nearly all of which are machine groomed, with one 19-km. backcountry trail. Lessons and cross-country gear, snowshoe and pulk sled rentals are available; you also can rent a backcountry cabin.

Kirkwood Cross-Country (209-258-7248) has 80 km. of machine-groomed tracks, skating lanes and three interconnected trail systems with three warming huts, including the 1864 Kirkwood Inn, a trappers' log cabin full of nostalgia. Rental gear includes cross-country, telemark, snowshoes and pulk sleds. Lessons are also available.

Hope Valley Cross-Country Ski Center (530-694-2266) is near the junction of Hwy. 89 and 88. It has about 100 km. of marked trails, a quarter of which are groomed. Trail fees are by donation. Lessons and rentals are available. The trails at **Sorensen's Resort** (800-423-9949; 530-694-2203) hook into this system.

Camp Richardson Resort (530-541-1801 or 542-6584) in South Lake Tahoe has a cross-country ski center with lessons, rentals and 35 km. of groomed trails along the Lake Tahoe shoreline. There are additional marked trails venturing into Desolation Wilderness. It's usually voted "Best Place to Cross-Country Ski" by Tahoe locals. You also can get full-moon guided tours, snowshoe rentals, and lodging/cross-country ski packages.

Sierra-at-Tahoe (530-659-7453) has more than 3 miles of groomed snowshoe trails complete with interpretive trail signs. Daily snowshoe rentals and guided tours available. There are no cross-country trails or tours here, but telemark skiers can get tours either in-bounds or into the backcountry, at Sierra's new Telemark and Backcountry Center. Telemark gear is available for rental.

 ## Accommodations

South Shore accommodations divide into four categories: the multistory casinos hugging the Nevada border for great views and nonstop nightlife; the top of Kingsbury Grade, near the base of Heavenly's Nevada side, for upscale condominiums and top-quality hotels; along the California lake shore for moderately priced motels; and at Kirkwood to escape the hustle and bustle. **Central Reservations for South Lake Tahoe** is (800) 288-2463.

If you plan to do all your skiing at Heavenly, **Heavenly Tahoe Vacations** (800-243-2836; 775-588-4584) can arrange an entire ski vacation including airfare, transfers, lessons, rentals, non-ski activities, skiing and lodging. If you can stay Sunday through Thursday nights, you can get extremely good deals. Lodging and lift packages can run as low as $69 per person, per night, double occupancy. If you're here Friday and Saturday, however, prices double or sometimes triple. South Shore has a wide variety of lodges and prices, however, so tell the agent how much you want to spend.

Many destination visitors like to be smack in the middle of the action. If you're in that group, try **Harveys Resort & Casino** (800-648-3361 from outside Nevada, 775-588-2411 from Nevada; $$–$$$) and **Harrah's Casino Hotel** (800-648-3353; 775-588-3515; $$–$$$$), which have everyone's highest ratings, from AAA to Mobil. Other casino-hotels within walking distance of the state line are **Caesars Tahoe** (800-648-3353; 775-586-2000; $$–$$$$) and the **Horizon Casino Resort** (800-648-3322; $$–$$$$). Ask for a lakeview room with a balcony at the Horizon.

On the California side, several beautiful resorts have been built in the past few years. The **Marriott Grand Residence Club** (866-204-7263; $$–$$$$) is in the Heavenly Village development at the base of Heavenly's gondola. It features in-suite kitchens, laundry service, a ski-check room, as well as a number of retail shops and the FiRE + iCE Restaurant (see *Dining*). It's also the closest hotel to Heavenly's gondola, which gives skiers and sightseers a jaw-dropping view of the lake on its 12-minute journey from downtown to the slopes.

Also near the gondola is one of our favorite places, the **Embassy Suites Lake Tahoe Resort** (800-362-2779; 530-544-5400; $$–$$$). Just 50 feet from the nearest casino, it has an indoor atrium, indoor pool and hot tub, an exercise center, on-site restaurant and lounge. Cooked-to-order breakfast and happy hour are included in the rates.

For the Nevada side of Heavenly accommodations, there are scores of condos at Stagecoach Base and Boulder Base areas. At the base of Kingsbury Grade on Hwy. 50 you'll find the **Lakeside Inn & Casino** (800-624-7980; 775-588-7777; $–$$), which offers some of the best deals. The rooms are simple and motelish.

The California side of South Lake Tahoe has many hotels and motels lining Hwy. 50. Among the best are two Best Western properties—**The Timber Cove Lodge** (800-528-1234; 530-541-6722; $–$$$), located on the beach; and **Station House Inn** (800-822-5953; 530-542-1101; $$–$$$), within walking distance of the casino area, on the California side of the border. Two miles from the casinos, **Inn By The Lake** (800-877-1466; 530-542-0330; $–$$$) sits almost at the shore (Hwy. 50 separates it from the shore). It has 100 guest rooms—including nine suites with kitchens, but many of the regular guest rooms are large and have refrigerators—plus a free continental breakfast with enough selections to keep you full until lunch, heated pool, and bi-level hot tub. It's also one of the stops on the free shuttle to the slopes.

Embassy Vacation Resorts (800-362-2779; 530-541-6122; $$$–$$$$) is a 300-suite resort with timeshare condos and all the amenities. At the intersection of Hwy. 50 and Ski Run Boulevard, it is close to the lake, the ferry dock and Heavenly's slopes.

For the rustic-minded, try the **Historic Camp Richardson Resort** (800-544-1801; $$–$$$). The cabins have large fireplaces, spacious living rooms and full kitchens. Perfect for couples traveling together or families who enjoy various outdoor sports. Onsite sledding, snowshoeing, cross-country trails and wilderness sleigh rides complete this seasonal resort. The historic hotel and beachside inn provide more "civilized" accommodations. A similar mountain paradise can be found on the Nevada side at **Zephyr Cove Resort** (775-588-6644; $$–$$$). The beachfront resort offers mountain cabins set amidst the pines, guided snowmobiling tours, cross-country skiing, plus it's the home of the M.S. Dixie II paddlewheeler, which operates year-round.

Adjacent to the Lakeside Beach is the funky **Royal Valhalla Motor Lodge** (800-999-4104; 530-544-2233; $–$$$), some rooms have kitchens and most, wonderful lake views. Just two blocks from the casinos, it sits in a quiet neighborhood.

Lakeland Village (800-822-5969; 530-544-1685; $$–$$$$) has a hotel and condominiums on the lake with shuttlebus service to Heavenly and Kirkwood. The units range from studios to a lakefront four-bedroom, three-bath unit. For those who want a room 150 yards from Heavenly's California base, the **Tahoe Seasons Resort**, with 160 suites, has received good reviews from everyone locally (530-541-6700; $$–$$$$). Another possibility is the **Holiday Inn Express** (800-544-5288; 530-544-5900; $$–$$$$).

One for couples only: The **Fantasy Inn** (800-367-7736; 530-541-4200; $$$–$$$$) has a wedding chapel and about 60 rooms designed for romance. Each room has one bed in a choice of several shapes (round, heart-shaped, water or regular mattress, king-size), a jetted tub for two, an in-room music system with 30 channels, adjustable peach-colored lighting and showers with double shower heads. Sixteen of the rooms have themes, such as Rain Forest (plants and rattan decor), Caesar's Indulgence (a sexy black decor), and Romeo and Juliet (the honeymoon suite). Theme suites are in the $245–$295 range. Ask about special ski and/or wedding package rates.

Dining (all area codes are 530 unless noted)

Evan's American Gourmet Cafe (542-1990; $$$) on Hwy. 89 has become one of the best-liked restaurants on the South Shore. The chef prepares California cuisine with an unusual flair. Expect to pay for his efforts, but they are well worth it. For a superb meal, great wine list and attentive service—with a beautiful view—head to **Friday's Station** (775-588-6611; $$$) at the top of Harrah's casino-hotel.

A small eclectic cafe with an island atmosphere (check out the salt and pepper shakers on each table), **Freshies** (542-3630; $) is another good bet for fresh, healthy food. In keeping with the name, the cafe offers half-off soups on powder days.

Other recommendations are **Fresh Ketch** (541-5683; $$$) for fish; **Dory's Oar** (541-6603; $$$) for steaks and seafood; or **ECHO Restaurant & Lounge** (543-2140; $$–$$$) in the Embassy Suites hotel for its delicious American fusion cuisine.

Beacon (541-0630; $$–$$$) at Camp Richardson is known for its blackened prime rib. **Nephele's** (544-8130; $$) serves California cuisine in a cozy setting. Next door to Nephele's is an outstanding restaurant called **Cafe Fiore** (541-2908; $$). It doesn't seat many, so reservations are a must. The food and the wine list are superb.

Several new restaurants have opened in Heavenly Village. The energetic and fun **FiRE + iCE** (542-6650; $–$$) at Marriott's Timber Lodge next to the gondola is an improvisational grill where you choose the ingredients for the chef to grill.

In April 2004 Sammy Hagar opened his second **Cabo Wabo Cantina** (775-588-2411; $$) in Harveys Resort Casino. Open for lunch and dinner, it specializes in authentic but creative Mexican dishes such as ahi tuna tacos and frozen margarita cake. When the clock strikes 10 p.m., it turns into a hopping nightclub.

Good reasonable restaurants include **The Cantina Bar and Grill** (544-1233; $) for Mexican; **Scusa** (542-0100; $$) for Italian (a local favorite); **Sato Japanese Restaurant** (544-0774 or 775-588-1914; $–$$) in the Horizon Casino for surprisingly good sushi specials; **Shoreline Cafe** (541-7858; $$) for good pasta specials and an extensive kids' menu; or **The Tudor Pub** (541-6603; $–$$), upstairs from Dory's Oar, for fish & chips and European beers on tap. Of the casinos' affordable buffets (and there are many), **Harveys** (775-588-2411; $) was reasonably priced, especially the seafood buffet and had large portions.

Del Soul (775-588-3515; $$) is a casual Mexican Grill. **Sprouts** (541-6969; $) is a local favorite. The extensive menu includes rice bowls, hummus melts and lasagna. Don't miss the smoothies, especially if you're ailing after a long night. A shot of wheatgrass might cure all.

For great breakfasts head to the **Red Hut Waffle Shop** (541-9024; $) where you can pack into a small room and listen to the talk of the town. Another branch is on Kingsbury Grade (775-588-7488; $), handy for skiers heading to the Nevada side of Heavenly. At **Heidi's** (544-8113; $), get anything from dozens of Belgian waffles to chocolate pancakes. If you're in over the weekend you must go to **Llewellyn's** (775-588-2411; $$) at Harvey's Resort Hotel for Sunday brunch; food is flavorful and the view breathtaking. If you're a jetlagged easterner and wake up at 4 a.m., head to one of the casino's 24-hour restaurants.

The Horizon's **Four Seasons** basic breakfast, or pick up a latte at **Starbucks** in the hotel lobby.

And just in case you crave a malt "so thick it holds the straw up," go to the **Zephyr Cove Resort.** Try the banana-chocolate shake. **Alpen Sierra Coffee Roasting Company**, at Hwy. 50 and Pioneer, is one of the area's best coffeehouses with locally roasted mountain coffee.

Dining: $$$$-Entrees $30+; $$$-$20-$30; $$-$10-$20; $-less than $10.
Accommodations: (double room) $$$$-$200+; $$$-$141-$200; $$-$81-$140; $-$80 and less.

On the mountains:

At Heavenly, table linen lunch service is offered at **Monument Peak Restaurant** ($–$$) at the top of the tram. **East Peak Lodge** ($) and the **Sky Deck** ($) both have outdoor lunch service and sun-drenched tables, but we recommend bringing your own food.

The best on-mountain lunch we had was at Sierra-at-Tahoe. We had a delicious Thai chicken wrap washed down with a Sierra Nevada Pale Ale at **The Sierra Pub** ($) in the day lodge. On weekends, there's live music on the sundeck. Another option is the **Grandview Bar & Grille** ($) at the summit, where you can chow down on Asian fare such as Kung Pao chicken and lettuce wraps while you drink in the views. Fresh-ground coffee and fresh-baked goods are sold in the **day lodge** ($).

Kirkwood and surrounding area:

If you're staying at Kirkwood, you'll probably discover the places to eat on your own—not a big selection, but all are pretty good. **Off the Wall Bar & Grille** ($$) in the Lodge at Kirkwood has California-style gourmet cuisine in a comfortable cozy atmosphere. **Bub's Sports Bar & Grill** ($–$$) across the street from the Cornice Express is where the locals eat, and you'll soon discover why. The burgers and sandwiches go a step beyond the usual bland slopeside cuisine. **Kirkwood Inn** ($$), built in 1864 and in operation ever since, features hearty meals such as steaks and seafood. Look for the bullet holes left in the walls from Prohibition days. A mile east of Kirkwood on Hwy. 88 is the **Caples Lake Resort** (209-258-8888; $$–$$$) for fine dining overlooking scenic Caples Lake. At the **General Store** ($) you can find inexpensive sandwiches and fresh cookies—great for a slope-side picnic.

Apres-ski/nightlife

At Sierra-at-Tahoe, the Sierra Pub is the place to swap tales, listen to live music and indulge in happy hour specials.

If your going near Heavenly, head to **Chevy's** immediately after skiing. If you want quieter apres-ski with a flickering fireplace, stop in at **Christiana Inn** across from the Heavenly ski area.

Later in the evening, blu in the **Montbleu Resort Casino and Spa** is a spectacle of light, sights and sounds as their DJs provide the rhythm track for an evening of hip-pswinging. **The Pub at Tahoe**, a great Irish pub near the state line, has terrific live music (listenable rather than danceable), pool tables on the first floor, and is packed every night.

If you've been to rocker Sammy Hagar's legendary **Cabo Wabo Cantina** in Cabo San Lucas, or always wished you could visit, you'll want to head to his Tahoe nightclub inside Harveys Resort Casino. Everyday drink specials make this a great gathering spot.

Another spot recommended by locals is **Mulligan's**. **The Goalpost Restaurant & Bar** in Stateline is the hot spot for the late-late crowd.

And of course, the casinos have musical reviews that are extravaganzas of sight and sound. Check a local newspaper for up-to-date listings.

Other activities

South Tahoe has lots to do, but space doesn't permit us to list all the options. Ask your hotel concierge for suggestions.

You can **ice skate** at the South Lake Tahoe Ice Arena (530-542-6262), open every afternoon from 1–5 p.m. and some evenings and mornings. Skates are available for rent. Call Lake Tahoe Balloons (530-544-1221) for **balloon rides** and Lake Tahoe Adventures (530-577-2940) for **snowmobiling**. The Husky Express (775-782-3047) takes people **dogsledding** in the Hope Valley. Camp Richardson (530-541-3113) has **sleigh rides** through meadows; reservations required.

Heavenly's Adventure Peak (775-586-7000) at the top of the gondola includes lift-accessed snow tubing. In the Heavenly Village at the base of the gondola (in the center of town), there is an **ice rink**.

At Kirkwood you can **ice skate** at the rink in the pedestrian village. Kirkwood also offers **dogsledding, sleigh rides, sauna and massage,** the **Swim Complex** with an Olympic-size pool and workout facilities, and a family **tubing hill.** Sierra-at-Tahoe has a **tubing hill** too.

There's art galleries and upscale **shopping** in Heavenly Village now that the new Village Center at Stateline is bursting at the seams with places to spend money. A few factory outlets are at "The Y" (the intersection of Hwys. 50 and 89 south of town).

For a **massage**, make an appointment with the Bodymind Studio (530-541-5041) in the Timber Cove Lodge. For **movies** head to the cineplex.

And of course, the **casinos** have musical reviews that are extravaganzas of sight and sound. Some shows run through the season; others are top-name singers and comedians who do one or two shows. Check a local newspaper for up-to-date listings.

Weddings aren't your everyday optional ski activity, but if you're thinking of getting married with little fuss, this is one of the best spots to do it. More than 20 wedding chapels dot the area, but probably the nicest ones are in the big hotels. Most have wedding concierges to plan every detail. You also can be married outdoors, either by the lake or on the slopes.

Getting there and getting around

By air: Reno-Tahoe International Airport has more than 100 nonstop flights a day from various parts of the country. The airport is 55 miles from South Lake Tahoe. The Lake Tahoe Airport, near South Lake Tahoe, has limited service from California. Buses and hotel shuttles take skiers to the resorts from both airports. Tahoe Casino Express (800-446-6128) runs 18 times daily between the Reno airport and South Shore.

By boat: The Tahoe Queen, an authentic Mississippi sternwheeler, double-decked and heated, takes South Shore skiers and snowboarders across Lake Tahoe to Squaw Valley (buses take skiers from the dock to the ski areas). Another paddlewheeler, the M.S. Dixie II, based at Zephyr Cove in Nevada, does daily cruises of Emerald Bay for adults and children, and Saturday night dinner cruises for adults during the winter. For fares and schedules, call Lake Tahoe Cruises at (530) 541-3364 or (800) 238-2463.

By bus: Shuttles run from almost every major hotel to the resorts. Check for schedules when you arrive. Most of the shuttles are free.

By car: Driving time from Reno is about 70 minutes. San Francisco is about four hours away on Hwy. 50. Sierra-at-Tahoe is 12 miles south of the lake on Hwy. 50. Kirkwood is on Hwy. 88 (follow signs from South Lake Tahoe). During storms, the California Highway Patrol doesn't let drivers come up the mountains without chains or a four-wheel-drive vehicle, so bring chains or be sure the car rental agency provides them. Or take the shuttle on snowy days.

Getting around: Drive a car if you intend to move frequently between the south and the north shores; otherwise, a car is optional. We'd say have one if you like to roam far afield at night. If not, you can walk to restaurants and nightspots near your hotel and use the ski shuttles during the day. Part of the redevelopment of South Tahoe also includes public transportation. BlueGo is a bi-state shuttle system intended to eliminate the need for private vehicles.

Dining: $$$$-Entrees $30+; $$$-$20-$30; $$-$10-$20; $-less than $10.
Accommodations: (double room) $$$$-$200+; $$$-$141-$200; $$-$81-$140; $-$80 and less.

Mammoth Mountain

June Mountain

California

Summit elevation:	11,053 feet
Vertical drop:	3,100 feet
Base elevation:	7,953 feet

Address: Mammoth Mountain, Box 24; Mammoth Lakes Visitors Bureau, Box 48; both Mammoth Lakes, CA 93546
Area code: 760
Ski area phone: 934-2571
and (800) 626-6684
Toll-free snow report/information:
(888) 766-9778
Toll-free reservations: (888) 466-2666
and (800) 626-6684
Fax: 934-7066
E-mail: 800mammoth@mammoth-mtn.com
Internet: www.visitmammoth.com (town);
www.mammothmountain.com (ski area)

Dining: ★★★
Apres-ski/nightlife: ★★★
Other activities: ★★★

Expert: ★★★★★
Advanced: ★★★★★
Intermediate: ★★★★★
Beginner: ★★★★
First-timer: ★★★★

Number and types of lifts: 28–3 gondolas, 1 high-speed six-pack chair, 9 high-speed quads, 1 quad, 6 triples, 5 doubles, 3 surface lifts
Skiable acreage: 3,500+ acres
Snowmaking: 33 percent
Uphill capacity: 50,000 per hour
Parks & pipes: 3 terrain parks, 1 halfpipe, 2 superpipes
Bed base: 30,000
Nearest lodging: Slopeside
Resort child care: Yes, newborns and older
Adult ticket, per day: $63–$78 (06/07 prices)

June Mountain Facts
Summit elevation: 10,135 feet
Vertical drop: 2,590 feet
Base elevation: 7,545 feet
Number and types of lifts: 7–2 high-speed quads, 4 doubles, 1 surface-lift
Skiable acreage: 500+ acres
Parks & pipes: 2 terrain parks, 1 superpipe
Uphill capacity: 10,000 per hour
Bed base: 2,000 local

No mountain is better named than Mammoth. When you stand at the base lodge and scan the mountain, you can't even see a quarter of the ski terrain. The encircling ridge, all above treeline, promises dramatic skiing, but what you can't see is even better. Lower peaks such as Lincoln Mountain, Gold Hill and Hemlock Ridge, all with groomed swaths and moguled canyons, stretch 6.5 miles in width. Mammoth is one of the nation's largest winter resorts in size, and at times it's the nation's busiest, with more than 14,000 skiers and riders swooping over its slopes on an average weekend.

Its season runs from early November through June—legitimately. Mammoth often relies on its 430 acres of snowmaking to be open by Thanksgiving, but snow often falls by early November. Skiing and riding here on the Fourth of July is a well-loved tradition among the diehards who haven't had enough.

Over the past few years a slopeside pedestrian village with 275 residential units and 140,000 square feet of retail space for shops, galleries, bars and restaurants has been developed. Visitors who stay in one of the three Village lodges, White Mountain Lodge, Lincoln House or Grand Sierra Lodge, can take advantage of the Mountain Center, a 17,000-square-foot skier services building in the center of the Village. It is connected to the Village Gondola, which whisks guests up to Canyon Lodge, eliminating the need for a car once you're in the town of Mammoth Lakes.

Up the road at the main base area, a labyrinthine base lodge houses the ski school, lift ticket windows, rental shops and hundreds of lockers for locals and visitors. The slopeside Mammoth Mountain Inn recently underwent a $1.5 million renovation, as did the third floor of the main lodge, where $4 million went into a compete cafeteria remodel including a sports bar that overlooks the snowboard park..

At the bottom of the mountain road lies the small but spread-out town of Mammoth Lakes. As the town grew to support the ski area's success, newcomers haphazardly trans-planted Southern California sprawl and mini-malls to the mountains. Since the Village was built three years ago, it has established the town center Mammoth has never really had. Most visitors come by car from Southern California, but the few who don't will feel the need for wheels—not much is within easy walking distance. However, there is a free town shuttlebus that runs day and night.

If size intimidates you, Mammoth's little sister June Mountain, a half-hour drive from Mammoth Lakes, will appeal to you. Its Old World village atmosphere in a sheltered canyon is on a more human scale. That is not to say it's a puny resort: it has seven chairlifts and a 2,590-foot vertical rise (as opposed to 3,100 feet at Mammoth).

 ## Mountain layout

This mountain is very, very large. No matter what ability level you're at, you won't be shortchanged. First-time visitors should pack a trail map. Seriously. Almost everything goes by number. The mountain is crisscrossed with a network of chairlifts numbered in the order they were built. It makes perfect sense to visitors who grew up with the mountain, but it's confusing to the first-time visitor who hears regulars planning their day football-quarterback style, "Take one to three, then back side to 23, down the ridge to 14, then to 13 and lateral to one." Now that the resort has installed several high-speed lifts and given them names, regulars still refer to the lifts by their former number, which makes it even more confusing for the first-time visitor. For the record, Chairs 1, 2, 3, 4, 6, 10, 11, 15, 16 and 17 all have names now, and exist only in the memories and automatic brain-recall of Mammoth regulars. Die-hards have been known to attempt a day of skiing the chairlifts in order—a hefty task that requires criss-crossing and careful planning, not to mention hiking.

If you're with a group, decide where to meet if you get separated. Pick a centrally located chair, rather than McCoy Station or the Main Lodge.

If you come on a weekend, avoid the Main Lodge at the top of the mountain road (unless you're staying at the slopeside Mammoth Mountain Inn). Tickets are sold (in order as you come up the road) at Eagle Lodge next to Juniper Springs Resort, Canyon Lodge, The Roller Coaster lift, Stump Alley Express and the Main Lodge. Eagle Lodge and the Canyon Lodge are actually off the main road to the ski area, so ask someone to direct you. To avoid weekend crowds, take Chairs 9, 25, 22, 21, 12, 13 and 14, listed from left to right on the trail map.

First-timers should go to Canyon Lodge or Main Lodge. Those with a little experience also can start at Eagle Lodge on the Eagle Express.

◆◆ **Expert:** Expert yaa-hoo skiers will strike out for the ridge, reachable by the gondola or a series of chairs. From the ridge, any chute or path will open into a wide bowl. Mammoth's signature run, a snarling lip of snow called Cornice Bowl, looms large in every expert's memory bank. Other runs dropping from the ridge are considered steeper and more treacherous. Reached from the gondola, Hangman's Hollow—Mammoth's toughest—is an hourglass-shaped chute hanging from the summit and bordered by wicked rocks. At its narrow part there's space for only one turn—a perfect one. Other expert shots are off Chair 22, and on powder days you can often find untracked or less-tracked snow on the far east Dragon's Back off Chair 9, or the far west (hiking access only) Hemlock Ridge above Chair 14.

♦ **Advanced:** One of the most popular advanced areas is the group of bowls available from Face Lift Express (formerly Chair 3). They're great warm-up runs for experts, but plan to get here early on weekends. The high-speed lift has helped lessen the formerly outrageous lines (that's our term; one of our favorite Mammoth employees describes it as "healthy"), but it is still busiest on weekend mornings around 9:30 a.m. Midweek, no problem.

A slightly less busy alternative is triple-Chair 5, the next chair to the left on the trail map, or Chair 14, to the far right on the map. Chairs 22 and 25, which provide access to Lincoln Mountain and its intermediate runs and advanced chutes, rarely have lines.

When you feel like attacking the ridge, head to Dave's Run. Off the gondola, traverse the ridge to trail-map left, then drop down when the pitch isn't sheer vertical. Dave's is still pretty steep, but of the single-black options off the ridge, it's usually the least crowded. If you have any doubts, ride the gondola back down to McCoy Station, or take the upper-intermediate ridge trail to more wide-open Scotty's or the Chair 14 area.

■ **Intermediate:** The middle part of the mountain is still above treeline, so those at this level have plenty of room to traverse on the single-black runs. Hidden canyons like Lower Dry Creek (off the Face Lift Express) are full of swoops and surprises, and require tighter turns. For long cruising, head to Eagle Express. Other intermediate playgrounds are served by the tree-lined runs from The Roller Coaster and Canyon express quads and Chairs 8, 20 and 21. At the other edge of the area is Chair 12 and the drop over to Chairs 13 and 14.

● **Beginner:** If you aren't a first-timer, but still practicing turns, the runs near Canyon Lodge are best. Trails such as Hansel and Gretel weave gently through evergreens, providing sheltered slopes for learning, away from the speed demons. When you're ready for the next step, Christmas Tree, a long run under Eagle Express, is pretty gentle. This part of the mountain gets soupy in the afternoon on warm days, however. If you're intimidated by crowds, and you're trying to step up to the intermediate level, avoid Stump Alley and Broadway, both usually packed with speeders.

●● **First-timer:** There are easy learning areas with carpet lifts at the Main Lodge (Discovery Chair), Canyon Lodge and Eagle Lodge, which is where the six-pack Eagle Express departs.

June Mountain: June Mountain doesn't have Mammoth's range of terrain, but most skiers and boarders will enjoy it. The pace at June is slower and the crowds considerably fewer. It is a very good choice for mid-winter Saturdays and holiday periods, as well as for families with young children who ski faster than their parents.

June Mountain has none of the high broad bowls that make Mammoth Mountain famous. The steepest terrain at June, The Face, is as steep as anything at Mammoth. Because it is on the lower mountain, it unfortunately doesn't keep the snow as long as the upper runs. Since June is more sheltered than Mammoth and none of its slopes is above treeline, June tends to hold powder longer than Mammoth's more exposed bowls and the snow doesn't crust up so quickly. There's a great view of June Lake from the upper runs.

Though June has a few expert drops, this level will be bored quickly. Intermediates will have a ball, however. Schatzi is a fantastic and long cruiser, and Matterhorn often is totally deserted. Beginners should stick to the mid-mountain, though Silverado is a gentle, long and uncrowded trail from the Rainbow Summit. June Mountain has two terrain parks covering 50 acres. For a small ski area, June is an impressively big player in terrain park innovation, with a top-notch superpipe that gets cut nightly, large jumps and tabletops, and rails of every variety.

Ride guide: So you're a leap-of-faith kind of rider? The plunge off Mammoth's summit ridge offers a slew of descents with one thing in common: All are so sickeningly steep you can easily reach out and touch the snow while turning. Want to test Newton's theory of gravity? Drop into the steeps of Climax, pop the cornice into Dave's Run, dance between the rocks in The Wipeout Chutes or huck into Hangman's Hollow. If you really want to shake up your innards, dart through the rocks at the top of Phillipe's and straight-shoot it all the way to the bottom. Mammoth is definitely one of the carving capitals of the West, so check out the arcs and deep trenches below while riding up the chair, and then slice some yourself. St. Anton, Stump Alley and Gremlin's Gulch are just three of the carving runs to hit. Just make sure to get up early if you expect freshies or perfect corduroy.

Parks and pipes

Mammoth puts mammoth amounts of money—more than $1 million—into 75 acres of parks and pipes. Main Park is often ranked one of the best freestyle areas in North America. Due to its proximity to the Southern California world of skate and surf culture, Mammoth is an industry leader so progressive that each season's new park features are kept mum until opening day. A ride on Thunderbound Express is entertainment in its own right, as most freeskiing and snowboarder pros pass though here — if they don't call it home. You'll find a 600-foot-long super-duper pipe—with walls that are a soaring 22 feet high—and a superpipe with 18-foot walls. Both are sculpted every single night. In addition to urban art-like features for top performance, including a 16' by 32' Wall Ride, kinked boxes, c-boxes, hits and tables as big as 80' in length, Mammoth also has fully developed parks for the smaller skill set. Two Family Fun Zones are located at both the Main and Canyon Lodge learning areas, and include low-to-the-snow rails and a mini-pipe with 5' walls. Mammoth has the intermediate South Park, on Roller Coaster West, and Jibs Galore on Carousel, where rails are tucked among the trees. One thing is for sure: with eight runs dedicated to parks, freeriders won't be bored.

 ## Cross-country and snowshoeing (see xcskiresorts.com for more details)

Twenty-five miles of groomed trails, actually summer roads, wind around four of the dozen or more high Alpine lakes for which the town of Mammoth Lakes is named. **Tamarack Lodge** (800-626-6684; 934-2442), a former summer hunting and fishing lodge now owned by Mammoth Mountain, maintains the trails. Rentals and lessons are available. On weekends it's advisable to reserve. Luxury and rustic cabins are available for rent. The Lakes Basin includes many trailheads into the backcountry, where no fee is charged. Stop into the lobby, where mulled cider is on hand and historical vibes radiate from the gigantic old stone fireplace. Special nighttime ski and snowshoe tours are offered under full moons, but because that's only three days per month, they tend to fill up quickly.

Lessons (06/07 prices)

Prices are for Saturdays and holidays; prices are somewhat lower Sunday through Friday. At Mammoth, lessons are available at the Main Lodge, the Canyon Lodge and Eagle Lodge. For Mammoth reservations or questions, call (800) 626-6684. For June Mountain Ski and Snowboard School, call 648-7733.

Group lessons: A three-hour lesson costs $67.

First-timer package: Rentals, lift ticket and three hours of lessons are $95 for skiers and snowboarders.

Private lessons: A one-hour early bird lesson costs $90; two hours in the afternoon cost $200; half day is $395 in the morning and $325 in the afternoon; full day is $515.

Special programs: There are many, including three-day camps for women that cost $395. Check the Mammoth website for dates.

Racing: Mammoth has a well-established racing heritage. It has hosted World Cup races, and several U.S. Ski Team coaches and executives call this resort home. Races occur almost every weekend, ranging from amateur ski club races to highly competitive events.

KidStuff (05/06 prices)

Child care: Ages newborn to 12 years old. Cost is $85 for a full day, $55 for a half day. Fees include snacks and lunch, except for infants. Day care can be combined with ski and snowboard school for ages 4–12. They get supervised activities, plus a lesson and rentals, for $130 ($140 holidays and weekends) for a full day; $70 for a half day. Reservations are advised for all child-care programs, at least three weeks ahead. Day care is at both The Small World Day Care Center at Mammoth Mountain Inn (934-0646), just across the street from the Main Lodge, and the child-care center at June Mountain (648-7609). Open from 8 a.m. to 4:30 p.m. Pager rentals available.

Children's lessons: The Woollywood Ski School teaches kids ages 4–12; snowboard lessons start at age 7. Full-day packages (lessons, lunch, lift ticket) for skiing or snowboarding cost $107 ($115 weekends and holidays). First-timers also can take a two-hour lesson for $42 ($51 weekends etc.). Helmets are required for all children in lessons.

Lift tickets (06/07 prices)

	Adult (19+)	Teen (13-18)	Child (7-12)
One day	$78	$59	$39
Three days	$193 ($64/day)	$145 ($48/day)	$97 ($32/day)
Four days	$258 ($62/day)	$187 ($46/day)	$125 ($31/day)

Who skis free: Children ages 6 and younger and seniors 80 and older ski free, as do first-timers taking a ski school lesson.

Who skis at a discount: Ages 65–79 ski for child prices.

Lift tickets may be used at either Mammoth or June; however, a June-only ticket (not valid at Mammoth) costs $60 for adults, $55 for ages 19–23, $48 for teens 13–18, $35 for kids 7–12 and seniors 65–79.

Note: The multiday rates listed here are non-holiday. If you visit midweek, multiday prices are a bit lower. During holidays, regular per-day rates apply, though you still can buy a multiday ticket.

Accommodations

Mammoth Mountain Inn (800-626-6684 reservations; 934-2581 front desk; $$–$$$$) at the main base is the most convenient to the mountain. The inn is owned by the ski resort, and includes a restaurant, two small sundries stores, and the resort's child-care facility. Lodging is deluxe to moderate and includes hotel rooms and condos. There is a rental shop right in the hotel.

The slopeside **Juniper Springs Lodge** and **Sunstone** (800-626-6684 reservations; 760-924-1102 front desk; $$$–$$$$) both feature deluxe condominium-style rooms with full kitchen, gas fireplaces and balconies, plus two heated outdoor pools, two hot tubs, a fitness center and underground parking. There's a coffee shop in the lobby, and next door in Little Eagle Lodge you'll find Talons Restaurant. There is a rental shop right in the hotel.

Lincoln House, **White Mountain Lodge and Grand Sierra Lodge** (800-626-6684 reservations; 934-1982 front desk; $$$-$$$$) make up the Village at Mammoth. Choose from studio to three-bedroom luxury lodge condos. Amenities include gas fireplace, DVD player, housekeeping and turndown service, equipped kitchens, slate floors and dining area. There are restaurants on site, gondola access to Canyon Lodge and a rental shop right in the hotel.

We list just a few of the places to stay in town. As a starting point, call **Mammoth Lakes Visitors Bureau** (888-466-2666) for a reservation referral. Generally, condos start at about $100 per night, while hotel accommodations—we use the term loosely, as Mammoth currently has more motels than true hotels—can be found for less than $80 per night. Sunday through Thursday stays are quite a bit cheaper than Friday and Saturday.

Mammoth Lakes has been called Condo City of the Sierras. Just beyond midtown, **Snow-creek** (800-544-6007; 934-3333; $$–$$$$) is its own wooded neighborhood. Units are spacious one-, two- and three-bedroom loft style condos. Closer to the slopes, next to The Canyon Lodge, are many large condominium complexes with a range of units. Try **Mountainback** (934-5000) or **1849 Condominiums** (800-421-1849; 934-7525; $$$–$$$$).

In the middle of town, only a walk to restaurants and a shuttle to the lifts, **Sierra Nevada Rodeway Inn** (800-824-5132; 934-2515; $–$$$) has hotel rooms and chalet units. Check out **Alpenhof Lodge** (934-6330; $–$$$) and the **Snow Goose Inn** (800-874-7368; $–$$$), one of a few B&Bs in town, decorated with antiques and a communal breakfast.

Mammoth has several inexpensive motels, including **Econo Lodge/Wildwood Inn** (934-6855; $–$$), **Motel 6** (934-6660; $-$$) and **Swiss Chalet** (934-2403; $–$$).

June Mountain: Double Eagle Resort & Spa (877-648-7004; 648-7004; $$$) in town has several two-bedroom cabins (all No Smoking), plus a restaurant called Eagle's Landing that serves delicious meals and has a magnificent view of the surrounding peaks.

June has two large condominium complexes — **Interlaken** has studios to three-bedroom units and **Edgewater** only has units that are suitable for six to nine people. Rates start at less than $100 midweek and $135–$150 weekends. All other lodgings at June are small and quaint, even funky. **The Haven** has studios for about $70 (648-7524). Call **June Lake Properties Reservations** at (800) 648-5863 or 648-7705. Also try **Fern Creek Lodge** (800-621-9146; $–$$$), **Whispering Pines** (800-648-7762; $–$$), or **Boulder Lodge** (648-7533; $–$$).

Dining

Mammoth Lakes has nearly 60 dining options, from gourmet French cuisine to delicatessen sandwiches and quick takeout. The best gourmet menu is at **Skadi** (934-3902; $$), with a romantic atmosphere and mountain views. **Petra's** (934-3500;

Dining: $$$$-Entrees $30+; $$$–$20-$30; $$–$10-$20; $-less than $10.
Accommodations: (double room) $$$$-$200+; $$$-$141-$200; $$-$81-$140; $-$80 and less.

$$) is a wine bar serving over 28 wines by the glass along with an ever-changing menu of appetizers served "tapas" style.

For the most romantic (and expensive) dining, head out to **Lakefront Restaurant at Tamarack Lodge** (934-2442; $$$) where the menu is basic but the presentation excellent. The atmosphere is Old World in a small dining room decorated with photos of movie stars who used to hang out here. Another top choice, with one of the best wine lists in town, is **The Restaurant at Convict Lake** (934-3803; $$$), 4 miles south of Mammoth Lakes on Hwy. 395. Look for the Convict Lake turnoff just south of the airport.

Side Door Cafe (934-5200) has a wine bar, panini sandwiches, crepes, retail wind and a coffee bar in the Village.

Nevados (934-4466; $$) has been one of Mammoth's top restaurants for more than 20 years. For steaks, prime rib and seafood, head to **Whiskey Creek** (934-2555; $$), **The Mogul Restaurant** (934-3039; $$) or the **Chart House** (934-4526; $$). Mogul has built its reputation as the best steak house, but we give it best marks for the grilled seafood as well.

A family spot serving famous ribs is **Angel's** (934-7427; $$).

Nik-N-Willie's Pizza (934-2012; $) has the best in town. Pizzas also are featured at **Giovanni's** (934-7563; $), **Perry's Italian Cafe** (934-6521; $), or **5 Boroughs Pizza** (924-1045; $). The best Mexican food is at **Roberto's** (934-3667; $) with homemade tortillas and big servings; or head to **Gomez's** (924-2693; $).

Grumpy's (934-8587; $) holds the distinction of the town's best fried chicken, also the best cole slaw, all presented in a big-screen TV, no-smoking, sports-bar atmosphere.

Shogun (934-3970; $) has Japanese cuisine and sushi. Try **Matsu** (934-8277; $) for inexpensive Chinese-American and **Thai'd Up** (934-7355; $) for Thai cuisine. **Austria Hof** (934-2764; $$) and **Alpenrose** (934-3077; $$) serve German and Austrian specialties.

The best breakfast in town is served at **Good Life Cafe** (934-1734; $). Locals also recommend **The Stove** (934-2821; $), with biscuits 3 or 4 inches high. Another restaurant with hearty breakfasts is **The Breakfast Club** (934-6944; $) at the intersection of Old Mammoth Road and Highway 203. Coffee lovers, your choices are **Looney Bean** (934-1345; $) in the Rite Aid shopping center; **Stellar Brew** (924-3559; $) on Main Street next to the Chevron station; **World Cup Coffee** (924-3629; $) on Old Mammoth Road across from the movie theater; **Paul Schat's Bakery and Cafe** (934-6055; $) on Main Street; and the **Old New York Deli and Bagel Co.** (934-3354; $). All have good pastries as well.

For full-service lunch or evening dining at the mountain, try the California cuisine at **Mountainside Grill** (934-0601) in the Mammoth Mountain Inn. Or head over to the more casual and crowded **Yodler** (934-0636). Other best bets for on-mountain lunch are the **Mill Cafe** at the base of Stump Alley Express, serving sandwiches and garlic fries, **Canyon Lodge** with its food court that solves any craving or **Parallax** in McCoy Station for fine luncheons highlighting Cal-Asian cuisine. Look for the notoriously "so-so cafeteria food" at the Main Lodge improved after a $4 million renovation in the summer of 2005.

In **June Lake**, the best dining is at the **Eagle's Landing Restaurant** (648-7897; $$) at the Double Eagle Resort and Spa. Other choices are **Tiger Bar and Cafe** (648-7551) for burgers and chicken; what there is of June nightlife happens at the Tiger Bar, as does breakfast — go figure, June's a small town. The **Sierra Inn Restaurant** (648-7774) has a slightly more upscale menu. The best dining is still in Mammoth Lakes.

Apres-ski/nightlife

Lively apres-ski gets under way across the parking lot from the Main Lodge at the **Yodler**. At the Canyon Lodge base area, try **Grizzly's** outdoor bar and BBQ. **Roberto's** upstairs bar in town is a popular apres-ski hangout; enjoy cool margaritas and four-dollar tacos. At **Sherwin's**, located at Sierra Meadows Ranch, there's live entertainment most weekends. Entertainment is also at Mammoth Mountain Inn's **Dry Creek Bar**.

Mammoth's longtime meet market (you may meet someone whose parents used to party hardy here in their younger days) is **Whiskey Creek,** which serves six microbrews. There's plenty of nighttime hoopla at **Grumpy's,** with five giant-screen TVs, pool, foosball, inexpensive chili and burgers. Visiting Brits like this place, and also hang out at the **Clock Tower Cellar** at the Alpenhof Lodge. For casual beer and pool, try **The Tap** on Main Street.

Lakanuki is a tiki-style bar that gets everyone up dancing and **Henessey's** is an Irish bar with a nice outdoor patio.

 ## Other activities

Snowmobiles can be rented from Mammoth Snowmobile Adventures (934-9645), DJs Snowmobile Adventures (935-4480); or Mammoth Polaris (924-3155). The area has about 300 miles of snowmobile trails, some signed and groomed, others not. **Bobsledding or tubing** down a designated track is available through Sledz (934-7533). **Dogsled rides** are offered by Dog Sled Adventures (934-6270).

Peruse local artisans' crafts, photography and artwork at **Edisto Gallery and Tea Room** on Old Mammoth Road, **Mammoth Gallery** or **Gallerie Barjur** (next door to one another in the Village). **Snowcreek Athletic Club** (934-8511) has a variety of indoor and outdoor facilities including an indoor swimming pool, tennis courts, daily yoga classes and racquetball.

Don't be fooled into thinking that the only **shopping** exists in the Village. Mammoth's shopping is oriented as much for the local population as for tourists. You won't find many trendy boutiques here, though there is a factory outlet center on Main Street, and many small shopping malls scattered throughout town. Mammoth Lakes also has a **movie theater** with two screens, Minaret Cinemas (934-3131). *The Mammoth Times*, the local weekly newspaper, is a good source for special events listings.

Getting there and getting around

By air: The nearest major airport is Reno, 165 miles away. Rent a car for the drive south, because ground transportation is spotty, and you probably will want a car in Mammoth. For the latest news, call the Mammoth Lakes Airport (934-3825), Mammoth Lakes Visitors Bureau, (888-466-2666) or consult the MLVB website (www.visitmammoth.com).

By car: Mammoth is 325 miles north of Los Angeles on Hwy. 395, and 165 miles south of Reno on the same highway. June Mountain is 20 miles north of Mammoth Lakes off Hwy. 395.

Getting around: The resort operates a free shuttle that runs throughout the town and to Mammoth's Main Lodge (4 miles out) and to the Canyon Lodge and Eagle Lodge. A Park and Ride lot is located on Old Mammoth Road across from the Chart House. A nightly shuttle makes loops around town until midnight during the week, 1 a.m. on Friday and Saturday nights, or call Mammoth Shuttle (934-3030) or Sierra Express (924-8294). Most visitors have a car.

Dining: $$$$-Entrees $30+; $$$-$20-$30; $$-$10-$20; $-less than $10.
Accommodations: (double room) $$$$-$200+; $$$-$141-$200; $$-$81-$140; $-$80 and less.

California regional resorts

Bear Valley, Bear Valley, CA; (209) 753-2301

Internet: www.bearvalley.com
10 lifts; 1,280 skiable acres; 1,900 vertical feet; 3 terrain parks; 1 halfpipe

Bear Valley is one of those word-of-mouth ski areas beloved by those who know it's at the winter terminus of Hwy. 4. This area has many things to like: 359 inches of snow annually; a town just big enough to provide lodging, food and alternate activities (cross-country skiing, ice skating and most snow sports); and an enticing advanced and expert area called Grizzly Bowl that makes up about 30 percent of the terrain. The Grizz is below the base area, and that's its drawback. With no snowmaking coverage and an elevation of 6,600–7,750 feet, Grizzly Bowl isn't always open. However, the upper mountain is covered by snowmaking and has a few black-diamond runs amid its great beginner and intermediate terrain. A good area for families, Bear Valley has daily child care starting at age 2. In July 2005, the ski area was purchased by Dundee Realty USA, which also owns Arapahoe Basin in Colorado, with plans for future development.

Lift tickets (05/06 prices): Adults, $46; young adult (13–19), $38; children (6–12), $16; seniors (65–74), $19; super seniors (75+), $10; kids 5 and younger, free. Weekday prices are lower.

Distance from San Francisco: About 190 miles east on I-580 and I-205, north on I-99, then east on Hwy. 4. Bear Valley is on the west slope of the Sierra Nevada and not accessible from Tahoe or Mammoth.

Lodging information: On the website, or press 5 after calling the recorded information line to get phone numbers for various hotels and condos. Two recommendations: Bear Valley Lodge (209-753-2327; $-$$$) is 3 miles from the slopes (as close as you can get) and smack in the center of the little town. About 25 miles down Hwy. 4 is The Dorrington Hotel & Restaurant (866-995-5800; 209-795-5800; $$), a charming shared-bath B&B in a historic house. The restaurant is worth a stop.

Badger Pass, Yosemite National Park, CA; (209) 372-1000

Internet: www.yosemitepark.com (listed in Activities)
5 lifts; 10 trails; 800 vertical feet

This is a tiny, 70-year-old ski area best suited for beginners, patient intermediates and families with young children. Though Badger Pass is charming (and the employees are wonderful), what makes it a great winter weekend destination is not the downhill skiing. It's special because it's inside Yosemite National Park. The park's legendary crowds disappear in the winter, so you'll share the majesty of the Yosemite Valley with a comfortable number of humans. Activities include naturalist-guided snowshoe walks, ice skating, snow tubing, sightseeing tours and lots more.

Yosemite has a renowned cross-country ski center headquartered at Badger Pass with lessons, 40 km. of machine-groomed track and another 150 km. of marked trails, including a 17-km. skating lane on the rim of the Yosemite Valley to Glacier Point.

Lift tickets (05/06 prices): Adults, $35; children (7–12), $18; seniors 65+ pay adult price

on weekends and holidays but ski free midweek/non-holidays; kids 6 and younger, free.
Distance from San Francisco: About 230 miles east on I-580, I-205 and Hwy. 120.
Distance from Los Angeles: About 290 miles north on I-5 and I-99, then east on Hwy.
41. Note: Hwy. 120 between Yosemite and Lee Vining is closed in winter, making Badger
Pass inaccessible from Mammoth.
Lodging information: (559) 253-5635 or on the website.

Big Bear Mountain Resorts, Big Bear Lake, CA; (909) 866-5766

Internet: www.bigbearmountainresorts.com (joint site)
Snow Summit: 12 lifts; 240 skiable acres; 1,200 vertical feet; 3 terrain parks; 1 halfpipe
Big Bear Mountain: 12 lifts; 198 skiable acres; 1,665 vertical feet; 1 terrain park; 1 superpipe;
1 halfpipe

Southern Californians just don't know how good they have it. On a sunny winter day,
it is entirely possible to spend the morning skiing at Big Bear (as the locals call it) and the
afternoon playing a round of golf in Palm Springs or surfing in the Pacific Ocean. These
neighboring ski areas, in the mountain town of Big Bear Lake, are less than a two-hour drive
from the fabled desert resort in one direction and the beach in the other.

The Big Bear areas, though at an altitude of between 7,000 and 8,800 feet, rely heavily on
snowmaking to cover the runs. Both are snowmaking experts and have a reliable water supply
from Big Bear Lake. Even if the season has been dry, you'll find surprisingly good snow on
the runs. And if the winter has been a wet one, the conditions can be quite good.

The terrain is largely intermediate, with a couple of runs at each that qualify as advanced,
but not expert. Snowboarding is hugely popular here, with boarders constituting more than half
of the business. Big Bear Mountain is actually one big terrain park with 150 jumps, 80 jibs,
one superpipe and one halfpipe. The features address every ability level and are scattered all
over the mountain, top to bottom. As if 195 acres of terrain features aren't enough, a shuttle
will take you to neighboring Snow Summit where you can play in another 45-acre park. The
town has many lodging and restaurant options and a charming, walkable downtown.

Neither area has child care; ski lessons start at age 4, snowboard lessons at age 6.

Lift tickets (04/05 prices): The resorts have a joint lift ticket. Adults, $49 ($62 holidays
and peak season weekends); young adults (13–21), $39 ($51 holidays etc.); child (7–12), $19
($25 holidays etc.); kids 6 and younger, free. Holiday rates also apply to Saturdays in January
and February. Night skiing lift tickets are available at Snow Summit.

Distance from Los Angeles: About 110 miles east on I-10, I-215, Hwy. 30, Hwy. 330
and Hwy. 18.

Distance from Ontario (nearest commercial airport): About 60 miles by I-10, I-215,
Hwy. 30, Hwy. 330 and Hwy. 18.

Lodging information: Big Bear Lake Resort Association's Lodging Referral Service,
(909) 866-5671 or (800) 424-4232; or its website, www.bigbearinfo.com.

Dining: $$$$-Entrees $30+; $$$-$20-$30; $$-$10-$20; $-less than $10.
Accommodations: (double room) $$$$-$200+; $$$-$141-$200; $$-$81-$140; $-$80 and less.

Aspen Snowmass

Colorado

Aspen Mountain
Buttermilk
Aspen Highlands
Snowmass

Address: Aspen Skiing Company,
P.O. Box 1248, Aspen, CO 81612 or
Snowmass Resort Association,
P.O. Box 5566, Snowmass Village, CO 81615
Area code: 970
Ski area phone: 925-1220 or (800) 525-6200
Snow report: 925-1221 or (888) 277-3676
Toll-free reservations: (800) 262-7736 or 925-9000
(Aspen); (800) 760-9627 (Snowmass)
Fax: 925-9008
E-mail: info@aspensnowmass.com (resort)
info@stayaspen.com (Aspen reservations)
info@snowmassvillage.com (Snowmass Village)

Internet: www.aspensnowmass.com (ski area)
www.stayaspensnowmass.com (lodging)
www.aspenchamber.org (visitor information)
www.snowmassvillage.com (Snowmass Village)
Bed base: 7,750; 13,050 within 10 miles (Aspen)
5,300 at base; 13,050 within 10 miles (Snowmass)
Nearest lodging: Slopeside, hotels, condos
Resort child care: 8 weeks to 4 years
Adult ticket, per day: $82 (06/07 prices)

Dining:★★★★★
Apres-ski/nightlife:★★★★★
Other activities:★★★★★

Ask a crowd of non-skiing Americans to name a ski resort, and you can bet a bundle that Aspen will be one of those they name, though they will probably know more about the rich and famous who frequent the resort than about its equally notable skiing. With four mountains within 12 miles of each other, offering a total of 43 lifts and more than 4,900 skiable acres, a trip to Aspen just for the skiing would be well worth it. But Aspen has much more.

Aspen fits a niche unique among North American ski resorts. Sure, other resorts attract wealth, but Aspen's wealth glitters and sparkles with a "look-this-way" flamboyance. Here, the well-to-do seem to want everyone else to know it. You'll see the newest ski and city fashions on beautiful women as they pass turn-of-the-century brick façades. Private jets wait for their owners on the airport tarmac. Paparazzi aim their lenses at every celebrity in town so that supermarket tabloids can keep their pages filled.

Don't head to Aspen purely to observe celebrities, however. You may not find any. They are most common during the Christmas-New Year holidays and March's sunshine days, but are difficult to spot when in ski clothes. If you want to mix with the upscale crowd, stay close to the Aspen Mountain gondola base, where the fanciest hotels and shops are clustered. You'll find a mixed crowd here, which combines expensive and reasonably priced restaurants and bars. Beyond downtown, the outward signs of wealth disappear.

If all your information about Aspen comes from *People* magazine, you probably think you can't afford to ski here. True, lift tickets are among the priciest in America, but it's a little-known fact that lodging and restaurants have a huge price range, starting out with inexpensive dorm accommodations and topping out at stratospheric luxury suites.

Perhaps due to Aspen's glamorous reputation, its adventurous nature is sometimes over-looked. Aspen also draws skiers and snowboarders who couldn't care less about the off-mountain scene. They come for the slopes, which have received rave reviews for decades. Aspen Mountain challenges intermediate through expert skiers and snowboarders. Buttermilk is the perfect beginner and cruising mountain, plus it's home to the 2005 ESPN Winter X Games

Ten and the Crazy T'rain Terrain Park, one of the longest in the country. Highlands is the most varied for its size, with terrain for experts and beginners, cruisers and bumpers. For 2005/06, Highlands is unveiling Deep Temerity, 180 new acres of advanced and expert terrain.

If you're determined to see celebrities at Aspen, three sightings are guaranteed on Aspen Mountain. Look for shrines for Elvis Presley, Marilyn Monroe and Jerry Garcia. The Elvis shrine is in a grove of trees just below Back of Bell 3. Marilyn's shrine is on a cat track above the Elvis shrine and Jerry is memorialized in a grove of spruce trees to skiers' right on Ruthie's Run after you unload from the FIS chair. Ask an Aspen ambassador for directions and be sure to take your camera. For a little romance, check out the Valentine's shrine between Walsh's and Hyrup's on Aspen Mountain, where you'll find a secluded "porch swing" to canoodle.

Snowmass

Though it is lumped into the Aspen experience by geography, Snowmass stands on its own as a winter destination. Snowmass ranks among the top 10 resorts in America in size, and it's the second-largest in Colorado (after Vail). It covers more than 3,100 acres—more than Aspen Mountain, Buttermilk and Highlands combined. And thanks to a surface lift to the top of the Cirque (formerly reached by a hike or snowcat), Snowmass lays claim to the longest vertical drop in the United States, 4,406 feet. (Big Sky, MT, has a 4,180-foot vertical; Jackson Hole, WY, 4,139 feet. Now you have your apres-ski bar conversation opener.)

The Snowmass Village Mall seems to stretch forever uphill with shops, restaurants, bars and skier services, but all are handicap accessible and if you are so inclined you can use hotel and public elevators (at 8,606 feet, you'll soon know why we added this). The resort has started construction on its new base village, due for completion in 2008. Improvements for 2005/06 include a new six-pack to replace the old Fanny Hill chair and a cabriolet lift connecting the new village and Snowmass Village Mall. The cabriolet between the villages helps overcome the elevation challenge, especially with kids before and after skiing.

Hundreds of condos line the lower part of the resort, and about 95 percent of the lodging is ski-in/ski-out. It doesn't get much more convenient than Snowmass. A note to those staying in a ski-in/ski-out condo: Make note of where you are before you head down to the lift for your first run. We had a heck of a time knowing where to cut off from the ski run to our unit in a sea of brown condos at the end of the day.

 ## Mountain layout

Aspen's four mountains are close to each other, but not interconnected. A free shuttle runs from base to base. ASC runs a very efficient equipment transfer program between its four mountains. For $5, you hand over your skis, poles or snowboard to an attendant in the base area at the end of the day, tell him/her where you're skiing the next day, and your gear will be waiting for you at that base area the next morning. It works very well.

♦♦**Expert: Highlands** is the best-balanced mountain of the three with slopes for every level, and it's the locals' favorite. The vertical rise is one of the highest in Colorado. Three high-speed quads whisk you to the summit so you're not wasting time on lifts.

From the top of Loge Peak, the run back to the base is an uneven series of steeps, cat tracks and gentle runouts. This mountain has some fantastic long cruises. The ridge, knifing directly to the summit, has thrilling pitches down both sides. Other than a few short blacks, such as Suzy Q and Limelight, the terrain makes a pronounced jump from intermediate to expert.

Experts should head for the steeps at the top of Loge Peak in the Steeplechase (sunny in

Aspen Mountain Facts
Summit elevation: 11,212 feet
Vertical drop: 3,267 feet
Base elevation: 7,945 feet
Number of lifts: 8–1 gondola, 1 high-speed quad, 1 high-speed double, 2 quads, 3 doubles
Snowmaking: 31 percent **Skiable acreage:** 673 acres
Uphill capacity: 10,775 per hour **Parks & pipes:** 1 park (open only in spring)
Expert:★★★★ Advanced:★★★★★
Intermediate:★★★★
Beginner/First-timer: Don't go here

Buttermilk Facts
Summit elevation: 9,900 feet
Vertical drop: 2,030 feet
Base elevation: 7,870 feet
Number of lifts: 9–2 high-speed quad, 3 doubles, 4 surface lift
Snowmaking: 25 percent **Skiable acreage:** 435 acres
Uphill capacity: 7,500 per hour **Parks & pipes:** 1 park, 1 pipe
Expert:★ Advanced:★★ Intermediate:★★★★
Beginner:★★★★★ First-timer:★★★★★

Aspen Highlands Facts
Summit elevation: 11,675 feet
Vertical drop: 3,635 feet
Base elevation: 8,040 feet
Number of lifts: 5–3 high-speed quads, 2 triples
Snowmaking: 14 percent **Skiable acreage:** 970 acres
Uphill capacity: 6,500 per hour **Parks & pipes:** None
Expert:★★★★ Advanced:★★★★★ Intermediate:★★★★
Beginner:★★★ First-timer:★★

Snowmass Facts
Summit elevation: 12,510 feet
Vertical drop: 4,406 feet
Base elevation: 8,104 feet
Number of lifts: 21–1 cabriolet, 1 high-speed six-pack, 6 high-speed quads, 1 triple,
6 doubles, 4 surface lifts, 2 moving carpets
Snowmaking: 6 percent **Skiable acreage:** 3,125 acres
Uphill capacity: 27,181 per hour **Parks & pipes:** 3 parks, 2 pipes
Expert:★★★★ Advanced:★★★★ Intermediate:★★★★★
Beginner:★★★ First-timer:★★

the morning) and Olympic Bowl (sunny in the afternoon) areas. These are very steep with no bail-out areas, so be sure you want to be here. Both areas have long cat tracks back to lifts.

Some of Colorado's steepest slopes stand above Loge Peak in Highland Bowl. You can reach the tops of the 40- to 45-degree slopes by hiking up the ridge for 20–60 minutes; or, if you happen to be at Loge Meadow between 11 a.m. and 1 p.m., hop on a free snowcat for a ride to the first access gate. The gladed runs here will keep you on your toes. The new Temerity triple means you can ski another 1,000 vertical feet down Highland Bowl and not hike out. The lift also accesses 180 new acres of chutes and trees, and the tree chutes off Loge Peak are now double in length.

Also check out the lower mountain. The Thunderbowl chair will take you from the base to the top of Bob's Glades or Upper Stein, or you can drop into double-black territory at several points along blue-square Golden Horn.

The basic guideline for **Aspen Mountain** is that the intermediate terrain is on the top knob around the summit and in the gullies between the ridges. The expert stuff drops from the ridges into the gullies. Of the blacks, take your pick and be sure you're up to it. These runs are very black. For bumps and trees, Bell Mountain right under the gondola is a good choice. Watch for the ski patrol to open Walsh's after a storm. It can be powder heaven, a run you can brag about all week. Guided "Powder Tours" are offered on the back side of Aspen Mountain; call (800) 525-6200 for information.

At **Snowmass,** the most extreme terrain is in the Hanging Valley Glades, which for years management was not comfortable opening. Accessed by the High Alpine lift, an ancient double chair, the options are countless, including steep chutes Possible and Baby Ruth into Hanging Valley Glades, or straight over the headwall to at least a dozen drops into the Hanging Valley.

Another extreme playground is the Cirque, a scooped-out place between Sheer Bliss and High Alpine lifts. This is served by a wind-powered surface lift that gets very popular on powder days, at the top of which you'll find the "Rocky Mountain High" run, named in memory of the late singer John Denver. Don't try this area unless you're comfortable on Hanging Valley Wall. The right side holds almost as many chutes as the Wall, and you'll need to make tight, jump turns at the top of Rock Island and KT Gully. Even more challenging is AMF at the top. A local says it stands for "Adios, My Friend," but we think he gave us the "this-is-a-family-guidebook" version.

♦ **Advanced:** If you consider yourself a very confident advanced skier, read the expert section. If you feel you have recently reached advanced status, read the intermediate section. In our experience, there's a big jump from intermediate to expert terrain at **Highlands** and **Aspen Mountain. Buttermilk's** marked advanced terrain is really more advanced-intermediate.

At **Snowmass,** look skier's left for chutes and drops and to the lower right side of the Sheer Bliss run to get the feel of the famous Cirque terrain without the heart-gripping fear of knowing you are not ready for that stuff. Skiers ready to burn up steep-pitched cruising will think they've found nirvana when they make the first descent into the Campground area. Here is a wonderful long run: To come off the top of Big Burn on Sneaky's, tuck to avoid the uphill stretch at Sam's Knob, cut south around the Knob and head into the blacks of Bear Claw, Slot, Wildcat or Zugspitze to the base of the Campground lift. The Campground runs on a deep powder day can make you thankful the chair at the bottom is not high-speed.

■ **Intermediate:** If you'd like to say you skied a black run on **Aspen Mountain,** Upper Little Percy or Red's Run are occasionally groomed. The ticket office or the on-mountain Concierge Center at the summit has a grooming report (you can check this at all the mountains, by the way).

Unsure if you can handle the terrain? If you can ski blues at other areas, do this: Ride the gondola to the top and ski the gentlest terrain, at the summit—runs such as Dipsy Doodle, Pussyfoot and Silver Bell. Keep riding the Ajax Express and Gentlemen's Ridge lifts. If any of those blue runs presents a challenge, ride back down in the gondola. The alternative to riding down is Copper Bowl or Spar Gulch, two narrow gullies that get packed late in the day as skiers funnel into them toward the base. Both runs join at Kleenex Corner—a sharp, narrow turn—then dump into Little Nell, a steep blue just above the gondola base. It's known as "Little Hell" because at day's end, it's crowded, usually a little slick and/or moguled, and smack in view of everyone.

The blue cruisers—led by North American—in sight of Bonnie's outdoor deck are a delight. If you're a confident intermediate, don't pass up skiing at Aspen Mountain.

At **Buttermilk,** intermediates with confident turns will have fun on Jacob's Ladder and Bear, which drop from the Cliff House to the main area, but the real playground is under the Tiehack chair. Much of this area is colored black on the trail map, but don't get too excited—it's just the toughest stuff on *this* mountain. You'll discover good upper-intermediate trails that make inspiring cruisers. In one day you can ride the Upper Tiehack chair a dozen times, taking a different cruise on each 1,500 vertical-foot run. Javelin is the best of the lot—a couple of tree islands to keep you awake and a lot of good dips and rolls. Smile in the evening when you overhear others scoffing about what a waste Buttermilk is for real skiers, and savor memories of 15,000 feet of vertical in just one afternoon.

At **Highlands,** intermediates will want to take these lifts: Cloud Nine, Olympic and Loge Peak. (The easiest of the intermediates are off Cloud Nine.) Don't miss Golden Horn and Thunderbowl on the lower mountain, very wide cruisers.

At **Snowmass,** intermediate terrain is literally everywhere, including from the summit (Cirque) and even the never-ending Green Mile, an upper intermediate run from High Alpine. There's a half-day's worth of intermediate options on each of Sam's Knob, Elk Camp, Two Creeks and Alpine Springs. The Big Burn is legendary cruiser fun. It's an entire side of a mountain that was allegedly set aflame by Ute Indians in the 1880s as a warning to advancing white settlers. The pioneers settled anyway, but the trees never grew back thickly, so the run, dotted by a few spruces, is a mile wide and a mile-and-a-half long. The new Fanny Hill six-pack whisks you from the Mall area directly to the Burn summit in less than 10 minutes. For an intermediate uncomfortable around trees, the Powerline Glades are a great primer. Two Creeks is largely a lodging access area, so it can be slow, but views of pricey real estate make it worth the ride. Alpine Springs feels like a separate, hidden ski area and also is home to the best on-mountain food at Gwyn's.

●● **Beginner: Aspen Mountain** may be the only mountain in America that has no designated green-circle runs. Don't try it if you're a beginner.

Buttermilk is all that Aspen Mountain isn't. Beginners can experience top-to-bottom runs as soon as they master snowplows. The beginner terrain concentrates under the Buttermilk West chair. Tom's Thumb, Red's Rover, Larkspur, Westward Ho and Blue Grouse will keep beginners improving. The Homestead Road turns back to the Savio chair and lazily winds its way to the Main Buttermilk area.

At **Highlands,** beginners are best served by the trails from the Exhibition chair—Prospector, Nugget, Exhibition, Red Onion and Apple Strudel.

At **Snowmass,** beginners have a wide gentle area parallel to the village. Fanny Hill eases down by the mall, Wood Run lift opens another easy glide around the Wood Road side of the village, and further to the left a long straightaway, Funnel, will give beginners the feeling they're really covering terrain. Beginners who want to see more of the mountain can head up to Sam's Knob and try the Top of the Knob, with its spectacular views and great menu, and head down a meandering trail bearing the names Max Park, Lunchline and Dawdler, which turns back to Fanny Hill. (Avoid the blue runs on the face of Sam's Knob because they are not for beginners.) The next step up would be Elk Camp, labeled blue but very gentle.

● **First-timer:** Take your first few lessons at **Buttermilk**. Of Aspen's four mountains, this is by far the best for a first day on skis or a snowboard. We would give the beginner terrain at **Snowmass** a higher rating but for one important fact: Many of the ski-in/ski-out condos are along the green runs, so at the beginning and end of the day, they often are used by skilled skiers and snowboarders in a hurry to get to either the lifts or the hot tub.

Ride Guide: At 673 acres, **Aspen Mountain** is not even one-fourth the size of Snowmass, but every acre is infinitely rideable. The mountain scenery is sublime—better, even, than Telluride or Crested Butte. This is a mountain for expert riders who respect and even revere a pristine Alpine playground. There are no beginner trails and scant few true intermediate runs. But if you have good skills, the mountain is replete with bumps, steeps, natural halfpipes and terrain features perfect for riders.

If you measure the quality of your riding by the perfection of the "esses" and the depth of the trenches you leave behind, **Buttermilk** is the place for you. Buttermilk has numerous constant-pitch, top-to-bottom fall line, groomed runs ideal for laying out one perfect carve after another. Larkspur can be one of the most fun carving runs on the mountain, but you'll go into the trees on either side if you don't keep your turns tight. Carve Larkspur nonstop, top to bottom, and we guarantee you'll be high-fiving your buddies. The mountain gets interesting over on Racer's Edge and Javelin; they'd probably be rated blues on other mountains, but they're labeled black diamonds here. These runs get groomed and they're steep enough to force even advanced riders to concentrate on working their edges. Cutting down from Tiehack Parkway are the Ptarmigan and Timber Doodle Glades. Here's where intermediate boarders can learn to ride in the trees. The terrain is steep enough not to stall out, yet the trees are spaced far enough apart to learn. There also are a lot of runs at Buttermilk with gully-like sides that riders of all ages can swoop up and down, such as Bear.

Highlands attracts riders who are interested in riding blacks and double-blacks. While the resort's quick to point out they actually have more green and blue terrain than black, if intermediate cruisers or a great terrain park is what you're looking for, you'll be happier at Snowmass or Buttermilk. Highlands is where advanced and expert riders go to go steep on big powder days. Get ready for a spectacular descent in the 12,500-foot Highland Bowl, 100 or more turns in champagne powder up to your waist—or higher. Your best bet is to do it your first time with a guide who has ridden it several times before. The new Deep Temerity triple chairlift means no more heinous traverse back to the lift.

Snowmass is so huge there's excellent terrain for riders of all levels—and persuasions—and generally little walking if you stay alert. Some areas to prepare for: the approach to Campgrounds, Two Creeks, Funnel and Alpine Springs lifts; the entire basin near the future base village on the way to the Makaha Terrain Park; the runs over the Trestle to the Sheer Bliss chair; Turkey Trot over to Elk Camp; and even the ride out below the Cirque can stop you in your tracks on powder days. Expert riders should head to the legendary Cirque. And from the top of High Alpine, ambitious riders hike 10 minutes to get hang time on Hanging Valley Wall. Advanced riders can play anywhere else, especially on Sam's Knob and the less-tracked Campground, as well as the Burn and rider's left along Sheer Bliss. Intermediate boarders seeking to get away from crowds on Fanny Hill should head for Elk Camp, where you'll find groomed intermediate slopes and a high-speed quad that lets you rack up the vertical. From the top of the Elk Camp lift, a short 5- to10-minute hike takes you to Long Shot, a backcountry-like, ungroomed run that winds 3 miles through the National forest—getting you even further away from the bubbas. For some big whoops, the Naked Lady offers some fun rollers.

Parks and pipes

The wild side of **Buttermilk** is the top-to-bottom Playstation 2 Crazy T'rain Terrain Park. Nearly 2 miles long, it features 30 rails and the only 15-foot superpipe in the four Aspen mountains. It's geared towards intermediates and better. At the bottom of the park a gigantic kicker allows tricksters with huge, and we're talking *huge*, air skills to put on a show for everyone at the base area. Hopefully, there's an ambulance standing by. **Highlands** doesn't have a halfpipe or terrain park; however, Prospector Trail is known locally as Grommets Gulch and is a natural halfpipe. Just a few yards away from the Sundeck restaurant on **Aspen Mountain,** former competitive skateboarder and snowboarder Othello partners with Aspen Skiing Company to teach rail riding in Othello's Rail Riders. Camp attendees learn how to get on a rail properly, how to balance and land, what not to do, tricks and terrain park etiquette. The camp also has a hut with video games, music, records and DVDs. Reservations are required; call the ski and snowboard school. For a long cruiser that forms a wild natural halfpipe, there's Spar Gulch, which cuts a steep "V" down the heart of the mountain to the patio of The Little Nell.

Snowmass' three terrain parks, Little Makaha, Midway Intermediate and Pipeline, cover the gamut of freestyle abilities, from first-timer to advanced trickster. Little Makaha, under the Funnel chair, is designed expressly for beginners and those ready to go the next step, with medium-sized bumps, boxes, rails, rollers and banks. A beginner pipe is on lower Velvet. The Midway Park now benefits from snowmaking and bigger jumps, more challenging boxes and more elements than the Makaha. The place for serious freestyle terrain elements is Pipeline Park on Sam's Knob. This is a continuous line of elements starting on Banzai Ridge, continuing on Coney Glade and finishing with Doddler Bowl. With a quick ride on Sam's Knob Express, this is a hardcore lap of quality hits and features. The superpipe can be found opposite Doddler at the end of the Coney Glade section.

 Cross-country and snowshoeing (visit xcskiresorts.com for more details)
Aspen/Snowmass has the most extensive free Nordic trail system in America, more than 65 km. of groomed trails called "Aspen's fifth mountain." The **Aspen Nordic Council's** (800-525-6200; 923-3148) free system is accessible from Aspen or Snowmass and includes easy golf-course skiing as well as more difficult trails rising up to Snowmass.

In addition to the free trails provided by Aspen's Nordic Council, **Ashcroft Ski Touring Unlimited** (925-1971) has 42 km. of groomed and set trails, and backcountry skiers can use summer hiking trails. Lessons and rentals are available. Other centers are the **Aspen Cross Country Center** (544-9246) on the Aspen Golf Course off Hwy. 82; **Ute Mountaineer** (925-2849); **Braun Hut System** (925-6618), which has information on trails to Crested Butte; and **Snowmass Cross Country Center** (923-3148).

Hut systems connect Aspen with Vail on the Tenth Mountain Trail and with Crested Butte over the Pearl Pass. Guides are available and recommended. Call Tenth Mountain Trail Association for more information, 925-5775, or send e-mail to huts@huts.org.

Snowshoeing is quite popular in town, so ask about those programs at any of the cross-country centers mentioned here. In conjunction with the Aspen Center for Environmental Studies (ACES), **Aspen Skiing Company** has naturalist-guided tours on Aspen Mountain and Snowmass. Tours include lifts, equipment and a snack; call 925-1220 or ACES at 925-5756 for reservations. You also can snowshoe up Aspen Mountain or Buttermilk at certain times and on certain runs. The lift ride down is free. Ask an Aspen Skiing Company concierge about this.

Lessons (05/06 prices)

For brochures and information, or to make reservations for ski and snowboard school programs, call 923-1227 or (877) 282-7736, or visit the website.

Group lessons: Adult small group lessons for Level 5 and up cost $119 a day. They are offered at all the mountains, and are limited to three per class for all levels. Unlimited extensions are $109 per day. Levels 1–4 take classes listed under the first-timer package.

First-timer package: Beginner's Magic is a package for Levels 1–4; offered at Buttermilk and Snowmass. Three-day ski/snowboard packages (including lessons, lift tickets, rentals) run $327. One-day programs are $129. Unlimited extensions of either program are $99 per day.

Private lessons: $365 for a half day for one to five people; and $2,400 for five full days. Other discounts are available. Reservations are required. Lessons are offered in several languages, and include ski storage, lift line privileges, and demo discounts. Offered every day on every mountain.

Special programs: Numerous, including clinics and/or ski and snowboard weeks for women, bumps, powder, off-piste, all-mountain, disabled skiers, video analysis, equipment assessment and many more.

Racing: NASTAR courses are on Silver Dip Swing at Aspen Mountain (daily), Nugget at Highlands (Wednesday–Sunday) and Cabin Trail at Snowmass (Monday, Wednesday, Friday, Saturday). Clinics also are offered.

KidStuff (05/06)

Child care: Ages 8 weeks to 4 years. Cost is $115 for a full day. Reservations are recommended. Child care in Aspen is offered by Kids' Club in the Yellow Brick Building, 315 Garmisch St. Call 925-3136. The state-licensed program offers indoor and outdoor (nonskiing) activities.

In Snowmass, the Snow Cubs program on the lower level of the Mall takes children ages 8 weeks to 3½ years. Cost is $65 half day, $98 for a full day with multiday discounts. Reservations required; call 923-0563 or (877) 282-7736.

Other options: Aspen Babysitting Company (948-6849) offers babysitting services at your hotel room or condo (insured and bonded). Little Red School House (923-3756) has licensed day care for ages 3–5. Baby's Away (800-948-9030; 920-1699) rents and will deliver baby needs to your lodge, such as crib, stroller, car seat and toys. Reservations are recommended for all of these services.

Children's lessons: Aspen Skiing Company has different children's programs, depending on the mountain. All kids 12 and younger *must* wear helmets while in ski and snowboard school. Helmets can be rented for $6 a day. Equipment rental is an additional $18. Lift tickets are extra for kids 7 and older. All-day programs include lunch. For more information about lessons, call 923-1227 or (877) 282-7736.

Ages 3–6 (Level 1–4) ski at Buttermilk, ages 5–6 (Level 5 and higher) ski at Aspen Highlands. Cost is $115 for a full day; $77 for a half day. Reservations are strongly recommended; if space is available for walk-ins, prices are higher. Ages 7–12 skiing and ages 8–12 snowboarding pay $80 per day at Buttermilk or Aspen Highlands. Kids 7-12 who are first-timers can take a lesson package that includes lesson, rentals and lift ticket for $95 (must be 8 years old to snowboard).

Snowmass programs are a bit different. Snow Cubs is for ages 8 weeks to 3½ years. Toddlers get daycare, lunch and brief ski lessons. Toilet-trained 3-year-olds take group lessons, while others must enroll in private lessons. The cost is $115 for a full day, plus $80 if a private lesson is needed. Ages 3½–6 years cost $115 for a full day; $77 for a half day. Ages 7–12 for skiing, and 8–12 for snowboarding, have full-day classes for $82. Teens who are first-timers can take a lesson package that includes lesson, rentals and lift ticket for $10.

Special activities: Children from 5th through 12th grade can mingle with local kids in the afternoons at the Aspen Youth Center (hotline with weekly activities information, 925-7091) in downtown Aspen. The center has **games, ping-pong, pool tables, movies** and a **dance room.** The center does special programs depending on the season. Admission is free.

Snowmass has some great free activities for kids once the lifts shut down. On Wednesdays, there's a **"Piñata Bash"** beginning at 3:30 p.m. in the middle of the Snowmass Village Mall. For **campfire sing-alongs and storytelling,** complete with free marshmallows and hot chocolate, meet at the firepit next to the Pokolodi Lodge at 4 p.m. Mondays and Wednesdays. Every night there are **magic and comedy shows** just for kids at the Tower Magic Bar and Restaurant. If you want a night to yourselves, **Night Hawks** is an evening child-care program (877-282-7736) for ages 3–10; $12/hour for the first child; half that price for additional children in the same family.

Lift tickets [05/06 prices]

	Adult	Youth (13-17)
One day (06/07)	$82	$75
Three days (out of 10)	$234 ($78/day)	$213 ($71/day)
Five days (out of 10)	$375 ($75/day)	$340 ($68/day)

Who skis free: Ages 6 and younger.

Who skis at a discount: Children (7–12) pay $49 per day for multiday tickets of four to seven days. Ages 65 to 69 pay youth rates for multiday tickets of four to seven days. Those 70 years and older get unlimited skiing or riding with The Silver Pass for $219 all season long. The best ticket prices are found by making a seven-day advance purchase. To purchase tickets, call (877) 282-7736 or buy online through the website.

Accommodations

Accommodations in Aspen range from luxurious and pricey to modest and inexpensive. **Stay Aspen Snowmass,** (800) 290-1325 or 925-9000, can reserve nearly all properties listed here. Multiday lift-and-lodging packages are the best deal. Log on to www.stayaspensnowmass.com for last-minute, discounted lodging packages.

Hotel Jerome (800-331-7213; 920-1000; $$$$) and the **Sardy House Residence & Carriage House Inn** (800-321-3457; 920-2525; $$$$), both on East Main Street, reflect Aspen's glory days. The Sardy House is a Victorian home transformed into a private residence club and inn. A modern addition with elegant rooms and suites has been tacked onto the rear. The Jerome—on the National Register of Historic Places—is a grand old hotel restored to more elegance than the silver barons ever knew. Even if you don't stay there, this Aspen landmark is worth a walk-through to view the antiques and old photos on the walls.

The **Little Nell** (888-843-6355; 920-4600; $$$$) is just steps from the Silver Queen Gondola at the base of Aspen Mountain. It has received the highest rating from several rating services, such as AAA and Mobil. All rooms have fireplaces, sofas, oversized beds with comforters, and marble bathrooms. There is a hot tub and a heated outdoor pool.

The **St. Regis Aspen** (888-454-9005; 920-3300; $$$$) has reinvented itself with major changes completed in 2004, including a 15,000-square-foot spa. Though the red brick building is just a few years old, it looks like it belongs to historic Aspen.

The **Residence** (920-6532; $$$$) has world-class European suites in an historic downtown landmark building. Also luxurious are the **SKY Hotel** (800-882-2582; 925-6760; $$$$) and the delightful award-winning **Hotel Lenado** (800-321-3457; 925-6246; $$$$) is another property of the Sardy House owners. It may be small, but it's huge in amenities, personality and service. A delicious hot breakfast is included in the room price, which drops into the $$$ category during shoulder seasons. Look for the funky-colored building on South Aspen Street.

The renovated **Snowflake Inn** (800-247-2069; 925-3221; $$–$$$), a block from the transportation center on East Hyman Avenue, is clean and roomy. It's within walking distance from the gondola, the buses to the other areas, and the downtown area. And it has a very friendly staff, laundry facilities, a heated pool and hot tub, and a free continental breakfast and apres-ski snacks. What more does one need?

One of our readers tells us **Hotel Durant** (925-8500; $$–$$$$) is one of his favorite "little hotels." Beautifully renovated in 1996, it's just two blocks from downtown and 1.5 blocks from Lift 1-A. The lounge fireplace and outdoor hot tub provide great ways to relax after a day on the slope and apre-ski wine and cheese are a nice plus.

Our favorite place in Aspen is a lodge of a kind that's disappearing all too fast: **The Mountain Chalet** (800-321-7813; 925-7797; $–$$$$). This place is just plain friendly to everyone, including families. If you can't stand a 3-year-old crawling over a lounge chair in the lobby or families howling over a game of Monopoly, don't stay here. Rooms come in all sizes, including bunks, and include a hearty breakfast served family-style. It's a few blocks from Aspen Mountain's Silver Queen gondola, and across the street from the transportation center. Pamper yourself with the outdoor heated pool, hot tub, sauna and steam room. Call early for rooms, because folks reserve space here well in advance. For the best prices, call directly.

Other places that treat guests very well are the **Mountain House Lodge** (920-3440; $$), the **Hotel Aspen** (800-527-7369; 925-3441; $$) and the **Molly Gibson Lodge** (800-356-6559; 925-3434; $$). Also try the **Limelight** (925-3025 or 800-433-0832; $$), and the **St. Moritz Lodge** (800-817-2069; 925-3220; $), a hostel only five blocks from the center of town.

You can still find inexpensive rooms at the **Christmas Inn** (925-3822; $$), **Innsbruck Inn** (925-2980; $$) renovated and reopening for winter '06, **Ullr Lodge** (925-7696; above left) and budget champion **Tyrolean Lodge** (925-4595 or 888-220-3809; $).

The **Heatherbed Lodge** (925-7077; 800-356-6782; $$) is a good place to stay near Aspen Highlands. Rates include a full breakfast.

Resort Quest and **Frias** are the largest condo management companies in the area. Resort Quest (720 East Hyman; 925-1400 or 800-222-7736), manages the **Fasching Haus** (925-2260) and **Durant Condominiums** (925-7910), both on the slopes. **Chateau Eau Claire** and **Chateau Roaring Fork** are two of their popular units. **Shadow Mountain** is not so luxurious, but has a ski-in/ski-out location. Frias (877-636-4626) books for the new **Hyatt Grand Aspen** and **St. Regis Residence Club** and also manage a large portfolio of privately owned condos. **Fifth Avenue** (925-7397) is also slopeside and is available through **StayAspenSnowmass** (888-290-1324). For luxury, three-bedroom condos on the slopes, try **Mountain Queen Con-**

Dining: $$$$-Entrees-$30+$; $$$-$20-30; $$-$10-20; $-less than $10.

Accommodations: (double room) $$$$-$200+; $$$-$141-$200; $$-$81-$140; $-$80 and less.

dominiums (925-6366). **The Gant** (925-5000 or 800-345-1471; above right) at the foot of Aspen Mountain is another choice.

Accommodations—Snowmass

Nearly half of the lodging at Snowmass is hotel rooms, and there are thousands of condominiums, many of which are slopeside.For other recommendations and reservations, call Snowmass Reservations (800-766-9627) or go to www.snowmassvillage.com.

The **Silvertree** (877-766-1999; $$$$) is the biggest hotel (260 rooms) with a conference center and feels like it inside. But it sits conveniently above the Snowmass Village Mall where most of the activity takes place.

Stonebridge Inn (; $–$$$; left), in the center of the village recently was renovated with $1 million in upgrades and added meeting space and a deck.

Less expensive hotel or lodge accommodations include the **Pokolodi Lodge** (800-666-4556; $–$$$); **Snowmass Inn** (800-635-3758; $–$$$); **Snowmass Mountain Chalet** (800-843-1579; $–$$$), which includes a full breakfast, delicious soup lunch and slopeside convenience (it just spent half a million in remodeling); or **Wildwood Lodge** (877-766-1999; $$–$$$$). Parking arrangements vary by property and can be inconvenient.

The **Crestwood Condominium Hotel** (800-356-5949; $$$–$$$$) is comfortable and roomy, right next to the slopes and well-designed for groups. Units have fireplaces, a bathroom for every bedroom, laundry facilities, new swimming pools and exercise room and airport shuttle service.

The **Sonnenblick** (800-525-9402; $$$$) has only large units, three or five bedrooms. For more moderate condos, try **Terracehouse** (800-525-9402; $$$–$$$$), a short walk to the lifts, or **Lichenhearth** (800-525-9402; $$$–$$$$), adjacent to the Fanny Hill lift. **The Top of the Village** (800-982-1311; $$$–$$$$; right) and the **Timberline** (800-922-4001; $$–$$$$) condos are a good 5- to 10-minute climb above the village mall. For economy condos, we like **Willows** (800-525-9402; $$$), two levels below the village mall.

Woodrun Place Condos and Conference Center (800-668-0401; $$$$) has had an extensive face-lift on its exterior to the tune of $12 million. The 33 townhomes at **Woodrun V** (800-718-3694; $$$$) have new exteriors and heated walkways, a new business center and other upgrades. The condos are right next to the midway loading station for the new Elk Camp Gondola. **Chamonix** (800-365-0410; $$$$) is another upscale condo complex.

Dining

We can't possibly review all the restaurants in Aspen, because the region's packed with worthy places to eat, but this list will get you started. Exotic ingredients and ethnic foods are definitely trendy in Aspen. Aspen is a place where you can enjoy the fine restaurants thoroughly, knowing that the next day you'll ski off those calories. But be careful—most menu items are separately priced and the bill can add up.

If cost is what you're worried about, many restaurants in Aspen have a "bar" menu. Bar menus are the locals' secrets to eating well and they aren't your usual hot wings and nachos. They're culinary delights running $8–$15, such as roast sirloin steak with gourmet mashed potatoes at **Cache Cache**, spinach-and-ricotta-cheese ravioli in a light smoked-ricotta-and-sage sauce at **L'Hostaria** or the Sambal shrimp quesadilla at **Elevation.**

Montagna (675 E. Durant; 920-6330; $$$$) at the Little Nell specializes in contemporary American Alpine cuisine. Executive Chef Paul Wade delights with an intricate blend of flavors, textures and colors. Montagna is a Grand Award recipient, the highest achievement from *Wine*

Spectator. Open for breakfast, lunch and dinner, as well as Sunday brunch.

Syzygy (520 E. Hyman Ave.; 925-3700, reservations required; $$$–$$$$) has a menu that combines French, Southwestern, Asian and Italian influences. Don't be put off by the hard-to-pronounce name (Siz-i-je) or the obscure explanation of its meaning on the menu. The food here is simply exquisite. The atmosphere is intimate yet casual, with live jazz performers who seem to make the food dance across your tongue.

Go to **Piñons** (second floor at 105 S. Mill; 920-2021; $$$$) to dine in what feels like a cozy Western ranch, with stucco walls, a leather bar and menus, and huge brass bowls. All meats and fish are grilled over mesquite and cherry wood. Desserts vary daily.

If you think that at these prices, you should be entertained and have your apartment cleaned for a year, one man will at least do the former. Owner Mead Metcalf has been playing to **The Crystal Palace** sellout crowds each evening at 6 and 9 p.m. for more than four decades (300 E. Hyman Ave.; 925-1455; $$$$, reservations may be necessary several weeks in advance). The Crystal Palace's talented staff not only cranks out a full dinner and bar service, but then belts out a cabaret revue spoofing the media's latest victims. You can choose from perfectly pink beef tenderloin with Madeira sauce, roast duckling, rack of lamb or prime rib. The food doesn't have to be good, but it is. Palace After Hours is a piano bar with New York City cabaret artist Michael McAssey (in the lounge following the dinner show).

World-renowned chef-owner Charles Dale should be commended for his newest venture, **Range** (304 E. Hopkins; 925-2402; $$$), where he lowered prices but didn't lower standards. Dale (who grew up in the palace in Monaco with Caroline and Albert) showcases Western ingredients such as salmon from Alaska's Copper River, Oregon morels and Idaho trout. The regional twist extends to the wines, which are all American.

Cache Cache (lower level of the Mill St. Plaza; 925-3835; $$–$$$) gets a thumbs-up from locals for French provincial cuisine, especially the half-price early-bird specials. The polenta nicoise, wild mushroom cannelloni and perfectly grilled yellowtail are favorites. **Rustique** (216 S. Monarch; 920-2555; $$–$$$) serves a wonderful cassoulet Toulousain with duck confit and sausage. It also has a child-friendly menu with 25 classic French favorites called "Small Plates."

Kenichi (233 E. Hopkins; 920-2212; $$$) and **Takah Sushi** (on the Hyman Avenue Mall; 925-8588; $$–$$$) are *the* locals' favorite for Pan Asian cuisine and sushi. Always crowded, reservations are a must, especially on Friday and Saturday nights.

Matthew Zubrod, who used to be executive chef at the Ritz-Carlton, opened **AspenDish** (430 E. Hyman; 925-1421; $$$) in the former Mogador Restaurant space on the Hyman St. Mall in spring of 2006. He serves creative American comfort foods like lobster corn dogs, truffle mac 'n cheese and C.L.T. sandwiches made of crab, lettuce and tomato.

Outstanding gourmet Italian restaurants are **Campo de Fiori** (205 E. Mill; 920-7717; $$–$$$) and Campo's cousin (same owner) **Gusto Ristorante** (415 E. Main; 925-8222; $$–$$$). Gusto's contemporary cuisine is refreshingly different than the classic dishes of Campo de Fiori and a tad less expensive. **Olives Aspen** (920-7356; $$$) at the St. Regis has a broad Mediterranean-inspired menu from award-winning Chef Todd English. Valet parking is complimentary.

The contemporary and casual **Elevation** (304 E. Hopkins; 544-5166; $$–$$$) serves New American cuisine with Asian influences. After dinner on weekends, Elevation turns into a hot nightclub, so you don't have to go back out in the cold till it's time to go back to your hotel. **Genre** (316 E Hopkins; 925-1260; $$–$$$), an intimate French bistro owned by local ski competitor Vince Lahey, has a strong local following, serving authentic French cuisine at

Dining: $$$$-Entrees $30+; $$$-$20-$30; $$-$10-$20; $-less than $10.
Accommodations: (double room) $$$$-$200+; $$$-$141-$200; $$-$81-$140; $-$80 and less.

reasonable prices. **L'Hostaria** (925-9022; $$–$$$) showcases decor and recipes direct from Italy. The specialty is a two-pound Chilean sea bass express-shipped daily and baked with olive oil, herbs, clams and mussels.

For more affordable dining, try **Asie** ($$), the "hottest place in town" for Asian fare and **Blue Maize** (308 S. Hunter; 925-6698, $$) for Southwest and Latin American food. How about a bistro in a bookstore—Explore Bookstore's upper level graduates into a smart vegetarian bistro with summa cum laude desserts and aptly named **Explore Bistro** (221 E. Main; 925-5338; $$). **The Steak Pit** (corner of Hopkins and Monarch; 925-3459; $$) has been in business since 1960, serving some of the best steaks in Aspen along with a sumptuous all-you-can-eat salad bar.

Little Ollie's (downstairs at 308 S. Hunter; 544-9888; $) has healthy Chinese food and offers take-out. **The Cantina** (corner of Mill and Main; 925-3663; $–$$) is a trendier Mexican alternative with the "best Mexican food north of San Antonio." **The Big Wrap** (544-1700; $) features burrito-like wraps but with a variety of exotic fillings. **Boogie's Diner** (534 E. Cooper; 925-6610; $) is a real '50s diner with oldies music, blue plate specials and meatloaf (great milkshakes, too).

For a real adventure, head out to the **Pine Creek Cookhouse** (925-1044; $$$), rebuilt in 2004. At an elevation of 9,725 feet, the log cabin is in the midst of towering pines beneath Elk Mountain peaks some 12 miles up Castle Creek Road. It is accessible by a 1.5-mile cross-country trek or by a sleigh drawn by a team of Percheron horses. Views are outstanding. Reservations are essential (at times two to four weeks in advance), as the logistics of running a kitchen not reached by road in winter is no small matter. The Cookhouse feeds several hundred people each day, and all that food (wild game is its specialty) comes in by snowmobile. Meals are prepared right in front of you in the open kitchen and are served by one of your cross-country guides.

Let's start with *the* place to eat breakfast, **The Wienerstube**, a.k.a. "the Stube" (633 E. Hyman and Spring; $). Come here for Eggs Benny, omelets, Austrian sausages and home-made Viennese pastries. Believe it or not, **Hickory House** (730 W. Main St.; $), known for its baby-back ribs, serves one of the best breakfasts around. **Poppycock's** (665 E. Cooper; $), a contemporary cafe with fancy pancakes, crepes and eggs, is delightful. **Main Street Bakery Cafe** (201 E. Main St.; $) has homemade baked goods, granola, fruit, eggs and great coffee. For the best coffee in town, head to **Bagel Bites** (710 E. Durant), or **Ink! Coffee** (inside the D&E Snowboard Shop in the Aspen Mountain Building).

Dining—Snowmass

If you are worried about staying in Snowmass and missing out on Aspen's fining dining atmosphere, do not fret. By the way, every restaurant in Snowmass has children's menus.

Known for its dogsledding and kennels, **Krabloonik** (923-3953; $$$$) has an even bigger reputation for its restaurant's wild-game selection and extensive wine list. In a rustic log house at Snowmass, this venue is the one Snowmass option where you can ring up Aspen-level dinner tabs. More down to earth are **Artisan Restaurant** (923-2420; $$$), in the Stonebridge Inn, with a superb menu of fish, seafood and vegetarian options in a homey rustic setting, and the Snowmass Club bistro, **Sage** (923-5600; $$$), which offers distinctive food with fixed-price options in a casual unpretentious atmosphere.

Most other eateries are in Snowmass Village Mall (if we don't tell you, that's where you'll find them). **La Provence** (923-6804; $$$) offers southern French fare accompanied by a very nice wine list and a view, though consistency can be an issue. **The Margarita Grill** (923-6803;

$$–$$$) serves southwestern cuisine influenced by Central America. **Il Poggio** (923-4292; $$–$$$) prepares classic Italian fare in two settings: an elegant experience complete with extensive wine choices, or casual with homemade pastas and hearth-baked pizzas. Service can be on the slow side in the more upscale dining room, where reservations are required.

Butch's Lobster Bar (923-4004; $$$), at the top of the village, is owned by a former lobsterman from Cape Cod; **Brothers' Grille** (923-8285; $–$$) in the Silvertree reportedly has the best hamburgers in the valley; and **Mountain Dragon** (923-3576; $–$$), one of the hottest spots for dinner or drinks, serves Chinese, sushi and free appetizers during happy hour.

The Stew Pot (923-2263; $–$$) features soups, tasty and unusual stews and sandwiches. The **Village Deli** ($) also serves healthy and inexpensive lunch options for those on the run. For pizza, steaks or hoagies, try **Taste of Philly** ($).

Spend a family evening at the **Burlingame Cabin** (923-0575; $$$) or the **Lynn Britt Cabin** (923-0460; fixed-price menu) nestled in aspen groves on Snowmass. At both, a heated snowcat and well-blanketed open-air sleigh transports guests to a cabin with wood stove, Western-style meal, bluegrass entertainment and sing-alongs.

For a quick breakfast on the way to the slopes, try **Paradise Bakery** ($) or **Fuel** (923-0091; $) for a breakfast burrito. **Brothers Grille** (923-8285; $–$$) has heaping helpings of morning food and **The Big Hoss Grill** (923-2597; $) serves everything from hearty "Hoss" breakfasts to barbeque-to-go.

Dining—on the mountains

The crown jewel of Aspen's on-mountain dining is the **Sundeck Restaurant** (429-6971; $$), housed in a magnificent lodge that replaces the old Sundeck building at the top of the gondola. It's a favorite spot for spectacular views, people-watching and innovative cuisine served from individual food stations. Check out the priceless old ski photos on the walls.

Ajax Tavern (920-9333; $$$), at the base of Silver Queen Gondola, boasts Tuscan influences in a richly wood-paneled room. Lunch is a hearty selection of Colorado lamb, roasted mussels, pastas, salads and sandwiches with a Napa Valley wine list and outdoor seating for primo people-watching. **Bump's** (925-4027; $–$$), at the Buttermilk base area, features foods from a wood-fired rotisserie, brick ovens and a pit smoker, as well as huge salads, pastas and stews. **Bonnie's** ($–$$), just above Lift 3 on Aspen Mountain, feeds some 1,500 hungry skiers per day between 9:30 a.m. and 2:30 p.m. Go before noon or after 2 p.m., unless you love lines. The double decks outside are *the* places to be during the day. Owner Bonnie Rayburn's gourmet pizza on freshly made crust is a huge crowd pleaser. Homemade soups, such as the Colorado white-bean chili, are served with large crusty pieces of fresh French bread. Save room for her world-famous apple strudel.

Other on-mountain options include the **Cliffhouse** ($) atop Buttermilk with an outdoor deck and serving its famous custom-cooked Mongolian Barbecue. **Cloud Nine**, a European-style bistro with a fixed-price menu, is decorated in early evacuation gear since it shares space with the Aspen Highlands ski patrol. It has killer views of the Maroon Bells, Aspen's world-famous peaks. Snowcats can bring you there for evening dining; call 544-3063. **Merry-Go-Round** ($), midmountain at Highlands, serves grilled bratwursts, burgers and Mexican fare, and is the location for the legendary jumping show on Freestyle Fridays.

The Village at Aspen Highlands is shaping up nicely, although it's a bit dark in color for our tastes and the buildings block the mountain view. Retail shops and restaurants are filling the empty spaces, and we like **Willow Creek** at the Ritz Carlton Club and **Iguana's** as alternatives for lunch and dinner.

Dining: $$$$–Entrees $30+; $$$–$20-$30; $$–$10-$20; $–less than $10.
Accommodations: (double room) $$$$–$200+; $$$–$141-$200; $$–$81-$140; $–$80 and less.

Snowmass Village excels with mountaintop cookery. **Gwyn's High Alpine Restaurant** (923-5188, reservations are essential), at the top of Alpine Springs (Lift 8), is among the best food in the region, on or off mountain. You can hike up for breakfast before the lifts open. **Krabloonik** (923-3953), mentioned earlier as a dinner choice, is also open for lunch. It's at the base of Campground off the Dawdler Catwalk. Another on-mountain option is **Up 4 Pizza** (923-0464; $) at the top of the Big Burn in Snowmass. For quick "power food," head to one of the **yurts** near the snowboard halfpipes and the terrain park, or at the bottom of Assay Hill. At the Two Creeks base area, chorizo and egg burritos start the day at **Two Creeks Mexican Cafe** ($). Fajitas, taco salad and burritos are typical lunch fare. The **Cirque Bar & Grill** ($–$$), slopeside at the Snowmass Village Mall, has a buffet breakfast for a fast exit to the slopes in the morning, and a more leisurely sit-down lunch and dinner service.

 ## Apres-ski/nightlife

Slopeside **Ajax Tavern** is a big draw for catching afternoon rays as the lifts start to close. If you don't find what you want there, the crowd spreads out to **The Terrace Room** at the Little Nell Hotel, **Mezzaluna, 39 Degrees** at the Sky Hotel, **Little Annie's, Cooper Street Pier,** the **J-Bar** (Jack Nicholson's hangout at the Jerome) and the **Red Onion.** Apres-ski comes in all varieties here, from **The Cantina**, with its very happy hour (have a margarita in the compadre size), to the quiet and genteel **Hotel Jerome Bar.** At Aspen Highlands, **Iguana's** is the place to be.

At night, the music and dance beat begin to take over. Earlier in the evening, the high-energy place to find out who's in town is **Mezzaluna**, with its brassy horseshoe-shaped bar. It's a good singles bar and gives you the best in upscale people-watching. **The Shadow Mountain Lounge** at the St. Regis has live music. **The Little Nell** bar and **Syzygy** have jazz. DJs rule at **Bar Aspen, The Speakeasy** and **The Lava Room.**

Jimmy's, an American restaurant and bar, is where the swank dinner crowd hits the dance floor on Saturday night for its signature Salsa Night. You'll also find what they claim to be one of the largest tequila menus in the country (more than 65).

Eric's Bar, Cigar Bar and **Aspen Billiards** all attract singles, and have lots of micro-brews on tap (great scotch, too). Another beer spot is **McStorlie's Pub.** A relatively mixed crowd congregates in the **Red Onion** and **Little Annie's. Cooper Street Pier** is very much a local and college student hangout.

There are many other night spots in town; pick up a copy of Aspen Magazine's Traveler's Guide for a list, or check local papers, The Aspen Times and The Aspen Daily News, for current happenings.

At Snowmass, you'll find most of the down-valley locals at the **Mountain Dragon** and **Butch's Lobster Bar** during apres-ski. The **Cirque Bar & Grill** has live music daily but tends to be crowded and somewhat rowdy. **Brothers' Grille** has five different draft beers and about a dozen hot drinks for quick warm-ups. **Zane's Tavern** is a sports bar with apres-ski drink specials. Renowned magician Doc Eason performs bar magic weekly at the **Stonebridge Inn** (923-2420). At night Snowmass Village is quiet.

 ## Other activities

Sleigh rides take place at the T-Lazy-7 Ranch (925-7040). The T-Lazy-7 also leads **snowmobile tours** around the Maroon Bells and through the ghost town of Independence. For winter **fly-fishing** trips call Aspen Outfitting Co. (925-3406), Oxbow Outfitting Co. (925-1505) or Aspen Sports (925-6332).

The 83,000-square-foot Aspen Recreation Center (544-4100) near the base of Aspen Highlands has an NHL-sized ice rink for public **ice skating** (skate rentals available), an aquatic area with a six-lane, 25-yard **competitive swimming pool, a leisure pool with a two-story water slide, hot tubs, steam rooms,** a 32-foot **climbing tower, weight room and batting cages.** There are locker rooms and a concession stand too. You also can **ice skate** across from the transportation center at Silver Circle Ice Rink (925-6360) and indoors at Aspen Ice Garden (920-5141).

The Aspen Center for Environmental Studies (925-5756) is a non-profit organization that holds many interesting programs, including **Naturalist Nights** every Thursday evening and **Potbelly Perspectives,** tales of travels and adventures, every Wednesday.

Cooking School of Aspen offers classes from Aspen's finest chefs for adults and kids (920-1879). You can make and paint your own **ceramics** at Kolor Wheel (544-6191) at 205 South Mill. It offers arts and crafts for adults and children.

The Wheeler Opera House (920-5770) hosts a variety of big-time entertainers throughout the season. **Belly Up Aspen** (450 So. Galena; 544-9800) is a live music venue for major attractions, such as Ben Harper, B.B. King, Joe Cocker, Jurassic 5.

When you're in Aspen you expect the best, the most state-of-the-art, the highest quality and the trendiest. SpaAspen delivers all that and more. By purchasing a SpaAspen service at the 77,000-square-foot **Aspen Club & Spa** (952-8900 or 866-484-8245), you have access to The Aspen Club for the day, which encompasses a health and fitness center and the Aspen Club Sports Medicine Institute. The facilities include everything you'd expect and more: 34 treatment rooms, swimming, tennis, child care, relaxation lounges and healthful food at the Club Cafe. Services include 17 types of massage, seven types of body treatments, numerous skin care programs and a full salon.

Remède Spa at the St. Regis Aspen (920-3300) is a 15,000-square-foot facility that includes a fitness center with on-staff certified trainers and nutritionists, full-service salon and full-service spa with 15 treatment rooms for massages, facials and body treatments.

Many winter visitors to Aspen never touch the slopes during their stay. This place is a shopper's paradise, and even if you can't afford the mostly high-end merchandise, browsing is part of the fun. High on the browsing scale is Boogie's, 534 E. Cooper St. In addition to funky clothes and other stuff, you'll find Elvis Presley's 1955 red Corvette (but not for sale). Les Chefs D'Aspen, on the corner of Cooper and Hunter, sells imported kitchenware plus local gourmet foods and coffee.

Clothing stores are abundant and filled with unusual items. Some of our favorites: Goldies and the Kids, 525 E. Cooper, for delightful kids' clothing; Gracy's at the Cooper Street Mall and Susie's Ltd. on E. Hopkins, to check out what the wear-it-once crowd has on consignment; Prada at 312 So. Galena; and Roots, near Prada, with Canadian imports.

Don't miss a visit to Explore Booksellers and Bistro, 221 E. Main. It's a legend in Aspen. Here you can pick up your favorite novel or ski guidebook and have dinner too.

Most of Aspen's 30 art galleries are within a four-by-three-block area between Spring and Monarch Streets and Hopkins Ave. and Durant St. Our favorites are Omnibus Gallery for vintage poster art; Galerie Du Bois for Impressionism; Highline Gallery for glass art; Pam Driscol Gallery for life-size bronze sculptures; and Baldwin Gallery for contemporary collections.

The Ultimate Taxi (927-9239) is a unique way to tour Aspen. This disco on wheels probably will top your list of Aspen memorable experiences.

Dining: $$$$-Entrees $30+; $$$-$20-$30; $$-$10-$20; $-less than $10.
Accommodations: (double room) $$$$-$200+; $$$-$141-$200; $$-$81-$140; $-$80 and less.

Other activities—Snowmass

Explore the wilderness around Snowmass on a leisurely guided two-hour **snowshoe tour** with an Aspen Center for Environmental Studies (925-5756) naturalist. Trips are daily 10 a.m.-1 p.m.; $45/adults; $29/kids and seniors 65 and older.

For a wilder time in the wilds of Snowmass, Maroon Bells or Independence Pass, go on a two- or four-hour **guided snowmobile tour**. Contact Blazing Adventures (923-4544), Western Adventures (923-3337) or T-Lazy-Seven (925-4614).

Krabloonik Kennels in Snowmass Village (923-4342) is known for its daily two-hour dogsledding tours through the Snowmass wilderness area, led by Iditarod-experienced huskies. Morning or afternoon rides include a four-course gourmet lunch at Krabloonik's restaurant.

Above It All Balloon (963-6148) and Unicorn Balloon (925-5752) are two Hot air balloon companies that can give you a bird's-eye view of the Elk Mountains and local wildlife year-round. (right)

Pokolodi Lodge hosts campfire sing-alongs (Mondays) and story-telling (Wednesdays) complete with hot chocolate and marshmellows from 4-5 p.m. Free for all ages. Let your kids get creative at a free hour of Kids Krafts near the ticket pavilion in the Snowmass Mall from 4-5 p.m. Tuesdays and Thursdays while you enjoy apres-ski of a different kind. While you're there, ask where the best sledding slope is.

Snowmass has the only **Zipline** (925-1220) in the world that picks you up while skiing or boarding and takes you on an 800-foot drop down the mountain. So far, it's also the only winter zipline in Colorado.

Snowmass Recreation Center (922-2240) is a brand new facility with lap pool and fitness center. Cost is $15 a day for non-residents or less with punch passes. The Aspen Rec Center (544-4100) sits between the town of Aspen and Snowmass and has more activities for the whole family, including climbing wall, pools with slides and a hockey rink. The Snowmass Club (923-5600) has a full-service spa.

The Anderson Ranch Arts Center (923-3181) in Snowmass Village exhibits work by visiting and resident artists during the winter.

 ## Getting there and getting around

By air: Aspen's Sardy Field, 3 miles from Aspen and 8 miles from Snowmass, is served by regular flights from four cities: Denver (United Express), Phoenix (America West Express), Memphis and Minneapolis/St. Paul (Northwest Jet Airlink) and Los Angeles (United Express). If you fly on major holidays, expect delays and carry on a well-packed bag.

Eagle County airport, about 70 miles away, is becoming the best-served airport for this resort. It hosts flights from Northwest, American, Continental, United Express, U.S. Airways and Delta. American has nonstop flights arriving from Dallas/Ft. Worth, Chicago, Newark, Los Angeles, New York La Guardia and Miami. Continental has nonstop service from Houston and Newark. Delta flies from Atlanta and Cincinnati. Northwest flies from Minneapolis/St. Paul. United Express flies daily connecting flights from Denver. U.S. Airways flies nonstop from Philadelphia, Charlotte and Denver. Colorado Mountain Express (800-525-6363) takes skiers from Eagle to Aspen.

If you find yourself in Aspen without your gear or outdoor clothing, make sure to ask the airlines for a voucher to rent what you need until they show up with your luggage. All the airlines hand out coupons for equipment in case yours is delayed. These vouchers are accepted at virtually every sports shop in town. If your luggage gets waylaid, call Lorenzo Semple at **Suit Yourself** (920-0295). He will be at your door with a van full of ski and snowboard clothing for you to rent during your stay. He takes airline vouchers.

Regular ground transportation also leaves the Denver International Airport for Aspen, but it's a four- to five-hour drive on I-70, about 220 miles away. Rental cars are available at both Denver and Eagle County Airport.

By train: Amtrak has service to Glenwood Springs, where skiers can get ground transportation for the 40-mile trip to Aspen.

Getting around: Aspen has a free bus system, RFTA, with several routes in town and to Glenwood Springs. There also is a separate, free shuttle between the various ski mountains during the day; there is a small fee after 4:30 p.m. Downtown is enjoyably walkable. Thank goodness a car is unnecessary, because parking is a pain.

Getting around Snowmass Village is a little more involved than getting around Aspen, so we'd like to share some tips based on our experience (and we still recommend that you use public transportation because of limited parking):

The (mostly) free bus system, RFTA, will shuttle you between Snowmass and Aspen. At Snowmass Village, you board the RFTA bus at the transportation center at the Snowmass Village Mall. Between 8 a.m. and 4:30 p.m., the RFTA bus is free. After 4:30 p.m., however, the charge is $3 per person, one way, between Aspen and Snowmass Village. If you have been skiing at one of the three mountains in Aspen and you relax in the bar afterward, keep a close eye on the clock so the charge doesn't take you by surprise.

Snowmass Village has a separate, free shuttle system with several routes that run throughout the village. To get to Aspen, you ride a Snowmass Village shuttle to the transportation center, then transfer to an RFTA bus. Although the system is very efficient (and you can't beat the price), it takes about an hour to get from a Snowmass Village condo to Aspen, and vice versa. If you expect to make two round trips per day into Aspen (one for skiing and the second for nightlife), stay in Aspen.

Nearby resorts

Sunlight Mountain Resort, Glenwood Springs, CO; (800) 445-7931

Internet: www.sunlightmtn.com
4 lifts; 470 acres; 2,010 vertical feet; 3 terrain parks

Not only is this a less pricey ski option if you're headed to nearby Aspen, but Glenwood Springs is the home of the world's largest hot springs pool, two blocks long and kept at a toasty 90 degrees. Most of Ski Sunlight is intermediate terrain, though the double-black-diamond Sunlight Extreme provides steep and gladed challenges for the best of skiers and riders.

Lift tickets (06/07 prices): Adults, $45; Junior (6-12) and Senior (60-69), $35; 70+ and younger than 6, $10.

Distance from Denver: About 222 miles west on I-70 and Hwy. 82. The closest airport is Vail/Eagle, about 30 miles east of Sunlight Mountain. Aspen is about 40 miles south. Glenwood Springs is a daily stop on Amtrak's California Zephyr route from San Francisco to Chicago.

Summit County
Colorado

Summit County Facts
Dining: ★★★
Apres-ski/nightlife: ★★★
Other activities: ★★★

Reservations: 800-530-3099 or 262-0817 (chamber)
E-mail: info@summitchamber.org
Internet: www.experiencethesummit.com (chamber)
www.townofdillon.com (Dillon)
www.townoffrisco.com (Frisco)
www.silverthorne.org (Silverthorne)
www.summitnet.com

Some winter vacationers aren't satisfied with skiing and riding at just one place. When they return to the office, they want to drop resort names and compare black-diamond plunges or best family vacations. For these skiers, we suggest Summit County.

Within Summit County, about a 90-minute drive from downtown Denver, are four well-known ski areas—Breckenridge, Copper Mountain, Keystone and Arapahoe Basin. Each resort—except A-Basin—has its own lodging, shopping and restaurants.

If you plan to do most of your skiing at just one area, stay at that resort. But if you want to experience them all, then set up your base camp in Dillon, Frisco or Silverthorne, three small towns off I-70 that surround Lake Dillon.

This tri-town area is smack in the center of the ski action. Breckenridge is about 9 miles in one direction, Copper Mountain is 5 miles in another, Keystone is 7 miles away in a third, and A-Basin just a little farther than Keystone. Having a car is nice, but not really necessary. The reliable Summit Stage, the free bus system subsidized by sales tax revenue, runs between the towns and the ski areas all day and into the night—until 2 a.m.

Summit County deserves its lofty name. It has a base elevation above 9,000 feet. (If you have problems with high altitudes, take note. If you like spring skiing, also take note: High elevations usually mean a longer ski season.) Each of these areas stays open until mid-April, and Arapahoe Basin—with its base lodge above 10,000 feet—often stays open until July 4.

Vail Resorts owns Keystone and Breckenridge. It has an interchangeable lift ticket that includes Vail, Beaver Creek, Keystone and Breckenridge, or you can buy a multiday ticket for just Keystone and Breckenridge for a little less. Your Keystone-Breckenridge ticket also is valid at Arapahoe Basin, or you can buy that ticket separately. You'll have to buy a separate ticket to ski at Copper Mountain.

This chapter lists accommodations, dining, nightlife and non-ski activities in the three towns of Frisco, Dillon and Silverthorne. Pick up information and helpful brochures at two Summit County Visitor Information Centers, one in Silverthorne at 246 Rainbow Dr. in the Silverthorne Factory Stores behind Wendy's and in Frisco at 916 N. Summit Blvd.

Separate chapters detail skiing, lodging, dining and nightlife at Breckenridge, Copper Mountain and Keystone. For information on skiing at A-Basin, see the Keystone chapter.

Accommodations

Frisco:

This is our first choice for a home base, for several reasons. One, it is the closest town to Breckenridge and Copper Mountain, and Keystone isn't far away. Two, its downtown area along Main Street has lots of funky shops and restaurants, perfect for a late afternoon or evening stroll. And three, we like friendly mountain inns, and found some good ones.

The **Galena Street Inn** (800-248-9138; 668-3224; $$-$$$), First Avenue and Galena Street (one block off Main Street), has a light and airy feel to it. Its 14 rooms have private baths, televisions and phones, and all are nicely furnished. A hot tub and sauna are among the amenities. A full breakfast with hot entree is included, as are apres-ski refreshments and home-baked treats. No smoking or pets.

Hotel Frisco (800-262-1002; 668-5009; $-$$$) was remodeled a few years ago. The cozy lodge, at 308 Main St., has 16 nicely decorated rooms, a huge river-rock fireplace in the lobby and an outdoor hot tub. Guests can access the Internet free via high-speed modems.

Frisco Lodge (800-279-6000; 668-5000; $$) at Fourth & Main has been hosting people since the 1800s when Frisco was a stagecoach stop. The staff members are long-time residents with insiders' knowledge of the area.

Cross Creek Resort (800-748-1849; 468-6291; $$-$$$) has 17 condos perched stream-side on Ten Mile Creek on the western edge of town. The resort, which is on the shuttle bus route, also has a clubhouse and conference center.

Chain hotels include **Best Western Lake Dillon Lodge** (800-727-0607; $$), **Holiday Inn** (800-782-7669; $$) and **Ramada** (668-87830), all clustered around Summit Boulevard. The budget motel **Alpine Inn** (800-314-3122; $) with continental breakfast sits behind the Best Western on the shuttle route. If you're looking for super-budget lodging, try **Just Bunks** (668-4757; $), a "home-style hostel" at 208 Teller St. that is drug-, alcohol- and smoke-free.

Dillon/Silverthorne:

There are chain hotels and motels, plus condos and chalets. The **Best Western Ptarmigan Lodge** (800-842-5939; 468-2341; $$-$$$) in the Dillon town center is one of the best bargains, particularly during the early and late seasons and in January. Another moderately priced motel is the **Dillon Inn** (800-262-0801; 262-0801; $$-$$$), which has an indoor pool. **The Lodge at Carolina in the Pines** (262-7500; $$-$$$$) is a B&B that overlooks Lake Dillon and has a serene setting.

Off the interstate in Silverthorne are side-by-side chain hotels: **La Quinta** (800-321-3509; 468-6200; $$-$$$) and **Days Inn** (800-329-7466; 468-8661; $$-$$$). The Summit Stage stops at their doors. **Comfort Suites** (513-0300; 276 Dillon Ridge Road; $$) is in the same vicinity off highway 9 in Dillon.

Budget travelers should stay at the **Super 8** (800-800-8000; 468-8888; $$-$$$) in Dillon, across from the Summit Place Shopping Center. Three of the best cheap restaurants are in this center. Or, try the **Alpen Hutte Lodge** (468-6336; $-$$) at 471 Rainbow Dr. Both the Greyhound bus from Denver and the Summit County buses stop there, and for about $27, you get a bed in an eight-person dorm room. Private rooms and family rooms are available. The lodge has a nice kitchen, is clean and it's walking distance from restaurants and shopping.

The towns have many more B&Bs, chain hotels, private homes and condos. For reservations, call **Summit County Central Reservations**, (800) 365-6365, or **Reservations for the Summit**, (800) 999-9510, or the **Summit Country Chamber**, (800) 530-3099 or 668-2051.

Dining
Frisco:

The newest contender for Frisco's best restaurant is **Samplings** (corner of 4th and Main, 668-8466; $$-$$$$). Choose gourmet dishes from six categories, all served on salad-size plates to taste and share (or not). Wines come from an impressive collection by the bottle, glass, or flight. A 20-foot-long community table adds friendship that comes with sharing meals. There's conventional seating, of course, in the casual rustic digs. It opens at 2 p.m.

Dining: $$$$-Entrees $30+; $$$-$20-$30; $$-$10-$20; $-less than $10.
Accommodations: (double room) $$$$-$200+; $$$-$141-$200; $$-$81-$140; $-$80 and less.

The Blue Spruce (20 Main St., 668-5900; $$$) is in an historic log cabin. Entrees include such dishes as veal picatta, steak Diane, and lamb chops with pestoDefinitely deserves to be at the top of anyone's dining list. Reservations recommended.

The '90s bistro atmosphere at **The Boatyard Pizzeria and Grill** (304 Main, 668-4728; $–$$) complements an extensive a la Carte menu that includes some of the best salad entrees in the county. Also serves specialty pizzas, pastas and American favorites. Ask to be seated in the back, away from the front-door draft.

Silverheels at the Ore House (603 Main St., 668-0345; $$–$$$) is a century-old dancehall legend with a history that serves Southwestern fare in the form of steaks and chops, seafood and to-die-for desserts like mud pie and Mexican caramel flan. Don't miss the tequila shots.

Farley's Chophouse (423 Main St.; 668-3733; $$) is famous for its prime rib and signature steak Filet Farley, but also serves chops, chicken and seafood.

Authentic Mexican restaurants are popping up and **Fiesta Jalisco** (450 W. Main, 668-5043; $$) is a good one. But the one locals are loving is **Carlos Miguel's** (720 N. Summit Blvd.; $-$$; 668-4900). It's fresh, fine Mexican food—tableside-prepared guacamole, ceviche de camaron, cochinita pibil—at affordable prices.

For good budget eats, **Deli Belly's** (275 Main St.; $) has giant sandwiches. If hot home-made soup sounds good after a cold day, take out a quart or three from **Mi Zuppa** in the Safeway shopping center on Summit Boulevard. In the same center, **Food Hedz World Cafe** offers an eclectic menu for the world's people. Locals love it too.

Halfway between Frisco and Breckenridge, in an area called Farmer's Korner, are neighboring restaurants that are quite different. **The Blue River Inn** (547-9928; $) is a no-frills local hangout with great burgers, inexpensive draft beers and a 10-ounce sirloin that is probably still less than $10. **The Swan Mountain Inn** (453-7903; $$$) at the intersection of Hwy. 9 and Swan Mountain Rd. offers an elegant, nightly four-course meal in a seven-table dining room with a fireplace. The inn also has a weekend brunch.

Dillon/Silverthorne:

A sea of fast-food chains pepper this area. But if you look (and follow this guide), you can find a few nice joints. A good choice for finer dining is **Ristorante Al Lago** (240 Lake Dillon, 468-6111; $$) with expertly prepared Northern Italian meals. Reliable food and service **Arapahoe Cafe and Pub** (626 Lake Dillon; 468-0873; $$) have made it a favorite in Summit County. The building is one of many that were saved when the reservoir was created.

For more casual dining in Dillon, try the **Dillon Dam Brewery** (262-7777;$-$$), which lives up to its slogan, "the best dam brewery in town." Get your name in early; the place jams on weekends. **Pug Ryan's** (Dillon town center, 468-2145; $–$$) is fantastic for steaks and microbrewed beer. **Wild Bill's Stone Oven Pizza** (Dillon town center, 468-2006; $) is a hit for—what else?—stone-oven pizzas. Old Chicago Restaurant (468-6200; $–$$; right) with 110 different beers and great happy hours is at Four Points by the Sheraton Hotel. **Jersey Boys** (149 Tenderfoot; 513-1087; $-$$) prepares "east-coast style" pizza and sandwiches to order, as well as other dinner dishes.

City Market serves as anchor for the Dillon Ridge Market Place. But a couple of good eateries here are worth trying. **Masato's** (262-6600; $-$$$) is an excellent Japanese restaurant and sushi bar (also in Avon, near Vail) and **Maxwell St. Grill & Pizzeria** (262-2020; $-$$), serving pizza, pasta and Chicago-style hot Italian sandwiches. There is also a **Starbucks**, if you need your fix (also in Breckenridge & Frisco).

In Silverthorne, you can cook your own meat over an open grill at **The Historic Mint** (347 Blue River Pkwy., 468-5247; $$). Or enjoy Tex-Mex food at **Old Dillon Inn** (468-2791;

$), which was relocated from the old town of Dillon just before it was flooded to create the lake. **Ti Amo** ($-$$$), our fave for Italian, has moved way north in Silverthorne near Target on Hwy. 9. The Italian owners keep the food authentic and consistently good. It's one of few Italian diners where we found gnocchi, and it's great!

For budget diners, the Summit Place Shopping Center on Hwy. 6 on the Dillon-Silverthorne border has several good restaurants, including **Sunshine Cafe** (468-6663; $), jammed with locals; and **Nick-N-Willy's** (262-1111; $) for very good bake-your-own take-out pizza.

 ## Apres-ski/nightlife

Mountain resorts and brew pubs seem to go hand in hand. Summit County has five, three in the tri-town area: **Backcountry Brewery** on the corner of Summit and Main in Frisco, **Pug Ryan's** and **The Dillon Dam Brewery**. (The others are in Breckenridge and Keystone.)

Blue Spruce Inn in Frisco, serves half-priced appetizers and daily $2 drafts from 4-7.

The leading sports bar in Frisco is **High Mountain Billiards**. This richly decorated bar in Dillon attracts a mostly over-30 clientele and is open till 2 a.m.

Old Dillon Inn in Silverthorne has live country & western music on weekends and great best margaritas. The building was pieced together from bits of defunct establishments and the whole collection was moved in 1961 when the old town of Dillon disappeared under the lake. Also in this area is **Murphy's** (501 Blue River Parkway) for Irish specialties and **The Mint,** Summit County's oldest bar at 347 Blue River Parkway.

Another popular choice is the Pub Down Under, underneath the Arapahoe Cafe in Dillon. **The Cala Inn in Summit Cove** (between Dillon and Keystone) is a new Scottish/Irish bar with great drink specials and delicious food, including a Guinness Steak Pie.

 ## KidStuff

Child care: Summit Sitters (453-7097) and **Resort Sitters** (748-8424) will come to your vacation home. Expect to pay about $14/hour with $1 more for each additional child.

Other options: Baby's Away of the Summit (800-984-9030; 668-5408) rents and delivers baby needs to your lodge, such as crib, stroller and toys.

Other activities

Exploring the old town of Breckenridge is great fun, either with a formal historical tour or on your own armed with a free guidesheet. Don't forget the **Main Street Historical Museum** with Breck's past in pictures and paraphernalia, the **Edwin Carter Museum** with its collection of Rocky Mountain fauna, and the **Barney Ford House Museum** with a fascinating history of a former slave who became the town's first black businessman. The new **Breckenridge Welcome Center** on Main Street is a 4,000-square-foot building that surrounds an historic mining cabin.

There are also mine tours and hut trips. For information, call the **Activities Center** (877-864-0868). **Breckenridge Dinner Sleigh Rides** (547-8383) fill up quickly, so call ahead. There are two ice rinks, one indoors, for drop-in hockey and free skating (547-9974). The **Breckenridge Recreation Center** (453-1734) on Airport Road north of town offers an array of indoor activities for non-ski days, such as swimming, tennis, racquetball, wall climbing, fitness center and basketball. They offer child care for kids ages 2 months to 5 years while you work out.

Dining: $$$$-Entrees $30+; $$$-$20-$30; $$-$10-$20; $-less than $10.
Accommodations: (double room) $$$$-$200+; $$$-$141-$200; $$-$81-$140; $-$80 and less.

Getting there and getting around

By air and car: Frisco, Dillon and Silverthorne are just off I-70, about 75 miles west of downtown Denver and 90 miles from Denver International Airport. Colorado Mountain Express vans transport from Denver International Airport (800-334-7433; 468-7600), as does Lift Ticket Limo (866-488-5280; 668-4899). The airport is about two hours away.

Getting around: Frisco is laid out nicely for walking along Main Street. The Summit Stage is a free bus system that links the towns with each other and the ski areas until 2 a.m. Summit Taxi (468-2266) provides transportation to the entire community.

A car is an option here; most distances are too far for walking, but the Summit Stage is reliable. Call 668-0999 for route info, or pick up a route map and schedule from the Summit County Chamber of Commerce, the two Visitor Information Centers or various stores. Note that the bus takes about an hour to get from one resort to another. If you really enjoy nightlife and want to do extensive exploration of the restaurants and bars, we recommend a car.

Nearby resorts

Loveland Ski Area, Georgetown, CO; (800) 736-3754 or (303) 571-5580

Internet: www.skiloveland.com

11 lifts; 1,365 acres; 2,410 vertical feet; 1 terrain park

You see the area as you approach the Eisenhower Tunnel along I-70 west from Denver. It looms into the distance right up to the Continental Divide, and spreads out on both sides of the interstate. A ski area in two parts, Loveland Basin and Loveland Valley are connected by a lift and a shuttle service. Loveland Valley, on the left as you approach the tunnel, is great for beginners, intermediates and anyone who wants to hide from the stiff winds that sometimes plague Loveland Basin. The Basin is a real stash, jammed with enough expert and advanced terrain to challenge the best and stuffed with intermediate runs and long cruisers, most of which you can't see from I-70. By the way—snowboarding accounts for more than 25 percent of lift ticket sales—the highest ratio of any Colorado area.

Experts can get high here—The Ridge, with its 400 acres of wild terrain, tops out at 13,010 feet, and is an above-timberline Alpine garden of glades, chutes and bowls. A few seasons ago the area opened Chair 9, the highest four-passenger chair lift in the world, so you no longer have to hike up to get the goodies. Advanced skiers should head for Chair 1 for bumps and chutes. Avalanche Bowl is a nasty short and sweet drop and Busy Gully demands tight turns right under the chair. Chairs 4 and 8 access the far right, a mix of wilderness-type bowls at the top, narrowing into tree bashing in the East and West Ropes and at Fail Safe. Intermediates and beginners can handle everything else, particularly Chairs 2, 4 and 6. The resort and Airwalk created a terrain park together with rails and funboxes.

Child care starts at 12 months. Telemark Clinics are scheduled throughout the season.

Lift tickets (06/07 prices): Adults, $52; children (6–14), $24; seniors (60–69), $39; ages 5 and younger ski free. Lower rates early and late season. Skiers 70 and older can buy an unrestricted season pass for $49. A four-pack ticket for $99 online can be used all in one day or spread out over the season. It has no blackout dates and is fully transferable.

Distance from Denver: 56 miles west via I-70 (about 80 miles from Denver airport).

Lodging information: (800) 225-5683. Lodging can be found in Georgetown, Idaho Springs or Dillon, each within 15 miles.

Breckenridge
Colorado

Summit elevation: 12,840 feet
Vertical drop: 3,240 feet
Base elevation: 9,600 feet

Address: Box 1058
Breckenridge, CO 80424
Area code: 970
Ski area phone: 453-5000 or
(800) 789-7669
Snow report: 453-6118
Toll-free reservations:
(877) 593-5260; UK: 0-800-89-7491
International: 0-800-272-00000
Fax: 453-7238
Toll-free foreign fax numbers:
UK: 0800-96-0055; Germany: 0130-82-7807;
Netherlands: 06-022-6653
E-mail: breckgst@vailresorts.com (ski area)
gobreck@gobreck.com (chamber)
cenres@gobreck.com (central reservations)
Internet: www.breckenridge.com (ski area) or
www.gobreck.com (chamber)

Number and types of lifts: 30–2 high-speed six-packs,
7 high-speed quads, 1 triple, 6 doubles, 5 surface lifts,
9 moving carpets
Skiable acreage: 2,208 acres
Snowmaking: 24 percent
Uphill capacity: 37,880 per hour
Parks & pipes: 4 parks, 4 pipes
Bed base: 25,000+
Nearest lodging: Slopeside
Resort child care: Yes, 2 months and older
Adult ticket, per day: $75 (05/06 prices)

Expert:★★★★
Advanced:★★★★★
Intermediate:★★★★
Beginner:★★ **First-timer:**★★★

Dining:★★★
Apres-ski/nightlife:★★★★
Other activities:★★★

Breckenridge is one of Colorado's mostpopular resorts and the second most visited in North America (after Vail). With a third of the trails ranked intermediate, four mountains, steep treelined gullies that collect feet of snow, and Alpine bowls that cap the mountain range, Breck has something for everyone. But it's Breckenridge the Town that sets this destination resort apart. It is richly colored by its gold mining history and still retains its Victorian charm and devil-may-care attitude of yesteryear. In fact, downtown Breckenridge is Colorado's largest historic district, with 171 vintage places of interest. In the evenings, locals and tourists congregate for happy hour, dinner, and maybe the theatre and late-night libations in the town's 39 bars and pubs (and 100 restaurants). Scores of skiing-starved Front Rangers—inhabitants of Denver and its suburbs—flock to the slopes. Even mid-winter, Breckenridge can get crowded. It's best enjoyed on non-holiday weekdays.

Although tourism is the heart of Breckenridge, it's not its soul. More than 3,000 residents live in Breckenridge year-round, and they care deeply about the town from a civic standpoint, making it feel more down-to-earth than some of Colorado's more chi-chi resorts. But new shops and restaurants do tend to cater to the upscale crowd. With Vail's ownership, this trend probably will continue. Restaurant and ski-area workers remain as friendly as ever, though, and some long-time Breckenridge locals still retain much of the casual attitude of their 19th-century predecessors, which helps balance out any stuffiness that the tourists may bring.

Mountain layout

Skiable terrain spans four interconnected mountains: Peaks 7, 8, 9 and 10 in the Ten Mile Range of Summit County. Skiers can load lifts from four base areas: The Village in town at the bottom of Peak 9; Beaver Run, also on Peak 9; the base of Peak 8 (this was the original ski area that opened in 1961); and the Snowflake base on Four O'Clock Road. Decide from which base you want to start and then hop a free shuttle from your closest stop in town or from the free parking lots. (Note: Close-in pay lots fill by 9:30 a.m. most days.) The Peak 8 SuperConnect makes peak-to-peak skiing easy. Free mountain tours are offered from the bases of Peaks 8 and 9 every morning.

◆◆**Expert:** Breckenridge boasts a very high percentage of black-diamond terrain (55 percent overall) and some of the highest in-bounds skiing in North America. The Alpine bowls of Peaks 7 and 8, the steep treed trails on the North Face of Peak 9, and the mogul runs spilling off the sides of Peak 10 make up most of the hundreds of acres of expert, steep terrain.

The new Imperial Express chairlift now carries skiers and riders to Imperial Bowl, crowning Peak 8 and topping out at nearly 13,000 feet. This lift will also dramatically shorten the hike to the top of Peak 7. If the lift is closed, you can still get to sensational snow on Peaks 7 and 8 via a long, curving T-bar. "Skiing the T-bar" all day is the expert's mantra during apres-ski.

The North Face on the back of Peak 9 also is expert territory. Powder builds up in the trees on its steep north side, and the 15-minute hike keeps it fresh. On Peak 10 you'll find Mustang, Dark Rider and Blackhawk sporting monstrous bumps.

◆ **Advanced:** Skiers looking for bumps and powder typically hang out on Peak 8, where they split their time between Chair 6—a separate area that is seldom crowded—and the above-treeline terrain off the T-Bar. The first four lines to skiers' right off the T-Bar are loads of fun. Lower Peak 8 has some good bump runs, including the double fall-line of Little Johnny, and High Anxiety and Rounders. Another good spot for bumps is off the E Chair on Peak 9. Peak 10 is evenly split between black and blue runs. Cimarron, marked black on the map, often is groomed because of race training that takes place here. The Burn, dropping to skier's left of the high-speed lift, offers short-but-sweet tree skiing and is great on a powder day.

■ **Intermediate:** The face of Peak 9 is ballroom skiing at its best. Consistently smooth grooming on perfectly pitched terrain makes it ideal for moderate ability levels on runs like Cashier, Columbia and Sundown. Avoid Bonanza, a slow-skiing area packed with practicing skiers. Advanced-intermediates enjoy the blue/black terrain of American, Gold King, Peerless and Volunteer, which often sprout mild bumps.

A few nice intermediate runs spill down Peak 8—North Star, Duke's and Claimjumper. Right next door the trails on Peak 7 rock and roll for excellent cruising. In a separate area, they funnel down to their own six-pack, the Independence—or the "Indie," as locals have dubbed it. That was the first name given to the mining town.

For steeper cruising, head to Peak 10 and alternate between Centennial, Doublejack and Crystal. The high-speed lift and mostly expert-marked terrain keeps crowds down here.

●● **Beginner/first-timer:** The beginner terrain on Peak 8 is shorter, but usually less crowded, than on Peak 9. The trails are away from traffic, offering a perfect place to practice turns and cruising. Peak 9 has the most terrain for beginners, but it can get very busy. The trails here are wide and gradual, especially Silverthorne. Watch out for fast skiers and boarders who cut through to get back to the base, especially at the end of the day. Stick to the Quicksilver lift and Chair A here; avoid the Beaver Run and Peak 8 SuperConnect lifts, they will take you higher to steeper terrain. Adventurous beginners might prefer to head to the blues on Peak 7.

The trails are never crowded, loads of fun, and are served by a six-pack chair.

First-timers will want to practice on the moving carpets at either Peak 8 or 9 before tackling anything off the other beginner lifts. You'll find the first-timer area separate and roped off on Peak 9, immensely reducing the intimidation factor.

Ride Guide: For steeps and deeps, head to the Imperial Express chairlift. Once hike-to terrain, it's where the locals head after a big dump. Some of the locals' favorites are The Lake Chutes, the Windows/Peak 9 Chutes and Imperial Bowl. Peak 10's got a few high-speed cruisers that will let you open up your board. For intermediates, practically the whole mountain is your canvas. Stay away from the mogul runs and you'll be smiling ear to ear. Beginners have the most beginner terrain in Summit County at your disposal. Peak 9 has the best terrain for a first snowboarding day. The resort has a snowboard-specific learning area on Eldorado, served by two conveyor belts. There's a learning terrain park here too.

Parks and pipes

Breckenridge has more than 20 years of experience courting snowboarders and has earned bragging rights as one of the top resorts for parks and pipes.

Three words for experts: Freeway Terrain Park. Peak 8's superpipe and terrain park have become legendary among snowboarders and freeskiers. Breckenridge was the first mountain in the country to build a superpipe—400 feet long with 18-foot walls—and it shows among the locals. The monster park is packed with rails, including rainbow rails and C rails, plus tabletops ranging from 35 to 62 feet, and a 55-foot stepup. On any given day, show up at the park and you'll quickly realize why you're *not* a pro rider. Breckenridge hosts the U.S. Snowboard Grand Prix the third weekend in December. This is the nation's first major snowboard competition of the season and world-class riders go head-to-head in the Freeway Park and superpipe.

If you're not ready for Freeway, then head to one of Breck's three smaller parks and pipes and start practicing. The resort's smallest park and pipe—best for learning—are on Eldorado on Peak 9. The next step up is the park and pipe on Peak 8 on Trygves (near Freeway), with small and medium-sized features and a small pipe. Before trying out Freeway, it's a good idea to go to Peak 9's Country Boy Terrain Park, with its medium-to-large-sized features and medium pipe. Breck is making it incredibly easy for you to progress according to your abilities.

Cross-country and snowshoeing (visit xcskiresorts.com for more details)

Breckenridge Nordic Center, Gold Run Nordic Center and Frisco Nordic Center provides about 100 km. of trails on one pass. The **Breckenridge Nordic Ski Center** (453-6855), near Peak 8 base on Ski Hill Road and on the free town bus route, has 30 km. of double-set trails for all abilities. Equipment rentals, lessons, and guided backcountry tours are available. The **Gold Run Nordic Center** (547-7889), off Tiger Run Road at the Breckenridge Golf Course, grooms 20 km. of trails for beginner through advanced skiers. Equipment rentals (including snowshoes), lessons, and guided backcountry tours are available. It's run by the town and has rolling ski trails and great views of the Ten Mile Mountain Range for photo backdrops. **Frisco Nordic Center** (668-0866), on Hwy. 9, has 46 km. of groomed classic and freestyle trails and 14 km. of snowshoe trails that traverse the peninsula of Lake Dillon. Rentals and instruction are available.

Lessons (05/06 prices)

Lesson packages for all abilities encourage spreading out learning: Choose from the Option Pack—one full-day lesson and two half-day lessons; the Two-Day Deal—two full days of lessons; or the Three-Day Deal—three full days of lessons (lessons can be taken anytime during vacation). We provide prices for regular season; rates are a bit lower during the value season.

Group lessons: $90 for a full day (five hours); half day costs $80.

First-timer package: A full-day lesson with ticket, rentals and lunch costs $205. Instructors meet you in the rental shop to guide you through the process, which can often be a bit daunting for first-timers. The instructor has lunch with your class to answer questions and help everyone feel more at ease. Snowboarders take a full-day class through the Burton Learn-to-Ride program, which offers lessons, lunch, ticket and special Burton equipment designed to "fast track" the learning curve for $235; reservations required.

Private lessons: $365 for three hours; $520 for a full day. Reservations recommended.

Special programs: There are many daily and multiday programs, including racing, telemark, bumps, parks and pipes, and lessons for disabled skiers. Women's camps include lunch, video analysis and updates on new women-specific gear. Women's Winter Week includes clinics (skiing, snowboarding and telemarking), demo days, spa treatments and a film festival. A two-day Prime Time seminar (50-plus age group) includes lift tickets, instruction, video analysis and a group dinner. For more information and rates, call (888) 576-2754.

Racing: NASTAR and self-timed courses are set up on Lower American on Peak 9.

KidStuff (06/07 prices)

Child care: Ages 2 months to 5 years. Cost is $105 a full day (regular season), with lunch. Reserve 24 hours ahead and deduct $10 per day per child.

Breckenridge has two children's centers: the Peak 9 center is in The Village complex, but if you're driving, use the Peak 8 center—it's larger and has more activities. At Peak 8, look for the center above the lift ticket windows; at Peak 9, it's in the lower level facing Maggie Pond. Reservations required; call (800) 789-7669, Ext. 3258 or 7449.

Other options: Another possibility for child care and instruction is Kinderhut (800-541-8779; 970-453-0379), a privately owned children's ski school and licensed day-care center. It accepts children 6 weeks to 6 years. Also see Summit County.

Children's lessons: Lessons are offered at the Peak 8 Kids' Castle and Peak 9 Village Center. Note: It's a short hike from the parking lot to the Kids' Castle, so allow extra time. An all-day program for ages 3–4 (must be toilet-trained) includes morning lessons, afternoon care, lunch and rentals for $119 (regular season). Children 5–13 get a full-day program with lift, lesson and lunch for $130. Ages 14 and older take adult lessons.

Breckenridge recommends the use of helmets for all kids taking lessons and parents are required to decline in writing if they so choose; helmet rentals are available. Reservations recommended for all programs, but required for ages 5–6 learning to snowboard; call (888) 576-2754 or reserve online.

Special activities: Kids Night Out is an evening of dinner and fun, while Kids Day Off includes lunch and activities. Call (970) 389-3211 for information and reservations.

Lift tickets (06/07 prices)

	Adult	Child (5-12)
One day	$78	$39
Three days	$234 ($78/day)	$117 ($39/day)
Five days	$390 ($78/day)	$195 ($39/day)

Who skis free: Ages 4 and younger.

Who skis at a discount: Seniors ages 65 and older pay $65 per day. Vail, which owns Breckenridge, offers PEAKS discounted tickets if you pre-purchase a three-day or more ticket at least 14 days in advance. Membership in PEAKS is free and you are automatically enrolled when you make an early purchase.

Interchangeability: Multiday lift tickets of three or more days also are valid at sister resorts Vail, Beaver Creek and Keystone, and at nearby Arapahoe Basin.

 ## Accommodations

The resort offers everything from fabulous private luxury homes to large hotels to dorm rooms. Many are within steps of a lift or right on the slopes for true ski-in/ski-out lodging. Those in town sit close to where the free bus stops. Early December, January and April-May are the most affordable times. Seasonal specials and last-minute deals can be found on the resort's website.

Breckenridge Central Reservations (877-593-5260) handles much of the resort's lodging, but numerous property management companies can help you find the best property and price for your needs as well. A few are **ResortQuest** (800-627-3766), **Ski Country Resorts & Sports** (800-633-8388), and **Great Western Lodging** (888-333-4535).

Four wonderful, upscale condo lodges are within steps of lifts and/or bus stops. They are **Grand Timber Lodge** (877-453-4440; $$$$), **Valdoro Mountain Lodge** (800-436-6780; 453-4880; $$$$), **Mountain Thunder Lodge** (800-800-7829; $$$$), a Vail Resorts property, and **The Hyatt at Main Street Station** (800-869-9172; 453-4000; $$$$). Main Street Station, with its open plaza, shops and restaurants, closes the gap between the town and the ski area in one of the best locations on the south end of town.

The Village at Breckenridge (888-346-5754; 453-2000; $$$–$$$$) wraps the Peak 9 base area and sits just below the Quicksilver Super chair. The units are spacious and nicely appointed, with a health club, heated parking and restaurants. Dog-friendly rooms are available.

Beaver Run Resort and Conference Center (800-525-2253; 453-6000; $$$–$$$$) is a slopeside complex on Peak 9 with restaurants, outdoor hot tubs, indoor/outdoor swimming pools, a giant indoor miniature golf course and a great game room for kids.

The Great Divide Lodge (888-346-5754; 453-4500; $$$$) recently remodeled each guestroom, the entire lobby and pool/hot tub area. But they didn't touch one of its best assets—its location, just across the road from the slopes. **The River Mountain Lodge** (888-627-3766; 453-4711; $$–$$$$) is a group of studio to four-bedroom suites in the heart of town. This is one of the town's most reasonable accommodations.

The Lodge and Spa at Breckenridge (800-736-1607; 453-9300; $$$–$$$$) perches on a cliff at 10,200 feet with a magnificent view. This intimate log inn houses a full-service spa and a very good restaurant. They provide a free shuttle to the ski area and are on the bus route.

Three distinctive B&Bs have found an instant audience with guests who appreciate the genteel side of Breckenridge. **Hunt Placer Inn** (800-472-1430; 453-7573; $$–$$$$) is a B&B off Ski Hill Rd. near Peak 8 named for the gold mining claim on the property. The decor in its eight elegant rooms (all with balconies, three with fireplaces) evokes various times in history. **Little Mountain Lodge** (800-468-7707; 453-1969; $$$–$$$$) is anything but little. This white-washed log home has an intimate staying-at-a-friend's-home feeling. The innkeepers add nice touches and tea at each guestroom door (there are 10) a half hour before breakfast. **Allaire Timbers Inn** (800-624-4904 outside Colorado; 453-7530; $$$–$$$$), a log inn on the south end, has great views. Each of the 10 guestrooms—all named after Colorado mountain

Dining: $$$$-Entrees $30+; $$$-$20-$30; $$-$10-$20; $-less than $10.
Accommodations: (double room) $$$$-$200+; $$$-$141-$200; $$-$81-$140; $-$80 and less.

passes—have private decks, and two suites come with their own hot tubs and fireplaces.

Several 19th-century homes in town have been converted into charming B&Bs, including: **Abbett Placer Inn** (S. French St., 888-794-7750; 453-6489; $–$$); **Barn on the River** (800-795-2975; 453-2975; $$–$$$); **Ridge Street Inn** (800-452-4680; 453-4680; $$); and **Fireside Inn** (N. French St., 453-6456; $–$$). The Fireside Inn is also a hostel with gender-segregated dorm rooms for $30–$38 per night, with two sets of bunk beds per room and shared baths.

If you like peace and quiet after a hard day of skiing, you'll love the B&Bs secluded in the pine and aspen forests away from town (you'll need a vehicle). **Muggins Gulch Inn** (800-275-8304; 453-7414; $$–$$$$) is a post-and-beam home on 161 acres 8 miles from town. Elegant English-country style defines **Colorado Pines Inn** (453-3960; $$–$$$), whose Australian-born owner believes "a good mattress and good food are essential." One of eight guestrooms caters to Fido with its own outside entrance. **High Country Lodge** (800-497-0097; 453-9843; $$–$$$) is a rustic inn 5 miles from town at 10,000 feet with amazing views of the Continental Divide. With 12 rooms, it specializes in family reunions and groups.

 ## Dining

Breckenridge has emerged from the dining doldrums. With the increase in upscale homes and overseas vacationers, we expect the trend to continue.

Pierre's Riverwalk Cafe (137 S. Main St., 453-0989; $$$–$$$$) stands alone in the field of excellent and expensive restaurants. Owner-chef Pierre Luc prepares French dishes with a California twist, consisting mostly of fish and game delicacies such as ostrich and pheasant.

The Cellar (200 S. Ridge St., 453-4777; $$–$$$$) has the same unique dining concept as Samplings in Frisco (see the *Summit County* chapter), where small plates of gourmet foods are shared with your companion diners. **Relish** (137 So. Main, 453-0989; $$$) is the town's newest eatery with one of the best mountain views. Chef/owner Matt Fackler has developed an eclectic menu with regional influences. **Top of the World Restaurant** (453-9300; $$$) in the Lodge & Spa is somewhat pricey, but consider the panoramic view as part of the meal. Grilled buffalo rib eye and Rocky Mountain trout are dishes they do well.

The Hearthstone (S. Ridge St., 453-1148; $$–$$$) is a stunning blue-and-white century-old house that sits prominently on the hill at the corner of Ridge and Washington. The Old World ambiance, balanced selection of meat, chicken and seafood and the killer desserts make this a very popular spot. **Cafe Alpine** (103 E. Adams St., 453-8218; $$–$$$) is the locals' favorite for fine dining, with an eclectic a la carte menu. This Victorian-home-turned-restaurant also serves excellent tapas at their Tapas Bar.

The Swiss Haven (325 S. Main St., 453-6969; $$–$$$) has cheese fondues, raclette and four types of rösti (a potato dish). As in Europe, they won't bring the bill until you ask for it, which can be pricey if you order soup, salad and the homemade apple tart. **The St. Bernard Inn** (S. Main St., 453-2572; $$–$$$), a long-time favorite, is in one of the historic buildings. They specialize in modern Northern Italian cuisine and make their own pasta and bread.

Carnivores should check out the **Spencer's** (620 Village Run, 453-8755; $$–$$$) at Beaver Run for all-you-can-eat prime rib; **Kenosha Steak House** (301 S. Main, 453-7313; $–$$$); or the **Steak & Rib** (N. Main St., 453-0063; $$–$$$), where New Zealand rack of lamb and West Indian baby back ribs are served in a rustic atmosphere that's a tad Caribbean. Try a tasty Breckenridge Mudslide in the downstairs bar. For things that swim (and some that don't), try **South Ridge Seafood Grill** (215 So. Ridge, 547-0063; $$–$$$).

Blue River Bistro (N. Main St., 453-6974; $–$$$) has it all, and is perfect for vegetarians, though a nice London broil and meat lasagne are also on the extensive menu. Salads as entrees are huge, and the many pastas like Linguine Portofino are divine. It's one of few restaurants that stay open until 2 a.m. with a late-night appetizer and dessert menu.

Salt Creek Steakhouse (110 E. Lincoln Ave., 453-4949; $$) has an Old West atmosphere and specializes in Texas-style barbecue—beef, chicken, sausage, turkey or ribs slow-cooked over post oak wood—as well as prime rib, steaks and seafood. **Quandary Grille** (Main Street Station, 547-5969; $–$$$) is known for its American grill items such as Ruby Red trout and barbecue ribs. Don't miss a fun experience with great down-home Bayou food at **Bubba Gump Shrimp Company** (231 Main St., 547-9000; $–$$.) If you like shrimp in all sizes, shapes and flavors served in a themed atmosphere, it's the perfect evening for you and your family.

For Mexican head to **Mi Casa** (Park Ave., 453-2071; $–$$), **Fiesta Jalisco** (224 S. Main, 547-3836; $–$$) or **Jalapeños** (110 S. Park Ave., 547-9297; $–$$). Other ethnic dining options are **Red Orchid** (206 N. Main, 453-1881; $–$$) for Chinese; **Mountain Flying Fish Sushi Bar and Asian Kitchen** (500 S. Main, 453-1502; $–$$$) and **Wasabi** (453-8311; $–$$) for Japanese; and **Giampietro's** (Lincoln Ave. and Main, 453-3838; $–$$) for award-winning pizza and Italian food—short on space but long on authentic flavor.

Also **Denzaemon Cafe** (216 So Main, 453-9809; $) serves noodle and rice bowl dishes with 540-year-old recipes from Japan. Go to **Giampietro's** (Lincoln Ave. and Main, 453-3838; $–$$) for award-winning pizza and Italian food—short on space but long on authentic flavor. Also try **Taddeo's** (505 S. Main St., 547-5959; $–$$$) for Italian family-style meals.

Beer lovers should try the **Breckenridge Brewery** (S. Main St., 453-1550; $) for typical brewhouse food, house-made beer on tap and lots of noise or **Burke & Riley's Pub** (upstairs at 500 S. Main, 547-2782; $–$$) for Irish specialties. **Rasta Pasta** (S. Main St., 453-7467; $) specializes in whimsical Jamaican-flavored pasta. **Angel's Hollow** (S. Ridge St., 453-8585; $) is great for a big-as-your-head burrito and burgers. **Euro Deli** (Lincoln Ave., 453-4473; $) has fab fresh sandwiches. The building that houses **Fatty's Pizzeria** (Ridge St., 453-9802; $) reveals its historic hotel background. The casual eatery remains a town favorite since 1975.

If you don't mind eating in a parking lot, **Windy City Pizza** (453-5570; $), next to City Market, has great deep-dish pizzas, a specialty. They also deliver. One the other side of the grocery store is **Mi Zuppa** (547-9791; $), a soup bar for sensational take-home soup and fresh bread. If you're in the mood for out-of-the-ordinary pizza pie, try **Extreme Pizza** (200 N. Main, 547-0399; $). They also deliver. **Downstairs at Eric's** (111 S. Main, 453-1401; $–$$), which has a sports bar with a massive beer list and video arcade, serves hot dogs and pizza until midnight.

La Francaise (411 S. Main, 547-7173; $) sells fabulous French pastries, crepes, quiches and breads are baked daily. They also serve sandwiches on a half baguette and salads, and will cater French specialties like a Boeuf Bourguignon dinner with 48-hour notice.

Don't feel like going out and don't want to cook? **Gourmet Cabby** (453-7788) delivers from a large group of town restaurants.

A toss-up for the breakfast winner is among **The Prospector** (S. Main St.; $), where the huevos rancheros will test your facial sweat glands; **Blue Moose** (S. Main St.; $), with a huge selection of egg favorites. A pancake's width behind is **Columbine Cafe** (S. Main St.; $), known for its generous omelets, eggs Benedict and specialty coffees. At **Daylight Donuts** (N. Main St.; $), locals love the pancakes, two eggs, and bacon for $3. For lighter fare and gourmet coffee, try **Clint's** (S. Main St.; $); **Cool River Cafe** (a few steps off Main in the 300 block; $); **Daylight Donuts** (N. Main St.; $); and **The Crown Cafe & Tavern** (upstairs at 215 S. Main St.; $).

Dining: $$$$-Entrees $30+; $$$-$20-$30; $$-$10-$20; $-less than $10.
Accommodations: (double room) $$$$-$200+; $$$-$141-$200; $$-$81-$140; $-$80 and less.

Apres-ski/nightlife

Nearly every restaurant offers Happy Hour with drink specials after the slopes close. Breckenridge's liveliest apres-ski bars are **Tiffany's** in Beaver Run, the **Breckenridge Brewery** for a great handcrafted brew, **Park Avenue Pub** in the Village, and **Mi Casa**, with thirst-quenching margaritas—or try their sangrias by the liter. **Bubba Gump's** has a heated outdoor deck with a smashing view of the mountain. **Fatty's** bar takes up the entire first floor and locals fill it to the brim. **The Maggie** holds her own among the apres-ski crowd with good drink specials.

Want to go where the locals go? Head to **Blue River Bistro** for the martini specials or to **South Ridge Seafood** for brews on tap.

If you're having trouble adjusting to the altitude, head over to the **O2 Lounge** in La Cima Mall, where you can enjoy an herbal martini and oxygen-enriched air in 10-, 20- and 30-minute increments.

While **Tiffany's** rocks until the wee hours, after dinner most of the action moves into town. At **Eric's** you'll find a rowdy crowd on TV sports nights. **Sherpa and Yeti's** on Main St. is the hot spot for live music and dancing, with a variety of bands playing blues, jazz, funk and reggae, plus local musicians' nights, all in an unfinished-sheet-rock atmosphere. This place really rocks, so if you packed your dancin' shoes, head here.

For a non-dancing, quieter time, try the **St. Bernard** on Main St. The cozy pub in the back is often packed with locals.

Salt Creek on E. Lincoln has live music and a huge upstairs dance floor that brings in the younger crowd. Thursday nights, $2 pitchers and 25-cent wings attract the locals. There's always a long wait line to get into the action. **The Dredge**, which is a replica of the dredge boats that churned the Blue River for gold in the early 1900s, has a classy bar.

Summit County's 9:1 male-to-female ratio dramatically improves at **The Quandary** on Monday nights when those with two X chromosomes get free beer.

The old **Gold Pan** on N. Main is the oldest continuously operating bar west of the Mississippi and was one of the wildest places in the Wild West, with a miner or two known to be thrown through the saloon doors. A long, century-old, mahogany bar presides over a now worn, dimly lit room with a pinball machine tucked into the back corner and a couple of well-utilized pool tables.

Cecelia's Bar makes great martinis, and recently expanded to add a dance floor and space for a DJ. **Liquid Lounge,** near Cecelia's, is a sure bet for great drinks and there's usually a DJ spinning tunes on the weekends. **The Crown** has cozy couches that are perfect for intimate apres-ski or late-night drinks, desserts or coffee. Nightlife ends with a visit to **Charlie Dog's** off Main St. at 111 Ski Hill Rd. When every other restaurant in town is closed, you can still satisfy your late-night cravings with a Chicago Dog or a sub.

 Other activities

Exploring the old town of Breckenridge is great fun, either with a formal **historical tour** or on your own armed with a free guidesheet. Don't forget the **Main Street Historical Museum** with Breck's past in pictures and paraphernalia, the **Edwin Carter Museum** with its collection of Rocky Mountain fauna, and the **Barney Ford House Museum** with a fascinating history of a former slave who became the town's first black businessman. The **Breckenridge Welcome Center,** on Main Street, opens in December 2005 as a 4,000-square-foot historic mining cabin, with the town's history on display inside, as well as exhibits of local ecology, geography, and the town's ski history.

Kids will get a kick out of the hands-on exhibits at **Mountain Top Children's Museum** (453-7878) in the village on Park Avenue. With special focus areas such as a Wonder Lab, Kidstruction Zone, and Tot Spot, the museum allows kids to create, dream and play.

Part of the town's history is with the Backstage Theatre (453-0199), performing award-winning **live shows** continuously since 1974. It shares a venue on Ridge St. — The Breckenridge Theatre for Performing Arts — with other groups as part of the Arts District

Good Times Adventure Tours (453-7604) offers thrilling **dogsled tours** and **snowmobile rides.** Good Times is very hands-on, letting customers run their own dogsled team or take their own snowmobile for a spin. Guides are professional and friendly, and prices are reasonable.

There are also **mine tours** and **hut trips.** For information, call the Activities Center (877-864-0868). **Breckenridge Dinner Sleigh Rides** (547-8383) fill up quickly, so call ahead. There are two **ice rinks**, one indoors, for drop-in hockey and free skating (547-9974).

The **Breckenridge Recreation Center** (453-1734) on Airport Road north of town offers an array of indoor activities for non-ski days, such as **swimming, tennis, racquetball, wall climbing, fitness center** and **basketball.** They offer child care for kids ages 2 months to 5 years while you work out.

If you happen to be in Breckenridge in mid-January, **Ullr Fest** with its parade and festivities is a great big hoot. Locals dress up in Nordic costumes, make a parade down the main street complete with naked streakers in sub-zero temps, throw candy and treats from the floats and make a family-wide festival out of the whole town. Don't miss it.

Breckenridge has a nice collection of spas. Twenty years combined experience stand behind the owners of **Blue Sage Spa** (547-5926), a small sensuous spa voted Best Day Spa by Summit County locals. At **Mountain Sanctuary Holistic Spa** (547-1610), each room resembles a Victorian bedroom, and upstairs is a large airy salon for wedding parties.

The full-facility **Grand Victorian Day Spa & Salon** (547-3624) is in the Grand Timber Lodge, you choose from a long list of head-to-toe therapies and services.

Downtown has scores of **boutiques.** The Breckenridge Arts District is between the corner of Main and Ridge on Washington Street. On an off-ski day, you can take a **workshop** at the Robert Whyte House. For **fine art galleries,** we recommend: Paint Horse Gallery for western art, Breckenridge Fine Art Gallery, Hibbard McGrath Gallery, and Highlands Gallery.

Breckenridge has bloomed as a destination for **weddings,** both summer and winter. For a wedding and honeymoon guide, call the Breckenridge Resort Chamber at (877) 864-0868. Also check the **Summit County** chapter for other activities.

Getting there and getting around

By air: Breckenridge is about 100 miles west of Denver International Airport. Colorado Mountain Express (800-525-6363) offers regular van shuttles connecting the resort with the airport, as does Lift Ticket Limo (866-488-5280; 668-4899).

By car: From Denver, take I-70 to Exit 203, then south on Hwy. 9.

Getting around: Nearly everything is within walking distance and free buses cruise the streets regularly. The Breckenridge Free Ride provides bus service throughout Breckenridge and some outlying areas. The Summit Stage provides free transportation between Dillon, Silverthorne, Keystone, Frisco, Breckenridge and Copper Mountain. Call 668-0999 for route information. Keystone and Breckenridge also operate a free inter-resort shuttle, the Ski KAB Express (496-4200), at varying times according to demand.

Dining: $$$$-Entrees $30+; $$$-$20-$30; $$-$10-$20; $-less than $10.
Accommodations: (double room) $$$$-$200+; $$$-$141-$200; $$-$81-$140; $-$80 and less.

Copper Mountain
Colorado

Summit:	12,313 feet
Vertical:	2,601 feet
Base:	9,712 feet

Address: P.O. Box 3001,
Copper Mountain, CO 80443
Area code: 970
Ski area phone: 968-2882
Toll-free information: (888) 229-9475
Toll-free reservations: (888) 219-2441
Reservations outside U.S.: 968-2882
Fax: 968-3156
E-mail: contactcenter@coppercolorado.com
Internet: www.coppercolorado.com
Expert:★★★★ **Advanced:**★★★★★
Intermediate:★★★★
Beginner:★★★★ **First-timer:**★★★★

Lifts: 22—1 high-speed six-pack, 4 high-speed quads,
5 triples, 5 doubles, 2 surface lifts, 5 moving carpets
Skiable acreage: 2,450 acres
Snowmaking: 16 percent
Uphill capacity: 32,324 per hour
Parks & pipes: 4 parks, 3 pipes
Bed base: 3,942
Nearest lodging: Walking distance
Child care: Yes, 6 weeks and older
Adult ticket, per day: $65-$69 (05/06 prices)
Dining:★★★
Apres-ski/nightlife:★★
Other activities:★★

Copper Mountain could be considered the model for the mythical book "Designing Ski Resorts for Dummies." It's easy to get to: just off I-70 from Denver. And it's easy to figure out: Thanks to the area's topography, trails are neatly organized by level of difficulty—left to right, facing the mountain, black diamond to blue square to green circle. Plus there's plenty of terrain to go around for all abilities. In fact, beginners aren't relegated to the lower slopes and, unlike many other areas, have an equal share of Copper's terrain.

Even the base areas are "separate but equal," with East Village serving the adrenaline hogs, The Village at Copper for the in-betweens, and Union Creek for beginners. OK, they don't check your skiing or riding skills before you sidle up to the bar at any of these areas, but be aware that meeting back at the base for a group with differing ability levels will include some planning. Fortunately, an efficient shuttle system connects the base areas, so if you can't find your way via the snow, you can via the bus.

While it doesn't take a lot of brain power to figure out the terrain layout, that doesn't mean that there isn't plenty of demanding skiing. Experts head to the summit, where chutes, cornices and double-diamond slits are worth studying in Copper's upper bowls. And because the terrain is so evenly distributed among ability levels, those wanting to improve and graduate with honors just have to work their way towards the other side of the mountain.

Copper Mountain is a paean to modern-day master planning. Born in 1972, the base area still has remnants of buildings that pay tribute to that decade of architectural aberrance. But taking an "if-you-build-it-they-will-come" attitude, resort developer Intrawest is now nearing the end of its intensive $500-million redevelopment plan, and Copper's base area is beginning to offer the "total resort" amenities that skiers and riders have come to expect.

That doesn't mean, however, that Copper's base is hopping. Either skiers are still hibernating in their condos at night or jumping back on that convenient I-70 and heading home, because they aren't out that much taking advantage of the increase in boutiques, restaurants, spas and apres-ski haunts, all within steps of the ski slopes. Now the resort's just waiting for skiers and riders to discover that it really does have it all.

Mountain layout

If you use lifts as meeting places, pay attention to the American *Eagle* and American *Flyer* chairs, which start in the same area but unload on different peaks.

♦♦ **Expert ♦ Advanced:** Copper's mountains are lofty, with Union Peak reaching 12,313 feet, Tucker Mountain 12,337 feet and Copper Peak 12,441 feet. And there, in the high Alpine, lie the double-diamond bowls. There's a lot to explore. Everything is gnarly, but we especially enjoyed Tucker's hike-to glades and chutes and the Enchanted Forest's untouched powder. Extra added attraction: Jump in one of the snowcats for laps to the top of Tucker Wednesdays through Sundays on a first-come, first-served basis. It's free (yes, you read that right).

If you survive Spaulding Bowl, you can choose from several very worthy runs to the bottom of the Resolution chair, where there's seldom a wait. The consistently good snow in Union Bowl under the Sierra lift gets even better when you hike to the top of the cirque. Not always so with Copper Bowl on the backside of Union Peak. Its slopes are south-facing, so ask around before you dive in. It could be ugly or divine.

The Super Bee six-pack accesses all terrain on the East Village side, including the relentless bumps on Far East, Too Much and Triple Treat under the Alpine lift. On a powder day, these runs are a real hoot! Be ready for the long trek out if the Alpine double isn't running. From the top of Super Bee you can slide down any of three short but sweet runs that parallel the Excelerator quad. Brennan's Grin will bring a smile to any serious bump skier's face.

■ **Intermediate:** Exit to the right of the American Flyer quad and zip down American Flyer, The Moz and Windsong, all wide groomed runs under the Timberline Express. After fresh snow, Copperfields gives a good challenge with perfectly placed, soft bumps. If you like trees, there are many places here to jump in, but be wary that some are thick. A stash of delightful unmarked woods under the American Flyer can be reached by taking High Point and bearing left before the steep pitch. It has nicely spaced trees all the way to Timberline Express.

Darting down any of the runs under the American Eagle quad will peg the fun meter, but beware that Main Vein and Bouncer seem to be the busiest. Off the Super Bee chair, try Andy's Encore, a worthy intermediate highway. Collage is also on this side of the mountain and has a few fun steep pitches. Or duck off Collage into 17 Glade—the farther right you go, the more open it gets. To avoid lifts at the area's base, take Excelerator on the upper mountain for a quick set of laps. Trails such as Ptarmigan are wide consistent runs back to the chair.

The bowls at Copper all offer "easier" ways down, and it will make your visit memorable, but think before you go. It's best if you're able to handle advanced terrain and conditions. Union Bowl is the ideal option because you'll specifically find that intermediate terrain and snow here is consistently good. The Spaulding Bowl dumps out into the Resolution area, which has steep and relentless bump runs down to the lift—if you don't like moguls, you won't have fun here. Copper Bowl can get nasty with weather.

●● **Beginner:** Make your way over to Union Creek and hop on the high-speed American Flyer (don't confuse it with the American Eagle) or High Point lifts. Nearly this whole side of the mountain consists of sweeping runs, perfect for the experienced beginner. For long runs to the bottom, from the American Flyer take Coppertone, an easy cruise. From both American Flyer and the High Point lifts, work your way to the Timberline Express quad chair, ride to the top and ski the delightful Soliloquy to Roundabout to the bottom.

You also can take the Rendezvous lift up top and enjoy the views while cruising Wheeler Creek and Union Park. Picnic tables provide plenty of opportunities to rest and check out the scenery. Avoid the Sierra lift here—it serves only blacks and blues.

● **First-timer:** Copper Mountain is a first-timer's dream mountain. The learning and beginner terrain is naturally separated from the gonzo's terrain on the other side. The Village at Copper and Union Creek both have areas served by moving carpets for those first few times on snow. Once you're comfortable on your gear, the Kokomo chair, in the Union Creek area, serves a super gentle, isolated area. When you have these runs conquered, the next step is the nearby Lumberjack lift, another chair with only beginner runs beneath it.

Ride Guide: Summit County's best-kept secret, Copper is a favorite of Colorado boarders. Copper Bowl is a true backcountry experience that's now lift-served. Then there's the Spaulding Bowl at the top of the Storm King Poma lift—provided you can deal with a Poma. The chutes here funnel down to the quad-exhausting bumps of Resolution Bowl (or "Rezo," as locals refer to it). Three runs and you'll be heading for a beer to chase away the lactic acid. If you dive into Far East, Too Much, Triple Treat or Formidable, you'll have quite the hike out if the Alpine double isn't running.

Parks and pipes

Copper is duly recognized as one of the top resorts for parks and pipes. The parks are groomed every night, while the pipes are cut every other night. The 20-acre Catalyst Terrain Park (Copper's main park) is on the Loverly trail and has three lines, one for each ability level. No matter how skilled you are, you'll appreciate watching what everyone else has up their sleeves—thrills and spills abound. Beginners have small kickers and rails here. Once you're confident in your landings, you'll find larger kickers and some jumps to up the challenge. As for the pros, go for as much air as you want on the shack jib, giant tabletops, hip features and an 8-foot wall ride set atop a 17-foot quarterpipe. The signature jump, The Shaft, is a 60-foot table. A section of rails includes a variety of flat, kinked and rainbow rails leading into the well-designed and maintained 430-foot-long superpipe, which has 18-foot-high walls.

If you like showing off, Copper's Main Vein Superpipe sits just above the base of the American Eagle lift and within view of the deck at Jack's. You can also watch pipe competitions and events from that vantage point.

Playground Kidz Park is full of small kickers, rollers and tables that provide the perfect venue to master your skills before moving on to the larger beginner features in the Catalyst Terrain Park. The resort also has a 200-foot-long minipipe with 6-foot-high walls. Night Rider is a park that's open on weekend nights.

Cross-country and snowshoeing (visit xcskiresorts.com for more details)

Through the activities center (968-2882), book overnight **tours to Janet's Cabin,** part of the 10th Mountain Division system and a gentle ski tour with a four-course progressive meal; various **women's clinics;** the **Backcountry Telemark Series;** and other **telemark camps.** Copper has a **cross-country trail map** available at Guest Services desks that identifies trails for differing abilities from beginner to expert. For more information, call 968-2318.

Snowshoers will find 21 km. of unmaintained and unpatrolled trails wandering through the woods at Union Creek. Another spectacular ungroomed option is the bike path that runs through Copper Village west to Vail Pass. A free **daily snowshoe tour** in the Union Creek area includes a guide, snowshoes and poles. Sign up at the Guest Services Desk in the Copper One Lodge in The Village at Copper.

Lessons (05/06 prices)

We list regular-season prices; value-season prices are a bit less. You can save 10 percent on all group lessons by either making advance reservations or by booking lodging with Copper Mountain.

Group lessons: $75 for a half day; $90 for a full day. Level Busters are three full-day sessions for the price of two sessions to get you to the next skill level and cost $180.

First-timer packages: An all-day package with lessons, lifts and rentals costs $123; half day is $108. First-time snowboarders take Burton Learn To Ride classes, with special equipment designed to help you learn more quickly.

Private lessons: For up to three people, a two-hour afternoon lesson costs $275; $340 for half day (three hours); $490 for full day (six hours). Family privates are available. Reservations for all private lessons are recommended.

Special programs: Women's Wednesdays, Bump Busters and Freestyle Fridays highlight the list. Call for details and prices.

KidStuff (05/06 prices)

Child care: Ages 6 weeks to 4 years. Full day with lunch costs $85; half day is $78 (morning only). Fun tip: In the "Belly Button" programs, the kids make chocolate-chip cookies to give to mom and dad when they return at the end of the ski day. Reservations required; call 968-2318, Ext. 38101; or (866) 841-2481. Walk-ins are accepted on a space-available basis and are charged an extra $10. Note: The child-care center, in The Village at Copper, is difficult to find. Ask for specific directions.

Other options: Copper offers **evening babysitting** in a guest's accommodations. Reservations required; call 968-2318, Ext. 38101. In-room babysitting services require 24-hour advance reservations or cancellations, and cost $12 per hour, plus $1 for each additional child.

Children's lessons: We list regular-season prices; value-season prices are lower. Full-day ski or snowboard programs (lunch, lesson, lifts) for kids ages 6–15 costs $107. Kids 3–5 have a full-day ski or snowboard program that includes off-snow activities for $124. Save 10 percent on lessons by either making advance reservations or by booking lodging with Copper.

Special activities: Kids' Night Out is filled with games, videos and pizza for kids up to age 10. It's free if parents spend $20 or more per child while shopping or dining at the resort.

Lift tickets (06/07 prices)

	Adult	Child (6-13)
One day	$79	$39
Three days	$237 ($79/day)	$117 ($39/day)
Five days	$395 ($79/day)	$195 ($39/day)

Who skis free: Ages 5 and younger always ski free.

Who skis at a discount: Early- and late-season prices are less. Seniors ages 60–69 pay $64 per day; ages 70+ pay $31. Beginners on green slopes payonly $10. For $20 you can upgrade to a BeeLine ticket for immediate access in designated lift lines.

Discounted Copper lift tickets are sold at hundreds of ski shops, grocery stores and convenience stores in Denver and the rest of the Front Range.

Note: Prices are higher during the Christmas holiday and early March 5–27.

Accommodations

Most of Copper's lodging is or seems brand new. Lodging through **Copper Mountain Reservations** (888-219-2441) includes hotels, condos and homes just steps from the slopes. Hotel rooms go for about $123–$369 per night; one-bedrooms, $154–$360; two-bedrooms, $225–$369; three-bedrooms, $357–$593; and four-bedrooms, $369–$689. All guests who book through CMR can use the Copper Mountain Racquet and Athletic Club.

The five buildings in **The Village at Copper** include everything from studios to three-bedroom condos. Some units have jetted tubs, gourmet kitchens and gas fireplaces; select buildings also have outdoor hot tubs and ski lockers. Wireless Internet access in the village costs about $10/day. The **Copper Springs Lodge,** a classic mountain lodge in East Village, has 108 units. **The Cirque** is luxury two- and three-bedroom condos near the Union Creek beginner area. With heated underground parking, two outdoor heated pools, hot tub, fire pit, kids' play rooms, fitness facility, and video room, it's a good choice for families.

As with all ski areas that manage property, Copper offers lift/lodging packages that can save considerably. Last-minute lodging discounts and special packages are available all season on Copper's website. Two other companies book accommodations: **Carbonate Property Management** (800-526-7737) and **Copper Vacations** (800-525-3887).

Dining

JJ's Rocky Mountain Tavern (968-2318; $–$$), in East Village's Copper Station day lodge, is named after J.J. Astor, husband of the Titanic's "Unsinkable" Molly Brown. It's reminiscent of an 1800s tavern and serves casual American fare; lunch, dinner and bar menus are available. If it's a nice day, sit on the deck at **McGillycuddy's** ($–$$), where you'll chow on authentic Irish fare and beverages while overlooking West Lake.

Popular for families staying in the Village is **Alpinista Mountain Bistro** (968-1144; $$) serving three squares a day of hearty bistro meals. Happy hour specials, a kids' menu, microbrews, wine-by-the-glass and a great patio make it perfect for every age and stage.

In the Foxpine Inn, the **Double Diamond Bar and Grill** (968-2880; $–$$) serves up the best burgers and soup around, and does a great job with pasta and its specialty, Colorado beef. A tip: Owner Dave Luthi hosts Friday Night Fish Frys all year long for only $5.95.

In The Village at Copper, **Endo's Adrenaline Cafe** ($), in the Mountain Plaza building. enjoys a strong following for great salads, burgers and fries. **Jack's Slopeside Grill** ($), at Copper One Lodge, is a market-style eatery serving a wide variety of food, including a deli, from 7 a.m. to 6 p.m. **Camp Hale Coffee** ($) is there when you need it, serving bean brews and pastries at wake-up call and throughout the day. Try **Salsa Mountain Cantina** ($) for Mexican and **Imperial Palace** (968-6688; $–$$) for Taiwanese and Szechwan Chinese. One local who used to live in Asia raves about the authentic deep-fried chicken wings and the great service at this family-owned eatery. At **Creekside Pizza** ($), hand-tossed pizza is the specialty, but you can get sandwiches and pasta dishes too.

Dinner sleigh rides (968-2232; reservations required) make a memorable event. A horse-drawn sleigh takes diners to a heated miner's tent for live entertainment and a gourmet meal. If you're at Copper during one of the winter full moons and want an adventure, sign up for the **Solitude Moonlight Dine and Ski** (968-2882). The evening begins with a ride up the American Eagle chairlift to Solitude Station for hot cider and a buffet dinner. After dessert, ski back to the village and finish with a cocktail.

Apres-ski/nightlife

JJ'sRocky Mountain Tavern, with its live entertainment and bar menu, is the hottest spot. It's in the East Village. Moe Dixon, a local entertainer, gets people dancing on the tables. Plus get with a free supersize of all draft beer from 3–6 p.m.

A popular hangout is **Endo's Adrenaline Cafe** in The Village at Copper, where you'll a sport-bar atmosphere. **Jack's Slopeside** at Copper One Lodge, with live entertainment Thursday to Saturday 3–5:30 p.m., headlines Lefty Lucy. Expect sing-alongs and more dancing on the bar. Jack's counterpart **Jill's Umbrella Bar** serves up Mojitos and Long Island Iced Tea among other thirst quenchers that you'll need for the Thursday afternoon Salsa dance lessons. **Storm King Lounge** features scotch and signature martinis, sushi, Sapporo and sake. Play pool and poker here while you imbibe.

With the Cold War over, the Russian-themed vodka bar and nightclub **Pravda** seems to be popular. A DJ keeps you thirsting for more of the exclusive list of 40 ice cold vodkas.

 Other activities

Other activities in and around the resort include **ice skating, tubing, sleigh rides, snowmobiling, dogsled rides** and **hot air balloon floats.** Copper Mountain Athletic Club (968-2882, Ext. 83025) has a **lap pool, sauna, steam room, hot tubs, cardiovascular equipment** and **racquetball courts.** When looking for the **Spa,** don't be put off by the club's workout feel. Past the weight room and locker rooms, the spa entrance is at the end of the hall. Once inside, you'll find the atmosphere warm and soothing, and the treatments, though limited to massage and facials, are excellent.

Make the rounds of the many **shops** at Copper Station, West Lake and The Village at Copper. Upper-end souvenirs, logo clothing and sports gear fill most of them. All American Goods sells USA- and Colorado-made products; 9600' specializes in outdoor clothing; and Rocky Mountain Chocolate Factory makes you-know-what. Also browse through the boutique shops on West Lake at Copper One Lodge.

For more activities see the Summit County or Vail chapters. Copper is about 20 miles from Vail and about 10 miles from the tri-town area of Dillon, Frisco and Silverthorne.

Getting there and getting around

By air: Copper Mountain is 90 miles west of Denver International Airport on I-70. Several ground transportation companies run vans between the airport and your lodge. Make arrangements when you reserve lodging, or call Colorado Mountain Express (800-525-6363) or Lift Ticket Limo (866-488-5280; 668-4899).

By car: Right off I-70 at Exit 195. You can see many of the trails from the freeway.

Getting around: If you plan to head over to Vail or to the other Summit County areas, you'll probably want a car, otherwise you don't need one. Copper Mountain's updated fleet of buses enhances an already superb (and free) shuttle service, running constantly between 8 a.m. and 11 p.m. Walking is also easy between the outlying condos and the village center. Free Summit Stage buses serve the three nearby ski areas, as well as the towns of Dillon, Silverthorne and Frisco. Warning: The buses make lots of stops, and it can take up to 90 minutes to make it down the road to the next resort. Good bus service links Copper Mountain and the nearest town, Frisco, including an express bus from the Frisco transfer station to Copper every half-hour. A multi-stop bus also runs so you can get a ride to Copper every half-hour during the day and early evening. If you are not staying at Copper, one warning about parking: All parking lots charge about $10 per day, except the outlying free Alpine lot near the highway.

Dining: $$$$-Entrees $30+; $$$-$20-$30; $$-$10-$20; $-less than $10.
Accommodations: (double room) $$$$-$200+; $$$-$141-$200; $$-$81-$140; $-$80 and less.

Keystone
Colorado

Address: Box 38, Keystone, CO 80435
Area code: 970
Ski area phone: 496-2316 or (800) 468-5004
Snow report: 496-4111 or (800) 468-5004
Toll-free reservations: (800) 468-5004
Toll-free foreign numbers:
UK (fax): 0800-89-6868
Germany (fax): 0130 82 0958
Netherlands (fax) 060 22 3972
Mexico (fax) 95-800-936-5633
Brazil: (fax) 000811-712-0553
Fax: 496-4343
E-mail: keystoneinfo@vailresorts.com
Internet: www.keystoneresort.com
Expert:★★ **Advanced:**★★★
Intermediate:★★★★
Beginner:★★★★ **First-timer:**★★★

Summit elevation (lift-served): 11,914 feet
Vertical drop: 2,630 feet
Base elevation: 9,284 feet

Number and types of lifts: 20–2 gondolas, 1 high-speed six-pack, 5 high-speed quads, 1 quad, 1 triple, 3 doubles, 1 surface lift, 6 moving carpets
Skiable acreage: 2,009 acres (plus 861 snowcat-served acres)
Snowmaking: 37 percent
Uphill capacity: 33,564 skiers per hour
Parks & pipes: 2 parks, 1 pipe
Nearest lodging: Slopeside, ski-in/ski-out
Bed base: 6,000
Resort child care: Yes, 2 months and older
Adult ticket, per day: $75 (05/06 prices)

Dining:★★★★★
Apres-ski/nightlife:★★★
Other activities:★★★

If you're looking for that quaint 19th-century Victorian mining-town charm that Colorado's renown for, you won't find it at Keystone. But if you're looking for a smoothly humming resort with buses shuttling to every corner, a child-friendly atmosphere, and one of the Rockies' largest snowmaking systems, you'll be pleased as pie.

The resort makes every effort to offer memorable family vacations with good customer service and easy planning for parents and kids. Everyone here is friendly, friendly, friendly. Keystone is known as a superb intermediate playground, but it has decent terrain at either end of the ability scale too. There aren't many surprises here and it's hard to get in over your head. Another attraction is Keystone's extensive night skiing, which means you don't have to get up early to get in a lot of vertical. A neat fact: Keystone uses wind power to light the trails and run the lifts at night.

For skiers and riders who feel uncomfortable in ungroomed snow, Keystone makes a concerted effort to keep its slopes smooth. They even stagger the opening of groomed trails to keep them smoother throughout the day. There is the common gripe, though, that all the snowmaking and grooming can sometimes make trails a bit slick. But Keystone doesn't get the natural snow its neighboring resorts do, so the snowmaking on it's lowest peak is a real plus. And with more than 1 million skier visits each year, they've got to do something to minimize the effects of all that skier traffic.

Keystone is owned by Vail Resorts, so there's plenty of money funneled into the amenities. The resort's largest base area is River Run, a pedestrian village that includes boutiques, coffee shops, restaurants and condominiums at the base of the River Run Gondola. Keystone was never known for its nightlife, but it seems to have remedied that quite a bit. But it still won't knock your socks off—this is mainly a family resort, after all.

Mountain layout

Keystone has three peaks, one behind another. In front is Dercum Mountain, named to honor Max and Edna Dercum, who pioneered the resort's founding. Dercum is laced with beginner and intermediate terrain, plus some expert glades on its backside. In the middle is North Peak, and finally, The Outback. Other than one snaking green-circle trail, these latter peaks have just blue and black terrain. This makes it easy to stay on trails where you belong, instead of ending up on a trail that scares you out of your wits.

♦♦ **Expert** ♦ **Advanced:** You won't find any double-diamonds here. For the most challenge, head to The Outback—a mix of open bowls, trails and glades. The quartet of Timberwolf, Bushwacker, Badger and The Grizz allow tree fans to pick how tight they want their forest. They also get massive bumps. Reach the two short black-diamond bowls here with a 10-minute hike from the top of the Outback Express. (This in-bounds terrain tops out at 12,408 feet, more than what's listed in the stat box, where we list lift-served terrain.)

North Peak is generally tamer than The Outback and is a great spot for working on technique and steeps. Star Fire, though rated blue, is a superb steep, groomed run, and a good warm-up for this area. Then head to black-diamond bump runs such as Ambush, Powder Cap or Bullet. Break your own tracks through the trees directly beneath the Santiago Express or duck into Bullet Glades for an adrenaline rush. Another stash of trees is called The Windows and requires a short hike from the bottom of the Outpost Gondola (off Dercum's back side).

Don't like to hike but still want to get into the backcountry? Keystone Adventure Tours operates two cats (weather dependent) for a little taste of a backcountry experience while staying in-bounds. Snowcats leave from both the top of the Outpost Gondola and The Outback, giving you two choices: Make reservations and ski with two guides in Bergman and Erickson Bowls, or take a snowcat to North Bowl and South Bowl for unguided descents. Either way, this is about the most affordable cat skiing you can get (see *Lift Tickets* for prices). While we can't attest to the terrain on the guided trips, the terrain in North Bowl is short and rather tame, though technical snow conditions can change that in a heartbeat. What makes it worthwhile is the lack of crowds, potentially finding some untracked snow and getting above treeline (there's no other way to do that at Keystone without hiking).

■ **Intermediate:** You have the run of the three mountains, with appropriate terrain on each. Dercum has runs such as Paymaster, Wild Irishman, Frenchman and Flying Dutchman that play with God-given terrain. The twists and natural steps on these cruisers represent trails at their best—they obviously did not have their character bulldozed out of them. Snowmaking covers the majority of Dercum's trails, and the grooming ranks among the best in the country.

The Mountain House base area has three chairlifts taking skiers up the mountain, and the other base area, River Run, is the lower station of the River Run Gondola. The gondola serves the night-skiing area. The resort says it's the largest single-mountain night ski operation in the United States, covering 10 runs and 315 acres of terrain.

Intermediates also can head to North Peak down Mozart, a wide blue run. Its width is essential, because it's the main pathway to the two rear peaks and can get crowded. On North Peak, Prospector and Last Alamo are the easiest of the blues, with Star Fire a good test for The Outback. If you think Star Fire is fun, not scary, head down Anticipation or Spillway to The Outback and play on the intermediate runs under the Outback Express chair. The advanced-intermediate glades to skier's left—Wolverine, Wildfire and Pika—are not as tough as the glades of the Black Forest, but also not a spot for timid intermediates.

●● **Beginner:** Stay on Dercum Mountain, where nearly a third of all beginner terrain lies. The best runs for beginners are the legendary and long Schoolmarm, plus Silverspoon and Spring Dipper. True beginners should beware of that first plunge off the top onto Spring Dipper—for a short pitch, it's blue, a bit steep and only for greenies graduating into their blue phase. Confident beginners who want the experience of spectacular views and lunch at the on-mountain restaurant at Outpost Lodge can ski down afterwards via Prospector on North Peak. Prospector is blue, but about two-thirds of it are in a slow zone so it's not too intimidating. Prospector merges with the slow zone on Mozart, but this trail is often crowded, so be alert.

● **First-timer:** Keystone has a learning center at the top of Dercum Mountain, with two learning runs and a triple chairlift. Instructors who teach first-timers highly recommend the Discovery Learning Area, home to a self-contained kids' ski school. It's a large, wide-open space protected from the wind and elements and is serviced by a chair and two moving carpets (a magic carpet replaced the T-bar for 2005/06). It's less crowded than the rest of the mountain and is completely closed off to all other skiers, so it's pretty darned safe.

Ride Guide: Experts seek out the powder on The Outback. Other than that, Keystone's steeps are mostly moguled, a major drawback for many advanced snowboarders. Intermediates have the run of the three mountains. However, riders find the cruisers rather crowded. First-timers and beginners will be glad to know gentle terrain is served by moving carpets and chairlifts, making it easy to get up the hill.

Parks and pipes

Keystone is in the running to be a heavyweight contender with a top-rated terrain park, a superpipe, various events, and the only legal night-riding in Summit County. The terrain park—A51—is in Packsaddle Bowl on Dercum Mountain, away from the mainstream runs, and has its own lift. To encourage snowboarders and freeskiers to claim this side of the mountain, the base area and Mountain House directly below it are designed with youth in mind.

A51 has three separate areas for beginners, intermediates and pros. The park features an 18-foot superpipe in the pro area that's sure to challenge even the best riders. Keystone has really stepped up to the plate with its rails and funboxes too. The resort tells us it's in the running for the most rails in the nation, but not all 51 of them are set up at one time—instead they're rotated to keep things entertaining. On any given day you might find a 150-foot-long rail, plus signature rails like the rollercoaster rail and the pro-restricted flaming barbecue rail. Next to A51 is the A51 Incubator, with smaller rails and features for those just learning to play in the park.

 ## Cross-country and snowshoeing (visit xcskiresorts.com for more details)

Keystone has extensive cross-country touring, with 16 km. of groomed trails around the resort, and an additional 57 km. of ungroomed backcountry skiing trails to ghost mining towns in the Montezuma area and around the region. The **Keystone Nordic Center** (496-4275) is at the River Course clubhouse off Hwy. 6. Lessons and rentals are available. Cross-country activities include cross-country ski workouts with a personal fitness trainer, guided moonlight tours and interpretive ecology tours. Snowshoe rentals also are available. The center has a map for trails in the region. The clubhouse has food service. For those who stay at Keystone Resort, the Adventure Passport in your lodging packet offers free trail access and discounts on rentals. For a door-to-door service ride, just call the E.A.S.E. bus (496-4200). **Adventure Point,** at the top of Dercum Mountain, is the place to head for guided snowshoe treks along the peak-to-peak trail to the top of North Peak.

Lessons (05/06 prices)

We provide regular-season prices. Value-season prices are a bit less.
Group lessons: A two-hour session, for skiers or snowboarders, costs $75.
Park and pipe lessons are available for the same price.

First-timer package: All-day ski or snowboard lessons start at 10:30 a.m. and cost $96 (add $11 for ticket; discounted rentals available). You can also take a half-day lesson for $86 (rentals additional)..

Private lessons: $365 for three hours and $520 for six hours.

Special programs: Clinics and camps are held for women and racing. Call for details.

Racing: NASTAR racing, clinics and a self-timed course are on Dercum Mountain.

KidStuff (05/06 prices)

Child care: Ages 2 months to 6 years. Cost is $95 for a full day, with lunch. Children ages 3 and older get outdoor snow play as part of the fun. The Keystone Children's Center has two locations: River Run and Mountain House. River Run is home to the Snow Play Program for ages 3–6; Mountain House is home to the 3-year-old Learn-to-Ski Program. Both facilities offer day care for ages 2 months–6 years, but Mountain House has a larger outdoor play area. Reservations required; call 496-4181 or (800) 255-3715, or make online reservations.

Other options: Baby's Away of the Summit (800-984-9030; 668-5408) rents and will deliver baby needs to your lodge, such as crib, stroller, car seat and toys.

Children's lessons: Three-year-olds can take a learn-to-ski program that includes lesson, lunch and crafts. Cost is $105 for a full day; rentals are an additional $15. Reservations are required; call (800) 255-3715. The full-day program for ages 4–12 includes lift ticket, lesson and lunch for $116; rentals are an additional $15. Snowboarding lessons start at age 5. Value-season prices are somewhat less. Helmets are recommended for all children enrolled in ski and snowboard programs; helmet rentals cost $12. A special one-hour lesson where parents can learn to teach their little ones is Mom, Dad & Me; cost is $80 and reservations are required. Keystone puts a big emphasis on families and children's lessons. Parts of the mountain are designated Children Only, and classes usually have no more than four students.

Lift tickets (06/07 prices)

	Adult	Child (5-12)
One day	$78	$39
Three days	$234 ($78/day)	$117 ($39/day)
Five of six days	$390 ($78/day)	$195 ($39/day)

Who skis free: Ages 4 and younger.

Who skis at a discount: Ages 65+ pay $65 per day. Prices are lower during early and late season. Keystone also has one of the country's largest night-skiing operations. A full-day ticket includes night skiing. Night-skiing-only prices are available. Vail, which owns Keystone, offers PEAKS discounted tickets if you pre-purchase a three-day or more ticket at least 14 days in advance. Membership in PEAKS is free and a pre-purchase automatically enrolls you.

Interchangeability: Multiday lift tickets of three or more days also are valid at Vail, Beaver Creek and Breckenridge and at nearby Arapahoe Basin.

Snowcat skiing and riding: Four hours of snowcat skiing and riding with guides costs $71 per person (in addition to lift ticket). Reservations recommended; advanced and expert skiers and riders only. A first-come, first-served 12-seat snowcat shuttle costs $5 per ride, picking up from the top of Outback Express and dropping off at the top of North and South Bowls (no guides).

Accommodations

Keystone Central Reservations (800-427-8308) books lodging, air transportation, lift tickets and other needs. Keystone is mostly a condominium community, but it also has two hotels and a quaint bed and breakfast that formerly was a stagecoach stop in the 1800s. Room or condo rates start at about $120 per night. Kids ages 12 and younger stay free with their parents, provided minimum occupancy is met and maximum occupancy not exceeded. All room reservations come with the Adventure Passport, a card that gives entry to more than $300 worth of activities (see *Other Activities*).

The quaint **Ski Tip Lodge** ($–$$$$), which was a stagecoach stop in the late 1800s, is a near-perfect ski lodge. Rooms are rustic in the best sense of the word with true ski history, the dining room is elegant and the sitting room is warm and inviting. The Ski Tip Lodge rents rooms with breakfast included. Private rooms have baths, and the dorm rooms share one. The rooms are small but comfortable and the food is outstanding. Don't plan on telephones, TVs or Internet access.

Keystone divides its lodging into seven "neighborhoods" and villages. Each group has a central swimming pool, shops and restaurants, and is serviced by excellent shuttlebus access. Generally, the closer the condo group is to the lifts, the nicer it is and the more interior amenities it has.

The main hub is the attractive **River Run Village**, which is walking distance from the River Run Gondola. The condos are spacious and convenient to the slopes and surround the best shopping in Keystone. A variety of outdoor concerts and events rock the plaza in winter. River Run is flanked by the neighborhoods of **East Keystone,** built around Ski Tip Lodge, and **North Keystone,** where the **Inn at Keystone** is located. From this neighborhood in the center of the resort, the views are spectacular.

Slopeside condos are truly ski-in/ski-out in the **Mountain House Neighborhood**, the second base area. The **Chateaux d'Mont** condos here are magnificent, luxurious and worth every penny. We strongly recommend trying to reserve one of these units.

To the west is **Lakeside Village** where shops, restaurants and the upscale **Keystone Lodge** hug the shores of the small lake and ice rink that is the focal point. **West Keystone**, close to the Conference Center, is the gateway to Keystone, where townhouses, private homes and condos greet visitors. The beautiful **Ranch** neighborhood follows the Snake River up the mountain toward The Keystone Ranch (see *Dining*).

Keystone's platinum collection of lodging properties continues to define luxury. When guests stay at one of these upscale condos or townhomes, they receive free ski check, welcome gifts, fresh flowers, a complimentary bottle of wine, personal concierge and daily newspapers. Be sure to ask about it if you're in the mood for pampering.

Dining

Keystone has gained a reputation for fine dining, thanks to the Colorado Mountain College Culinary Institute based there. Qualified students apprentice for three years in the resort's restaurants under world-renowned chefs before receiving degrees in culinary arts from the American Culinary Federation. So, lucky Keystone visitors get to sample the fruits of their labors.

All of Keystone's restaurants require reservations, which you can make before leaving home by calling the activities/dining toll-free number, (800) 354-4386. If you're staying at a resort property, dial Ext. 4386. If you're staying elsewhere in Summit County, call 496-4386. Use these numbers for all the restaurants we list here.

Keystone has three dining experiences not to be missed—**Alpenglow Stube**, perched at 11,444 feet on North Peak and the highest gourmet restaurant in the country; **Ski Tip Lodge**, the cozy inn where all of Keystone's history oozes from every log; and **Keystone Ranch**, named one of Colorado's Best Restaurants by the Zagat Survey. All are sophisticated gourmet restaurants in charming settings, perfect for romantic dinners or groups of adults (and not at all suitable for noisy young children). The chefs at each have a friendly rivalry, which helps to keep the standards high. Save room for dessert and appetizers.

Alpenglow Stube ($$$) in The Outpost features rough-hewn timbers, massive fireplaces, vaulted ceilings and expansive windows. The Stube serves what we rate as the best on-mountain dinner available in the U.S. The adventure begins two valleys away with a ride on two gondolas suspended over the lighted slopes of Dercum Mountain. The restaurant is a large but cozy room that looks as if Martha Stewart's Swiss cousin was the decorator. The menu features a six- to eight-course menu (for a fixed price of $95 per person) of such fare as wood-grilled salmon, grilled wild game and slow-roasted duck. Figure about another $40 a bottle for wine. Everything from the setting to cuisine is perfect—even more amazing considering that every bit of fresh food on your plate was transported via gondola or snowcat.

Renowned among discerning clientele in Summit County, **Ski Tip Lodge** ($$$) is a cozy and inviting place with a standard for service that all restaurants strive for yet not all achieve. Formerly an 1800s stagecoach stop, and now a bed and breakfast, the lodge for a time was the private home of Keystone founders Max and Edna Dercum. It serves a fixed-price, four-course meal for adults and a three-course meal for children 12 and younger. The creative menu changes daily, and delights constantly.

Keystone Ranch ($$$) is a restored log ranch house, built in the 1930s as a wedding present to Bernardine Smith and Howard Reynolds. Reportedly, the only completely original part of the house is the fireplace, yet you feel as if you're dining at the home of an intimate friend. American regional cuisine is prepared with Rocky Mountain indigenous ingredients—such as piñon-encrusted lamb or elk with wild mushrooms.

You say your kids want to ride the gondolas for dinner too? Take the family to **Der Fondue Chessel** ($$$), also at The Outpost at the top of North Peak. Enjoy fondue, raclette and wine (not for the kids, of course) with music by a Bavarian band.

In Lakeside Village, Keystone Lodge's **Champeaux** ($$$) brings a taste of Provence to the Rockies. Indulge in southeastern French cuisine while taking in the panoramic views of Keystone Lake and the Snake River Valley. For a Western meal to satisfy a big hunger, head to the **Bighorn Steakhouse** ($$–$$$), renowned for its cuts of tender prime rib and its 16-ounce Cowboy Rib Eye Steak, handcut and served on the bone in barbecue butter. The atmosphere is casual and relaxed. The **Summit Seafood Company** ($$), in the Keystone Inn, specializes in—what else?—fresh seafood, including mahi mahi, swordfish and even local trout.

For truly casual dining, we got a tasty individual-sized pizza and a draft beer sitting at the bar in the **Snake River Saloon.** Across Hwy. 6 in the Mountain View Plaza is **Dos Locos** (262-9185; $–$$), a Mexican restaurant (no surprise there) that is especially popular during happy hour—the margaritas are extremely refreshing.

At River Run, try **Kickapoo Tavern** ($–$$) for appetizers or light fare such as the turkey chili (a house specialty), burgers, soup or low-priced salads. **The Great Northern**

Dining: $$$$–Entrees $30+; $$$–$20-$30; $$–$10-$20; $-less than $10.
Accommodations: (double room) $$$$–$200+; $$$–$141-$200; $$–$81-$140; $-$80 and less.

Tavern ($$$) is anything but your ordinary tavern. The chefs are creative across the board, from appetizers of salmon papaya tostadas and panko vegetable rolls to entrees of Hawaiian mero sea bass, sweet Thai ahi tuna and Colorado lamb T-bones with puttanesca raisin sauce. **Paisano's ($–$$)** is a family-friendly, casual Italian restaurant. Dinner favors pastas, pastas and more pastas. Breakfast here is known for building your own fritattas and Italian scrambles, or a sinful breakfast of Italian toast stuffed with mascarpone. Have a Bloody Mary, a Grey Goose Screwdriver or a Monday Morning Mimosa. For a lighter breakfast, pick up a wrap or bagel sandwich at the **Inxpot ($)**.

Dinner Sleigh Rides take you the scenic route to a festive Western-style dinner and entertainment; reservations are required.

Apres-ski/nightlife

Keystone's apres-ski and nightlife used to be limited, but now you'll find new bars and clubs in River Run. Be sure to check out happy hour and apres-ski at the Jimmy Buffet-style **Parrot Eyes** in River Run. Hang out on the deck, delve into burritos, tacos, nachos or tamales, and wash it all down with margaritas. Live music five nights a week keeps the apres-ski lively.

Other places for apres-ski activity include **Last Lift Bar** in the Mountain House at Dercum Mountain base, or **Snake River Saloon,** one of Keystone's older establishments that rocks on weekends with live music for dancing. **Tenderfoot Lounge,** in Keystone Lodge, has comfy couches and chairs, piano entertainment and a 15-foot fireplace.

At River Run, **Kickapoo Tavern** draws a crowd on its patio on sunny days, and inside on snowy ones. Don't miss the Kickapoo Mountain Joy Juice, a surprisingly potent blend of rums and fruit juices. **The Great Northern** is Keystone's only brewery and chophouse, and its handcrafted brews make it another favorite apres-ski scene in River Run. The **Inxpot** brews specialty teas, gourmet coffees and offers a full-service bar. Part coffeehouse, part bar, part bookshop, it's the kind of place that makes you feel like a local.

A "don't miss" is the **Goat**—the true locals' hang out. The Goat recently opened a dining room and more upscale/sleek bar adjacent to the old, smoky dive that locals seem to still prefer. At the original Goat, catch a game of foosball, grab a Pabst Blue Ribbon and soak up the local scene. Warning: The decor is something you'd find in the basement of a fraternity house or at a garage sale in the 1970s. Live music adds even more entertainment.

Sports fans will enjoy **Pizza on the Plaza** in Lakeside Village, where you'll find flat-screen TVs, HDTVs and a big plasma screen. You name the sport, surely it's playing on one of the screens. To dance till you drop, head to Keystone's only nightclub, **Green Light,** in River Run, where the day lodge morphs into a dance party. It's open every weekend until 2 a.m.

Other activities

The **Adventure Passport** is free with a stay at Keystone Resort's lodging properties. It gives you free activities on and off the mountain, which in the past have included **yoga, wine tastings, horse-drawn sleigh rides, ice skating, snowshoeing** and more. Make sure to take advantage of it. All non-skiing activities are booked by calling the **Adventure Center** at (800) 354-4386 or 496-4386.

Adventure Point, at the top of Dercum Mountain, is the place to head for frighteningly fast **tubing** and **snowbiking**. Two-hour **guided snowmobile tours** travel through the National Forest. Take control and be the driver, or simply ride along as a passenger. Reservations are required. **Ice skating** in the middle of Keystone Village is open every day and night. The outdoor lake, reportedly the largest Zamboni-maintained outdoor skating lake in North America, is smoothed twice a day. Skate rentals are available. The fitness center at Keystone Lodge features **massages, steam room, outdoor heated pool, cardio and weight rooms,** and a **hot tub.**

Summit County's newest full-service day spa, **Serenity Spa & Salon** (513-9002), uses natural products from Aveda. Therapists, treatments and service here match the excellence one expects from a salon carrying the world-renowned name. For warmth after the cold, try the Floating Massage with warm water cushions cradling your body. The spa menu lists a full array of salon services, including manicures for men. The **Spa at Keystone Lodge** (496-4118) features specialized massages, facials and body treatments for every pampering need. Create your own experience from the signature collection for an hour or an entire day; even have a massage in the privacy of your own room.

River Run Village has some very good **shops,** mostly selling upscale costume jewelry, Native American pottery and crafts, and elegant clothing. Gorsuch is the standard for a classy retailer of ski merchandise. You'll also find the standard souvenir and T-shirt shops in Keystone Village. Other good shopping is in nearby Breckenridge or the Silverthorne Factory Stores.

Getting there and getting around

By air: Denver International Airport is 90 miles away via I-70. Transportation between the airport and the resort can be booked with the central reservations number, (800) 427-8308. Colorado Mountain Express (800-525-6363) and Lift Ticket Limo (866-488-5280; 668-4899) have regular vans between the resort and airport.

By car: Take I-70 west from Denver, through the Eisenhower Tunnel, to Dillon at Exit 205. Head east for 6 miles on Hwy. 6.

Getting around: Within Keystone an excellent free shuttle system runs continuously starting at 7:30 a.m. In the evenings the shuttles run every 20 minutes until midnight on weeknights, and until 2 a.m. on Fridays and Saturdays. Bartenders and hotel doormen will call the shuttle to ensure pickup in the evenings and late at night, 496-4200. If you are staying and skiing mostly at Keystone, you won't need a car. The Summit Stage provides free transportation between Dillon, Silverthorne, Frisco, Breckenridge and Copper Mountain. Call 668-0999 for route information.

Nearby resorts

Arapahoe Basin, Arapahoe Basin, CO; (888) 272-7246
Internet: www.arapahoebasin.com
6 lifts; 490 acres; 2,270 vertical feet; 2 terrain parks

Arapahoe Basin—or A-Basin, as the locals call it—is legendary for many things. It has the highest skiable terrain in North America (the summit tops out at 13,050 feet). It has some of the steepest terrain inside a resort's boundaries. It has one of the longest ski seasons in North America (usually ending in June, sometimes July). It offers some of the best backcountry and avalanche awareness clinics in North America. Yet it has a relaxed, no-frills attitude—the type of place where few strive to wear matching ski outfits.

Two above-timberline bowls dominate the upper half of the mountain, which tops out on the Continental Divide. On a clear day, the view is amazing. But the real gestalt of A-Basin lies to the right of the Pallavicini Lift. The super-steep "Pali" side of A-Basin is for the strong and hardy who brave rocks, bumps, and gullies. It's not unusual to see skiers and riders zip along the ridge, launch off the cornice into the bowl, and rip big lines till they're out of sight. Making it down Pali is a rite of passage. On the other side of the mountain, the entire East

Dining: $$$$-Entrees $30+; $$$-$20-$30; $$-$10-$20; $-less than $10.
Accommodations: (double room) $$$$-$200+; $$$-$141-$200; $$-$81-$140; $-$80 and less.

Wall has chutes, gullies and steeps that experts regularly explore, but it requires hiking or a hair-raising traverse. Don't be fooled by the reported skiable acreage, this mountain skis big and A-Basin doesn't count the East Wall.

For all its gnarly reputation, A-Basin has excellent intermediate and beginner terrain. With its central base area, kids can't get lost, and stress is minimal because it's rarely crowded. The highest chairs, Lenawee Mountain Lift and Norway Lift, serve a slew of delightful intermediate trails. The above-treeline slopes mean runs are wide open, and you can let your skis choose your path. A-Basin does a great job of grooming, but there's plenty of ungroomed terrain for those who like it *au natural*. The beginner trails wind down from the Exhibition chairlift. Wrangler is a very wide, flat trail that builds confidence. Chisholm and Sundance are the next steps up. First-timers start on their own lift at the Molly Hogan Learning Center, and the flat, nearly separate area beneath it. You can buy a ticket to use only this lift for $10 and upgrade it to an all-mountain ticket if you feel up to more challenging runs.

This is high-elevation territory, with a base at 10,780 feet above sea level, so snow is usually plentiful. One of the best times to visit A-Basin is in the spring, when the mountain becomes the "beach," with barbecues and volleyball games providing the ambiance. "Beachin' at the Basin" is a spring ritual in May enjoyed by anyone who loves soft snow, cool bands, hot barbecue and sun.

Not surprisingly, this is a tele-skier's dream mountain. Perhaps it's the laid-back attitude, perhaps it's the proud touting of its purist roots, perhaps it's the terrain that mimics the nearby backcountry. Whatever the reason, 15 percent of A-Basin's guests are telemark skiers.

As for snowboarders: Forget spring break in Mexico. There's nothing like A-Basin's spring corn snow, with a frequent overnight dose of powder. Riding varies from cornice jumps off of the Norway Lift to sweeping beginner and intermediate runs. With a quick hike, the East Wall delivers treeless powder runs with an intermittent jump or two. Bigger air hits can be found in the Rock Garden off of the Pallavicini Lift, along with some rowdy, tree-lined chutes. On the lower part of the mountain, North Fork's natural berms and bumps are also worth a diversion. There are no treacherous runouts to avoid, as every trail winds nicely back to the base (though sometimes Pali Wog out of the Pali side can be daunting).

A-Basin's main terrain park, Mutha' Hucker, has rails, tabletops, boxes and a Huckster Jump for catching big air. The park is usually open into June and really rocks then. For beginners, a new park will be built on Sundance for the 2005/06 season.

The ski area has a respected ski school and classes are small, so you'll get plenty of individual attention. For those who consider skiing and riding "more of a passion and expression than a sport," A-Basin offers the High Adventure Series, excellent clinics and seminars on backcountry skiing, skiing the steeps, telemarking and avalanche awareness. Children's lessons start at age 4 for skiing, 8 for snowboarding.

New for 2005/06, a 7,200-square-foot building will house the rental and repair shop; terrain park clinics will be added to the ski school's High Adventure Series; and more snow guns will help with early-season snow conditions..

Lift tickets (2005/06 prices): Adults, $51; youth (15–19) and seniors (60–69), $41; child (6–14), $22; and 70 and older, $10; ages 5 and younger, free. One child skis free with a full-price adult lift ticket. Prices for adults and youth/seniors are lower during spring. Though Vail Resorts doesn't own A-Basin, it has arranged for Keystone/Breckenridge lift tickets to be valid at A-Basin too.

Lodging information: Summit County Chamber, (800) 530-3099 or (970) 262-0817.

Beaver Creek
Colorado

Summit elevation:	11,440 feet
Vertical drop:	4,040 feet
Base elevation:	7,400 feet

Address: P.O. Box 7
Vail, CO 81658
Area code: 970
Ski area phone: 845-9090 or (800) 404-3535
Snow report: (800) 404-3535
Toll-free reservations: (800) 404-3535 (See Vail chapter for foreign toll-free phone numbers.)
Fax: 496-4980
E-mail: bcinfo@vailresorts.com
Internet: www.beavercreek.com
Expert:★★★
Advanced:★★★★
Intermediate:★★★★
Beginner:★★★★
First-timer:★★★

Number and types of lifts: 16—10 high-speed quads, 2 triples, 3 doubles, 1 surface lift
Skiable Acreage: 1,625 acres
Snowmaking: 43 percent
Uphill capacity: 30,739 per hour
Parks & pipes: 3 parks, 1 pipe
Bed base: 3,741 in resort; 4,000 in Avon
Nearest lodging: Slopeside, hotels and condos
Resort child care: Yes, 2 months and older
Adult ticket, per day: $83 (06/07 price)

Dining:★★★★
Apres-ski/nightlife:★
Other activities:★★

Beaver Creek has grown up to become a mountain village and is celebrating its 25th anniversary this year. What started out as a series of seemingly random hotels and condominiums has been knit together with a series of walkways to create a village atmosphere with a European flair. It has a real soul and can rightfully take its place as one of the country's top luxury resorts.

The central complex is pedestrian only—with snow-free walkways—and shops and restaurants are scattered throughout. The Vilar Center for the Arts features top entertainment, and forms the focus of the development along with the outdoor Black Family Ice Rink. Covered escalators whisk skiers and snowboarders from the shuttle drop-off point to the lifts. Attention to detail includes warm chocolate-chip cookies handed out after each day on the slopes and collector postcards to be mailed free of charge anywhere in the world. More upscale than big sister Vail, the Beaver Creek experience is carefully scripted to appeal to the A-list guests and wannabes it draws. At the same time, those of more modest means won't feel out of place here anymore.

Those with a taste for being pampered are plopped squarely in the lap of luxury—at a price. Beaver Creek's unofficial motto used to be, "If you aren't worth a million dollars, don't even bother coming here." No one will ask for a copy of last year's tax return to verify your earnings, of course. Yet it's clear that this isn't a place for penny-pinchers, or even the budget-conscious. The art galleries, gift shops and outfitters feature prices that are fitting for visitors with six-figure incomes.

Beaver Creek attracts the Fortune 500 crowd and many of the condominiums are corporate-owned. The corporate owners have worked hard to create an exclusive air, with prices as upscale as its visitors. If you can afford it, the experience come with all the bells and whistles.

But you don't *have* to go broke to truly enjoy the Beaver Creek experience. Just don't stay in the village. Surprisingly, the regular resort amenities such as apres-ski and dining are all very affordable. Staying in a nearby town such as Avon, with a good shuttle system plus a lift in Beaver Creek Landing, makes this a resort for Everyman.

The rich and famous as well as the common folk will find very good skiing and snow-boarding for all ability levels here. Visitors can ski or snowboard between Beaver Creek, Arrowhead and Bachelor Gulch. A ski-way connects Bachelor Gulch back to Beaver Creek Landing near the parking lots at the base of the resort. Complimentary shuttles also make the loop, but not as frequently as you might like.

 ## Mountain layout

Much of the Beaver Creek terrain is expertly groomed. An enthusiastic fleet of snowcats patrols the mountainside 20 out of every 24 hours, grooming half the mountain's terrain each day. To ski intermediate and beginner trails at Beaver Creek is "to ski on corduroy." If you're an expert or advanced skier, don't let this scare you away. Beaver Creek leaves your terrain alone, so you'll find plenty of challenge.

♦♦**Expert ♦Advanced:** When Beaver Creek opened in 1980, its first runs were mostly beginner and intermediate. Some still think of it—mistakenly—as a cruiser mountain. Not so: Advanced skiers and experts should spend at least a day here, maybe more. Our advice is to choose a weekend, when the lines are long at Vail, yet are nonexistent here.

What's surprising is the amount of truly tough stuff. The Birds of Prey runs rival anything Vail offers—all long, steep and mogul-studded. If you want to feel like a world-class racer, the downhill course, one of the most difficult in the world, is groomed as often as possible for a long and super-fast double-diamond cruiser. While somewhat shorter, Ripsaw and Cataract in Rose Bowl, and Loco in Larkspur Bowl, are equally challenging. New for 06/07 east of Rose Bowl are Stone Creek Chutes scooped out of short but steep pitches of up to 45 degrees. Grouse Mountain is strictly for black-diamond types, no matter what the trail map may suggest. Only in spring, when slushier snow slows skiers down, should such runs as Screech Owl, Falcon Park and Royal Elk Glades be attempted by thrill-seeking advanced skiers.

■ **Intermediate:** Beaver Creek is an excellent resort for intermediates at every level. For those intermediates bordering on advanced, the runs under the Centennial Express lift are long and have a moderately steep pitch—enough to be exciting, but not the kind to scare you out of your bindings. If you can catch these runs after a grooming, the black-diamond-designated sections are definitely within the abilities of upper-intermediates. Centennial, the main run in this area, is not the best choice for a warm-up if the resort hasn't had snow in a while. It's in the shade early in the morning, and everyone uses it, so the surface can get skied off and a bit slick (but it's a super run under good conditions). Harrier is a locals' favorite where you'll often find yourself skiing solo. Don't miss Harrier when it's been groomed. Another great intermediate route is Redtail to the Larkspur Lift, then descend down Larkspur Bowl.

Early in the morning, the runs under the Strawberry Park lift are in the sun. We recommend Pitchfork for your warm-up, and a couple of the runs in the Bachelor Gulch area for a follow-up. Bachelor Gulch's runs are shorter and gentler than the ones above Beaver Creek Village—perfect for those in the middle of the intermediate ability range. Arrowhead is another good choice for intermediates, though its southerly exposure means thin snow at the tail end of dry spells.

If you're on the lower end of the intermediate scale, try the runs at the top of the Cinch Express. Trails to avoid unless you have lots of confidence (or it's a soft-snow spring day) are the blue trails on Grouse Mountain.

●● **Beginner:** The easiest runs are at the top, accessed by the Centennial Express and Cinch Express lifts. Once you reach the top, head over to Red Buffalo, Mystic Island and the other runs in the Slow Zone. Ride the Drink of Water lift again and again, because this area has no intermediate or expert runs where faster skiers zip past at high speeds. Flattops, Piney and Powell, to the other side of the Cinch lift, are wide and gentle. A bonus: You get to see the same magnificent summit view that everyone else does. You get back to Beaver Creek Village on a long, clearly marked beginner run (it's really a cat track) called Cinch. One thing beginners should watch out for: Beaver Creek has sudden shifts from beginner to expert terrain. The trails are well-marked, but when you're moving fast and trying to concentrate, the signs can fly by. The Arrowhead section also is good for beginners.

● **First-timer:** Beaver Creek's learning area is at the base, served by two lifts.

Ride Guide: Riding at "The Beav" is an experience all its own. With so much grooming and round the clock snowmaking, the runs can have a consistency that's sometimes almost too perfect. Don't worry, though, because the natural deep powder can still be found almost all season—just look in the woods. The woods are actually Beaver Creek's number-one asset to snowboarders. Powder lines, world-class log slides that will make any skateboarder envious and cliff lines abound, making The Beav one of the favorites among Colorado locals in the know. Be sure to check the trail map for snowboard gladed zones.

Intermediates should let it rip down one of America's best unheralded cruisers, Centennial, which dips and turns down the lower half of the mountain. Beginners should stay away from Cinch. It's a beginner's nightmare. Intermediate and advanced riders should have no problem maintaining their speed on this cat track, but to the first-time rider, it's literally a speed death-sentence. Don't learn to jump on the family runs off Latigo—ski patrol will not hesitate to pull your pass for airing in a family area.

Parks and pipes

Centennial brings you right to the Moonshine Terrain Park, which has definitely stepped up to the plate in the past few years. With every type of rail imaginable, logslides, hips, spines and some nice-sized tabletops—plus a yurt with foosball, cable TV and beverages—Moonshine Terrain Park is great for everyone from the intermediate on up. The superpipe is at the top of the intermediate Latigo run. From the expert who's working on backside rodeos, to the advanced rider learning how to do frontside airs, it's the ideal pipe to perfect your style and to get away from the crowds that some of the other mountains draw.

Zoom Room is a progressive beginner to intermediate park. It begins with smaller introductory features—including rollers, small tables and small rails—and moves to progressively larger features and rails. Park 101 has rollers, dots and other terrain features that allow lower-level riders and skiers of all ages to learn weighting and unweighting of boards and skis.

 Cross-country and snowshoeing (visit xcskiresorts.com for more details)
For a different Nordic experience at an Alpine ski area, head to McCoy Park at the top of the Strawberry Park Express Lift. Instead of skiing on the flats (usually a golf course) at the base of a ski area, you'll be on a 32-km. system at the summit, 9,840 feet, with spectacular views in every direction. Groomed and tracked for both skating and classic skiing, the trail system has one advanced (and exciting) loop, the Wild Side trail, but is basically beginner and intermediate. An ungroomed single track for snowshoers is called the Upper Atlas Traverse. Skiers and snowshoers can take one of several trails to the base, download on the Strawberry Park Express Lift or take the very

gradual Home Comfort trail (6 km.) all the way down—fun with new snow to slow you down but speedy if there isn't.

Tours, lessons and rentals are available. The park also has snowshoe rentals and tours. For more information on Nordic activities, call the Beaver Creek Nordic Center at 845-5313.

Lessons [05/06 prices]

Lessons meet at the base area near the Centennial Express lift. Instruction is available in nearly 30 languages. Call the Ski and Snowboard School at (800) 475-4543 or 845-5300. Unless otherwise indicated, we list regular season prices; value season prices are lower.

Group lessons: A full-day group is $120. A great deal, available only during select times, is the 3-Peat Series: three consecutive adult lessons of any ability level for $189.

First-timer package: A full-day lesson with lift ticket and rentals costs $193. A great deal available during the value season is the First Time Series, offering three consecutive full days of lessons with lift tickets for $190 ($240 with rentals).

First-time snowboarders also can take a Burton Learn to Ride clinic that uses special Burton snowboards, bindings and boots designed to reduce the difficulty of learning to ride. The goal is to get students linking toeside and heelside turns on the very first day and significantly reduce the number of falls. Call for prices of the lift/lesson/rental package.

Private lessons: $405 for a half-day, and $595 for a full day (for one to six people). One-hour lessons, when available, are $150. Reservations are highly recommended.

Racing: Two NASTAR courses and a coin-op course are next to the Centennial run.

KidStuff [06/07 prices]

Child care: Ages 2 months to 6 years. Full-day program costs $107 during regular season. Reservations required; call 845-5325. Hours are 8 a.m. to 4:30 p.m. Free pagers are available. The ski school and child-care center are right in the base village, although the Small World Play School is a bit hard to find. After crossing the covered bridge that leads into the village, turn left and walk down the stairs until you see the sign to your right.

Other options: The Park Hyatt (949-1234) offers programs for children, as well as babysitting. Baby's Away (800-369-9030; 926-5256) rents and delivers baby needs.

Children's lessons: Lessons are available for children as young as 3 years old (toilet-trained). Ski lessons are offered for kids 3–12; snowboarding lessons are for ages 7–12. Cost is $153 during regular season and includes lesson, lift and lunch. Teens 15–18 can take all-day lessons for $125 plus lifts and lunch. Reservations are not required, except for kids ages 3–6. Register for all lessons at 8 a.m. or pre-register the day before; you also can register online at the website. Call 845-5464 for information about all children's lesson programs.

Skiing with your kids: Like Vail, Beaver Creek is sprinkled with Kids Adventure Zones. Kids can search out such haunts as the Tombstone Territory or the Hibernating Bear Cave. Most are off Cinch near the top of the Centennial Lift.

Lift tickets [06/07 prices]

	Adult	Child (5-12)
One day	$83	$52
Three days	$249 ($83/day)	$150 ($50/day)
Five days	$415 ($83/day)	$250 ($50/day)

www.skisnowboard.com   Telephone area code: 970

Who skis free: Ages 4 and younger.

Who skis at a discount: Ages 65+ pay $73 per day. Pre-purchase your lift tickets online and you'll receive a discount. Vail offers PEAKS discounted tickets if you pre-purchase a three-day or more ticket at least 14 days in advance. Membership in PEAKS is free and you are automatically enrolled when you make your early purchase. Prices are lower during early and late season, and higher during holidays.

Interchangeability: All lift tickets purchased at Vail or Beaver Creek also are valid at sister resorts Keystone and Breckenridge, as well as at nearby Arapahoe Basin. Only multiday tickets of three or more days purchased at Keystone or Breckenridge are valid at Vail and Beaver Creek. All lift tickets purchased at Keystone or Breckenridge also are valid at nearby Arapahoe Basin.

 ## Accommodations

Beaver Creek lodging is expensive. It's tough to find a room for less than $200 per night, unless you want to vacation off season.

The ski-in/ski-out **Park Hyatt Beaver Creek Resort & Spa** (800-233-1234; 949-1234; $$$$) features the 20,000-square-foot Allegria spa. All rooms have free Internet access and wireless keyboards with flat screens. A ski ambassador gives guests lessons and tours (fee), and storyteller Frank Doll, a third-generation Vail Valley resident, weaves tales fireside. There's also a heated outdoor pool. The five restaurants and lounges address all styles of dining.

Chateau Residence Club (949-1616; $$$$) offers private luxury hillside condos with all the amenities of a hotel: concierge, daily maid service, a great restaurant and lounge, etc. It echoes the castle-like elegance of the Banff Springs Hotel with suites starting at $750 per night with a three-night minimum. The staff is warm and welcoming no matter whether you're wearing a floor-length mink or fleece vest.

The **Ritz-Carlton, Bachelor Gulch** (800-241-3333; 748-6200; $$$$) promises seclusion, luxury and excellence. If you can imagine the amenity, it is probably here. Also available are a full-service and fully equipped 21,000-square-foot spa, outdoor heated pool, and Ritz Kids program. Dogs are surprisingly welcome. But if you left Fido at home and need a canine fix, take Bachelor, the hotel's yellow lab, for a walk or snowshoe, compliments of Loan-A-Lab.

The **Pines Lodge** (800-859-8242; $$$$), Rock Resorts condo-hotel property near the Strawberry Park lift, is a member of Preferred Hotels and Resorts Worldwide. Guests can enjoy a hot tub, heated outdoor pool, fitness room and massage therapy. Don't miss its award-winning Grouse Mountain Grill restaurant (see *Dining*). The **Inn at Beaver Creek** (800-859-8242; $$–$$$$), ski-in/ski-out lodging on a far smaller scale than the Park Hyatt, has 37 rooms and eight suites with a free hot gourmet breakfast. Cocktails, cappuccinos and a light menu are offered apres-ski. Guests also have a sauna and steam room.

The **Beaver Creek Lodge** (800-525-7280; 845-9800; $$–$$$$) is the only all-suite resort in the Vail Valley. The 71 units have living rooms, fireplaces, wireless Internet access, and TVs with VCRs. Onsite amenities include a fitness center, indoor/outdoor pool, hot tub, steam room, sauna and ski lockers.

The **Centennial Lodge** (800-845-7060; $$$$) claims to have the best prices on the mountain, but doesn't provide full hotel service. It has underground parking and a pool. This lodge has some condos and three hotel rooms. Both the **Centennial Lodge** and **Creekside Lodge** (949-7071; $$$$) are in the village. **The Poste Montane** (800-497-9238; 845-7500; $$–$$$$) is in Beaver Creek Resort Village, as is **St. James Place** (800-859-8242; 845-9300; $$$$). **The Borders Lodge** (800-846-0233; 926-2300; $$–$$$$) is a comfortable ski-in/ski-

Dining: $$$$-Entrees $30+; $$$-$20-$30; $$-$10-$20; $-less than $10.
Accommodations: (double room) $$$$-$200+; $$$-$141-$200; $$-$81-$140; $-$80 and less.

out condominium complex next to the Elkhorn lift, within easy walk of the village. Its condos range in size from one to three bedrooms and the list of facilities includes two outdoor hot tubs and year-round pool.

Elkhorn Lodge (888-833-5018; 845-2270; $$$$) has studios and one- to four-bedroom condos and penthouses with ski-in/ski-out convenience adjacent to the Elkhorn lift. Amenities include fully equipped kitchens, fireplaces, balconies, spa tubs in the bathrooms, two outdoor hot tubs and a fitness area.

The Charter (800-525-6660 or 949-6660; $$–$$$$), which bills itself as having "all of the conveniences of a condominium with all of the luxuries of a world-class hotel," gives guests more of the typical Beaver Creek amenities—wonderful wood-paneled interiors, European decor, fireplaces and stunning mountain views. One- through five-bedroom units are available. Two restaurants offer menus to suit anyone's tastes.

If your budget won't support accommodations inside Beaver Creek's gates, head to the nearby town of Avon for the valley's best condo deals at the **Christie Lodge** (800-551-4320; 949-7700; $$–$$$$). Or, you can stay in the town of Edwards, about 5 miles from Beaver Creek. One possibility there is **The Inn at Riverwalk** (888-926-0606; 926-0606; $$–$$$). VailNet (www.vail.net) has a very good lodging search feature that will suggest lodging according to location, amenities and price.

Dining

Beaver Creek is infatuated with the term "gourmet." Everything, right down to the garden-variety burger, is designated gourmet. Plus, these Colorado chefs do love their spices. The dishes we tried featured gratuitous amounts of onions, garlic and exotic flavors.

Splendido at The Chateau (845-8808; $$$$) is very popular with locals, especially for special occasions. Many regulars come for the piano player, Taylor Kundolf, but chef David Walford has a huge following for his succulent game. The wine cellar is vast. It's one of the most richly elegant yet accessible properties in Vail or Beaver Creek.

Mirabelle (949-7728; $$$–$$$$), a longtime local favorite at the bottom of the resort access road in an old farmhouse, serves well-prepared Belgian-influenced nouvelle cuisine.

SaddleRidge (845-5450; $$$–$$$$) showcases the country's largest private collection of Western artifacts outside of a museum. It's open for dinner with a game-dominated a la carte menu prepared by executive chef Geordy Ogden, who presented at the prestigious James Beard House. After dessert take a look at the saddle with Buffalo Bill's sketch impressed into the leather—the image is his own handiwork.

Grouse Mountain Grill (949-0600; $$$$), adjacent to the Pines Lodge, serves Rocky Mountain cuisine, featuring such dishes as Colorado lamb and pretzel-crusted pork chops. The elegant interior is intimate, all the more so because of the nightly jazz pianist who performs during dinner. Zagat's repeatedly names the restaurant as one of the best in the region.

In Market Square, follow your nose to **Toscanini** (845-5590; $$–$$$$), a busy Italian restaurant overlooking the outdoor ice rink featuring excellent seafood and pasta dishes. Special children's menu selections are available.

Beaver Creek Chophouse (845-0555; $$$) serves certified Angus beef and live Main lobster in a slopeside location with a fantastic view.

A fairly new addition to the village center is **Foxnut Asian Fusion & Sushi** (845-0700; $$$). Its trendy interior of bright pink walls hung with Asian magazine ads, chartreuse booths and hanging lanterns deviates from the elegant Beaver Creek norm, but sushi fans love it. **Rocks Modern Grill** (845-1730; $$$) is in the newly remodeled Beaver Creek Lodge and serves classic American food for breakfast, lunch and dinner. Dinner in the private wine room can be set up with a reservation.

By Beaver Creek standards, **traMonti** (949-5552, $$–$$$) is one of the more inexpensive places to eat. It serves pastas and risottos, and Northern Italian-prepared veal, steak, chicken and seafood. The family-friendly menu in the slopeside **Bivans** (949-1234; $$–$$$) in the Park Hyatt Beaver Creek encourages sharing with a focus on informality.

Besides moving to a new location in the Poste Montane and expanding its space, the **Blue Moose** (845-8666; $$-$) also expanded its menu from pizza to a variety of Italian dishes.

The **Golden Eagle** (949-1940; $$–$$$) is a less costly, though not less exotic, place to dine. With entrees such as medallions of Australian kangaroo and roast loin of elk on the menu, guests can take a culinary world tour without leaving their seats.

In Avon try **The Vista Brasserie** (949-3366; $$) for good American fare and **Fiesta Jalisco** (845-8088; $$) for tasty Mexican meals. **Masato's Sushi Bar** (949-0330; $$–$$$), in the Chapel Square complex, has great sushi chefs and reasonably priced Japanese food. **Ti Amo** (845-8153; $$–$$$) is Avon's best for good-value Italian. Or try the town of Edwards, just west of Avon. The **Gore Range Brewery** has outrageous salads, wood-fired thin-crust pizza, and peel-and-eat shrimp. There's also a hip sushi restaurant called **Sato** (926-7684; $–$$).

Beaver Creek has a wonderfully memorable dining experience, a night at **Beano's Cabin** (949-9090, book early; $$$$). Groups are bundled onto a 40-person sleigh and pulled up the mountain under the stars by a snowcat. The cabin (a bit of a misnomer, since the building is fairly large) is upscale-rustic on the outside and elegant inside, with a roaring stone-hearth fire, log beams and well-prepared cuisine. The five-course meal concludes with remarkable desserts. The cost is per person, including the sleigh ride but not the wine, tax or gratuity. Equally delightful is **Zach's Cabin** (845-6575, book early; $$$–$$$$), up on the mountain between Arrowhead and Bachelor Gulch Villages. Similar in concept to Beano's Cabin, this 13,000-square-foot cabin is nestled in a grove of aspen trees and guests arrive on a snowcat-drawn sleigh.

Apres-ski/nightlife

Asked what nightlife was worth a look, one worker first told us, "There isn't anything," then after a bit of thinking, amended her response to, "Well, there are some meeting places." The first place to stop on the way back to town from the Larkspur Bowl is **The Talons Deck at Red Tail Camp,** where revelers gather to begin apres-ski. In the spring, the deck is packed and Sundays mean live entertainment al fresco.

The Coyote Cafe would surely qualify as a meeting place, particularly among locals such as the Beaver Creek Ski Patrol, at the end of the day. This Mexican cantina/watering hole caters to locals, and with well-drink and draft-beer specials at the end of the day, its prices are reasonable. Bartenders can whip up a margarita to get you in the apres-ski mood, and the staff is intentionally informal—in contrast with the rest of Beaver Creek. Don't plan on staying out late—it closes at 11 p.m. (as late as 1 a.m. on hopping nights). If you're young and looking for apres-ski, this is it.

McCoy's is the places to go for live apres-ski entertainment as soon as you leave the slopes. Also try the **Dusty Boot Saloon**, where you'll find mondo 46-ounce margaritas and a comprehensive tequila list. **The Blue Moose** has great pizza and a fun atmosphere, and the lowest prices in Beaver Creek Village.

Dining: $$$$-Entrees $30+; $$$–$20-$30; $$-$10-$20; $-less than $10.
Accommodations: (double room) $$$$-$200+; $$$-$141-$200; $$-$81-$140; $-$80 and less.

The Park Hyatt's **Whiskey Elk** bar, which stays open until 2 a.m., features entertainment from local musicians and serves small batch bourbons, single malt scotch, ports and wine by the glass. At night, when the stars are out, it's a dazzling display for tired skiers and riders.

The best deck in Beaver Creek might be at the **Chophouse** (845-0555). While you watch the sunset with drinks and occasional live music, a magician entertains kids and adults six afternoons a week.

Other activities

The **Vilar Center for the Arts** (888-920-2787; 845-8497) is a 528-seat performing arts center snugged under the ice rink in Beaver Creek. It's modeled after a turn-of-the-century theater in Munich and presents world-class entertainment four to six nights a week. The year-round outdoor **Black Family Ice Rink** is in the heart of Beaver Creek. Ice skating exhibitions are held here periodically in the winter.

If you need to restore mind and body (like those sore skiing legs), visit one of Beaver Creek's **spas.**

Every Thursday night, level-five and higher skiers are invited to join in on **Thursday Night Lights,** a ski-down with glow sticks followed by a huge fireworks show. Register at the Children's Ski and Snowboard School. The resort concierge (845-9090) can make reservations for other activities, such as **dogsledding, snowmobiling, snowshoeing, fly fishing, ice fishing, hot-air ballooning** and **sleigh rides.**

Beautiful **boutiques** line the pedestrian walkway in the heart of the resort. A special stop on your list should be The Golden Bear, just west of the skating rink in Beaver Creek. It's owned by local women whose logo is the golden bear (it's Vail's logo too), which you can find in all forms of jewelry and art. Great stylish clothes and other special gifts tempt the wallet. The Golden Beaver, in the Beaver Creek Lodge, sells golden beaver jewelry, Beaver Creek's insignia.

Getting there and getting around

By air: Flights land at the Vail/Eagle County airport, about 35 miles west of Vail, and the Denver International Airport, 110 miles east. Eagle County airport is served by American, Northwest, Delta, Continental, United Express and United.

Ground transportation between Denver and Vail is frequent and convenient. The trip to Vail takes about 2.5 hours. Contact Colorado Mountain Express at (800) 525-6363; Vail Valley Taxi (476-8294); or Airport Transportation Service (476-7576). Though flights into Denver may be a bit less expensive than Eagle, also consider the cost of round-trip ground transportation, where per-person rates from Denver are about double those from Eagle.

By car: Beaver Creek is right on I-70, 100 miles west of Denver and 140 miles east of Grand Junction. Beaver Creek is 10 miles west of Vail and just 3 miles south of Avon.

Getting around: Beaver Creek is very self-contained. A complimentary shuttle takes you anywhere within Beaver Creek between 6 a.m. and 2 a.m. daily. The shuttle is like a taxi, so ask your concierge or restaurant hostess to call (949-1938), and allow 10–15 minutes for pickup. Shuttles between Beaver Creek and Vail cost $3.

Here's something that's pretty tough to pass up: **BMW's Complimentary Mountain Driving Tour** operates out of the Pines Lodge. All Beaver Creek guests are invited to reserve a BMW for a test drive or for an entire evening. Call the Pines Lodge at (970) 845-7900.

Crested Butte
Colorado

Summit elevation (lift-served):	11,875 feet
Vertical drop:	2,775 feet
Base elevation (lowest lift):	9,100 feet

Address: P.O. Box 5700, 12 Snowmass Road
Mt. Crested Butte, CO 81225
Area code: 970
Ski area phone: 349-2333
Snow report: (888) 442-8883
Toll-free reservations: (800) 810-7669
Toll-free foreign numbers: 0800 894085 (U.K.)
Fax: 349-2397
E-mail: info@cbmr.com
Internet: www.skicb.com (ski resort)
crestedbuttechamber.com (chamber of commerce)
Expert:★★★★★
Advanced:★★★★★ **Intermediate:**★★★★
Beginner:★★★ **First-timer:**★★★★

Number of lifts: 15—3 high-speed quads,
2 quads, 3 triples, 3 doubles, 2 surface lifts, 2
moving carpets
Snowmaking: 37 percent (300 acres)
Skiable acreage: 1,125 acres
Uphill capacity: 19,160 per hour
Parks & pipes: 2 parks, 2 pipes
Bed base: 5,550
Nearest lodging: Slopeside
Resort child care: Yes, 6 months and older
Adult ticket, per day: $63–$69 (05/06 prices)
Dining:★★★★★
Apres-ski/nightlife:★★★★
Other activities:★★★

Crested Butte has long been hailed as the "anti resort" of Colorado—that is, anti-glitz, yet with all of the amenities and spectacular scenery for which the state is famous. It can be hard to get locals to divulge the secrets of their mountain, but that isn't a big hurdle because just about every run, chute and tree line is a gem in itself.

Extreme terrain is Crested Butte's signature, and for good reason. With an expanse of more than 500 acres of double-black terrain, it's a lift-served backcountry experience. In fact, locals who have skied and snowboarded here for years claim to not have had enough time to fully explore the possible lines. But beginners and intermediates also can find plenty of excitement. The mountain is laid out in such a way as to keep the less-skilled skiers and riders safely on easier runs, where there is no fear of accidentally getting in trouble..

If Crested Butte has a downfall, it is that compared with other legendary extreme resorts, it doesn't have as many powder days as the locals would like. But it averages more snowfall than most of the state, so it's easy to get the feeling that the locals are a bit, shall we say, spoiled? And the 2004/05 season brought a particularly excellent snow experience, with the best conditions in 10 years.

Funky, laid-back and friendly are oft-heard descriptions of the Crested Butte experience. When you walk into any restaurant or bar in town, it doesn't matter if you're a janitor or a Fortune 500 CEO, you'll be treated with the same warmth and respect—as long as you leave your "big-city" attitude outside. Award-winning wine bars mingle with cook-your-own hot dog stands. Five-star lodging overlooks local hangout shacks nestled in the woods. The apres-ski scene is rich at the resort's base, especially in spring, when lounging is best on the numerous large, sunny decks. Just down the road, the National Historic District of the town of Crested Butte reeks of charm and authentic Wild West.

Crested Butte is snowboard friendly—both in attitude and terrain. It is also host to some of the most entertaining competitions in the West, including the 15th Annual SAAB U.S. Extreme Freeskiing Championships, the U.S. Freeskiing Telemark Championships, and the and the 3rd Annual SlushHuck.

The new Mt. Crested Butte base village called "Mountaineer Square," which includes a conference center, aquatic/civic center, visitor center and upscale lodging, is open for this season. Also new for 2006/07, a high-speed quad which will replace the East River chair.The beginner and first-timer areas will also see more improvements. Planning is underway for terrain expansion to neighboring Snodgrass Mountain.

Mountain layout

Our base elevation in the stats box is at the point of the lowest lift, East River. The base area where the facilities are is about 200 feet higher, at 9,375 feet. Also, our stats reflect lift-served terrain—you can hike to the 12,162-foot level for a 3,062-foot vertical descent.

♦♦ **Expert:** The overwhelming sense of "feeling exposed" is the first hint that Crested Butte is no ordinary mountain. Then watch skiers work their way through rocky chutes to launch themselves off 40-foot cliffs and you know you are among some of the most elite skiers on the planet. You'll find some of the toughest in-bounds terrain on the continent here, much of it serviced by a T-bar ride. And while you don't have to traverse or hike, you'll find yourself doing so anyway in search of yet more fresh tracks, the best lines and more adrenaline thrills.

It's advisable to make friends with a local or a mountain guide before venturing off into Crested Butte's steeps. They are filled with cliff bands, so be sure to know your line before jumping in. The hardcore runs are the infamous Extreme Limits, comparable to their more famous counterparts across the boarders in Utah and Wyoming. Pitches average 39 to 44 degrees, almost 50-percent steeper than a typical "most difficult" ski area run.

Note: Hire a mountain guide for the North Face for $25 per person—a steal of a deal.

♦ **Advanced:** Crested Butte's single-blacks are long, bumpy and fun. The well-traveled ones are under the Silver Queen lift, but the Twister lift is the local secret. Try anything off of that. While it is in the middle of everything, it doesn't get the traffic you would expect. The Double-Top Glades served by the East River Lift are also an experience to be had.

■ **Intermediate:** Crested Butte has added intermediate terrain, all linked by conveniently placed lifts, making it easy to work your way across the mountain to get to increasingly more demanding runs. Warm up on the Gold Link and Prospect lifts, exclusively serving intermediates. From here, head to the Teocalli and East River lifts for yet more isolation from faster skiers. Advanced-intermediates can manage most of the runs down from the Silver Queen high-speed quad. The short and steep Twister and Crystal both have good bailout routes.

Kids can find plenty of fun in the glades off the Gold Link, Prospect and Red Lady lifts—they're more like luge runs though the trees. Keep an eye out for the signs with cartoon characters pointing the way. Be sure to pick up a kids' trail map too.

● **Beginner:** Red Lady Express accesses a nice variety of beginner trails. Wide-open green-circles are plentiful here. For solid beginners and beginner-intermediates this is heaven—all fun runs with no chance of getting in over your head, and few encounters with yahoos going too fast. For a change of scenery, head up Painter Boy Lift and take Gunsight Pass around the back of the mountain to the Teocalli Lift, which drops you off at the top of the same area served by Red Lady Express. Be sure to stop by the midmountain cabin and outdoor seating at the top of the Painter Boy lift when you need a break.

●● **First-timer:** The resort has a terrific learning setup. First-timers are separated into one area for adults and another for kids, each served by a moving carpet. Kids also have a small snow play zone where they can get used to moving around on skis. Practice for a day or two on the three trails off Peachtree Lift before attempting the Red Lady Express. When you're ready for Red Lady, try Houston first since it's the gentlest. Houston also takes you to Painter Boy Lift.

Ride Guide: Crested Butte as a town harbors no prejudice against those who approach the world a little differently—and that reflects in its attitude toward snowboarders. Welcome. Now strap in and get ready for a frickin' ride. Anywhere experts go off the T-bar is good. Just beware, the lift was designed by a sadist—it's a steep, awkward ride, and if you've never done it before, chances are it will bail you on your first try (the resort swears that the new T-bar here will make the ride easier, but that remains to be seen, so we're giving you fair warning). The bonus is that only those truly worthy of riding this terrain make it to the top. The farther out you traverse from the top of this lift, the less likely you are to see people. The downside is that if you want to do laps all the way to the bottom, it'll take you an hour to get back, because you have to ride the slo-o-ow East River Chair. An excellent choice for true hardcores off the T-bar is the 40-degree Headwall. Once again, the farther you traverse, the less likely you are to cross tracks. But *don't* go out here if you are not really a seasoned expert. The 12-inch-by-12-inch sign that reads "Cliff Area" actually means that there is a 400-foot-long cliff band below you. If Teocalli Bowl is open, go there immediately.

Flats are unavoidable here, as they are most everywhere. The really annoying one, though, is near the base of the mountain at the Red Lady Express side. Keep your speed or you'll get stuck on a heinous flat—a quarter-mile long flat.

Parks and pipes

As if the steeps and cliffs aren't enough, Crested Butte has an awesome advanced park along the lower Canaan run. The Canaan Terrain Park, above the Paradise warming house, is long, with good sequences of tabletops, rails and kickers—including a 55-foot monster—that allow for creativity. The wall ride is where you'll really find out just how good you are. Because the park's beneath the Paradise lift, it's the perfect place to collect a bunch of cheers—or jeers—depending on your style.

Crested Butte's 420-foot-long superpipe is also off the Paradise chairlift on Forest Queen. The Zaugg cuts it to be 55 feet wide and 18 feet high with a slope of 17 degrees.

Painter Boy Park at the top of Painter Boy offers solace to those who aren't ready to jump in with the big contenders, -though you'll see some kid riders and skiers here who are pretty hot. Kids as well as adults come here to ride the smaller features and get a feel for tabletops, rail slides and the minipipe.

 ## Cross-country and snowshoeing (see xcskiresorts.com for more details)

Crested Butte is linked with one of the most extensive cross-country networks in Colorado. The **Crested Butte Nordic Center** (349-1707) is located at the edge of town, on 2nd Street between Sopris and Whiterock Streets. About 70 km. of Nordic tracks begin a few yards from the Nordic Center. The center also has an outdoor rink and sledding hill for apres-Nordic activity. There are more than 100 miles of backcountry trails. Group lessons, half-day and all-day tours are scheduled several times each week, but private lessons and special tours must be requested two days in advance.

Snowshoe activities are offered. Snowshoe and cross-country rentals are available. There are also hut-to-hut cross-country and snowshoe trips.

Snowshoe tours at Crested Butte Mountain Resort (800-444-9236; 349-2211) depart from the Crested Butte Mountain Schools. Tour takes about 2.5 hours and includes a snack break. The price includes snowshoe rentals, lifts, guides and snacks. Moonlight snowshoe tours are a fun evening activity for people of all ages and abilities. Cost includes snowshoe rental, snowcat ride and guided tour. The tours are offered only during the full moons.

Lessons (05/06 prices)

Registration and reservations for all programs are at the Ski and Snowboard Instruction desk in the Gothic building, 349-2252 or (800) 444-9236. Most of Crested Butte's professional instructors have received the "New Skiers Retention Accreditation" from the Rocky Mountain Division of the PSIA. Skills acquired through this program let instructors deliver the best first-time lesson possible.

Group lessons: Ski and snowboard clinics are for skill levels 2–5 and cost $73 for a 2.5-hour lesson. Higher levels take specialized workshops to address personal goals, such as turning fundamentals, parallel turns, all terrain, telemark, and racing; cost is $90 for 2.5 hours with a four-person maximum.

First-timer package: A three-hour novice ski or snowboard lesson with lift ticket and rentals costs $99.

Private lessons: $225 for two hours. Each additional person costs $45. A six-hour (all day) private for two to five people is $510.

Special programs: The Family Adventure Clinic is a 2.5-hour lesson for the entire family in which an instructor is a guide to the resort's best attractions. Families choose what's right for them, whether to ski and/or snowboard, play in the terrain parks, try out the bumps, venture into the "Extreme Limits," or cruise the corduroy. Offered daily, the price is $275 for parents and kids.

Kim Reichhelm, a renowned extreme ski champion and former U.S. Ski Team member, teaches multiday women's workshops here. We know Kim and can vouch for her ability to improve women's technique and confidence without scaring them to smithereens. Women's Ski Adventures are offered in February with lodging at The Grand Lodge. The program includes clinics with video analysis, daily off-slope fun, gift bags, product demos, welcome and award dinners, breakfasts and lunches, lift tickets, lodging and more. Call (888) 444-8151.

There are also daily North Face tours for extreme skiers that guide you through some of Crested Butte's most challenging terrain; cost is $30 per person, beginning at 9:45 a.m.

Racing: NASTAR races cost $6 for two runs and $1 for each additional run. Race workshops are offered at the Crested Butte Mountain Schools. NASTAR races are held daily from 10 a.m.–3 p.m. (weather permitting) on Smith Hill and Canaan.

KidStuff (05/06 prices)

Child care: Ages 6 months to 7 years. For ages 6-18 months, cost is $95 for a full day, or $14 per hour. For ages 19 months through 7 years, cost is $92 for a full day, or $12 per hour. The program includes crafts, games, snow play and other activities, but no ski lessons; toddlers have separate programs from the older children. Reservations are strongly recommended; registration and information are in the Kid's Ski & Snowboard World in the Whetstone Building at the base of the Silver Queen Lift; 349-2259 or (800) 600-7349.

Children's lessons: Programs for ages 3–7 include ski rental and supervised day care after the lesson; $107 for a full day (with lunch) or $97 for half day (no lunch). More experienced kids have classes separate from beginners. For ages 8–12, a full day for skiing or snowboarding is $107 (includes lunch); half-day is $97 (no lunch); these prices do not include lift tickets or rental equipment. The all-day Rip Session and Parks and Pipes Session are for ages 8–15, Level 8 and 9 skiers and snowboarders; cost is $175. Race workshops are offered for children. Register at the ski and snowboard school desk. Helmets are required for all children ages 12 and younger who are enrolled in lessons; rentals available.

Special activities: Kids can join ski instructors for a torchlight skiing party down green runs. They'll return to Kid's World for a pizza party, games and kids-only fun. The party goes from 3:45-8 p.m. and costs $30. Kid's World can arrange a "Kid's Night Out" with food, fun and games upon request for groups of five or more. It's offered from 3:45-10 p.m. and costs $45. More evening programs are available; call Kid's World for information and reservations.

Lift tickets [06/07 prices]

	Adult	Child (7-12)
One day	$74	$37
Three days	$213 ($71/day)	$108 ($36/day)
Five days	$340 ($68/day)	$170 ($34/day)

Who skis free: Ages 6 and younger always ski free.

Who skis at a discount: Teens (13–17) pay $56 for one day; $159 for three days; and $255 for five days. Seniors (65+) pay $55.50 for one day; $159.75 for three days; and $255 for five days. Early- and late-season prices are lower.

Accommodations

Most of the accommodations are clustered around the ski area in Mt. Crested Butte. The historic town has a handful of lodges and quaint B&Bs, but they aren't as convenient to the slopes. However, they are less expensive and closer to the nightlife, and offer a taste of more rustic Western atmosphere. A free bus service takes you right to the slopes every 15 minutes, so the primary inconvenience of in-town lodging is the short bus ride. Make sure to ask about lodging packages that include lift tickets.

Crested Butte Vacations (800-544-8448) can take care of everything from your plane tickets to lodging, lift tickets and lessons. It also offers some of the best packages available. Before you make any arrangements, call and ask for the best possible deal.

The Grand Lodge Crested Butte ($$$–$$$$), formerly the Sheraton, is 200 yards from the lifts in the center of the base village. It's the only full-service hotel other than Club Med and the new owners are investing $5 million in renovations, converting half of it into condominium units and renovating the remaining hotel rooms. You'll find an indoor/outdoor swimming pool, hot tub, fitness room, concierge, room service, gift shop and business center here.

Black Bear Lodge (800-544-8448; $$$$), the newest luxury property, features three-bedroom condominiums only 30 yards from the Peachtree lift. The custom condos are spacious and include a gourmet kitchen, fireplace, outdoor hot tub and covered parking.

The Plaza ($$$$), only 80 yards from the Silver Queen superchair, features one of the most luxurious and roomy condominium units in Mt. Crested Butte. There are two hot tubs, a sauna and covered parking. There's also a great pizza joint and pub here, The Firehouse Grill. Kid's World is just 50 yards away.

Treasury Point ($$$$) features luxury four-bedroom townhomes that are spacious and beautifully furnished, and include a garage and a complex with an outdoor hot tub.

The Villas ($$$$), the most luxurious townhouses in Mt. Crested Butte, are just across from the lifts. The units are tastefully decorated and have private balconies.

The Buttes ($$$–$$$$) are well-appointed condos close to the lifts. Rooms range in size from studios to three bedrooms. **The Gateway** ($$$–$$$$), across from the Peachtree lift and about a two-minute stroll from the Silver Queen, may be the best luxury of any condo on the slopes when you trade price for space and amenities.

Wood Creek and **Mountain Edge** ($$–$$$$) are convenient to the lifts, and the **Columbine** is a more moderate ski-in/ski-out property. These three, together with nine others within shuttlebus distance of the lifts, are managed by several agencies, so it's best to book through Crested Butte Vacations (800-544-8448).

The Crested Butte Club Boutique and Spa (349-6655; $$–$$$$) on Second St. in town is the upscale, old-world elegance champion of the area. Seven suites have been individually furnished with Victorian furnishings including double sinks and beautiful four-poster or canopied beds and a fireplace. The amenities include the fitness club, with heated swimming pool, two steam baths, three hot tubs, weight room, and massage and weight trainer. This is a no-smoking property.

The Claim Jumper (349-6471; $$–$$$), 704 Whiterock St., is a historic log-home bed & breakfast and the class act in town. It's filled with a collection of memorable antiques. Bedrooms have themes and are furnished with brass or old iron beds. There are only six rooms rooms, all with private bath. Room rates include a full breakfast. The Claim Jumper can arrange catered weddings and special-occasion receptions.

The Christiana Guesthaus (800-824-7899; 349-5326; $–$$), 621 Maroon Ave., is only a block from the ski shuttle and a five-minute walk from downtown. This has a mountain inn atmosphere and most of the guests manage to get to know one another. The rooms are small, but guests spend a good deal of time in the hotel's living rooms so this doesn't really matter. Let the owners know if you need quiet, because some rooms get quite a bit of traffic from the owner's family and folk using the washers and dryers.

The Elk Mountain Lodge (349-7533; $$–$$$), around the corner from the Forest Queen on 2nd Street, has simple but comfortable rooms, all with private baths. Ask for Room 20 on the third floor with lots of space, a balcony and a great view.

Other recommended B&Bs in town, both of which serve hot gourmet breakfasts, are the flowery Victorian **Elizabeth Anne** (349-0147; 703 Maroon Ave.; $$$) and **The Ruby of Crested Butte** (800-390-1338; 624 Gothic Ave.; $$), newly opened and classy yet dog-friendly.

PR Property Management (349-6281), at 214 6th Street, has rentals in private homes as well as condominiums. For something out of the ordinary, ask for their advice.

Dining

Crested Butte is blessed with more excellent, affordable restaurants than any other resort in the West. One writer noted that the fine dining per capita is highest here of any resort in Colorado. You can dine on gourmet French cuisine in an intimate setting, or chow down on platters of family-style fried chicken and steaks.

The WoodStone Grille (349-8030; $$$) at The Grand Lodge Crested Butte serves well-prepared contemporary cuisine for breakfast and dinner. For a quick lunch, **WoodStone Deli** ($) is good for soup, pizza and specialty sandwiches.

For a full-service lunch, you'll find first-rate Italian fare from soups to desserts at **Rustica Ristorante** (349-2274; $–$$) in the midmountain Paradise Warming House. On warm days, sit out on the deck for spectacular views. Rustica has happy hour, from 2:30 to 3:30 p.m. For a special evening, make reservations for **Dinner@10,000 Feet** (349-2211). A snowcat pulls you in an open sleigh up the mountain for a four-course dinner at Rustica.

For an on-mountain gourmet lunch experience, you'll be delighted by the creative culinary practices at the **Ice Bar and Restaurant** (349-2275; $$–$$$). It's true that "sexy ice babes" serve specialty martinis and by-the-glass fine wines at the deckside bar sculpted from ice. Make reservations for Last Tracks Dinners here through Guest Services (349-2211).

Butte 66 Roadhouse BBQ (349-2999; $–$$) showcases everything from auto grills to sporting gear and whacky signs. It serves breakfast, lunch and dinner.

The Avalanche ($) is another good lunch stop, especially for burgers and grilled sandwiches, and has killer cookies. It also serves hearty breakfasts and some great dinner deals.

Camp 4 Coffee ($) is the locals' favorite hangout and serves the "Best Coffee in Town" with tasty breakfast items, from pastries to breakfast burritos. Find it in the mountain village or at the top of Painter Boy Lift, where it also sells lunch items.

Another option: Make reservations for a **First Tracks Breakfast** (349-2378), where you'll meet at 8:15 a.m. at the Red Lady Express lift for first tracks on the mountain and an all-you-can-eat breakfast buffet.

In town:

The Timberline Restaurant (201 Elk Ave., 349-9831; $$$) mixes a trendy bar downstairs with Mediterranean decor upstairs. Chef Tim Egelhoff combines seasonal products to create a Cafe French Cuisine, whose roots are classic French with a pinch of California and a dash of the Rockies. The menu changes often. The early bird menu, served nightly from 5:30 to 6 p.m., offers a $15 three-course meal. Open Mon-Sun from 5:30–10 p.m.

The Buffalo Grill (349-9699; $$–$$$), near the four-way stop at 435 Sixth St., 349-9699; $$–$$$), specializes in buffalo and beef steaks, free range and organic entrees served with a Western flair. Make reservations—the place is tiny, but filled with atmosphere and one not to miss.

Le Bosquet (Majestic Plaza at Sixth and Bellview, 349-5808; $$$–$$$$; left) serves signature dishes including Colorado roast rack of lamb, hazelnut chicken, and portabella Wellington. This is possibly Crested Butte's finest for formal French cuisine. The early bird menu, served nightly from 5:30 to 6:30 p.m., offers a $20 three-course meal. There's also a bistro menu at its bar.

Soupçon Restaurant (349-5448; $$$) is hidden in the alley behind Kochevar's Bar. This log cabin started at half its current size in 1916 as a private residence to the Kochevars. Soupçon dates back more than a quarter of a century. This place is as romantic as it gets. Chef-owner Scott Greene has created an innovative French cuisine, with menu items posted daily on a chalkboard. Reserve two to three days ahead for one of two seatings, 6 p.m. and 8:15 p.m.

Idle Spur Steakhouse and Crested Butte Brewery (349-5026; $$–$$$) is always crowded and noisy. It offers hand-cut steaks, burgers (including vegetable and elk—sounds better than it is), Mexican entrees and a selection of fresh fish, all reasonably priced.

The chef-owned **Bacchanale** (349-5257; $$–$$$) creates delightful Northern Italian dishes of veal, salmon and homemade pastas. Desserts are fabulous. The antique bar, wrought-iron railings, photography and prints on the walls contribute to a comfortable, classy experience.

Dining: $$$$-Entrees $30+; $$$-$20-$30; $$-$10-$20; $-less than $10.
Accommodations: (double room) $$$$-$200+; $$$-$141-$200; $$-$81-$140; $-$80 and less.

Lobar (349-0480; $$) is like nothing you'd expect to find in Crested Butte, yet for some reason, it fits perfectly. Hidden away in a cellar, this urban sushi and tapas lounge is ultra-chic but also laid-back. Food is exquisitely prepared.

For hard-to-beat group and family dining, head to **The Slogar** (349-5765; $$). It used to be the first bar the miners hit when returning home. Slogar's offers a skillet-fried chicken dinner with mashed potatoes, biscuits, creamed corn, ice cream and even some other extras for a flat price. It also offers a family-style steak dinner. Reservations are recommended.

For other substantial meals, head down Elk Avenue to **Donita's Cantina** (349-6674; $$), where the margaritas are giant and strong and Mexican food comes in heaping portions. Be early or be ready to wait. No reservations. For a quick meal, try **The Last Steep** (349-7007; $–$$), very popular with locals and known for everything from sandwiches to "BBQ Rib Night."

Pitas in Paradise (349-0897; $) is reminiscent of a sandwich shop, only it serves blues on the radio and Greek specialties such as gyros, falafel, wraps and baklava. It has a full coffee bar, wine and beer in addition to your standard drink options. Even after you add a side, you're still coming in under $10, and with huge portions, you won't leave hungry.

There's no doubt that the best hearty, traditional breakfast is found at the **Paradise Cafe** (349-6233; $).

 ## Apres-ski/nightlife

Here nightlife means wandering from bar to bar. The immediate apres-ski action is centered in **Rafters** at the base of the lifts or **The Avalanche**. The slopeside **Coors Light Butte 66 Roadhouse BBQ** in the Treasury Building has apres-ski drink specials and live entertainment. It has the largest and sunniest deck at the base area and the best slopeside mountain view of Crested Butte Mountain.

Then the action begins to move downtown to the **Wooden Nickel**, with some wild drinks, and **The El Dorado**, known around town as "The Eldo" and, according to one local, it has a "smokin' dance floor." **Talk of the Town** is a smoky locals' place with video games, shuffleboard and pool tables. **Kochevar's** is another local favorite where Butch Cassidy and the Sundance Kid used to saddle up to the bar. **The Crested Butte Brewery/Idle Spur** is a microbrewery with live music and dancing on weekends. Brewery tours 2-5 p.m. daily during happy hour.

Duck into the cellar entrance of **Lobar** and discover the uptown side of Crested Butte. Lounge in cushy seating, sidle up to the long bar for drinks and sample sushi and tapas while DJs and live music keep you entertained. On weekends, folks come here to kick up their heels on the dance floor.

The **Princess Wine Bar** at 218 Elk Ave. is the place to finish your night on the town. This *Wine Spectator* award-winning establishment offers a limited menu of appetizers, and a few tempting desserts to enjoy with cappuccino or a fine dessert wine. With no doubt the best selection of quality wines by the glass, the Princess also carries a full list of cognacs, ports and single malts. Come relax by the fire. Open daily from 10 a.m. to "whenever."

 ## Other activities

A **tubing hill** at the base area is open daily after the lifts close. For information on resort activities, call 349-2211. Other winter activities include **snowmobiling, dogsledding, ice skating, sledding, winter horseback riding** with Fantasy Ranch, and **sleigh rides** (with and without dinners) through Just Horsin' Around. Call the Crested Butte Chamber of Commerce at 349-6438 for brochures and information.

Crested Butte Mountain Guides (877-455-2307; 349-5430) offers avalanche safety courses, backcountry guiding, ice climbing, and backcountry gear rentals (beacons, shovels, backpacks and more). Backcountry gear can also be rented at **The Troutfitter** (349-1323).

There are loads of great **shops and boutiques** at the resort and especially in town. Among them: Diamond Tanita Art Gallery for jewelry, glass, ceramics, paper, forged iron and other functional art pieces; Cookworks, Inc., a gourmet kitchen shop; The Book Store, with local maps, Western art and collectibles; and the Milky Way for unique women's apparel and lacy things. The Alpineer has outdoor gear for mountaineering, biking, hiking and backpacking, plus guide services and rentals.

Getting there and getting around

By air: Despite its seemingly isolated location, Crested Butte is quite convenient to reach. The nearest airport is Gunnison/Crested Butte Airport, 30 miles away. It services both jets and commuter planes. New for 2005/06, American Airlines will fly a daily non-stop 757 from Dallas to the Gunnison/Crested Butte Regional Airport. United Airlines offers daily Airbus jet and prop service from Denver International Airport..

Alpine Express (800-822-4844; 641-5074) meets every arriving flight and takes you directly to your hotel or condo. For reservations, call Crested Butte Vacations or the company directly.

By car: Crested Butte is at the end of Hwy. 135, about 30 miles north of Gunnison. Hertz, Budget and Avis operate at the Gunnison/Crested Butte Airport. It's about 230 miles from Denver via Hwys. 285, 50 and 135. From Colorado Springs, take Hwys. 24 West, 285 South, 50 West, then 135 North to Crested Butte.

Getting around: No need for a car. Crested Butte's free town-resort shuttle, running every 15 minutes, is reliable and fun to ride, thanks to some free-spirited and friendly drivers. Town taxi for after-hours travel is available at 349-5543.

Nearby resorts

Monarch, Monarch, CO; (888) 996-7669; (719) 530-5000
Internet: www.skimonarch.com
5 lifts; 670 acres; 1,170 vertical feet

Monarch, smack on the Continental Divide and at a high altitude, is known for powder and more powder. It gets about 350 inches of snow a year, but only about 170,000 skier visits (many Colorado destination resorts get that in just a couple of weeks). That means a lot more untracked snow to play in. The resort caters to families, and has groomed beginner and intermediate terrain for those who don't like the steep and deep. Experts can opt for snowcat skiing and riding on more than 900 acres of backcountry terrain. This area is fairly isolated and without many off-slope activities. Child care starts at 2 months.

Lift tickets (06/07 prices): Adults, $49; children (7–12), $19; seniors (62–69), $26. Children 6 and younger, and seniors 70 and older, free.

Distance from Denver: About 160 miles southwest via Hwys. 285 and 50.

Distance from Gunnison (closest airport): About 35 miles east on Hwy. 50.

Lodging information: (800) 332-3668. Monarch has an overnight lodge 3 miles away; other lodging is in Salida, 18 miles east.

Dining: $$$$-Entrees $30+; $$$-$20-$30; $$-$10-$20; $-less than $10.
Accommodations: (double room) $$$$-$200+; $$$-$141-$200; $$-$81-$140; $-$80 and less.

Purgatory at Durango Mountain Resort
Colorado

Summit elevation: 10,822 feet
Vertical drop: 2,029 feet
Base elevation: 8,793 feet

Address: One Skier Place,
Durango, CO 81301
Area code: 970
Ski area phone/Snow report: 247-9000
Toll-free reservations: (800) 982-6102
E-mail: info@durangomountain.com
Internet:
www.durangomountainresort.com (ski area)
or www.durango.com (town)
Expert: ★
Advanced: ★★★
Intermediate: ★★★★★
Beginner: ★★★★★
First-timer: ★★★★★

Number of lifts: 10–1 high-speed six-pack, 1 high-speed quad, 4 triples, 3 doubles, 1 moving carpet
Snowmaking: 30 percent
Skiable acreage: 1,200 acres
Uphill capacity: 15,600 per hour
Parks & pipes: 2 parks, 1 pipe
Bed base: 3,120 near resort; 7,000 in Durango
Nearest lodging: Slopeside
Resort child care: Yes, 2 months and older
Adult ticket, per day: $59 (06/07 prices)

Dining: ★★★
Apres-ski/nightlife: ★★★
Other activities: ★★★★

Purgatory at Durango Mountain Resort is a hidden gem. It's tucked away in Southwest Colorado in the four corners area, closer to Albuquerque than it is to Denver. It doesn't draw celebrities or the crowds that you encounter at resorts west of Denver. What you will find are more bluebird days than any other resort in Colorado, plus snow that's usually good and often great. And you'll seldom wait in lift lines.

Durango draws heavily from New Mexico, Arizona and Texas. Skiers wearing jeans and cowboy hats, whooping and hollering their way down beginner runs aren't uncommon. The preponderance of intermediate skiers means Purgatory's advanced trails are sparsely skied, so fresh powder remains untracked even longer. Boarders will love the mountain's many terraced runs.

The ski area reaches back from the highway like a 2-mile-long shoulder stretching up a glaciated valley—extensive in its choices once you start exploring. The mountain's only downside is that it's 25 miles north of town, which is where the action is.

Durango's historic downtown is full of great restaurants, brew pubs and galleries. It's a college town as well as a ski town. So if you and your group can't have fun in Durango, well, you'd better just stay home. Inexpensive motels line Main Avenue, and rates for a single can dip as low as $29 a night during the ski season. Families, students, and others on a budget can enjoy a very low-cost ski vacation here.

Purgatory Mountain receives an average of 260 inches of snow per year. Early-season snowmaking efforts here focus on covering a few runs well rather than a large area. The best snow conditions are typically in February and March.

Mountain layout

Thousands of years ago glaciers scraped out the Animas Valley, leaving behind terraced mountainsides. The effect is like a roller coaster ride. The roller coaster effect lures those who love to catch air (yes, there are warnings all over the place, but who can resist?), and those who need a breather will appreciate the flat rest stops. We counted, and you'll get about 10 to 15 turns in before the pancake, keeping terror to a minimum and forgiving the less athletic among us.

◆◆**Expert:** Only experts looking for extremes will be disappointed here. The toughest trail on the mountain is Bull Run, a double-black route that starts off rather gently. Once you're on the lower part of it, there's no getting off. It has a tough pitch as well as funnels and moguls. Bottom's Chute is a nasty surprise. Also try the powder stashes between Peace and Boogie. Tree fans will like the aspens between Pandemonium and Lower Hades.

◆**Advanced:** From the top of the six-pack, what starts out as Paradise soon turns into Pandemonium, a black diamond that gets steeper and bumpier. Likewise, Upper Hades also starts out mild, but turns hellacious once you drop over the headwall onto Lower Hades. Styx, next to the ski area boundary, can be heavenly after a fresh snowstorm.

On the back side of the mountain, Snag, perhaps the most terraced run on the mountain, leads skiers to challenging chutes leading back to the Hermosa Park lift. The Legends lift, as far away as you can go, is home to most of the black diamonds. Poet's Glade and Paul's Park offer nice glade skiing, Elliott's has a nice sustained pitch.

■ **Intermediate:** Despite the mountain's name, this is intermediate paradise—such are the variety and plenitude of trails. Intermediates enjoy endless options for whoop-de-doing at high speeds. There are occasional frustrating flats—some folks call the resort "traversatory"—but for the most part you'll find plenty of fun.

Intermediates seem to prefer the terrain served by the Hermosa Park Express lift. Regularly groomed runs include Peace, Boogie, Where, Zinfandel, and Airmail. Want to ratchet it up a notch? Head down Legends toward Dead Spike, which is frequently split-groomed, with good intermediate "starter bumps" on the ungroomed side.

●● **Beginner:** After graduating from the bunny hill, beginners should head for the Twilight double chair. It serves terrain ideally suited for beginners and families with small children. You won't be endangered by a lot of fast skiers here. The easiest trail is Pinkerton Toll Road, a winding cat track. Divinity and Angel's Tread are wide runs. Columbine winds through several stands of trees, giving beginners the feeling of being deep in the woods. If this terrain is simply too easy, you may want to cut over on Salvation to the Hermosa Park Express, where you'll find groomed intermediate terrain.

● **First-timer:** First-timers have the secluded Columbine Learning Area, with its own lifts, directly across from the lower parking lots. After a couple of lessons on the slopes under the Columbine lift, beginners can ride the Graduate lift to the base area. The "Family Ski Zone" under the Twilight chair is the logical place for beginners to head next, rather than taking the Purgatory Village Express to the top of the mountain. Two cat tracks take you back down to the Columbine beginner area (both trails cross an underpass beneath Sheol Street). There's also a moving carpet for young beginners off of chair 4 in the base area next to Hoody's Base Camp.

Ride Guide: The signature run is Snag, an exciting roller-coaster ride of steep, moderate, steep, moderate pitches—all the way down! Rider-constructed hits can often be found here and at various places beneath the Legends triple. On days with freshies, locals head for the Legends triple, where powder hounds can head into the trees on Poet's Glade or Paul's

Park. From the Grizzly double, a delightful powder pocket can often be found hidden away on Cathedral Tree Way (rider's left off Bull Run). Paradise offers wide-open corduroy for laying out sick carves. Beginners should head for Sa's Psyche, beneath the Engineer lift. It's nicely groomed, gentle-pitched terrain, with only one flat spot. Snowboarders generally avoid the Twilight lift because of lack of suitable terrain.

You'll find flat traverses connecting the front and back side. Getting to the back side requires carrying lots of speed on Hermosa Parkway. Reaching the maze at the bottom of the Hermosa Park lift without having to unstrap and skate requires executing a kamikaze-style run. To return from the back side, avoid the much-too-flat BD&M Expressway. Instead, zigzag: Take Path to Peace, ride up the Hermosa Park Express, Silver Tip it to either black-diamond Cool It or blue-square The Bank, then continue past the bottom of the Engineer lift to Demon. The right side of Demon is a gully that provides a natural halfpipe, but be extremely careful of beginners finding their way home after lunch.

Parks and pipes

Paradise Freestyle Arena features 10 consecutive hits with a 50-foot Big Air competition jump, plus jibbing features with boxes, a rainbow rail, two street rails, a balance beam and "The Serpentine," a 45-foot S-rail. The halfpipe is 400 feet long with 15-foot walls. The park is on the front side of the mountain and runs parallel to the Purgatory Village Express chairlift, with plenty of opportunities to "wow" the crowd. The Pitchfork Terrain Garden, behind the Powderhouse near the Engineer lift, has hits and features for those just starting out or looking to refine their skills in the park.

Cross-country and snowshoeing (visit xcskiresorts.com for more details)

The **Nordic Center** (247-6000 Ext. 114 or 385-2114), maintained by the Durango Nordic Ski Club, is just north of the ski area and across Hwy. 550. There are 16 km. of groomed trails for classic and skate skiing. Nordic skiers find the same undulating terrain as Alpine skiers do, with appropriate terrain for various ability levels. The center offers clinics, races, group and private lessons, rentals, children's programs, daytime and moonlight tours. As part of Purgatory's Total Adventure Ticket™, one Alpine ski day can be exchanged for the Nordic package. There are also guided backcountry and full-moon snowshoe tours, which can be booked through Durango Mountain Resort Ski Concierge in the Purgatory Village Center.

Lessons (05/06 prices)

Reservations are recommended for all lessons; call 385-2169.
Group lessons: $45 for a 2.5-hour morning lesson.
First-timer package: First-time skiers and snowboarders get a full-day group lesson, beginner lift ticket and rentals for $104. The resort guarantees you'll be able to ski or snowboard from the top of the mountain after two lessons or the next lesson is free. Snowboarders also can take the Burton Learn to Ride Program, an all-day lesson with lift ticket and rentals for $104.

Private lessons: $169 for two hours; $249 for three hours; $419 for a full day. A Family & Friends Private for up to four people costs $219 for two hours; $299 for three hours; $499 for a full day.

Special programs: The resort offers clinics for snowboarding, racing, telemarking and mogul techniques. Call for details. The Adaptive Sports Association (385-2163, November–

April) runs one of the nation's leading adaptive skiing programs here. Programs include lift ticket, adaptive equipment and lessons for the visually, physically or mentally impaired.

Racing: NASTAR racing occurs daily at the Paradise Events Arena. Skiers can also opt for self-timed racing for $1 per run.

KidStuff [05/06 prices]

Child care: Ages 2 months to 3 years. Cost is $78 for a full day with lunch and $60 for a half day. Toddlers (ages 2-3) get outdoor snow play, arts and crafts, games, movies and story time. Reservations required; call 385-2149 or (800) 525-0892. If you're not sure whether to put your child in day care or lessons, Durango Mountain's Kids Central, on the second floor of the Village Center, will help assess your child's abilities and interests, then escort him or her to the appropriate spot. **Note:** The day-care staff can recommend a babysitter while you enjoy a night out.

Children's lessons: Ski lessons are available for kids 3-12 years old, snowboarding lessons are for kids 6-12. Full-day programs, including lift ticket, rentals and lunch, cost $79; half day, $63. The program for 3-year-olds includes lunch, indoor activity, and an introduction-to-ski lesson with special skis that attach to snowboots (included in cost). Reservations are required for all ages.

Special activities: The Snowcoaster Tubing hill is the place where kids congregate after skiing and riding, or check out Family Movie Nights in the Community Center.

Lift tickets [06/07 prices]

	Adult	Child (6-12)
One day	$59	$29
Three days	$168 ($56 per day)	$87 ($29 per day)
Five days	$280 ($56 per day)	$145 ($29 per day)

Who skis free: Ages 5 and younger.

Who skis at a discount: Teens (13–18) and seniors (62–69) pay $40 for one day; $123 for three days; $205 for five days. Ages 70+ pay $15 per day. Skiers who book packages through the resort receive discounted lift tickets.

Note: There are early/late season discounts. Holiday day tickets cost $62 for adults; $45 for teens and seniors; $32 for children; and $19 for ages 70+. The resort offers a Total Adventure Ticket™: Guests purchasing a four-day or more ticket can apply credit for a day of downhill skiing against a day of cross-country skiing or one of several vacation activities in southwest Colorado. Call for details.

Accommodations

Durango Mountain Resort has three primary lodging areas. The condos at the base area are the most expensive. A limited number of resort hotels and condos within 10 miles of the ski area are slightly less. Motels in Durango can cost as little as $29 per night, but are 25 miles away. Except on holidays, motel reservations are seldom needed in town. All Durango and Durango Mountain Resort lodging can be booked through **Durango Mountain Resort Reservations,** (800) 525-0892, or the **Durango Area Reservations** (800) 525-8855. Check lodgings online at www.durango.org. Several Durango properties are listed at **Vacation Rentals by Owner,** www.vrbo.com.

Base-area lodging is available at the **Purgatory Village Condominium Hotel** (800-

Dining: $$$$-Entrees $30+; $$$-$20-$30; $$-$10-$20; $-less than $10.
Accommodations: (double room) $$$$-$200+; $$$-$141-$200; $$-$81-$140; $-$80 and less.

693-0175; 385-2100; $$-$$$$), and the following condo complexes: **Angelhaus** (247-8090; $$-$$$$), **Brimstone** (259-1066; $$-$$$$), **East Rim** (385-2100; $$-$$$$), **Edelweiss**, **Graysill**, **Sitzmark** and **Twilight View** (all $$-$$$$). Condos are full-service units with kitchens and fireplaces.

Several other full-service resorts are within 10 miles of the ski area: **Cascade Village** (800-525-0896; $$-$$$$), **Silver Pick** (800-295-4820; $$-$$$$) and **Lodge at Tamarron** (259-2000; $$-$$$$). Most of these outlying complexes offer free shuttles to the ski area.

In-town lodging can be found at the **Hampton Inn** (247-2600), the **Doubletree** (259-6580), which accepts pets, and the **Marriott Residence Inn** (259-6200). A plethora of older, less-expensive motels line North Main Avenue, including the **Day's End** (259-3311). The **Spanish Trails Inn** (247-4173) offers kitchenettes and is across the street from City Market.

Five historic lodging properties are worth mentioning. **The Strater Hotel** (800-247-4431; $$$) and the **General Palmer Hotel** (800-523-3358; $$-$$$) are multistory, brick hotels that date back more than 100 years. Both are in the heart of the walkable downtown area. The Strater has a great Victorian-style hot tub area that would be the envy of many larger, more sophisticated properties and its Diamond Belle Saloon is a classic that's now no-smoking. **The Leland House Bed & Breakfast** and **The Rochester Hotel** (800-664-1920 for both; $$–$$$ for both), across the street from each other on East Second Avenue in the heart of the downtown historic district, are owned by the same family. The Rochester has two dog-friendly rooms. The Leland House has a Durango history theme, with the rooms named after local historic figures. The Rochester Hotel has a Hollywood theme, with each room named for a film shot at least in part in Durango. "Butch Cassidy and the Sundance Kid," "Around The World in 80 Days" and "City Slickers" were all filmed in this region. **Jarvis Suites** (800-824-1024; 259-6190; $$-$$$) at 10th and Main are recently redecorated with a killer view of the action on Main Avenue. Built in 1888, the hotel is on the National Register of Historic Places.

Two B&Bs between Durango and the ski area bear mention: the **Apple Orchard Inn** (247-0751; $$), on Hwy. 203 near Trimble Hot Springs, and **Country Sunshine** (247-2853; $$) near where Hwy. 250 runs into Hwy. 550N. Staying at either would drastically reduce the amount of driving you do.

Dining

There are several options at the base area. **Purgy's Pub** ($) serves burgers, Mexican and pizza in a bar atmosphere. Savor the hearty homemade soups and stews at the **Mountain Market Deli** ($), a local's favorite lunch spot. **Village Coffee Co.** ($) is the requisite coffeehouse and bakery. **Creekside Cafe** ($) serves up breakfast and lunch in a family-friendly atmosphere.

Dante's, at the Grizzly midway station, serves lunch. Upstairs, **Cafe de los Pinos** has gourmet lunches with great views of the slopes and a nice bar. **The Powderhouse Restaurant** beneath the Hermosa Park quad serves lunch fare along Italian themes.

There is good dining along the highway between town and the area. For fresh fish and local game, try the rustic **Cascade Grill** (259-3500; $$$), 2 miles north of the resort. The **Hamilton Chop House** (259-6636; $$$), 10 miles south of the resort in the Lodge at Tamarron, serves excellent wild game, prime beef and seafood. **The Sow's Ear** (247-3527; $$-$$$) at the Silverpick Lodge is famous for its large hand-cut steaks. The **Aspen Cafe** (259-8025, $-$$) in the Needles Country Square is small and casual, but the owner cooks up a fine dinner.

You'll find restaurants of almost every persuasion downtown. Most don't require, nor do they accept, reservations.

Chez Grand-mere (247-7979; $$$) is a delicious taste of France in the Colorado Southwest. Owner and Chef Michel Poumay is one of only 33 living Master Chefs of Belgium's Culinary Society. The little building near the train depot is hard to find, so look behind the Polo Store and the Gaslight Theatre.

Seasons (764 Main Ave., 382-9790; $$$) features rotisserie-roasted dinners (sea bass, trout, chicken, lamb). **Ken & Sue's** (636 Main Ave., 259-2616; $$) is a favorite among locals. Continental fare with a homey twist make for memorable meals. **Ariano's** (150 East College Dr., 247-8146; $$-$$$) serves northern Italian cuisine. Swanky **Randy's** (247-9083; $$-$$$) next door serves just about the nicest prime rib in town and is one of the few restaurants in Durango that accepts reservations. Ask for a curtained booth for a romantic dinner.

The Ore House (147 College Dr., 247-5707; $$-$$$) is an Old West steak house, rustic and casual. **The Red Snapper** (144 East 9th St., 259-3417; $$-$$$) has fresh seafood, by far the nicest salad bar in town, along with an exotic saltwater-aquarium decor. **The Cyprus Cafe** (725 E. Second Ave., 385-6884; $$) offers delicious Mediterranean dishes at quite reasonable prices. Their lamb dishes are to die for.

Award-winning **Francisco's Restaurante Y Cantina** (619 Main Ave., 247-4098; $$) has a Southwestern menu and has been a Durango landmark since 1968. Hidden-away **Gazpacho** (431 E. Second Ave., 259-9494; $$) rivals Francisco's with authentic New Mexican cuisine. **Tequilas** (948 Main Ave., 259-7655; $$), where the waiters all pretend not to speak English, is another local's favorite and serves the finest margarita in town, made with fresh-squeezed limes. Ask for an Especial. **East by Southwest** (160 E. College Dr., 247-5533; $$) has a full sushi bar and Pan Asian cuisine.

Olde Tymer's Cafe (1000 Main Ave., 259-2990; $-$$), is tops for a good hamburger. Monday is burger night, Friday is the taco special. **Christina's** (21382 Hwy. 160 West, 382-3844; $$) offers very reasonably priced continental cuisine. The parking lot is always full, telling you something!

Carver's Brewing Co. (1022 Main Ave., 259-2545; $-$$) is the best place in Durango for breakfast; muffins and bagels are baked fresh daily. Carver's has a nice children's menu—their meals are served on a Frisbee they get to keep. **College Drive Cafe** ($) bakes the best homemade cinnamon rolls (closed Monday and Tuesday). If you prefer the eggs-and-bacon-type breakfast, head for the **Durango Diner** (957 Main Ave., $). Sunday brunch at the **Doubletree Hotel** ($$) is outstanding. Or start the day off at the **Steamin' Bean** ($) a hangout for coffee, chess and chai. **Oscar's** in the City Market South Center is famous for decadent French toast.

 ## Apres-ski/nightlife

After the lifts close, some people meet at **Purgy's Pub,** which sometimes has a band. **Shakers Martini Bar** on the 2nd floor at Purgy's, features top shelf liquors, jumbo shrimp and olive skewers. In general, however, apres-ski is found in town, not on the mountain.

The "locals" spot here is the **Schoolhouse Cafe**, a small and friendly hangout 2 miles south of the resort across the road from the Needles Country Store. This is where the lift ops, ski patrollers and other insiders fill up on beer and calzones the size of footballs. The music rocks, and the pool table is free.

A wa-aay popular apres-ski spot that's available on trade with your Total Adventure Ticket™ is **Trimble Hot Springs** (247-0111), 8 miles north of Durango on the way back from the ski area. Natural mineral springs bubble into two outdoor therapy pools, one heated to 90 degrees and the other to 105. A heated outdoor 50-meter pool awaits lap swimmers.

Dining: $$$$-Entrees $30+; $$$-$20-$30; $$-$10-$20; $-less than $10.
Accommodations: (double room) $$$$-$200+; $$$-$141-$200; $$-$81-$140; $-$80 and less.

If you really want to party, go to downtown Durango—depending on the time of year, it's either jumping or mildly hopping. Spring Break, which goes on for several weeks in March, packs 'em in and the bars schedule lots of entertainment.

Carver's Brewing Co. offers several beers brewed on-site along with a full dinner menu. **Steamworks**, a brew pub on the corner of 8th Street and East Second Avenue, pours award-winning beer and serves moderately priced food in a party atmosphere. **Lady Falconburgh's Barley Exchange** has 20 microbrews on tap and more than 80 different bottled beers. Their Philly Cheese Steak is excellent. **El Rancho** is Durango's old standby. You've got to stop and have at least one drink there, along with a bowl of free popcorn. Other bars have come and gone but "The Ranch" has served liquid refreshment since the days when Jack Dempsey fought his first fight there, although historians now say the fight actually occurred across the street. A mural on the side of the old Central Hotel depicts Dempsey's first TKO.

Durango has quite a variety of musical entertainment. Flyers posted around town will tell you who's playing where. The **Wild Horse Saloon** has dancing and live music. **Solid Muldoon's** is primarily a dance and pool-shoot spot for the college crowd, but worth a visit for the decor. **Coloradaponga's** is a smoky pool hall. **Scoot'n Blues** dishes up soul, jazz, and, of course, blues, blues, blues. Over at the **Diamond Belle Saloon** in the Strater Hotel, a ragtime piano player plunks out hit tunes from the Gay '90s—1890s, that is. The Diamond Belle's waitresses wear vintage-era costumes that are worth the price of a drink to see! Another favorite is **The Office** at the Strater, where the three-martini apres-ski is *de rigueur*. Check out the $11,000 chandelier.

 # Other activities

If you haven't had enough on-slope time, the resort has a SnowCoaster **tubing** hill. Book activities such as **winter fly-fishing, snowmobiling** and **dinner sleigh rides** through the Durango Mountain Resort Ski Concierge.

Durango has two **snowcat operations:** The San Juan Ski Company (259-9671; closed Tuesdays) takes skiers and boarders to 35,000 acres of powder; El Diablo (877-241-9643; 385-7288) provides tours in the San Juan Mountains, including Molas Pass, near Silverton, a quaint Victorian mining town. Reservations are strongly recommended for both.

Durango has a couple of off-slope activities unique in the ski industry. Nearby is one of America's finest national parks, **Mesa Verde.** Anasazi Indian cliff dwellings dating back more than 800 years have been preserved here. Plan an early start for a day trip to Mesa Verde; it's about an hour west of Durango but over a mountain pass.

Another unique activity is the **Durango & Silverton Narrow Gauge Railroad** (www.durangotrain.com). Durango was founded in 1880 by the Denver and Rio Grande Railroad when the line to Silverton was extended in order to haul ore to a smelter being built on the river in Durango, near local sources of coal. Today, the train hauls tourists. Daily in winter, it goes halfway to Silverton then returns to Durango, a five-hour round trip. Though the cars are enclosed, warm clothing is highly recommended. If you purchase a Total Adventure Ticket™, you can exchange a day of skiing for the train ride. The train leaves at noon and arrives back in Durango at 5 p.m., with wine, cheese and hot cider served at the Cascade Wye. Check the schedule ahead of time, just in case.

If you don't have time for the train ride, consider just visiting the **Railroad Museum**. There are antique photographs, locomotives, handcars and putt-putts and rare W.H. Jackson photos. There are several other museums in Durango to visit (call for days and hours). The **Animas Museum** (259-2402), 31st St. & W. 2nd Ave., shows exhibits on area history and

Indian cultures. **Children's Museum of Durango** (259-9234), 802 E. 2nd Ave. upstairs in the Durango Arts Center, has hands-on exhibits for kids ages 2-11. Call for winter hours.

The Sky Ute Lodge and Casino offers gambling and some 380 Vegas-style slots.

Durango's **shops** smack of shabby chic, Old West and unique custom designs. We like The Tulip Tree, a gift shop at 600 Main Ave., and Durango International Fine Arts Gallery on College Avenue for collectibles. The Bookcase, 601 E. Second Ave., offers a fine inventory of used and collector books. The Rocky Mountain Chocolate Factory, which has branches at every Colorado resort, started in this location at the south end of Main Avenue. Durango Custom Hats & Saddles (formerly O'Farrell Hat Company), on Main near the General Palmer Hotel, makes what are acknowledged as the world's finest cowboy hats. You'll have to dig deep in your pocketbook to put one of their hats on your head, though. Real deep. The **art galleries** are first rate. Among our favorites: Sorrell Sky Gallery on Main (on the corner of 9th), Durango Arts Center Gallery Shop at 802 E. 2nd Ave. for local artistry, and Toh Atin Gallery at 145 W. 9th St. for Southwestern art.

Getting there and getting around

By air: The Durango-La Plata County Airport is 40 miles south of Durango Mountain Resort and about 15 miles from downtown. Daily flights on regional jets and prop planes arrive from Denver on United and Phoenix on America West.

By car: The resort is 25 miles from Durango, 350 miles southwest of Denver, 232 miles northwest of Albuquerque and 470 miles northeast of Phoenix. There are no major mountain passes from the south or west. In summary, Durango is a four-hour drive from Albuquerque. It's six-plus hours from Denver in the winter over numerous mountain passes, which frequently close when it snows. Chains or four-wheel drive are occasionally required on Hwy. 550N heading from Durango to the resort during and immediately after major snowstorms; however, 99 percent of the time front-wheel drive is all that's needed.

Getting around: Visitors have several ground transportation options: (1) Rent a car. If possible, request four-wheel drive. The Durango airport has a number of rental agencies. Cars can also be rented at the Strater and Doubletree hotels. Ask about transportation when making a reservation. (2) Some of the larger hotels offer shuttle service to and from the slopes. Others offer free or low-cost airport shuttles. Some lodges on the north end of town offer free nightlife shuttles for guests. (3) Mountain Transport shuttles between town and the slopes, with two departures each morning and two every afternoon. Cost is $10 round trip. Call the resort for departure times and places. (4) Durango Transportation (259-4818) provides on-call taxi service as well as airport pick-ups. (5) Durango Transit buses and trolleys, red minibuses decorated to resemble antique trolleys, provide service within city limits. The trolley trolls Main Avenue. Bus fare is $1, trolley fare is 50 cents.

Downtown Durango is delightfully walkable. Here's something to know when trying to find a Durango street address: Nearly all of Durango's streets have numbered names. The streets parallel to Main are "Avenues" and the numbers usually are spelled out (Second Avenue, for example). The streets that intersect Main all are "Streets" and the number is seldom spelled out. Most tourists hang out on Main between 5th and 11th, and occasionally venture onto Second Avenue. 6th Street is better known as "College Drive."

Nearby resorts

Wolf Creek Ski Area, Pagosa Springs, CO; (970) 264-5639

Internet: www.wolfcreekski.com

6 lifts; 1,600 acres; 1,604 vertical feet

Wolf Creek is the "non-resort" where skiers and riders go to drown themselves in fresh powder, explore the trees and launch off cliffs. Most of the time, you're not on a marked trail and fresh tracks can be found days after storms. This isn't a destination resort with endless groomers, cute shops and activities for non-skiers. It's a gateway to the backcountry.

Because of the tremendous amounts of snow, avalanche control is a big issue. There are gates to access the ridgeline between Treasure Chair and Boundary Bowl, the Waterfall area, Montezuma Bowl, the Knife Ridge Chutes and Horseshoe Bowls. Unlike bigger resorts, Wolf Creek doesn't go out of its way to dynamite every rock, pull every stump, or remove every downed tree, all of which actually improve the stability of the snow pack. They just let the snow bury it all.

The facilities at the base of family-owned Wolf Creek are limited: a ticket office, a cafeteria and bar, a restaurant, restrooms, a tiny ski shop and an even tinier rental shop. But Wolf Creek has a wonderful feel to it. In the cafeteria you'll enjoy homemade soups served from crockpots, and fresh egg salad sandwiches rather than frozen production-line, hockey-puck burgers. On sunny days the patio is popular, and brown-bagging is welcome.

Holy Moses, visible from the lift, only begins to give advanced skiers and riders a taste of what's available. For an even bigger taste, try black diamonds Prospector and Glory Hole. The Waterfall area is served by the new Alberta Lift (formerly served by snowcat). To access the gates leading here, ride Treasure Chair, then follow Navajo Trail or shortcut down lower Glory Hole. Stay slightly skier's right to get to Alberta Lift, which serves only expert terrain off Knife Ridge. The only other way to reach the intermediate Burn Area farther down the bowl is Park Avenue, an intermediate run that's available as an escape route. A bit of hiking will take extreme skiers and riders over to Horseshoe Bowl, the resort's eastern-most bowl.

Advanced-intermediates should head for Silver Streak, Treasure, Alberta and Tranquility off Treasure Chair. Lower-level intermediates will enjoy trails like Charisma, Powder Puff and Windjammer off Bonanza chair. Snowboarders: Don't bother looking for a halfpipe and terrain park; there are none. Take advantage of the natural terrain features instead. Beginners should stick to Dickey Chair and either Bunny Hop or Kelly Boyce trails. First-timers have a moving carpet and beginner's lift in front of the lodge.

We suggest you stay in either South Fork or, preferably, Pagosa Springs (as in Pagosa Hot Springs). Once you get past the slight sulfur smell, Pagosa's 11 different pools, all at different temperatures, are about the finest apres-ski experience there is. They're on the river, suitable for an icy plunge to make your skin tingle. Pagosa Springs has an old-world charm that's hard to describe. And it's inexpensive compared to destination resorts.

Lift tickets (04/05 prices): Adults, $43; children (6-12) and seniors (65 and older), $25; kids 5 and younger, free.

Driving distances: From Durango, 72 miles east on Hwy. 160; from Pagosa Springs, 23 miles; from South Fork, 18 miles. You'll need a four-wheel drive vehicle.

Lodging information: The resort does not have lodging and it doesn't handle lodging reservations, but you'll find a complete listing of nearby accommodations on the resort website. Other resources: Pagosa Springs Chamber, (800) 252-2204 or www.pagosaspringschamber.com; South Fork Business Association, (800) 571-0881 or www.southfork.org/lodging.

Steamboat
Colorado

Summit elevation:	10,568 feet
Vertical drop:	3,668 feet
Base elevation:	6,900 feet

Address: 2305 Mt. Werner Circle
Steamboat Springs, CO 80487
Area code: 970
Ski area phone: 879-6111
Snow report: 879-7300
Toll-free reservations: (800) 922-2722
Fax: 879-7844
E-mail: info@steamboat-ski.com
Internet: www.steamboat.com

Expert:★★★
Advanced:★★★★
Intermediate:★★★★★
Beginner:★★
First-timer:★★

Number and types of lifts: 20—1 8-passenger gondola, 4 high-speed quads, 1 quad, 7 triples, 5 doubles, 2 surface lifts
Skiable acreage: 2,965 acres
Snowmaking: 15 percent
Uphill capacity: 32,158 per hour
Parks & pipes: 2 parks, 3 pipes
Bed base: 18,917
Nearest lodging: Slopeside
Resort child care: Yes, 6 months and older
Adult ticket, per day: $79 (06/07)

Dining:★★★★
Apres-ski/nightlife:★★★
Other activities:★★★★★

More than three hours from Denver, Steamboat isn't just one mountain. It covers a whole mountain range. In the valley below is Steamboat Springs, a classic Western mining and ranching town that now beats to the heart of tourism. Unlike other Colorado ski resorts, Steamboat's expansive terrain -- 3,668 vertical feet covering almost 3,000 acres -- is below timberline, meaning there are no take-your-breath-away bowls or steep rocky chutes.

Steamboat's geographic location near the Wyoming border has several advantages. At the Western foot of Rabbit Ears Pass, the resort is a haul from Colorado's Front Range, so the day-trippers who crowd the Summit County resorts don't fill the liftlines here.

Venture into downtown Steamboat Springs—about five minutes by car and 15 minutes by a free shuttlebus from the mountain—and you may see cowboys sauntering down the main drag. Northwest Colorado still has cattle ranches, so they'll probably be the real thing. But the only horse you'll likely see is a life-sized statue that stands on the sidewalk outside F.M. Light & Sons, a clothing store that has been open (and in the same family) since 1905.

New for 2006/07, resort management has replaced the Sunshine triple chair with a solar/wind-powered high-speed detachable quad—cutting ascent time in half—and added a new trail and expanded snowmaking in this section of the mountain. The resort also added new grooming equipment, including a Zaugg superpipe cutter. Travelers arriving by air will find the Yampa Valley Regional Airport significantly expanded and renovated.

Mountain layout

◆◆ Expert ◆ Advanced: Expert descents here mean trees, bumps in trees and short, sweet bump runs. There are a handful of double-diamond tree runs off Mt. Werner, but they're short, and, while a bit unnerving, totally do-able. Drop over Storm Peak to the Morningside lift to avoid hiking to this terrain. For classic Steamboat trees, look to skier's right off the Sundown Express chair. These aspen and pine groves have been expertly thinned, both by humans and Mother Nature. Sundown Liftline and Shadows seem never-ending.

Elsewhere on the mountain, don't be shy about ducking into the trees, like the space between Concentration and Vagabond on the lower part of the mountain or the "Twisticane" trees between Twister and Hurricane. Once you start looking, you'll see that the entire mountain is one big skiable forest.

The 260 acres that make up Pioneer Ridge off the Pony Express lift have gained a local fan club with long, winding runs. It's fun because Steamboat shied away from the straight-down cut and went with the terrain angles here.

■ **Intermediate:** Among the great cruisers are the blue trails from the Sunshine and Sundown Express lifts (locals call this area "Wally World"), Sunset and Rainbow off the Four Points lift and Vagabond and Heavenly Daze off Thunderhead Express. The Sunshine Chair blues also have spots where beginning tree skiers can practice. If crowds build in any of those areas, take laps on the intermediate runs reached by the Bashor and Christie chairs, which often are deserted.

Longhorn, off Pioneer Ridge, is a locals' favorite with unparalleled views of the Yampa Valley. Skiers and riders can duck in and out of the lodgepole pines that border both sides of this run as they cruise off the Pony Express lift to the base of the Storm Peak Express lift.

On many of the black-diamond runs, although the terrain has steep spots and the moguls get pretty high, the trails are generally wide, allowing ample room for mistakes and recoveries. Westside, a black trail below Rendezvous Saddle, is steep but usually well groomed. It's a good starting point for intermediates who wonder if they can handle the other black runs. If you're learning to do moguls, head for Concentration, marked black on the map, or Surprise, marked blue. Often half of these runs are groomed, while the other half is left to build bumps.

●● **Beginner:** With the exception of some gentle terrain served by the Bashor and the two Christie chairs, most of the green trails above the base area are cat tracks. Wally World's gentle runs often attract classes, though, and you have to forgive skiers and riders who can't turn and stop. Many of the green runs are narrow. Some intersect higher-ability runs where bombers sometimes use the intersection as a launching pad for the next section, and a few have slightly intimidating drop-offs on the downhill side. If beginners are part of your group, encourage them to enroll in a clinic so they will have a pleasant experience.

● **First-timer:** A successful first-time experience—especially for adults—depends on two things: great instruction and suitable, uncrowded terrain. In the past, we've said Steamboat rates highly on the former, but not on the latter. However, the resort has re-shaped the learn-to-ski terrain and improved the grade of the slope and fall line. This learning terrain, at the base of the mountain and separated from other traffic, lets novices totally concentrate on the fun.

Ride Guide: Steamboat's trademark Champagne Powder® snow, which seems to fall in well-timed weekly accumulations, makes this a tree boarder's paradise. Shadows, with its steady pitch and widely spaced aspen trees, is possibly the most perfect tree run in Colorado. And Pioneer Ridge, below Storm Peak, invites exploration, although the long run-out makes a little hiking likely. When the pow blows out (as if), enter The Twilight Zone between the Sunshine and Sundown lifts. It's a difficult gladed run studded with moguls.

If you're lucky, you might run into Banana George Blair, Steamboat's 90-something snowboard ambassador and barefoot water skier extraordinaire. Always clad in yellow, Banana was extreme before the term was coined; he learned to snowboard at age 75. He's cooler than you, so share the love.

For beginning snowboarders, a moving carpet serves the learning area. This section, at the base of the mountain is separated from other traffic so novices can focus on their fun.

Parks and pipes

Steamboat is ranked in the Top 10 in the country for its parks and pipes by several ski and snowboard magazines. Even its "vibe" gets high ratings. The Bashor lift serves both the Mavericks Superpipe and the SoBe Terrain Park. Mavericks Superpipe is a big hit. The resort claims it's currently the longest superpipe on the continent (650 feet long, 50 feet wide and 15-foot walls with 17-foot transitions). There's a mega music system and snowmaking. A 50-foot quarterpipe finishes off the superpipe ride. The SoBe Terrain Park is chock full of features for all ability levels. You'll find 11 jumps with different landings, hips, tables and mailboxes, plus 11 rails including a flat bar, flat-down, rainbow, S-rail and crazy double barrel. Mini-Mav is a 200-foot-long minipipe version of Mavericks with 10-foot walls for beginner riders. There's also a kids-only terrain park, the Beehive, at Rough Rider Basin.

Cross-country and snowshoeing (visit xcskiresorts.com for more details)

The **Steamboat Ski Touring Center** (879-8180) at 2000 Clubhouse Drive has about 30 km. of groomed set tracks along Fish Creek and the surrounding countryside. The touring center has group and private instruction, rentals, a restaurant, and backcountry guided tours. Snowshoeing also is available on 10 km. of trails.

Steamboat offers on-mountain snowshoe tours that meet each Monday through Saturday from the top of the Gondola and are guided by the Steamboat Ambassadors. Bring your own shoes or rent from Steamboat Ski Rentals (879-5444).

Track skiing is available at **Howelsen Hill** in downtown Steamboat Springs (879-8499) and at **Vista Verde** (879-3858; 800-526-7433), **High Meadows Ranch** (736-8416; 800-457-4453) and **Home Ranch** (879-1780). All guest ranches are 18–25 miles from Steamboat Springs. The latter trio cater to overnight guests, but day visitors also are welcome. Vista Verde's 30-km. system is especially good for beginners—most of the terrain is quite gentle. High Meadows grooms about 12 km., with additional trails groomed as needed. Home Ranch has 40 km. of groomed track, and it offers cross-country, backcountry and telemarking.

For a real thrill, take a tour to **Rabbit Ears Pass** (guided tours available through Steamboat Touring Center and Ski Haus, 879-0385); you'll be skiing on the Continental Divide. The marked backcountry ski trails range from 1.7 to 7 miles, from relatively gentle slopes to steep and gnarly, but on a clear day you can see forever. Call or visit the **U.S. Forest Service** (29587 W. US 40 in Steamboat Springs, 879-1722) to get current ski conditions and safety tips. Other popular backcountry areas are **Buffalo Pass, Pearl Lake State Park, Stagecoach State Recreation Area** and **Steamboat Lake State Park**.

Lessons (05/06 prices)

Group lessons: For intermediate and advanced skiers or snowboarders, lessons cost $80 for a full day and $62 for a half day during regular season; cost is $73 for all day and $57 for a half day during value season. Beginners get a first-timer package.

First-timer package: For first-timers and beginners, an all-day lesson, lift and rental package for skiers and snowboarders costs $99 regular season; $94 value season. Half-day lesson, lift and rental package costs $94 regular season; $89 value season. The resort allows novices to repeat the first lesson at no charge until they've learned to descend from the Preview lift in a controlled manner.

Private lessons: During regular season, cost is $170 for a 90-minute Early Bird Special starting at 8:30 a.m., $280 for two hours, $290 for a half-day afternoon, $340 for a half-day morning, $525 for all day. Value season prices are $160 for Early Bird Special, $250 for two hours, $260 for half-day afternoon, $310 for half-day morning and $490 for all day. Reservations required; call (800) 299-5017.

Special programs: First Tracks, Bumps, and Parks & Pipe clinics last from 1.5 to three hours and cost $35–$85. Three-day women's programs cost $330. The Mount Werner Challenge program—a day's instruction in skiing steeps, bumps, trees and powder. The program is available Thursdays and Saturdays for $90. Also new is the Telemark Saturdays program, which introduces you to freeheel skiing. Cost is $90 for the day clinic.

Racing: Steamboat is home to 56 Olympic and world medalists, so it's a natural for racing and competition programs. The resort boasts one of the largest race facilities in the world with NASTAR racing open to the public from 10:30 a.m.-12:30 p.m., Wednesdays through Sundays in the Bashor Race Arena. A daily pass (unlimited runs) costs $10/day. Also in the race arena is a dual race-training course—fun if you've always told your buddies that you would dust them in a race. The course is open from 9:30 a.m. to 3:30 p.m. at $1 per run.

Steamboat also has the Billy Kidd Performance Center, which offers one-, two- and three-day camps on specific dates for adults who are at least of intermediate ability. The camps refine technique in the bumps, through race gates and on tough terrain. One-day camps (Monday or Thursday) cost $225; two-day camps (Thursday–Friday) are $450 and three-day camps (Monday–Wednesday) are $675.

KidStuff (05/06 prices)

Child care: Ages 6 months to kindergarten (usually age 5). Cost is $99 all day with lunch, or $72 half day ($92 all day, $68 half day during value season). Multiday discounts are available. Parents must provide lunch for kids younger than 18 months. Reservations are required for all care programs, and must be prepaid. Cancellations must be 24 hours in advance to avoid being charged. Call the Kids' Vacation Center, 879-6111 or (800) 299-5017. Steamboat's children's programs have been very highly rated over the years by various magazines.

Other options: Baby's Away (800-978-9030; 879-2354) rents and will deliver baby needs to your lodge, such as crib, stroller, car seat and toys.

Children's lessons: Ages 2–5 can opt for a one-hour private lesson and all-day child care for $220, including lunch ($200 value season). Ages 3½–4 who want more time on snow can take all-day clinics that have two to four hours on snow plus playtime and lunch for $104 ($97 value season). Ages 4–kindergarden can get even more time on skis in either a half-day program at $79 ($75 value season) or full-day for $104 ($97 value season). No lift ticket is required for kids ages 5 and younger.

However, lift tickets are extra for all programs listed below (see *Lift Tickets* to see which kids need to pay for a ticket and who skis free). Ages 6–15 pay $99 for an all-day lesson with lunch, or $72 for a half-day afternoon lesson ($92 all day, $67 half day during value season). Classes are grouped according to age and ability. Kids 8 and older who are at least intermediate skiers and riders can take a half-day freestyle park and pipe clinic for $85. Children and teens also have a Desperado Ski and Snowboard Week program for $495 ($460 during value season). The lessons are all day and lunches are included. Kids stay with the same instructor the entire week. Ages 13–17 who are at the intermediate level or higher can join the "Steamboat Teen Ski Challenge" an all-day program (with lunch) offered at select times. The cost is $99 per day. Steamboat also has the Billy Kidd Performance Center for ages 8 and older who are at least of intermediate ability (see *Adult Lessons*).

Group tracking: Kids enrolled in children's programs are issued a Steamboat Mountain Watch, a Wi-Fi tracking device that allows parents to follow their location throughout the day. Kiosks for tracking your child can be found on the mountain and around the resort.

Skiing with your children: Steamboat has five kids-only lifts and two special teaching areas with their own moving carpets. More advanced children have kids-only ski terrain at Rough Rider Basin with its own lift, plus Indian teepees, a frontier-style fort and the Beehive kids' terrain park. One child 12 or younger rents gear free with each five-day parental adult rental; certain restrictions apply. Rentals are available at the Kids' Vacation Center. Helmet rentals also are available.

Special activities: Kids Adventure Club offers a "Kids Adventure Club at Night" for ages 5–12 years every Tuesday through Friday evening from 6–10 p.m. Held in the Kids' Vacation Center, it's a camp environment with supervision, pizza, snacks, games, movies and rest time. Children ages 5–7 can go tubing and children 8–12 are involved in a variety of activities including tubing, a climbing wall and swimming. Reservations are required by 4:30 p.m. on the day of the requested date. Walk-in guests are accommodated on a space-available basis. Cost is $45 per child.

 ## Lift tickets [06/07 prices]

	Adult	Child (6-12)
One day	$79	$49
Three days	$237 ($79/day)	$147 ($49/day)
Five days	$395 ($79/day)	$245 ($49/day)

Who skis free: Children 5 and younger always ski free. One child up to age 12 skis free the same number of days when the parent or grandparent buys a five-day or longer lift ticket. Two kids, two parents, both kids ski free. Three kids, two parents, the third kid buys a ticket at the regular child rate. No blackout periods, even during Christmas. Bring proof of age.

Who skis at a discount: Teens 13–18 ride lifts for $59 a day for up to five days; six or more days, teens pay $55 per day; ID required. Ages 65–69 pay $61 per day; ID required. Ages 70 and older pay $31; ID required.

Note: Early-, late-, and mid-season prices are lower; holiday rates are higher.

Accommodations

In general, staying in the Steamboat mountain village is more expensive than in town. Condos outnumber hotel and motel rooms. Rates vary throughout the season: Before mid-December and after March 31 are cheapest; January comes next, and Christmas and Presidents' Weekend are most expensive.

Steamboat Central Reservations (800-922-2722; 879-0740) will make suggestions to match your needs and desires. Let the reservationist know the price range, location and room requirements (quiet location, good for families, laundry or other special amenities).

The Sheraton Steamboat Resort and Conference Center (800-848-8878; 800-848-8877 in Colorado; 879-2220; $$-$$$), a luxury full-service hotel, sits 60 feet from the Steamboat

Gondola. The Morningside tower condominiums here have two- to four-bedroom units. We love the views and open design of the main living areas.

With spacious one, two- or three-room suites complete with full kitchen, the fairly new **Steamboat Grand Resort Hotel and Conference Center** (877-269-2628; 871-5500; $$$-$$$$) is a great bet for extended families. Traditional hotel rooms and bigger penthouses also are available. For Internet junkies, there is high-speed wireless, but it can be a little pricey ($40 for five days). The hotel is working on extending wireless to all rooms in time for 2005/06. The Grand has a game room, heated pool, complete fitness center and a full-service spa.

Nearly all the other lodging at the ski area is condominiums—hundreds of them surround the base. **Torian Plum** (800-228-2458; 879-8811; $$$-$$$$) is one of the best, with spotless rooms and facilities, an extremely helpful staff, the ski area out one door and the top bars and restaurants out the other. Torian Plum's sister properties, **Bronze Tree** and **Trappeur's Crossing,** have similar prices. Bronze Tree has two- and three-bedroom units. Trappeur's Crossing is about two blocks from the lifts, but offers a free private shuttle from 7 a.m. to 11 p.m. **Timberline** at Trappeur's Crossing and **Creekside** at Torian Plum (800-228-2458; 879-8811). We were knocked out by the mountain-facing views, mountain-style furnishings and the ski-in/ski-out location at Creekside. Ditto (except for views) at Timberline, two blocks from the Gondola, with on-call shuttle service.

Generally, prices are based on how close the property is to the lifts. Among those in the expensive category are the **Best Western Ptarmigan Inn** (800-538-7519; $$$) at the base of the Gondola, **Storm Meadows Townhomes** (800-262-5150; 879-5151; $$$), **Norwegian Log Condominiums** (800-525-2622; 879-3700; $$$) and **Thunderhead Lodge and Condominiums** (800-525-5502; 879-9000; $$$).

Others in this price category are **Timber Run Condominiums** (800-525-5502; 879-7000; $$$) with three outdoor hot tubs of varying sizes; **The Lodge at Steamboat** (800-525-5502; 879-6000; $$$); and **The Ranch at Steamboat** (800-525-2002; 879-3000; $$$), with great views of the ski hill and the broad Yampa Valley.

Moving Mountains Chalet (877-624-2538; 870-9359) has luxury chalets adjacent to the ski area for groups up to 14 people. They arrange all travel, lodging, dining and recreation details ahead of time, including a personal chef and pre-programmed cell phones.

Economy lodging includes **Alpiner Lodge** (800-538-7519; 879-1430; $$) downtown, **Shadow Run Condominiums** (800-525-2622; 879-3700; $$), 500 yards from lifts, and **Alpine Meadows Townhomes** (800-525-2622; 879-3700; $$), just a bit further.

The Steamboat Bed and Breakfast (879-5724; $$$), just a few years old, is at 442 Pine St. This B&B has rooms filled with antiques. Rates include breakfast. No children or pets allowed. **Caroline's Bed and Breakfast** (870-1696; $$), 838 Merritt St., is another good choice for those who like B&Bs.

Travelers who enjoy remote rural elegance will be delighted by a stay at **The Home Ranch** (879-1780; $$$$) in the town of Clark, a 40-minute drive north of Steamboat. This is one of a handful of Relais et Chateaux properties in the U.S. Eight wooden cabins are nestled in the aspens with views of the surrounding mountains. Each is distinctly decorated and has a hot tub on the porch and a wood stove inside. Explore the cross-country and snowshoe trails here.

Between town and the mountain is the pleasant **Iron Horse Inn** (879-6505; $$) offering recently renovated suites with kitchenettes (small but functional) and a two-story building of clean and comfortable hotel rooms.

Some chain motels have shown up in the last couple of years. They're generally scattered in a row along Hwy. 40 just before the turnoff to the mountain. The newest is the **Marriott**

Fairfield Inn & Suites (870-9000; $$). Sixty-five no-frills rooms are a half-mile from Gondola Square on the free bus route. Others include **Holiday Inn** (879-2250; $$), **Hampton Inn & Suites** (871-8900; $$), Inn at Steamboat (879-2600; $$), **Bunkhouse Lodge** (871-9121; $$), and **Super 8 Motel** (879-5230; $$). Or you can stay downtown in the **Rabbit Ears Motel** (800-828-7702; 879-1150; $$) across the street from the hot springs pools. Look for the neon lights in the shape of a bunny's head.

Another option out of town is **Strawberry Park Hot Springs Cabins** (879-0342; $), about 10 miles north of Steamboat at the mineral hot springs. Both covered wagons and cabins are available for overnight stays. Lodging price includes a hot springs pass—lovely soaking outdoors on a winter night. Also on the road to the hot springs, six miles from the ski area, are the **Steamboat Log Cabins** (879-1060; $$) at Perry-Mansfield, complete with kitchens and woodburning stoves.

Dining

Steamboat has great variety: more than 75 restaurants and bars, including one or more Cajun, Chinese, French, Italian, and Scandinavian. Look for the Steamboat Dining Guide in your hotel or condo—it has menus and prices.

One of the most impressive evenings in Steamboat is found at **Hazie's** (879-6111; reservations required for dinner, available Friday through Sunday and holidays; $$$) at the top of Thunderhead via the gondola. Hazie's serves a special continental dinner, with unbeatable views. Cost is $59 for adults, $45 for teens 13–18, and $30 for children 6–12; not appropriate for children 5 and younger. Cost includes gondola ride. You also can have lunch (reservations recommended) daily from 11:30 a.m. to 2:30 p.m. Choose from an assortment of soups and salads, entrees and burgers.

For elegant dining, it's hard to beat **The Cabin** (871-5550; $$$) on the lobby level of the Steamboat Grand. It features contemporary Colorado cuisine for breakfast and dinner and specializes in native Colorado wild game and "jet-fresh" seafood.

Ragnar's (879-6111; reservations required for dinner and suggested for lunch; $$–$$$) at Rendezvous Saddle halfway down the High Noon ski run features Scandinavian and continental cuisine. Start with the baked Camembert tivoli or gravlax with mustard dill sauce. Or, perhaps, try the excellent Norwegian salad with proscuitto, or the traditional Norwegian seafood chowder. Entrees include daily specials. Three nights a week (Friday through Sunday), Ragnar's offers a fixed-price Scandinavian menu at $79 for adults, $65 for teens 13–18, and $50 for children 6–12; not appropriate for children 5 and younger. The evening starts at Gondola Square, but once off the gondola at the top of Thunderhead, you climb into a snowcat-drawn sleigh to continue your journey to Rendezvous Saddle. Price includes gondola and sleigh ride. We recommend a mug of hot spiced glögg before relaxing to music and enjoying the meal.

Western BBQ Nights (871-5150; reservations required; $$$), Friday through Sunday, feature live country-western entertainment, dancing, an all-you-can-eat buffet and a full cash bar, all on the third floor of the Thunderhead Building at the top of the gondola. Cost is $37 for adults, $28 for teens 13–18, $16 for children 6–12, and free for ages 5 and younger.

The **Rendezvous Saddle** building, halfway down the High Noon ski run, has a two-level contemporary food court and large ground level deck where you can get BBQ. **Stoker Bar** (871-5150; $-$$), on the first floor of the Thunderhead Building (at the top of the Gondola), has full-service lunch of soups, chili, sandwiches, microbrews and specialty drinks. **The Bear River Bar & Grill** (formerly known as Buddy's Run), at the base across from the Gondola bay entrance, has very quickly gotten very popular.

Dining: $$$$-Entrees $30+; $$$-$20-$30; $$-$10-$20; $-less than $10.
Accommodations: (double room) $$$$-$200+; $$$-$141-$200; $$-$81-$140; $-$80 and less.

Saketumi (870-1019), pronounced "sock-it-to-me," is a hip spot on the mountain for sushi and Asian fusion cuisine. Open for lunch and dinner.

For Steamboat's pinnacle of French dining, try **L'Apogee** (911 Lincoln Avenue, 879-1919; $$$). While the food cannot be too highly praised, it is the wine list that is truly impressive. This crew also services the more casual **Harwigs Grill** (same address, no reservations; $–$$). Here, the menu reflects a passion for Southeast Asian flavors.

Another fine-dining choice is **Antares** (57-1/2 Eighth St., 879-9939; $$$). Not coincidentally, all the principals are alums from L'Apogee. Serving new American cuisine, this restaurant—named for a star in the Scorpio constellation—is housed in the historic Rehder building, built in the early 1900s. Open daily 5:30 p.m. to 10:30 p.m.

For more than Mex, don't miss **La Montaña,** (2500 Village Drive, 879-5800; $$–$$$). The inventive menu goes way beyond tacos and fajitas. Their guacamole sauce is the house special and, as the song says, simply irresistible.

The **Cottonwood Grill** (701 Yampa Avenue, 879-2229; $$-$$$), downtown on the Yampa River, is owned by Chef Michael Fragola (formerly of La Montaña) and features vibrant Pacific Rim cuisine blending American and Asian flavors with traditional favorites.

A popular seafood restaurant is the **Steamboat Yacht Club** (811 Yampa Ave., 879-4774; $$) overlooking the river. It is perfect for watching night skiing or Wednesday night ski jumping on Howelsen Hill. Its menu is designed to mix and match fish, cooking techniques and sauces to suit your tastes. The Yacht Club is one of the best restaurants for the price in town.

The **Steamboat Smokehouse** (912 Lincoln Ave.; $–$$) has a no-credit card, no-reservations, no-nonsense atmosphere, with some of Colorado's best Texas-style hickory-smoked barbecued anything—you name it—brisket, sausage, turkey, chicken, ham and more. We love that we can toss our peanut shells on the floor and the beer mugs are iced.

Dos Amigos (879-4270; $$) serves Tex-Mex food and sandwiches and is part of the infamous "Steamboat Triangle" apres-ski circuit along with **Tugboat Grill & Pub** ($-$$) and **Slopeside** ($$). **Cafe Diva** (871-0508; $$) is an upscale wine bar with elegant cuisine in the Torian Plum Plaza.

Family recipes are shared at **Mambo Italiano** (870-0500; $$), an inexpensive but excellent diner with 19 different pastas. If you're lucky, the pizza chef will sing for you. **Johnny B. Good's Diner** (870-8400; $), a fifties-style soda fountain, is best known for its chocolate milkshakes and quick service. Also great for breakfast.

Old West Steakhouse (879-1441; $$) has packed in the crowds for years with its generous portions of steak and seafood. You easily could make a meal out of the appetizers. **Giovanni's** (879-4141; $$) has not only Brooklyn-style Italian fare, but also what may be the largest collection of Brooklyn memorabilia this side of the borough. For more casual Italian, head to **Riggio's** (879-9010; $$) on Lincoln. Seafood and veal are especially good, and be sure to leave room for their homemade desserts.

Ore House at the Pine Grove (879-1441; $$–$$$) has served steaks, seafood, elk and buffalo for more than 30 years. **Yama-Chans** (879-8862; $$) is Steamboat's first Japanese restaurant and sushi bar. **Tequilas Family Restaurant** (879-5500; $$) is an authentic Mexican eatery. The helpings are generous (a plate for two actually feeds three with leftovers). Warning: The food is spicy. **Braun's Bar & Grill** (870-1441; $–$$) serves a variety of creative grilled sandwiches and other dishes (Penalty Box burger, anyone?). Think of it as an upscale sports bar. **Mahogany Ridge Brewery & Grill** (879-3773; $–$$), Steamboat's only brew pub, has great brews and superior pub grub.

If you're in town for breakfast or lunch, try the **Creekside Cafe and Grill** (879-4925;

$). Homemade soup, sandwiches and salads are served along with soothing classical music. For some quiet-time and a light lunch (sandwiches, homemade pasta salads and soups) head to **Off The Beaten Path** bookstore and coffeehouse (879-6830; $).

Other good downtown breakfast spots are **Winona's,** where the lines form early and often, or **The Shack Cafe. The Tugboat Grill & Pub** at the base area is also good. For high-carb breakfasts try **Market on the Mountain,** in the same complex as La Montaña, for homemade muffins, cinnamon rolls and bagels (and deli sandwiches for lunch); **Mocha Molly's,** serving muffins, bagels and designer coffees at both the ski area base and in town; or **Jitter's** in Gondola Square for smoothies, designer coffees, bagels and bagel sandwiches. Avid skiers can board the gondola at 8 a.m. and have breakfast at **The Early Bird Breakfast Buffet** up top until the slopes open. Biscuits and gravy are a specialty, with other high-fuel fare.

 ## Apres-ski/nightlife

Dos Amigos, as already noted, is one leg of the "Steamboat Triangle." Have margaritas here, then head for **Slopeside** and **The Tugboat Grill & Pub** for beer or mixed drinks. **Chaps,** in the Steamboat Grand, is a Western-themed bar and grill with live entertainment most evenings throughout the winter. A quieter apres-ski on the mountain can be found at **Three Saddles** in the Sheraton. Formerly HB's, it had a makeover a few years ago and is now a wide-open, great-view kind of place. Downtown, the **Old Town Pub** and **Mahogany Ridge** have great-apres ski.

Sandwiched between Dos Amigos and Tugboat is a three-tiered building that you never have to leave. The main floor houses **Wired,** an Internet cafe by day and a martini bar by night. After 5 p.m. you can slurp a Mango Tango Tini, Dreamsicle or Slippery Banana from an extensive menu. Jocks can hit the sports bar, **Lupo's,** on the second level; and later the third story comes alive at **Levelz Nightclub,** where live bands play for late-night dancing. Downtown, the lively spots include **The Tap House, Steamboat Smokehouse, Mahogany Ridge** and **The Old Town Pub**.

Other activities

Steamboat has so much to do off the mountain, it's tempting to skip the skiing. Here is a mere sampling:

Soak in the natural thermal waters at **Strawberry Park Hot Springs** (879-0342), about 10 miles north of the ski area. Unless you have four-wheel drive, spend extra for a tour that includes transportation—the road to the springs is narrow, slick, steep and winding, and parking is extremely limited. It's open from 10 a.m. to 10 p.m. during the week and stays open a little later on weekends. Helpful info: After dark, many bathers go without suits (unless it's a moonlit night, you won't see much), and Wednesdays are often designated as "clothing optional" days/nights. The only place to change is an unheated teepee, so wear your swimsuit under your clothes. Many people bring a plastic bag to store their clothes; otherwise steam from the pools combined with the cold air may freeze them. Water shoes will protect your feet from the rocky entry. Beverages are OK as long as they aren't in a glass container.

Families might prefer the Steamboat Health and Recreation Center (879-1828) in downtown Steamboat, with lockers, **workout rooms, hot springs pools, lap pools** and a huge **waterslide.**

Day spas we recommend are Rocky Mountain Spa (870-9860) on Burgess Creek Rd. at the mountain; Life Essentials (871-9543) downtown; Sol Day Spa (871-9765) in the Sheraton Hotel; and Bear River Therapists (879-8282). The Steamboat Grand (871-5514) also has a

Dining: $$$$-Entrees $30+; $$$-$20-$30; $$-$10-$20; $-less than $10.
Accommodations: (double room) $$$$-$200+; $$$-$141-$200; $$-$81-$140; $-$80 and less.

full-service spa. Ask for their signature treatments and enjoy.

Learn to drive on slick roads at the **Bridgestone Winter Driving School** (800-949-7543; 879-6104). Half-day, full-day and multiday lessons on a specially constructed course are a unique experience, one that could save your life.

Steamboat Powdercats (877-624-2538; 870-9359) offers **deep powder cat skiing and boarding** in the Steamboat vicinity. Runs vary in length from 600 to 1,600 vertical feet and in steepness from 20 to 45 degrees.

Other activities include weekend **theater** from the Steamboat Community Players (879-3254), **dogsled rides** (879-4662), **ice skating** at Howelsen Ice Arena (879-0341), **ice climbing** (879-4857), **indoor climbing** (879-5421), **indoor tennis** (879-8400), **snowmobile touring, tubing, horseback riding** and **hot-air balloons** (several businesses offer these last two activities, ask when you get into town), and far too many more to list. You can make reservations for activities through **Steamboat Central Reservations** (800-922-2722; 879-0740), or **Windwalker Premier Tours** (800-748-1642; 879-8065).

Shopping opportunities are many and varied, both in the village and downtown. The Sports Stalker (879-0371) at Gondola Square rents ski clothes, mainly courtesy of the airline that lost your luggage. Steamboat's **movie theaters** are downtown and at the mountain.

Getting there and getting around

By air: Yampa Valley Airport at Hayden, 22 miles away, handles jets. American, Continental, Delta, United and Northwest have nonstop flights from nine U.S. cities, plus one-stop connecting service from many more. Three ground transportation companies provide service from the airport and from Denver International Airport—Alpine Taxi/Limo (879-2800), Western Coach 4x4 Limo (870-0771), and Mountain Luxury Limousine (879-0077). Avis, Budget and Hertz have cars available at the Yampa Valley Airport.

By car: Steamboat is 157 miles northwest of Denver. Take I-70 west through the Eisenhower Tunnel to exit 205 at Silverthorne (allow extra time if you want to stop at Silverthorne's factory outlet mall), north on Hwy. 9 to Kremmling, then west on Hwy. 40 over Rabbit Ears Pass to the resort.

Getting around: A car is optional. Steamboat has an excellent free bus system between town and ski area running every 20 minutes. Call 879-5585 for information.

Telluride
Colorado

Summit elevation:	12,260 feet
Vertical drop:	3,535 feet
Base elevation:	8,725 feet

Address: 565 Mountain Village Boulevard
Telluride, CO 81435
Area code: 970
Ski area phone: 728-6900
Snow report: 728-7425
Toll-free reservations: (866) 287-5016
or (800) 525-3455
Fax: 728-6228
Internet: www.tellurideskiresort.com (resort)
www.telluride.com (visitors' guide)

Expert:★★★★★ **Advanced:**★★★★★
Intermediate:★★★★
Beginner:★★★★★
First-timer: ★★★★★

Number and types of lifts: 16—2 gondolas,
7 high-speed quads, 2 triples, 2 doubles,
2 surface lifts, 1 moving carpet
Skiable acreage: 1,700 acres
Snowmaking: 15 percent
Uphill capacity: 21,186 per hour
Parks & pipes: 2 parks, 1 pipe
Bed base: 5,300
Nearest lodging: Slopeside
Resort child care: Yes, 2 months and older
Adult ticket, per day: $73-$76 (05/06)

Dining:★★★★
Apres-ski/nightlife:★★★
Other activities:★★★★

Telluride is at the crossroads of colliding worlds. The bottom of the box canyon in which Telluride sits is red-rock desert, while the mountains tumbling into town are snowcapped and craggy Alpine granite. There's the Old West town of Telluride and the contemporary Mountain Village. One is a pageantry of Victorian buildings wearing bright and bold colors. The other is formed from rock and log, dressed in muted earth tones.

Mountain Village, partway up the mountain, is hunkered in at 9,540 feet above sea level, while the town of Telluride rests at the very bottom of the trails at 8,725 feet. Skiing down any of the front runs that drop into town feels as if you're going to land on someone's doorstep. The free 2.5-mile gondola links the town of Telluride with Mountain Village, making it a cinch to go back and forth between the two for shopping or dining.

Telluride certainly is one of the most breathtaking environments for a ski resort. Be prepared for recreating at high altitude, with lifts dumping you off as high as 12,260 feet. Perhaps the most delightful surprise about Telluride is that it's one of the few North American resorts that can truly be a remarkable vacation for just about everyone, regardless of skill level. From a copious amount of gentle learning terrain to ideal powder training grounds for intermediates, it seems downright greedy to ask for more. As for advanced skiers and riders, whether you get your thrills ripping down steep trails that spit you out into town, or you long for the solitude of high-mountain peaks with no hint of civilization, it's here waiting. Those venturing into the backcountry have much to choose from, too, including a couple peaks topping 14,000 feet.

Everyone here is quick to spin tales about Telluride's fascinating history, from Butch Cassidy robbing the bank to the first miners strapping on a pair of 7-foot-long skis to glide down the mountain. It's all woven into the fabric of life and as authentic as it gets. Skiing replaced the ailing mining industry in the early 1970s, saving the small community from becoming a ghost town. It also saved its rich past, preserving the entire town in a National Historic District that's worth the visit alone.

Mountain layout

♦♦ Expert ♦ Advanced: Ask locals where to head first, and you'll get a split decision: Some recommend the front face that drops into town, which put Telluride on the skiers' map in the first place. Others steer you to Gold Hill and Prospect Bowl, newer terrain that practically guarantees Telluride will *stay* on the skiers' map. Frankly, wherever you start, you'll end up doing it all and having a ball, so in the end, it's a moot point.

If you start on the front face, The Plunge and Spiral Stairs will make you or break you. This duo is as challenging a combination of steep bumps as you can find anywhere. The best part is the audience on the chair. The Plunge is normally split-groomed, creating one of the steepest and most daringly exciting snow highways we've seen, and if your knees give out, you can bail out. Whatever you do, don't let the jaw-dropping view into town distract you. The face is swathed in other worthy double- and single-diamond trails as well, most with VW-sized bumps, so go ahead and give those knees a real workout.

If you prefer more of a backcountry experience, Gold Hill and Prospect Bowl will suit you just right. The 450 acres of glades and above-timberline skiing on Gold Hill are sure to please. Do laps on these double-diamond runs by riding the Gold Hill lift, which dumps you off at the 12,260-foot mark, Telluride's highest lift-served terrain. If it's a clear day after a big storm, take a nanosecond to admire the magnificent view before dropping in. In Prospect Bowl, the expert terrain is off Prospect Ridge and Bald Mountain, and it's all hike-to but within bounds. On a powder day, the blues back here are delightful even for more accomplished skiers and riders. Keep an eye out for trees to duck in and out of. For those who are properly equipped, Telluride also has backcountry access points off the top of the Gold Hill and Prospect Bowl chairs.

■ Intermediate: It's hard to complain when several lifts are pretty much dedicated solely to intermediate terrain. On a powder day, confident intermediates should make a beeline to Prospect Bowl. Here you'll get a lift-served backcountry experience that will make you feel like a highly accomplished skier or rider. Sandia, Magnolia and Stella let you rock 'n roll down the middle of the bowl, with sections of glades to explore if you're game.

See Forever—Telluride's aptly named signature run—is a glorious glide down the mountain, almost 3 miles top to bottom. If you're tired, it seems like it takes forever, but there's plenty of superb spots to stop and enjoy the view. On a clear day you can see the mountains of Utah.

The terrain off the Palmyra and Village chairs can keep you happy all day long. With names like Peek-a-Boo, Misty Maiden and Butterfly, you've just gotta let 'em run! If you want to try your luck in powder, Prospect Bowl is about as good as it gets.

If the single-diamonds on the front face have been groomed, they are acceptable for strong intermediates ready to improve their skills. If they haven't been groomed, the moguls make these steep runs really tough and you'll want to stick to the blues instead.

●● Beginner: Telluride is one of the top spots on the continent for beginners. Ute Park—the learning area in Prospect Bowl—has trail names that tie into the resort's mining past, like Galloping Goose, May Girl, Nellie and Little Maude. The Sunshine chair serves terrain that's a great ego booster once you've learned to link your turns. The runs are long and very gentle, allowing you to meander back to the lift.

● First-timer: The Meadows is about as perfect a novice area as you can find. It's completely separated from other terrain. The lift here is a Chondola, a hybrid high-speed quad with gondola cars also on the cable.

Ride Guide: For advanced gladed areas, check out the trees between Allais Alley and Silver Glade. For riders who get their fix with bowl skiing and deep powder, Gold Hill and Prospect Bowl give you the ultimate in big-board freeriding. Near the bottom of Prospect Bowl, you'll want to carry your speed so you don't end up hoofing to the lift. Intermediates will enjoy short runs off the Palmyra chair including Dew Drop (look for hits), Ophir Loop and Silver Tip. Avoid Cake Walk when you're done riding this lift. Instead, ride it back to the top then stay rider's right and pick up the Apex chair. You can then ride See Forever back to the gondola or drop off the front into town. Too-flat runs for snowboarders to avoid include Bridges and Galloping Goose off the Sunshine chair.

Parks and pipes

Telluride's Air Garden Terrain Park, with three distinct lines for all ability levels, has more than 11 acres and 480 vertical feet of berms, banks, rails, funboxes, A-frames, tombstones and tabletops. There's also a superpipe with 18-foot walls. Get there by riding the Village lift or the gondola. The Air Garden Yurt is at the top of the superpipe and offers riders a crankin' stereo system and excellent views of the park while taking a break. Newbies might want to get their park baptism in a learning park with rollers and berms off the Ute Park lift.

If you want, you can skip the manmade and head to the Plunge lift. East and West Drains form two natural halfpipes that are 2,000-feet and 4,000-feet long respectively. In addition, there's a 1,200-foot natural quarterpipe on Bushwhacker.

Cross-country and snowshoeing (visit xcskiresorts.com for more details)

The spectacular scenery in Telluride makes cross-country skiing pure joy to experience. For high-mesa cross-country skiing this area is tough to beat. The **Telluride Nordic Center** (728-1144) offers a 30-km. network of groomed trails around town and the ski area.

Lessons, rentals and full-day backcountry tours are available. If you'd like to ski the intermediate and advanced groomed Nordic trails at Magic Meadows at the top of the Sunshine chair, buy a ticket at the downhill-ski-area ticket windows.

The San Juan Mountains set the stage with spectacular scenery for guided tours of a five-hut, 68-mile network of intermediate and advanced trails. While the **San Juan Hut System** (728-6935) is recommended for intermediates, you should really be a strong intermediate in good physical shape. You can tour the entire route or make individual huts your destination. Huts, about 6 miles apart, are equipped with padded bunks, propane cooking appliances and big potbelly stoves. Skiable terrain around the huts ranges from bowls, chutes and trees to gentle slopes. Guides are available for groups, with a maximum of eight skiers.

Lessons (05/06 prices)

Telluride's school has a good reputation. A successful learning experience requires two things: good instruction and appropriate terrain. Telluride has both. Clinics operate out of the Mountain Village Activity Center, a one-stop facility that has lift tickets, lessons, full-service rental shop, overnight equipment storage, children's ski school and child care. Peak/holiday rates are higher. A computer system links Telluride Sports' six rental shops and permanently stores client information so future rentals can be paperwork-free and equipment can be returned to any shop.

Group lessons: All-day group lessons cost $98; two-hour morning clinics are $50.

First-timer package: $119 for skiers or snowboarders, includes a full day of lessons, lifts and rentals; three-day program costs $189. Nordic and telemark are offered only on certain days; call for specifics.

Private lessons: $225 for early bird or late riser; $315 half day; $515 full day.

Special programs: Many, including a highly acclaimed Women's Week program that offers lifts, races, video analysis, seminars, parties and more. Call for dates and cost; reservations required. Adaptive and telemark clinics also available; call for details.

Racing: Run the NASTAR course for $3 per run or $9 for five runs. The course is near the Smuggler Express lift. A self-timed course is $1 per run.

KidStuff (05/06 prices)

Child care: Ages 2 months to 3 years. Cost for infants 2–11 months, $79 for a full day with lunch; $62 for a half day. For toddlers 1–3 years old, $72 for a full day with lunch; $55 for a half day. Reservations are required; call 728-7531 or (800) 801-4832 at least 24 hours in advance or make reservations at telluridekids.com. Children's ski and day-care programs are in the Village Nursery and Children's Center in the Mountain Village Activity Center. There's one staff person for every two infants and one staff person for every five toddlers. The activity center's glass kiosk atop the nursery's central playroom allows parents to peer down at their little ones without being seen.

Other options: Travelin' Tots (728-6618) is a retail store that rents cribs, linens, toys, joggers and more to avoid packing hassles; evening child-care referrals also are available.

Children's lessons: The Children's Ski & Snowboard School teaches kids ages 3–12 (snowboard lessons are offered for kids 7–12). Lessons, lift and lunch are $105–124 a full day, with multiday discounts. With lessons, rentals cost an additional $20. Half-day lessons are available. Helmet rentals cost $7. Reservations required for lessons; call (800) 801-4832 or make reservations at telluridekids.com.

Special activities: A supervised program called Afternoon Kids Club is available after ski school programs; it's free for those enrolled in ski school. It runs from 3–4 p.m. and reservations are required. Wildlife Day introduces kids to animals from the Rocky Mountain Ark, a wildlife rehabilitation facility and licensed non-profit organization. Kids are exposed to rehabilitated wild animals in a safe, fun and informative environment. Houdini, a prairie dog, or Liberty, a bald eagle, are just a few of the creatures the children might encounter during lunch hour. Weekly and holiday story readings are held throughout the year at the Wilkinson Public Library(728-6613). The library also has computers with a selection of interactive CDs and Internet access.

Lift tickets (05/06 prices)

	Adult	Child (6-12)
One day	$76	$45
Three days	$228 ($76/day)	$135 ($45/day)
Five days	$365 ($73/day)	$225 ($45/day)

Who skis free: Ages 5 and younger.

Who skis at a discount: Seniors 65 and older pay $54 per day (rounded to nearest dollar). To get discounts on multiday tickets, you must book them online at least seven days in advance, in which case, adults pay $217 ($72/day) for three days and $323 ($65/day) for five days.

Accommodations

In Telluride you can stay down in the historic town or in the Mountain Village. We start with some of our favorite spots in town; lodging in the mountain village is listed afterwards. Both **Telluride Resort Reservations** (866-287-5016) and **Telluride Central Reservations** (800-525-3455) are good places to start if you're not sure where you want to stay. Make sure to ask about lodging packages and specials. The resort's website also carries lodging deals.

Franklin Manor (800-537-4781; 728-3001; $$$–$$$$) could say its middle name is romance. Named for artist Richard Franklin, the manor showcases his neo-classical works in a gallery and all five uniquely decorated bedrooms. **The San Sophia Inn & Condominiums** (800-537-4781; 728-3001; $$–$$$$) is near the gondola and the Oak Street lift. This cozy inn is considered one of Telluride's best, with exceptional service.

A luxury spot is **The Hotel Columbia** (800-201-9505; 728-0660; $$$–$$$$), right at the Telluride base of the gondola. It was built to look historic, but with the space and amenities of modern hotel rooms, such as fireplaces, big beds, a rooftop hot tub and luxurious bathrooms. The hotel has an office for guests' use, equipped with fax, copier and computer.

Ice House Lodge & Condominiums (800-544-3436; 728-6300; $$$$), a block from the gondola, showcases custom furniture, antique Navajo rugs and 6-foot tubs. Adjacent condos have full kitchens and two or three bedrooms. Amenities include a continental breakfast, apres-ski goodies, outdoor heated pool, hot tub and steam room. In stark contrast to the town's prevalent Victorian theme, **Camel's Garden Resort Hotel & Condominiums** (888-772-2635; 728-9300; $$$$), in the gondola plaza, is a contemporary structure. The ski-in/ski-out luxury property sports understated elegance with handcrafted furniture, Italian marble bathrooms, oversized tubs and fireplaces. Views from the outdoor 25-foot hot tub are spectacular.

The elegant **Hotel Telluride** (866-468-3504; 369-1188; $$$–$$$$) is on the western edge of town. Be prepared to be pampered, from the featherbed and down comforter to the granite countertops and Italian tile in the bathrooms. A spa is on the premises (see *Other Activities*), as well as a bistro.

The **New Sheridan Hotel** (800-200-1891; 728-4351; $$–$$$$) was lovingly restored for its 100th birthday in 1995. Rich dark colors, period Victorian furniture and black-and-white pictures from Telluride's past make a stay here feel authentic. Breakfast, an open pantry with snacks and drinks, and free Internet access are included in the price. **Bear Creek Inn** (800-338-7064; 728-6681; $$–$$$$), in a brick building on Colorado Avenue, has 10 rooms with private bath and TV, roof deck, sauna and steam room. Continental breakfast is included.

The Victorian Inn (800-611-9893; 728-6601; $$–$$$$), one block from the gondola, recently remodeled 14 of its 32 rooms, some with kitchenettes. Amenities include a complimentary continental breakfast, outdoor hot tub and sauna.

If you like seclusion, the **Skyline Ranch** (888-754-1126; 728-3757; $$) is 8 miles outside of Telluride. Choose between no-smoking rooms and cabins. The meals are outstanding. Hot full breakfast and apres-ski munchies are included in the price. Even if you don't stay here, come one night for a sleigh ride dinner; it's a tradition. Transportation into Telluride is provided.

All the condos below are managed by **ResortQuest at Telluride,** (877) 826-8043. **The Riverside Condos** ($$$–$$$$) are perhaps the nicest in town and near the base of the gondola. **Manitou Riverhouse** ($$$$) is just as close to the lifts, but be ready for lots of stairs if you rent here. Around the Coonskin Base check into **Viking Lodge** ($$$–$$$$), **Etta Place** ($$$–$$$$) and **Cimarron Lodge** ($$$$), where you can almost literally fall out of bed and onto the lifts.

Dining: $$$$–Entrees $30+; $$$–$20-$30; $$–$10-$20; $-less than $10.
Accommodations: (double room) $$$$–$200+; $$$–$141-$200; $$–$81-$140; $-$80 and less.

In the Mountain Village

Everything in the Mountain Village is recently built and luxury is a given.

Smartly showcasing its Southwestern flair, **The Peaks at Telluride** (800-789-2220; 728-6800; $$$$) pampers with spacious rooms, down bedding, terrycloth robes, oversized tubs and marble double-sink vanities. The ski-in/ski-out resort hotel has one of the largest full-service spas in the country and guests have daily spa access (see *Other Activities*). Children 16 and younger stay free in their parents' room. Pets are permitted, and the spa has programs just for them.

The highly praised **Inn at Lost Creek** (888-601-5678; 728-5678; $$$$) is a rustic, yet classic, slopeside lodge with 32 unique rooms that include fireplaces, jetted tubs and steam showers, plus two roof-top hot tubs, topnotch guest service and the 9545 restaurant (see *Dining*). The great room, crafted of stone and weathered timber, is warmly inviting. **Aspen Ridge Townhomes** (888-707-4717; $$$$) feature three-bedroom units with saunas, steam showers, hot tubs and fireplaces. **Bear Creek Lodge** (866-538-7731; $$$$) looks like a high-Alpine chalet crossed with a rustic mountain lodge with its peaked roofs mimicking the mountain peaks around it. Each unit has a jetted tub, washer and dryer, and a gourmet kitchen. Plus it also has two outdoor hot tubs and a heated pool, a fitness center and an indoor hot tub.

Mountain Village has many **condos,** some of which start at $200 per night (double that for the ones closest to the lifts) and top out around $800. Call **ResortQuest Telluride** (877-826-8043) for more information.

Regional Lodging Program

Telluride has a Regional Lodging Program with seven neighboring towns. If you stay in one of these spots, you can get discount lift tickets throughout the season, saving up to 41 percent. The towns, their distance from Telluride and the number to call are: Cortez/Dolores/Rico/Mancos, four towns 25–70 miles away, (800) 253-1616; Montrose, 65 miles, (800) 348-3495; Ouray, 47 miles, (800) 228-1876; and Ridgeway, 37 miles, (800) 754-3103. Durango, which is nearer to Purgatory at Durango Mountain Resort, also is part of this program, (800) 228-1876. Durango is 125 miles from Telluride and just 25 miles from Durango Mountain Resort. If you want to do both resorts on one trip, it might be worth a call to this program.

Dining

Dining in Telluride and the Mountain Village is as much of an inspiring experience as the skiing and riding. It's hard not to have a good meal here, even in the simpler restaurants and cafes.

In town

An award-winning wine list, elegant surroundings and New American creations make **Harmons** (728-3773; $$$) in the train depot a perennial favorite. The menu changes often.

Chef-owner Mark Reggiannini and his wife Mairen have taken over **La Marmotte** (728-6232; $$$) after the death of its longtime owner. It continues to serves French cuisine, but with a modern twist that's influenced by the chef's New England roots. **221 S. Oak** (it's both the name and address; 728-9507; $$$), in a peach-walled Victorian house, is subtly chic with regional American dishes that vary nightly according to the freshest ingredients available.

Chef-owner Chad Scothorn, known for making Beano's in Vail such a treasure, is at the helm of **The Cosmopolitan & Tasting Cellar** (728-1292; $$$) in the Hotel Columbia at the gondola base. His eclectic American fare is influenced by French, Southwestern and Thai flavors and served in generous portions. **Rustico Ristorante** (728-4046; $$–$$$), on Telluride's main street, is run by Italian natives and has authentic food at good prices. In addition to pasta, it serves homemade foccacia and a tiramisu worth the fat grams. You can even practice your *grazies* and *pregos* with the waiters.

Dine on seafood and steaks at **The Bluepoint Grill** (728-8862; $$), then go downstairs to The Noir Bar, a cozy after-hours martini and wine lounge with leather and faux-fur furniture. **New Sheridan Chop House** (728-9100; $$$) has a relationship with Niman Ranch, known for delectable naturally raised meats, so it's no surprise that the beef, pork and lamb dishes here are excellent. It's a delightful extra that the seafood and wild game are just as tasty.

Excelsior Cafe (728-4250; $$) has good-value North Italian cuisine and a late-night menu. **Sofio's** (728-4882; $$) is a long-time Mexican tradition, but be prepared for a wait. It's worth it—have a margarita. The only brewpub in town is **Smuggler's** (728-0919; $–$$) where pub grub is served in an historic mining warehouse. Friday and Saturday nights are "Rib Nights" with prime rib or baby back ribs. **Shanghai Palace** (728-0882; $$) has a humongous Chinese menu.

Looking for French pastries, Belgian chocolates, homemade soups and sandwiches, or an apres-ski glass of wine? You'll find it at **Wildflour** (728-8887; $–$$), a gourmet bakery in Camel's Garden Resort Hotel by the gondola. **Baked in Telluride** (738-4775; $–$$), known by its acronym B-I-T and more than 25 years old, is a bakery in a century-old warehouse. It's great for pastries (especially the chocolate eclairs), bagels and deli sandwiches.

Coffeehouses have hit Telluride, and visitors have several to choose from: **The Steaming Bean, Maggie's,** and **Between the Covers Book Store** are all on Colorado Avenue.

In the Mountain Village

Indulge in the exquisite cuisine at **Allred's** (728-7474; $$$) while you drink in the staggering views. The timber-and-stone dining room with towering windows overlooks the 14,000-foot peaks and the historic town twinkling 1,800 feet below. The menu changes frequently, but expect inspirational dishes. You'll either get drunk by the natural high or by choosing from the 8,000 bottles in the wine cellar. A special tasting menu is a treat for guests who wish to pair a selection of fine wines with several signature dishes.

The Inn at Lost Creek houses a restaurant named for Mountain Village's altitude, **9545** (728-6293; $$–$$$). Specializing in organic cuisine for both lunch and dinner, it boasts the most extensive single-malt scotch selection in Telluride. **La Piazza del Villaggio** (728-8283; $$–$$$) is the sister to Rustico in town. Same family, same great food. **That Pizza Place** ($–$$) is a funky pizzeria at the base of the gondola that serves Sicilian-style pizza.

Legends ($–$$), in Wyndham Peaks, is open for breakfast and lunch only. It serves light fare, grilled specialties and great burgers. The Express Skiers luncheon buffet makes lunch quick and healthy. Golden Spa cuisine also is available here.

The **Telluride Coffee Company** began as a coffee cart in the village and has grown enough to need an indoor location—just steps away from the slopes. Choose from traditional coffee and espresso drinks, chai tea, iced coffee, juices, sodas and fresh pastries. The old coffee cart in Heritage Plaza is still open for a rich cup of joe on the go. **Skiers Union** at the bottom of the Village chair has great juices and coffee.

On-mountain

Gorrono Ranch, mid-mountain on Misty Maiden, is a restored Basque sheepherder's homestead with American favorites and delicious barbecue on a sunny deck known as "the Beach." **Giuseppe's**, at the top of the Plunge lift, is the place for Italian fare with killer views. **Big Billie's,** named after the town's madame who died in 1957, specializes in Southwestern and barbecue at the base of the Chondola and Sunshine chair.

Dining: $$$$–Entrees $30+; $$$–$20-$30; $$–$10-$20; $–less than $10.
Accommodations: (double room) $$$$–$200+; $$$–$141-$200; $$–$81-$140; $–$80 and less.

Apres-ski/nightlife

For immediate apres-ski, stop at "the Beach" at Gorrono Ranch, the mid-mountain spot for sun and microbrews. Or pop into **West End Tavern** near the Coonskin lift. For inspiring views of Wilson Peak at sunset, sink into an oversized couch or chair and sip an apres-ski drink in the **Great Room at the Wyndham Peaks Resort** in the Mountain Village. A bar menu that includes spa cuisine is available. **Eagle's Bar and Grille** on Colorado Avenue has a huge bar and great happy-hour prices.

For live music and dancing go to the **Fly Me to the Moon Saloon** with entertainment Thursday through Saturday. **The Last Dollar Saloon** (known to locals as 'The Buck") has the best selection of imported beer in Telluride, plus pool tables and dart boards. It's a bit of a manly-man beer bar—not many women hang out. The old Victorian **New Sheridan Bar** is one of the "must sees" in Telluride to experience the essence of the Old West. It would be no surprise to have Butch Cassidy and the Sundance Kid come sauntering in.

 ## Other activities

The mountain offers **snowbiking, tubing** and **snowskating** (wheel-less skateboards designed for snow) at Thrill Hill, an outdoor activity center at the base of Lift 2 and accessible from Mountain Village. It's open from 2:30–7 p.m., Wednesday–Sunday. For indoor fun, go to Plaza Arcade to play **video games, foosball, air hockey** and **pinball,** or the Xbox Arcade next to That Pizza Place to play **Xbox games.**

You can go on **sleigh rides** at Skyline Guest Ranch (888-754-1126); **horseback riding** with Roudy at Telluride Horseback (728-9611); **winter fly fishing** with Telluride Outside (728-3895); **hot-air ballooning** with San Juan Balloon Adventures (626-5495); **dogsledding** with Winter Moon Sled Dog Adventures (729-0058); **snowmobile tours** of Telluride's mining past with Telluride Snowmobile Adventures (728-4475) or Dave's Snowmobile tours (728-7737); and **helicopter skiing and riding** with Telluride Helitrax (728-8377; 866-435-4754). There's a pond in Mountain Village and another in town for **ice skating**. It isn't every town that has a colorful past like Telluride's, so **Boling's Historical Tour of Telluride** (728-6639) is well worth the time, and entertaining too, since local performer Ashley Boling dresses the part.

Non-skiers and those who need a break might enjoy stretching their creative muscles at the **Ah Haa School for the Arts** (728-3886), which offers weekly and daily classes on painting, silk dyeing and more. **First-run films** are shown nightly at the Nugget Theatre and sometimes at the Sheridan Opera House. Speaking of the **Sheridan Opera House,** it was originally a vaudeville theater and is the stage for many events. Check the calendar and see if any local theater productions are scheduled during your stay, because the locals are ripe with talent. The old hospital has been turned into the **Telluride Historical Museum,** which depicts the mining past of the Victorian town.

The fabulous **Golden Door Spa** (800-772-5482; 728-2590) at the Wyndham Peaks Hotel is a 42,000-square-foot facility on four levels. Sister spa to the Golden Door in Escondido, Calif., the spa provides sanctuary in the tradition of the ancient Honjin inns of Japan. The spa has 44 treatment rooms where you can be treated to a wide variety of massage techniques, facials, body treatments and signature treatments. A 50-minute massage begins at $120. We highly recommend the three-hour Breath of Life package for people not used to being at high altitude. You'll spend 20 minutes in the Oxygen Bar, be slathered in a re-mineralizing body mask to exfoliate and rehydrate your skin, take a break for a delectable spa lunch and end with an oxygen facial treatment. Wyndham guests have complimentary use of the fitness level

(Cybex weight room and cardiovascular deck), the men's and women's kivas, saunas, steam rooms, indoor and outdoor hot tubs, an indoor lap pool connected by a water slide to the lower indoor/outdoor pool, squash and racquetball courts, and indoor climbing wall.

Telluride has great shopping in one-of-a-kind **boutiques** and more than a dozen **art galleries.** Some of our favorites, all on Colorado Avenue: Lizard Head Mining Co., for its extraordinary custom-made jewelry; At Home in Telluride, with distinctive housewares and gifts; Picaya, with some nice and inexpensive jewelry and clothing; the Scott White Contemporary Art Gallery, showcasing renowned contemporary artists (affiliated with San Diego's distinguished gallery); Overland Sheepskin & Leather for clothing, footwear, accessories and home products; and Telluride Antique Market. A nice souvenir is a hat from Horny Toad Activewear, a national outdoor clothing company headquartered here. If you decide you'd like a Nordic wool-and-felt hat like a lot of locals wear, call Kim Chapin-Richard, a member of the ski patrol and hat maker (728-3443). She'll need a few days' notice.

Getting there and getting around

By air: Telluride has a small, weather-plagued airport 6 miles from town, served by United Express from Denver and America West Express from Phoenix. Montrose, 65 miles away, is where most visitors arrive, either by plan or by a weather diversion from Telluride. Continental has daily nonstop jet service to Montrose from Houston, four days a week from Los Angeles (daily during peak times), and on Saturdays from Newark. American Airlines offers daily nonstop jet service to Montrose from Dallas/Forth Worth and Chicago. United has daily jet service from Denver, and often from other cities as well.

If you fly into the Telluride airport, no matter what the weather, pack a carry-on with enough essentials to get you through 24 hours. These small planes fill with people, then add as much luggage as they can safely transport. This is a sound policy, but it also means that your bags may be delayed. If you arrive without your bags, check with your airline to see if it will provide a voucher for rental clothing and gear at local sporting goods stores. Ways around the problem: 1) Fly to Montrose. The drive is farther, but you'll have your bags with you. 2) Send your bags early via UPS or Federal Express to Mail Boxes Etc. in Telluride, which will arrange for your bags to be delivered to your lodging (inbound and outbound). Allow 10 business days for shipping. Call 728-8111 for complete details.

Ground transport is provided by Telluride Express (728-6000), Mountain Limo (728-9606) and Alpine Luxury Limo (728-8750). Call 24 hours in advance for Montrose airport pickups.

By car: Telluride is 335 miles from Denver via I-70 west, and Hwys. 50, 550, 62 and 145. From the southwest, it is 125 miles from Durango via Hwys. 160, 184 and 145. From the Montrose airport head south on Hwy. 550 to Ridgway, then take Hwys. 62 and 145 to Placerville and Telluride.

Getting around: A car is unnecessary. The town is just 12 blocks long—you can walk anywhere. If you have them, bring boots with at least an ankle-high cuff. During warm spells, the snowmelt on the side streets can get quite deep. A free bus service runs in town, and the free gondola makes the commute between town and the Mountain Village simple. If the gondola is not running, call Dial-A-Ride (728-8888) when you get to the base of the gondola in Mountain Village, and a van will ferry you without charge to destinations in the Mountain Village.

Vail

Colorado

Summit elevation:	11,570 feet
Vertical drop:	3,450 feet
Base elevation:	8,120 feet

Address: P.O. Box 7
Vail, CO 81658
Area code: 970
Ski area phone: 845-2500
Snow report: 476-4888 or (800) 404-3535
Toll-free reservations: (800) 404-3535
Fax: 845-2609
E-mail: vailinfo@vailresorts.com
Internet: www.vail.com (resort)
www.snow.com (corporate)
www.vailalways.com (Vail Valley)

Number and types of lifts: 33—1 12-person gondola, 14 high-speed quads, 1 quadchair, 3 triple chairs, 4 double chairs, 10 surface lifts
Skiable acreage: 5,289 acres
Snowmaking: 10 percent
Uphill capacity: 53,381 per hour
Parks & pipes: 3 parks, 1 pipe
Bed base: 11,059 within 10 miles
Nearest lodging: Slopeside, condos & hotels
Resort child care: Yes, 2 months and older
Adult ticket, per day: $81 (05/06 prices)

Expert:★★★★
Advanced:★★★★★
Intermediate:★★★★★
Beginner:★★★ **First-timer:**★★★

Dining:★★★★★
Apres-ski/nightlife:★★★★★
Other activities:★★★★★

Vail opened on Dec. 15, 1962, boasting one gondola, two chairs, eight ski instructors and a $5 lift ticket. Today Vail is a *complete* area, lacking none of the essential ingredients that form the magical stew of a world-class winter resort. Vail was conceived as a transplanted Austrian village with condominium convenience, raucous nightlife and quiet lounges, fine dining and pizzeria snacking. It's a small city at the base of a huge mountain. Its off-slope activities are unsurpassed—shopping, skating, movies, museums, sleigh riding and so much more—everything money can buy. Bring lots of money—temptations abound, and bargains are few.

But village and expenses aside, there is above all Vail Mountain—a single, stoop-shouldered behemoth. Though it does not have ultra-steeps or deeps, what it does have is three distinct experiences: There's a huge front face of long and very smooth cruisers, an enormous back-bowl experience of wide-open adventure unlike anything this side of the Atlantic, and Blue Sky Basin providing lift access to a backcountry-style experience.

Vail lays claim to the biggest single ski mountain in North America. Fortunately, it's segmented: You can concentrate on separate bowls and faces for a morning or afternoon and always have the choice of a new path down. And none of these runs seems intimidating, although there is plenty of challenge for every level of skier. Vail's network of 14 high-speed quads is also the largest in the country. Combined, the mountain and its system of 33 lifts let you do more skiing and less back-tracking than almost any other resort you can name.

But be aware—Vail is continuing its five-year, $500-million redevelopment plan with construction of Vail Square in the LionsHead area. When completed in 2007, Vail Square will be home to a luxury hotel, full-service spa, condominiums, ice skating plaza, restaurants, shops, and skier and guest services. In the meantime, hotels, restaurants, and shops in Lions-Head may have limited access (or even be closed) at certain times during construction. Check www.newvail.com for construction updates and road closures.

Mountain layout

If you're skiing with a group, arrange a meeting place in case you get separated. This is one big mountain. After a week here, you'll still be discovering new pitches and trails. By the way—locals call the lifts by their numbers rather than their names. If you want to play with them, do the same.

♦♦**Expert** ♦**Advanced:** We give the expert and advanced terrain here a thumbs-up because of the "sheer volume" quotient. That is, advanced and better can comfortably spend a week working out kinks in trees and bumps, and if you luck into a powder day, doing laps on Genghis Kahn alone will test your mettle. Overall, nothing should scare the bejeebers out of you, but you *will* have to sweat.

On the front side, as you face the hill, check out the double-black diamonds named Blue Ox, Highline and Rogers Run. Nearby Prima, off Northwoods Express, is tougher still, and the best skiers like to make the Prima-Pronto run their endurance test. Pronto drops right down to Northwoods Express and gets its share of oglers in line. The Prima Cornice can get you sucking air at the top, but it needs plenty of snow to open. The only authentic gut-suckers on the front face are the tops of South and North Rim off the Northwoods lift, leading to a tight but nice Gandy Dancer, and even those are short and sweet.

Under the Vista Bahn, when there's enough snow, The Chutes beckon. It's a bit of work to get to them, and the payoff is brief, straight timber bashing. LionsHead has only three very short sections of advanced terrain. Simba's steep stretch at the bottom often bumps up, as does Minnie's Mile, a run that pops out onto the cruiser Born Free, and Lower Ledges.

Solid skiers, of course, will also want to explore Vail's famous Back Bowls. Stretching 6 miles across, they provide more than 2,734 acres of choose-your-own-path skiing. On a sunny day, these bowls are about as good as skiing gets.

You'll certainly want to try the steeps and glades in Blue Sky Basin for a taste of lift-served backcountry skiing. The secret in Blue Sky Basin is that it's north facing, so the snow stays better here longer and there's a lot more of it.

■ **Intermediate:** Intermediate skiers and riders will run out of vacation time before they run out of trails to explore. Few other mountains offer an intermediate expansive terrain and seemingly countless trails, and Vail promises to groom 1,500 acres on average each night. Especially worthy cruising areas include the long ride down the mountain under and to the right of the Eagle Bahn Gondola, almost any of the runs bordering the Avanti express chair, the Northwoods run, and the relatively short but sweet trio down to Game Creek Bowl. Our vote for best run on the mountain, and one available to advanced-intermediates (though parts are rated black), is the top-to-bottom swath named Riva Ridge.

LionsHead is all about intermediate skiing. The trails tend to roll from the top of the gondola down to the valley like ribbon candy—each trail has a steeper section followed by an easier stretch. Simba is a long swooping run, good anytime, and often chosen as the last run. But beware, it can resemble a freeway of skiers "heading to the barn" for apres-ski. Born Free is another classic intermediate run that loops lazily to the valley floor.

Confident intermediates also can enjoy the Back Bowls, but stick close to groomed trails in China Bowl and Tea Cup Bowl. (Poppy Fields in China Bowl often is groomed during the day.) If you get tired or frustrated with the natural conditions, you can bail out easily.

In Blue Sky Basin, at least one trail is groomed daily, so low-intermediates can enjoy this peaceful and secluded remote area. Only strong intermediates who can handle powder and some trees should try the ungroomed trails. Pete's Express Lift runs up the eastern-most point of Blue Sky Basin in Pete's Bowl to access more than 125 acres of intermediate terrain.

●● **Beginner:** The best areas are at Golden Peak and the top of the gondola, and a group of short green runs under the Sourdough Lift on the top left of the trail map. Unfortunately, Vail doesn't have a large area of concentrated green runs. Most lifts on the front face have one or two green-designated trails, a bunch of blue trails and one or two blacks. Take a trail map and pay attention to the signs.

Vail is one of the few resorts with beginner slopes at the top of the mountain. Take the Eagle Bahn Gondola. At the top, the beginner area offers inspiring 360-degree views. A group of short green runs are served by a chairlift to skier's right (east) of the gondola, and you can do laps on this chair. The best part is beginners are the only ones using the chair. You can follow a series of cat tracks with names like Cub's Way and Bwana Loop that crisscross the mountain. If cat tracks make you nervous, Vail's trail map marks them with dotted lines so you'll know where they are. However, it's tough to avoid them here, unless you ride the gondola back down.

● **First-timer:** There are small learning areas in the Golden Peak base area and the top of the Eagle Bahn Gondola at Adventure Ridge. From Adventure Ridge, you can return to the valley via the gondola.

Ride Guide: Let's make it easy: If you're going to ride Vail, we mean really *ride* the mountain, it's time to ignore trail names. What you want to do here is focus on the kind of terrain you want to ride, then stick to the chair that accesses it. This way you avoid always traversing the mountain. By the way, riding the trees is the most direct way to avoid taking cat tracks and multiple lifts.

On the front side of the mountain, experts are going to want to ride the Northwoods lift a lot. On a powder day this is a great place to hit—rocks, steep lines and cliff gaps are every-where—but once it's tracked, get out of there. Head rider's right of the Vista Bahn, or to The Riva Bahn and Vail's world-class terrain park and superpipe. Advanced riders who prefer trees enjoy Riva Glade and Hairbag Alley. Both are tight trees where snowboarders rule.

The back side of the mountain is where Vail really shines. Start at the top of Game Creek Express, where you can access the Cornice with a five-minute walk. Drop in off the cornice, then head down to the motocross jumps, which are exactly that, three giant windlips that form natural tabletops perfect for throwing down new tricks. The lift-accessed backcountry experi-ence in Blue Sky Basin is a rider's paradise—and since it's very remote, you won't have to ride a sequence of chairs once you get there.

This mountain was really designed for intermediates. The Avanti Chair and the gondola will be equal to heaven for you. Everything can be found there: Long high-speed cruisers, woods runs, gaps, kickers and logs. Golden Peak is it for beginners and first-timers. All the cat tracks can be tough when you're first learning to ride because you can't carry your speed yet. Vail has an excellent beginner instruction program, so take advantage of it.

Parks and pipes

Vail puts a lot of effort and commitment into its parks and superpipe. Spread out among its three parks, you'll find countless tabletops, rails and log rails. The superpipe is 425 feet long with 18-foot walls. The Golden Peak Terrain Park is sweetly set up, starting off with a nicely groomed superpipe so you can hit the massive pipe in succession with the tabletops in one run, rather than having to choose one or the other. Below the jumps is the rail park, with rails of varying sizes and shapes. There are an abundance of rails and jumps, mostly tabletops with two approaches, that let you decide if you want to go big or bigger. If you're not an experienced jumper, you will probably end up landing flat on the tabletop, since most of them require major distance to make it to the landing. All the rails are for more advanced rail riders too. Also, tucked in some trees off Mule Skinner you'll find hand-carved log rails. If you're less experienced in the parks, try Mule Skinner Terrain Park, which is on an adjacent trail and includes smaller features that are less intimidating than the main lines in the advanced park.

Bwana Park in LionsHead has a variety of smaller jumps and low-to-the-ground rails to provide a progressive learning experience for those who are developing their skills. For the kids, or the kids at heart, go to Chaos Canyon, a kid's adventure zone and terrain park. It's under Mid-Vail Lodge, off Lion's Way. There are some fun features here, starting out with a series of banked turns winding through the woods. There are groomer-width tracks, as well as kid-width tracks that might be a little harder to navigate on a board, much better for the skiers. Boarders, stick to the wider paths. About three-quarters of the way down the banked turns is a very small beginners' jump to practice getting air under your board.

 ## Cross-country and snowshoeing (visit xcskiresorts.com for more details

Two cross-country centers serve Nordic skiers and snowshoers, one at **Golden Peak** and one at the **Vail Golf Course.** Both offer lessons, tours and rentals. Call the Golden Peak Center at 479-3210. Vail has beefed up its Cross-Country, Telemark and Snowshoe Adventure Center at Golden Peak, where guided tours and instruction are available through the Vail Nordi Ski School. Instructors specialize in cross-country skiing, telemark skiing, snowshoeing and skate skiing.

 ## Lessons (05/06 prices)

The ski school has offices and meeting places at Vail Village near the base of the Vista Bahn Express, at LionsHead next to the gondola, at Golden Peak next to Chairs 6 and 12, at Mid-Vail next to Chairs 3 and 4, and at the top of the gondola. Private lessons meet at Vail Village. Call the ski school at 476-3239. Prices we provide are for regular season.

Group lessons: $110 for a full day. Vail offers a wide variety of lesson-lift-and/or-rental packages for skiers and snowboarders too detailed for us to list here.

First-timer package: Full-day lesson and beginner lift cost $145; with rentals, $175. The First Time Skier Series is three consecutive full days of lessons that cost $240 for lessons, lifts and rentals.

First-time snowboarders also can take a Burton Learn to Ride clinic that uses special Burton snowboards, bindings and boots designed to reduce the difficulty of learning to ride. The goal is to get students linking toeside and heelside turns on the very first day and significantly reduce the number of falls. Call for prices of the lift/lesson/rental package.

Private lessons: One to six people cost $160 for one hour, $275 for two hours, $405 for a half-day, and $595 for the day.

Special workshops: Focus is on specific skills or snow conditions, such as parallel skiing or bumps. Most are afternoon three-hour sessions for $85.

"Her Turn" Adventure Workshops for Women are three-day programs. Breakthroughs are common in the supportive small-group atmosphere. The Telemark Workshop Series is also a personal favorite. Scheduled on weekends, it focuses solely on the on-snow experience for a single day, and comes in unisex, kids, and women-only varieties. Call the resort for prices.

Pepi's Wedel Weeks were created in the European tradition, allowing skiers to start off the ski season with an inexpensive lesson package. These are held for three weeks only, in December and January. It's a seven-day, all-inclusive program. Call (800) 610-7374.

ReTreat Yourself is a women's snowboarding program with pro rider Barrett Christy that includes coaching, board tuning clinics, yoga and more. Call (800) 475-4543.

Racing: Vail has quite a recreational racing complex near the bottom of the Avanti Express lift with two NASTAR courses, two coin-operated courses, two courses reserved for groups, a course for teaching clinics and a Sybervision area. A surface lift serves the courses.

KidStuff [05/06 prices]

Child Care: Ages 2 months to 6 years. Supervised playroom and non-skiing programs cost $92 regular season. Reservations required; call 479-3285 or make online reservations. The state-of-the-art Small World Play School is in the Golden Peak base area. Free pagers are available.

Other options: For **babysitters,** call 476-7400. **Baby's Away** (800-369-9030; 926-5256) rents and delivers baby needs, such as crib, stroller, car seat and toys to your lodge.

Lessons: Lessons are available for children as young as 3 years old (toilet-trained). Ski lessons are offered for ages 3–14; snowboarding lessons are for ages 7–14. Cost is $132 during regular season and includes lesson, lift and lunch. Holiday Camps are offered during holidays for kids ages 7–14 who are intermediate skiers and better. Call for prices and details.

Register for all lessons at 8 a.m. or pre-register the day before; you also can register online at the website. Reservations are not required. Vail encourages kids younger than age 14 enrolled in ski and snowboard programs to wear helmets. Rentals are available. If you don't want your child to wear a helmet, you must decline in writing in order for your child to participate. Children's Ski and Snowboard Centers are located at both LionsHead and at Golden Peak. Both centers offer "one-stop shopping" for lessons and rentals.

Skiing with your kids: The resort is sprinkled with Kids Adventure Zones. Chaos Canyon features weather-theme trails Ricochet Ridge, Tornado Alley and Thunder Lane. Thunder Cat Cave has a replica of a wildcat hovering over a cave entrance. Inside, kids will find ecological information about the Rocky Mountains' four-footed predators. A Kids Adventure Map highlights most of the zones so kids can find them, but some are left up to discovery. With the help of Vail mascots, Ranger Raccoon and Crazy Coyote, children also learn about SKE-Cology™, highlighting environmental awareness and responsibility on the mountain. Kids even have their own restaurant at Mid-Vail called Chaos Canyon Kids' Cafe.

Special activities: Night Owls is a supervised evening of dinner and activities at Adventure Ridge for kids ages 7–14. Meet at 4:30 p.m. to head up the mountain. Cost is $70 regular season ages 7–12; $80 for ages 13–18. Make reservations at the children's ski and snowboard school.

Lift tickets [05/06 prices]

	Adult	Child (5-12)
One day	$81	$49
Three days	$243 ($81/day)	$147 ($49/day)
Five days	$405 ($81/day)	$245 ($49/day)

Who skis free: Ages 4 and younger.

Who skis at a discount: Ages 65+ pay $71 per day. Vail offers PEAKS discounted tickets if you pre-purchase online a three-day or more ticket at least seven days in advance. Membership in PEAKS is free and you are automatically enrolled when you make your early purchase. Prices are lower during early and late season, and higher during holidays.

Interchangeability: All lift tickets also are valid at sister resorts Beaver Creek, Keystone and Breckenridge, as well as at nearby Arapahoe Basin.

Accommodations

Vail's lodging choices are so vast we can't even begin to list them here. Before you call Central Reservations, know your price range, what amenities you need and which ones you want, how close you'd like to be to the lifts and how close you'll settle for if you find nothing in your budget within that distance. Prices dip from 25 to 40 percent before Christmas and in April. But if you come at that time, be sure the bus system is in full operation or that you're within walking distance of necessities; otherwise rent a car.

Vail's premier properties are clustered in Vail Village at the base of the Vista Bahn Express. Selecting the best place in town is a virtual toss-up between four hotels.

The Lodge at Vail (800-331-5634; 476-5011; $$$$) is the original hotel around which the rest of the resort was built. It is only steps away from the lifts, ski school and main street action. The Lodge serves a great buffet breakfast. **Gasthof Gramshammer** (476-5626; $$$$) is at the crossroads of Vail Village. Our favorite and the most economical within this group of hotels is the **Christiania** (800-530-3999; 476-5641; $$$$). **Sonnenalp Resort** (800-654-8312; 476-5656; $$$$) is a group of buildings that exude Alpine warmth and charm. The spa is the place to head for sore muscle relief.

In LionsHead, the **Marriott's Mountain Resort at Vail** (800-648-0720; 476-4444; $$$–$$$$) is top of the line and a three-minute walk from the gondola. **Lion Square Lodge** (476-2281; $$$–$$$$) is steps from the Eagle Bahn Gondola and Born Free Express lift.

The slopeside **Vail Cascade Resort & Spa** (800-420-2424; 476-7111; $$$$) lodges guests in rooms, suites and condominiums. A $20-million remodel involved spending $5 million to elegantly refinish all 292 rooms and suites plus other interior spaces in rich colors. The multi-award-winning property includes the Aria Spa & Club, the Vail Valley's largest fitness facility, as well as two ski shops, two movie theaters and its own chairlift accessing Vail's slopes. There's free shuttle service to Vail Village and LionsHead, and ski valet service. An excellent restaurant means dining here is a "can't miss" (see *Dining*).

Condominiums are plentiful in the Vail region. The most reasonable for those who want to be on the shuttlebus route are in LionsHead, clustered around the gondola, and in East Vail at **Vail Racquet Club** (800-428-4840; 476-4840; $$-$$$).

The Fabulous Vailglo Lodge (476-5506; $$-$$$) in LionsHead is a 34-room Best Western hotel that operates like an elegant B&B. It has easy access to the slopes and town. For other relatively more affordable lodging, try **Antlers** (476-2471; $$-$$$$) in LionsHead and **Manor Vail Resort** (800-950-8245; 476-5000; $$-$$$$) in Golden Peak, with hotel rooms, suites and condos. A great value can be found at the remodeled **Apex at Vail/Holiday Inn** (800-543-2814; 476-2739; $$) in West Vail. Rooms are a nice surprise, a hot tub and fitness center are on hand, plus you'll get a complimentary breakfast and ski shuttle. A recommended B&B is the **Savory Inn** (866-728-6794; 476-1304; $$$-$$$$), where you'll stay in a wonderfully elegant log cabin lodge along the Gore Creek that also offers cooking classes with world-class chefs of the Cooking School of Vail.

Dining

Eating out in Vail is as much of a tradition as skiing the Back Bowls. Always make reservations. More than 80 bars and restaurants offer the spectrum of options from pizza to exquisite gourmet dining.

La Tour (476-4403; $$$-$$$$) and **The Left Bank** (476-3696; $$$-$$$$), both French, have long been considered Vail's best. Another standby, **Sweet Basil** (476-0125; $$$-$$$$), is

Dining: $$$$-Entrees $30+; $$$-$20-$30; $$-$10-$20; $-less than $10.
Accommodations: (double room) $$$$-$200+; $$$-$141-$200; $$-$81-$140; $-$80 and less.

consistently good with creative dishes. **Terra Bistro** (476-6836; $$$) is on the east end of the Vail Mountain Lodge. Although difficult to find (the sign is very small), this upscale, eclectic restaurant specializing in "fusion cuisine" is a local favorite. **Chap's Grill and Chophouse** (476-7014; $$$-$$$$), in the Vail Cascade Resort & Spa, serves some of the best steaks, wild game and seafood in the Vail area. We like **Lancelot** (476-5828; $$-$$$) for prime rib, **Montauk** (476-2601; $$$) for seafood, and **Wildflower** (476-5011; $$$-$$$$) in **The Lodge** for contemporary American and an excellent wine list.

Less expensive but just as scrumptious is the legendary **Pepi's** (476-5626; $$) for the best goulash and white veal bratwursts; and **Campo de Fiori** (476-8994; $$-$$$), with fine Italian fare and a friendly staff. **Cucina Rustica** (476-5011; $$-$$$) serves Tuscan-style Italian in The Lodge. If you're willing to drive west to a locals' favorite in Eagle-Vail, **Ti Amo** (845-8153; $$-$$$) won't disappoint. **Sapphire Restaurant & Oyster Bar** (476-2828; $$$) serves creative seafood, Vail's only oyster bar menu, and some meat and fowl specialties. **Billy's Island Grill (476-8811; $$)** in LionsHead serves killer mango margaritas.

Those on a budget should try **Pazzo's** (476-9026; $) for pasta and create-your-own-pizza. **Bart and Yeti's** (476-2754; $$) in LionsHead is great for lunch or light dinner. **Moe's Barbecue** (479-7888; $-$$) in LionsHead is a local's favorite for pulled pork sandwiches, chicken and such. For an inexpensive lunch, try the **Clark's Market Deli** (476-1199; $) in Vail Village. Enjoy sandwiches, tofu, tabouli, Santa Fe rice and beans, and other tasty treats in a small seating area facing the front slopes of Vail.

On the mountain, have lunch at the **Two Elk Restaurant** (479-4560; $-$$) above China Bowl, with its log lodge frame, Ute Indian motif and views of the Gore Range. Go early or late, because finding a seat at prime time is tough. Or try the sophisticated lunches at **Larkspur** (479-8050; $$-$$$) in the Golden Peak base lodge. It's also one of our top choices for dinner, where you're able to pair your French-influenced American seasonal cuisine with one of the 4,000 bottles of wine. **Mid-Vail's food court** has moderate (for Vail) prices—$10 buys a huge potato with toppings, a local beer and a piece of fruit.

Game Creek Restaurant & Club (479-4275) is extremely exclusive, with only 350 members (Ross Perot, Charles Schwab and so on). Don't try to eat lunch here, it's members-only. But it's open to the public for dinner, and it's just a snowcat ride from the top of the Eagle Bahn. For about $90 per person, sans alcohol and gratuity but including the transportation, you get a six-course gourmet meal—a choice of game, seafood, veal, steak and lamb—and a gorgeous view of the valley below. Make your reservation to coincide with sunset.

For breakfast, the best deal in town is at **D.J. MacAdams** ($) in LionsHead's Concert Hall Plaza, a tiny diner where you'll watch cooks make heaping plates of omelets, scrambletts (like an omelet only using scrambled eggs) and blintzes. Wash it down with a fruit smoothie. It's open 24 hours, except Mondays (reopening at 7 a.m. Tuesday). **West Side Cafe** ($) in West Vail is a locals' favorite for coffee and bagels or breakfast burritos. If you're looking for a buffet breakfast (continental or hot) in a fine-dining atmosphere, head to **Chap's Grill** ($$) in the Vail Cascade Resort & Spa or the **Mountain Grille Restaurant** ($$) at the Marriott's Mountain Resort at Vail. You can also get a la carte items at both.

Down Valley

If you have a car, drive west to exit 171 and turn off at old town Minturn where the **Minturn Country Club** (827-4114; $$$) lets you grill your own meat or fish steak. Just across the street, the area's best Mexican food is dished out at the raucous **Saloon** (827-5954; $-$$)—a favorite of World Cup racers—or **Chili Willy's** (827-5887; $-$$). The **Turntable**

Restaurant (827-4268; $-$$) wins accolades for its green chili.

Further down valley, past the Beaver Creek exit about 4 miles, keep an eye out for **Balata's at Singletree Golf Club** (926-3528; $$-$$$) on your right. You'll find a lovely high-end continental cuisine restaurant where you can go dressed up and enjoy the fabulous sunsets behind the New York mountain range.

Discover the locals' favorite, **Juniper Restaurant** (926-7001; $$), in the Riverwalk Center in Edwards. "Comfort Fusion" cuisine blends with the bistro atmosphere for a relaxing gourmet meal.

At the Edwards exit, left off the highway, check out the valley's oldest restaurant and bar, **The Gashouse** (926-3613; $-$$). Seafood, homemade soups, steaks, wild game and award-winning chili are served in a rustic 50-year-old log cabin. Apres-ski it's good for lobster tails, little-neck clams and jumbo lump crab cakes. The best sports bar and grill could be **Paddy's** (949-6093; $-$$) on Hwy. 6. The house specialty prime rib is big and fat.

In Edwards, look for the **Gore Range Brewery** (926-2739; $-$$). There's also Chinese, Thai, Japanese and Vietnamese cuisine all over the place. The margaritas at **Fiesta's Cafe & Cantina** (926-2121; $-$$) are yummy (20 tequilas to choose from) and the chicken enchiladas in white jalapeño sauce are the house specialty. At **Markos** (926-7003; $) in the Edwards Business Plaza, you'll find pastas, pizzas and Caesar salads at rock bottom prices. Stop by **Bonjour Bakery** (926-5539; $) to pick up several loaves of to-die-for bread, but call for winter hours before you make the trip.

 ## Apres-ski/nightlife

Apres-ski is centered in the Village or in LionsHead. **The Red Lion** has a deck, live music and great nachos. In the Village, try **Los Amigos** at the base of the Vista Bahn and join the viewers on the deck watching late-day skiers make their way down the steep Pepi's Face. **Vendetta's** in the Village is a locals' favorite. **Mickey's** at the Lodge at Vail has the top piano bar. Several restaurants have house entertainers who are long-time career musicians. In LionsHead, **Garfinkel's** has a great sunny deck overlooking the slopes. Gather your buddies and try their shot wheel.

Bart & Yeti's, named after the owner's late dogs, is like a classic Western tavern, studded with rustic logs, wagon wheels, photographs depicting the Wild West, and stuffed birds. It's a tried-and-true locals' hangout with little fanfare.

For later nightlife, **The Tap Room** on Bridge Street caters to a movin' and groovin' mature crowd, while a few doors away, **Samana** attracts a young crowd with loud rock'n'roll. **The Club** normally offers acoustic guitar music. **8150** has live alternative music.

 ## Other activities

Adventure Ridge at the top of the gondola is an on-mountain activity center, open from 2 p.m. to 9 p.m. Enjoy the **ice-skating rink, kids' snowmobile track, lift-served tubing hill, ski-biking** and other activities here. If you haven't tried ski-biking, do so. It is a hoot to go careening down the mountain at night with a light strapped to your head; just be prepared for exhausted legs. Blue Moon Restaurant & Bar serves affordable family dinners. The gondola cabins are heated and lighted.

Vail has a number of **athletic clubs** and **spas**. The Aria Spa & Club (spa 479-5942, club 476-7400) at the Vail Cascade Resort has 14 treatment rooms including a couple's spa suite. The athletic facilities are the best in Vail and include a pool; cardio equipment; free weights; indoor track; and basketball, volleyball, racquetball and squash courts. The Spa at Vail Moun-

Dining: $$$$-Entrees $30+; $$$-$20-$30; $$-$10-$20; $-less than $10.
Accommodations: (double room) $$$$-$200+; $$$-$141-$200; $$-$81-$140; $-$80 and less.

tain Lodge (476-7960) also has fitness facilities in Vail Village and the only climbing wall in the Vail Valley. The Vail Racquet Club (476-3267) in East Vail has indoor tennis, squash and racquetball courts, swimming pool and weight room.

Take a ride on the Vail Golf Course with **Steve Jones Sleigh Rides** (476-8057). The **Colorado Ski Museum** in the Vail Transportation Center traces the history of skiing in the state. Admission is free. Vail also has several **movie theaters,** an indoor **ice-skating rink,** several **hot-air balloon companies** and many other things to do. Call the Vail Activities Desk at 476-9090 for the complete list.

Cooking classes with world-class chefs are taught at **Cooking School of Vail** (866-728-6794 or 476-1304). The school is at the Savory Inn.

Vail's unique **boutiques and shops,** mostly upscale, can keep your credit card active for days. Late March is the best time to find bargains in skiwear and winter clothes.

Getting there and getting around

By air: Flights land at the Vail/Eagle County airport, about 35 miles west of Vail, and the Denver International Airport, 110 miles east. Eagle County airport is served by American, Northwest, Delta, Continental, United Express, United and U.S. Airways (from Philadelphia and Charlotte).

Ground transportation between Denver and Vail is frequent and convenient. Contact Vail Valley Transportation at (800) 882-8872; Colorado Mountain Express at (800) 525-6363; Airlink Shuttle at (800) 554-8245; or Vail Valley Taxi (Eagle airport only) at 476-8294. Though flights into Denver may be a bit less expensive than Eagle, also consider the cost of ground transportation—about $60 per person round trip from Eagle and about $115 from Denver.

By car: Vail is 100 miles west of Denver and 140 miles east of Grand Junction.

Getting around: Most parts of Vail are very self-contained, and the free, reliable bus service runs throughout town from East to West Vail. Visitors and locals ride the bus, because parking is very limited and expensive. Shuttles to Beaver Creek cost $3 one way and depart from the Transportation Center above the parking structure in Vail Village.

Winter Park
Colorado

Summit elevation: 12,060 feet
Vertical drop: 3,060 feet
Base elevation: 9,000 feet

Address: P.O. Box 36, Winter Park, CO 80482
Area code: 970
Ski area phone: 726-5514
Denver line: (303) 892-0961
Toll-free reservations: (800) 729-5813;
(970) 726-5587 (outside the U.S. and Canada)
Fax: (970) 726-5993
E-mail: wpinfo@skiwinterpark.com
Internet: www.skiwinterpark.com,
www.winterparkresort.com, www.ridewinterpark.com
(ski area) or www.winterpark-info.com (town)
Expert:★★★★ **Advanced:**★★★★
Intermediate:★★★★
Beginner:★★★★
First-timer:★★★★★

Number of lifts: 24–1 high-speed six-pack, 7
high-speed quads, 4 triples, 7 doubles, 2 surface
lifts, 3 moving carpets
Snowmaking: 10 percent
Skiable acreage: 2,762 acres
Uphill capacity: 36,000 per hour
Parks & pipes: 3 parks, 2 pipes
Bed base: 12,500
Nearest lodging: Slopeside
Resort child care: Yes, 2 months and older
Adult ticket, per day: $72 (05/06 prices)

Dining:★★★
Apres-ski/nightlife:★★
Other activities:★★★

In the early 1900s, when the Moffat Tunnel through the Rockies was completed, Denverites began to ride the train here. The shacks first built for the tunnel construction crews made perfect warming huts for hardy skiers who climbed the mountains and schussed down on 7-foot-long boards. The ski area now is part of the Denver public parks system (owned by the city and county of Denver). Today, Winter Park ranks as one of the largest ski areas in Colorado.

This is a great mountain with a wonderfully easy-going atmosphere. The ski area and most of the lodging are tucked into the woods off the main highway, which retains this town's rural feel. Winter Park also has several traditional mountain inns—the kind with large common rooms where people can read, talk or play board games. They are tough to find these days. We like them, and you'll find descriptions in the Lodging section.

But, the times are changing. The Zephyr Mountain Lodge, with shops and a restaurant on the ground floor and condos above, has brought upscale slopeside lodging to Winter Park. And there's more to come. In May 2006 the resort will began construction on condos, a shopping area and a parking garage. For now, Winter Park is still charmingly funky, affordable and low-key, with lodging designed with families in mind, plus one of Colorado's most respected ski schools. The children's and disabled-skier programs are among the biggest, most advanced and most respected in the nation.

Although Winter Park maintains a great family reputation, it is a surprisingly good destination for singles. The town benefits from having only a few, but good, nightlife centers. Meaning that you get to meet most of the other skiers in town if that's what you want; and the mountain inn lodging gives singles a great opportunity to meet other vacationers over dinner and drinks, or while enjoying the hot tubs. If you're looking for a solid good time without the fanfare, Winter Park presents you with one of the best opportunities.

Mountain layout

Though the mountain is completely interconnected by lifts, it has separate base areas: Mary Jane and Winter Park.

♦♦ **Expert:** Visitors who have read about Winter Park arrive expecting a good intermediate resort with plenty of lower-intermediate and beginner trails. Yes, that's all here. What is surprising is the amount of expert terrain. Vasquez Cirque has nearly 700 acres of steep chutes and gladed powder stashes accessed by a hike along the ridge from the Timberline chairlift. Mary Jane is where you'll find the famous bumps and super-steeps. Try the chutes accessible only through controlled gates.

♦**Advanced:** For advanced skiers, the most popular lift on the Winter Park side is the Zephyr Express. It provides access to Mary Jane (via Outhouse), or the advanced runs on the Winter Park side—Bradley's Bash, Balch, Mulligan's Mile, Rhetta's Run, Outrigger and Hughes. From the top of Zephyr, Outhouse is now a split-groomed trail, offering fans of big bumps *or* steep groomers a route to the base of Mary Jane.

At Mary Jane, head for the black runs off the Summit Express. If you're still standing, you're ready for the runs off the Challenger chair—all black diamond, all ungroomed with monstrous moguls, and all tough as a bag of nails.

■ **Intermediate:** Parsenn Bowl has more than 200 acres of open space. If you hit Parsenn on a good day, you're in for a treat. The upper part is above treeline, medium-steep with spectacular views, while the gladed bottom is a delight, especially if you're just learning to ski between trees. Though rated blue and blue-black on the trail map, wind and weather conditions can make the bowl a workout.

Vasquez Ridge on the Winter Park side has an excellent collection of cruising runs. Avoid the long runout down the Big Valley trail by taking Buckaroo. To change mountains, green-circle Gunbarrel takes skiers to the High Lonesome Express quad and the Mary Jane area.

The Sunnyside lift on the Mary Jane side has excellent intermediate runs. If you can handle these with no trouble, try Sleeper, one of Winter Park's "blue-black" designated runs.

●●**Beginner:** The Winter Park base area serves most of the beginner trails. Beginners can ride to the top of the mountain to Sunspot and then ski down March Hare, or you can ski all the way back to the base using the Cranmer Cutoff to Parkway. When these become easy, try Cranmer, Jabberwocky and White Rabbit.

● **First-timer:** Winter Park is one of the best ski areas in the nation for novices. Discovery Park is 26 acres of gentle, protected learning terrain served by a double, a triple and a high-speed quad, which slows down for loading and unloading. Another 5 acres of beginner/teaching terrain can be found next to the Gemini Lift. Two moving carpets and one surface lift allow children *and* adults to make runs without getting on and off a chairlift.

Ride Guide: While Mary Jane is famous for its bumps, it also boasts smooth glades and chutes off of the Summit Express and Challenger lifts. Catch them on a powder day and you'll feel like a hero. Overall, the Mary Jane terrain is ideal for experts and advanced-inter-mediates, plus it's easy to negotiate with no flat runouts. A note of caution: While the Winter Park side is better suited for beginners, it can be a challenge for riders because it has some flats and runouts. Take the Zephyr Express and Eskimo Express lifts to avoid most of them. Although you have to endure some flats, the Pioneer Express lift also offers some interesting intermediate terrain for riders, notably Upper Sundance to Buckaroo. On the way back to the Winter Park base, just be sure to take Parkway Trail or Larry Sale to avoid Turnpike at all costs—*ALL COSTS.* It's longer and flatter than Kansas.

Parks and pipes

Winter Park takes the freeriding freenzy to an elevated level with a superpipe and three terrain parks. Rail Yard Terrain Park on Allan Phipps trail is the place for experts. It's packed with 25 rails—including a couple 30-foot banked C rails and a 15-foot trapezoid—and 16 components such as kickers and spines. The 450-foot superpipe is 50 feet wide at the base and has 18-foot walls. From the outdoor decks of Snoasis, guests have a great view of skiers and snowboarders catching huge air on the bottom three jumps. The terrain park on Jack Kendrick trail has rails and features for intermediate riders. The under-vert minipipe here allows you to get a feel for edging and flow technique in a pipe. Discovery Park has small entry-level features for beginners to get used to being in the air and shifting weight.

 ## Cross-country and snowshoeing (visit xcskiresorts.com for more details)

Devil's Thumb Cross-Country Center (726-8231) has great views of the mountains and 105 km. of trails groomed for both skating and gliding. The center is near Tabernash on County Road 83. Rentals and lessons are available. You'll also find 20 km. of marked, groomed snowshoe trails.

Snow Mountain Ranch (887-2152), 8 miles west of Winter Park on Highway 40, offers 100 km. of groomed trails through a variety of terrain—open, wooded, hilly and flat. The system includes a lighted 3-km. loop for night skiing. The instruction staff includes national-level coaches and racers. Ski lessons, rentals, lodging, dining and child care are available. Snow Mountain Ranch is also a YMCA with inexpensive dorm and cabin lodging.

Arapahoe National Forest contains more than 600 km. of backcountry Nordic and snowshoeing trails, and the **Fraser Experimental Forest Ranger Station** is the take-off point for marked trails suitable for all skiing levels of skiers, with no trail fees, but also no facilities.

On-mountain snowshoe tours are offered several times daily from the base of **Winter Park Resort.** The two-hour guided tour includes a chairlift ride to the tour's starting point, rental snowshoes, and information about native plants and animals.

Winter Park and the Fraser Valley's extensive mountain biking trails are used in winter for snowshoeing. The **Winter Park/Fraser Chamber of Commerce** has maps.

 ## Lessons (05/06 prices)

The Ski & Snowboard School desks are in Balcony House at the Winter Park base. We provide regular-season prices; value-season prices are lower. You can save up to 10 percent if you book online.

Group lessons: $65 for 2.5 hours, for all levels.

First-timer package: A half-day package with lessons, lifts and rentals costs $49.

Private lessons: $429 for a full day; $319 for three hours; $259 for two hours.

Special programs: Two mult-day examples: Women's Progressive Ski Clinics, $225; Women's Ski & Ride Weekend, $169. Also offered are multi-session telemark, moguls and parks & pipes clinics.

Winter Park's National Sports Center for the Disabled, the world's leader in disabled ski instruction, has a full-time race-training program for disabled skiers. Instruction is available for all levels, and the race program is open to advanced intermediates or above.

Racing: NASTAR, daily on the Cranmer Trail above Snoasis Restaurant. It costs $5 for two runs for adults or $7 for all day, and $3 for two runs for kids (12 and under) or $5 all day. Drop-ins are welcome in the Masters (25 and older) race-training program.

KidStuff (05/06 prices)

Child care: Ages 2 months through 6 years. All day, including lunch, costs $91; half day is $71 (no lunch). Complimentary use of a beeper/pager is included. Reservations are required for child care; reservations for add-on private lessons are strongly recommended, especially on weekends. Reservation forms are required and reservations can be made by calling (800) 420-8093. Reserve early, as the Winter Park child-care program sometimes hits capacity. Note: Winter Park has always been a leader in creative children's ski programs. Its multistory Kids Adventure Junction handles more than 600 children on some days and does it very well. The Center is open from 8 a.m. to 4 p.m.

Children's lessons: We provide regular season prices. You can save 10 percent if you book in advance by calling (800) 729-7907. All-day programs for children ages 3–17 years, including all-day lift ticket, complimentary use of a helmet, lunch, instruction and supervision, cost $114 without rentals; $129 with rentals. Snowboard lessons are available for ages 6–17 years. If you think a full day on snow is too much for your child, a combination ski lesson and day care program for ages 3–6 costs $114 (includes rentals). Reservations for add-on private lessons are strongly recommended, especially on weekends.

Lift tickets (05/06 prices)

	Adult	Child (6-13)
One day	$72	$36
Three days	$216 ($72/day)	$108 ($36/day)
Five days	$360 ($72/day)	$180 ($36/day)

Who skis free: Kids 5 and younger always ski free; seniors 70 and older ski free Monday–Thursday only.

Who skis at a discount: Ages 65–69 pay $58. Seniors 70+ pay $58 Friday–Sunday only. Half-day tickets are offered for mornings or afternoons. Beginner lift tickets on the Galloping Goose lift at Mary Jane cost $5 per day.

If you purchase your multiday tickets online at least three days in advance, you'll save 10 percent. Winter Park offers discounts through select Front Range businesses, such as Safeway, that save about $10 per day (the days aren't specified, so you can buy as many tickets for as many days as you plan to ski/ride).

Note: Prices are higher for holidays and during most of March.

Accommodations

Winter Park Central Reservations, (800) 729-5813, can book 150 different lodging properties, plus air transportation, lift tickets and special activities.

This resort has a group of mountain inns unique in Colorado. They all serve meals family-style so guests easily meet one another. Most inns have meal plans included and have transportation to and from the slopes. The food is usually good and plentiful, and the owners go out of their way to please guests. These inns are perfect for travelers who want to meet others.

Perhaps the most upscale mountain inn is the **Gasthaus Eichler** (800-543-3899; 726-5133; $-$$$). The inn is very European and the rooms are well decorated with down comforters on the beds. Each bathroom is equipped with a jetted tub. It's perfect if you want quiet, elegant lodging in the center of town within walking distance of restaurants and nightlife.

Arapahoe Ski Lodge (800-754-0094; 726-8222; $–$$$), also downtown, is a pleasant, friendly, no-smoking mountain inn that feels like home. The rooms have private baths. It features a spa and indoor pool. Prices include breakfast, dinner and transport to the slopes.

The Woodspur Lodge (800-626-6562; 726-8417; $–$$$) has a massive living room with a fireplace, soaring roof and plenty of space. The rooms here are of two types—newly restored and old style. Ask for one of the updated rooms if you are staying as a couple and one of the older rooms for larger groups. The lodge is served by local buses as well as lodge vans that shuttle skiers to the area and the town. Rates include breakfast and dinner.

The Timber House Ski Lodge (800-843-3502; 726-5477; $–$$$) is tucked into the woods at the edge of the area. A private trail leads directly back to the lodge. Meet other guests in the giant living room with its stone fireplace or in the outdoor hot tub. Meals are included.

The other mountain inns and B&Bs are outside of town toward Tabernash.

The Wild Horse Inn (800-729-5813; $$–$$$) is the most elegant of the local B&Bs and is built with large pine logs. The seven rooms each have a private bath and private balcony. Special attractions include a hot tub, an on-site masseuse, and endless freshly baked cookies.

Whistle Stop Bed & Breakfast (800-729-5813; 726-8767; $–$$) is a casual B&B just a block from the train station in Fraser. Two of the rooms have private baths and two have shared baths. Each guest room is on a different level of the inn for increased privacy.

The Outpost Inn (800-430-4538; 726-5346; $–$$$), a B&B, is comfortable and homey. Vans shuttle skiers to and from the ski area. A spa becomes a social center in the evenings. A maximum of 20 guests at a time stay at the inn. Rates include breakfast, but no dinner.

Winter Park also has many condo complexes. The Zephyr Mountain Lodge (800-729-5813; 726-8400; $$$-$$$$) is a luxury condo-style hotel at the base, with generous rooms, full kitchens and free high-speed Internet access. The Iron Horse Resort Retreat (800-621-8190; 726-8851; $$-$$$$) has a swimming pool and a fitness center. Iron Horse is about 2 miles outside of the town center near the base of the slopes, but has excellent shuttle service.

Winter Park Mountain Lodge (866-726-5473; 726-4211; $–$$$) is across from the ski resort and is part hotel, part ski lodge. It is an attractive and affordable choice for those who want to be close to the slopes. It has an indoor pool, hot tubs, brew pub and game room.

The Vintage (800-472-7017; 726-8801; $$-$$$$) is slightly out of the center of town but right next to the ski area. It features a restaurant, fitness room, swimming pool and good shuttle service into the town. The beautiful wooden bar came from a London pub.

For condos in town, try either the Snowblaze (800-729-5813; 726-5701; $$$-$$$$) or Crestview Place (800-729-5813; 726-9421; $$$-$$$$), across the street from Cooper Creek Square. Snowblaze has a modest athletic club. Studio units have Murphy beds, and two- and three-bedroom units have baths for each bedroom, private saunas and fireplaces. Crestview Place does not have an athletic club or private saunas, but has fireplaces and full kitchens.

One of the most popularly priced condominium complexes is the Hi Country Haus (800-729-5813; 726-9421; $$$-$$$$). These condos are spread out in a dozen buildings and share a recreation center with four hot tubs, sauna and heated swimming pool.

A couple of unusual alternatives outside of town are perfect for Nordic skiers. Devil's Thumb Ranch (800-729-5813; 726-5632; $-$$) has undergone a major renovation, adding the county's first full-service spa, new upscale cabins and a gourmet restaurant featuring organic dishes. Also try the Snow Mountain Ranch (970-887-2152; Denver line, 303-443-4743), which has Nordic trails, plus dorm facilities and cabins. It's owned by YMCA of the Rockies, and it conducts year-round recreational programs.

Dining: $$$$-Entrees $30+; $$$-$20-$30; $$-$10-$20; $-less than $10.
Accommodations: (double room) $$$$-$200+; $$$-$141-$200; $$-$81-$140; $-$80 and less.

Dining

Winter Park isn't packed with high-priced restaurants; instead, the emphasis has always been on good solid cooking. Recently, local bistros have gotten away from homestyle, stodgy cooking and are leaning toward new, innovative cuisine.

The **Ranch House Restaurant at Devil's Thumb** (726-5633; $$$) has rocketed to the top of the "must try" dining experiences in Winter Park. Tenderloin steaks, rack of lamb, and fresh seafood are prepared in this rustic dining room with views of the Continental Divide.

The **Gasthaus Eichler** (726-5133; $$–$$$) in the center of Winter Park has an Austrian/German-influenced menu. Locals all rave about **The Shed** (726-9912; $$) on Hwy. 40, which has one of the most imaginative menus with an emphasis on Southwestern cuisine, and **Fontenot's Cajun Cafe** (726-4021; $$), with fresh fish dishes prepared New Orleans style.

The **Untamed Steakhouse at Wildcreek** (726-1111; $$–$$$) serves Wood Fire Prime Rib and other cuts of beef, as well as poultry and seafood.

Smokin' Moe's (726-4600; $$), in Cooper Creek Square, has established itself as *the* place to load up on spicy barbecued ribs, hot links, chicken and "Okie baloney." For Mexican fare try **Fiesta Jalisco** (726-4877; $$), which serves so many entrees it's difficult to pick just one. **Deno's** (726-5332; $–$$), a locals' favorite, has several good pasta dishes as well as chicken, steak and shrimp selections. **Base Camp Bakery & Cafe** (726-5530; $–$$) is a tiny place that makes excellent breakfasts, baked goods, and nice sandwiches.

In Fraser, **DeAntonio's** (726-9999; $) makes good pizza and take-out food. **Randi's Irish Saloon** (726-1172; $–$$$) in downtown Winter Park is a good family restaurant with plenty of traditional pub food served at lunch and dinner.

Hernando's Pizza & Pasta Pub (726-5409; $–$$), with its central fireplace, is recommended by locals, and is often crowded—you can opt for free delivery. Great thick-and-chewy-crust pizza with unusual topping combinations are the specialty. Also try the **Winter Park Pub** (726-4929; $$), downtown on Hwy. 40, which offers traditional pub fare, 15 beers on tap, and "Mystery Beer Night." There are a lot of 20-somethings here.

For the best eggs-and-bacon breakfast in town head straight to **The Mountain Rose** (726-9940; $), but only if you aren't pressed for time. **Carver's Bakery & Cafe** (725-8202; $–$$) behind Cooper Creek Square serves breakfasts, amazing cinnamon rolls and superb sandwiches.

On the slopes, the best lunch is in the smallish, cozy **Club Car** (726-1442; $) at the Mary Jane base area. Be sure to save room for dessert—particularly the mud pie. The **Lodge at Sunspot** (726-1446; $–$$) atop the mountain is a spectacular setting for a gourmet lunch.

Condo dwellers and others who want to gather their own provisions will find a large **Safeway** supermarket (970-726-9484) in Fraser; it can be reached by the free shuttlebus.

 Apres-ski/nightlife

After a dramatic remodeling and revitalization, the slopeside **Derailer Bar** and its deck are *the* place to be for apres-ski. **The Shed,** in downtown Winter Park, has happy hour deals on margaritas and appetizers, and is popular with locals and visitors alike. **The Pub** is best described as "hardcore local," while **Mirasol Cantina,** a Mexican spot, is a good happy hour locale with two-for-one drinks and $1.50 tacos from 4–6 p.m.

For sports events, go to **Deno's Mountain Bistro** with half-a-dozen TVs, plus more than 100 types of beer and 200 wines. **Kickapoo's** is a tavern/restaurant at the base of the slopes, with two outdoor decks for drinks and dining on sunny days.

The Untamed Steakhouse at **Wildcreek** frequently has live music—this place really moves after 10 p.m. You can play pool here too. **Randi's Irish Saloon** also features live music that draws the dancing crowd after dinner. For a quiet drink without the loud music, head to **Tipper's Tavern** in the Vintage Hotel or **Eichler's. The Iron Horse** sometimes has a guitar player in the bar, and a Comedy Club every other Wednesday in ski season. **Higher Grounds** in downtown Winter Park has established its reputation on its excellent martini and sushi bar.

Diehards using public transportation, take note: After midnight, the free shuttle service is finished, but **Home James** (726-5060) has taxi service available until 2 a.m.

 ## Other activities

Devil's Thumb Outfitters (726-1099) and Dashing Through the Snow (726-5376) have old-fashioned **sleigh rides** with a stop for refreshments around a roaring campfire. Devil's Thumb Ranch (726-8231) has **winter horseback riding, sleigh rides** (including a dinner ride) and **ice skating.** Grand Adventures (726-9247 or 800-726-9257), with **dogsled rides** pulled by spirited Siberian huskies, go through miles of spectacular backcountry. Dog Sled Rides of Winter Park (726-8326) is another option.

Trailblazer (726-8452 or 800-669-0134) or Grand Adventures (726-9247 or 800-726-9257) offer **snowmobile tours.** The ski resort offers an evening dinner tour where riders go up the ski runs.

For **snow tubing,** go to the Fraser Valley Tubing Hill (726-5954). **The Base Camp 9000 Indoor Climbing Wall** is a 750 square-foot, state-of-the-art apparatus in the West Portal Station building.

There are a few **shops,** especially for sports equipment and clothing.

 ## Getting there and around

By air: Denver International Airport is a hub for several major airlines. Home James vans take skiers from the airport to Winter Park. Reserve through Central Reservations, or contact the van lines directly. Home James: 726-5060 in Colorado; or (800) 729-5813.

By car: Winter Park is 85 miles northwest of Denver International Airport on Hwy. 40. Take I-70 west to Exit 232, then head toward Winter Park and Fraser on Hwy. 40.

By train: Amtrak's California Zephyr, which runs between Chicago and San Francisco, makes a stop in Fraser, only a few miles from the ski area.

The Ski Train is an unusual treat. Operating for more than 60 years, during the season it brings 750 passengers daily from Denver directly to the Winter Park base area. It chugs along 56 miles, climbs 4,000 feet, and snakes through 28 tunnels and across canyons, ravines, and ice-crusted rivers. For Ski Train information and reservations, call (303) 296-4754.

Getting around: Rent a car for any extensive restaurant or bar hopping. If you plan to stick close to your lodging at night and your lodge transports you to the slopes, you won't need a car. Taxi service is available by calling 726-5060.

Dining: $$$$-Entrees $30+; $$$-$20-$30; $$-$10-$20; $-less than $10.
Accommodations: (double room) $$$$-$200+; $$$-$141-$200; $$-$81-$140; $-$80 and less.

Nearby resorts

SolVista Basin at Granby Ranch, Granby, CO; (970) 887-3384; (888) 283-7458

Internet: www.solvista.com

5 lifts; 406 acres; 1,000 vertical feet

SolVista Basin caters to families and is well suited for them, with ski-in/ski-out condos, gentle terrain, one central base lodge and many off-slope activities (be aware that they do not have child care). SolVista's ski area is comprised of two interconnected mountains. East Mountain is primarily for beginners and intermediates, while West Mountain's terrain is mainly intermediate and advanced with limited beginner access. Bear Bahn Park is a separate learn-to-ski park. All lifts radiate from a central base lodge making it easy for families and groups to ski together. Groups can rent SolVista for private night-skiing parties. The resort also has 25 km. of groomed Nordic track adjacent to the base lodge.

Lift tickets (2005/06 prices): Adults, $44–$46; Juniors (6–12), $21–$24; Seniors (61–69), $29–31; 70+ and younger than 6, free.

Distance from Denver: About 80 miles west via I-70 and Hwy. 40. It's 15 miles north of Winter Park.

Lodging information: SolVista Reservation and Travel (888-283-7458; 887-3384) is the central booking agency for more than 20 properties that include condominiums, family-style mountain inns, hotels, bed and breakfasts, motels, and property management companies.

Eldora Mountain Resort, Nederland, CO; (800) 444-0447; (303) 440-8700

Internet: www.eldora.com

12 lifts; 680 acres; 1,400 vertical feet; 1 terrain park; 1 superpipe

Eldora's stats are misleading: This skis and rides like a bigger mountain and draws significant crowds from Denver, Boulder and the Midwest states. Actually four mountains, the area lays out nicely according to ability level. In the back, experts and advanced skiers head for Corona Bowl's black- and double-black-diamond terrain. Runs like the West Ridge are definitely challenging, and the chutes and glades are for experienced skiers only. Indian Peaks and Challenge Mountain are laced with wide-open cruisers such as everyone's favorite first run, Hornblower, while Little Hawk Mountain is the beginner and family skiing and riding zone. Tricksters can play in a terrain park with rails, rollers, table jumps and boxes or head to the 600-foot-long superpipe.

Because this is the closest skiing to Denver, weekends can get crowded. But then, you won't have to drive crowded I-70 to get to Eldora—a fact that balances out the occasional lift lines. The resort has excellent kids' and family programs and the most popular Nordic trail system in the state. The 16,000-square-foot lodge, built of logs and natural indigenous rock, is centrally located and houses the rental shop, child care, ski school registration and dining services.

Lift tickets (2005/06 prices): Adult, $53; juniors (6–15), $33; seniors (65–74), $35; kids 5 and younger, and seniors 75 and older, $5.

Distance from Denver: Eldora is 65 miles from Denver International Airport, 45 miles from Denver via Hwys. 36 and 119, and 21 miles from Boulder. Eldora is the only ski resort with daily scheduled bus service via the Regional Transportation District, (303) 299-6002.

Lodging information: (800) 444-0447 (Boulder Convention and Visitors Bureau). Accommodations are in the historic mining town of Nederland, plus Boulder and Denver.

Schweitzer Mountain Resort and Silver Mountain, Idaho

Coeur d'Alene Region Facts

Dining:★★★
Apres-ski/nightlife:★★★
Other activities:★★★

Phone: (208) 664-3194
Toll-free information: (877) 782-9232
Internet: www.coeurdalene.org (visitors bureau)
E-mail: info@coeurdalene.org
Bed base: 1,500 rooms

Families and friends who have gone to the Central Rockies for years for their annual ski vacations, in their quest for something new, are gravitating to the Selkirks at the western edge of the northern Rockies. That means the Idaho panhandle, snuggled between Montana and Washington, home to Schweitzer and Silver mountain resorts.

Schweitzer Mountain Resort is big—3,000 skiable acres—and it's coming on big in the minds of destination skiers. It's especially favorable to skiers who like a resort where one skier per acre is a crowded day. That makes it equally delightful for experts and beginners alike. Named for a Swiss hermit who once settled on the mountain, it's one of Idaho's largest resorts. It overlooks a huge lake, Lake Pend Orielle, and also has an attractive mountain village at its base area. As if being in northern Idaho isn't remote enough, with a 9-mile access road, you really are getting away from it all here.

As for Silver Mountain, well, in 1989, an Associated Press story announced the bad news: "Liability risks and increased costs of maintaining a dangerous mountain road have prompted Kellogg's City Council to close Silverhorn Ski Area this winter." It went on to announce the good news: "The hill will reopen next year under the new name of Silver Mountain and with a new $13-million gondola." The resort and its north-facing slopes went from zero in 1989 to Snow Country Magazine's Top 50 ski resorts in four years. It's certainly worth getting to know now, before it gets even bigger. Management says an adjacent 32,000 acres of private land is available for future development.

Both mountains are roughly equidistant from the lakeside city of Coeur d'Alene, a fun place to stay. It's thriving with plenty of dining, nightlife and shopping. The lake, one of 55 in the area, is more than 25 miles long. Near town are plenty of parks and hiking trails, and the Coeur d'Alene Resort has a floating boardwalk over the water that's almost a mile long.

Schweitzer Mountain Resort

Schweitzer is one of Idaho's largest ski areas, but it's still uncrowded. One skier per acre (3,000 acres) is a good-sized crowd here. Its acreage is the second biggest in Idaho (Bogus Basin is slightly larger), and its vertical drop is second only to Sun Valley's 3,400 feet. It's been known to the region for 42 years as a true skiers' mountain, but now that the word is out nationally, things will change annually.

A European-style village with shops, restaurants and lodging provides creature comforts, with more development to come. However, many visitors stay in Sandpoint, 11 miles away on the shore of beautiful Lake Pend Oreille. This is the sort of place that people visit, then try to figure out a way to move here. Nestled between the Selkirk and Cabinet Mountains, overlooking Lake Pend Oreille, Sandpoint was originally a lumber town on the water. The shoreline, with its fjords, small inlets and peninsulas, resembles Washington state's San Juan Islands.

Schweitzer has mostly east-facing terrain. Compared to Rocky Mountain resorts, the elevation (6,400 feet) is not high, but it gets plenty of snow from its position in the Selkirks. When storms come from the north, the snow is dry and fluffy, but more often it's wet and dense. It's drier than the Cascade Concrete that falls on Washington and Oregon areas, but still wet enough to have earned the local term, Panhandle Premix.

Schweitzer cut its trails like Salt Lake City built its streets—wide enough to turn around a team of oxen. You wouldn't want to try that on Schweitzer's slopes, but rest assured that there is plenty of room to execute your turns. When the skies are clear, the vistas are outstand-

Schweitzer Mountain Resort Facts

Summit elevation:	6,400 feet
Vertical drop:	2,400 feet
Base elevation:	4,700 feet

Address: 10,000 Mountain Road, Sandpoint, ID 83864
Area code: 208
Ski area phone: 263-9555; (800) 831-8810
Snow report: 263-9562
Toll-free reservations: (800) 831-8810
E-mail: ski@schweitzer.com
Internet: www.schweitzer.com
Number of lifts: 9—1 high-speed six-pack, 1 quad, 4 doubles, 2 surface lifts, 1 moving carpet
Snowmaking: 47 acres
Skiable acreage: 3,000 acres
Uphill capacity: 8,092 per hour
Parks & pipes: 1 park, 1 pipe
Nearest lodging: Slopeside
Resort child care: Yes, 4 months and older
Adult ticket, per day: $41-$45 (05/06 prices)

Expert:★★★
Advanced:★★★
Intermediate:★★★★
Beginner:★★ **First-timer:**★★★

Dining: ★★★
Apres-ski/nightlife: ★★
Other activities: ★★

Silver Mountain Facts

Summit elevation:	6,300 feet
Vertical drop:	2,200 feet
Base elevation:	4,100 feet

Address: 610 Bunker Ave., Kellogg, ID 83837
Area code: 208
Ski area phone: 783-1111; (800) 204-6428
Snow report: 783-1111
Toll-free reservations: (866) 344-2675
E-mail: infosm@silvermt.com
Internet: www.silvermt.com
Number of lifts: 7—1 high-speed gondola, 1 quad, 2 triples, 2 doubles, 1 surface lift
Snowmaking: 35 acres
Skiable acreage: 1,590 acres (plus extensive off-piste)
Uphill capacity: 10,000 per hour
Parks & pipes: 1 park, 1 pipe
Nearest lodging: Gondola Base Village
Resort child care: Yes, 2 years and older
Adult ticket, per day: $40 (05/06 price)

Expert:★★★
Advanced:★★★
Intermediate:★★★★
Beginner:★★
First-timer:★★

Dining: ★★
Apres-ski/nightlife: ★
Other activities: ★★

ing: From the summit, skiers can look east into Montana's Cabinet Range and north to the Canadian Selkirks. And the view of big Lake Pend Oreille is memorable.

Mountain layout

♦♦ **Expert:** Schweitzer's runs and chutes are steepest at the top of its two broad bowls, North and South. The bowls are separated by the Great Divide, a long wide ridge that gives you a continuous option to drop into either bowl. Some double-black terrain tumbles off the South Bowl rim, but most experts head up the Great Escape and turn right to North Bowl, where steeps are studded with cliff bands and trees. Patient trekkers are rewarded with the Siberia Chutes.

♦ **Advanced:** A whole bowlful of chutes await in the South Bowl. There are so many, they're lettered rather than named, as in A Chute, B Chute, and so forth. Upper Stiles and the adjacent Headwall Chutes are favored by those going for quick turnaround times. Off Stella The Six-Pack Chair are two adjacent single-black runs—No Joke and Revenge—that would be double-blacks anywhere else. They both are short thrills, but stay away on icy days. Make sure to check out the resort's new lift-served terrain in "Little Blue."

■ **Intermediate:** You can wend your way down from the South Bowl summit, but unload midway on the Snow Ghost chair for North Bowl because the upper terrain is tougher. Stella The Six-Pack Chair goes to the ridge of the Northwest Territory, where you'll find 150 acres of gladed and groomed terrain. Intermediate favorites here are Cathedral Aisle, Timber Cruiser and Zip Down.

●● **Beginner:** No beginner runs come down from the top, but get a nice view by unloading midway up Chair One and heading down blue-square Gypsy. The Enchanted Forest and Happy Trails are perfect for children. Both run the length of the Musical Chairs chair, which goes right by the windows of the 40,000-square-foot Headquarters Day Lodge, so parents can check out their kids. The Enchanted Forest, with kid-high, widely spaced mounds that children can go over or around, is barred to adults and jealous snowboarders.

● **First-timer:** A wonderful learning area, completely isolated from other traffic, is served by a chair and a new moving carpet. Better yet, it's below the base area, so first-timers can start out skiing and snowboarding, rather than sidestepping up the hill or riding a lift.

Ride Guide: Schweitzer is pretty much riders' heaven, even beyond the terrain park. The chutes and bowls are all blues and blacks with easy access and return. One exception is the "Cat Track to Village" that crosses under the Sunny Side lift—there's a bit of uphill toward the end. Ridge Run, left from the top of the Great Escape Quad, is very wide and gently sloped, so you might stall out in deep, ungroomed snow. Outback Bowl is choice for tree-running—try Glade-iater from the top of the Stella six-pack.

Pipes and parks

Stomping Grounds Terrain Park is accessed from the Chair One midstation. It's 50 acres of freeriders' fun, with beginner, intermediate and expert terrain featuring jumps, rails and tabletops. Weekly jam sessions and coaching events take place throughout the year. It's also open for night riding.

Lessons (05/06 prices)

Group lessons: Custom group lessons are limited to three per class, so you'll get plenty of attention from the instructor. One-hour lessons cost $35. A package including lessons, gear and lift ticket costs $70; a three-day package costs $165.

First-timer package: First-time skiers and riders get a lesson with beginner lift ticket and rentals for $59. A three-day package costs $99. Each lesson is between one and two hours long, depending upon number of students.

Private lessons: $65 for one hour; $150 for a half day; $300 for a full day. First or last lesson of the day costs $55. Each additional person costs $15.

KidStuff (05/06 prices)

Child care: Ages 4 months to 12 years. For kids in diapers, cost is $55 for a full day; $45 for a half day. For kids out of diapers, cost is $45 for a full day; $35 for a half day. A hot lunch costs $5. Reservations strongly recommended; call (800) 831-8810, Ext. 2374.

Children's lessons: Kinder Kamp, for ages 4–6, includes a morning and afternoon lesson, rentals and an indoor recreation break and costs $85. All-day programs for ages 7–12 include lessons, lift ticket and lunch for $75; half day, $45 (without lunch). Snowboard lessons are available only on weekends and holidays.

Lift tickets (05/06 prices)

	Adult	Child (7-12)
One day	$45	$30
Three of four days	$127 ($42/day)	$85 ($28/day)
Five of seven days	$207 ($41/day)	$138 ($28/day)

Who skis free: Nobody.

Who skis at a discount: Youth (13–17) pay $35 for one day. Seniors (65+) pay $40. Children 6 and younger pay $5.

Note: Prices have been rounded to the nearest dollar. Peak/holiday prices are higher.

Cross-country and snowshoeing (visit xcskiresorts.com for more details)

Schweitzer has more than 32 km. of trails, most groomed and track set. A snowshoe trail lets you explore Hermit's Hollow. Rentals and trail passes are available in the village at The Ski & Ride Center.

Accommodations

On the mountain, **Selkirk Lodge, White Pine Lodge** and **Schweitzer Resort Condos** (800-831-8810; $$$–$$$$) are all ski-in/ski-out properties with full amenities.

In downtown Sandpoint, lodging is inexpensive (many rooms less than $100 a night) and fairly basic. Try the four-room, lakeside **Coit House B&B** (866-265-2648; 265-4035; $$) for a romantic getaway that includes a hot breakfast. Right across the street, the same owners operate **K-2 Inn** (263-3441; $–$$), a no-smoking motel featuring rooms, suites and apartments with fridges and microwaves, plus a hot tub. **La Quinta Inn** (800-282-0660; 263-9581; $$) has 68 rooms, including three suites, serves a complimentary breakfast and welcomes pets.

Dining

Ivano's Ristorante (263-0211; $–$$$), a gracious Italian restaurant in Sandpoint, has been in business for more than 20 years and is one of the locals' favorites. An extensive entree selection includes pasta, fresh seafood, buffalo, beef, chicken, veal and vegetarian.

Cafe Trinity (225-7558; $–$$$), one of Sandpoint's newest culinary additions, specializes in Creole cooking. Just two of many favorites are the spunky crawfish chowder and the pecan-crusted chicken salad. **Swan's Landing** (265-2000; $–$$$), a premiere steakhouse on the south end of the Long Bridge, pairs fabulous sunsets with Black Angus beef.

Chimney Rock Grill (255-3071; $$), in the Selkirk Lodge at the mountain, is known for its regional cuisine and serves an $18 seafood boil to die for. It includes three kinds of mussels, three kinds of clams, tiger shrimp, French bread, corn on the cob, and potatoes, accompanied by salad and finished off with huckleberry cheesecake.

For breakfast or lunch and great views, try **Cabinet Mountain Coffee** in the Lakeview Lodge. **Stella's Provisions** in the village is a one-stop, no frills sandwich shop with just what you need to keep you on the go.

If you have a car, visit **The Lodge on Hidden Lakes** (263-1642: $$–$$$), 8 miles east of Sandpoint. The kitchen offers homemade soups, breads, views and a warm atmosphere with food to match.

 ## Other activities

Sightseeing is a delight in this picturesque area. Sandpoint is on the northwest shore of the ear-shaped Lake Pend Oreille, which is 43 miles long. The name is French for "pendant of ear," and is so called because the local Indians during white settlement wore ear pendants.

Sandpoint's **Winter Carnival**, usually held the third week in January, has snow sculpture extravaganzas, ice skating parties, a "Taste of Sandpoint" on the Cedar Street Bridge, a Parade of Lights and a host of special events on Schweitzer Mountain. For information, call the Greater Sandpoint Chamber of Commerce at (800) 800-2106 or 263-2161.

Train buffs, more properly called **railfans,** consider Sandpoint to be a paradise. Railroad tracks here are called "The Funnel" because all 50 trains per day funnel onto the one track that goes through town. Sandpoint is at the convergence of the former Great Northern and Northern Pacific Railroad mainlines. They merged into the Burlington Northern system in 1970. Train watching is a never-ending source of amusement. A good photo opportunity is the Pend d'Oreille transfer yard, which is used daily by Burlington Northern, Union Pacific and Montana Rail Link.

In the Selkirk Lodge on the mountain, **Heaven, the Spa** (263-8107) pampers guests with everything from hot rock treatments to Thai massage and more.

Shopping includes some culinary delights. Coldwater Creek (263-2265), in downtown Sandpoint in a beautiful facility on Cedar Street Bridge, is a huge signature store with a deli and wine bar. Be sure to visit the bargain attic on the second floor. Don't miss the Pend d'Oreille Winery (265-8545), just a few blocks from Coldwater Creek. You can have four free tastings. More tastings are free if you buy a bottle of wine. The gift shop is full of off-beat and interesting items—you can even buy "retired" oak barrel planters. Sandpoint is home to Litehouse Bleu Cheese Factory (263-2030), which has its full line and samples at its local retail store.

Dining: $$$$-Entrees C$30+; $$$-C$20-$30; $$-C$10-$20; $-less than C$10.
Accommodations: (double room) $$$$-C$200+; $$$-C$141-$200; $$-C$81-$140; $-C$80 and less.

Silver Mountain

Silver Mountain, above Kellogg in Idaho's Silver Valley, is rapidly becoming another ex-mining-town-turned-successful-ski-mountain story, just like Park City, Aspen, Telluride and Ketchum. Like Red Mountain in British Columbia, skiers come here for a few days and never leave. The attitude is cheerful, upbeat, and everyone understands why skiers and snowboarders spend all day—day after day—on the slopes.

Silver Mountain's original name was Jackass Ski Bowl and it's been hard to market ever since. The name honored the discoverer of the metal that brought riches to the valley more than a century ago. Local legend says a donkey got away from its owner, scampered up a hill, and was standing on a rock with a silvery glint when the owner caught up with it. Bunker Hill Mine, which also took lead, zinc and copper from the hillsides, ran the ski area for employee recreation and changed the name to Silverhorn. But in the early 1980s silver prices plunged and Bunker Hill closed. What the company left behind was a white-knuckle road up to the ski area (later condemned by the city) and a Superfund cleanup site of astounding proportions. Kellogg took over what is now Silver Mountain and taxed itself $2 million to build the 45-tower, 3.1-mile gondola, the longest in the world. It rises out of the parking lot a quarter mile from I-90.

The gondola descends low over the houses and yards of the town of Wardner before climbing to Silver's "base area," called Mountain Haus, at 5,700 feet. A hefty portion of Silver's terrain is below the Mountain Haus, which gives the area its 2,200-foot vertical drop. There are no trails down to the base, though, so the gondola is the only way in and out.

The 1,590 skiable acres descend from two mountain peaks of the Bitterroots—Kellogg Peak and Wardner Peak. Like British Columbia's Red Mountain, Oregon's Mt. Bachelor and Idaho's Bogus Basin, there is a bit of 360-degree skiing around Kellogg Peak to the Sky Way Ridge that gets skiers to the Chair 4 trails of Wardner Peak.

This guarantee can't be beat: If snow conditions don't please you, return your lift ticket to the gondola base within an hour and a half and get a pass for another day.

Mountain layout

Silver has two connected peaks, Kellogg and Wardner. The gondola deposits skiers and snowboarders at Mountain Haus on Kellogg. Skiers and boarders fan out in several directions. Most stay on the Kellogg side, so to avoid even a mirage of crowds, head to the Wardner side. Lift lines are rarely a problem, but the gondola queue can back up for downloading at closing time (remember, you can't ski to the gondola base). To avoid morning clog, ride up a half-hour early for breakfast at Mountain Haus.

◆◆**Expert:** Experts come for the steep glades of giant Ponderosa pines and the open-boundary policy. Take the Wardner Peak Traverse to an inspirational knob with a stupendous view of the Silver Valley below. Some challenging black-diamond runs go back down to the Shaft and Chair 4. Terrible Edith, off Noah's and under Chair 5, is one of those runs that makes you feel like you're skiing down a globe. The farther down you go, the steeper it gets, until finally you see the cat track below—and that's only half-way down.

◆**Advanced:** For advanced skiers, the run rating always depends on snow conditions. On fresh powder days, take Silver Belt to Rendezvous on the Kellogg side. For great thrills on the Wardner side, cut down anywhere from the early section of the Wardner Peak Traverse. The best skiing on powder days is off the scree slopes between the tops of Chairs 4 and 2. Pass Midway and keep going down through the Shaft to the Chair 4 base. Day fog can cause night ice when the thermometer dips. Until it softens up, stay on the groomed runs (most of the Kellogg side). Centennial and Tamarack, both blues, are safe bets on the Wardner side.

■ **Intermediate:** Silver Belt, from the triple Chair 2, is a wide and terrific intermediate warm-up run. At the Junction you can turn down Saddle Back for a bumpier ride, or take a hard left on the Cross Over Run to the Midway load station on Chair 4 for a ride to Wardner Peak. From the top there are several trails back to Midway.

●●● ● **Beginner/First-timer:** Chairs 1, 2, 3, and 5 at the Mountain Haus base area all serve beginner terrain. Below the lodge, Ross Run is a wide beginner favorite, allowing crossover to Noah's and back again, ending on Dawdler with a choice to return to Chair 5 or Chair 3.

Ride Guide: After snowboarders ripped through yards in little Wardner under the gondola, it's now illegal to ski or snowboard in town. But there's plenty of space on the mountain.

Parks and pipes

Silver's terrain park on Lower Quicksilver run has jumps, pools, wave walls and a halfpipe.

Lessons (05/06 prices)

Reservations are recommended for all lessons.

Group lessons: 90-minute lessons cost $20; three-hour lessons, offered only on weekends and holidays, cost $39.

First-timer package: First-time skiers and riders get a 90-minute lesson with beginner lift ticket and rentals for $49. A three-day package costs $99.

Private lessons: $49 for one hour; $129 for three hours; $199 for a full day. Early-bird lesson starts at 9 a.m. and costs $29. Each additional person costs $10.

KidStuff (05/06 prices)

Child care: Ages 2 to 6. Cost is $39 for a full day; $25 for a half day; $7 per hour. Add a one-hour private lesson for $39. Private child care is available for younger children by special arrangement. The child-care center is in the Mountain Haus and is open 8:30 a.m. to 4 p.m. daily, plus during night-skiing hours on Friday and Saturday. Reservations strongly recommended; call (800) 204-6428.

Children's lessons: All-day programs for ages 5–12 include lessons, rentals, lift ticket and lunch for $65; half day, $55 (without lunch). Snowboard lessons start at age 8. Multiday discounts are available.

Lift tickets (05/06 prices)

	Adult	Child (7-12)
One day	$40	$20
Three days	$114 ($38/day)	$54 ($18/day)
Five days	$190 ($38/day)	$90 ($18/day)

Who skis free: Children 6 and younger.

Who skis at a discount: Youth (13–17), seniors (60–69) and college students with a valid ID pay $27 for one day; $78 for three; $125 for five. Super Seniors 70 and older pay $19 for one day; multiday discounts apply. Silver Mountain offers reciprocal complimentary and discount ticket privileges to season passholders of Mission Ridge, Ski Banff@Norquay, Big White, Silver Star and White Pass.

Note: Prices are higher for peak/holiday periods.

Accommodations

Morning Star Lodge (800-344-2675; $$–$$$) at the Gondola Base Village has condos with full amenities, spacious facilities and rooftop hot tubs.

The Mansion on the Hill (786-4455; $$$), a B&B in Kellogg that also owns The Veranda (see *Dining*), offers rooms, cottages and breakfast in a cozy setting. A day spa is on the premises.

The most affordable place to stay is at the base of the gondola at the **Baymont Inn** (800-785-5443; 783-1234; $–$$). It's next to the gondola base, extremely clean, with an indoor pool, hot tub and serves a continental breakfast in the lobby. **Silver Ridge Mountain Lodge** ((800-435-2588) is close to the gondola village. **The Trail Motel** (784-1161; $-$$), clean and comfortable with restaurants nearby, is half a mile from the gondola village.

Silverhorn Motor Inn & Restaurant (738-1151; $-$$) six blocks from the gondola village, has an indoor hot tub, restaurant, movie library and a free laundry.

Dining

Rumor has it that **The Veranda** (783-2625; $$), in a beautifully restored home with a country French theme, has the best dinner in Kellogg. **Terrible Edith's** ($–$$), named after a lady of the night from the mining-boom era, is at the gondola base and features Italian food and microbrews. They also serve a mean and reasonable breakfast. Locals say the best breakfast in town can be had at **Sam's** ($), across the highway from the gondola. Order hash browns and eggs or omelets and tell them the local secret: "Brian sent us."

The Mountain House Grill at the Mountain Haus base area at the top of the gondola has great cafeteria-style chili, soup, pizza, burgers and quick snacks. Stop in at **Mountain Tapas Cafe** in the gondola village for espresso. Stop in on your way down, too. They also serve tapas, fine wines and microbrews on tap. **CJ's Cafe** in Kellogg, three minutes from the resort, serves breakfast and lunch. Bring your lift ticket for a free espresso.

The Enaville Resort (682-3453; $–$$), off I-90 Exit 43A, is always a real treat for visitors new to the Kellogg area. Known locally as the Snake Pit, it's more of a destination dinery than a resort. Over its 125-year history, the Snake Pit accommodated a lot of people for a lot of purposes, but sleeping through the night was never one of them. Sorry, no overnighters these days. While you're wondering who those people dressed in camouflage are, enjoy an appetizer of Rocky Mountain oysters before moving on to buffalo burgers and barbecue.

Other activities

Silver Mountain has a scenic 5 km. **snowshoe trail** that's a nice break from skiing. Rent snowshoes at the resort's rental shop. **Snowmobiling** is very big in Wallace—where it's legal on city streets—10 miles east of Kellogg on I-90, and also at Lookout Pass, 10 miles past Wallace on the Montana border. Lookout has a snowmobile camp and access to 600 miles of snowmobile trails. Call (800) 643-2386 for more information (Best Western Wallace Inn, a headquarters of sorts, for snowmobiling with free security snowmobile storage).

Silver Mountain's **Mardi Gras** party, normally the last Saturday in February, has a scavenger hunt for kids, face painting, children's snow castle and ice sculptures along with fun games. Later on it's time for the adults to cut loose with live music, drink specials, costume contest and a lot of crazy Mardi Gras attire and bead wear.

Perhaps symbolic of the new Kellogg spirit are the life-sized **sculptures-from-scrap** that are placed around downtown. They were made by Dave Dose, a high school teacher and county commissioner with a sense of humor.

At Cataldo, 24 miles east of Coeur d'Alene on I-90 (Exit 39), sits the **Mission of the Sacred Heart**, Idaho's oldest building. It was hand built, without nails, and the walls are a 1-foot-thick mixture of mud, clay, willow saplings and straw, covered with boards inside and out. Jesuit priests supervised up to 300 Coeur d'Alene Indians at a time during the 1850-53 construction. Guided or self-guided tours are available. The mission is open year-round.

You'll find a variety of **shops** at the Gondola Base Village and in downtown Kellogg.

Coeur d'Alene

Coeur d'Alene, in the center of Northern Idaho, is a central base for exploring the area. It offers all the features of big-town life with a small-town ambience. The downtown area is alongside Lake Coeur d'Alene, which has 135 miles of shoreline. Many cruise boats offer lake trips to watch eagles, take in the scenery, eat dinner or visit the Famous Floating Golf Green and dozens of quiet coves. The cruises are on hiatus for most of the winter, but from Thanksgiving to New Year's, they tour around the area lakeside properties, which are festively lighted for the holiday season.

If you plan to ski at Silver Mountain or Schweitzer, make your base at the world-class **Coeur d'Alene Resort** (800-688-5253; 765-4000; $$-$$$$). The Resort is in the heart of downtown, on the lakeshore. It boasts a full-service spa, fitness center and four restaurants, including the newly renovated **Beverly's** ($$$–$$$$), an elegant, prize-winning, top-floor restaurant with spectacular views and a million-dollar wine inventory. Transportation is available to both mountains; an airport shuttle also is available.

Don't leave this city without a visit to **Hudson's Hamburgers** ($) for a "Huddy Burger." Just a block from the Coeur d'Alene Resort, it's an institution. Opened in 1907, the small diner-like restaurant with a simple, long counter lined by stools has been in the Hudson family for three generations. They offer three choices—hamburgers with pickles, onions and/or cheese—and each burger is made from scratch. They also offer three special sauces, which you can buy for a reasonable price (the hot spicy mustard is a treasure if you like hot and spicy).

The best breakfast around is at the Coeur d'Alene Resort at **Dockside** ($). It also has the best view. Everyone's favorite is the Sunday brunch at $25. Other great breakfasts can be had at **Michael D's** ($) at the end of Main Street and at **The Breakfast Nook** ($), known for crab omelets and hash browns.

Getting there and getting around

By air: Spokane International Airport, in Spokane, Wash., is the nearest major airport. For ground transportation, call Moose Express (676-1561). Car rentals are available at the airport. The airport is 86 miles from Schweitzer, 75 miles from Silver Mountain and 40 miles from Coeur d'Alene.

By rail: Amtrak's Empire Builder stops in downtown Sandpoint, with connections to Seattle, Portland, St. Paul and Chicago. Car rentals are available in Sandpoint.

By car: Schweitzer is in Sandpoint, 90 minutes from Spokane. Take I-90 to Coeur d'Alene, then Hwy. 95 north to Sandpoint. The 9-mile access road to the ski area has six hairpin switchbacks and can be a bit hairy. Silver Mountain is in Kellogg, about 75 minutes from Spokane and right off I-90 east of Coeur d'Alene. If you make home base in Coeur d'Alene, Silver is 40 miles away and Schweitzer is 50 miles. Coeur d'Alene is off I-90, be-

Dining: $$$$-Entrees C$30+; $$$-C$20-$30; $$-C$10-$20; $-less than C$10.
Accommodations: (double room) $$$$-C$200+; $$$-C$141-$200; $$-C$81-$140; $-C$80 and less.

Sun Valley
Idaho

Summit elevation:	9,150 feet
Vertical drop:	3,400 feet
Base:	5,750 feet

Address: Sun Valley Resort,
1 Sun Valley Rd., Box 10, Sun Valley, ID 83353
Area code: 208
Toll-free reservations: (800) 786-8259 (resort) or (800) 634-3347 ext. 1 (Sun Valley/Ketchum Central Reservations)
Snow report: 622-2093 or (800) 635-4150
Fax: 622-3700 (resort) or 726-4533 (visitors' bureau)
E-mail: ski@sunvalley.com (resort) or info@visitsunvalley.com (visitors' bureau)
Internet: www.sunvalley.com (resort) or www.visitsunvalley.com (visitors' bureau)
Expert:★★★★ **Advanced:**★★★★★
Intermediate:★★★★★
Beginner:★★★ **First-timer:**★★★

Number of lifts: 19–7 high-speed quads, 5 triples, 4 doubles, 2 surface lifts, 1 moving carpet
Snowmaking: 73 percent of groomed terrain
Skiable acreage: 2,054 acres
Uphill capacity: 26,780 per hour
Parks & pipes: 1 pipe
Bed Base: 4,500
Nearest lodging: Walking distance, condos
Resort child care: Yes, 6 months and older
Adult ticket, per day: $66-$69 (05/06 price)

Dining:★★★★★
Apres-ski/nightlife:★★★★
Other activities:★★★★

Sun Valley may provide America's perfect ski vacation. It has a European accent mixed with the Wild West. It is isolated, yet comfortable; rough in texture, but also refined; Austrian in tone, cowboy in spirit.

Ageless would be the one word to describe Sun Valley Village, America's first ski resort, built in 1936 by Union Pacific tycoon Averell Harriman. It exudes restrained elegance with the traditional Sun Valley Lodge, village, steeple, horse-drawn sleighs and steaming pools. Sun Valley does low-key with perfection. In contrast, the town of Ketchum is all-American West, a flash of red brick, a slab of prime rib, a rustic cluster of small restaurants, shops, homes, condos and lodges. It's the nearby town of Ketchum that actually curls around the broad-shouldered evergreen rise of Bald Mountain, known as Baldy to locals. Each snow ribbon dropping from the summit into the valley leads to the streets of Ketchum.

This is Hemingway country. When he wasn't hobnobbing with the glitterati of the day, he wrote most of "For Whom The Bell Tolls" in the Sun Valley Lodge, where photos show Hollywood celebrities who first made the place famous. Sun Valley has developed many famous winter-sport athletes: the late Gretchen Fraser, who was the first American Olympic ski champion in 1948; Christin Cooper, a 1984 silver Olympic medalist; Picabo Street, who won a silver at the 1994 Olympics and a gold in the 1998 Olympics; and Muffy Davis, 2002 three-time Paralympic silver medalist and overall World Cup Champion.

The Sun Valley Company keeps the skiing as up-to-date as any in America: The resort has a large computerized snowmaking system and seven high-speed quads, including one that rises a whopping 3,144 vertical feet in 10 minutes. Its day lodges have won raves from skiers and architectural awards from the ski industry. The newly built 26,000-square-foot day lodge at Dollar Mountain makes it easy for families and beginners to set up base camp.

And yet, it is the celebration of its history that makes Sun Valley stand out from the rest of America's ski areas. If you enjoy history, you must stay at the Sun Valley Lodge, a beautifully preserved property with a pronounced mid-20th-century feel. The elegance of a bygone era is encountered in the details: uniformed doormen; a formal dining room; a large second-floor "drawing room" with the piano in the center, overstuffed chairs and sofas in the middle, and fireplaces at either end; and an immense "hot tub" swimming pool that dates to the early days of the resort. "Sun Valley Serenade," a 1941 movie starring Sonja Henie and John Payne, is as corny as can be when you see it at home but it's lots of fun when you see it in Sun Valley, especially when you later try to track down the exact filming locations on the mountain and in the lodge.

Mountain layout

Sun Valley is split between two mountains separated by a 15–20 minute bus trip. Bald Mountain (called "Baldy") is best suited for intermediate and advanced skiers, while beginners and first-timers should stick to Dollar. If you are in a group of mixed abilities, plan to ski in separate groups all day and meet later for apres-ski activities.

♦♦ **Expert ♦ Advanced:** Baldy's terrain is best known for its long runs with a consistent pitch, rather than flats, cliffs and walls. Mile-long ridge runs lead to a clutch of advanced and intermediate bowls. The Mayday chair reaches this great bowl skiing.

Limelight is a long, excellent bump run. Holiday is no vacation. The Exhibition plunge is one of the best known black-diamond descents. Fire Trail, on the ski area boundary, is a darting, tree-covered descent for those who can make quick, flowing turns. The Seattle Ridge trail with hypnotic views curves around the bowls. The bowl area below is a joy. The downhill skier's right is a little easier, skier's left a little tougher, and you can catch the sun throughout the day. There are sections where you can do 50-yard-wide turns, but there is no easy terrain where you can relax your quads. The only flats are on top.

■ **Intermediate:** Baldy is good for this level. Trails are not quite as wide as at other Rocky Mountain resorts, but they're a lot wider than New England trails, and most are very long.

The best warm-ups are either the Upper and Lower College runs leading to the River Run area, or the Warm Springs run. Both descend from the top and head to the base, though College takes a little jog and joins with River Run near the bottom. Warm Springs is labeled blue-square and College is labeled green, but frankly, we didn't observe that much of a difference. Both are long, moderately steep, very well groomed and loads of fun. Other good spots are Cozy, Hemingway and Greyhawk in the Warm Springs area, often less crowded because the trail map shows a black-diamond entry (there's an intermediate cat-track entrance a little farther down that isn't as obvious on the map), as well as the Seattle Ridge runs, marked green but definitely intermediate level.

If you want to follow the sun, start your day in the River Run area, then shift to the runs dropping off Seattle Ridge and finish up cruising the Warm Springs face.

●● **Beginner:** Do not be fooled by the green-circle markings on the Baldy trail map. Beginners should not ski Baldy. Repeat: Beginners should not ski Baldy. The runs are seriously underrated for difficulty. Yes, yes, we're well aware that the green-blue-black ratings system reflects the relative difficulty of the trails at each individual resort. Sun Valley followed the rules and marked the "easiest" runs on Baldy with green circles. Compared to other resorts, however, these runs are blue—royal blue, deep blue. If you are at all tentative about your skills, start out on Dollar. However, this means you'll be isolated for lunch and apres-ski from family and friends who are skiing Baldy.

● **First-timer:** Skiing parents can enroll their children in ski school at the River Run Lodge and Skier Services building at the base of the River Run trail on Baldy. The ski school will transport children enrolled in novice lessons to Dollar. Adult first-timers should head directly to Dollar. The terrain here is perfect for learning and good for starting out in powder.

Ride Guide: Baldy's terrain is best known for its long runs with a consistent pitch, great for turning perfect arcs. Be prepared for the mile-long ridge runs that lead to several advanced and intermediate bowls, but don't avoid them or you'll miss out on some prime terrain. If you're an intermediate planning to sample the Warm Springs terrain, just be aware that the intermediate entrance is a cat track.

Parks and pipes

A 400-foot-long halfpipe with 12-foot-high walls can be found in the Warm Springs area, to rider's left just below Race Arena.

Cross-country and snowshoeing (visit xcskiresorts.com for more details)

The Sun Valley/Ketchum area has about 210 km. of trails overall. The closest facilities are at the **Sun Valley Nordic Center** (622-2250 or 622-2251), within walking distance of the Sun Valley Lodge, where 41 km. of cross-country ski trails are groomed and marked for difficulty; 4 km. are dog friendly. Lessons are available. The Atlas Snowshoe Center rents snowshoes for the 6 km. of free designated snowshoe trails.

The Blaine County Recreation District grooms the **North Valley Trails**, which have more than 100 km. of groomed trails in the Sawtooth National Recreation Area supported by set trail fees or donations. Dogs are welcome to accompany you on 30 km. of designated groomed trails. The largest center is **Galena Lodge** (726-4010; grooming report, 726-6662) with 56 km. of trails, a full restaurant and a ski shop. It also has a 15- km. snowshoe trail and snowshoe rentals. A popular event is dinner followed by moonlit skiing, or star gazing dinners with local astronomers. Galena is 24 miles north of Ketchum on Hwy. 75. There is a bus that runs from Sun Valley North to Galena at 10 a.m. and then returns at 2 p.m., so that there is no need to bring a car to access the North Valley Trails.

Wood River Trails features 30 km. of trails stretching north of Ketchum to Hailey and Bellevue. **Lake Creek** has 15.5 km. of trails, and three other areas have less than 10 km. each. The **Boulder Mountain Trail** stretches 30 km. from the Sawtooth National Recreation Area headquarters 8 miles north of Ketchum to Easley Hot Springs and Galena, and is groomed all winter, snow conditions permitting.

Avalanche and snow condition reports are available 24 hours a day from the Ketchum Ranger District at 622-8027. North Valley Trails maintains a **grooming hotline,** 726-6662.

For backcountry tours through the largest wilderness area outside Alaska, contact either **Sun Valley Trekking** (788-1966) or **Sawtooth Mountain Guides** (774-3324). Both feature hut-to-hut skiing and the opportunity to stay in yurts as well.

Lessons (05/06 prices)

Call the Sun Valley Ski School (622-2289) for more information.
Group lessons: $50 for two hours, with multiday discounts, for skiing and snowboarding.

First-timer package: A two-hour lesson, all-day rentals and lift ticket cost $95.

Private lessons: $102 for one person for one hour; all-day costs $460. Discounts are available for multiple hours (cheaper in the afternoon) and additional people in lesson.

Special programs: Master racing clinics run three hours per day for $70. A multiday women's clinic is held several times each season—call for exact dates.

KidStuff [05/06 prices]

Child care: Sun Valley's Playschool in the Sun Valley Village offers care for kids 6 months to 6 years, but the upper age limit is not strictly enforced, should you have a 7-year-old who doesn't ski or ride. Ages 6 months–2 years, cost is $92 full day, $74 for a half day. Toilet-trained and older are $76 all day, $65 half day. Reservations required, and priority is given to guests in Sun Valley resort hotels and condos. Call 622-2288.

Other options: Super Sitters (788-5080) has screened sitters trained in CPR and first aid who do in-room babysitting. **Baby's Away** (800-327-9030; 726-0199) rents and will deliver baby needs to your lodge, such as crib, stroller, car seat and toys.

Children's lessons: A four-hour ski session, including lunch, is $110 for kids 4–12 years old; snowboard lessons are for kids 7–12. Tiny Tracks is a ski lesson from noon to 1 p.m. for kids 3–4 years old; cost is $60. Discounts are available for multiple days in all children's programs. Lift tickets are extra.

Special activities: Boulder Mountain Clay Works (726-4484) runs children's classes for throwing clay on the wheel and painting pottery. Cottonwood Catering (726-0606) has cooking classes for children throughout the year. A popular free activity is sledding down Penny Hill, across from the Sun Valley Barn.

Lift tickets [05/06 prices]

	Adult	Child (Up to 12)
One day	$69	$40
Three of four days	$204 ($68/day)	$114 ($38/day)
Five of six days	$330 ($66/day)	$180 ($36/day)

These are prices for tickets at Baldy.

Who skis free: Children 15 and younger ski and stay free when they are with a parent (one child per parent) in a Sun Valley Resort hotel or condo or any participating property in Ketchum, Elkhorn or Warm Springs. Blackout periods for this offer are the Christmas/New Year holiday, all of February and the first week of March; call (800) 786-8259 for specific dates.

Who skis at a discount: Ages 65 and older pay $50 per day. Prices for those who ski only at Dollar/Elkhorn are: adult $30, child $24. Ticket prices are lowered early and late season.

Note: The Exchange Lift Program allows the exchange of multiday tickets (three days or more) for other events and activities. One of the days can be exchanged for your choice of select activities.

Accommodations

For information or reservations, call (800) 634-3347, Ext. 1.

Built in 1936, the **Sun Valley Lodge & Sun Valley Resort** (800-786-8259; $$–$$$$) is the heart of the resort, though it is not slopeside. A skating rink once ruled by ice queen Sonja Henie is just outside the doors. The village is a 3,800-acre Alpine enclave of pedestrian walkways, wall paintings, snow sculptures and spruce foliage. Because the Lodge was built well before the time of group tourism, each room is unique: pricing depends on room size and added factors such as view and balcony. The Tyrolean-style

Sun Valley Inn (800-786-8259; $$–$$$$), about a hundred yards from the Lodge, is a bit less expensive but offers most of the same amenities. Both the Lodge and the Inn have just received first-class facelifts. French-country rooms have marble baths and large-screen plasma TVs. Condos and suites are available; ask about packages.

Knob Hill Inn (800-526-8010; 726-8010; $$$$) was recently accepted into the exclusive Relais et Chateaux group. It looks Old World Austria on the outside, but inside the rooms are quite modern and spacious—especially the jetted tubs.

Pennay's at River Run (800-736-7503; 726-9086; $$$–$$$$) is a cluster of family-perfect condos within walking distance of River Run lifts. There is a big outdoor hot tub, and units have VCRs. A snowmobile-drawn carriage whisks guests to and from the River Run lifts.

Best Western Tyrolean Lodge (800-333-7912; 726-5336; $$), only 400 yards from the River Run lift, has an Alpine atmosphere with wood-paneled ceilings and down comforters. A champagne continental breakfast is served. **Best Western Kentwood Lodge** (800-805-1001; 726-4114; $$) with an indoor pool is in the middle of town, convenient to everything. The rates here are a bit higher than at the Tyrolean. **Clarion Inn** (800-262-4833; 726-5900; $–$$), a hotel with a large outdoor hot tub and continental breakfasts, has rooms with simple decor that open to outdoor walkways. It can be quite rowdy during spring break and holidays.

Christophe CondoHotel (800-779-1394; 726-5601; $–$$$$) has roomy condos with underground parking and heated pool. Make sure you know exactly how to get to your room; the outdoor walkways are somewhat confusing. **Tamarack Lodge** (800-521-5379; 726-3344; $$) is smack in the middle of town with a hot tub and indoor pool. Good for families, the lodge is equipped with microwaves, refrigerators and coffee makers. It doesn't get any more convenient than this for nightlife and dining. Rooms with fireplaces cost more.

Povey Pensione (128 W. Bullion St., Hailey; 800-370-4682; 788-4682; $) is a century-old residence maintaining the original character of its builder, John Povey, a British carpenter, who built and lived in the house when Hailey was a mining town. This Pensione is about 13 miles south of Ketchum. If you stay here, rent a car. Children younger than 12 are not allowed.

Lift Tower Lodge (800-462-8646; 726-5163; $) gets its name from a section of an old ski lift and is very close to the River Run base. All rooms have two beds, a refrigerator, TV and phone, and the lodge has a hot tub. Complimentary breakfasts include bagels, coffee and orange juice. The free bus stops in front. During value season the price of a room can be halved.

High Country Resort Properties (800-726-7076) has an extensive selection of homes, townhomes and condominiums for short- and long-term rentals in the greater Ketchum-Sun Valley area. Choices range from cozy cabins to luxury homes. Special services available include car rental, shuttle bus, airport pick-up, dinner reservations and activity booking. For private home rentals, you also can call **ResortQuest Sun Valley** (800-521-2515; 726-5601) or **Premier Resorts** (800-635-4444; 727-4000). Both have rentals near the lifts, downtown, out at Elkhorn Village near the Dollar Mountain lifts, and homes that offer privacy and isolation.

Dining

On the mountain:

The **Warm Springs, Seattle Ridge** and **River Run day lodges** have excellent restaurants. Skiers can settle down to a lunch of prime rib, salmon, stone-fired pizza and many other delights, all while enjoying panoramic views. The deck at Seattle Ridge is gorgeous. Deli and gourmet cafeteria-style clusters are the latest in on-mountain dining, and Sun Valley has these, too. The **Round House** is one of the original mountaintop restaurants. The **Lookout Restaurant** is often hidden under a mound of snow, which keeps lunchtime crowds small. It's the mountain's *original* restaurant and it looks like a blockhouse, but it serves a good range of soups, tamales, hot dogs and sandwiches. Brown-bagging is OK at the Lookout too. Eating after 1:30 p.m. to avoid the crowds. The **Dollar Cabin** at the base of Dollar Mt. has been replaced with a new building.

In Sun Valley Village:

The **Sun Valley Lodge Dining Room** (622-2150; $$$–$$$$) has old-time elegance and is the only spot in the area with live music and dinner dancing. Try the Steak Diane, Chateaubriand Bearnaise Bouquetiere, and fresh Idaho trout or poached salmon.

The **Ram** (622-2225; $$$), attached to the Sun Valley Inn, serves elegant European and French specialties ranging from grilled New York strip loin to fish and seafood. **Gretchen's** (622-2144; $$) in the Lodge has a fine dinner menu, including Idaho lamb and beef, and serves breakfast and lunch too ($). Recent additions are **Bald Mountain Pizza and Pasta** (622-2143; $$) for dinner and the new **Inn Lobby Lounge** (622-2266; $$) in the Sun Valley Inn for a light meal. At **Sun Valley Deli** (622-2060) pick up sandwiches and quick snacks.

The **Konditorei** (622-2235; $) has an Austrian flavor and excellent lunches, such as hearty soups served in a bread bowl next to a mountain of fruit. Follow up your meal with a stop at the **Chocolate Foundry** (622-2147; $) and take home something to satisfy your sweet cravings. The **Boiler Room** (622-2148) in the Village has great apres-ski along with comedy acts for the evening crowd.

At the Sun Valley Lodge, **Gretchen's** (622-2144; $) has plentiful breakfast fare with moderate prices and **Konditorei** (622-2235; $) in the Sun Valley Village has good breakfasts. The **Lodge Dining Room** (726-2150; $) serves an excellent Sunday brunch.

In Ketchum:

Ketchum has some of the best restaurants of any ski resort in America. Anyone with fine dining on his or her mind will not be disappointed. The region's real gourmet action takes place here. The price ranges we give here are a rough guide.

These restaurants all vie for "best of Ketchum." **Michel's Christiania** (726-3388; $$$), run by Michel Rudigoz, serves fine French cuisine. **Felix's** (726-1166; $$$), which has moved to 380 1st Ave. North, offers a continental menu in a very international setting. **Evergreen Bistro** (726-3388; $$$) has an elegant atmosphere of wood, crystal and glass and quite possibly the town's best wine list. **Chandler's** (726-1776; $$$) serves gourmet meals in a series of tiny rooms. Ask to be seated near the fireplace if you are with a group; couples should ask for the small alcove off the main fireplace room. The three-course "prix fixe" meal is one of Ketchum's best bargains.

Bistro 44 (726-2040; $$$) serves authentic French cooking prepared by chef-owner Alain Gilot. It's open for lunch and dinner is prepared in two seatings nightly, Monday through Saturday. Reservations are required for dinner. For trattoria-style cuisine, handmade pastas and excellent fish specials, head to the **Baci Italian Cafe and Wine Bar** (726-8384; $$).

Dean's Restaurant (726-8911; $$), formerly the Coyote Grill and Wine Bar (same owners, same place, just a new name), has a very romantic setting. Filled with couches and overstuffed chairs snuggling tiny tables, the rooms accentuate the creative grill cuisine.

The **Pioneer Saloon** (726-3139; $$), a local hangout going back into Ketchum history, is known for its prime rib and baked potatoes. **Ketchum Grill** (726-4660; $$) has a daring, innovative menu with flavor mixtures that will keep your tastebuds tingling. The restaurant participates in the Chef's Collective to buy only locally grown/hunted or organic produce. **Rico's Pizza and Pasta** (726-7426; $$) is the local's favorite spot for take-out Italian dishes, which leaves the dining room empty and quiet.

Dining: $$$$-Entrees $30+; $$$-$20-$30; $$-$10-$20; $-less than $10.

Accommodations: (double room) $$$$-$200+; $$$-$141-$200; $$-$81-$140; $-$80 and less.

Sushi on Second (726-5181; $$) has Japanese fare. Locals say **Globus** (726-1301; $$) has good Chinese/Thai food. **Panda Chinese Restaurant** (726-3591; $) serves Chinese meals from several regions.

Ketchum Kantina (726-5072; $$) and **Desperado's** (726-3068; $$) are family-friendly Mexican restaurants. **Warm Springs Ranch Restaurant** (726-2609; $$) serves a wide-ranging menu including children's specials, and mountain trout swim in pools near the cozy cabin. **Sawtooth Club** (726-5233) has good grub overlooking the fireplace.

Grumpy's (no phone, we're told; $) is the locals' favorite for great burgers and beer; it's on Warm Springs Road just down from Backwood's (and next door to a laundromat, in case you need to wash a few clothes). **Smoky Mountain Pizza & Pasta** (622-5625; $) has great, very affordable Italian fare and massive salads. And the **Burger Grill** (726-7733; $$) serves up thick hamburgers, mounds of fries and frosty shakes.

For breakfast head to the **Kneadery** (726-9462; $) on Leadville Street with a cozy woodsy atmosphere. It's open for lunch as well. **Java on Fourth** (726-2882; $) has daily specials, excellent food and an unusual atmosphere.

Directly across the street from the Warm Springs Lodge at the base of Baldy is a Ketchum institution, **Irving's Red Hot** stand, where you can get great hotdogs. "The Works" (a dog smothered in fixings and chips) for only $2 is a lunch bargain that can't be beat.

One evening dining adventure that should not be missed is the horse-drawn sleigh ride dinner at **Trail Creek Cabin** (622-2135; $$$). The cozy rough-hewn cabin dates from 1937 and can be reached by sleigh, car or cross-country skis. For the sleigh ride, make reservations 72 hours in advance, but you can always check for open space; call 622-2135. The sleigh ride costs $22. Entrees are $19–$25. Be warned, however—if you don't speak up, an accordionist may play somebody else's old favorites during dinner. **Galena Lodge** (726-4010) also offers moonlight and star gazing dinners in the warmth of a rustic lodge.

Apres-ski/nightlife

If your skiing ends in Warm Springs, **Apples** is the spot for a mountainside debriefing. Overall, Warm Springs is the top base for slopeside revelry. Just remember not to take beverages on the bus; drivers are quick to enforce the rules.

The **Boiler Room** at Sun Valley has the Mike Murphy comedy show every afternoon at 5:30 p.m. for a small charge. Check the schedule for "Sun Valley Serenade" and Warren Miller movies at the **Opera House** in Sun Valley starting at 5 p.m. And the **Duchin Room** in the Lodge has music starting at 4 p.m. On Thursdays, head to **River Run Lodge** for entertainment.

At the western-bar-themed **Whiskey Jacques,** a favorite Hemingway haunt, patrons can listen to live music and dance inside an authentic log building. The **Pioneer Saloon** gets very crowded very early on weekends. **Grumpy's** fills with locals ordering schooners.

The **Casino** is so named because there used to be slot machines where the tables now stand. **Cellar Pub** is an authentic Irish pub. It's a locals' favorite that's smoke-free and ambiance-rich. You can get a hearty plate of fish & chips until 10 p.m.

The **Sun Valley Wine Company** has a wine cellar, reportedly the largest wine selection in Idaho, and offers a light lunch and dinner menu. It is above the Ketchum state liquor store on Leadville Street. Choose a bottle of wine from its large inventory, then enjoy it in a quiet, conversation-oriented environment next to a fireplace.

It's **Lefty's Bar & Grill** for locals, darts and draft beers. As the unofficial post-game headquarters of the Sun Valley Suns ice hockey team, this hole-in-the-wall packs a crowd.

If you are staying in Sun Valley or Warm Springs and plan on partying in Ketchum, the

KART bus system stops running at midnight, but A-1 Taxi (726-9351) is available.

Other activities

Snowmobiling is available through Smiley Creek Lodge (774-3547). The Sun Valley Resort outdoor rink is open for **ice skating** year round. **Tubing** enthusiasts should head to Dollar Mountain. **Ice hockey** fans can catch home games of the Sun Valley Suns three times a month.

Sun Valley Heli-Ski (622-3108) offers **backcountry ski adventures** for all levels of skiers. **Paragliding** with Fly Sun Valley (726-3332) gets you floating over the mountains. **Ice fishing/fly fishing** is offered by Silver Creek Outfitters (726-5282) and Lost River Outfitters (726-1706).

The Sun Valley Athletic Club (726-3664) with daily and weekly rates is open to visitors with **child care, massage, aerobics, weights and swimming.** Also try High Altitude Fitness (726-1959). Sacred Cow Yoga Studio (726-7018), next to the Sun Valley Garden Center, offers a variety of **yoga** and **meditation** at varying levels throughout the week.

Shopping is extensive. The Sun Valley Village is full of boutiques and shops offering everything from Bogner and jewels to handmade chocolates. A few shops worth highlighting: The Toy Store, for unique toys from around the globe; Barry J. Peterson Jewelers, for Limoges collectors' boxes and unique jewelry; and The Country Cousin for low-priced accessories and gifts. Pick up some secondhand bargains at the Gold Mine Thrift Shop—because this supports the The Community Library in Ketchum, residents give their (sometimes barely) used clothing and sporting goods to this store. The **library** is a gem. It has an amazing history section.

Sun Valley Center for the Arts has performances and showings during the ski season. Call 726-9491 for a schedule or the Chamber & Visitors Bureau, 726-3423. **Art galleries** are another center of Ketchum and Sun Valley's cultural life.

Getting there and getting around

By air: The closest airport is Friedman Memorial, 12 miles south in Hailey. It's served by Horizon Air with daily non-stop flights from Los Angeles, Oakland and Seattle, and Delta Airlines, with multiple flights daily from Salt Lake City. Weather sometimes closes it. Another option is Twin Falls, about 90 minutes away (Delta Airlines), or Boise, about 155 miles and 2.5 hours away.

Several properties provide transportation, or use one of the following companies, most of which will pick you up in Hailey, Twin Falls or Boise: Sun Valley Stages, (800) 574-8661; Sun Valley Chauffeur, 725-0880; or Sun Valley Express, (800) 622-8267 or 342-7795.

By car: Sun Valley/Ketchum is 82 miles north of Twin Falls on Hwy. 75, and 152 miles from Boise.

Getting around: You don't really need a car if you're staying in Sun Valley Village or near the KART bus routes, which link Sun Valley, Ketchum and Baldy, running about every 20 minutes. For schedule information, call 726-7140.

Dining: $$$$-Entrees $30+; $$$-$20-$30; $$-$10-$20; $-less than $10.
Accommodations: (double room) $$$$-$200+; $$$-$141-$200; $$-$81-$140; $-$80 and less.

Idaho regional resorts

Bogus Basin, Boise, ID; (208) 332-5100; (800) 367-4397

Internet: www.bogusbasin.com

7 lifts; 2,600 skiable acres; 1,800 vertical feet; 1 terrain park

Bogus Basin is much more than the day hill skiers would expect of a seven-chair mountain so close to a city (16 miles from Boise). Bogus is a community-owned, full-service destination resort. Boise's Amtrak station brings in the destination skiers, and lodging both at the base and on the mountain keeps them on the slopes. Basically, Bogus is big.

And, like British Columbia's Red Mountain, Bogus has 360-degree skiing around its highest peak. Shafer Butte, at 7,582 feet, is reached on the front side by the Superior lift, and on the back by Pine Creek lift. Don't miss the back side. It's like the front, only pumped up. The other peak, 7,070-foot Dear Point, is accessed by the Deer Point lift from Bogus Creek Lodge, and via the Showcase lift.

What about the name Bogus Basin? Legend has it that fool's gold—iron pyrite—was mined there and marketed to gullible city folks as the real thing. There was real stuff in the area, however, and all the ski runs are named after legitimate mines.

The mountain also has two restaurants, Nordic skiing and the 70-unit, mid-mountain Pioneer Inn. Child care starts at 10 months. The 800-foot tubing runs give you a good run for your money. All tubers must be at least 36 inches tall. Tubing is a great kick-in-the-pants if you haven't done it in a while, especially on a groomed course without the pesky trees that normally get in the way. Even getting back up the hill is made easy—the paddle tow does the work while you kick back in the tube and watch the scenery unfold.

Lift tickets (05/06 prices): Adults, $42; children (7–11), $20; ages 6 and younger and ages 70 and older, free.

Distance from Boise: About 16 miles north. Coming east or west on I-84, take the City Center Connector to River Street exit, then 15th Street to Hill Road to Bogus Basin Road.

Lodging information: Pioneer Condominiums (800-367-4397; $$–$$$$) are on the mountain. In Boise, the elegant Grove Hotel (800-426-0670; $$$) is central to downtown.

Brundage Mountain, McCall, ID; (208) 634-7462; (800) 888-7544

Internet: www.brundage.com Snow report: (888) 255-7669

5 lifts; 1,300 acres; 1,800 vertical feet; 1 terrain park

Brundage is definitely one of those underrated resorts. Payette Lake, which Brundage overlooks, is beautiful and sparsely populated, with many outdoor activities. From the top of the mountain, you also can see the Salmon River Mountains, Oregon's Eagle Cap Wilderness and the Seven Devils towering over Hells Canyon, America's deepest river gorge. The skiing is pleasant and uncrowded, with occasional challenging drops, but mostly cruisers. Intermediates find this mountain a real delight. Advanced and expert skiers and riders should head into the trees or chutes of the Hidden Valley area.

A latte shack at the bottom of the Bluebird high-speed quad near the lodge will gas you up when you get tired. No Starbucks for the Potato State though—the coffee will be a special brew just for Brundage that's made by Idaho's own White Cloud Coffee. The Bear's Den, a yurt at the top of the mountain serves snacks, hot drinks, beer, wine and spirits.

Brundage has a reputation for some of the lightest powder in the Pacific Northwest, and the mountain offers guided skiing via snowcat in a permit area of more than 19,000 acres in the Payette National Forest. Child care starts at 6 weeks.

You might want to add on a side trip to nearby Tamarack Resort.

Lift tickets (05/06 prices): Adults, $40; junior (12–18) and senior (65–69), $30; youth (7–11), $20; ages 6 and younger and 70+, free.

Distance from Boise: About 110 miles north via Hwy. 55. The drive is quite scenic.

Lodging information: McCall Central Reservations, (800) 844-3246. Recommended: Luxury lodging, with individually decorated rooms, jetted tubs and bay windows, can be found at The Ashley Inn (866-382-5621; $$–$$$$) in Cascade on Hwy. 55, 23 miles south of McCall and 75 miles north of Boise. Or try the modern, comfortable The Hunt Lodge—Holiday Inn Express (800-465-4329; $$–$$$$) in McCall.

Tamarack Resort, Donnelly, ID; (208) 325-1000; (877) 826-7376

Internet: www.tamarackidaho.com

7 lifts; 2,100 skiable acres; 2,800 vertical feet; 2 terrain parks; 1 superpipe

When you arrive at Tamarack Resort, don't think you've taken a wrong turn when all you see are a couple of nice big yurts and some chairlifts, but no permanent buildings in sight. Tamarack is very much a project in motion, and it's all infrastructure so far. Workers are busy all around this resort, which might remind you of a mini Lake Louise in Alberta, Canada.

Winter 2004/05 was the first lift-served ski season at Tamarack—the first four-season resort to be built in the U.S. in 22 years. Tamarack, which averages 300 inches of snow each year, is 100 miles north of Boise, west of the village of Donnelly and beside Cascade Lake in Idaho's gorgeous and largely untouched Long Valley. The first two seasons, Tamarack offered only snowcat-serviced terrain, enough to familiarize skiers and riders with the mountain's bounty and make them want to come back for more.

The summit of the 7,700-foot-high West Mountain is above treeline, but not by much. The top third of the bowls are sparsely treed, but farther down the mountain, trails lace their way through the forest. Eventually the resort plans to have seven high-speed lifts and numerous surface lifts. New for 2005/06, a high-speed quad (the resort's third) opens up advanced trails and glades on a north-facing peak; a fixed-grip quad provides ski-in/ski-out access to the Whitewater area lodging; and improvements to snowmaking focus on high-traffic areas.

The resort base sits at 4,900 feet and the "village" is currently several big yurts functioning as a day lodge, rental and repair shop, and restaurants. The atmosphere is sure to bring out a sense of adventure in you. The resort's development schedule is at least a year behind, but they seem back on track now, concentrating on recreational activities, with plans to begin construction of the base village soon. Tamarack also has 30 km. of groomed trails for Nordic skiing and 10 km. of snowshoe trails. Lessons are available for both Nordic and Alpine skiing and snowboarding. The resort limits tickets to 1,500 people per day.

Tamarack Resort was granted a 49-year lease of about 2,100 acres of Idaho State Endowment Land, where the skiing and riding takes place. The resort owns 1,500 adjacent acres, where homes, chalets, condos and the golf course will be built. The last U.S. resorts of comparable size to be constructed were Beaver Creek, Colo., and Deer Valley, Utah. Developers have been trying to build this resort in west-central Idaho for more than a decade, but they fell by the wayside until now. You might want to add on a day or two at nearby Brundage Mountain.

Lift tickets (05/06 prices): Adults, $57; juniors (7–17), $29; seniors (65+), $40; ages 6 and younger, free.

Distance from Boise: 100 miles from Boise Airport on Hwy. 55. Sun Valley Stages will provide a van shuttle between the airport and resort.

Lodging information: (877) 826-7376 for Tamarack Resort Central Reservations.

Big Mountain
Montana

Summit elevation:	7,000 feet
Vertical drop:	2,500 feet
Base elevation:	4,500 feet

Address: P.O. Box 1400. Whitefish, MT 59937
Area code: 406
Ski area phone: 862-2900; (800) 858-4152
Snow report: 862-7669
Toll-free reservations: (800) 858-4152
E-mail: bigmtn@bigmtn.com
Internet: www.bigmtn.com
or www.skiwhitefish.com (resort)
www.stayatbigmountain.com (lodging)

Expert:★★★★
Advanced:★★★★
Intermediate:★★★★★
Beginner:★★
First-timer:★★★

Number and types of lifts: 11–2 high-speed quads, 1 quad, 5 triples, 1 double, 2 surface lifts
Skiable acreage: 3,020 acres
Snowmaking: 5 percent
Uphill capacity: 13,800 per hour
Parks & pipes: 1 park
Bed base: 1,600 on mountain
Nearest lodging: Slopeside, hotels and condos
Resort child care: Yes, infants and older
Adult ticket, per day: $45–$49 (05/06 prices)

Dining:★★★
Apres-ski/nightlife:★★★
Other activities:★★★

Big Mountain, a comfortable and unpretentious resort in Montana, just up the hill from Whitefish, enjoys and suffers eclectic weather and snow conditions from fluff to fog to soup to cement. It's a mix of the western side of the Rockies and Pacific Northwest maritime, called "inland maritime," producing plenty of fluffy powder along with plenty of challenging conditions, depending on the weather.

This resort is still a bit of a secret, it has been discovered by skiers and riders drawn here not just by the remoteness, but also by the no-frills, laid-back spirit of its people. The resort, in the far northwest corner of Montana near the Canadian border, is as big as its name, especially since it has a generous out-of-bounds policy. The uninhabited territory surrounding the ski area is also vast. Every which way you look, Glacier National Park, the Bob Marshall Wilderness Area, the Flathead National Forest and the Canadian Rockies thrust jagged peaks into the sky, split by wide valleys filled with lakes and rivers.

The mountain is well-balanced for all abilities, particularly now that the resort is redesigning the beginner area. Families will find Big Mountain resort to be an absolute joy. Mixed groups can ski together, since advanced and expert terrain drop off intermediate trails and eventually meet back up again near the base. While beginners can't ski from the summit, they have an isolated area that friends and family can easily access to check in, share a few runs and meet for lunch before heading back to their respective runs.

The ski area base, Big Mountain Village, hosts a cluster of hotels and condo properties along with a number of restaurants and historic bars. This base area is currently under redevelopment and will offer extended facilities once their new Master Plan is put in place. Whitefish, a quaint historic railroad town just 8 miles down the mountain, is part of the Big Mountain Ski Resort experience. The town is home base for many visitors and is well-equipped to handle a broad variety of travelers.

The weather here is a mix of the western side of the Rockies and Pacific Northwest maritime, called "inland maritime." Weather on the eastern side of the Rockies is what's reported on the Weather Channel — ignore it — where all the "...degrees below zero" occur. Toward the summit, spectacular "snow ghosts," are created — trees encased in many layers of frost and snow. If you forget your sunscreen, you'll probably survive, but don't forget your goggles. Pack your sunglasses. When the sun shines, the views and the the skiing are both spectacular.

The biggest news for 2006/07 is that a new, larger day lodge will open on the site of the old Outpost Lodge, near the beginner area. The full-service lodge will have ticket sales, rentals, the Kids' Center, the Snowsports Center and a cafeteria. In conjunction with this development, another beginner chair will be installed and more beginner terrain added. This expansion is in addition to regrading done in 2005 to make beginner trails easier. A moving carpet for first-time skiers and riders will also make a debut. All this development is part of the new Master Plan to create a more unified base village and skier plaza.

 Mountain layout

Big Mountain's Ambassador Program offers free tours of the mountain, open to intermediates and above, at 10 a.m. and 1 p.m. The main access to Big Mountain is The Glacier Chaser.

♦♦**Expert** ♦**Advanced:** Big Mountain's generous out-of-bounds policy and the abundance of tree skiing make this resort a delight for expert and advanced skiers. Within the boundaries are 3,000 acres of sprawling terrain; another 1,000 acres are in the U.S. Forest Service permit area. Intermediate trails here follow the ridges and all advanced and expert lines drop off those ridges.

Most experts make a beeline to East Rim to tackle First Creek and North Bowl Chute (a.k.a. N.B.C.). This area has cliffs, but nothing you can't get around. You could easily spend all day here and not explore it all. Don's Descent, farther down off Russ's Street, is heavily treed. The other double-diamond area that's fun is Picture Chutes. It's not obvious because it's out of bounds, but shoot up to Radio Tower off Gray Wolf to find deep powder in short steeps that drop you back onto Gray Wolf, then shoot into the trees on and around Bighorn for more untracked steep and deep adventure.

Throughout the entire Good Medicine, North Bowl and Hellroaring Basin areas you'll find fields of powder and thousands of trees. Want dense trees that open up into some rollicking powder fields? Try The Back 9, Connie's Coulee and Fault 2 or Fault 3 into Haskill Slide. If you don't want to see any wide-open spaces, head to Stumptown, Window Pane or Teepee.

■ **Intermediate:** It's tough for intermediates not to have fun here. Half the mountain is rated just for you. Go straight off The Glacier Chaser for Chair 7 on the North Side, or make a U-turn to reach Toni Matt, The Big Ravine, Inspiration and MoeMentum (named for Olympic downhill champ Tommy Moe), all perfect for top-to-bottom power cruising with wide GS turns. Hellfire, the resort's longest trail is 3.3 miles.

If visibility is low at the summit, dip into the tree-lined 1,000 Turns, just off Toni Matt, which dumps you back onto the lower part of The Big Ravine. It's also easier to see on the North Side, off Bigfoot T-bar or in the area around Chair 2, simply because these parts of the mountain are not above treeline.

Advanced-intermediates should be able to tackle any of the groomed single-diamonds or the Ptarmigan Bowl, which has easy bailouts.

●● **Beginner:** For 2006/07, Big Mountain is making huge improvements to the beginner area, including a new day lodge—with the Kids' Center and Snowsports Center—a new lift and more terrain. The bulk of the beginner trails are here and under Chair 3, a bit higher on the mountain. The runs in the beginner area inspire confidence and smiles. If you're adventurous, work your way over to Chair 3, Easy Rider and Heaven's T-bar, where you'll also find the main base village. When you want to return to the day lodge, take the meandering Home Again run.

●**First-timer:** First-timers have an excellent learning area, separate from other skiers, on the gentle trails under Chair 6 (which costs nothing to ride, by the way).

Ride Guide: It's no wonder why Big Mountain is consistently rated highly by snowboard magazines, as it makes an honorable attempt to cater to riders. It sponsors its own snowboard team and has a handful of seasonal events. From the top of Glacier Chaser, the hardest choice is deciding on which wide-open, rolling, impeccably groomed trail you should lay out a string of razor sharp, horizontal-flying Euro carves. A hint: There's no wrong answer, but just be sure to keep your speed on the cat track at the bottom. After a few warm-ups, duck into the trees almost anywhere across the mountain for some smooth powder turns, or head to the expansive out-of-bounds areas.

Parks and pipes

Big Mountain has a terrain park on Silvertip that serves up tabletops, hits, gap jumps, rails, boxes and berms.

Cross-country and snowshoeing (visit xcskiresorts.com for more details)

Big Mountain Nordic Center (862-2900) is adjacent to the Outpost Lodge. It has 16 km. of groomed trails for classic and skate skiing. Downhill ski pass holders can use the cross-country trails for free. Trail passes, maps and rentals are available at the Outpost Lodge or the Big Mountain Sports in the base village.

Grouse Mountain Lodge (862-3000) in Whitefish has 15 km. of groomed cross-country trails and night skiing with 2.4 km. lighted. The **Izaak Walton Inn** (888-5700), 62 miles east on Hwy. 2 (also an Amtrak flag stop), has 30 km. of groomed trails as well as guides.

Glacier National Park provides a natural cross-country paradise. Here the unplowed park roads and trails provide kilometer after kilometer of ungroomed passages. Check with the Communications Center (888-7800) or the park rangers for weather and snow conditions.

Lessons (05/06 prices)

Group lessons: Half day, $35; full day, $50.

First-timer package: Beginner lift ticket, rentals and two-hour lesson for skiing or snowboarding is $45; add $15 to upgrade to a full day.

Private lessons: One or two people, half day costs $160 ($50 for each additional person); full day costs $310 ($55 for each additional person). One-hour Quick Tips costs $80 (as available). Reservations are recommended.

Special programs: Big Mountain has two-hour clinics for bumps, steeps and powder for $30. Telemark workshops and Teen Camp are by appointment only, $45. Women-only and men-only workshops and advanced skiing seminars are taught at select times. Call the Snow Sports Center at 862-2909 for dates and prices.

Racing: A NASTAR course is open off Chair 3 on Saturdays and Sundays, 11 a.m.–3 p.m. Cost is $5 for two runs and $1 for each additional run.

KidStuff (05/06 prices)

Child care: Ages newborn to 12 years. Full day, 14 months and older, costs $55 including lunch. Full day for infants younger than 14 months is $80, not including lunch; hourly rate is $9. The day-care facility is open three nights a week until 10 p.m. for babysitting at $10 per hour for 14 months and older. The facility has room for just three infants at a time, so reserve far in advance. Discounts available for families with multiple children. Reservations are required for infants and recommended for toddlers, 862-1999.

Children's lessons: Skiers ages 4–5, and snowboarders ages 6–7, can take an all-day program with day care, rentals and lunch for $130; half day costs $70. No more than five kids per class. Full day for kids ages 6–14 includes four hours of lessons (two sessions) for $50; half-day, $35. Lift tickets, rental gear and lunch are not included in the price. Learn to Ski (ages 6–14) and Learn to Snowboard (8–14) is a half-day lesson, limited lift ticket and rentals for $45; add $15 to upgrade to full day.

Lift tickets (06/07 prices)

	Adult	Junior (7-18)
One day	$52	$36
Three days	$156 ($52/day)	$108 ($36/day)
Five days	$260 ($52/day)	$180 ($36/day)

Who skis free: Kids ages 6 and younger; seniors 80 and older. Night skiing costs $14, but is free with a day or multiday ticket. Chair 6 is free each day for skiing and snowboarding.

Who skis at a discount: Ages 65–79 and college students with ID pay $42 a day. Night skiing costs $14 a night.

Accommodations

All lodging in Big Mountain Village and Whitefish can be reserved by calling **Big Mountain Reservations** at (800) 858-4152 or the **Whitefish Chamber** at (877) 862-3548. Rates are lower before Christmas, in January and in April; rates are higher during the Christmas/New Year and Presidents' Day holidays.

The **Kandahar Lodge at Big Mountain** (800-862-6094; 862-6098; $$–$$$$) looks like a mountain lodge should—log decor, spacious public areas and a soaring stone fireplace. The rooms are large and the food outstanding. The Wellness Center has an indoor hot tub, dry sauna and steam room. A free shuttle takes guests to the base area and at the end of the day skiers and riders can glide right to the door.

The **Alpinglow Inn** (800-754-6760; 862-6966; $$) sits at the center of the village, with beautiful views from the restaurant and perhaps the most convenient location for skiers. Amenities include his and her saunas, two outdoor hot tubs overlooking the valley and laundry facilities. **The Hibernation House** (800-858-4152; $$) is touted as the "friendliest lodge on the mountain." Big Mountain's best hotel lodging value, it is complete with a large indoor hot tub, laundry room and buffet breakfast. Rooms have a queen bed, twin bunks and a private bath. A groomed run leads to the door by the ski room and it's a short walk to the trails and lifts.

Morning Eagle (800-858-4152; $$$$) is the newest ski-in/ski-out development in the village. The two-story lobby with large stone fireplace and lounge is inviting. Studios and one- to

Dining: $$$$-Entrees $30+; $$$-$20-$30; $$-$10-$20; $-less than $10.
Accommodations: (double room) $$$$-$200+; $$$-$141-$200; $$-$81-$140; $-$80 and less.

three-bedroom units have full kitchens, washers and dryers, complimentary high-speed Internet access in each living room, plus an outdoor hot tub on the top floor and a fitness facility.

Kintla Lodge (800-858-4152; 862-1960; $$$–$$$$) at the base of Chair 3 is a premier ski-in/ski-out condominium property with elevator access, underground parking, a lounge and large deck, ski lockers, outdoor hot tub, sauna, fireplaces in all living rooms and some master bedrooms, and complimentary high-speed Internet access. **The Edelweiss** (800-858-4152; $$–$$$$) has studios, one- and two-bedroom condos, each with a fireplace (fire logs provided), full kitchen, and balcony or patio. Common areas and services include hot tub and sauna, use of the Swim Center, coin-operated laundry, and high-speed Internet access in the lobby (laptop and cable connection required)

A variety of lodging is 8 miles away in Whitefish. Many properties offer ski packages, which include lift tickets, and free transportation to and from the mountain.

The biggest and most convenient hotel is the **Grouse Mountain Lodge** (800-321-8822; $$–$$$). It has an indoor pool, two restaurants and a spacious bar. A free shuttle takes guests to the mountain every morning, as well as downtown for those who don't want to walk the short distance. Cross-country skiing on the golf course is right out the back door. **The Pine Lodge** (800-305-7463; $–$$$) boasts an indoor-outdoor pool with connecting swim channel, hot tub and free continental breakfast. The **Best Western-Rocky Mountain Lodge** (800-862-2569; $–$$$) includes a continental breakfast and features an outdoor pool and hot tub.

For B&Bs, the **Garden Wall Inn** (888-530-1700; $$–$$$) is on the free S.N.O.W. bus route and within walking distance of downtown. It's an impeccably restored 1920s house-turned-inn featuring five guestrooms furnished with antiques. A three-course gourmet breakfast is included. **Good Medicine Lodge** (800-860-5488; $–$$) is built of cedar timbers and has a rustic atmosphere. **Hidden Moose Lodge** (888-733-6667; $$–$$$) showcases Montana-themed guestrooms with with rich mountain colors and local art on the walls. Relax after skiing in the outdoor eight-person hot tub. Rates include full breakfast and evening beverages.

The pet-friendly **Holiday Inn Express** (877-270-6405; 862-4020; $$–$$$), remodeled in June 2005, has an indoor pool with a 90-foot waterslide, two outdoor hot tubs, a breakfast bar and fresh-baked cookies every evening.

For rock-bottom prices, try the clean and comfortable **Cheap Sleep Motel** (800-862-3711; 862-5515; $), which is farther from town; or the European-like hostel, **the Bunk House Traveler's Inn and Hostel** (862-3377; $) in town.

Dining

The **Summit House** (862-1971; $$$), with new furniture and a revamped menu, hosts Moonlight Dine & Ski evenings, plus breakfast and lunch. The high-speed Glacier Chaser quad chairs are replaced by gondola cars to whisk evening diners up the mountain.

For a special evening, and definitely the best meal on the mountain, try **Cafe Kandahar** (862-6098; $$–$$$) in the base village. Chef Andy Blanton prepares modern American cuisine with classical French and traditional Louisiana influences. The wine list is extensive.

The Hellroaring Saloon (862-6364; $$), a 50-year-old, log-decor building, was the original base lodge. All food on the menu is homemade. It serves lunch and dinner. **Moguls Village Pub** (862-1980; $$) is at the base of Chair 2 and serves breakfast, lunch and dinner. The **Alpinglow Restaurant** (862-6966; $$) has the best view of the Flathead Valley.

Most restaurants are in Whitefish and offer a surprising variety. The finest dining in the area is at the **Whitefish Lake Restaurant** (862-5285; $$–$$$). In an historic log building, it's known for excellent steaks and prime rib. **The Grill** and the more upscale **Wine Room** (862-3000; $$-$$$) are in the Grouse Mountain Lodge.

On Central Avenue, the New Orleans-influenced **Tupelo Grill** (862-6136; $-$$$) always has fresh fish on the menu. For topnotch sushi and inventive Asian dishes, head to **Wasabi Sushi Bar & Ginger Grill** (863-9283; $-$$$).

The family-run **Mambo Italiano** (863-9600; $$-$$$) is just plain fun. Come here for lively wait staff, music and lots of wine to complement your meal, which is made with the freshest of ingredients. Portions are enormous, so expect leftovers to finish off another time.

McGarry's Roadhouse (862-6223; $$-$$$) has an open kitchen with a constantly changing menu of daily specials that reflect the flavors of the season. **Corner House Grille** (862-2323; $$$) pairs French, Pan Pacific and New American foods with an extensive wine list.

For local color, try **Truby's** (862-4979; $-$$) for wood-fired pizza and great steaks. **Paddle & Axe Saloon** (862-7550; $-$$) is a good place for steaks and pasta.

The **Quickie Sandwich Shop** ($-$$) offers East Coast subs and great sandwiches. Locals and tourists sip espresso at the **Montana Coffee Traders** or eat in "the Buff," at the **Buffalo Cafe** (862-2833; $). At the latter spot, try the Buffalo Pie—layers of hashbrowns, ham, cheese and poached eggs. It's open for lunch as well. **Baker Street Bistro** (862-6383; $), on the town-mountain road, is an excellent breakfast spot with homemade bagels.

 ## Apres-ski/nightlife

The Hellroaring Saloon serves some of the best apres-ski nachos anywhere. Best deal: If you buy a Hellroaring baseball cap you get your second beer free every day you wear it to the bar. Also on the mountain, **Moguls Village Pub** has entertainment nightly. The **Bierstube** offers free beer every Wednesday at 5:30 p.m. to celebrate the Frabert Award, presented each week to the employee or visitor who commits the biggest goof-up.

It's worth a visit to the **Palace Bar** in Whitefish just to see its turn-of-the-century carved mahogany bar. Microbrew fans can head for the **Great Northern Bar & Grille** on Central Avenue. They have live music from Thursday to Saturday and acoustic open-mic on Tuesday. Locals come for the burgers and wide selection of microbrewery beers and stay for the music and general debauchery. For more free beer, stop by the **Great Northern Brewery,** home of Buckin' Horse Beer, with a friendly tasting room open to the public.

Dire Wolf is a favorite hangout for Big Mountain's boarders and teleskiers. It's just outside town on the road down from the ski area. On Central Avenue choose from the no-smoking **Truby's; Casey's,** in the oldest building in town; and the sports bar (high school sports, that is) **Bulldog Saloon.**

Like martinis? Then head to **Paddle & Axe Saloon,** Whitefish's newest bar and restaurant with a great dinner menu to boot. For a more mellow time, try the adult lounge at the **Grill** in the Grouse Mountain Lodge.

For later night carousing, try the **Remington** or the **Palace Bar**, both on Central Avenue. For a no-glitz, real cowboy evening—complete with live foot-stomping music and longneck beer bottles—head to the **Blue Moon Nite Club** in Columbia Falls at the intersection of Hwys. 2 and 40.

 ## Other activities

Adrenaline junkies should try **snow cycles,** similar to full-suspension mountain bikes but with skis on the bike and mini-skis on your feet. A real blast! Lift-accessed **snow tubing** is offered in the "Snow Toy" area along with a

Dining: $$$$-Entrees $30+; $$$-$20-$30; $$-$10-$20; $-less than $10.
Accommodations: (double room) $$$$-$200+; $$$-$141-$200; $$-$81-$140; $-$80 and less.

small **sledding** hill. **Snowcat skiing and riding** is offered in backcountry areas outside the resort's eastern boundary; call 862-2909 for information.

Downtown in Whitefish **sleigh rides** leave the Grouse Mountain Lodge (862-3000) for a 20-minute ride to a camp near Lost Coon Lake. **Snowmobiling** is a favorite pastime of Montanans, so plenty of guide services are available. Canyon Creek Cat House (800-933-5133) is in nearby Columbia Falls, with more than 200 miles of groomed trails. Flathead Convention and Visitors Association at (800) 543-3105 has a list of additional guide services. Backcountry snowmobile tours are available from Big Mountain's summit (862-2900).

Learn about the fascinating history of Whitefish by visiting the tiny Stumptown Historical Society Museum at the Railway Depot. For starters, it will help you figure out why Whitefish was originally called Stumptown. The museum is run by some very dedicated townspeople who love sharing what they know about the region. While there, pick up a Whitefish Historical Tour pamphlet to take a self-guided tour of the downtown area.

Shopping in Big Mountain Village continues to expand, with a variety of specialty shops along the Kintla shopping pavilion and Morning Eagle boardwalk including clothing, gear, kids items, photography, and custom jewelry. Whitefish's Central Avenue has many **art galleries** and stores that stock Western clothing, jewelry and crafts. Montana Coffee Traders, on Hwy. 93 south of town, has many Montana food gift items, such as huckleberry syrup.

Big Mountain has a terrific **Guest Services and Information** center in the base village where you can find out more about other activities. Call 862-2900.

Getting there and getting around

By air: Glacier Park International Airport in Kalispell, 19 miles south of the resort, is served by Delta, Horizon/Alaska Air, Northwest and America West airlines. Call Flathead Glacier Transportation (892-3390) for ground transportation or check with your hotel for guest shuttle availability.

By car: Big Mountain is 8 miles from Whitefish at the junction of Hwys. 2 and 93.

By train: Amtrak's Empire Builder stops in Whitefish daily from Seattle and Portland to the west and from Chicago and Minneapolis to the east. Kids ride free. Call (800) 872-7245 for information.

Getting around: If you stay and play at the mountain, you won't need a car. The S.N.O.W bus makes free daily runs between Whitefish and the mountain. The last run back up the mountain is around 11 p.m. Wednesday through Saturday. However, most lodges have free shuttle service available for guests and taxi service also is available. A car is essential if you plan to explore.

Nearby resorts

Blacktail Mountain offers panoramic views of Glacier National Park and Flathead Lake. The parking lot is at the top of the mountain so you get to ski before you ever board a lift. Blacktail Mountain offers three lifts, 24 runs on 200 acres with a vertical drop of about 1,500 feet. Lift tickets (2006/07 prices) are $34 for adults; $25 for students ages 13–18; $15 for children ages 8–12; $15 for seniors 70 and older; and free for ages 7 and younger. The 17,000-square-foot lodge at the "base" area houses everything—the ski shop, ski school, bar and restaurant all are in the three-story building. Day care is available. The ski area is in Lakeside, about 45 minutes south of Kalispell, which itself is about half an hour from Whitefish. Phone: 406-844-0999; Internet: www.blacktailmountain.com.

Big Sky
Montana

Summit elevation:	**11,150 feet**
Vertical drop:	**4,350 feet**
Base elevation:	**6,800 feet (Lone Moose)**
	7,500 feet (Mountain Village)

Address: P.O. Box 160001,
1 Lone Mountain Trail, Big Sky, MT 59716
Area code: 406
Ski area phone: 995-5000 (Hotel guest calls
and switchboard)
Snow report: 995-5900
Toll-free reservations: (800) 548-4486
Fax: 995-5001
Internet: www.bigskyresort.com

Expert:★★★★★
Advanced:★★★★
Intermediate:★★★★
Beginner:★★
First-timer:★★

Number and types of lifts: 18–1 aerial tram,
1 four-passenger gondola, 4 high-speed quads,
1 quad, 3 triples, 5 doubles, 1 surface lift,
2 moving carpets
Acreage: 3,600 acres
Snowmaking: 10 percent of trails
Uphill capacity: 20,000 per hour
Parks & pipes: 1 park, 1 pipe
Bed base: 4,250
Nearest lodging: Slopeside, hotel and condos
Resort child care: Yes, 6 months and older
Adult ticket, per day: $63–$69 (06/07 prices)

Dining:★★★ **Apres-ski/nightlife:**★★
Other activities:★★

If you find yourself at an uncrowded mountain, surrounded by stunning wilderness and polite Argentinians, don't be surprised that you're vacationing at Big Sky in Montana. It seems avid skiers and riders from the Andes have discovered a resort that many of us in North America have never visited. Maybe it's time to put this resort on your must-visit list too.

From the moment you land at Bozeman's Gallatin Field, which feels more like a private rancher's massive lodge than an airport, you know you're in for a different kind of vacation. Here you can expect lots of friendly employees in cowboy hats holding open doors for you, a genuine laid-back atmosphere, spectacular scenery and plenty of challenging terrain.

Big Sky, with its impressive Matterhorn-shaped peak scraping the heavens at 11,166 feet, is a serious skier's mountain from the summit, yet it has excellent cruisers closer to the base. Indeed, the intermediate groomers are such a delight that experts who wear themselves out on the tougher terrain still have plenty to grin about as they swoop down the lower trails with friends and family.

An aerial tram with two 15-passenger cars whisks you up to the 11,150-foot mark on Lone Peak, giving you a stomach-in-your-throat close-up of the craggy mountain just before coming in for a landing. If you get to the top and find that the chutes, couloirs and steeps are more than you can handle, no problem—admire the views of the nearby Spanish Peaks Wilderness area and ride back down.

Big Sky attracts about 300,000 skier visits each season; however, they're all swallowed up by the 3,600-acre terrain. A big daily turnout is 4,000 people, meaning short lines for the lifts and roughly one skier per acre. With about 400 inches of snowfall, powder days are frequent and last much longer than the first run. Most visitors don't consider their vacation complete until they've spent at least a day in Yellowstone, only an hour away (see *Other Activities*).

Mountain layout

♦♦ Expert ♦ Advanced: The runs from the Lone Peak summit are a test of who is an expert and who wants to be. Most are rated double-black diamond—none are easier than a single diamond—and justifiably so. Above-treeline exposures beckon anyone looking for powder, chutes, steep pitches and wide-open terrain. Want a really long run that will leave you weak in the knees? Start with the steeps of Lenin to wide-open Liberty Bowl to Dakota Gully to the delightful trees of Bavarian Forest. Hippy Highway then funnels you back from the boundary edge to the Shedhorn lift.

The more adventurous must register with the ski patrol to challenge the A-Z Chutes, the Pinnacles and Big Couloir, all out of bounds. (The latter is 42 degrees steep and half-a-mile long). If you want to try this terrain, you have to bring a transceiver, a shovel and a partner.

If the tram line is long, take Turkey Traverse and explore South Wall to your heart's content. The vast area on Lone Mountain's north side is where many locals play. The Challenger chair climbs 1,670 steep vertical feet to open hair-raising in-bounds terrain. Steep, long pitches drop down Big Rock Tongue, trees pepper narrow chutes on Little Tree and Zucchini Patch, and untracked lines are often found as you traverse toward's Ray's Ridge.

Andesite Mountain is a gem of a secret for advanced and expert terrain. It's all below treeline, so you'll find glades like Rock Pocket, Snake Pit and Bear Lair, as well as some bump runs like Mad Wolf and Broken Arrow that will make your legs scream for a break.

When hunting for the last of the powder, try the glades off the Challenger lift, head to Andesite, especially off the Lone Moose Triple, or leap into Buffalo Jump and Rice Bowl under the Swift Current lift.

■ Intermediate: Big Sky has two mountains, Lone Mountain and Andesite, that connect at the base. The blue-rated trails on both have a wide range in pitch and grooming. Some are kind and rolling, but others—such as the blues in the Shedhorn area—lean toward black. Not all the blue trails are groomed, and some have cat-track runouts or are simply too short.

On Lone Mountain, fine-tune your technique on the groomed cruisers under the gondola and the Swift Current chair, such as Calamity Jane, Huntley Hollow and Lobo. If you want to try some bowl skiing, head to Upper Morningstar. For advanced-intermediates, trails off the Shedhorn lift are south-facing and get plenty of sun at times when the lower mountain is in the shade. Upper Sunlight to Sunlight is absolutely delightful. Views are of the backcountry and you'll feel a world away from the rest of the resort.

On Andesite, skis run fast and long on Big Horn, Elk Park Ridge, Elk Park Meadows and Ambush. The manicured slopes of Tippy's Tumble and Silver Knife have some steep sections. During the spring, make sure to hit the trails off the Thunder Wolf quad early in the day before the sun has turned them into heavy mashed potatoes.

●● Beginner: The south side of Andesite Mountain is great for beginners because of the wide, gentle slopes and because it gets a lot of sun. Enjoy runs such as Sacajawea, El Dorado and Ponderosa from the Southern Comfort chair. Fewer hot shots ski on Andesite, a comfort if you get unnerved when someone passes by closely at high speed. On the way back to the base village, the winding Pacifier lets you admire awesome views.

On Lone Mountain, you can reach gentle rollers such as Mr. K, White Wing and Lone Wolf via the gondola or the Explorer chair. Mr. K gets high traffic as the lifts close down for the day, but it's nice and wide. If you're with people who are more accomplished than you, convince them to take a few runs on Mr. K and Lone Wolf, they'll enjoy it too.

● First-timer: Though not physically isolated from the rest of the terrain, the learning area, at Lone Mountain's base, is away from high traffic until the end of the day. A moving carpet transports you up the slope to learn your first turns. For the youngest ones, a smaller moving carpet is in a fenced-off area in the base area used by children's ski school.

Ride Guide: For some ridge riding and above-treeline faces, head to the top of Lone Mountain at 11,150 feet. The South Face isn't as steep as the chutes under the tram, but you'll still find yourself leaning into the mountain when you're "taking a breather." If you like catching air time with the locals, there's often a group of them building jumps on Screaming Left, at the bottom of Liberty Bowl. If you prefer the woods, Bavarian Forest is a great romp. After the woods and runs below the face, try to stay central to avoid most of Cow Flats (1.5 miles of flats) and Hippy Highway—end up as close to the Shedhorn lift as you can. Also try to avoid Middle Road when working your way back to the mountain village. This mountain's great for laying out arcs too. Pick any groomer to your left off the Swift Current chair and gondola.

Parks and pipes

Big Sky has a well-kept halfpipe and terrain park on Andesite by Ambush Meadows. The halfpipe is just after the Ambush entrance and just before Tippy's Tumble. After watching skilled riders in the park, newbies should head left of the pipe, to the beginner terrain park's hits and a 6-inch-high rail slide. Intermediate and expert park riders will find the bulk of the terrain park and rail slides directly below the halfpipe. Several kickers range in difficulty depending on speed, the direction you go into the hit and the direction you land. The rail slides, funboxes and wall ride here are all shapes and sizes. Several tabletops are near the bottom, with plenty of spectators watching from the base area and the lift, so don't blow it. On Lone Mountain, there's a natural halfpipe on Lower Morningstar and another on Buffalo Jump.

 Cross-country and snowshoeing (visit xcskiresorts.com for more details)
Lone Mountain Ranch (995-4644; 800-514-4644) offers more than 65 km. of international-caliber Nordic skiing for all levels, with groomed and skating lanes. The trail system winds through open meadows and forested canyons. The Ranch teams with Alpenguide Tours of West Yellowstone to offer a variety of backcountry skiing, including snowcoach tours into Yellowstone. Tours also are available into the Spanish Peaks. Cabins with fireplace and full bath can be rented for a week, including all meals, trail pass and evening programs. The Ranch has a Nordic shop, rentals and lessons.

Big Sky has a marked and separated snowshoe trail up a portion of Lone Mountain called Moose Tracks—it starts at the base of Andesite and Lone Mountains. Rent **snowshoes** from Grizzly Outfitters (995-2939) or Big Sky Ski Rental (995-5841).

 Lessons [06/07 prices]
Group lessons: Half-day ski lessons cost $49, morning or afternoon. Snowboarders take a 2.5-hour morning or afternoon lesson for $55.
First-timer package: A half-day lesson with learning area ticket and rentals costs $77. Upgrade to a beginner chair ticket for an additional $25.

Private lessons: Two hours (up to three guests) cost $220 in the morning, $205 in the afternoon, $315 for a half-day afternoon, $300 for a half-day morning, $495 for a full day. Guide services cost the same. A private one-hour telemark lesson is $90.

Special programs: Advanced clinics concentrate on Lone Peak's steeps and tackle moguls, powder or other conditions du jousr, $60.

Racing: Check in with the ski school daily for details.

KidStuff (06/07 prices)

Child care: Ages 6 months and older. For ages 6–23 months, cost is $85 for a full day. For 2–8 years old, $87 for a full day, $62 for a half day. Reservations are required and parents will need to bring some things, so call ahead, 995-2335. The bright, airy facility is at slopeside Snowcrest Lodge.

Children's lessons: Ages 3–4 can take a 45-minute introduction to skiing in the afternoon, $65 (day care and rentals extra). Mini Camp, for ages 4–6, is $126 and includes all-day ski lessons, activities and lunch. Ski Camp, for ages 6–14, is $105 and includes all-day ski lessons, activities and lunch. Mini Rider Camp, for ages 6–9, is $142 and Snowboard Camp, for ages 10–14, is $106. Snowboarders 15 and older can take a 2.5-hour lesson for $50. Prices do not include lift ticket and rentals for kids 11 and older. Helmets are available for rental, $5. For information on lessons, call 995-5743.

Special activities: Kid's Club, based in the Huntley, is a very popular kids' program that's available from 3–5 p.m. Monday through Friday. The clubroom is full of toys, games, arts and crafts materials and stuff for all kinds of fun activities. The program is free, but advance registration is required because space is limited. Kids love to meet the Ski Patrol rescue dogs and watch the impressive demonstration of their skills in performing searches (see Other Activities for details.) A free fireworks show lights up the sky every Saturday at 8 p.m.

Lift tickets (06/07 prices)

	Adult	Junior/Student (14–21)
One day	$69	$48
Three days	$197 ($66/day)	$144 ($48/day)
Five days	$325 ($65/day)	$255 ($48/day)

Who skis free: Two children (up to age 10) ski free per paying adult.

Who skis at a discount: Youth (11–13) costs $25 per day. Seniors 67 and older pay $35 per day. College students must have ID to get college rates.

Accommodations

Big Sky is divided into three areas serviced by a free shuttle system. **Big Sky Central Reservations**, (800) 548-4486, can book most lodging.

In the Mountain Village:

The Summit at Big Sky ($$$–$$$$) is a ski-in/ski-out condo-hotel with one- to three-bedroom units, plus eight penthouses, all with mountain views. This is low-key luxury—an artful blend of craftsmanship and comfortable furnishings. The exterior looks more like a European hotel than one in America's Wild West, but the common areas are reflective of a rancher's home, with oversized leather and animal-print furniture, artwork depicting Montana's history and natural beauty, soaring stone fireplaces and polished wood. Spacious rooms in earthy colors have a variety of options including fireplaces, oversized showers, jetted tubs, full kitchens, hot tubs and wet bars. The Summit also has a sauna, steam room, pool-size hot tub with views of the mountain (part indoor, part outdoor), fitness facilities and day spa. **Alpenglow** ($$$$) is the newest condo complex with great views and contemporary western decor.

The ski-in/ski-out **Shoshone Condominium Hotel** ($$$$) has spacious condos with kitchens, fireplaces and jetted tubs, plus a lap pool, indoor hot tub, health club, steam bath and more. **The Huntley** ($$–$$$$), also ski-in/ski-out, includes a buffet breakfast and has an outdoor pool, two hot tubs, sauna, workout room and game room.

Mountain Village has many condo complexes, and guests have access to The Huntley's hot tubs and pool. **Lone Moose Meadows** ($$$$) is slopeside. If you want luxury, try **Snowcrest, Beaverhead** and **Arrowhead Condominiums** with two to four bedrooms ($$$$). Or try the more moderately priced **Stillwater** ($$–$$$$), which has studios and two-bedroom units.

The slopeside **Mountain Inn** (877-995-7858; 995-7858; $$–$$$$) has 90 suites with fridges and microwaves. Amenities include an indoor pool, two hot tubs and an exercise room, plus a continental breakfast. Children 18 and younger stay free in their parents' room.

ResortQuest of Big Sky (800-548-4488; 995-4800) and **Big Sky Chalet Rentals** (800-845-4428; 995-2665) also rent condos and homes in Mountain Village.

In the Meadow Village (6 miles away):

River Rock Lodge (800-695-8284; 995-2295; $$–$$$$) is a "boutique-style European hotel" built of stone and log with beautiful interior decor. Rates include continental breakfast.

East West Resorts (800-845-4428; 995-2665) manages several condo complexes here, including **Hidden Village** ($$$$), units set in the forest with in-house hot tubs and garage, and **Park** ($$$–$$$$), with head-on views of Lone Peak. **ResortQuest of Big Sky** (800-548-4488; 995-4800) rents many condos on the cross-country trail system.

In the Canyon (3 miles from the Meadow Village, in the beautiful Gallatin River Canyon, 9 miles from the lifts, serviced by the shuttle):

Buck's T-4 Lodge (800-822-4484; 995-4111; $$$–$$$$) is not your ordinary Best Western. The former hunting lodge retains its rustic appeal. Relax in the two pool-sized outdoor hot tubs, hang out by the large stone fireplace and eat a memorable meal at its restaurant specializing in wild game (see *Dining*). Rates include a hot breakfast buffet. Free high-speed Internet access is available. Ski packages are offered with Big Sky and Moonlight Basin.

The Rainbow Ranch Lodge (800-937-4132; 406-995-4132; $$$–$$$$) is on the Gallatin River. A luxurious western-ranch lodge, it has 12 rooms with private baths, and an excellent bar and restaurant (see *Dining*). Ski packages are available.

The **Comfort Inn** (800-228-5150; 406-995-2333; $–$$$) is clean, though it has little charm. The nicest budget accommodations are at the **Corral Motel** (406-995-4249; $).

Dining

In the Mountain Village:

For a memorable meal, try **The Cabin Bar & Grill** (995-4244; $$–$$$), which specializes in regional cuisine. Leave the kids behind and enjoy an outstanding meal for all its worth. **Peaks** (995-8000; $$$), in The Summit, showcases a menu of new Western cuisine in an elegant but casual setting. The breakfast buffet is very good but a bit pricey.

M.R. Hummers (995-4543; $$–$$$) aces its baby back ribs, prime rib and steaks, served in nice-sized portions by attentive staff. **Huntley Lodge** (995-5783; $$–$$$) is fine dining in a rustic lodge setting. Yet another very good breakfast buffet and more reasonably priced.

Bambu Bar & Asian Bistro (995-4933; $$) gets crowded quickly with noisy patrons and serves average-quality Asian dishes, including sushi. **Dante's Inferno** (995-3999; $$–$$$) has slope views and Italian cuisine that's budget-busting for what you get. **Black Bear Bar 'n' Grill** (995-2845; $–$$) is a casual spot for breakfast or dinner.

In the Meadow Village:

Lone Mountain Ranch Dining Room (995-2782; $$–$$$), in a stunning log lodge with elk antler chandeliers and a massive stone fireplace, serves first-rate American regional cuisine. Sleigh-ride dinners are offered; call ahead as space is limited.

Dining: $$$$-Entrees $30+; $$$-$20-$30; $$-$10-$20; $-less than $10.
Accommodations: (double room) $$$$-$200+; $$$-$141-$200; $$-$81-$140; $-$80 and less.

La Luna (995-3280; $–$$) satisfies cravings for authentic Mexican food, from simple to fancy dishes. Guinness on tap and terrific pesto pizza can be found at **Uncle Milkies Pizza and Subs** (995-2900; $-$$). **Allgoods Bar & Grill** (995-2750; $–$$) serves hickory-smoked ribs, chicken, pork, homemade stews and burgers. For hearty sandwiches, try **The Wrap Shack** (995-3099; $), **Slider's Deli** (995-2566; $), and the **Hungry Moose Market & Deli** (995-3045; $). For breakfast, stop in at the **Huckleberry Cafe** (995-3130; $), which has the best reputation in town, or the **Blue Moon Bakery** (995-2305; $), also great for lunch.

In the Gallatin Canyon:
You probably don't know this, but just about the best resort dining in North America is hidden away in Montana at **Buck's T-4 Restaurant** (995-4111; $$$–$$$$). This rustic former hunting lodge plays funky folk or cool jazz while your taste buds bliss away. You can't go wrong with any choice you make—the chef is brilliant in his use of subtle flavors and creative blends. **The Rainbow Ranch Lodge** (995-4132; $$$–$$$$) is known for elegant dining overlooking the Gallatin River. An imaginative menu focuses on wild game, fresh seafood and vegetarian.

 ## Apres-ski/nightlife

Check the local newspaper, *The Lone Peak Lookout*, for entertainment. The hub of night activity is the Mountain Village. Happy hour kicks off in **Chet's Bar** in the Huntley Lodge, with the Crazy Austrian show (just go see it). Chet's also has poker games. The **Carabiner** in the Summit is a wonderful place to relax with a drink in oversized chairs. Mellow live entertainment provides background music. If you have the chance to hear Michael Haring on the acoustic guitar, make sure to also check out his wonderful wildlife photography and maybe bring something home as a memento.

Black Bear Bar & Grill and **Dante's Inferno** both rock hard and long. Other places to check out are **Alpine Lounge,** where the locals get wild, and **Bambu Bar,** where the 20-somethings gravitate for drinks. In the Meadow Village, it's quieter, but **Allgoods Bar & Grill** is likely to attract crowds at night. Allgoods also has a pool table, darts and poker.

In the canyon, check out the **Buck's T-4** game room, with pool tables, foosball and video games. Locals like the **Corral** and **The Half Moon Saloon**, with darts and pool. Both are roadhouse-style Western bars.

Other activities

Yellowstone National Park is a big attraction, and yes, it's open in winter. A bus runs daily from Big Sky to West Yellowstone, where snowcoaches pick up riders for guided tours of the park to see wildlife, thermal pools and Old Faithful. Expect to encounter buffalo, elk, bald eagles, trumpeter swans and coyotes. Wildlife is rather abundant in winter since cold weather and snow force them down into the valley for food. The family-owned **Snowcoach Yellowstone** (800-426-7669; 646-9564) has modern comfy snowcoaches and engaging guides. For more information on the area and all its recreation choices, call the **West Yellowstone Chamber of Commerce** (646-7701).

Snowmobiling in Yellowstone National Park is quite popular. Guides are required by law, and most snowmobile shops offer a 10 percent discount with a Big Sky lift ticket and provide bus service from the resort and West Yellowstone. Try Rendezvous Snowmobile Rentals, (800-426-7669; 646-9564); Yellowstone Tour & Travel, (800-221-1151); or Two Top Snowmobile, (800-522-7802; 646-7802). You don't need a guide if you plan to snowmobile outside the park boundaries, where you'll find hundreds of miles of forest trails.

Dogsled rides are offered by Spirit of the North Dog Adventures (995-4644), Lone Mountain Ranch (995-2783) or 320 Ranch (995-4283). **Dinner sleigh rides** also are available. **Winter fly fishing** on the Gallatin River can be booked through Gallatin Riverguides (995-2290) or East Slope Anglers (995-4369), who have licenses, equipment rentals and supplies.

The full-service **Solace Spa at Big Sky** (995-5803) has three treatment rooms in the Huntley and two in The Summit. It provides a full range of professional therapy including massage, body wraps, facials, beauty enhancements, and aromatherapy.

If you have the opportunity to attend a weekly **avalanche search and rescue demo** by the ski patrol and their dogs, don't miss it. It's fascinating, and someday these dogs just might save your life. The Huntley Lodge shows free **movies** in the amphitheater at night. The Mountain Village and Meadow Village have many **shops** and **boutiques,** as well as **grocery stores.**

Getting there and getting around

By air: Bozeman Gallatin Field Airport is served by Horizon Air, United Express, Delta, Northwest and Big Sky Airlines. The resort is an hour from the airport. Car rentals are available. Karst 4X4 Stage (800-287-4759; 556-3540) shuttles passengers between the airport and the resort. If you're staying in a condo and don't plan to rent a car, call Mountain Taxi (800-423-4742), fax them your grocery list, and they'll shop before you arrive, then transport you from the airport to your condo.

By car: Big Sky is 45 miles south of Bozeman on Hwy. 191 along the Gallatin River.

Getting around: If you stay at the Mountain Village, a car is unnecessary unless you plan to do a lot of sightseeing. A free shuttlebus runs between the Big Sky villages 7 a.m.–11 p.m., starting in mid-December through the winter.

Nearby resorts

Moonlight Basin, Big Sky, MT; (406) 995-7600

Internet: www.moonlightbasin.com
6 lifts; 1,680 skiable acres; 2,720 vertical feet

Moonlight Basin is on the north face of Lone Mountain and first opened in December 2003. Since then, it's been adding new lifts, trails and amenities every season. At build-out, the resort will have 3,500 acres of skiable terrain and up to 12 lifts. For the 2005/06 season, the resort is installing the Headwater lift to serve steep terrain previously accessed only by hoofing it, and cut another 30 acres of new trails and glades. Skiers and riders will find a vertical descent of 2,720 feet that's lift-served. Those who want to earn their turns will find in-bounds, hike-to terrain topping out at 3,850 feet of vertical.

The resort's base area revolves around the very upscale Moonlight Lodge and Spa ($$$$), which has four ski-in/ski-out luxury penthouse suites, and is home base to the two- and three-bedroom Saddle Ridge Townhomes and two-bedroom log cabins in Cowboy Heaven. The lodge has a full-service spa, shops and an outdoor ice rink too. The resort offers ski and snowboard lessons. Child care starts at age 6 months.

Lift tickets (06/07): Adults, $47; juniors (11–17), $35; college students/seniors (70+), $35; kids 10 and younger, free with paid adult. A joint ticket with Big Sky is available.

Distance from Bozeman: The resort is 47 miles south of Bozeman on Hwy. 191 along the Gallatin River. It's 1.2 miles past Big Sky.

Lodging information: Bookings are handled by EastWest Resorts, (866) 212-0612.

Dining: $$$$-Entrees $30+; $$$-$20-$30; $$-$10-$20; $-less than $10.
Accommodations: (double room) $$$$-$200+; $$$-$141-$200; $$-$81-$140; $-$80 and less.

Ski Santa Fe

New Mexico

Summit elevation:	12,075 feet
Vertical drop:	1,725 feet
Base elevation:	10,350 feet

Address: 2209 Brothers Road, #220
Santa Fe, NM 87505
Area code: 505
Ski area phone: 982-4429
Snow report: 983-9155
Toll-free reservations: (877) 737-7366
Within New Mexico: 747-5557
Fax: 986-0645
E-mail: info@skisantafe.com
Internet: www.skisantafe.com
Expert:★★
Advanced:★★★
Intermediate:★★★
Beginner:★★★★ **First-timer:**★★★

Number and types of lifts: 6–1 quad, 2 triples, 2 doubles, 2 surface lifts
Skiable acreage: 660 acres
Snowmaking: 50 percent
Uphill capacity: 7,800 skiers per hour
Parks & pipes: None
Bed base: 5,500 in Santa Fe
Nearest lodging: About 15 miles away
Resort child care: Yes, 3 months to 3 years
Adult ticket, per day: $44-$49 (05/06)

Dining:★★★★★
Apres-ski/nightlife:★★
Other activities:★★★★

At Ski Santa Fe, snow-covered trails curl through towering Ponderosa pines in the Sangre de Cristo mountains, only 16 miles from the city of Santa Fe, the very heart of Southwestern style. Take the bright sunlight of the high desert, fresh powder snow and a skier-friendly mountain, then add pre-Columbian Indian Pueblos, Spanish architecture, art galleries and top it with a renowned regional cuisine — you have the savory mix that makes up a unique ski vacation.

Santa Fe (elevation 7,000 feet) offers interesting contradictions. It is old and new, high mountains and flat desert, with cool winters that surprise out-of-staters who think of New Mexico as hot and dry. Skiing in this state is unlike anywhere else on the continent. To get a more foreign-feeling ski vacation, you'd need a passport.

Some skiers think Taos Ski Valley is the only New Mexico ski area worth a long plane ride—not so. If your main interest is racking up vertical feet, then by all means head for Taos, but Santa Fe (just an hour north of Albuquerque) is a better destination for those who prefer a balanced ski-and-sightseeing vacation. Santa Fe is one of the most culturally fascinating cities in the United States. It is loaded with great restaurants, superior art galleries, a variety of activities, and the ski area is a lot bigger than most people imagine. Though the mountain is known as a day-area destination for Santa Fe and Albuquerque skiers, out-of-town visitors will find a surprising amount of terrain.

Founded by Spanish conquistadors in 1607, more than a dozen years before the pilgrims landed in Plymouth, Santa Fe is North America's oldest capital city. It is rich in history and culture, but of a different kind from mining-town ski areas.

When the Spanish arrived, the area was already populated with 100,000 Native Americans who spoke nine languages and lived in some 70 multi-storied adobe pueblos, some still inhabited today. For the next 150 years Santa Fe grew as a frontier military base and trading center, where Spanish soldiers and missionaries, Anglo mountain men and Native Americans mixed. In 1846, during the Mexican War, New Mexico was ceded to the United States. Santa Fe, at the end of the Santa Fe Trail, became a frontier town, hosting the likes of Billy the Kid and Kit Carson. In the early part of this century, Santa Fe took on a new flavor. It became a magnet for men and women of the arts and literature. Today this city of 60,000 people is home to one of the world's premier art colonies.

Ski Santa Fe has one of the highest lift-served elevations in the nation—12,000 feet on top, 10,350 feet at the base. If you're susceptible to altitude problems, take note; however, all lodging is in Santa Fe, and some people are fine if they sleep at a lower elevation.

Mountain layout

◆◆ Expert ◆ Advanced: For the most part, the mountain's expert terrain is to the left of the Tesuque Peak chair. With fresh snow, locals go first to Columbine, Big Rocks and Wizard. These runs all check in as very steep and are for advanced skiers only. Roadrunner is the expert bump run directly under the Tesuque chair. Tequila Sunrise and Easter Bowl have the best glade skiing. On the far side of the mountain, reached by the Santa Fe Super Chief quad, Muerte and Desafio have isolated trail skiing for advanced skiers.

The Big Tesuque Bowl attracts the intrepid, who enter this area via Cornice. (Once skiers leave Cornice, they are outside the ski area's permitted boundary.) Big Tesuque skiers find natural powder, bowl skiing and trees. The bowls empty onto the area's entrance road, three miles below the base area, leaving you to hitchhike back up. First-timers should go with a local who knows this area: It's genuine backcountry, it's big and people occasionally get lost.

■ **Intermediate:** On a fresh powder day (once a week on average), local intermediates and advanced skiers head straight for the Tesuque Peak triple chair, up to 12,000 feet and the top of the mountain. To the right of the lift (as the trail map reads) is Gayway, a glorious, groomed pitch with several spicy turns that gives new meaning to the term "spectacular scenery." On a clear day, you almost get the feeling of flying, thanks to the 150-mile vista as the trail drops away. Parachute, which parallels Gayway, is a groomed black diamond with a somewhat steeper pitch. On the far side of the mountain, reached by the Santa Fe Super Chief quad, Middle and Lower Broadway have isolated trail skiing for intermediate skiers.

●● **Beginner:** This level will be happiest on the lower part of the mountain, on the wide boulevard of Easy Street. Advanced-beginners will find more challenges and a slightly steeper pitch on Open Slope and Upper and Lower Midland. If you're feeling adventurous, try Lower Burro for an exhilarating, winding trip through the trees on a mild pitch.

● **First-timer:** Good terrain at the mountain's base served by Pine Flats lift is protected by snowfences. For children Chipmunk Corner lift provides a tucked-away learning area.

Parks and pipes

Ski Santa Fe does not have any formal parks or pipes.

Cross-country and snowshoeing (visit xcskiresorts.com for more details)

Santa Fe has no groomed or tracked trails. However, there are maintained backcountry trails in the **Santa Fe National Forest. Aspen Vista Road,** 2 miles below the ski area, is a popular and moderately difficult 7-mile trail. **Black Canyon Campground,** 8 miles up the ski road, is a popular area for beginners. Maps and information on conditions in the Santa Fe National Forest are available from the National Forest Service at 988-6940. For ski area information only, call 982-5300.

Lessons (06/07 prices)

Group lessons: Adult lessons cost $35. A second session on the same day only costs an extra $20.

First-timer package: Two group lessons, beginner lift and rentals is $65 for skiers, $78 for snowboarders.

Private lessons: $70 per hour; $119 for two hours; discounts for multiple hours.

Special programs: Among them are a women's program, classes for ages 50 and older, mogul clinics, telemark lessons and powder workshops. Check with ski school, 982-4429.

Racing: A coin-op race course is open Thursday through Sunday.

KidStuff (06/07 prices)

Child care: Ages 3 months to 3 years. All-day program costs $66; $50 half day; $14 per hour. Ages 3 and 4 who are completely toilet-trained can register for Snowplay, a program that is "an introduction to the skiing environment." This program, which includes indoor and outdoor activities, is $66 all day and $50 half day. Reservations required; call 988-9636. Only full-day packages for child care are sold during holiday periods.

Children's lessons: Ages 4–9, all day including lunch and lift ticket, $84 with rentals. Half-day programs are $68 with rentals. Four-year-olds have a morning lesson with play activities in the afternoon; others have lessons in both morning and afternoon.

Lift tickets (06/07 prices)

	Adult	Teen (13-20)	Child (12 and younger)
One day	$51	$41	$37
Three days	$142 ($47+/day)	$114 ($38/day)	$103 ($34+/day)
Five days	$227 ($45+/day)	$182 ($36/day)	$165 ($33/day)

Who skis free: Skiers age 72 and older and kids shorter than 46 inches in ski boots.

Who skis at a discount: Ages 62–71 pay the child rate. A ticket valid only on the beginner lift is $25.

Accommodations

Ski Santa Fe has no base lodging, but even if it did, you'd want to be in Santa Fe for dining, shopping and the museums. More than 70 hotels, motels, inns, condominiums and B&Bs serve Santa Fe visitors. Winter is low season in this region, but the increase of visitors trying to take advantage of this have actually caused prices to rise from bargain to a moderate level during the past few years. Expect to pay about $75–$110 a day, per person, for a ski-stay package at one of the many hotels on Cerrillos Road and 25 to 50 percent more downtown.

Lift-and-lodging packages are the best deal; call **All Santa Fe Reservations** (877-737-7366) for lodging or the **Santa Fe Visitors Bureau,** (800) 777-2489 for general information. Downtown is where the best restaurants, shopping and nightlife are concentrated, although we do recommend a few great dining options outside the Plaza area.

The Inn of The Five Graces (866-992-0957; 992-0957; $$$$, above and left) is one of America's most unusual and unique luxury hotels. It is a delightful and surprising compound of one- and two-story adobe and river-rock buildings, with 22 suites and tranquil garden courtyards. Room doors open to a warren of walkways and patios under the Santa Fe sky.

Every corner of the property is resplendent with surprises and inspired touches.

La Posada de Santa Fe (800-727-5276; 986-0000; $$–$$$), restored in 1999, is a short walk from the Plaza. On the grounds is the Staab House, a Victorian mansion serving as the restaurant. **Inn and Spa at Loretto** (800-727-5531; 988-5531; $$$) provides fabulous rooms only steps from the Plaza. None of the 157 rooms are identical and the hotel has excellent meeting facilities. A curving pool, the gourmet El Fuego restaurant and the Avanyu Spa add a opportunity to refresh both your body and soul. **La Fonda Hotel** (800-523-5002; 982-5511; $$$–$$$$) is the historic place to stay. An inn of one sort or another has been on this site for 300 years (Billy the Kid worked in the kitchen here washing dishes). If you don't stay, at least stroll through and take a look—they don't make them like this anymore.

The way they make them now is across the Plaza from La Fonda. **The Inn of the Anasazi** (800-688-8100; 988-3030; $$$–$$$$) is the politically correct place to stay. The hotel's restaurants use vegetables grown by local organic farmers. Leftovers are given to a homeless shelter and everything is recycled. The Southwestern decor and furnishings are immaculate.

Eldorado (800-955-4455; 988-4455; $$–$$$$) is the city's largest hotel with 219 rooms. It has just undergone an extensive rennovation, has opened a new spa and rates right up with best in town. The **Hotel Plaza Real** (877-901-7666; 988-4900; $$$) is convenient and comfortable. Of the 56 hotel units, 44 are suites with fireplaces. An ample continental breakfast is included. We also enjoyed the adobe **Inn on the Alameda** (888-984-2124; 984-2121; $$$), which is handy to Canyon Road and offers a continental breakfast. In a village of adobe cottages, most featuring their own Indian kiva fireplaces,

Excellent B&Bs are **Adobe Abode** (983-3133; $$$–$$$$), **Alexander's Inn** (888-321-5123; 986-1431; $$–$$$), the spacious **Dancing Ground of the Sun** (800-745-9910; 986-9797; $–$$$) and the classy **Water Street Inn** (800-646-6752; 984-1193; $$–$$$). The B&B Association of New Mexico does not have a website, but it can be reached at 982-3332.

Other accommodations to consider are the historic **Hotel St. Francis** (800-529-5700; 983-5700; $$), the **Hilton of Santa Fe** (800-336-3676; 988-2811; $$$) and the **Hotel Santa Fe** (800-825-9876; 982-1200; $–$$$), partly owned by the Picuris Pueblo. Families should try the **El Rey Inn** (800-521-1349; 982-1931; $$–$$$), **Garrett's Desert Inn** (800-888-2145; 982-1851; $$), the **Campanilla Compound** condominiums (800-828-9700; 988-7585; $$$), and the **Otra Vez** condos (988-2244; $$–$$$).

The closest lodging to the ski area is **Fort Marcy Hotel Suites** (800-745-9910; $–$$), just off the ski area road. They have 80 condominiums from one to three rooms and are only four blocks from the Plaza.

Many of the chain hotels, such as **Comfort Inn** ($$), **Days Inn** ($), **Holiday Inn** ($$) and **Hampton Inn** ($), have adopted the local adobe architectural style and are a little less expensive. They are conveniently located on Cerillos Road, which makes them handy for getting to the ski area, but out of walking range for downtown.

Dining

On the mountain, skiers have two choices. **La Casa Cafeteria** in the base lodge called La Casa Mall, and **Totemoff's Bar and Grill** at the base of the Tesuque Peak Chair. La Casa, with a French chef, offers a variety of options including a pasta bar and a daily special such as fresh salmon with lemon tarragon. Its breakfast burrito is wicked good, but only for brave palates. Totemoff's features burgers, salads, pasta, cocktails and a sun deck.

Back in the city, Santa Fe cooks and you're in for a treat. Including fast food, Santa Fe

Dining: $$$$-Entrees $30+; $$$-$20-$30; $$-$10-$20; $-less than $10.
Accommodations: (double room) $$$$-$200+; $$$-$141-$200; $$-$81-$140; $-$80 and less.

has nearly 200 places to strap on the feed bag. From traditional New Mexican cuisine to steaks and seafood, Santa Fe has more food variety than you could consume in a year and far more good restaurants than we have room to recommend.

Fuego (986-0000; $$$$) at La Posada de Santa Fe has award-winning fine dining with a fabulous wine list. **Geronimo** (724 Canyon Rd., 982-1500; $$$$) is the spot for that special night out, with crisp linens, attentive staff and wonderfully prepared eclectic cuisine. **315 Restaurant and Wine Bar** (986-9190; $$$) serves memorable meals with a French Provencal flair and excellent wines.

Two main hotel restaurants shouldn't be missed. We recommend the spectacular dining room at La Fonda, **La Plazuela** (992-5511; $$$). Breakfast lets you enjoy the colorful dining room for more reasonable prices. **Baleen at the Inn at Loretto** (984-7915; $$), only steps from the Plaza, serves food that is surprisingly reasonable in price and delightfully inventive.

Coyote Cafe (132 W. Water St., 983-1615; $$$) has a fixed-price menu and modern Southwestern cuisine in its main dining room; those in the bar can order a la carte. **Pasqual's** (121 Don Gaspar, 983-9340; $$$) is great for breakfast, but it's good anytime for delicious and beautifully presented New Mexican cuisine. Call for dinner reservations or expect to wait a long time. If you want to meet people, ask to be seated at the communal table. **La Casa Sena** (125 East Palace Ave., 988-9232; $$$) is tastefully continental. Don't miss the adjacent **Cantina** ($$), where waiters and bartenders sing cabaret between food and drinks. If you want to nibble tapas instead of dinner, this is the place to do it. **Julian's** (221 Shelby, 988-2355; $$$), favored by locals, is very upscale Italian.

At **Maria's New Mexican Kitchen** (555 W. Cordova Rd., 983-7929; $), you'll probably meet the affable owner, Al Lucero, who wrote *Maria's Real Margarita Book* featuring history and recipes of the more than 100 "real" margaritas served in the restaurant. Robert Redford, a frequent customer when he's in town, wrote the foreword. The food is wonderful also, especially the posole and green-chile stew.

Locals flock to **The Shed** (113 ½ Palace Ave., 982-9030; $$) and **La Choza** (905 Alarid St., 982-0909; $$) but watch out for the green chile—it could burn a hole in your ski boots. If you dare to try the chile, make sure you get lots of garlic bread to ease the pain.

The Pink Adobe (406 Old Santa Fe Trail, 983-7712; $$) is Santa Fe's oldest restaurant, a local favorite and sometimes difficult to even get reservations (which are necessary). They specialize in New Mexican and Creole foods. Prices are moderate to expensive. Next door, **The Dragon Room** is a favorite of locals and visitors alike for cocktails. **El Farol** (808 Canyon Rd., 983-9912; $$$) is the oldest Spanish-food restaurant and dates back to just a few years after the Pink Adobe. Specialties include a variety of curry dishes, hot and cold tapas as well as one of the best selections of Spanish wines in the U.S.

For a romantic evening try **Andiamo** (322 Garfield St., 995-9595; $$). It is a little off the beaten track but serves unique pasta dishes with candlelight ambiance.

The Cowgirl Hall of Fame (319 S. Guadalupe, 928-2565; $–$$) is what the name implies with authentic Texas-style barbecue with kid's menu, play area and a to-go area for their barbeque. Don't hesitate to join the tourists at **The Ore House** (upstairs at 50 Lincoln Ave., 983-8687; $$) on the Plaza for free apres-ski snacks. On Canyon Road, **Celebrations** (613 Canyon Rd., 989-8904; $$) is in the heart of gallery row and is jammed at lunchtime. **Tomasita's Cafe** (500 S. Guadalupe, 983-5721; $) is fast food with a twist. Portions are large, service is friendly, and it's a favorite of Santa Fe families, so be prepared to wait. It is inexpensive, and has some of the best New Mexican fare in town.

The Plaza Restaurant (54 Lincoln, 982-1664; $) is a throwback to diner days; regulars swear everything is good and very affordable. **Zia Diner** (326 South Guadalupe, 988-7008; $) is an easy 15-minute walk from the Plaza and features All-American favorites (New Mexican style, of course) such as meat loaf stuffed with piñon nuts, basic pastas and soups. **R&B Ribs, Burgers, Rhythm & Blues** (709 Don Cubero, 992-8002; $) is also recommended.

Atomic Grill (103 E. Water St., 820-2866; $) serves wood-fired pizza, pastas and hamburgers together with about 80 bottled beers. There's take-out and delivery too.

For vegetarian head to the **Annapurna Chai House** (988-9688). for Chinese (if you've had it with Southwestern stuff) head to **Little House Chinese Cuisine** (1965 Cerrillos Road, 983-1558; $). **Khonami** (next door to the Cowgirl Hall of Fame) has Japanese food.

For breakfast with the movers and shakers in downtown Santa Fe, head to **Tia Sophia** (210 W San Francisco St, 983-9880; $). The **Tecelote Cafe** (1203 Cerrillos Rd., 988-1362; $-$$) is a good place for breakfast just like Mom used to make if your mother liked using spices.

 ## Apres-ski/nightlife

For elegant apres-ski (you can go in ski clothes), head for **Inn of the Anasazi** or **La Posada,** both close to the Plaza.

Swig (135 West Palace Ave.; 955-0400; $$$) is the pick-up spot and serves great martinis. With its "global" cuisine and Asian tapas, this spot was designed to intoxicate the senses.

A wonderful place to mix dinner with entertainment is at **La Cantina** (988-9232) in the historic Sena Plaza, a stately adobe built as a family home in the 1860s. The restaurant features New Mexican specialties and singing waiters and waitresses. For about $20, you can eat, drink and hear an exceptional dinner theater show, belted out between courses. Children are welcome, reservations a must.

El Farol (983-9912) on Canyon Road, is Santa Fe's oldest bar with live entertainment every night and Flameco on Wednesdays.

The **Catamount Bar & Grill** (125 E. Water St.; 988-7222) is a teeming sports bar featuring big-screen TV, pool tables and specials like "Jägermeister Night." **Second Street Brewery** (982-3030) has ales, bitter and stout every night and music most nights. **Blue Corn Cafe and Brewery** (438-1800) is a kinda franchise sports bar that makes its own brews.

Club Allegria (471-2324) brings the latin beat to Santa Fe.

Willees Blues Club (982-0117) normally had great music action with plenty to drink. However, they serve even a potato chip.

 ## Other activities

The **museums** in Santa Fe are first rate. Buy a four-day pass for $15, which will admit you to five of the best: the Museum of International Folk Art (strong in Spanish art of the area), the Palace of the Governors (for local history), the Museum of Indian Arts and Culture, the Museum of Fine Arts, and the Museum Of Spanish Colonial Art. The Georgia O'Keeffe Museum has its own entry fees.

You should consider touring the eight **Indian pueblos** near Santa Fe. The San Ildefonso Pueblo, famous for its distinctive pottery style, is the most scenic. Its annual festival to honor its patron saint is in late January and features traditional clothing and dances. If you have a car, and especially if you are driving north on U.S. Hwy. 84/285 to Taos, be sure and take the Hwy. 503 turnoff at Pojoaque and drive east to Chimayo, site of the Santuario de Chimayo, famous for its dirt thought to have healing powers. At the end of the church parking lot, you'll find Leona's, a funky little walk-up where the tamale pie and burritos are exceptional. On the way to Taos you wind through foothills and into high mountain Hispanic villages like Truchas

Dining: $$$$-Entrees $30+; $$$-$20-$30; $$-$10-$20; $-less than $10.
Accommodations: (double room) $$$$-$200+; $$$-$141-$200; $$-$81-$140; $-$80 and less.

and Las Trampas. For beautiful woven blankets, stop at Ortega's in Chimayo, where family members still practice a craft brought to New Mexico in the 1600s by their ancestors.

An initial warning: It will be much cheaper to ski all day than venture into Santa Fe's many tempting **shops** and **galleries.** That warning given, more than 250 galleries feature Native American crafts and art, as well as fine art on a par with galleries in New York, Florence or Paris. Local artisans sell their wares on blankets in front of the 390-year-old Palace of the Governors, a long-standing Santa Fe shopping tradition.

Canyon Road is the world-famous strip of galleries featuring wonderful art of all styles, for all tastes. The walk from the Plaza area is pleasant. The Waxlander Gallery features wonderful pastel still-life works of J. Alex Potter. Our favorite is Nedra Matteucci's Fenn Galleries, 1075 Paseo de Peralta, just south of Canyon Road. The day we visited, we counted four Zuniga sculptures starting at $80,000 each. Don't miss the garden.

If you feel a little woozy after pricing Zuniga artwork, head to **Cloud Nine Oxygen Bar** (410 Old Santa Fe Trail, between Pink Adobe & Rio Chama; 470-3494) for an oxygen-aromatherapy-elixer pick-me-up.

How can you *not* indulge yourself in Santa Fe? Compared with many resorts, spas here are almost affordable. For an extensive list check out skisnowboard.com.

Call the **Santa Fe Visitors Bureau** (955-6200; 800-777-2489) for more information on these and other activities.

Getting there and getting around

By air: Albuquerque has the nearest major airport, 60 miles away. Private pilots can use the Santa Fe Regional Airport. For shuttles from the airport in Albuquerque to Santa Fe, call 474-5696.

By car: Santa Fe is north of Albuquerque on I-25, an easy hour's drive. The ski area is 16 miles from town on Hwy. 475.

Getting around: Getting around Santa Fe and to and from the ski area is difficult without a car, though a shuttle service is available from the airport to major hotels. The airport in Albuquerque has the leading rental car agencies.

Taos

with Red River and Angel Fire
New Mexico

Summit elevation:	11,819 feet
Vertical drop:	2,612 feet
Base elevation:	9,207 feet

Taos Ski Valley

Address: Box 90,
Taos Ski Valley, NM 87525
Area code: 505
Ski area phone: 776-2291
Snow report: 776-2916 **Fax:** 776-8596
Toll-free reservations: (866) 250-7313
E-mail: tsv@skitaos.org
Internet: http://skitaos.org/
Expert:★★★★★
Advanced:★★★★★
Intermediate:★★★★
Beginner:★★
First-timer:★

Number of lifts: 12–4 quads,
1 triple, 5 doubles, 2 surface lifts
Snowmaking: 46 percent
Uphill capacity: 15,000 per hour
Total acreage: 1,096 acres terrain, 687 acres trails
Snowboarding: Not allowed
Parks & pipes: 1 terrain park, 1 quarterpipe
Bed base: 3,705 at base and in town
Nearest lodging: Slopeside; hotels, condos
Resort child care: Yes, 6 weeks to 2 years
Adult ticket, per day: $54-$57 (05/06 prices)

Dining (Including town):★★★★
Apres-ski/nightlife:★★
Other activities:★★★

Northern New Mexico has some of the best skiing to be found in the United States. Taos has long been legendary for its steeps and deep powder, and nearby Red River and Angel Fire both offer excellent and different ski experiences. Most of the information in this chapter concentrates on Taos, which is a true destination resort, but we'll also give you a flavor of Red River and Angel Fire (see *Nearby Resorts* at end of chapter).

Taos Ski Valley is a little piece of the Alps, founded by a Swiss native and surrounded by hotels and restaurants built by Frenchmen and Austrians. It's near the town of Taos, a rich mix of Spanish and Indian cultures, blended over the centuries to produce the Southwestern style. This style isn't trendy here; it's the way things have always been.

Taos Ski Valley holds another distinction: While many resorts walk a delicate marketing tightrope, touting whatever expert terrain they possess while trying not to scare anyone off, Taos seems to enjoy its tough reputation. It advises visitors to meet the challenge by enrolling in Ski Better Week, a package of lessons, accommodations, meals and lift tickets. Just about everybody staying at the mountain enrolls in ski school. If you aren't part of a class, you feel like the kid who didn't get chosen for the baseball team. Apres-ski talk centers on Ski-Better-Week anecdotes, leaving independents to sit at the bar with little to add to the discussion.

Fifty-one percent of Taos' runs are rated expert, and half of the expert runs are double-black diamonds. Intermediates will have a field day with great steep cruising. Taos can be an extremely rewarding ski experience *because* of its challenge. The runs demand you give it your best. Beginners and intermediates will find 100 percent of their terrain is covered with snow-making. By the way, Taos is one of the last resorts in the nation to still ban snowboarding.

The town of Taos is 18 miles from Taos Ski Valley. Long a haven for artists, the town has galleries, shops, restaurants and hotels ranging from luxurious to pedestrian.

Mountain layout

Taos has something for everyone in the intermediate, advanced and expert levels. Every good skier will be challenged every day.

♦♦**Expert:** For tree skiers, Taos has a special challenge, the twin runs Castor and Pollux. They hardly look like runs, just steep wooded parts of the mountain, unskiable, where some joker put a sign that looks just like a trail marker. The trees are 2 to 15 feet apart, and advanced classes regularly train here. Also, the tree thinning off of West Basin Ridge has increased skiable terrain for experts.

Powder skiing lasts on Highline Ridge and Kachina Peak, for two reasons: They are double-black diamonds and Kachina Peak is reachable only after a 75-minute hike from the top chair at 11,800 feet to the ridge at 12,481 feet (top to bottom, you'll rack up 3,244 vertical feet). You can, however, ski off Highline Ridge and West Basin Ridge after only a 15-minute hike. Skiers are advised to go with an instructor or a patroller on your very first time.

♦**Advanced:** Advanced skiers won't be disappointed. All of the tree skiing is an effort and the black-diamond trails are as advertised. Hunziker, isolated by a short climb, provides good bumps that narrow about halfway down the trail. Otherwise test yourself on some of the off-trail skiing dropping from the ridges.

■ **Intermediate:** Taos has a lot of terrain at this level. Smooth bowls are found off the Kachina quad chair. Other good intermediate terrain is under Chairs 7 and 8. Anything marked as a blue trail is a blast, with plenty of length for cruising. Some at this level may feel pushed; if you're in that group, go ski the greens for a while and keep your head held high. Better yet, sign up for a class.

●● **Beginner:** Taos has some nice isolated beginner terrain, such as Honeysuckle, which descends the skier's right side of the ridge. Bonanza and Bambi give beginners a way down on the other side of the ridge. The main problem is negotiating either White Feather or Rubezahl when they are crowded with skiers coming back into the village. Despite the slow-down efforts of ski hosts stationed every 20 feet or so, both runs resemble the Hollywood Freeway at rush hour, except that the faster skiers aren't stalled in traffic. They zip around the slower ones, who are gingerly making their way home. On busy days it's a mess. Timing is important: Come down early, or better yet, be one of the last to descend.

● **First-timer:** Only athletic novices should attempt to learn here. Despite the highly regarded ski school, the jump from the tiny learning area to the mountain is enormous. Better learning terrain is at nearby Angel Fire or Red River.

Ride Guide: Snowboarding is not permitted. Head to Angel Fire or Red River.

Parks and pipes

Taos knows that skiers like terrain parks too, so step right up. The Out to Launch Terrain Park features two huge airs, a hip, a quarterpipe, and rails. The park, on Maxie's run under Lift 7, is groomed nightly.

Lessons [06/07 prices]

Group lessons: Two hours, morning or afternoon, $46. Some lessons at Taos concentrate on specific skills, such as moguls or telemarking.

First-timer package: Novice lift ticket, 4.5-hour lessons and rentals for $77; two days cost $115.

Private lessons: For up to four skiers, costs are $130 for an hour, $200 for two hours,

$285 for a half day, and $460 for a full day.

Special programs: Ski Better Weeks are the core of the Taos ski experience, developed by former French Junior Alpine champion and ski school technical director Jean Mayer. Participants are matched for six mornings of intensive lessons, and they ski with the same instructor all week. Sixty-five percent of the participants are intermediate or higher. Ski Week normally costs $210 for six days (lift ticket extra), but is $105 during the Half Price Sale and only $60 during the January Special Sale (Jan 7, 14, 21 and 28). Many lodging properties offer the Ski Better Week as a package with meals and accommodations. There are Specialized Ski Week programs for teens and for ages 50 and older at select times during the season.

Specialized Super Ski weeks for advanced skiers are offered on select dates. They includes six two-hour morning lessons and four two-hour afternoon sessions, Monday through Thursday with the afternoon sessions having a special focus which varies with the week. This is not a program for the timid or late-night party types, but most will find their skills much improved by the end of the week. It's offered at select times. Prices range from $210-$360.

Taos Ski Valley also has shorter programs that concentrate on specifics, such as Moguls designed to aid advanced and expert skiers.

KidStuff [06/07 prices]

Child care: Ages 6 weeks to 2 years. Full day with lunch is $70; a half day costs $50. Toddlers get indoor activities and snow play. Reservations required; call 776-2291. There is one staffer for every two infants.

Children's lessons: The Kinderkäfig children's center is unfortunately an inconvenient distance from the main base area. A full-day program for ages 3–15, including lesson, lunch and afternoon supervised skiing, costs $99 a day. (Ages 3–5 get a program that combines lessons, snow play and indoor activities.) Reservations are recommended; call 776-2291.

Lift tickets [06/07 prices]

	Adult	Child (7-12)
One day	$59	$36
Two days	$112 ($56/day)	$68 ($34/day)
Five days	$280 ($56/day)	$170 ($34/day)

Who skis free: Ages 80 and older. Any child 6 or younger skis free when an accompanying adult purchases a lift ticket.

Who skis at a discount: Ages 70–79 ski for $44, but if they plan to ski here for more than two days, it's better to purchase a season pass which costs $88 for seniors. Ages 13–17 ski for $46 a single day; $44 multiday. Taos reduces its ticket prices in the early and late seasons.

Cross-country and snowshoeing (visit xcskiresorts.com for more details)

Southwest Nordic Center (758-4761) has cross-country lessons, tours and yurt trips. **Enchanted Forest Cross-Country Ski Area** (754-2374) is 40 miles northeast of Taos by Hwys. 522 and 38. It has 34 km. of backcountry trails, some groomed, and an elevation of 10,300 feet, from which you have great views of the Moreno and Red River valleys. At the Miller's Crossing headquarters in downtown Red River, you can rent equipment (including pulks) and pick up trail maps.

Accommodations

Taos' Ski-Better-Week packages include up to seven nights lodging (Saturday to Saturday), six lift tickets and six morning lessons. In some cases, meals are included, too. Almost all Taos properties offer packages. Prices range from about $794 to about $1,900 per person, double occupancy. If price or specific amenities are concerns, call Taos Valley Resort Association (800-776-1111 or 776-2233) or Southern Rockies Reservations (866-250-7275) to book lodging or ski-stay-air packages. Taos has lodging ski & stay specials throughout the season that are worth checking out too.

The Inn at Snakedance (800-322-9815; 776-2277; $$$$) has been renovated and renamed the **Snakedance Condominiums and Spa**. The new facility plans to reopen on December 15, 2005 and will have 24 ski-in/ski-out rooms. Amenities will include a spa with hot tub, sauna, exercise and massage facility; a bar; and a restaurant serving continental cuisine with a Southwest flair.

The Bavarian Lodge (770-0450; $$$$) is about as good as it gets on the mountain when it comes to the German/Austrian good life. The interior art was created by Swiss artist Reto Messmer and the building features Bavarian antiques.

Hotel St. Bernard (776-2251; $$$) managed by the ski school technical director Jean Mayer, offers the flavor of Europe. The cuisine and ambiance are both legendary.

Edelweiss Condominium Resort and Spa (800-458-8754; 776-2301; $$–$$$$) is at the base of the village. It has just been totally renovated. **The Powderhorn** (800-776-2346; 776-2341 $$$) has bright, clean and spacious rooms steps from the lifts. **Sierra del Sol** (776-2981; $$) has a series of studio, 1BR and 2BR condos. **The Alpine Village Suites** (800-576-2666; $$–$$$$) is one of the newest accommodations available on the mountain. Most suites have private balconies with streamside or mountainside views.

Austing Haus (800-748-2932; 776-2649; $$; left) is 1.5 miles from the base of Taos Ski Valley and is an unusual structure. It is the tallest timber frame building in the United States and owner Paul Austing is justifiably proud of the 24-unit lodge he helped build himself. The food in the glass dining room is very good. Next door, **The Columbine** (888-884-5723; 776-5723; $$) is a twin of the Austing Haus with 20 rooms and some small conference facilities. Both have regular shuttle service to the lifts. Between the ski area and town is a bed-and-breakfast inn, the **Salsa del Salto** (776-2422; $$–$$$).

The town of Taos offers a wide range of accommodations. Prices are generally less expensive than staying at Taos Ski Valley.

El Monte Sagrado (800-828-TAOS; 758-3502; $$$$) is the luxury king of the area. It is one of the Leading Small Hotels of the World and is at the top of the best travel magazine resort lists.

The Fechin Inn (800-911-2937; 751-1000; $$–$$$$) is the next most luxurious place to stay. The **Historic Taos Inn** (800-826-7466, spells TAOS-INN; $–$$$$) is the cultural center of Taos. The lobby, built around the old town well, is a gathering place for artists. Rooms feature adobe fireplaces, antiques and Taos-style furniture built by local artisans. **The Sagebrush Inn** (800-428-3626; 758-2254; $$$–$$$$) is an historic inn with a priceless collection of Southwestern art in the lobby and some of the best nightlife in town.

At the lower end of the price range are **El Pueblo Lodge** (800-433-9612; $–$$$), **Indian Hills Inn** (800-444-2346; $), and often, rooms in the chain hotels, such as Holiday Inn or Ramada. The least expensive is the skiers' hostel, **The Abominable Snowmansion** (776-8298; $) in Arroyo Seco, 9 miles from the Village, where the rates are about $25–$60.

We also enjoyed four other B&Bs in Taos, which seems to have an unusual number of fine choices: **Hacienda del Sol** (758-0287; $$) owned by John and Marcine Landon; the **Old Taos Guesthouse** (758-5448; $–$$), owned by Tim and Leslie Reeves (who are fun to ski with); and **Inn on La Loma Plaza** (758-1717; $$–$$$$), owned by Peggy Davis and her husband, Jerry (both former mayors in Vail and Avon, CO). **Alma del Monte** (776-2721; $$), halfway between the hubbub of the plaza and Taos Ski Valley, is managed by Suzanne Head. B&Bs can be booked through the Taos B&B Association, (800) 876-7857.

The **Inger Jirby Guest Houses** (758-7333; $$$$), a creation of an artist from Sweden, are eclectically decorated, luxurious and only two blocks from the plaza.

Dining

Because so many properties here offer Ski-Better-Week packages, which include meals, most restaurants are operated by the lodges. The best independent eateries in the village are **Rhoda's Restaurant** (776-2005; $$), serving very affordable entrees such as salmon stir fry, peppercorn steaks and tiger shrimp scampi; and **Tim's Stray Dog Cantina** (776-2894; $$) where you can find green chile everything. On the **deck at the St. Bernard** you can get the best value on the mountain. If you have a chance to eat at the St. Bernard, do so. It is an experience that typifies the old-world ski lodges.

The **Bavarian** (770-0450; $$–$$$; right), at the bottom of the Kachina Lift, is one of the best lunch spots in the ski valley, for that matter at any ski resort. They serve wonderful spätzle, wienerschnitzel and strudel. The **Hondo Restaurant** ($$–$$$) at Snakedance Condominiums and Spa is open for dinner and features winemaker dinners with California vintners. Dinner is stellar featuring a tasty collection of small dishes and a spectacular wine list with bottles ranging from $20 to hundreds. **Edelweiss Spa and Condominiums** ($$–$$$) also serves three meals daily to the general public.

About a mile-and-a-half down the mountain road is **X-Treme Steaks** (776-2451; $$–$$) in the Amizette Lodge. They serve melt-in-your-mouth elk filets and well-prepared steaks. The place is BYOB, so come with a bottle of wine if that is what you expect to drink.

On the road into the valley, the **Momentitos de la Vida** (776-3333; $$$) specializes in exceptional American and Continental cuisine. **OBL** (Old Blinking Light) (776-8787; $–$$) is known for its steaks and chile and its giant margaritas. A new restaurant, **Sabroso** (776-3333; $$) in Arroyo Seco has one of the best atmospheres in the area and the food is good too.

The town of Taos has great variety when it comes to restaurants. **The Trading Post** (758-5089; $$) has a bit of everything—Cajun, New Mexican, Italian, steaks. **Joseph's Table** (751-4512; $$$) in the Hotel la Fonda de Taos on the square has been a gourmet establishment for years. The menu at the **Apple Tree Restaurant** (758-1900; $$–$$$) lists Southwestern dishes, such as barbequed duck fajitas and mango chicken enchiladas, and continental cuisine, such as salmon alfredo. On the historic plaza, **The Garden Restaurant** (758-9483; $$–$$$) offers New Mexican as well as American, Italian and French entrees.

Other good dining can be found at **Lambert's** (758-1009, $$$) three blocks from the Plaza, and at the **Downtown Bistro** (737-5060; $$) just south of town on the road to Santa Fe. For two spots full of colorful locals head to **Ogelvies** (758-8866; $$), right on the plaza, and **Doc Martin's** in the Taos Inn (758-1977; $$) just off the plaza on the main street through town.

Michael's Kitchen (758-4178; $) has phenomenally large and excellent breakfasts. Or head to **El Taoseño** (758-4142; $) for a great breakfast burrito. In Taos Ski Valley try the **Blueberry Blue Corn Pancakes** or Tim's fine Breakfast Burrito at **Tim's Stray Dog Cantina** (776-2894; $$).

Dining: $$$$-Entrees $30+; $$$-$20-$30; $$-$10-$20; $-less than $10.
Accommodations: (double room) $$$$-$200+; $$$-$141-$200; $$-$81-$140; $-$80 and less.

Apres-ski/nightlife

When lifts close at Taos Ski Valley, skiers head to the deck of the **Hotel St. Bernard**, the **Martini Tree Bar** at the Resort Center, or to drink German beer at **The Bavarian**. The place to be and be seen is the **Edelweiss Bar** where Craig, Julia Robert's personal Taos margarita maker will create a personal fresh-squeezed concoction. For entertainment, your best bet is the Martini Tree or the Edelweiss Bar both with live music.

It's livelier in Taos town, but not wild (unless you hit the Alley Cantina on a good night). The **Alley Cantina** has a live band and wild dancing some nights. Check the schedule, you'll love it. **The Sagebrush Inn** has country and western dances. **Ogelvie's Bar and Grill** in Taos Plaza hops. For microbrew fans, **Eske's Brew Pub** off the Taos Plaza is the spot. Be sure to try the unique Green Chile Beer at least once. Skiers and local artists mix at the **Adobe Bar**, the living room for artsy locals. At the Taos Pueblo there is gambling at the **Taos Mountain Casino**. The *Taos News* has a weekly entertainment guide.

 ## Other activities

Taos is quite historic. The **Martinez Hacienda,** built in 1804, is a monument to the Spanish Colonial era in Northern New Mexico. **Kit Carson** is buried in Taos and his home and museum are open to the public. The **Millicent Rogers Museum** has a fantastic collection of Indian jewelry and art. The **Fechin Institute** is worth a visit to see the Russian artist's art and architecture.

Adventure Tours in Taos (758-1167) has **sleigh rides** and **snowmobile tours. Taos Ice Arena** (758-8234) is open Thanksgiving through February. **Fly fishing** tours are offered in winter on the Red River by Los Rios Anglers (758-2798). For **snowmobiling** in Red River call BobCat Pass Adventures (754-2769), Sled Shed (754-6370) or Fast Eddie's (754-3103). Roadrunner Tours (377-6416) offers **horse-drawn sleigh rides** to a sheepherders' tent with a dinner cooked over an open fire.

In Red River there is a unique **Night Sky Adventure** (754-2941) that provides a powerful telescopic universe tour that takes advantage of the altitude and the clear winter skies.

Visit the **Taos Pueblo,** the 700-year-old home of the Tiwa Indians. Visitors are welcome to the pueblo, workshops, ceremonies and sacred dances, except for a four- to six-week period each winter when the pueblo is closed for religious reasons. For exact dates, call the Taos Chamber of Commerce (800-732-8267). The pueblo is open from 9 a.m. to 4:30 p.m.

Georgia O'Keeffe and R.C. Gorman have made Taos legendary with art lovers. Eighty **galleries** are here. Get a list from Taos Chamber of Commerce, 758-3873 or (800) 732-8267.

 ## Getting there and getting around

By air: Albuquerque is the nearest major airport, 135 miles south. Rental car agencies are at the airport. For ground transportation, contact Faust's Transportation, 758-3410 in Taos, or 843-9042 in Albuquerque; or Pride of Taos, 758-8340.

By car: I-25 north to Santa Fe, then Hwys. 285, 84 and 68 to Taos. Taos Ski Valley is 18 miles farther north on Hwy. 150. For Red River head north on Hwy. 522 and east on Hwy. 38. For Angel Fire go east on Hwy. 64.

Getting around: If you stay in Taos Ski Valley village and have no desire to go into the town of Taos 18 miles away, you won't need a car. If you want to visit the town, or aren't staying at the ski area, you'll need one. In Red River you won't need a car, but you'll need one to get there. The same goes for Angel Fire, where you can park your car and forget it.

Nearby Resorts

Angel Fire Resort, Angel Fire, NM; (505) 377-4200; (800) 633-7463

Internet: www.angelfireresort.com

5 lifts; 450 skiable acres; 2,077 vertical feet; 4 terrain parks; 1 superpipe, 1 halfpipe

Angel Fire is a modern, purpose-built resort about a half-hour—22 miles—east of Taos. The accommodations are all very close to the slopes and the mountain has been created for families and mellow skiing with touches of challenge.

This resort is especially good for beginners and intermediates. You have to go out of your way to get into trouble. It's about as good as it gets for families and those who want to take it easy. The resort has added some expert terrain, but it's tucked away where no one will accidentally get into trouble. **Beginners** will want to take Headin' Home from the top of the high-speed Chile Express quad. Stay on the trail or drop down Bodacious and wend your way back to the base area. Beginners can also experience the back bowl by winding down Highway, then dropping off Hallelujah or La Bajada to end up at the base of the Southwest Flyer, another high-speed quad. **Intermediates** will have fun on Fat City, Fire Escape, Mother Lode and Arriba in the back bowl. We recommend staying in the back bowl. On the front side you can cruise down some good intermediate trails such as I-25, Prospector and Jasper's, but all end in a long runout to the base area. **Advanced/Expert** levels will find meager offerings but they can be fun. A cluster of black runs under Lift 6 provides a challenge. To the far skier's right of the back bowl, a series of advanced runs were recently added to Detonator and Nitro.

Angel Fire has snapped up the opportunity to become New Mexico's premier snowboarding destination, thanks to Taos' steadfast refusal to allow snowboarding. The Chile Express high-speed quad whisks boarders to the top of the 10,677-foot mountain. Sound systems pump out great tunes underneath the lifts. Angel Fire has a young feel to it, unlike the conservative, staid atmosphere of some larger resorts.

There are four terrain parks with tabletops, rail slides and spines. Two are high up on the mountain. Liberation Park is reached by its own chair, Lift #3. Badlands Park is on Fat City and can be reached by Southwest Flyer or Lift #3. Cayenne Park is on Exhibition near the base of the mountain, served by Lift #2. The Junkyard Park, also on Exhibition, includes jumps, rails, tabletops, ramps and sliders and is open to skiers, snowboarders and snowskaters. Angel Fire has the only superpipe and halfpipe in New Mexico. The resort hosts world-famous shovel racing in February, after which the course is transformed for a slopestyle competition held each March.

Angel Fire has an excellent ski school that focuses on beginner and intermediate skiers as well as children. Their snowboarding instruction is consistently highly rated too. The resort recently expanded its children's ski and snowboard school with a 6,000-square-foot building designed specifically for kids. Angel Fire Resort Day Care (800-633-7463), housed in a new state-of-the-art facility near the kids' ski school, is open 8 a.m. to 5 p.m. Full-and half-day programs provide activities for children ages 6 weeks through 10 years. Costs range from $35 to $78 for day care and children's lesson programs.

Adventure Park, at the base, has a day tubing hill. At the summit, you'll find 22 km. of cross-country and snowshoe trails with beautiful views of New Mexico's highest mountain, Wheeler Peak. Lessons and rentals are available.

Lift tickets (2006/07): Adult, $52; youth (7–12), $40; multiday discounts apply. Ages 6 and younger and ages 70 and older ski free.

Accommodations: The Angel Fire Resort Hotel (800-633-7463; $$–$$$) has standard

Dining: $$$$-Entrees $30+; $$$-$20-$30; $$-$10-$20; $-less than $10.

Accommodations: (double room) $$$$-$200+; $$$-$141-$200; $$-$81-$140; $-$80 and less.

and deluxe rooms and suites. The resort has managed **condominiums** ($$–$$$) and has a full program of ski packages. The hotel is slopeside and the condos have a shuttlebus.

Dining/apres-ski/nightlife: Dining is a resort affair. There aren't many choices outside of the base area. The top spot is **Aldo's Cafe and Cantina** (377-6401; $$), with Italian bistro cuisine, right next to the Chile Express lift. **Branding Iron** (337-4201; $) serves breakfast and dinner in the resort hotel. **Jasper's Bar** ($) in the resort hotel has a bar menu. **Zebadiah's** (377-8005; $–$$) is off the resort and has a good family restaurant. The **Roasted Clove** (337-0636; $$) cooks fine continental dishes but is difficult to spot. Be sure to ask for directions. For pizza call the **Pizza Stop** (337-6340; $), just off the mountain and specializing in freshly made crust and sauces, **Beverly's** (377-2337; $) or the new **Grapevine Gourmet** (377-2884), both in town. For the best barbecue in town, try **Willy's Smokehouse** (377-2765). The new **Bear's Den** (377-1113) at the entrance of the resort is serving breakfast, lunch and dinner. On the mountain, go to the **Summit Haus** for brats and burgers and **Village Haus** on the base area deck for snacks and grilled items. Both have full-service bars. Angel Fire snoozes in the evenings, but **Village Haus** has live entertainment, 3–7 p.m. every weekend. There is also a bit of an apres-ski buzz in **Jasper's**.

Other activities: After a long day on the slopes you may wish to recharge with a Leg Anti-Fatigue Treatment at **Sage Skin and Body Care** (377-5959). Roadrunner Tours (377-6416) offers **winter horse rides** and old-fashioned **sleigh rides.** Try your hand at **ice fishing** in nearby Eagle Nest through the Eagle Nest Marina (337-6941). For solitude and meditation visit the **Vietnam Veterans National Memorial** (337-6900), the first memorial built to honor the men and women serving in Vietnam.

Red River Ski Area, Red River, NM; (505) 754-2223

Internet: www.redriverskiarea.com

7 lifts; 290 skiable acres; 1,600 vertical feet; 1 terrain park

Red River, about an hour drive—37 miles—north of Taos, has no pretensions about Indians or the Spanish. This once was a down-and-dirty mining town with saloons and bordellos lining the streets. Today, Red River is one of the prettiest ski towns and most convenient to be found in the U.S. Two main lifts drop right into town and most hotels and condos are within walking distance of them. If you don't want to walk, take the town trolley that makes its rounds every 15 minutes.

This is a fun mountain, a lot of fun. Red Chair and Copper Chair reach the summit from different spots in town. This is not high-speed quad territory; all these lifts are fixed-grip. There's a terrain park for those who like tricks and air. From the highest point, Ski Tip, **beginners** can drop to the other side of the peak to test about a dozen easy runs served by a double chair. Beginners can also ski all the way back to the base area along Cowpoke Cruise, which meanders down the entire 1,600 feet of vertical. **Intermediates** have the entire skier's right of the mountain for fun and games. These trails are the definition of cruiser delights. **Advanced and expert** skiers can head to skier's left from Ski Tip. Here, those seeking challenge will find a mix of trees and black-diamond trails.

Red River claims to be one of the great teaching mountains. It has an excellent ski school that focuses on beginner and intermediate skiers as well as children. Red River's Youth Center and Buckaroo Child Care is open from 8 a.m. to 4:30 p.m. Children from 6 months to 4 years are accepted for child care; $30 for half day, $48 for full day. Kids ages 4–10 have lessons and indoor activities, and are grouped in classes according to age and ability. Costs range from $35 to $87, depending on number of hours and whether lunch and rental equipment is included.

Lift tickets (2006/07): Adult, $53; teen (13–19), $47; juniors and seniors, $38. Multiday discounts are available.

Accommodations: Almost all hotels are relatively close to the lifts and the town. For **lodging information,** call (800) 331-7669 or 754-2366. **Lifts West Condo/Hotel** (800-221-1859; 754-2778; $–$$) has spacious rooms and a wild second-floor hot tub. For European charm, stay at the **Alpine Lodge** (800-252-2333; $$$) or **Edelweiss** (800-445-6077; $$-$$$) with its heated swimming pool. **The Auslander Condominiums** (800-753-2311; 754-2311; $$), **Black Mountain Lodge** (800-825-2469; 754-2469; $$), **Copper King Lodge** (800-727-6210; 754-6210; $–$$) and **The Riverside** (800-432-9999; 754-2252; $) are all almost ski-in/ski-out. Groups and large families can find great deals on cabin and townhouse rentals through **Red River Real Estate** (800-453-3498; $$-$$$$) or **Bandanna Red River Properties** (800-521-4389; $$-$$$$).

Dining/apres-ski/nightlife/other activities: Don't come here looking for fancy gourmet fare. This town is focused on good down-home meals with quantity. That said, **Brett's** (654-6136; $$) has an elegant dining room and a menu where everything from seafood to lamb is spiced with gourmet phrases. **Texas Reds Steakhouse and Saloon** (754-2922; $$) is everything a cowboy steakhouse should be. From the newsprint menu to the charbroiled beef, this is a carnivore's paradise. **The Lodge at Red River** (754-6280; $$) has a good family restaurant with plenty of steaks, but you can find trout and shrimp as well. **Timbers** (754-3090; $$) is another western-style steakhouse. For Tex-Mex head to **Sundance** (754-6271; $) or to **Angelina's** (754-2211; $). The new **Roberto's** (754-6270) inside Lift's West specializes in highly recommendable Old Mexican food. For N.Y.-style pizza and other Italian meals try **Pappa's** (754-2951; $). For breakfast head to **Mountain Village Diner,** across from the Chamber of Commerce, for an all-you-can-eat feast, to the **Alpine Lodge** for their breakfast burritos, or to **Shotgun Willie's** for the "Mountain Man Breakfast."

Red River is the nightlife capital of the region. If you want a rocking time, this is the spot to come. The town is normally packed with a young college crowd that loves to dance and sing. Head to the **Motherlode Saloon** for a chance to two-step and hear great live music. **The Mineshaft Theater** has concerts. **Texas Reds** often has singers in the bar. And the **Bull O'The Woods Saloon** has cowboy karaoke. **The Lonesome Pine Pub** serves eight New Mexico microbrews on tap; check their hours before you head there. **Chubbies Tavern** rocks during apres-ski with the college crowd.

Residents of Red River have an excellent sense of humor—and mischief. In November it's **BYOT** (bring your own turkey) for the annual Turkey Toboggan, where competitors race down the slope seated on the frozen beasts. February brings fully costumed **Mardi Gras** celebrations with awards for best and most unique masks. **St. Patrick's Day** is celebrated with a big ol' party. From mid-March to the end of the season, spring break **"Beach Days"** is the biggest celebration of the year with beach music, hula hoop contests, the flashlight parade for kids 12 and younger, a sand volleyball court and events all up and down the main street. This is a good party town.

Dining: $$$$-Entrees $30+; $$$-$20-$30; $$-$10-$20; $-less than $10.
Accommodations: (double room) $$$$-$200+; $$$-$141-$200; $$-$81-$140; $-$80 and less.

Ski Apache, Ruidoso, NM, (505) 336-4356; (505) 257-9001 (snow report)

www.skiapache.com

11 lifts, 750 acres, 1,900 vertical feet, 1 terrain park

Ski Apache, where trails cruise through the pines of the Mescalero Apache Indian reservation, sits at the end of a dramatic access road high above the cowboy town of Ruidoso in south-central New Mexico. This is the southernmost major destination ski area in North America, only 120 miles north of the Mexican border.

The region with the town and the resort occupies an oasis of pine-covered mountains surrounded by the sprawling New Mexican desert. From the Lookout Snack Bar, at the top of the gondola, the panorama is one of the most expansive to be found at any ski resort in North America. The view takes in the White Sands National Monument, the site of the first atom bomb explosion, the forest where Smokey Bear was rescued and the Old West towns where Billy the Kid roamed.

Trail names echo the Apache heritage—Geronimo, Screaming Eagle, Chino and Ambush. Skiers from Texas, Germans from nearby Holloman Air Force Base, and Mexican visitors all mix with the Mescalero Indians who make the resort work. You'll find no condo developments and no ski-in/ski-out hotels at the ski area—this is a pure ski resort. The elevation between 9,600 and 11,500 feet guarantees snow and the location in southern New Mexico tempers the weather and favors plenty of sunny days.

This is an intermediate's playground, but advanced levels won't be disappointed. Beginners will be pushed for all they're worth—the shift from mellow terrain to more significant steeps is a big one. Sometimes it's hard to tell the blues from blacks. They're both tough.

Twelve miles from the snowfields of Ski Apache and about 3,000 feet below the sacred Sierra Blanca peak, the town of Ruidoso spreads along a valley floor surrounded by gentle pines. This town is mainly a summer resort with the focus on Ruidoso Downs—home of quarter-horse racing, five golf courses and a full May-to-October program of music and cultural events. This makes winter the bargain time for most B&Bs, motels and hotels.

Mountain layout: Bounded by two ridges, Ski Apache is divided roughly in half by a third center ridge that runs parallel to the boundary ridges. The area's gondola runs along the center ridge from the base to the summit. At the top of the area on trail-map left, expansive Apache Bowl has wide-open skiing from 11,500 feet with about 650 feet of vertical. Most of the rest of the slopes are off the center ridge, which has a long intermediate trail running along the crest with expert and intermediate trails dropping to trail-map right. The rest of the skiing is near the bottom of the left boundary ridge. Again, a blue cruiser snakes along the crest and black-diamond pitches fall toward the base area.

♦♦**Expert** ♦**Advanced:** Experts may want to head elsewhere for extreme terrain, but you can find some challenge in the steeps and glades. For advanced skiers, there are plenty of moguls and steep pitches on all of the north faces. Apache Bowl and The Face (which drops into the bowl from the center ridge) offer great powder skiing when the conditions cooperate. Those who want to stay in the bowl can upload using a triple chair that allows them to stay right in the bowl without working their way back down to the base.

■**Intermediate:** This is a great resort for intermediates looking to improve. The blues are mellow and the blacks reach some excellent pitches. For cruising, stick to the ridges, or take your first runs on Ambush, Chino or Meadows, to the right as you unload from the gondola. For showoff time, take a few zips along Capitan, the blue-square run that drops right to the base area—it is a joy. For bumps head to The Terrible and Incredible. Plan to be challenged.

●●**Beginner:** Beginners have their own area served by Chair 7. Those shifting from beginner to intermediate should try Lower Deep Freeze and Snowpark.

●**First-timer:** The learning area is off Chairs 3 and 5 at the base. This area is fenced off so those taking first-time lessons are not subjected to more advanced skiers and snowboarders zipping through their classes.

Ride Guide: Apache Bowl is a favorite spot when powder falls or is blown over the ridge. Do laps off the lift that exclusively serves the bowl, then toss in some variety by riding up The Face and dropping off the ridge trails. The terrain forms natural halfpipes known locally as "the fingers" in the center of Apache Bowl. Yee-haw, as the Texans would say!

Lift tickets (06/07 prices): Adults (13–61), $51; children (7–12), $32; seniors 70 and older, ski free; ages 5 and younger, free.

Distance from Ruidoso: About 16 miles on Mechem Drive and Ski Run Road.

Lodging information: There are more than 70 lodging properties in the Ruidoso area. For a complete listing, see ruidoso.net.

The Inn of the Mountain Gods (257-5141; 800-545-9011; $$), is a massive casino set on one of the Indians' sacred lakes with picture windows that open to reveal the ski area on their sacred mountain in the far distance.

For luxury amidst beautiful art, head to the **Hurd Gallery & Guest Homes** (800-658-6912; 653-4331; $$$$) in San Patricio near the junction of Hwys. 70 and 380, about 30 miles from Ruidoso. Spectacular lodging starts at $200 a night.

Hawthorn Suites (258-5500; 866-211-7727; $$) is Ruidoso's newest upscale choice in lodging. It features all suites with amenities including indoor pool, hot tub and massages.

Swiss Chalet Inn (258-3333; 800-477-9477; $-$$), perched above town, is one of the last lodges before the turnoff to the resort. Views from the restaurant are beautiful.

Enchantment Inn (378-4051; 800-435-0280; $) is a full-service hotel. **Shadow Mountain Lodge** (257-4886; 800-441-4331; $-$$) is designed for couples, with king-size beds, fireplaces and hot tubs. **Holiday Inn Express** (257-3736; 800-257-5477; $-$$) includes breakfast. **Sitzmark Chalet Motel** (257-4140; 800-658-9694; $) offers inexpensive packages including lift tickets.

Condotel (800-545-9017; 258-5200) offers a large selection of two- to six-bedroom condos, cabins and private homes. These lodging choices can be viewed and booked online at www.ruidosoreservations.com.

Dining: Try **Pasta Cafe** (257-6666; $–$$) for Italian specialties and **Le Bistro** (257-0132) for faux French. **The Cattle Baron** (257-9355; $$) is the place to head for steaks. **The Texas Club** (258-3325; $–$$) also serves great steaks and all-American fare.

Tinnies Silver Dollar (653-4425; $$) provides dining with a step back in time about 30 miles from Ruidoso toward Roswell. The yesteryear dining rooms are lined with paintings harking back to the Old West or showcasing the Hurd/Wyeth family art. **The Green House** (354-0373; $$), in nearby Capitan, serves good grub fresh from its own greenhouse. Both are worth the drive.

Cafe Rio (257-7746; $–$$) on downtown's main drag serves a curious Mediterranean mixture (Italian, Portuguese, Greek) of pizza, pasta, soups and seafood in diner-like surroundings. **Terraza Camanario Restaurant** (257-4227) and **Casa Blanca** (257-2495; $) offer Tex-Mex. **Farley's** (258-5676; $) has a good family atmosphere with fajitas and burgers.

Dining: $$$$-Entrees $30+; $$$-$20-$30; $$-$10-$20; $-less than $10.
Accommodations: (double room) $$$$-$200+; $$$-$141-$200; $$-$81-$140; $-$80 and less.

Oregon regional resorts

Timberline Lodge, Timberline, OR; (503) 622-7979

Internet: www.timberlinelodge.com

7 lifts; 1,430 lift-served acres; 3,590 feet vertical; 2 terrain parks; 1 halfpipe

Timberline is known for its summer skiing and beautiful, historic lodge. Timberline was the continent's first ski area to offer lift-served summer skiing, and now more than 50,000 skiers come each summer. The Palmer Snowfield, at 8,500 feet above sea level, has a steady pitch at the advanced-intermediate level. It's challenging enough that you'll find World Cup ski racers from several countries practicing technique. A high-speed quad, Palmer Express, allows Timberline to keep the terrain open nearly the entire year, and gives the area the greatest vertical drop in the Northwest—3,590 feet. The deep snows of winter sometimes require cat drivers to dig out the lift, the upper terminal of which is inside the mountain. Spring skiing is incredible off this lift. Palmer runs through Labor Day every year, conditions permitting (and they usually do).

Half of Timberline skiing is still below treeline and the main lodge, but few experiences in the skiing world match a ride up the Magic Mile Super Express and the Palmer Express to the top of the Palmer Snowfield. The original Magic Mile lift was the second ski lift in the country, after Sun Valley's. Silcox Hut, which served as the original top terminus and warming hut, has been restored and is open to overnight groups. Below the Timberline Lodge are many blues and greens, with a few short blacks. The trail system between the trees makes each run feel like a wilderness excursion.

Timberline has two terrain parks to challenge everyone from the amateur to the professional level. The parks and halfpipe are accessed by the Stormin' Norman high-speed quad.

Lift tickets (05/06 prices): Adult day tickets, $43; children (7–12), $26; ages 6 and younger and 72 and older, free with ID.

Distance from Portland: 68 miles.

Lodging information: (800) 547-1406. Inquire about the historic slopeside **Timberline Lodge** ($–$$$) and the mountaintop **Silcox Hut** ($$).

Mt. Hood Meadows, OR; (503) 287-5438 in Portland or (503) 337-2222 at mountain

Internet: www.skihood.com

14 lifts; 2,150 lift-served acres; 2,777 feet vertical; 3 terrain parks; 1 superpipe

Mt. Hood Meadows has by far the most varied terrain of the Mt. Hood ski areas and is as big as many Western destination resorts. The Vista Express quad lift gets you to terrain that is not much used. Slopes to skier's right off the lift are regularly groomed and are some of the best and most diverse terrain on the mountain. Perhaps the name should be changed from the Badlands to the Goodlands. It's full of expert powder caches, pitches, cruisers and some beginner runs. Freestylers can now get to the Vista Park plus South Park and the superpipe in one run.

Heather Canyon, when it is open, has always been the favorite for experts. Three of its entry runs—Twilight, Pluto and Moon Bowl—are winchcat-groomed, which means advanced and upper-intermediate skiers can go where they once had feared to tread. Snowcat skiing adds another 1,020 feet of vertical drop. To start way high with the runs into Super Bowl, you must take the Super Bowl Snow Cat from the top of Cascade Express. The ride costs

www.skisnowboard.com has detailed writeups about these resorts

www.xcskiresorts.com has details about nearby cross-country trails

$10 per trip.

Meadows has a lot of what you'd have to call "free range" terrain. Most anywhere is good for riding and most of the mountain rides big. The east-facing runs between the Cascade Express and the boundary—more of a face actually—are all smoothies, good for swooping back and forth. Between the Cascade Express and the Mt. Hood Express are six little bowls and patches of trees—all single-black runs. For the real deal, head to the experts-only Heather Canyon. Absolute Magnitude is the best to jump into from the Shooting Star Ridge. For the upper canyon, you have to take Cascade Express and turn right. Things are steeper up here.

A favorite intermediate area is under the Hood River Express chair, called "Hurry" (for its initials—HRE). The entire HRE pod is designated slow speed for families and novice skiers and snowboarders. Beginners have the runs under the Daisy, Buttercup and Red chairs. Mitchell Creek Boulevard, reached from the Red chair, is particularly great for kids. Night skiers are served by four chairlifts near the lodge, one of them a high-speed quad.

Lift tickets per shift (06/07 prices): Adult tickets, $49; juniors (7–12) and seniors (65+), $29; ages 6 and younger, $6. (Shifts are 9 a.m.–4 p.m., 11 a.m.–7 p.m., and 1–10 p.m.)

Distance from Hood River: 35 miles.

Lodging information: (800) 754-4663.

Mt. Hood SkiBowl, OR; (503) 272-3206

Internet: www.skibowl.com

9 lifts; 960 lift-served acres; 1,500 feet vertical; 1 terrain park; 1 halfpipe

Mt. Hood SkiBowl is gaining a reputation for challenging ski runs with the addition of its Outback area and 1,500 feet of vertical reached from Upper Bowl. The mountain is now rated at 60 percent expert, but the 65 runs have enough variety for all skills. Beginners have some nice terrain, although the unloading ramps on the Multorpor side can be steep and intimidating for those at this level. The Multorpor side and the Outback are favorites for snowboarders.

The Terrain Park, on Lower Surprise, features a halfpipe, hips, lips, rollers and spines. The Stump Garden is a boardercross course, accessible from the Cascade chair.

Mt. Hood SkiBowl is one of America's largest night-skiing areas. It illuminates 34 runs, including some truly steep black-diamond runs. It also emphasizes ski racing, with programs for a variety of age groups.

Lift tickets (05/06 prices): Adult day tickets, $36; children (7–12) and seniors (65+), $20; ages 6 and younger and seniors 72 and older, free.

Distance from Portland: 53 miles.

Lodging information: (800) 754-2695; or visit the resort's website.

Mt. Bachelor, Bend, OR; (541) 382-2442

Internet: www.mtbachelor.com

13 lifts; 3,683 lift-served acres; 3,365 feet vertical; 2 terrain parks; 1 superpipe; 1 halfpipe

Mt. Bachelor is not your typical mountain. At other resorts, the highest point often is difficult to distinguish from neighboring summits, which may be just a few feet higher or lower. But Mt. Bachelor, a stately volcanic cone that is part of the Cascades mountain range, rises from Oregon's high desert and is visible for miles in every direction.

On the eastern side of the Cascades, where snow falls lighter and drier than at other Northwestern resorts, Mt. Bachelor has become a popular destination for Western skiers and snowboarders. Despite no on-mountain lodging and little nightlife, Mt. Bachelor attracts visitors with its dependable snowpack, clear dry air, average daytime winter temperatures of

Dining: $$$$-Entrees $30+; $$$-$20-$30; $$-$10-$20; $-less than $10.

Accommodations: (double room) $$$$-$200+; $$$-$141-$200; $$-$81-$140; $-$80 and less.

26 degrees, and fine skiing and snowboarding from early November into July.

Visitors should keep in mind that all that snow results from a lot of storms, and winds often close the Summit Express chair, a high-speed quad to the 9,065-foot treeless summit. An average stormy day brings winds of 60 to 70 miles per hour, which can kick up ground blizzards where the snow swirls into a whiteout six feet high. (Visibility is usually better lower on the mountain, where the ski trails are protected by trees.) But when the weather is clear and you're standing on top, you can see California's Mt. Shasta 180 miles to the south.

Between the Outback and Red chairs is an unusual geologic feature, a lone cinder cone. It's not lift-served, so powder lasts there until it's wind-packed. By getting up a head of steam from Leeway, skiers can swoop up nearly two-thirds of the way and climb the rest.

Mt. Bachelor's Northwest Express Quad serves 400 acres of tree skiing and open-bowl terrain in an area called the Northwest Territory. When the Summit Express is open, experts should head for it. The steepest descent is through The Pinnacles, a jagged rock formation reached by a 150-foot hike from the top of the lift, then across the broad, ungroomed expanse of Cirque Bowl. Next might be Cow's Face, far to the left of Summit Chair, steep but smooth. Because it's unknown to many skiers, it doesn't get carved into moguls, but wind packs it hard. You can find moguls on Grotto, Canyon and Coffee Run, off the Pine Marten chair.

This mountain is best suited to intermediates. The Outback Express, with a 1,780-foot vertical rise, serves excellent intermediate runs. From this chair, Boomerang is the only run rated black, and it parallels the lift. One blue run, Down Under, often is left ungroomed for mogul enthusiasts. Other popular chairs for intermediates are the Pine Marten Express and the Skyliner Express. Old Skyliner, off the Pine Marten chair, has marvelous dips and rolls—far more fun than the usual freeway design of many intermediate trails.

For beginners, green-circle trails descend from every lift except the Summit and Outback chairs. More difficult trails are on either side, funneling the faster skiers away from those still learning to control their turns. Novices have their own terrain at both base lodges. Adjacent to the West Village Day Lodge is a short high-speed quad chair, Sunshine Accelerator. The runs it serves are called Milky Way and Home Run, a clear giveaway of the terrain's gentleness. At the Sunrise Lodge the Carrousel Triple chair gets riders to the Carnival and Marshmallow runs.

The resort has a superpipe built to Olympic specifications, 400 feet long with 17-foot walls. You'll find it next to the Pine Marten lift. A superpipe cutter keeps it in tip-top shape. On the other side of the Pine Marten Express is the Mt. Bachelor Slopestyle Arena. The Air Chamber Terrain Park covers the entire DSQ run near the Skyliner Express and is about 6,300 feet long and spread across 20 acres. It includes jumps, quarterpipes, spines, hips, tabletops and Signature Rails by the Mt. B Freeride Team. Parks and pipes beginners will find both an appropriately sized park near the bottom of the Sunshine Accelerator as well as a minipipe.

Most freeriding takes place in the Outback, which is loaded with trees and fall-line runs. For your final run in the Outback, try to take the Outback Express back up to Pine Marten Lodge. If you take the Northwest Express Quad up, you have to traverse the Northwest Crossover, and it's a bit flat. The New Summit Express gets you to the Peak of Mt. Bachelor, well above treeline. There are some good steeps in The Cirque. Everything else up there to the left of the Express is gentle terrain.

Lift tickets (05/06 prices): Adult day tickets, $49; children (6–12), $30; teens (13–18), $39; 5 and younger and 70+, free.

Distance from Portland: 162 miles. **Distance from Bend:** 21 miles.

Lodging information: (800) 829-2442.

www.skisnowboard.com has detailed writeups about these resorts
www.xcskiresorts.com has details about nearby cross-country trails

Utah skiing

and staying in Salt Lake City

Salt Lake City Facts
Dining: ★★★★
Apres-ski/nightlife: ★★★★
Other activities: ★★★★★

Bed base: 17,366
Area code: 801
Reservations: (800) 541-4955 or 521-2822 (Salt Lake Convention & Visitors Bureau)
E-mail: slcvb@saltlake.org
Internet: www.visitsaltlake.com (Salt Lake Convention & Visitors Bureau) and www.skiutah.com (Ski Utah)
Visitor Information Centers: Salt Palace Convention Center, 90 South West Temple, open daily (main location); Salt Lake City International Airport, open daily

Cosmopolitan city or an outdoor recreation destination? Salt Lake City is both in one. Recently named as one of Outside magazine's "18 perfect towns that have it all," Salt Lake, with all its snowsports options, also has pro basketball plus a symphony, opera, dance companies and live theater, not to mention the Mormon Tabernacle Choir. The choices of what to do when not on the slopes or trails are almost endless and include gourmet dining, rollicking brew pubs, comedy clubs, shopping, art galleries, and did we mention stuff like bobsledding, Nordic jumping and speed skating? You'd better stay an extra week.

Hosting the 2002 Olympics helped to enhance and show off the city and the nearby canyons. The quantity and quality of the snow has to be experienced in person to be truly appreciated. Yes, they must have inclement days, but it certainly seems that the snow comes mostly at night, leaving skiers and riders with feathery powder on beautiful bluebird days. In fact, rumour has it that it snows at Big and Little Cottonwood Canyon resorts on average every third day.

Salt Lake shouts wide open spaces and Western scope with its distinctive streets built wide enough for a wagon with a team of oxen to make a U-turn, yet it is connected by non-stop flights to more than 90 destinations. This means skiers and boarders can have breakfast at home and take advantage of free skiing at Alta from 3 to 4 p.m. that afternoon. The towering Rockies and fantastic skiing and boarding are a mere 35 minutes from downtown. (For in-depth information on getting around the region, see Getting there.)

While the altitude – as high as 11,000 feet at some of the resorts – means drink lots of water and get plenty of sleep, there are those who have enough energy to go out on the town after attacking the slopes all day. Hooray, drinking is allowed in Utah. Microbreweries are everywhere. and martini bars are springing up for those who want their alcohol high-test. Add in jazz clubs, country western hangouts, piano bars and live music and staying in Salt Lake means skiers and riders will have a well-rounded winter resort experience in the middle of a happening city.

 ## Accommodations

Salt Lake City has about 100 lodging facilities, so we can't possibly list them all. This should give you a good start, though. Although rates are a little higher downtown than in outlying parts of the city, it is worth the extra few bucks to be close to Salt Lake City's major attractions. Make sure to ask about ski-and-stay packages.

Most Salt Lake hotels also sell the Ski Salt Lake Super Pass—an interchangeable voucher good for day passes at Alta, Brighton, Solitude or Snowbird—for as little as $45 (includes complimentary public transportation from downtown to the resort).

The Grand America Hotel (800-621-4505; 258-6000; $$$$) is the most recent property of Earl Holding, who also owns Sun Valley Resort, Snowbasin Ski Resort and the Little America Hotel chain. Elegantly appointed with authentic antiques, paintings, sculptures and carpets, this hotel could be listed as a museum. Ask about arrangements for an art tour when you visit. There is a full-service spa on the premises as well as a pool and hot tub. Enjoy afternoon tea in the beautifully decorated lobby. The staff understands the meaning of service.

The **Hotel Monaco** (877-294-9710; 595-0000; $$–$$$), a glamorous boutique hotel, is in an historic bank building. Definitely not a cookie-cutter property, the Monaco will deliver a pet goldfish to your room at your request and serves up free back and neck massages during the complimentary evening wine reception. And don't be surprised if you see your favorite rock star or NBA team in the lobby. The lively Bambara, an award-winning bistro-type restaurant, serves an eclectic menu of fabulous dishes just off the lobby.

The upscale **Marriott Salt Lake City Downtown** (888-236-2427; 531-0800; $$–$$$) has spacious rooms that are tasteful and comfortable with an indoor pool, hot tub, sauna and health club on the premises. Parking costs $10 per day. **Marriott Salt Lake City Center** (866-961-8700; 961-8700; $$–$$$), adjacent to the Gallivan Plaza, showcases a great ice-skating rink and cultural events. It has the same amenities, and parking is $10 per day.

Hilton Salt Lake City Center (800-445-8667; 328-2000; $–$$$) is one block farther south on West Temple. The Hilton spent $12 million to renovate the hotel and give it a new look. The **Peery Hotel** (800-331-0073; 521-4300; $–$$$), historic, elegant, and once a bordello. Enjoy architecturally distinct rooms with pedestal sinks, marble, and period furniture.

The tasteful **Little America Hotel and Towers** (800-453-9450; 363-6781; $–$$$), a sister property to Grand America Hotel, has some of the largest rooms we've seen in a hotel—great for spreading out all the gear that skiers carry. **Embassy Suites Hotel** (359-7800; $–$$$) has two-room suites with a free cook-to-order breakfast, plus there's a hot tub, indoor pool and sauna. The **Marriott University Park Hotel** (581-1000; $–$$$) is near the University of Utah, farther from downtown but closer to the resorts. It is at a higher elevation than downtown, so it has a dandy view of the city from its glassed-in hot tub.

Downtown, **Red Lion Hotel Salt Lake Downtown** (800-733-5466; 521-7373; $–$$$) has nicely appointed deluxe rooms, an outdoor heated pool, exercise facilities and free parking. For budget lodging, try the **Salt Lake City Center Travelodge** (531-7100; $), **Travelodge Temple Square** (533-8200; $–$$), or **Deseret Inn** (532-2900; $).

Three B&Bs in historic buildings are clustered about seven blocks from Temple Square, each with wonderfully decorated rooms. **The Anniversary Inn** (800-324-4152; 363-4900; $$–$$$$) is as romantic as it sounds, with themed rooms that cover everything from a mansion suite to a jungle safari and a sultan's palace. **The Armstrong Mansion Bed &Breakfast** (800-708-1333; 531-1333; $$–$$$$), built by a mayor of Salt Lake City for his bride in 1893, is a Queen Anne-style mansion on the National Register. It's been restored to its original appearance and each room is romance-themed with luxurious bedding. Some rooms have jetted tubs. The **Anton Boxrud Bed & Breakfast** (363-8035; 800-524-5511; $–$$) is a small mansion resplendent with polished wood, beveled glass windows, antiques and hand-woven lace.

A good, cheap place to stay the night before you fly out, is the **Days Inn Airport** (800-329-7466; 539-8538; $–$$) includes continental breakfast with make-your-own Belgian waffles. There's also an indoor hot tub and pool. It's just minutes away from the airport, too.

 **Dining**

Downtown Salt Lake City has restaurants in nearly every food category you can name, including Afghan, Peruvian and Thai.

Metropolitan (173 W. Broadway, 364-3472; $$$) is Utah's most-awarded restaurant and has world-class New American gourmet cuisine that rivals some of the best of any other major city. It also serves vegetarian entrees. There's live jazz here on Saturday evenings.

Bambara (202 S. Main St., 363-5454; $$$) specializes in fresh, seasonal foods with Italian, French and Asian influences in a nouveau bistro setting in the Hotel Monaco.

Casually elegant Italian dining can be found at **Baci'Trattoria** (134 W. Pierpont Ave., 328-1500; $$). **Xiao-Li** (307 W. 200 South, 328-8688; $$) in the warehouse district features award-winning authentic Mandarin and Szechuan dishes and has a low-key, elegant atmosphere, with Oriental screens, high-backed rosewood chairs, and Chinese prints and scrolls on the walls. **Mikado** (67 W. 100 South, 328-0929; $$) has fresh fish and sushi, and has been in business for four decades. **Golden Phoenix** (1084 S. State St., 539-1122; $$) has been recognized as one of the top Chinese restaurants.

There are a wealth of choices for steak and seafood. **New Yorker** (60 W. Market St., 363-0166; $$$) is elegant, though you'll see people dressed in just about anything, including jeans. American cuisine is beautifully presented and don't be surprised if you see the mayor here, since it's the "in" place to dine. The more casual **Market Street Grill** (322-4668; $$) and the colorful **Market Street Oyster Bar** (531-6044; $$) focus on fresh seafood, but also serve steaks and pastas. (Market Street Grill has great breakfasts, by the way.) For understated elegance, go to **Christopher's Seafood and Steakhouse** (100 W. Broadway, 519-8515; $$). Big appetites will love the **Rodizio Grill** (459 Trolley Square, 220-0500; $$), an authentic Brazilian-style steakhouse. Kids younger than 9 eat free. **Lamb's Grill Cafe** (169 S. Main, 364-7166; $$) is Utah's oldest restaurant, dating to 1919, plus it serves a great breakfast.

The Garden Cafe (555 S. Main, 258-6000; $$) at the Grand America Hotel serves Seasonal Cuisine using fresh produce, seafood and game. Sunday brunch here is acclaimed.

At the base of Little Cottonwood Canyon is **La Caille** (942-1751; $$$), which gets rave reviews for its French cuisine, serving staff and setting. It's built to look like a French chateau and surrounded by gardens filled with swans, peacocks, rabbits and other animals. Make reservations; this place is *tres chic.* There's a B&B on premises.

Red Iguana (736 W. North Temple, 322-1489; $-$$) gets lots of rave reviews from locals for the top Mexican featuring a half-dozen moles and a great chile verde. **Cafe Pierpont** (122 W. Pierpont Ave., 364-1222; $–$$) is a festive and noisy Mexican restaurant reminiscent of a town square with wandering Mexican guitar players and women making tortillas from scratch near the entrance. Portions are huge here. The crab enchiladas suiza are fabulous. **Rio Grande Cafe** (270 S. Rio Grande, 364-3302; $) in the historic Rio Grande Train Station is another of downtown's best bets for Mexican.

Salt Lake City has three brew pubs and they're all worth checking out. **Squatters Pub Brewery** (147 W. Broadway, 363-2739; $-$$) entices with a broad, eclectic menu and everything sounds delicious. We suggest you select one of their dishes with beer as an ingredient. You'll also find good pub fare and beer at the other brew pubs: **Desert Edge Brewery at the Pub** (273 Trolley Square, 521-8917; $), in an old trolley building, and **Red Rock Brewing Co.** (254 South 200 West, 521-7446; $-$$), in a converted warehouse with many meals cooked in a wood-fired oven.

Dining: $$$$-Entrees $30+; $$$-$20-$30; $$-$10-$20; $-less than $10.
Accommodations: (double room) $$$$-$200+; $$$-$141-$200; $$-$81-$140; $-$80 and less.

Apres-ski/nightlife

Utah's liquor laws: Baby-boomer skiers remember when getting a glass of wine meant a trip to the state liquor store before going to a restaurant, then paying a setup fee before you could consume your own brown-bagged bottle. Now it's much easier, but here are a few tips:

Restaurants that have liquor licenses (most do) can serve alcohol from noon to midnight "to customers intending to dine." Wine and liquor menus are delivered along with your dining menu, and many restaurants promote their drink specialties on table cardholders. Some restaurants are still designated as private clubs, which means you'll have to pay a small temporary membership fee to get in.

Bars don't exist in Utah, at least not by that name. If you are planning just to drink, not eat, you'll have to do so at a private club. Don't be deterred by restaurant or nightclub advertising that has phrasing like this: "A private club for the benefit of its members." You, too, can become a member. Utah residents buy an annual membership costing up to $35 for each club. Visitors pay $5 for a membership, valid for three weeks for the visitor and seven guests. Annual members can bring guests, too. Just think of it as a cover charge.

You can also purchase beer, wine and liquor very easily. Grocery and convenience stores sell beer. Sixteen state liquor stores in the Salt Lake area sell wine, spirits, and beer (closed on Sundays). Wine lovers will want to visit the Utah State Wine Store, 255 South 300 East, which has more than 3,000 different varieties of wine.

After a day of skiing at Alta or Snowbird, check out **Cafe Trio** (733-6600), on your left at the southeast end of the Salt Lake Valley at the bottom of the mountains, for high-end brew, pub food and great apres-ski atmosphere.

For an unusual happy hour, stop by the **Cotton Bottom Inn** (2820 E. 6200 South; 273-9830) at the base of Big and Little Cottonwood Canyons. This is a raucous, sawdust-on-the-floor tavern with great garlic burgers and an earthy crowd. It is just off of Exit 7 on Hwy. 215.

Green Street (in Trolley Square) is apparently favored by Salt Lake City's career crowd. The Olympics brought a host of dance clubs to Salt Lake including **Vortex** and the **W Lounge**, both within a one-block radius on West Temple Street, across from the venerable **Port o' Call Social Club** (400 East and West Temple). **The Red Door**, Salt Lake's most sophisticated martini bar, is next door to Bambara and the Hotel Monaco. If you want to visit an establishment that's surely making the local Mormon population a bit crazed, the **Crazy Goat Gentlemen's Club** is a euphemism for Salt Lake's you-know-what…wink, wink (Arrow Press Square, 119 S. West Temple, in the rear).

If you like movies and microbrews, head to **Brewvies** (677 South 200 West; 322-3891). This establishment combines second-run (movies that already have been shown but aren't yet in video stores), independent and classic films with a gourmet-pizza-and-beer restaurant. Many people come to eat or drink, then decide whether to hang around for the movies being shown on four screens. You must be 21 years old.

For a more complete list of nightlife, pick up a free copy of *This Week Salt Lake*. This excellent guide tells you what is happening within a two-week period.

Other activities

Experienced skiers can ski to six different resorts via backcountry routes on the all-day **Interconnect Adventure Tour** (534-1907; reservations required). Mountain guides lead three to 12 skiers and some traversing and walking are necessary, so you need to be a confident skier and in good physical condition. The four-area tour (Solitude, Brighton, Alta and Snowbird) is offered three days a week, while the six-area tour (those four plus Park City Mountain Resort and Deer Valley) goes the other four days. Each tour costs $175 (05/06 price), including return transportation and lunch.

If your legs are beat from skiing and snowboarding in too much powder, take a day off to visit **Antelope Island State Park** (801-773-2941 for entrance gate or 725-9263 for visitor center). The island is home to free-roaming herds of bison, bighorn sheep, mule deer and antelope, as well as smaller animals such as bobcats and coyotes.

This isn't the typical ski-town nighttime activity, but classical music lovers shouldn't miss the free 8 p.m. Thursday night rehearsals of the **Mormon Tabernacle Choir** at Temple Square. You also can attend Sunday when the choir broadcasts live from 9:30 to 10 a.m. Seating ends at 9:15 a.m. and you must stay seated for the duration of the half-hour program.

You can check out your ancestors at the **FamilySearch Center** at the Mormon computer center inside the restored historic Hotel Utah (15 ES Temple St.). Be sure to bring a list of family ancestors, names and dates to make your free search worthwhile. You can also do a free search at the nearby **Family History Library** (35 NW Temple St.), also run by the Mormons.

Some other unusual ski town activities include attending a **Utah Jazz** (355-3865) basketball game, or getting all dressed up for **theater, symphony, dance** or **opera** performances.

Shopping here is extensive. At Trolley Square, beautifully restored trolley barns contain shops, art galleries and restaurants, plus a movie theater. The Gateway Plaza is a two-story outdoor pedestrian mall that surrounds the restored Union Pacific Depot, originally built in 1908 and featuring French Renaissance architecture. This isn't your ordinary shopping mall. In addition to shops, restaurants and a movie theater, you'll also find a planetarium here. Two giant contemporary malls, Crossroads Plaza and ZCMI Center, are across from each other near Temple Square.

Utah is home to five spectacular **national parks,** all within about four hours of Salt Lake: Arches, Bryce Canyon, Canyonlands, Capitol Reef and Zion. A side trip is worthwhile.

 Getting there and getting around

By air: Salt Lake City is a major airline hub. Ground transportation is well organized. You can go directly to the shuttle desks in the airport.

By train: Amtrak's California Zephyr stops in Salt Lake City (at 4 a.m. coming from the West Coast, but the fare is cheap. From Chicago, the train arrives at midnight). Call (800) 872-7245 or consult the Amtrak website, www.amtrak.com.

Getting around: Rent a car if you want to cover a lot of ground in the evening; otherwise, use public transportation. Getting to the resorts is a snap: Several ground transportation companies operate shuttles to the ski areas from Salt Lake City. Ask your lodging about them.

You can take the Utah Transit Authority light rail (known as UTA TRAX) from downtown and transfer to a UTA ski bus to take you to any of the Cottonwood Canyon resorts. This is very convenient and affordable, and the rail cars and buses are remarkably clean. It costs $6 round trip for a Ski Pass. Plan for about an hour total travel time. The only drawback: On Sunday, TRAX doesn't run from downtown until after 10 a.m. If you want to get to the resorts early, you can call a cab (about $25 one way; still cheaper than renting a car) to take you to the ski bus stop. Ride the Utah Transit Authority ski buses for $3 round trip from the park-and-ride at the canyon's mouth to any of the Cottonwood Canyon resorts (exact fare is required).

UTA also has a free fare zone downtown, convenient for sightseeing and evening activities. Buses run at night downtown until about 11:30 p.m., but only about once per hour. Call 287-4636 for more info. There are several taxi companies available, too.

Dining: $$$$-Entrees $30+; $$$-$20-$30; $$-$10-$20; $-less than $10.
Accommodations: (double room) $$$$-$200+; $$$-$141-$200; $$-$81-$140; $-$80 and less.

Nearby resorts

Sundance, Sundance, UT; (801) 225-4107; (800) 892-1600

Internet: www.sundanceresort.com

3 lifts; 450 acres; 2,150 vertical feet

Though this ski area has been owned by actor-director Robert Redford for more than 30 years, it has never been highly marketed—and that's on purpose. Skiing and snowboarding are not the resort's main event. Rather Redford has achieved a balance between outdoor recreation of all kinds, the arts and an intimate environment. Set on the slopes of breathtaking 12,000-foot Mt. Timpanogos, Sundance is regarded as the most beautiful ski area in Utah. To experience the challenging and varied terrain, get there early because the ski area limits lift tickets to 1,200 per day. Locals comprise 80 percent of the skier/snowboarder visits. Even when the 105 guestrooms are full, there is never a crowd on the mountain. Lodging packages offer many different possibilities like free lift tickets and full breakfasts in the Foundry Grill.

The area has a full-service Nordic Center featuring 40 km. of groomed cross-country trails and 10 km. of snowshoe trails. You'll also find two excellent restaurants, an eco-friendly gift shop, the historic Owl Bar, and the Sundance Art Shack offering a full schedule of classes, retreats and workshops throughout the year. Guests also enjoy screenings of award-winning films from past and present Sundance Film Festivals. (This annual event, held in larger Park City during late January, celebrates the achievements of independent filmmakers.)

Lift tickets (05/06 prices): Adults, $44 ($32 midweek); children 12 and younger, $20; children 5 and younger, free; seniors 65 and older, $12.

Distance from Salt Lake City: About 50 miles south via I-15, east on Hwy. 52, north on Hwy. 189, then a short hop west on Hwy. 92.

Lodging information: 225-4107 or (800) 892-1600.

Brian Head, Brian Head, UT; (800) 272-7426; (435) 677-2035

Internet: www.brianhead.com

8 lifts; 500+ acres; 1,320 vertical feet; 4 terrain parks; 1 halfpipe

Brian Head, in Utah's southwest corner near Bryce and Zion national parks, holds two distinctions among Utah resorts: It is one of very few *not* within an hour of Salt Lake City airport, and it draws virtually all its customers from Southern California and Southern Nevada. For these skiers, Brian Head is very accessible (all freeway until the last 12 miles) and has an excellent variety of mostly intermediate terrain covered by that famous dry Utah powder.

Child care starts at 6 weeks, and the town has several condo complexes, restaurants and a hotel. A tubing hill is open daily, and also at night every Friday and Saturday, plus during holiday periods. Brian Head also has night skiing on weekends and holidays. However, this is a quiet area in the evenings.

Lift tickets (05/06 prices): Adults, $40; children (6-12) and seniors (65+), $27; ages 5 and younger, free with paying adult.

Distance from Las Vegas: About 200 miles north by I-15 and Hwy. 143.

Distance from Salt Lake City: About 4 hours south via I-15 and Hwy. 143.

Lodging information: (800) 677-2810; www.brianheadutah.com.

Alta
Utah

Summit elevation: **10,550 feet**
Vertical drop: **2,020 feet**
Base elevation: **8,530 feet**

Address: P.O. Box 8007
Alta, UT 84092-8007
Area code: 801
Ski area phone: 359-1078
Snow report: 572-3939
Reservations: 742-0101
or (888) 782-9258
E-mail: info@alta.com
Internet: www.alta.com
Expert:★★★★★
Advanced:★★★★★
Intermediate:★★★★
Beginner:★★★★
First-timer:★★★

Number and types of lifts: 11–2 high-speed quads,
1 high-speed triple, 1 triple, 3 doubles, 4 surface lifts
Skiable acreage: 2,200 acres
Snowmaking: 3 percent (50 acres)
Uphill capacity: 11,284 skiers per hour
Snowboarding: Not allowed
Parks & pipes: 1 park
Bed base: 1,136
Nearest lodging: Slopeside, inns
Resort child care: Yes, 6 weeks and older
Adult ticket, per day: $44-$49 (05/06 prices)
Dining:★★★
Apres-ski/nightlife:★★
Other activities:★

Alta sits at the top of Little Cottonwood Canyon in a high-Alpine basin where the ski experience is much like it was in 1938. That year, Alta opened with one rickety chairlift—which actually didn't carry any skiers until January 15, 1939—and one not-quite-finished lodge to house overnight guests. A few modern conveniences have found their way into the basin since then—such as three high-speed chairlifts and free wireless Internet access at most lodges. But the gestaldt of the place has remained the same.

The fact that Alta calls itself a ski area, not a resort, is telling. Here, it's all about the skiing—and only skiing; snowboarding is still prohibited. Rates at the five lodges include breakfast and dinner because Alta guests are here to eat, sleep and ski, and not necessarily in that order. There are no trendy nightclubs, shops or restaurants in Alta, although the dining in the lodges is excellent. Skiers save their energy for the slopes. The Rustler Lodge even has stools in front of its bathroom sinks, lest a skier be too weary to brush his or her teeth.

For many, Alta is love at first sight and the ski area attracts an enormous repeat following. The lodges report that 70 to 80 percent of their guests return. And it's not just the old-fashioned ambiance that's the lure. The basin is blanketed on average with over 40 feet of dry Wasatch powder each year. Skiing in this much light, fluffy snow is not only intoxicating, it's addictive. The steep headwalls spill onto rolling alpine meadows that cascade to the canyon floor. This mixture of terrain keeps it interesting. If the powder is tracked in the Ballroom, there are hundreds of acres of hidden nooks and crannies—like the trees off the Wildcat lift—to explore.

But Alta's reputation for steep-and-deep belies its gentler side. The ski area is as much gently rolling alpine meadow with wide groomed swaths as it is heart-stopping headwall with waist-deep snow. It has some of the best beginner terrain in Utah and its children's programs are also excellent. Only 11 of 116 total named trails are rated for beginners, but they are long rolling slopes that drop over 800 vertical feet—far longer than the average learning piste. It's also a beginner's paradise.

A great option for anyone staying here for at least a week: Purchase an AltaSnowbird ticket and enjoy the two resorts' combined terrain. To reach Snowbird, look for the gate in the saddle off Alta's Sugarloaf chairlift. A gatekeeper won't let anyone pass who doesn't have a combined ticket. Drop down the beginner and intermediate trails of Mineral Basin, then either return to the saddle via the Baldy Express chairlift, or take the Mineral Basin quad to Snowbird's Hidden Peak.

One other thing: It's pronounced AL-ta, like the name Al, not AHL-ta. Pronounce it correctly, and Alta regulars might just show you their favorite lines.

 ## Mountain layout

The ski area has front and back sides with two base stations. Wildcat base area is the first one you reach. It has basic facilities—ticket office, restaurants, restrooms and ski patrol.

The Albion base area houses the Children's Center, Ski School, restaurant, retail and rental operations. Albion is where you'll find beginner slopes, but it also has intermediate and expert terrain at higher elevations. Albion and Wildcat bases are connected by a long, horizontal, two-way transfer rope tow: Just grab the rope and let it pull you along.

From the top of Germania Pass, the runs down the front side return you to the Wildcat base area; runs down the back go to Albion, or give access to the Sugarloaf and Supreme lifts.

◆◆**Expert** ◆**Advanced:** Alta's trail map shows no double black diamonds. That's your first clue to the local attitude. If you're good enough to ski challenging terrain, you shouldn't need differentiation between advanced and expert. Yes, there is double-diamond terrain; it's up to you to figure it out.

At the Wildcat base, the Wildcat and Collins lifts serve intermediate and advanced runs—narrow trails, bump runs, open powder fields and many glades. Even on powder days, only one lift ride is required to reach the reward.

From the Collins lift, skiers can access an entirely different ridge, West Rustler. Off High Traverse, a dozen-plus blacks fall on both sides of the ridge. Eagle's Nest, North Rustler and High Rustler descend the ridge's front face back to the Collins lift. On the backside, the East Greeley area highlights a seemingly endless series of broad bowl routes, including Greeley Hill, High Greeley and Eddie's High Nowhere—all leading to the Sunnyside lift or the Transfer Tow that traverses the base area. Stay high from Collins along blue-rated Devil's Way to reach short, steep shots on Keyhole Gulch, Glory Hole and Yellow Tail.

On powder days, regulars line up to the right of the Collins unloading station. They're waiting for the patrollers to drop the rope to Ballroom, a wide bowl that's initially rated blue but grows steeper as it's traversed until it reaches the black-rated Baldy Shoulder, Stimulation and Johnson's Warm-Up. All those people rushing past you on the traverse? They're locals who know exactly where the powder's best. Follow those people.

Far to skier's right runs the Supreme lift, accessed via Supreme Access off Razor Back (this is flat, so carry your speed). On powder days, go to the Albion base instead of the Wildcat base and head up to the Supreme lift, which drops you off at 10,595 feet. Once off the lift, where all but three runs are black-rated, drop in wherever you want; you can't go wrong. Some of Alta's best tree skiing is off this lift. The terrain is steep, the snow holds for days and trees are more abundant than the map shows.

Experts hunting a unique Alta experience should seek Alf's High Rustler, named after one of the founding fathers of Alta. Getting there is adventure enough for some. Ride the Collins lift and take the high traverse. Stay on the traverse as it crosses the ridge toward Greeley Bowl, and keep on traversing. The traverse becomes narrow, the drop-offs precipitous on each side. Eventually it spirals around the mountaintop knoll, and opens to High Rustler, a beautiful, steep run that is little skied, enjoys breathtaking views of the valley, and spills right out into the lodges at the bottom.

■ **Intermediate:** Intermediate skiers experience a certain special heaven at Alta—well-groomed trails, ungroomed powder fields and friendly pitches with wide-open and un-peopled runs. Not even any lift lines! And remember, no snowboarders.

Start on the Albion side where intermediates have the most extensive terrain under the Sugarloaf lift. Find groomed cruisers plus a few very gentle pitches off to one side that don't get groomed—a super place to take some powder turns. Devil's Elbow is a real hoot, as is Roller Coaster. There's one nice intermediate run off the Supreme lift—Upper Big Dipper—but don't plan to ski this lift unless you want lots of challenging blacks.

On the Wildcat side, intermediate trails take you from the top of both the Wildcat and Collins lifts. Mambo and Main Street are loads of fun. Just watch for the steep top of Main Street. If you want a delightful powder field, head to Ballroom. Don't traverse too far, as the terrain gets steeper the farther you go (don't worry, you can see when it gets steeper).

●● **Beginner** ● **First-timer:** Although Alta is well-known for its extremely difficult terrain, it also boasts exquisite grooming of the best snow in the region. This may come as a surprise, but Alta has the best beginner terrain in all of Utah.

The best beginner and first-timer terrain is at the Albion base. If you're staying at the Wildcat Base, take the transfer tow over to the Albion Base for warm ups and confidence-builders. The Albion and Sunnyside lifts access gentle slopes. This first-timer area is fairly safe and protected from faster skiers, but watch out for speeders on Home Run as it crosses the beginner runs.

Sunnyside has been upgraded to a bit more of an advanced-beginner run, but the rest are pure beginner runs. The mile-long run, Crooked Mile, takes you gently back to the bottom of both the Albion and Sunnyside lifts.

Ride Guide: Snowboarding is not permitted. Head next door to Snowbird.

Parks and pipes

Always wanted a terrain park just for skiers? Then Alta is the place for you! Alta built a terrain park at the top of the Sunnyside lift on the Albion side of the mountain. The park is wide open with features including small and medium jumps, a luge, a box and rails. It's open when weather and snow permit.

Cross-country and snowshoeing (visit xcskiresorts.com for more details)

Alta (742-9722) has 5 km. of groomed track for skate and classic skiing near the transfer tow. The Alta Nordic center at the Wildcat Base offers gear rental, including snowshoes and telemark, plus there's an espresso bar as well as a retail shop with clothing and accessories.

Lessons (05/06 prices)

Bearing the name of Alf Engen, the Norwegian ski jumper who came to Utah in 1930, the ski school is recognized in the industry for its contributions to the development of professional ski instruction. Lower-level ski lessons meet at the base of the Albion lift, while upper-skill levels meet below the base of the Germania lift. For all ski school programs, call 359-1078.

Group lessons: Levels 1–5 take two-hour lessons, $42. Levels 6 and up get 2.5-hour workshops that focus on specific skills such as parallel turning, moguls or powder, $54.

Private lessons: A one-hour lesson costs $75; additional person, $23. An early-bird lesson from 8:30–9:30 a.m. costs $85; additional person, $33. Two hours, $150; additional person, $46. Three hours, $225; additional person costs $69. All day, $450; additional person, $69.

Special programs: A 2.5-hour telemark workshop is offered Tuesdays, Thursdays and Sundays for $54. Diamond Challenge is a 2.5-hour afternoon workshop for Level 9 (true expert) skiers for $54. The instructor gives pointers, but mostly acts as a guide to Alta's steeps.

Racing: Alta's race course is at the Sunnyside lift; Friday and Saturday from 11 a.m. to 3 p.m. Pay at the race arena or at the ticket office.

KidStuff (05/06 prices)

Child care: Ages 6 weeks to 9 years. All-day infant care by reservation only is $80. All-day child care (3 and older) with lunch is $60. All-day child-care with a two-hour ski lesson is available for skill levels 1–2 for $85 (includes lunch). Alta's child-care center is a state-licensed facility owned and operated by Redwood Preschool, Inc. Space is limited, so reservations are highly recommended; call 742-3042 or book online.

Children's lessons: For beginner and intermediate skiers (skill levels 1–6), ages 4–12: All Day Adventure for skill levels 1–2 is $85 (with lunch); for skill levels 3–6, it's $99 (including lunch and lift ticket). Half Day Adventure for levels 1–6 is $40. For advanced and expert skiers (skill levels 7–9), ages 7–teens: All Day Explorer costs $115 (with lunch and lift); Afternoon Explorer costs $50. All children's lessons meet at the Albion base.

Special activities: Most lodges at Alta offer supervised children's programs, both during the day and after the lifts close, though some are only during holidays and peak times. Inquire when making lodging reservations.

Lift tickets (06/07 prices)

	Adult	Child (12 and younger)
One day	$52	$23
Three days	$150 ($50/day)	$69 ($23/day)
Five days	$235 ($47/day)	$115 ($23/day)

Who skis free: Ages 80 and older. All surface lifts are free, any time, any day. After 3 p.m. every day, skiing is free on the Sunnyside lift.

Who skis at a discount: Skiers pay $28 to use the beginner lifts in the Albion area. The AltaSnowbird ticket that allows you to access both resorts' terrain costs $71 a day; multiday AltaSnowbird tickets cost $64/day for three to four days, $60/day for five or more days.

Accommodations

Alta is one of the few ski areas that still has traditional ski lodges where breakfast and dinner are included in the cost. This is a super way to meet new people, particularly if you are traveling alone. Most of these lodges also have either dorm rooms or single occupancy rates available. Ask whether your room has a private bath, since some rooms do not. Rates are lower in value season, which is prior to mid-December, most of January, and April to closing.

It doesn't get any better than the luxurious **Alta's Rustler Lodge** (742-2200; 888-532-2582; $$-$$$$). Recently remodeled, it's rich in colors and textures reminiscent of a private club yet, at the same time, conveying the inviting feeling of home. It has an outdoor heated pool and hot tub, plus a eucalyptus steam room, workout room and full-service spa. The elegant restaurant and bar have picture windows looking right out onto the mountain. Prices include a sumptuous breakfast and a savory gourmet dinner accompanied by live dinner music.

The Alta Lodge (800-707-2582, reservations only; 742-3500; $$–$$$$) is a 57-room inn with saunas, hot tubs, and several common areas, including the popular Sitzmark Club bar with its views of the slopes. By guest preference over the years, the lodge has only one television, a large-screen unit with satellite and a video/DVD library. Eighty percent of the guests are repeat customers who return each year and know each other on a first-name basis. The same chef has been in the kitchen for more than 30 years and the food is very good.

Alta Peruvian (800-453-8488, reservations only; 742-3000; $$–$$$$) has a heated outdoor pool and hot tub, sauna, and movies each night. The rates include lift passes, breakfast, lunch and dinner (food's great, by the way). It's a short walk from the Wildcat base or you can take the lodge's free shuttle.

Goldminer's Daughter (800-453-4573, reservations only; 742-2300; $$–$$$$), named after a huge mining claim, is closest to the Wildcat lift. The outside resembles 1960s Soviet housing, but on the inside, it's quite pleasant and has everything you need. Extensive renovations revamped the lobby in 2003 and rooms in 2004. Complementary wireless Internet is available in the lobby, lounge and cafe. Prices include breakfast and a remarkably good dinner.

Snowpine Lodge (742-2000; $$–$$$) is Alta's oldest and smallest lodging. It was extensively renovated in 1990 to help it retain its charm, warmth and homey atmosphere. It has an outdoor hot tub and a Scandinavian sauna. Price includes breakfast and dinner.

Two large condominium complexes, **Hellgate** (742-2020; $$$–$$$$) and **Blackjack** (800-343-0347; 742-3200; $$–$$$$), are between Alta and Snowbird, with Blackjack better situated for skiing between the two resorts. Both have van service to the ski areas. Studios, one-bedrooms sleeping four, two-bedrooms sleeping six and three-bedrooms are offered.

Canyon Services (800-562-2888) rents luxurious condos and homes with fully equipped kitchens, washers and dryers, and cable TV.

Dining

For one of the best gourmet meals anywhere, go to **Alta's Rustler Lodge** (742-2200; $$$) for a four-course, fixed-price dinner. There's a kid's meal for children 7 and younger. Reservations are required. You also can eat breakfast and lunch here ($). A close second is **Alta Lodge** (742-3500; 322-4631 from Salt Lake; $$$), another restaurant that serves a four-course, fixed-price dinner. Sunday buffet dinners and the Kids' Dinner also are popular. Reservations are required for dinner. Grab a bite to eat for lunch as well ($).

The award-winning **Shallow Shaft** (742-2177; $$$), a restaurant on Alta's main road, is open for dinner only and has innovative Southwest cuisine featuring wild game, seafood, steak, pasta and chicken entrees. Reservations required.

On the mountain: For a tasty sit-down lunch on the mountain, head to the **Collins Grill** ($-$$), upstairs in the mid-mountain Watson Shelter. You'll have great views of the mountain and skiers too. We had lobster ravioli and carrot ginger soup and both were fabulous. There are three on-mountain **cafeterias.** The **Albion Grill** ($) at the Albion base is not your average resort cafeteria. You'll find a great salad bar, homemade soups, chili and baked goods. Plus it serves a mean Reuben and fries. Wash it down with one of the microbrews. You can get hearty breakfasts here too. At the Wildcat base, everyone seems to congregate for breakfast and lunch at the **Slopeside Cafe and espresso bar** ($) at Goldminer's Daughter Lodge.

See the Salt Lake City chapter for other options.

Dining: $$$$-Entrees $30+; $$$-$20-$30; $$-$10-$20; $-less than $10.
Accommodations: (double room) $$$$-$200+; $$$-$141-$200; $$-$81-$140; $-$80 and less.

Apres-ski/nightlife

Bring your own. There's nothing going on but what visitors cook up—either in their condo or the lodge's common rooms. That doesn't mean there's nothing to do, though, because the lodges all offer plenty of activities for their guests. That said, the best nighttime gatherings we found were at the **Alta Peruvian Lodge bar,** where guests and locals gather (with a cover charge on weekends) for drinks at a lively bar or around the fire. The dog curled around the couch is the local mascot. Local lore has it that the bookshelves at the Alta Peruvian have been voted the best nightlife in Alta. The **Sitzmark Bar** at the Alta Lodge is also good for apres-ski story swapping. **Goldminer's Daughter Alpine Lounge** hops after the lifts close and has a good selection of beers. The **Eagle's Nest Lounge** at Alta's Rustler Lodge is the most upscale lodge bar and has killer views of the sunset over the mountains.

 ## Other activities

Alta offers **snowcat skiing** on 325 acres in Grizzly Gulch, adjacent to the ski area. Runs average 1,500 vertical feet, with the highest elevation at 10,500 feet. Cost includes an orientation, continental breakfast and guides. Both skiers and snowboarders are welcome, must be advanced or experts (but the ski area is still closed to snowboarders). For reservations, call 359-1078, Ext. 271 or 742-3333, Ext. 271.

Alta attracts those who like to ski from morning 'til the last lift shuts down, so there aren't many non-skiing activities. A 45-minute **guided interpretive ski tour** is given by a Wasatch-Cache National Forest ranger on weekends and holidays at 1:30 p.m. Meet at the sign at the bottom of Cecret lift. Little Cottonwood Canyon has spectacular **helicopter skiing** with Wasatch Powderbird Guides (800-974-4354; 742-2800), based between Snowbird and Alta.

To revitalize yourself after a day on the slopes, go to **Alta Day Spa** (742-2200) at Alta's Rustler Lodge or have a masseuse visit your room from **Wasatch Mountain Massage** (742-3313). A few **shops** in the Little Cottonwood Canyon area have local handicrafts, artwork and books, but skiers don't come to Alta for the shopping. Note, however, that one of our staff writers found a replacement lens for his goggles in the general store at Alta Lodge—no other shops in the region carried them.

See the Salt Lake City chapter for other options.

 ## Getting there and getting around

By air: Salt Lake City is a major airline hub, so flights are numerous from every corner of the continent. Many companies provide ground transportation, which is well organized. When you make lodging reservations, ask about ground transportation arrangements and most lodges will make them for you. You also can go directly to the shuttle desks in the airport.

By train: Amtrak's California Zephyr stops in Salt Lake City (at 4 a.m. coming from the West Coast, but the fare is cheap. From Chicago, the train arrives at midnight). Call (800) 872-7245 or consult the Amtrak website, www.amtrak.com.

By car: Alta is 25 miles southeast of Salt Lake City in Little Cottonwood Canyon on Hwy. 210. The most direct route from downtown and the airport is to go east on I-80, south on I-215, take 6200 South exit (turns into Wasatch Blvd.), then follow the signs to Alta.

Getting around: If you fly in, don't bother renting a car. Most lodges have free shuttles to get you to the slopes or to neighboring restaurants. A free bus links Alta and Snowbird. If you plan to ski a lot of other Utah areas, stay in Salt Lake City (see Salt Lake City chapter). Public transportation makes it easy to get from Salt Lake City to the resorts.

Snowbird
Utah

Summit elevation: 11,000 feet
Vertical drop: 3,240 feet
Base elevation: 7,760 feet

Address: P.O. Box 929000
Snowbird, UT 84092-9000
Area code: 801
Ski area phone: 933-2222
Snow report: 933-2100
Toll-free reservations: (800) 453-3000
Fax: 947-8227
Internet: www.snowbird.com
Expert: ★★★★★
Advanced: ★★★★★
Intermediate: ★★★
Beginner:★★★
First-timer: ★★

Number of lifts: 13—1 aerial tram,
3 high-speed quads, 7 double chairs, 2 rope tows
Snowmaking: Minimal
Skiable acreage: 2,500-plus acres
Uphill capacity: 16,800 per hour
Parks & pipes: 2 parks, 1 pipe
Bed Base: 1,800+
Nearest lodging: Slopeside, hotel
Resort child care: Yes, 6 weeks and older
Adult ticket, per day: $48-$62 (05/06 prices)
Dining: ★★
Apres-ski/nightlife: ★★
Other activities: ★★

Snowbird is to skiing and snowboarding what Oahu's North Shore is to surfing. Snowsports lovers come to this hallowed canyon to push their limits and ride hard.

Snowbird ski resort UtahWith almost 3,000 vertical feet of steep bowls and tree-lined chutes, all covered in almost 500 inches of light Wasatch powder each year, Snowbird is a "must experience" mountain for any expert.

You get the sense of what this mountain is all about from Snowbird Center, a narrow spot in Little Cottonwood Canyon where the 8-minute tram ride starts. The slopes rise straight up from the canyon floor to Hidden Peak at 11,000 feet. The view from the tram, as it travels above the canyon wall, then high above the Cirque, will make experts quiver in anticipation and everyone else quiver in fear. Everything within view is a potential line and the only easy way down is an exposed serpentine cat track. On a powder day, people charge off the tram as if someone has yelled "Fire!"

Snowbird is certainly not an experts-only mountain. The Creekside Lodge, which opened in 2006, sits below a wide gulley of easier terrain. And Mineral Basin, accessible from Hidden Peak, as well as a tunnel off the new Peruvian Express high-speed quad, is tamer than Snowbird's front side. It gets the dawn's early rays, so many head there for the day's first turns. But Snowbird is still a challenging mountain and not for the faint of heart. It is humbling to all—even those who huck its steepest chutes—but exhilarating and inspiring as well. For beginners and experts alike, technique always improves.

Snowbird used to be Alta's backcountry—the resorts share Mount Baldy's flanks. It was the brainchild of Alta Lodge worker Ted Johnson who bought a mining claim at what is now Snowbird's base. Johnson envisioned an entirely different resort than laid-back, retro Alta—one with modern conveniences like a tram and large hotel. He convinced Texas oilman and rancher Dick Bass to finance the project. Snowbird opened in December 1971 with the tram, three other lifts and the Lodge at Snowbird. Two years later, the first wing of the massive

Cliff Lodge opened. With concrete as the primary building material, Snowbird's base area—it's a stretch to call it a village—feels almost industrial. But in an avalanche-prone canyon, the solid buildings provide guests a high level of safety and comfort.

Inside the concrete edifices are all the amenities of a world-class resort. The Cliff Lodge's 11-story atrium is adorned with massive oriental rugs hung by rock climbers. Some of the best dining in Utah is found here. The Cliff Spa, high atop the Cliff Lodge, has an outdoor hot tub and heated pool, a steam room and massage therapists waiting to rejuvenate sore muscles so you can enjoy another day of knee-deep powder or turns down the Gad Chutes.

A great option for anyone staying here at least a week: Purchase an Alta/Snowbird ticket and enjoy the two resorts' combined terrain (snowboarders must either don telemark or Alpine skis or stick to Snowbird, since snowboarding is not allowed at Alta). The two resorts are connected by a ridgetop trail between Snowbird's Mineral Basin and Alta's Albion Basin. The gate takes you into the beginner and intermediate trails of Mineral Basin, and the intermediate and advanced trails of Albion Basin. You also can take a free ski bus between the two resorts.

 ## Mountain layout

Snowbird is divided into three distinct areas: Peruvian Gulch, Gad Valley and Mineral Basin. A good suggestion is to warm up in Mineral Basin, where the sun shines and warms early in the day. After a couple runs in the bowls, head over to Gad Valley for a leisurely 3,000-vertical-foot drop down to the Gadzoom high-speed quad. A northeast exposure on the Peruvian Gulch side keeps The Cirque's steep runs good all day, a treat for the late morning or early afternoon.

Mineral Basin is this mountain's saving grace for beginners and intermediates. The terrain there is aptly rated and provides the opportunity to improve your skills without being scared stiff. The single diamonds here also can be confidently tackled by advanced intermediates.

◆◆**Expert:** Unlike many mountains that are steep near their summits, then flatten into more gentle run-outs, Snowbird is palm-sweating steep from the first turns off 11,000-foot Hidden Peak to leg-aching steep about 3,000 vertical feet later when the base area finally comes into view, looking like buildings at the base of a cliff.

The 125-person tram is the most direct route to Hidden Peak. When the first tram arrives at the summit on powder days, there's a mad dash for the slopes. Skiers and snowboarders hurl their equipment and then themselves over the docking station's railings to make first tracks. If you're the first on the Cirque Traverse or Mineral Basin's Pathway to Paradise, a long traverse to the basin's steeper sections, be prepared for faster, hungrier powder hunters to mow you over. Join the race. Or wait until others have departed, then go where they don't.

If the bowls, chutes, and trees look intimidating, the easiest ways down from Hidden Peak are Chip's Run, a narrow zigzagging cat track that winds down Peruvian Gulch's headwall, then spills into the more forgiving bottom of the Gulch, or the airy Road to Provo.

But most experts will want to test their legs in The Cirque, a wide-open plunge that tumbles into even steeper bowls and chutes.

The Peruvian Express quad opens for the 2006/07 season, and it will change how experts ski and ride Snowbird. On a powder day, many will still head for the tram. But the Peruvian quad takes you 2,600 vertical feet into Peruvian Gulch and is a good way up the mountain when the tram line is long. Although the Cirque's steeps aren't accessible from here, it's a quick four-minute trip through a tunnel to Mineral Basin. Or follow the traverse on skier's right to the gladed double-diamond chutes and trees on the west-facing wall of the Gulch.

Mineral Basin is a great place to start your day because the sun shines here first.

♦**Advanced:** Advanced skiers who choose routes thoughtfully can find plentiful challenges and thrills at the right ability level. Off the tram, Regulator Johnson, a wide-open snowfield, presents the most obvious choice. It can be skied repeatedly from the Little Cloud lift, but it's a crossroads for many other routes and tends to chop up quickly. Johnson is black-rated, but it does have a wide groomed swath down the center, and this descent can be easier than Chip's sharp and crowded switchbacks, even though Chip's is rated blue.

Going to skier's right from the tram, follow Primrose Path all the way down, or branch off onto Adager or lower Silver Fox, for an incredibly long top-to-bottom slide.

Mineral Basin can be reached from the top of the Little Cloud chair, the top of the tram, or via the tunnel from Peruvian Gulch. From the top of the tram or Little Cloud lift, take the Path to Paradise. This is a narrow ledge worn into the hillside and the traffic on it can resemble a mad scramble on the San Bernardino Freeway or N.J. Turnpike.

Nash Flora Lode and Silver Dipper, found about two-thirds of the way across Path to Paradise, create perhaps the best drop-in for advanced skiers; Junior's Powder Paradise offers a gentler blue/black descent. Mineral Basin's far side (skier's right) is strictly expert territory. Skiing to Mineral Basin in the opposite direction off the tram, along Chips Access, leads to Double Down and Chamonix Chutes, two good runs for advanced skiers.

Runs like Gadzooks, S.T.H., Black Forest and Organ Grinder, reached from the Gad 2 lift, are often overlooked. They aren't too long, present a nice challenge, and some gladed secrets can be found between them. Or, try Tiger Tail for a longer challenge.

Way off to skier's left by the Baby Thunder lift—and nearly forgotten—Tiny Tiger offers a short challenge, and double-black rated Lazy Susan and Alice Avenue create an opportunity to try expert runs that are short enough to forgive any skills shortcomings.

■ **Intermediate:** If you can ski Emma with ease, you have several options for the next test. Any of the blue-square runs off the three Gad chairs will be fun. Bananas and Election off Gad 2 are as exhilarating as it gets on skis. If you can handle these, you should be ready to tackle the easiest runs off the tram. Adventurous intermediates should try some of the short ungroomed pitches off Chip's for some extra challenge.

For others, the Baby Thunder area helps to bridge the steepness gap between Snowbird's novice slope and Big Emma, so head here for easier terrain. You can also work on technique on the greens under the Wilbere chair.

Mineral Basin is a wide-open bowl with a backcountry feel to it. Wilderness and a peaceful quietness surround you here, don't miss it. Meander your way down via Lupine Loop (green on the map) to figure out your comfort zone here. The blues are aptly rated. If you're learning to ski powder, you'll find the edges of the greens off Baldy Express are just the right pitch to give you that floating sensation without making you feel as if you're going too fast. There are also some widely spaced trees here to boost your confidence. If you're feeling bold, take the Bench Traverse and try the bowl. New for 2006/07, you can reach Mineral Basin via the Peruvian Express, then the tunnel from Peruvian Gulch, thereby eliminating the need to take the tram, which can feel airy to those not accustomed to such heights.

●●**Beginner & ● First-timer:** The beginners' ski school with rentals, lift tickets and instruction is at the Snowbird Center base area, below The Cliff Lodge. Just beside The Cliff Lodge is the best lift for first-timers and beginners. The Chickadee run, with a gentle pitch and friendly lift operators, is guaranteed to be smoothly groomed.

After a bit of a hike—and there seem to be quite a few to get around Snowbird—daring beginners can ski down Ski School Lane to the Wilbere Lift. The Mountain School Learning Area is just off the top of the Wilbere Lift, so you know it's got to be beginner-friendly.

Big Emma is a favorite cruiser when it's groomed. It's a bit steep and can be crowded. You can venture farther to the Baby Thunder Lift and ski the green Easy Street run, but this is mainly a blue and black area, so be aware of both the difficult runs and the fast skiers in this area. The Mid-Gad Lift also accesses some green areas, but again, be aware of crowded and craggy conditions.

For a memorable experience beginners can't find at most mountains, take the tram up to Mineral Basin, where you can get a view of the backcountry. Lupine Loop, an airy path that winds down Mineral Basin, will take you to Baldy Express. This lift feeds runs marked green on the map, but keep in mind that they will challenge most beginners. When you want to return to the base lodge, simply take the tram back down (do not even think about skiing down the front side, there is no easy way down).

Ride Guide: For the advanced rider, a trip to Utah without riding Snowbird would be like going to Hawaii and not surfing in the ocean. This big mountain is what freeriding is all about and if it dumps snow, plan on some runs of a lifetime. When it comes to the ultimate freeriding resort in Utah, Snowbird is the place. With a vertical drop over 3,000 feet, Snowbird offers steep, long, gnarly lines that can push anybody to the next level.

Riding up the tram will immediately put the magnitude of this mountain into perspective. The lower half of the tramline highlights endless steep tree shots. The upper half gives a bird's-eye view of the famous Cirque. Take advantage of the ride up to check out some lines or cliffs that look good.

At the top of Hidden Peak the riding options are unlimited. To the east lies Mount Baldy, a 15-minute hike to giant chutes and cliffs.To the west is the treeless Little Cloud bowl. For an even more technical line cruise out the Cirque Traverse to Lone Pine. Here on rider's right are multiple chutes and cliffs. On rider's left are big shots with scattered trees and rocks. If you drop in here, you'll eventually end up at the Gad Valley and the Gadzoom quad. The Gad Valley is much mellower with wide-open groomers braiding all over the mountain. However, there are still some good steep chutes and drops right under the lift.

Runs to rider's left of Gadzoom leads to the Little Cloud double. This area is divided into five wide-open bowls. On a powder day, it's wise to head here first because at times it quickly gets tracked out.

On the backside of the mountain is Mineral Basin, a massive, south-facing paradise. Vast bowls, all-sized cliffs and some smooth, rolling groomers are all waiting to be hit. This side of the mountain resembles a big, natural terrain park. There is even an unofficial jump run which has hips, rollers, and a few cat track gaps. Just follow some locals to figure out the drill. Another section worth checking is Powder Paradise. From the top stay high on the right traverse to the boundary gate and hike to the goods from there.

Parks and pipes

Each year Snowbird's parks have been getting bigger and better. The area served by the Baby Thunder lift is dedicated to the terrain park. The Tiny Tiger trail has the biggest tabletops on the mountain. Most of these jumps have a few different lips which can throw riders 10 to 60 feet down to the transitions. Depending on snow conditions, it can be hard to make it to the tranny, so check it out first or let someone else be the guinea pig. Past the hits there are a few really fun boxes and a couple of decent rails. Another run off Baby Thunder is Alice's Avenue. This is the intermediate park where the consequences aren't as high. Small to mid-size tabletops are found here with a few rides on boxes and rails.

Upper Blue Bell is home to a boardercross course with a luge, an intermediate hip jump and a couple of intermediate tabletops. Lower Blue Bell has five large expert rails and fun-boxes. Snowbird's second boardercross course, with six intermediate jumps and tabletops, is on Tiny Tiger.

The Snowbird superpipe lives on the Big Emma run. The pipe is 400 feet long, 50 feet wide and has walls up to 17 feet. The super big transitions make this pipe pretty user-friendly. Next to the pipe there is a smaller beginner park with a few super-mellow jumps. With the resort's huge selection of tabletops, boxes, rails and the superpipe, there are perfect hits for everyone from beginners to pro riders.

Cross-country and snowshoeing

Snowbird does not offer cross-country skiing. However, it does offer **snow-shoe tours** and snowshoe rentals. Call 933-2147 for more information.

Lessons (05/06 prices)

Snowbird Mountain School has four one-stop locations for ski and snowboard school registration and buying lift tickets (tickets are not included in the lesson price). The offices are on Level 1 of the Cliff Lodge, the Plaza Deck of the Snowbird Center, the Cottonwood Room on Level 2 of the Snowbird Center, and in the new Day Lodge in Gad Valley. For more information or reservations, call 933-2170.

Group lessons: A half-day class costs $65 (open to all levels morning or afternoon); it's $100 to take both classes on the same day. Advanced-intermediates and better can take an all-day Mountain Experience for $100.

First-timer package: First-time skiers and snowboarders get a half-day group lesson, lift ticket and rentals for $70. Two sessions on the same day cost $105; a three-day program with one half-day lesson each day costs $210.

Private lessons: For one person, half day is $295; full day is $495. For two to five people, half day is $350; full day is $575. Customized group sessions are available for six to eight people, call for details.

Special programs: Women's Ski & Snowboard, Snowbird University, and Wild Mountain Yoga are all four-day camps. Skiing and snowboarding are separate women's seminars. There are also steeps camps for skiers and riders. Call for prices and dates.

KidStuff (05/06 prices)

Child care: Ages 6 weeks to 12 years. These prices are for regular season; value season prices are lower. It costs $90 a day with lunch for ages 6 weeks to 3 years; $85 for ages 3 years (toilet-trained) to 12 years. Half-day and multi-day discounts are available. Evening babysitting is $15 an hour, a little more for an additional child, but you must be staying in a Snowbird lodge to use this service; 48-hour advance reservation required. Reservations suggested for all child care; reservations two weeks in advance are required for infants and toddlers. Call Camp Snowbird at (801) 933-2256 or reserve when you book your vacation. A non-refundable $25 cancellation fee for infant/toddler reservations is applied toward your final day.

Children's lessons: A program for 3-year-olds includes a one-hour private lesson with a half-day session of child care for $95 (with lunch and rentals). Kids 4–6 get a program that combines a morning and afternoon lesson with indoor activities for $150 (with lunch and rentals). For ages 7–15, a full-day program with lunch and lessons costs $100; half day is $65 (no lunch). Ability levels are separated. Reservations are required for all children.

Special activities: Kids' Night Out is for ages 4–6 and includes crafts, movies, outdoor play and dinner. Adventures After Dark is for ages 7–15 and includes outdoor activities such as snowshoeing, tubing, movies and dinner. Both programs are offered Wednesday and Saturday from 6:30-10 p.m.; reservations required. Wednesday nights cost $30, with second child in same family for $25; Saturday nights cost $40, second child in same family, $35. Board games and playing cards are available at the front desk of all of Snowbird's hotels. Snowbird also has arcades throughout the Snowbird Village—in the Iron Blosam Lodge on Level 2, in the Cliff Lodge on Level A, and in the Snowbird Center on Level 1.

Lift tickets (05/06 prices)

	Adult	Child (12 and younger)
One day	$62	Free (see below)
Three days	$156 ($52/day)	
Five days	$240 ($48/day)	

Who skis free: Two children 12 and younger ride the chairs free when an accompanying adult purchases a lift ticket. (Tram access costs $15.) Children of lodging guests ski the entire mountain free, and there's no limit on the number of children for Snowbird lodging guests.

Who skis at a discount: Seniors 65 and older ski for $49. A ticket only for the Chickadee chair is $15.

Note: These are the prices with tram access. For chairs only, the one-day prices are $51 for adults; $40 for seniors. Don't buy tram access if you don't plan to use it; you can always upgrade a day's ticket to include the tram for $11. The AltaSnowbird ticket that allows you to access both resorts' terrain costs $69 a day; multiday AltaSnowbird tickets cost $62 per day for three to four days, $58 per day for five or more days.

Accommodations

All lodging at Snowbird is within walking distance of the base lifts, and can be reserved by calling **Snowbird Central Reservations** (800-453-3000). Winter season is mid-December through early April; value season is before and after those dates. Snowbird also has added a January value season, where rates are between the high and low seasons. Snowbird's season is a long one, lasting well into May most years. Lodging also is plentiful in Salt Lake City.

The Cliff Lodge ($$$–$$$$) spreads like an eagle's wings at the base. The concrete-and-glass behemoth belies the luxury that awaits inside. There's an 11-story atrium, a renowned spa (see *Other Activities*), and a glassed-in rooftop with a heated pool overlooking the slopes. The pool complex has a trio of hot tubs and an outdoor heated pool, and a nearby fruit-juice bar. The lodge showcases an enormous Oriental rug collection, including at least one in every room. Mountain-view rooms have picture windows from the shower that peer into the sleeping area and out to the view beyond (there's a shower curtain you can pull for modesty). The Cliff Lodge also has suites. Children younger than 12 stay and ski free with adults.

The Lodge at Snowbird ($$–$$$$), **The Inn** ($$–$$$$), and the **Iron Blosam Lodge** ($$–$$$$) are three condominium complexes with similar layouts. Not as elegant or as expensive as the Cliff Lodge, but they are well maintained, roomy and comfortable. Amenities include outdoor swimming pools, indoor hot tubs and saunas. Rates start at $125 for an efficiency or studio during value season, and top out at $539–$819 for a one-bedroom with loft during winter season.

Dining

The Aerie (933-2160; $$$; reservations recommended; right) on top of the Cliff Lodge is considered one of Utah's best restaurants, for good reason. The Asian decor is elegant and tasteful, the views from the large picture windows spectacular and the food and house piano player are excellent.

The adjacent **Aerie Sushi Bar** ($–$$) serves fresh hand-rolled sushi. At ground level of the Cliff Lodge's atrium, the **Atrium Restaurant** ($–$$) is fine for baked goods and espresso, a lunch buffet or snacks. **El Chanate** ($–$$) on Level A of the Cliff Lodge is the place for Mexican fare.

At the Iron Blosam Lodge, **The Wildflower** (933-2230; $$; reservations recommended) features outstanding Mediterranean cuisine. **The Lodge Bistro** ($$–$$$) in the Lodge at Snowbird has a cozy atmosphere with an eclectic bistro menu. **The Steak Pit** ($$$) in the Snowbird Center at the base of the mountain specializes in hand-cut steaks and seafood. There's usually a wait, but it's worth it.

The rest of the eateries in the Snowbird Center cater to the ski crowd, serving breakfast and lunch. For sit-down service, **The Forklift** ($) has great sandwiches and salads, plus a large fireplace. For the best lunch value, go to the pasta bar at **The Rendezvous** cafeteria where you can order huge servings of made-to-order hot pasta dishes that are absolutely yummy for just $7.95.

There's also a well-stocked salad island and the usual cafeteria fare. **Pier 49 San Francisco Sourdough Pizza** has sourdough pizza with lots of toppings. **Birdfeeder** has gourmet coffees, including espressos and light snacks.

At **Snowbird Center** you'll find a grocery and deli with a take-out breakfast and lunch counter. Its liquor store is closed on Sundays and holidays.

See the Salt Lake City chapter for other options.

 ## Apres-ski/nightlife

Snowbird's nightlife is very quiet. For the liveliest apres-ski, try the **Tram Club**, on the bottom floor of the Snowbird Center, with retro decor and a picture-window view of the tram's huge operating gears. It's your best bet if you want to dance. Sporting events are showcased on about a dozen TVs. **The Wildflower Lounge** is mellow and has a good bar menu. **The Aerie** has a bar with live jazz several nights a week. There's the usual bar menu, plus apres-ski specials on fresh sushi. **Keyhole Cantina,** which specializes in margaritas and is home to Utah's largest selection of premium tequilas, also is a great place for Utah microbrews. Watch sports events on four TVs, listen to live acoustic music, or spin tunes on the jukebox. Apres-ski specials are served daily until 5:30 p.m.

Remember: The nightspots are "private clubs" that charge a $4 three-week membership fee. If you are staying at a Snowbird lodge, the membership is included with your accommodations; however, the Tram Club is owned separately and requires a separate membership. At night, you can take the free Snowbird shuttle to and from the Snowbird Center and the various restaurants and nightspots at the lodges. If you're staying at the Cliff Lodge, you can walk down some stairs and across the Chickadee novice slope to get to the Snowbird Center; however, we recommend the shuttle, which runs until 11 p.m. (sometimes later). The walking route is slippery, and you'll be dodging skiers and others who use that slope at night.

See the Salt Lake City chapter for other options.

Dining: $$$$-Entrees $30+; $$$-$20-$30; $$-$10-$20; $-less than $10.
Accommodations: (double room) $$$$-$200+; $$$-$141-$200; $$-$81-$140; $-$80 and less.

Other activities

Snowbird operates a **tubing hill** daily from 1 to 8 p.m. **Ice skating** is available at the Cliff Lodge on an outdoor rink; skate rentals available. You can go **night skiing** for free on the Chickadee novice slope outside the Cliff Lodge on Wednesday, Friday and Saturday until 8:30 p.m. **Snowmobile tours** zip you through the awesome backcountry of Mineral Basin. Snowbird also offers **guided backcountry tours** with the resort's ski patrollers. All tours are dependent upon weather conditions, ability level and time availability; reservations required. Or be adventurous in-bounds with **First Tracks,** a guided tour of the mountain for a select few before the lifts open to the public, starting at 7:45 a.m. The program is designed for experts; reservations required. For all activities at the resort, call the Activity Center (933-2147) for information and reservations. They also can help arrange off-mountain activities.

Snowbird is doing an important part to promote backcountry safety awareness: A **Rescue Training Center,** which simulates finding buried avalanche victims, is free for anyone who wants to practice. Users select the number of "victims" for their practice session at the control panel and then receive computer-generated feedback at the completion of their search for buried transmitters. Hey, it's free, and your life—and your friends' lives—are worth more than that, so take advantage of it.

Little Cottonwood Canyon has spectacular **helicopter skiing** available from Wasatch Powderbird Guides (800-974-4354; 742-2800), based between Snowbird and Alta.

The 27,000-square-foot **Cliff Spa and Salon** (933-2225 for the spa, 933-2268 for the salon), on the top floor of the hotel, has 23 treatment rooms and a variety of treatments for body, face, hair and nails. You'll also find an exercise facility, a rooftop pool and hot tub, and yoga classes.

For information on entertainment, contact **Entertainment & Special Events** (933-2110). A champion browser will finish off the dozen or so **shops** in half a day. However, the Salt Lake Valley, where you'll find more extensive shopping, is a short drive away.

See the Salt Lake City chapter for other options.

 Getting there and getting around

By air: Salt Lake City is a major airline hub, so flights are numerous. Many companies provide ground transportation, which is well organized. When you make lodging reservations, ask about ground transportation arrangements and most lodges will make them for you. You also can go directly to the shuttle desks in the airport.

By train: Amtrak's California Zephyr stops in Salt Lake City (at 4 a.m. coming from the West Coast, but the fare is cheap. From Chicago, the train arrives at midnight). Call (800) 872-7245 or consult the Amtrak website, www.amtrak.com.

By car: Snowbird is 25 miles southeast of Salt Lake City in Little Cottonwood Canyon. The most direct route from downtown and the airport is to go east on I-80, south on I-215, take 6200 South exit (turns into Wasatch Blvd.), then follow the signs to Snowbird.

Getting around: If you fly in, don't bother renting a car—Snowbird is entirely walkable. A free Snowbird shuttle also will get you to various points within the resort complex. Free bus service links Alta and Snowbird. If you plan to ski a lot of other Utah areas, stay in Salt Lake City (see Salt Lake City chapter). Public transportation makes it easy to get from Salt Lake City to the resorts.

Brighton Ski Resort

Big Cottonwood Canyon
Utah

Summit elevation:	10,500 feet
Vertical drop:	1,745 feet
Base elevation:	8,755 feet

Address: 12601 Big Cottonwood Canyon Road Brighton, UT 84121
Area code: 801
Ski area phone: 532-4731
Snow report: 532-4731
Toll-free information: (800) 873-5512
Internet: www.brightonresort.com
E-mail: info@brightonresort.com

Expert:★★★
Advanced:★★★★
Intermediate:★★★★
Beginner:★★★★
First-timer:★★★★

Number of lifts: 7–3 high-speed quads, 1 quad, 1 triple, 2 doubles
Snowmaking: 20 percent
Skiable acreage: 1,050 acres
Uphill capacity: 11,500+ per hour
Parks & pipes: 3 parks, 1 pipe
Bed base: About 50 (resort); 17,366 (Salt Lake City)
Resort child care: No
Nearest lodging: Walking distance
Adult ticket, per day: $44 (05/06 price)

Dining:★★
Apres-ski/nightlife★
Other Activities:★

Founded in 1936, Brighton is Utah's oldest resort. It still retains its old-time charm, even though there have been many modern updates. The people here are low-key and friendly, and it just feels like home.

The views from the summit are spectacular and include the Great Salt Lake and Mt. Timpanogos, soaring to 11,700 feet. The resort's two "sides" offer distinctly different experiences. New Englanders will feel like they're back home when they're on the Majestic side, a forest of evergreens with winding and twisting narrow trails. In fact, Brighton offers the most extensive tree skiing of the four Cottonwood Canyons resorts. You can spend all day in the woods, only coming out for meals and lift rides. The Millicent side is more like what you'd expect out West, with bowls, cliffs and wide-open spaces.

Brighton has some true expert terrain, but it is not nearly as exhaustive as the other Cottonwood Canyons resorts. It does, however, provide access via its open-boundary policy to some of the best backcountry terrain in Utah. If our expert rating included the out-of-bounds terrain, it would be at least four, if not five, stars. We recommend that out-of-staters head into the backcountry only with a local guide. And always stop by the ski patrol shack to get the latest news on avalanche danger and words of wisdom for the day.

Brighton was one of the first Utah resorts to embrace snowboarding and, as a result, snowboarders remain quite loyal. The combination of exciting terrain, fabulous terrain parks, lots of snow and low prices adds to the resort's popularity with riders. In fact, we heard rumors that "everyone at Brighton snowboards" but we skied here on a weekend and there weren't any more boarders here than at any of the other resorts (except, of course, Alta).

The neighboring resort in Big Cottonwood Canyon is Solitude. Together, these two resorts offer an incredible variety and depth of terrain. Brighton and Solitude offer a joint lift ticket allowing you to ski/ride both mountains, so make sure to inquire if you are interested. Brighton also has night skiing and riding, with 20 lighted runs that include the parks and pipes.

The huge Brighton Center houses lift ticket sales, rental and retail shops, as well as restrooms and lockers. Its cleanly utilitarian, Western appearance is appealing—a cross between log cabin and military barracks. There isn't much to do here once the lifts close, but Brighton regulars like it that way. People come to ski or snowboard, period. In fact, this resort reminds us of one of our favorite Eastern resorts, Jay Peak—only on growth hormones.

 ## Mountain layout

Brighton regulars refer to the "Majestic" side, served by the Majestic and other chairs, and the "Millicent" side, served by the Millicent and Evergreen chairs.

◆◆ **Expert** ◆ **Advanced:**Nearly forty percent of Brighton is rated advanced or expert. The major portions of that terrain are found on the far side of skier's right (Majestic) and skier's left (Millicent) at higher elevations.

Millicent has less intermediate-level skier/rider traffic. The area holds some terrific inbounds bowl and cliff skiing, including some smaller natural features perfect for those who are not overly daring or who are new to backcountry-style sliding. Steep open lines are found on Scree Slope and Lone Pine. Precipitous pitches can also be found on Spaghetti, while Captain Hook presents sharp pitch amongst trees.The Cliff Area offers genuine out-of-bounds territory that's readily accessed from Millicent. But, even though it's within eyeshot of the marked pistes, it pays to go in with someone who knows the territory.

The Millicent chair itself, it seems only fair to note, has no safety bar and moves slowly. We who have vertigo issues were extremely uncomfortable when it traversed—and stopped over—the 200-foot drop about two-thirds of the way up.

The Majestic side, too, offers excellent challenges, highlighted by a short, heart-stopping run called Hard Coin off the Snake Creek Express. The trees are sometimes so thick you can hardly pick a line. It's exhilarating. A bit of hiking leads to the gladed Snake Bowl.

From the Great Western Express quad, four sheer, open-sloped challenges can be accessed: Endless Winter, Rein's Run, Clark's Roost and True Grit; each is a bit shorter than the last, but all get the legs pumping.

Some tree-skier favorites: Sawbuck and the trees between it plus Doyle's Dive, both off the Snake Creek Express; from the Crest Express Chair, the trees off skier's left of Wren Hollow (don't go too low, or you'll have to hike out of Cliff Area) and off Pacific Highway, just past Tantamount; from the Great Western Express quad, the glades between trails (scope it out from the lift) and those just outside the boundary line (careful: cliffs).

Brighton maintains an open-boundaries policy, allowing experts to ski/ride the backcountry as they wish. Just don't go alone, carry the appropriate equipment (minimally a beacon, probe and shovel), ask about current avalanche conditions and make sure someone knows where you've gone.

Advanced sliders are well-served, too. The Millicent and Evergreen chairs access fine adventures on Devil's Dip, Chute 2, Boll Weevil, Exhibition and a long gallivant down Evergreen. On the Majestic side, the Great Western quad accesses Elk Park, which connects to Aspen Glo, Golden Needles, Silver Spur Desperado and Elk Park Ride, creating long, delightfully textured scrambles that mostly finish with generous intermediate cruises to the bottom. For moguls, try Rockin'R.

■ **Intermediate:** Intermediates have the run of practically the whole area. The Majestic side has trails with gentler pitches while the Millicent side is a bit steeper and more wide-open. On the Majestic side, Western Trail, off the Great Western quad, has fabulous views. Thor, off Snake Creek Express, is a rolling and rollicking trail that gets you whooping and hollering. Pioneer, off Snake Creek, is a great cruiser. The Elk Park Ridge run descends 1,745 feet, summit to base, from the Great Western chair. The lower section is single-diamond because once you reach the end of the ridge, you'll have ungroomed snow. If you don't like skiing the ungroomed, branch off at Golden Needle for the rest of the way down.

If you're interested in testing out the trees, try any of the woods near the bottom of the mountain such as those off Hawkeye and Scout. Once you get comfortable there, dip in and out of the woods wherever it looks fun.On the Millicent side, Backdoor, Christy Bowl and Perris Bowl are all sure to put a smile on your face.

●● **Beginner:** From the Brighton Center base, good beginner runs like Mary Back and Lost Maid descend from the Majestic chair. From the top of the Majestic, make your way over to the Snake Creek Express which goes to the top of Preston Peak. Beginners should keep an eye out so they don't get onto an intermediate trail: Greens and blues do a lot of intertwining here. Grooming, which is usually seamless, can make all the difference.

● **First-timer:** Brighton has a stellar reputation as the place where Utah skiers learn. One of the reasons is that skiers 10 and younger ski free and Utah families tend to be large in number. The Explorer chair serves two trails on a gentle slope apart from general traffic and is a great area for first-timers and beginners as well. Best for beginners to stay away from the Great Western Express and Millicent chairs, as they serve mostly black and double blacks with no easy way down. There's a green run down from the Evergreen chair, Main Street but this two-seater is only open on the weekend.

Ride Guide: Snowboarders like the Millicent side for its bowls, cliffs and ledges, plus you can hike from the top of the lift to Elevator, at the peak's summit. The Majestic side is one big stash of woods waiting to be discovered. If you like to play on natural terrain features, try Thor off Snake Creek Express, and Backbone and Backdoor off the Millicent chair. Pioneer off Snake Creek is great for ripping arcs. Brighton is an excellent mountain for trying new kinds of terrain to push your envelope: glades, ungroomed, and gradually increasing steeps.

The Majestic side has a considerable flat area about mid-mountain that runs across the girth of the mountain and again as you near the bottom. A few runs and you'll know exactly where you need to let it rip to carry your speed, though many riders like to duck into the woods to avoid the flats. If you're heading from the Majestic side to the Millicent side via Milly Access, be prepared for the hoofing that's required at the end.

Brighton has a solid reputation as the place where Utah snowboarders learn. The Explorer chair serves two trails on a gentle slope apart from general traffic. With Brighton's abundant beginner and intermediate terrain, it's an excellent mountain for learning to link those turns. Start off the Explorer chair—busy speeders stay elsewhere on the mountain, so you can practice without looking over your shoulder all the time. Head next to the gentle runs off the Majestic chair. Once you have some confidence, go for the top of the Snake Creek Express. You'll be on top of the world.

Parks and pipes

Brighton's parks and pipe have been going off for more than a decade.Years before most resorts even allowed snowboarding, Brighton was building and grooming tabletops and pipes for its riders.

Off the Majestic lift lives "Big Bertha," a 30- to 50-foot tabletop. On a typical sunny day many locals will be spinning 7s and rodeos while flying 50 feet through the air. After Bertha there usually is another tabletop that leads to the superpipe. The superpipe is about 500 feet long with walls up to 14 feet. As it runs due north, the sun hits it evenly through out the day.

Another option after Bertha is to go rider's right toward a rail and box section.This area was designed and built by Jarred Winkler, the pipe and park creator. Winkler is responsible for making all the rails, boxes and walls at Brighton as well as for a lot of the other resorts in the West. The park is constantly evolving so, depending on the mood of the crew, the set up is always changing. There are usually 15 to 20 features on this run which can all get gnarly.

Getting off the Crest Express, head toward the My-Oh-My park. Here there are three tabletops in a row, all with three different-sized lips. These lips range from a foot or two of air, to 15 to 25 feet. The My-Oh-My section drains out to "Candy Land." This spot houses 10 to 15 rails and boxes and is the area to fine tune technical jibbing skills.

Off the backside of the Majestic lift is the learner park where beginners can experience hitting jumps or rails for the first time. Easy, low-consequence boxes and rails are set up here and tiny tabletops are available to learn technique and style.

Cross-country and snowshoeing (visit xcskiresorts.com for more details)

At 8,700 feet between Solitude and Brighton, the **Solitude Nordic Center's Silver Lake Day Lodge** (536-5774) is a spectacular setting for cross-country skiing and snowshoeing. It has 20 km. of prepared trails for both classic and skating styles, plus ski and snowshoe rentals, lessons (including telemark), light snacks and guided backcountry tours. During full moons, you can do moonlight cross-country skiing.

Lessons (05/06 prices)

Group lessons: $30 for two hours; $55 for four hours. Also offered on Thursday nights for $30 (includes lift ticket at night). "The Works" package includes a group lesson, all-day ticket and all-day rentals for $85.

First-timer package: Includes a full day of rentals, beginner lift ticket and a group lesson—$65 for skiing and snowboarding.

Private lessons: $70 for one hour, with each additional person $25. A 2.5-hour lesson costs $155; additional person, $50. All-day with lift pass is $295; additional person, $75.

Special programs: Includes clinics for women, Burton Method Center Learn-to-Ride, parks and pipe, telemark, adaptive and advanced technique.

KidStuff (05/06 prices)

Child care: Brighton does not provide child-care services.

Children's lessons: A full-day program with lesson, lunch and lift ticket for ages 4–7 costs $90; half day, $55. Two-hour ski or snowboard lessons also are available for $40. Ages 8–12 can take an all-day ski or snowboard program for $80; half day, $50. Two-hour ski or snowboard lessons also are available for $35. Rentals are an additional $15.

Lift tickets (05/06 prices)

Ages 11 to 69 pay $41. Brighton does not sell multiday tickets. Twilight and Super Day tickets are available when lifts are running into the evening. Brighton has about 200 acres of night skiing every day except Sunday.

Who skis free: Ages 10 and younger, two children per paying adult with no restrictions or blackout dates.

Who skis at a discount: Ages 70 and older pay $10. A beginner lift pass, good on two lifts, is $27. A single-ride ticket is $10. Night skiing and riding costs $27.

Accommodations

The **Brighton Lodge** (800-873-5512; 532-4731; $$–$$$) is small, cozy, has a hot tub and is at the base of the lifts. Continental breakfast is included. Kids 10 and younger stay and ski/ride free (limit two per adult). **Mount Majestic Properties** (888-236-0667) rents a tremendous selection of cabins and chalets right on the Brighton Circle with the easiest access to the resort. **Silver Fork Lodge** (888-649-9551; 533-9977; $$–$$$) just down the road is a peaceful, rustic mountain retreat. There's a sauna, weight room, ping pong and foosball table, and a common room with a TV.

Dining/apres-ski/other activities

Dining: The **Alpine Rose** ($) is the main slopeside cafeteria. If you like big hearty breakfasts, you won't be disappointed. You can get lunch and dinner here too. When the weather's good, try the barbecue on the sundeck. The **Brighton Chalet** ($), at the base of Mt. Millicent, serves quick meals. The slopeside **Molly Green's** ($–$$) is the place for sit-down pub service and local brews. Try the Evergreen Dip with tortilla chips and crustini bread washed down with a microbrew. The Mt. Millicent wrap, with hummus, assorted veggies and a chopped veggie patty, also is very tasty. Locals like to head to the **Silver Fork Lodge** (533-9977) just down the road for their meals, no matter whether it's breakfast ($), lunch ($) or dinner ($$–$$$). You name it, it's on the menu. See the Solitude chapter for other nearby dining options.

Apres-ski: Head to the slopeside **Molly Green's,** a rustic A-frame filled with chatter.

Other activities: There's nothing here at the mountain. See the Salt Lake City chapter.

Getting there and getting around

By air and train: Salt Lake City is a major transportation hub, so flights are numerous. Amtrak also serves the city. Many companies provide ground transportation and it is well organized. When you make your lodging reservations, ask about ground transportation arrangements and most will make them for you. You also can go directly to the shuttle desks in the airport.

By car: Brighton is about 25 miles southeast of Salt Lake City in Big Cottonwood Canyon on State Hwy. 190 (Big Cottonwood Canyon Rd.). The most direct route from downtown and the airport is to go east on I-80, south on I-215, take 6200 South exit (turns into Wasatch Blvd.), then follow the signs to Solitude and Brighton.

Getting around: During the day, UTA buses run between Solitude and Brighton for $1.25 each way (exact fare required). If you want to really explore and go back and forth between Salt Lake City and the resort, a car is your best bet. If you don't like to eat at the same place twice, or you like nightlife, we recommend staying at the bottom of the canyon or in Salt Lake City. There is no public transportation at night between Salt Lake City and the canyon. If you stay in Salt Lake City, it's easy to get to the mountain during the day using public transportation. See the Salt Lake City chapter for details.

Dining: $$$$-Entrees $30+; $$$-$20-$30; $$-$10-$20; $-less than $10.
Accommodations: (double room) $$$$-$200+; $$$-$141-$200; $$-$81-$140; $-$80 and less.

Solitude Mountain Resort
Utah

Summit elevation:	10,035 feet
Vertical drop:	2,047 feet
Base elevation:	7,988 feet

Address: 12000 Big Cottonwood Canyon
Solitude, UT 84121
Area code: 801
Ski area phone: 534-1400
Snow report: 536-5777
Toll-free reservations: (800) 748-4754
Fax: (435) 649-5276
E-mail: info@skisolitude.com
Internet: www.skisolitude.com
Expert:★★★★
Advanced:★★★★
Intermediate:★★★★
Beginner:★★★★ **First-timer:**★★★★

Number of lifts: 8–1 high-speed quad, 2 quads,
1 triple, 4 doubles
Snowmaking: 150 acres
Skiable acreage: 1,200
Uphill capacity: 12,550 per hour
Parks & pipes: 1 park
Bed base: 425 (resort); 17,366 (Salt Lake City)
Resort child care: None, babysitting available
Nearest lodging: Slopeside, condos & hotel
Adult ticket, per day: $47 (04/05 prices)
Dining:★★★
Apres-ski/nightlife:★
Other activities:★

The modernization of Solitude has created one of Utah's best compact winter destinations with great terrain for every level of skier and rider.

Solitude Ski Resort, UtahSolitude is aptly named. Tucked away in Big Cottonwood Canyon with neighboring Brighton, it doesn't get the attention of say Snowbird and Alta just one canyon over. There are only 425 beds at the base, so it hardly qualifies as a big resort. all of which is excellent news for those few visitors seeking the trademark solitude and skiing.

"Cozy" might be an over worked adjective, but it certainly applies here. Solitude is family-owned and it shows. Loyal guests come back here year after year and staff members demonstrate the same loyalty (the director of slope-side maintenance, for example, has worked here since 1986).

The base itself suggests an old European mountain town in miniature, complete with a Bavarian-style inn, central clock tower, low-rise condo blocks and stores. Despite its newness, there is an old-world feel. It's quiet during the day and even quieter in the evening when the guests—mostly families—leave the one apres-ski spot, the Thirsty Squirrel, and drift along the snow-banked lanes, first to the small selection of restaurants, and then to an early night in the luxurious condos.

But don't be fooled by its size. Especially when combined with Brighton (both resorts are covered in a single lift ticket), Solitude offers a variety and depth of terrain.

Mountain layout

Big Cottonwood Canyon's Solitude has excellent terrain for all levels. Skiers and snowboarders easily can progress here. One disadvantage to the trail layout for some groups: If your group includes people at the opposite ends of the ability scale, you'll likely spend your day on different parts of the mountain, but you can always meet up for lunch.

To help new visitors get a better feel for the resort, Solitude's trail map has helpful yellow notes on it. Although the quips are a bit trite—"Honeycomb Canyon: Two words: True Solitude"—the notes really do help decipher the trail map.

♦♦ **Expert ♦ Advanced:** Solitude gets far less traffic than the Little Cottonwood Canyon resorts, so the dry Wasatch powder can stay untouched even two days after a storm. Experts should head straight to the Summit or Powderhorn chair. The double-diamonds are short, palm-sweating steeps through the trees, and even the single-diamonds don't leave much room for error. For longer runs, hike the ridge above Honeycomb Canyon. But check conditions first and never hike alone. The tree runs off of Eagle Ridge—Navarone and Here Be Dragons—are steep, tight, and sometimes set-up.

Honeycomb Canyon is a great place for advanced skiers to hone powder skills. From the traverse, drop in wherever the pitch and powder looks right. Advanced skiers will also enjoy the bowl-like runs from the top of the Powderhorn chair; Paradise, Vertigo and Paradise Lost are open, airy, and leg-screaming steep.

For fast, steep corduroy—and it usually stays as untracked corduroy well into the day—head to the right off the Eagle Express, the first high-speed chairlift installed in Utah. Challenger is reportedly the steepest groomed run in Utah. Fast turns here are as close to freefalling as many of us want to get. Serenity/F.I.S. feels even steeper, with ungroomed moguls on one side to slow the freefalling feel.

■ **Intermediate:** Intermediates have wonderful terrain to choose from. The Powderhorn and Eagle Express chairs have no green runs, just blue and black. If you're at the high end of the intermediate level, you'll like this terrain. If you're new to the intermediate level, try the Sunrise or Apex chairs. Sunshine Bowl is wide open and groomed, so you'll be carving some huge arcs on this one. Other places to let 'em rip: Rumble, Grumble and Stumble. Gary's Glade is a great introduction to glade skiing. You can duck in and out of the trees here. A hidden jewel of glades: the unnamed trees under the Apex chair.

The Summit chair has upper-intermediate runs like Dynamite and Liberty. Eventually you'll meet the runs off the Sunrise chair, which head back to the base. Want a taste of the backcountry? Woodlawn is a marked run that follows the floor of Honeycomb Canyon. On the map it's rated black and blue. Check the grooming report before you head in: When groomed, it's a great advanced-intermediate run—otherwise, it's advanced all the way, with some hefty mogul fields and a short but extremely steep section that looks like it might be a small waterfall in the summer. It's thrilling to watch the higher-level skiers tackling the canyon sides.

●● **Beginner ● First-timer:** Novices start on the Link chair, a slow-moving lift that serves a nearly flat, very wide, isolated run called Easy Street. This is at the base of the New Moonbeam Lodge and the Snowsports Academy ski school, where all facilities are convenient for beginners. Look for Solitude's Director of Skiing, veteran Olympian Leif Grevie. He's always on site in a handsome Norwegian sweater providing gracious and helpful tips.

Once you conquer the gentle Easy Street run off the Link chair, graduate to the Moonbeam chair, where Little Dollie, Pokey Pine and Same Street will easily take you back down to the base. The Sunrise chair, out of the Village at Solitude, has one green trail, North Star, surrounded by lots of gentle blues that afford variety.

Don't worry about hotshots on your beginner trails. However, the green slopes tend to be crowded, so be aware of beginning skiers who might not always be in control.

The Apex chair is a good place for advanced-beginners. All the trails are rated blue here, but they are gentle and some are wide open, so if grooming is good, advanced-beginners should have no trouble.

Ride Guide: To sum up Solitude Resort, it's all in the name—secluded, and all to yourself. This mountain has steeps, bowls, tight tree shots and backcountry access to some of the sickest lines around.

Starting on the west side of the resort off the Eagle Express quad there's a group of several wide intermediate groomers. Staying far rider's left hooks up with Challenger, one of the steepest groomed runs in Utah. Dropping the fall line off the quad runs into the Sunshine Bowl, which is probably the most open shot the mountain has.

Half way up the Powder Horn lift, some unbelievable lines start to come into view. Steep, perfectly spaced tree shots are right under the lift. As the lift approaches the top, another area comes into sight with about six black diamond runs off to the rider's left. On a powder day this is the spot to fly as fast as possible laying out a wide turn or two every hundred vertical feet or so.

The terrain off the Summit lift is unreal. On the left side of the chair is the Evergreen ridge hike that separates Solitude from Brighton Resort. The lines off this ridge are all north facing and consistently have the best snow on the mountain. Choose lines carefully because it is easy to get cliffed out.

At the midpoint of the Summit lift the views get intense. On the lift's left lies a good-size pitch of steep glades called the Headwall Forest—at the bottom of this shot, keep a lot of speed to make it through a long flat spot. However, if you don't make it, there is only about a one- to two-minute walk that is well worth the sick shot. Additionally, on the lift's right, giant cliff bands and a few chutes are visible and these are only a few minutes away.

Once the Summit lift ride is over, prepare to be blown away by the view into Honeycomb Canyon. Fantasy Ridge climbs up and down the far end of Honeycomb Canyon and is accessed from this point when open. This ridge hike is crazy. It is really exposed and hairball—a slip in the wrong section would definitely result in a run to the nearest hospital. However, after completing the hike the rewards are sweet. Cirque-sized chutes and bowls are everywhere. It would take years to explore all of the possibilities found in this area of the resort.

Another option is to take the traverses left or right. The left traverse usually is not snowboard friendly, but the right traverse is a little better. With some skating, sidestepping and walking it is possible to reach the amazing lines of the Black Forest. This is another north-facing gem at Solitude and it contains some of the most perfectly spaced trees one could ask for. Dropping anywhere in this paradise will be killer and will eventually empty out at the Honeycomb quad. From here, the short lift ride reaches the ridge back to the front side of the resort.

To hit this shot again it's mandatory to take the Powder Horn and Summit lifts to the top. This sequence is definitely a time-consuming lap, but it also helps to conserve the powder days after a storm.

Figuring out how and where to ride this mountain is half the fun of the Solitude experience. Pay attention and follow some locals, and the payoffs will be good.

Parks and pipes

Solitude has an excellent beginner park. Almost all of the hits and features have low consequences and are perfect for novice freestylers and kids. There are a few little to mid-size tabletops and a few ride-on rails and boxes. If the park seems a little mellow just start exploring the natural terrain park, which is all over the mountain.

Cross-country and snowshoeing (visit xcskiresorts.com for more details)

At 8,700 feet between Solitude and Brighton, the **Solitude Nordic Center's Silver Lake Day Lodge** (536-5774) is a spectacular setting for cross-country skiing and snowshoeing. It has 20 km. of prepared trails for both classic and skating styles, plus ski and snowshoe rentals, lessons (including telemark), light snacks and guided backcountry tours. During full moons, you can do moonlight cross-country skiing.

Lessons [05/06 prices]

Group lessons: $50 for two hours. All-day lessons are $70.

First-timer package: Rentals, beginner lift ticket and a half-day morning lesson costs $100. An afternoon class costs $90.

Private lessons: One hour costs $85 for one to three people; $165 for four to six. A one-hour lesson at 9 a.m. or 3 p.m. costs $77 for one to three people; $150 for four to six. Half-day lesson costs $210 for one to three people; $290 for four to six. All-day lesson costs $350 for one to three people; $450 for four to six.

Special programs: Back Tracks is a guided daylong trip into the backcountry that includes lift ticket, lunch, transceivers and other backcountry gear. For groups up to 10 people; guides are Solitude Professional Ski Patrollers. Call for details and reservations, (801) 536-5705 or (800) 748-4754.

Racing: Solitude has an electronically timed, side-by-side dual course on the Main Street trail, open every day, weather permitting.

KidStuff [05/06 prices]

Child care: Solitude does not provide any child care. However, an offsite company, **Guardian Angel** (598-1229), offers babysitting services and will come to your room.

Children's lessons: Ski lessons are for kids ages 4–12; snowboard lessons are for ages 7–12. Full-day program with lift ticket and lunch is $85; a half-day without lunch is $55. Multiday packages available. Rentals cost $15 per day. A learn-to-ski or -snowboard package includes all-day lesson, rentals, lift ticket and rentals for $100. Private one-hour ski lessons for kids ages 2½–4 and private snowboard lessons for kids 4–7 cost $60; reservations required.

Lift tickets [05/06 prices]

	Adult (11-59)	Child (7-13)
One day	$50	$28

* Multiday tickets are available through lodging and are typically tied into lodging specials.

Who skis free: Ages 6 and younger ski for free, but need to get a ticket.

Who skis at a discount: Seniors (60-69) pay $40. Ages 70+ pay $10. A beginner lift ticket, valid on the Link and Moonbeam II chairs, is $36.

Note: Solitude has a Ride Access Card, an electronic ticketing system that allows skiers to pay by the run. It's completely transferable (so parents can swap), usable on any day during the season and better than purchasing a multiday ticket. The maximum number of rides the system will take off in a day is 10. Ten rides cost $48; 20 rides, $94; 30 rides, $141; 40 rides, $188; 50 rides, $235. Remember: Help keep ticket costs down by recycling your card when leaving the resort; drop it at any of the convenient locations resort-wide.

Dining: $$$$-Entrees $30+; $$$-$20-$30; $$-$10-$20; $-less than $10.

Accommodations: (double room) $$$$-$200+; $$$-$141-$200; $$-$81-$140; $-$80 and less.

Accommodations

Solitude has beautiful Alpine-inspired, base-area lodging. Everything is slopeside. Most are ski-in, but none are ski-out since you have to walk a few yards to the lifts. All on-mountain guests have access to Club Solitude, in Eagle Springs East. Lodging can be booked by calling (800) 748-4754.

Eagle Springs West and **Eagle Springs East** ($$$–$$$$) both feature luxurious one- to three-bedroom condominiums with hand-finished furnishings and generous gourmet kitchens. Heated sidewalks surround a large outdoor heated swimming pool with a waterfall, plus a waterslide for kids of all ages. On each side of the pool are 18-person hot tubs.

The Inn at Solitude ($$$$) has 46 spacious rooms, most with two queen beds (though kings and suites are available). All have terry-cloth robes to wear to the outdoor pool and hot tub, hair dryers, mini-refrigerators, TV with VCR (tape rentals available), and daily newspaper delivery. The Inn also has a full-service spa.

Creekside at Solitude ($$$$) has 18 condos ranging in size from one to three bedrooms. The condos are spacious and well-appointed, and share an outdoor rooftop hot tub. The three-bedroom units have a jetted tub and four bathrooms, so the person sleeping on the living room sofa has a bathroom, too. **Powderhorn Lodge** ($$$–$$$$) has one-, two- and three-bedroom condos with gas fireplaces, full kitchens and laundry facilities. There's an outdoor hot tub and a pool table in the lobby.

Dining

St. Bernard's (536-5508; $$$; reservations) in the Inn is Solitude's fine-dining restaurant, where you'll enjoy fireside meals in an intimate setting. Classic American cuisine has an inspired blending of tastes. You'll find great wines to accompany your meal. It also serves the resort's only sit-down breakfast ($), with both a continental buffet and made-to-order specialties.

Creekside Restaurant (536-5785; $$–$$$), on the first floor of the Creekside condos, serves lunch and dinner. We dined on appetizers to get a full sense of the menu. Everything is creative and tastes wonderful. The baked polenta with woodland mushrooms is absolutely out of this world. Entrees range from wood-fired pizzas to pasta, lamb and veal.

Dinner at the **Solitude Yurt** (536-5709) is very popular. Twenty people cross-country ski or snowshoe to a yurt for a five-course gourmet meal and then ski or snowshoe back (it's a beginner trail both ways and the equipment is included in the cost). The cost is $80, and no children younger than 8 are allowed. Reservations are a must, and it's hard to get in.

Solitude's cafeteria, **Last Chance Mining Camp** ($), is on two levels and can seat about 400 people. **Sunshine Grill** ($), open for lunch, features a lively grill adjacent to the best people-watching on the mountain, affectionately called "the beach." **The Moonbeam Day Lodge** has a new restaurant for 2005/06. Another place for a quick bite is the **Stone Haus**, a grocery store in the village, or the **Thirsty Squirrel** ($), which serves panini, nachos and pizza.

Apres-ski/nightlife

The **Thirsty Squirrel** is the place to head to swap stories, eat, drink and be merry. There's a pool table, wide-screen TV and local beer sold by the pitcher. There's also a beer bar at the **Last Chance Mining Camp** and a bar in the new **Moonbeam Day Lodge**. The village's **Stone Haus** is a state liquor store, if you want to stock up for your condo.

Remember: The nightspots are "private clubs" that charge a $4 three-week membership fee. If you are staying at a Solitude lodge, the membership is included with your accommodations. For the lowdown on Utah's liquor laws, including the "private club membership" you'll need if you aren't a lodging guest, see the Salt Lake City chapter.

Other activities

After the lifts close, it's very mellow here. You can go **ice skating** at an outdoor rink in the village center; skate rentals are available. Club Solitude in Eagle Springs East offers complimentary activities to all on-mountain guests that include a **large-screen movie** in the media room, a **fitness room, billiards,** an **outdoor hot tub and pool,** and a **kids' playroom with board games, X-Box, foosball table, and computers with games.** There's also a **fireside lounge** that's great for relaxing.

Essentials Spa (801-535-4137 ext. 5510) in the Inn at Solitude is a full-service spa offering facials, body treatments and massages. There are also sessions in yoga, pilates and Thai stretching.

Getting there and getting around

By air and train: Salt Lake City is a major transportation hub, so flights are numerous. Amtrak also serves the city. Many companies provide ground transportation and it is well organized. When you make your lodging reservations, ask about ground transportation arrangements and most will make them for you. You also can go directly to the shuttle desks in the airport.

By car: Solitude is about 25 miles southeast of Salt Lake City in Big Cottonwood Canyon on Hwy. 190 (Big Cottonwood Canyon Rd.). The most direct route from downtown and the airport is to go east on I-80, south on I-215, take 6200 South exit (turns into Wasatch Blvd.), then follow the signs to Solitude and Brighton.

Getting around: If you're staying at the resort, you can walk to everything within the village. During the day, UTA buses run between Solitude and Brighton for $1.25 (exact fare required). If you want to really explore and go back and forth between Salt Lake City and the resort, a car is your best bet. If you don't like to eat at the same place twice, or you like nightlife, we recommend staying at the bottom of the canyon or in Salt Lake City. There is no public transportation at night between Salt Lake City and the canyon. If you stay in Salt Lake City, it's easy to get to the mountain during the day using public transportation. See the Salt Lake City chapter for details.

Ogden Region

Snowbasin and Powder Mountain

Ogden Facts
Dining: ★★★
Apres-ski/nightlife: ★★
Other activities: ★★

Area code: 801
Area information: (800) 255-8824
E-mail: info@ogden.travel
Internet: www.ogden.travel (Ogden Convention & Visitors Bureau) and www.skiutah.com (Ski Utah)

About 40 miles north of Salt Lake City is the growing ski city of Ogden. It is becoming a center for the ski and snowboard industry and is the city host for two excellent ski areas.

Ogden, envisioned as a Mormon town, was eventually developed by workers for the railroad in 1869. It has one of America's most picturesque and storied main streets, "Historic 25th Street," plus several hotels and plenty of dining options. In addition, the town is a center for the arts with galleries, theater, opera and orchestra performances throughout the winter.

Above Ogden, Utah, lies Eden in a hidden mountain valley at the end of a spectacular narrow canyon bordered to the north and south by giant ski and snowboard areas blessed with what many call the world's best snow. They have what are among the world's best views too—from their tops you can see four states: Utah, Wyoming, Idaho and Nevada.

The thinly-settled Upper Ogden Valley gently spreads around the Pineview Reservoir with a smattering of less than a thousand condominiums and private homes with limited restaurants, hotels and almost no nightlife. Once a trading post for fur trappers and pioneers, the valley is slowly beginning its controlled development towards destination resort status.

Powder Mountain extends across the northern border of the local county into Cache County and to the south Snowbasin's shoulders drop into Morgan County. These mountains are expansive, uncrowded and have excellent powder. But that is where their likeness disappears.

Snowbasin, Huntsville, UT; (801) 399-1135

Internet: www.snowbasin.com
11 lifts; 2,650 acres; 2,950 vertical feet; 2 terrain parks

Snowbasin, home to the men's and women's Olympic downhill, Super G and combined races in 2002, is new with a tram, two gondolas, a high-speed chairlift and a handful of fixed grip chairs. Groomed trails crisscross the area. Earl's Lodge at the base lodge and Needles and John Paul Lodge at the top of the high-speed lifts are spectacular, modern, massive log buildings. The resort also claims the largest and most modern automatic snowmaking system in the country.

Snowbasin stretches along the southern edge of Ogden Valley. The ski and snowboard area has three distinct sections.

The John Paul Express lift and the Mt. Allen Tram serve Allen's Peak and the No Name area. This sector is rugged with expert slopes dropping steeply through trees. Here is where the downhill courses raged down almost 3,000 unrelenting and twisting vertical feet of terrain.

The center of the resort and the original heart of the trail system traces the mountain from Needles through Middle Bowl and Wildcat Bowl. The Needles Express gondola whisks skiers and riders up 2,310 feet from the base lodge. The degree of steepness declines a touch from that found at Allen's Peak and trails are a bit wider.

The final sector is beneath Strawberry peak served by a gondola, where wide open 2,472 feet of vertical terrain presents expansive bowl skiing and riding.

Lift tickets (06/07 prices): Adults, $60; children (7–12), $37; senior (65–79), $84; ages 80+ ski free and children 6 and younger, free with paying adult.

Powder Mountain, UT; (801) 225-4107; (800) 892-1600

Internet: www.powdermountain.net
7 lifts; 5,500 acres; 2,522 vertical feet

Powder Mountain is a throwback to the way skiing used to be with four chairs and three surface lifts that serve more than 5,500 acres of terrain with most of the resort left untouched by grooming machines. The mountain is replacing their double Hidden Lake chairlift to the top with a detachable high-speed quad which will open for the 2006-07 season. The lodge is rustic, small and cozy with basic soups, salads, scones and burgers. And snowmaking? Forget about it. Nature provides plenty of the real stuff.

This is a massive resort that's bigger than Snowbird and Alta combined. The lifts are few (four chairlifts and three surface lifts) and far between, however they link well with each other. A shuttlebus picks up skiers who drop over the backside. There are only a couple of groomed trails dropping down from the top of each lift. But what you see, you can ski or ride. There is also night skiing at the Sundown Lift from 4 – 10 p.m.

Every morning at 10 a.m., complimentary guides leaving from the Timberline Sports Shop are available to take skiers and riders on tours of the mountain to give everyone an orientation to the massive mountain. These orientation groups are popular and many of the skiers and riders end up signing up for a guide to take them to the best powder at the resort.

Lift tickets (06/07 prices): Adults, $50; children (6-12), $30; seniors (62–69), $40; seniors (70–79), $20; ages 5 and younger and 80+, free.

Acommodations

The real bed base for both of these mountains is Ogden, only about 20-30 minutes down the mountain through the Ogden Canyon or around Snowbasin looping to the south. All this is only a half-hour north of the Salt Lake City airport. There is a cluster of lodging options in the Upper Valley closer to the ski areas. We start with the Upper Valley. Call (800) 554-2741.

UPPER OGDEN VALLEY: Columbine Inn (801-745-3772 x146; $$), at the base area of Powder Mountain, has affordable rooms ranging from basic double rooms with pull-out couch to three-BR condos with fireplaces right at the base area.

PowMow Condos (801-458-9112),Powder Ridge Condos and Sundown Condos (801-745-3722) have condominiums at the base area as well.

Red Moose Inn (877-745-0333; $$) combines motel convenience, hotel-style amenities and B&B atmosphere. Built in the grand lodge style, even standard rooms are spacious. Most rooms have minimal cooking facilities, but some have full kitchenettes.

Moose Hollow Condominiums (877-745-0333) on the road to Powder Mountain and under the same ownership as Red Moose Lodge, are new and upscale, ranging in size from two to five bedrooms. All have free, high-speed Internet, satellite TV and gas fireplace.

Lakeside Village (800-939-2030), on the shores of Pineview Reservoir, is the collection of condominiums most convenient to Snowbasin that provide real luxury in the Upper Valley. Most units have large whirlpool tubs in the master bath and a large outdoor hot tub on the deck. All have extremely well-equipped kitchens (right down to coffee grinders) and

Dining: $$$$-Entrees $30+; $$$-$20-$30; $$-$10-$20; $-less than $10.
Accommodations: (double room) $$$$-$200+; $$$-$141-$200; $$-$81-$140; $-$80 and less.

washer/dryers; most have fireplaces, and many have garages.

Snowberry Inn (745-2634 or 801-745-2634; $$) is a comfy B&B just 15 minutes from either Snowbasin or Powder Mountain. All rooms (some are pretty small) have private baths; best value is the family suite with kitchen. A full breakfast and afternoon refreshments are included, and there's a billiards table, darts, TV and outdoor hot tub

Jackson Fork Inn (800-609-9466 or 745-0051; $-$$), in Huntsville, has seven knotty pine 2-story suites in a converted dairy barn with complimentary continental breakfast.

All rooms at the riverside **Alaskan Inn** (801-621-8600 or 621-8600; $$$-$$$$) have an Arctic theme. Rates include a full breakfast, delivered to the room or cabin.

OGDEN CITY DOWNTOWN:

Marriott Ogden (888-825-3163; 627-1190; $$) 292 rooms in the middle of the action in downtown Ogden on 24th Street, with high-speed internet access, pool and fitness center. It's the only full service hotel in the area with a restaurant and private club for apres-ski.

Hampton Inn & Suites (800-486-7866 or 394-9400) is built in an historic downtown building. Free high-speed internet and local phone calls, plus a hot tub and fitness room.

Best Western High Country Inn (800-594-8979 or 394-9474) sits at Exit 347 off I-15 at 12th Street. It's only 35 minutes to the SLC airport and also to the ski areas. The hotel has a heated outdoor pool and hot tub. **Comfort Suites** (800-462-9925 or 621-2545; left) off 21st Street is a well appointed place with 142 rooms with an indoor pool and hot tub. It is within 30 minutes of the airport and the major ski areas.

Also check out the **Historic Ben Lomond Hotel**, (877-627-1900) and Holiday Inn Express (800-465-4329) in the Ogden area.

Dining

Dining at Powder Mountain

Dining here is a throwback to the 1970s in both atmosphere (rustic is a kind description) and offerings. The **Powder Mountain Restaurant** at the Resort Center, the largest restaurant on the mountain, serves cafeteria style at the main base area. It's famous for its scones, soups and sandwiches, but don't look for anything green on the menu. Downstairs in the same building the **Powder Keg** is the local watering hole with a selection of draft beers, good burgers, grilled and fried chix sandwiches. **Hidden Lake Lodge**, at the top of the Hidden Lake lift, serves burgers, fries, chili and similar fare along with spectacular views. **Sundown Lodge**, at the base of the Sundown lift, serves a limited menu of cold and hot sandwiches, fries and snacks.

Dining at Snowbasin: Dining here is a cut above the normal mountain fare found at many American resorts. **Earl's Lodge** at the base is framed of Canadian spruce with spectacular views of the mountain. It serves a sit-down meal or upscale cafeteria food.

John Paul Lodge and the **Needles Lodge** on the mountain serve lunches from several self-service stations. Select from soups and sandwiches, pizza and pasta or a daily entree. The lodge is designed in an octagonal layout reminiscent of the Round House at Sun Valley.

Dining in Ogden

The **Roosters Brewing Company and Restaurant** (627-6171; $-$$) is one of the town's best places to for a casual meal at a great value. The local homebrews are excellent.

Everyone raves about **Tona Sushi Bar and Grill** (622-8662; $-$$) and are amazed to find a sushi place of this quality is in Ogden. Sushi fans visit numerous times over a visit.

Union Grill (621-2830) in Union Station under the same ownership as Roosters is another local hot spot. The menu is basic American with steaks, chops and soups.

Prairie Schooner (392-2712 or 621-5511; $$–$$$), downtown next to the Ogden Archway, serves steaks, prime rib and seafood in an atmosphere of mini-Conestoga wagons.

La Ferrovia (394-8628) serves good Italian meals right on 25th Street.

The Athenian Restaurant (621-4911) on 25th Street, is the place for Greek food in town with the added attraction of belly dancing Thursdays through Saturdays.

Two-bit Street Cafe (393-1225), started by a New York transplant, serves breakfast at its long bar. This is the only antique store/restaurant on 25th Street.

For breakfast in town head to **Jeremiah's** (394-3273), considered one of the best places in Ogden with wonderful pancakes and cinnamon rolls.

Dining in the Upper Valley

Wolf Creek Resort Restaurants (866-0111 or 745-3737) are on the road to Powder Mountain. **The Grille** provides fine dining and good wines. **The Rusty Cactus** serves basic and filling Tex-Mex meals. **Tracks** is the breakfast spot with huge breakfast burritos.

Gray Cliff Lodge (392-6775), halfway up the Ogden Canyon, is an Ogden institution serving excellent lamb and mountain trout as well as steaks and seafood.

The Oaks (394-2421) also sits in the Ogden Canyon, just above the rushing river. It has been in operation for more than 100 years. Must be some good cookin'.

Jackson Fork Inn (745-0051; $$) serves good brunch on Sundays and dinner during the week. The menu is basic American with a few Italian entrees.

Yukon Grille (745-9293), in Huntsville right on Trappers Village Square, serves meals in a "Western antiques" atmosphere. Breakfast is creative with a Martini Omelet or chicken fried steak and eggs. They also have good Mexican food.

Eats of Eden (745-8618) serves pasta, pizza and sandwiches.

No trip to Ogden's Upper Valley is complete without a visit to the **Shooting Star Saloon** (745-2002),the oldest, continuously running tavern in Utah. While here dare to try a Star Burger, a burger-and-sausage combo that screams heart attack, but they say is harmless. Go, if only to see the stuffed critters, including a jackalope and, yes, a St. Bernard, and the ceiling of $1 bills and to listen to crooners on the jukebox. It is closed on Mondays and Tuesdays.

Red Dog Grill (745-2400) on the road to Snowbasin, is a choice place for breakfast.

Alpine Pizza (745-1900), run by a Chicago native, serves prize-winning pies ranging from the basics to their award-winning Carbonara with Alfredo sauce. Try the subs/hoagies, the salads and homemade Italian ice as well. They deliver to most places in the Upper Valley.

 ## Nightlife/Apres-ski

The Shooting Star Saloon (745-2002) Utah's oldest, in the Upper Valley, is a place skiers must have at least one drink. Avoid snacking on a Star Burger if you are planning to dine later in the evening. Don't miss the St. Bernard trophy on the wall. You'll never see another like it.

At Powder Mountain head to the **Powder Keg** for a brew right after skiing or riding. The place will be packed with instructors and others talking about their secret runs.

In downtown Ogden on Historic 25th Street, **Roosters Brewing Company** is on one side of the main street at 253 and **Brewskis** is on the other at 244. **The Wine Cellar** (2550 Washington Blvd.; 399-3600) has jazz most nights. **The City Club** is on 25th Street. **Angelo's Tavern**, also on 25th Street, has live music and a beer garden. **Mojo's** fills with a young crowd for music on Friday and Saturday nights, but no drinking. **Kokomo Club** on 25th Street has pool tournaments and big-screen TV.

Dining: $$$$-Entrees $30+; $$$-$20-$30; $$-$10-$20; $-less than $10.
Accommodations: (double room) $$$$-$200+; $$$-$141-$200; $$-$81-$140; $-$80 and less.

Park City, Utah

Deer Valley

Park City Mountain Resort

The Canyons

Regional Facts
Toll-free information:
(800) 453-1360 (Park City Chamber)
Fax: 649-0532 (lodging)
Internet: www.parkcityinfo.com (town)
Dining:★★★★
Apres-ski/nightlife:★★★★
Other activities:★★★

Walk outside the No Name Saloon at dusk, just as the lights of Main Street begin to twinkle seductively and the sidewalks fill with apres-ski traffic, and you can almost hear the clank of spurs. Squint your eyes and the strolling figures become the miners and cowboys who roamed this same street a hundred years ago, swaggering through 30-odd saloons in what was once one of the country's largest silver mining towns. Soon the vision is gone, and the people are once again modern-day funseekers. Yet the flamboyant atmosphere of the silver rush remains.

Park City originally was founded by soldiers who had been sent west to discourage Brigham Young from ending the Utah Territory's association with the Union. Park City boomed during the mining era, then almost became a ghost town during the Depression and World War II. Now Park City can be counted among the world's top winter resorts. This is the most accessible destination resort of its caliber in the country, just 30 miles from Salt Lake City via a major freeway. Skiers and snowboarders from across the country can leave home in the morning and be making turns at one of the region's resorts that afternoon.

Three world-class resorts surround the mountain city. Each has its own personality and caters to different clientele. Deer Valley doesn't allow snowboarders and banks on exclusivity, perfect service and flawless grooming. Park City Mountain Resort, with lifts right into town, caters to more of the middle- to upper-middle-class intermediate crowd with long, wide cruising trails highlighted with pockets of expert terrain. And The Canyons has carved out a niche for wide-open slopes and good out-of-bounds skiing. They all share the Old West mining atmosphere of Park City and the fine Utah powder.

This chapter is organized with the three resort descriptions leading off, together with supporting mountain-related information such as lessons, lift tickets, child care, and so forth for each of the three mountains. The general Park City information follows, such as town dining, accommodations, apres-ski and other activities.

Park City interchangeable lift ticket (05/06 prices)

The Silver Passport gets you on the lifts at Deer Valley, Park City Mountain Resort and The Canyons. You must advance-book at least three nights of lodging to purchase the pass. You can use the pass at one resort each day. Snowboarders may not use Deer Valley's lifts, and the pass is not valid the week between Christmas and New Year's. Adults pay $213 for three days ($71/day), $272 for four days ($68/day), $330 for five days ($66/day); children ages 6–12 pay $123 for three days ($41/day), $148 for four days ($37/day), $185 for five days ($37/day). Discounts for longer stays are available. More information: Deer Valley Central Reservations, (800) 558-3337, Park City Mountain Reservations, (800) 222-7275 or The Canyons Reservations, (888) 226-9667.

Deer Valley Resort Facts

Summit elevation: **9,570 feet**
Vertical drop: **3,000 feet**
Base elevation: **6,570 feet**

Address: P.O. Box 1525, Park City, UT 84060
Area code: 435
Ski area phone: 649-1000
Snow report: 649-2000 **Fax:** 645-6939
Toll-free information: (800) 424-3337
Toll-free reservations: (800) 558-3337
Internet: www.deervalley.com

Expert:★★★★
Advanced:★★★★
Intermediate:★★★★
Beginner:★★ **First-timer:**★

Number of lifts: 21–1 gondola, 9 high-speed quads, 2 quads, 7 triples, 2 doubles
Snowmaking: 27 percent
Skiable acreage: 1,825 acres
Uphill capacity: 43,500 per hour
Snowboarding: Not allowed
Parks & pipes: 1 park
Nearest lodging: Slopeside
Resort child care: Yes, 2 months and older
Adult ticket, per day: $74-$76 (05/06 prices)

Deer Valley Resort

Deer Valley is one of North America's most exclusive resorts. Everything is top notch from the manicured snow conditions to the gleaming brass and glass cafeterias and gourmet restaurants. Deer Valley is as upscale as it gets in America, but without any snobbery that might affect other expensive places in the country. Here, locals and staff really care about sharing this mountain with their guests and know the meaning of the word service. This is one of four American resorts that is for skiers only. This noticeably affects the ambiance of the mountain.

The resort itself is just a couple of miles from the historic mining town of Park City. Deer Valley is a cluster of condominiums and lush hotels huddled around a spectacular ski area. You can lounge in luxury up on the mountainside or head downtown to have fun in one of America's best ski towns.

Deer Valley is renowned for pampering its guests with top-flight meals, palatial accommodations, attentive service and impeccable slopes. Guest service attendants lift skis off car racks when you drive up to unload, tissues are at every lift, restaurants make a gourmet salivate, a free ski corral service lets you can safely leave your best equipment and grooming crews comb the snow so pool-table smooth that everyone skis smoother and better.

Experts who might scoff at the daily slope manicure can ditch the main drag. Scoot directly to the chutes and bowls off Empire Canyon or bumps off the Sultan and Mayflower chairs for advanced terrain. Deer Valley fills a marvelous niche in the ski world, satisfying those who enjoy elegance and are willing to pay a little more for their privileges.

Mountain layout

Keep in mind that there are really four mountains here, ranging from Bald Eagle at 8,400 feet to the top of Empire Canyon at 9,570 feet.

◆◆ **Expert:** Empire Canyon, topping out at 9,570 feet, is not only the highest point at Deer Valley, but also the gnarliest. The double-diamond Daly Chutes, the Daly Bowl and the Anchor Trees are short, steep and superbly challenging. Single-diamond terrain at Lady Morgan Bowl in Empire adds some nice vertical. The Empire Express accesses the 500 acres of eight chutes and three bowls.

Flagstaff Mountain, with both bump and cruising runs, is easy to navigate and a good rendezvous when several members of your group ski at different ability levels. Experts take a short traverse to the left off the top of this lift to Ontario Bowl's double-diamond tree skiing.

♦ **Advanced:** The Mayflower Lift, to the far left on the trail map, supplies respectable single-diamond terrain on both sides of the lift. Moguls on Morning Star, Fortune Teller, Paradise and Narrow Gauge are a delight. The long trails are bordered by glades—great places to drop into and out of on a whim. While Mayflower and its neighboring chair Sultan feature ungroomed runs, the bumps rarely grow too big. Orient Express and Stein's Way are advanced cruisers with good pitch, and Perseverance, coupled with the initial steeper sections of Thunderer, Blue Ledge and Grizzly, is good for those entering advanced status. Look for the glades at the bottom of the Empire Canyon and Flagstaff area too.

■ **Intermediate**: Deer Valley offers both intermediate and advanced-intermediate terrain, though we're hard pressed to tell the two apart. If you want to have plenty of company and beautiful scenery, the best runs are Sunset, Birdseye (both on Bald Mountain) and Success (on Bald Eagle Mountain). Areas with the most intermediate runs are served by the Wasatch Express, Sterling and Northside Express chairs. Run after run down trails such as Legal Tender, Wizard, Nabob, Sidewinder and Hawkeye are a blast. The runs under the Northside Express are farther from the base areas, so they're not as crowded as the Wasatch Express area.

The Empire Canyon and Deer Crest areas also have some fun slopes for this level—in particular, try the advanced-intermediate bowls Conviction, Solace and Orion. The view of the Jordanelle Reservoir from the Deer Crest area is fabulous; however, the Jordanelle run has one wicked narrow part that may intimidate newly intermediate skiers, and don't even think about taking a beginner down it, assuming it'll be easy to get to the gondola base parking lot. A fun place to test your intermediate tree- and bump-skiing legs is in the unnamed area on Flagstaff off the Ontario trail, or by sneaking through the trees at the top of the Quincy Lift. They're marked, but not named (as of this printing), and are worth a giggle.

Other great areas are Flagstaff Mountain and Bald Eagle Mountain, known as the "lower mountain." Last Chance passes by a lot of spectacular homes, perfect for lookie-loos. If you are a timid intermediate, stick to Deer Valley's green-circle runs at first. We find the greens here to be a bit turquoise, just a shade easier than the true blues.

●● **Beginner:** Deer Valley's offerings at this level have improved in past years. Best spots are the outside runs on Flagstaff Mountain, Ontario and Mountain Daisy/Banner. If you are a timid beginner, read the first-timer advice. If you're a brave soul who just needs some practice, we especially recommend Sunset, a gentle, scenic route that descends from the top of Bald Mountain—but head back to the base before day's end or you'll find yourself in the role of a human slalom pole, being passed at close range by fast skiers. There's also the Little Chief Family Ski Area in Empire Canyon, which is one run that hardly seems worth the traverse and chairlift experience to get there.

● **First-timer:** The novice area is gentle enough, but it's a big step to the next level. Some of Deer Valley's green runs also access trails and runouts that better skiers use to reach the base area. A novice might feel as though he or she is riding a scooter on a freeway, which can be intimidating in this land of speed and curve.

Ride Guide: Snowboarding is not allowed.

Parks and pipes

Deer Valley built a skiers-only terrain park called Tricks 'N' Turns (TNT) Park. It's in the Empire Canyon area, off the Little Chief chair, and is geared toward intermediate-level, family-oriented fun. The Ore Cart Rails include funboxes, double barrels, single rails, small jumps and some surprises. The Ore Cart Rails are adjacent to the Skier Cross Course on Nugget. The Skier Cross Course is a timed course, $2 per run, with large banked turns, jumps and rolls.

Lessons (05/06 prices)

Reservations are essential for all programs; call (888) 754-8477 or (435) 645-6648, or book online.

Semi-private lessons: Semi-private Max 4 lessons, limited to four students, have replaced group lessons. A semi-private (all levels) costs $115 and lasts three hours.

First-timer package: None. Take semi-private or private lessons.

Private lessons: Beginners get a one-hour lesson for $105 (up to two skiers). All other ability levels pay $125 for one hour, $355 for three hours, $585 all day (up to two skiers).

Special programs: Women and men have three-day clinics at certain times in the season for $430 (lift ticket extra). Mahre Training Center Camps are three-day and five-day camps held in December and January. Camps are taught by Deer Valley instructors, with some coaching from Olympic racers Steve and Phil Mahre. Call the resort for details and reservations.

Racing: A race program called Medalist Challenge is held on the Race Course above Silver Lake Lodge, reachable by the Sterling or Wasatch Lifts. The cost is $10 for two runs and the daily chance to earn a medal. About once a week, Deer Valley's Ambassador of Skiing, Heidi Voelker, a three-time Olympian and 12-year veteran of the U.S. Ski Team, runs the course so you can compare your time to hers.

KidStuff (05/06 prices)

Child care: Ages 2 months to 12 years. Full day for ages 2–12 years, with lunch, costs $90. Full-day infant care, ages 2 months–8 months, including lunch if appropriate, $90. Reservations are essential. Call 645-6648 or reserve when you book lodging. Half-day is sold on space-available basis and cannot be reserved.

Children's lessons: Full-day programs for ages 3–12 cost $140 for lessons, lift ticket and lunch. Four-year-olds (potty-trained) have a program that is a combination of day care and a 2.5-hour ski lesson. Three-year-olds have a program that is a combination of day care and a one-hour private lesson. Reservations are essential for all programs; call (435) 645-6648 or (888) 754-8477, or book online.

Lift tickets (05/06 prices)

	Adult	Child (4–12)
One day	$74	$42
Three days	$210 ($70/day)	$111 ($37/day)
Five days	$335 ($67/day)	$175 ($35/day)

Who skis free: No one.

Who skis at a discount: Kids 3 and younger pay $19 per day. Skiers 65 and older pay $52 for a single day; $144 for three days; $230 for five days.

Note: Adults pay $76 during the holiday season. For seven or eight days between Christmas and New Year's, Deer Valley's multiday discounts are suspended. However, ticket sales are limited, so on holidays the extra few bucks to ski Deer Valley are worth it. You can make ticket reservations when you book your lodging, and this is highly recommended during the Christmas period and the February Presidents' Day holiday week.

Accommodations—Deer Valley Resort

At Deer Valley the lodging has a decidedly upscale flavor—and tariffs to match. Even in the value season the least expensive starts at about $200 per night. Accommodations have the same high quality one finds at the resort itself, and much of it is slopeside. If it's in your budget, book it. If not, stay in Park City—only a short ride away on a frequent shuttlebus.

Top dog is the **Stein Eriksen Lodge** (800-453-1302 or 649-3700; $$$–$$$$). Think of any luxury or service and you will probably find it—heated sidewalks between buildings, fireplaces in the rooms, fresh terrycloth robes, floor-to-ceiling windows. A $42-million expansion recently added 11 lavish condominiums and a conference center. The lodge also added a 4,340-square-foot, full-service spa that's open for both guests and the public.

Other places to stay on the mountain include the **Stag Lodge**, **The Chateaux at Silver Lake**, **The Lodges at Deer Valley**, **Black Diamond Lodge**, **Trail's End Lodge**, **Silver Lake Village** and the more economical **Snow Park**, all with similar luxurious amenities and all bookable through Premier Resorts at (800-453-3833; 615-2600; $$$$). Call reservations for individual property details. **The Goldener Hirsch Inn** (800-252-3373; 649-7770; $$$$) offers the elegance and service of a top Austrian hotel at midmountain in Deer Valley.

The **Pinnacle Condominiums** ($$$$) have spacious and well-appointed interiors, and they aren't too far from the bus stop. Closer to the lifts—actually ski-in/ski-out properties—are the **Pine Inn** ($$$$) and **La Maconnerie** ($$$$). All units have private hot tubs.

For reservations in Deer Valley, call **Deer Valley Lodging,** which also manages numerous lodges, condominiums and private homes (800-453-3833; 649-4040), or **Deer Valley Central Reservations** (800-558-3337; 649-1000).

Dining—Deer Valley Resort

Deer Valley's dining mirrors the overall high quality (and cost) of the resort, but the variety of exquisite places to eat may make it difficult to figure out which will be the site for that special evening. From Park City, take the free Park City Transit buses, which run until 10 p.m. To make advance dinner reservations (recommended) from anywhere in the United States, call (800) 424-3337.

The **Mariposa** (645-6715; $$$) at Silver Lake Lodge is the gourmets' top choice. To really get the full "taste" of The Mariposa's treats, try either the Chef's Vegetable Tasting or The Mariposa Tasting.

The **Glitretind Restaurant** (649-3700; $$$) at Stein Eriksen Lodge offers creative, but very American fare. Glitretind's all-you-can-eat skier's lunch buffet with made-to-order pasta dishes, a carving table, various salads and delectable desserts is not outrageously expensive.

The **Seafood Buffet** (645-6632; $$$) at Snow Park Lodge, spread out Mondays through Saturdays, is magnificent. Every type of seafood you can think of is here, and it's all you can eat—a real bargain. You won't want to miss the Dungeness crab and tiger shrimp. By the way, there's a gorgeous roast beef for landlubbers.

A unique dining experience is a three-course meal served at the the **Fireside Dinner at Empire Canyon Lodge** every Wednesday and Thursday (645-6632; reservations suggested). Each couse is served in front of a different fireplace, and the evening is topped off with a caramel or chocolate fondue. Dinner is $40 per person for adults and $20 for children younger than 12.

Park City Mountain Resort Facts

Summit elevation: 10,000 feet
Vertical drop: 3,100 feet
Base elevation: 6,900 feet

Address: P.O. Box 39, Park City, UT 84060
Area code: 435
Ski area phone: 649-8111
Snow report: 647-5449 or (800) 222-7275
Toll-free information: (800) 222-7275 (resort)
Toll-free reservations: (800) 927-7694 (Park City Mountain Reservations)
Internet: www.parkcitymountain.com and pcride.com

Number of lifts: 14–4 high-speed six-packs, 2 high-speed quads, 4 triples, 4 doubles
Snowmaking: 14 percent
Skiing acreage: 3,300 acres
Uphill capacity: 27,200 per hour
Parks & pipes: 4 parks, 1 pipe
Bed base: 21,500 (town)
Nearest lodging: Slopeside, condos
Resort child care: None; lessons start at age 3½
Adult ticket, per day: Rates change daily; see Lift Ticket section
Expert: ★★★★
Advanced: ★★★★
Intermediate: ★★★★
Beginner: ★★★ **First-timer:** ★★★

The **Goldener Hirsch Inn** (649-7770; $$$) in Silver Lake Village serves breakfast, lunch and dinner in an Austrian setting. Traditionalists will find weinerschnitzel, handmade bratwurst and raclette cheese, and others can enjoy the regional American specialties. The interior of the restaurant is a replica of one in Salzburg, while the inn is styled after an Austrian mansion.

For a great breakfast value, head to the buffet at the **Snow Park Restaurant** and for lunch go to the **Silver Lake Restaurant** or **Empire Canyon Grill**. These cafeteria-style restaurants glisten with shiny brass and sparkling glass. P.S. You've got to have the turkey chili. Then go to the shop where you can buy the ingredients to take home and make your own huge pot.

Park City Mountain Resort

Park City's mining heritage is quite evident at the resort, where old mine ruins dot the slopes. The Park City Historical Society has put up signs describing each of the sites, so skiers and boarders can get a sense of history as they enjoy the day.

Most reviews of Park City Mountain Resort characterize it as a cruisers' paradise, which is true enough. While it may not have as many steeps as Snowbird or Alta, its bowl skiing and chutes are serious—even on the expert scale. It doesn't have a huge amount of lower-end terrain, but beginners can get high enough to see the views—unlike at many resorts.

The Town Bridge that links Park City Mountain Resort to the heart of Park City allows skiers and riders direct on-snow access to the Main Street hub of Park City. This means you can ski or ride straight to Main Street, have a choice of some 100 restaurants and shops to visit during lunch, and then ride back up the mountain on the Town Lift.

Mountain layout

The Town Lift triple chair loads from the lower part of Park City's Main Street to the base of the Bonanza lift partway up the mountain. Even on holidays or peak periods, the Town Lift is often empty, so you may want to take the free shuttle here and avoid the crowds. If Payday has a line, try the Eagle chair (to the far right of the base area) and head down blue-square Temptation to the King Con chair.

♦♦ **Expert:** Start off with a trip to the top of Blueslip Bowl off the Pioneer Lift. Report-

---

Dining: $$$$–Entrees $30+; $$$–$20-$30; $$–$10-$20; $–less than $10.
Accommodations: (double room) $$$$–$200+; $$$–$141-$200; $$–$81-$140; $–$80 and less.

edly, when this was the boundary of the ski area, resort workers regularly slipped under the ropes and made tracks down the bowl. The management passed out blue (you're fired) slips to anyone caught floating through this powder bowl. If you can ski Blueslip with confidence, then try Jupiter Bowl and its neighboring bowls—McConkey's, Puma and Scott's.

Jupiter Bowl has steep expert terrain. To reach the Jupiter lift, take the Jupiter access road from the top of the Pioneer or Thaynes lifts. It's a long, flat traverse. To the left as you get off the Jupiter lift are wide-open faces, especially on the West Face, the easiest way down (a relative term). The West Face can be covered with windblown crust; ask about conditions. Narrow gullies and chutes drop vertically between tightly packed evergreens. Head to the right as you get off the chair and try Portuguese Gap, a run more akin to having the floor open below you, or traverse to Scott's Bowl. Main Bowl, closer to the lift, also offers some nice turns.

The adventurous (and those with parachutes) will find definite thrills in McConkey's Bowl and Puma Bowl. McConkey's is served by McConkey's Hi-Speed Six-Pack. Puma still requires a long traverse across a ridge and some hiking from either the Jupiter or McConkey's lifts to reach its steep faces and chutes on the backside of Jupiter Peak.

♦ **Advanced:** If you're looking for steeps or moguls, try the blacks off the Motherlode triple or the neighboring Thaynes double. Glory Hole, Double Jack and the like offer a good challenge. Or, ski the front face on the runs off the Ski Team Lift. Most of the deliciously long trails here are left *au naturel*, but Willy's is on the occasional grooming list. Hit it on the right day, and it's *fun*. For a steep cruiser that is groomed daily, head down nearby Silver Queen. Or try out Silver King, a steep, smooth boulevard used by Resort Ski Ambassador Picabo Street to train back from rehab before the 2002 Winter Games.

■ **Intermediate:** Choices are mind-boggling. If you want to start with a worthy cruiser, take Payday from the top of the lift by the same name. The views are spectacular, and at night it becomes one of the longest lighted runs in the Rockies.

Probably most popular are the 11 trails served by King Consolidated (called "King Con" by just about everyone). These runs have a steep, wide, smooth pitch. Both intermediates and advanced skiers will enjoy the runs under the Silverlode chair. To avoid crowds, try the four blues under the Pioneer chair. Or, board McConkey's, enjoy the spectacular view, and take the intermediate ridge routes down from the top. If you want to test yourself, look for a grooming report to find out which black-diamond runs have been groomed.

●● **Beginner:** Even those just getting into their snowplow turns can take the Payday and Bonanza chairs to the Summit House and descend the 3.5-mile-long, easy run appropriately named Homerun. For an adventure and to see a different part of the mountain, take the Mid-Mountain Run to the Pioneer chair, where you can have lunch and watch experts head down Blueslip Bowl.

The only complaint about the beginner runs here is that everyone else uses them too. The upper parts of the green-circle trails are used as access routes, while the bottoms are the end runs for skiers coming off more advanced terrain. The greens here are wide and gentle, but they wind in and around tougher stuff. If you're just starting out and concerned about getting in above your head, carry a trail map and pay attention to the signage. And head to the bottom well before day's end if you like plenty of room.

● **First-timer:** The First Time high-speed quad, which slows down during loading and unloading to help ease apprehensions of getting on and off the lift, serves two nice and easy trails. The Three Kings chair takes you a bit higher to more good learning terrain.

Ride Guide: Park City Mountain Resort has some long, nearly flat runs that snowboarders will want to avoid. The two worst ones are Jupiter Access and Thaynes Canyon, both of

The Canyons Resort Facts

Summit elevation: **9,990 feet**
Vertical drop: **3,190 feet**
Base elevation: **6,800 feet**

Address: 4000 The Canyons Resort Drive
Park City, UT 84060
Area code: 435
Ski area phone: 649-5400
Snow report phone: 615-3456
Toll-free information: (800) 754-1636
Toll-free reservations: (888) 226-9667
Fax: 649-7374
Internet: www.thecanyons.com

Expert:★★★★★
Advanced:★★★★★
Intermediate:★★★★
Beginner:★★ **First-timer:**★
Number of lifts: 16–1 high-speed Cabriolet, 1 gondola, 5 high-speed quads, 4 quads, 2 triples, 1 double, 2 surface lifts
Snowmaking: 4+ percent (160 acres)
Skiable Acreage: 3,500 acres
Uphill capacity: 25,700+ per hour
Parks & pipes: 2 parks, 1 pipe
Bed base: 1,200+ slopeside, 12,000 (town)
Nearest lodging: Slopeside
Resort child care: Yes, 6 weeks ad older
Adult ticket, per day: $61–$69 (05/06 prices)

which are used primarily to reach other parts of the mountain. In particular, Jupiter Access road from the top of the Pioneer or Thaynes lifts is a long, flat traverse, so don't lose your speed. You can avoid the worst traverses with advanced planning. However, snowboarders have a bit of an advantage in Park City's hike-to powder bowls, because they get to hike to the best stuff in soft boots.

The best all-around freeriding area is below Home Run between the Claim Jumper and Parley's Park runs. Three lifts can get you there: Silverlode Hi-Speed Six-Pack, Motherlode Lift and Bonanza Hi-Speed Six-Pack. There are some good cuts through the trees, plenty of bumps and some wide smoothies good for kicking up the speed.

Parks and pipes

Both the Town Lift and the Payday Hi-Speed Six-Pack deposit you above the huge terrain park on Payday. The park has a sound system and is lighted for night riding. You'll also find a superpipe on Eagle, similar to the one used in the 2002 Winter Olympics. Three additional terrain parks spread out the tricksters on Pick N Shovel, Jonesy's and the King's Crown Superpark. If you're lucky, you'll see the Park City All-Star riders and skiers jibbing in the parks.

Lessons (05/06 prices)

Prices below are for regular season, which covers most of the season. Value season has lower prices.

Group lessons: For beginners and intermediates, $75 for three hours (ski or snowboard). Intermediate skiers and better choose from skill workshops such as fine-tuning parallel turns, tackling black-diamond terrain, learning moguls, and advancing to all-mountain skiing, $75 for 4.25 hours. Advanced skiers and better can take a two-hour Power Clinic to become stronger, technical skiers in all terrain, $35. Advanced snowboarders and better can choose between freeriding or park and pipes workshops, $75 for three hours.

First-timer package: The Learn to Ski VIP Experience uses specially designed skis and is limited to five students. The Learn to Ride VIP experience uses specially designed snowboards and is limited to four students. These all-day programs cost $175 for lesson, beginner lift ticket and rentals. Reservations required; call (800) 227-2754. A three-hour group lesson is also available for $75 (beginner lift ticket included; rentals extra).

Private lessons: For one person: $120 for one hour, $220 for two hours; $315 for three hours; $525. Discounts are available for up to six people.

Racing: NASTAR is on the Blanche trail Wednesday through Saturday. Two runs cost $6; each additional run is $1. Park City Dual Challenge is set up on Clementine nearly every day. The cost is $1 per run; $5 for seven runs.

KidStuff (05/06 prices)

Child care: The resort does not provide child-care services. The Park City Chamber of Commerce can refer **child-care facilities** or **babysitting services.** Call (800) 453-1360 or locally, 649-6100. The "angels" of **Guardian Angel Babysitting Service** (783-2662) guard in-room, plus rent baby gear and shop for your groceries. **Baby's Away** (800-379-9030; 645-8823) rents and will deliver baby needs to your lodge, such as cribs, strollers and toys.

Children's lessons: Prices are for regular season, which covers most of the season; prices during value season are lower. Ages 6–13, $125 for a full day including lift ticket and lunch; snowboard lessons start at age 7. A parks and pipes program is available for advanced snowboarders for the same cost. Children ages 3 1/2–5 have a program that includes lesson, lift ticket, rentals, lunch and indoor activities for $140 (three kids per instructor). Discounts for multiday lessons are available.

First-timers must take the Children's Learn to Ski/Snowboard Preferred Experience, a full-day group lesson that costs $175 with lift ticket and rental of gear designed to help them learn. This class is limited to five students and success is guaranteed; if your child isn't riding the chair and turning on the beginner runs by the end of the day, another lesson is free.

Lift tickets

	Adult	Child (7-12)
One day	* See Notes	* See Notes

Who skis free: Kids 6 and younger.

*Notes: Park City Mountain Resort uses a variable pricing structure depending upon conditions (snow, weather, crowds, etc.). This means if you buy tickets at the window, you will most likely pay a premium rate. The only way to get a guaranteed price is to purchase tickets at least seven days in advance; good on multiday tickets only. A good way to estimate what you might pay at the ticket window on any given day is to note the cost of a two-day advance-purchase ticket and expect to pay at least that price. To purchase multiday tickets, call Guest Services at (800) 222-7275 or book online.

Early-season and value-season prices are lower. The resort has night skiing and riding from 4–7:30 p.m. Call for prices.

The Canyons

The Canyons Resort is the first resort you pass on the way into Park City. It's just a few miles away from the historic downtown area and is connected by a free shuttle service. The American Skiing Company (ASC) bought The Canyons in 1997 and has transformed the resort. Just about every lift and building has been replaced, rebuilt or otherwise improved. With eight mountain peaks, The Canyons Resort is now one of the nation's top five largest resorts.

The Grand Summit Resort Hotel is the focal point of the base development. It appears as if ASC has finally tossed aside the cookie-cutter design used in their eastern Grand Summit hotels. This hotel is actually worthy of the adjective "grand." The circular base village with its arched entrance is warm and inviting, creating a cozy feel to an area that opens up to a humongous amount of terrain and awesome vistas.

The local motto is "If you can see it, you can ski it." Gates to out-of-bounds skiing have serious signs warning of avalanche danger. Lives have been lost in recent years by people who didn't heed the warnings. There is so much expert and advanced terrain within bounds at The Canyons that you can literally explore the mountain until you drop from exhaustion and still not get to everything during a weeklong vacation. Experts from the East Coast who prefer tree skiing and riding won't be disappointed—woods are as tight as anything back home. Intermediates have plenty to choose from, and this is a great mountain if you want to improve to the next level. Beginners and first-timers have seven acres set aside specifically for them.

Mountain layout

The skiing and riding at The Canyons is spread across eight peaks.

♦♦ **Expert** ♦ **Advanced:** Most of The Canyons' terrain is not visible from the base area. What you can't see are chutes and gullies as extreme as any in Utah. Most of The Canyons' real expert terrain is in the trees off the Ninety Nine 90 Express, Tombstone Express and the Super Condor Express. These lifts follow ridges and the trees and snow drop away on either side. Ninety Nine 90 has heart-stopping chutes off to the right, like Red Pine and Charlie Brown. Peak 5 terrain is touted as intermediate tree skiing, but the trees—lots and lots of trees—make this area more of an expert's playground. The Condor chair takes you to terrain that is very steep, such as the South Side Chutes, or the dense glades of Canis Lupis. Head to the top of Murdock Peak for ungroomed bowl descents.

■ **Intermediate:** Every chair gets you to blue runs, but sometimes only one or two. The best trails are in the center of the resort, under the Saddleback Express (Snow Dancer is quite nice), The Snow Canyon Express (wide paths here) and the lower mountain. The blue runs under the Condor and Tombstone chairs are fun intermediate challenges, especially the double-blues like Cloud 9 (running the length of the Tombstone Express) and Apex Ridge next to the Super Condor Express. Ski Aplande, which takes off from Apex Ridge, a few times and you may feel ready to move on to black runs like Devil's Friend and Rendezvous Ridge.

●● **Beginner** ● **First-timer:** The Canyons has seven acres of beginner terrain near the top of the Flight of The Canyons gondola. The area is set aside from skier traffic and is framed by trees that separate beginners from main trails. There are also beginner trails off the High Meadow and Saddleback lifts and in the Dreamscape area. We suggest you enroll in lessons to have a guide keep you out of trouble.

Ride Guide: Way back when The Canyons was ParkWest, it was the first Park City ski area to allow snowboarding. The policy never changed, even though the area's name did a few times. Utah boarders are loyal because of that support, plus they know incredible terrain when they ride it. For riding in the trees, Peak 5 is a good option. Also try the steeps and chutes off the Ninety Nine 90 Express chair. A 20-minute hike from the top of Super Condor Express to Murdock Peaks' 9,602-foot summit will get you freshies in Murdock Bowl, The Saddle Chutes or One-Hundred Turns. If you're looking for wide groomers, the runs off Snow Canyon Express will get your board screaming and warm you up for trails off the Super Condor Express.

Parks and pipes

The Canyons' award-winning 18-acre terrain park, which caters to all abilities with several lines of features, is off Snow Canyon Express. The elevation is high here, so the park has pretty consistent natural snow coverage. You'll find more than 30 components, including boxes, rails and various hits, plus the halfpipe.

The Canyons has seven natural halfpipes too. Nearest the base area are two that can be reached via the Golden Eagle chair. The higher of the two, The Tube, runs off Broken Arrow next to Grizzly. The lower, The Black Hole, cuts off Super Fury and comes out on Flume, below the Snow Canyon Express. A long narrow creek bed/halfpipe runs next to Spider Monkey. It's a beginner's terror. Perhaps the most well-known natural pipe is adjacent to Upper Boa and called Canis Lupis. Two more natural halfpipes can be accessed via Saddleback Express: The first is part of Pine Draw, which is the beginner/intermediate terrain park, and the second is to rider's left of the trail CIA. Then there's the steep drainage off Ninety Nine 90 in Talus Garden: The tight, windy pipe is a challenge several thousand feet long.

Lessons (05/06 prices)

Group lessons: Clinics are 2.5 hours and cost $65; a full day costs $110.
First-timer package: First-timers get a full-day lesson, lift ticket and rentals for $100. Reservations are highly recommended.

Private lessons: For one or two people, $120 for one hour, $201 for two hours, and $496 for all day. For three to five people, $215 for two hours and $551 for all day.

Special programs: Women's Workshop, a three-day program with U.S. Olympian Holly Flanders, is offered several times during the season. Olympian Sean Smith teaches two-day Mogul Clinics. For both programs, call for details and required reservations, 615-3449.

KidStuff (05/06 prices)

Child care: Ages 6 weeks to 6 years. Full day for kids 2–6, with lunch, costs $75; half day, $55 with lunch. Full day for ages 6 weeks to 2 years old costs $82; half day, $62. Day care is offered 8:30 a.m.–4:30 p.m. No hourly rates are available. Parents should supply a change of clothes and snow clothes. Reservations are recommended at all times but essential during holiday periods. For advance reservations, call 615-3402. For same-day reservations, call 615-8036. The Day Care Center keeps a list of independent babysitters.

Children's lessons: The most-requested program is a full day that includes lunch, lift ticket and equipment, plus indoor play time for younger children. It costs $122 for Canyon Cats, ages 4–6, skiing only, and $138 for Canyon Carvers, ages 7–12, skiing or riding. Reservations are recommended; call 615-3449. Canyon Cubs, ages 2–3, get full day care plus a 90-minute private lesson for $177—reservations are required; call 615-8036. Special teen lessons for ages 13–18, split into groups by ability, cost $110 for a full day; lunch and lift tickets are not included. Call or check the website for dates.

Lift tickets (05/06 prices)

	Adult	Junior (7-12)
One day	$69	$41
Three days	$195 ($65/day)	$117 ($39/day)
Five days	$305 ($61/day)	$195 ($39/day)

Who skis free: Ages 6 and younger.

Who skis at a discount: Skiers 65 and older pay junior prices. Check out the American Skiing Company ticket website at www.meticket.com for other deals.

Note: Early- and late-season prices are lower; peak prices are higher.

Accommodations—The Canyons

A few steps from the Flight of The Canyons gondola, **The Grand Summit Resort Hotel** (888-226-9667; 615-8040; $$$$) has luxurious penthouses, one- to three-bedroom condos, studios and hotel rooms. Most of the 360 rooms have balconies, fireplaces, jetted tubs and full kitchens. The hotel also offers full-service health club, including a heated outdoor pool with hot tubs, steamroom, sauna and massage. The hotel has an on-site restaurant, bistro and lounges.

The 150-room **Sundial Lodge** (888-226-9667; $$$$) is in the heart of The Canyons Resort Village. The condominium lodge offers guestrooms and one- and two-bedroom condominium-style accommodations with kitchens and jetted tubs. Most condominiums have fireplaces and balconies. Guests have access to a rooftop hot tub and plunge pool.

Dining—The Canyons

The Canyons has three on-mountain lodges for dining: **Red Pine Cafe** ($), at the top of the Flight of The Canyons gondola, serves healthy grilled food, pizza and deli sandwiches; **Sun Lodge at Snow Canyon** ($–$$) serves Asian and Mexican dishes; and the award-winning **Lookout Cabin** ($$), at the top of Lookout chairlift, has a table-served luncheon menu of grilled fish, meats and salads and a full-service bar (not only is the food wonderful here, the mountain views are spectacular). **Doc's at the Gondola** ($–$$), in the Grand Summit, is good for lunch and apres-ski. Also in the base area, **Smokie's Smokehouse** ($–$$) serves family-style barbecue and Cajun fare and has an unobstructed view of the terrain park.

Cross-country and snowshoeing (visit xcskiresorts.com for more details)

White Pine Touring (615-5858) offers 20 km. of track and skate skiing, plus track, skate and telemark lessons at the Park City golf course and an adjacent dairy farm. For those who want to get off the flats, half-day snowshoe (Wednesday and Sunday) and ski (Tuesday and Friday) tours in the Uinta Mountains are available. If you venture out on your own, this is a good stop for advice and maps of the local mountain bike trails that are perfect for snowshoeing (many are accessible from downtown Park City).

The Homestead Resort (654-1102; 800-327-7220), 14 miles southeast of Park City in Midway, has 12 km. of skiing at Homestead Golf Course and 18 km. at Wasatch Mountain State Park. Snowshoeing and snowmobiling also are available. Nearby **Soldier Hollow,** site of the 2002 Olympic cross-country competitions, offers 26 km. of both track and skate skiing for all levels.

KidStuff—Park City Region

Other options: The Park City Chamber of Commerce can refer visitors to **child-care facilities** or **babysitting services.** Call (800) 453-1360 or locally, 649-6100. **Baby's Away** (800-379-9030; 645-8823) rents and will deliver baby needs to your lodge, such as crib, stroller, car seat and toys.

Accommodations

In and around Park City are bed & breakfasts, country inns, chain hotels and condominiums. Park City's lodging is roughly grouped either in the old town surrounding the Resort Center Complex or in the Prospector Square area. A wonderful newer part of town is Lower Main (also called South Main), which surrounds the base of the Town Lift. All areas are served by the free shuttlebus system.

Downtown and at the Park City Mountain Resort base:

In old Park City the best is the **Washington School Inn** (800-824-1672; 649-3800; $$–$$$$). This is a very elegant 15-room (including three suites) country inn built in a former schoolhouse. Each room has a private bath and is named to honor a former Park City teacher. Everything is definitely first-class. It has a hot tub and steam bath, and is steps away from the center of the old town. If you are on your honeymoon, ask for the Miss Urie Room. Room rates include breakfast and afternoon tea. No children younger than age 12.

The **Blue Church Lodge & Townhouses** (800-626-5467; 649-8009; $$–$$$$) are constructed around an old church a block from Main Street. Listed on the National Register of Historic Places, it is a grouping of seven condominiums ranging from one to four bedrooms in the church, with four additional townhouses across the street. A continental breakfast is included, but it doesn't fit the category of B&B in the classic sense. It has indoor and outdoor spas and laundry facilities.

If the key to lodging, as in real estate, is location, location, location, then **Treasure Mountain Inn** (800-344-2460; $$–$$$$) at the top of Main Street is a winner. These are studio, one- and two-bedroom condos with kitchens. Each of the three buildings has a coin-operated laundry and there is a hot tub in the courtyard. Rooms are quiet, but step outside and you are smack dab in the middle of the nighttime action. Another spot on Main Street is the **1904 Imperial Hotel** (800-669-8824; 649-1904; $$$), a B&B in an historic old house. All rooms have their own bath, telephone and TV. There's a big hot tub for everyone to use (guests also can reserve private hot-tub time). Lizzie, the hotel's ghost, turns lights on and off and rings bells to get attention (she never appears in person). Legend is that Lizzie was killed in the Mayflower Room by a jealous lover. The hotel's sister property, **The Old Miners' Lodge** (800-648-8068; 645-8068; $$–$$$) is two blocks from Main Street on Woodside Avenue. Intermediate skiers can ski to the back door, but it's a long walk down a hefty flight of stairs to get to the Town Lift. The lodge is historic and quiet (it's a member of Select Registry), with rooms that all have private baths but no TV or in-room phones.

The bargain spots are dormitory digs and hotel rooms in the **Chateau Apres Lodge,** "A Skier's Ski Lodge" (800-357-3556; 649-9372; $–$$). Stay at **Base Camp Park City** (888-980-7244; $) to save money and be close to all the best nightlife. Bathrooms, a lounge and a kitchenette are shared, but there are private ski lockers.

The South Main area is the newest hot spot in town. The **Marriott Summit Watch** (800-845-5279; 647-4100; $$$–$$$$) is smack in the middle of this pedestrian complex with restaurants, shops and the Town Lift right outside the door. A draw is the Marriott's Aquacade, a pool and activities center built under old trestles. Every evening there's something scheduled for kids, such as crafts, movies or an ice skating excursion, ranging in cost from $15 to $30.

Near the Resort Center you'll find another cluster of hotels and condos. The best is the **Silver King Hotel** (800-331-8652; 649-5500; $$$–$$$$). This condo hotel is about 100 yards from the lifts and at the hub of the transportation system. Some units have private hot tubs. **The Lodge at the Mountain Village** (888-727-5248; 649-0800; $$$–$$$$) is the second choice for luxury. It literally surrounds the base area lifts for true ski-in/ski-out. It has lots of amenities—hot tubs, health club, pool, steamroom and concierge.

Shadow Ridge Resort Hotel & Conference Center (800-451-3031; 649-4300; $$–$$$$) is the other top property near the lifts. It has a sauna, hot tub and laundry, plus underground parking. Choose from hotel rooms to three-bedroom condos. **Snow Flower Condominiums** (800-852-3101; 649-6400; $$–$$$$) is 100 feet from the beginner area and offers studios to five-bedroom units. Each unit has single-person jetted tubs and underground parking.

For more economical condos, try the **Edelweiss Haus** (800-245-6417; 649-9342; $$–$$$$) across the street from the lifts and the Silver King Hotel. Extras include a heated outdoor pool and hot tub. Hotel rooms to two-bedroom condos are available.

Other locations in town:

The **Inn at Prospector Square** (888-870-4386; 649-7100; $$–$$$$) is a group of condos that includes use of its athletic club in the rates. **The Yarrow Resort Hotel** (800-927-7694 or 649-7000; $$–$$$$) is considered good family lodging. Children younger than 12 stay free and the hotel, with a year-round heated outdoor pool, sits amid shopping, movies and restaurants. It is on the shuttlebus route, about a five-minute ride from Park City's Main Street.

The 199-room **Park City Marriott** (800-754-3279; 649-2900; $$–$$$$) is an absolutely gorgeous full-service resort hotel. There are refrigerators and coffeemakers in every room, plus double phone lines and desks with built-in outlets for those who must combine work with pleasure. It also has an atrium pool, sauna and hot tub. The bus stop is right outside the door.

For luxury condos and houses at affordable prices as well as a chance to get some last-minute or off-peak bargains in the entire Park City area, call **AAA Lodging & Ski Reservations** (800-522-7669; 649-6225).

Dining

Park City's restaurants get better every year—and more expensive. Pick up one of the two free dining-guide magazines to get menus, but be aware that not all the restaurants are listed. Main Street is where you'll find many of the best restaurants in town: The top four are **Grappa, Chimayo, Zoom** and **Riverhorse.**

If you can pay the freight, the Northern Italian menu, wine list and ambiance are outstanding at chef Bill White's **Grappa** (645-0636, $$$). It's in a 100-year-old building; try to get a table by the fireplace. Many locals recommend **Chimayo** (649-6222; $$$), also owned by chef Bill White, for its inventive Southwestern cuisine (don't miss the dark-chocolate flan). **Zoom Roadhouse Grill** (649-9108; $$$) is housed in the old train depot. Owned by Robert Redford, whose Sundance Film Festival transforms the town each January, it serves "plain folks food." Finally, the **Riverhorse Cafe** (649-3536; $$$–$$$$) is a can't-miss choice for anyone who enjoys contemporary American continental food in a low-key, elegant atmosphere. Every year since 1995, it's received the DiRoNa Award for excellence in dining.

Cisero's Ristorante (649-5044, $$$) is known for its fresh pastas and after-dinner live bands. The muted colors of **Cafe Terigo** (645-9555; $$$) are relaxing and everything on the contemporary Italian menu sounds delectable so it's hard to make a choice. **Grub Steak** (649-8060; $$–$$$) gets high marks for steak and seafood and has a 35-item salad bar.

Asian restaurants are popular, with **Bangkok Thai** (649-8424; $$$) the choice for Thai and **Taste of Saigon** (647-0688; $$) for Vietnamese food. Park City also has four Chinese restaurants. **China Panda** (649-5593; $$) is the spot for your Chinese fix. Many Park City restaurants offer excellent take-out. After a wipe-out day on the slopes and a soak in the hot

Dining: $$$$–Entrees $30+; $$$–$20–$30; $$–$10–$20; $–less than $10.
Accommodations: (double room) $$$$–$200+; $$$–$141–$200; $$–$81–$140; $–$80 and less.

tub, we devoured a tender Moo Goo Gai Pan and a tasty mixed vegetable dish from **Szechwan** (649-0957; $$). Take a free shuttle into town for pick up or have food delivered for an additional 20 percent of the total.

The hot spot is Lower Main. **Wahso** (615-0300; $$$), again owned by the ubiquitous Bill White, is where to go for classy Asian food. The dining here is elegant and reminiscent of Shanghai in the 1930s.

Off Main Street, one restaurant that vies for best-in-town honors is **Adolph's** (649-7177; $$$). The Swiss chef-owner prepares European-inspired cuisine. Hidden on Park Avenue, **Chez Betty** (649-8181; $$$) in the Copperbottom Inn serves excellent American/French cuisine in a formal setting.

The Claim Jumper Steak House (649-8051; $$–$$$) is casual for families and has a children's menu, while **Prime Steak House** (655-9739, $$$) is an upscale night out.

Head to **Nacho Mama's** (645-8226; $–$$) for tasty Southwestern/Mexican food and margaritas that go down far too smoothly and **Baja Cantina** (649-2252; $–$$) at the Resort Plaza for a festive atmosphere, huge burritos and Tex-Mex made with fresh ingredients. The lowest-priced Mexican restaurant is **El Chubasco** (645-9114; $–$$), in Prospector Square, where you'll get real Mexican food with quick service but no atmosphere.

The Eating Establishment (649-8284; $) is a locals' cheap-eats favorite for meals any time of day, as is **Main St. Pizza and Noodle** (645-8878; $).

For breakfast, **The Eating Establishment** ($) on Main Street is the leader for hearty-meal fans (the menu includes some trendy selections, such as smoked salmon Eggs Benedict). **Off Main Cafe and Bakery** ($) does omelets and pancakes in the Prospector Square area. For a lighter breakfast, try **Einstein Brothers Bagel Bakery** ($) in the Prospector Square area for a huge variety of bagels and spreads, as well as great coffee, or **Wasatch Bagels** ($) on Kearns Boulevard next to Dan's Grocery Store. For funky local ambiance and a cheap breakfast special ($3.89 for egg, ham and cheese on a bagel), hit **The Main Street Deli** ($). The **Morning Ray Cafe** ($) or **Mountain Air** ($) are the places to share a java with the locals.

 ## Apres-ski/nightlife

Park City has some of the best nightlife of any ski town. Immediate slopeside apres-ski centers are **Deer Valley's The Lounge**, where live singers perform on the weekends; **Legends Bar & Bistro** and **The Brew House**, both in the Legacy Lodge at Park City Mountain Resort base; and **The Forum** at The Canyons.

According to locals, **O'Shucks** is the place to be on Main Street for the younger folks (skiers and boarders). **Harry Os,** half way down Main, is a giant warehouse of a bar, complete with six pool tables, a big-screen TV and a boisterous younger crowd. It is the place on Saturday nights. **The No Name Saloon**, next door, is your basic bar with a shuffleboard table, loud juke music and louder conversation. **Mother Urban's**, named after a famous bordello madam, is a cellar version of a knotty-pine mining shack that sells 101 beers and features live jazz Tuesdays, Thursdays and Fridays. Also try the **Wasatch Brew Pub** at the top of Main Street, where you can watch the brewing process even as you reap its yeasty rewards. **The Spur** on Main Street offers a comfortable, no-smoking setting with live music. **Adolph's**, with piano music, has been recommended for quieter evenings in the newer section of town.

When the **Egyptian Theater** performs plays, as it often does during the winter, it makes a nice evening's entertainment. **The Eccles Center**, which opened in 1998, houses two live stages and is a year-round focal point for the performing arts in Park City. For weekly arts and entertainment events, call 647-9747 or 655-3114.

Other activities

Park City offers some rare sports treats: **ski jumping, luge and bobsled** at the Utah Olympic Park (658-4200). The park hosted the 2002 Olympic competition in those events. Yes, you can fly off the end of a ramp just like the Olympians do (you'll be on much smaller ramps, but it will feel like the 120-meter jump, let us assure you). You can take jumping lessons (required rental helmets included), or ride on the Olympic luge/bobsled track in a neophyte-friendly luge "ice rocket" or as a passenger in a four-person bobsled. (They supply the driver.) Schedules are different each day, and not every activity is offered every day, so call for specifics and prices. Definitely call in advance for a spot in the bobsled—the 48-second ride of your life, wild and rugged. You won't be disappointed. The park is open daily. It's worth a tour even if you don't participate in the sports, particularly with the recent opening of its museum celebrating Utah's ski history, from the first jumping competitions to XIX Olympic Winter Games.

Experienced skiers can ski to six different resorts via backcountry routes on the all-day **Interconnect Adventure Tour** (534-1907; reservations required). Mountain guides lead six to 14 skiers and some traversing and walking are necessary, so you need to be a confident skier and in good physical condition. The six-area tour (Deer Valley, Park City Mountain Resort, Solitude, Brighton, Alta and Snowbird) costs $175 (05/06 price), including return transportation and lunch.

The Adventures Desk (649-9619) at the Grand Summit Resort Hotel is the easiest and most direct way for guests at The Canyons to book guided outdoor adventures. Activities include **snowmobiling, dogsledding, snowshoeing, hot air ballooning,** and **fly fishing.** If you are not a guest at The Canyons, you can reserve these kinds of activities by calling one central number at **ABC Reservations Central,** (800) 820-2223 or 649-2223. There is no fee and most adventures provide free shuttle service.

Gorgoza Park, a tubing park owned by Park City Mountain Resort, is about five minutes out of town off of I-80. You'll find family fun on **eight lanes of tubing** and **mini-snowmobile rides.** The resort also has **sleigh rides** and **snowmobile tours** for family activities. Park City has local **skateboard park,** complete with lights for night skating.

Stop by the Church of Jesus Christ of Latter-Day Saints' **Family History Center** at 531 Main Street (Mormon church). Computers are available for genealogy checks for anyone free of charge. **The Park City Museum** on Main Street details local history, and is excellent. Admission is by donation, and it is open every day, at varying times.

Park City's calendar has some unusual events. Park City Mountain Resort will kick off the season with a **women's professional snowboard slopestyle competition.** The resort also will host the **World Superpipe Championships.** Deer Valley will be hosting the **Sprint Grand National World Cup** event the last weekend of January. Robert Redford's **Sundance Film Festival** is in late January, showcasing new films from around the world.

The 30,000-square-foot **Papillon the Spa,** at the Westgate Park City Resort & Spa (655-2266) at The Canyons, has 17 treatment rooms (13 massage and facial, two wet rooms, a couples room and treatment suite); private men's and women's locker facilities with relaxation lounges, saunas, steamrooms and showers; and a coed hot tub with cascading waterfall. Services include massages and body and facial treatments emphasizing native desert and mountain botanicals. Full salon services, fitness facility, exercise studio and yoga studio are available.

Align Spa (647-9300) is a full-service day spa on the lobby level of Shadow Ridge Hotel and Conference Center. Massages, facials and body treatments are available.

Dining: $$$$-Entrees $30+; $$$-$20-$30; $$-$10-$20; $-less than $10.
Accommodations: (double room) $$$$-$200+; $$$-$141-$200; $$-$81-$140; $-$80 and less.

Park City has two popular **shopping** areas: Historic Main Street in downtown Park City and a factory outlet center on the edge of town. The outlets include Eddie Bauer, Brooks Brothers, Gap, Nike and Polo, among many others. You can jump on a free shuttle or take a cab for $6 round trip per person. Park City's free shuttlebus system now operates in town and out to Kimball Junction/Factory Outlet Mall (including The Canyons Resort). Take an hour or two and walk Main Street to find **museums, art galleries** and fine and funky shops. A must-see is Silver Junction Mercantile with every nook and cranny crammed full of old stuff, from rusty license plates and political buttons to Elvis and Beatles memorabilia. Nativo offers high-end young clothing and avant-garde jewelry. The Park City Clothing Company in the Main Street Mall sells vintage Pendleton clothing at vintage prices.

Don't miss Changing Hands, a consignment shop way off the beaten track in the back of Galleria Mall. Great high-fashion ski clothes during the season and higher-end labels for the rest of the inventory. Hard to find, but well worth it. If you are traveling with your pet or had to leave him at home, stop at the Love Your Pet Bakery to bring home a treat.

You can't go to Deer Valley without shopping at Deer Valley Signatures Stores, where you'll find a variety of Deer Valley logo items and exclusive merchandise, including apparel, blankets, accessories and glassware, as well as specialty Signature food items from Deer Valley's kitchens (including that fabulous turkey chili). There are three locations, open daily: Snow Park Lodge, Silver Lake Village and at 625 Main St. in downtown Park City.

Getting there and getting around

By air: The drive from the Salt Lake City International Airport to Park City takes 45 minutes. Ground transportation makes frequent trips between the airport and Park City. Providers include Lewis Brothers Stages (800-826-5844; 649-2256); Park City Transportation (800-637-3803; 649-8567); and All Resort Express (800-457-9457; 649-3999). If you arrive without reservations, go to the transportation counter at the airport and you'll ride on the next available van.

By car: Park City is 36 miles east of Salt Lake City, by I-80 and Utah Hwy. 224.

Getting around: If you're staying close to the town center or near a stop on the free bus line, you can do without a rental car. The town bus system has five routes with service every 20 minutes, if not more frequently, from 7 a.m. to 1 a.m. If you take a side trip to one of the Cottonwood Canyons ski resorts, Lewis Brothers Stages and Park City Transportation have shuttles. Lewis Brothers offers a Canyon Jumper package to Solitude and Snowbird, including transportation and lift ticket. Prepay the evening before you wish to ski.

Crystal Mountain
Washington

Summit elevation:	7,012 feet
Vertical drop:	2,612 feet
Base elevation:	4,400 feet

Address: 33914 Crystal Mountain Blvd.,
Crystal Mountain WA 98022
Area code: 360
Ski area phone: 663-2265
Reservations: No central reservations
Snow report: (888) 754-6199
Road conditions: (800) 695-7623
Fax: 663-3001
E-mail: comments@skicrystal.com
Internet: www.skicrystal.com (resort);
www.staycrystal.com (lodging)
Expert:★★★★
Advanced:★★★★
Intermediate:★★★★★
Beginner:★★★
First-timer:★★★★★

Number and types of lifts: 10–2 high-speed
six-pack chairs, 2 high-speed quads, 2 triples, 3
doubles, 1 moving carpet
Skiable Acreage: 2,300 acres (including 1,000
backcountry)
Snowmaking: 1.3 percent
Uphill capacity: 19,110 per hour
Parks & pipes: 1 pipe
Bed base: About 350 (176 rooms)
Nearest lodging: Slopeside, cabins
Resort child care: None
Adult ticket, per day: $53 (06/07 price)

Dining:★★★
Apres-ski/nightlife:★★
Other activities:★

When the weather is right and the snow is deep, hardcore skiers from all over the West Coast beam themselves to Crystal for unparalleled skiing. The terrain is steep and thrilling, and there's enough of it to keep the adrenaline rushing all day. There's enough snow too, often 12 feet deep at the top. It snowed 65 inches one record-breaking day during a recent season—and the average annual snowfall is 380 inches.

It's Washington's only destination Alpine ski resort, just a 90-minute drive from Seattle. The on-mountain condos, lodges and restaurants delight local skiers who would otherwise have to leave the state for a vacation. The new 12,500-square-foot Campbell Basin Lodge at the top of the Forest Queen lift means skiers and snowboarders can grab a nice lunch without having to go all the way to the base area. And there's more to come, since the U.S. Forest Service approved a 12-year Master Development Plan.

 ## Mountain layout

◆◆**Expert** ◆**Advanced:** Experts may only see one-third of the trails designated for them, but they'll find their real thrills in the patrolled backcountry terrain here. Seven days a week (conditions permitting), a shuttle bus picks up at the backcountry return every half hour. And there's something to be said for skiing and riding a mountain dwarfed by nearby 14,410-foot Mt. Rainier.

Black-diamond runs are a whopping 43 percent of the terrain. That high percentage is because of the 1,000 skiable acres in the in-bounds backcountry areas, most of which is not lift-served. It's the kind of terrain that is out of bounds at most ski areas—woods, chutes and steep bowls. With the new winch-cat groomers, expect to see corduroy on runs like Iceberg Gulch, Green Valley and Deer Fly.

■ **Intermediate:** Blue runs make up another 37 percent of Crystal's 2,300 acres. However, runs are fairly short, such as Lucky Shot, Little Shot and Gandy's Run, all from Summit House. For a longer run, ski Green Valley from the right of Summit House to the base of the Green Valley chair and continue to the base area on Kelly's Gap Road.

●●**Beginner** ●**First-timer:** Beginners can have fun on Broadway and Skid Road, both served by the base-area lift, The Chinook Express. First-timers have their own Meadow and Fairway runs served by the Discovery chair. Child novices now have a moving carpet lift called the Kid Conveyor instead of a handle tow.

Ride Guide: Crystal has woods, ridges, carving slopes and legal backcountry that keep freeriders coming back. A lot of intermediate and advanced riders enjoy the up-mountain area off Green Valley Chair, reached by taking Chinook and Rainier Express chairs.

Parks and pipes

For the acrobatically inclined, a halfpipe screams for action next to the Quicksilver Chair. The resort built an in-ground halfpipe that's 250 feet long, 50 feet wide, and has 18-foot walls. Not quite to superpipe standards, but the U.S. Forest Service prevents the larger dimensions.

Lessons (06/07 prices)

Group lessons: $40 for a two-hour session, $50 for four hours. With all-mountain lift ticket and gear rental, it's $95 for a two-hour lesson and $105 for a four-hour lesson, for both skiing and snowboarding.

First-timer package: Two-hour lesson, beginner lift ticket and rental gear, $45, skiing or snowboarding. The four-hour version is $10 more.

Private lessons: For up to two people, one hour, $70; two hours, $130; three hours; $180; full day, $330. A one-hour lesson before 10 a.m. or after 2 p.m. costs $60. Add $10 per hour for each extra person.

KidStuff (06/07 prices)

Child care: The resort does not offer non-skiing child care.

Children's lessons: Ages 4–11 for skiers and ages 7–11 for snowboarders. Includes lift, lesson and supervision. Lunch is included in the full-day session. Full day $80; half day $60. Rental equipment costs $12.

Lift tickets (06/07 prices)

	Adult	Youth (11-17)
One day	$53	$48

Who skis free: No one.

Who skis at a discount: Ages 10 and younger, $5. Seniors 70 and older, $28. Beginner-only lift tickets (Discovery Chair) are $33. Crystal Mountain does not sell multiday tickets, but a book of five adult all-day vouchers saves about $5 per day. The vouchers can be used by anyone and are sold at the mountain and at Puget Sound ski shops. Night skiing is available January through February, 4 p.m.–8 p.m.

Accommodations

Lodging is walking distance from the slopes. Three hotels and more than 100 condominiums are run by three operations. For the three hotels—**Alpine Inn** ($$–$$$), **Quicksilver Lodge** ($$–$$$) and **Village Inn** ($$)—call Crystal

Mountain Hotels (888-754-6400; 663-2262). At the legendary Alpine Inn, units range from a small room for two with a shower down the hall to a deluxe with two double beds. The lobby is a cozy gathering spot. The Quicksilver Lodge is a comfortable Camay soap/plastic cup kind of lodging with no-smoking rooms and feather duvets. The large open lobby with a piano, games and comfy furniture makes it very popular with families. It's a five-minute walk to the base. The Village Inn has queen and twin rooms with fridges.

For country-inn-themed chalet suites, call **Alta Crystal Resort** (800-277-6475; 663-2500; $$$–$$$$). Amenities include an outdoor heated pool and hot tub. For condos, call **Crystal Mountain Lodging Suites** (888-668-4368; 663-2558; $$$–$$$$). All units have kitchens, some have fireplaces. Individual amenities, sleeping arrangements and furnishing vary with suite sizes and locations.

The lower parking lot has 42 **RV hookups,** first-come, first-served, $20 per night.

Dining/apres-ski/nightlife

Restaurants cater to both the white-linen and take-out crowds, with rustic dining, a cafeteria and apres-ski lounges in between. **Summit House** ($–$$), a rustic dining lodge on the mountain, is at the top of the Rainier Express lift (6,872 feet). You'll find gourmet pizzas and pastas along with soups and salads, but the main attraction is the view of Mount Rainier. **Campbell Basin Lodge** ($) has a nice food court with stations for pasta, soup, grilled sandwiches, burritos and wraps, gourmet pizza and stir-fry. Back down at the base area, the **Alpine Inn Restaurant** (663-7727; $$–$$$), open for breakfast and dinner daily, is a Crystal legend serving fine foods and wines. The Alpine also serves a great breakfast with traditional eggs Benedict, florentine, rancheros and even a tofu scramble.

The **Bullwheel Pub & Grill,** upstairs in the main base lodge, has full cocktail service, the tastiest burgers at Crystal and a great view of the slopes. The **Snorting Elk Cellar** downstairs in the Alpine Inn is like a Bavarian Rathskeller. It's always the place to gather after a great day on the slopes. Try to settle in near the cozy fireplace. Dance to the live bands on the weekends if you can squeeze your booty into the crowded, popular bar. The Elk has a terrific selection of microbrews, full cocktail service and expanded food service to the bar from its own deli.

Find all your essential grocery, bakery, beer and wine needs at **The Market at Crystal Mountain.** Bonus: The **Espresso stand** next to the Market not only serves espresso but every kind of gourmet hot dog you could ever imagine—king dog, queen dog, black dog, Chicago dog, ball park dog, Big Red—you get the picture. Pick your poison.

Other activities

You'll find a hot tub, sauna, showers and game room at **East Peak Massage and Fitness** (663-2505), next to the Alpine Inn above Parking Lot C. With adaptive ski equipment, **SKIFORALL** (425-462-0978) offers training for and fun on the snow for children and adults with disabilities.

Getting there and getting around

By air: Seattle-Tacoma airport is served by most major airlines.
By car: Crystal is 76 miles southeast of Seattle and a 64-mile drive from Sea-Tac Airport. Drive south on I-5 from Seattle, take Exit 142 east to Auburn, Hwy. 164 to Enumclaw, and Hwy. 410 east to Crystal Mountain Boulevard.
By bus: Service from Puget Sound is available on the Crystal Mountain Ski & Snowboard Express on Saturdays and Sundays from December to March. Call (800) 665-2122, 8 a.m. to 5 p.m.

Dining: $$$$-Entrees $30+; $$$-$20-$30; $$-$10-$20; $-less than $10.
Accommodations: (double room) $$$$-$200+; $$$-$141-$200; $$-$81-$140; $-$80 and less.

Washington State Regional Resorts

Mt. Baker, Bellingham, WA; (360) 734-6771; (360) 671-0211 (snow reports)

Internet: www.mtbaker.us
9 lifts; 1,000 acres; 1,550 vertical feet; 1 terrain park; 1 halfpipe

Mountain resorts need snow, and this resort in northwest Washington State gets more of it than any other. This is not hype. Mt. Baker holds the world record, certified by the National Oceanic and Atmospheric Administration, for a winter season's snowfall of 1,140 inches.

In an era when smaller ski hills and non-destination resort ski areas are disappearing, Mt. Baker's success is an exception. Location, location and location—Baker draws skiers and snowboarders from both Vancouver, British Columbia, one hour north and Seattle, two-and-a-half hours south—has a lot to do with it, but the main ingredients are the average annual 645-inch snowfall and its "non-corporate" style of management. It's just funky.

Mt. Baker's improvements in the past few years include a second Cascadian-style day lodge, five more quad lifts and expansion of its intermediate terrain. Now, even on record days, lift lines never top five minutes. Mt. Baker's four-year upgrade plan to replace all double chairs is now in the last phase.

The mountain offers all-day possibilities to skiers and snowboarders alike, with plenty of faces and woods that bring out the pioneer spirit. This is truly snowboarder heaven, where the hardcore insist "snowboarding was born."

One drawback to the ski area's low elevation is that the freezing level can yo–yo, and marginally cold days can turn snow to rain without notice. Ski patrollers keep a few sets of dry clothes in their hut for themselves. Bring a change of clothes for yourself, it's good insurance.

The Pan Dome side, served by Chairs 1, 2, 3 and 6, is for the mogul bashers and chute shooters. Hot skiers can play here endlessly challenging the steep and deep. Every time experts take one run, they are sure to find another just as hairy. Shuksan has more wide-open, powder bowl type of terrain. Experts-only runs include Gabl's Run under Chair 5 and The Chute. The Chute, a horrific, straight-down run under Chair 1, is where a staff writer once ended up in a tree well after a body slam with an unknown opposite-sex skier. The folks on the lift were well entertained and it took some creative maneuvers for the victims to extricate themselves. Make sure there's enough snow before you try this one.

The out-of-bounds areas are extremely attractive at Mt. Baker and many pass the caution signs and do the hikes at the top of Chair 8. But avalanches are a problem out of bounds, and sometimes people die. You must have an avalanche transceiver and know how to use it. Plus, have a partner, a shovel, and know your route, the terrain, avalanche conditions and predictions.

Nearly 70 percent of Mt. Baker's terrain is labeled blue or green. On soft snow days, intermediates can go just about anywhere on the mountain with confidence, minus the chutes, of course. On icy days, however, definitely avoid Razor Hone Canyon. It becomes a long series of shelves. North Face and Honkers get unforgiving too, with their boulderish bumps. Probably the most fun for intermediates is the terrain off Chair 8, especially Oh Zone and

Daytona. The ride up rivals Blackcomb's Jersey Cream Express Chair for the majestic view of the mountain ridges past the area boundary at Rumble Gully.

The beginner terrain is all at the bottom of the mountain. Chair 7 expands the Shuksan possibilities, but not much. Beginners will probably want to avoid Chair 8 for the time being—its terrain is mostly intermediate.

On the Pan Dome side, beginners can easily get back to the lodge on the Austin and Blueberry runs, even though they are labeled intermediate. The signs are good, but don't follow tracks or other skiers if you don't know where they're going. You may end up on steep Pan Face or unmapped places called Rattrap and Gunbarrel. The ski patrol performs rescues on icy crags that are best avoided. The learning areas are near the Heather Meadows base lodge and the White Salmon Day Lodge. The greatest variety is found at the Heather Meadows side. The slopes are long and gentle, not sectioned off, but not used by more accomplished sliders. Snowboard novices—some of whom feel immortal rather than timid—use this area. Timid novices probably are better off learning elsewhere.

Ride guide: The entire mountain is challenging fun for snowboarders. There is not much in the way of flats. Without speed from the top of Chair 3 to load onto Chair 2, you might have a short walk. The only in-bounds climb, maybe 50 yards long, is from the ends of Chair 6 and Chair 7 if you're heading to the Austin run or the Blueberry Cat Track to return to the upper lodge, Heather Meadows Day Lodge. The Sticky Wicket woods give good ride until the snow is flatted out. From the woods there are a few choice access steeps into Razorhone Canyon. There are several good chutes, especially in the spring, from Gabl's run into the little valley under Chair 5.

Parks and pipes: The huge terrain park is under Chair 8. It's 600 feet long, 80 feet wide and has anywhere from six to 12 features, depending upon snowpack. The permanent halfpipe is just to rider's right of Chair 7 on the White Salmon side. There's still the natural halfpipe—starting from the top of Chair 5, it follows a creek bed for a few hundred yards and is normally buried under 20 feet of snow.

Lift tickets (05/06 prices): Weekend/Holiday: adults (16–59), $38; youth (7–15), $29; senior (60–69), $32. Weekday: adults (16–59), $30; youth (7–15), $24; senior (60–69), $27. Kids 6 and younger ski free & seniors 70+ pay $11 all season.

Distance: The Mt. Baker Ski Area is at the end of the Mt. Baker Hwy., 56 miles east of Bellingham, I-5, Exit 255. The drive from Bellingham takes about 90 minutes; from Seattle, allow three hours; and from Vancouver, B.C., two hours.

Lodging information: Mt. Baker Lodging (800-709-7669; 599-2453; $$–$$$$), in Glacier, rents vacation houses. The **Mt. Baker Chalet** (800-258–2405; 599-2405; $–$$$$), at Mile Post 33 on the Mt. Baker Hwy. at the west end of Glacier, has 20 cabins and condos. The **Snowline Inn** (800-228-0119; 599-2788; $–$$) rents studio units and condo loft units. **Glacier Creek Lodge** (800-719-1414; 599-2991; $–$$$) has motel and cabin units.

There are a lot of small, charming B&Bs in the Glacier area with two or more rooms that are all in the same price range. **The luxurious Inn at Mt. Baker** (599-1776; $$), just east of Glacier, was specifically built in 2000 to be a bed & breakfast.

The Summit, Snoqualmie Pass, WA; (425) 434-7669; (206) 236-1600 (info line)

Internet: www.summit-at-snoqualmie.com

25 lifts; 1,916 acres; 2,310 vertical feet; 5 terrain parks; 1 superpipe

The Summit comprises four separate ski areas, all within a mile of each other on Snoqualmie Pass. Three are connected by trails, and the fourth, Alpental, is a mile away on

Dining: $$$$-Entrees $30+; $$$-$20-$30; $$-$10-$20; $-less than $10.

Accommodations: (double room) $$$$-$200+; $$$-$141-$200; $$-$81-$140; $-$80 and less.

another face. The four areas—Alpental, Summit West, Summit Central and Summit East—share an interchangeable lift ticket and offer a free shuttle so skiers can get from one to the others. Our stats reflect the combined lifts and acreage, while the vertical listed is for Alpental. The vertical drop at the other three areas varies from 900 to 1,080 feet.

Alpental has the most rugged reputation. Summit West features gentle green and blue runs, plus it's home to two terrain parks and a snowdeck/snowskate park. Summit Central has mostly gentle terrain with a few serious black-diamond drops off the ridge, as well as the flagship terrain park and 400-foot-long superpipe with 17-foot-high walls. The pipe has a sound system and is lighted for night riding. Summit East has some great tree runs among its attractions. At least one of the areas is closed every weekday, sometimes two are, but the entire complex is open weekends and holidays (call or visit the website for the specific schedule).

Child care starts at 6 months and is offered at Summit West; make reservations. Night skiing operates until 10:30 p.m. (9 p.m. Sundays) on any mountain open that day. Night child care is available by reservation. A Nordic ski area offers 50 km. of trails.

Lift tickets (06/07 prices): Adults (13–61), $46; youth (7–12)/senior (62–69), $31; children 6 and younger & super seniors 70+, $9 (taxes are not included).

Distance from Seattle: About 50 miles east on I-90.

Lodging information: Visit the resort's website for a listing of lodging and private homes available for rent.

Stevens Pass, Skykomish, WA; (206) 812-4510; (206) 634-1645 (info line)

Internet: www.stevenspass.com

10 lifts; 1,125 acres; 1,800 vertical feet; 2 terrain parks; 1 superpipe

The snow here is tough to beat. Geographical elevation combined with dry wind from the east make the snow conditions at Stevens Pass nearly perfect throughout the winter season. Annual average snowfall is 450 inches, providing an average snowpack of 110 inches.

The upper-front of Big Chief Mountain is steep and dense with Alpine conifers and a few skinny runs, providing the most challenging terrain at Stevens. The lower-front of Big Chief has one open intermediate run. The backside of Big Chief, called Mill Valley, faces south and has lots of very open runs and is popular among Stevens die-hards. On the front of Cowboy Mountain lies the most intermediate runs and lit night-skiing terrain. From the top of Cowboy, amazing scenery and backcountry access is possible, as well as more challenging experts terrain. In the heart of the base area is the beginner terrain and tubing hill.

The night terrain offers something for everyone—two high-speed quads combined with four additional lifts offer access to 12 major runs through 400 acres. Night operations run seven nights a week from 4–10 p.m. Tube City is also lighted until 9 p.m.

There is child care for kids ages 3–12 (must be toilet trained). The Stevens Pass Nordic Center, 5 miles from the resort on Hwy. 2, has 28 km. of cross-country and snowshoe trails.

Lift tickets (06/07 prices): Adults (13–61), $52; children (7–12), $33; senior (62–69), $35; seniors 70 and older, $9; ages 6 and younger, $6. (Prices are rounded to nearest dollar.)

Distance from Seattle: About 78 miles northeast on Hwy. 2.

Lodging information: The closest is SkyRiver Inn (800-367-8194; 360-677-2261; $$) in Skykomish. Leavenworth, a tourist town with an Alpine Bavarian theme, is 35 miles east of Stevens Pass. For lodging information in Leavenworth, call Bavarian Bedfinders (800-323-2920) or the Leavenworth Chamber Of Commerce (509-548-5807).

Grand Targhee Resort

Wyoming

Summit elevation:	10,000 feet
Vertical drop:	2,000 feet
Base elevation:	8,000 feet

Address: P.O. Box SKI, Alta, WY 83414
Area code: 307
Ski area phone: 353-2300
Fax: 353-8148
Toll-free snow report: (800) 827-4433
Toll-free reservations: (800) 827-4433
E-mail: info@grandtarghee.com
Internet: www.grandtarghee.com

Number of lifts: 5–2 high-speed quads, 1 quad, 1 double, 1 moving carpet
Snowmaking: None
Skiable acreage: 2,000 lift-served acres
Parks & pipes: 2 parks
Bed Base: 432 pillows (96 lodging units)
Nearest lodging: Slopeside, hotel and condos
Resort child care: Yes, 2 months and older
Adult ticket, per day: $54–$57 (06/07)

Expert:★★★
Advanced:★★★★
Intermediate:★★★★★
Beginner:★★★★
First-timer:★★★

Dining:★★★
Apres-ski/nightlife:★
Other activities:★

If you were looking for an intermediate's Shangri-La, it would sit on large rounded mountains sprinkled with just enough trees to make it look like Who-ville during the holidays. Snow would regularly blanket the slopes, often leaving the trees looking like Seussian gnomes. Yet it would have a few groomed swaths lying like ribbon candy on the mountains' flanks. The base area would be small yet have everything you need, from strong coffee to amusing T-shirts ("I've run out of sick days, so I'm calling in dead") and the usual array of ski accessories. And everything would be run by friendly folks. From the summit, this intermediate haven would have views so awesome that even the locals stop to gawk. And it would have out-of-bounds terrain for those who get their joneses from more than caffeine. It would look like Grand Targhee Resort.

Sitting as it does on the windward side of the Grand Tetons, Grand Targhee is much more than the perfect intermediate resort. Whenever it snows—which is often, about 500 inches of snow falls here each winter—it's not an intermediate resort at all. The seemingly boundless open terrain becomes one huge powder stash. And the groomers aren't keen on packing it down. No-sir-ee. This Shangri-La designates beginner, intermediate and advanced *powder* areas on its trail map, with fresh ungroomed snow left on the gentle rolling terrain where powder puppies can cut their first turns.

The Sacajawea high-speed quad takes you to 500 acres of terrain on Peaked Mountain that could previously only be reached by snowcat. About a third of this terrain is groomed. The rest is pristine glade skiing and open bowls left untouched for fresh tracks. Better yet, on adverse weather days, Peaked Mountain provides protection from the wind and low clouds. And if you're looking for an out-of-bounds peak called Mary's Nipple, well, just look for the signs pointing to Mary's. All written references to anatomical features were dropped in spring

2003 so as to not offend guests. Presumably, the potentially offended don't speak French ("Regardez, les montagnes ressemblent a des grands tetons!").

The best part of this powder paradise is you won't have to share it with the masses, because this resort is grandly isolated. Grand Targhee is in Wyoming, but the only way to get here is through Idaho. Its huge bowls of snow are on the western slope of the Tetons, which hug the border between the two states. Targhee usually gets double their famous neighbor Jackson Hole's snowfall. And with days where there are maybe 800 people on the mountain, and two-plus feet of powder, it's worth every dime.

No ski area is perfect for everyone, though. If you go stir-crazy without a variety of restaurants and other things to do, we suggest you stay in Jackson and spend one day of your vacation here. But if you'd like to completely unwind, ski during the day, read a good book at night and head home new and invigorated, this is the perfect place.

Mountain layout

◆◆ **Expert:** Grand Targhee does not have much for experts, but that doesn't necessarily mean you'll be bored here, especially if you hit it after a big dump when the entire mountain becomes one big powder puff. Experienced powderhounds will want to opt for snowcat skiing on Peaked Mountain. Ten skiers per snowcat, with two guides, head out to enjoy this snowy playground. The longest run is 3.2 miles and covers slightly more than 2,800 vertical.

If you can't afford the cat, don't stress over it. Head for the treed chutes off Rock Garden, which are short but loads of fun. If—and only if—there's no snowcat running, you can hike above the Sacajawea lift and access some gnarly unnamed cliffs that drop you off into the ever-so-long Teton Vista Traverse. Or ask a local where to find Parking Lot Rocks and Toilet Bowl. You can follow the signs to Mary's no-longer-mentioned-anatomical-feature too. The resort provides excellent backcountry access and since most expert terrain here includes cliffs, but not many steeps and chutes to speak of, many experts choose to hike for the goods.

◆ **Advanced:** Fred's best advanced shots are found skiers' right off Rock Garden in a series of treed chutes called The Good, The Bad, The Ugly and The East Woods, all leading into Chief Joseph Bowl. To skiers' left, Instructors Chute and Patrol Chute are rewarding, but require a long green-rated runout on Teton Vista Traverse. For fast groovin'-on-groomed, try The Face to Ladies Waist.

The Sacajawea lift takes you to 500 acres of glades, bowls and a few groomed runs on Peaked Mountain. Most terrain here is intermediate-rated, but the groomed runs Northern Lights and Shadow Woman (both rated blue/black) present some nice pitches. The secret here is to pass through the gates along Dreamweaver to skiers' right and pick a line in the steeps through the trees that links to Powder Reserve Traverse and back to the main base. Best for advanced: Go just beyond the last gate to a line called Das Boot—it's not *that* steep. Some fun is also found in the glades to skiers' right of the chair.

■ **Intermediate:** Fred's Mountain offers boundary-to-boundary skiing and riding. On snowy days, which come often, its blue runs and the trees between them are perfect pitches for pillows of powder. Chief Joseph Bowl, Blackfoot Bowl and the runs under Dreamcatcher Chair are, well, dreamy. On non-powder days, you can fly on the screaming groomers. Since the locals usually show up only when there's freshies, you'll have unbroken corduroy to yourself all day. If you want to try going off-piste, leftovers that have softened in the sun are fun on fat skis. The gladed terrain on neighboring Peaked Mountain was snatched from the cat-skiing area, corralled in-bounds and designated for intermediates. You can do laps here since this secluded patch of paradise boasts its own lift, Sacajawea.

●● **Beginner** ● **First-timer:** The completely separate beginner area makes Targhee a recommended learning resort. While the beginner terrain appears limited as you look at the trail map, the trails have glades and fun themes, plus rollers and wide-open cruisers. They offer surprising variety that can keep children and adult beginners both challenged and occupied until their skills increase. Conveniently located near the ski school office, the area is served by the Shoshone quad lift and, for first-timers, a moving carpet. The only downside for beginners is that the rest of the mountain has just one green-circle trail, the very long Teton Vista Traverse. Upper-level beginners can give it a try from the top of the Dreamcatcher quad, but be prepared for some narrow turns and fast skiers blowing by as they merge from other trails and make their way to the base.

Ride Guide: The traverse from Peaked Mountain to the main area may cause problems for riders who aren't skilled in carrying speed. Just stay aware. For first-time snowboarders, Grand Targhee is one of the best places to learn. Where else can you learn how to ride slamming into a pillow of powder rather than a hard-packed slope? The moving carpet that takes you up the hill in the learning area is much easier for snowboarders to use than rope tows or surface lifts too.

Parks and pipes

"Trick Town" terrain park—geared towards intermediates and advanced-intermediates—has 15 features, including eight rails, and has been a big hit with riders and freeskiers on those days when they aren't out chasing fresh tracks. The park is near the base area, on Big Scout just to the left of the Dreamcatcher quad, and is served by the Shoshone quad. The "North Pole Park" is perfectly suited for youngsters, beginners, low-intermediates and families. It's in the "Fun Zone," also off the Shoshone quad. The resort does not have a halfpipe (unless you count the natural halfpipe under Dreamcatcher lift—it's called Ladies Waist).

Cross-country and snowshoeing (visit xcskiresorts.com for more details)

Grand Targhee Nordic Center (800-827-4433; 353-2300) has 15 km of track groomed for touring and skating. The trails wind through varied terrain, offering beautiful vistas of the Greater Yellowstone area as well as meadows and aspen glades. The majority of trails are in the Ricks Basin area to the north of the base area, but the system also includes a beginner track called Hamster Loop. The sandwich board at the lift-ticket kiosk lists the grooming report for the Nordic area.

Grand Targhee has an unusual set-up: Rather than taking care of everything in a Nordic center, you get your rental equipment in the main lodge's rental center, then buy your trail pass and lessons at the Snowsports School building. The ski school teaches telemarking as well as touring and skating techniques.

Snowshoe in the Caribou-Targhee National Forest with Resort Naturalist Andy Steele and learn about winter ecology, animal tracks and native vegetation. He tells stories about the wilderness that only 30 years in the Forest Service could provide. Tours start at 10:30 a.m. and 2:30 p.m., Thursday through Sunday. Each two-hour session has a three-person minimum. This tour is free, but all tips go to support a non-profit wilderness organization. Andy's log cabin is right at the ski area base, where you can find him most days. No reservations are necessary, but it would be courteous to let him know when you'd like to trek with him. Snowshoe rentals are available; wear your own boots.

Lessons (06/07 prices)

Many instructors have been with the Ski Training Center since its first season in 1969, so you're in good hands.

Group lessons: $48 for adults, at 10 a.m. and 1 p.m.

First-timer package: Two-hour lesson with beginner lift ticket and rentals costs $99.

Private lessons: $80 for one hour, $130 for two hours, $180 for three hours, $280 for all day ($25 for each additional person).

Special programs: In-bounds Adventure for a tour of the mountain's hidden stashes and some coaching too. Cost: $40 per hour. The resort has several special clinics such as Extreme Skiing, Women Ski The Tetons, snowboarding and telemark. Call for details and prices.

KidStuff (06/07 prices)

Child care: Ages 2 months to 5 years. Kids 2 months to 2 years cost $51 per day, $39 per half day. Ages 3 to 5 cost $46 per day, $34 per half day. The program includes two snacks and lunch for the full day; just a snack for a half day. Packages are available with one-hour private or group ski lessons. The kids' clubhouse is near the beginner skiing terrain and moving carpet lift. It has a homey, log-cabin feel with separate rooms for quiet movie watching and active playtime. Reservations required; call (800) 827-4433. Babysitting services are available outside of regular day care; ask at the main lodge front desk.

Children's lessons: Ski programs for ages 4–5 cost $95 for a full day with lessons, lifts, lunch and day-care activities; $59 for a half day. Ages 6–16 cost $90 for a full day with lessons, lunch and lift ticket; $45 for a half day. Snowboarding lessons begin at age 8.

Lift tickets (06/07 prices)

	Adult	Junior (6-14)
One day	$57	$35
Three days	$165 ($55/day)	$99 ($33/day)
Five days	$270 ($54/day)	$160 ($32/day)

Who skis free: Ages 5 and younger.

Who skis at a discount: Ages 62 and older pay $36 for one day. Those who ski more than one day at Grand Targhee probably are staying here too. In those cases Targhee's lodging-lift packages are the most economical and practical. On all Targhee lodging packages, children ages 14 and younger stay and ski free, one child per paying adult.

Note: A full day of snowcat skiing, including lunch, snacks and beverages served in a Snowcat Skiing souvenir mug, costs $299; a half day is $225. Here's a great deal: Book a three-day or longer package stay from opening (mid-November) through Dec. 24, 2006, and get a free day of snowcat skiing; on a seven-day package, you'll get two days on the cat free.

Accommodations

The small village sleeps about 450 people at **two hotel-type lodges and a 32-unit, multistory condo building.** All are within an easy walk to lifts and base facilities. Most units come packaged with lift tickets, but you can rent rooms and condos without buying lift tickets (though frankly, we have no idea why you'd want to). Try to stay at Targhee Lodge, Teewinot Lodge or the Sioux Lodge Apartments. Nightly rates per room at the lodges run $69 to $212; at the condos $79 to $494. The absolute best deal is Teewinot Lodge, where Sunday through Thursday it costs as low as $74 per night all season (holidays excluded). Kids 14 and younger are always free on lodging packages.

Packages that include ski tickets and two group lessons are offered for seven nights and six days, five nights and four days, and three nights and three days. Value Season brings significant savings. If you book a package from opening day to mid-December, not only will you save on your lodging, tickets and lessons, you'll also get the free snowcat skiing described in the *Lift Ticket* section (conditions permitting).

Dining

There's not much variety in this small village, but there's a lot of quality. **Targhee Steakhouse** ($$–$$$) is Targhee's finest restaurant, with entrees such as rack of lamb, whiskey chicken, shrimp scampi and poached salmon. It also serves breakfast and lunch. **Snorkel's** ($) is the spot for gourmet pizza and pasta for the family. Breakfast here features sinful pastries and espressos. **Wild Bill's Grille** ($) has breakfast, pizza, a soup and salad bar, sandwiches and Mexican food. The **Trap Bar** ($) serves a fine Idaho potato with all the trimmings, basic grilled sandwiches, burgers and chicken, plus apres-ski snacks. **Dinner sleigh rides** cost $35 for adults and $15 for kids (14 and younger).

Apres-ski/nightlife/other activities

This is not Targhee's strong point, but you'll be too tired after a powder day to really care. **Snorkel's** has apres-ski with varietal wines by the glass, microbrew beers and upscale appetizers in a relaxed atmosphere. The **Trap Bar** is livelier, with live music, plus great apres-ski snacks like the spilling-over nachos basket. Don't miss their specialty Targhatini, made with local huckleberries and local vodka in a trendy sugared glass—sweet but refreshing.

Outdoor activities include a **tubing park** and a free **ice skating rink** (rental skates are available). For some extra excitement, grab a pair of goggles and **mush a dogsled** through an hour-and-a-half backcountry trip that includes a trail snack and beverage. Or you can take a **sleigh ride** or go **snowmobiling**. You'll also find a **heated swimming pool** and **hot tubs.**

Dreamchasers Spa (353-2300 ext. 1358) is a cozy, three-treatment-room spa where you can indulge in massages, herbal and mud wraps, baths, a sauna and aromatherapy.

Shopping in this small village includes a smart boutique, a general store, a hard-goods shop, snowboard shop, rental and ski repair shop, and a ski clothing shop. Be sure to visit A Touch of the Tetons, a boutique that showcases a large selection of locally made jewelry .

Getting there and getting around

By air: Targhee is served by airports in Jackson, Wyo., and Idaho Falls, Idaho. Resort shuttles pick up guests by reservation. There's non-stop daily service from Salt Lake City, Denver, Chicago, Minneapolis and Houston, plus weekend non-stop service from Atlanta and Dallas. You can rent cars at either airport.

By car: Targhee is just inside the Wyoming border on the west side of the Tetons, accessible only from Idaho. Be forewarned: Travel at primetime and you're in a parade of bumper-to-bumper traffic, both up and down the mountain.

By bus: The Targhee Express bus picks up in Jackson and at Teton Village. It's $63 for round trip and full-day lift pass; call 733-3135.

Getting around: Don't rent a car—there's nowhere to drive.

Dining: $$$$-Entrees $30+; $$$-$20-$30; $$-$10-$20; $-less than $10.
Accommodations: (double room) $$$$-$200+; $$$-$141-$200; $$-$81-$140; $-$80 and less.

Jackson Hole
Wyoming

Summit elevation: 10,450 feet
Vertical drop: 4,139 feet
Base elevation: 6,311 feet

Address: P.O. Box 290
Teton Village, WY 83025
Area code: 307
Ski area phone: 733-2292
Toll-free snow report: (888) 333-7766
Toll-free reservations: (800) 443-6931
Fax: 733-2660
E-mail: info@jacksonhole.com
Internet: www.jacksonhole.com (resort)
www.jacksonholetraveler.com (region)
Expert:★★★★★
Advanced:★★★★★
Intermediate:★★★★
Beginner:★★
First-timer:★★★★

Number and types of lifts: 12–1 aerial tram,
1 eight-person gondola, 2 high-speed quads, 4
quads, 2 triples, 1 double, 1 moving carpet
Skiable acreage: 2,700 acres
Snowmaking: 11 percent
Uphill capacity: 12,000+ per hour
Parks & pipes: 1 park, 2 pipes
Bed base: 10,000 in valley, 3,200 at base
Nearest lodging: Slopeside
Resort child care: Yes, 6 months and older
Adult ticket, per day: $73 (06/07 prices)

Dining:★★★★
Apres-ski/nightlife:★★★
Other activities:★★★★

If you're like many skiers and riders arriving in Jackson Hole, your very bumpy plane landing is just a precursor to the adventure waiting for you on the mountain. Might as well get used to that feeling of slight jitters, because it'll probably be with you for much of your stay.

True, Jackson Hole isn't all about taking routes that scare the pants off you, but you'll get the most out of the two mountain peaks if you go a bit beyond your comfort zone.

Rendezvous Mountain has some of the steepest in-bounds terrain around, with much of it swathed in well-deserved designations as black- or double-black-diamond runs. Adjacent Apres Vous Mountain and the lower elevations of Rendezvous are gentler, with fabulous intermediate slopes and a top-notch learning area. And wherever you look, the views are astonishing. Jagged peaks soar out of a narrow flat plain that's spliced by the winding Snake River. It is with an inspiring sense of wonder that you realize Jackson and its surrounding wilderness are part of the 1.7-million-acre Bridger-Teton National Forest and adjacent to Grand Teton National Park.

Teton Village, at the base of the mountain, has grown up to be a respectable home base for your vacation. The village offers everything you need, including a grocery and liquor store. Lodging ranges from what must be the cheapest slopeside lodging in the states, at Hostel X, to several posh mountain retreats and a multitude of condos. Add restaurants serving everything from burgers to sushi to wild game, and a smattering of nightlife, and you could easily spend your vacation right here.

But wait. No trip to Jackson Hole is complete without visiting the town of Jackson, 12 miles down the road. The impression here of the Western frontier is authentic—Jackson is still as remote and wild as it ever was and those cowboys ambling down the street are local ranchers and ranch hands (although a few tourists think they can fake it, you'll notice they stick out like sore thumbs). The original town of Jackson was home to mercantile stores, cafes, saloons, hotels, bordellos, and even a jail. Today, many of those buildings remain, but now house gourmet restaurants, rowdy bars, Victorian inns, upscale boutiques, art galleries and coffeehouses. And all this revolves around one of the prettiest town squares anywhere, defined by elk antler gateway arches.

Women have always made a big impact on Jackson and in 1920, the town elected one of the first all-women town councils in the U.S., which The New York Times dubbed the "petticoat government." Now many of Jackson's women dominate mountain sports, ripping lines down big mountains and climbing distant peaks, carrying on the tradition of women who can do anything just as well as, or better than, a man. So, when you're riding up the lift, look closely—many of those hot skiers and riders are women, and often they are proudly wearing feminine colors to show they're not afraid to have someone say, "Hey, that's a girl!" You betcha, it is!

News for 2006/07: the old aerial tram has just been retired but 100% of the mountain is still accessible, thanks in part to the new East Ridge Chair rising from the top of Sublette to just below Corbet's Cabin on the summit. Capacity to the base of the upper mountain has been increased by adding 18 more cabins to the Bridger Gondola. Sixteen more chairs have been added to the Thunder Chair.

Another new addition this season is the Bridger Restaurant, due to open at Christmas at the top of the Bridger Gondola (elevation: 9,095 feet). Among its various eateries is the Couloir, a 100-seat, waiter-service restaurant serving lunch and, as of mid-January, dinner (see dining section).

Mountain layout

No mistake about it. Jackson Hole is not for the faint of heart or the weak of quads. It's steep, often deep and the trees are tight. Apres Vous Mountain is best known for its groomed intermediate cruisers as well as the black Saratoga Bowl. Rendezvous Mountain has a handful of groomed runs; most of the blues here would be blacks anywhere else. As you ride the chairs or tram, you'll see skiers and riders hucking themselves off cliffs, snaking lines through seemingly impenetrable trees and treating monstrous moguls as mere debris in the trail.

♦♦**Expert** ♦**Advanced:** If you're looking for steep (and often deep), Jackson is your mountain. Fully half of the resort's 2,700 acres is marked with one or two black diamonds, and you can now reach 3,000-plus backcountry acres from on-mountain access gates. Board the big red tram for the 12-minute trip to the top of Rendezvous Mountain. The tram unlocks the soul of Jackson, so this will set you up for the rest of the day. From the top, you have two choices. If you have something to prove, head down the ridge to the infamous Corbet's Couloir, a narrow, rocky chute that requires a 10- to 20-foot airborne entry. Or take the "easier" way down, Rendezvous Bowl.

Below Rendezvous, drop into Cheyenne Bowl. If it hasn't snowed in a couple of days, try the bumps and trees on the north side of the bowl near Bivouac. Then yo-yo on the Sublette Quad until you've made lines down the Alta Chutes—some of the steepest marked terrain at Jackson—and the Expert Chutes below Tensleep Bowl. Don't miss Paint Brush into the unmarked Toilet Bowl, or the narrow, stump- and rock-filled Tower Three Chute. For an out-of-bounds experience (while remaining in-bounds), a 15- to 20-minute hike takes you to the Headwall. The Crags above the Casper Lift area offers 200 acres of bowls, chutes and trees to explore. The hike is 25–35 minutes.

If it's a powder day, don't miss the Hobacks—accessed off the Rendezvous Trail. But don't head here if it hasn't snowed in a while—unless, of course, you like crusty crud. Saratoga Bowl, off Apres Vous Mountain, is an often-overlooked playground of trees and gullies. For the ultimate in gullies, try your new-school moves in Dick's Ditch, a natural halfpipe.

■ **Intermediate:** Concentrate on the runs skier's left of the tram, using the gondola and the Apres Vous Quad to access the wide-open groomers like Gros Ventre, Werner and Moran. The shorter runs down Casper Bowl—like Sleeping Indian and Wide Open—provide plenty of opportunities to try your luck in the trees.

Follow the solid blue lines for groomed terrain and the broken blue lines for ungroomed powder or bumps. As long as you're willing to ski ungroomed stuff, you'll run out of gas before you run out of terrain. Complimentary orientation tours for intermediate-level skiers depart the Mountain Host building daily at 9:30 a.m.

●● **Beginner:** Jackson Hole's easiest terrain is served by two dedicated lifts, the Eagle's Rest double and the Teewinot Quad. The green-rated runs are appropriately gentle, and some present interesting meanders among the trees. Kids will love the informal single-tracks that squiggle into the woods. But the amount of beginner runs is limited, advanced-beginners will grow bored rather quickly, and it's a big step from those gently undulating slopes to Jackson Hole's blues. Even the wide, groomed slopes of Apres Vous and Casper Bowl have a much steeper pitch than blues at other resorts and can be intimidating for advanced-beginners. The Sweetwater triple chair makes it easy to access the Casper Bowl area of lower-intermediate terrain when you think you're ready. But if you're leaning toward the advanced-beginner category, our advice is to take a lesson or two. The resort has a program just for you (*see Lessons*)

● **First-timer:** Jackson Hole's excellent learning terrain surprises most people. At the base of Apres Vous Mountain, along the Eagle's Rest trail, stands a fenced-in area that's served by a moving carpet. Faster skiers can't get in, so those just learning won't get nervous. The transition to the adjacent green runs is made easy by dedicated beginner lifts. Parents should take note that Jackson Hole's "Rough Riders" kids' offering combines day care and children's instruction in one of the most innovative programs for young first-timers we have seen.

Ride Guide: The mountain is swathed in traverses that allow a snowboarder with any momentum an easy way down. And riders have the advantage over skiers when it comes to hoofing up to the hike-to terrain. That said, in Saratoga Bowl veer rider's right as you head down or you'll have an awful traverse, perhaps even a hike, out.

Parks and pipes

Apres Vous on it's own could hold itself as a very strong freeriding mountain, which is why you'll find the superpipe here, along with various hits and kickers built by the locals. We don't recommend building your own kickers; if you're busted, they'll pull your ticket. Luckily there are natural booters and kickers all over the place; try following some local riders around for the inside line. And don't miss Upper Dick's Ditch, where you'll find a natural quarterpipe and halfpipe.

The superpipe now has a surface lift, so it's easy to get back to the top. The terrain park, served by the Apres Vous Quad, is next to the superpipe and has 10 components including jumps, rails, bumps and a small quarterpipe. Just like Jackson Hole's natural terrain, the park features are intended for those with some experience and are not really designed for first-timers. Take care and pay attention to the signs. There is a dedicated park and pipe staff always on hand to give advice, so make sure to check out conditions with them before you launch any air.

Cross-country and snowshoeing (visit xcskiresorts.com for more details)

Nordic skiers can strike out for marked trails in **Grand Teton or Yellowstone National Parks,** or try one of the three touring centers in the valley.

The **Saddlehorn Activities Center** (800-443-6139; 739-2629), also called the Jackson Hole Nordic Center, has 17 km. of groomed track in Teton Village, next to the Snake River Lodge. The majority of trails are on the North Meadow, mostly flat with hills on the outer edge. The South Meadow has 7 km. of trails where dogs are permitted. The center also offers telemark lessons, snowshoe rentals and dogsled rides.

Teton Pines Country Club (733-1005) has 14 km. of groomed skating and classic lanes on a gentle golf course with more ups and downs than you'd expect. The **town of Jackson** grooms about 30 km. each week in Game Creek Canyon, Cache Creek Canyon and the Snake River Dike. Call 739-6789 for the current grooming conditions. Also, **Grand Teton National Park** grooms a 32-km. trail between the Bradley-Taggart Lakes parking area and the Signal Mountain parking area once a week, usually on Thursdays.

The **Hole Hiking Experience** (690-4453) provides naturalist- or wildlife-biologist-guided snowshoe tours in the Bridger-Teton National Forest or Grand Teton National Park.

Lessons (05/06)

The ski/snowboard school is not only the place to get instruction, it's also the place to engage a knowledgeable mountain guide. Jackson Hole's nooks and crannies can best be enjoyed with someone who knows them. Make reservations for ski school programs including mountain guides by calling 739-2610 or (800) 450-0477.

Group lessons: Full-day lessons cost $80 for beginners and $90 for intermediates. Jackson Hole has a special class, "Turn it Up," for those bored by the beginner trails but intimidated by the blues, for $90. Jackson Hole offers packages for all these classes that include lift tickets and rentals.

First-timer package: Jackson Hole's Learn To Turn program is $85 and includes a guarantee that learners will be able to control speed and make turns after one day of lessons. Beginners can repeat these lessons for free until they "get it." For snowboarders, the resort offers Burton's innovative Learn-To-Ride program for $95.

Private lessons: Three morning hours cost $345 and three afternoon hours are $295 for up to five skiers. Early "Tram Privates" start at 8:30 a.m. with four hours costing $415; a full day is $520 (the same as hiring a backcountry guide).

Special programs: There are many, such as instruction for the disabled (adaptive lessons questions are answered via a special adaptive hotline during the season), Steep & Deep ($820, four days, separate skiing, snowboarding and tele sessions), Backcountry Camp ($560, three-day program), and women ski and women snowboard programs ($820, four days). These multi-day camps include coaching, lifts, video, some meals and more.

Racing: There's a NASTAR course off the Casper Bowl Triple Chair. The resort offers race-training clinics.

KidStuff (05/06 prices)

Child care: The Kids Ranch Wranglers group is for ages 6 months to 2 years. Cost is $110 for a full day. The flexible program also has two half-day options, one in the morning from 8:30 a.m. through 12:30 p.m. for $95; the other, 12:30 p.m. through 4:30 p.m., for $85. Toddlers get lunch and a snack; parents must provide food for infants. Reservations (307-739-2691) and a copy of your child's immunization records are required. Kids Ranch children's programs are based at the Cody House, just above the gondola base.

Other options: For babysitting at your hotel or condo, call Babysitting Service of Jackson Hole (800-253-9650; 307-733-0685) or Childcare Services (307-733-5178).

Children's lessons: Rough Riders is for ages 3–6 (must be toilet-trained) and includes lift tickets and rentals. A full day with lunch is $125; half day in the afternoon is $95. Little Rippers is a semi-private snowboard lesson for ages 5–6 and costs $190 for a full day (lift, lesson, rentals and lunch); $115 for a half day in the afternoon.

Explorers (ages 7–14) is $145 for full day with lift ticket, rentals and lunch; $110 for a half-day afternoon lesson. Team Extreme (ages 12–17) is a full-day program for advanced skiers and riders offered at certain times of the year. It includes lift ticket, rentals and lunch for $155.

Special activities: Kids Night Out is a supervised dinner followed by indoor games and movies. Call for times and cost; reservations required.

Lift tickets (05/06 prices)

	Adult	Young Adult (15-21)	Child (6-14)
One day	$70	$56	$35
Three days	$201 ($67/day)	$162 ($54/day)	$101 ($34/day)
Five days	$330 ($66/day)	$265 ($53/day)	$165 ($33/day)

Who skis free: Children 5 and younger.

Who skis at a discount: Ages 65 and older pay children's prices. Beginners pay a minimal ticket fee for the beginner lifts.

Notes: A photo ID is required to obtain young adult and senior rates. Christmas prices are higher; early-season prices are lower.

Accommodations

Choose from three locations: Teton Village at the base of the slopes; the town of Jackson, with lots of eating, shopping and partying but 12 miles from skiing; or hotels, condos and some fine resorts between the two. Bus transportation between Jackson and the ski area is readily available.

We haven't listed all of the available lodging, so call **Jackson Hole Central Reservations** (800-443-6931) for more information. This agency can book your entire trip.

Many hotels here have combined "Jackson Hole" with "Inn," "Lodge" or "Hotel." Another popular name is "Teton." If you book one, pay attention to the exact name and the location, or your ground transportation could easily drop you and your luggage in the wrong place.

Teton Village

The following properties are all within steps of the slopes and each other, so the choice is on facilities or price rather than location. Most of these properties have ski packages.

The luxurious, ski-in/ski-out **Four Seasons Resort Jackson Hole** (800-295-5281; 734-5040; $$$$) has rooms and suites with natural wood, stone and local art that reflect the region's Western and Native American influences. The hotel has an outdoor heated pool, three outdoor hot-spring-style hot tubs, a restaurant (see *Dining*), two lounges, shops and a full-service spa. Children younger than 18 stay free if they're in the same room with parents.

Snake River Lodge & Spa (800-445-4655; $$$-$$$$), just steps from the tram and gondola, has double rooms to three-bedroom suites. There's also an excellent restaurant (see *Dining*) and comfy lobby lounge. See *Other Activities* for information about its spa.

Teton Mountain Lodge (800-801-6615; 734-7111; $$$$) is appointed in the classic Western style featuring stone fireplaces, kitchens and jetted tubs. High-end amenities include indoor/outdoor pools, fitness facilities and spa, and a decent restaurant (see *Dining*).

The Bavarian-style **Alpenhof Lodge** (800-732-3244; 733-3242; $$–$$$$) is the closest lodging to the lifts and a classic in Teton Village. It has an outstanding dining room (see *Dining*). The casual Bistro, open for lunch and dinner, is also popular for apres-ski.

The Best Western Inn at Jackson Hole (800-842-7666; 733-2311; $$–$$$$) is about 100 yards from the tram. Rooms are spacious, and many have kitchenettes, fireplaces and/or lofts. Two drawbacks: Soundproofing between rooms is minimal and exterior corridors mean that every time you leave your room, you step outside.

Village Center Inn (800-443-8613; 733-3990; $$), next to the tram, has 16 one- and two-bedroom units, some with lofts. **Crystal Springs Lodge** (800-443-8613; $$$) is a newly remodeled luxury condo property in Teton Village just 50 yards from the aerial tram.

The Hostel X (733-3415; $) is family-owned and has some of the most inexpensive slopeside lodging in the United States. Rooms are spartan, but have private baths and maid service. Amenities include ping pong and pool tables, game area and laundry facilities.

Condominiums and **private homes** are available through Jackson Hole Resort Lodging (800-443-8613) and Jackson Hole Central Reservations (800-443-6931; 733-4005). Rates range from $115–$850 per night.

Jackson

Many of these accommodations also offer ski packages. All listed here are within a block or two of the public bus service to Teton Village unless noted.

One of the best is the **Wort Hotel** (800-322-2727; 733-2190; $$$–$$$$), an 1880s-style hotel that blends elegance with Wild West. It's home to the Silver Dollar Bar (see *Apres-ski/nightlife*).

Snow King Resort (800-522-5464; 733-5200; $$–$$$) is a find for families. The full-service hotel and condominiums are slopeside to the Snow King ski area (see *Nearby resorts* at the end of this chapter). Relax in the lounge while the kids burn excess energy night skiing, snow tubing, skating on the indoor ice rink, splashing in the outdoor heated pool or hanging in the arcade. Babysitting is available. It's an easy walk to Town Square. **Love Ridge Resort Lodges** (800-533-7669; 733-5200; $$$) are the newest luxury condos at Snow King, with all the amenities you'd expect in a high-end property plus those of the nearby hotel. Ask about "Ski 3" packages that allow you to ski at Snow King, Jackson Hole and Grand Targhee.

The Quality Inn 49er Inn and Suites (733-7550; $$–$$$) is a three-building complex at the edge of town and a stone's throw from an express bus stop. Suites are spacious and feature fireplaces, large bathrooms, excellent fitness facilities and a hot tub. At the **Parkway Inn** (733-3143; $$-$$$) bed & breakfast, the decor is decidedly Old World Victorian.

Teddy bears slumber upon fluffy white duvets at the **Rusty Parrot Lodge and Spa** (800-458-2004; 733-2000; $$$$), a classy, in-town B&B with a renowned restaurant (see *Dining*) and spa (see *Other Activities*). Rates include a full breakfast and all-day refreshments served fireside. The bus to Jackson Hole stops outside the front door (passes are provided).

At **The Grand Victorian Lodge** (800-584-0532; 739-2294; $$–$$$), you get breakfast in bed so you can laze away the morning or gulp it down while you rush to get ready for a powder day. The Victorian decor and down comforters make for inviting rooms.

Dining: $$$$-Entrees $30+; $$$-$20-$30; $$-$10-$20; $-less than $10.
Accommodations: (double room) $$$$-$200+; $$$-$141-$200; $$-$81-$140; $-$80 and less.

The **Bunkhouse Hostel** (733-3668; $), a no-frills dorm in the basement of a motel, comprises one 25-bed room, a separate room with couches for lounging and a kitchen area with microwave and refrigerators. There are separate men's and women's lavatories, and a laundry is available. The rate is $25 per night, first-come/first-served.

Between downtown and the ski area

The **Red Lion Wyoming Inn of Jackson** (800-844-0035; 734-0035; $$–$$$$) and **The Best Western Lodge at Jackson Hole** (800-458-3866; 739-9703 $–$$$) are across the street from one another on Broadway (Hwy. 89). Red Lion Wyoming Inn is decorated with antique reproduction furniture, but has no pool or hot tub, though some rooms have jetted tubs. It serves a continental breakfast. The Best Western Lodge at Jackson Hole (there also is a Jackson Hole Lodge, which is quite different) is a delight for children with carved, painted bears and raccoons that hang from poles and peek from behind benches. It has a swimming pool and hot tub. The Gun Barrel Steak House is next door.

Spring Creek Ranch (800-443-6139; 733-8833; $$$–$$$$) is distinguished by jaw-dropping views, primo service, one of the area's best restaurants (see *Dining*) and a secluded location atop the East Gros Ventre butte. Choose from hotel rooms, condos and luxurious executive homes. The decor is Western elegance. Despite the seclusion and amenities, it's not stuffy or pretentious. Also on site are a spa (see *Other Activities*), Nordic center and stables. Free airport, town and ski shuttles provided. Hotel rates include breakfast.

Next door is the ultra-exclusive **Amangani** (877-734-7666; 734-7333; $$$$). If you've got mega bucks, stay here; it has everything you could imagine wanting and then some, but if you have to ask, fuggedabowdit.

On Teton Village Road a few miles from the ski area and town is **Teton Pines Resort** (800-238-2223; 733-1005; $$$–$$$$).

The **Jackson Hole Racquet Club** (800-443-8613; $$–$$$$) is a relatively inexpensive condo cluster. It's just 4 miles to Teton Village and has a grocery store on the premises as well as a restaurant, bar and liquor store. The resort runs a free shuttle to the mountain.

Just below Teton Village is the log-cabin-style **Wildflower Inn Bed & Breakfast** (733-4710; $$–$$$$), with fireplaces, a shared hot tub and fitness area, and fabulous breakfasts. One of the top romantic inns in the nation, it's just five minutes from the ski area.

Dining

We'll start with the selection at the ski area, and work our way toward town. If you're staying in Teton Village, be sure to spend at least one evening in town, if only to see the lighted elk-horn arches in the town square.

Teton Village

Alpenrose at the Alpenhof Hotel (733-3462; $$$-$$$$) is a quiet, genteel place. You might begin with seared St. Jacques scallops and move onto roasted baby pheasant or walleye with French cockles. **Dietrich's Bar & Bistro** (733-3242; $$), also at the Alpenhof, brings the price down a notch and specializes in Alpine favorites such as fondues, bratwurst, sauerbraten and wienerschnitzel. They also serve entrees such as wild game loaf, fish and chips, and lamb cassoulet in a casual setting.

At **GameFish** (732-6040; $$$) in the Snake River Lodge and Spa, the emphasis is on native game and fish, with traditional and creative renditions of each. A skilled wait staff, good wine list and exquisite desserts—don't miss the chocolate souffle—make it a comfortable place to while away a leisurely meal.

Cascade Grill House & Spirits (732-6932; $$$-$$$$), with a menu of "new Western" cuisine and an atmosphere to match, is in the Teton Mountain Lodge. If you go, leave your pacemaker at home. A red-blooded menu is big on grilled meats and heart-stopper desserts like Mile High Brownie Sundae and Molten Chocolate Volcano Cake.

The Best Western Inn at Jackson Hole has two noteworthy restaurants. **Masa Sushi** (733-2962; $-$$) is a tiny restaurant that serves stunning sushi; reservations are essential. **Vertical** (734-2375; $$-$$$) has classic black-&-white photos of movie stars on its walls, an enormous glass wine storage rack climbing 20 feet of vertical behind the bar, and a very modern vibe with its chrome, aluminum and glass interior. Be chic and nibble on a selection from the cheese menu while sipping on a glass of wine, or be sated and try the succulent seafood pasta with a pineapple jalapeño margarita. Its menu changes nightly.

The Four Seasons Resort has a restaurant and two lounges. The **Westbank Grill** (734-5040; $$-$$$) focuses on flavors and ingredients of the American West. The **Lobby Lounge** and **The Peak** both serve light meals that are quite affordable for lunchtime skiers.

The very funky **Mangy Moose** (733-4913; $-$$) is a three-fold find. Head downstairs to The Rocky Mountain Oyster for a bargain breakfast or lunch; to the restaurant for steaks, chicken, game, fish and a salad bar; and to the Saloon for pizza, burgers and apres-ski.

For a truly unique dinner experience, make reservations well in advance for the **Solitude Cabin Dinner Sleighrides** (739-2603; $$$). The price ($54.95 adults; $33.95 children younger than 10) includes a sleigh ride to the cabin and a four-course meal; choose from roast prime rib or broiled salmon filet. Live musical entertainment adds to the fun. Drinks aren't part of the fixed price, but you can bring your own (as long as you can handle the $5 cork fee).

New for 06/07: **The Couloir**, part of the new Bridger Restaurant (located at the top of the Bridger Gondola at 9,095 feet) will be open for dinner from mid-January onwards. After dinner in the rustic-elegant Couloir you take a star-lit ride back to the valley in the Gondola.

You can grab a breakfast or lunch bagel in the **Bridger Center** locker area. For heartier quick morning eats, try the tramline burrito at **The Village Cafe**. Eat upstairs for fast service, or head down for a more leisurely meal and choices for the health conscious. You can get good food here for lunch. You'll find bagels, sandwiches and hot soup specials at **Bridger Bagels & Espresso** on the first level of Bridger Center. **Jackson Hole Sports** on the second level of Bridger Center is the place for coffee, espresso and Danish pastries.

Jackson

Soft lighting, a roaring fire, and an open kitchen accent the intimate **Wild Sage Restaurant** (744-0935; $$$) at the Rusty Parrot Lodge. Many locals consider it Jackson's finest restaurant. The setting is elegant yet unpretentious, the wine list is excellent and the service is professional. The pan-seared Alaskan halibut and the seared elk tenderloin are can't-miss choices.

Off Broadway Grille (733-9777; $$-$$$) features entrees such as lamb tenderloin with a Mediterranean black olive tapenade, Thai-steamed seafood with Asian flavors or sauteed sea scallops and leeks in a creamy tomato-saffron sauce. **The Blue Lion** (733-3912; $$-$$$), hidden away in a blue-clapboard house with several intimate dining rooms, is known for its roast rack of lamb, which we describe as cooked a la shake 'n' bake.

Locals all seem to love **Rendezvous Bistro** (739-1100; $-$$). The well-prepared home-style menu defies the moderate prices. Salads and sandwiches satisfy lighter appetites, while entrees, such as a mouth-watering free-range half chicken, confit of duck, rustic lamb stew and curry vegetables with wonton strips, satisfy those who've worked up an appetite. The atmosphere can be boisterous—its name is certainly fitting.

Another that earns accolades from locals is **Koshu** (733-5283; $$) where an Asian-inspired

Dining: $$$$-Entrees $30+; $$$-$20-$30; $$-$10-$20; $-less than $10.
Accommodations: (double room) $$$$-$200+; $$$-$141-$200; $$-$81-$140; $-$80 and less.

menu showcases such items as kumamoto oysters, ahi tartare, and Peking duck breast.

The small but sophisticated **Nikai** (734-6490; $-$$), two blocks north of Town Square, is where the younger, smarter crowd goes for sushi and Asian cuisine.

Try the **Cyprus Restaurant** (733-8220; $$–$$$$) a block off the main street with Mediterranean dishes like lamb and cous cous and a signature dish the locals call lobster mac & cheese. Belly dancers entertain guests every Friday night.

The **Cadillac Grille** and **Billy's Burgers** (733-3279; $$-$$$) right on the town square, with plenty of meat and game but also eclectic entrees like goat cheese ravioli. Billy's Burgers serves, well, burgers—best in town, say the locals. And if you just want a drink, it's 2-for-1 every night, 5-7 p.m.

For casual inexpensive dining, the local classic is **Bubba's** (733-2288; $-$$), with heaping plates of "bubbacued" ribs, chicken, beef and pork. Bubba's doesn't take reservations. Be prepared to wait, and while you do, send a member of your party to the liquor store—Bubba's is BYOB and they encourage you to bring your own bottles.

Another casual place is **Mountain High Pizza Pie** (733-3646, $) and they deliver when you can't quite get it together to go out. **Nani's Genuine Pasta House** (733-3888; $$), two blocks north of Broadway, and **Anthony's** (733-3717; $$), near the Wort Hotel, get raves from locals for authentic Italian regional cooking. For Mexican, head to **The Merry Piglets** (733-2966; $-$$); for Thai, it's **Thai Me Up** (733-0005; $-$$) a block from the town square.

The hearty-breakfast king is **Bubba's** ($). For tamer breakfast fare try **The Bunnery** (733-5474; $) with excellent omelets, whole-grain waffles and bakery items, and **Jedediah's Original House of Sourdough** (733-5671; $) for superb sourjack pancakes.

Between town and the ski area

Set high on a butte with a wall of windows framing the Tetons, the **Granary at Spring Creek** (733-8833; $$$-$$$$) lets you drink in the views along with your elk tenderloin or hazelnut-encrusted trout. Desert tones provide a neutral background for the top-notch food and views. You may want to take a sleigh ride before dinner (reservations are required). Come early on Fridays for the jazz happy hour. Note: This isn't a good choice for vegetarians.

Another top choice is **The Grille at Teton Pines** (733-1005; $$–$$$) at the Teton Pines Resort, with a beautiful dining room and extensive wine list. **Stiegler's** (733-1071; $$) has specialties from chef-owner Peter Stiegler's home in Austria.

For casual dining, try the **Calico Italian Restaurant & Bar** (733-2460; $$), halfway between Jackson and Teton Village at a bus stop on Village Road and very popular with the locals. If you're headed to Grand Targhee, rustic **Nora's Fish Creek Inn** in Wilson (733-8288; $$ for dinner) is a local favorite for any meal, especially breakfast.

For more ideas, pick up a copy of the *Jackson Hole Dining Guide* or browse through the rack of business-card-sized menus at your hotel.

Apres ski/nightlife

The Mangy Moose is by far the rowdiest spot in Teton Village for apres-ski and nightlife. It's also one of the best spots in all of skidom. Have fun testing both your endurance and your coordination twirling around on the small dance floor while trying not to bump into everyone crammed in around you. Big-name entertainers often provide an intimate concert here, so check the newspaper listings. **The Village Cafe** near the base of the tram is crowded with locals at the end of the day. **Cascade Grill House & Spirits** in the Teton Mountain Lodge is a local favorite and delivers great apres-ski atmosphere. **Dietrich's**

Bar & Bistro at the Alpenhof Lodge attracts a sedate group, as does the lobby bar in **Snake River Lodge**, where you can curl up in an oversized chair by the fire. **The Peak** in the Four Seasons is busy and a surprisingly good value—the perfect place to swap stories over table games and TVs broadcasting sporting-event coverage. Fine wine and cheeses from around the world set the tone for the ultra-modern setting at **Vertical**, in the Best Western Inn.

In town, **The Million Dollar Cowboy Bar** attracts tourists who love saddle bar stools and line-dancing to live country & western bands. Try it, corny as it sounds, it's a hoot. The crowd tends to be 40 and older. It's cash-only, so leave the credit card at home. **The Silver Dollar Bar**, at the Wort Hotel, is similar, with 2,032 uncirculated 1921 silver dollars embedded in the curving bar. It serves great buffalo burgers plus, on Sunday nights, all-you-can-eat pizza.

Cadillac Grille has the best happy hour in town—two-for-one drinks every night from 5-7 p.m. Try their "signature" cosmopolitan. At **Nikai,** the "in spot" for sushi lovers, a DJ turns Friday night into hip-hop night. The young set that likes to party hard heads to the **Log Cabin Saloon** to shoot pool, play foosball and darts, and drink heavily. Another hot spot is the **Rancher** where drafts are $1 and mixed drinks $2 during Tuesday night Town Meetings. **The Shady Lady Saloon** at the Snow King Resort has live entertainment several nights a week.

The local crowd heads to the **Snake River Brewing Co.** for award-winning, yet afford-able, hand-crafted lagers and ales as well as sandwiches, pastas and wood-fired pizza. **Koshu** is a tiny, laid-back wine bar.

Another local hangout is the **Stagecoach**, in Wilson. The busiest times are Thursdays for disco night (honest!) and on Sundays, when the legendary house band performs its mix of country & western, bluegrass and swing.

The Bull Moose Saloon (877-498-7993), 35 miles south of Jackson in Alpine, has mechanical bull riding every Wednesday, Friday and Saturday night. Ladies ride free; men pay $3 per ride, $10 for the whole night. The saloon also brings in exotic dancers about once a month, $10 admission.

 Other activities

To book most activities, call Jackson Hole Reservations at 739-3076.

Many guests make the time to visit nearby **Grand Teton** and **Yellowstone National Parks.** Several unusual activities center around Jackson's abun-dant wildlife. Plan to spend a half day at the **National Museum of Wildlife Art** (800-313-9553; 733-5771) combining a museum tour with lunch in the cafe and a sleigh ride onto the National Elk Refuge. The museum houses the nation's premier collection of fine wildlife artwork in varied media. Lunch is a treat. The semi-self-serve cafe, operated by Spring Creek Ranch, dishes delicious soups, salads, sandwiches and kids' favorites. The cafe overlooks the **National Elk Refuge** (733-9212), where 7,000 to 9,000 elk winter. You can take a one-hour horse-drawn sleigh ride, accompanied by a refuge biologist, out to the herd to view wildlife in its natural setting. Combination museum and sleigh-ride tickets are available. An outstanding educational tour is offered through **Wildlife Expeditions of Teton Science School** (733-2623). You ride with a biologist to help note the location and numbers of various birds and animals. Half-day, full-day and multiday tours, some into Yellowstone National Park, are offered. We spotted bison, elk, eagles, moose, deer, bighorn sheep and trumpeter swans. Everyone gets to use binoculars and a powerful spotting scope for up-close viewing.

Horse-drawn **dinner sleigh rides** are offered by Spring Creek Resort (733-8833) and Solitude Cabin (739-2603). Bar-T-Five (733-5386) operates the sleigh rides on the National Elk Refuge and also has a **winter show** with a barbecue dinner and "yarn-spinnin'. "

Dining: $$$$-Entrees $30+; $$$-$20-$30; $$-$10-$20; $-less than $10.
Accommodations: (double room) $$$$-$200+; $$$-$141-$200; $$-$81-$140; $-$80 and less.

The Jackson Hole Nordic Center (739-2629; 800-443-6139) has hour-long **dogsled tours.** Mush with Billy Snodgrass at Continental Divide Dogsled Adventures (800-531-6874), the main dogsled outfitter in the region.

The **Snow King Center** (800-522-5464; 733-5200) houses a regulation ice rink, open to the public, where the local hockey team plays regularly. The center also hosts regular concerts and shows by big-name entertainers. Check local papers for events.

Other activities include **guided snowmobile excursions**. Most outfitters, and there are many, provide transportation to and from your lodging. Llama Louie's Reservations (733-1617), conveniently in the Mangy Moose, arranges snowmobile trips without a charge.

High Mountain Heli-Skiing (733-3274) offers **helicopter skiing** on untracked powder in five mountain ranges surrounding Jackson Hole. These folks have been operating for more than 25 years. Rendezvous Ski and Snowboard Tours gives daily **backcountry tours** in Grand Teton Park, Teton Pass and other locations, while Snow King Mountain Guides operates trips off the back of Snow King and Teton pass for Nordic and alpine skiers.

The small, but full-service **Wilderness Adventure Spa at Spring Creek Ranch** (733-8833) is designed to incorporate feng shui principles of harmony and balance as well as to reflect Native American influences. Facilities include women's and men's steam rooms and a co-ed hot tub overlooking the mountains.

The full-service, five-story **Avanyu Spa** (800-445-4655; 732-6070) at the Snake River Lodge has a free-form indoor-outdoor heated pool with waterfall hot tub in addition to rain and Swiss showers, hot tub, sauna and steam room in the locker rooms. A spa menu is available.

In town, **The Body Sage Day Spa** (733-4455) at the Rusty Parrot Lodge offers traditional spa therapies including massage, facials and scrubs and exclusive treatments integrating local ingredients, such as rose petals.

Shopping is plentiful. You can easily while away an afternoon browsing the boutiques, factory outlets and art galleries in Jackson. As a general rule, you'll find the farther you get from Town Square, the less expensive the prices are. The covered wooden sidewalks encourage window shopping, even when it snows.

If you're a fan of classical music, the **Grand Teton Music Festival** (733-1128) stages a monthly concert series in Walk Festival Hall in Teton Village.

You can pick up culture, shopping, dining or vacation-planning guides at the Wyoming information center on the north edge of town, or call the Jackson Hole Chamber of Commerce (733-3316).

Getting there and getting around

By air: Four major carriers now serve Jackson Hole with jets: American, United, Northwest and Delta. There's non-stop daily service from Salt Lake City, Denver, Chicago, Dallas and Minneapolis, plus weekend non-stop service from Atlanta and Cincinnati. Check with the resort central reservations for air bargains. This is a small airport, surrounded by towering mountains, with pretty good chances of delayed flights. It may be a wise idea to build an extra day into your schedule heading in and out, especially if your travel requires several plane changes. And if weather grounds you, remember to ask about distressed traveler rates at local lodgings.

By car: Jackson is on Hwys. 89, 26 and 191 in western Wyoming. The town is 10 miles south of the airport, and Teton Village is 12 miles farther by Hwys. 89, 22 and 390. Driving, Jackson Hole is five hours from Salt Lake City and 10 hours from Denver.

To stem the tide of traffic into Teton Village, Jackson Hole has opened the Stillson Parking Lot, which offers free parking about 7 miles from the base area with free open-air shuttles to and fro. All other parking at the base area is paid, up to $10 per day, unless you are riding with at least four or more in your car—then it is free anywhere.

Getting around: The rule in the past was rent a car. But for visitors to Jackson Hole who are staying at the ski area and focused on skiing and snowboarding, the mountain village has everything you need to stay busy for a week. You can use the shuttlebus to get into town, and taxis between the village and town are only about $10. If you are staying in town, a car may be more convenient and will save lots of time. While buses run regularly, they can add up to 45 minutes to your commuting time during the busy apres-ski period, and at night, buses from town to Teton Village run only once an hour. If you're headed to nearby Grand Targhee, unless you're used to driving steep Rocky Mountain passes, we recommend that you take the Targhee Express (733-3101) in snowy weather. It's $15 well spent.

Motorists, take note: Highway signs say little about the ski areas. From town, follow signs to Teton Village to get to Jackson Hole Mountain Resort, and to Wilson when driving to Grand Targhee.

Southern Teton Area Rapid Transit (START) buses run frequently between Jackson and Teton Village to 10 p.m. in ski season for a small fee. Study the bus schedule and get on an express bus if you want to minimize your commute. Another good deal: books of bus passes sold at most resorts. They can save you a few bucks off the published fare. Five companies provide taxi services and airport shuttles: Jackson Hole Transportation (733-3135), Gray Line (733-4325), Buckboard Cab (733-1112), All-Star Taxi (733-2888) and All Trans (733-1700). Check websites for discount coupons on airport shuttles.

Nearby resorts

Snow King Resort, Jackson Hole, WY; (800) 522-5464
Internet: www.snowking.com
4 lifts; 400 acres; 1,571 vertical feet; 1 terrain park; 1 halfpipe

Snow King, Wyoming's oldest ski area, is in downtown Jackson, about 12 miles from Jackson Hole Ski Resort. Despite its in-town location, crowds don't exist here except for special events. The north-facing slopes plunge 1,571 feet, with some trails literally dropping out from under you. The steep, consistent pitch makes it a favorite for European World Cup teams, who often train here before events at Park City, for visitors who like to open throttle on manicured groomers and for local powder pigs who head here instead of fighting the tram crowds at Jackson Hole. Sixty percent of the mountain's 400 acres is rated advanced, and that includes some bump runs and glades; Bearcat to Bearcat Glades is a corker. Beginners and lower intermediates have a few gentle runs on the lower mountain. Another plus: The "Wow!" views from the 7,808-foot summit.

The resort includes a hotel and condominiums (see *Accommodations* above). The Snow King Center houses a regulation ice rink where you can skate, watch semi-pro hockey and perhaps even take in a concert by luminaries such as B.B. King. Snow King also has a multilane tubing park open weekdays, 4 to 8 p.m., and weekends, noon to 8 p.m.

Lift tickets (06/07): $35 adult; $25 for ages 14 and younger and 60 and older. Note that lifts open at 10 a.m. If your flight lands early enough, consider warming up here with a two-hour ticket, $17 adult, $12 juniors/senior. Or, combine a two-hour ticket with Sunday Brunch at Rafferty's, the hotel restaurant. Night skiing Tuesday through Saturday costs $15 adults, $10 junior/senior.

Canadian Resorts

Canada is a prime destination for a ski or snowboard vacation. Generally, the giant mountains and vast snowfields are in the West, while the narrow trails and quaint ski towns are in the East, just as they are in the U.S. But a Canadian ski/snowboard vacation also has some very attractive differences. Some examples:

• Some of Canada's leading winter resorts are in national parks. Banff and Jasper National Parks have four ski areas within their boundaries. The scenery is magnificent and wild animal sightings are common.

• You can stay in an opulent, historic hotel, even if you're on a budget. The Fairmont chain includes several grand hotels built to accommodate late 19th- and early 20th-century luxury rail travel. In summer these castle-like hotels are jammed with tourists willing to pay premium rates, but in winter, prices plummet.

• In Quebec, the French influence provides a European flavor to a vacation. Yet, English also is spoken so Americans shouldn't feel too overwhelmed.

• We provide prices in Canadian dollars, which, at press time in September 2006, was about C$1.10 for each U.S. dollar and C$1.42 for each euro. Canada has a Goods and Services Tax (GST) of 7 percent, and we note whether it is included in listed prices, which are rounded up to the nearest dollar. Foreign tourists can get a GST refund for goods they take out of the country and on hotel rooms they pay for themselves (but not on rooms prepaid through a travel agent). You can't get refunds for meals or services such as transportation or lift tickets. Most hotels have refund forms. The amount spent must be more than C$200 and visitors must get proof of export upon leaving Canada.

Canada can be as cold as you've heard, or warmer than you imagined. We've skied in windbreakers in January, and huddled into fleece neck-warmers during a sudden April snowstorm. Our advice is to plan for everything.

Though it is not yet law, authorities in the U.S. and Canada strongly urge U.S. citizens to carry a passport if they have one. If not, U.S. citizens must have citizenship and residency proof. A birth or naturalization certificate is sufficient. A driver's license alone is not. It's best to have at least two forms of ID. These requirements are more for return to the U.S. than for entry into Canada, especially given the increased border security since Sept. 11, 2001. A passport is always required for citizens of countries other than U.S. and Canada.

Single and divorced parents, take note: In an effort to prevent child stealing, Canadian immigration requires that any parent entering Canada alone with his/her child show proof of custody, such as a notarized letter from the other parent. Anyone traveling with someone else's child (grandparents, uncles and aunts, friends) must present a notarized letter signed by both of the child's parents. If you're driving with friends in separate cars, be sure kids are matched with parents when crossing the border. Sometimes you'll breeze through without being asked for proof, but it's best to be prepared.

Banff, Canada
Sunshine Village
Banff@Norquay

Banff Region Facts
Dining:★★★★
Apres-ski/nightlife:★★★★
Other activities:★★★★★

Internet: www.skibig3.com (tri-area skiing)
www.banfflakelouise.com (tourism bureau)
www.canadianrockies.net (townsite)
Bed Base: 10,000 in Banff

While flying into Calgary during the day provides awe-inspiring views of the Canadian Rocky Mountains, perhaps the best surprise is to arrive late at night, when everything is enveloped in pitch black, and make the hour-and-a-half-long drive to Banff. That way, the next morning when you draw back the curtains, the massive craggy mountains are suddenly right there, in your face. What a wake-up call!

Banff is home to three resorts—Sunshine Village, Ski Banff @ Norquay and Lake Louise. The three mountains provide very different ski experiences, just one of the reasons Banff makes a fabulous ski trip. For those who have never skied out West, it's easy to be overwhelmed by the massive amount of terrain and the steep craggy peaks. You can plan your vacation accordingly to start at the smallest of the resorts and work up to the larger and more difficult ones: Spend your first day at Ski Banff @ Norquay, the next at Sunshine Village, then head to Lake Louise. There is a sense of being swallowed up by the wilderness—embraced by Mother Nature and then gently released to be part of her bountiful gifts here. Wildlife is plentiful, sightings of elk herds in town are common. Mule deer and bighorn sheep live in the Bow Valley, and sometimes bears and wolves can be seen along less-traveled roads.

The completion of the coast-to-coast railway in 1885 made one of the most picturesque and remote pockets in the Rocky Mountains suddenly accessible. This virgin landscape—formerly known only to Canada's Aboriginal peoples, fur traders and explorers—was now open to tourists. That same year, Canada established its first national park, Banff. Later, four other national parks were created nearby: Yoho, Jasper, Kootenay and Glacier, which explains why much of the region's rugged beauty remains essentially unspoiled. The scenery is still as magnificent as it was to the train travelers of the late 1800s with snow-capped mountain ridges, cliff faces pocked by glaciers, mountain lakes and hot springs.

Contrast this with the beautifully designed, compact, yet very cosmopolitan town of Banff , filled with excellent restaurants, nightclubs, shops and lodging. The atmosphere is a uniquely Canadian blend of quaint and rustic, set amid some of the most rugged scenery in the Rockies.

Because summer is the high season in the park, crowds diminish in winter and lodging prices are rock bottom, even at the most luxurious hotels. The temperature can be numbingly cold, or pleasantly warm if a Chinook wind blows. Unlike the Canadian resorts closer to the Pacific Ocean, ski areas in Banff receive a dry, fluffy powder that is the best thing this side of Utah.

Tri-Area Lift Passes (05/06 prices, without tax)

The Banff/Lake Louise Region has an interchangeable lift ticket. It can be used at Sunshine, Ski Banff@Norquay and Lake Louise, and includes a free shuttle between most Banff/Lake Louise hotels and the ski areas. It also includes a free night-skiing ticket (Fridays only) when used at Ski Banff@Norquay to make up the price difference. It's easy and convenient. Prices are lower when purchased with a vacation package. (Prices rounded to nearest dollar.)

	Adults	Children (6–12)	Youth (13–17)/Seniors (65+)
Three of four days	C$204	C$96	C$182
Five of seven days	C$340	C$160	C$304
Seven of nine days	C$469	C$224	C$425

Sunshine Village Facts

Summit elevation:	8,954 feet
Vertical drop:	3,514 feet
Base elevation:	5,440 feet

Address: Box 1510, Banff, Alberta, Canada T1L 1J5
Area code: 403
Ski area phone: 762-6500
Snow report: 760-7669
Toll-free reservations: (877) 542-2633
Fax: 762-6513
Internet: www.skibanff.com
Number of lifts: 12–1 high-speed 8-passenger gondola, 5 high-speed quads, 2 quads, 1 triple, 1 double, 2 moving carpets
Snowmaking: None
Skiable acreage: 3,358 acres
Uphill capacity: 22,000 per hour
Parks & pipes: 1 park, 1 pipe
Nearest lodging: Slopeside, hotel
Resort child care: Yes, 19 months and older
Adult ticket, per day: C$56-C$63 (04/05, without tax)

Expert:★★★★
Advanced:★★★★
Intermediate:★★★★
Beginner:★★★★ **First-timer:**★★★★

Ski Banff@Norquay Facts

Summit elevation:	7,000 feet
Vertical drop:	1,650 feet
Base elevation:	5,350 feet

Address: P.O. Box 1520, Banff, Alberta, Canada T1L 1B4
Area code: 403
Ski area phone: 762-4421
Snow report: 760-7704
Fax: 762-8133
E-mail: info@banffnorquay.com
Internet: www.banffnorquay.com
Number of lifts: 5–1 high-speed quad, 2 quads, 1 double, 1 moving carpet
Snowmaking: 85 percent
Skiable Acreage: 190 acres
Uphill capacity: 7,000 per hour
Parks & pipes: 1 park, 1 pipe
Nearest lodging: Base of access road–ski-in only
Resort child care: Yes, 19 months and older
Adult ticket, per day: C$49 (04/05, without tax)

Expert:★★★★
Advanced:★★★★
Intermediate:★★★
Beginner:★★
First-timer:★★

Sunshine Village

Sunshine Village has long been known for its winding gondola ride that carries you almost 1,650 vertical feet from the parking lot—along the walls of a valley and box canyon—to the village base area and the rest of the lifts. On this 13-minute ride to the rest of the lifts (or 6 minutes to Goat's Eye mid-station), you have plenty of time to survey the slopes where the real thrill rides begin. Much of the skiing on Sunshine's three peaks is wide-open, bowl-type skiing, but the bottom half of the slopes are covered in evergreens for those who like their runs cut through trees.

Though a restaurant and rental shop are near the parking lot at the gondola base, the real "base area" for Sunshine is at the top of the gondola at 7,082 feet, where you will find a mountain village with a lodge, rental shop, general store, restaurant and the only slopeside lodging in the national parks. From this point lifts take off in all directions. Most people never head all the way down until the end of the day and some not until the end of their vacation.It's worth noting that Sunshine has the longest ski season in the region, running from the middle of November through the middle of May. If the weather is clear, the views across and down the canyon are nearly as breathtaking as the runs.

Mountain layout

The 3-mile Banff Avenue—which takes you from the village down to the parking lot at the end of the day—is a long, luscious trip for beginners, but it will seem tame for many intermediates. Advanced skiers can play on drops to the left, but they're short and eventually rejoin the trail. An alternative way down is Canyon Trail, which starts out intermediate and turns into a single-black diamond. You catch it near the base of the Jackrabbit Quad.

♦♦Expert ♦Advanced: There's plenty of terrain to explore. If you can't stand the thought of even a 13-minute gondola ride, plus another lift ride before being able to hit the slopes, get off at the Goat's Eye station and board the Goat's Eye Express. It whisks you to the top of 9,200-foot Goat's Eye Mountain and 1,900 vertical feet of black and double-black routes. There are even a couple of excellent blue cruisers thrown into the mix. The skiing at the top is steep and wide-open until you crest a ridge into the glades, at which point the runs are cut fairly wide through trees with plenty of pitch.

The runs under the Angel Express Quad—especially Ecstasy—have good pitch. At the top, the skiing is wide-open and above treeline, with spectacular views. Those in search of the steep-and-deep will not be disappointed, as towards the midway point the run splits into multiple fingers. Some are short but quite steep chutes.

Heading right at the top of the Angel Express will take you into a fairly steep bowl. Shoot down to the Continental Divide High-Speed Quad. This lift takes you a soaring 1,450 feet to the almost-summit of Lookout Mountain. At the top you cross the Continental Divide from Alberta to British Colombia. These descents also are wide-open, with moguls on North Divide and powder and open skiing in the Bye Bye Bowl, which is convex instead of concave. Make sure to carry your speed at the bottom to get out of the bowl.

From the top of the Continental Divide Quad, skiers can climb a short distance for some truly extreme skiing on the Northface of Lookout Mountain, in the chutes of Delirium Dive. Here, three rules are strictly enforced: 1) All skiers/riders must wear an avalanche transceiver; 2) All skiers/riders must carry a rescue shovel; and 3) You must ski or ride with a partner. Ask about renting transceivers and shovels at the ski area. Helmets are recommended. Be forewarned: The entrance is remarkably steep, though fairly wide. But after the first 30 or 40 yards, Delirium opens up into one of the finest and least-skied bowls in the Rockies. Instead of dropping in off the cornice, you can climb backwards down a metal stairway but friends told us it was scarier than just sucking it up and "diving in." The resort's other extreme terrain, The Wild West, is on Goat's Eye and has the same restrictions.

■ **Intermediate:** There's terrain from every lift for intermediates; however, be sure you are confident at this ability level if you try the runs on Goat's Eye or the peak of Lookout Mountain. Think twice if the weather's socked in, too. Lack of visibility can be nerve-wracking and downright dangerous. It's a blast playing on the blues off the Strawberry Triple on Mt. Standish. The grade's just right on Boutry's Bowl for those learning to ski powder. Carry your speed and cut through the woods to get back to the chair.

You'll find some short black runs off the Wolverine Express and the JackRabbit Quad You can enjoy this area any time of the day, then either ride the gondola to the top from its midstation or take Miss Gratz to the Tee Pee Town chair.

●● **Beginner:** The Strawberry Triple Chair and the Wolverine Express high-speed quad have gentle wide slopes good for those still perfecting their technique. The Angel Express serves longer, narrower slopes that loop around the steeper faces.

● **First-timer:** First-timers learn near the base village, where a moving carpet carries you to the top of a short gentle slope that is off to one side. The Strawberry Triple Chair and the Wolverine Express high-speed quad have gentle wide slopes.

Find green runs off the Continenetal Divide Chair as well, but if it's foggy, it might be a bit of a challenge. When the skies are clear, it's worth the trip to the top of the divide where two provinces, Alberta and British Columbia, are visible. Then follow the greens to the bottom of the Strawberry Triple.

Ride Guide: If you like to hike for your turns, there are plenty of choices. You'll find lots of awesome cliffs, chutes and gullies, plus wide-open bowls. Start off with hiking up from the tops of Standish Express, Wawa quad and Goat's Eye Express. The marked trails in these areas are also favorites with snowboarders.

Sunshine Village has one serious flat on Lookout Mountain when you're coming out of Bye Bye Bowl or South Divide. You need to really carry your speed, and even then, you'll probably have to hoof up the last section, which is actually a little hill that then drops you back into the main area so you can work your way to the lifts. Perhaps this is why so many riders avoid the top part of Lookout Mountain. Other flats and runouts you should be aware of (you'll be fine as long as you're ready for them): The beginning of Banff Avenue as you head out of the Village back toward the base and the bottom section of Sunshine Coast, where all the runs on Goat's Eye dump you on the way back to the lift.

Pipes and parks

Mt. Standish is a huge hit with riders. The Dell Valley is a natural halfpipe near the Strawberry Triple Chair. The triangle formed by the Wawa quad and the Standish Express is a natural terrain park with lots of air, natural hits, a quarterpipe, lips and drops. The SilverBullet Half-pipe is on lower Strawberry Face. On lower Lookout Mountain, you'll find the terrain park, with kickers, ramps and rails. The boardercross is here too. Sunshine makes snow only in its halfpipe and relies on Mother Nature to provide enough snow for its terrain park, so some features may not be available till later in the season.

Lessons (05/06 prices, with tax)

Group lessons: Daily Group Workshops are full-day programs available to all ability levels. Levels 1–3 pay C$130 and groups are limited to six people. Levels 4–6 pay C$155 and groups are limited to four people.

First-timer package: A full-day program with lesson, rentals and lift ticket is C$145. A three-day package costs C$390.

Private lessons: For up to five people, C$355 for three hours; C$535 for a full day.

Special programs: Sunshine Village encourages the traditional Ski Week, a weeklong stay at the slopeside Sunshine Inn, by providing packages including classes with the same instructor. Groups can be divided by ability level or by family, and include evening activities. Camps for women, adventure skiers and tackling Delirium Dive are available; call (877) 542-2633 for dates and prices. Sunshine Village participates in Club Ski and Club Snowboard, a three-day program featuring lessons with the same instructor and group, skiing one day each at three resorts (see *Lessons* in the Lake Louise chapter for details).

 ## KidStuff (05/06 prices, with tax)

Child care: Ages 19 months to 6 years. Full day with lunch is C$55. Reservations recommended; call (877) 542-2633.

Children's lessons: Ages 3–6 can get a combo ski-and-play program. A full day with lunch and lift ticket costs C$80. Ski rentals are extra. Reserve through day care. Kids Kampus is an all-day program for kids ages 6–12, skiing or snowboarding. The price for a full day with lunch is C$95; multiday discounts available. Mountain Riders for kids 13–17 costs C$100 for a full day with lunch. Lift tickets and rentals are extra. Sunshine Village participates in Club Junior, a three-day program featuring lessons with the same instructor and group, skiing one day each at three resorts (see *KidStuff* in the Lake Louise chapter for details).

Special activities: There are daily apres-ski activities for children staying at the Sunshine Inn. Activities include garbage-bag sledding, movies, games and hot tub parties.

 ## Lift tickets (05/06 prices, without tax)

	Adult	Child (6-12)
One day	C$65	C$24
Three of four days	C$186 (C$62/day)	C$72 (C$24/day)
Five of seven days	C$311 (C$62/day)	C$120 (C$24/day)

Note: Prices have been rounded to the nearest dollar.

Who skis free: Children ages 5 and younger.

Who skis at a discount: Youth ages 13–17 pay C$45 for one day. Ages 65 and older pay C$51. Multiday discounts apply.

Ski Banff@Norquay

This small, but challenging, ski area is just a 10-minute drive from Banff and boasts some of the best grooming in Western Canada. It also has some of the gnarliest bump runs we've ever skied. There are virtually no lift lines here, so you can really rack up the vertical. The winding mountain road that takes you up to the base lodge can be fairly intimidating, but the views are incredible as you climb above the town of Banff. Be sure to look out for elk; we saw dozens of them.

The 24,000 square foot Cascade Lodge at the base was built in 1996 after the previous lodge burned down. This beautiful post & beam lodge includes an excellent restaurant, a bar, three large stone fireplaces and the other usual services.

Mountain layout

♦♦**Expert** ♦**Advanced:** The view of Banff and the Bow Valley from the North American chair is fabulous. This is the lift that takes you to those ribbons of bumps tumbling down the mountainside. It's an old slow chair that rarely has a line. Be positively sure you want to be here. This is very tough stuff, with no blue or green ways down. That said, we *must* tell you that these are quite possibly the most fun bump runs in all of skidom. And they are *long*! The bumps can get so big, folks of short stature can barely see over them. By the way, look closely at the tea house at the top of the lift—it's built to have avalanches roll right over the top of it.

Upper Lone Pine is the name of that double-black mogul belt that plunges down a 35-percent gradient. There's a daily contest (when the lift is open) called Club 35,000 to see who can make the most consecutive runs in eight hours on this 3,500-foot-long, skeleton-jarring wall. It takes 10 runs to make the club—many have done it, which says a lot for local physical fitness. Off the Mystic Express Quad, some chutes drop you off into a gully that feeds you back to the lifts. Black Magic and Ka-Poof are screaming cruisers.

Another appeal for the adventure seeker is a chute called Valley of the Ten, a narrow drainage perfect for thrills. To get to it, skiers at the top of North American chair drop off to the left into a drop-out called Gun Run, the steepest thing on the mountain. The easiest way down from this chair is Memorial Bowl, and it's still a tough black with monster moguls.

■ **Intermediate:** Three chairs climb up ridges that serve the area's beginner and mostly intermediate runs. The terrain off the Pathfinder Express Quad, unseen from the base area, is mainly groomed intermediate. The intermediate runs here are pretty steep by most standards, so they're not for the timid, but excellent grooming makes them truly delightful. The mellower terrain is found off the Spirit quad. Start out on Hoodoo and work your way up to the tougher trails. Intermediates wanting to stay in the sun all day have a challenge. At midday none of the Pathfinder trails gets sun except the front two runs, Black Magic and Ka-Poof, which are both blacks.

●● ● **Beginner/First-timer:** The Cascade quad chair serves most of the sheltered beginner terrain. It connects to Spirit and the long Pathfinder Express quads, once you get those legs under you. There's a big jump from beginner terrain to intermediate terrain here, so be forewarned.

Ride Guide: Many snowboarders hate moguls, and if you're one of them, you won't find much black terrain unless you hike for it. The exceptions are Black Magic, Excalibur and Ka-Poof, off the Mystic Express Quad. However, if you consider moguls to be a challenge that will only improve your riding skills—and give you some true bragging rights—make a beeline for the bumps off the North American double chair. The intermediate trails here are groomed to perfection, meaning lots of fun for riders who like to carve arcs or just let it rip. Some of the trails are rolling rides with occasional lips for catching air. It's easy to get around the mountain, since riders here don't have to worry about flats and traverses.

Parks and pipes

The terrain park has a halfpipe, tabletops, rails, jib boxes, gap jumps and more. The park is groomed at least five nights a week, so you'll get the best riding experience they can give you. The park is conveniently located near the base and served by the Cascade Quad Chair;

a reduced-rate Cascade lift ticket is available (see *Lift Tickets*). You'll find some fun natural hits around the mountain if you look for them. Bruno's Gully is a must-try.

Lessons [05/06 prices, without tax]

Group lessons: Levels 1–3 pay C$60 for a half day skiing or snowboarding; C$80 for a full day. Levels 4–6 pay C$70 for a half day.

First-timer package: C$56 for a two-hour group lesson, lift ticket on the Cascade chair and rental equipment for skiers or snowboarders. Additional two-hour lesson in the afternoon, C$30. A two-day program costs C$140 and a three-day program costs $210.

Private lessons: C$90 for one hour; C$250 for a half day; C$400 for a full day. Each additional person costs C$30, maximum of four.

Special programs: Ski Banff@Norquay participates in Club Ski and Club Snowboard, a three-day program of lessons with the same instructor and group, skiing one day each at three resorts (see *Lessons* in the Lake Louise chapter for details).

KidStuff [05/06 prices, without tax]

Child care: Ages 19 months to 6 years. Full day, without lunch, is C$35. Half day, either morning or afternoon, is C$25. You can add an introductory ski lesson for $25. Lunch is C$6. Prices have been rounded to the nearest dollar. Reservations recommended; call 760-7709.

Children's lessons: Ski and snowboard programs are available for children ages 6-12. Full day is C$77 (lunch included); two hours, C$55. A child's beginner package (lift, two-hour lesson and rentals) is C$56. Ski Banff@Norquay participates in Club Junior, a three-day program of lessons with the same instructor and group, skiing one day each at three resorts (see *Lessons* in the Lake Louise chapter for details).

Lift tickets [05/06 prices, without tax]

	Adult	Child (6–12)
One day	C$52	C$17
Noon-4 p.m.	C$41	C$14
Two hours	C$29	C$11

Who skis free: Children 5 and younger ski free when an adult buys a lift ticket.

Who skis at a discount: Youth ages 13-17 and seniors 65 and older ski for C$40. If you only want to use the terrain park, a ticket for the Cascade lift costs C$35 for adults, C$12 for children, C$26 for seniors and students with ID. Ski Banff@Norquay has the region's only night skiing. It's on Fridays and C$24 for adults, C$12 for children, C$22 for seniors and students with ID.

Although Ski Banff@Norquay also sells multiday tickets, we've given you the ticket prices we think destination visitors are most likely to use. The area sells hourly tickets for two to five hours, ranging in price from C$29 to C$47 for adults (discounts for kids, youth and seniors). Our recommendation: Use the Tri-Area Lift Pass at Lake Louise and Sunshine Village, and buy a two- or three-hour ticket here. If you want to ski here again after two hours (and you may—it's a fun place, yet small), *then* use a day on your Tri-Area Pass.

Cross-country and snowshoeing (visit xcskiresorts.com for more details)

There are some lovely, easy loops **along the Bow River.** Take Banff Avenue to the end of Spray Avenue, or turn left and cross the river. Trails wind through the whole area. **Parks Canada** puts out a very informative booklet on the extensive Nordic skiing and snowshoeing in Banff National Park; you can get a copy for a small fee at the Banff Information Center, 224 Banff Ave., 9 a.m. to 5 p.m.

The Ski Stop (762-5333) in **The Fairmont Banff Springs** rents skis and skates. You also can get trail maps and information.

Several sports shops rent snowshoes; ask your lodging concierge. **White Mountain Adventures** (678-4099) is just one of many guide outfits that offers naturalist-guided snowshoe treks, guided backcountry tours and cross-country skiing tours.

Accommodations

Banff has accommodations to meet every taste and every budget. Rooms can be found for as little as C$50. Even the premier locations are within most budgets. In addition to the 7 percent GST, Alberta also has a 5 percent lodging tax. **Banff/Lake Louise Central Reservations** (800-661-1676) books lodging in Banff, Lake Louise and Jasper. **Ski Banff-Lake Louise-Sunshine Reservations** (877-754-7076) books ski packages including the tri-area lift tickets and lodging at more than 30 Banff and Lake Louise properties. Packages are customized and can include Club Ski, Club Snowboard and Club Junior lessons, rentals, air and other activities. Also visit online at www.skibig3.com.

The Sunshine Inn (762-6500; 800-661-1676; $$–$$$), at 7,200 feet in the center of Sunshine's base village, is the only slopeside lodging in Banff National Park. The resort recently renovated the lobby area, restaurant, lounge and some guestrooms. It's reached by riding the gondola up from the parking lot. Rooms are neat and simple. There's a giant outdoor hot tub where you and 19 others can relax while watching skiers and riders on Lookout Mountain. You'll also have access to a dry sauna, massage and chiropractic services, a family and game room, and an exercise room. All nightly rates include lift tickets. The inn also runs a Ski Week program.

Decore Hotels purchased Norquay's Timberline Inn, renamed it **The Juniper** (877-762-2281; 762-2281), completed extensive renovations and opened in December 2004. It's at the bottom of Norquay's access road, so technically it's Banff's only ski-in hotel. You can ski in along a 1.5-kilometer trail, but you'll need the hotel's shuttle to take you to the lifts. The hotel also has a restaurant.

Other lodging is in Banff. We strongly recommend the experience of staying at **The Fairmont Banff Springs** (800-441-1414 in the U.S. and Canada; 762-2211; $$$–$$$$), the wine-colored, Scottish-influenced castle perched on a small hill, a short walk from downtown. You have seen this classic, rundle-rock monolith in many photos with its pointed, green-copper roofs rising from the nine-story walls, framed by evergreens and craggy peaks. Its public areas are expansive, designed for turn-of-the-century mingling—we're talking a ballroom for 16,000. The hotel has a magnificent, newly-renovated spa (available at an additional fee) with private mineral pool and waterfall pools, saunas, steam rooms and hot tubs as well as a fitness room, salons and treatment areas. There are also indoor and outdoor pools available free for all guests, plus shops and restaurants and scheduled activities, such as dogsledding and snowshoeing with guides. Rates during the winter are a bargain compared to the summer. Ask about the Ski with Breakfast package, including lodging, lift tickets, ski shuttles, valet parking and gratuities for two.

"An enclave of civility" is how the **Rimrock Resort Hotel** (800-661-1587; 762-3356; $$$$) describes itself, and we agree. It's posh, sophisticated, elegant and refined, with a full-service spa and fitness center, an excellent restaurant, comfortable lounge and views to match. It is one of only five Canadian members of the Leading Hotels of the World, a group of luxury hotels.

Families should stay at the **Douglas Fir Resort & Chalets** (800-661-9267; 762-5591; $$–$$$$). There are condo-style units with wood-burning fireplaces and full kitchens, two- and three-bedroom chalets, and a few suites. Kids love the two indoor waterslides here. We're not talking little-dinky kiddy slides, we're talking huge, winding, fast waterslides like you would normally find at an outdoor water park. Parents can sit in the steam room, or the hot tub, or the wade pool at the bottom of the slides and watch them whoop it up. Or play on the waterslides with the kids. The waterslide area is open to the public for a cost, but it's free for hotel guests. In a separate area, for guests only, you'll find an indoor swimming pool, hot tub and saunas. There are also a coin laundry and a convenience store.

The **Mount Royal Hotel** (800-267-3035 Western Canada only; 762-3331; $$–$$$$) has a great location in downtown Banff, an excellent choice for those who enjoy nightlife. It gets a fair amount of street noise from Banff Avenue and has an exceptionally good restaurant.

The Inns of Banff (800-661-1272; 762-4581; $$–$$$$), a modern, multi-level lodge with balconies in most rooms, is a 15-minute walk from downtown. **High Country Inn** (800-661-1244; 762-2236; $$–$$$) on Banff Avenue, two blocks from downtown, is one of the least expensive and has a pool and an Italian/Swiss Restaurant.

Banff Alpine Centre—HI (866-762-4122; 762-4123; $) on Tunnel Mountain Road and part of Hostelling International, recently added a 66-bed wing with rooms that have two or four beds and private bathrooms. In the older rooms, showers are shared. Facilities include a laundry, kitchen and pub-style restaurant.

SameSun Backpacker Lodge (762-5521; $) 449 Banff Avenue, sports a friendly, funky atmosphere. What used to be Global VIllage Banff, this newly renovated dowtown lodging caters to those who are comfortable in a hostel environment. The lodge offers most amenities available in higher-priced hotel/motels: WiFi and web access with no curfew, no lockout, ski packages and ski shuttles right outside your door.

If your flight home is early in the morning, you can't beat the **Delta Calgary Airport Hotel** (291-2600 or 800-268-1133; $$$). Roll out of bed, then walk out the front door of the hotel and into the terminal. It also has a pool and fitness center, lounge and two restaurants. The food is good and the service excellent.

Dining

For those staying at Sunshine Village, the **Eagle's Nest Dining Room** ($$) in the Sunshine Inn offers fine dining with lobster and filet mignon. **The Chimney Corner Lounge** ($-$$), the inn's fireplace lounge, serves a very good sit-down lunch. Try the barbecued beef and a local-brewed ale. Ask to sit in the sunroom so you can watch the skiers and riders on Lookout Mountain. The **cafeteria** has the best cafeteria food and selection for a ski area in this region. The **Creekside Restaurant** ($) at the base of the gondola serves a hearty breakfast, or choose a la carte. Ask for a flavored cappuccino. Take time to wander around the restaurant to look at pictures from Sunshine's past—during the early glamorous days of skiing—as well as Native American relics and antique outdoor winter gear.

On-mountain at Ski Banff@Norquay, the food is tasty and affordable in the **Lone Pine Pub** ($), upstairs in the main lodge with gorgeous views. Try the lemon pepper salmon burger,

Dining: $$$$-Entrees C$30+; $$$-C$20-$30; $$-C$10-$20; $-less than C$10.
Accommodations: (double room) $$$$-C$200+; $$$-C$141-$200; $$-C$81-$140; $-C$80 and less.

the Alberta wild mushroom and bison stew, or the chicken souvlaki wrapped in a pita. The children's menu (ages 12 and younger) is C$5.50 for your choice of peanut butter & jelly, grilled cheese, chicken fingers, cheeseburger or hot dog.

In the town of Banff, diners have a tremendous choice of restaurants. You will find almost every variety of ethnic food, as well as the familiar steak-and-seafood restaurants. Many restaurants here, especially those on Banff Avenue, are on the second floor above the shops. Sometimes the entrances are obvious, sometimes not, so keep an eye out.

The Fairmont Banff Springs alone has 10 restaurants. The **Banffshire Club** (762-6860; $$$$), The Fairmont's premium dining experience, evokes the intimacy of a rich yet understated private club. Tapestries, wrought-iron light fixtures, vaulted ceilings, archways, leather, fine linens, bone china and crystal set the stage for cuisine prepared by Executive Chef Daniel Buss. The four-course, prix fixe menu has a French influence, with entrees changing by the season to make the best use of fresh regional specialties. Wine aficionados will appreciate the wine list representing more than 2,000 labels; scotch fans have a list of 75 scotches. **Castello Ristorante** (762-6860; $$) specializes in Italian dinners. The expansive lunch buffet at the **Bow Valley Grill** (762-2211, Ext. 6841; $$–$$$) is worth a visit. Choose from a wide selection of salads, soups, side dishes and entrees as well as stir-fry and pasta stations. A dessert buffet is available for C$5 more. An a la carte menu is also available, but the best value is the buffet. Austrian, German and Swiss fare, including schnitzels and fondues, are the specialties at **Waldhous** (762-6860; $$), a Bavarian escape within a former golf clubhouse. Rich woodwork, a huge fireplace and Bavarian accents complement the menu. **Grapes** (762-2211, Ext. 6660; $$), a 21-seat wine bar, serves light meals.

Le Beaujolais (corner of Banff Avenue and Buffalo Street, 762-2712; $$$) receives high praise for its French cuisine. Meals can be ordered a la carte, but the restaurant specializes in fixed-price three- or five-course meals. You are likely to see diners in coats and ties, though neither is required. The dining room at **Buffalo Mountain Lodge** (Tunnel Mountain Road, 762-2400; $$$) offers relaxed elegance with hand-hewn beam construction and a massive fieldstone fireplace. Rocky Mountain cuisine is its specialty, with a variety of wild game and fish. The wine list was awarded *Wine Spectator's* "Award of Excellence" several years in a row.

Tiki bar meets the Wild West at the smoky **Grizzly House Restaurant** (207 Banff Ave., 762-4055; $$-$$$$). Alberta beef and exotic game meats are the specialties, fondues and hot rocks are the preferred preparations, and smokers are welcome. Take a walk on the wild side and stretch your wallet and tastebuds by ordering the exotic fondue dinner, with shark, alligator, rattlesnake, ostrich, frogs legs, buffalo and venison.

For gourmet Italian, you can try **Giorgio's Trattoria** (219 Banff Ave. 762-5114; $$), which serves Northern Italian pastas and pizzas, or **Guido's** (116 Banff Ave. above McDonald's, 762-4002; $$) for American Italian food such as spaghetti, lasagna and chicken parmigiana. **Ticino Swiss-Italian Restaurant** (415 Banff Ave., 762-3848; $$–$$$) specializes in dishes from the Italian part of Switzerland.

Bumper's The Beef House (603 Banff Ave., 762-2622; $$–$$$), with a cozy log interior, has been serving Alberta beef since 1975. Try the melt-in-your-mouth prime rib (which comes in four cuts). Watch out, the horseradish sauce is very hot. The chicken cafoosalum has a very tasty maple sugar-lime sauce. The meal comes with a good salad bar; try the mango jalapeño salad dressing or the creamy cucumber. If you save room for dessert, order a large nut sundae and serve three people. There's a good kids' menu, plus they will take most adult choices and make a smaller portion for children 12 and younger.

Not surprisingly, steaks and chops dominate the menu at the second-floor **Saltlik, A Rare**

Steakhouse (221 Bear St., 762-2467; $–$$), where tables surround a copper, central fireplace. Veggies and potatoes are priced separately, and served as sides.

Typhoon (211 Caribou St., 762-2000; $$–$$$) is the place for eclectic Asian cuisine served in a colorful dining room. Make a meal from the all-day appetizers or choose from entrees such as green Thai chicken curry, spicy tiger prawns, and pork & beef satay, each listed with a wine recommendation. Or choose from more than a dozen beers, half from Asia.

The intimate **Cafe Soleil** (208 Caribou St., 762-2090; $–$$$) is a Mediterranean tapas and wine bar. Choose from an all-day tapas menu, with more than two dozen tantalizing but affordable choices, or a Big Tapas menu after 6 p.m., with a half-dozen choices of more expensive delicacies such as lamb tajine, beef tenderloin and seared ahi tuna. Paninis, pizzas and pastas are available too. Have fun trying to pair the right wines from the wine bar with your tapas selections.

The popular **Coyotes Deli & Grill** (206 Caribou St., 762-3963; $$–$$$) specializes in tasty Southwestern meals, including vegetarian and pasta dishes. Try the smoked chicken burrito or the roasted vegetable and shaved asiago pizza. Open for breakfast, lunch and dinner. Dinner reservations are recommended and if you're 15 minutes late, you lose it. If you want a natural meal to complement all that natural beauty, head to the **Sunfood Cafe** (Sundance Mall at 215 Banff Ave., 760-3933; $) for vegetarian fare such as stir fry, Swiss cheese roesti, smoked tofu and zucchini pasta. If you have food allergies, the restaurant promises to prepare the food according to your needs.

Earl's (229 Banff Ave. at Wolf Street, 762-4414; $$) gets rave reviews for moderately priced Canadian beefsteak, fresh salmon, pasta and thin-crust pizza. **St. James Gate Olde Irish Pub** (205 Wolf St., 762-9355; $–$$) specializes in hearty Irish pub food that warms the heart on a cold winter day. **Wild Bill's Saloon** (201 Banff Ave., 762-0333; $$–$$$) is a big ol' saloon and dance hall that serves big ol' burgers made from beef, elk, buffalo and boar, as well as seafood, steaks and chicken.

Aardvark Pizza & Sub (304 Caribou St., 762-5500; $–$$), "the locals' choice in homemade pizza for over a decade," makes a great thick-crust pizza. The buffalo wings are mighty tasty and come in mild, medium, hot or suicide (mild is an accurate description). Open 11 a.m.–4 a.m. Delivery is free and there's a money-back guarantee if you're not satisfied.

One of the most fun places to eat breakfast, lunch or an informal supper is **Joe Btfsplk's Diner** (221 Banff Ave. 762-5529; $). Set in a 1950s-style diner decor complete with jukebox and Elvis posters, this restaurant serves huge portions.

For gourmet coffee, the best hot chocolate in town, delicious pastries and darn good chicken sandwiches, visit **Evelyn's Coffee Bar** (210 Banff Ave.; $) and its sister shops **Evelyn's Too** (229 Bear St.; $) and **Evelyn's Three** (119 Banff Ave; $). **Second Cup** (Cascade Plaza Mall at 317 Banff Ave.; $) serves coffees, pastries and atmosphere that are anything but second-rate. Enjoy stuffed chairs and a cozy ambiance.

Apres-ski/nightlife

Things really start hopping at night. Younger crowds probably will enjoy Banff nightspots, while older skiers might be happier at The Fairmont Banff Springs' many bars and lounges. The Happy Bus shuttles skiers to nightspots around Banff until midnight for C$2, or you can walk between most lodging and town.

Apres-ski, head to **The Paddock** at The Mount Royal Hotel. Crowds also gather at **The Rose and Crown**, an English-style pub with draft ale, a fireplace, pool table, darts and live entertainment. **St. James Gate Olde Irish Pub,** built in Dublin and assembled in Banff, is

Dining: $$$$-Entrees C$30+; $$$-C$20-$30; $$-C$10-$20; $-less than C$10.

Accommodations: (double room) $$$$-C$200+; $$$-C$141-$200; $$-C$81-$140; $-C$80 and less.

a traditional Irish pub with 33 draft beers and more than 65 single malt scotches. **Tommy's Neighbourhood Pub** on Banff Ave. is popular with the locals. **Magpie & Stump** serves up great nachos and some of Banff's best apres-ski.

Retreat after skiing into the cozy and justifiably popular **Cafe Soleil,** a Mediterranean tapas and wine bar. Snag a seat by the window for people watching, settle in by the fireplace or grab a bar stool and chat up the barkeep about the wide-ranging wine list, with many available by the glass. Nibble on selections from the all-day tapas menu, with more than two dozen choices, each more enticing than the previous.

In The Fairmont Banff Springs, the **Rundle Lounge** has quiet music for hotel guests. At the **Waldhaus** by The Fairmont Banff Springs Golf Course, Happy Hans and Lauren, on accordion and trumpet, get everybody singing.

At night, **Bumper's Loft Lounge** has a casual crowd, with live entertainment and ski movies. The lively **Saltlik Lounge** is where you can often hear live blues and jazz or watch sporting events on six large-screen TVs. **Wild Bill's Legendary Saloon** on Banff Avenue has both country & western and rock bands and a huge dance floor. Locals flock to **Barbary Coast** on Banff Avenue for what is repeatedly hailed as the best live music, usually rock/blues. **The Aurora,** in the basement of the Clocktower Mall, features a lounge, cigar bar and dance floor with DJs and bands. This is the dance bar where everyone goes after every place else in town closes. Finish off your night on the lower level at 110 Banff Ave.

Other activities

Banff has so much to do, we can only begin to do it justice. We can't imagine anyone coming here and not finding the time to explore the natural beauty of the region and view the abundant wildlife. Just a few of the ways to do that: Go **dogsledding** (Howling Dog Tours, 678-9588) or **ice fishing** (Banff Fishing Unlimited, 762-4936); take a **sleigh ride** (Warner Guiding and Outfitting, 762-4551); or take an introductory course in **ice climbing** or **ski mountaineering** (Yamnuska; 678-4164).

Take the **Johnston Canyon Icewalk** (White Mountain Adventures, 678-4099) and learn about the canyon's history, wildlife and habitat from a local guide. At the end of the canyon, watch ice climbers work their way up the frozen waterfall. You should be in good physical shape for this icewalk, since you are hiking along the canyon on paths that go up, down and around natural formations.

One of the most famous **heli-skiing** companies, Canadian Mountain Holidays, is headquartered here (762-7100). Plus RK Heli-Ski does day heli-ski trips from Banff (762-3771). You also can go **helicopter sightseeing** with Alpine Helicopters (678-4802) to view the magnificent mountain peaks. On a clear day, take the **Sulphur Mountain Gondola** (762-2523) for a beautiful vista of the Bow Valley.

If you aren't staying at the Douglas Fir Resort & Chalets (762-5591), you can still use their **two giant indoor waterslides, kiddie pool, hot tub, steam room, fitness room, arcade and pool tables** (see *Accommodations*). This is a great way to meet other families and for your kids to make new friends on vacation. Cost is C$8 per person for non-guests of the hotel; kids 3 and younger are free.

The **Banff Upper Hot Springs** (762-1515) is a wonderful way to wind down after a day on the slopes. Natural hot mineral waters fill a huge outdoor pool, and you're surrounded by beautiful mountain scenery. Cost is C$7.50 for adults, C$6.50 for children and seniors. Winter hours are 10 a.m.–10 p.m., Friday and Saturday until 11 p.m. A restaurant and gift shop are on site. There's also the full-service **Pleiades Massage & Spa** here (760-2500 for spa reservations).

For culture vultures and those who want to discover the softer side of town, the **Culture Walk Banff Trail Guide** maps and describes more than a dozen art galleries, museums and cultural organizations in town, most within a few blocks walk of each other. Worth seeking out are Canada House Gallery, The Quest Gallery and About Canada. Not on the map is Very Canada, with merchandise that reflects Canada's culture and history.

Museums of note: Banff Park Museum for the story of early tourism and wildlife management, and a taxidermy collection of animals indigenous to the Park; Cave & Basin National Historic Site, where the hot springs were first discovered; Whyte Museum of the Canadian Rockies, for historic and contemporary art and historic homes; and the Buffalo Nations Luxton Museum, for Plains Indians history.

In the townsite, **shopping** is almost an athletic activity, with hundreds of shops lining Banff Avenue and its side streets. Most shops are clustered in little malls where you can enter the store from the inside on crummy days, or from the outside in good weather. Worth a drop-in: The Hudson's Bay Company, a department store famed for its blankets and Canada's oldest company, founded in 1670; and Roots Canada, for fine leather-and-cloth backpacks and handbags, and casual clothing.

For non-kitschy Canadian souvenirs: Orca Canada or Great Northern Trading Company (clothing, jewelry, knickknacks), Rocks and Gems (inexpensive jewelry made from native Canadian gemstones), and A Taste of the Rockies (smoked salmon, jams and honeys).

The Fairmont Banff Springs has 18 specialty and boutique shops, featuring designer jewelry, toys and clothing. Our favorite in the hotel is The Canadian Pacific Store, with items that reflect the bygone elegance of luxury train travel.

Getting there and getting around

By air: Calgary Airport is served by major airlines. Rocky Mountain Sky Shuttle (888-762-8754; 762-5200), Brewster Transportation (762-6767) Greyline Transportation (762-9102) and Banff Airporter (762-3330) will get you from the airport to Banff.

By car: Banff is 85 miles west of Calgary on the Trans-Canada Highway, a 90-minute drive. Ski Banff@Norquay is on Norquay Road, one exit past the Banff townsite. The Sunshine Village exit is 5 miles west of Banff; it's 5 more miles to the gondola base parking area. Free shuttles pick up skiers at 11 Banff hotels and the bus depot. Check the website for updates on pic-up sites, schedules and fares.

Getting around: It is possible to ski Banff and Lake Louise without a rental car by using free shuttlebuses offered with the Tri-Area Lift Ticket to the ski areas. The Happy Bus takes you within the town and region (noon to midnight only between Oct. 1 and April 30, C$2 a ride). Taxis are available too, but that can add up quickly. For spectacular sightseeing and exploring, it's best to have a car.

Lake Louise Ski Area

Banff Region, Alberta, Canada

Summit elevation:	8,650 feet
Vertical drop:	3,250 feet
Base elevation:	5,400 feet

Address: P.O. Box 5, Lake Louise Alberta, Canada T0L 1E0
Area code: 403
Ski area phone: 522-3555
Snow report: 762-4766 (Banff)
Toll-free reservations: (800) 258-7669
Fax: 522-2095
E-mail: info@skilouise.com
Internet: www.skilouise.com (resort)
www.skibig3.com (tri-area skiing)
www.banfflakelouise.com (tourism bureau)
Expert:★★★★ **Advanced:**★★★★
Intermediate:★★★★
Beginner:★★★★
First-timer:★★★★

Number and types of lifts: 12–1 6-person gondola, 1 high-speed six-pack, 2 high-speed quads, 1 quad, 1 triple, 2 doubles, 4 surface lifts
Skiable acreage: 4,200 acres
Snowmaking: 40 percent
Uphill capacity: 18,790 per hour
Parks & pipes: 1 park, 3 pipes
Bed base: 10,000 in Banff
Nearest lodging: About 2 miles away
Resort child care: Yes, 3 weeks and older
Adult ticket, per day: C$64 (05/06 without tax)

Dining:★★★
Apres-ski/nightlife:★★
Other activities:★★★★ (includes Banff region)

One visit is usually all it takes for Lake Louise to make virtually *everyone's* top 10 list of mountain resorts. It doesn't have a glitzy Vail persona. Instead, Lake Louise is down home, warm and friendly. It's a wonderful destination for families and groups with different ability levels. Its vast terrain provides plenty of fun and challenge for everyone. Lake Louise has some truly steep terrain, but that's balanced nicely with groomed intermediate runs that are enough fun for experts to *want* to join their friends and family members who prefer this kind of terrain. That says a lot. Top that off with delightful beginner and first-timer terrain, and everyone's bound to be happy.

The 24,000-square-foot Lodge of the Ten Peaks, and the corresponding remodeling of the original base lodge, are the first things you see when you pull up to the resort. The massive, split-beam log buildings are one of the most handsome in the Rockies: Think of a log cabin built by Paul Bunyan. The lodge is constructed of some 2,500 fir, pine and spruce logs, most of them thinned from the Ptarmigan slope to open glade skiing and riding.

Mountain layout

Lake Louise is comprised of four mountain faces that create three distinct areas: the Front Face, the Back Bowls and the Larch Area. The trail map has an excellent synopsis of where different ability levels should head.

If you want sun all day and want to ski the whole area, go to the Back Bowls in the morning, Larch midday and end up on the Front Face. Take a free guided tour by the Ski Friends, a volunteer group, two times daily starting at Whiskyjack Lodge.

◆◆**Expert** ◆**Advanced:** On the Front Side, give the Men's Downhill or Ladies' Downhill a try to get an idea of what the big boys and girls ski when Lake Louise hosts World Cup races in early December. Plenty of runs directly below the Grizzly Express Gondola, Top of the World Express and especially the Summit Platter have excellent pitch and grade, as evidenced by the liberal smattering of black diamonds on the trail map.

The Summit Platter is a Poma lift that on windswept or icy days can become an expert challenge all by itself. Whatever you do, don't skip Brown Shirt, it holds freshies for a week. The resort's steepest chutes, the Whitehorn 2 gullies, are off this lift too; they're not for the weak of heart and helmets are recommended.

After Whitehorn 2, probably the next-most-hair-raising area of the mountain is The Diamond Mine, accessed off the Paradise Chair. The special attractions here include cornices and some of the steepest chutes in the area. Yowza! Cornice-hoppers should go to the headwalls at the ER3 and ER7 gullies. Parachutes optional.

Sample the double- and single-black diamonds under the Ptarmigan Chair. These tend to be steep, long and full of moguls. Bark-eaters should aim for the Fall Line Glades, a slew of glades to the right of Ptarmigan Chair. Awesome!

From the top of the Larch Chair, you'll see that some powder freaks have hiked up to the summit to drop down Elevator Shaft, between two rock outcroppings. For a more modest thrill in a less traveled area, exit left off Larch Chair, then stay right and high on a gladed traverse until you find a deep powder bowl under Elevator Shaft. Called Rock Garden, it's a hidden playground of loops, swoops, moguls and Cadillac-sized rocks.

There's great tree skiing on Lookout Chutes and Tower 12. If you think you're up for another run, you'll find major bump thrills on Lynx.

■ **Intermediate:** On the Front Face, don't miss Meadowlark and Wapta, reached by the Eagle Chair; or Homerun and Gully, reached from Top of the World. The Front Face has a good web of intermediate trails served by the Olympic, Glacier and Friendly Giant.chairs. There are some great Front Face drops down Skyline to Sunset Terrace and then back to the lifts. This run gives intermediates plenty of opportunities to dip into the ungroomed stuff.

Intermediates can reach the Back Bowls via the Top of the World chair or the Summit Platter, which will take you a little higher on the back side to a run called Boomerang, an immensely fun cruiser. If the weather is socked in, however, skip Boomerang.

The Larch Area has the best intermediate skiing, accessed by a high-speed quad. Wolverine, Larch and Bobcat are all long cruisers. We like the middle-of-nowhere feel here too. Ready to try some bumps? Lynx has a black-diamond moniker, but can be handled by most adventurous intermediates and it's short enough that you can see the end if you get exhausted. There are some trees you can dip in and out of too.

Advanced-intermediates can tackle the Back Bowls. After some initial trepidation, you should be completely comfortable with skiing and riding the single-diamond runs here.

●● **Beginner:** Those with a little experience can ride the Friendly Giant or Glacier quad chairs and head down Wiwaxy, a 2.5-mile cruiser. Next step is Eagle Chair.

If you're getting pretty confident and would like to try the Back Bowls, ride the Grizzly Express Gondola and take Pika down the back. You also can descend from the Top of the World chair on Saddleback, a cat track that can be a bit intimidating, especially if the snow's iffy. Definitely don't try Saddleback on a low-visibility day—there are no trees to guide you, and you must negotiate a couple of narrow spots. Beginners have a pair of nice runs in the Larch Area, Marmot and Lookout.

● **First-timer:** Novices enrolled in lessons will start on the Sunny T-Bar, which serves an excellent beginner area separated from the rest of the runs.

Ride Guide: The Summit Platter is a Poma lift that's an expert challenge all by itself for snowboarders (and on windy or icy days, yikes!). If you can get over the trials and tribulations of riding the Platter—and you *really* should—there are some great hikes off the top to your left. Want guaranteed freshies? Head to the Back Bowls and stay far left to Brown Shirt. It's worth it to work your way over to it. While you're there, hike to Upper Boomerang, North Cornice and Wild Gully. The runout from the Back Bowls is kind of a drag, but it does have some pitch, so just carry your speed and you'll be fine. Off Larch Chair, hike in whichever direction draws you, you can't go wrong. Carvers will find fresh cord on groomed runs for ripping arcs. Try Meadowlark, Home Run and Gully on the Front Side, and Larch in the Larch Area. First-timers enrolled in lessons will start on the Sunny T-Bar, which serves an excellent beginner area separated from the rest of the runs. Too bad it's a T-Bar, a nightmare for snowboarders.

Parks and pipes

Lake Louise gets huge kudos for its terrain park and superpipe. The resort has one of the largest terrain parks in North America—Showtime—served by a high-speed quad. It features tabletop jumps ranging from 15 to 75 feet, more than 25 rails and funboxes, and two immense quarterpipes. The superpipe, higher on the mountain on Upper Juniper, is linked to the terrain park so you can hit both in one continuous run.

Cross-country and snowshoeing (visit xcskiresorts.com for more details)

The Fairmont Chateau Lake Louise (800-441-1414; 522-3511) has about 50 km. of groomed trails and access to hundreds of miles of backcountry trails. The ungroomed, well-marked, 7-mile trail to Skoki Lodge, a rustic log cabin (meaning no electricity, no plumbing, wood-burning stove), starts near Temple Lodge at the ski area. If you're not up for skiing so far into the wilderness, follow the gentle Shoreline Trail at The Fairmont Chateau Lake Louise. Skiing *on* Lake Louise is not recommended.

A complex 20-km. network called **Pipestone Loops** starts 4 miles west of the Lake Louise Overpass on the Trans-Canada Highway. Although all are marked beginner, some are suitable for the intermediate.

About 25 miles from Lake Louise, just over the border into British Columbia, is **Emerald Lake Lodge** (343-6321 or 800-663-6336). It has a 40-km. network of groomed trails with views of the Presidential Range, lodging in comfortable cabins and activities such as skating, snowshoeing and a games room. The lodge has a shuttle to the Lake Louise ski area.

Before setting out on any of the trails, check trail conditions at a park warden's office. Be aware that trail classification is done by healthy Canadians in good shape.

Lessons [05/06 prices, without tax]

Group lessons: For skiers or snowboarders, levels 2-3, it costs C$79 for 2.5 hours or C$109 for an all-day lesson. Levels 4-6 pay C$99 for 2.5 hours or C$129 for an all-day lesson that includes video analysis.

First-timer package: C$69 includes a full-day lesson, equipment rental and beginner lift ticket for skiers or snowboarders. A three-day package including lessons, rentals and lift ticket costs C$349; program starts on Sunday or Thursday.

Private lessons: One hour costs C$139; one hour after 3 p.m., C$89; First Tracks (1.5 hours starting at 8:30 a.m.) costs C$99; two hours, C$229; full day, C$499.

Special programs: Lake Louise has several special clinics, some for two hours, others for several days, including Performance Plus Workshops, women's camps and more.

The Club Ski program and Club Snowboard program operate at Lake Louise, Sunshine Village and Ski Banff @ Norquay. Groups of similar interest and expertise ski or ride together with the same instructor for four hours a day at each of the three areas. The program starts Sundays and Thursdays, and one benefit is lift-line priority. For 2005/06, the three-day program costs C$234 (plus tax, lift tickets and rentals).

Racing: A dual-slalom NASTAR course is available for group bookings.

KidStuff [05/06 prices, without tax]

Child care: Ages 3 weeks to 6 years. Toddlers have their own play area. A full day is C$56 for infants to 19 months. Ages 19 months to 36 months cost C$45 for a full day; C$25 for a half day. Ages 36 months and older cost C$39 for a full day; C$25 for a half day. Ask about discounts for multiple children. Free snacks are provided; lunch is available by request for C$7. Infants younger than 19 months require reservations; no reservations are taken for other ages. Call 522-3555.

Children's lessons: The Kinderski program for ages 3–6 provides supervised day care, one ski lesson and indoor and outdoor play. Cost is C$20 for one lesson, or C$29 for two one-hour lessons; must book through day care. All-day ski programs for children ages 5–12 and snowboard programs for kids 7–12 cost C$76. Lift tickets are an additional $18; rentals are C$13; lunch is C$13. All children in ski and snowboard programs must wear helmets; rentals available for C$7. Club Junior (fashioned after the adult's Club Ski and Club Snowboard programs) is a three-day program featuring group lessons and skiing one day each at the three Banff resorts; C$234 for 2005/06 (plus tax, lift tickets and rentals).

Lift tickets [05/06 prices, without tax]

	Adult	Child (6-12)
One day	C$64	C$20
Three days	C$192 (S64/day)	C$60 (S20/day)
Five days	C$320 (S64/day)	C$100 (S20/day)

Who skis free: Children younger than 6.

Who skis at a discount: Youth ages 13–17 pay C$45 for one day; ages 65 and older pay C$51. Skiers and boarders interested in visiting other Banff ski areas should buy the Tri-Area Pass (see Banff Region chapter for prices).

Accommodations

Banff/Lake Louise Central Reservations (800-661-1676) books lodging in Banff, Lake Louise and Jasper. **Resorts of the Canadian Rockies Inc.** (800-258-7669), which owns Lake Louise, books ski packages and lodging for these Western Canada resorts: Lake Louise, Nakiska, Fernie and Kimberley. **Ski Banff-Lake Louise-Sunshine Reservations** (877-754-7076) books ski packages including the tri-area lift tickets and lodging at more than 30 Banff and Lake Louise properties. Packages are customized and can include Club Ski, Club Snowboard and Club Junior lessons, rentals, air and other activities.

The Fairmont Chateau Lake Louise (800-441-1414; 522-3511; $$$–$$$$) nests on the shore of Lake Louise, with the spectacular Victoria Glacier in the distance. This hotel dates back to a log chalet built in 1890. It has nearly 500 guestrooms, restaurants, shops, Nordic ski center, masseuse and free ski shuttles.

The Post Hotel (800-661-1586; 522-3989; $$$–$$$$) is a cozy, beautifully furnished, 93-room log lodge with great views on all sides. It's personal and quiet, with the warmth and elegance provided by Swiss innkeepers. The buffet breakfast is a board of tasty delights.

If you like staying in lodging of a quieter, gentler era, **Deer Lodge** (800-661-1595; 522-3747; $$$) will help your blood pressure drop 20 points. Rooms have no television, but you can read by a roaring fireplace in the enormous common room. There's no elevator, but friendly bellhops will carry your luggage. It's old and rustic, many rooms have no phones, some are small, but all are beautifully decorated with antiques and made for romance. It has a great rooftop hot tub too.

Lake Louise Inn (800-661-9237; 522-3791; $$–$$$$) is a simply decorated hotel that's good for families. Rooms range in size from economy double (two double beds) to superior lofts that sleep six. Amenities include heated indoor pool, hot tub, steam room and arcade room.

The **Canadian Alpine Centre & International Hostel** (522-2200; $), on Village Road, is bright, spotless and modern. Its lounge, with comfy chairs and Internet kiosks, is nicer than those at many hotels. Nightly rates start at $23; three-day ski packages, including tickets at Lake Louise, shuttles and breakfast, begin at $185.

If you've got a car and want a rustic lodge experience in a wilderness setting, check into the **Simpson's Num-Ti-Jah Lodge** (522-2167; $$–$$$). It's in the middle of prime territory for backcountry skiing, about a half-hour's drive from Lake Louise. This funky stone-and-log hotel sits on the shores of Bow Lake, and on clear days you can see the glaciers.

Dining

For breakfast on the mountain, the **Great Bear Room** ($) in the Whiskyjack Lodge serves a yummy and affordable breakfast buffet (however, beverages are extra, which took us by surprise). On-mountain lunch options are **The Powder Keg** ($$) with nachos, sandwiches and pizza; the **Great Bear Room,** with very affordable hot and cold luncheon buffets; and **Sawyer's Nook Restaurant** ($$) in Temple Lodge.

By far, the most enjoyable time we've ever had dining on a mountain is at the **Lake Louise Torchlight Dinner & Ski,** with an extensive buffet dinner held at the midmountain Whitehorn Lodge on Mondays and Fridays (522-3555; reservations required). Flamboyant live entertainment, doing the limbo for your meal, eating at communal tables and skiing down by torchlight make a memorable evening. Cost is C$53 per adult, C$25 per child.

On Saturday evenings, the **Brewster Cowboy's Barbecue & Dance Barn** (800-691-5085; 762-5454; $$$) provides a hearty cowboy dinner of a "Hip of Beef" served on a pitchfork, baked beans, baked potatoes, soup, salad and pie. Enjoy Western entertainment from mid-December to early April. This adventure includes a sleigh ride to the barn where you'll slap your thigh to a live country band, and dance if that's your passion. Package price is C$48 plus tax per adult (13 and older); C$28 for kids 12 and younger.

For dinner in **The Fairmont Chateau Lake Louise** (522-3511 for reservations at all its restaurants), the most elegant dining room is the **Edelweiss** ($$$), serving such entrees as salmon and duckling. The **Walliser Stube Wine Bar** ($$–$$$) specializes in Swiss cuisine such as raclette and fondue. **The Poppy Room** is a family restaurant, the only one open for breakfast in winter, aside from the 24-hour deli. **Glacier Saloon** ($$) has steak sandwiches, finger food and salads. The Chateau's **deli** is a good choice for a quick light breakfast or lunch. It also can pack a lunch to go.

The Post Hotel (522-3989; $$$) is recognized as serving the finest Continental cuisine in Lake Louise. For a special occasion, this is a wonderful place. **Deer Lodge** (522-3747;

$$$) has homemade breads as well as innovative specials and pastries.

Lake Louise Station (522-2600; $$–$$$) is a restored railway station with views of the mountains and freight trains that rumble past. The menu is quite extensive, with pastas, lamb, Alberta steaks and fresh salmon, among other dishes. Couples might like a table in the Killarney car, which was the private railroad car of a Canadian Railroad president.

If you're itching for a change of scenery, take the half-hour drive up the Icefields Parkway to get a taste of the Rocky Mountain cuisine at the **Elkhorn Dining Room** (522-2167; $$$) at Simpson's Num-Ti-Jah Lodge. Try to identify the animal trophy heads lining the walls while dining on fresh trout or hunter-style venison.

What a find! **Bill Peyto's Cafe** (522-2200; $) at the Canadian Alpine Centre & International Hostel promises great food at affordable prices and delivers it. The menu, posted on a chalkboard, is long and varied, with an emphasis on healthy, wholesome food. Breakfast is served until 2 p.m.

 ## Apres-ski/nightlife

Sitzmark Lounge is the apres-ski spot at the mountain. It's in the Whiskeyjack Lodge and has live entertainment on weekends. On sunny spring days, hang out on the deck of the **Glacier Gazebo** near the base lifts.

Apres-ski and nightlife in town center in the hotels. At The Fairmont Chateau Lake Louise, **The Glacier Saloon** has a lively atmosphere and dancing, while the **Walliser Stube** is a bit more subdued. For those who quit the slopes early, high tea (C$48 for two) in the Chateau's **Lobby Bar** or **Lakeview Lounge** is an experience that invites lingering. Quiet conversation is possible at **The Explorer's Lounge** in the Lake Louise Inn and The Post Hotel's **Outpost.** Explorer's offers DJ and karaoke nights during the week too.

 ## Other activities

Kingmik Sled Dog Tours (877-919-7779; 763-8887), operating since 1982, offers trips ranging from a 30-minute introduction to the two-hour Great Divide Experience to the Alberta/British Columbia Great Divide, during which participants get a chance to drive the team. Each sled holds up to two adults and one child.

The Banff/Lake Louise area has many opportunities for other winter sports such as **skating, ice fishing** and **ice climbing,** as well as more relaxing activities such as **sightseeing, hot springs** and **museums.** See the Banff chapter for details.

 ## Getting there and getting around

By air: Calgary Airport is served by major airlines, including Air Canada. Rocky Mountain Sky Shuttle (888-762-8754; 762-5200), Brewster Transportation (762-6700), Greyline Transportation (762-9102) or Banff Airporter (762-3330) will get you from the airport to Banff or Lake Louise.

By car: Lake Louise Village is 115 miles west of Calgary and 36 miles from Banff.

Getting around: Bus service is available from the airport directly to most hotels. The Lake Louise shuttlebus is free and operates from most hotels to the base of the ski lifts. Buy the Tri-Area ski pass and your bus transportation is included. We really recommend a car for extensive sightseeing.

Dining: $$$$-Entrees C$30+; $$$-C$20-$30; $$-C$10-$20; $-less than C$10.
Accommodations: (double room) $$$$-C$200+; $$$-C$141-$200; $$-C$81-$140; $-C$80 and less.

Marmot Basin

Jasper, Alberta
Canada

Summit elevation (lift-served):	**7,970 feet**
Vertical drop:	**2,400 feet**
Base elevation:	**5,570 feet**

Address: P.O. Box 1300
Jasper, AB, Canada T0E 1E0
Area code: 780
Snow report: 488-5909 (Edmonton)
Ski area phone: 852-3816 **Fax:** 852-3533
Toll-free reservations: (877) 902-9455 and
(800) 473-8135
E-mail: info@skimarmot.com
Internet: www.skimarmot.com or
www.skiingjasper.com (resort)
www.jaspercanadianrockies.com (tourism bureau)
Expert:★★★★
Advanced:★★★★
Intermediate:★★★
Beginner:★★★ **First-timer:**★★★

Number and types of lifts: 9–1 high-speed quad, 1
quad, 1 triple, 3 doubles,
2 surface lifts, 1 moving carpet
Skiable acreage: 1,675 acres
Snowmaking: 1 percent
Uphill capacity: 11,931 skiers per hour
Parks & pipes: 2 parks
Bed base: 5,500
Nearest lodging: About 11 miles away in Jasper
Resort child care: Yes, 19 months and older
Adult ticket, per day: C$42-C$59 (06/07, without tax)

Dining:★★★
Apres-ski/nightlife:★★★
Other activities:★★★★

Far into the northland and separated from the hustle of Banff by a three-hour drive, Jasper is far enough north, and far enough from a major airport (Edmonton: four hours), that people aren't here by mistake or on a whim. People come to Jasper National Park for the scenery, the remoteness, the wonder of a herd of elk outside their hotel and the call of Canadian geese swooping over Lac Beauvert in the spring while the ski area still has winter snow.

Marmot Basin's base lodge, Caribou Chalet, is a beautiful 32,000-square-foot building that blends in with its surroundings. The terrain is fairly evenly divided among ability levels, with appropriate challenge, so everyone will enjoy themselves. If you're looking to improve your skills, Marmot is a perfect choice.

Marmot continues to open new terrain every year. Most recent was Cornice Run, off Marmot Peak, accessed by a short hike from the top of the Eagle Ridge Chair. Eagle Ridge, previously accessed only by hiking, is now serviced by a quad chair. Eagle Ridge has two faces: Eagle East and Chalet Slope. The 22 runs off the ridge include expert, advanced and intermediate terrain, as well as one novice trail that winds its way down the mountain. Eagle East provides a wilderness experience with the convenience and safety of staying within the boundaries of the ski area. In addition to the prime tree skiing in Eagle East, two huge bowls of advanced and expert terrain are here. The resort also opened Outer Limits, accessed off the back of the Paradise Chair, for another wilderness experience.

Mountain layout

The area's one high-speed quad, Eagle Express, serves as the primary chair to the upper-mountain lifts. It can get somewhat crowded during peak loading times. Try Caribou Chair on the lower mountain, far to the right, where there's rarely a wait. It has terrain for all abilities and also will get you to the upper-mountain lifts. You can purchase lift tickets at the hut near Caribou Chair on the weekend, so you can bypass the lines at the base ticket windows. To reach it, drive past the main lodge and head for the farthest parking lot (fourth lot). Or park in any of the lots in this area and ski down to the base to buy your ticket. If you want to learn about the local history while you explore the mountain, join a mountain host for a complimentary tour.

♦♦**Expert ♦Advanced:** Marmot has tree-lined runs toward the bottom and wide-open bowls at the top. Generally, the higher you go, the tougher the skiing gets. The Knob Chair takes you to the highest lift-served terrain. From the top of that lift, the hardiest hike the last 600 feet up to Marmot Peak. (Our vertical-foot and summit stats reflect the *lift-served* terrain, while those advertised by the area include this hike.) It's all Alpine bowls up here, and they are really sweet.

Experts will want to drop into the fine powder in outrageously large Dupres Bowl, with Dupres Chute dividing it from Charlie's Bowl, which is even steeper and stays untracked longer. Charlie's Bowl has a 50+-degree entrance that mellows out to perhaps 42 degrees.

Another good choice for bowls and untracked powder is to stay high and to the right of The Knob (facing down the mountain). Experts have several different playgrounds all to themselves here—including McCready's Choice and Thunder Bowl.

On Eagle Ridge, Chalet Slope is a vast area of glades that are some of the most challenging and grin-inducing we've ever skied. Powder lasts the longest here. The chutes, bowls and glades on Eagle East are an experience like no other at Marmot, with warning signs to sober you. Once you drop off the back side, you have no idea you're still at the resort. It's a true backcountry experience.

There's also excellent glade skiing off the Paradise Chair and Kiefer T-bar, both of which serve Caribou Ridge. Off to the right, facing downhill, you'll have an absolute blast in the trees in a black area misnamed Milk Run. Caribou Knoll is a real hoot too. Further down the mountain, drop into any woods that look tempting, especially those off green-circle Old Road. Outer Limits is an off-piste experience similar to Eagle East off the back of the Paradise Chair. Plan for at least 30 minutes to make your way out along the rather flat Whistler Creek Trail, which dumps you back out next to the third parking lot below the Caribou Chair.

■ **Intermediate:** Every lift has an intermediate way down, even The Knob. Punch Bowl and Paradise are especially delightful runs. The Knob Traverse takes you high on the mountain where you'll have incredible views.

On blustery days, stay low on the mountain, where trees provide shelter from winds that sometimes block visibility on the naked summit. The intermediate runs on Chalet Slope off Eagle Ridge, which also hold snow longest, are excellent choices.

●●**Beginner ●First-timer:** The three lifts at the base serve most of the lower-level terrain. Beginners have expansive mountain access, with 1,100 vertical feet on Eagle Express after you master terrain from the School House T-bar. You can even head up to Caribou Ridge for an above-treeline thrill where a wide trail, Basin Run, takes you safely back to the lower slopes. A novice run on Chalet Slope off Eagle Ridge provides gorgeous views from the top before you wind down the mountain.

Ride Guide: Most riders come here for the freeriding. Off the Knob Chair, you can hike another 600 feet to catch freshies in Upper Basin or choose Peak Run to scoot over to the gully below Thunder Bowl (carry your speed on this traverse). Don't skip Charlie's Bowl—there are so many lines here, it's possible to spend all day. Carry your speed to make it from the top of Knob Chair to the entrance of Charlie's Bowl, and there's a rather flat runout at the bottom, so you might have to hoof it a bit on both ends. Eagle East is a true backcountry experience with positively heart-thumping terrain. The drop-ins to this area can be intimidating and often require long traverses to get you where you want to go; just suck it up. Pay attention to boundary signs funneling you back toward the trails or you'll have a long hike out. Very nice beginner terrain is at the base of the mountain, but it's served by a T-bar, which can be a nightmare for snowboarders. Intermediates have great choices all over the mountain. There's very nice beginner terrain at the base of the mountain, served by a Platter lift which can be difficult for snowboarders. Head higher up the mountain via the Paradise and Kiefer chairs for the Marmot Terrain Park located on Marmot Run in the Upper Area.

Parks and pipes

The terrain park is on Marmot Run in the upper area of the mountain. It's a respectable size park with tabletops, hips, spines and rails. There's a nice natural quarterpipe on Marmot Run too. During early season, before Mother Nature provides enough snow to build big terrain park features (the resort relies on all-natural snow), Marmot terrain park staff install a smaller rail park on an old road, just above the loading station of the Eagle Ridge quad.

Cross-country and snowshoeing (visit xcskiresorts.com for more details)

This is prime ski touring and snowshoeing country with scenery guaranteed to delight. For a complete winter trail listing and guide, stop by Jasper National Park's Information Center or call 852-6176.

Jasper Park Lodge trails, about 19 km., are unparalleled for beauty and variety. The gentle, groomed and easily accessible trails wind around lake shores, Alpine meadows and forests. The easiest is Cavell, a 5 km. loop with the elk. The perimeter loop samples a little of everything the Jasper Park Lodge trails offer.

Near Jasper Townsite, a good level, nighttime-lit beginner trail is 4.5km Whistlers Campground Loop, 4.5 km. Pyramid Bench Trail, 4.7 km. rated intermediate, overlooks the Athabasca River Valley. Patricia Lake Circle, 5.9 km. intermediate (follow the trail clockwise), provides stunning views of Mt. Edith Cavell, the region's most prominent and dramatically sloped peak. Most lodges have trail maps. .

For **guided cross-country skiing, backcountry and snowshoeing tours,** contact Edge Control, 852-4945; Beyond the Beaten Path, 852-5650; Overlander Trekking & Tours, 852-4056 (snowshoe tours only); or Alpine Art, 852-3709. Ask about rentals and/or instruction.

A full day's ski over Maccarib Pass from the Marmot Basin Road on the north shore of Amethyst Lake leads to Tonquin Valley Lodge, hearty home-cooked meals and welcome beds. Contact **Tonquin Valley Ski Tours,** Box 550, Jasper, Alberta T0L 1E0; 852-3909.

Lessons (05/06 prices, without tax)

Group lessons: "Ski and Snowboard Improvement Clinics" are for all abilities, C$46 for two hours.

First-timer package: Includes lift pass, two-hour lesson and ski or snowboard equipment for C$69.

Private lessons: C$65 for one hour hour, with multihour lessons available.

Special programs: Ski Week packages are for all ability levels and include three days of lift tickets, three two-hour sessions, three days of rentals plus video analysis and an optional dinner with your instructor; cost is C$380.

KidStuff [05/06 prices, without tax]

Child care: Ages 19 months to 6 years. All-day care costs C$45. Lunch is an additional C$6. Per hour rate is C$7; each additional child in family, C$6 per hour. For reservations, call 852-3816.

Children's lessons: Ages 4–5, one-hour group lesson in morning or afternoon for those who have been on skis, C$37; introduction to skiing includes one-hour lessons, lift ticket and rentals, C$65. For ages 6–12, there are several options. A full-day program, ski or snowboard, costs C$115 (includes lunch). A two-hour group lesson, ski or snowboard, costs C$37. Learn-to-ski or snowboard lessons including lift ticket and rentals are C$59. One-hour private lessons are C$65. Ski & Snowboard Weeks include three days of lessons, lift tickets, rentals, video analysis and an optional dinner with the instructor for C$280. Kids 13 and older do not have full-day programs; instead they take lessons through the adult ski school.

Lift tickets [05/06 prices, without tax]

	Adult	Junior (6-12)
One day	C$59	C$21
Three days	C$172 ($57/day)	C$62 ($21/day)
Five days	C$286 ($57/day)	C$104 ($21/day)

Who skis free: Children 5 and younger.

Who skis at a discount: Youth/student prices (ages 13–25) and seniors (65+) are C$47 for one day, with multiday discounts; college-age students must be full time and present a valid student ID. Early season rates are lower. During the Jasper in January winter festival, everyone 13 and older pays C$42 per day, juniors pay C$21.

Accommodations

The resort does not have mountainside lodging. Stay in nearby Jasper which offers a variety of accommodations from downtown rooms to family-style units with kitchens to private lakeshore cabins. Many of the lodges listed have ski packages, so be sure to ask..

Jasper Tourism and Commerce (Box 98, Jasper, Alberta, T0E 1E0; call 780-852-3858) will send a ski vacation planner that includes rates. Central reservations at (877) 902-9455 has a wide selection of accommodations, activities and tours, transportation and ski packages. For the Jasper area in particular, call **Ski Jasper** at (800) 473-8135 October through April.

The Fairmont Jasper Park Lodge (852-3301 or 800-441-1414; $$–$$$$) is located on 900 acres a few miles from town. Traditional log cabins from the 1920s and cedar chalets with spacious modern suites are all elegantly rustic and sensuous. The older buildings have all been renovated and are thoroughly modern in the areas that count, such as bathrooms. Everything is linked by pathways along Lac Beauvert to the main building, which is reminiscent of a great hunting lodge and houses all the restaurants, night spots and shops. The lodge suggests all the best qualities you'd expect from someone's wilderness summer camp, combined with the amenities you'd expect from a fine resort. We found delightful staff, fabulous food, and enchanting rooms with beds that gave us one of the best night's sleep we've ever had.

Pyramid Lake Resort (888-852-4900; 852-4900; $$–$$$$) began its life as a local fishing village. The 7-km. road from downtown Jasper winds through woods, revealing glimpses of the mountains along the way. The resort's wilderness setting is stunning, ideal for backcountry skiing fans and others who prefer quiet, remote places. Most of the modern chalets have lovely

Dining: $$$$-Entrees (C$30+; $$$-C$20-$30; $$-C$10-$20; $-less than C$10.
Accommodations: (double room) $$$$-C$200+; $$$-C$141-$200; $$-C$81-$140; $-C$80 and less.

lake views, kitchenettes and fireplaces, plus there's a 10-person outdoor hot tub.

The upscale **Chateau Jasper** (852-5644; 800-661-9323; $$–$$$$) is about a 15-minute walk from "downtown" Jasper and has an indoor pool and hot tub. The Chateau offers a shuttle to town.

In town, **Jasper Inn Alpine Resort** (852-4461; 800-661-1933; $$–$$$$) has spacious standard rooms, studios, suites, loft units and one- to two-bedroom condo-style units. There's an indoor pool, steam room, sauna, hot tub and coin laundry, plus a very good restaurant.

The Sawridge Inn & Conference Center Jasper (852-5111; 800-661-6427; $$–$$$$) offers everything from deluxe standard rooms to luxury parlor suites that reflect a Canadian Native American flair. It has an indoor pool, outdoor hot tubs, Finnish sauna and laundry facilities. The European Beauty & Wellness Center here is a full-service spa.

The Astoria (852-3351; 800-661-7343; $$) is a small hotel of character with charmingly renovated guestrooms. **Whistlers Inn** (852-3361; 800-282-9919; $$) has nice standards, deluxes and suites, some recently renovated. It has a steam room, outdoor rooftop hot tub, two restaurants, pub and a gift shop.

Marmot Lodge (852-4471; 888-852-7737; $–$$$) has rooms with kitchens and fireplaces. Indoor pool, sauna and hot tub are on the premises. Children younger than 12 are free. **The Athabasca Hotel** (852-3386; 887-542-8422; $–$$), one of Jasper's original lodgings, blends mountain influences with a Victorian theme and is close to the bus and VIA RAIL station.

If you fly into or out of Edmonton, stay at the **Fantasyland Hotel** (800-661-6454; 444-3000; $$$–$$$$). Every floor is decorated in a theme such as Hollywood, Canadian Pacific Railway, and so forth. It's an experience. The hotel adjoins the West Edmonton Mall.

Dining

On the mountain, Marmot Basin has six places to eat. Upstairs in the Caribou Chalet, the **Caribou Bar & Grill** ($–$$) serves excellent sandwiches, burgers and salads. There's also a **cafeteria** ($) in the base lodge. **Paradise Chalet** at mid-mountain has a cafe and lounge ($), as well as a nice deck. On busy days, eat lunch at their **Charlie's Lounge** before 11:45 a.m. or after 1:15 p.m. **Eagle Chalet** ($–$$) at mid-mountain is a cozy rustic restaurant with a fireplace to warm you. Both Paradise Chalet and Eagle Chalet have fabulous views of Jasper National Park.

Jasper has some excellent and varied restaurants. Canadian, Chinese, French, Greek, Italian, Korean, Japanese, Mexican, continental and family-style dining are all available.

The lakeview **Edith Cavell Dining Room** (852-6052; $$$) in The Fairmont Jasper Park Lodge specializes in elegant informality. The dress is resort casual, the setting is china on white linen, the service is attentive and the food is the best in the area. The menu showcases continental cuisine (save room for dessert). For breakfast, **The Meadows** ($–$$) serves wholesome food in a country setting; try the excellent breakfast buffet.

A stone fireplace, soaring ceilings and spectacular views overlooking Pyramid Lake set the stage at **The Pines** (852-4900; $$–$$$) at Pyramid Lake Resort. Enjoy Rocky Mountain mushroom bisque, rack of lamb and smoked chicken and shrimp carbonara.

In Jasper, The Inn Restaurant (852-4461; $$; right) at Jasper Inn offers a cozy, casual atmosphere. The creative menu includes such appetizers as citrus-marinated chicken brochettes, pernod-soaked scallops and various pasta entrees. Also choose from Alberta beef, salmon, fish and chicken.

Andy's Bistro (852-4559; $$), downtown, is very popular—especially with locals. The moderately priced menu emphasizes Swiss and Canadian cuisine. Locals recommend the mixed salad and the lamb. A C$25 special some nights includes an appetizer, entree and dessert.

Walter's Dining Room (852-5111; $$) in the Sawridge Inn specializes in tasty Canadian and continental dishes. Check out the stuffed wildlife as you dine. Save room for dessert.

Tonquin Prime Rib Village (852-4966; $$) serves steaks, prime rib and seafood. The Greek-style lamb chops are, well, you just have to try them for yourself. The restaurant has a bar and a beautiful view. Make reservations. **Fiddle River Seafood Company** (852-3032; $$–$$$) gets raves for creative fresh fish cooking. **Embers Steakhouse** (852-4471; $$) serves light and healthy cuisine (beef, local fish) in a casually elegant restaurant. **Sorrentino's Bistro Bar** (852-5644; $$$) in the Chateau Jasper features authentic Italian fare.

L&W Restaurant (852-4114; $$), with an atrium setting and remarkably broad menu is a very good Greek restaruant; also choose from steaks, seafood, pasta and pizza. **Whistlestop Bar** (852-3361; $) at Whistlers Inn serves a bar menu. **Something Else Restaurant** (852-3233; $$) is also a good choice for families.

The area's best sushi is served at **Oka Sushi** (852-3301; $$) in the Fairmont Jasper Park Lodge, but also popular is **Denjiro** (852-3780; $$), with Japanese entrees and a sushi bar.

Miss Italia (852-4002; $$) is the spot for Italian cooking. **Mountain Foods Cafe** (852-4050; $), a sit-down or take-out restaurant, has affordable prices for its deli items. For pizza by the slice, head to the local's favorite, **Truffles and Trout** (852-9676; $). Pizza and other Italian dishes are served at **Jasper Pizza Place** (852-3225; $).

The **Soft Rock Cafe** ($), with Internet service, serves the area's best breakfast and serves it all day. Don't miss **Papa George's Restaurant** (852-3351; $–$$) in the Astoria Hotel on the main drag. It has a rich, lengthy history in Jasper and serves some of the best Italian food in the Rockies. **Bear Paw's Bakery** (852-3233; $) sells freshly baked goods daily.

Coco's Cafe (852-4550; $), downtown on Patricia Street, is a locals' favorite with awesome little dishes, pastries and Jasper's best coffee.

 ## Apres-ski/nightlife

Jasper is not known for rocking nightlife, but you can certainly find some action. The **Atha-B Club** in Athabasca Hotel has the liveliest dancing in town. The hotel also has **O'Shea's**, an Irish pub. **Whistle Stop** at Whistlers Inn is a good pub-type nightspot with darts, pool and big-screen sports. **De'd Dog Pub** in the Astoria Hotel is a locals' hangout that draws folks of mixed ages; light food is available. **Fireside Lounge** in Marmot Lodge has nightly entertainment. **Pete's** attracts a younger crowd with disco and occasional live music. **Downstream** is a bar with good chicken wings.

At Fairmont Jasper Park Lodge, the **Emerald Lounge** has hearty apres-ski snacks, and **Tent City Sports Lounge** recalls the history of the lodge and has lively entertainment.

 ## Other activities

Visitors come to Jasper National Park to ski but also to enjoy the pristine wilderness and wildlife. There are a variety of ways to do the latter. Here are just a few:

Jasper in January is the area's annual winter festival. Lift tickets drop considerably, as do lodging rates. Activities include demo days, a mountain-to-valley relay race, ice and snow sculpting, canyon crawls, snowshoeing, tobogganing, chili cook-off, taste of the town food sampler, ice rescue demonstrations and more.

One of the most unusual adventures is a **Maligne Canyon Icewalk,** a guided tour through Maligne Canyon. You'll hike a little more than a mile through a 6- to 20-foot-wide gorge on

Dining: $$$$-Entrees C$30+; $$$-C$20-$30; $$-C$10-$20; $-less than C$10.
Accommodations: (double room) $$$$-C$200+; $$$-C$141-$200; $$-C$81-$140; $-C$80 and less.

the frozen river past ice caves, frozen waterfalls and towering canyon walls. We cannot recommend this experience highly enough. Call Overlander Trekking & Tours, 852-4056. Tours also provided by Beyond the Beaten Path, 852-5650, or Jasper Adventure Center at 852-5595.

Ice skating on a lake and **sleigh rides** are available at Fairmont Jasper Park Lodge. Or rent **snowbikes** at Marmot Basin. Go **dogsledding** with Overlander Trekking & Tours, 852-4056, or the Jasper Adventure Center, 852-5595. **Heliskiing** in Valemount, B.C., 56 miles away along a scenic drive, is available mid-February to mid-April. Book through Overlander Trekking & Tours, 852-4056; also Robson HeliMagic, 566-4700. Snowfarmers (250-566-9161) in Valemont has, get this: **snowmobile-serviced skiing and riding.** Maximum six guests. Snowfarmers also provides **snowmobile touring.**

Jasper Activity Center (852-3381) on Pyramid Lake Road has **swimming, curling, squash, racquetball, a weight room** and **indoor skating. Minor league hockey games** are held on Saturdays and Sundays.

Sightseeing companies run bus tours to the Icefields Parkway. Call Brewster Transportation, 852-3332, or Jasper Adventure Center, 852-5595. Plan to take one day to drive along the Icefields Parkway (Hwy. 93)—you won't be sorry.

Wildlife spotting is a must-do: You're very likely to see mule deer, bighorn sheep, mountain goats and elk; if you're lucky, you'll also see moose, caribou, wolves and coyotes. The exhibits at **Jasper-Yellowhead Museum and Archives** (852-3013) highlight Jasper's history and human heritage, such as the early explorers, the fur trade, the railway and skiing.

Make sure to pick up a **free winter guide** for a complete overview of activities and attractions in Jasper.

Getting there and getting around

By air: Calgary and Edmonton are the primary gateways to the Canadian Rockies. These International airports provide non-stop and direct flights and connectors. If you don't rent a car, Greyhound operates daily service from Edmonton and Vancouver; call 421-4211.

By car: From Edmonton, Jasper is 225 miles west on Hwy. 16. The ski area is 12 miles south of Jasper via Hwy. 93, 93A and Marmot Basin Road. Jasper is about 170 miles north of Banff.

By train: VIA RAIL (888-842-7245) operates service to Jasper from Edmonton and Vancouver on its restored '50s-style art deco train, the Canadian. U.S. travel agents have more information. Ask about the Snow Train to Jasper.

Getting around: A car is best here. The ski area is a few miles from the town and lodging. Inquire about the daily shuttlebus from Jasper hotels to Marmot Basin. Sun Dog Tours (780-852-4056 or 888-786-3641) provides the Jasper–Banff Daily Connector.

Big White Ski Resort and Silver Star Mountain Resort

British Columbia, Canada

From British Columbia's west coast, the mountain ranges roll east in ascending waves until they reach the Rocky Mountain peaks on the Continental Divide. The British Columbia highlands and plateaus take moisture from the Pacific storms that drop dryer snow in the Monashees, Selkirks, Kootenays and Purcells on their way to the Rockies. It's here that you'll find the resorts of Interior British Columbia. The skiing experience in western Canada has its own fingerprint, its own special flavor with an inviting appeal to skiers from eastern North America, Europe and Australia. Big White and Silver Star are under the same ownership and with one lift ticket, skiers and snowboarders have access to almost 6,000 acres of skiable terrain.

Big White Ski Resort

Big White, Canada's largest completely ski-in/ski-out resort village, overlooks the spectacular Monashee Mountain Range. Though it's been around for more than 40 years, it's been only in the last decade that it's grown into full resort status.

Big White is big and getting bigger. The newly built Snow Ghost Express, paralleling the current Ridge Rocket Express, services Big White's most popular runs and terrain from the main base near the Ridge Day lodge. A free gondola carries guests down from the main village plaza to Happy Valley, home to a day lodge, rental shop, high-end gift shop, a skating trail and rink, Nordic center, beginner's learning center and a humongous tubing park. Several luxury condominium projects are completed, including The Timbers, Perfection Ridge, The Crescent, and The Aspens Phase 2.

The Okanagan Valley is the hot winter destination in the West, and many advise getting here soon while it's still relatively affordable. For Australians, Big White is the second-biggest destination ski resort in B.C., behind Whistler Blackcomb. The village sits at 5,760 feet (B.C.'s highest base area) and lifts carry skiers up to 7,606 feet. That's about the same elevation as Whistler Blackcomb, but the air and snow are considerably dryer this far inland. One of Big White's signature features is its tree skiing. Night skiing with 1,624 vertical feet is open Tuesday through Saturday; the terrain park is lighted as well.

Mountain layout

♦♦**Expert** ♦**Advanced:** Experts normally like the Gem Lake Express runs, which are nice and long. Goat's Kick, left of the Ridge Rocket Express, is an especially fun challenge. Going to the right from the Alpine T-bar gets you into Parachute Bowl. Don't miss Big White's Pegasus and the double-black extreme playground, The Cliff, off the same lift. You'll have quite a ski-out to the Black Forest Express, but the initial double-black rush is worth it. Plus a chair in The Cliff area means you can do laps here before heading down.

Natural hits and drops fall off Perfection, Falcon Glades and around Westridge. For

Big White Ski Resort Facts

Address: Box 2039, Station R,
Kelowna, B.C., Canada V1X 4K5
Area code: 250
Ski area phone: 765-3101
Snow report: 765-7669
Fax: 765-1822
Toll-free reservations: (800) 663-2772
E-mail: bigwhite@bigwhite.com (information)
or cenres@bigwhite.com (reservations)
Internet: www.bigwhite.com
Expert:★★★
Advanced:★★★★
Intermediate:★★★★
Beginner:★★★★ **First-timer:**★★★

Summit elevation: 7,606 feet
Vertical drop: 2,550 feet
Base elevation: 5,706 feet (Village base);
4,950 feet (Westridge base)

Number of lifts: 17–1 8-passenger high-speed gondola, 1 high-speed 6-pack, 4 high-speed quads, 1 quad, 1 triple, 3 doubles, 1 T-bar, 2 moving carpets, 1 handle tow, 2 tube lifts
Snowmaking: Only in terrain park
Skiable acreage: 2,765 acres
Uphill capacity: 28,000 per hour
Parks & pipes: 2 parks, 2pipes
Bed base: 14,000
Nearest lodging: Slopeside lodging, all ski-in/ski-out
Resort child care: 18 months and older
Adult ticket, per day: C$58-C$64 (05/06, without tax)
Dining:★★★

bumps, try Dragon's Tongue to the left of Ridge Rocket Express.

■ **Intermediate:** Good warm-up runs are the Sun Run from the top of the Alpine T-bar, Exhibition, Highway 33, Serwas and Sundance. There's also fine terrain off the Rocket and Powder chairs. Roller Coaster, Blue Sapphire and Kalinas Rainbow come recommended. International is an intermediate bump run. The blue ratings in the Black Forest are low-end. An entire area off Gem Lake Express is dedicated solely to intermediate runs, making it worthwhile to venture to this out-of-the-way part of the mountain.

●● **Beginner:** Millie's Mile, named after the owner's granddaughter, runs alongside the Black Forest Express. All lifts serve at least one green run.

● **First-timer:** A complete learn-to-ski facility, in a private and secluded teaching area, is snuggled in at the base of the free Happy Valley gondola, a short ride down from the Village Plaza. Hummingbird, served by the Plaza Chair, is designated for first-timers only. Woodcutter is also excellent, but mind the traffic.

Ride Guide: Riders have a good time most anywhere on the mountain. Particularly popular are the Sun-Rype Bowl and the adjacent Black Bear run, both reached by the Gem Lake Express. The bowl is a big gentle swoop of a run that can get you into some trees known as the Black Bear Glades. Also reached from Gem Lake Express is the single-black Blackjack, a good long fall-line run. The only double-blacks are reached by the Alpine T-bar, which many snowboarders find difficult to ride, and the new double chair to The Cliff and East Peak area. There are some gentle runs down from the top of the T-bar if you change your mind.

Parks and pipes

Big White invested $2.5 million to build TELUS Park, with an on-mountain lodge and chairlift, so it can be used as a training and competition facility for snowboarding and freeskiing. But don't worry, ordinary folks can use it too. The 50-acre park area centralizes the terrain parks, rail garden, pipes, boardercross and family fun-race area. An Olympic-sized, 500-foot-long superpipe, with 17-foot transitional walls, meets World Cup FIS and X Games standards. If that's too intimidating for you, try the 400-foot-long halfpipe with 12-foot walls. Look for an intermediate terrain and rail park, an advanced terrain and rail park, and a boardercross course capable of hosting Olympic FIS qualifying events. Within the terrain parks, you'll find assorted mailbox sliders, step-up jumps and hips. Rails include minis, flats, rainbows, kinks and wide rails. Snowmaking covers the park area, making it easier to open everything earlier in the season. The park is lit for night skiing and riding and the on-mountain lodge here—with food and beverage facilities, large deck and washroom—provides a place by the park to take a break.

Cross-country and snowshoeing (visit xcskiresorts.com for more details)

Big White has 25 km. of cross-country trails. The beginners' trail is a 4.3-km. loop from the Plaza Chair. Cross-country skiing is included with lift tickets.

Lessons [05/06 prices, without tax]

For lesson information and reservations, call 491-6101; 765-3101.

Group lessons: A two-hour lesson costs C$45; multiday rates are available.

First-timer package: A two-hour learn-to-ski or -snowboard lesson, including Plaza lift ticket and rentals, costs C$55. A three-day package costs C$149.

Private lessons: For up to three people, all day costs C$350; half-day afternoon, C$179; half-day morning, C$229; two hours, C$169; a 1.5-hour early-bird private starting at 8:30 a.m. costs C$125. Add an additional person to a private for C$45. Reservations are recommended for all private lessons and are required for an all-day lesson.

Special programs: Ski/Board Weeks are four-day programs with two-hour lessons, video analysis, fun race, souvenirs and a wrap-up luncheon for C$160 (start in December on Mondays). Additional programs offered: Free Ride Weekend Camps, TELUS Park Flight School and Heavy Metal Shop. Check specialty programs with the reservation desk.

KidStuff [05/06 prices, without tax]

Child care: Ages 18 months to 6 years. It costs C$60 for a full day (lunch included); C$36 for a half day. Multiday discounts are available. Hourly rate is C$14. Ages 3–4 can add a lesson to the child-care program; C$99, including child care. Located in the Village Plaza, the Kids Centre recommends reservations; 765-3101, ext. 233. Parents/guardians must provide proof of birth date (either birth certificate or passport), immunization history and health insurance number. The resort accommodates dietary needs based on allergies and also requests that no nut products are brought into the child-care center. Big White's child-care program is recognized world-wide as top-notch.

Children's lessons: Ages 4–12, a full day costs C$86 and includes lunch; half day costs C$48. Program for kids ages 4–6 includes indoor play time; snowboard lessons start at age 7. Private lessons are available and range from C$99 to C$350, depending upon the length of time. The resort recommends all children wear helmets; rental is free but supplies are limited. A note about the kids' instruction center: It's recognized as a top program for kids. Security is tight. Parents are given pagers.

Special activities: The Kids' Centre offers Kids After Dark, supervised evening programs including Pizza and Movie Night, Craft Night, Torchlight Parade, Carnival Night, and Skating and Tubing Parties. Bookings can be made at the Kids' Centre prior to 3 p.m. on the day offered.

Dining: $$$$-Entrees C$30+; $$$-C$20-$30; $$-C$10-$20; $-less than C$10.
Accommodations: (double room) $$$$-C$200+; $$$-C$141-$200; $$-C$81-$140; $-C$80 and less.

Lift tickets (05/06 prices, without tax)

	Adult	Youth (13-18)	Child (6-12)
One day	C$64	C$55	C$32
Three days	C$178 ($59/day)	C$151 ($50/day)	C$82 ($27/day)
Five days	C$292 ($58/day)	C$247 ($49/day)	C$132 ($26/day)

Who skis free: Children 5 and younger.

Who skis at a discount: Seniors 65+ and Canadian college students pay youth prices.

Note: Prices are rounded to the nearest dollar. Big White has night skiing, 5 p.m.–8 p.m., Tuesday to Saturday, from mid-December to end of March.

Accommodations

Lodging in the Big White mountain village ranges from hostels, hotels and condos to private chalets, all ski-in/ski-out. **Big White Central Reservations** (800-663-2772 in North America) is a one-stop shop for accommodation and package vacation needs. You can also visit the website for accommodation details.

Chateau Big White ($$–$$$$) is close to services in the Village Plaza. All rooms have gas fireplaces and kitchenettes with microwaves and fridges. The hotel has a lounge, four-star restaurant, day spa, underground parking and hot tub. The **Inn at Big White** ($$–$$$$), across the street from the Chateau, has 100 rooms, an outdoor pool and hot tub, fitness room, restaurant and lounge. **White Crystal Inn** ($$–$$$$), a European-style hotel in the heart of the village, features cable TV, room phones, an outdoor hot tub and a great slopeside lounge.

Condominiums and vacation homes, all new or recently built, range in size from one to four bedrooms, and feature full bathrooms and kitchens. Some units have gas fireplaces, balconies and private hot tubs. Choose from **Stonebridge Lodge** ($$$–$$$$), **Trappers' Crossing** ($$$–$$$$), **Timber Ridge** ($$$–$$$$), **Tree Tops** ($$$–$$$$), **Black Bear** ($$$–$$$$), **Grizzly Lodge** ($$$–$$$$) and **Blacksmith Lodge** ($$$–$$$$).

Chateau On The Ridge ($$–$$$) features condos with kitchens, gas fireplaces and outdoor common hot tubs. **Das Hofbrauhaus** ($–$$$) is slopeside with an indoor pool, hot tub and racquetball courts. **Eagles Resort** ($$–$$$) offers 20 three-bedroom condos with gas fireplace and kitchens, plus a large hot tub on the property. **Graystoke Inn** ($$) has one- and two-bedroom condos, plus a common outdoor hot tub.

The **Monashee Inn** ($$–$$$) gives an unsurpassed view of the Monashee Mountains. The **Ponderosa Inn** ($–$$$), on the Easy Street trail, is family-oriented and has a hot tub and sauna. In the heart of the village, the **Whitefoot Lodge** ($–$$) features a hot tub, sauna, cold plunge, and laundry. Some rooms have kitchenettes.

The slopeside **SameSun Backpacker Ski Lodge** (877-562-2783; 545-8933; $) is a hostel with dorm rooms, private rooms and deluxe rooms. Recent renovations included upgrading all the private rooms and adding hardwood floors throughout.

Dining

Unlike most other ski resorts, you don't have to drive or even walk more than a block or so to find a great meal.

Beano's (491-3558; $), in the middle of the main ticket/rental building, serves the best coffee, soup and sandwiches in the village. Beano's owners are usually on site waiting on friendly Big White owners, managers and ski school directors enjoying their morning javas. Big White's owners and family live just across the street and like to check out what's happening with their guests and staff each morning. Drop by and say hello, give a compliment or lodge a complaint. They'll be glad you did. Surf the Internet with your latte upstairs at the **TELUS E-Loft.**

Snowshoe Sam's (765-1416; $$-$$$) is a legend at Big White. This multistoried establishment, up a flight of steps in the village, concentrates mainly on steaks and chops, although the seafood and pasta are quite good. You'll need dinner reservations, especially on the weekend. It gets packed. Their claim to fame is their Gunbarrel Coffee. It's as much of a show as it is an after-dinner drink. Your waiter pulls up alongside your table with a shotgun and pours flaming Grand Marnier down the barrel into a glass with brandy, cacao and whipped cream. The restaurant, which originated in Apex, sells the most Grand Marnier in Canada.

The **Swiss Bear Dining Room** (491-7750; $$-$$$) in the Chateau Big White serves authentic Swiss cuisine, specializing in delicious fondues. Reservations are recommended.

The Inn Restaurant (491-0221, ext. 407; $-$$), in the Inn at Big White, is a great family restaurant with a wonderful view that serves breakfast, lunch and dinner with an interesting menu (some good veggie choices).

Coltino's Ristorante (765-5611; $$), at Das Hofbrauhaus, serves Italian fare as well as Alberta beef. **Raakel's** next door has apres-ski where they serve some mean salads, burgers and pizzas. They also offer the usual pub fare of wings, fries, even poutine—that typical French-Canadian dish of French fries topped with cheese curd and steaming hot gravy.

Frank's Chinese Laundry (765-7866; $$) in the Whitefoot Lodge prepares good Chinese food with a quick in–and-out lunchtime buffet. Ride the gondola down to the **Kettle Valley Steakhouse** (491-0130; $$-$$$) for steak, stylish wine bar and comfy surroundings.

 Apres-ski/nightlife

Big White has seven lounges and bars. Live bands perform regularly. **Snowshoe Sam's** is commonly thought of as the best ski bar in Canada, and we agree. It has DJ, live bands and games of chance. Their legendary "Gunbarrel Coffee" show is a must. **Raakel's Ridge Pub,** in Das Hofbrauhaus, has dancing and a nightly party atmosphere. **Happy Valley Bar,** just a gondola ride down from the village, parties with live DJs and theme nights. It's a great place for family groups and get-togethers. In Whitefoot Lodge, there is a **market** (765-7666) with everything from liquor to video rentals.

 Other activities

The Happy Valley Adventure Centre at the bottom of the gondola offers the **Mega Snow Coaster tube ride** with 10 lanes and two lifts, **snowmobile tours, sleigh rides, ice skating** and **snowshoeing.** For more information or to book activities, visit the Activities Desk in the Village Centre Mall or call 491-6111.

Weekly activities include **A Taste of Big White Welcome Party** every Monday, **Torchlight Parade and Fireworks, Carnival Night** and **Bingo Night.**

The **Whitefoot Medical Clinic** (765-0544) operates in the village from 3–6 p.m. for medical services. Appointments are preferred, but not required.

Silver Star Mountain Resort

First-time visitors to Silver Star love the frontier ambience of the 1890s Victoria Gaslight village. With a street full of unique wooden buildings in surprising colors, and no cars, Silver Star has a compact touch of elegance, even with eight hotels, restaurants, plenty of shopping and an aquatic center.

Dining: $$$$-Entrees C$30+; $$$-C$20-$30; $$-C$10-$20; $-less than C$10.
Accommodations: (double room) $$$$-C$200+; $$$-C$141-$200; $$-C$81-$140; $-C$80 and less.

The mountain and its village are highly rated for family skiing. It's the fourth-largest downhill ski resort in British Columbia, behind Whistler Blackcomb, Sun Peaks and Panorama. Silver Star is usually the first British Columbia ski resort to open. The south-facing Vance Creek area consists of gentle slopes and nicely groomed cruisers, while the Putnam Creek face is renowned for its deep powder and challenging black-diamond terrain. After dark, the Summit Chair is lighted up, top to bottom, for night skiing. The town of Vernon is 14 miles away.

Silver Star recently developed the northwest-facing Silver Woods area by adding an express quad to access more than a dozen trails and glades for all ability levels. Silver Star and Big White are under the same ownership and with one lift ticket, skiers and snowboarders have access to almost 6,000 acres of skiable terrain.

 ## Mountain layout

Silver Star's terrain covers two very different mountain faces. For families: the Vance Creek area served by the Summit Chair and the Comet Six-Pack Express. For the more adventurous: the Putnam Creek area accessed by the Powder Gulch Express and the Summit Chair. The backside is steep and challenging; the front side is beginner-friendly. From the top of the Summit Chair and the Comet Express, you can see Sun Peaks and Big White.

♦♦**Expert:** Don't delay—head straight to the Putnam Creek side and scout the Back Bowl. Look for Free Fall, Where's Bob, Black Pine and Kirkenheimer. Three Wise Men, White Elephant and Holy Smokes will smoke your thighs. Then work your way over to the other side of the Powder Gulch Express to 3 Wisemen, Headwall and Chute 5.

♦**Advanced:** There are plenty of single-blacks on both sides of the mountain. Be sure to test yourself on Caliper Ridge, a trail that runs under the Powder Gulch Express.

■**Intermediate:** Gypsy Queen, reached via Aunt Gladys from Paradise Camp, is the most popular blue run on the mountain. Another really great one, on the opposite side of the Powder Gulch Express, is Sunny Ridge. It takes off to the left just before Paradise Camp.

Silver Star Mountain Resort Facts

Summit elevation:	**6,280 feet**
Vertical Drop:	**2,500 feet**
Base elevation:	**5,280 feet**

Address: Box 3002,
Silver Star Mountain, B.C., Canada V1B 3M1
Area code: 250
Ski area phone: 542-0224
Snow report: 542-1745
Toll-free reservations: (800) 663-4431
Fax: 542-1236
E-mail: star@skisilverstar.com
Internet: www.skisilverstar.com
Expert:★★★★ **Advanced:**★★★
Intermediate:★★★★ **Beginner:**★★★
First-timer:★★★★

Number of lifts: 9–1 high-speed six-pack chair, 2 high-speed quads, 1 quad, 1 double, 2 T-bars, 2 moving carpets
Snowmaking: No
Skiable acreage: 3,065 acres
Uphill capacity: 14,700 per hour
Parks and pipes: 1 park, 1 pipe
Bed base: 3,500 on mountain; nearby RV camping
Nearest lodging: Slopeside, all ski-in/ski-out
Resort child care: Newborn and older
Adult ticket, per day: C$58–C$64 (05/06, without tax)

Dining:★★★
Apres-ski/nightlife:★★
Other activities:★★★

●● **Beginner:** If you want to get high on the mountain, you can't go wrong taking the Powder Gulch Express. From the top, Bergerstrasse/Aunt Gladys make a sweet 5-mile green run. You can also grab the Home Run Tee from there and take the Main St. Skiway straight to the village.

● **First-timer:** Discovery Park is served by the moving carpet and is fenced to keep out the speedy interlopers, so it's a good place to make those initial turns. Once confident, head to the Silver Queen Chair for longer beginner runs.

Ride Guide: On the Putnam side, watch out for the Bergerstrasse flats above Paradise Camp. Once beyond it though, there are plenty of single- and double-black runs that will keep your inner freerider happy. The runs all are served by the Powder Gulch Express. Just take Aunt Gladys and pick your chute off to the left.

Parks and pipes

TELUS Park Silver Star is a halfpipe and terrain park on Big Dipper. TELUS Park has features for all riders and skiers, from small lanes with fat boxes to learn to slide on and mini-hits to learn how to catch your first air, to a large park lane with kinked rails. For advanced riders, long boxes and killer s-rails are coupled with large hits for big air..

Cross-country and snowshoeing (visit xcskiresorts.com for more)

Silver Star's cross-country trails attract skiers from around the world. Many are Olympic athletes in training who come for the Month of Nordic Festival. There are two fully certified biathalon ranges here. Lessons are available daily; cross-country ski camps are held in November. The 38 miles of trails at the resort are skating and classic groomed, and 2.5 miles are lit for night skiing. Guided snowshoe tours also are available.

Lessons (05/06 prices, without tax)

To make reservations for ski school programs, call 558-6065.

Group lessons: A two-hour lesson, beginning at 10 a.m., C$45.

First-timer package: Discover Skiing and Discover Snowboarding include lift, two-hour lesson and rentals, C$54. A three-day package costs C$149.

Private lessons: One-hour lesson, C$99; two-hour lesson, C$169; half day, C$229; full day, C$350. Discounts for up to three additional people. Reservations highly recommended.

Special programs: Ski Weeks include five two-hour group lessons, social events, a fun race and video analysis for C$199. Call for details and reservations.

KidStuff (05/06 prices, without tax)

Child care: Ages newborn to 6 years. For infants up to age 3, cost is C$76 for a full day; C$45 for a half day. For ages 3–6, a full day costs C$60; a half day costs C$36. Full days include lunch; half days have a C$12 lunch option. For reservations, call 558-6028.

Children's lessons: Ages 4–12 get a full-day program (with lunch) for C$86; half day, C$48. Snowboard lessons start at age 8. A full-day package for Adventure Week includes five four-hour lessons and lunches, C$299; a half-day program of five two-hour lessons, C$199. Youth ages 13–18 have lessons tailored after adult programs: two-hour group lesson, C$45; Discover Skiing and Discover Snowboarding include lift, two-hour lesson and rentals, C$54; Ski Weeks include five two-hour group lessons, social events, a fun race and video analysis for C$199. Reservations required for all programs. For kids 12 and younger, call 558-6028;

for kids 13 and older, call 558-6065.

Special activities: "Kids Night Out" is a supervised evening at Tube Town. The program runs Thursday only from 5 p.m. to 7:30 p.m. For ages 6–12, it's tubing and dinner for C$19; ages 3–5 get a movie and dinner for C$16. Reservations required; space subject to availability.

Lift tickets [05/06 prices, without tax]

	Adult	Youth (13-18)	Child (6-12)
One day	C$64	C$55	C$32
Three days	C$178 ($59/day)	C$151 ($50/day)	C$82 ($27/day)
Five days	C$292 ($58/day)	C$247 ($49/day)	C$132 ($26/day)

Who skis free: Children 5 and younger.

Who skis at a discount: Seniors 65+ and Canadian college students pay youth prices.

Note: Prices are rounded to the nearest dollar. Night skiing is available Thursday through Saturday, 3:30–9 p.m.

Accommodations

All Silver Star hotels are centered around the main village. Lodging can be booked through **Silver Star Holidays,** (800) 663-4431.

The **Lord Aberdeen Apartment Hotel** (800-553-5885; 542-1992; $$$–$$$$) offers private-entrance, one- and two-bedroom apartments, each with a full kitchen. The hotel has a sauna and outdoor hot tub. The **Silver Lode Inn** (800-554-4881; 549-5105; $$–$$$) is a Swiss-style hotel with 38 rooms, some with kitchenettes, fireplaces and jetted tubs.

The Victorian-themed **Silver Star Club Resort** (800-610-0805; 549-5191; $$–$$$$) has three buildings with outdoor hot tubs and a variety of accommodations, from standard rooms to two-bedroom units with full kitchens and fireplaces.

The **Pinnacles Suite Hotel** (800-551-7466; 542-4548; $$$$) sits on the edge of the ski runs and has units with up to four bedrooms. **Putnam Station Inn** (800-489-0599; 542-2459; $$–$$$) features a railroad atmosphere, plus an outdoor hot tub under the water tower.

These units all can be booked through **Silver Star Accommodation** (877-630-7827; 558-7825) or **Mountain Vacation Homes** (800-489-0599; 542-2459): **Creekside** condominiums ($$$–$$$$) have one- and two-bedroom units, with kitchens, fireplace and an outdoor hot tub. The **Grandview** ($$$) condominium complex has 33 two-bedroom units, each with a view of the Monashee Mountains. Rent a private **vacation home** ($$$$) in the Knoll Area on-mountain with easy access to lifts and village.

SameSun Backpacker Ski Lodge (877-562-2783; 545-8933; $–$$) offers ski-in/ski-out private, family and dorm rooms with hot tubs, free breakfast and linen service.

Dining

Craigellachie Dining Room (542-2459; $$–$$$), in the Putnam Station Inn, showcases train memorabilia. It has a full Okanagan wine list and a menu with everything from pasta to buffalo steak and wild Arctic char. It serves breakfast, lunch and dinner. Also in the Putnam, **The Wine Cellar** ($$) is an intimate wine bar with full meals. The **Silver Lode Inn Dining Room** (549-5105; $–$$$) features Swiss and international cuisine and a buffet dinner on Thursday evenings.

In the Silver Star Club Resort you'll find the most upscale restaurant, **Clementine's Dining Room** (549-5191; $$–$$$$), with special prime rib Thursdays and buffet Sundays; **The**

Italian Garden (558-1448; $–$$), with pick-up and delivery; and the **Vance Creek Saloon** (503-1452; $–$$), serving light meals and snacks until midnight.

Don't miss the **Lord Aberdeen Bistro** (542-1992; $), where soups are a specialty and there's a wide variety of homemade fare. **Long John's** Pub (549-2992; $$) at the Lord Aberdeen Hotel offers pub fare, lunch, dinner and drinks; families are welcome.

Bugaboos Bakery Cafe (545-3208; $–$$), noted for its award-winning strudels and coffee, is a European-style cafe beside the Town T-Bar on the Vance Creek boardwalk. **Francuccino's Mountain Bakery & Cafe** (558-6032; $–$$), owned by the same couple, also serves delicious European baked goods, plus gourmet dinners three nights a week (reservations required). **Paradise Camp** (558-6087; $–$$), at the Powder Gulch Express midstation, is good for an informal lunch or snacks. Some ski writers think it's the best place on the continent to enjoy a beer on the outdoor sundeck in the spring. In the Town Hall day lodge, the **Town Hall Eatery** (558-6024; $) is the locals' hangout featuring soups, sandwiches, burgers and more.

 ## Apres-ski/nightlife

Be sure to check out the Weekly Events Calendar when you check in. It lists the special apres-ski activities that vary from week to week. Meanwhile, head over to the **Vance Creek Saloon** where there's entertainment to be had Wednesday to Saturday. **Charlie's Bar** is quieter and cozier. It's off the Silver Lode Inn Dining Room. In the lower level of Putnam Station is a fantastic little **Wine Cellar** featuring various wines and meals. **Long John's** at the Lord Aberdeen Hotel has live entertainment four nights a week.

Other activities

Silver Star's Adventure Park has a lift-served **Tubetown, skating pond, Mini-Z snowmobile park** for kids, **horse-drawn sleigh rides, snowmobile tours and snowshoe excursions.** The National Altitude Training Center has a **climbing wall** (lessons available). On Thursday nights in the auditorium, the locals and staff put on an extravaganza of music, comedy and entertainment called **Silver Star Snow Show**—don't miss it. Guided **snowmobile tours** are available.

Getting there and getting around

By air: Kelowna International Airport is about an hour's drive from Big White and Silver Star, and less than an hour's flight from Vancouver, Calgary or Seattle. Non-stop flights from Toronto are available. U.S. Customs is at the Kelowna Airport. Big White and Silver Star's airport shuttles serve the ski areas; seats must be reserved 72 hours in advance. For Big White Central Reservations, call (800) 663-2772. For Silver Star Central Holidays, call (800) 663-4431. Big White has a Budget rental agency on the mountain. One-way rentals to and from the airport can be booked through Big White Central Reservations.

By car: Silver Star and Big White are in the heart of the Okanagan Valley. Big White is 35 miles southeast of Kelowna, and Silver Star is 40 miles northeast of Kelowna. The two resorts are 59 miles apart. The resorts are about 4.5 to 5.5 hours from Vancouver and Spokane, and six to seven hours from Seattle.

Getting around: No car is needed at Big White or Silver Star unless you plan to explore. At Silver Star, a taxi loops continuously throughout the resort until 10 p.m. daily. Inter-resort shuttles provide transfers between Big White and Silver Star so you can ski for a day or split your stay between the resorts.

Dining: $$$$-Entrees C$30+; $$$-C$20-$30; $$-C$10-$20; $-less than C$10.
Accommodations: (double room) $$$$-C$200+; $$$-C$141-$200; $$-C$81-$140; $-C$80 and less.

Fernie Alpine Resort
British Columbia

Summit elevation:	6,316 feet
Vertical drop:	2,816 feet
Base elevation:	3,500 feet

Address: 5339 Fernie Ski Hill Rd., Fernie, British Columbia, Canada V0B 1M6
Area code: 250
Ski area phone: 423-4655
Snow report: 423-3555 or (800) 258-7669
Toll-free eservations: (800) 258-7669; (866) 633-7643
Fax: 423-6644
E-mail: info@skifernie.com
Internet: www.skifernie.com
Expert:★★★★★
Advanced:★★★★★
Intermediate:★★★★
Beginner:★★

Number and types of lifts: 10–2 high-speed quads, 2 quads, 2 triples, 4 surface lifts
Skiable acreage: 2,504 acres
Snowmaking: 5 percent (125 acres)
Uphill capacity: 13,716 skiers per hour
Parks & pipes: 1 park, 1 pipe
Bed base: 4,368 (mountain); 6,754 (town)
Nearest lodging: Slopeside, ski-in/ski-out
Resort child care: Yes, newborn and older
Adult ticket, per day: C$64 (05/06, without tax)

Dining:★★★
Apres-ski/nightlife:★★
Other activities:★★★

Perhaps you've heard the fervent whispers about Fernie already: You'll find some of the steepest terrain you'll ever see in-bounds, and what's out-of-bounds is free for the taking too. The snow is unbelievable—deep and light and almost magical. The terrain seems unlimited—if you see it, and can get to it, you can ski it. There are no crowds, so you have the mountain practically to yourself. Of course, all this tantalizing lore is shared with the necessary forewarning, "We're only telling you this because we know you'll keep it to yourself."

Well, diehards really have nothing to worry about, because Fernie is not for the faint of heart. While every bowl has some groomed terrain, most terrain is left the way Mother Nature made it—and that's the way Fernie's fans want it to be. Fernie has some of the steepest in-bounds terrain you'll find at any resort in North America. Because of that, there are many in-bound areas prone to avalanches. These areas are well marked, but you should know what to look for. If you suddenly come upon warning signs, pay close attention. Literally, one section can be marked green to go, while just a few hundred feet farther, you'll find danger signs telling you to steer clear. About 60 professional patrollers, all trained in avalanche safety and explosives, keep Fernie under watchful eye, so make sure to thank them for paying such attention to life-saving details.

When we visited in March, we woke up one morning to powderhounds drooling over the thigh-deep dump. Fortunately we were signed up for the First Tracks program so we snorkled snow—and giggled uncontrollably—for an hour before the rest of the horde hit the slopes. Some friends who stayed longer enjoyed two more days of freshies before dragging their heels back home.

Fernie, tucked into the craggy Lizard Range of the Canadian Rockies, is several hours from civilization and caters to a casual crowd that comes here for one thing and one thing only:

the allure of the mountain. It can easily be lumped in with other resorts known to worship the zen of skiing: Red Mountain, Alta, Snowbird, Crested Butte, Jay Peak. In fact, it is reminiscent of Red Mountain and Rossland, only a bit more grown up. Much of the mountainside village is just a few years old and includes lodging, restaurants, apres-ski bars, coffee shops and a grocery store. Fernie, owned by Resorts of the Canadian Rockies, has plans for expansion both in the slopeside village and on the mountain. Fortunately, there isn't a lot of room for village expansion, so this resort should stay as intimate and laid-back as it is right now.

The turn-of-the-century coal mining town of Fernie is just 3 miles away. The main street, 2nd Avenue, is actually parallel to the road you'll travel on into town. Fernie burned down twice during the early 1900s and, when it was rebuilt in 1910, builders were required by code to use brick and stone. The result is a colorful blend of shops, restaurants, clubs and bars.

Fernie is ripe with legends, including the powder-making Griz, honored with an annual winter carnival, and the curse-bearing Ghostrider, who appears in the shadows of Mount Hosmer. Ask any local, they love to share their history.

Mountain layout

Fernie consists of five seemingly limitless bowls of pure delight that dump you into gut-wrenching steeps and chutes, gnarly trees, gentle glades and thrilling trails. All have terrain for all abilities; it's really a matter of taking the time to explore each and deciding on your favorite. It's easy to spend all day exploring one bowl. If you can see it, you can ski it—and sometimes you can't see it till you work your way *to* it! It's a good idea to take a complimentary mountain tour on your first day so you can become familiar with how to travel the mountain. Meet at the carousel in front of Guest Services at 9:30 a.m. and 1 p.m.

♦♦**Expert ♦Advanced:** What can we say? It doesn't get better than this. Explore to your heart's content. Some traverses cross very steep terrain and if you're prone to vertigo, be prepared, but it's worth getting over it. We're sure we don't have to tell you that the best goods don't have names, but we'll start you off with some suggestions. Find the "idiot's traverse" in Timber Bowl and head to some sweet trees off Diamond Back and in Anaconda Glades and Gotta Go, or head to Cedar Bowl and jump into King Fir and Cedar Ridge. Bootleg Glades have a sphincter-tightening drop-in, but you'll enjoy the goods once you overcome it. Surprize got its name after an avalanche etched it into the mountain.

After a storm, take the Lizard Traverse at least halfway across before dropping into wide-open, floatable powder. Siberia Bowl has some great powder stashes too. On clear days after a snowfall, follow the "leaping lemmings" line out of Currie Bowl and up to Polar Peak. And for days after, when much of the mountain is skied off, don't despair, you'll still find powder in the trees off Decline, leading into Easter Bowl and Lizard Bowl. Skip the chutes off the ridge between Currie and Lizard bowls if there hasn't been a fresh snowfall—otherwise they are guaranteed death slides. Check with the ski patrol before going into the out-of-bounds Fish Bowl; rescues are often necessary there.

If you're a powderhound, it's worth paying extra to join the First Tracks program—you'll ski freshies while others have to wait in line for the lifts to open.

■ **Intermediate:** If you're an intermediate who loves long cruisers, you'll get bored rather quickly. But if you're ready to test your skills and move to the ungroomed and trees, this is the mountain for you. All of the bowls have very nice intermediate terrain, just search for what you want: small bumps, ungroomed, semi-steep or trees. It's easy to dip in and out off the groomed trails as you gain confidence. You'll have great fun on Currie Powder and

Currie Glades, wandering farther afield as you get more adventurous. The trees in Timber Bowl and Currie Bowl are fabulous ego-boosters. Dancer, Cascade and Bow in Lizard Bowl are wide-open slopes perfect for learning powder.

●●**Beginner:** While Fernie has excellent beginner terrain that's nicely separated from other ability levels, it's still adventurous by most standards. Your best bet is to join a ski week group, where instructors can help you overcome any trepidation you may have.

●**First-timer:** The word on the street is that if you learn to ski here, you'll advance more rapidly than at most other resorts. This is a very challenging mountain. First-timers should join a ski week program to avoid being overly intimidated.

Ride Guide: Fernie's natural terrain is a big draw to snowboarders. However, you'll find Fernie a challenge simply because of all the traverses. To access the best-kept secrets, you'll have to follow some harrowing traverses that are lo-o-ong excursions. However, the snowboarders we talked to all said the great terrain is worth every bit of the agony it requires to get to it. Your best bet is to explore each bowl thoroughly before moving on to the next one so as to minimize some of the traversing (such as to get back from the Haul Back T-bar). You definitely want to avoid the very long run-out at the bottom of Falling Star, where you'll end up walking out—most riders only use it when they return from hiking in the backcountry on this side of the mountain.

Parks and pipes

Fernie has a meticulously groomed halfpipe good for all ability levels that is served by the Deer Chair. A terrain park with rails and hits on Upper Falling Star is accessible by the Timber Bowl Express Quad. But most skiers and riders come here for the natural terrain.

Cross-country and snowshoeing (visit xcskiresorts.com for more details)

Fernie Alpine Resort has 10 km. of trails in a figure-eight loop, good for both skating and classic. Trail usage is free. Lessons and guided cross-country tours are available. Fernie does not rent equipment, so bring your own. At the **Fernie Golf & Country Club** trails are beginner to intermediate.

Guided snowshoe tours with a naturalist are a great aerobic workout, plus you'll be entertained with local legends and lore. Did you know that Fernie burned down twice and you can see exactly where those fires stopped on the mountain by looking at the tree growth? Book through Guest Services.

The network of **mountain biking trails** found throughout Fernie are excellent for snowshoeing. Pick up a copy of the trail guide at local retailers.

Lessons (05/06 prices, without tax)

Group lessons: Skiers and snowboarders levels 1–4 pay C$59 for a half-day lesson; C$89 for a full day. Levels 5–6 pay C$79 for a half day; C$89 for a full day.

First-timer package: The package, which includes a beginner lift pass, rentals and half-day group lesson (skiing, telemarking or snowboarding), costs C$69; a full day costs C$79. We recommend the learn-to-ski or -snowboard week package to help first-timers feel comfortable here: Three-day programs start on Sunday or Thursday and include rentals, full lift pass and Ski Week lessons (*see Special Programs* below) for C$349; youth (13–17) pay C$319.

Private lessons: Skiing, snowboarding or telemarking lessons (three people maximum) cost C$229 for two hours; C$299 for three hours; C$499 for six hours (all day). An early-bird lesson for 1.5 hours that starts at 9 a.m. costs C$125; a two-hour late-day lesson costs $129.

Special programs: Ski & Snowboard Weeks will help you rise to the challenge of the mountain and are highly recommended. The three-day program gives you the same instructor every day and includes a NASTAR race, video analysis and apres-ski reception. Programs start Sunday and Thursday. A full-day program costs C$249.

First Tracks is an early-start program (7:45 a.m.) with lift line priority only available on days that have fresh powder, C$79 (lift ticket extra). Book the night before. Skiers and riders who are intermediates or better can hire a mountain guide for the day and get lift-line priority too (minimum of two people per guide, ages 10 and older). Cost is C$99 per person.

KidStuff [05/06 prices, without tax]

Child care: Ages newborn to 6 years old. For infants up to 18 months, a full day is C$56; no half-day care is available. For ages 19 months up to 3 years, a full day is C$45; half day, C$25. For ages 3-6 years, a full day is $39; half day is $25. Ask about discounts for multiple children. Free snacks are provided; lunch is available by request for C$7. A late fee of C$7 is charged for every 15 minutes late. Kids 3-4 years old can take a one-hour group lesson, booked through day care, for C$18. Reservations are recommended, especially for infants, at least 24 hours in advance. Resort Kids Daycare is a safe, licensed facility for children and is in the Cornerstone Lodge.

Children's lessons: Full-day programs (skiing and snowboarding) for ages 5–12 cost C$79; half-day morning, C$59 (three hours); half-day afternoon, C$39 (two hours). Supervised lunch, C$14. Rental gear is extra. All children in ski school programs are required to wear helmets; rentals are available. The first-timer package, including a beginner lift pass, rentals and half-day group lesson, costs C$49; full day costs C$89. Kids Adventure Camps, for ages 5–12, are three-day programs that include a NASTAR race, video analysis and apres-ski party. Three days cost C$189 (starts on Sunday and Thursday). Supervised lunch, C$14 per day.

Special activities: Kids Activity Night is a supervised evening of activities (6–9 p.m. Wednesdays and Saturdays) for ages 6–12. Register for specific activities—such as meeting the horses that pull sleighs—or join for a whole week of fun (arts and crafts, snow soccer and more). Register with ski school by 5 p.m. that day, C$30 per child (dinner included).

Lift tickets [05/06 prices, without tax]

	Adult	Child (6-12)
One day	C$64	C$20
Three days	C$192 (C$64/day)	C$60 (C$20/day)
Five days	C$320 (C$64/day)	C$100 (C$20/day)

Who skis free: Ages 5 and younger.

Who skis at a discount: Youth (13-17) pay C$45 and seniors (65+) pay C$51 for one day; multiday discounts kick in on four or more days.

Accommodations

Fernie's Central Reservations, (800) 258-7669 or (403) 209-3321, creates custom packages including lodging, lift tickets, flights and car rentals. Most of the mountain village accommodations are newly built, providing state-of-the-art amenities and luxuries.

The magnificent riverstone-and-log **Lizard Creek Lodge** (877-228-1948; 423-2057;

Dining: $$$$-Entrees C$30+; $$$-C$20-$30; $$-C$10-$20; $-less than C$10.

Accommodations: (double room) $$$$-C$200+; $$$-C$141-$200; $$-C$81-$140; $-C$80 and less.

$$$–$$$$), just steps away from the Elk Quad chairlift, does a marvelous job of blending luxury with rustic splendor. Each unit has a fully equipped kitchen, fireplace and balcony. The complex has an outdoor heated pool, spa, fitness center, lounge and gourmet restaurant.

Cornerstone Lodge (423-6871; $$–$$$$) is in the middle of the slopeside village near the Deer Chair and has a bird's-eye view of the halfpipe. All rooms are comfortably furnished deluxe suites with gas fireplace, kitchen, washer and dryer, and balcony.

Kerrin-Lee Gartner's Snow Creek Lodge (800-667-9911; $$–$$$$) is another excellent mountainside choice, where you'll find studios, one- and two-bedroom suites, and cabins built in the style of early Canadian architecture with stone and logs. Guests have a heated outdoor swimming pool, two hot tubs and a fitness room.

Griz Inn (800-661-0118; 423-9221; $$–$$$$), built in 1982 as the second on-hill accommodation, has hotel rooms, studios, and one-, two- and three-bedroom suites with lofts. Suites include full kitchens. Amenities include an indoor pool, outdoor hot tub and sauna.

If you're on a budget but want to be on the mountain, stay at the older but comfortable **Wolf's Den Mountain Lodge** (800-258-7669; 423-4655; $$), where standard hotel rooms have coffee makers and small refrigerators. Guests can use two indoor hot tubs, an exercise room and a game room, as well as common laundry facilities.

Rocky Mountain Vacations (877-423-7905; fax 250-423-7995; $$$–$$$$) manages many private luxury chalets and condos with all the goodies. Choose from mountainside, town and rural locations.

Various **townhouse and chalet** options also are available, so be sure to inquire about them if you'd rather stay in lodging of this kind.

In town:

If you really enjoy nightlife and dining out, you may prefer to stay in town 3 miles away instead of at the mountain.

The upscale **Best Western Fernie Mountain Lodge** (423-5500; $$–$$$) has deluxe guest rooms, some with kitchenettes, as well as themed hot tub suites. The lodge has an indoor pool, hot tubs, fitness center and common laundry facilities. Choose from standard hotel and junior studio rooms at the stone-and-log **Park Place Lodge** (888-381-7275; 423-6871; $$). Some rooms have kitchenettes and mini-refrigerators. The lodge has an indoor pool and hot tub.

Riverside Mountain Lodge (877-423-5600; $–$$$$) offerings range from value-priced hotel rooms to luxury chalets. **Cedar Lodge** (800-977-2977; 423-4622; $–$$) is an older property with prices to reflect it; microwave and fridge in rooms. **Three Sisters Motel** (877-326-8888; 423-4438; $–$$) gives a basic motel experience.

Fernie also has two hostels, **SameSun International Hostel** (877-562-2783; 423-4492; $), part of a chain that also packages guided tours, and **The Raging Elk Hostel** (423-6811; $). Seasoned hostelers told us SameSun has nicer beds but can be noisy, while Raging Elk is less polished but has a separate common area for people who party or just want to stay up late.

 **Dining**

For such a remote and tiny town, you'll find a remarkable choice of good dining, both on the mountain and in town. We suspect that as Fernie becomes a bigger blip on the radar screen, more skilled chefs will find their way here.

On the mountain:

You'd be missing out on a special gourmet experience if you don't eat at **Lizard Creek Lodge** (423-2057; $$$; reservations recommended). Ask to be seated near the grand riverstone fireplace. The Chilean sea bass and filet mignon were both superb. The fondue lunch, served in the lounge, is said to be excellent.

Another gourmet experience is **The Wood on the Hill** (423-4597; $$), with a lively jazz-and-blues-influenced ambiance. They serve only British Columbia wines with their creative menu. The Alberta beef tenderloin gets raves from locals. It's open noon to midnight.

Gabriella's Little Italy Restaurant (423-7388; $) serves heaping plates of pasta and sandwiches on focaccia. **Kelsey's Restaurant** (423-2444; $–$$), in Cornerstone Lodge, is a chain pub-style restaurant with a rustic interior and a broad menu.

Slopeside Coffee and Deli (423-2440; $) is the place to go for Starbucks coffee and pastries, light lunches and deli products. **The Griz Bar** ($) lays out a mean salad bar, plus you'll find a basic bar menu for lunch. Downstairs is the **cafeteria.** For a quick energy fix, check out **Spuds "eh,"** a meals-on-wheels food truck that drops anchor in front of the ticket window and serves handcut fries with several types of sauces. The Yamagoya (423-0090; $$) is decidedly Japanese with a full sushi bar, private tatami rooms and sake bar.

In town:

A real culinary surprise is **The Curry Bowl** (423-2695; $$), a tiny restaurant owned by a couple in their 20s. They specialize in "enlightened Asian cuisine," of Thailand, India and Japan. They don't take reservations, and it is at least an hour wait, but worth it.

If you're interested in a rare dining environment, go to **The Old Elevator** (423-7115; $$–$$$; reservations recommended), a grain feed store and grain elevator built in 1908 that have been lovingly refurbished. Music of the '20s, big band and swing add to the step-back-in-time impression, and stained glass windows add mystery to the mountain views.

Las Tres Hermanas (423-3215; $$) in the Northern Hotel is a festive Mexican restaurant specializing in authentic regional dishes and, of course, margaritas.

Locals recommend "Pasta Tuesdays" at **Boston Pizza** (423-2634; $–$$) where you'll get heaping plates of pasta for less than C$10. **The Pub Bar & Grill** (423-6871; $) in the Park Place Lodge is the place for pub grub. Choose from three Chinese restaurants with take-out; locals tell us the best is **Ginger Beef** (423-4611; $).

Relax with a cup of gourmet coffee, cappuccino or espresso at **Cappuccino Corner** on 2nd Avenue. We can't help but rave about the black raspberry mocha. Homemade soups and baked goods round out the choices. Board games and six computers with Internet access make this more than a coffee shop.

Apres-ski/nightlife

Crowds start gathering at **The Grizzly Bar** even before the lifts shut down, and it revs up to a loud hum with tall tales of the day's skiing and riding. There's live music and dancing on weekends from 3 - 6 p.m. plus Saturday nights 9 p.m. to midnight. **Kelsey's** is the other on-mountain destination for a lively crowd. A more sedate crowd heads to the **Lizard Creek Lodge Lounge,** where you can be swallowed up by leather chairs and couches while you watch night fall over the mountain or watch the big-screen TV. Appetizers and a menu are available here.

In town, play pool, foosball, ping pong or watch your favorite sports on scattered TV screens at the **Pub Bar & Grill** in the Park Place Lodge. **The Eldorado Lounge** is the town's most aerobic nightclub, with a dance floor that's hopping every night but Sunday. Or head to **Eschwig's** at The Northern Hotel. For those who want a quieter evening, there's a **movie theater.** Fernie was well known for its beer brewing till 1960 and the new **Fernie Brewing Company** hopes to revive that history. Local restaurants and pubs serve the company's microbrews.

Dining: $$$$–Entrees C$30+; $$$–C$20-$30; $$–C$10-$20; $–less than C$10.
Accommodations: (double room) $$$$–C$200+; $$$–C$141-$200; $$–C$81-$140; $–C$80 and less.

Other activities

You can book a slew of activities through the resort's Guest Services (423-4655): **horse-drawn sleigh rides, torchlight run & barbecue, snowmobiling tours, wildlife viewing, ice fishing, backcountry tours,** and **dogsledding.**

Choose from three **cat-skiing** operations: Island Lake Lodge (888- 422-8754) only allows 36 guests per tour. Powder Cowboy Cat-Skiing Tours (423-3700 or 888-422-8754) has its own Bull River Ranch, with terrain. Fernie Wilderness Adventures (423-6704) takes you to terrain that's great for first-time cat-skiers.

This is one small town that believes in staying healthy in mind, body and spirit. Unwind after a hard day on the slopes at the Spa at Lizard Creek Lodge (423-2057), with treatments including **aromatherapy, hydrotherapy** and **massages.** You'll also find a hair salon and esthetician here. In town, choose from Fernie Mountain Massage Therapy Clinic (423-5522), Hydrotherapy Spa & Massage Therapy Clinic (423-7667), Jade River Healing Center Chinese Medicine Clinic (423-7667) and Fernie Chiropractic (423-4800). Hospital: (423-4453).

If you're interested in learning about Fernie's history, pick up a copy of the **Heritage Walking Tour** booklet from the Fernie Information Center in town. You'll also find enough **shops** along 2nd Avenue to spend an afternoon browsing. There are several Alpine sports stores, all worth checking out. If you're looking for unique gifts, we recommend Stephanie's Glass & Art Studio for custom-made stained glass and work by local artists, Ghostrider Trading Co. for handcrafted items by local artisans and mountain-lifestyle clothing, and Carosella Artworks for home decor and jewelry (they have a shop in the mountain village too).

Pick up a copy of the *Fernie Guide* for other activity suggestions.

Getting there and getting around

By air: Most people fly into Calgary International Airport because it's served by most major airlines. It's about a three-hour drive to Fernie. The smaller Cranbrook Airport, served by Air BC, is an hour away. You also can fly into Glacier International Airport in Kalispell, Mont., which is about two hours away. If you use the Rocky Mountain Sky Shuttle (888-762-8754 in U.S. and Canada, or 403-762-5200) from Calgary, make sure to ask your driver for local lore and wild tales of living in the rugged British Columbia wilderness. We found both our drivers to be Fernie locals who were very entertaining. Mountain Perks (423-4023) runs another Calgary-Fernie shuttle service.

By car: If you drive, be watchful for moose, deer, elk and bighorn sheep, which often wander into the road. From Calgary: South on Provincial Hwy. 2 to Crowsnest Hwy. 3, west on Hwy. 3 until you reach the town of Fernie. If the weather is nice, you can take a slightly shorter, more scenic route: south on Hwy. 2 to Hwy. 7, west on Hwy. 7 to town of Black Diamond, south on Hwy. 22, west on Hwy. 3.

From Kalispell, go north on Hwy. 93 through the United States-Canada border. Continue on Hwy. 93 to its end, at the junction of Crowsnest Hwy. 3, then go east on Hwy. 3. After passing Morrissey, look for the turnoff to Fernie Alpine Resort on your left.

Getting around: Kootenay Taxi runs a ski shuttle between the mountain and town. During the day, a one-way trip costs C$3; four one-way rides, C$10; a Frequent Rider Card (10 rides), C$25. In the evening, a free shuttle runs between 6:15 and 11:10 p.m. We found the shuttle schedule to be somewhat inconvenient and ended up calling for a taxi (423-4408) to return to the mountain each time (about C$18 1-waywith tip). To do any kind of exploring, rent a car.

Kicking Horse Mountain Resort
British Columbia, Canada

Summit elevation:	8.033 feet
Vertical drop:	4,133 feet
Base elevation:	3,900 feet

Address: Kicking Horse Mountain Resort, 1500 Kicking Horse Trail, Box 839, Golden, BC, Canada V0A 1H0
Area code: 250
Ski Area Phone: 439-5400
Snow report: 439-5400
Toll-free reservations: (866) 754-5425
Fax: 439-5401
E-mail: guestservices@kickinghorseresort.com
Internet: www.kickinghorseresort.com
Expert: ★★★★★
Advanced: ★★★★★
Intermediate: ★★★
Beginner: ★★★ **First-timer:** ★★

Number and types of lifts: 5–1 8-person gondola, 2 quads, 1 double, 1 moving carpet
Skiable acreage: 2,750 acres
Snowmaking: No
Uphill capacity: 14,000 per hour
Parks & pipes: None
Bed base: About 314 slopeside; 1,100 in Golden
Nearest lodging: Ski-in/ski-out
Resort child care: Yes, 18 months and older
Adult ticket, per day: C$54–C$59 (05/06, without tax)

Dining: ★★★
Apres-ski/nightlife: ★★
Other activities: ★★

Kicking Horse Mountain Resort in interior British Columbia is a jeweled crown in the making—a true work in progress. It's on Highway 1, just 48 miles west of Lake Louise between Kootenay and Glacier national parks in the town of Golden. The once locally owned day hill is undergoing a huge infusion of money from its new owners, the Netherlands-based construction giant Ballast Nedam International, a company that traditionally builds dams and bridges.

Originally run by local volunteers and known as Whitetooth, Ballast Nedam renamed this potentially world-class ski area Kicking Horse and transformed the site, adding two new lifts including a bottom-to-top gondola, two ski lodges, its first slopeside lodging and other amenities. Their goal is to make this resort one of the largest ski areas in North America.

Kicking Horse Mountain Resort's peaks were once prime heliskiing terrain, a vast wilderness ripe with other peaks that are still used for heliskiing and snowcat skiing. What Mother Nature has provided in her "eagle eye" views from the top of the ski area combined with its natural ski terrain make it hard for skiers and riders to resist.

The resort is situated amongst three mountain ranges—the Purcells, the Selkirks and the Canadian Rockies, a region full of national parks in every direction—Banff, Jasper, Glacier, Kootenay, Yoho and Mt. Revelstoke.

The resort has a hardcore reputation. As with many other resorts with steep terrain, the avalanche danger at Kicking Horse is ever present, so ski and ride with care and respect for the mountain. The resort benefits from its location by missing wetter weather that can plague its southern B.C. neighbors. It gets lots of snow, though it can be heavy powder.

Full build-out of the $300-million, 10-year development is planned for 2010. The goal is to make this resort one of the largest ski resorts in North America. The resort has a 4,133-foot vertical drop, second in Canada only to Whistler Blackcomb. When its skiable acreage increases from 2,750 to 4,005 at build-out, Kicking Horse will join the ranks of Vail, Squaw Valley and Whistler Blackcomb, all monstrous when it comes to lift-accessed terrain. The resort also will soon reap the benefits of a government investment of $125 million in roadway improvements. The funding will be used to augment the highway to four lanes, improving access to the resort from the East.

Down the road, Golden is a logger's village in the throes of a failing timber industry that just happens to sit at the foot of a developing ski hill with a very bright future. The influx of outside private and local provincial money promises to change Golden's fortunes forever.

Beginner and lower-intermediate terrain is greatly improved by grooming and access. The addition of a midstation on the beginner Catamount chair accesses shorter runs. The first phase of a child-care facility offers a convenient guest service for those with kids. The resort continues its real estate development as well. Kicking Horse Resort has extreme potential and its new owners have the vision to make it happen.

 ## Mountain layout

For the 20 years prior to the Golden Eagle Express Gondola, heli-skiing was the main way to enjoy the higher reaches of the resort. Now, everyone can enjoy the high Crystal Bowl. If it's springtime, see if Boo, the grizzly, is showing himself at the midmountain bear refuge.

◆◆**Expert** ◆**Advanced:** Experts and advanced skiers and riders, this is your mountain. Even without riding the Golden Eagle Express Gondola to the 7,700-foot top of the main peak, there are black-diamond runs to the bottom. The Pioneer double chair, at the head of the parking lot, gets you to all the serious lower-mountain runs. A good warm-up is Race Place. It's the longest of the lower runs and is normally groomed. Bumpsters will want to drop into Pioneer right under the lift.

The trail map of the higher peaks can be misleading, since most of the terrain is unnamed. The marked trails are merely "suggestions" to guide you. Turn right or left as you get off the gondola and drop into whichever bowl beckons. These were heli-skiing runs with steep headwalls before the gondola was built. To the left is Bowl Over, reached by tight trees off CPR Ridge, the super-fun Flying Dutchman, or hiking up to Terminator Peak.

To the right of the gondola is Crystal Bowl. When heading to the bottom, steer skier's left of the chair to avoid It's a Ten cat track, hooking up instead with several single-diamond trails that drop you off right at the parking lot, or blue cruisers that dump out at the base lodge.

When heading to the hike-to terrain, check in with ski patrol, ask about conditions and tell them where you're going. Rescues off the higher peaks can be harrowing because of cliffs.

■ **Intermediate:** Intermediates can take any lift to access good terrain. To get into Bowl Over, take Sluiceway from the top of the gondola. It veers left as you get off the lift, follows a gentle ridge for a moment and then descends into Bowl Over. Continuing past treeline, the run becomes Knee Deep, aiming back toward the gondola, eventually joining It's a Ten. As you glide along It's a Ten, you have a choice of four blue runs to the bottom, plus a few blacks if you're feeling adventurous and a few greens.

If you want to stay up on the higher mountain for several runs, enter Crystal Bowl from the top of the gondola. You can do laps in Crystal Bowl off the Stairway to Heaven lift.

●● **Beginner** ● **First-timer:** Beginners have a way down from all of the lifts except Stairway to Heaven. You can get on the gentler part of It's a Ten from the top of the Catamount quad chair, or simply go down Big Ben, where you'll find a slew of green trails going in all directions. All the terrain off Catamount is gentle and delightful. After some warm-up runs here, confident beginners can take the gondola to the top and ski down the longest run on the mountain—the 10-km.-long cat track It's a Ten. Check to see if it's been groomed before you go. First-timers will *not* want to do that. Instead, stay on the Pony Express carpet until you're feeling comfortable enough to try some longer trails off the Catamount quad. The lift's new midstation makes it easier for novices to work their way up to longer trails.

Ride Guide: The jump-offs into the bowls are gut-sucking even for skilled riders, and there are a lot of steep shots off the ridges. Many a rider has had to be rescued off cliff areas here because it's impossible to change directions, so be careful and pay attention to your route. Make sure to ride the Stairway to Heaven for access to the black-diamond My Blue Heaven area. Intermediates too have great choices all over the mountain. The mid-bowls are comprised of blue and green runs and a ride out and down Terminator will peg your fun meter for sure.

The most thrilling trees are under the Stairway to Heaven lift, but the woods lower down the mountain are also big and thick. Beginners will be comfortable in the Catamount lift region, where there are several green runs mixed with blues..

Parks and pipes

Kicking Horse has no plans to add terrain parks or pipes, but who needs 'em when most of the resort has above-Alpine heli-skiing-quality snow and terrain for the price of a lift pass? If you must, have a ball in the woods between Bubbly and Euphoria, where you'll find a natural halfpipe and terrain park.

Cross-country and snowshoeing (visit xcskiresorts for more details)

Dawn Mountain Nordic Ski Trails at the resort's base has 14 km. of classic track-set trails, including 1.5 km. of skating track. There are beginner loop trails, plus intermediate and expert trails. A trailside warming hut sits 1 km. into the course. A donation is suggested for use of the trails. Cross-country equipment and snowshoes can be rented from **Canyon Creek Outfitters.**

Lessons (05/06 prices, without tax)

Group lessons: Group lessons cost C$139 per person for a full day (10 a.m. to 3 p.m.) and include lunch at the Eagle's Eye Restaurant. Morning-only lessons cost C$99. The maximum size of the group is six skiers or riders.

First-timer packages: First-timers are offered the Discover Program. Cost is C$150 for a full day from 9:30 a.m. to 3 p.m. Lesson, lunch, rentals and beginner lift ticket are included. Morning-only lessons cost C$110. The maximum group is three people.

Private lessons: Private lessons cost C$460 for a full day and C$270 for a half day. Lessons are for up to five participants, offer lift line priority, and overnight ski storage for multiday lessons. Video analysis is included in a full-day private and costs an additional C$20 for a half day. Two-hour lessons in the afternoons are available an a space-available basis.

Fresh Tracks is available with instructors from 9–10 a.m., Over Lunch is from 12–1 p.m. and Last Call is at 3 p.m. These one-hour lessons each cost C$70, are limited to three people and offer lift line priority.

Special programs: Guides take groups on "Rips, Tips and Tours" of the mountain to help skiers and riders discover the mountain's secret stashes. A two-hour tour in the a.m. or p.m. costs C$40. Performance Camps prepare advanced and experts for big-mountain skiing, as well as snowcat skiing and heli-skiing trips. Full-day camp with clinic, video analysis and lunch at Eagle's Eye Restaurant costs C$230; maximum of three students.

KidsStuff (05/06 prices, without tax)

Child care: Ages 18 months to 5 years. A full day, including lunch and snacks, costs C$55. A half day (up to 3.5 hours, morning or afternoon) costs $40 and includes a snack; add lunch for C$10. Pre-registration is required; information can be found at Guest Services in the Day Lodge. The child-care center is in the Day Lodge and is open daily from 9 a.m. to 4:30 p.m. **Children's lessons:** For children 6–12, a full day costs C$85 (with lunch); half day costs C$50. Lift and rentals are extra; helmets are provided free. Children are grouped according to ability levels. Tiny Tykes, for ages 3–5, costs C$80 for a full day (with lunch); C$60 for a half day. Cost includes lift pass, helmet and tip clips for skis.

Special activities: Kid's Night Out, offered Friday and Saturday evenings, costs C$10 per hour with a minimum two-hour stay. A variety of activities will keep kids busy while parents get some time out.

Lift tickets (05/06 prices, without tax)

	Adult	Child (7-12)
One day	C$59	C$27
Three days	C$168 (C$56/day)	C$75 (C$25/day)
Five days	C$270 (C$54/day)	C$120 (C$24/day)

Who skis free: Kids 6 and younger.

Who skis at a discount: Youth (13-18) and seniors (65+) pay C$49 for one day; three days, C$141; five days, C$224.

Sightseers: For C$17, you can ride the gondola up and down for lunch or dinner and savor the food and the spectacular views. Children cost C$10.

Accommodations

Kicking Horse Mountain Resort has a toll-free reservations number for most area properties, (866) 754-5425. You can also pre-book tickets and transportation. Development of the mountain village is quite recent, so all lodging is new or like new. All the small lodges are owned by delightful couples who know how to make a vacation relaxing and special. Developments for the 2006-07 season include a luxurious 48-unit Palliser Lodge, a lodge in Gondola Plaza adding 50 units, retail and shopping, Cabins of Kicking Horse and other town homes and upscale homes.

Glacier Lodge (877-754-5486; 439-1160; $$–$$$$) is a ski-in/ski-out condo lodge with 56 units as large as three bedrooms with loft. Designed to blend into its Rocky Mountain surroundings with its stone and timber architecture, it's just steps from the gondola. Each unit has a full kitchen, washer/dryer, gas fireplace and mountain views. Leather couches and chairs make relaxing by your fireplace a no-brainer. Other amenities include outdoor hot tub, sauna, steam room and fitness center. Friendly staff manage the front desk. The nearly identical Mountaineer Lodge has another 51 units, is owned by the same company and is right next door.

Copper Horse Lodge (877-544-7644; 344-7644; $$$), an intimate and classy 10-room inn, has all the modern conveniences in its spacious rooms: multi-jet spa showers, terry robes, featherbeds, Internet access, phones, bar fridges and flat-screen TVs with DVD players. The one deluxe room has a jetted tub. Other amenities include a common area with soaring fireplace and game table, an outdoor hot tub, a bar (bartender will deliver drinks to guests in the common areas), and a very good restaurant (see *Dining*). Prices include a full hot breakfast.

It's a short walk to the lifts.

The rock-and-timber **Vagabond Lodge** (344-2622; $$$; 344-2622), with 10 suites and comfy common areas for guests to mingle, is stunning and inviting—like a fancy European pension. Rooms are spacious, with featherbeds and armoirs. The lodge is an adult environment and features a breakfast room for complimentary continental breakfast, library and games room, media room with a large TV and Internet access, lounge area with fireplace, and an outdoor hot tub. Suites do not have TVs or phones. It's a short walk to the lifts.

Whispering Pines (344-7188; $$–$$$) has luxurious three-bedroom townhouses providing ski-in/ski-out lodging just a few minutes' away from the day lodge and near the gondola. All units have kitchens, fireplaces, washers and dryers, outdoor hot tub and maid service. Depending on the unit, up to eight guests can be easily accommodated.

There is another option for staying (literally) on-mountain: the exclusive C$875 per room, per night "Winter Getaway" at **Eagle's Eye Suites** (866-754-5425; $$$$). Just upstairs above the Eagle's Eye Restaurant at 7,700 feet, two lovely two-person suites with private balconies overlook the Columbia Valley and three mountain ranges. Amenities include pretty much anything you'd expect for that price, including your own 24-hour valet/concierge service, personalized dining menus, lift tickets, guaranteed first tracks, private ski instructor, champagne, gift basket and other take-aways. The most exclusive part of this package is the VIP gondola cabin with leather seats, CD player and wine bucket for those 12-minute rides.

The town of Golden offers comfortable chain properties and a number of inns and B&Bs. Many Golden properties have shuttle service available to the ski area as needed for a small charge.

The Prestige Inn (866-754-5425; $$–$$$), not as swanky as rumored but still decent, is a hotel with kitchenettes, fridges, an indoor pool and hot tub. A day spa and liquor store also are on the premises. **Best Western Mountainview Inn** (866-754-5425; $–$$) includes an indoor pool, coin laundry room and extra-large, family-sized rooms. **Ramada Limited** (800-593-0511; 439-1888; $–$$$) has an indoor pool, hot tub, coin laundry, business center with Internet access and kitchenette suites. Complimentary continental breakfast is included.

The **Golden Rim Motor Inn** (877-311-2216; $) is a real treasure, with thoughtful staff making the stay highly memorable. You'll find a waterslide, hot tub, indoor pool, saunas and recreation room.

Hillside Lodge & Chalets (344-7281; $$), owned and operated by the Baier family, is a B&B located about 15 minutes west of Golden, just north of Hwy. 1 on the Blaeberry River. Guestrooms have private baths and include sumptuous breakfasts. Sonja and Hubert Baier also serve dinner. Five chalets each have twin or queen beds, private baths, handcrafted furnishings, wood stoves, and fridges. Coffee and tea are provided.

Tschurtschenthaler Lodge (pronounced Church-en-Taller; 344-7325; 866-344-8184; $$) is five minutes south of Golden. Guest rooms have private baths. Breakfast, a sauna hut and breathtaking views are all included. **Cedar House Cafe & Restaurant** (344-4679; $$), just 15 minutes from the resort, rents a cabin that sleeps four and includes laundry, kitchen and TV.

Alpine Meadows Lodge (344-5863; $$), on a scenic benchland just outside Golden, has 10 guestrooms overlooking the great room and serves full hot breakfasts. The **Golden Kicking Horse Hostel** (344-5071; $) has beds for C$20 per night, full kitchen facilities, free parking, other amenities and no curfew.

Dining: $$$$-Entrees C$30+; $$$-C$20-$30; $$-C$10-$20; $-less than C$10.
Accommodations: (double room) $$$$-C$200+; $$$-C$141-$200; $$-C$81-$140; $-C$80 and less.

Dining

Hands down, the most spectacular and elegant dining at Kicking Horse is at **Eagle's Eye Restaurant** (866-754-5425; $$$$ for dinner; $$ for lunch), just a gondola ride up to the 7,705-foot summit. Billed as "Canada's Most Elevated Dining Experience," it's the highest restaurant in Canada and equally fabulous for lunch and dinner. Ambitious entrees run the gamut from a vegetarian roasted pepper with polenta to fish, duck, buffalo and wild caribou. Begin the meal with sumptuous starters like lox, mussels, buffalo carpaccio and foie gras. The wine selection is quite varied and features many British Columbia labels. It's open for lunch every day, for dinner only on Friday and Saturday. The Cascadian architecture and the views are both breathtaking.

In the mountain village, **Corks Restaurant** (344-6201; $$$), at Copper Horse Lodge, serves contemporary mountain cuisine, such as maple-glazed wild coho salmon, in a bistro setting. A take-out menu highlights its gourmet pizzas. Our favorite is the bizzaro pizza with spicy sausage, spinach, chicken and mango chutney. **Sushi Kuma** ($–$$), at Glacier Lodge, is tiny, but the chefs create big tastes, whether you choose sushi, noodles, rice bowls or dinner boxes.

You can grab a quick bite to eat at **Heaven's Door Yurt** ($) at the base of the Stairway to Heaven lift in Crystal Bowl. The **cafeteria** ($) at the Day Lodge serves great made-to-order omelets for breakfast, and soups, salads, sandwiches and burgers for lunch.

Off the mountain in Golden, **Cedar House Cafe & Restaurant** (344-4679; $$–$$$$) has an open concept kitchen and features a vegetarian menu alongside the obligatory Alberta beef, pork, salmon and lamb. The chef uses wild, sustainable fish, free-range meats and organic produce. **Kicking Horse Grill** (344-2330; $$–$$$), owned by two Dutch cousins, is in an old log cabin that belies its interior of burled logs, white tablecloths, candlelight, and jazz playing in the background. The laid-back staff members, called "culinary tour guides," are knowledgeable and courteous. The delectable menu changes every three months to showcase international dishes. **Eleven22** (344-2443; $$–$$$) is a bright and cheerful bistro with several small rooms that create an intimate setting. It specializes in vegetarian Thai dishes, pastas and a variety of meats. Open nightly for dinner, Thursday through Saturday for lunch.

Apres-ski/nightlife

Apres-ski revs up at the **Day Lodge** every afternoon. On Fridays and Saturdays only, end up at the **Eagle's Eye** at the summit for drinks and starters, and ride the gondola back down. **Corks** at the Copper Horse Lodge gets chatty with local beers, wine and contemporary music playing in the background. Try some of the tasty appetizers to tide you over.

For some raucous nightlife, head into Golden to The Lodge. Locals refer to it as a "peeler" bar and tell us that "fresh meat" Mondays are the rowdiest since that's opening night on the circuit for the new "peeler" of the week (if you don't know what a "peeler" is, think "better than a wet T-shirt contest").

Mad Trapper is a pub with pool tables and lots of locals. **Packers**, a dance bar, spotlights live bands on weekends, djs on Thursdays and Fridays, playing danceable rock and Top 40 tunes. If you hate to dance, vie for the pool tables. Otherwise, downtown Golden hasn't grown into its apres-ski and nightlife britches. Yet.

Other activities

This region is the destination for world-class **heli- and snowcat-skiing operators,** as well as **backcountry guided tours.** One you might not have heard of yet, but should consider, is Chatter Creek Mountain Lodges (344-7199), owned by two local loggers who also happen to be passionate about skiing and riding. The skilled staff is laid-back and friendly, the lodges are simple but comfortable, and the emphasis is on great skiing and riding in a pristine and spectacular environment. The remote lodges are accessed solely by helicopter. All terrain is accessed via snowcat, but plans are to add heli-terrain, which ranges from a base of 4,900 feet to a summit of 9,600 feet, with some skiing and riding on glaciers. When other operators were closed in January 2005 due to inclement conditions during the Pineapple Express that hit the area, Chatter Creek skiers enjoyed thigh-deep powder, with most days benefiting from fresh overnight snow.

Guided snowmobile tours are available through SnowPeak Rentals & Tours (888-512-4222; 344-8385) and Kinbasket Adventures (344-6012).

Cedar & Sage Spa (290-0018; 344-7990), a privately owned day spa in the Prestige Inn, offers wraps, massages, masks, facials, manicures, pedicures and hair care. Just-for-men treatments also are available.

The scenery in the region is simply amazing, with frequent **wildlife sightings,** and places worth day visits include **Lake Louise, Radium Hot Springs, Revelstoke,** and the surrounding **six national parks.** Make sure to pick up free area road maps, most accommodations have them on site.

For **shopping,** you'll find a few shops in the mountain village and a few more downtown. Not surprisingly, emphasis is on outdoor recreational products.

Getting there and getting around

By air: Calgary International Airport is your gateway to Kicking Horse Mountain Resort, which is about 3 hours west along the Trans Canada Highway in Golden, B.C. The airport is served by all major airlines. The Rocky Mountain Sky Shuttle (888-762-8754; 403-762-5200) makes trips from the airport to Golden twice a day.

By bus: A daily shuttle service goes from the Calgary Airport to Calgary's Greyhound depot, where you can catch a bus to Golden. Call (888) 438-2992 for the airport shuttle's details and schedules. The Powder Express bus (800-644-8888; 403-762-4554) goes from Banff and Lake Louise hotels to Kicking Horse for a day trip; cost includes bus ride and lift ticket.

By car: If you rent a car at the airport, life gets much easier. From Calgary, take the Trans Canada Highway and travel west, past Banff and Lake Louise to Golden, about a 3-hour drive along a scenic route. The pass through the Rockies can be treacherous in bad weather, so be sure to check road conditions. Follow signs to Golden Town Centre.

Getting around: Snow Shuttles run from Golden accommodations to the resort for C$6. A one-way taxi ride between Golden and the resort is costly. Be sure to have the correct Canadian currency for fare or you'll be charged a lot more in American dollars—the cabbies don't seem to have a handle on the exchange thing. It's easy to get around by car, and we recommend one so you can explore this beautiful region.

Dining: $$$$-Entrees C$30+; $$$-C$20-$30; $$-C$10-$20; $-less than C$10.
Accommodations: (double room) $$$$-C$200+; $$$-C$141-$200; $$-C$81-$140; $-C$80 and less.

Panorama Mountain Village
British Columbia, Canada

Summit elevation:	**7,800 feet**
Vertical drop:	**4,000 feet**
Base elevation:	**3,800 feet**

Address: Panorama Mountain Village, Panorama, BC, Canada V0A 1T0
Area code: 250
Ski area phone: 342-6941
Snow report: 342-6941
Toll-free reservations: (800) 663-2929
Fax: 341-4199
E-mail: paninfo@panoramaresort.com
Internet: www.panoramaresort.com

Expert: ★★★
Advanced: ★★★
Intermediate: ★★★★
Beginner: ★★★
First-timer: ★★★

Number of lifts: 9-1 8-person village gondola, 2 high-speed quads, 1 quad, 1 triple, 1 double, 2 surface lifts, 1 moving carpet
Skiable acres: 2,847 acres
Snowmaking: 40 percent
Uphill capacity: 8,500+ per hour
Parks & pipes: 2 parks, 1 pipe
Bed base: 3,500 at the base
Nearest lodging: Slopeside, ski-in/ski-out
Resort child care: Yes, 18 months and older
Adult ticket, per day: C$50-C$59 (05/06 without tax)

Dining: ★★★
Apres-ski/nightlife: ★★★
Other activities: ★★★

Panorama Mountain Village is two hours south of Banff on the west side of the Continental Divide, which separates Alberta from British Columbia. Just think about the massive snowfall from clouds trying to rise over the Divide. Yum. British Columbians figure they get the best of the winter deal.

Panorama is now one of the Canadian Rockies' premier winter vacation destinations. With the addition of ski terrain, high-speed lifts, restaurants, giant slopeside hot pools, accommodations and a village gondola, life is looking pretty good on the western slope of the Rockies. The resort has almost 3,000 patrolled acres, including bowls, backcountry terrain in Taynton Bowl, the gladed Extreme Dream Zone, terrain parks and an FIS-regulation halfpipe. Panorama is known for its high percentage of intermediate, advanced and expert runs and, since everything is below treeline, it has an abundance of glade skiing.

Mountain layout

At the very top, the Summit Hut and Taynton Takeout wait for you to enjoy the "view of a thousand peaks." First-time visitors can learn their way around with a free guide service.

◆◆ **Expert** ◆**Advanced:** The resort has almost 1,000 acres of backcountry-style terrain in Taynton Bowl. The bowl used to be strictly heli-skiing territory and provides loads of wide-open and naturally gladed runs. The main chutes are more than 1,700 vertical feet. Also head to Millennium (a fall-line run off the top of the Champagne Express), the gladed Extreme Dream Zone and the wide-open Sun Bowl. Tight Spots, Schober's Glades and Hideaway also ramp up the fun meter.

■ **Intermediate:** Intermediates favor Alive Glades and Sun Bowl. Some may think the one blue-square run from the summit is appropriately named Getmedown. Most intermediates will want to stay below the Summit Quad. Adventurous intermediates should test themselves on the single-blacks lower on the mountain before heading to the top.

●● **Beginner** ● **First-timer:** Beginners should stick to the learning area and the Mile 1 Quad Express to get comfortable before trying any of the other chairlifts. The learning area, with a platter, moving carpet and a chair, is in the lowlands, away from the hubbub.

Ride Guide: While most riders give the manmade stuff a thumbs up, they really come here for the natural terrain. This resort rocks for intermediate, advanced and expert riders. Check out almost 1,000 acres of backcountry in the Taynton Bowl: You'll find chutes, glades and wide-open runs here. Be forewarned: It's a long trudge out of the bowl.

Parks and pipes
In the Showzone Terrain Park, experienced riders and skiers will find multiple tabletops, kickers, spines, rails, funboxes and an FIS-regulation halfpipe. Little rippers and freestyle newcomers will be happy in Blue Park, with its scaled-down versions of all the elements found in Showzone to ensure a fun and safer experience for kids and intermediate snowboarders. Both terrain parks are lit for night sessions and piped-in DMX music adds to the ambience.

Cross-country and snowshoeing (visit xcskiresorts.com for more details)
The Greywolf Nordic Centre (342-6941 ext. 3840) offers 20.5 km. of groomed cross-country trails for classic and skate skiing, plus 6.6 km. for classic only. The Nordic clubhouse (the Greywolf Golf Course Clubhouse in the summer season) has rental equipment, waxing service, lessons and refreshments, plus changing rooms, lockers and showers. Trail fees are $10 adults, $7 teens, $6 juniors.

Lessons (05/06 prices, without tax)
The Bilodeau School of Skiing and Snowboarding is highly regarded.
Group lessons: Diamond Cutters is a one-day clinic (four hours) for intermediate and advanced skiers that teaches route selection and advanced skills. Cost is C$89 and includes lunch at the Elkhorn Cabin. Group lessons for beginner and intermediate skiers last 1.5 hours and cost C$49. Group lessons for beginner and intermediate snowboarders are 1.5 hours and cost C$39.

First-timer package: First-time skiers can take a MagicTrax Group Lesson with specially trained MagicTrax instructors and "shortcut" shaped skis. The three-day program includes rentals and a 3.5-hour lesson each day for C$189. First Run Snowboard (or Second Run for novices) is a two-hour group introduction to snowboarding; cost is C$49.

Private lessons: One-hour lessons cost C$89, 1.5 hours cost $109.

Special programs: Confidence Club for skiers is a three-day group clinic designed to help you master the blue runs. Cost is C$179 for 10.5 hours of instruction.

KidStuff (05/06 prices, without tax)
Child care: Ages 18 months through 5 years old. Cost is C$65 for all day; C$35 half day. Lunch is an additional C$7. For Wee Wascals reservations, call 341-3041. Telus Mobility call-in stations are located on the mountain for parents to check in on their wee ones. Evening babysitters are available by arrangement.

Children's lessons: There are extensive lesson offerings for children. Register in advance with the ski school for all children's lessons, (888) 767-7799 or 342-6941. The Snowbirds program is an introduction to skiing for kids 3-4 years old. Lessons are at 9:15 a.m. or 3:15

p.m. and cost C$29; most children spend the rest of the day in child care. The all-day Adventure Club (10:30 a.m. to 3 p.m.) is for skiers ages 5–14 and snowboarders ages 8–14. It costs C$69 (includes lunch) for one day; C$189 for three consecutive days; each additional day costs C$55.

First-time skiers ages 14 and older can take a MagicTrax Group Lesson with specially trained MagicTrax instructors and "shortcut" shaped skis. The three-day program includes rentals and a 3.5-hour lesson each day for C$189. First Run Snowboard for kids 8 and older teaches the basic skills of sliding, turning on an easy slope and lift riding. The two-hour lesson starts at 10 a.m. or 2:30 p.m. and costs C$49.

Skiing with kids: The "kids only zone" is just off the Mile One quad chair. The Secret Forest is a magical place including a mid-mountain wooden fort and park where kids can kick off their skis and play.

Special activities: Horse-drawn sleigh rides take you along Toby Creek to Trappers Cabin, an old-time ranch where there's a roaring fire, hot chocolate and s'mores. Winter Wonderland is the place to go every Saturday night for a kid's parade, story telling and the snow dance. Another option is to drop into the Panorama Springs Hot Pools for a game of "Hot Pool Bingo." There are even magic shows on some nights. "Kid's Nights" include indoor games, activities and crafts for children ages 5-12. Older kids can go to Teen Movie Night or the Core Lounge and E-Zone games arcade. The Glacier nightclub also hosts Teen Club Nights on Thursday and Sunday nights. Check in at Guest Services for more details and cost.

Lift tickets [05/06 prices without tax]

	Adult	Child (7-12)
One day	C$59	C$27
Three days	C$159 (S$53+/day)	C$74 (S$25+/day)
Five days	C$249 (S$50+/day)	C$119 (S$24+/day)

Who skis free: Ages 4 and under.

Who skis at a discount: Teens (13-18) pay C$54; three days, C$139; five days, C$199. Seniors 65 and older pay teen prices. Children ages 5-6 pay C$12 per day with multiday discounts.

Accommodations

Panorama has more than 600 slopeside condos and townhomes, plus a 102-unit hotel. Call 800-663-2929 for all slopeside lodging reservations, or book online at www.skipanorama.com.

Wolf Lake, Aurora, Riverbend and **Hearthstone Townhomes** ($$$–$$$$) feature superior ski-in/ski-out access. These one- to three-bedroom lodgings throughout the village have full kitchens, fireplaces and VCRs.

1,000 Peaks Lodge and Summit, Ski Tip Lodge, Tamarack Lodge, Panorama Springs Condo/Hotel and **Taynton Lodge** ($$–$$$) are condos. All were recently built slopeside in the heart of the upper village surrounding the hot pools.

Horsethief Lodge and **Toby Creek Lodge** ($$) are family-style studio condos with one to three bedrooms, some with lofts, in the lower village. Units have full kitchens, fireplaces, VCRs, underground parking and easy ski and upper village access.

The Pine Inn ($–$$) has budget hotel rooms with full bath, television and coffeemaker. **The Elkhorn Cabin Bed & Breakfast** (888-767-7799; $$$$) overlooks Toby Creek valley and Mount Nelson. It's rustic, romantic and very comfortable. The package includes a fireplace, bed quilts, big pillows, washbasin, soap and towels, plus dinner and breakfast prepared in advance.

 ## Dining

With eight restaurants in the village, plus more down-mountain in Invermere, the dining options are plentiful. **Wildfire Rustic Grill** ($$–$$$), with its wood-and-stone interior, big fireplaces and great views of the mountain, specializes in casual contemporary cuisine. Try the grilled maple-bourbon-glazed salmon. **Ferrari's on Toby Creek** ($$–$$$), underneath the grocery store, serves tasty seafood, Alberta beef, wild game and very imaginative pastas. **Crazy Horse Saloon** ($$-$) is good too.

 ## Apres-ski/nightlife

Outdoor hot tubs are available, plus the **Panorama Springs** giant slopeside hot pools. Have some inside fun at the **Crazy Horse Saloon, Jackpine Pub**, **T-Bar & Grill**, **Heli-Plex Bar & Grill** (try the jumbo heli wings and the heli soup!) and the **Glacier Nite Club**.

 ## Other activities

In Ski Tip Lodge, the Mountain Adventure Centre (341-3044) is a complete information and booking service for activities and events, including **hot springs tours; dinner shuttle to Invermere restaurants; day trips to Lake Louise, Kimberley and Kicking Horse Mountain Resort; games arcade; skating; sleigh rides; snowmobile tours; massage therapist** and more.

Adjacent to the ski area is **R.K. Heli-Ski Panorama Inc.** (342-3889 or 1-800-661-6060), with one-day heli-skiing packages from about C$600. The company has 2,000 square kilometers of runs that include glaciers and glades, all between 5,500 and 11,000 feet of elevation.

Toby Creek Adventures (342-5047 or 888-357-4449) offers **guided snowmobile tours,** specializing in hourly and multiday guided tours in the Columbia Valley between Fairmont Hot Springs and Radium Hot Springs.

The nearby town of Invermere on the Lake has **shopping** and **working art studios.** Taxi and shuttle service are available.

 ## Getting there and getting around

By air: Calgary International Airport is the gateway to Panorama. The airport is 185 miles from Panorama and is served by all major airlines. There is daily shuttle service from both Calgary International Airport and Banff. Transfers must be pre-booked with accommodations. Cranbrook Airport, 75 miles north of Panorama, is served by regional air carriers.

By car: From Calgary, take TransCanada Hwy. 1 west through Banff to the Hwy. 93 junction with Kootenay Parkway (about 12 miles past Banff). Take Hwy. 93 south to Radium, BC (63 miles). From Radium, drive south about 8 miles on Hwy. 95 to the town of Invermere, then continue 11 miles from Invermere directly to Panorama Mountain Village.

Getting around: While a car is certainly not needed at Panorama, the reality is that most visitors arrive by car, and they're handy for getting into Invermere on your own schedule.

Dining: $$$$-Entrees C$30+; $$$-C$20-$30; $$-C$10-$20; $-less than C$10.
Accommodations: (double room) $$$$-C$200+; $$$-C$141-$200; $$-C$81-$140; $-C$80 and less.

Red Resort
British Columbia, Canada

Summit elevation:	6,800 feet
Vertical drop:	2,900 feet
Base elevation:	3,888 feet

Address: P.O. Box 670
Rossland, B.C., Canada V0G 1Y0
Area code: 250
Ski area phone: 362-7384
Toll-free information: (800) 663-0105
Snow report: (800) 663-0105
Reservations: 362-7013
Toll-free reservations: (877) 969-7669
Fax: 362-5833
E-mail: info@redresort.com
Internet: www.redresort.com
Expert: ★★★★★
Advanced: ★★★★★
Intermediate: ★★★
Beginner: ★★ **First-timer:** ★★

Number and types of lifts: 6–3 triples, 1 double,
1 T-bar, 1 moving carpet
Skiable acreage: 1,585 acres
Snowmaking: None
Uphill capacity: 7,500 per hour
Parks & pipes: 1 park
Bed base: 400 rooms within 6 miles
Nearest lodging: Slopeside
Resort child care: Yes, 18 months and older
Adult ticket, per day: C$48–C$52 (05/06, without tax)

Dining: ★★★
Apres-ski/nightlife: ★
Other activities: ★★

By Western standards, Red Resort is rather small, only 1,585 acres. So how can you possibly get lost here? Who knows, but it happens.

The trail map is a moot point—until the end of the day. That's when you sit down with a cold beer and try to figure out just exactly where you've been that day. Sure there are plenty of trails, but the reason to come here is for the phenomenal tree skiing and riding—deep and steep to wide and sweet. Trails signs? Not for most of Red's true gems, even if it's marked right there on the map. Ask locals and they'll tell you to look for the four-by-four post to your right off the cat track (Beer Belly) or the round red reflector nailed to a tree on your left at the top of the saddle (Short Squaw). That's why it's a genuine surprise to be gliding through a prime piece of woods and suddenly see a small sign in the middle of the glade that says "Powder Fields." OK, so you're not really lost after all, *someone's* been here before you.

Red Resort will take you back to the good ol' days when skiing was glamorous, romantic and adventurous. This retro ski area is indisputably a step back in time—even beyond its established ski area days to its pioneering golden era. If you didn't see the full-on view of the mountain rising in the background, you might not even know you're at a resort. This small town of 4,000 residents has no traffic lights, making it hard to believe that back in 1897, when thousands came hoping to prosper from the gold mines, this was British Columbia's largest city. Now you'll find a simple mining town with a touch of class that is sure to catch the unsuspecting visitor by surprise. Spend an afternoon wandering the town, shopping at the shops and chatting with the friendly locals.

Red Resort was recently sold to avid skier and part-time Rossland resident Howard Katkov, who has plans to carry it into the future without losing the retro appeal of its past. He wants to triple the resort's skiable terrain, but retain the tree skiing for which it's renowned.

The resort added a moving carpet for those just learning to ski and ride, about 400 acres of gladed terrain, a terrain park and a cross-country skiing/snowshoe loop starting at the base area. The mid-mountain Paradise Lodge also had a facelift. Construction is underway for a development of 67 slopeside condos right at the base.

Mountain layout

The ski area consists of two mountains: Red Mountain, an extinct volcano and the original site of the ski area, and Granite Mountain, which includes the Paradise area and mid-mountain lodge. Both peaks offer 360 degrees of skiing terrain. The ski area is exceptional for advanced-intermediates to experts. Red is, after all, where Olympic Gold Medallist Nancy Greene and dozens of other Canadian Olympians did their training. Solid intermediates will be pushed to their limits. Lower-intermediates and beginners may be discouraged by the lack of gentle slopes, but adventurous souls will thrive here. Snow Hosts give free guided tours of the mountain every day at 9 a.m. and 1 p.m.

♦♦ **Expert** ♦ **Advanced:** Tree skiing and riding is the big draw here; remember to double up in the woods. No point in choosing a favorite shot through the woods, because you may never find it again—skiers who have worked here for years still find new routes. Locals are known to come up in the summer and cut their own trails.

Red has a few short and steep runs at the tippy top. Don't forget to check out the gladed area of widely spaced trees between Sally's Alley and War Eagle. Experts will want to head to Granite for fabulous tree skiing, chutes, bowls, steeps and cliff bands. The trees on Granite are mostly towering pines with smatterings of younger evergreens and some hardwoods lower down the mountain. The tight and steep trees of both Short Squaw and Beer Belly dump into hidden steep bowls. The Powder Fields spread across the front of the mountain, with ledges and cliffs. For some unnamed woods that are probably known primarily by locals, try the trees off Ruby Tuesday, Gambler Towers, the lower part of Boardwalk near Paradise Lodge, and anywhere off Southside Road before reaching the roped-off area at Ledges Traverse.

Bump enthusiasts can test their skills on the long and unforgiving Slides, which soften up nicely in the sun but can be littered with boulders (near the bottom of Buffalo Ridge, you'll need to tuck straight up the ridge ahead of you to get here). Centre Star is another favorite for moguls—in full view of everyone on the lift.

■ **Intermediate:** On Red, take in the views overlooking town as you wind down Sally's Alley or let 'em rip down Face of Red and Back Trail.

This is a marvelous resort for learning to ski and ride in the woods. The trees are evergreens, and mostly large ones, with plenty of space in between them.

On Granite, head to the Paradise Chair. Groomed runs such as Southern Belle, Southern Comfort, and Gambler—among others—let you cruise and take a dip into the trees where you feel comfortable. Mini Bowls and Meadows have widely spaced trees. Drop in anywhere after passing Southern Comfort.

Ruby Tuesday and Gambler Towers are single-black runs, but groomed, so advanced-intermediates should have no problem navigating down them. Maggie's Farm is the next step for tree skiers and riders after you've become comfortable in the woods.

●● **Beginner:** The beginner area is nicely separated from the rest of the mountain. Stick to the T-bar or the Silverlode triple chair for good spots to practice the basics. Confident beginners should ride to the top of Granite and cruise the 4.5-mile Long Squaw, which winds around the mountain and affords staggering views. The beginner trails in the Paradise area are quite nice, but it's a long cat track returning to the base. You might want to end your day early to avoid the rush back when the lifts close. Avoid Red, except to use the T-bar—there's no easy way down from the top. Terrain for those shifting from beginner to intermediate is limited.

● **First-timer:** Plenty of skiers and riders learn here. A moving carpet at the base area near the T-bar serves the learning terrain. The area is fenced off so faster skiers and riders aren't intimidating. Once you're comfortable linking turns, try the Silverlode triple and T-bar.

Ride Guide: The woods here are what appeal to freeriders. Caution: Many trails through the woods are unmarked, ungroomed and unpatrolled. Don't ride alone. This is one mountain where hiring a local guide can make a big difference in your vertical day. On Granite, the tight and steep trees of both Short Squaw and Beer Belly open into hidden steep bowls.The Powder Fields spread across the front of the mountain with challenging ledges and cliffs.

Most of the goods are off cat tracks that require carrying speed, and even then, there may be some hiking. Of note: To get to anything around Powder Fields and The Orchards, shoot across Boardwalk at the top of Granite and carry speed along a ridge and most likely walk the last section because there's a short hill at the end. To get to The Slides, as you near the bottom of Buffalo Ridge, rip straight up the ridge ahead. Ridge Road, which gives access to the Paradise area, Beer Belly and Doug's Run, is a bit flat in parts. Beer Belly, The Slides, Short Squaw and the rest of the diamond-rated trails around them finish at the end of Long Squaw and Easy Street, which are pretty flat near the end. Coming back from the Paradise area on Southside Road requires paying attention to speed. Groomed runs such as Southern Belle, Southern Comfort, and Gambler—among others—let you cruise and take a dip into the trees. For starters, try Meadows, Mini Bowls, and Inagadadavida. Mini Bowls and Meadows have widely spaced trees. Drop in anywhere after passing Southern Comfort. Beginners should stay on the open slopes or practice off the T-bar. Beginners like Long Squaw, a 4.5-mile cruiser that wraps around Granite Mountain. The green trails in the Paradise area are friendly for beginners, but it's a long cat track returning to the base.You might want to end your day early to avoid the rush back when the lifts close. Avoid Red, except to use the T-bar—there's no easy way down from the top of this peak. Terrain for those shifting from beginner to intermediate is limited. A moving carpet at the base area near the T-bar serves the learning terrain. The area is fenced off from faster skiers and riders. Once you're comfortable linking turns, try the Silverlode triple and T-bar.

Parks and pipes

The resort built a terrain park on skier's left of the T-Bar, in full view of everyone sitting outside on the base lodge's deck. Jeff Patterson, a world-renowned terrain park designer, is the creative force behind it. It's designed for all ability levels, including a fenced-off beginner section, and includes 15 rails, funboxes and tabletops.

 Cross-country and snowshoeing (visit xcskiresorts.com for more details)

Blackjack Cross Country Ski Club (362-7163), across the road, has 40 km. of trails. About 30 km. are groomed, both double-tracked and for skating. Trails wind past hemlock stands and frozen beaver ponds. The network has three shelters, including a cabin at the trailhead. Rentals and instruction are available through High Country Sports at the base of Red Resort.

The Cross-Country and Snowshoe Loop, accessible from the base area, connects to the Centennial Trail which winds its way from the mountain to Rossland's city center. Tracks are also set after snowfalls and open to cross-country skiers and snowshoers. Rentals are available through Red Resort's rentals. Free cross-country skiing on tracks set after every snowfall is available 28 km. north of Rossland (on Hwy. 3B) in the Nancy Greene Provincial Park. The 45 km. of trails are maintained by the Castlegar Nordic Ski Club.

Lessons (05/06 prices, without tax)

For lessons or guides, call (800) 663-0105 ext. 235.

Group lessons: C$44 for two hours, skiing or snowboarding.

First-timer package: C$52 for the first and second day of skiing or snowboarding (includes beginner lift ticket, lesson and rentals).

Private lessons: One hour, C$79; half day, C$189; full day is C$325.

Special programs: Guiding costs C$169 for three hours and C$289 for a full day. Guiding is for expert skiers and snowboarders only. Three-day women's camps with freeskiing champion Kirsty Exner are offered at select times for intermediates and better; call for details.

KidStuff (05/06 prices, without tax)

Child care: Ages 18 months to 6 years. Full day costs C$40; half day (less than 4 hours), C$25. Most bring lunch, but lunch is available for an extra cost. Reservations required; call (800) 663-0105 ext. 237. The child-care center also can provide a list of babysitters.

Children's lessons: For ages 3–6, a three-hour morning or afternoon lesson with hot cocoa break is C$33. Kids 7–12 get full-day group ski lessons for C$60 (lunch is an additional C$6); a two-hour group lesson is C$33. Reservations are required for kids' programs.

Lift tickets (05/06 prices, without tax)

	Adult	Junior (7-12)
One day	C$52	C$28
Three days	C$150 (C$50/day)	C$78 (C$26/day)
Five days	C$240 (C$48/day)	C$120 (C$24/day)

Who skis free: Children ages 6 and younger; seniors ages 75 and older.

Who skis at a discount: Seniors (65–74) pay C$34 for one day, C$96 for three days and C$150 for five days. Teens (13–18) pay C$42 for one day, C$120 for three days and C$190 for five days. A beginner-only ticket is C$20 for adults and teens, C$15 for juniors and seniors.

Accommodations

Red Resort Central Reservations: (877) 969-7669; (250) 362-7013.

Carolyn's Corner, The Lofts, Copper Chalets, Red Robs and **White Wolf Cabins** (866-475-4733; $$$–$$$$) are luxury condominiums with one to four bedrooms at the base of the mountain. They all include hot tub, full kitchen, heated bathroom floors, pre-ordered groceries, gas fireplaces, garage and full laundry. The condos are ski-in with a short walk to the lifts (just on the other side of the parking lot).

Ram's Head Inn (877-267-4323; 362-9577; $$), artfully blending Scandinavian and Native American motifs, is a short walk from the base area. The sauna and outdoor teak hot tub provide the perfect wind-down at day's end, or simply lounge by the stone fireplace.

The funky, Swiss-chalet-style **Red Shutter Inn** (362-5131; $–$$), right in the ski area parking lot, has six rooms, plus an outdoor hot tub and cedar sauna. Multiday stays include breakfast and dinner, served family-style.

In town, the full-service **Prestige Mountain Resort** (877-737-8443; $$$–$$$$) has brand new deluxe guestrooms, suites, kitchenettes and theme suites. Formerly the Uplander

Hotel, this newest addition to the Prestige Hotels & Resorts chain has undergone a complete renovation, including a new lobby, day spa, cappuccino bistro, sports bar and lounge, and restaurant (see *Dining*). The pet-friendly **Thriftlodge** (800-663-0203; 362-7364; $–$$$) is a bit out of the center of town, but has comfortable rooms, large outdoor hot tub, free shuttle to the mountain, and free continental breakfast. The simple **Rossland Motel** (877-362-7218; 362-7218; $) has rooms with kitchens; perfect for families.

Rossland also has a few B&Bs. Try **Angela's B&B Guesthouse** (362-7790; $–$$), with its witty and friendly hostess who is sometimes your personal mountain tour guide, or **Black Bear B&B** (877-362-3398; 362-3398; $$), one of Rossland's heritage homes with original rich woodwork and leaded stained-glass windows.

Mountain Shadow Youth Hostel (888-393-7160; 362-7160; $) has rooms for C$20 a night. Most bunks are shared with five others but there are a couple of private rooms. Kitchen facilities are open to all.

 ## Dining

Rossland is a major surprise when it comes to dining. Several of the restaurants serve diverse, upscale and contemporary cuisine that seems out of sync with the rustic mining town. The food is so darn good at the top restaurants that many guests willingly go back for more. With broad menus, the food doesn't get boring.

The finest cooking is found at **Gypsy at Red** (362-3347; $$–$$$), at the base of Red Resort in the Red Robs. It's best described as California bistro meets the British Columbia mountains, with fireside leather couches and boldly colored, mountain-inspired art. From creative entrees of seared Ahi tuna and braised lamb shank to an extensive tapas menu, you can't go wrong. Top it off with dessert, perhaps the bourbon orange pecan tart with bourbon cream.

Munro's Restaurant (362-7375; $$–$$$) at the Prestige Mountain Resort, formerly the Louis Blue Dining Room, promises "Excellence In Dining" with prime rib, seafood and pasta dishes. **Idgie's Restaurant** (362-0078; $$) specializes in food from around the world—curry, Creole and lots of garlic.The tiny restaurant is dressed in bright yellows and blues and filled with the buzz of clientele. Fresh fish and pastas dominate the menu.

The **Flying Steamshovel** (362-7323; $) is a lively pub and Mexican restaurant with great views. **Sunshine Cafe** (362-7630; $) has basic burgers and pasta in major portions. **Rock Cut Pub & Restaurant** ($–$$), between the mountain and town, serves average pub fare but its breakfasts get a thumbs up.

Clansey's is the locals' hangout and offers a full breakfast and lunch menu. **Alpine Grind Coffee House** dishes out hot and cold breakfasts to go with its gourmet coffees and teas. On weekends, try the awesome Belgian waffles. **Sourdough Alley** in the base lodge is also a good stop for breakfast.

 ## Apres-ski/nightlife

For immediate apres-ski, head to the retro **Rafter's Lounge** upstairs in the base lodge, originally an old mining building. From old-timers to young freeriders, everyone lines up for cold drafts and launches into the day's tall tales, all the while surrounded by historical ski paraphernalia. Or try the more refined **Gypsy at Red** in the Red Robs to indulge in some mouth-watering tapas and wash them down with the drink of your choice. By 5 p.m., the action has headed to Rossland, and it's mostly wherever you and your friends get together. **Rock Cut Pub,** just down the road, is apparently where all the locals go to get wild. It's got a big deck with an in-your-face view of the mountain, a billiards table and arcade games, and ski movies or other sports-related programming on the TVs. Free appetizers every Friday from 4-6 p.m.; buy a jug of beer, get 10 free wings, every day. Bands get the crowd rocking on weekends. **Buffalo Ridge Sports Bar & Lounge** at The Prestige Mountain Resort and **Flying Steamshovel** are other gathering spots.

Other activities

The Rossland Arena has **hockey games, curling matches** and public **ice skating.** You can book a sheet at the **curling club** (minimum two sheets or 16 people); call The Hub at the mountain (ext. 233). High Mountain Adventures (362-5342) has **snowmobile tours** and rentals.

Snowwater Heli-Skiing and Snowcat-Skiing (866-722-7669), with 80,000 acres just outside of Nelson, specializes in multiday **heli- and cat-skiing** packages in a custom-built mountain lodge with fabulous gourmet meals, though single-day trips also are available. Heli-skiing for overnight guests is backed up by snowcat skiing if weather prevents flying.

The guides at Rossland Mountain Adventures (877-550-6677) provide **backcountry tours** and **clinics.** They have a variety of tours to choose from: single day, yurt and lodge touring, women only, and custom packages, to name a few. They also teach **courses in orienteering, avalanche awareness** and **wilderness first aid.**

Rossland has a small collection of **shops.** Browse through Mainstage Gallery for local art, Gold Rush Books & Espresso for you know what, The Cellar for Canadian-made gifts, and both the Legacy Gift Room and Feather Your Nest for unique home products. For on-mountain renting and shopping, Red Sports, formerly LeRois Sports, provides rental, retail and customer service at the base of Red.

The biggest party of the year is the **Winter Carnival** for three days near the end of January with a snow sculpture contest, parade, dances and other festivities. Call 362-5399.

If you have a car, take a day trip to **Nelson,** about an hour away. Another town ripe with mining history, Nelson is the central administrative center for the Kootenays, but rather surprisingly has an artsy aura. It's packed with colorful Victorian homes and magnificent stone administrative buildings. You can easily spend a day here walking along the main street and its offshoots exploring shops, cafes and restaurants.

Getting there and getting around

By air: The airport in Castlegar, 20 miles north, is served by Air Canada Jazz from Vancouver and Calgary. Hotel pickup and rental cars are available, or call Castlegar Taxi, 365-7222. The nearest airport with U.S.-carrier service is Spokane, 125 miles south. The Red Express shuttle offers round-trip ground transportation between Red Resort and Spokane Airport and other airports listed here. Call resort reservations at (877) 969-7669. Red Mountain also partners with Dollar Rent-a-Car if you'd like to rent a vehicle. Kelowna Airport is a 3 to 3 1/2 hour drive and Trail Airport is a 15 minute drive.

By car: Red Resort is 3 miles from the town of Rossland; only 10 miles from the Canada-U.S. border on Hwy. 3B. From Spokane, take Hwys. 395 and 25 north to Rossland.

Getting around: We recommend a car for off-slope exploring. If you're staying up at the mountain and want to eat in town, you're out of luck without a car. The town bus and hotel shuttles only go to the mountain around 8:30–9:30 a.m. and have pickups when the lifts close around 3:30 p.m.

Dining: $$$$-Entrees C$30+; $$$-C$20-$30; $$-C$10-$20; $-less than C$10.
Accommodations: (double room) $$$$-C$200+; $$$-C$141-$200; $$-C$81-$140; $-C$80 and less.

Sun Peaks
British Columbia, Canada

Summit elevation: **6,824 feet**
Vertical Drop: **2,891 feet**
Base elevation: **3,933 feet (Burfield)**
4,117 feet (Village)

Address: #50-3150 Creekside Way, Sun Peaks, B.C., Canada V0E 1Z1
Area code: 250
Ski area phone: 578-7842
Snow report: 578-7232
Toll-free reservations: 800-807-3257
Fax: 578-7843
E-mail: info@sunpeaksresort.com
Internet: www.sunpeaksresort.com
Expert:★★★
Advanced:★★★★
Intermediate:★★★★
Beginner:★★★ **First-timer:**★★★

Number of lifts: 12–3 high-speed quads, 2 quad, 1 triple, 6 surface lifts
Skiable acreage: 3,678 acres
Snowmaking: 40 acres
Uphill capacity: 11,000 per hour
Parks & pipes: 2 parks, 1 pipe
Bed base: 5,000
Nearest lodging: Slopeside, ski-in/ski-out
Resort child care: 18 months and older
Adult ticket, per day: C$57–C$60 (06/07; without tax)
Dining:★★★★
Apres-ski/nightlife:★★
Other activities:★★★★

Sun Peaks is a huge resort in the heart of heli-skiing country that seems to have appeared out of nowhere, with rapid development in the past few years. Locals began the ski area in 1961, with volunteers carving many of the runs that are skied today. Its strides toward the future of skiing began with Nippon Cable's purchase of the former Tod Mountain in 1992. More than C$450 million has been invested so far, C$10 million this year.

With a recently built first-class hotel and a third mountain adding almost 1,000 acres, Sun Peaks is in the big leagues. The resort's slogan is "Three Mountains, One Village" and the third mountain has made all the difference. The resort is now ranked the largest ski area in the interior and the second largest in British Columbia behind Whistler.

Al Raine and his Olympic ski-champion wife, Nancy Greene Raine, who together helped build Whistler to the international destination it is today, now call Sun Peaks home, and Nancy is both the director and ambassador of skiing here. The resort has one of five North American detachable quads with a bubble, the 1.5-mile Sunburst Express, smack in the middle of the main village. Off to its right are six single-diamond steeps, all in a row, plus four steep blues off to the left. And that's not all. The Sunburst Ridge alone has 15 different trails, plus countless glades. Sun Peaks has a new fifth quad for the 2006-07 season. It's to the right of the Sunburst Express and services great expert territory as well as blue and green runs down from the top. Beginners have their own separate area near the Village Day Lodge in front of Nancy Greene's hotel, Cahilty Lodge. It's very much out of the way of busy skier traffic, affording first-timers a measure of safety.

Sun Peaks now uses a second winchcat for grooming steep terrain and increased its snowmaking capacity for more even coverage during the early season, including the terrain parks and halfpipe.

Mountain layout

Just a warning: If you use lifts as meeting places, be aware that Sun*dance* and Sun*burst* chairs unload at different points.

♦♦ Expert ♦ **Advanced:** Head to the top for bowls, chutes and headwalls. Hat Trick, to the right of the Crystal triple chair, dumps you unceremoniously into the woods. Challenger and Expo runs on the lower Burfield area are thigh-burning mogul monsters. The six runs to the right of the Sun*burst* Express are big favorites for advanced skiers, but you'll have a fine ol' time in the Burfield Quad region. Off Juniper Ridge to the left are several challenging runs and Spillway down the upper east face always holds great snow. If there are intermediates in your group, you can head with them to Mt. Morrisey and play on four short trails that dump off Delta's Return. Spin Cycle makes you feel like you'll land on the village roofs below. The new quad chair from the bottom of Cariboo allows quicker return to the Crystal Chair with entree to popular runs like Chute, Spillway, Green Door and the Headwalls.

■ **Intermediate:** The Sun*dance* Express to the right gets you to the top of Sundance Ridge where three blue runs (Grannie Greene's, Sun Catcher and Sunrise) begin. If you take the Sun*burst* Express, you'll find four long, steep, cruising blue runs on the left. Higher up, in Crystal Bowl, there are lots of blue runs. The recently opened Mt. Morrisey is mostly easy intermediate terrain. The new quad chair at the bottom of the Cariboo accesses blue runs Distributor and OSV as well as green runs Cahilty and Crystal Lane down to the base. Four new intermediate runs on the lower part of Orient Ridge provide easier access to the East Village development.

●● **Beginner:** The beauty of Sun Peaks is that there are green runs descending from every lift. One of the most fun is the 4-mile run that starts at the top of the Burfield Quad and goes all the way down to the village. If you want to do it again, be sure to take the Burfield Outrun to skier's right under the Sunburst Express and back to the bottom of the lift.

● **First-timer:** The Village Platter area is next to the village, yet out of the way of through traffic, and it's all for you. Its Gentle Giant run is perfect for beginners. In fact, these three beginner runs—Sunbeam, Gentle Giant and Cowabunga—cannot terrorize you, guaranteed.

Ride Guide: Snowboarders love Sun Peaks. There are virtually no traverses, with the exception of the Mt. Morrisey Connector run. Freeriders can choose everything from long, fall-line groomers to an incredible number of gladed runs. Even a rookie powder boarder will enjoy the Cahilty Glades. If you're looking for excitement, do the Chute trees, the Pink Flamingos or hike into the Gils backcountry.

Parks and pipes

Sun Peaks is a popular stop on the FIS Grundig Snowboard World Cup. The 2,500-foot-long terrain park covers 30 acres just to the left of the Sundance Express. There's an excellent half-pipe right underneath the lift. It's 325 feet long with an average slope of 20 degrees, maintained with a HPG 12-foot radius grinder. A well-designed half-mile-long permanent boardercross course leads down from the halfpipe to the terrain park. Improvements to the terrain parks on Sundance Mountain include rails, jumps and fun boxes, an expanded green/blue terrain park and a new edge park bully grooming machine.

Cross-country and snowshoeing (visit xcskiresorts.com for more details)

Sun Peaks has 40 km. of cross-country trails, half wilderness trails and half track-set trails and skating lanes. Rentals and lessons are available. Snowshoeing, alone or with a guide, follows dedicated trails with bird feeding stations, wildlife viewing and a snow cave. Rentals include snowshoes, gaiters and an interpretive map. Tours include snowshoes, gaiters and headlamps for evening tours.

Just 25 minutes from Kamloops is **Stake Lake Trails** (fax, 579-5653; snow phone, 372-5514), with 45 km. of well-groomed classic and skating tracks. It's run by the Kamloops Overlander Ski Club.

Lessons [05/06 prices, without tax]

Group lessons: Breakthrough lessons for beginners cost C$45 for two hours. Explorer programs for intermediates cost C$65 for four hours; C$45 for two hours. Top of the World Clinics for advanced skiers are two hours, C$55.

First-timer package: A two-hour lesson plus rentals and lift ticket costs C$55.

Private lessons: For a one-hour lesson, C$99 (C$30 for additional person); a two-hour lesson, C$150 (up to three people; C$30 for additional person); a half-day lesson, C$210 (up to five people; C$30 for additional person); an all-day lesson, C$375 (up to five people; C$30 for additional person). Early risers and those skiing during lunch can take a one-hour lesson for C$79 (C$30 for additional person).

Special programs: Thursday is Ladies Day, a fun-filled program with lunch and prizes that features the resort's top female instructors; cost is C$45. A one-hour private lesson with Olympic-champion Nancy Greene costs C$175 (C$30 for an additional person).

KidStuff [05/06 prices, without tax]

Child care: Ages 18 months to 5 years. Full day costs C$55 with lunch; half day is C$30 with snacks only. Reservations recommended; call 578-5433.

Children's lessons: Sun Kids lessons are for ages 6–12. Full day with lunch, C$65; half day, C$40. Lift ticket and rentals are extra. Sun Tots, for ages 3–5, offers full- or half-day group ski lesson programs that cost between C$30 and C$85, and can include lunch, lessons and snow play. Lifts are complimentary; gear rentals, C$8.

First-timers take a Discover program that includes lifts, two-hour lessons and rentals for C$45. Lessons start at either 10 a.m. or 1:30 p.m. Ski programs are for ages 6–12; snowboard programs are for ages 8–12.

Special activities: The Kids Adventure Park is and it includes tobogganing, a miniature snowmobile track. a lift-served tubing park with two lanes and a skating rink.

Lift tickets [06/07 prices, without tax]

	Adult	Youth (13-18)	Child (6-12)
One day	C$60	C$51	C$33
Three days	C$171 (C$57/day)	C$138 (C$46/day)	C$81 (C$27/day)
Five days	C$270 (C$54/day)	C$230 (C$46/day)	C$135 (C$27/day)

Who skis free: Children 5 and younger.
Who skis at a discount: Seniors 65 and older, C$45 for one day.

Accommodations

All hotels are ski-in/ski-out; many other properties are as well. **Central Reservations** (800-807-3257; 578-5594) can arrange everything.

Nancy Greene's Cahilty Lodge (800-244-8424; 578-7454; $$–$$$$), practically on the slopes, is a condominium lodge with hotel rooms, studio units and large family units. Nancy's gold and silver Olympic medals are displayed in the lobby. The lodge has laundry facilities, a reading room, fitness center, hot tub and restaurant and bar are also on the premises. Complimentary underground parking.

Sundance Lodge (578-0200; $$–$$$$) sits right at the base of the beginner platter lift, and a short walk to the Sundance Express. Some units have kitchens, and all have coffee makers and microwaves. You'll find a fitness center, hot tub, restaurant and shops.

The 226-room **Delta Sun Peak Resort** (800-552-5516; 578-6000; $$–$$$$) is a full-service hotel that includes shops, a business center, an indoor/outdoor pool, three hot tubs, fitness center, spa, steam room and sauna, babysitting, game rooms, restaurant and a nightclub.

The **Hearthstone Lodge** (888-659-2211; 578-7878; $$–$$$) and **Woodlands Fireside Lodge** (578-8588; $$–$$$), across from Cahilty Lodge, are both condominium hotels with deluxe studios and suites, plus a fitness center. All suites have kitchens or kitchenettes and fireplaces. **The Heffley Inn** (578-8343; $$) is a 26-room, European-style hotel in the center of the village with a hot tub, sauna and steam room. The **Sun Peaks International Hostel** (578-0057; $), a large rustic lodge at the base of the Burfield lift, offers slopeside accommodation from C$20 per person. There is also a hostel in Kamloops. A stately brick building, once the provincial courthouse, houses the **Old Courthouse Hostel** (866-782-9526; $).

Dining

Put **Mantles Restaurant & Bar** (578-6000; $$–$$$) in the new Delta Sun Peaks Resort on your "must-visit" list for its full menu of Pacific Northwest cuisine,tasty appetizers and wide selection of beers, wines and drinks.

A high-end restaurant with sterling hospitality is **Powder Hounds** (578-0014; $$–$$$) in the Fireside Lodge. The Hearthstone Lodge is home to two fine dining venues: **Baggio's Ristorante** (578-8832; $$–$$$) serves authentic Italian cuisine with daily fresh-made pasta and **Servus on Creekside** (578-7383; $$–$$$) features a European flair in an intimate, romantic setting. **Toro's** (578-7870; $$), in the Heffley Inn, specializes in Asian flavors, including Thai, Chinese and Japanese. Prices are reasonable and take out is available. The Steakhouse at Sun Peaks Lodge (578-7878) has a great kids menu. Reservations recommended.

Masa's Bar & Grill ($–$$) in the Village Day Lodge is a casual pub and family restaurant. **Bottom's Bar & Grill** ($–$$) in Sundance Lodge is invitingly noisy with good food that hits the spot after a day on the mountain. You'll quickly learn to trust the local McDonnell brothers' eclectic fusion menu at **Macker's Bistro & Bar** ($–$$) in Nancy Greene's Cahilty Lodge. It features warm service in a casual and fun atmosphere.

Bento's Day Lodge ($), east of the Village Day Lodge, is an OK quick cafeteria stop in your busy ski day. You can eat "bring your own" meals here too. For the best coffee on the mountain, go to **Bolacco Cafe** ($) in the Sundance Lodge in the village. **Cafe Soleil** in the Village Day Lodge serves gourmet coffees, baked goods, soups and sandwiches. The mid-mountain **Sunburst Restaurant** ($) is the only on-mountain cafeteria. It's at the top of the Sunburst chairlift and has great soups, salads and burgers—and, of course, great views.

One last sinful stop is **Baggs Sweets**, a great place in the Hearthstone Lodge to indulge in thirst-quenching coffees, desserts and chocolates, or to get a panini sandwich.

Apres-ski/nightlife

Things used to be kind of quiet here at the end of the day, but now have livened up quite a bit. Two apres-ski favorites are **Bottom's Bar & Grill** and **Masa's Bar & Grill,** for a chatty pub-style atmosphere. Or try the nightclub **MackDaddy's,**

Dining: $$$$–Entrees C$30+; $$$–C$20-$30; $$–C$10-$20; $–less than C$10.
Accommodations: (double room) $$$$–C$200+; $$$–C$141-$200; $$–C$81-$140; $–C$80 and less.

just around the corner and downstairs from the Delta Sun Peaks Resort entrance in the Delta building. There's a $10 cover, full bar and a large, busy dance floor. You'll hear live music on many weekends. The clientele ranges from "way young" to seniors, but everyone is both welcome and comfortable. It's THE place to be and be seen. **Mantel's Bar** in the Delta Resort also sees an age range in customers, but it's a quieter ambiance (no dance floor) catering to an older crowd.

Other activities

At Sun Peaks' **Annual Icewine Festival**, started in 1999 and held in late January, participants slip and stroll between village hotels and restaurants, with glass in hand, on a progressive wine-tasting adventure. At least 20 Okanagan Valley wineries are featured, with more than 100 wines. Festival events include wine tastings, a gourmet winemasters' dinner, seminars and an awards presentation. Festival activities are scheduled for the late afternoon and evening to allow for skiing, dogsledding, snowshoeing, ice skating, snowmobiling and other winter fun. For an adrenaline rush, try catskiing or **snowbiking.** An Olympic-size, flood-lit **skating rink** offers drop-in hockey, skate rentals, stick rentals, and more. When you're done skating, relax at the nearby Sports Centre in the **outdoor pool** or **hot tub**.

Special activities that children will especially enjoy are **mini-snowmobiles,** a **bungy trampoline, tobogganing** and a lift access area for **tubing** and **night skiing and boarding** that's open until 8 p.m.

One-hour **dogsled rides** leave from the horse barn at the east end of the village. You can even mush your own team if you're age 14 or older. Tours are offered Tuesday to Sunday at 10 a.m., noon and 3 p.m. Visit the **Resort Activity & Information Centre** in the Village Day Lodge for tickets, or phone 578-5542. **Sleigh rides** leave from the Village Day Lodge. Choose between valley tours or evening dessert rides.

Sun Peaks Snowmobile Tours supplies helmets with visors and all exterior clothing (except gloves). Drivers must have a driver's license; passengers need only be adults, or have parental consent.

Getting there and getting around

By air: Kamloops Airport is the nearest airport. For shuttle service from the Kamloops Airport to Sun Peaks, call 319-3539.

By car: Sun Peaks is a 45-minute drive from Kamloops. From Kelowna it's 2.5 hours, from Vancouver it's 4 hours, from Seattle it's 5.5 hours, and from Banff it's 6 hours.

Getting around: You don't need a car if you plan to spend all your time at the resort. Regular shuttles (Mondays, Wednesdays & Saturdays; 800-244-8424) provide transportation to and from Whistler. Shuttles also connect with the Kelowna Airport as well as other BC Ski Country resorts (800-807-3257).

Whistler Blackcomb
British Columbia, Canada

Whistler Blackcomb Resort Facts

Address: 4545 Blackcomb Way, Whistler, BC, Canada V0N 1B4 (resort)
4010 Whistler Way, Whistler, BC, Canada V0N 1B4 (Tourism Whistler)
Area code: 604 (Note: Use the prefix when dialing local telephone numbers within Whistler)
Ski area phone: 932-3434; (800) 766-0449 (within North America); 0800-587-1743 (from the UK)
Snow report: 932-4211 or (800) 766-0449
Toll-free reservations: (888) 284-9999 or (800) 944-7853 (within North America); 0800-731-5983 (from the UK)
Internet: www.whistlerblackcomb.com (resort) or www.tourismwhistler.com (Tourism Whistler)
Bed base: 5,418 **Nearest lodging:** Slopeside, hotel and condos
Resort child care: Yes, 3 months and older
Parks & pipes: 5 parks, 3 pipes
Adult ticket, per day: C$73 (05/06, without tax)

Dining: ★★★★★ **Apres-ski/nightlife:** ★★★★★★ **Other activities:** ★★★★★★

Whistler Mountain Facts

Base elevation:	**2,140 feet (Creekside)**
	2,214 feet (Village)
Summit elevation:	**7,160 feet**
Vertical drop:	**5,020 feet**

Number of lifts: 22–1 10-person high-speed gondola, 1 6-person high-speed gondola, 7 high-speed quads, 2 triples, 1 double, 5 surface lifts
Snowmaking: 4.5 percent
Skiable acreage: 4,757 acres
Uphill capacity: 29,895 per hour
Expert: ★★★★★ **Advanced:** ★★★★★
Intermediate: ★★★★★
Beginner: ★★★ **First-timer:** ★★★

Blackcomb Mountain Facts
Base elevation: 2,214 feet (Village)
Summit elevation: 8,000 feet
Vertical drop: 5,786 feet
Number of lifts: 17–1 eight-person high-speed gondola, 6 high-speed quads, 3 triples, 7 surface lifts
Snowmaking: 10 percent
Skiable acreage: 4,414 acres
Uphill capacity: 29,112 per hour
Expert: ★★★★★ **Advanced:** ★★★★★
Intermediate: ★★★★★
Beginner: ★★★★
First-timer: ★★

Whistler Blackcomb has consistently been rated in ski and travel magazine surveys as the most popular ski resort in North America. There are several reasons for this: two mountains with the largest vertical drop on the continent, 5,280 feet; tremendous bowl skiing; and runs that wind down the mountain seemingly forever—the longest run on each mountain is 7 miles. To top it off, the town has a people-friendly, five-village base area with lodging, restaurants and nightclubs, much of which is within walking distance. The main areas of Whistler Village are designed for pedestrian-only traffic.

The resort is huge, and its myriad attractions, both on-slope and off, have helped it to become one of North America's favorite international ski spots. Visitors flock here from Australia, Asia, Europe and Latin America, as well as North America.

While Whistler generally gets rave reviews, one drawback that comes up most often by word of mouth sounds worse than it really is. And that is Whistler's weather. Close to the Pacific Ocean at a low base altitude just over 2,000 feet, Whistler can at times get heavy rain or dense fog. But, the weather at the bottom isn't always what's at the top—it may be raining in Whistler Village, but snowing (or even sunny) on the summit. Crystal-clear, sunny days are a frequent surprise, especially later in the season. Whistler is a destination resort with a local population of about 10,000. But, as resorts go, this one ranks among North America's largest. Built in a European style, it has more than 120 restaurants and bars, more than 200 shops, plus more than 100 condos, B&Bs, lodges and hotels offering nearly 5,400 units.

Now that the International Olympic Committee has chosen Whistler (and Vancouver) to host the 2010 Winter Olympics and Paralympics, their winding Sea to Ski Highway seems paved with gold but has "not nearly enough passing lanes," according to Canada's news magazine, *Maclean's*. Major highway upgrades are now in progress to the tune of C$600 million, as well as improved marine, coach, air and train service. Whistler will host Alpine and Nordic skiing, ski jumping, biathlon, luge, skeleton, bobsled, sledge ice hockey and curling. Snowboarding, freestyle skiing and the opening and closing ceremonies will be celebrated in Vancouver

Mountain layout

Whistler doesn't give you a trail map. They give you a trail atlas. Tips: There are more tree runs, more cut trails on Blackcomb. Whistler has more Alpine bowls. If you're facing a snowstorm, you can often navigate better on Blackcomb. On sunny days, Whistler has more spectacular views, especially in the bowls. On snowy days, if you're skiing Whistler, just ride Big Red and Garbanzo.

But ski both mountains. Part of the appeal is to stand on one mountain and look across the steep Fitzsimmons Valley at the runs of the other—to chart out where to go or gloat over where you've been. Both mountains offer complimentary tours for intermediates and experts, which may be the best way for those new to this resort to learn their way around. Tours meet outside the Roundhouse Lodge on Whistler (at the top of the Village Gondola) and at the Rendezvous on Blackcomb (at the top of the Solar Coaster) at 11:30 a.m. The tour guides are seasoned skiers at both mountains so you'll get some history with your adventure.

◆◆ **Expert** ◆ **Advanced:** At Whistler, start at the Whistler Village Gondola and take a speedy ride up 3,800 vertical feet to the Roundhouse Lodge. Ascending over so much terrain, you'll think you're at the summit, but one glance out the gondola building reveals a series of five giant bowls above the treeline. These spread out from left to right: Symphony Bowl, Harmony Bowl, Flute Bowl, Glacier Bowl, Whistler Bowl and West Bowl (plus the unseen Bagel Bowl, far to the right edge of the ski boundary), all served by the Harmony Express, Peak Chair and the new Symphony Express lift which serves 1,000 acres of inbounds back-country terrain now called Symphony Amphitheatre. On busier days, take the Fitzsimmons quad out of the Village, then the Garbanzo Express to get up on the mountain. Ski the top, especially late morning. Stay in the Alpine to avoid the crowds and stop for a late or early lunch for the same reason.

Experts will pause just long enough to enjoy the view and then take the Peak Chair to the 7,160-foot summit, turning left along the ridge. Navigate the tricky entrances to The Cirque or The Couloir, and you'll be on some of Whistler's steepest terrain. Or continue down the ridge and drop into Glacier Bowl via the Saddle, which is often groomed. Or turn right off the chair and drop into Whistler Bowl. There are no marked runs here—it's wide open. Be creative and let fly. A groomed path rips down Whistler Bowl and Shale Slope to the bottom of the Peak

Chair—the steepest winch-groomed terrain in North America. Don't miss the new high speed Symphony Express which accesses 1,000 acres of high alpine. This area can be reached from the top of the Peak chair or the top of Harmony Express. Flute Peak will remain a hike-in, in-bounds backcountry experience, but this new lift eliminates the hike out.

Though most of the expert playground is above treeline, the lower mountain has a few advanced challenges, most notably the Dave Murray Downhill, which starts at the top of Garbanzo Express (and Orange Chair) and drops more than 3,300 vertical feet to the Whistler Creekside base. Hook up with a local and explore the midmountain glades here—especially on snowy days. The glades are significant in this region of the mountain—try the trees off Seppo's or the glades of Club 21 and Side Order—all accessed by the underused Garbanzo Chair.

The west side of Whistler Mountain gives you 400 acres in the Peak to Creek area. Jump in to huge Alpine bowls, glades and wide runs cutting between monster trees on the ride to the valley floor. Named runs for advanced and experts here are Dusty's Descent, Big Timber and Home Run. Flute Bowl , now accessed by the new Symphony Express high speed quad, is an in-bounds backcountry experience. The 700-acre bowl starts in the Alpine and transitions into glades.

But wait, there's more—another whole mountain. Blackcomb's gondola, Excalibur, is right next to the Whistler Village Gondola in the village. Take it to the Excelerator and Glacier Express high-speed quads. Now you're almost at the top. Take the Horstman T-bar to reach Blackcomb's outstanding 7th Heaven Zone. If you're staying in the Upper Village, either ski down to the Excalibur gondola or hop on the speedy Wizard Express, a quad with an aerodynamic Plexiglas windscreen that also keeps out the rain, which can be a soaking menace at the 2,200-foot base area. Then hop on Solar Coaster. At Rendezvous, laze your way down Expressway to the 7th Heaven Express. This south-facing Alpine zone has advanced and intermediate terrain for sun-loving skiers and riders.

Or from the top of the Horstman T-bar, drop down onto Horstman Glacier on Blue Line. Keep to the left and peer over the cornice into the double-black-diamond chutes. Just seeing the abyss—or seeing someone hurl himself into it— gives quite a rush. The best known of these severe, narrow chutes is Couloir Extreme. The entry requires a leap of faith and skill. For chutes that will give you a thrill but not a heart attack, find Secret Chute or Pakalolo, which is narrow and steep with rock walls on either side..

Experts and advanced skiers won't want to miss the Blackcomb Glacier Zone, accessed from the Showcase T-bar. Drop into the Blowhole, a wind-carved halfpipe between the glacier and a rock wall. Or if this gives you weak knees, keep heading out to the glacier itself, rated blue, but stay high and skier's left under Blowhole to get to more challenging terrain. Beware the 5-kilometer runout at the end. For Blackcomb's true "extreme"—considered some of the best expert skiing in North America—head to the bowls off Spanky's Ladder.

■ **Intermediate:** For intermediate skiers, the general rule of thumb says that Whistler Mountain caters to low-end intermediates while Blackcomb suits upper-intermediates. Therefore, this ability group should begin its Whistler experience on Whistler Mountain. Don't hesitate going straight to the peak at 7,160 feet or to Little Whistler Peak at 6,939. Here is where you'll find the best snow and some of the finest and most scenic blue runs.

Left off the Peak Chair is The Saddle, an ultra smooth ride on a glacier. Because glaciers keep the snow refrigerated, it stays cold and dry. To the right is Highway 86, a long ridgeline cruiser that takes you down to Big Red Express. This lift takes you to a slew of blue runs and to Harmony Express, which carries you to Harmony and Symphony Bowls, where you can happily play all day. Burnt Stew Trail skirts the upper boundary where the views are divine.

Then sail down Harmony Ridge, and if you're feeling frisky, drop into Low Roll for some soft sweet bumps that provide a nice change of pace. The Symphony Express takes you to spectacular high alpine intermediate terrain. Access it from the top of the Peak chair or Harmony Express for wide-open bowls, high-intermediate gladed areas and two conventionally cut trails for low-intermediates.

When you're ready to ski to Creekside, take the famous Franz's Run, a 5-mile peak-to-creek cruiser that begins above timberline and ends in the village. Look for a plaque identifying the run just to the right of the T-bar above Roundhouse Lodge. It's one of the longest runs in North America. Or carve your way from top to bottom on Peak to Creek, which is the resort's longest intermediate run and groomed regularly.

At Blackcomb for upper intermediates, the same rule applies: stay high. Three express lifts—7th Heaven, Jersey Cream and Solar Coaster—will keep you smiling on runs like Cloud Nine, Southern Comfort and Panorama. The snow on Jersey Cream and Cougar Milk is as smooth as cream cheese, and the pitch of Ross's Gold, Cruiser and Springboard is perfect for cruising. If there hasn't been any new snowfall and if hardpack or crud are not your favorite conditions, check the grooming charts at the top of each lift.

Do take at least one trip down Blackcomb Glacier via Glacier Express and Showcase T-bar. The snow on top is always light and dry, but be ready for a long runout (part of which is over a frozen lake). Take a look down the scary-looking, expert-rated Blowhole before heading into the intermediate wide-open bowl. It's steep at the top, but the width means that even lower intermediates can manage it without too much trepidation. Horstman Glacier is another option for intermediates who want bragging rights of skiing on a glacier. Below the glaciers, Ridge Runner provides a nice way home or access to Excelerator Chair and more blues.

Catch the sun by heading over to the 7th Heaven Bowl (Glacier Express to the Horstman T-Bar). With options to pick the degree of steepness you want to tackle, 7th Heaven is a perfect place for a group with abilities from lower- to upper-intermediate to ski, all meeting at the 7th Heaven Express. From the Crystal Chair, take a rollicking ride down Rock'N'Roll—the trail starts off steep, then twists and rolls down the hill. Other great trails on this side include Twist & Shout, Ridge Runner, and Zig Zag, with the only negative being that all but Zig Zag end at the Blackcomb Glacier Road runout. To get to the base, be sure to read the map and take the trails on skier's right to get to the Blackcomb side or skier's left to make your way to Whistler Village.

●● **Beginner:** The good news on the Whistler side is that there's plenty of green-rated skiing higher up on the mountain. The bad news is that skiing back to the base at day's end can be a navigation and traffic nightmare. On a beginner's first day, it's best to start with Whistler's midmountain. Take the Whistler Village Gondola to its top at Roundhouse Lodge. Good routes can be found by following Ego Bowl under the Emerald Express lift to either Pig Alley or Lower Whiskey Jack, back to the Emerald Express chair. Ride the chair back up to Roundhouse Lodge. Other nice choices from there are, on skier's left, Upper Whiskey Jack to Lower Whiskey Jack, which then presents two options: Continuing past the Emerald Express on down Upper Olympic to the Gondola's midstation stop; or crossing under the Emerald Express at the top which winds into the Green Acres Family Zone that empties out onto Sidewinder and takes you back to Emerald Express.

If you're a bit more intrepid and want to see things from nearer the high peaks, the options are either Pika's Traverse from Harmony Chair to the top of Emerald Express, or Burnt Stew, a long, winding run down the perimeter designed just so beginners can experience being above treeline. On sunny days, Burnt Stew will make a beginner's day.

You'll find green-circle routes to the base village from the Roundhouse. But, pay close attention to signs, check the daily grooming report before you launch—and take a trail map. Once you're on an intermediate trail, there's usually no escape. Local tip: For the ski down to the village, Crabapple, when groomed, is a great option since few people ski it. When descending at the end of the day, however, the best advice is to download on the gondola.

Blackcomb offers exhilarating runs for the experienced beginner. Fearless adventure-seekers looking for views should make their way to 7th Heaven and take the Green Line all the way down. Green Line does get quite narrow and winds across a number of intermediate and expert runs. Just take your time. Ditto for Crystal Road, which runs from the Crystal Hut.

If you need lots of room to play, ride the Solar Coaster Express lift and glide along the Expressway to Easy Out. This run ends at the top of the Wizard Express, where you may pick up the tail end of Green Line to the base. For short, mellow runs take the Magic Chair at the Upper Village.

● **First-timer:** At Whistler, the first-timer area and Children's Learning Center are at the gondola's midstation, about 1,000 feet higher than the base. Although both mountains are sensitive to first-timers, this area is more secluded than Blackcomb's, and an entire class can fit into one gondola. It's not only an easier and more secure experience for the total novice, but you get to be "up on the mountain," something that's relatively unusual for skiers of this level. The Olympic Chair runs at an easy-to-use slow speed and serves only first-timer terrain. Whistler's nearby Family Zone on the Emerald Express offers great terrain for family members just starting out. Kids should check out the kids-only treehouses in the Emerald Forest.

New skiers may be overwhelmed by some of the green traverse runs on Blackcomb's higher elevations. It is best to build confidence by sticking to the learning areas at the Blackcomb base. When ready for traffic and quicker turns, trek to Blackcomb's Magic Castle and Adventure Center near the Solar Coaster (especially kids).

Ride Guide: Most riders, especially freeriders, prefer the Blackcomb side because of the fall-line runs. The Whistler side was originally designed with the mountain's contours in mind, but a lot of fall-line runs have been added in recent years to even the score.

To get out of the crowds and up to the goods on Blackcomb, from the base take Excalibur Gondola or Wizard Express, depending on which is closer. From either, take Excelerator Chair. To access the real extremes above treeline, take the Glacier Express. It seems like an endless chain of chairlift rides, but once at the top of Glacier, taking in the stunning views and over-abundance of rideable acreage, you'll realize it's all well worth it!

From the top of 7th Heaven or Horstman T-bar, drop down into Couloir Extreme, Big Bang, or Pakalolo, some of the more extreme chutes on this mountain. If you're not quite up for that challenge just yet, Secret Bowl is a nice open area to taste some extremes without having to navigate your turns through a tight rocky space. Secret Chute (stay right) is a single-black chute if you decide the Couloir is a little much. Also from Glacier Express you can do a short hike to Spanky's Ladder, which opens to the "Gem Bowls"—Garnet, Diamond, Ruby and Sapphire Bowls—all double-black-diamond bowls and very intense riding.If you want to do some terrain above treeline but aren't ready for the extremes, from Glacier Express ride the Horstman T-bar over to the 7th Heaven Zone, where you'll find an array of ways down. There is even a green trail down, although it may be a bit more difficult than the typical green trail, so beginners be forewarned. This section of the mountain gets a lot of sun, so even on non-powder days the snow is soft and edgeable. If you want to continue to enjoy the sun and views from this part of the mountain, almost all of the trails here end up back at the 7th Heaven Express so you can easily do laps.Blackcomb cruising runs like those around the Jersey Cream

Express chair and the Jersey Cream Wall have some nice little jumps when the snow is fresh. Some flats to avoid, unless you just *must* go across to the 7th Heaven Express, are 7th Avenue and Expressway to rider's right of the Catskinner Chair.

From Whistler Village, you can ride Whistler Mountain by taking the gondola to the Roundhouse to 6,069 feet. This is just above treeline and to stay above it, head either left to the Harmony Express chair for intermediates and advanced riders, or right to the Peak Chair for experts. If you're an intermediate and have mastered T-barism, head right to the T-bars that run up between T-Bar Run and the Headwall. The big bowls are reached from the Harmony Express.Below treeline, the Orange Chair region is a favorite for snowboarding but is usually open only for events. Check before heading here. If Orange is closed, try Big Red instead. Intermediates favor Banana Peel and Orange Peel, runs tolerated by advanced riders till they lead into Wild Card and Jimmy's Joker. These are the runs responsible for the t-shirts that said, "Real men ski Whistler" back when Blackcomb first opened. While beginners can take a green run down from any chairlift (do it for the views on a sunny day), you'll want to practice near the Olympic Chair. It can be reached via the Fitzsimmons Express from the Village. But you've got your own bowl riding too—Ego Bowl just below the Roundhouse, reached by the gondola.

Parks and pipes

Talk about making it simple: Whistler Blackcomb's park rating system runs S-M-L-XL. If you're just beginning on the freestyle terrain, start with the Terrain Garden on Blackcomb, rated S. Then try the Habitat Park on Whistler Mountain, rated S-M, M-L. The Nintendo Park—rated M, L—and the Highest Level Terrain Park—rated XL—are both on Blackcomb. If you're unsure of yourself in the halfpipe, try the Whistler halfpipe, rated M, before moving on to the superpipes on Blackcomb, both rated L.

If giant parks and pipes are what you're seeking, look no further than Blackcomb Mountain. The Nintendo Superpipe is near the Highest Level Terrain Park. The Super Night Pipe—meeting World Cup specifications at 490 feet long with 16-foot-high walls—is on Lower Cruiser in the Base II area, providing easy viewing for spectators. It's open during Whistler Blackcomb's Night Moves on Thursday, Friday and Saturday nights from 5-9 p.m. Access is from Blackcomb's Base II parking lot, or via the Magic Chair.

The huge Nintendo Terrain Park will satisfy the best freestyle riders and intermediate jibbers too. Just below and to rider's left of the Rendezvous Lodge—accessible from Jersey Cream Express, Solar Coaster Express and Catskinner Chair—enter the gate into banked turns, boardercross style, that dump you to a line of different-sized rails to choose from. Here is where the separation begins. Those who want to go huge, stay to the left and go into the next gate labeled the Highest Level. However, be prepared to be denied access unless you've gotten yourself a special Highest Level Pass and are wearing a helmet (both required for entering this section). You can obtain one of these C$15 passes, good for the season, at Guest Relations in the Whistler Village Gondola building. If you need a helmet, the Mountain Adventure Centre rents them. After entering the checkpoint you'll find yourself in a world of giants, with tabletops, ramp jumps and rails—all designed for very experienced riders.

If you are not quite up to pro status, stay to the right of Nintendo Terrain Park, where the special pass is not required, and find yourself hucking from still significantly large features including spines, jumps and rails of all sizes and widths, plus a funbox. If you want to keep riding the park, take the Catskinner Chair, which runs the length of the park. Unfortunately, you can't hit the Nintendo Superpipe if you want to catch Catskinner back up. At the bottom of the terrain park to the right is the Nintendo Superpipe. This is the most immaculate pipe we have ever seen. There's also a snowcross course, designed for intermediate to expert riders. Beginners haven't been left out, the Big Easy Terrain Garden here will let you get a feel for catching air.

Take note of the music playing: There are no swear words. That's a clue to your expected behavior. The tunes are pretty mellow in the morning and grow harder as the day wears on. People riding up the Catskinner Chair can hear the music quite well, and since the Catskinner is considered a family chair…well, you get the picture.

On Whistler Mountain, at the top of Emerald Express Chair, you'll find the Whistler Halfpipe. It has walls about 14 feet high and is nicely maintained. The intermediate Nintendo Habitat Terrain Park is just below the halfpipe. The 600-foot-vertical park is packed with at least 15 rails, including a wide rainbow rail and a wide stepdown rail, plus a long funbox, rollers, hip jumps and a jib-proof picnic table. A sound system keeps the beat to your tricks.

 Cross-country and snowshoeing (visit xcskiresorts.com for more)
Nordic skiing is nearby and easily accessible on the municipal **Lost Lake Trails,** 32 km. of double-tracked trails with a skating lane. At night, a 4-km. stretch of trail is lit until 10 p.m. The log hut at Lost Lake is a great rest stop. For conditions or information, call Cross Country Connection at 905-0071.

Another local trail network is at **Nicklaus North Golf Course Trails,** with 6 km. of easy trails at the foot of Old Mill Road. Trail tickets and rental equipment are available at the Meadow Park Sports Centre (935-7529), just 4 miles north of the village off Hwy. 99. Your trail pass covers a hot tub, steam, sauna or swim at the center. **Whistler Cross Country Ski & Hike Ltd.** (932-7711), a local outfitter for lessons or guided cross-country ski tours at the golf course, operates out of Whistler Village and runs a shuttle back and forth.

Many avid cross-country skiers travel north to the Cariboo region and the **100 Mile House,** with more than 150 km. of groomed tracks. Call 435-5622 for more information.

The outdoor adventure playground west of Whistler called Callaghan Country features more than 8,000 acres of high Alpine terrain, unlimited ski touring, Nordic skiing, snowshoeing or snowmobiling with 36 feet of guaranteed natural snow and no altitude problems. Guests of the **Callaghan Backcountry Lodge** (938-0616) are transported to this adventure in the mountains, old growth forest and Alpine meadows via helicopter, snowmobile or snowcat. Guides, transportation, food, equipment and lodging are included in the lodge's packages. Callaghan Country will be the site of the Olympic biathalon, cross-country skiing, Nordic combined and ski jumping competitions, as well as the Paralympic events. Plans are to build a Nordic Centre, an athlete's village, a media village and stadiums.

Snowshoeing in Whistler can be done on any of the local hiking trails. More isolated and easy snowshoeing on your own can be done along the **Cheakamus River,** accessed at Function Junction on the west side of Hwy. 99. The 12-km. hiking trail along the river is quite scenic. Cross Country Connection (905-0071) rents snowshoes and it's on the Whistler trail network, which can be reached day or night right from the village. The **Lost Lake Loop** is a popular and gentle trail that takes about 45 minutes to snowshoe.

Outdoor Adventures at Whistler (932-0647) offers an introductory snowshoeing experience that travels from the Whistler Gondola midstation back to the gondola base, primarily following a trail used for mountain biking in summertime. Other tours, ranging from 1.5 to three hours, travel beyond the ski resort and vary in degrees of difficulty from easy to challenging; some include snacks or lunch, and there is an evening fondue dinner tour.

Lessons (05/06 prices, without tax)

Prices provided are for regular season and are lower for value periods. It's best to call ahead for information and to reserve a space in a class, (800) 766-0449, or locally, 932-3434. Whistler Days offers 50% off including Supergroups for 11 weeks during the season. Check for details.

Group lessons: Supergroups, limited to three students, are for skiers and snowboarders of all ability levels. A full-day program for beginners costs C$210; intermediates and higher levels pay C$249 (lift ticket and rentals extra). Half-day lessons are available. Wednesday and Friday ski sessions include video analysis. Summit Sessions, for intermediates and better, focus on snow conditions and terrain of the day, such as bumps, powder and steeps. Cost is C$89 for a half day, C$99 for a full day. Snowboarders take a full-day program for C$99.

First-timer package: The ski program is a full-day class using special Rossignol short skis; cost includes lesson, rentals and lift ticket. One day costs C$143, three days cost C$349. Snowboarding lessons for adult beginners use specially designed Burton boards and cost C$143 for one day and C$359 for three days; includes lessons, lift ticket and rentals.

Private lessons: Skiers and snowboarders pay C$399 for a half day in the morning and C$299 for a half day in the afternoon; full day, C$579.

Special programs: Single-day and multiday camps aim at women, skiers and riders wanting to reach a higher level, backcountry, racing, parks and pipes, and other topics. Visit the resort's website for details and prices.

Racing: Whistler Mountain offers a free drop-in race course at the Pontiac Race Center under the Emerald Express chairlift.

KidStuff (05/06 prices, without tax)

Child care: Ages 3 months to 4 years. A full day is C$98 (includes lunch and snacks). Whistler Kids has three day-care locations and provides parents with pagers—just in case. The playrooms are bright and tidy, and the sitter to child ratio is 1:4 with a maximum of 10 children per room. The center in Westin Resort at Whistler Village accepts kids 18 months through 4 years; the center at the base of the Wizard Express (Upper Village Blackcomb) accepts ages 18 months through 3 years; and the center at Creekside accepts ages 3 months through 3 years. Unless you are staying in Creekside, you'll need to take the bus or shuttle. Reservations are strongly encouraged; mandatory during holidays and special events. Call (800) 766-0449 or 932-3434.

Other options: The Nanny Network (938-2823) and **Babysitting Whistler** (888-906-2229; 902-2229) both offer 24-hour service with a minimum three-hour sitting, C$15 per hour. Early booking can ensure the same sitter throughout your stay. For an additional charge Babysitting Whistler will provide a pager to keep you in touch with your caregiver. Both groups have crib, highchair and stroller rentals, though some of these items may be available through your lodging. **Teddy Bear Daycare** (935-8415) at Maurice Young Millennium Place in Village North watches children 7 a.m. to 7 p.m. and offers full-day (C$75) and half-day rates (C$40) for toddlers 2½ years old through school age. Parents must provide lunch; snacks and juice are included. The **Whistler Activity Center** (877-991-9988; 938-2769) can refer you to other babysitting services. Look for the **Kid Friendly!** designation for businesses and community groups that provide child and youth-friendly amenities and programs. Depending upon the activity, you may not need to tuck your child in day care.

Children's lessons: Full-day programs are available for ages 3–12 years for skiing and ages 6–12 for snowboarding. Ages 3–4 years pay C$108; ages 5–12 pay C$104. Lunch is included, but rental equipment and lift tickets are extra. Children's rental package includes a helmet. A popular program for ages 3–12 is a five-day Adventure Camp that starts each Monday; call for prices (there are two-day Adventure Camps offered on weekends). Teen programs (ages 13–17) are offered daily, C$104 for a full day including lunch. Five-day teen camps cost C$520 (lessons only). Reservations for all lessons are strongly recommended; call 800-766-0449 or 932-3434.

Special activities: Whistler Kids offers a Kids Night Out program 6–10 p.m. Thursdays and Saturdays for ages 5–12. Cost is C$45; reservations required.

Lift tickets (05/06 prices, without tax)

	Adult	Child (7-12)
One day	C$73	C$39
Three days	C$219 (C$73/day)	C$117 (C$39/day)
Five days	C$365 (C$73/day)	C$195 (C$39/day)

Who skis free: Children ages 6 and younger.

Who skis at a discount: Youth (13–18) and seniors 65 and older pay C$63 for one day, C$189 for three days, C$315 for five. Super seniors (75+) can purchase a C$99 season pass with unlimited use, a great buy even for destination visitors planning to make one multiday trip for the season.

Note: Tickets are good at either mountain. Prices are rounded to the nearest dollar. Prices are higher for Christmas/New Year's; prices are lower in January and late-season.

Accommodations

No matter what your budget, whether luxury or no-frills, you can find some bargains off-season or with lift-and-lodging packages. The best starting point is **Whistler Central Reservations,** (800) 944-7853, or **Resort Reservations,** (888) 284-9999. Since there is such variety in lodging, you'll be a happier camper if you query first about details. Don't assume you'll always be at the base of major lifts. During holiday periods (generally late December), seven-night minimum stays are given priority. The online vacation planner allows guests to book all aspects of a vacation. For those of you traveling with Fido, check out Puppyzone.com, a listing of hotels that take dogs (you'll find quite a few).

In order to help you get oriented, we've separated accommodations into the five villages that comprise Whistler Blackcomb, starting with the southern-most Creekside and working our way north through Whistler Village, Village North (including Marketplace), Upper Village and Blackcomb Benchlands.

Creekside:

First Tracks Lodge at Whistler Creek (938-9999; $$$–$$$$), Whistler's most exclusive suite experience with a 24-hour concierge, is about 11 yards from the base of the Creekside Gondola to the back door. **Legends** (938-9999; $$–$$$$) is about 30 yards from the gondola. Both feature upscale ski-in/ski-out lodging, and are right in the middle of the revamped Creekside development. **Whistler Resort & Club** (932-5756; $$–$$$), an older property, has standard hotel rooms and suites. With 24-hour check-in and a funky, friendly atmosphere, it's a five-minute walk across the highway to the Creekside Gondola base. You can hop a municipal bus from any of these lodgings to the central Whistler Village every 15 minutes for C$1.50.

Dining: $$$$-Entrees C$30+; $$$-C$20-$30; $$-C$10-$20; $-less than C$10.
Accommodations: (double room) $$$$-C$200+; $$$-C$141-$200; $$-C$81-$140; $-C$80 and less.

Whistler Village:

The 419-unit, all-suite **Westin Resort & Spa** (888-634-5577; 905-5000; $$$–$$$$) is mountainside with ski-in/ski-out access to both mountains, a world-class spa and health club. This four-star/four-diamond property features a 24-hour front desk, concierge and is a 30-second walk to the Whistler Blackcomb gondola base.

You can roll out of bed and practically onto either the Blackcomb or Whistler gondolas from the **Pan Pacific Lodge** (888-905-9995; 905-2999; $$$–$$$$; *left and above right*). This chic hotel boasts one of the best locations for skiers and riders and we can't argue. Studios, one- and two-bedroom units all have full kitchens and fireplaces. Amenities include outdoor heated pool and hot tubs, exercise room, guest laundry, spa services, in-resort shuttle service and a pub restaurant. Its new tower opened in July 2005. Pan Pacific has recently opened a second Whistler property, **Pan Pacfic Whistler Mountainside** (888-905-9995; $$$–$$$$), an 83-room, all-suite luxury boutique hotel. Located in the heart of Whistler Village, near the Pan Pacific Lodge, this property features fold-away tables, breakfast bars, kitchens and efficient use of space. Amenities are similar to the Pan Pacific Lodge and include a lap pool, hot tubs, spa, fitness room, complimentary breakfast and evening hors d'oeuvres.

The **Crystal Lodge** (800-667-3363; 932-2221; $$$–$$$$; *below right*) added 22 rooms in an extensive renovation for a total of 159 rooms. Cozy common areas around the fireplaces give a European atmosphere. This lodging in the center of the village has 24-hour front desk service, elevators and is a two-minute walk to the Whistler Blackcomb gondolas. Underground parking is C$12 per day.

Hearthstone Lodge (800-663-7711; 932-4161; $$–$$$$), **Best Western Listel Whistler Hotel** (800-663-5472; 932-1133; $$$–$$$$), and **Blackcomb Lodge** (888-621-1177; 932-4155; $$–$$$), which recently underwent a $5-million renovation, all offer good accommodations with 24-hour front desk service, elevators and some walk-ups. All are within three minutes walking distance of the main village and the gondolas.

The **Holiday Inn SunSpree Resort** (800-229-3188; 938-0878; $$$–$$$$) is in Whistler Village Centre. Its suite design is very imaginative, and maids are not allowed to use sprays in certain "allergy-free" rooms. It has a concierge, 24-hour front desk service and is a three-minute walk to the main gondola base. One of the newer properties in the heart of Whistler Village is **Adara Hotel**, (866-23272; $$$-$$$$) a 41-room boutique hotel at 4122 Village Green close to shopping, restaurants and nightlife. Expect 24-hour front desk service with concierge, all guest services and five star amenities.

The **Coast Whistler Hotel** (800-663-5644; 932-2522; $$$) is well placed, across the road from Whistler Village. The rooms are small but the staff friendly. The pool and hot tub are busy every night. Kids stay free. This property seems to be popular with the younger set and is on the outskirts of the main village, about a five-minute walk from the gondola base.

If you don't mind a longer walk to the village center, the **Tantalus Lodge** (888-633-4046; 932-4146; $$$–$$$$) is a comfortable suite alternative to staying in the heart of the village. This property has a heated outdoor pool and hot tub that require a short outdoor walk across the parking lot. It offers a shuttle during ski hours to the Whistler Blackcomb gondola base (or about a seven-minute walk over a hill). All 76 units have two bedrooms, two baths, full kitchen, fireplace and balcony. Good for couples traveling together or families with teens.

Upper Village:

Opened in June 2004, the **Four Seasons Resort Whistler** (888-935-2460; 935-3400; $$$–$$$$) raised the elegance bar in Whistler. This premier resort hotel features 242 spacious guest rooms, suites and townhomes. All units are decorated in rich colors blended with wood accents and have gas fireplaces; most have balconies. Amenities include a spa featuring special therapies for men and unusual, local organic seaweed treatments; a health club; outdoor free-form pool and hot tubs; restaurant and bar. The Four Seasons also offers a full-service ski concierge facility at the Blackcomb base. The resort is on the shuttle route and within walking distance to lifts and the main Whistler Village.

The Fairmont Chateau Whistler (800-606-8244; 938-8000; $$$–$$$$) is another premier property. It has 550 rooms in 12 stories, an expansive sun deck stretching below the high turrets next to the indoor/outdoor pool and hot tub, two restaurants, an expanded lounge off the lobby for great apres-ski, an extensive health club and renovated world-class Vida wellness spa, high-speed Internet connections in most rooms at C$14/day and prime ski-in/ski-out access to Blackcomb. The ambience is distinctly upscale and the service outstanding.

The **Glacier Lodge** (888-898-9208; 905-0518; $$$–$$$$), centrally situated at the Blackcomb base across from The Fairmont Chateau Whistler, features suites with kitchens, gas fireplaces, balconies, living rooms, dataport telephones, duvets and all the usual high-end amenities. It's a two-minute walk from the base of the Blackcomb Wizard lift. **Le Chamois** (888-560-9453; 932-8700; $$$–$$$$), just down the plaza from The Fairmont Chateau, is another upscale property with all the usual amenities. The European-style hotel houses a topnotch restaurant (see *Dining*), and is a brief walk to the base of the Blackcomb Wizard lift.

Village North:

Delta Whistler Village Suites (800-268-1133; 905-3987; $$$–$$$$) includes amenities such as kitchen facilities, pool, indoor/outdoor hot tubs, and workout room. It's a 10-minute walk to the gondolas or you can take a complimentary shuttle.

The **Summit Lodge** (888-913-8811; 932-2778; $$$–$$$$), nestled in the heart of Whistler's Marketplace and a 10-minute walk to either Blackcomb or Whistler, is a boutique retreat with 81 fireplace suites, covered balconies, soaker tubs, kitchenettes, down duvets, terrycloth robes and dataport telephones. This is not your cookie-cutter lodging. The hotel recently opened an exclusive Javanese spa and an adjacent restaurant, Elements. Summit Lodge also features an outdoor heated pool, hot tub, sauna, workout room and shuttle service to the ski lifts.

Pinnacle International Resort (888-999-8986; 938-3218; $$$–$$$$), on Main Street in Village North Centre, bills itself as Whistler's first "boutique/romance hotel." It has suites with queen beds and double hot tubs close to the fireplace. It's an eight-minute walk to the gondola base or take a free shuttle.

Glacier's Reach (800-777-0185; 932-1154; $–$$$) condos are owner-owned and some of the better value properties in Whistler. Many have kitchens and private outdoor hot tubs—their big claim to fame. It has underground parking (C$12 per day), but no elevators, plus a pool and common hot tub. They offer an "extras" package with a resort calling card, no charge for local calls and many complimentary rentals and services throughout the villages. It's a 10-minute free village shuttle ride to and from either base. A grocery store and many shops are across the street in Marketplace.

Benchlands:

Marriott-Residence Inn Whistler/Blackcomb (800-331-3131; 905-3400; $$$–$$$$) is secluded on the Blackcomb side beside the Wizard Express lift. Ski out to the Wizard Express in the Upper Village and ski in back to the hotel. Good bear sightings in this neighborhood.

Accommodations Outside Main Villages

Edgewater Lodge (888-870-9065; 932-0688; $$$–$$$$) is on a peninsula of Green Lake, bordering a golf course and the River of Golden Dreams—great for those who want

Dining: $$$$-Entrees (C$30+; $$$-C$20-$30; $$-C$10-$20; $-less than C$10.
Accommodations: (double room) $$$$-C$200+; $$$-C$141-$200; $$-C$81-$140; $-C$80 and less.

luxury and no village bustle. It has 12 rooms, six of them suites, cross-country skiing and snowshoeing. It's a 10-minute drive from the village base.

Two dormitory lodges and a youth hostel have beds for less than C$40 a night and private rooms for about C$80 a night. **Fireside Lodge** (932-4545; $) is about 4 miles south of the main village, a five-minute walk to the bus stop and another five-minute bus ride to the Whistler Blackcomb main base. **AMS/UBC Whistler Lodge** (932-6604; $), about a mile from Creekside Village, is a "bring-your-own bedding" lodging (though you can rent bedding too). It has a hot tub, sauna, common kitchen and laundry areas and is a short municipal bus ride or 20-minute walk to the Creekside base. **Whistler Hostel** (932-5492; $) is about 6 miles west of Whistler Village. Its desk is open mornings and afternoon/evenings only.

Whistler also has upscale B&Bs. These are in residential areas and usually have no more than eight rooms. Most have private baths. Rates start at about C$125 and include breakfast. Ask for those with B.C. Accommodations approval.

Durlacher Hof (932-1924; $$$–$$$$) is the genuine B&B article for skiers wanting an Austrian lodging experience. At the door, you swap your boots for boiled-wool slippers. Each of the eight rooms has its own bath and extra-long beds. They can accommodate 16 to 20 guests total. Breakfasts are always spectacular, as only the Austrians can do, and on occasion, visiting celebrity chefs prepare dinner on the weekends. It's about a five-minute transit bus ride to the main village.

Dining

For years locals have recommended the **Rimrock Cafe and Oyster Bar** (932-5565; $$$–$$$$) in Highland Lodge as the best restaurant in town. Entrees such as blue marlin and roasted northern muskox loin grace the menu, complemented by an extensive wine list. Leave room for the exquisite desserts. **Le Gros** (932-4611; $$$; reservations) is another local favorite for the best in modern European fare with a decidedly French twist. It's about a mile south in Twin Lakes Village, serves dinner only (seven nights a week) and is not usually listed in restaurant guides.

Bearfoot Bistro (932-3433; $$$–$$$$) is a high-end French restaurant offering a fixed-price gourmet chef's menu that begins with a French tradition called "sabering." Guests can "saber" a bottle of champagne in a celebratory ceremony by running a sword along the seam of a champagne bottle and blow the cork against a distant wall to cheers of other diners. There's a less formal (and less expensive) wine bar with the same kitchen and a simpler bistro menu here too.

Fifty Two 80 Bistro (935-3400; $$–$$$$) at the Four Seasons Resort Whistler specializes in seafood and fun comfort foods such as shapely potatoes and massaged chicken. Whether you're in the mood for the seafood bar or a delectable five-course meal, all are accompanied by exemplary service, an atmosphere of elegant informality and a very nice selection of local wines. The name signifies Blackcomb's vertical drop: 5,280 feet.

Aubergine Grill (935-4344; $$$) at The Westin features magnificent views and specialty seafood menus from their executive chef. If you're into beef, don't miss the classic **Hy's Steakhouse** (905-5555; $$–$$$; reservations recommended) near the entrance to the village off Hwy. 99. Its slogan is "tender steaks and stiff drinks" and they're not kidding. **Val d'Isere** (932-4666; $$–$$$), in the Town Plaza and open for dinner only, features fine French cuisine and has a strong local reputation.

Umberto Menghi, a flamboyant Italian chef whose TV cooking show is popular in Canada (locals call Umberto "our Emeril"), has two restaurants in Whistler. **Trattoria Di Umberto**

(932-5858; $$), inside the Mountainside Lodge, offers elegant and traditional Italian fare in a casual, relaxed atmosphere. **Il Caminetto Di Umberto** (932-4442; $$$), open for dinner only, features more formal Italian Tuscan cuisine. You can take home his private-label olive oil and Bambolo wines from Tuscany. Reservations recommended at both.

Mario Enero, once Umberto's longtime head chef, owns **La Rua** (932-5011; $$$–$$$$; dinner only, reservations recommended) in Le Chamois Hotel. This fine Italian restaurant features great food and elegant service. If you like extensive wine lists and a sommalier to make recommendations for each course, then you'll enjoy **Araxi Restaurant & Bar** (932-4540; $$$–$$$$; reservations recommended), which serves creative fish, meat, vegetarian and pasta dishes. The chef uses local and organically grown food. Save room for dessert. It's the hip place to dine and, since it's on the village square, it's a great place to people-watch.

Quattro at Whistler (905-4844; $$–$$$$), in the Pinnacle Hotel, is one of the most popular Italian/Mediterranean restaurants in Village North. It has an innovative kitchen and a 600-plus wine list. Especially notable are the antipasti and the house-made pastas. The pressed cornish game hen was the best dish during a week of excellent dining. **Edgewater Lodge** (932-0688; $$$) requires reservations for a high-end dining experience from escargot to schnitzel to lamb to venison…and everything in between. The lakeside setting is stunning.

When eating at **Wildflower** (938-2033; $$$), in The Fairmont Chateau Whistler, start with an icewine martini, then delve into the innovative regional cuisine that is the specialty of this award-winning restaurant. Don't forget to check out the wine room.

Get a taste of Austria at **Bavaria** (932-7518; $$$), where schnitzels and fondues rule. The atmosphere amid a rich wood interior is warm, welcoming and somewhat sophisticated—but you can still order a burger for your kid.

Elements Tapas Lounge (932-5569; $$), attached to The Kimpton-owned Summit Lodge in Village North is an intimate 40-seat room with a warm atmosphere and the stunning culinary quality that a Kimptom property always provides. The tapas menu offers exotic cold and warm plates of salad, seafood, meats and veggies as well as sweets, all at reasonable prices. The hotel holds its complementary wine-tasting here each evening

Visiting Japanese tourists means excellent Japanese restaurants. **Sushi Village** (932-3330; $$–$$$) on the second floor of the Sundial Hotel at the Whistler Blackcomb gondola base is legion. We found the service excellent, the sushi fresh, and the prices reasonable. A good introduction to sushi is the combo A plate, with salmon, cucumber and tuna maki rolls; split that and a bowl of noodle soup and you've got a meal for two for less than C$16. Tempura and noodle soups are available, too. For steaks cooked Japanese steakhouse-style, it's **Teppan Village** (932-2223; $$–$$$) in the Delta Resort at the Whistler Blackcomb base or the very popular **Sushi Ya** (905-0155; $$–$$$) in the Marketplace area above McDonald's. They do take-out as well. There's a good sushi restaurant, **Zen** (932-3667; $$$), in First Tracks Lodge at Creekside serves sushi in a sleek modern atmosphere.

For good food at a good price, head to **The Brew House** (905-2739; $$). It boasts about its wood-fired pizza oven and rotisserie, yet also delivers a surprisingly wide menu of well-prepared foods. Entrees range from bad-ass beef ribs (you better be really, really hungry) to Shanghai noodle bowl to cedar-planked salmon. It's a casual place, a bit loud, but with good service and, of course, excellent brews made on the premises.

At the streetside entrance to the Le Chamois Hotel is a locals' favorite Thai restaurant, **Thai One On** (932-4822; $$), featuring nicely priced dishes for eat-in or take-out. **Zeuski's Taverna** (932-6009; $$), in the Whistler Town Plaza, has moderately priced Greek food. They also do take-out.

Dining: $$$$-Entrees C$30+; $$$-C$20-$30; $$-C$10-$20; $-less than C$10.
Accommodations: (double room) $$$$-C$200+; $$$-C$141-$200; $$-C$81-$140; $-C$80 and less.

On some travelers' top-10 list you'll find the **Splitz Grill** (938-9300; $$) in the Alpenglow Building. It features burgerzburgerzbergerz: chicken, salmon, Italian sausage, lentil, veggie, smokies and whatever else you can dream up. It also has a great kids menu and a variety of ice cream banana "splitz."

Caramba Restaurant (938-1879; $–$$), in Town Plaza, is a favorite of our staff Whistler experts. It is "Mediterreaneanish," with a great putanesca pasta, wood-fired pizzas, and a Caramba salad (chicken, butter lettuce, peanut sauce), all at very reasonable prices. It's a busy, noisy and happenin' place. It's pub-fare-plus with a casual flare. Don't miss a visit to **Kypriaki Norte** (932-0600; $–$$) for traditional Greek food including moussaka, souvlaki, spanakopita and saganaki. They also offer paella and fish and salmon entrees.

Cinnamon Bear Bar (966-5060; $), near the Hilton, serves typical bar fare, burgers, pizzas and salads from 11 a.m. to 1 a.m. **The Keg** (932-5151; $–$$) at Whistler Village Inns and Suites has good steaks, seafood and basic American food. **Hoz's Pub & Sports Bar** (932-5940; $–$$), in Whistler Creekside, is big on the typical snacks, burgers, fish and chips menu. They also feature stir fry, chicken, steak and pasta options.

Four and Twenty (935-1743; $–$$), above the Royal Bank in the village, serves good value for the Whistler dollar. Known as the home of savory meat and veggie pies, soups and sweets, this Brit establishment offers comfort food for a reasonable price. **Portobello** (938-2046; $$) has a la carte dining at tables where you order from a menu, but also has an extensive deli counter where you can eat-in or take-out.

Get great Kung Pao chicken at **Earl's** (935-3222; $–$$) and watch hockey in the country that claims the sport. The desserts are massive. **Milestones** (938-4648; $–$$) has a huge family-style menu, plus the **Palomino Bar** ($$).

In the Pan Pacific Mountainside Lodge, **Dubh Linn Gate Old Irish Pub** (905-4047; $$), an authentic Irish pub, has a country feel with offerings of stews, steak & kidney pie, fish & chips and the best draft beer selection in Whistler. Choose from 50 whiskies and 16 beers on tap while you dig the live music. **Crêpe Montagne** (905-4444; $$) at Market Pavillion serves French everything: music, language and savory crepes. Fondue and raclette are also available. Both are cozy gathering spots for breakfast as well. **The Amsterdam Cafe** (932-8334; $$) is a primo people-watching spot, facing Whistler Village Square, the heartbeat of Whistler.

A Whistler favorite of youth and those looking for a quick but tasty bite is **Zogs Dogs** ($), an outdoor fast food stand in Mountain Square in front of Showcase, the snowboard retail store. Zogs features chili and cheese hot dogs, various flavored Beavertails (a Canadian fried pastry) and French fries with gravy and other fixings. Outdoor and heated seating are provided.

Ric's Grill (932-7427; $) in the Crystal Lodge is one of Whistler's lower-priced restaurants that locals and families patronize. Fare includes ribs, salads, stir fry, and various barbeque specialties with steak fries or foot-high onion rings. Pizza is available in either Chicago deep dish or thin crust.

Auntie Em's Kitchen (932-1163; $), in the Village North Marketplace, is a way-above-average deli with a deep menu featuring monster vegetarian sandwiches, matzo-ball soup, breakfast all day, and good breads and sweets, especially the cranberry-date bar. For a simple, cozy meal, sneak into **Gone Bakery & Soup Co.** (905-4663; $), just off the main Village Square behind the best bookstore in the village (Armchair Books) and right on the square. It has a reader board of daily deli specials where you can order at the counter and either take out or park yourself in their comfy chairs. Moderate prices and great food.

Ciao-Thyme Bistro (932-7051; $), in the Upper Village across from The Fairmont Chateau, where owner Chef Bernard was formerly head chef, is known for its decadent cinnamon pecan buns. The cafe is tiny, so it's a good place to order breakfast to go. Locals say this bistro is the best breakfast in Whistler. Creative sandwiches for lunch are a specialty too. **Ingrid's Village Cafe** (932-7000; $) on Skier's Approach near Village Square, is a local legend in Whistler, in business since 1986. Enjoy a huge, best-in-Whistler breakfast for cheap in their cozy deli. Open 7:30 a.m. to 6 p.m. so you can get more than breakfast. **Dubh Linn Gate** (905-4047; $–$$) serves large portions of pancakes, porridge, eggs and omelettes. Perfect, unless the thought of eating breakfast in a bar makes your head spin. **Evergreens** (932-7346; $–$$) in the Hilton Whistler Resort has a fine daily buffet breakfast for less than C$20.

Riverside Junction Cafe & Internet (905-1199; $), 2.5 km north of the village at the Riverside Campground, offers all-day breakfast, also lunch and dinner for a great value, especially for nearby campers. It's open 7 a.m.–9 p.m. with licensed premises and offers hard-wired and wireless Internet connection. Other Internet cafes in the village include **Cyber Web Internet Cafe**, **Hot Box Coffee and Internet** and **The Hub**.

Sleigh Ride Dining

Enjoy a sleigh ride under the evening stars and then a fondue dinner in **The Chalet** (932-0647) at The Fairmont Chateau Golf Club. Reservations required. **Whistler Outdoor Experience** (932-3389) offers a number of sleigh rides and dinner combinations in the Whistler area.

On-mountain Dining

There's good food on the mountains too. Two unique dining experiences that shouldn't be missed: Waffles at **The Crystal Hut** and ribs at **Dusty's Bar & BBQ**. **The Crystal Hut** ($–$$) on Blackcomeb Mountain is fit for a king—or at least a prince. England's Prince Charles brunched on its signature homemade waffles, and so should you. It's on the ridge just above the Crystal Chair and, on a clear morning, the views vie with the waffles for the blue-ribbon prize. Canadian Snowmobile Adventures offers a Mountaintop Fondue Ride to the Crystal Hut, where you'll indulge in a candlelit cheese and broth fondue, as well as refreshments, dessert and live entertainment. **Dusty's** (905-2171; $–$$), in Creekside, has awesome buckets of ribs and great apres-ski. Don't miss it.

For fine Alpine dining, stop for lunch at **Christine's** (938-7437; $$–$$$) in Rendezvous Lodge on Blackcomb. Choose from excellent salads and entrees including salmon and creative tapas. The portions are small but tasty, perfect in the middle of the day so you can ski or ride afterward without hitting the post-lunch wall. Reservations are a good idea here.

At the Glacier Creek Lodge, you can choose from market-style fare at the **International Plaza** ($–$$) or grab a taste of West Coast specialties at the **BC Eatery** ($–$$).

The Roundhouse Lodge at the almost-top of Whistler boasts four restaurants (all 905-2373) including **Pika's** ($–$$), perfect for families craving burgers and fries or gourmet baked potatoes and home-made soup. Try **Steeps Grill** ($–$$) for a simple menu of signature seafood chowder, salads and entrees. **Mountain Market** ($–$$) offers open market-style dining with your pick of Thai, wraps, fish & chips, salads and deli sandwiches. **Paloma's** ($–$$) features Italian fare including pastas and pizza.

Chic Pea ($), at the top of the Garbanzo Express on Whistler, is a neat midmountain cabin where you can get creative pizzas whole or by the slice, scrumptious freshly made subs, and ooey-gooey cinnamon buns. Eager skiers and riders can board the Whistler Village Gondola at 7:15 a.m. for **Fresh Tracks buffet breakfast** ($$, lift ticket extra; through mid-April) at the Roundhouse Lodge and first rights to the runs. It's a basic buffet—you're *really* getting early access to the slopes.

Dining: $$$$-Entrees C$30+; $$$-C$20-$30; $$-C$10-$20; $-less than C$10.
Accommodations: (double room) $$$$-C$200+; $$$-C$141-$200; $$-C$81-$140; $-C$80 and less.

Condo renters

The Grocery Store in the village will deliver groceries to your condo for your arrival. Prices are higher than your local grocery store, but reasonable. Call 932-3628 with a grocery list. Other options for groceries: **Food Plus** (932-6193), open 24 hours, is in Creekside; **Marketplace IGA** (938-2850) in the Marketplace; and **Nester's Market & Pharmacy** (932-3545) 1 km. north of the village—"Where the locals shop." Nester's will also deliver for a C$75 order or more.

Apres-ski/nightlife

Apres-ski spills out onto the snow from **Garibaldi Lift Co. Bar and Grill** at Whistler Village Gondola base and **Merlin's** at Blackcomb. Both are beer-and-nachos spots with lively music. The outdoor patio at **Longhorn Saloon & Grill,** in the Carleton Lodge at the base of the village gondolas, always seems to be jammin' with people of all ages, whether it's for lunchtime, apres-ski or late-night revelry. Music pumps, the draft beer flows and you can even grab a bite to eat here. It's known for its 29 burgers. **Dubh Linn Gate Old Irish Pub,** an Irish pub in the Pan Pacific Mountainside Lodge, is another place for immediate fun when the lifts close. Enjoy a rousing atmosphere with Celtic music, 50 whiskies and 16 beers on tap. **Citta's,** in the center of Whistler Village, has an atrium and is another good apres-ski spot.

Whistler Blackcomb has happening nightlife, from hot and heavy to sweet and subdued. **Amsterdam Cafe** in Village Square is Whistler's funkiest local hangout for nighttime mingling. Drop into a deep couch or pull up a bar stool beside a famous local athlete. **Tommy Africa's** is in the main Whistler Village, under the Rexall Drugstore and behind the zebra poles. If keeping in step with the go-go girls is too tough, belly up to one of the two bars for fuel. **Buffalo Bill's,** after 16 years one of Whistler's favorite nightspots, has pool tables, video games and a crowded but friendly dance floor. It's just across from the conference center.

The Savage Beagle favors funk and acid jazz in a double-decker, double-loud lounge right in the middle of downtown Whistler. Open until 2 a.m. Search out the legendary **Garfinkel's,** pumping music for the younger crowd in the Delta Whistler Village Suites. It's a popular locals' bar that features electronica nights and brings in very good live acts.

Dusty's Bar & BBQ at Creekside is still the locals' choice. Recently renovated, Dusty's is home to stellar live music. Now here's some local lore: The DJ station in the bar houses one of the original gondolas named for Seppo, another original who actually set up the first Whistler gondola in 1966.

For a more civilized apres-ski or evening drink, snuggle in at The Fairmont Chateau Whistler's **Mallard Bar** just off the hotel lobby with a view of Blackcomb Mountain. The Four Seasons' **Fifty Two 80 Bar** is a relaxing place for a specialty martini or glass of local wine. The **Firerock Lounge** at the Westin Resort & Spa is in the heart of Whistler Village and is an intimate spot to have a brew and some Northwest cuisine. **Black's Pub** on the square in the Sundial Hotel is also in Whistler Village, just 20 yards from the gondola bases. You'll get 180-degree views and have your pick of 99 beers and 45 scotches.

Check *The Pique* or *The Whistler Question* for the weekly entertainment listings.

Other activities

Whistler Heli-Skiing (932-4105) and Coast Range Heliskiing (800-701-8744; 894-1144) in Pemberton are the local experts in **heli-skiing.** Venture beyond the ski area boundary for one or more days. Daily and multiday **backcoun-**

try ski and snowboard tours are available through Whistler Alpine Guides (938-9242) and Callaghan Country Wilderness Adventures (938-0616). Whether you're new to the sport or an experienced climber, **ice climbing** with Whistler Alpine Guides (938-9242) will provide a once-in-a-lifetime experience.

Hundreds of miles of logging roads are accessible for **snowmobiling**. Cougar Mountain Wilderness Adventures (932-4086) and Blackcomb Snowmobiles Ltd. (932-8484) have tours several times a day, and evening rides. Canadian Snowmobile Adventures (938-1616) offers luxury evening dinner tours up Blackcomb Mountain. Cougar Mountain Wilderness Adventures now offers **dogsledding**. Make reservations as early as possible.

Ziptrek Ecotours (866-935-0001; 935-0001) offers a 2.5-hour tour, year round, that sends you whizzing along five ziplines at speeds up to 40+ miles/hour about 200 feet above the creek. Zipsters are attached by body harness and carabiner to a steel pulley system—very safe—and the trip is as fun as anything you'll do at Whistler. **Whistler Bungee** (938-9333) lets you take a dive off a 160-foot pedestrian bridge—and live to tell the tale.

Ice skating, swimming and drop-in **hockey** take place at Meadow Park Sports Centre (935-8350) a few miles north of the village. **Sleigh rides** are offered by Blackcomb Sleighrides (932-7631) and Whistler Outdoor Experience Co. (932-3389). If the weather's bad, or for apres-ski, visit the indoor **Great Wall Climbing and Guiding Centre** (905-7625) where you can literally climb the wall (in the Sundial Hotel, lower level).

Whistler Activity Central (877-935-4528; 935-4528) provides information and reservations for these and other activities. Or try **Explore Whistler Adventures** in the Westin Resort & Spa (935-3445).

Whistler has several **full-service spas.** Many hotels offer **in-room massages** and many salons offer limited **spa services** as well. You can even get a **Shiatsu massage** in some of the on-mountain lodges during peak lunch hours. Check out our website at www.skisnowboard.com for detailed spa information.

Getting there and getting around

By air: Most major airlines fly to Vancouver. Allow plenty of time in the Vancouver Airport, both arriving and leaving, for customs declarations and currency exchange. Helijet (800-665-4354; Vancouver, 273-1414) flies twice daily from the Vancouver airport to Whistler, a 35-minute trip.

Perimeter's Whistler Express (877-317-7788; Whistler, 905-0041; Vancouver 266-5386) connects the Vancouver Airport to Whistler nine times a day, with the last bus leaving at 11: 30 p.m. Reservations are required by noon, one day prior.

By car: From Vancouver, follow Hwy. 99 north all the way to Whistler. For part of the trip, Hwy. 99 merges with Hwy.1 (Trans Canada Highway). Keep an eye out for Exit 2, where Hwy. 99 splits off to go to Whistler.

By bus: Greyhound Canada (800-661-8747; 932-5031) operates from the Vancouver bus depot at Main and Terminal.

Getting around: You don't need a car in Whistler. But unless you're staying in Whistler Village or Upper Village, you'll probably rely on the free shuttle (932-4020) to get around. Buses run throughout the resort town with the "primary" route looping from the Village to Marketplace (Village North) to the Upper Village and the Blackcomb Mountain base lodge from 6:15 a.m. until 1 a.m. All buses go through the village loop. However if you are going between the Benchlands and Creekside, or between Creekside and the Meadow Park Sports Centre, you need to transfer onto another bus at the village bus loop. For local cabs, call Whistler Taxi (932-3333). Many of the upscale hotels offer free shuttle service also.

Quebec City, Canada
Mont-Sainte-Anne, Stoneham, Le Massif

Quebec City Facts

Address: Greater Quebec Area Tourism and Convention Bureau, 835, avenue Wilfrid-Laurier, Quebec (Quebec) G1R 2L3
Toll-free reservations: (800) 665-1528
Dining:★★★★★
Apres-ski/nightlife:★★★★★
Other activities:★★★★★

Area code: 418
Phone: 641-6290
Fax: 522-0830
E-mail: info@quebecregion.com
Internet: www.quebecregion.com
Bed base: 11,200

Quebec is a city that not only embraces winter, it celebrates it. Founded in 1608 by the French navigator, geographer and explorer Samuel de Champlain, Quebec is the only walled city in North America outside of Mexico. Perched atop a 350-foot-high cliff overlooking the St. Lawrence River, it immerses North American visitors in French history and culture, providing a taste of Europe without the jetlag.

Drive down Grande Allee, enter Old Quebec through Porte (gate) Saint-Louis and descend into the 18th century. The narrow streets are lined with stately old homes, many of them now gourmet restaurants and boutique hotels. You half-expect to see horse-drawn carriages clacketty-clacking along les rues. Don't worry if your French is rusty (or nonexistent); almost everyone on the front lines of tourism speaks at least some English. And here's a real plus: Winter is low season in Quebec City. With the exception of Winter Carnival weekends, lodging rates are at their lowest.

Although you may have the city to yourself in the low season, you'll feel a certain *joie de vivre*. Everywhere you turn there's an activity: tobogganing, sleigh rides, ice skating, ice climbing, snow rafting, dogsledding, cross-country skiing, you name it. Quebec is alive with culture, too. The calendar is punctuated with festivals, and the city dotted with 27 museums. With more than 4,900 restaurants representing 85 different ethnic styles, the city is also renowned for its cuisine.

Beginning the last weekend in January, Winter Carnival is a 17-day party presided over by the jolly snowman ambassador, Bonhomme. Nearly everyone wears the colorful sash that is the signature of Quebec, and the city is full of dancers, singers, bands, ice sculptures and parades. Perhaps the craziest, but most hotly contested, event is the çanoe race across the ice-choked St. Lawrence.

Don't miss Quebec's little Champs Elysees, Grande Allée, near the Parliament. Private homes once owned by judges and members of Parliament have been converted to discos, restaurants and other outlets for nightlife. Cartier Avenue is great for shopping, and Petit Champlain, one of North America's oldest shopping streets, is lined with boutiques and galleries and feels like pure Europe. It can be reached by the funicular, a cable car straight down from outside Fairmont Chateau Frontenac, for C$1.50 each way, or the infamous Breakneck Stairs.

Mont-Sainte-Anne, the largest ski resort in eastern Quebec, and Stoneham are each about 30 minutes away, while Le Massif is a little shy of an hour-long drive. Each resort has its own

Mont-Sainte-Anne Facts

Summit elevation: **2,625 feet**
Vertical drop: **2,050 feet**
Base elevation: **575 feet**
Address: 2000, Beau Pre
Beaupre (Quebec) Canada G0A 1E0
Area code: 418
Ski area phone: 827-4561
Snow report: (888) 827-4579 or 827-4579
Fax: 827-3121
Toll-free reservations: (800) 463-1568
or (418) 827-5281
E-mail: info@mont-sainte-anne.com
Internet: www.mont-sainte-anne.com

Number and types of lifts: 13–1 high-speed
8-passenger gondola, 2 high-speed quads, 1 quad,
1 triple, 2 doubles, 6 surface
Skiable acreage: 450 acres
Snowmaking: 80 percent
Uphill capacity: 18,560
Parks and pipes: 3 parks, 2 pipes, 1 junior
Bed base: 2,000
Nearest lodging: Slopeside
Resort child care: Yes, 6 months and older
Adult ticket, per day: C$48-53(05/06 without tax)
Expert:★★★★
Advanced: ★★★★
Intermediate: ★★★★★
Beginner: ★★★ First-timer: ★★★★

---

nearby lodging, though without the big-city activities. A three-area ticket, Carte Blanche, is a multiday, multidestination ticket between Mont-Sainte-Anne, Stoneham and Le Massif for about C$50 per day, per adult. With Carte Blanche, visitors staying in downtown hotels can also use the Winter Express shuttle to get to the mountains for just a few dollars more.

Mont-Sainte-Anne

Drive east along the St. Lawrence, and you'll soon reach Mont-Sainte-Anne. With 2,050 feet of vertical, it's impressive, big-mountain skiing with a lift system to match. Trails drop from summit to base at a near-constant pitch, with only a short runout to the lift. Trail ratings aren't inflated here, and experts won't get bored; eight of the mountain's trails are true double diamonds, some with challenging bumps and/or glades, and 10 are F.I.S.-approved race trails. But this isn't to say beginners and intermediates will be intimidated. There are plenty of wide cruising runs and gentle beginner trails spread across the mountain's three faces. All that and an excellent terrain park make it a good choice for all ability levels. In general, the slopes increase in difficulty as you move from east to west.

The South Side faces the St. Lawrence River, where all base facilities are located. It also bakes under the sun, so the snow is often heavier here. The North Side, or the backside, has a high-speed quad and a small lodge. The West Side is dedicated to backcountry skiing and riding on natural snow.

Mont-Sainte-Anne's riverside location delivers plenty of snow, an average of 160 inches a year. When the wind whips up the river, though, it's a bone-chilling and damp cold, so go prepared.

This resort lets you get a good taste of winter Quebecois-style. Don't miss the sugar-house on the La Pichard trail, where you can taste such treats as maple sugar on snow. You can try paragliding, ice skating, snowshoeing or dogsledding, all served with a French accent. Mont-Sainte-Anne's cross-country center is the largest in Canada and second largest in North America.

Mountain layout

◆◆**Expert ◆Advanced**: West of the gondola on the South Face is an expert's playground, with serious single- and double-black trails and glades. This is steep terrain with a continuous fall line. La Super S is long and smooth and steep; its evil twin, La S, is the same, but with bumps. For even more challenge, head into the woods on La Brunelle or try La Triumph in the new Black Forest glade. Two lifts—La Trip and La Sainte-Paix—service this area, but it's faster to shoot to the base and take the gondola. For a backcountry experience, head to the West Side.

On the South Side, take La Crete to La Beauregard for a long, steep, fast cruise. These are two of the 10 FIS-certified race trails on the mountain. La Pionniere, just east of the gondola, has the feel of an old-style New England trail as it twists its way down the upper third of the mountain. On the North Side, L'Archipel and La Surprenante are good choices. To escape the crowds, take L'Amarok on the West Side, served only by a T-bar. If your passion is bumps, work those knees on La Gondoleuse, under the L'Etoile-Filante gondola. For a backcountry experience, head to the West Side.

■ **Intermediate**: While experts and advanced skiers head west off the gondola, inter-mediates should head east (on the South Side), or over the top to the North Side. Warm up on Le Gros Vallon or La Beaupre on the South Side. Be sure to take at least one run on La Pichard to stop by the sugar shack for a maple-syrup treat. On cold days, ride either the gon-dola, L'Etoile-Filante, or L'Express du Sud, a high-speed quad with a bubble cover to shield the wind. Don't miss the North Side's great cruising trails and the intermediate-level glades, La Vital-Roy and La Sidney-Dawes. The snow is often softer here.

●● **Beginner ● First-timer**: The eastern edge of the mountain on both the South and the North sides is where you'll find the easiest trails. Take the gondola up, then work your way down La Familale on the South Side, L'Escapade and La Ferreolaise on the North Side, then return to the South Side on Le Chemin Du Roy, which wraps slowly and gently from the North Side summit to the South Side base. La Foret Enchantee, off La Ferrelolaise, is a fun trail through the trees for children. Choose from three free surface lifts in the ski school area at the mountain's base. After mastering these, take the gondola to the summit and meander down the mountain's longest trail, Le Chemin du Roy.

Parks and Pipes

Mont-Sainte-Anne's 282,500-square-foot, mountain-top terrain park, La Grande Allee, is perfectly situated under the La Tortue quad chair on the South Side. This is a fun park, with numerous jumps of varying types and difficulty, a few rails and a fun box. It's a good idea to take a run-through to check the jumps before hitting them full speed, as many are not what they first appear. The park has a fairly mellow pitch, so you'll want to maintain speed; expect to miss some hits if you fall, as you'll need time to build speed again. The park is also home to Dragon's Cradle, a beginners' halfpipe. The halfpipe and the terrain park are open at night.

Cross-country and snowshoeing (visit xcskiresorts.com)

Superlatives are all one hears for the **Mont-Sainte-Anne Cross-Country Centre**, 7 km. from the downhill area. With 224 km. of trails through the Laurentian forest, this center is the largest in Canada, second only to Cali-fornia's Royal Gorge in North America, and not to be missed just for the *joie de ski* Canadians exude on cross-country trails.

The Mont-Sainte-Anne Cross-Country Centre has plenty of trails for all abilities. A choice of varying length trail loops make it easy to adjust your outing to your ability and stamina. Skating skiers will find a whopping 135 km. of groomed trails.

The area's base lodge has an extensive ski school, a small cafeteria, a waxing room and a cross-country boutique with rentals, which include a baby glider to pull along your youngster, if you choose not to leave him or her at the Alpine area day care.

A day trip for the not-faint-of-heart is the trek along the powerline (Sentier du Versant Nord) to the base of the north side of Mont-Sainte-Anne Alpine area. Though it's about a 7 km. trek, *all uphill*, the reward is the superb scenery along the way and a nice lunch at the Chalet du Versant Nord. And then there's skiing downhill all the way back to the base lodge.

Mont-Sainte-Anne also has 20 km. of snowshoeing trails. Try the guided tours with a Swiss fondue dinner at the Summit Lodge, on Wednesday and Saturday nights.

Lodging at the cross-country area include the unique B&B, L'Auberge du Fondeur (827-5281; 800-463-1568) right on the trails, or the Ruisseau Rouge and Le Chaudron shelters along the trails. These rustic shelters each can accommodate up to eight skiers and are equipped with a woodstove so skiers can cook their own meals. Reservations are required (827-4561, Ext. 408), but there is no charge for their use with purchase of a two-day or more ski pass.

Lessons (05/06 prices, without tax)

Group lessons: A 2.25-hour session is C$53 (mornings only). During holiday and school break periods, only Adult Ski Week is available at C$179 for four mornings (must pre-register seven days in advance). Ski Week includes lessons, fun races, video, cocktail parties and other activities.

First-timer package: Discover Skiing and Snowboarding is a three-step beginner program, with each lesson lasting two hours. Initiation is C$55 and includes equipment for the day and access to beginner slopes. Practice is a second lesson in the beginner area and costs C$55 with rentals. Discovery is C$79 and includes rentals and a full-mountain lift pass.

Private lessons: One person for two hours is C$189. First Tracks one-hour private clinics, offered for intermediate and advanced levels, cost C$66 for one or two people, and include access to the lift 15 minutes before it officially opens. Last Tracks one-hour private clinics are available after 3 p.m. for C$66 for one or two people. A Pro for the Day costs C$320 for up to three students. An afternoon semi-private is C$107 for two hours.

KidStuff (05/06 prices, without tax)

Child care: Mont-Sainte-Anne's award-winning Children's Centre takes children ages 6 months to 14 years. It houses a nursery, day care, ski and snowboard lessons, Kinderski program, equipment rental, a trail reserved exclusively for children, indoor and outdoor playgrounds and a video and music hall. The fee is C$57 per day for the first child in a family (the cost decreases for each additional child from the same family). Hourly rate is C$15. Meals are C$6.

Child care is wisely split into two sections: the day-care center for ages 2–10 and the nursery for babies ages 6–24 months. Day care in the nursery without skiing is available for children 7 months–6 years. Open 9 a.m. (8:30 on weekends) to 4:15 p.m., the Children's Centre is in the same building as the Ski & Snowboard School (note: it is a bit of a climb for a little one). There is at least one caretaker for every three babies, who have their own nap, play and feeding area. The nursery can accommodate up to 12 children daily.

Children's lessons: Ages 4–14 take a program from 9:30 a.m. to noon for C$52. Adventure Week is a four-day camp with lessons, fun races, videos, parties and other activities for C$230; pre-register seven days in advance. All instructors speak both French and English. Note: All prices are rounded up to the nearest dollar.

Lift tickets (05/06 prices, without tax)

Weekend prices	Adult	Young Adult (14-22)	Seniors 65+	Child (7-13)
One day	C$53	C$43	C$28	C$43
Three days	C$153	C$124	C$80	C$115
Five days	C$242	C$196	C$127	C$196

Who skis free: Children age 6 and younger. Beginners ski on three lifts at no charge.

Who skis at a discount: Disabled skiers and riders.

Note: Night skiing, half-day and other tickets are available. Ticket prices have been rounded to nearest dollar.

Tri-Area Lift Ticket: The Carte Blanche is a multiday lift ticket valid at Mont-Sainte-Ann, Stoneham and Le Massif. It includes several perks, such as a free shuttle between Mont-Sainte-Anne and Le Massif, and night skiing at Mont-Sainte-Anne and Stoneham. Adults pay C$156 for three days, C$245 for five days; ages 65+ pay C$126 for three days, C$200 for five days; ages 13–17 pay C$117 for three days, C$185 for five days; ages 7–12 pay C$81 for three days, C$125 for five days.

Accommodations at the resort

The suites at the full-service, ski-in/ski-out **Chateau Mont-Sainte-Anne** (800-463-4467; 827-5211; $–$$$), next to the gondola base, is starting to show its "crow's-feet" and could use some refurbishing. Rooms are spacious and all have balconies and kitchenettes; loft suites also have fireplaces. You'll find a health club, indoor pool, hot tub and sauna, restaurants and lounges as well.

The family-friendly **Hotel Val-des-Neiges** (888-554-6005; 418-827-5711: $–$$) is five minutes from the base lodge (shuttles available to Le Massif) and has an indoor pool, whirlpool and sauna, lounge with deli menu, dining room and full-service spa. The hotel has whirlpool baths in most of its 200+ rooms. Suites with fireplaces and condos are also available.

For condominium lodging, try **Chalets Mont-Sainte-Anne** (800-463-4395; 827-5776; $–$$), next to the Chateau; the ski-in/ski-out **Village Touristique Mont-Sainte-Anne** (800-463-7775; $–$$); the Swiss-style **Chalets Montmorency** (800-463-2612; $–$$), 800 yards from the lifts and with a free shuttle; or the stone Quebecois-style **Chalets Village** (800-461-2030; $–$$), each chalet with fireplace, double hot tub or sauna and multiple bedrooms and bathrooms. If you have need to house a large party, The Manor has 28 rooms.

Dining

Snowshoe from the top of the gondola to **La Crete Lodge** (827-4561, Ext. 0; $$$) for Swiss fondue on Wednesday and Saturday nights. Ride the gondola to the summit, then snowshoe to the lodge for a fondue dinner. It's a great family activity.

Auberge Boudreault (826-1333; $$–$$$) serves regional fine cuisine, fresh pastas, veal and game. **BeauRegard** (827-5211; $$$$) has won awards for its food and wine selection.

In Beaupre: **L'Aventure** (827-5748; $–$$) is a lively bar and restaurant with an excellent view of the mountain. It serves an eclectic selection including Mexican and Italian favorites. The menu at **Le St-Bernard** (827-6668; $–$$) lists steaks, pizzas and pastas. **Auberge La Camarine** (800-567-3939 or 827-1958; $$$) serves progressive French cuisine.

Apres-ski/nightlife

At Mont-Sainte-Anne, the place to head immediately after skiing is the **Chouette Bar**, in the main lodge at the base of the mountain. It has pool tables, music and dancing to a disc jockey. The **T-Bar** in Chateau Mont-Sainte-Anne is a good spot to stop later on for a relaxing drink in a more genteel atmosphere. On Wednesday through Saturday nights, entertainment is provided by a singer or musician.

 ## Other activities

Mont-Sainte-Anne has a **skating rink** at the base. **Skating, dogsledding, paragliding and sleigh rides** can be arranged at the area. **Snowmobiling** is available nearby. For information on all, call 827-4561.

The Charlevoix region has deep roots in its Catholic religious heritage. In every parish you can visit the church of each village, but don't miss a trip to the spectacular **Basilica Sainte-Anne-de-Beaupre** (827-3781) on your route between Quebec City and Mont-Sainte-Anne. It's one of 20 pilgrimage shrines in Quebec. The original burned to the ground in 1927. This replacement is magnificent, immense and there's a fair touch of whimsy in the floor tiles depicting the seven deadly sins.

 ## Getting there

Take Rte. 138 from Quebec City to St.-Anne-de-Beaupre, then Rte. 360 to the resort.

Stoneham

Stoneham is just 20 minutes north of Québec City. As you near Stoneham, don't be fooled. The resort is much larger than the few trails you see directly ahead. Thirty-two trails stretch across three mountains. The emphasis here is not on how big the vertical drops are (they range from 1,140 to 1,380 feet), but on how much terrain the connected mountains deliver. Stoneham has terrain from double-diamond glades to leisurely cruisers. Advanced skiers on multiday vacations will soon want to escape to Mont-Sainte-Anne or Le Massif. Kids will find a lot of activities to keep them occupied. And terrain park addicts will have met their match.

Situated in a sun-filled, wind-protected horseshoe valley, Stoneham attracts locals when the temperatures drop or the wind howls. The emphasis here is on having fun, whether on the slopes or in the restaurants and bars. Don't let the very English sounding name of the mountain mislead you; Stoneham is *tres* French, with many of its patrons speaking only French (most mountain personnel are bilingual, however). But that's good news, because as one regular Stoneham skier puts it, "The French know about food, and they know about fun."

Sixty percent of the mountain is open for night skiing, and that includes a lighted half-pipe and snow-tubing area. With its party reputation, a visit for the nighttime skiing (and the refreshments afterwards) is a must for anyone on a ski vacation to the Quebec City region.

 ## Mountain layout

♦♦**Expert** ♦**Advanced:** Experts will want to head straight for Peak Four. Little grooming is done here, and the trails are steep, skinny and bumped. Well-named trails Le Zipper, Le Kamikaza and Le Monstre are legitimate double blacks. They are left *au natural*, so you want to be on the look out for stumps, rocks, cliffs and other such obstructions in lean snow years.

Dining: $$$$-Entrees (C$30+; $$$-C$20-$30; $$-C$10-$20; $-less than C$10.
Accommodations: (double room) $$$$-C$200+; $$$-C$141-$200; $$-C$81-$140; $-C$80 and less.

Stoneham Facts

Summit elevation:	**2,075 feet**
Vertical drop:	**1,380 feet**
Base elevation:	**695 feet**

Address: 1420, Chemin du Hibou, Stoneham, PQ, Canada G0A 4P0

Area code: 418

Ski area phone: 848-2411

Snow report: 848-2415

Toll-free reservations: (800) 463-6888

Fax: 848-1133

Internet: www.ski-stoneham.com

Expert: ★ **Advanced**: ★

Intermediate: ★★★★

Beginner: ★★★★

First-timer: ★★★★

Number and types of lifts: 8-1 high-speed quad, 2 quads, 1 double, 3 surface lifts, 1 moving carpet

Skiable acreage: 326 (daytime); 184 (nighttime)

Snowmaking: 86 percent

Uphill capacity: 14,200 per hour

Parks and pipes: 4 parks, 1 pipe

Bed base: 500 at base; 10,000 in Quebec City, 20 minutes away

Nearest lodging: Slopeside

Resort child care: Yes, 1 month and up

Adult ticket, per day: C$43 (05/06) without tax)

Stoneham is primarily a family mountain and even double-black-diamond trails La Panoramique and La Bomba, though steep, are maneuverable for upper-intermediate skiers. If you like glades, head for La Sapinere.

■ **Intermediate:** The entire mountain is an intermediate's playground. Even the bump runs, glades and, as mentioned earlier, the groomed double-black-diamond trails should be tried and conquered. Undulating terrain and wide-open trails call for lots of top-to-bottom giant-slalom runs. For challenging fun, try La Chute and Bossanova, both are long with steep pitches that mellow then drop again for little adrenaline rushes.

●● **Beginner** ● **First-timer:** Although considered a family mountain, Stoneham is surprisingly lean on true beginner terrain. Peaks One and Two have a couple of top-to-bottom green-circle trails (La Randonnee off Peak 1; La Laurentienne off peak 2), but even these have places that may challenge real beginners. The wide-open area served by a quad and two Poma lifts right in front of the main base lodge gives a nonthreatening place for beginners and first-timers.

Parks and pipes

Our riders loved Stoneham, which has some of the best terrain features we've seen in the East. It boasts a huge, well maintained superpipe as well as numerous terrain parks. A beginner's terrain park, with super-easy rails and jumps, is on the edge of Les Cantons. For more advanced features, cut over to La Traverse and head down Les Merisiers to La Fabuleuse. For continuous fun, just do laps on the A quad and the superpipe, with 17-foot walls. A Kokanee bus is buried in the park. There's also a mile-long boardercross course on La Rock-n-Roll.

Even adults have fun in Casimir's Enchanted Journey, a children's terrain park with large wooden animal and character cut-outs in the trees off Le Petit Champlain. Sous Bois is a natural terrain park. This wide, long glade is full of little hits, chutes through the trees, rolling turns and a few gentle moguls.

Lessons (05/06 prices, without tax)

All lessons are by reservation only, call (418) 848-2415, ext. 537.

Group lessons: The Head Tyrolia Snow Sports Academy provides focused sessions for intermediate and expert skiers 19 and older. Two-hour morning sessions are offered on Monday, Friday, Saturday and Sunday for C$39.

First-timer package: A private one-hour lesson with equipment rental and lift ticket is C$61 for skiers, C$67 for snowboarders. A 1.5-hour group lesson is C$42 for skiers (C$29 for a night lesson), C$48 for snowboarders (C$35 for a night lesson).

Private lessons: C$40 for one hour for one person, plus C$20 for each additional person; C$66 plus C$28 for a two-hour lesson; C$96 plus C$42 for a three-hour series; C$150 plus C$49 for a five-hour series. Discounted equipment rental rates are available. You also can arrange for a one-hour video coaching session for C$40 for one person, C$20 for each additional student.

Note: Prices rounded to nearest dollar.

KidStuff (05/06 prices, without tax)

Child care: For ages 1 month–12 years. Cost for the first child for one day is C$28 with lunch; the second child from the same family costs C$22. The hourly rate is C$10 for infants 18 months and younger; C$8 for those older than 18 months. Day care has bilingual caregivers, but most of the children on any given day speak only French. Open from 8:30 a.m.–5 p.m., the center is just a few steps from the main base lodge, but the walk to the actual skiing can be a bit of a trek for little ones. It has a large game room and separate sleeping and eating rooms, as well as a nifty adjacent outdoor playground. The center will arrange babysitting if you call ahead. Reservations are recommended.

Children's lessons: Kidz Island has programs designed for children ages 3–6. A full-day (8:30 a.m.–5 p.m.) with a four-hour lesson, rentals, two snacks, lunch and day care is C$55. Multiday rates are available. For children just starting out, the ratio is four to six children per instructor. **Note**: we've rounded prices up to the nearest dollar.

Lift tickets (05/06 prices, without tax)

Weekend prices	Adult	Student (14-22)	Seniors (65+)	Youth (7-13)
One day	C$43	C$32	C$35	C$18
Evening	C$25	C$22	C$22	C$14
Three days	C$123	C$90	C$99	C$51

Note: Because of night skiing, Stoneham offers a variety of tickets including the longer day ticket (9 a.m. to 6 p.m.), a day-to-evening ticket (12:30 p.m. to closing), a half day ticket (12:30 to 4:30) and an evening ticket (3 p.m. to closing). Consecutive multiday tickets include night skiing and may be bought to seven days.

Who skis free: Children ages 6 and younger.

Accommodations at or near the resort

The practical **Hotel Stoneham** ($–$$) is an anchor in the ski area's mini-village and has 60 spacious rooms where children younger than age 18 stay for free when sharing a room with their parents. The ski area also rents out about 100 condos through Condominiums Stoneham; the **Condo du Village** are most convenient. These vary in size from studios to four bedrooms and are at the base of the slopes. Attractive ski-and-stay packages are available. For reservations, call (800) 463-6888 or 848-2411.

Le Manoir du Lac Delage (866-222-3810; 848-2551; $–$$) is 10 minutes from the slopes, yet feels a world away. It's a meticulously appointed country inn, with an excellent dining room overlooking the lake, a full spa and an indoor pool.

Dining

The tiny outpost lodge at the base of Peak Four has crepes, soup and sandwiches. Lunch and light snacks are in **Le Bar Le 4 Foyers** (the bar of the four fireplaces) in the base lodge. **Le Pub St-Edmond** ($–$$) serves delicious smoked-meat sandwiches in an English pub atmosphere. **The Feu Follet** ($$), attached to the base lodge and adjacent to Le Bar Le 4 Foyers, is open for breakfast, lunch and dinner.

For an elegant meal, go to **Le Gourmet Champetre** (848-2551) at the Le Manoir du Lac Dulage overlooking the lake. Entrees include striped bass, grilled sea scallops and braised lamb. A four-course table d'hote is $32.95. **L'Incontournable** ($–$$), also at Le Manoir, is a bar with fireplace, TV and pool table. It serves a light menu of burgers, salads and pizzas.

Apres-ski/nightlife

Because the base area is so small, it may be hard to believe that the Quebecois leave Quebec City and head here to have fun, but that's what they do. **Le Bar Le 4 Foyers**, a funky Irish pub, brings in a wide range of musical performers, including the requisite rock bands and a disco night on Thursdays. It serves basic pub fare and screens nonstop snowboard flicks on the TV. There's also a pool table in the back room. **Le Pub St-Edmond**, on the other end of the village (a three-minute walk), offers a little more mellow fare, with folk and oldies plus a wide selection of beers. Skiers will find that even with a language barrier—many of Stoneham's regular skiers speak no English—apres-ski conviviality prevails, and trying to make your French understood after a few drinks is actually fun.

Other activities

Stoneham has three slopes that are specially equipped for **tubing**, with a lift and a cabin shelter and snack area designed for the enjoyment of this activity. **Ice skating** as well as an **indoor climbing wall** are available. For **snowmobiling**, go to Lac Beauport to Nord Tour (841-2810) for rentals.

The Spa Le Manoir du Lac Delage (800-463-2841 or 848-0691) offers body care, massages, skin care, facials, back treatment and programs for hands and feet. Massages are C$40 for 30 minutes, C$65 for 60 minutes and C$85 for 90 minutes. Indulge yourself with a Leisure Package including a health assessment; use of the indoor pool, sauna and whirlpool; relaxation massage; fresh juice or herb tea; therapeutic bath; and pressure therapy for C$90. A four-hour package adds a body wrap and facial to the mix for C$150. After your treatment, splurge on dinner here.

Shopping: The mini-village has two small stores: Boutique Sports Alpins offers gifts and interesting ski items, and La Shop is for snowboarders.

Getting there and getting around

Stoneham is 20 minutes from Quebec City via Rte. 73 North, taking the Stoneham exit.

Le Massif

Perched on the edge of the St. Lawrence River, Le Massif is a must-visit resort. It is one of eastern Canada's great secrets, but not for long. Once accessible only via school bus, Le Massif has transformed itself into one of eastern Canada's most eco-friendly resorts. With the addition of a second high-speed quad , Le Massif became the site of Canada's national training center for downhill and Super G. And the changes keep coming. The new owner Daniel Gauthier has invested C$5 million in the replacement of a double chair with a high-speed quad, six new intermediate and advanced trails, widened glades and increased snowmaking capacity.

The spectacular summit lodge is built to take advantage of the endless views up and down the St. Lawrence. From the moment you step out of your car at the summit area you are struck with the awesome views and the resort's natural beauty. It's calm, quiet, peaceful. And the trails appear to just plunge 2,500 feet directly down into the ice-choked St. Lawrence, referred to as the sea, given its greater than 10-mile width here. As you descend La Petite-Riviere, a classic first-run trail, a fishing trawler or cargo ship might pass silently right beneath you. Little wonder that Le Massif and its surroundings are within a UNESCO World Biosphere Reserve. Le Massif's owners have honored this beauty by developing the area in harmony with nature. The lifts are, for the most part, hidden in the trees, and the trails follow the natural fall lines of the three connected mountains.

Le Massif has Canada's highest vertical drop east of the Canadian Rockies. Because of its riverfront location, it receives abundant snowfall. Legend has it that when the area's mascot owl, Le Grand Duc, circles, the area will receive at least 30 centimeters of snow within 48 hours.

When you visit, don't pack a lunch. The cafeteria food here is among the best and the most reasonably priced we've seen: On our last visit, we had escargot over angel-hair pasta and Charlevoix sausage with fresh local cheeses, and samplings of Charlevoix-region gourmet. Two pubs, one at the summit, the other at the base, serve a good selection of beers and wines.

Be forewarned, that the farther east you head from Quebec City, the less English you hear. A little bit of patience goes a long way when trying to speak with locals at some of the inns and restaurants where little English is spoken. But don't let that deter you. The Charlevoix Region will likely steal your heart.

Mountain layout

♦♦**Expert** ♦**Advanced:** La "42," an ungroomed, natural-snow trail, snakes its way down the eastern edge of the mountain. It's punctuated with bumps, stumps, narrow chutes and steep drops, and clinched with the area's trademark jaw-dropping views of the St. Lawrence. Le Sous-Bois ("glades" in French) is relatively tame by comparison. La Tremblay, a single black, can be challenging since it's rarely groomed. For a short, steep thrill, take the plunge on La Pointe.

Le Massif's 2001 expansion added a new peak with a summit that was built up using rocks dug out of what's become a nearby lake. The trails here boast a sustained pitch that quickly accelerates you to rocket speed as you hurtle toward the river. The double-black Le Charlevoix is the training trail.

■ **Intermediate**: With nary a bump in sight, this mountain is nirvana for cruisers. The black diamond and blue square designations seem almost arbitrary. Three-fourths of the runs are meticulously groomed, and only occasional steep pitches give pause to an intermediate skier. The runs are long (2.36 miles, the longest), so rest stops allow for spectacular views of the ice-capped St. Lawrence. Concentrate your efforts on Le Grande-Pointe Express quad

Dining: $$$$-Entrees C$30+; $$$-C$20-$30; $$-C$10-$20; $-less than C$10.
Accommodations: (double room) $$$$-C$200+; $$$-C$141-$200; $$-C$81-$140; $-C$80 and less.

Le Massif facts

Summit elevation: 2,645 feet
Vertical drop: 2,526 feet
Base elevation: 118 feet
Expert: ★★★ **Advanced:** ★★★★
Intermediate: ★★★
Beginner: ★★
First-timer: ★
Address: 1350 Rue Principale, C.P. 47, Petite-Riviere-Saint-Francois, Quebec, Canada G0A 2L0
Area code: 418
Ski area phone: 632-5876; (877) 536-2774
Snow report: 632-5876; (877) 536-2774
Fax: 632-5205

Toll-free reservations: (866) 435-4160
E-mail: info@lemassif.com
Internet: www.lemassif.com
Number and types of lifts: 5–3 high-speed quads, 2 surface lifts
Skiable acreage: 302 acres
Snowmaking: 60 percent
Uphill capacity: 8,700 per hour
Parks & pipes: 2 terrain parks
Bed base: 873
Nearest lodging: One-half mile
Resort child care: Yes, 2 years and older
Adult ticket, per day: $50 (05/06 without tax)

chair for the best vertical and choice. La Petite-Riviere, a blue, is a sweet way to launch your day with spectacular drop-dead views of the river.

●● **Beginner** ● **First-timer:** Stick to the beginner trails off the double chair. The leap from first-timer to intermediate is a big jump, on the main mountain. Trails that start out fine for beginners all finish along narrow trails where upper-level skiers race back to the lift. It is unsettling. We're told improvements to the snowmaking system and new advanced trails to the base will help reduce this problem.

First-timers have a rope tow just below the summit day lodge.

Ride Guide: Le Massif is ideal for carving deep arcing turns. Early in the season, the traverse over to the Le Maillard high-speed quad, Lift C, is a miserable hike. Instead, ride down La Richard or L'Archipel to get to the Maillard Express mid-station.

Parks and pipes

A big-air terrain park is in the area served by the new Camp Boule Express.

Cross-country and snowshoeing (visit xcskiresorts.com for more details)

Le Sentier des Caps is developing a 65-km. cross-country network at the top of the ridge, about a mile behind the new ski lodge with a base on the access road from Quebec City.

For those near Malbaie, 160 km. of cross-country and snowshoeing possibilities are extensive and well developed in the **Parc Regional du Mont Grand-Fonds**. Trails for every level of Nordic skier loop around lakes and past four chalets where skiers can rest and imbibe.

Lessons (05/06 prices, without taxes)

Group lessons: Le Massif only offers private and semi-private lessons.
Private lessons: A one-hour private lesson costs C$49 for one person; C$43 per person for two people; C$39 per person for three people. Two hours cost C$85 for one person; C$69 per person for two people; C$55 per person for three people. A private first-timer lesson costs C$89 for one person for 1.5 hours; C$74 per person for two people for 1.5 hours; and C$69 per person for three or more people for two hours.

KidStuff [05/06 prices, without taxes]

Child care: Le Massif has a day-care center at its mountaintop lodge. It comprises one large room and can handle 21 children. Comfortable furniture is set about, and a crib area is cordoned off by curtains. Equipment rental is across the hall. Day care is available for ages 2–10 years. The full-day program with lunch runs from 8:30 a.m.–4:30 p.m. and costs C$28; half-day (8:30 a.m.–12:30 p.m., or 12:30 p.m.–4: 30 p.m.) is C$20. Hourly day care is available for C$8; a separate lunch can be bought for C$7. Reservations are required; call 632-5876 or (877) 536-2774.

Children's lessons: A one-hour semi-private lesson can be added to the day-care program for C$15. The resort has a beginner area that's convenient to the children's room.

A group program for ages 7–16 is C$57. All include lesson, lift ticket and equipment rentals for the day; program runs from 10 a.m. to 3 p.m. Discounts available for multiple days.

Lift tickets [05/06 prices, without tax]

Weekend	Adult	Young Adult (17-23)/Sr. 65+	Junior (7-16)
One day	C$50	C$40	C$26
Three day	C$139	C$109	C$71
Five day	C$232	C$182	C$118

Who skis free: Children ages 6 and younger.

Note: Rates are rounded up to the nearest dollar.

Accommodations and dining near the resort

Le Massif offers skiing packages at B&Bs, inns and motels as well as chalets and villas in nearby towns; most include dinner for guests and are also open to the public for dinner, which is why we've combined dining and lodging.

Baie-Saint-Paul is the largest town and offers the best variety of dining and lodging as well as nightlife. For regional information, call (800) 667-2276. **Maison Otis** (800-267-2254; 435-2255; $$–$$$) pampers guests with one of the region's best dining rooms, a full-service spa, a cozy lounge, a lively cafe and even a discoteque. It also has an indoor pool, saunas and whirlpool tub. Rooms vary greatly, from cozy to sprawling; some have fireplaces and hot tubs. Rates include a choice-of-menu breakfast and a four-course dinner. **Auberge La Grande Maison** (800-361-5575; 435-5575; $–$$), built in 1913, was previously a hospital and is now a charming bed & breakfast. **Auberge La Pignoronde** (888-554-6004; 435-5505; $–$$) overlooks the town and bay and is some of the closest lodging to Le Massif. It's a good choice for families. It has a good restaurant, with a variety of meal plans available, and an indoor pool. **Hotel Baie-Saint-Paul** (800-650-3683; 435-3683; $) has spacious, although basic, rooms, an indoor pool and a restaurant.

La Malbaie, 45 minutes east of Le Massif, has an excellent selection of chic lodging as well as a small ski area, Grand Fonds (see *Nearby Skiing,* below). The grandest lodging is at **Le Manoir Richelieu** (800-866-5577;665-3703; $$–$$$), a four-star, five-diamond Fairmont resort with all the amenities you would expect, as well as a casino, indoor and outdoor pools and full spa. Other on-site activities include cross-country, snowmobile and snowshoe trails, a skating rink, sleigh rides and dogsledding. The resort sits on the bank of the St. Lawrence River, providing magnificent views from many rooms.

Auberge des 3 Canards (800-461-3761; 665-3761; $$$–$$$$) is just down the hill from the Manoir Richelieu. All rooms have spectacular views to the river and its acclaimed dining, prepared by long-time Chef Eric Betrand from Strasbourg, France, has won numerous awards.

Deluxe rooms come with jetted tub for two and a fireplace.

L'Auberge des Peupliers (888-282-3743; 665-4423; $$$–$$$$) sits high atop a hill overlooking the St. Lawrence River and is one of the oldest guesthouses in the region. Rooms are a pleasant mix of antique and rustic, but include all the modern amenities you're accustomed to having. Sauna and indoor jetted tub, plus spa services are available upon request. Breakfast and a five-course regional dinner prepared by a renowned chef are included.

One of the best reasons to visit Canada in the winter is to get low-season rates at high-end resorts. One such place is the Relais & Chateaux property **La Pinsonniere** (800-387-4431; 665-4431; $$–$$$$), a country inn hugging the shore in La Malbaie. Impeccable service, fine cuisine and a flair for romance define its character. An impressive collection of masterpieces from regional artists hangs on the walls of the dining room and throughout the inn.

 ## Other activities

The Charlevoix region abounds with outdoor activities. **Snowmobiling** is extremely popular here, as is **dogsledding**. Your hotel should be able to make arrangements. The Fairmont Manoir Richelieu has a **casino.**

The **Centre Sante Beaute Francine Thibeault**, in Baie-Saint-Paul (435-6028), offers a full range of **spa and salon services**. Among the services at the **Amerispa** (800-699-7352; 665-2600) at the Fairmont Manoir Richelieu, are Vichy shower massage, body wraps and back treatment. Massage begins at C$95. Be forewarned, not a lot of English spoken here.

Take a **scenic drive** along the St. Lawrence River from Pointe-au-Pic to Baie-Saint-Paul, through St. Irenee, known for the famous music academy Le Domaine Forget, and its river beaches. A spectacular descent brings you to the tiny 200-person town of Saint-Joseph-de-la-Rive, where a free ferry plies the route to Isle-aux-Coudres. Try the pastries at Boulangerie Laurentide, visit the Maritime Museum and see handcrafted papermaking at Papeterie Saint-Gilles. In Baie Saint-Paul, stop at the La Laiterie Charlevoix (435-2184) and La Maison D'Affinage Maurice Dufour (435-5692), where you can see **cheesemaking** in process and purchase fresh cheese. A must-top for chocoholics is the Chocolaterie Cynthia, on rue St. Jean-Baptiste (435-6060). For a break, enjoy lunch at surprising Joe's Deli Bar Smoked Meat, where the sandwiches are massive and tasty (and Joe is friendly and speaks English).

The Charlevoix region's scenery and intriguing light attracts many important painters. Dozens of **art galleries** dot the entire route from La Malbaie. Baie-Saint-Paul has 20 galleries, although not all are open in winter. Many artists are represented at Galerie d'Art Iris, 30 rue St. Jean-Baptiste. La Maison de Rene Richard is worth a visit to see the development of one of Canada's most renowned artists. Le Centre d'Art has changing exhibits. Guy Pacquet often opens his home studio to visitors; the views are breathtaking, the artwork spectacular.

 ## Getting there

Le Massif is 45 miles east of Quebec City on Rte. 138. If you are staying in downtown Quebec City and don't have a car, take the **Winter Express Shuttle** (525-5191) to Le Massif; round trip cost is about C$25. Reservations are required.

Nearby resorts

Parc regional du Mont Grand-Fonds, La Malbaie, Charlevoix (Quebec); (418) 665-0095

Internet: www.montgrandfonds.com
3 lifts: 1 quad, 2 T-bars; 14 trails; 1,095 vertical feet

Mont Grand Fonds, just 15 minutes from Le Manoir Richelieu, skis bigger than it actually is. Crowds are rare, which is a good thing since there's only one quad and two T-bars. The atmosphere is laid back, the views over the St. Lawrence are terrific, and the trails were cut for maximum sun exposure. Trails to the right of the lifts, as you look up at the mountain, are primarily intermediate, with a few gentle beginner trails, while those to the left provide more challenge. Glades start out open and inviting, but get tighter and steeper as you descend. This is an excellent family mountain. Its proximity to the fabulous Manoir is ideal.

Note: Lifts open at 10 a.m. on weekdays, 9 a.m. on weekends. Day care is available at the area. Grand Fonds also has 160 km. of groomed cross-country trails with four heated warming huts and a bird-watching area and 16 km. of snowshoe trails. A tubing park has its own lift.

Lift tickets (04/05): Adults, C$35; student (16–22), C$25 ; child (6-15) C$23.

Distance from Quebec: 90 miles via Rte. 138.

Lodging information: See Le Manoir Richelieu in *Accommodations* on page 527.

Accommodations—Quebec City

Fairmont Le Chateau Frontenac (800-441-1414; 692-3861; $$–$$$$), perched on the edge of the Cap Diamant promontory in Old Quebec's upper town, is the grande dame of Quebec City. It is historic, formal, elegant and full-service. Rooms vary greatly, from small to spacious, some offering magnificent views of the St. Lawrence. Most packages here include the hotel's bountiful buffet breakfast, enough to fuel you through most of the day. The hotel has a health club with indoor pool and a full-service spa. Also full service are the **Quebec Hilton** (800-445-8667; 647-2411; $$–$$$$), and **Hotel Loews Le Concorde** (800-235-6397; 647-2222; $$–$$$$), both in old Quebec, but outside the city walls.

Some of the top hotels in town are termed boutique hotels. The following five, all in the Vieux-Port area, are among the city's best places to stay.

Hotel Dominion 1912 (692-2224; $$–$$$), perhaps the best of the lot, is ultra-modern yet hidden in an old factory. Glass showers and sinks highlight the bathrooms, and the beds are covered with mounds of down. The spacious rooms have Bose Wave Radios and 27-inch TVs. Breakfast is a non-stop continental affair.

The intimate **Auberge Saint-Pierre** (888-268-1017; 694-7981; $–$$$) is a treat. Guest rooms range from the *petite economique* ones with barely enough room to set down a suitcase, to grand suites, with elaborate whirlpool tubs for two. There's a nice bar and a quiet living room with fireplace.

The **Auberge Saint-Antoine** (888-692-2211; 692-2211; $–$$$), is a luxurious retreat in the heart of a lively, attractive, 18th-century neighborhood with museums, art galleries, antique shops, boutiques and restaurants. Rooms are spread out in 300-year-old buildings on an important archaeological site. Artfully displayed artifacts throughout the hotel provide a glimpse into the life of Quebec's first inhabitants. Some of the 95 rooms have views on the St. Lawrence River, others of Quebec's fortifications and many have a terrace and/or fireplace.

Hotel Le Clos Saint-Louis (694-1311; $–$$) is a romantic 25-room hotel filled with

Dining: $$$$–Entrees (C$30+; $$$–C$20-$30; $$–C$10-$20; $-less than C$10.
Accommodations: (double room) $$$$–C$200+; $$$–C$141-$200; $$–C$81-$140; $-C$80 and less.

period antiques. Rooms are spacious, each with private bath, and the hotel, built as a stately home in 1844, opens directly onto one of the old city's main streets.

Hotel Le Priori (692-3992; $–$$) has small rooms but much larger suites.

Small hotels within the city walls are the **Hotel Clarendon** (888-554-6001; 692-2480), the **Hotellerie Fleur-de-Lys** (800-567-2106; 694-0106; $$–$$$), and the **Manoir de l'Esplanade** (694-0834).

Hotel Acadia (800-463-0280; 694-0280; $–$$) serves a continental breakfast and also has packages with Mont-Sainte-Anne.

The **Hotel Manoir Victoria** (800-463-6283; 692-1030; $–$$$), in the old city, is a good choice for families. Also popular with families is **L'Hotel du Vieux-Quebec** (800-361-7787; 692-1850; $–$$$).

Auberge Louis-Hebert (525-7812; $), on the Grande Allee, the heart of Quebec City's nightlife, also has a good restaurant, and rates include breakfast. As is true of much of old Quebec, the comforts are modern within 17th-century walls.

Small inns and bed & breakfasts are clustered around the Frontenac and offer simple rooms, usually with breakfast, at affordable rates. Try the **Hotel Manoir de la Terrasse** (694-1592; $), **the Manoir Sainte-Genevieve** (694-1666; $–$$) or the **Chateau Bellevue** (800-463-2716; 692-2573; $–$$)

Three hostels provide bottom-dollar lodging: **Auberge International de Quebec** (694-0755; $), a member of Hostelling International, which has a cafeteria and 279 beds in various configurations, including private and family rooms; **Auberge de la Paix** (694-0735; $), which has 14 rooms with two to eight beds, a kitchen and breakfast; or **Association du YWCA de Quebec** (683-2155; $), with shared bathrooms, swimming pool and self-service kitchen.

For something completely different, consider one night at the **Ice Hotel** (www.icehotel-canada.com; $$$). Constructed and furnished completely of snow and ice, it opens in January and closes about three months later, when it melts. Sleeping bags are guaranteed to keep guests warm to 30-degrees below zero; it's a lot like winter camping, only fancier.

Dining—Quebec City

You have to work to get a bad meal in this city. Almost all restaurants post their menu outside the door, and most include a *Table d'hote*, or set menu, usually with appetizer, entree and dessert, for a fixed price.

For traditional Quebecois cooking like *grandmere* used to make—pea soup, onion soup, meat pies, fish and game dishes and for dessert, maple syrup pie—dine at **Aux Anciens Canadiens** (692-1627; $$$–$$$$). Five cozy dining rooms on two floors have been built in one of the oldest houses in the city, Maison Jacquet. The building was constructed between 1675-76 with thick stone walls, wainscoting and recessed cupboards. The lunch menu (normally less than C$15) is served from noon until 6 p.m., making for an affordable and hearty early supper for skiers returning from the slopes.

Next door, **Restaurant Continental** (694-9995; $$$–$$$$) prepares Quebec's only true upscale French cuisine with flambe tableside service. The other top spot in the upper old town is **Le Saint-Amour** (694-0667; $$$$).

One of our favorite restaurants in Vieux-Quebec is **Auberge du Tresor** (694-1876; $$$) which serves mussels (*moules*) that were the best we've eaten this side of the Atlantic Ocean. **Au Parmesan** (692-0341; $$$), with an accordionist and lots of singing locals, serves homemade pasta. **Gambrinus** (692-5144; $$$), overlooking the Place d'Armes, is an excellent Italian restaurant with a French flair and good seafood. A strolling musician performs at night.

At **47ieme Parallele Resto International** (692-1534; $$$), you'll find home-style European and exotic dish presentations.

There's no graffiti at **Graffiti**, (1191 Cartier Ave; 529-4949; $$$), but an eclectic array of art adorns the brick and warm wood walls. French and Italian cuisine make up the two menus—a la carte and table d'hote. Don't miss the apple tart with maple sauce. Brunch in the atrium room is a popular Sunday event. We're told this is one of the city's best.

Another good choice is **Initiale** (694-1818; $$$$), which serves fine French cuisine. **Laurie Raphael** (692-4555; $$) emphasizes fresh Quebecois-style cuisine. The more casual art deco **L'Echaude** (692-1299; $$$) serves a mix of traditional and nouvelle French cuisine. **Cafe du Monde** (692-4495; $$–$$$), with its bistro atmosphere and affordable wines, fills with locals each evening. **Piazzetta** (692-2962; $$) only steps away is an inexpensive choice for creative focaccio and pizzas (we loved the apple-and-pork pizza).

Rue du Petit-Champlain has several good eateries. Stone walls and a fireplace create an intimate setting at **Marie-Clarisse** (692-0857; $$$$), at the base of the funicular and the bottom of the Breakneck Stairs. It serves excellent fish and seafood in two intimate dining rooms. **Cochon Dingue** ($$) offers a wide-ranging, bistro-style menu that's good for families and it serves excellent breakfasts. Kids younger than 10 pay C$5 for a complete meal. Three Cochon Dingue restaurants are at 46, boul. Champlain (692-2013); 46, Rene-Levesque O. (523-2013); and 1326, av. Maguire (684-2013). **Le Petit Cochon Dingue** (OK, Cochon Dingue means Crazy Pig; 694-0303) is a traditional pastry shop with a bakery, cafe and sandwich shop. The donuts are, well, old-fashioned, and you can't beat the raisin buns anywhere. **Le Lapin Saute** (692-5325; $$–$$$) is popular for breakfast, but avoid it for dinner.

In the old train station, **Gare du Palais**, **l'Aviatic Club** (522-3555; $$$–$$$$) looks like an officers' mess and serves specialty foods from five continents. Stay awhile and join the nightlife.

Along the Grande Allee, start the night with dinner at **Louis-Hebert** (525-7812; $$–$$$) and you'll be well situated to enjoy this street's hearty nightlife afterward. This is where the cognoscenti dine, such as the Members of Parliament and other creme de la creme. Allow a long evening for your dining experience and don't be afraid of asking for special plates. There is also a boutique hotel above the cookery.

Cosmos (640-0606; $$), on the Grande Allee, is *the* place to see and be seen. It has a fantastic Quebecois menu at a reasonable price. It's a trendy bistro with a vast offering from around-the-world salads to great sandwiches, pastas, frites, poutine and huge dessert menu.

Take in a view of the whole city from **L'Astral** (647-2222; $$–$$$$), the revolving restaurant atop Loews Le Concorde hotel. It takes about one hour for it to make a complete circle. A buffet is served Saturday night, and the Sunday brunch is in a class of its own. Reservations are a must. For a carbo feed, head to the **Place du Spaghetti** (694-9144).

For simple, Mediterranean-style fare, head to **Freres de la Cote** (692-5445; $$), a lively restaurant with an open kitchen and wood-burning ovens. The eclectic menu ranges from tenderloin horsemeat to sweetbread to European pizza to osso bucco. **Portofino Bistro Italiano** (692-8888; $–$$), in the center of Old Quebec, is a good choice for pizza. The Pizza Grizzly (with smoked salmon) is particularly tasty.

If you're a bit adventurous, visit a **sugar shack**: Follow signs for a *cabane a sucre*. Most open only when the sap is running. The fare usually includes crepes, eggs, meat pies, meats, toast, baked beans, all topped with maple syrup and flavored with music and dancing.

Dining: $$$$-Entrees C$30+; $$$-C$20-$30; $$-C$10-$20; $-less than C$10.
Accommodations: (double room) $$$$-C$200+; $$$-C$141-$200; $$-C$81-$140; $-C$80 and less.

Apres-ski/nightlife—Quebec City

The Grande Allée is lined with bars and restaurants and is the number one choice for nightlife in the city. Next to the Lowes Le Concorde, at 575 Grande Allée, there is a complex of nightlife. The top floor has a lounge called **Charlotte**, the second floor is a disco called **Maurice**, the ground floor is a bar called **Cosmos**. They were all filled on the Friday night we visited. The bar at street level fills first, then Charlotte's Lounge starts up about 10 p.m. followed by Maurice around midnight.

The Clarendon Hotel has good jazz music. **St. Jean Street** offers a number of bars with traditional French music including La Playa that serves 75 different martini drinks to accompany Mexican food (go figure).

Le Capitole features a Las Vegas-style dinner show. Don't miss having a drink at the **Bar St-Laurent in Le Chateau Frontenac**. **Le Pape George** is a bistro with French singers.

Down in the vieux-port district at 37 Quai Saint-André is **L'Inox**, a large, smoky brew pub with pool tables and loud music that attracts a young crowd.

Other activities

Quebec City has so much to offer you could spend most of your ski vacation in the city without even venturing to the slopes. We've selected just a sampling of what you can do.

On the Terrasse Dufferin there is a not-to-be-missed, exciting **toboggan** ride that is open most days from 11 a.m to 11 p.m. Cost is only C$2 per rider. You can **ice skate** for C$5 at a rink nearby.

The **funicular** (692-1132) is the shortest link between Dufferin Terrace at the Chateau Frontenac and Quartier Petit Champlain in the lower city. This landmark and unique transportation vehicle provides commanding views of the St. Lawrence River. It is wheelchair accessible. Take a **ferry ride** across the river for a spectacular perspective of the walled city. It leaves every half hour during the day and every hour at night (644-3704).

The frozen falls at **Montmorency Falls Park** (663-3330) are one-and-a-half times higher than Niagara Falls. Cable cars, bridges lookouts and trails make it possible to get close to the falls. For **ice climbing**, L'Ascensation (647-4422) rents equipment and provides guides.

At Village Vacances Valcartier (844-2200), 20 minutes north of the city, *go* **snow rafting, sliding** and **tubing** on 38 slides; **skate** through a forest; **race go-karts** on an ice-covered track; **snowmobile, ride horseback, dogsled** or take a **sleigh ride**.

In the city, you can **cross-country ski** on the Plains of Abraham (649-6476 for information; 648-4212 for trail conditions) or **snowshoe** or take a **sleigh ride** (687-0707). Station Touristique Duchesnay, surrounding the Ice Hotel, 20 minutes north of Quebec, has 150 km. of cross-country trails that wind almost exclusively through evergreens. Side-by-side tracks make cross-country for couples enjoyable. In the spring a stop at the sugar house is a good time.

The Greater Quebec area is home to 1,512 km. of **snowmobile trails**. For rentals and guided tours, try Laurentides Sports Service Inc. in Charlesbourg (849-2824); Location S.M. Sport in Loretteville (842-2703); or Dion Moto (337-2776).

The history and culture of the region is captured in many **museums and interpretation centers** throughout Old Quebec City. Begin with a three-site ticket (C$8.50) for the Musee de la civilisation (85 rue Dalhousie, 643-2158), Musee de l'Amerique francaise (2 cote de la Fabrique, 692-2843) and Centre d'interpretation de Place-Royale (27 rue Notre-Dame, 646-3167). You'll be swallowed up in human adventure, the origins of the French-speaking world and 400 years of Place-Royale—the first permanent French settlement in North America, established in 1608. (Winter hours: 10 a.m.–5 p.m. Tuesday–Sunday; admission is free every Tuesday). Also worth visiting: Musee national des beaux-arts du Quebec (643-2150), the national art gallery partly housed in a former prison annexed to the 1933 museum by a glassed-in space (Wednesday has evening hours); Musee du Fort (692-2175) with a sound-and-light show on the famous battles of the city; and Musee d'art Inuit Brousseau (694-1828), the first museum dedicated exclusively to Inuit art and culture. The Citadelle (694-2815) is the largest military fortification in North America still occupied by regular troops and the official residence of Governor General of Canada. It was built in 1820-1832 to protect the city from invaders.

The narrow streets of Le Quartier Petit Champlain, in Vieux-Quebec, are lined with ancient stone buildings housing **boutiques** with traditional and contemporary Canadian artwork, crafts, clothing and more. Artists sell their work on the pedestrian alleyway, Rue du Tresor, off Place d'Armes. The Galeries de la Capitale not only has 250 shops, but an amusement center. Boutique Metiers d'art at 29, Notre-Dame, has a vast collection of local and regional art. Potenciel L'Art de la Table, 27 rue du Petite Champlain, is a cook's heaven of upscale tools, cookbooks and trinkets for the kitchen. Zazu Boutique, 31, rue du Petite Champlain, just down the narrow street, features one-of-a-kind Montreal and Quebec designer women's clothing, such as hand-stitched parkas and coats with fur hoods and fashionable outer clothing for the below-zero temperatures in Quebec.

Getting there and getting around

By air: Fly into Quebec City's Jean-Lesage International Airport. HiverExpress operates a winter shuttle from the airport to the city for C$24.50 each way; or take a cab, call 525-5191; or rent a car.

By car: Stoneham is 20 minutes from Quebec City via Hwy. 73N, taking the Stoneham exit. To get to Mont-Sainte-Anne, take Rte. 138 from Quebec City to St.-Anne-de-Beaupre, then Rte. 360 to the resort. It's about a half hour away. Le Massif is 45 miles east of Quebec City. Take Route 138 to Petite-Riviere-Sainte-Francois, then follow signs to Le Massif.

Getting around: For those without a car, the HiverExpress runs shuttles from downtown hotels to Mont-Sainte-Anne from mid-November to April. It costs about C$25 round trip or C$20 one way; call 525-5191. Shuttles leave Quebec City at 8 a.m. and 10 a.m. and return at 4:30 p.m. For the return trip, shuttles leave the ski area at 9 a.m. and return at 3:30 p.m. Reservations are compulsory (before 7 a.m. on the day of the trip) and may be made through your hotel. Shuttles to Stoneham also are offered; and another shuttle connects at Mont-Sainte-Anne to Le Massif. The Orleans Express operates between Mont-Sainte-Anne and Quebec City on Fridays, Saturdays and Sundays; call 525-3000.

Dining: $$$$-Entrees C$30+; $$$-C$20-$30; $$-C$10-$20; $-less than C$10.
Accommodations: (double room) $$$$-C$200+; $$$-C$141-$200; $$-C$81-$140; $-C$80 and less..

Tremblant
Quebec, Canada

Summit elevation:	3,001 feet
Vertical drop:	2,131 feet
Base elevation:	870 feet

Address: 1000, Chemin des Voyageurs
Mont-Tremblant, Quebec, Canada J8E 1T1
Area code: 819
Ski area phone: 681-2000
Snow report: (819) 681-5778
Toll-free information : (866) 356-2242
Toll-free reservations: (866) 829-7722
Fax: 681-5999
E-mail: info_tremblant@intrawest.com
Internet: www.tremblant.ca
Expert: ★★★
Advanced: ★★★★
Intermediate:★★★★
Beginner: ★★★★
First-timer: ★★★★

Number and types of lifts: 13–1 high-speed,
eight-person gondola; 5 high-speed quads; 1 quad;
2 triples; 3 moving carpets; 1 cabriolet
Skiable acres: 628 acres
Snowmaking: 77 percent
Uphill capacity: 27,230 skiers per hour
Parks & pipes: 3 parks; 2 pipes
Bed base: 3,500-plus at resort base
Nearest lodging: slopeside, hotel & condos
Resort child care: Yes, 12 months and older
Adult ticket, per day: $56 (without tax)
Dining: ★★★★
Apres-ski/nightlife: ★★★★
Other activities: ★★★★

Heading north out of Montreal, it's hard to believe that you're anywhere near mountains worth skiing. Montreal is flat, flat, flat. But about 30 minutes into your drive, you catch glimpses of oddly shaped hills bursting out of the flatness, almost like giants trying to punch their way through the ground to catch a breath of fresh air. Suddenly, you are surrounded by these funky hills, and it occurs to you: Ski trails are etched among the trees, and beautiful homes dot the hillsides (see end of chapter for a description of these five ski areas).

Tremblant is the highest peak in the Laurentians. Tremblant, a French word that has its roots in Algonquin legend, means Trembling Mountain: The mountain shook, as though by an angry god, from the Laurentian Shield's release by the weight of the Arctic glacier. The tiny town of Tremblant is a few miles from the resort, but slopeside you'll find a European-style village that gives you everything you need while vacationing here (but don't miss a visit to the nearby town). When the multi-colored tin roofs of the mountain village glisten in the sunlight, they look like a bag of Skittles candy spilled across the snow. Village designers wanted to blend manmade structures with nature, to provide intimate surprises with every turn, and they succeeded. The landscape changes with virtually every step: glimpses of the mountain, or the lake at the foot of the mountain, or courtyards and colorful balconies, or rooftops descending the mountainside resembling dominos leading towards the lake.

This is one of skiing's historic peaks. It began in the 1930s—in 1932, if you count Tremblant's founding from the first Kandahar downhill ski race; or in 1938, the hectic year that Philadelphia millionaire Joe Ryan hiked to the top of Mont-Tremblant, purchased it and opened North America's second true winter resort (Sun Valley was the first, two years earlier).

The complete resort experience includes the old village of Tremblant and the picturesque town of St. Jovite, dripping with Quebecois culture. Though the employees speak English, the native language here is French, and you will earn big smiles from locals if you give it a try.

The entire experience is steeped in romance, so you'll win extra brownie points if you bring your lover here. Plus, there's little or no jet lag for North Americans. Keep in mind though, that the summit consistently registers the coldest temperatures south of Hudson Bay.

 ## Mountain layout

Tremblant is a hulk of a mountain with skiing on four faces. The trail map proclaims North and South sides, but these would be more accurately portrayed with designations Northeast and Southwest. It is easy for skiers to follow the sun: Simply ski on the North Side in the mornings to catch the sun and then move to the South Side for the afternoons.

The resort recently added a true south face, Versant Soleil, with 15 intermediate and advanced trails and glades. Most trails are groomed daily, but since 60 percent of the area consists of glades, don't expect buffed snow in the woods.

Most skiers and boarders start from the South Side, where the base village is located. On crowded days, many savvy locals make the 15-minute drive to the parking lot on the North Side, where they can avoid the crowds and get first crack at skiing in the sun.

♦♦**Expert:** The most challenging sections are in The Edge and Versant Soleil. The Edge is reached by the Letendre trail, which starts halfway down the North Side and brings skiers to the base of the Edge quad chair. This chair serves only expert and advanced terrain. Only one trail, Action, is cut; the other descents are through the trees. Reaction and Sensation are cut wide enough for strong intermediates, but the glades dropping to the right down Emotion will push experts to their limits. For bumps, try Dynamite, one of the steepest trails in eastern Canada, and Expo, beneath the lift and wide enough for big wipeouts. The drop down Devil's River and into the woods at Boiling Kettle is a rush.

Versant Soleil, accessed by the Le Soleil lift, is 80-percent expert with the bonus of sunshine. Black and double-black runs take you through fall-line glades. We didn't find any truly tough glade skiing here, but it was all rollicking fun.

♦**Advanced:** For the most part, the single blacks are excellent choices for advanced skiers and riders. It should be noted that we found quite a range among Tremblant's single-black diamond trails: some a challenge worthy of the rating, such as Banzai and Le Tunnel; others that could have been rated blue-square cruisers, such as Geant; and Dernier Cri, which we thought barely deserved a blue rating.

Kandahar is a ripping groomed cruiser. There are steep drops off La Crete down Vertige (a double-diamond) and Dunzee (both get bumped in spring). Ryan is one of the original trails, narrow and twisting with short, very manageable stretches of steeps that earn its lower section a double diamond. If you think Ryan is challenging at the top, you can bail out on blue-square Charron before you get to the narrow part.

■ **Intermediate:** On the South Side, Grand Prix, Beauvallon and Alpine are great wide-open cruising runs. The Cure Deslauriers trail, toward the lower part of the mountain, has been contoured to form snow waves. Kandahar, though rated black, is groomed. It has one fairly steep section, but is a good choice for upper-intermediates. At the end of the day, Johannsen—a short blue stretch at the base that funnels everyone off the mountain—gets bumped and/or mushy, depending on temperatures.

The North Side appears tough on the trail map, but is more intermediate than advanced. Stick to the far right or far left and you can't go wrong. Geant, Saute-Moutons and Duncan Haut are all fine for confident intermediates, and in some respects, are better than Beauchemin and Lowell Thomas, which are rated blue and get a lot more traffic.

Franc Sud and Toboggan are challenging runs that allow intermediates a frightening glimpse of some gnarly Versant Soleil terrain. Le Soleil high speed quad provides welcome relief back to the North Side.

●● **Beginner:** Le P'tit Bonheur takes beginners from the top of the North Side to the easiest mid-mountain trails. Still, most will stick to the South Side. From the top of the Flying Mile lift, beginners head left to La Passe and Nansen bas or they can head right down Standard and Biere-en-bas (named after a shortcut secretly cut by a racer when the staff would race down at the end of the day for beers; winner got to drink for free). Finally, take the big step to the top of the mountain and head down La Crête and all of Nansen. This is a fantastic area to start, but stick to Nansen or Roy Scott at the end of the day to avoid the crowds.

● **First-timer:** Novices start on the carpet lifts near the bell (the ski school meeting place). After first-timers master that terrain, they advance to the Flying Mile lift and Nansen.

Ride Guide: Riders should try to avoid Geant; it has a very long run-out.

Parks and pipes

Tremblant has dedicated about 40 acres to its three terrain parks and superpipe. The 420-foot superpipe is on the North Side, as is North Park, which also is known as the Intermediate Park. The area is groomed by a state-of-the-art Scorpion snowpark grooming machine and has rollers, tabletops, spines, bankturns and rails. The park and pipe are reached by, and run alongside of, the Lowell Thomas lift, in full view of the lift. The Progression Park and the Advanced Park are off the South Side's Flying Mile lift. Features include rails, tabletops and jumps and music. Major competitions take place here since it's in full view of the base area.

 Cross-country and snowshoeing (visit xcskiresorts.com for more details)
Canadians have serious winters, so they take their winter sports seriously. Case in point: the abundant and varied cross-country choices available to visitors to the Tremblant region. More than 260 km. of cross-country trails are scattered in the region, most of which are found in Parc National du Mont-Tremblant (688-2281; park admittance fee). Trails wind through maple and birch forests and provide views of wildlife and lakes. This vast reserve offers two reception centers, complete with ski and snowshoe rentals and 150 km. of trails, 49 km. of which are marked. Pack a lunch and ski out to one of the heated huts. Choose among trail loops of varying degrees of difficulty and length may be chosen. If you're lucky, trail guides will stop by a hut to tell you more about the history and the wildlife of the region. The park also has 17 km. for snowshoeing.

The **Centre de Ski de Fond** (425-5588), owned by the town, offers a network of more than 100 km. of trails, with 50 km. double-tracked and 12 km. skate-groomed. The undulating trails are known for their magnificent vistas. The majority of these vista vantage points are on diamond and double-diamond trails. The La Diable network has nine trails totaling 49 km. with six heated huts along the way. The Jack Rabbit network has seven trails, 30 km. altogether, with two heated huts. Skis and snowshoes are available for rent, and you can also arrange a trip on marked but ungroomed trails to backcountry bunkhouses.

Choose in-village, inn-to-inn trails in the Mont-Tremblant/St.-Jovite region, a wilderness trek in the nearby Parc du Mont-Tremblant. Or, experience the longest linear park in North America, the 200-kilometer "Le P'tit Train du Nord," that runs from St.-Jerome through Mont-Tremblant to Mont-Laurier. St.-Jerome to Ste. Agathe is for cross-country skiing, and Ste. Agathe to Mont-Laurier is for snowmobiling.

Popular choices for the average cross-country skier, who will still get his or her share of magnificent views and occasional sightings of wildlife, include the winding Domaine St. Bernard, the Jack Rabbit and skiing on the Gray Rocks golf course. A portion of Le P'tit Train du Nord linear park is also incorporated into these trails.

Snowshoeing trails on Tremblant's summit can be accessed from the gondola. A three-hour **guided deer-observation snowshoe** tour departs Tuesday, Wednesday and Friday afternoons from the Activity Centre. Full-day trips also are available. **Full Moon Snowshoe Outings** are offered once a month by La Source (681-3000 ext. 46533).

Lessons (05/06 prices, without tax)

Group lessons: C$57 for a 90-minute session, with two sessions offered each morning; C$50 for afternoon.

Private lessons: A 90-minute private lesson, from 8:30 a.m. to 10 a.m. is C$118. One hour of private lesson, in the morning, is C$106.

First-timer packages: The Learn to Ski /Ride programs are 90-minute lessons that include lift ticket and rentals for C$69 at 9:15 a.m. or 11 a.m. and C$59 if taken at 1:15 p.m.

Special programs: Ski Week includes three hours of lessons daily, all with the same instructor; C$233 for four days; teens 13-17, C$243. The program also includes a fun race, photo souvenir, video analysis and a farewell dinner. Book at least seven days in advance for a discount; call (888) 857-8043.

First Tracks allows boarding the Express gondola at 7:15 a.m., have a buffet breakfast at the Grand Manitou summit chalet and begin skiing at 8 a.m. for C$18 plus your lift ticket.

KidStuff (05/06 prices, without tax)

Child care: The Kidz Club and day-care center is at the Sommet des Neiges. It provides care for children ages 12 months to 6 years for C$49 for a half day; C$57 for a half day with lunch; C$79 for a full day with lunch. Reservations, (888) 857-8043. Or check with your hotel or condo concierge for babysitting services that come to your room.

Children's lessons: Adventure Day is a full-day lesson with lunch for children 3–12 (ski) and 7–12 (snowboard). Ages 3–4 pay C$104 for a full day, including lunch; ages 5–12, C$102. Kids Ski Weekends (seven hours over two days, with lunch) cost C$200 for ages 3–4; C$184 for 5–12. Ski Weeks (four days with lunch) cost C$359 for ages 3–4; C$339 for ages 5–12. Prices for all children's programs are lower if pre-booked; call (888) 857-8043.

Lift tickets (05/06 prices, without tax)

	Adult	Child (6-12)
One day	C$56	C$33

Note: Multiday lift tickets are sold through various promotions; see the website.

Who skis free: Children 5 and younger. The moving carpet beginner's lift is free.

Who skis at a discount: Skiers 65 and older pay C$49. Students 13–17 pay C$42.

Note: Prices are rounded up to the nearest Canadian dollar.

Dining: $$$$-Entrees C$30+; $$$-C$20-$30; $$-C$10-$20; $-less than C$10.
Accommodations: (double room) $$$$-C$200+; $$$-C$141-$200; $$-C$81-$140; $-C$80 and less.

Accommodations

Intrawest Central Reservations (866-829-7722) can book all lodging and has good travel, lodging and ski packages. We list lodging choices in the base village, but there are less expensive alternatives nearby.

At the upper end of the village, the luxurious **Fairmont Tremblant** (866-829-7722; 681-7000; $$$–$$$$) is a magnificent stone-and-timber structure with ski-in/walk-out access, shops and restaurants, and a health club with indoor and outdoor heated pools.

Le Westin Resort & Spa (866-783-5630; 681-8000; $$$$) is a high-end condo-hotel with ski-in/ski-out access, featuring 126 rooms, an outdoor saltwater pool, 24-hour room service and a world-class spa. Lots of mahogany and rich colors throughout make it inviting. **Ermitage du Lac** (681-2222, $$$$) is a boutique hotel near the base of the Cabriolet lift at the lower end of the original village. The rooms include a continental breakfast, and the hot tub in front of the hotel sees lots of spirited action.

The all-suite **Le Sommet des Neiges** (866-783-5630; 681-2000; $$$$) is just 100 feet from the Express Gondola. Suites have one to three bedrooms and include fireplace, fully equipped kitchens, washer and dryer. It has an exercise room, outdoor hot tub and indoor parking too.

The **Marriott Residence Inn, Manoir Labelle** (866-829-7722; 681-4000; $$$–$$$$) is at the lower end of the village. Price includes a continental breakfast. **La Tour Des Voyageurs** (866-783-5630; 681-2000; $$$–$$$$) is a condominium hotel with ski-in/ski out access, a swimming pool and exercise room. **Le Country Inn & Suites by Carlson** (866-783-5630; 681-2000; $$$–$$$$) has comfortably appointed rooms, most with fireplaces and full kitchens,plus sauna, outdoor hot tub, exercise room and indoor parking. The slopeside **Lodge de la Montagne** (866-783-5630; 681-2000; $$$–$$$$) houses country-style condominium units, many with gas fireplaces and kitchens, plus sauna, outdoor whirlpool, exercise room and indoor parking.

Three- to four-story buildings line the cobblestoned street between the Fairmont to La Tour Des Voyageurs, housing restaurants and shops, and the roomy and beautifully furnished **Saint Bernard, Johannsen and Deslauriers condos** (866-783-5630; $$–$$$) above.

Other condo complexes are within 2 miles and have shuttle service to the slopes. **Pinoteau Village** (800-667-2200; $$$–$$$$) and **Condotels du Village** (800-567-6724; $–$$) have kitchens, balconies and fireplaces. Pinoteau Village has cross-country trails outside its doors, while the Condotels has a clubhouse with a sauna, hot tub and exercise

Intrawest Central Reservations also can book the **Club Tremblant** (800-567-8341; $$$–$$$$), where rates include breakfast and dinner and lifts; **Gray Rocks** (800-567-6767; $$–$$$$), which has its own small ski area and specializes in the all-inclusive, heavy-on-socializing Ski Week; the luxurious **Intrawest Resort Club** (800-799-3258; $$–$$$$); or several condos, inns, motels and historic lodges in the villages of Mont-Tremblant and St.-Jovite.

Hotel packages at the resort can include an exclusive passport in the value season. This includes either a 30-minute massage and one day of New Generation ski or snowboard rental; or 90 minutes of refreshing your skills with an instructor and an hour in a sleighride. Advanced reservations are required.

For budget travelers, The 84-bed **Mont-Tremblant Youth Hostel** (425-6008; $) offers four- to 10-bed dorm rooms as well as private rooms; all with shared baths. The lodge is in the village, about 2 miles from the mountain, and a shuttle (fee charged) stops at the front door. A fully-equipped kitchen is available, but the hostel offers an inexpensive continental breakfast. Guests can relax in a common room with TV, a library and Internet access.

Dining

Most of the restaurants have moderately priced food, and you can have lunch-type foods for supper, if you like. At the foot of the Gondola Express in the pedestrian village, there are a number of **outdoor barbecue venues**, in the springtime. At outside grills you can get a hot dog with chips, hamburgers or grilled chicken for less than C$5. Most restaurants on the Place St. Bernard have an outdoor grill blazing on sunny days.

Near the Place St. Bernard: The **Cafe Johannsen** serves soups, bagels, salads, beers, coffee and muffins. **L'Oberoi** (681-4555; $–$$) is a deli offering cheeses, pates and cold cuts, sandwiches, fresh breads and other dishes. For the town's best coffee and a good selection of pastries, visit **Au Grain de Cafe** (681-4567; $), just off the plaza.

New in 2006-07 is a Cajun-style bistro called **Fat Mardi's Restaurant** (681-2439; $$–$$$). Some authentic Lousiana cooking to warm up a winter evening. **Le Shack** (681-4700; $–$$) has a breakfast buffet and is the spot for people-watching during lunch or an apres-ski beer or two.

In Vieux-Tremblant, **Plus Minus Cafe** (681-4994; $–$$), is the best restaurant in the resort, indeed in Quebec, boasting some of the most exclusive wines in Canada. The three owners of **Creperie Catherine** (681-4888; $–$$) used to cook aboard ships. Now, they offer Bretonne-style crepes with any kind of filling you could possibly dream up in a delightful indoor/outdoor building. It's a great stop for breakfast and desserts.

Microbrasserie La Diable (681-4546; $–$$) serves light meals of European sausages with its six unique craft beers, brewed on the premises.

La Savoie (681-4573; $$–$$$) serves traditional French Alpine meals. Everything on the menu is "all-you-can-eat," and prices are per person. The communal dining experience is great. If you sit next to the cheese warmer, you'll become an expert in preparing raclette.

La Grappe a Vin (681-4727; $$–$$$) is an intimate wine bar where you can order 40 wines by the glass and another 130 by the bottle, or choose from 43 ports and madeiras, 50 scotches and 30 imported beers. In addition, an oyster bar, wild game pates, local cheeses, fresh soups and salads are available. It's fun apres-ski and perfect for a light dinner.

If you're after a true feast, the high-end **U Restaurant Sushi Bar** (681-4141; $$$), in Le Westin Resort, specializes in Japanese cuisine with emphasis on sushi, sashimi and maki.

Windigo at the Fairmont Tremblant (681-7685; $$–$$$) lays out a sumptuous and tasty theme buffet Thursday through Saturday and also serves Sunday brunch.

The Pizzateria (681-4522; $–$$) has such enticing flavors floating from their doors, you'd be hard-pressed not to stop in. Order to take out or be seen on their strategically placed outdoor deck, perfect people-watching territory. The house specialty at **La Chouquetterie** (681-4509; $), which translates as "sugar tree," is the cream puff, Tropez style. **Queues de Castor** (681-4678; $), also known as BeaverTails®, is a tiny take-out spot. The traditional Canadian pastry—similar to fried dough—is called a Beavertail because that's what it looks like, and it's sinfully yummy. **The Coco Pazzo Deli** (681-4774; $) sells cheeses, salamis, prosciutto and dry pastas. It's around the corner from its restaurant, also called **Coco Pazzo** ($$$), where the menu includes rack of lamb, grilled veal and herb-encrusted sea bass.

Les Artistes (681-4606; $–$$) is a traditional French bistro food. Sample offerings at the wine bar or sit on their terrace overlooking Lake Miroir. Smoked meats are a specialty in the Laurentians, and **Moe's** (425-9821; $–$$), in nearby St.-Jovite, has the best in the region.

On the hill: For lunch, the non-smoking **Grand Manitou**, on top at 3,000 feet (the highest peak in the Laurentians), should satisfy most appetites. It features a meal of the day, for $7 or $10, sandwiches to order, salad bar, pizza, fries and hot dogs.

Dining: $$$$-Entrees C$30+; $$$-C$20-$30; $$-C$10-$20; $-less than C$10.

Accommodations: (double room) $$$$-C$200+; $$$-C$141-$200; $$-C$81-$140; $-C$80 and less.

Apres-ski/nightlife

Since many of the hot spots also are restaurants, see the *Dining* section.

On sunny days, the best apres-ski is in the **Place St. Bernard,** where a stage often is set up with a live band cranking out the tunes. People sit in chairs with a brew and enjoy the sun, listen to the music and watch everyone looking for their friends.

La Grappe a Vin is the place to go for fine wine or liquors and light fare. The mountain-top bar in the **Grand Manitou** is open for apres-ski. **Microbrasserie La Diable** has canned music, good sausages for late-night snacks and six beers brewed on the premises. Blues bands play every Friday and Saturday.

Le Shack is a bit louder and often has a live band on the weekends. The whimsical decor of trees and flying geese overhead makes you feel like you're outdoors. The dancing never stops, so be prepared for a lot of apres-ski exercise. Shooters are served in the traditional Quebec miniature glass ski boot.

Cafe d'Epoque in Vieux-Tremblant sports strobe lights, loud live music (also CDs) and lots of bodies pressed together on the crowded rustic wood dance floor. OK at night, but a bit of a pit when exposed to daylight. **P'tit Caribou,** also in Vieux-Tremblant, consistently gets high ratings from Canadian magazines. Great, loud music and bar-top dancing by go-go girl wannabes. The people and the noise create the wild party ambience. Be ready to stay up far too late into the night.

 Other activities

You can take a **sleigh ride,** go **ice skating** on Lac Miroir, go for a **dogsled ride** (you can mush the dogs yourself) or a **horseback ride,** go **ice climbing** or zip around on a **snowmobile.** There's a **tubing** park in St. Jovite. Visit nearby **Le Scandinave** (425-5524) and wallow in the Scandinavian baths. The theory is simple: warm up your body, then close your skin's pores by chilling the body rapidly, then relax. Start in a Finnish sauna or steam bath, then plunge into cold water by running under a waterfall, diving into a pool or dipping into the river. To warm back up, sit in the outdoor hot tub or return to the sauna or steam bath. Repeat all this as necessary!

The **Spa-sur-le-Lac at Club Tremblant** (425-8341) offers a more traditional experience with 11 body-care and aesthetic rooms and a beauty salon. The **Amerispa Le Westin Resort Tremblant** (681-7080) and **Fairmont Tremblant** (681-7680) offer complete spa services including facials, manicures, and massages.

Aquaclub La Source (681-5668), billed as "A Lake in the Laurentians," lets guests escape winter. This family-oriented spa includes an exercise room and a lake complete with beach, waterfall and Tarzan-style rope swing. The **Spa** at the Activity Centre (681-4848) has sauna, steam bath, outdoor hot tubs, massage and other services for those age 18 and older.

The village has about 45 **shops.** Some of the fanciest are in the Fairmont Tremblant. Chocoholics will want to make fast tracks to the Rocky Mountain Chocolate Factory, where they'll find creamy fudge and crunchy toffee. The village also has a two-screen **movie theater.**

To book any activity, call the Activity Center, (866) 356-2242 or 681-4848. For more information, you can reach the Mont-Tremblant Tourism Office at 425-2434.

Getting there and getting around

By air: The nearest major airport is Montreal, 75 miles away, served by most major airlines. In high season, charter and package flights are offered direct into Mont Tremblant International Airport from Toronto and New York/Newark. Call (877) 425-7919.

By car: From Montreal, take autoroute 15 north to Sainte-Agathe, where the 15 merges with 117. Continue on autoroute 117 north past St.-Jovite. About five kilometers (a little less than three miles) past the town, take exit 119 and turn right on Montee Ryan (there's an Ultramar gas station on the left). Follow signs to Tremblant.

Getting around: Most visitors arrive by car, so rent one if you fly into Montreal. And then to get some use from the car, we suggest side trips to Mont-Tremblant Village and St.-Jovite. Remember, the farther you drive from Montreal, the fewer signes in English you will see.

Nearby skiing

Gray Rocks, Mont-Tremblant (Quebec); (819) 425-2771; (800) 567-6767
Internet: www.grayrocks.com
5 lifts: 1 quad, 3 doubles, 1 surface lift; 22 trails; 620 vertical feet

Gray Rocks is a mouse compared to Tremblant: When you stand at Tremblant's summit, you can see Gray Rocks' 22 compact runs a few miles in the distance. It may look small, but Gray Rocks is a mouse that roars. Good trail planning and maintenance make Gray Rocks feel like a much bigger mountain. Trails wrap around it, rather than plunge straight down, and they incorporate natural terrain features.

This is one of the best learning mountains in North America, and Gray Rocks has capitalized on that strength by carving out a big slice of the student skier market. The success of its Learn-to-Ski Week is overwhelming, with thousands of North Americans taking lessons every season. Lessons are not only for timid first-timers. Skiers of every level are faced with a challenging week of perfecting technique. Ski Weeks have been offered since 1951 and include everything: lodging, meals, instruction, video analysis, lift tickets, access to Le Spa fitness center and indoor pool, gratuities, a souvenir pin and photo and full social calendar and activities.

Part of the success is creating group camaraderie, on and off the slopes. Since people learn best when they are relaxed and having fun, Gray Rocks considers its off-slope program as important as the lessons on the hill. Nightly entertainment, oui. But après-ski also has such creative alternatives as a cooking course, French lessons, wine-and-cheese get-togethers, classical guitar concerts, sleigh rides, a spa and fitness center-the list goes on. Gray Rocks has a day care and "Ski'N'Play" program for children, and it even has a pet kennel.

Gray Rocks also offers an all-inclusive "ski getaway" (room, meals, entertainment, gratuities, skiing, fitness center), with the option to add lessons and clinics. Ski or Snowboard Week (03/04 prices) rates begin at C$1,362 per adult and vary with season and accommodation. A program with lessons at Tremblant also is available.

The Valley of Saint-Sauveur Resorts

Saint-Sauveur des Monts (Quebec); (450) 227-4671; (514) 871-0101

Internet: www.montsaintsauveur.com
(Note: Telephone numbers link a caller to anything from mountain information to lodging reservations. Although the message is in French, there is an option to choose English. It works.)

The Valley of Saint-Sauveur encompasses five ski resorts in a big French *cafe au lait* cup: Mont Saint-Sauveur, Mont Avila, Ski Morin Heights, Mont Olympia and Ski Mont Gabriel. These five mountains collectively have 107 runs served by a total of 31 lifts and are linked by a free shuttlebus service. One lift ticket is good at all five areas. With 67 illuminated slopes and 3,000,000 watts of lighting, they comprise one of the largest night-skiing/snowboarding terrains in the world. When the sun goes down, every hill in the valley comes alive with a sparkling circular blanket of light. This is a true family destination. Each area has its own character and small base village, but they all share extensive snowmaking and proximity to the charming little 100-year-old Quebec village of Saint-Sauveur, about 45 minutes north of Montreal. More than 60 restaurants feature international cuisine for every budget. Packages are available at most lodging facilities, which range from four-star hotels to affordable condos and family-run B&Bs. Nearly 80 shops, fashion boutiques and warehouses satisfy the need to shop, and there are three supermarkets in the village for condo guests wanting to cook in. In the evening, rue Principale is the "buzz" with bars, bistros, discos and live music.

Mont Saint-Sauveur and Mont Avila

Mont Saint-Sauveur: 8 lifts; 38 trails; 142 acres; 699 vertical feet
Mont Avila: 3 lifts; 11 trails; 35 acres; 615 vertical feet

Mont Saint-Sauveur and Mont Avila are considered two separate resorts, but they are actually linked together across the face of three hills with only a property-line boundary. Mont Saint-Sauveur is the «in spot» of the Valley with the highest vertical and most skiable acres. It has the most advanced and intermediate trails of the five with snowmaking on all 142 acres, so if you like to cruise, this is for you. It holds the record for the longest ski season in Quebec with about 180 days thanks to high-tech snowmaking.

Mont Avila also has a snow park for snow tubing and snow rafting, as well as ice-skating and snowshoeing opportunities. Like many Laurentian ski resorts, this hill opens a window on the Quebequois culture, with the «Erabliere» sugar shack where the traditional maple syrup on snow is served. The village of Saint-Sauveur is at the base.

Ski Morin Heights

6 lifts; 23 trails; 90 acres; 656 vertical feet

Ski Morin Heights is characterized as the best-kept secret in the Laurentians. The resort offers a mix of snowsport activities: skiing, snowboarding, back-country telemarking, cross-country and snowshoeing. If you enjoy expert glade skiing, Kicking Horse (skier's right on the edge of the area) will keep you grinning. Or move over a bit to eight more expert runs right next door. Although it accommodates all levels, this is the hill for the advanced and expert skier. It has the most double-blacks/blacks in the five-resort area. The village of Morin-Heights is at the base adjacent to the largest cross-country ski facility in the area, with 175 km.

Mont Olympia

6 lifts; 23 trails; 140 acres; 656 vertical feet

Mont Olympia has the best selection of trails for beginners and youngsters. Most of the runs are greens and blues, but with three double-blacks and three blacks, experts will find challenging terrain, so it's a great family hill. Mont Olympia gets more sun than any of the other Valley resorts and is best known for its Snow School and Olympic skier Jean-Luc Brassard.

Ski Mont Gabriel

7 lifts; 18 trails; 80 acres; 656 vertical feet

Ski Mont Gabriel is the only resort in the Valley to have a dedicated snowboarding mountainside with a terrain park and jumping site accessed by its own T-bar. The official site of the Canadian Freestyle Championships, this resort is also a great place to learn. The area between its two mountains (simply named Mountain 1 and Mountain 2) has a big green area for the first-timers and beginners. Mountain 2 is snowboarder's heaven, but there are also some blue runs down from the top. This is the warmest ski area of the five resorts.

Eastern Townships, Canada
Mont Orford, Mont Sutton, Owl's Head and Bromont

The Eastern Townships' marketing efforts would have you believe that the four ski areas in the region—Sutton, Orford, Bromont and Owl's Head—are right next door to each other, but in reality they are from 20 to 45 minutes away from each other on dry roads.

If you're planning to visit all the areas, consider the interchangeable Townships Ski Ticket. Reserve when booking your lodging or purchase at any of the participating resorts.

Mont Orford; (819) 843-6548; (866) 673-6731
Internet: www.orford.com
8 lifts—2 quads, 1 triple, 3 doubles, 2 surface lifts; 244 skiable acres; 1,772 feet vertical drop.

Mont Orford is operated under a long-term lease on government land within Parc du Mont-Orford. The resort is spread across three separate mountain peaks and has fabulous terrain for all abilities. Adventurous skiers will be challenged here, and you'll be completely surprised by that because at first glance, the mountain looks rather tame. The trails are long, giving skiers and riders maximum use of the vertical drop, and follow the contours of the mountain.

Triple-diamond labels are a bit hyped, but experts won't be disappointed either. Take La Quatuor lift to the top of Mont Giroux, and "warm up" on Slalom: When we skied it, there was new powder and the workout left us huffing and puffing with screaming quads. Riding up Le Quad du Village, you'll realize what you're up for as you look at the bodies littered across Sherbrooke below you (probably thought they'd take a break from the glade skiing—hey, it's a trail, how hard can it be?).

For those who prefer trails to woods, don't worry, be happy. Trois-Ruisseaux and Maxi on Mont Orford are especially delightful, and both are groomed in the middle of the day, which is a special treat since these are popular trails. Trois-Ruisseaux is a winding trail, narrow in spots with nice steep pitches. Maxi, on the other hand, is steep and goes straight down the mountain. Watch out, you'll pick up lots of speed before you know it.

The intermediate trails on Mont Alfred-Desrochers are winding and rolling, sometimes narrow, but with a steady pitch and no unexpected steeps. A wonderful experience! Because the chair is a bit out of the way, you'll find these trails relatively uncrowded.

Sutton My Mountain Resort!; (450) 538-2545; (866) 538-2545
Internet: www.sutton.ca
9 lifts—1 high-speed quad, 2 quads, 6 doubles; 174 skiable acres; 1,500 feet vertical drop.

A trip to Sutton is a step back in time. The resort made its debut in 1960 and still has some of its original chair lifts, which you board after working your way through a lift line of wooden fences and passing ticket-checker booths that look like little red-trimmed log cabins. All around you, skiers and riders decked out in the latest gear and apparel chatter away in French. Which reminds us to tell you that Sutton and the nearby town may just be one of the friendliest places we've ever visited. Everyone seems to know everyone, and if they don't know you, they act like they do. By the way, just say bonjour or merci and everyone happily switches to English (yes, your accent will give you away!).

At first glance, Sutton appears to be a small area, but it skis like a large resort. Trails and glades take you all over the mountain before reaching the bottom. Ability levels are generally separated from each other: Beginner terrain is on the far right; intermediate terrain is in the middle; expert terrain is to the far left. Two lifts in the middle of the mountain also serve beginner terrain.

Glades, or sous-bois, clearly set this mountain apart from others. They are thinned enough to groom—not often, because they're most fun in the powder. The glades were cut in 1960, long before other resorts even thought of such a thing. Trails follow the true fall line. You're constantly winding your way down the mountain. Trails are also usually left au naturel—only 13 are groomed nightly, and fewer than that on a powder day. Are you getting the message yet? This charming retro resort gets a lot of powder, and that's what the skiers here like, so the owners don't mess with it. Speaking of the owners, the same family that opened the resort still runs it, with great affection and respect for the mountain and its guests.

Ski Bromont; Bromont (Quebec); (450) 534-2200; 1-866 BROMONT (276-6668)
Internet: www.skibromont.com
6 lifts–2 high-speed quad, 3 quads, 1 surface lift; 250 skiable acres; 1,329 feet vertical drop.

Bromont, the Eastern Townships ski area closest to Montreal, can be a very busy place, particularly at night. Québécois are well-known for their love of night skiing, and Bromont fills that fancy very well. About 75 percent of the terrain, including the terrain park, is lighted for night skiing, which goes till 10 p.m. Sunday through Thursday and 10:44 p.m. Friday and Saturday.

The close proximity to Montreal ensures steady business and a lively night life. Indeed, six times during the season the resort stages Nuit Blanche, or "white night," in which you can ski or ride from 7 p.m.– 3 a.m. for C$21.75 (plus tax). These events are extremely popular, especially with the college and 20-something set, with high-powered dancing and partying in the bar until the wee hours.

Although the trail map is dominated by diamonds, the trails are really intermediate. Experts and advanced skiers will find that the cruisers are a great way to give tired legs a break after skiing hard all week at Mont Orford or Mont Sutton. Grooming is meticulous, and on weekends, trails are groomed three times a day. Most skiers will want to spend only a day here because of limited terrain, but the area's expansion onto its eastern face, in a section called Versant du Lac, helps to add texture and terrain.

The mountain has a lower elevation than other resorts in the area, so it often rains here when it snows elsewhere. Bromont gives you 30 minutes to test conditions—if you're not pleased, exchange your ticket for a coupon to return at no extra charge.

Owl's Head; Mansonville (Quebec); (800) 363 3342 for lodging reservations
Internet: www.owlshead.com or info@owlshead.com
8 lifts–3 high-speed quads, 1 quad, 4 doubles; 14,400 skiers/hr uphill capacity; 1,772 feet vertical.

Owl's Head is named after the Abenaki Indian's greatest chief, Owl, whose spirit will live forever through the naming of the mountain in his honor. The minute you get off the lift, any lift, you'll be awestruck by the views. Lake Memphremagog is below the base, and you often feel as if you'll ski right off the edge of the mountain into the lake. No kidding: The magnificent views are comparable to skiing in the Tahoe region of California. This is a lovely mountain; perfect for families and groups that want gentle skiing and nicely groomed trails.

This is a lovely little mountain that's perfect for families and groups that want gentle skiing and nicely groomed trails. However, it is small and most will not want to ski here for an entire week unless you have young children.

Index
downhill and cross-country
resorts alphabetically